ESPERANTO-ENGLISH DICTIONARY

ESPERANTA-ANGLA VORTARO

Compiled by
Paul Denisowski

Edited by
Michael Everson

evertype
2012

Eldonita de/*Published by* Evertype, Cnoc Sceichín, Leac an Anfa, Cathair na Mart, Co. Mhaigh Eo, Éire / Irlando. *www.evertype.com*.

Teksto © 2012 Paul Denisowski, permesita laŭ la permesilo Krea Komunaĵo Atribuite 3.0 Neadaptita.
Text © 2012 Paul Denisowski, *licensed under a Creative Commons Attribution 3.0 Unported Licence.*

Ĉi tiu unua eldono/*This edition* © 2012 Michael Everson.

Ĉiuj rajtoj rezervitaj. Neniu parto de ĉi tiu eldonaĵo povas esti reproduktita, konservita en retrovsistemo, aŭ transmisiita, laŭ ia ajn formo aŭ pere de ia ajn rimedo, elektronika, mekanika, fotokopia, registra, aŭ alia, sen skribita antaŭpermeso de la Eldonisto, aŭ kiel eksplicite permesata laŭleĝe, aŭ laŭ kondiĉoj kontraktitaj kun la organizaĵo respondeca pri reprografikorajtoj.
All rights reserved. No part of this publication may be reproduced, stored in a retrieval system, or transmitted, in any form or by any means, electronic, mechanical, photocopying, recording, or otherwise, without the prior permission in writing of the Publisher, or as expressly permitted by law, or under terms agreed with the appropriate reprographics rights organization.

Katalogorikordo pri ĉi tiu libro estas havebla de la Brita Biblioteko.
A catalogue record for this book is available from the British Library.

ISBN-10 1-78201-006-8 (hardcover)
ISBN-13 978-1-78201-006-7 (hardcover)

ISBN-10 1-78201-007-6 (paperback)
ISBN-13 978-1-78201-007-4 (paperback)

Dezajno kaj komposto/*Typesetting and design*: Michael Everson.
 Presliteroj/*Set in* Baskerville, Everson Mono, & **Collegiate**.

Kovrilo/*Cover*: Michael Everson.

Presita de/*Printed by* LightningSource.

CONTENTS

Antaŭparolo al la eldono presita de 2012 iv
Preface to the 2012 printed edition vi
Preface to the 2012 online edition viii
La dek ses reguloj de Esperanta gramatiko x
The sixteen rules of Esperanto grammar xi
Affixes xvi
Dictionary 1
   A 1
   B 57
   C 84
   Ĉ 89
   D 96
   E 119
   F 143
   G 165
   Ĝ 177
   H 180
   Ĥ 190
   I 191
   J 205
   Ĵ 209
   K 210
   L 254
   M 270
   N 309
   O 325
   P 334
   R 372
   S 391
   Ŝ 431
   T 437
   U 459
   Ŭ 462
   V 463
   X Y Z 478

ANTAŬPAROLO AL LA ELDONO PRESITA DE 2012

Pluraj Esperantaj vortaroj ekzistas por anglaparolantoj, variante laŭ grandeco kaj kvalito. La *Comprehensive English-Esperanto Dictionary* de Peter Benson plenumas bone la esperojn de sia titolo; la *English-Esperanto-English Dictionary* de John C. Wells estas pli konciza sed montriĝas tre utila, kaj kompreneble havigas tradukajn ekvivalentojn en ambaŭ direktoj. La superba *Esperanto-English Dictionary* de Montagu Butler tro longe estas elĉerpita, kaj kvankam mi opinias ke nova eldono profitus de nova kompostado kun malpli da arbitraj mallongigoj, eĉ neŝanĝita represaĵo estus bonvena por multaj lernantoj. La malnova *Esperanto-English Dictionary* de Fleming Fulcher kaj Bernard Long estas certe utila, kaj enhavas iujn obskurajn vortojn kiuj ne troviĝas en Benson aŭ Wells. Multaj lernantoj eble nun denove malkovras la *English-Esperanto Dictionary* de John Charles O'Connor kaj Charles Frederic Hayes, nun kiam ĝi fariĝis havebla pere de Project Gutenberg.

Kompreneble la *Plena Ilustrita Vortaro* nun haveblas rete ĉe **vortaro.net**, sed la bezono por moderna Esperanta-angla vortaro restas akra por multaj esperantistoj. La *Esperanto-English Dictionary* de Paul Denisowski eble helpas plenigi parton de tiu bezono, almenaŭ surbaze de sia grandega amplekso. Dirinte tion, estus plej bone montri ambaŭ la fortojn kaj malfortojn de ĉi tiu vortaro, kaj klarigi kion ĝi faras kaj ne faras.

Kion ĝi *ja* faras estas doni rapidan aliron al angla gloso por pli ol 52.000 kapvortoj. Kion ĝi *ne* faras estas proponi grandan kvanton da subtileco, rilate al parentezaj notoj pri la uzado aŭ preciza signifo de multaj el la tradukaj ekvivalentoj. Kiel Denisowski rimarkas en sia antaŭparolo al la reta eldono, la libro estis kompilita uzante jam ekzistantajn glosarojn kaj ankaŭ multajn glosarojn, kiujn li mem preparis. Kiel tia, la korpuso de ESPDIC pli funkcias kiel glosaro ol kiel pli kompleksa speco de vortaro. Sed ĉar ĝi estis kompilita de glosaroj kreitaj de uzantoj, la vortaro enhavas vortojn kiuj eble ne troviĝas en pli malgrandaj vortaroj. Ĝi enhavas grandan nombron da sciencaj terminoj, ekzemple, precipe el la fakoj de medicino kaj matematiko.

Iom da ripetado troviĝas en ĉi tiu vortaro, eble ĉar multaj el la vortoj enhavitaj estas neologismoj, anstataŭ vortoj oficialigitaj de la Akademio de Esperanto, tiel ke iliaj ortografio kaj morfologio ankoraŭ ne estas formale fiksitaj. Estas dividstrekitaj kunmetaĵoj, nedividstrekitaj kunmetaĵoj, kaj seninterrompaj kunmetaĵoj kun **-a** aŭ **-o** mankanta. Loknomoj aparte montras multan ortografian variadon. Bona ekzemplo estas 'Saud-Arabio', kiu aperas kiel **Sauda Arabio**, **Sauda Arabujo**, **Saud-Arabio**, **Saudarabujo**, **Saudiarabio**, **Saudiarabujo**, **Saŭda Arabujo**, kaj **Saŭdarabujo**.

ESPERANTA-ANGLA VORTARO

Tia variado povus inspiri Esperantistajn vortaristojn normigi la terminologion por tiaj frazeroj. Valora aldono al la vortaro eble estos indiki vortojn kiuj estas inkluzivitaj en la *PIV*.

Dum Paul Denisowski prizorgas sian retan ESPDIC-korpuson, mi provos konservi la aktualecon de ĉi tiu vortaro, eldonante aldonojn kaj korektojn ĉe **evertype.com/books/espdic.html**. Preparante ĉi tiun eldonon, mi jam sendis al Paul pli ol 800 proponitajn aldonojn kaj korektojn de diversaj specoj, inkluzive de multaj korektoj de literumaj eraroj en la anglaj glosoj.

Mia propra redakta praktiko estis sufiĉe minimuma. Mi klopodis normaligi la anglajn tradukojn laŭ ortografio oksforda, pro tio, ke la fontdosieroj enhavas ambaŭ britajn kaj usonajn literumojn por multaj vortoj. Mi alfabete ordigis strikte, do streketoj kaj punktoj estas ignoritaj en la ordigo: **F-klefo** aperas post **fjordo** kaj antaŭ **flagaĵo**, kaj **k.t.p.** aperas post **ksisto** kaj antaŭ **Kualalumpuro**. Frazoj konsistantaj el du aŭ pli da vortoj apartigitaj per spacoj ĝenerale estas kungrupigitaj en paragrafon kun kapvorto; ĉi tiuj paragrafoj kutime inkludas pluralojn kaj akuzativojn por substantivoj kaj adjektivoj, kaj tempojn kaj imperativojn por verboj. Derivaĵoj sekvas la kapvortajn formojn ene de iliaj paragrafoj, eĉ kvankam tio ne estas ĝustadire laŭ alfabeta ordo:

> **bona** good, nice, OK, kind. **bona ordo** well-ordering. **bonaj manieroj** good manners. **bonan matenon!** good morning!
> **ekesti** to arise, start to be. **ekestis ventego** a storm blew up.
> **sidiĝi** to become seated, sit down. **sidiĝu!** sit down!

Mi volas esprimi mian dankemon al John C. Wells, kiu donis al mi sian permeson bazi la sekcion "Affixes" en la antaŭa materialo sur la sekcio "Affixes and Endings" en lia *Concise Esperanto and English Dictionary*. Lia prezentaĵo estas konciza kaj ekzakta, kaj mi ne povus fari ĝin pli bone.

Dankon mi ankaŭ ŝuldas al Patrick H. Wynne por lia provlegado de la antaŭa materialo kaj precipe por lia zorgado, ke la Dek Ses Reguloj estu prezentitaj ĝuste.

Fine mi ŝatus danki al la kompilinto, Paul Denisowski, pro la grandega kvanto de laborado kiun li faris, kaj pro sia grandanima kuraĝigo, ke mi havebligu tiun laboradon en presita formo. Mi fidas ke ĉi tiu libro montriĝos bonvena kaj utila ilo por studantoj de Esperanto.

Michael Everson
Vestporto, la 26-an de julio 2012

PREFACE TO THE 2012 PRINTED EDITION

Several Esperanto dictionaries exist for English-speakers, varying in size and quality. Peter Benson's *Comprehensive English-Esperanto Dictionary* lives up to its title very well; John C. Wells' *English-Esperanto-English Dictionary* is more concise but has proved to be very useful, and of course gives translation equivalents in both directions. Montagu Butler's magnificent *Esperanto-English Dictionary* is too long out of print, and although I think that a new edition could benefit from new typesetting with fewer arbitrary abbreviations, even an unchanged reprint would be welcomed by many learners. Fleming Fulcher and Bernard Long's older *Esperanto-English Dictionary* is handy enough, and sports the odd obscure word not found in Benson or Wells. Many learners may now be rediscovering John Charles O'Connor and Charles Frederic Hayes' *English-Esperanto Dictionary* now that it has been made available via Project Gutenberg.

Of course the *Plena Ilustrita Vortaro* is now available online at **vortaro.net**, but the need for a modern Esperanto-to-English dictionary remains keen for many Esperantists. Paul Denisowski's *Esperanto-English Dictionary* may help to fill a part of that need, on the basis of its sheer size alone. Having said that, it is best to point out both the strengths and the weaknesses of this dictionary, to make plain what it does and does not do.

What it *does* do is give quick access to an English gloss for over 52,000 headwords. What it *doesn't* do is offer a huge amount of subtlety, in terms of parenthetical notes on the usage or precise meaning of many of the translation equivalents. As Denisowski notes in his preface to the online edition, the book was compiled from existing glossaries as well as from many glossaries he himself prepared. As such, the ESPDIC corpus functions more as a glossary than as a more complex kind of dictionary. But because it was compiled from user-created glossaries, the dictionary contains words which may not be found in smaller dictionaries. It contains a large number of scientific terms, for instance, especially from the fields of medicine and mathematics.

A certain amount of duplication is found in this dictionary, perhaps because many of the words it contains are neologisms, rather than words sanctioned by the Akademio de Esperanto, and so their spelling and morphology have not been formally established. There are hyphenated compounds, unhyphenated compounds, and run-on compounds with **-a** or **-o** omitted. Place-names in particular show a great deal of variability in spelling. A good example is 'Saudi Arabia', which appears as **Sauda Arabio**,

ESPERANTO-ENGLISH DICTIONARY

Sauda Arabujo, **Saud-Arabio**, **Saud-arabujo**, **Saudiarabio**, **Saudi-arabujo**, **Saŭda Arabujo**, and **Saŭd-arabujo**. Such variation may inspire Esperantist lexicographers to standardize the terminology for such items. A valuable addition to the dictionary might be to indicate words which are included in the *PIV*.

As Paul Denisowski maintains his online ESPDIC corpus, I will attempt to keep this dictionary up-to-date, publishing additions and corrections at **evertype.com/books/espdic.html**. In preparing this edition I have already forwarded to Paul over 800 suggested additions and corrections of various kinds, including a large number of corrections to spelling errors in the English glosses.

My own editorial practice has been fairly light-handed. I have endeavoured to normalize the English translations to Oxford spelling, since the source files present both British and American spellings for many words. I have alphabetized strictly, so hyphens and full stops are ignored in sorting: **F-klefo** appears after **fjordo** and before **flagaĵo**, and **k.t.p.** appears after **ksisto** and before **Kualalumpuro**. Phrases consisting of two or more words separated by spaces have generally been concatenated into a paragraph with a headword; these paragraphs usually include plurals and accusatives for nouns and adjectives, and tenses and imperatives for verbs. The derived forms follow the headword forms within their paragraphs, even though this may not be strictly speaking alphabetical:

> **bona** good, nice, OK, kind. **bona ordo** well-ordering. **bonaj manieroj** good manners. **bonan matenon!** good morning!
> **ekesti** to arise, start to be. **ekestis ventego** a storm blew up.
> **sidiĝi** to become seated, sit down. **sidiĝu!** sit down!

I would like to express my gratitude to John C. Wells for giving me his permission to base the section "Affixes" in the front-matter on the "Affixes and Endings" section in his *Concise Esperanto and English Dictionary*. His presentation is concise and accurate, and I could not have done better.

My thanks are also due to Patrick H. Wynne for reading through the front-matter and in particular for taking care that the Sixteen Rules had been presented correctly.

Finally I would like to thank the compiler, Paul Denisowski, for the massive amount of work he has done, and for his generosity in encouraging me to make that work available in a printed form. I trust that this book will prove a welcome and useful tool for students of Esperanto.

Michael Everson
Westport, 26 July 2012

PREFACE TO THE 2012 ONLINE EDITION

The purpose of the ESPDIC project is to create an electronic Esperanto-English dictionary in the form of a single Unicode (UTF8) text file with the following format: "Esperanto : English", that is: Esperanto entry, space, colon, space, English definition—one entry per line). In some cases, a semicolon is used to show different definitions for Esperanto homonyms, e.g. "kajo : conjunction; quay, wharf". The simple formatting is designed to facilitate the integration of the ESPDIC dictionary into other applications (which is highly encouraged).

One of the main purposes of this project is to make a large, comprehensive, and updatable Esperanto-English dictionary available to the public in a wide variety of formats and applications. To this end, ESPDIC (Esperanto English Dictionary) by Paul Denisowski is licensed under a Creative Commons Attribution 3.0 Unported License. What this means is that anyone can use, transmit, or modify ESPDIC for any purpose, including commercial purposes, as long as the source is properly attributed.

History: Based on the experiences I had with the CEDICT (Chinese-English Dictionary) project I started in the late 1990s, I decided to do something similar for Esperanto. The core of this dictionary was made up of vocabulary lists I created from various Esperanto textbooks as well as word lists I found on the Internet. The dictionary was then augmented by vocabulary lists I made from reading both print and online sources. In the early part of 2011 I believed that the dictionary had reached a sufficient size (about 30,000 entries) and I went through the dictionary from start to finish trying to catch the most obvious errors, formatting issues, etc. Any remaining errors or issues (and I'm sure there will always be some) are of course my own responsibility.

My goal is to continue to add to this dictionary on a regular basis, as well as to integrate any contributions made by the community at large. Contributions were a major factor in the growth of the CEDICT project and are warmly welcome. Please also see the release history at the end of this file.

Based on some requests I'm also offering .mobi (Amazon Kindle, etc.), .epub, and .pdf versions of ESPDIC. This is still somewhat experimental, so please contact me if you have any issues, suggestions, etc.

If you have any questions, comments etc. about the project or the dictionary, please send them to me at paul@denisowski.org and I will answer them as quickly as I am able. Questions about Esperanto in general and other questions not specific to the dictionary would best be directed to one

ESPERANTO-ENGLISH DICTIONARY

of the excellent Esperanto forums on the Internet, such as *Lernu!* (**lernu.net**) or the *Esperanto League of North America* (**esperanto-usa.org**).

"Vortaro, tio estas la tuta universo laŭ alfabeta ordo" – Anatole France

Paul Denisowski

RELEASE HISTORY :
- 26 Feburary 2012: 52,323 entries—Additions and corrections
- 15 January 2012: 32,718 entries—Additions and corrections
- 24 August 2011: 32,140 entries—Additions and corrections
- 27 June 2011: 31,479 entries—Additions and corrections
- 02 June 2011: 30,404 entries—Additions and corrections
- 04 May 2011: 28,988 entries—Initial release of the dictionary

LA DEK SES REGULOJ
DE ESPERANTA GRAMATIKO

A. ALFABETO.

Aa	[a]	Ll	[l]
Bb	[b]	Mm	[m]
Cc	[ts]	Nn	[n]
Ĉĉ	[tʃ]	Oo	[o]
Dd	[d]	Pp	[p]
Ee	[ɛ]	Rr	[r] aŭ [ɾ]
Ff	[f]	Ss	[s]
Gg	[g]	Ŝŝ	[ʃ]
Ĝĝ	[dʒ]	Tt	[t]
Hh	[h]	Uu	[u]
Ĥĥ	[x]	Ŭŭ	[w]
Ii	[i]	Vv	[v]
Jj	[j]	Zz	[z]
Ĵĵ	[ʒ]		
Kk	[k]		

Rimarko 1. La litero **ŭ** estas uzata nur post vokaloj.

Rimarko 2. Presejoj, kiuj ne posedas la literojn **ĉ**, **ĝ**, **ĥ**, **ĵ**, **ŝ**, **ŭ**, povas anstataŭ ili uzi **ch**, **gh**, **hh**, **jh**, **sh**, **u**. [Nuntempe oni pli ofte anstataŭigas ambaŭ supersignojn ˆ kaj ˇ per **cx**, **gx**, **hx**, **jx**, **sx**, **ux**, kiam surogata skribsistemo estas bezonata. —Redaktoro]

B. PARTOJ DE PAROLO.

1. Artikolo nedifinita ne ekzistas; ekzistas nur artikolo difinita (**la**), egala por ĉiuj genroj, kazoj kaj nombroj.

   Rimarko. La uzado de la artikolo estas tia sama, kiel en la germana, franca kaj aliaj lingvoj. La personoj, por kiuj la uzado de la artikolo prezentas malfacilaĵon, povas tute ĝin ne uzi.

2. Substantivoj estas formataj per aldono de **-o** al la radiko. Por la formado de la pluralo oni aldonas la finiĝon **-j** al la singularo. Kazoj ekzistas nur du: nominativo kaj akuzativo. La radiko kun aldonita **-o** estas la nominativo, la akuzativo aldonas **-n** post la **-o-**. La ceteraj kazoj estas esprimataj per helpo de prepozicioj: la genitivo per **de**, la dativo per **al**, la instrumentalo (ablativo) per **per**, aŭ aliaj prepozicioj laŭ la senco. Ekz. radiko **patr-**, **la patro**, **al la patro**, **de la patro**, **la patron**, **por la patro**, **kun la patro**, **la patroj**, **la patrojn**, **per la patroj**, **por la patroj**.

THE SIXTEEN RULES OF ESPERANTO GRAMMAR

A. THE ALPHABET

Aa	[a] like *a* in English *father*	**Ll**	[l] like *l* in English *line*.
Bb	[b] like *b* in English *bin*.	**Mm**	[m] like *m* in English *man*.
Cc	[ts] like *ts* in English *tsetse*.	**Nn**	[n] like *n* in English *name*.
Ĉĉ	[tʃ] like *ch* in English *chin*.	**Oo**	[o] like *oa* in English *boat*.
Dd	[d] like *d* in English *din*.	**Pp**	[p] like *p* in English *pin*.
Ee	[ɛ] like *e* in English *bet*.	**Rr**	[ɾ] with a single tap as in Scottish English or Spanish, or [r] with a trill.
Ff	[f] like *f* in English *fin*.		
Gg	[g] like *g* in English *game*.		
Ĝĝ	[dʒ] like *g* in English *gin*.	**Ss**	[s] like *s* in English *sin*.
Hh	[h] like *h* in English *him*.	**Ŝŝ**	[ʃ] like *sh* in English *shin*.
Ĥĥ	[x] like *ch* in Scottish English *loch*.	**Tt**	[t] like *t* in English *tin*.
Ii	[i] like *ee* in English *beet*.	**Uu**	[u] like *oo* in English *boot*.
Jj	[j] like *y* in English *yam*.	**Ŭŭ**	[w] like *u* in English *bout* (used in diphthongs)
Ĵĵ	[ʒ] like *zh* in the Russian name *Zhivago*.		
		Vv	[v] like *v* in English *vane*.
Kk	[k] like *k* in English *kin*.	**Zz**	[z] like *z* in English *zone*.

Note 1. The letter **ŭ** is used only after vowels.

Note 2. Printing houses that do not have the letters **ĉ, ĝ, ĥ, ĵ, ŝ, ŭ** can use **ch, gh, hh, jh, sh, u** instead. [Nowadays it is more common to replace both diacritics ^ and ˘ with **cx, gx, hx, jx, sx, ux** when a fallback representation is needed.— Editor]

B. PARTS OF SPEECH

1. There is no indefinite article (English *a, an*); there is only a definite article (English *the*), **la**, the same for all genders, cases, and numbers.

    Note. The use of the article is the same as in German, French, and other languages. People for whom use of the article presents a difficulty may forego its use entirely.

2. Substantives are formed by adding **-o** to the root. To form the plural, the ending **-j** is added to the singular. There are only two cases: nominative and accusative. The root with an added **-o** is the nominative, the accusative adds an **-n** after the **-o-**. Other cases are formed with prepositions: the genitive by **de** *of*, the dative by **al** *to*, the instrumental (ablative) by **per** *by means of*, or other prepositions as the sense demands. E.g. root **patr-** *father*; **la patro** *the father*; **al la patro** *to the father*; **de la patro** *of the father*; **la patron** *the father* (obj.), **por la patro** *for the father*; **kun la patro** *with the father*; **la patroj** *the fathers*; **la patrojn** *the fathers* (obj.); **per la patroj** *by the fathers*; **por la patroj** *for the fathers*.

ESPERANTA-ANGLA VORTARO

3. Adjektivoj estas formataj per aldono de **-a** al la radiko. Kazoj kaj nombroj kiel ĉe substantivoj. La komparativo estas farata per la vorto **pli**, la superlativo per **plej**. Post la komparativo la vorto *than* (angle) tradukiĝas per **ol**, kaj post la superlativo la vorto *of* (angle) tradukiĝas per **el**. Ekz. **pli blanka ol neĝo; mi havas la plej belan patrinon el ĉiuj; mi havas la plej bonan patrinon.**

4. La bazaj numeraloj (ne deklinaciataj) estas: **unu** (1), **du** (2), **tri** (3), **kvar** (4), **kvin** (5), **ses** (6), **sep** (7), **ok** (8), **naŭ** (9), **dek** (10), **cent** (100), **mil** (1000). La dekoj kaj centoj estas formataj per simpla kunigo de la numeraloj. Por la ordaj numeraloj oni aldonas la adjektivan finiĝon **-a**; por la multiplikaj, la sufikson **-obl**; por la frakciaj, **-on**; por la kolektivaj, **-op**; por la distribuaj, la vorton **po**. Krom tio povas esti uzataj numeraloj substantivaj kaj adverbaj. Ekz. **kvincent tridek tri** (533); **kvara, unua, dua; triobla; kvarono, duono; duope, kvarope; po kvin; unuo, cento; sepe, unue, due.**

5. La pronomoj personaj estas: **mi, vi, li, ŝi, ĝi** (por bestoj aŭ aĵoj), **si, ni, ili, oni** (senpersona plurala pronomo). Pronomoj posedaj estas formataj per aldono de la adjektiva finiĝo **-a**. La deklinacio de la pronomoj estas kiel ĉe substantivoj. Ekz. **min, mia, la viaj.**

6. Verbo ne estas ŝanĝata laŭ personoj nek nombroj; ekz. **mi faras, la patro faras, ili faras.**

Verbaj formoj:
a) La tempo prezenca finiĝas per **-as**; ekz. **mi faras.**
b) La tempo preterita per **-is**; ekz. **vi faris, li faris.**
c) La tempo futura per **-os**; ekz. **ili faros.**
ĉ) La modo kondicionala per **-us**; ekz. **ŝi farus.**
d) La modo imperativa per **-u**; ekz. **faru, ni faru.**
e) La modo infinitiva per **-i**; ekz. **fari.**

Participoj (kaj gerundioj):
Estas du formoj de participo en la internacia lingvo, la deklinaciebla aŭ adjektiva, kaj la nedeklinaciebla aŭ adverba.

f) La participo aktiva prezenca finiĝas per **-ant**, ekz. **faranta, farante.**

g) La participo aktiva preterita per **-int**, ekz. **farinta, farinte.**

ĝ) La participo aktiva futura per **-ont**, ekz. **faronta, faronte.**

h) La participo pasiva prezenca per **-at**, ekz. **farata, farate.**

ĥ) La participo pasiva preterita per **-it**, ekz. **farita, farite.**

i) La participo pasiva futura per **-ot**, ekz. **farota, farote.**

ESPERANTO-ENGLISH DICTIONARY

3. Adjectives are formed by adding **-a** to the root. The numbers and cases are the same as in substantives. The comparative is formed with the word **pli** *more*; the superlative by **plej** *most*. After the comparative the word *than* is rendered by **ol**, and after the superlative the word *of* is rendered by **el**. Examples: **pli blanka ol neĝo** *whiter than snow*; **mi havas la plej belan patrinon el ĉiuj** *I have the most beautiful mother of all*; **mi havas la plej bonan patrinon** *I have the best mother*.

4. The basic cardinal numerals (which are not declined) are: **unu** (1), **du** (2), **tri** (3), **kvar** (4), **kvin** (5), **ses** (6), **sep** (7), **ok** (8), **naŭ** (9), **dek** (10), **cent** (100), **mil** (1000). The tens and hundreds are formed by simple junction of the numerals. Ordinals are formed by adding the adjectival ending **-a** to the cardinals; multiplicatives add the suffix **-obl**; fractionals add **-on**; collective numerals add **-op**; distributives add the word **po**. In addition, numbers can be used as nouns (with **-o**) and adverbs (with **-e**). E.g. **kvincent tridek tri** (533); **kvara** *fourth*, **unua** *first*, **dua** *second*; **triobla** *threefold, triple*; **kvarono** *a fourth, a quarter*, **duono** *a half*; **duope** *by twos*, **kvarope** *by fours*; **po kvin** *five apiece*; **unuo** *unit*, **cento** *a hundred*; **sepe** *seventhly*, **unue** *firstly*, **due** *secondly*.

5. The personal pronouns are: **mi** *I*, **vi** *you*, **li** *he*, **ŝi** *she*, **ĝi** *it* (for animals or things), **si** *self*, **ni** *we*, **ili** *they*, **oni** *one* (impersonal pronoun). Possessive pronouns are formed by adding the adjectival ending **-a**. The declension of the pronouns is like that of substantives. E.g. **min** *me* (obj.), **mia** *my, mine*, **la viaj** 'yours'.

6. The verb does not change its form for person or number, e.g. **mi faras** *I do*; **la patro faras** *the father does*; **ili faras** *they do*.

Verbal forms:
a) The present tense ends in **-as**, e.g. **mi faras** *I do*.
b) The past tense ends in **-is**, e.g. **vi faris** *you did*, **li faris** *he did*.
c) The future tense ends in **-os**, e.g. **ili faros** *they will do*.
ĉ) The conditional mood ends in **-us**, e.g. **ŝi farus** *she would do*.
d) The imperative mood ends in **-u**, e.g. **faru!** *do!* **ni faru** *let us do*.
e) The infinitive mood ends in **-i**, e.g. **fari** *to do*.

Participles (and gerunds):
There are two forms of the participle in the international language, the declinable or adjectival, and the indeclinable or adverbial.

f) The active present participle ends in **-ant**, e.g. **faranta** *doing*; **farante** *doing*.

g) The active past participle ends in **-int**, e.g. **farinta** *having done*; **farinte** *having done*.

ĝ) The active future participle ends in **-ont**, e.g. **faronta** *going to do*; **faronte** *about to do*.

h) The passive present participle ends in **-at**, e.g. **farata** *being done*, **farate** *being done*.

ĥ) The passive past participle ends in **-it**, e.g. **farita** *having been done*; **farite** *having been done*.

i) The passive future participle ends in **-ot**, e.g. **farota** *to be done*; **farote** *about to be done*.

ESPERANTA-ANGLA VORTARO

Ĉiuj formoj de la pasivo estas formataj per helpo de responda formo de la verbo **est-** kaj prezenca aŭ preterita participo pasiva de la bezonata verbo; la prepozicio ĉe la pasivo estas **de**. Ekz. **ŝi estas amata de ĉiuj** (participo prezenca: la afero fariĝas); **la pordo estas fermita** (participo preterita: la afero jam estas farita).

7. Adverboj estas formataj per aldono de **-e** al la radiko. Gradoj de komparado estas la samaj kiel ĉe adjektivoj. Ekz. **mia frato pli bone kantas ol mi**.

8. Ĉiuj prepozicioj per si mem postulas la nominativon.

C. ĜENERALAJ REGULOJ

9. Ĉiu vorto estas legata, kiel ĝi estas skribita. Ne estas neelparolataj literoj.
10. La akcento estas ĉiam sur la antaŭlasta silabo.
11. Vortoj kunmetitaj estas formataj per simpla kunigo de la vortoj (radikoj) (la ĉefa vorto staras en la fino); ili estas kune skribitaj kiel unu vorto, sed, en elementaj verkoj, disigitaj per streketoj (|). La gramatikaj finiĝoj estas rigardataj ankaŭ kiel memstaraj vortoj. Ekz. **vaporŝipo** estas formita de: **vapor**, **ŝip**, kaj **-o** (finiĝo de la substantivo).
12. Se en frazo estas alia nea vorto, la vorto **ne** estas forlasata. Ekz. **mi neniam vidis, mi nenion vidis**.
13. En frazoj respondantaj al la demando **kien?**, la vortoj ricevas la finiĝon de la akuzativo. Ekz. **kie vi estas?**, **tie** (en tiu loko); **kien vi iras? tien** (al tiu loko), **mi iras Parizon, Londonon, Varsovion, domon**.
14. Ĉiu prepozicio havas en Esperanto difinitan kaj konstantan signifon, kiu fiksas ĝian uzon; sed se ni devas uzi ian prepozicion kaj la rekta senco ne montras al ni, kiun prepozicion ni devas preni, tiam ni uzas la prepozicion **je**, kiu ne havas memstaran signifon; ekz. **ĝoji je tio**, **ridi je tio**, **enuo je la patrujo**, **malsana je la okuloj**. La klareco neniel suferas pro tio, ĉar en ĉiuj lingvoj oni uzas en tiaj okazoj iun ajn prepozicion, se nur la uzado donis al ĝi sankcion; en la internacia lingvo ĉiam estas uzata en similaj okazoj nur la prepozicio **je**. Anstataŭ la prepozicio **je** oni povas ankaŭ uzi la akuzativon sen prepozicio, se oni timas nenian dusencaĵon.
15. La tiel nomataj vortoj "fremdaj", t.e. tiuj, kiujn la plimulto de la lingvoj prenis el unu fremda fonto, estas uzataj en la lingvo internacia sen ŝanĝo, ricevante nur la ortografion kaj la gramatikajn finiĝojn de tiu ĉi lingvo. Tia estas la regulo koncerne la bazajn vortojn, sed ĉe diversaj vortoj de unu radiko estas pli bone uzi senŝanĝe nur la vorton bazan kaj formi la ceterajn derivaĵojn el tiu ĉi lasta laŭ la reguloj de la lingvo internacia. Ekz. **tragedio**, sed **tragedia**; **teatro**, sed **teatra** (ne: **teatricala**), k.t.p.
16. La finiĝo **-o** de substantivoj kaj la **-a** de la artikolo povas esti iafoje forlasataj kaj anstataŭataj de apostrofo pro belsoneco. Ekz. **Ŝiller'** (Schiller) anstataŭ **Ŝillero**; **de l' mondo** anstataŭ **de la mondo**; **dom'** anstataŭ **domo**.

ESPERANTO-ENGLISH DICTIONARY

All forms of the passive are rendered by the respective forms of the verb **est-** *to be* and the present or past passive participle of the required verb; the preposition used with the passive is **de** *by*. E.g. **ŝi estas amata de ĉiuj** *she is loved by every one* (present participle: the action is being done); **la pordo estas fermita** *the door is closed* (past participle: the action has already been done).

7. Adverbs are formed by adding **-e** to the root. The degrees of comparison are the same as in adjectives. E.g., **mia frato pli bone kantas ol mi** *my brother sings better than I*.
8. All prepositions take the nominative case.

C. GENERAL RULES

9. Every word is pronounced exactly as it is written. There are no silent letters.
10. The stress is always on the penultimate syllable.
11. Compound words are formed by the simple junction of roots, (the principal word standing last); they are written as a single word, but in elementary works may be separated by a small line (|). Grammatical endings are also considered as independent words. E.g. **vaporŝipo** *steamboat* is composed of the roots **vapor** *steam*, and **ŝip** *a boat*, with the substantival ending **-o**.
12. If in a sentence there is another negative word, the word **ne** is left out. E.g. **mi neniam vidis** *I never saw*, **mi nenion vidis** *I saw nothing*.
13. In phrases answering the question **kien?** *whither? to where?*, the words take the accusative. E.g. **kie vi estas?** *where are you?* **tie** *there* (in that place); **kien vi iras?** *where are you going?* **tien** *there* (to that place); **mi iras Parizon, Londonon, Varsovion, domon** *I am going to Paris, to London, to Warsaw, home*.
14. Every preposition in Esperanto has a definite and constant meaning, which fixes its use; but if we need to use some preposition, and it is not quite evident from the sense which it should be, then we use the preposition **je**, which has no definite meaning; e.g, **ĝoji je tio** *to rejoice over it*; **ridi je tio** *to laugh at it*; **enuo je la patrujo** *a longing for one's fatherland*; **malsana je la okuloj** *having a sickness of the eyes*. This does not diminish clarity in any way, for in every language different prepositions, sanctioned only by customary usage, are employed in these dubious cases; in the international language the preposition **je** alone is always used in similar cases. Instead of the preposition **je**, the accusative without a preposition can also be used, when there is no danger of confusion.
15. The so-called "foreign" words, i.e. words which the majority of languages have derived from the same source, undergo no change in the international language, save for taking on the orthography and grammatical endings of this language. Such is the rule with regard to basic words; but with various words derived from one root it is better to use only the basic word without change, and to form other derivatives from this according to the rules of the international language. E.g. **teatro** *theatre*, but **teatra** *theatrical*, (not **teatricala**), etc.
16. The ending **-o** of substantives and the **-a** of the article can sometimes be dropped and replaced by an apostrophe for the sake of euphony. E.g. **Ŝiller'** *Schiller* for **Ŝillero**; **de l' mondo** for **de la mondo** *of the world*; **dom'** for **domo** *house*.

AFFIXES

GRAMMATICAL ENDINGS
-a *adjective*: **ama** of love, loving; **telefona** telephonic.
-as *verb, present tense*: **mi amas** I love; **li telefonas** he telephones.
-e *adverb*: **ame** lovingly; **telefone** by telephone, telephonically.
-i *verb, infinitive*: **ami** to love; **telefoni** to telephone.
-is *verb, past tense*: **mi amis** I loved; **li telefonis** he telephoned.
-j *plural*: **novaj telefonoj** new telephones.
-n *accusative*: **mi amas lin** I love him; **li amas mian filon** he loves my son; **kien?** where to? whither?
-o *noun*: **amo** love; **telefono** a telephone.
-os *verb, future tense*: **mi amos** I shall love, I'll love; **li telefonos** he will telephone, he'll be telephoning.
-u *verb, imperative*: **amu!** love! **li telefonu** let him telephone.
-us *verb, conditional*: **mi amus** I would love (if...); **li telefonus** he would telephone.

PARTICIPIAL FORMATIVES
-ant- *present active participle*: **skribanta** writing.
-at- *present passive participle*: **skribata** being written.
-int- *past active participle*: **skribinta** having written.
-it- *past passive participle*: **skribita** written.
-ont- *future active participle*: **skribonta** going to write.
-ot- *future passive participle*: **skribota** going to be written.

OFFICIAL PREFIXES
There is no real criterion for distinguishing prefixes from other roots. All of the following are accordingly entered and exemplified in the body of the dictionary, together with other roots sometimes regarded as prefixes (such as **ĉef-**, **vic-**) and certain unofficial technical prefixes (such as **but-**, **mikro-**).

bo- *relative by marriage*, -in-law.
dis- *separation, dispersal*, dis-.
ek- *commencement, suddenness.*
eks- *former, late*, ex-.
ge- *both sexes taken together.*
mal- *direct opposite.*
mis- *wrongly*, mis-.
pra- *primordiality, remoteness of relationship.*
re- *return, repetition*, re-.

ESPERANTO-ENGLISH DICTIONARY

OFFICIAL SUFFIXES

-aĉ- *disparagement*: **domaĉo** hovel; **skribaĉi** scrawl.

-ad- *action, particularly prolonged, repeated, or habitual action*: **naĝado** swimming; **pafado** shooting; **kuradi** keep on running.

-aĵ- (1.) *a concrete manifestation of an abstraction*: **novaĵo** a novelty; (2.) *the external manifestation of an activity*: **segaĵo** sawdust; (3.) *a characteristic piece of behaviour*: **infanaĵo** a childish act; (4.) *the flesh of an animal*: **bovaĵo** beef.

-an- *member (of a group), inhabitant (of a place or country)*: **kursano** a course member; **vilaĝano** villager; **Kristano** Christian.

-ar- *collective, group*: **arbaro** wood, forest; **homaro** mankind.

-ĉj- *forms masculine pet-names, either on the root or more usually to a shortened part of it; thus, from* **Vilhelmo** William, *the pet-name is* **Vilĉjo, Vilheĉjo, Viĉjo** Will, Billy. *Note also* **paĉjo** Dad *from* **patro** father.

-ebl- *possibility*, -able, -ible: **legebla** legible; **portebla** portable.

-ec- *abstract name of quality*: **blankeco** whiteness; **profesoreco** professorship; **silkeca** silky.

-eg- *augmentative*: **bonega** excellent; **petegi** beseech.

-ej- *place allotted to or characterized by*: **kuirejo** kitchen; **lernejo** school.

-em- *disposition, tendency*: **komprenema** understanding; **parolema** talkative; **mortema** mortal.

-end- *passive obligation*, to be -ed, that must be -ed: **pagenda** payable.

-er- *small particle of a whole*: **panero** crumb; **ĉenero** link.

-estr- *leader, head*: **staciestro** station-master.

-et- *diminutive*: **dormeti** doze; **libreto** booklet.

-id- (1.) *the descendent of*: **Izraelido** Israelite; **reĝido** prince; (2.) *the young of an animal*: **hundido** puppy; **katido** kitten.

-ig- *causative*, make, render: **purigi** clean, purify; **ebligi** make possible; **bindigi** have bound; **starigi** stand *tr.*

-iĝ- become, get: **edziĝi** get married; **pliboniĝi** improve *intr.*; **enlitiĝi** get into bed; **ruliĝi** roll *intr.*

-il- *tool, implement, means*: **hakilo** axe; **ŝlosilo** key.

-in- *female*: **ĉevalino** mare; **patrino** mother.

-ind- *worthiness, merit*: **laŭdinda** praiseworthy; **aminda** loveable.

-ing- *socket, holder*: **glavingo** scabbard; **plumingo** pen-holder.

-ism- (1.) *theory, system*, -ism: **platonismo** Platonism; **protektismo** protectionism; (2.) *characteristic behaviour pattern*, -ism: **alkoholismo** alcoholism; **magnetismo** magnetism; **fetiĉismo** fetishism; **anglismo** anglicism.

-ist- *person habitually occupied with something*: (1.) *professional*: **instruisto** teacher; (2.) *enthusiastic amateur*: **biciklisto** cyclist; (3.) *adherent, partisan*: **marksisto** Marxist.

-nj- *forms feminine pet-names, either on the root or more usually to a shortened part of it; thus, from* **Sofio** Sophia, *the pet-name is* **Sonjo, Sofinjo** Sonya, Sophie. *Note also* **panjo** Mum, Mom.

-obl- *multiple*: **duobla** double; **kvaroble** fourfold.

-on- *fraction*: **duono** half; **sesono** sixth.

ESPERANTA-ANGLA VORTARO

-op- *collective numeral*: **unuope** one by one; **kvaropo** quartet.

-uj- *thing regularly filled with something*: (1.) *container, receptacle*: **monujo** purse; **knedujo** kneading-trough; (2.) *country*: **Anglujo** England; (3.) *tree*: **pomujo** apple tree (*although in this third sense a compound with* **-arb-**, *thus* **pomarbo**, *is perhaps preferable as less open to ambiguity*).

-ul- *person*: **junulo** youth, young man; **drinkulo** drunkard.

-um- *no fixed meaning*: **malvarmumi** catch cold; **plenumi** fulfil; **plandumo** sole (of shoe); **krucumi** crucify.

TECHNICAL AND UNOFFICIAL SUFFIXES

-ac- (*botany*) *name of family*: **rozacoj** Rosaceae.

-al-[1] (*botany*) *name of order*: **likopodialoj** Lycopodiales.

-al-[2] (*chemistry*) *aldehyde*: **etanalo** acetaldehyde.

-algi- (*medicine*) *pain*: **lumbalgio** lumbago.

-an- (*chemistry*) *paraffin hydrocarbon*: **pentano** pentane.

-at- (*chemistry*) *salt of -ic acid*: **nitrato** nitrate.

-ator- *piece of machinery*: **levatoro** hoist, lift; **generatoro** generator.

-ed- (*zoology*) *name of family*: **cervedoj** Cervidae.

-en-[1] (*chemistry*) *unsaturated hydrocarbon*: **propileno** propylene.

-en-[2] (*zoology*) *name of subfamily*: **mustelenoj** Mustelinae.

-esk- (*literary*) -esque: **japaneska** Japanesque.

-i- *name of a country, derived* (1.) *from that of a river or town*: **Alĝerio** Algeria; (2.) *from that of the inhabitant*: **Anglio** England (*Note: in spite of being rejected in favour of* **-ujo** *by the Lingva Komitato, this use of* **-io** *is extremely common, particularly for the names of East European countries*: **Ĉeĥoslovakio**, **Jugoslavio**, **Bulgario** *etc.*).

-icid- (*biology*) -icide, -killer: **herbicido** herbicide, weed-killer.

-id- (*chemistry*) -ide: **klorido** chloride.

-ik- (*chemistry*) *salt*, -ic: **ferika klorido** ferric chloride.

-il- (*chemistry*) *alkyl*, -yl: **butilo** butyl.

-ilion- *British, but not US*, -illion: **duiliono** 10^{12}, *British* billion, *US* trillion; **kviniliono** 10^{30}.

-in- (*chemistry*) *acetylenic hydrocarbon*, -yne: **butino** butyne.

-istik- *art, science, or skill, whose practitioner is an* **-isto**: **lingvistiko** linguistics.

-it-[1] (*chemistry*) *salt of -ous acid*: **nitrito** nitrite.

-it-[2] (*medicine*) *inflammation*, -itis: **apendicito** appendicitis.

-iv- *capability*: **pagiva** able to pay, solvent; **produktiva** productive.

-iz- -ize: (1.) *provide with*: **najlizi** furnish with nails, stud; (2.) *technical or scientific procedure*: **hipnotizi** hypnotize.

-metr- -(o)meter: **ampermetro** ammeter; **spektrometro** spectrometer.

-metri- -(o)metry: **spektrometrio** spectrometry.

-ograf- -ographer: **leksikografo** lexicographer.

-ografi- -ography: **leksikografio** lexicography.

-oid- -oid: **elipsoido** ellipsoid; [*also* **-ojd-**].

-ol- (*chemistry*) -OH *compound*: **etanolo** ethyl alcohol.

-olog- -ologer, -ologist: **leksikologo** lexicologist.

ESPERANTO-ENGLISH DICTIONARY

-**ologi-** -ology: **leksikologio** lexicology; **Esperantologio** the scholarly study of Esperanto, Esperantology.

-**om-** (*medicine*) *tumour*: **fibromo** fibroma.

-**on-** (*chemistry*) *ketone*: **propanono** propanone.

-**oskop-** -oscope: **spektroskopo** spectroscope.

-**oskopi-** -oscopy: **spektroskopio** spectroscopy.

-**oz-**[1] (*chemistry*) *salt*, -ous: **feroza klorido** ferrous chloride.

-**oz-**[2] (*medicine*) *disease*, -osis: **tuberkulozo** tuberculosis.

-**oz-**[3] *abundance of, full of*: **poroza** porous; *to avoid possible confusion with other senses of* -**oz-**, *forms with no suffix, or with* -**hav-** *or* -**riĉ-** *are to be preferred:* **pora**, **porhava**, **porriĉa** porous.

-**ul-** (*zoology*) *group of animals with a particular characteristic*: **mamulo** mammal; **rampulo** reptile (*This is probably best considered an extension of the ordinary sense of* -**ul-** *rather than a special technical suffix.*).

Note: this list is by no means exhaustive, particularly in the field of medicine. There are many terms, furthermore, whose analysis is uncertain in that they can be regarded either as derivatives, formed by affixation, or as separate roots—for example: **apendicito** (**apendic-ito**), **etileno** (**etil-eno**), **generatoro** (**gener-atoro**).

A

a name of the letter A.
Aarono Aaron.
Abadono Abaddon (biblical, a compartment of Gehenna).
abaĵuro lampshade.
abako abacus, ball frame, counting frame, calculating frame, chart.
abakteria abacterial.
abaktio abactio.
abampero abampere.
abandoni to relinquish.
abandonito abandoned person.
abandono abandonment, relinquishment.
abasido Abbasid.
Abaso Abbas.
abata abbatial. **abata jurisdikcio** abbacy.
abateco abbacy, abbotship.
abateja abbatial.
abatejo abbey.
abatina abbatial.
abatineja abbatial.
abatinejo abbey.
abatino abbess.
abatiso barricade of trees or branches, abatis.
abatlando abbacy.
abato abbé, abbot.
abazia abasic, abatic.
abazio abasia (inability to walk caused by lack of muscular coordination).
abceso abscess.
abdika abdication.
abdikado abdication.
abdikanto abdicant, abdicator.
abdikebla abdicable.
abdiki to abdicate, resign.
abdiko abdication.
abdomena abdominal.
abdomeno abdomen, belly, lower part of the body.
abdukcia abducent. **abdukcia muskolo** abductor.
abdukcii to abduct.
abdukcio abduction.
abduktado abduction.
abdukti to abduct.
abdukto abduction.
abduktoro abductor.
Abdulo Abdul, Abdullah.
abeke aback.
abela[1] Abel's, Abelian, commutative (group).
  abela kriterio Abel test.
abela[2] related to bees. **abela kolonio** bee colony, settlement.
abelaro swarm of bees.
abelbredado beekeeping.

abelbredisto bee keeper.
abelĉelaro beehive.
abelĉelo bee cell.
abeldomo apiary.
abeledoj Apidae.
abeleja apiarian.
abelejo apiary.
abelino queen bee.
abelisto beekeeper.
abelkesto beehive (box-style).
abelkolonio bee colony.
abelkorbo beehive (basket-style).
abelkulturado beekeeping.
abelkulturisto apiarist, beekeeper.
abelkulturo beekeeping.
abelmanĝulo bee-eater.
Abelo Abel, Abell.
abelo bee.
abelreĝino queen bee.
abelsvarmo swarm of bees.
abelŝedo bee-shed.
abeluja of a beehive.
abelujo beehive, hive.
abelujoforma beehive-shaped.
abelvakso beeswax.
abelveneno bee poison.
abelviro drone.
aberacia aberrant, deviant.
aberacii to deviate.
aberacio aberrance, aberrancy, aberration.
Aberdaŭgledo Milford Haven.
aberdenano Aberdonian.
Aberdeno Aberdeen.
Aberduro Aberdour.
Aberfeldo Aberfeldy.
Aberfojlo Aberfoyle.
Abergaveno Abergavenny.
Abergvaŭno Fishguard.
aberi to aberrate.
Abermaŭo Barmouth.
Abertaŭo Swansea.
abevilio Abbeville.
abĥaza Abkhazian.
Abĥazio Abkhazia.
abĥazo Abkhazian.
Abĥazujo Abkhazia.
abia deal.
abiarbaro fir forest, fir wood.
abiaro fir forest, fir wood.
Abida Abida.
abidarmo abhidharma.
abiejo fir forest, fir wood.
abietinacido abietin acid.
abietino abietin.
abieto spruce (tree), fir (tree).

1

abifrukto fir cone.
abikonuso fir cone.
Abimael Abimael.
Abimeleĥ Abimelech.
Abintono Abington.
abio Abies, fir (tree).
abioarbaro fir forest, fir wood.
abiofrukto fir cone.
abiogenezo abiogenesis.
abiokonuso fir cone.
abiopiceo Norway Spruce tree.
abiopinglo fir-needle.
abiotika abiotic.
abiotrofio abiotrophy.
abiozo abiosis.
abipiceo Norway Spruce tree.
abipinglo fir-needle.
abisena Abyssinian, Ethiopian.
Abisenio Abyssinia, Ethiopia.
Abiseno Abyssinian, Ethiopian.
Abisenujo Abyssinia, Ethiopia.
abisma abysmal.
abisme abysmally.
abismejo (the) abyss.
abismo abyss, chasm, gulf, precipice, oblivion.
abiturienta baccalaureate; related to high school graduation. **abiturienta diplomo** leaving certificate. **abiturienta ekzameno** final examination, leaving examination.
abiturientekzameno (secondary or high school) exit examination.
abiturientino femals certificated secondary school leaver, female high school graduate.
abituriento certificated secondary school leaver, high school graduate.
abjudiki to abjudicate.
abjudiko abjudication.
abĵurado abjuration.
abĵuri to abjure, abnegate.
abĵuro abjuration.
ablacia ablative. **ablacia aĝo** ablation age.
ablacii to ablate.
ablacio ablation.
ablaktaciado ablactation.
ablaktacio ablactation.
ablaktado ablactation.
ablakti to wean.
ablativa ablative.
ablativo ablative.
ablaŭto ablaut, apophony.
ablefario ablepharia, ablephary.
ablucio ablution.
abnegacia abnegation.
abnegacianto abnegator.
abnegacii to abnegate, deny oneself.
abnegacio abnegation, self-denial, renunciation.
Abnero Abner.
abnorma abnormal.
abnormaĵo abnormality.
abnorme abnormally.
abnormeco abnormality.
aboclibro book of ABCs.
aboco ABC, alphabet, basics, fundamentals, primer, rudiments.
abocolernanto abecedarian.
abocolibro book of ABCs.
abolanto abolisher.
abolebla abolishable.
aboli to abolish, abrogate.
abolicii to abolish, abrogate.
aboliciismo abolitionism.
aboliciisto abolitionist.
abolicio abolition, abrogation.
abolicionismo abolitionism.
abolicionisto abolitionist.
abolismo abolitionism.
abolisto abolitionist.
abolo abolition, abrogation.
abomaso rennet-stomach.
a-bombo atom bomb, atomic bomb, A-bomb.
abomena abominable, dismal, dreary, hideous, horrible, nasty, detestable, loathsome, revolting.
abomenadi to avoid, abhor.
abomenado abhorrence, abomination.
abomenaĵo abomination, atrocity.
abomenanto abominator.
abomene abominably.
abomeneco abomination.
abomenego strong aversion.
abomeni to abhor, abominate, detest, loathe.
abomeniga abhorrent.
abomenige abhorrently.
abomenigi to disgust, deter, repel.
abomeninda abhorrent, abominable, alien, awful, hideous, horrible, revolting.
abomenindaĵo abhorrence, abomination, atrocity, horror.
abomeninde abominably.
abomenindeco abominableness.
abomenindulo abominable person.
abomeno abhorrence, abomination, horror, disgust, loathing.
abomenulo villain, scoundrel.
abona subscription-related.
abonantaro subscription base.
abonanto subscriber.
abonantoj subscribers.
abonbileto commutation ticket, season ticket.
abone by subscription, with a subscription.
abonebla available by subscription.
abonejo subscription office.
aboni to have a subscription, subscribe to.

abonigi to sign someone up for (a subscription).
abonilo subscription form.
abonkarto commutation ticket, season ticket.
abonkosto subscription price.
abono subscription.
abonpago subscription payment.
abonprezo subscription price.
aborala aboral.
aborigena aboriginal.
aborigeneco aboriginality.
aborigeno aborigine, aboriginal (person).
aborta abortive.
abortaĵo miscarriage, abortion, stillborn or aborted foetus.
aborteco abortiveness.
abortema inclined to abort.
aborti to abort, fail, miscarry.
abortiga abortion-inducing.
abortigi to abort, quash, wreck, bring about an abortion.
abortigilo method of abortion.
abortigisto abortionist.
abortigo abortion.
abortitaĵo aborted or stillborn foetus.
abortito aborted foetus.
aborto abortion, failure, miscarriage.
abortrimedo abortifacient.
abortulo aborted child.
abrada abrasive.
abradaĵo abrasive substance.
abradi to abrade.
abrado abrasion.
abrahama Abrahamic, Abrahamitic.
Abrahamo Abraham.
abrakadabro abracadabra.
abrakio abrachius.
Abram Abram.
Abramo Abram.
abrazia related to an abrasion.
abrazii to abrade.
abraziiĝi to cave in.
abraziilo abrasive.
abrazio abrasion.
abreviacio abbreviation.
abrikota related to apricots.
abrikotarbo apricot tree.
abrikotbrando apricot brandy.
abrikotfloro apricot blossom.
abrikotfolio apricot leaf.
abrikoto apricot.
abrikotujo apricot tree.
abrogacia abrogative.
abrogacianto abrogator.
abrogacii to abrogate.
abrogacio abrogation.
abrogi to abrogate.
abrogo abrogation.

abrotano southernwood (Artemisia abrotanum).
Abruco Abruzzo (region of Italy).
abrupta abrupt.
abruptaĵo something abrupt, an abrupt thing.
abrupte abruptly.
abrupteco abruptness, off-handedness, rudeness.
abrupto haste, abruptness.
abruptulo abrupt person.
Abruzoj Abruzzo (region of Italy).
abscedi to discharge pus.
abscesa abscessed.
abscesi to abscess.
absceso abscess.
abscisa akso axis of abscissae, x-axis.
absciso abscissa, x-coordinate.
absejli to abseil.
absida apsidal.
absideto apsidiole.
absido apsis, apse.
absinta absinthic, absinthinian, abstemious, abstinthial.
absintaĵo absinth.
absintismo absinthism.
absintlikvoro absinth.
absinto absinth, wormwood.
absoluta absolute, stark, unconditional.
   absoluta adreso absolute address. **absoluta alteco** height above sea level. **absoluta aŭdo** absolute pitch. **absoluta ekstremumo** absolute extremum. **absoluta monopolo** absolute monopoly. **absoluta sonsento** absolute pitch. **absoluta valoro** absolute value.
absolute absolutely.
absolute konverĝa absolutely convergent.
absolute ne not at all, by no means, anything but. **absolute ne!** absolutely not!
absoluteco absoluteless.
absolutigi to absolutize.
absolutisma absolutist.
absolutismo absolutism.
absolutisto absolutist.
absoluto an absolute.
absolva absolutory, absolvent, absolving.
absolvanto absolver.
absolvebla absolvable.
absolvi to absolve, acquit, pardon.
absolvo absolution, acquittal.
absorba absorbent (for a person's attention).
absorbi to absorb, engross, occupy, preoccupy. **absorbita de** absorbed in.
absorbiga absorbing. **absorbiga pensado** absorbing thoughts.
absorbige absorbingly.

absorbiĝi to be absorbed, engrossed. **absorbiĝi en sia laboro** to be absorbed in one's work.
absorbiĝo bemusement, immersion, preoccupation.
absorbilo absorbent.
absorbita de absorbed in.
absorbiteco bemusement, immersion, preoccupation.
absorbo absorption.
absorbospektro absorption spectrum.
abstemia abstemious.
abstemio teetotalism, (total) abstinence.
abstemiulo abstainer.
abstina abstemious.
abstinado abstinence.
abstinanto teetotaler, total abstainer.
abstineco abstinence.
abstinema abstemious, abstinthial.
abstinemo will to abstain.
abstinenco abstinence, teetotalism, total abstinence.
abstinenculo abstainer (from pleasures), teetotaler, total abstainer.
abstini to abstain.
abstino abstention.
abstinulo abstainer (from pleasures).
abstrakta abstract. **abstrakta datumtipo** abstract data type. **abstrakta komputilo** abstract machine.
abstraktado abstraction.
abstraktaĵo abstraction.
abstraktatema abstract. **abstraktatemaj pensantoj** abstract thoughts.
abstrakte abstractly.
abstrakteco abstractness.
abstrakti to abstract.
abstraktigi to make abstract.
abstraktismo abstractism.
abstrakto abstract.
absurda absurd.
absurdaĵo absurdity, nonsense, rubbish.
absurde absurdly.
absurdeco absurdity.
absurdo absurdity.
Abŝalomo Absalom.
Abudabio Abu Dhabi.
Abudabo Abu Dhabi.
Abuĝo Abuja.
abulejo wild beehive.
abulio lack of will.
abunda abundant, affluent, ample, copious, plentiful, profuse, rich, bountiful.
abunde abundantly.
abundeco abundance.
abundega superabundant.
abundege very abundantly.
abundegi to superabound.
abundegiĝo bonanza.
abundego cornucopia, superabundance, surfeit.
abundi to abound.
abundo abundance, plenty, bounty.
abundokorno cornucopia.
abutilo abutilon (genus of broadleaf evergreens).
abutmento supporting wall, abutment.
abvolto abvolt.
acefala acephalous.
acefalo acephalan, acephalous organism.
acefaloj acephalans.
acenafteno acenaphthene.
acera maple, of a maple.
aceracoj maple family.
acerba acerbic, acid, acrid, harsh, sour, tart.
acerbe acridly, harshly, sourly.
acerbeco acerbity.
acerbigi to acerbate, acidulate.
acerbranĉo maple branch, branch of a maple tree.
acero maple, sycamore.
acersiropo maple syrup.
acersukero maple sugar.
aceta acetic.
acetablo acetabulum.
acetabula acetabular.
acetabulo acetabulum.
acetacido acetic acid.
acetaldehido acetaldehyde.
acetatigi to acetylate.
acetato acetate.
acetbakterio acetobacteria.
acetigi to turn into vinegar.
acetigo acetification, acetifying.
acetil- acetyl-.
acetila acetyl.
acetileno acetylene.
acetili to acetylate.
acetilizi to acetylate.
acetilkolino acetylcolene.
acetilo acetyl.
acetilsalicila acido acetylsalicylic acid.
acetilsalicilatacido acetylsalicylic acid.
acetilsalicilato acetylsalicylate.
aceto acetic acid, vinegar.
acetometro acetometer, acetimeter.
acetona acetonic.
acetonemio acetonemia.
acetonilo acetonyl.
acetono acetone.
acetonurio acetonuria (excessive acetone in the urine).
acida acerbic, acid, sour, tart, acidic. **acida ĉerizo** morello. **acida indico** acid number, acid value.
acidadolĉa bittersweet.
acidaĵo acid.
acidbano acid bath.

acide

acide sourly, tartly, acidicly.
acideco acidity.
acideta tart, sour, aciduous.
acidetigi to make sour.
acidetigo acidulation.
acidgrado acidity.
acidi to be acid, be sour.
acidigebla acidifiable.
acidigi to acidify, sour. **acidigi lakton** to sour milk.
acidigo acidification.
acidiĝi to acidify, (grow) sour, become acidified.
acidiĝo acidification.
acidimetrio acidimetry.
acidimetro acidometer.
acidimuna acid-proof.
acidizi to acidulate.
acidkremo sour cream.
acidmezurado acidimetry.
acidometrio acidimetry.
acidmordi to acid burn.
acidnombro acid value, acid number.
acido acid.
acidofara acid-forming.
acidometro meter for acid.
acidoza acidotic.
acidozo acidosis.
acidpluvo acid rain.
acidrezista acid-fast, acid-proof, acid-resistant.
acidrostaĵo sauerbraten (sour roast).
acidsalo acid salt.
acidsukeraĵo acid drop.
acidujo acid container.
acikla acyclic.
acina acinar, acinose, acinous, aciniform.
acino acinus.
acinoforma aciniform.
acinoza acinar, acinose, acinous, aciniform.
acipenseredoj Acipenseridae (a family of fish).
acipenserformaj Acipenseriformes (order of fish).
acipensero sturgeon.
Aciso Acis (mythological character).
Acoroj the Azores.
activa active.
active actively.
activo asset.
aĉa lousy, rotten, poor in quality, ugly, wretched, no good.
aĉaĵaro horrible year.
aĉaĵo disgusting thing.
aĉakaturo acciaccatura, crushed note, short grace note.
aĉe miserably, poorly.
aĉetadi to buy, keep buying, continue to buy.

adapti

aĉetado acquisition, purchase, shopping, purchasing.
aĉetaĵo acquisition, purchase.
aĉetakiri to acquire, buy, purchase.
aĉetanta regiono market, outlet.
aĉetantino female shopper, female buyer.
aĉetanto buyer, client, purchaser.
aĉetĉareto shopping cart, shopping trolley.
aĉetebla for sale.
aĉetejo shop, store.
aĉetfervoro interest.
aĉeti to acquire, buy, purchase, take over. **aĉeti aŭkcie** to buy at a public sale.
aĉetiĝi to be(come) purchased.
aĉetinto buyer.
aĉetisto buyer, purchasing agent, purchaser (professional).
aĉetkorbeto shopping basket.
aĉetlisto shopping list.
aĉeto acquisition, buy, purchase, taking over.
aĉetpovo buying power, purchasing power.
aĉetrulkorbo shopping cart.
aĉetsako carrier bag.
aĉetsumo cost, cost of purchase, purchase money.
aĉettaŝo shopping bag.
aĉetumi to go shopping.
aĉeŭleo Acheulean era of prehistory.
aĉi to be awful, rotten, terrible.
aĉigi to cause to be bad, cause to be worse.
aĉiĝi to become bad, become terrible, become worse.
aĉodora malodorous, bad-smelling, stinking, smelly.
aĉulo wretch (despicable person).
Ada Ada.
ada continual.
adaĝa adagio.
adaĝe adagio.
adaĝete adagietto.
adaĝo adagio.
adalberto Adalbert.
Adalberto Adalbert.
adama Adamic, Adamical.
adamantino enamel.
adamasko damask.
adamito adamite.
Adamo Adam.
adampomo Adam's apple.
Adampomo Adam's apple.
adamtero ruddle.
adapta adaptative.
adaptado adaptation.
adaptaĵo adaptation.
adaptebla adaptable.
adaptebleco adaptability.
adapti to accommodate, adapt, adjust, attune, fix, fit, mount, place, tune. **adapti por orkestro** to orchestrate, score.

5

adaptigo accommodation.
adaptiĝebla adaptable.
adaptiĝema adaptable.
adaptiĝemo adaptability.
adaptiĝi to accommodate oneself, adapt oneself.
adaptiĝo adaptation, adjustment.
adaptilo adapter, controller.
adaptinto adaptor.
adaptita adapted.
adaptiteco adaptedness.
adapto adaptation, adjustment. **adapto por orkestro** orchestration.
adaptometrio adaptometry.
adaro Adar.
Adaro Adare.
adasismo suffix rhyme.
Adbeel Adbeel.
AdE → **Akademio de Esperanto**.
ade continually, continously, repeatedly, often.
adekvata adequate, appropriate, sufficient.
adekvate appropriately, in a fitting way, adequately.
adekvateco adequacy.
Adelaido Adelaide.
Adelajdo Adelaide.
Adelilando Adélie Land.
Adelo Adele.
Adelstano Aethelstan, Æþelstán.
aden- adeno- (denoting a gland).
Adena Aden. **Adena Golfo** Gulf of Aden.
adeneca adenoidal.
adenektomio adenectomy.
adenino adenine.
adenito adenitis.
Adeno Aden.
adeno gland, ade-.
adenoida adenoidal.
adenoidaĵoj adenoids.
adenoidismo adenoidism.
adenoidito adenoiditis.
adenoido adenoid.
adenoidoj adenoids.
adenokarcinomo adenocarcinoma.
adenomo adenoma.
adenopatio adenopathy.
adenovirusa adenoviral.
adenoviruso adenovirus.
adenozilo adenozyl.
adenozino adenozine.
adenpatio adenpathy.
adepti to adapt, fit.
adeptigi to indoctrinate, recruit.
adepto acolyte, adept, adherent, supporter, initiate, follower.
adhera adhesive, (point) of adherence, (point) of closure, limit (point), sticky.
adheraĵo adherent, adherence, closure.

adhereco adherence, adhesiveness.
adherema adhesive.
adheremo adhesiveness.
adherenzo adhesive.
adheri to adhere, stick to.
adherigaĵo adhesive.
adhero adherence, adhesion.
adherumi to adhere.
adherumo adhesion.
adhezi to adhere.
adi to keep (on), continue.
adiabata adiabatic.
adiabato adiabatic condition.
adianto maidenhair fern.
adiaŭ adieu, farewell, bye, good-bye.
adiaŭa goodbye, farewell.
adiaŭbankedo farewell banquet.
adiaŭdeklamo farewell speech.
adiaŭdiri to say good-bye.
adiaŭdiro (word of) good-bye, saying good-bye.
adiaŭe in good-bye, as a farewell, in parting.
adiaŭi to say farewell, say good-bye, take leave from, log out.
adiaŭkisi to kiss good-bye.
adiaŭo farewell, good-bye.
adici to add.
adicia additive. **adicia grupo** additive group.
adiciato addend.
adiciebla additive.
adicieska simbolo adding operator.
adicii to add (up), count in.
adiciilo adding machine.
adicimaŝino adding machine.
adicio addition.
Adiĝo Adige river.
adinamia adynamic.
adipa adipose.
adipeco adiposity, adiposeness.
adipo adeps, animal fat.
adipociro adipocere.
adipoĉelo adipocyte, adipose cell.
adipogenezo adipogenesis.
adipoza adipose.
adipozo adipose.
Adis-Abebo Addis Abeba.
Adisabebo Addis Ababa.
adisona Addisonian. **adisona malsano** Addison's disease.
Adisono Addison.
adito adytum.
adjektiva adjectival.
adjektivigi to make into an adjective, turn into an adjective.
adjektivo adjective.
adjekto adjunct, adverbial.
adjudanto adjutant, aide-de-camp.
adjudike by tender.

adjudiki to invite tenders (for), put out to tender.
adjudiko (invitation to) tender.
adjunkta adjunct.
adjunkto adjunct, assistant, aide, aide-de-camp.
adjuracio adjuration.
adjutanteco adjutancy.
adjutanto adjutant, aide.
Adma Adama.
adminiklo adminiculum.
adminisracia administrative.
administra administrative. **administra aparato** machine of government. **administra jaro** financial year. **administra ofico** stewardship. **administraj kostoj** administrative expenses.
administracia administrative.
administracie administratively.
administraciejo administration.
administracio administration, management.
administrada informsistemo management information system.
administrado administration, governance, management, running.
administrantaro administration, management, administrative unit.
administranto administrator, manager.
administraro administration, administrative staff.
administratoro administrator, manager.
administre administratively.
administrejo administrative office.
administri to administer, manage.
administristaro administration, management.
administristino female administrator.
administristo administrator.
administro administration, management.
admira admiring.
admiradi to admire.
admirado admiration.
admiraĵo admiration.
admirala of an admiral, of an admirality.
admiralaro admiralty.
admiraleco admiralship.
admiraledzino admiral's wife.
admiralejo admiralty.
admiralitato admiralty.
admiralo admiral.
admiralŝipo admiral.
Admiraltoj Admirality Islands.
admirantino (female) admirer.
admiranto admirer.
admire admiringly.
admirego awe.
admiri to admire.
admirinda admirable.

admirinde admirably.
admiro admiration.
admitanco admittance, reciprocal impedance.
admona admonitory.
admonanto admonisher.
admoni to admonish, advise, censure, exhort, scold, reprimand, tell off.
admonletero dunning letter, (debt) collection letter.
admono admonition, exhortation.
adoba adobe.
adobo adobe.
adoleska adolescent.
adoleskanteco adolescence.
adoleskantino adolescent, teenage girl.
adoleskanto adolescent.
adoleskeco adolescence, puberty.
adoleski to be an adolescent.
adolesko adolescence.
adoleskulino adolescent.
adoleskulo adolescent.
Adolfo Adolf.
adolta of an adult.
adolteco adulthood.
adoltiĝi to come of age, become an adult.
adoltiĝo becoming an adult, maturity.
adolto adult.
adonido pheasant's eye.
Adoniso Adonis.
adoniso apollo.
Adono Adonis.
adopta adoptive. **adoptaj gepatroj** foster parents.
adoptado adoption.
adoptanto adopter.
adoptato adoptee.
adopte by adoption.
adoptebla adoptable.
adopti to adopt.
adoptinto adoptive parent.
adoptita adopted, adoptive.
adoptito adoptee, adoptive child.
adopto adoption.
adoptulo adoptive child.
adora adoring.
adoradi to worship, adore.
adorado adoration, worship.
adorantino adorer, female adorer, worshipper, female worshipper.
adoranto adorer, worshipper.
adoratino adored one.
adorato adored one.
adorejo centre of worship, place of worship.
adori to adore, worship, idolize.
adorinda adorable.
adorinde adorably.
adorindeco adorableness, adorablility.

adorkliniĝi to prostrate oneself, bow in worship.
adoro adoration, worship.
adoroado worship.
adrenalino adrenaline.
adrenalo adrenal gland, suprarenal gland.
adresado addressing.
adresanto shipper, sender.
adresaparato addressing machine, addressograph.
adresareto mailing list.
adresaro address book, address list, directory.
adresato addressee, receiver, recipient.
adresatribuo address assignment.
adresbuso address bus.
adresebla addressable.
adresetikedo address label.
adresi to address (a letter, person), send (by mail).
adresiga maŝino addressing machine.
adresigilo addressing machine.
adresilo address pointer, addressing machine.
adresinto addresser, sender.
adresita addressed.
adresito addressee, person addressed.
adreskarto dispatch note.
adreslibro directory.
adresmaŝino addressing machine.
adresmetodo addressing technique.
adresnivelo location counter.
adreso address.
adresobuso address bus.
adresparto address field.
adrespresilo addressing machine.
adresreĝistro address register.
adresspaco address space.
adressubstituo indirect addressing.
adresŝanĝo change of address.
adresulo addressee.
Adria Adriatic. **Adria Maro** Adriatic Sea.
Adriano Adrian.
Adrianopolo Adrianople.
adriatika Adriatic. **Adriatika Maro** Adriatic, Adriatic Sea.
Adriatiko Adriatic, Adriatic Sea.
adsorba adsorbent, adsorptive.
adsorbado adsorption.
adsorbaĵo adsorbate.
adsorbanto adsorbent.
adsorbeco adsorption.
adsorbi to adsorb.
adsorbiga adsorbent.
adsorbige adsorbently.
adsorbiĝi to adsorb.
adsorbiĝo adsorption.
adsorbilo adsorbent.
adsorbo adsorbtion.
adstringa acerbic, acid, astringent, harsh, tart.

adstringantaĵo astringent.
adstringe astringently, harshly.
adstringeco acerbity.
adstringi to make dry.
adstringilo astringent.
adukcia adducent. **adukcia muskolo** adductor.
adukcii to adduct.
adukcio adduction.
adukti to adduct.
adukto adductor.
aduktora adductor.
aduktoro adductor.
adulacio adulation.
adulado adulation.
Adulamano Odollamite.
adulanto adulator.
adulario moonstone.
adulema adulatory.
aduli to adulate.
adulta adulterous.
adultado adultery.
adultaĵo adult.
adultanto adulterer.
adulteca adulterous.
adultema adulterous.
adultera adulterant.
adulteri to adulterate, dilute, weaken.
adulterilo adulterant.
adultero adulteration.
adulti to commit adultery.
adultigi to cause someone to commit adultery.
adultintino adulteress, adulterous woman.
adultinto adulterer.
adulto adultery.
adultulino adulteress.
adultulo adulterer.
advaŭso advowson.
advekcio advection.
adventa Adventual.
adventica adventitious.
adventico advential.
adventismo Adventism.
Adventismo Adventism.
adventisto Adventist.
Adventisto Adventist (religious denomination).
adventiva adventive.
adventivulo adventive.
Advento Advent.
advento advent.
adverba adverbial.
adverbe adverbially.
adverbeco adverbiality.
adverbigi to adverbialize.
adverbo adverb.
adversa adverse.
adverse adversely.

adversulo adversary, antagonist.
advokata advocatory, barristerial. **advokata profesio** the legal profession.
advokataĉo bad lawyer, immoral lawyer.
advokataro advocacy.
advokateco advocation.
advokatejo law office.
advokati to advocate.
advokatiĝi to be accepted to the bar.
advokato advocate, barrister, counsel, intercessor, lawyer, solicitor, attorney.
adzo adze.
aedo aoidos.
aera aerial, overhead, airborne. **aera defendo** air defence. **aera rezisto** air resistance.
aeramaso air mass.
aerarmea bazo air base.
aerarmeo air force.
aeratako air raid, air strike.
aerbano air bath.
aerbatalo air battle.
aerbazo air base.
aerbezona in need of air.
aerbezonanta in need of air.
aerblovilo blower.
aerblovo draught, gust of air.
aerboato airboat.
aerbremso air brake.
aerbrosi to airbrush.
aerbroso airbrush.
aerbuso airbus.
aercirkuligo air circulation.
aerdefenda artilerio ack-ack, anti-aircraft guns.
aerdefendo air-defence, anti-aircraft defences.
aerdinamiko aerodynamics.
aerdukto air duct.
aere aerially, airy, through the air. **aere malvarmigata** air-cooled.
aereca airy.
aereldukto air outlet.
aerellasa vlavo bleeding valve.
aeremio air embolism.
aerendukto air intake.
aereskadro air squadron.
aerfendo air pocket (aviation).
aerfiltrilo air filter.
aerfloto air fleet.
aerfluo air flow.
aerfoto air view.
aerfotografado aerial photography.
aerfotomapo aerial map.
aerfreŝigilo air freshener.
aerfusilo air rifle.
aerĝustigilo air regulator.
aerhaveno aerodrome, airport, airdrome.
aerhelico airscrew.

aeri to air.
aerimuna air tight.
aerizolita anaerobic.
aerkamero air chamber.
aerkastelo castle in the sky.
aerkavo air pocket.
aerkerna air-bearing (as an air-bearing spindle).
aerklapo air valve.
aerklimatizita air-conditioned.
aerkluzo airlock.
aerkompresoro air compressor.
aerkondiĉigilo air conditioner.
aerkondukilo air duct.
aerkoridoro air corridor, air lane.
aerkuseno air cushion.
aerlinia piloto airline pilot.
aerlinio airline, airway.
aerlito air mattress.
aermalpurigo air pollution.
aermalsana airsick.
aermalsano airsickness.
aermapo aerial map.
aermaso air mass.
aermatraco air mattress.
aermeĥanikisto flight engineer, flight mechanic.
aernavigado aeronautics, aviation.
aernetolera air-intolerant.
aernetoleranta air-intolerant.
aero air.
aerobatika acrobatic.
aerobatike acrobatically.
aerobatiko acrobatics.
aerobia aerobic, aerobiotic.
aerobie aerobically.
aerobiko acrobatics.
aerobio aerobe, aerobium.
aerobiologio aerobiology.
aerobuso airbus.
aeroĉelo aerocyst, air cell.
aerodefendo air defence.
aerodinamika aerodynamic, streamlined.
aerodinamike aerodynamically.
aerodinamiko aerodynamics.
aerodino aerodyne.
aerodromo aerodrome, airdrome, airfield.
aerofagio aerophagy.
aerofiziko aerophysics.
aerofloto air fleet.
aerofobio aerophobia.
aeroforo acrophore.
aerofoto air view.
aeroframo airframe.
aeroglita having the property of gliding on air.
aerografio aerography.
aerogramo aerogram, air letter.
aerohaveno airport.

aerokondukilo air duct.
aerolita aerolitic.
aerolito meteoric stone, meteorite, aerolite.
aerolitologio aerolithology.
aerologia aerologic, aerological.
aerologiisto aerologist.
aerologio aerology.
aerologo aerologist.
aeromancio aeromancy, austromancy.
aerometria aerometric.
aerometrio aerometry.
aerometro aerometer.
aeronaŭta aeronautic, aeronautical.
aeronaŭtika aeronautic, aeronautical.
aeronaŭtike aeronautically.
aeronaŭtiko aeronautics.
aeronaŭto aeronaut, airman.
aeronavigado aeronautics.
aeropafilo blowgun.
Aeropago areopagus.
aeroplano aeroplane, airplane, plane.
aeroporta aeriferous.
aeropoŝto air mail, airmail.
aeropremo air pressure.
aeropumpilo air pump.
aeroskopo aeroscope.
aerosolo aerosol.
aerospaco air space.
aerostatika aerostatic.
aerostatiko aerostatics.
aerostato (air) balloon, aerostat.
aeroterapio aerotherapeutics.
aerpafilo air gun.
aerpejzaĝo airscape.
aerpejzaĵo aerial view.
aerpeniko airbrush.
aerpilkego balloon (plaything).
aerpirato skyjacker.
aerpistolo airgun.
aerplano aeroplane.
aerpolucio air-pollution.
aerpompilo air pump.
aerponto air bridge, airlift.
aerportado airlift.
aerporti to airlift.
aerpoŝta letero air letter, aerogram.
aerpoŝte via air mail.
aerpoŝtmarko air mail stamp.
aerpoŝto airmail.
aerprema bremso air brake.
aerpremo air pressure.
aerprovizo air supply.
aerpumpilo air pump.
aerputo air well.
aerrapido airspeed.
aerregado air supremacy.
aerregilo air regulator.
aersako airbag.
aersoldato airman.

aerspaco airspace.
aerstevardino air hostess, stewardess.
aerŝakto air shaft.
aerŝarĝo air freight.
aerŝipo airship.
aerŝtono aerolite, meteorite, meteor.
aertaksio air taxi.
aertiro drag (in aviation).
aertolera air-tolerant.
aertoleranta air-tolerant.
aertransportado air transport.
aertransporto air transport.
aertruo air pocket.
aertubo inner tube, tube.
aerujo air canister.
aeruma airy. **aeruma krado** air grid.
aerumado aeration.
aerumi to aerate, air out, give an airing, ventilate.
aerumilo aerator.
aervalvo air valve.
aerveturado aeronautics, aviation, air travel.
aerveturanto aeronaut.
aerveturilo airship.
aerveziketo air blister, air bubble.
aerveziko air bladder.
aervido air view.
aerviva aerobic.
aervojo airway.
afabla amiable, nice, affable, friendly, good-natured, kind, user-friendly.
afablaĵo a courtesy.
afable kindly, affably.
afableco affability, kindness, friendliness.
afablega most charming.
afablege in a very friendly manner.
afablulo affable person.
afagio aphagia.
afaniptero aphaniptera (the group of insects that includes the flea).
Afaro Sof Omar Caves of Ethiopia.
afazia aphasic.
afazio aphasia.
afaziulo aphasiac.
afekcia emotional, sentimental.
afekcie emotionally, sentimentally.
afekcii to affect, influence.
afekciita affected.
afekciite affectedly.
afekcio affection, affect.
afekta affected, artificial, assumed, prim.
afektado affectation.
afektaĵo affectation, pose, mannerism.
afekte primly, showily, artifically. **afekte milda** bland, sugary.
afekteco affection.
afektema affected, artificial, assumed, pretentious.
afekteme showily.

afekti to be affected, pose, put on airs, feign, pretend.
afektita inflated.
afektiva affective, emotional.
afekto affectation.
afektulino emotional woman.
afektulo poseur, show-off.
afelio aphelion.
afera related to business, related to objects/things.
afereca business-like.
aferema business-like.
aferenta afferent.
afereto little thing, small matter.
aferezo a word formed by truncating its initial sound.
aferisto businessman, businessperson.
aferkoncerneco relevance.
aferlisto agenda.
afero affair, business, deal, case, matter, thing, object. **afero de gusto** matter of taste.
aferpaperoj business mail.
aferstato state of affairs.
aferŝarĝito chargé d'affaires.
aferulo businessman.
afervojaĝo business trip.
Afgana Afghan.
afgana Afghan.
afganhundo Afghan, Afghan hound.
Afganino Afghan woman.
Afganio Afghanistan.
Afganistano Afghanistan.
Afganlando Afghanistan.
Afgano Afghan.
afgano afghani.
Afganujo Afghanistan.
afhanhundo Afghan hound.
afidavito affidavit.
afidedo aphid.
afidedoj Aphididae.
afido aphid, aphis, greenfly.
afidomanĝa aphidivorous.
afiksa affixal.
afiksi to attach, put up.
afikso affix.
afina affine, having affinity. **afina ebeno** affine plane. **afina geometrio** affine geometry. **afina hiperebeno** affine hyperplane. **afina rekto** affine line. **afina rotacio** affine rotation. **afina spacio** affine space. **afina spaco** affine space. **afina subspacio** affine variety. **afina subspaco** affine variety.
afinacii to refine (metal).
afinacio refining (metallurgy).
afineco affinity.
afini to have affinity.
afino affinity.

afiso greenfly.
afiŝejo bulletin board, bulletin board system.
afiŝhomo sign-carrier, placard-carrier, poster-carrier.
afiŝi to placard, post, post up. **afiŝi mesaĝon** post.
afiŝisto bill poster.
afiŝkolono advertising pillar.
afiŝo notice, placard, poster, bill, sign, article.
afiŝtabelo bulletin board.
afiŝtabulo billboard, notice board.
aflabla amiable.
aflable amiably.
aflikta distressing, grievous, painful, troublesome.
afliktado affliction, ordeal, trial.
aflikte painfully.
aflikti to afflict, grieve, distress.
afliktiĝi to become afflicted.
afliktiĝo sadness.
afliktita sad.
aflikto affliction.
afonia aphonic, aphonous.
afonio aphonia.
aforisma aphoristic.
aforisme aphoristically.
aforismo aphorism.
aforisto aphorist.
aframerika Afro-American.
aframerikano Afro-American.
afranki to prepay, put on stamps, frank.
afrankita post-paid, stamped.
afrankite postage prepaid.
afranko postage.
afranktarifo postal rates.
afrazia Afro-Asian.
afraziano Afro-Asian.
afrika African.
afrikanino African woman.
afrikano African.
afrikansa Afrikaans.
Afrikansa Afrikaans. **afrikansa lingvo** Afrikaans, Afrikaans language.
afrikanso Afrikaner, Afrikaans (language).
afrikata affricative.
afrikato affricate, affricative.
afrikazia Afro-Asian.
afrikigi to africanize.
afrikismo africanism.
Afriko Africa.
afrito afreet, afrite.
Afrodita Aphrodite.
afrodita of Aphrodite.
Afrodito Aphrodite.
afrodito Aphrodite.
afrodizia aphrodisiac.
afrodiziaĵo aphrodisiac.
afrodiziako aphrodisiac.
afrodizigilo aphrodisiac.

afrodiziiga aphrodisiac.
afrodiziigaĵo aphrodisiac.
afrodiziigilo aphrodisiac.
afrodizio sexual excitement, arousal, aphrodisia.
afta aphthous ulcer. **afta febro** foot and mouth disease.
afto aphtha, aphthous ulcer, mouth ulcer.
aftozo hoof-and-mouth disease.
afusto carriage, gun carriage.
afustovosto gun carriage stock.
aga active.
agaca acerbic, acrid, tart.
agace acerbically, acridly, tartly.
agaceco acerbity.
agaci to aggravate, annoy, irritate, set on edge.
agaciga tart.
agaciĝi to be set on edge.
agaco irritant.
agadi to act, occur, take place.
agado action, activity.
Agago Agag.
agama officious.
Agamedo Agamedes (mythology).
Agamemno Agamemnon.
Agamemnono Agamemnon.
agamia agamic (biology).
agamio Agami heron, Chestnut-bellied heron.
agamo agamid lizard.
aganto agent.
agao aga.
agapanto agapanthus (flower).
agapo agape, love feast.
agaragaro agar, agar-agar.
agarika agaricaceous, agaricoid.
agarikacoj Agrucis family.
agariko agaricus (species of mushroom).
agaro agar.
agata agate.
agatido agathis (genus of evergreens, botany).
agatigi to agatize.
agato agate.
Agatoklo Agathocles.
agava agave.
agavbrando tequila.
agavo agave, American aloe.
agavvino agave wine.
agawo agave.
agebla operative.
Agejno Again River.
agema active.
ageme actively.
agemo activity.
agendo agenda, appointment book, engagement diary, memorandum book, notebook.
Agenoro Agenor.

agenta agential.
agenteco agency.
agentejo agency.
agento agent.
agenturo agency.
agerato whiteweed.
Agesilauso Agesilaus.
agi to act, move, take action, do. **agi laŭ** to act on, act upon, follow, observe. **agi sub la influo de** to act under the influence of.
agigi to actuate.
agistrodono moccasin.
agita agitational, inflammatory.
agitacio agitation, excitement, flutter.
agitadi to shake (up).
agitado agitation, commotion.
agitanto activist, agitator.
agitatoro agitator.
agitfolio polemic pamphlet.
agitgrupo action committee, action group.
agiti to abet, agitate, incite, stir up.
agitiĝi to become agitated.
agitiĝo agitation, commotion.
agitilo agitator.
agitismo activism.
agitisto agitator.
agitkomisiono action committee, action group.
agito agitation, commotion, disturbance, excitement, flutter, turmoil.
agitvorto slogan (esp. political).
agla of an eagle. **agla nazo** aquiline nose.
agleca aquiline, eagle-like. **agleca nazo** aquiline nose.
aglejo eyrie.
aglibero elbow room.
aglido eaglet.
Aglo Aquila.
aglo eagle.
aglobuteo eagle buzzard.
aglofiliko eagle fern.
aglofloro eagle flower.
agloko action spot.
aglokula eagle eye.
aglomera agglomerative.
aglomerado agglomeration.
aglomeraĵo agglomerate.
aglomerato agglomeration.
aglomeri to agglomerate, mass.
aglomeriĝi to agglomerate.
aglomero agglomeration.
aglonaza beak-nosed.
aglonesto eyrie.
aglutina agglutinative.
aglutini to agglutinate, bond.
aglutiniĝi to agglutinate.
aglutinilo binding agent.
aglutinino agglutinin.
aglutino agglutination.

aglutinogeno agglutinogen.
agmaniero behaviour.
agnata agnate, agnatic.
agnateco agnation, kinship.
agnato agnate (paternal relative).
Agneso Agnes.
Agnio Agni, Hindu god of fire.
agnoski to acknowledge, recognize (as official).
agnoskita acknowledged, recognized.
agnosko acknowledgment.
agnostika agnostic.
agnostikismo agnosticism.
agnostikisto agnostic.
agnostikulo agnostic.
agnozio agnosia.
Agnuso Agnus Dei.
ago achievement, act, action.
agogia agogic.
agonia agonizing.
agonii to be dying, suffer the throes of death, agonize, be near death.
agonio agony, death throes.
agonistiko agonostics.
agorafobio agoraphobia.
agordaĵo setting (as in a computer setting).
agordaro profile.
agorde in unison.
agordforko tuning fork.
agordi to configure, customize, tune, attune.
agordiĝemo manageability, tractability.
agordiĝi to be tuned (up).
agordilo tuner (device), tuning fork, setup program, (software), wizard (software).
agordisto tuner (person).
agordo accord, agreement, consonance, customization, options, setup, settings, mood, tuning.
agordoforko tuning fork.
agordotubo tuning pipe.
agoro agora.
agpotencialo action potential.
agrabla agreeable, enjoyable, lovely, nice, pleasant.
agrablaĵo fun things or activities.
agrable agreeably, comfortably, pleasantly.
agrableco pleasantness.
agrablega very pleasant, extremely agreeable.
agrabligi to make pleasant, make comfortable, make pleasing.
agrablo amenity.
agrablodora pleasant-smelling.
agrafa fermilo hooks and eyes.
agrafi to clamp together, clasp.
agrafio agraphia.
agrafo binding, clasp, hook, fastener.
agramatismo agrammatism.
Agrao Agra.

agrara agrarian, agricultural, farm-.
agrega aggregate.
agregacio agrégation (French academic qualification).
agregaĵo aggregate.
agregato aggregate.
agregi to aggregate.
agregiĝi to aggregate.
agresa aggressive.
agresanto aggressor, attacker, assailant.
agrese aggressively.
agresema aggressive.
agreseme aggressively.
agresemo aggression.
agresi to aggress, attack, commit aggression.
agresinto aggressor, attacker, assailant.
agresiva aggressive.
agreso aggression.
agresonto aggressor.
agrikultura agricultural. **agrikultura ekspozicio** agricultural exhibition. **agrikultura instruado** agricultural instruction. **agrikultura lernejo** agricultural school. **agrikultura produktaĵo** agricultural product.
agrikulturista ligo farmers' union.
agrikulturisto agrarian, farmer.
agrikulturo agriculture, farming, tillage.
agrimonio agrimony.
Agripino Agrippina.
Agripo Agrippa.
agro arable land, cultivated field, field.
agrobakterio agrobacteria.
agrobiologio agrobiology.
agrokultivo agriculture.
agrokultura agricultural.
agrokulturisto agrarian, farmer.
agrokulturo agriculture.
agronomia agricultural.
agronomiisto agronomist.
agronomio agriculture, agronomics, agronomy.
agronomisto agronomist.
agronomo agriculturist, agronomist.
agropiro couch grass, dog grass.
agrostemo corn cockle.
agrostido bent grass.
agroturismo farm holidays.
agutio agouti (species of rodent).
aĝa aged.
Aĝario Adzharia.
aĝi to be the age of.
Aĝinkurto Agincourt.
aĝio agio, exchange premium.
aĝiotado stock-jobbing.
aĝioti to speculate in stocks.
aĝiotisto stock jobber.
aĝioto stock-jobbing.
aĝlimo age limit.

aĝo age (how old someone or something is).
aĝolimo age limit.
aha aha.
Ahasvero Ahasuerus, the Wandering Jew.
Ahazio Ahaziah.
Ahazo Ahaz.
Ahijaho Ahijah.
Ahimeleĥo Ahimelech.
Ahitofelo Ahithophel.
ahmadismo Ahmadism.
Ahmedo Achmed.
Ahuramazdo Ahura-Mazda.
aĥ (interjection).
Aĥabo Ahab.
aĥaja Achaean.
aĥajano Achaean, Achaian.
Aĥajo Achaea, Achaia.
Aĥaŝveroŝ Ahasuerus.
Aĥaŝveroŝo Ahasuerus, Ahashverosh.
aĥemenida Achaemenian.
Aĥemeno Achaemenes.
Aĥeno Aix-la-Chapelle.
Aĥerono Acheron.
aĥi to gasp, whimper.
aĥila tendeno Achilles tendon.
aĥilkalkano Achilles' heel.
Aĥilo Achilles.
aĥiltendeno Achilles' tendon.
Aĥmedo Ahmed.
Aĥnaŝino Achnasheen.
aideso AIDS.
aidoso AIDS.
aidosulo AIDS patient.
aidozo AIDS.
aikido aikido.
ailanto Ailanthus, tree of heaven.
aina Ainu.
Aino Ainu.
Aja Aia.
Ajaco Ajax.
Ajaio Aeaea.
Ajakso Ajax.
ajapano ayapana.
ajatolaho ayatollah.
ajatolo ayatollah.
ajdeso AIDS.
ajgena eigen.
ajgeno eigenvalue.
ajgenspaco eigenspace.
ajgenspaco characteristic subspace.
ajgensubspaco characteristic subspace, eigensubspace.
ajgenvaloro eigenvalue.
ajgenvektoro eigenvector.
Ajitiso Aeetes.
ajkso Aix.
ajla garlicky.
ajlero garlic bulb.
ajlo garlic, leek.
ajlobulbero garlic clove.
ajlobulbo garlic bulb.
ajmara Aymarian.
ajmaro Aymara.
Ajmeo Amy.
ajn ever.
ajna arbitrary, any (at all).
ajne arbitrarily.
ajnlitera wildcard.
Ajnsvorto Ainsworth.
ajnulo John Doe (some arbitrary person).
ajnuo Ainu.
Ajro Ayr.
ajugo bugle.
ajurvedo Ayurveda.
ajuto nozzle, jet.
ajzi to bend.
aĵeto little thing.
aĵgenro inanimate gender, neuter gender.
aĵo thing.
aĵoj stuff, things.
aĵura open-work, pierced-work, perforated, fretted.
Ak. → **Akademio**.
a.K. → **antaŭ Kristo** before Christ, BC.
akacio acacia.
Akad Achad.
akada Akkadian.
akadano Akkadian.
akademia academic.
akademiano academician, academian, academist, academy member.
akademie academically.
akademio academy. **Akademio de Esperanto** Esperanto Academy.
akademiulo academic, scholar.
akadia Acadian.
akadiano Acadian.
Akadio Acadia.
Akado Accad, Akkad.
Akadujo Acadia.
akadujo Akkadia.
Akajo Achaea.
akajunukso cashew nut.
akaĵuarbo cashew.
akaĵunukso cashew nut.
akaĵuo cashew apple, cashew-nut.
akaĵupomo cashew apple.
akaĵuujo cashew tree.
Akan Acan.
Ak-ano → **akademiano**.
akanto acanthus.
akantopagro bream.
akapari to corner (the market), monopolize, usurp.
akaparo hoarding, monopoly.
akaro maggot, mite.
akaŝa akashic.
akcela accelerative.

akcelado

akcelado acceleration.
akcelajo accelerant, accelerator.
akcelanta accelerative.
akcelanto promoter, promotor.
akcelego spurt.
akcelenzo accelerant, accelerator.
akceli to accelerate, advance, further, hasten, promote, speed up.
akceliĝi to accelerate, pick up.
akceliĝo acceleration.
akcelilo (super)collider, accelerator (pedal), particle accelerator.
akcelmezurilo accelerometer.
akcelo acceleration.
akcelometro accelerometer.
akcelpedalo accelerator (pedal), gas pedal.
akcenta accented, emphasized, stressed.
akcentado accentuation.
akcentega emphatic.
akcentege emphatically.
akcentegi to accentuate, emphasize.
akcentego emphasis.
akcenti to accentuate, emphasize, accent, stress.
akcentita accented, emphasized, stressed.
akcento accent, stress, emphasis.
akcentperdo loss of accent.
akcentsigno stress mark.
akcepta accepting.
akceptadi to keep accepting.
akceptado accepting.
akceptaĵo acceptance.
akceptanto acceptor.
akcepte acceptingly.
akceptebla acceptable.
akcepteble acceptably, reasonably.
akceptebleco acceptability.
akcepteblo acceptability.
akcepteco admissibility.
akceptejo reception (area, desk).
akceptema receptive.
akcepteme receptively.
akcepti to accept, accredit, admit, receive, take (in). **akcepti la respondecon pri** to account for. **akcepti oficiale** to do the honours. **akcepti solene** to welcome. **akcepti vizitantojn** to entertain, receive.
akceptigi to win acceptance for. **akceptigi obstine** to drive through.
akceptiĝi to be accepted.
akceptiĝo reception.
akceptinda acceptable.
akceptindeco acceptability, susceptibility.
akceptistino receptionist.
akceptisto receptionist.
akceptita accepted.
akceptkvitanco receipt.
akcepto acceptance, admission, reception.
akceptoro acceptor.

akiremo

akceptosalono reception room.
akceptpoŝtĝirilo giro payment slip.
akceptsalono reception room.
akcesora accessory, secondary. **akcesora fako** subsidiary subject. **akcesora nervo** accessory nerve. **akcesora tono** overtone.
akcesoraĵo accessory, side issue.
akcesorajoj accessories.
akcesorulo accessory.
akcia joint-stock. **akcia kompanio** company with share capital, joint-stock company, corporation. **akcia societo** company with share capital, joint-stock company, corporation.
akciaro share capital.
akcidenco accidence, adjunct.
akcident accident.
akcidenta accidental.
akcidente accidentally.
akcidentema accident-prone.
akcidenti to have an accident.
akcidentiĝi to suffer an accident.
akcidento accident, mishap.
akcidentrisko accident risk.
akcihavanto shareholder.
akcimerkato stock-market.
akcio corporate share, share (finance), stock. **akcio de navigacia kompanio** shipping share. **akcioj** shares, stock.
akcipitredoj Accipitridae family.
akcipitro accipiter, goshawk, hawk.
akcipitroherbo hawkweed.
akciuleco shareholdership.
akciulo shareholder.
akcizi to levy an excise tax.
akcizisto actionary.
akcizo excise, excise duty, excise tax.
akĉento accent.
a.K.E. → **antaŭ la Komuna Ero** before the Common Era, BCE.
akebio akebi (eastern Asiatic vine).
akejlognato bitterling.
Akemeno Achaemenes.
Akeno Aix-la-Chapelle.
akeo sloth.
Akerono Acheron.
Akerso Akers.
akileo Achillea, yarrow, milfoil.
akilkalkano Achilles' heel.
Akilo Achilles.
akiltendeno Achilles' tendon.
akinezio akinesia.
akiradi to acquire, obtain.
akirado acquirement, acquisition.
akiraĵo accession, acquisition, gain, booty.
akirebla obtainable.
akirema acquisitive.
akiremo acquisitiveness.

akiri

akiri to achieve, acquire, attain, get, obtain. **akiri lertecon en** to acquire skill in. **akiri pene** to reclaim.
akiristo sales representative, travelling salesman.
akiritaĵo possessions, acquisitions, belongings.
akiro accession, acquisition, asset, acquirement, attainment, gain, spoil (booty).
aklamado acclamation.
aklame by acclamation.
aklami to acclaim, applaud, hail.
aklamo acclaim, acclamation, approval.
aklimatizi to acclimatize.
aklimatiziĝi to acclimate, acclimatize.
akmeo acme.
akna spotty, zitty.
akneo acne.
aknero pimple, blemish, spot, zit.
akno acne, pimple, blemish, spot, zit.
aknozo acne.
akolio acholia.
akolito acolyte.
akomodebla adjustable.
akomodi to accommodate, adapt, adjust.
akomodiĝi to accommodate, adjust.
akomodiĝo accommodation.
akomodo accommodation.
akompana attendant.
akompanadi to accompany.
akompanado accompaniment.
akompanaĵo accompaniment.
akompanantaro entourage, suite, train.
akompanantino chaperon, duenna.
akompananto accompanist, companion.
akompanate de accompanied by.
akompane al accompanied by.
akompani to accompany, attend. **akompani varte** to chaperon.
akompanisto accompanist.
akompano accompaniment, escort.
akonitino aconitine, aconitic.
akonito aconite, monkshood, friar's caps, wolf's bane.
akorda compatible, consistent. **akorda kun** in accordance with.
akorde in accordance. **akorde al** in accordance with. **akorde kun** in accordance with.
akordi to (be in) accord, agree, match. **akordi kaze kaj nombre** to agree in number and gender.
akordiga conciliatory.
akordigebla reconcilable.
akordigi to place in accord, bring into agreement.
akordigo conciliation.
akordiĝema manageable, tractable.

akrocianozo

akordiĝi to accord, come in accordance, come to an agreement.
akordionisto accordionist.
akordiono accordion.
akordo accord, accordance, agreement, chord, concord, concurrence, concurrency, consonance.
akoro calamus.
akra abrasive, acrimonious, acute, lurid, sharp, keen, poignant. **akra sento** penetration. **akra sono** grating noise. **akra tono** tartness.
akraema bitter.
akraflanka angular, sharp-edged.
akraĵo cutting edge, blade, peak, point.
akratona abrasive, acrid, acrimonious, sharp-toned, shrill, snappy, tart.
akratoneco acrimony.
akre sharply, abrasively.
akreaĵo acreage.
akrearo acreage.
akreco acerbity, acrimony, acuity, sharpness.
akreditaĵo credentials.
akreditato authorized representative.
akrediti to accredit.
akreditilo credentials.
akreditivi to arrange a credit.
akreditivo letter of credit, request for credit.
akredito accreditation.
akrega very sharp.
akreo acre.
akresona shrill.
akretema acrimonious.
akretona sharp-toned, piercing.
akrevida lynx-eyed.
akrevidanto sharp-sighted person, person with sharp vision.
akridedo acridid.
akridedoj Acrididae.
akrido Acridium, grasshopper, locust.
akrigi to sharpen, whet.
akrigilo sharpener.
akrigrimeno strop.
akrila acrylic. **akrila acido** acrylic acid. **akrila rezino** acrylic resin.
akrilato acrylate.
akrilo acryl.
akrilonitrilo acrylonitrile.
akro acre.
akrobata acrobatic.
akrobatado acrobatics.
akrobataĵo acrobatics.
akrobate acrobatically.
akrobatiko acrobatics.
akrobato acrobat.
akrocefala acrocephalic.
akrocefaleco acrocephalia.
akrocefalulo acrocephalic.
akrocianozo acrocyanosis.

akrodora acrid.
akrogena acrogenic, acrogenous.
akromata achromatic.
akromateco achromaticity, achromatism.
akromatigado achromatization.
akromatigi to achromatize.
akromatino achromatin.
akromatopsia colour blind.
akromatopsio achromatopsia, colour-blindness.
akromegalia acromegalic.
akromegalio acromegaly.
akromio acromion.
akroniĉo acronychia, yellow-wood.
akronimo acronym.
Akropolo Acropolis.
akrostiĥo acrostic.
akrostika acrostic.
akrostiko acrostic.
akrotero acroter, acroterium.
akrulino cat.
akrupi to buck.
aksa axial.
Aksa el-Aqsa-mosque.
akse axially.
aksela axillar, axillary.
akselburĝono axillary bud.
akselkavo armpit.
akselo armpit, crotch (of a tree), underarm.
aksesoraĵo accessories.
aksingo hub, nave, stock (of a wheel), socket.
aksinito axinite.
aksinomancio axinomancy.
aksiologio axiology.
aksioma axiomatic.
aksiomaro axiom system, axiomatic system.
aksiomo axiom. **aksiomo de indukto** axiom of complete induction. **aksiomo de matematika indukto** axiom of complete induction.
aksisa axial.
aksiso axis.
aksisoido axis, axis deer.
akslagro axle bearings.
akso axis, axle, pivot, spindle, alliance.
aksoido axoid.
aksokrucoj axes of coordinates.
aksolotlo axolotl.
aksono axon.
aksopinto pivot, spindle.
aksujo bearing, pillow-block.
aktaro dossier.
aktebero baneberry.
akteo baneberry.
aktia of Actium.
aktina actinic.
aktinio actinium; sea-anemone.
aktiniserio actinium series.
aktinismo actinism.

aktiniumo actinium.
aktinofago actinophage.
aktinoida actinide.
aktinoido actinide.
aktinokemio actinochemistry.
aktinolito actinolite.
aktinologio actinology.
aktinometra actinometric.
aktinometrio actinometry.
aktinometro actinometer.
aktinomiceto actinomycete.
aktinomicetozo actinomycosis.
aktinomiko actinomycete.
aktinomikozo actinomycosis.
aktinono actinon.
aktinoterapio actinotherapy.
Aktio Actium.
aktisto actuary, recorder, clerk.
aktiva active, in action. **aktiva voĉo** active voice.
aktivaĵo activity, something active.
aktive actively.
aktiveco activity, vigor.
aktiviganto activating agent, activator.
aktivigenzo activating agent, activator.
aktivigi to activate, put on, start, switch on, turn on.
aktivigilo activator.
aktivigo activation.
aktiviĝi to act up.
aktivismo activism.
aktivisto activist.
aktivo active (voice), assets.
aktivoj assets.
aktivularo activists.
aktivulo activist.
akto act, certificate, diploma, document, deed.
aktora actor's.
aktorado recitation, acting.
aktoraro acting company, acting troupe.
aktori to act.
aktorino actress.
aktoro actor.
aktuala contemporary, current, present, present-day, topical, up-to-date, live. **aktuala malfinio** actual infinity.
aktualaĵo topic.
aktuale at present.
aktualeco topicality.
aktualigi to update.
aktualigo updating.
aktuaria actuarial. **aktuaria scienco** actuarial science.
aktuario actuary.
aktuaro actuary.
aktujo brief case, portfolio.
akuala topical, up to date.
akuleo aculeus.

akumeno acumen.
akumula accumulative.
akumulado accumulation.
akumulaĵo accumulation.
akumulanto accumulator.
akumulatorejo battery room.
akumulatoro accumulator, battery, storage battery, rechargeable battery.
akumulejo accumulator.
akumuli to accumulate, heap, pile up, stack, hoard.
akumuliĝa accumulation (point), cluster (point).
akumuliĝanta accumulative.
akumuliĝi to accumulate.
akumuliĝo accumulation.
akumulilo accumulator, battery, storage battery.
akumulinto accumulator.
akumulo accumulation.
akumulonto accumulator.
akupunkturisto acupuncturist.
akupunkturo acupuncture.
akurata accurate, on time, prompt, punctual, exact, precise,.
akurate exactly, sharp.
akurateco accuracy, exactitude, precision, exactness, punctuality.
akustika acoustic. **akustika gitaro** acoustic guitar. **akustika modemo** acoustic modem.
akustikaujo resonance box.
akustiko acoustics.
akuŝa maternity.
akuŝantino woman in labour, woman giving birth.
akuŝarto birthing technique.
akuŝbufo midwife toad, alytes.
akuŝdoloro labour pain.
akuŝejo birthing centre, maternity ward (of a hospital, e.g.).
akuŝi to (be in) labour, be in the process of giving birth.
akuŝigi to deliver, cause to be born, induce labour.
akuŝigistino midwife, obstetrician.
akuŝigisto obstetrician.
akuŝiĝa labour, relating to childbirth.
akuŝiĝo labour, time of giving birth.
akuŝilo forceps.
akuŝintino woman who has just given birth.
akuŝistino midwife, person assisting in the delivery of an infant.
akuŝisto obstetrician.
akuŝlito childbed.
akuŝo accouchement, childbirth, delivery.
akuŝoĉambro lying-in room.
akuŝologio obstetrician.
akuŝpeno labour.

akuta acute, penetrating.
akutangula acute (acute-angled).
akutangulo acute angle.
akute sharply, acutely.
akuteco acuteness.
akutimigi to accustom.
akuto acute accent (´).
akuza accusatory.
akuzado accusation.
akuzaĵo accusation, charge, complaint, indictment.
akuzakto bill of indictment.
akuzanto accuser.
akuzativa accusative.
akuzativigi to put into the accusative.
akuzativo accusative. **akuzativo de tempo** accusative of time.
akuzato accused.
akuzi to accuse, allege, charge. **akuzi pri** to accuse of, charge with, impeach of, indict for, tax with.
akuzisto accuser, prosecutor.
akuzito accused, defendant.
akuzo accusation.
akva aquatic, of water, aqueous, watery.
akvado watering.
akvafalo waterfall.
akvafortado etching.
akvafortaĵo etching.
akvaforti to etch.
akvaforto etching, aqua-fortis.
akvamarina aquamarine.
akvamarino aquamarine.
akvaraneo water spider.
akvarelo aquarelle, watercolor painting.
akvario aquarium.
akvaro the waters.
akvatintaĵo aquatint.
akvatinto acid washing, aquatint.
akveca aqueous, watery.
akveco wetness, moisture.
akvedukto aqueduct.
akvemetita alluvial.
akvenergio hydroenergy.
akvero drop, drop of water.
akvi to irrigate, water.
akvifoliacoj Aquifoliaceae.
akvifolio holly.
akvilegio aquilegia, columbine.
akvilo watering can.
Akvilono Aquilon.
akvimuna watertight, waterproof.
Akvisto Aquarius (zodiac).
Akvitanio Aquitaine.
akvitano Aquitanian.
Akvitanujo Aquitaine.
akvo water.
akvobaraĵo dam.
akvobarilo weir.

akvoblua water-blue.
akvobubalo water buffalo.
akvocervo sambar.
akvoĉefkondukilo water-main.
akvodinamiko hydrodynamics, fluid dynamics.
akvodislimo water parting, watershed, divide.
akvodivenisto water-diviner.
akvodividejo watershed.
akvodukto aqueduct.
akvoenergio hydroenergy.
akvofalego cataract.
akvofalo waterfall, cascade.
akvofarbo water colour.
akvofluejo watercourse.
akvofonto spring.
akvoglaso water glass.
akvoguto drop, drop of water.
akvohorloĝo water clock.
akvoimuna waterproof, watertight.
akvokirleto backwater.
akvokirlo whirlpool.
akvokloŝo diving bell.
akvokoko coot.
akvokondukilo hose, pipe.
akvokonduko aqueduct.
akvokonduktilo aqueduct.
akvokreso watercress.
akvokultivado aquaculture, aquiculture.
akvokulturo aquaculture.
akvokuraco hydropathy.
akvolilio water lily.
akvomalsano dropsy.
akvomarko watermark.
akvomelono watermelon.
akvomoligilo water-softener.
akvonaĝulo aquanaut.
akvonecesejo water closet.
akvopentraĵo watercolor.
akvopipo water pipe, bong.
akvopistolo water-pistol.
akvoplaneo aquaplane.
akvoplanto aquatic plant.
akvopoloo water-polo.
akvoprovizi to irrigate, provide water to.
akvopulmo aqualung.
akvoputo wellspring.
akvorado water wheel.
akvoralo water rail.
akvorezervujo reservoir.
akvoriĉa abounding in water.
akvosciencisto hydrologist.
akvoscienco hydrology.
akvoskiado water-skiing.
akvoskianto water-skier.
akvoskii to water-ski.
akvoskio water-ski.
akvosoldato water soldier.

akvostacio water station, water tower.
akvoŝprucilo sprinkler.
akvoŝtopilo dam.
akvoŝvelo dropsy.
akvotaksio water taxi.
akvotelero marsh pennywort.
akvotrairi to wade.
akvotrinkiga for watering, for providing drinking water.
akvotruo pool.
akvotubo drain, water-pipe.
akvoturnejo maelstrom, whirlpool.
akvoturniĝo eddy.
akvoturno whirlpool (in water).
akvoturo water tower.
akvovaporo vapour.
akvoveturilo water vehicle.
akvovojo waterway.
akvujego reservoir.
akvujo cistern, tank, water tank, reservoir, water body, basin.
akvumado watering.
akvumi to flush, drench, irrigate, water, rinse.
akvumilo watering can.
akvumtubo water hose.
akzerci to exercise, practice.
akzui iun pri murdo to accuse someone of murder.
al at, to, toward, towards. **al donacita ĉevalo oni buŝon ne esploras** don't look a gift horse in the mouth. **al Kristnasko** at Christmas (time). **al la afero!** to business!.
al si reciproke to one another.
ala alar.
alabama Alabaman, Alabamian.
alabamano Alabaman, Alabamian.
Alabamo Alabama, Alabama River.
alabastra alabaster.
alabastro alabaster.
Aladeno Aladdin.
Aladina kavo Aladdin's cave.
Aladina lampo Aladdin's lamp.
Alaho Allah.
alaĵo addendum.
alambiko alembic.
Alandinsuloj Aalands Islands.
alanino alanine.
Alano Allan.
Alanponto Bridge of Allan.
alaranĝebla adaptable.
alaranĝi to adapt, adjust.
alarma alarming. **alarma novaĵo** alarming (piece of) news.
alarmbremso communication cord.
alarme alarmingly.
alarmejo battle station.
alarmi to alarm, raise the alarm, sound the alarm.

alarmilo alarm.
alarminstalajo alarm.
alarmisto alarmist.
alarmo alarm, alert.
alarmpafo warning shot.
alarmsignalo alarm, alarm signal.
alarmsireno alarm siren.
alarmsonorilo alarm bell.
alarmŝtuparo fire escape.
alaska Alaskan. **Alaska Duoninsulo** Alaska Peninsula. **Alaska Golfo** Gulf of Alaska.
alaskano Alaskan.
Alasko Alaska.
alastrimo alastrim.
alaŭdedoj Alaudidae, larks, passeriformes.
alaŭdfalko hobby, wet-nurse.
alaŭdo lark, skylark.
alaŭdosprono delphinium, larkspur, knight's-spur.
albana Albanian. **albana lingvo** Albanian, Albanian language.
albanino Albanian, Albanian woman.
Albanio Albania.
albano Albanian.
Albanujo Albania.
albatiĝi al bang into, bump into.
albato collision.
albatredoj albatrosses, procellariformes.
albatro albatross.
albatroso albatross.
albedo albedo.
albergo inn, hotel.
Albertio Alberta.
Albertlago Lake Albert.
Alberto Albert.
albigensa Albigensian.
albigensismo Catharism (religious movement in the 12th and 13th centuries).
albigenso Albigensian.
albineco albinism, albinoism.
albinisma albinistic.
albinismo albinism.
Albino Albin.
albino albino.
Albiono Albion.
albito albite.
albizio Albizzia (a tree genus).
albo alb.
alboji to bark at, bay at.
albordigi to bring to shore.
albordiĝa haveno port of call.
albordiĝejo landing stage, pier.
albordiĝi to land.
Albreĥto Albert.
albruli to burn.
albugineo albuginea.
albugo albugo.

albumeno albumen, white of egg, endosperm (of seeds).
albumfolio album page.
albumina albuminous.
albumino albumin.
albuminoida albuminoid.
albuminoido albuminoid.
albuminurio albuminuria, Bright's disease.
albumkovrilo album cover.
albumo album.
albumozo albumose.
alburno[1] alburnum, sapwood.
alburno[2] alburnus, bleak (type of fish).
alcedo halcyon, kingfisher.
alcelafo hartebeest.
alceli to chase, hunt after, hunt for, pursue.
alceliri to zero in.
alcentrigi to centre, centralize.
alcentrokura centripetal.
alceo hollyhock.
Alcibiado Alcibiades.
alcionedoj Alcedinidae (family of birds).
alciono halcyon, kingfisher.
alĉapo headpiece, covering.
alĉemilo lady's mantle, rosacea.
Aldebarano Aldebaran.
Aldeburgo Aldeburgh.
aldehida aldehydic.
aldehido aldehyde.
aldermano alderman.
Aldernejo Alderney.
aldhobojo cor anglais.
aldirekti to head for.
aldiri to address, speak to, add.
aldisto alt, contertenor.
aldo alto, contralto (voice), viola.
aldona additional, supplementary.
aldonado addition.
aldonaĵo addendum, addition, additive, appendage.
aldone additionally, in addition. **aldone al mi** in addition to me. **aldone al tio ke** in addition to the fact that.
aldonfolioj addendum.
aldoni to add (to), append, supplement.
aldoni akvon al to dilute, weaken (with water).
aldoniĝi to accrue.
aldoniĝo accrual.
aldonita accompanying.
aldoniteco devotion, self-sacrifice.
aldono addendum, addition, adjunct, appendix, rider, supplement.
aldonvalora imposto value added tax, VAT.
aldosterono aldosterone.
aldoviolono viola.
aldozo aldose.
aldulino alto, contralto.

aldulo

aldulo alto.
aldviolono viola, alto.
aleatora aleatory.
aleatore by chance.
Aleĉjo Alex.
aleego avenue.
Aleganoj Alleghanys.
alegoria allegoric.
alegorie allegorically.
alegorio allegory.
alegre allegro.
alegrete allegretto.
alegreto allegretto.
alegro allegro.
aleksandra verso alexandrine.
aleksandria alexandrian.
Aleksandrianismo Alexandrianism.
Aleksandriano Alexandrian.
Aleksandrio Alexandria.
Aleksandro Alexander. **Aleksandro la Granda** Alexander the Great.
aleksandro alexandrine verse.
aleksino alexin.
Aleksio Alexis.
Alekso Alex, Alexei.
alektromancio alectromancy.
alelekti to co-opt.
alelo allele.
alemana Alemannic.
aleno awl.
aleo avenue, passage, way, (garden) walk, path, alley, boulevard.
Alepo Aleppo.
alergena allergenic.
alergeno allergen.
alergia allergic.
alergie allergically.
alergiiga allergenic.
alergiisto allergist.
alergio allergy.
alergiologio allergology.
alero penthouse, shed.
alerono aileron.
alesti to be present.
alesto attendance, presence.
aletŝraŭbingo wing-nut.
aleuta Aleutian. **Aleutaj Insuloj** Aleutian Islands.
aleutano Aleut.
aleuto Aleut. **Aleutoj** Aleutian Islands.
aleŭrito candlenut tree.
aleŭromancio aleuromancy.
Aleŭtoj Aleutian Islands.
aleveni to arrive.
alezi to ream, bore (a cylinder).
alezilo reamer.
alfa alpha (Aα). **Alfa Centaŭro** Alpha Centauri. **alfa-partiklo** alpha particle.

algebra

alfa-radiado alpha radiation. **alfa testado** alpha testing.
alfabeta alphabetical. **alfabeta ordigo** alphabetical order. **alfabeta ordo** alphabetic.
alfabete alphabetically.
alfabetigi to alphabetize.
alfabetigo alphabetization; teaching someone to read.
alfabeto alphabet.
alfabetumi to spell.
alfabetumo ABC book, book of ABCs.
alfaldi to tuck up.
alfanumera alphanumeric.
alfanumere alphanumerically.
alfao alpha.
alfaradioj alpha rays.
alfarado adaptation.
alfari to accommodate, adapt.
alfaŭki to bark at.
alfenido alfenide (an alloy of nickel and silver electroplated with silver).
alfiksado application.
alfiksaĵo appendage.
alfiksi to affix, attach. **alfiksi al** to attach to.
alfiksiĝi to attach.
alfiksita attached.
alfiksitaĵo attachment, attached object.
alfikso attachment.
alfitomancio alphitomancy.
alfluanto tributary (of a river).
alflugdirekto approach path, approach route.
alflugi to approach, fly.
alflui to come flocking in, flow towards, rush towards, stream towards, incoming.
alfluo flow, influx, flood, flux, high tide, incoming tide.
alfo[1] alpha (Aα).
alfo[2] stipa grass, hafta, esparto grass (Stipa tenacissima).
Alfonso Alphonse.
Alfonzo Alphonse, Alphonso.
alforĝi to weld.
alformi to form (to fashion).
alformiĝi en to transform (oneself) into.
alfortikigi to fasten, attach.
Alfredo Alfred.
alfrontado confrontation, facing.
alfrontema confrontational.
alfronteme confrontationally.
alfronti to confront, face.
alfundigi to deposit.
alfundiĝi to sink.
alga algal.
algardi to guard.
algebra algebraic. **algebra dualo** full dual space. **algebra frakcio** algebraic fraction.

algebre

algebra prezento algebraic form. **algebra strukturo** algebraic structure.
algebre algebraically. **algebre fermita** algebraically closed (field).
algebristo algebraist.
algebro algebra.
algida algid.
alglui to paste, paste up, placard, post, post up.
algluiĝema sticky.
algluiĝemo adhesiveness.
algluiĝi to stick.
algluiĝo adhesion.
algo alga, seaweed.
algoj algae.
Algolo Algol.
algologiisto algologist.
algologio algology.
algologo algologist.
algonkena Algonquian, Algonquin.
algonkeno Algonquian, Algonquin.
algonkia Algonkian.
algonkina Algonquin.
algonkino Algonquin.
Algonkio Algonkian.
algoritma algorithmic. **algoritma lingvo** algorithmic language.
algoritmo algorithm.
alĝebro linear algebra.
Alĝerano Algerian.
alĝeria Algerian.
alĝerianino Algerian woman.
alĝeriano Algerian.
Alĝerio Algeria.
Alĝerlando Algeria.
Alĝero Algeria, Algiers.
alĝustigebla adjustable.
alĝustigeble adjustably.
alĝustigeti to tinker, tweak.
alĝustigeto tweak.
alĝustigi to adjust, put right, correct.
alĝustigilo adjuster, adjustment knob.
alĝustigo adjustment.
alĝustiĝi to adjust.
Alhambro Alhambra.
alhasti to hurry towards, hasten towards.
alĥemia alchemic, alchemical.
alĥemiisto alchemist.
alĥemio alchemy.
alia other, another (one), different, else.
aliaflanke on the other side.
aliaĵo something else.
alialoke elsewhere.
aliam at another time, at some other time.
aliamaniere differently, otherwise.
alianca allied.
aliancana allied.
aliancano ally.
Aliancanoj Allies.

aliigi

alianci to align, ally.
alianciĝi to ally, form an alliance, side with.
aliancito ally.
alianco alliance.
alianculo ally.
alianome alias, also known as, otherwise, otherwise called.
aliaranĝi to rearrange.
aliario garlic mustard, hedge garlic, jack-by-the-hedge.
Alibabo Ali Baba.
alibio alibi.
Alicao Alice.
alidado alidad, alidade.
alidire in other words.
alidirekti to redirect.
alie differently, else, otherwise, in another way, or else. **alie dirite** in other words.
aliena mentally ill.
alienanto alienor.
alienebla alienable.
alieneco alienation.
alieni to dispose of, sell.
alienisto psychiatrist, shrink.
alieno alienation.
alies another man's, other people's.
aliesnomo allonym.
alifata aliphatic.
alifato aliphatic.
aliflanke on the other hand. **aliflanke de** on the other side of.
alifoje another time.
aliformi to reconfigure, change, alter, transfigure.
aliformigi to transfigure, transform, transmute.
aliformigiiĝo transform.
aliformigo recreation, refashioning, regeneration, transformation.
aliformiĝi to be transformed.
aliformiĝo metamorphosis, transformation.
aligatoredoj Alligatoridae, alligators.
aligatori to converse with another Esperantist in a language other than one's own or Esperanto.
aligatoro alligator.
aligentulo other person, person of another group.
aligi to affiliate, join. **aligi al** to ascribe, attribute.
aliĝanto disciple.
aliĝformularo application form.
aliĝi to join, enrol, become affiliated.
aliĝilo application form, registration form.
aliĝinto supporter.
aliĝo accession, adhesion.
aliĝulo adherent.
aliiga klavo ALT key.
aliigi to alter, change, turn, modify.

aliigo

aliigo alteration.
aliiĝi to alter, change, undergo modification.
aliiĝo alteration, change, conversion, transformation.
alikvanto non-aliquot part.
alikvota aliquot.
alikvoto aliquot part.
alila allyl.
alilanda exotic, foreign.
alilandano alien, foreigner, citizen of another country.
alilande abroad.
alilando foreign country.
alilandulo alien, foreigner.
aliloke elsewhere.
aliloken elsewhere.
alimaniere differently.
alimenta alimentary.
alimento alimony, maintenance (grant, allowance).
alimenttubo alimentary canal.
alinei to indent.
alineo paragraph, indentation.
Alino Aline.
alinome alias, otherwise, otherwise called.
alinomita differently named.
alinomite alias, otherwise, otherwise called.
alinomo alias.
Alio Ali.
alio something else.
Alio-Babo Ali Baba.
aliokaze otherwise.
aliparte in another part, in another place.
Alipaŝo Ali Pasha.
alirebla accessible.
alireblo access.
alirejo access, approach, gateway.
alireligiulo dissenter.
aliri to advance, approach, come on.
aliro access, approach.
alirvojo access road.
aliseksema heterosexual.
aliseksemo heterosexuality.
aliseksemulo heterosexual.
alismo water plantain.
aliso alyssum.
Alisono Allison, Alison.
alispeca another kind of, of another kind.
alistrukturi to rearrange, restructure.
aliŝtatano alien.
alitempe another time.
aliteracia alliterative.
aliteracii to alliterate.
aliteracio alliteration.
aliula infano someone else's child.
aliulo other (person), another (person), someone else.
alivesti to disguise.
alivorte in other words, put another way.

alkoholentenanta

alizarbo common whitebeam.
alizarino alizarin.
alizeo trade-wind.
alizo whitebeam berry.
alizujo common whitebeam.
aljuĝado tender.
aljuĝi to adjudge, award.
aljuĝiĝi to be awarded, be granted.
aljuĝo adjudication.
aljungi to put.
alĵeti to hurl.
alĵuri to swear (to something).
alkado alcade.
alkadrigi to justify (text).
alkadrigo justification, right alignment, right justification.
alkaja Alcaic.
alkala alkaline.
alkaleca alkaline.
alkaleco alkalinity.
alkalibluo alkali blue.
alkalio alkali.
alkalizi to alkalinize, alkalize.
alkalkuli to impute.
alkalo alkali.
alkaloido alkaloid.
alkalozo alkalosis.
alkano alkane, alkene.
alkanolo alkanol.
alkanserio alkane series.
alkantilopo eland.
alkao auk.
alkateni to chain, tie up with chains, fasten with chains.
alkazaro alcazar.
alkekengo bladder-cherry, Chinese lantern, Japanese lantern, winter cherry.
alkemia alchemic, alchemical.
alkemiisto alchemist.
alkemilo lady's mantle.
alkemio alchemy.
alkido baby elk.
alkino female elk.
Alkinoo Alcinous.
alklaki to click.
alklako click.
alklimatigi to acclimatize.
alklimatiĝi to acclimate, acclimatize.
alklimatiĝo acclimatization.
alko elk, moose.
alkohola alcoholic, spirituous.
alkoholaĵmalpermeso ban on liquor.
alkoholaĵmaniulo alcoholic.
alkoholaĵo alcohol, booze, liquor, spirits, strong drink.
alkoholaĵoj alcoholic drinks, spirits, liquor.
alkoholato alcoholate.
alkoholemio alcoholaemia.
alkoholentenanta alcoholic.

alkoholhava

alkoholhava alcoholic.
alkoholigi to spike (something with alcohol).
alkoholismo alcoholism.
alkoholisto alcoholic.
alkoholizmo alcoholism.
alkoholmetro alcoholometer.
alkoholmisuzo alcohol abuse.
alkoholo alcohol, spirit.
alkoholtitro alcoholic content.
alkoholulo alcoholic.
alkolektiĝi al sia popolo to be gathered to one's people.
alkonduki to bring.
alkondukita lead to.
alkonformigi to standardize, adapt, make something conform.
alkonformigo accommodation.
alkonformiĝemo adaptability.
alkonformiĝi to accommodate oneself, adapt oneself.
alkonformiĝo adaptation.
alkonstrui to add.
alkonvena fitly, appropriately, conveniently.
alkova fenestro bay window.
alkovo alcove, recess.
alkrementi to increment.
alkreska adnate.
alkreskado accretion.
alkreskaĵo accretion.
alkreski to accrete.
alkreskigi to accrete.
alkreskigo accretion.
alkroĉi to hasp, hitch on, hook on.
alkroĉiĝi to cling to, get caught on.
alkroĉiĝi al to board.
alkrustiĝi to fur.
alkrustiĝo fur, scale.
alkudri to sew, sew on.
alkulturigi to acculturate.
alkulturigo acculturation.
alkuri to have recourse to, run to.
alkuro crush.
alkutimaĵo habit, trick.
alkutimigi to get someone used to something.
alkutimiĝi to get in the habit of, become accustomed.
alkutimiĝo adjustment.
allasebla admissible.
allaseble admissibly.
allasi to admit.
allaso admission, admittance.
alligfosto bollard, dolphin, mooring-mast.
alligi to attach, fasten, moor, tie, tie on, lash, make fast. **alligi per ŝnurego** to moor a ship.
alligilo tether.
alligitaĵo attachment.
alligiteco adherence, attachment.

almozulejo

alligo attachment.
alliniigi to align.
alliniigo alignment.
alloga attractive.
allogaĵo attraction, bait.
alloge persuasively.
allogeco attraction, attractiveness, charm.
allogi to attract, draw, entice, ensnare.
allogo attraction.
allokigi to place.
allokigo placement.
Almagesto Almagest, Almagest.
almanaĥo almanac.
almanako almanac.
almanĝaĵoj hors d'œuvre(s).
almanito toadstool.
almare seawards, towards the sea.
almarĝenigi to sideline.
almarĝenigo marginalization.
almarŝi to advance, march on.
almarŝo advance.
almatano resident of Almaty.
Almato Almaty.
almenaŭ at (the very) least, if nothing else.
almeo alma, almeh.
almetaĵo appendage, attachment.
almeti to apply, put on, attach.
almeto application.
almezuri to adjust, take a measurement.
almiksado admixture.
almiksaĵo admixture.
almiksi to admix.
almikso admixture.
almiliti to conquer.
Almo Alma.
Almodad Elmodad.
almontri to point out, point at.
almordi to bite, rise to the bait, take the bait.
almovi to move towards.
almozdonema charitable.
almozdoneme charitably.
almozdoni to give alms.
almozi to beg.
almozisto almsman, mendicant, beggar.
almozkesto poor box.
almozmonaĥo mendicant friar.
almozo alms, charity, handout, charitable relief. **almozon peti** to beg (alms).
almozordeno mendicant order.
almozosako charity bag.
almozpetado begging.
almozpetanto beggar.
almozpeti to beg.
almozpeto beggary.
almozpetulo beggar.
almozsako beggar's bag.
almozujo alms-box.
almozulejo almshouse, workhouse, poorhouse.

almozulino

almozulino beggar woman.
almozulo beggar, pauper.
alna alder, of an alder.
alnaĝi to be washed ashore.
alnajli to nail down, nail something to the floor.
alnika alnico.
alniko alnico.
alniveligi to level something, reduce to a certain level.
alno alder (tree).
alnomo alias, nickname, surname.
alo branch, wing.
aloa stratioto common water soldier.
aloaĵo aloe.
aloarbo aloe-tree.
alobazo base of arm, base of wing.
alobrogo Allobroge.
alodo alodium.
alofona allophonic.
alofono allophone.
aloino aloin.
aloji to alloy.
alojiĝi to alloy.
alojo alloy.
alojsio lemon grass.
aloligno eaglewood.
alomorfa allomorphic.
alomorfo allomorph.
alonĝo allonge, extension.
aloo aloe.
alopatia allopathic.
alopatio allopathy.
alopato allopath.
alopecio alopecia, baldness.
alopekuro foxtail grass.
aloritmio allorhythmia.
alosimila aloetic.
Alosto Alost.
alosukeltiristo aloe juice collector.
alosuko aloe juice.
alotriomorfa allotriomorphic, xenomorphic.
alotrofio allotrophy.
alotropa allotropic.
alotropeco allotropism, allotropy.
alotropio allotropism, allotropy.
alotropo allotrope.
alozo shad (fish).
alpa alpine. **alpa montaro** the Alps.
alpago extra fee.
alpako alpaca (animal, wood).
alpano alpine dweller.
alpara at par.
alpardo alpenglow.
alpare at face value, at par.
alpareco parity.
alparo face value, nominal value, parity, par.
alparolebla approachable, communicative.
alparolegi to harangue.

alsalto

alparoli to address, speak to.
alparolo intervention, message, speech.
alpaŝi to approach, deal with, tackle. **alpaŝi al** to approach. **alpaŝi rekte al la afero** to get right to business, cut to the chase, not beat around the bush.
alpaŝo approach.
alpatrujigo repatriation.
alpbastono alpenstock.
alpendaĵo appendage.
alpendigaĵo appendage.
alpendigi to append.
alpherbejo alp, alpine pasture.
alpingli to pin up.
alpinismo mountaineering.
alpinisto alpinist.
alpismo mountaineering.
alpisto Alpinist, climber, mountain climber, mountaineer.
alpkapro ibex.
alpo alp, mountain pasture. **Alpoj** Alps.
alpokapro ibex.
alportadi to give, bring as an offering.
alportado arrival, arrivals, supply.
alportanto bearer.
alporti to bring, fetch, convey.
alportiĝi to be carried.
alporto offering.
alpostenigi to assign.
alpostenigo assignment.
alpreĝi to pray to, invoke.
alpremi to clasp.
alpreni to adopt, espouse, assume (a value), take (a value). **alpreni ion al la koro** to take something to heart.
alpreno adoption, assumption, espousal, uptake.
alproksimigi to bring close together.
alproksimiĝado convergence.
alproksimiĝi to advance, come close, come closer, come on, approach.
alproksimiĝo approach.
alpromesi to promise (something to someone).
alproprigi to assimilate, grab. **alproprigi al si** to abstract.
alproprigo appropriation, assimilation, takeover.
alprunti to lend, loan.
alpuŝiĝi to be pushed on(to).
alrajdi to ride, run towards.
alrigardi to look at.
alrigidiĝi to stick to, seize upon.
alsaca Alsatian.
alsacano Alsatian.
Alsaco Alsace, Elsass. **Alsaco-Loreno** Alsace-Lorraine.
alsalti to pounce.
alsalto pounce.

alsendi to send to.
alsendo sending.
alsino Stellaria.
alskribaĵo appended writing.
alskribi to ascribe.
alspiro aspiration.
alstrata fenestro window facing the street.
alsuprado ascent.
alŝipi to send by boat.
alŝovi to push (toward, on).
alŝoviĝi to draw up to the table, sit down to table.
alŝtatigo nationalization.
alŝteligi to approach stealthily.
alŝultrigi to shoulder.
alŝultriĝi to aim, take aim.
alŝuti to upload.
alŝvebi to float.
alta high, lofty, tall, alto. **alta frekvenco** high frequency. **Alta Kanto** Canticles, Song of Solomon, Song of Songs. **alta protektado** sponsorship. **alta protektanto** sponsor. **alta tajdo** high tide.
altabliĝi to sit down at the table.
altagrada advanced.
Altairo Altair.
altaja Altaic. **altaja lingvo** Altai language. **Altaja lingvofamilio** Altai language family.
Altajo Altai, Altai Mountains.
altaĵeto hillock.
altaĵo elevation, height(s), eminence, rise, ascent.
altakrobato aerialist.
altano overlook, terrace.
altarbildo altarpiece.
altarejo chancel, presbyterium, sanctuary.
altarkandelo altar candle.
Altaro Ara.
altaro altar.
altarpentraĵo altarpiece.
altarŝtupoj altar steps.
altartabulo altarpiece.
altartapiŝo altar carpet.
altartuko altar cloth.
alte highly. **alte flugi** to soar.
altebenaĵo plateau, a high place, a place at a high elevation .
alteco height, altitude.
altecofobio acrophobia.
altefluga high-flying.
altega lofty, sublime.
altegiĝi to soar.
altejo high place, elevated place.
altekosta expensive.
altempigi to tune.
alten into the heights.
alteni to bind (closely to).
alteniĝa adhesive, sticky.
alteniĝi to adhere, stick.
alteniĝo adherence, adhesion.
alteno blocking, closure.
alteo althea, marsh mallow, hibiscus.
altepreza costly, expensive.
altera landward(s), towards land.
altere landward(s), towards land.
alterigi to beach, land (a boat).
alteriĝa vojeto airstrip.
alteriĝi to land (an aeroplane, etc.).
alteriĝo landing.
alterna alternate, alternating.
alterna grupo alternating group.
alterna kurento alternating current.
alternado alternation.
alternanco half period.
alternanta elektra fluo alternating electrical current.
alternativa alternative.
alternative alternatively, instead.
alternativo alternative, option.
alternatoro alternator.
alterndirekta half-duplex.
alterne alternately, alternatively.
alterneco alternation, variation.
alterni to alternate.
alternigado alternation.
alternigi to alternate.
alternigo alternation.
alternilo alternator.
alternklavo ALT key, alternate key.
alterno alternation.
altestime yours faithfully, yours sincerely, yours truly.
alteŝatata valuable, precious.
altfluga high-pitched.
altforno blast-furnace.
altfrekvenca high-frequency.
altgrada advanced.
altgrade extremely, greatly, highly, in a large measure.
altgradigi to upgrade.
altgradigo upgrade.
alti to lift, raise, make high.
altigi to elevate, shrug, raise.
altigo rise.
altiĝanta rising.
altiĝi to rise.
altiĝo rise.
altimetro altimeter.
altiplano plateau.
altira attractive. **altira forto** attraction.
altire attractively.
altiri to attract.
altiro attraction.
altirpovo (power of) attraction.
altituda altitudinal.
altitudo altitude.
altklasulo someone of the upper class.

altkreska

altkreska tall.
altkvalita high quality.
altlernejo academy, college.
altlevi to lift up, raise up, uplift.
altmaro high tide.
altmontarano Highlander.
altmontaro high mountain range.
altnivela high-level. **altnivela programlingvo** high level programming language.
alto altitude, height.
altoangulo angle of elevation.
altocentro orthocenter.
altofobio acrophobia.
altoindikilo altimeter, altitude gauge.
altokumuluso altocumulus.
altometro altimeter.
altostratuso altostratus.
altpremilo autoclave.
altpreza pricey, priceless, invaluable.
altranĉi to tailor, cut to form.
altranga high ranking.
altrangulo high-ranking person.
altreliefo high relief.
altrudi to force, impose upon.
altrudo imposition.
altruisma altruistic.
altruismano altruist.
altruisme altruistically.
altruismo altruism, unselfishness.
altruista altruistic.
altruisto altruist.
altruita al forced on.
altstatura lanky, of high stature, tall.
alttaksi to highly esteem, value greatly.
alttemperatura high-temperature.
alturniĝi to turn towards.
altvalora costly, valuable, precious, expensive, of great value.
aluda indirect, allusive.
alude indirectly.
aludi to allude, hint, refer to. **aludi al** to advert (to). **aludi kalumnie** to insinuate.
aludo allusion.
alumetisto matchmaker.
Alumetlago Allumette Lake.
alumeto match (fire).
alumetujo match box.
aluminaĵoj aluminiumware.
aluminato aluminate.
aluminia aluminic, aluminium, aluminous.
aluminiato aluminate.
aluminiika aluminic, aluminium.
aluminio aluminium.
aluminioza aluminous.
aluminizi to aluminize.
alumino alumina.
alunejo alunite mine.
alunito alunite.
aluno alum.

amanitino

aluntero alumina.
aluvia alluvial.
aluviaĵo alluvial deposid.
aluvio alluvion, alluvium.
aluzi to use.
Alvan Alvan.
alvenadi to arrive.
alvenanto person arriving, thing arriving.
alveni to arrive, end up, get.
alvenigi to cause someone to come.
alveninto arrival.
alveno arrival.
alventabelo arrival board, arrival schedule.
alveola alveolar.
alveolara alveolar.
alveolaro alveolar.
alveolhava alveolate.
alveolito alveolitis.
alveolo alveolus, cavity, socket.
alveoloza alveolate.
alveoluloj Alveolata.
alveturejo access, approach, drive, sweep.
alveturi to arrive (by vehicle), collide, run.
alveturigi to bring, convey, supply.
alviciĝi to follow, be lined up, be arrayed.
Alvo Alva.
alvojo access, approach, coming.
alvokadi to call (towards), call upon.
alvokado invocation.
alvoki to appeal to, invoke. **alvoki iun kiel atestanton** to call someone as a witness. **alvoki preĝe** to invoke.
alvokiĝo vocation.
alvoko call, invocation.
alvuso fry, restocking fish, spawned fish.
alzaca Alsatian.
alzacano Alsatian.
Alzaco Alsace.
alzano auburn.
ama fond.
amabla dainty, kind, nice, pretty.
amaĉi to make love.
Amadeo Amadeus.
amafero affair (romantic), love affair.
amaĵanto paramour.
amaĵema flirtatious.
amaĵi to make love.
amaĵistino courtesan, mistress.
amaĵisto courtesan, geisha.
amaĵo love affair.
Amalek Amalech.
Amalekido Amalecite.
Amaleko Amalech.
amalgami to amalgamate.
amalgamiĝi to amalgamate.
amalgamo amalgam.
Amalio Amalia, Amelia.
amando almond.
amanitino amanitine.

amanito amanita (mushroom).
Amano Amman.
amanta affectionate, loving.
amante affectionately, lovingly.
amantino lover, mistress.
amanto lover, suitor, sweetheart.
amao aum.
amara acerbic, acrimonious, bitter.
amaraĵo bitters.
amaranta amaranthine.
amaranto amaranth (genus of herbs).
amare bitterly.
amareco acerbity, bitterness.
amarigi to make bitter.
amariĝi to become bitter.
amarilidacoj crinum.
amarilido amaryllis, belladonna lily.
amariliso amaryllis.
Amarilo Amarillo.
amaro acrimony, bitterness.
amasa heavy, mass, massive.
amasaĵo heap, pile.
amasbuĉado massacre, slaughter, slaughtering.
amasbuĉi to massacre, slaughter.
amasdemonstracio demonstration, rally.
amasdetrua armilo weapon of mass destruction.
amase in large numbers, en masse.
amasega multitudinous.
amasegaro swarms, hordes.
amasego great quantity.
amaseto small quantity.
amasfabrikado mass production.
amasfabriki to mass produce.
Amasiaso Amaziah.
amasigi to accumulate, amass, heap, pile up, collect.
amasigo accumulation.
amasiĝanta accumulative.
amasiĝi to accumulate.
amasiĝo accumulation, assembly.
amasinformilo mass media.
amaskomunikilo (instrument of) mass media, mass communication.
amaskomunikiloj media.
amaskuregi to stampede.
amaskurego stampede.
amasloĝejo mass accommodations.
amasmortigado carnage.
amasmurdi to commit mass murder.
amasmurdisto mass murderer.
amasmurdo mass murder.
Amaso Amasa.
amaso accumulation, body, crowd, heap, mass, multitude, pile, swarm, hoard, mob, throng, troop. **amaso da** a mass of.
amastombejo mass grave.
amata loved, beloved.

amataĵo hobby, pastime.
Amateraso Amaterasu.
amatino beloved, loved one, lover, sweetheart, well-beloved.
amato beloved, loved one, lover, sweetheart, well-beloved.
amatora amateur.
amatora radio amateur radio.
amatoraĉa amateurish.
amatoraĵo amateur handicraft, pottering, trifling work.
amatore in an amateur way.
amatoreca amateurish, small-time.
amatoreco amateurishness.
amatoro amateur, enthusiast, fancier.
amaŭrozo amaurosis.
amazona Amazon, Amazonian. **Amazona Riverego** Amazon, Amazon River.
Amazonbaseno Amazon Basin.
Amazonio Amazonas.
Amazono Amazon.
amazono Amazon, Amazon River.
ambasadejo embassy.
ambasado diplomatic mission, embassy.
ambasadonaro embassy.
ambasadora ambassadorial.
ambasadoreco ambassadorship, embassy.
ambasadorejo embassy, embassy building.
ambasadorino ambassador, female ambassador.
ambasadoro ambassador.
ambaŭ both.
ambaŭdekstra ambidextrous.
ambaŭdekstre ambidextrously.
ambaŭdekstreco ambidexterity.
ambaŭdirekta bidirectional, duplex. **ambaŭdirekta implikacio** bidirectional implication. **ambaŭdirekta kanalo** circuit.
ambaŭflanka reciprocal, bilateral.
ambaŭflanke on both sides. **ambaŭflanke de** on both sides of. **ambaŭflanken** to both sides.
ambaŭflanki to straddle.
ambaŭseksa bisexual.
ambaŭseksema bisexual.
ambaŭseksemo bisexuality.
ambaŭseksulo hermaphrodite.
ambaŭtranĉa two-edged.
ambicia ambitious.
ambicie ambitiously.
ambicii to have the ambition to.
ambicio ambition.
ambiciulo careerist, ambitious person.
ambidekstra ambidextrous.
ambifikso ambifix.
ambigua ambiguous.
ambiguaĵo ambiguity.
ambigue ambiguously.
ambigueco ambiguity.

ambiguo

ambiguo ambiguity.
ambivalenca ambivalent.
ambivalence ambivalently.
ambivalenco ambivalence.
ambivertiteco ambiversion.
ambivertito ambivert.
Amblarduo Muir of Ord.
ambli to amble.
ambliopa amblyopic.
ambliopio amblyopia.
amblo amble.
ambona Amboinese.
ambonano Amboinese.
ambono ambo, pulpit, platform; Amboina.
ambosbeko beak of anvil.
amboso anvil.
ambosoĉizilo hardy.
ambro amber, ambergris, grey amber.
ambrozia Ambrosian, ambrosial.
ambrozio ambrosia.
ambulancisto ambulance driver.
ambulanco ambulance, field hospital.
ambulatorio outpatient care facility.
amdeklaro declaration of love.
ame fondly, lovingly.
ameba amoebic.
amebla lovable.
ameble lovably.
amebo amoeba.
amebocito amoebocyte.
ameboida amoebous.
ameco fondness, tenderness.
amegi to adore, dote, idolize.
amelazo amylase.
ameli to starch.
amelo amylum, farina, starch.
amema amorous, tender, affectionate.
ameme amorously, tenderly, affectionately.
amemo tenderness.
amenda amendatory.
amendamento amendment.
amendi to amend.
amendo amendment.
ameno amen.
amenoreo amenorrhoea.
amenta amentaceous.
amento amentum, catkin.
amentoforma amentiform.
americio americium.
amerika American. **Amerika Ekspreso** American Express (company).
amerikanino American woman.
amerikanismo Americanism.
Amerikano American.
amerikano American.
Ameriko America.
amesprimo declaration (of love).
ameti to have a crush on, like.
ametista amethyst, amethystine.

amikto

ametisto amethyst.
ametropa ametropic.
ametropeco ametropia.
ametropio ametropia.
amfetamino amphetamine.
amfiartro amphiarthrosis.
amfibia amphibious. **amfibia veturilo** amphibious vehicle.
amfibie amphibiously.
amfibio amphibian.
amfibioj Amphibia, amphibians.
amfibiologio amphibiology, amphibology.
amfibolo amphibole, hornblende.
amfibologio amphibology.
amfibraĥa amphibrachic.
amfibraĥo amphibrach.
amfibraka amphibrachic.
amfibrako amphibrach.
amfiktiona amphictyonic.
amfiktionaro amphictyony.
Amfiktiono Amphictyon.
amfiktiono amphictyon.
Amfimedono Amphimedon.
amfiokso amphioxus.
Amfiono Amphion.
amfipodo amphipod.
Amfipolo Amphipolis.
amfiteatra amphitheatric, amphitheatrical.
amfiteatro amphitheatre, lecture hall.
Amfitriono Amphitryon.
amfiumo blind eel.
amforo amphora. **Amforo** Aquarius (zodiac).
amfotera amphoteric.
amhara Amharic.
amharo Amharic.
ami to love, cherish.
amiantio flypoison.
amianto amianth, amianthus.
amido amide.
amidolo amidol.
amiga endearing.
amigdalo amygdala.
amige endearingly.
amigi to endear.
amika friendly.
amikaĵo good office, kind turn.
amikaro circle of friends.
amike in a friendly manner.
amikeca affectionate, amiable.
amikece affectionately.
amikeco amity, friendship.
amikema friendly.
amikemo friendliness.
amiki to be friends, be on good terms.
amikiĝi to become friends, make friends.
amikino friend (female).
amiko friend.
amikto amictus.

amila amyl.
amilalkoholo amyl alcohol.
amilazo amylase.
amilo amyl.
amina amino. **amina acido** amino acid.
aminacido amino acid.
aminda affectionate, lovable, amiable.
aminde affectionately.
amindeco amiability, sweetness.
amindo charm, sweetness.
amindumado courtship.
amindumeti to flirt.
amindumi to court, woo, make love to.
amindumisto wooer.
aminfenolo aminophenol.
amino amine.
aminoacido amino acid.
aminofenolo aminophenol.
aminotolueno anisidine.
amintrigo (secret love) affair.
amio bowfin.
Amirantoj Amirants.
amisto gallant, wooer, lover.
amiŝa Amish.
amiŝismo Amishism.
amiŝo Amish.
amitozo amitosis.
amkandidato suitor, potential lover.
amletero love letter.
amnestii to amnesty, pardon.
amnestio act of grace, amnesty.
amnezia amnesiac.
amnezio amnesia.
amneziulo amnesiac.
amnia amniotic.
amnio amnion (of embryo).
amniocentezo amniocentesis.
Amnono Amnon.
amo affection, love.
amofilo marram grass.
amoke amuck.
amoki to run amok.
amoko amuck.
amomo cinnamon.
amonia ammoniacal. **amonia klorido** ammonium chloride.
amoniaka ammoniacal.
amoniakeca ammoniacal.
amoniakizi to ammoniate.
amoniako ammonia, anhydrous ammonia.
Amonido Ammonite.
amoniklorido ammonium chloride.
amonio ammonia, ammonium.
amonito ammonite.
Amono Ammon, Amon, Amun.
amoplena affectionate.
amora amatory, amorous, risqué.
amorado lovemaking.
amorantino (female) lover.
amoranto lover.
amoreto cupid.
amorfa amorphous.
amori to make love, have sex.
Amorido Amorrhite.
amoristino hooker, prostitute, whore.
amoristo hooker, prostitute, whore, gigolo.
Amoro Amour, Cupid, Eros.
amoro love, sex, sexual love.
amorspektemulo voyeur.
amortizebla redeemable, repayable.
amortizi to amortize, deaden, damp.
amortiziĝi to depreciate.
amortizilo shock absorber.
amortizo redemption, sinking fund.
amorveka hot, sexy.
amovendistino escort, hooker, prostitute, whore.
amovendisto prostitute, whore, gigolo.
ampelopso ampelopsis creeper, Virginia creeper.
amperhoro ampere-hour.
ampermetro ammeter.
amperminuto ampere-minute.
ampero ampere, amp.
amperometro ammeter.
ampersekundo ampere-second.
ampervolvo ampere turn.
ampleko extent.
ampleksa ample, bulky, extensive, comprehensive.
ampleksaĵo bulkiness.
amplekse comprehensively.
ampleksi to comprise, cover, extend to, include, embrace.
ampleksigi to amplify, enlarge.
ampleksigo enlargement.
ampleksiĝi to enlarge.
amplekso amplitude, bulk, dimension, extent, size, scope, magnitude, range.
amplena full of love.
amplene full of love.
amplifa amplificatory.
amplifatoro amplifier.
amplifi to amplify.
amplifika amplificative, amplificatory.
amplifikatoro amplifier.
amplifiki to amplify.
amplifikilo amplifier.
amplifiko amplification.
amplifilo amplifier.
amplifo amplification.
amplitudo amplitude.
amplitudregilo amplitude regulator.
ampola ampullaceous, ampullary.
ampolingo bulb socket.
ampolo (light) bulb, ampoule, ampulla.
ampolosimila ampullaceous, ampullary.
ampoltubo pipette.

amputado amputation.
amputi to amputate.
amputito amputee.
amputo amputation.
Amrafel Amraphel.
amrakonto love story.
Amramo Amram.
amrendevuo (amorous) rendezvous.
amrilato romantic relationship.
amsterdama Amsterdam.
amsterdamano inhabitant of Amsterdam, native of Amsterdam.
Amsterdamo Amsterdam.
amu atomic mass unit.
Amudarjo Amu Darya, Amudaryra, Oxus.
amuleto amulet, charm, talisman.
Amuro Amur.
amuza amusing, entertaining, funny.
amuzadiĝi to have a good time.
amuzado fun, amusement.
amuzaĵo entertainment, hobby, pastime, funny thing.
amuzaoĵo amusement.
amuze amusingly.
amuzejo amusement park.
amuzi to amuse, divert, entertain, unbend, relax. **amuzi nin** to enjoy ourselves. **amuzi sin** be amused.
amuziĝadi to be on the spree.
amuziĝi to enjoy oneself, have a good time, have fun.
amuziĝo amusement, spree.
amuzilo plaything, toy.
amuzisto entertainer.
amuzo amusement, fun.
amuzparko fun fair.
amuzrakonteto funny story.
anabaptismo Anabaptism.
anabaptisto Anabaptist.
anabata ascending.
anabazo Anabasis.
Anabelo Annabel, Annabelle.
anabiozo anabiosis.
anabola anabolic.
anabolismo anabolism.
anabolo anabolism.
anaerobia anaerobic.
anaerobio anaerobe.
anaerobiozo anaerobiosis.
anafazo anaphase.
anafilaksia anaphylactic.
anafilaksio anaphylaxis.
anaforo anaphora.
anagalo pimpernel.
anaglifa anaglyphic, anaglyphical.
anaglifo anaglyph.
anagramo anagram.
anakampto pyramidal orchid.
anakardiacoj Anacardiaceae (plant family).
anakardio cashew nut.
anakinezio anakinesis.
Anako Anak.
anakoluto anacoluthon.
anakondo anaconda.
anakoreta anchoritic, anchoritical.
anakoretino anchoress.
anakoreto anchorite.
anakreona Anacreontic.
Anakreono Anacreon.
anakreono Anacreon.
anakronisma anachronistic.
anakronisme anachronistically.
anakronismo anachronism.
anakruzo anacrusis, upbeat.
Anaksagoro Anaxagoras.
Anaksimandro Anaximander.
Anaksimeno Anaximenes.
anala anal. **anala seksumo** anal sex.
analagmatika anallagmatic.
anale anally.
analekto analecta.
analeptika analeptic.
analeptiko analeptic.
analfabeta illiterate.
analfabeteco illiteracy.
analfabetismo illiteracy.
analfabeto analphabetic, illiterate.
analfabetulo illiterate.
analgezia analgesic.
analgeziko analgesic, painkiller.
analgezio analgesia.
analisto annalist.
analitika analytic, analytical. **analitika funkcio** analytic function. **analitika geometrio** analytical geometry. **analitika modelo** analytical model.
analitiko analysis, analytics, calculus.
analiza analytical.
analizebla analyzable.
analizema analytic, analytical.
analizi to analyse, assay, construe, parse.
analizilo analyser.
analizisto analyst, analytical chemist.
analizo analysis.
analo annals, record, chronicle(s).
analoga analogue, analogous. **analoga komputilo** analogue computer, analogue machine. **analogaj datenoj** analogue data.
analogaĵo analogue.
analogcifereca analogue-digital.
analoge by analogy with, on the analogy of.
analogeco analogousness, analogy.
analogia analogical, analogous.
analogio analogy.
analogo analogue.
analoj annals.
anama Annamese.
Anamido Anamim.

anamnezo anamnesis.
Anamo Annam.
anamorfoza anamorphic.
anamorfozo anamorphosis.
ananaso pineapple.
ananassuko pineapple juice.
ananasujo pineapple.
Ananiaso Ananias.
ananimo ananym.
Anao anna.
anapesta anapestic, anapaestic.
anapesto anapest, antidactylus.
anarĥia anarchic, anarchical, anarchist, chaotic.
anarĥie anarchically.
anarĥiismo anarchism.
anarĥiista anarchistic.
anarĥiisto anarchist.
anarĥio anarchy.
anarĥiulo anarchist.
anarkia anarchic, anarchical, anarchist, chaotic.
anarkiismo anarchism.
anarkiista anarchistic.
anarkiisto anarchist.
anarkio anarchy.
anarkisindikatismo anarcho-syndicalism.
anarkisma anarchic, anarchical.
anarkismo anarchism.
anarkista anarchistic.
anarkisto anarchist.
anarkiulo anarchist.
anaro adherents, disciples, following, party, supporters, company, troop, membership.
anasa duck, duck-, duck's, of a duck. **anasa ovo** duck egg.
anasaĵo duck, duck meat.
anasarko anasarca.
anasbleki to quack (duck).
anasedoj Anatidae (bird family).
anasido duckling.
anasino duck.
anasiri to waddle.
Anaso Annas.
anaso duck.
anaspaŝi to waddle.
Anastaziao Anastasia.
Anastazio Anastasia.
anastigmata anastigmatic.
anastigmato anastigmat, anastigmatic lens.
anastomoza anastomotic.
anastomozo anastomosis.
anastrofo anastrophe.
anatazo anatase.
anatema anathematic.
anatemi to curse, anathematize.
anatemo anathema, ban, excommunication.
anatifo barnacle.
anatolia Anatolian.

Anatolio Anatolia, Asia Minor.
anatolo Anatolia.
anatomia anatomical.
anatomie anatomically.
anatomiisto anatomist.
anatomio anatomy.
anatomo anatomist.
anatropa anatropal, anatropous.
anêo reed (of a musical instrument).
anĉovo anchovy.
anda Andean.
andaluza Andalusian.
andaluzia Andalusian.
andaluziano Andalusian.
andaluzino Andalusian woman.
Andaluzio Andalusia.
andaluzo Andalusian.
Andaluzujo Andalusia.
Andamanmaro Andaman Sea.
Andamanoj Andaman Islands.
andante andante.
andantete andantino.
andanteto andantino.
andantino andantino.
andanto andante.
andezito andesite.
Andoj Andes.
andora Andorrian.
andoranino Andorrian woman.
andorano Andorrian.
Andoro Andorra.
Andreaso Andreas.
Andreo Andrew.
androdioika androdioecious.
androfobio androphobia.
androforo androphore.
androgena androgenic, androgynous.
androgeno androgen.
androgina androgynous.
androgino androgyne.
androika androecious.
Androklo Androclus, Androcles.
andromaĥo Andromache.
Andromedo Andromeda.
andromonoika andromonoecious.
Androniko Andronicus.
androsterono androsterone.
andujo andouille.
aneco membership.
anekdota anecdotal.
anekdotaro collection of anecdotes.
anekdotisto anecdotist.
anekdoto anecdote.
aneksa accessory.
aneksado annexation.
aneksaĵo annex.
aneksi to annex.
aneksismo annexationism.
aneksisto annexationist.

anekso annexation, annex.
aneli to let down.
anelido annelida.
anelidoj annelids.
anelo anellus.
anemia anaemic.
anemio anaemia.
anemiulo anaemic.
anemofila anemophilous.
anemografio anemography.
anemografo anemograph.
anemogramo anemogram.
anemometrio anemometry.
anemometro anemometer, wind gauge.
anemona anemonic.
anemono anemone.
anemoskopo anemoscope.
aneroida aneroid.
aneroido aneroid, barometer.
anerojda aneroid.
anesteza anaesthetic.
anestezado anaesthesia.
anestezaĵo anaesthetic.
anestezaparato anaesthesia apparatus.
anestezenzo anaesthetic.
anestezi to anaesthetize.
anestezilo anaesthetic.
anesteziologio anaesthesiology.
anesteziologo anaesthesiologist, anaesthetist.
anestezisto anaesthetist.
anestezo anaesthesia.
aneto dill.
aneŭrino aneurine, thiamine.
aneŭrisma aneurysmal.
aneŭrismo aneurysm.
anfrakta anfractuous.
anfrakto cavity, anfractuosity.
Angaro Angara.
angeliko angelica.
Angeliko Angelica.
Angelino Angela.
Angelo Angelo.
angia vascular.
angigenezo angiogenesis.
angiledoj Anguillidae (fish family).
angilforkego eelspear.
angilforma anguilliform, eel-shaped.
angilglata slippery as an eel.
angilhaŭto eelskin.
angilkaptado eel fishing.
angilkesto eel-preserve, eel-trunk.
angilkorbo eel-basket, eel-pot.
angilnaso eel-pot, eel-trap.
angilo eel.
angiloforma anguilliform, eel-shaped.
angiloformaj Apodes.
angilokaptado eel-fishing.
angilpasteĉo eel-pie.
angilsimila eel-like.

angilulo eelworm.
angilvendisto eel-monger.
angino angina, quinsy.
angio blood vessel, vessel.
angiogenezo angiogenesis.
angiomo angioma.
angioplastio angioplasty.
angiosarkomo angiosarcoma.
angioskopo angioscope.
angiosperma angiospermatous, angiospermous.
angiospermo angiosperm.
angla English. **angla lingvo** English, English language. **angla scilo** bluebell, common bluebell.
anglalingva in English, English-language.
anglalingve in English.
anglamika anglophile, pro-English.
anglaparola Anglophone.
anglaparolanto Anglophone.
angle in English.
angleparolanto Anglophone.
anglicismo Anglicism.
angligi to Anglicize, anglicize.
angligo Anglicization.
anglikana Anglican.
anglikanismo Anglicanism.
anglikano Anglican.
anglino English, Englishwoman.
Anglio England.
anglismo Anglicism.
anglo Englishman.
anglofobio anglophobia.
Anglolando England.
anglomanio Anglomania.
anglonormanda Anglo-Norman.
anglosaksa Anglo-Saxon.
anglosakso Anglo-Saxon.
Anglujo England.
angola Angolan.
angolanino Angolian woman.
angolano Angolese.
Angolo Angola.
angora distressed, oppressing.
angorego agony.
angoreta slightly worried.
angori to feel distressed.
angorigi to anguish.
angoro agony, anguish, fear, distress, angst.
angorŝvito cold sweat.
angosturo angostura.
angstromo angstrom.
angula angular, gaunt. **angula distanco** angular distance, angular separation. **angula koeficiento** angular coefficient, slope. **angula movokvanto** angular momentum. **angulaj krampoj** angle brackets (〈 〉).
angulaĵo angle iron.

anguleca angular.
anguleco angularity.
angulen around the corner.
anguleto nook.
angulfero angle-iron.
angulfidela conformal (transformation).
angulhava angular.
anguligi to angle.
anguliĝi to angle.
angulilo set square.
angulmezurilo protractor.
angulo angle, corner.
angulrelo angle iron, angle bar.
angultrabo angle iron, angle bar.
angura Angora. **angura kato** Angora cat.
Anguro Angora, Ankara.
angusturo angostura.
Angvilo Anguilla.
angvisedoj Anguidae.
angviso blindworm, slow-worm.
anĝela angelic. **anĝela saluto** angelic salutation.
anĝelapero angelophany.
anĝele angelically.
anĝeleca angelic.
anĝeleco angelhood.
anĝelino female angel.
anĝelo angel.
anĝelogardanto guardian.
anĝelosimila angelic.
anĝeluso angelus.
anheli to be out of breath, pant, hyperventilate.
anhelo breathlessness, panting, gasping.
anhidra anhydrous, waterless.
anhidrido anhydride.
anhidrito anhydrite.
anĥo ankh.
anigi to affiliate. **anigi al** to become a member of.
anigu insert.
aniĝi to accede, affiliate, join.
aniĝilo application, application form.
aniĝo enrolment.
anihilacii to annihilate.
anihilacio annihilation.
anilinnigro aniline black.
anilino aniline.
anilo anil.
anima of the soul, spiritual.
animaciaĵo animation, animated work.
animacio animation.
animado animation.
animala animal. **animala odoro** animal smell.
animalo animal (as opposed to vegetable or mineral). **animaloj** Animal kingdom.
anime mentally.
animeco animation.
animeo anime (Japanese animation).
animi to animate, enliven, vitalize, inspire.
animilo animus.
animisma animistic.
animismo animism.
animisto animist.
animita animated.
animkonflikto conflict of conscience.
animo soul, spirit.
animstato mood, state of mind.
animzorgado chaplaincy.
animzorganto chaplain.
aniono anion.
anizlikvoro anisette.
anizo anise, aniseed.
anizokorio anisocoria.
anizometropio anisometropia.
anizoplanto anise.
anizosfigmio anisosphygmia.
anizosukeraĵo candy-coated aniseed.
anizotropa anisotropic, anizotropic.
anizotropia anisotropic.
anizotropio anisotropia.
anizsemo aniseed.
anizujo anise.
anjona anionic.
anjono anion.
Ankaro Ankara.
ankaŭ also, likewise, too, moreover. **ankaŭ mi** to me too.
ankero anchor.
ankilostomo hookworm.
ankilozigo anchylosis.
ankiloziĝi to be affected by anchylosis.
ankilozo anchylosis, stiffness of joints.
ankoneo anconeus.
ankono ancon, Ancona.
ankoraŭ again, not yet, still, yet, anew. **ankoraŭ kvin-ses jaroj** five or six more years. **ankoraŭ iom da** some more. **ankoraŭ ne** not yet, still not. **ankoraŭ unu** one more, another.
ankoraŭfoje once more.
ankradejo anchorage.
ankrado anchorage.
ankraĵo anchorage.
ankrejo anchorage, moorage, mooring.
Ankrenviso Ancrene Riwle.
ankreto grapnel.
ankri to anchor.
ankriĝi to be anchored.
ankriĝo anchorage.
ankro anchor.
ankroĉeno anchor cable.
ankrokablo anchor rope, anchor hauser.
ankrotarifo anchorage fee.
ankrovinĉo windlass.
ankrumi to (ride at) anchor.
anksia anxious, apprehensive.

anksie

anksie anxiously.
anksieco anxiety.
anksio anxiety.
ankuzo alkanet.
Annao Ann.
Anneto Annette.
Anno Anne.
ano member, supporter.
anobiedoj Anobiidae.
anobio death-watch beetle, bookworm.
anoda anodal.
anodina anodyne.
anodino anodyne.
anodizi to anodize.
anodo anode.
anofelo anopheles (mosquito).
anoksemio anoxemia.
anoksio anoxia.
anolito anolyte.
anomalia deviating, divergent.
anomalio abnormity, anomaly.
anonarbo Annona cherimola.
anoncado announcement, notification, notice.
anoncanto proclaimer, advertiser.
anonceto (small) advertisement, want ad.
anonci to advertise, announce, give notice, profess. **anonci laŭtvoĉe** to call over. **anonci sin** to apply.
anoncîĝi to announce.
anoncistino announcer.
anoncisto announcer.
anonco ad, advertisement, announcement.
anonctabulego billboard.
anonctabulo announcement board, bulletin board.
anonima anonymous. **anonima FTP** anonymous FTP. **anonima kompanio** limited liability company. **anonima societo** limited liability company.
anonime anonymously.
anonimeco anonymity.
anonimo anonymous author, anonymous letter.
anonimulo anonymous writer.
anono cherimoya.
anonujo Annona cherimola.
anopsio anopsia.
anorakjako anorak jacket.
anorakkapuĉo anorak hood.
anorako anorak, parka, windbreaker.
anoreksia anoretic, anorexic.
anoreksio anorexia.
anoreksiulino anorexic.
anormala abnormal.
anortita anorthitic.
anortito anorthite.
anosmio anosmia.
anse akimbo.

antaŭ

Anselmo Anselm.
ansera anserine, anserous.
anserajô goose (meat).
anserhaŭto goosebumps, gooseflesh, goosepimples.
anserido gosling.
anserina anserine, anserous.
anserino goose.
ansero goose.
anseroformaj Anseriformes (order of birds).
anservice single file.
anserviro gander.
anshava ansate.
anso handle, knob, latch.
anst. → **anstataŭ**.
anstataŭ in lieu of, in place of, instead of.
anstataŭa acting, ad interim, alternate, deputy, surrogate, ersatz, substitute, replacement. **anstataŭa rado** spare tyre.
anstataŭaĵo substitute, replacement, surrogate.
anstataŭanto second (in a duel).
anstataŭe instead.
anstataŭi to replace, substitute, supersede, take the place of, supplant, stand in, supplant.
anstataŭiga replacement, substitute. **anstataŭiga skribreĝimo** overtype mode, overwrite mode.
anstataŭigaĵo replacement.
anstataŭigi to replace, make a substitution, put in place of.
anstataŭigo replacement, substitution.
anstataŭiĝi to be replaced.
anstataŭilo surrogate, substitution.
anstataŭo replacement, substitution, surrogate.
anstataŭulo proxy.
anstromo angstrom.
antagonisma antagonistic.
antagonisme antagonistically.
antagonismo antagonism, antithesis, contradistinction, contrast, opposition.
antagonistigi to antagonize.
antagonisto adversary, opponent, antagonist.
Antareso Antares.
antarkta Antarctic. **antarkta aŭroro** southern lights, Aurora Australis. **Antarkta Oceano** Antarctic Ocean.
antarktika Antarctic. **Antarktika Oceano** Antarctic Ocean.
Antarktiko Antarctic.
Antarktio Antarctic, Antarctica.
Antarkto Antarctic, the Antarctic.
Antaro Antares.
antaŭ above, above, before, in front of, to, ago. **antaŭ ĉio** above all, especially. **antaŭ kelkaj jaroj** several years ago. **antaŭ**

kelkaj tagoj a few days ago, some days ago. **antaŭ Kristo** before Christ, BC. **antaŭ la endormiĝo** before going to sleep. **antaŭ la Komuna Ero** before the Common Era, BCE. **antaŭ nelonga tempo** not long ago. **antaŭ ne longe** lately, recently, since. **antaŭ nelonge** not long ago, recently. **antaŭ ok tagoj** a week ago. **antaŭ ol** before, previous to, ere. **antaŭ rajdanto** scout. **antaŭ tri monatoj** three months ago. **antaŭ tri tagoj** three days ago. **antaŭ unu jaro** one year ago.
antaŭ- advance, fore-.
antaŭa advance, advanced, antecedent, anterior, earlier, former, forward, past, preceding, previous, prior. **antaŭa flanko** façade, front, obverse. **antaŭa grajpo** forward grapple. **antaŭa kaj posta** former and latter. **antaŭa kovrilo** front cover. **antaŭa kruro** front leg. **antaŭa lampo** headlamp. **antaŭa masto** foremast. **antaŭa nomo** first name. **antaŭa nulo** leading zero. **antaŭa parto** prow. **antaŭa piedo** foreleg, front paw. **antaŭa steveno** stem. **antaŭa tago** eve, day before.
antaŭaj nuloj leading zeros.
antaŭaĉeti to buy in advance.
antaŭafero preliminary.
antaŭafikso prefix.
antaŭaj nuloj leading zeros.
antaŭaĵo antecedent, precedent, front, prelude.
antaŭamplifikatoro preamplifier.
antaŭamplifilo preamplifier.
antaŭanonci to preannounce, announce in advance.
antaŭanto predecessor.
antaŭaranĝi to prearrange.
antaŭarango prearrangement.
antaŭaverti to forewarn.
antaŭbraka antebrachial.
antaŭbrako forearm, lower arm.
antaŭĉambra antechamber, of an antechamber.
antaŭĉambro antechamber, anteroom.
antaŭĉuro precum.
antaŭdati to antedate.
antaŭdatiĝi to antedate, predate.
antaŭdatumi to antedate.
antaŭdecidi to predetermine.
antaŭdecido predetermination.
antaŭdestini to predestine.
antaŭdestinismo predestination.
antaŭdestinita predestined.
antaŭdestino predestination.
antaŭdifini to predefine.
antaŭdiluva antediluvian, very ancient.
antaŭdirebla predictable.
antaŭdireble predictably.

antaŭdiri to forecast, foretell, prophesy, predict, augur, prophesy.
antaŭdiristino fortune teller.
antaŭdiristo fortune teller.
antaŭdiro prediction.
antaŭe ahead, formerly, previously, before, beforehand, forward, in advance, in front.
antaŭecindikatoro priority indicator.
antaŭeco precedence, priority.
antaŭedziĝa antenuptial.
antaŭen ahead, forth, forward(s), on(ward).
antaŭen puŝi to impel, propel.
antaŭenema forward-thinking, progressive.
antaŭenigi to advance, move forward, promote.
antaŭenigi to advance.
antaŭenigo advancement.
antaŭeniri to advance, go forward.
antaŭenirigi to advance.
antaŭeniro advance.
antaŭenkliniĝi to bend forwards.
antaŭenmarŝi to march forward.
antaŭenmova advancing.
antaŭenmovi to advance.
antaŭenpaŝi to step forward.
antaŭenpuŝi to push forward.
antaŭenpuŝo impetus.
antaŭenrajdi to ride fowards.
antaŭenrigardi to look forwards.
antaŭenrigardo forward look.
antaŭensalti to leap forward.
antaŭensendi to send on.
antaŭenveni to come forward.
antaŭfabrikita domo prefabricated house.
antaŭfari to prepare, do something in advance.
Antaŭfasta Mardo Shrove-Tuesday.
antaŭfenestro windshield.
antaŭfiguri to foreshadow, prefigure.
antaŭfiksi to predetermine, prearrange, set in advance.
antaŭfiksita predetermined. **antaŭfiksita tempo** predetermined time.
antaŭfinala semifinal.
antaŭfinalisto semifinalist.
antaŭfinalo semifinal.
antaŭflari to smell something coming.
antaŭforigi to avoid, evade. **antaŭforigi akcidenton** to avoid an accident.
antaŭgarda precautionary, preventive.
antaŭgardi to guard, preserve, protect, save.
antaŭgardo protection.
antaŭgardoado preservative.
antaŭgeedziĝa antenuptial.
antaŭglaco windshield.
antaŭgusto foretaste.
antaŭgvardio vanguard.
antaŭĝoji to look forward to. **antaŭĝoji pri** to look forward to.

antaŭĝui to look forward to.
antaŭhaltigi to forestall, obviate, prevent.
antaŭhieraŭ the day before yesterday.
antaŭhistorio prehistory.
antaŭi to precede.
antaŭigi to substitute.
antaŭiĝanto leader.
antaŭiĝi to stand out.
antaŭiĝo lead.
antaŭira leading. **antaŭira nulo** leading zero. **antaŭira spaceto** leading space.
antaŭiranto precursor.
antaŭiri to go before, precede, press forward.
antaŭjuĝa biased.
antaŭjuĝemo bias.
antaŭjuĝi to prejudge.
antaŭjuĝo prejudice.
antaŭkalkuli to precalculate, calculate in advance, estimate.
antaŭkambrio pre-Cambrian.
antaŭkanti to sing in public, perform.
antaŭkapablo predisposition.
antaŭkompakta precompact (set).
antaŭkomplico accessory before the fact.
antaŭkondiĉo precondition, prerequisite.
antaŭkongreso pre-congress.
antaŭkonsenti to prearrange, agree on in advance, make a prior arrangement.
antaŭkonsentita dato prearranged date.
antaŭkonstruaĵo forebuilding.
antaŭkontrolo de datenoj data validation.
antaŭkorto forecourt.
antaŭlasta last but one, penultimate.
antaŭlegi to pronounce.
antaŭlerneja pre-school.
antaŭlonge long ago.
antaŭludaĵo prelude.
antaŭludi to perform in public.
antaŭludo prelude, foreplay.
antaŭmalhelpa pre-emptive.
antaŭmalhelpi to prevent.
antaŭmanĝaĵo appetizer.
antaŭmarŝanto scout.
antaŭmasto foremast.
antaŭmenciita aforementioned, aforesaid.
antaŭmendi to reserve.
antaŭmendo booking.
antaŭmeta operaciskribo prefix notation.
antaŭmeti to serve.
antaŭmetistino waitress.
antaŭmilita antebellum.
antaŭmontro preview.
antaŭmorta ante-mortem.
antaŭnaska antenatal.
antaŭnelonge a short while ago, not long ago.
antaŭnoktomeza dormo beauty sleep.
antaŭnomo first name.
antaŭo fore. **antaŭo posten** back to front.

antaŭombri to adumbrate.
antaŭopinia preconceived.
antaŭopinii to anticipate, judge in advance.
antaŭopinio preconception.
antaŭpage in advance.
antaŭpagi to prepay.
antaŭpago advance payment, advance.
antaŭparoli to give a speech.
antaŭparolo foreword, introduction, preface, preamble.
antaŭparto forepart, steerage, stem (of ship).
antaŭpaska antepaschal.
antaŭpatro forefather.
antaŭpendaĵo antependium.
antaŭpensi to think about in advance, to consider ahead of time.
antaŭpensita premeditated.
antaŭpiedo forefoot.
antaŭplado appetizer.
antaŭplano foreground.
antaŭplenumi to fulfill in advance.
antaŭposteno outpost.
antaŭpremisi to presume, presuppose.
antaŭpreparo preliminary.
antaŭprezentaĵo trailer.
antaŭprezenti to preview.
antaŭprezento preview.
antaŭpripensi to consider in advance, think through ahead of time.
antaŭrajdanto postilion.
antaŭrakonti to relate in advance.
antaŭrangi to outrank, be superior in rank.
antaŭrevolucia pre-revolutionary.
antaŭrimeda precautionary.
antaŭrimedo measure, precaution.
antaŭripeti to repeat.
antaŭsalono antechamber.
antaŭsavi to warn.
antaŭscii to know in advance.
antaŭsciiga premonitory.
antaŭsciigi to portend.
antaŭscio foreknowledge.
antaŭsenti to have a premonition.
antaŭsento foreboding, presentiment.
antaŭsigni to foreshadow, foretell, foretoken, presage.
antaŭsigno foreshadower, indication, omen, portent, precursor, presage, sign, prognostic.
antaŭskizi to adumbrate.
antaŭskribaĵo prologue.
antaŭstari to stand before, in front of.
antaŭstato status quo.
antaŭstomako antestomach.
antaŭsupozi to presume, presuppose.
antaŭsupozo presumption, presupposition.
antaŭtagmeza a.m., morning.
antaŭtagmeze in the morning.
antaŭtagmezo morning.
antaŭtago eve.

antaŭtegmento

antaŭtegmento penthouse, shed.
antaŭtempa premature, untimely.
antaŭtempe prematurely.
antaŭtempi to be premature, early.
antaŭteni to present.
antaŭtimi to be apprehensive.
antaŭtimo fear, apprehension.
antaŭtraktado preprocessing.
antaŭtraktilo preprocessor.
antaŭtuko apron.
antaŭulo forerunner, harbinger, precursor, predecessor.
antaŭurba suburban.
antaŭurbo suburb.
antaŭvelo foresail.
antaŭvenanto precursor.
antaŭvenda advance.
antaŭveni to precede.
antaŭveninto forerunner.
antaŭveno lead-up.
antaŭverko prologue.
antaŭvespero dusk, twilight.
antaŭvida prospective.
antaŭvidebla foreseeable, measurable.
antaŭvideble predictably, unsurprisingly.
antaŭvidi to anticipate, foresee.
antaŭzorga thoughtful.
antaŭzorge carefully.
antaŭzorgi to take care beforehand, take precautions.
antaŭzorgo foresight, forethought, preservation, thoughtfulness, providence, precaution.
antecedento antecedent.
antecedentoj antecedents, record.
antefikso antefix.
antelikso anthelix.
antemido dog-fennel, mayweed.
antemo anthem.
antena antennal.
anteneto antennule.
antenkomutilo antenna switch.
antenkonektilo antenna terminal.
anteno aerial, antenna, feeler.
antenteme expectantly.
antentinda relevant.
antenturo antenna tower.
antera antheral.
anteridio antheridium.
anteriko Saint Bernard's lily.
antero anther.
anterozoido antherozoid.
anterozoo antherozoid.
anthelikso anthelix.
anthelio anthelion.
antiacido antacid.
antiamerika anti-American.
anti-antikorpo anti-antibody.
antiarrezino antiar.
antiartrita antiarthritic.

antikvisto

antiaviadila antiaircraft.
antibakteria antibacterial.
antibiotika antibiotic.
antibiotiko antibiotic.
anticiklono anticyclone.
anticipa advance, expectant.
anticipado look ahead.
anticipe in anticipation.
anticipi to anticipate, expect, think ahead.
anticipo anticipation.
antideprima antidepressant.
antiderivativo antiderivative.
antideŭterono antideuteron.
antidorko springbok.
antidota antidotal.
antidoto antidote.
antielektrono antielectron.
antiemetiko antiemetic.
antienzimo antienzyme.
antifebra antifebrile, antipyretic.
antiferomagneta antiferromagnetic.
antifona antiphonal.
antifono antiphony, antiphon, anthem.
antifrazo antiphrase.
antigena antigenic.
antigeno antigen.
Antigona Antigone.
Antigvo Antigua. **Antigvo kaj Barbudo** Antigua and Barbuda.
antihemofilia antihemophilic.
antiheroo antihero.
antihidrofobia antihydrophobic.
antihipnota antihypnotic.
antihipokondria antihypochondriac.
antihistamino antihistamine.
antihisteria antihysteric.
antiklerikala anticlerical.
antiklimaksa anticlimactic.
antiklimakso anticlimax.
antiklinala anticlinal.
antiklinalo anticline.
antikoagulenzo anticoagulant.
antikoncipa contraceptive.
antikonvulsia anticonvulsive.
antikorpo antibody.
Antikostio Anticosti Island.
antikrezo antichresis, assignment of profits.
antikristo Antichrist.
antikva ancient, antique, antiquated, rare, old. **antikva tempo** antiquity.
antikvaja antiquarian.
antikvajbutiko antique shop, antique store.
antikvaĵejo antique shop, antique store.
antikvaĵista antiquarian.
antikvaĵisto antique dealer.
antikvaĵo relic, antique.
antikvarko antiquark.
antikveco antiquity.
antikvisto antiquary.

antikvulo ancient one.
antila Antillian.
antilano Antillian.
antilogaritma antilogarithmic.
antilogaritmo antilogarithm.
Antiloj Antilles.
antilopo antelope.
antimalaria antimalarial.
antimaterio antimatter.
antimisila antimissile.
antimonika antimonic.
antimono antimony.
antimonoza antimonous.
antineŭralgia analgesic.
antineŭtrino antineutrino.
antineŭtrono antineutron.
antinomio antinomy.
Antioĥio Antioch.
Antioĥujo Antioch.
antipapo antipope.
antiparaliza antiparalytic.
antipartiklo antiparticle.
antipartikulo antiparticle.
Antipaso Antipas.
antipatia antipathetic, nasty, repugnant, averse.
antipatie uncongenially.
antipatii to antipathize.
antipatio antipathy, aversion, dislike, revulsion.
antipatioeco repugnance.
Antipatro Antipater.
antiperistalta antiperistaltic.
antiperspirilo antiperspirant.
antipirino antipyrine.
antipoda antipodal.
antipodo antipode(s).
antipodoj antipodes.
Antipodoj Antipodes, the Antipodes.
antiprotono antiproton.
antipsikoza antipsychotic.
antirakita antirachitic.
antirino snapdragon, antirrhinum.
antirisko beaked parsley.
antirusta antirust.
antisemidismo anti-Semitism.
antisemita anti-Semitic.
antisemitismo anti-Semitism.
antisemito anti-Semite.
antisepsa antiseptic.
antisepsaĵo antiseptic.
antisepsi to disinfect.
antisepsilo antiseptic.
antisepso antisepsis.
antisero antiserum.
antisimetria antisymmetric.
antiskorbuta antiscorbutic.
antisocieta antisocial.
antispasma antispasmodic, antispastic.

antistrofo antistrophe.
antitanka antitank.
antiteza antithetical, antithetic.
antitezo antithesis.
antitoksino antitoxin.
antitrado antitrade.
antitrusta antitrust.
antitusa antitussive.
antivirusa antiviral, antivirus.
antiviruso antivirus.
antivitamino antivitamin.
antologio anthology.
Antoneno Antoninus.
antonima antonymous.
antonimo antonym.
Antonineto Antoinette.
Antonio Antony.
Antono Anton.
antonomazio antonomasia.
antozoo anthozoan.
antraceno anthracene.
antracito anthracite.
antrakinono anthraquinone.
antrakonito anthraconite.
antrakozo anthracosis.
antrakso anthrax, carbuncle.
Antrimo Antrim.
antrisko beaked parsley.
antro antrum.
antropocentra anthropocentric.
antropofaga anthropophagous.
antropofagio anthropophagy.
antropofagismo anthropophagy.
antropofago anthropophagite, anthropophagus.
antropofobio anthropophobia.
antropoida anthropoidal.
antropoido anthropoid.
antropoidoj Anthropoidea.
antropologia anthropologic, anthropological.
antropologie anthropologically.
antropologiisto anthropologist.
antropologio anthropology.
antropologo anthropologist.
antropomancio anthropomancy.
antropometria anthropometric.
antropometrio anthropometry.
antropomorfa anthropomorphic.
antropomorfigi to anthropomorphize.
antropomorfismo anthropomorphism.
antropopiteko chimp, chimpanzee.
antropozofio anthroposophy.
antuso pipit.
antverpena Antwerp.
Antverpeno Antwerp.
Anubo Anubis.
anuitato annual installment, installment, repayment, annuity.

anunciacio annunciation. **Anunciacio** Annunciation, Lady Day.
anura anuran, anurous.
anurio anuria.
anuro anuran.
anuroj Anura.
anusa anal. **anusa seksumado** anal sex.
anuse anally.
anusfiki to sodomize.
anuskoito anal sex.
anuso anus, ass.
aoristo aorist.
aorta aortic.
aorto aorta.
apaĉa Apache.
apaĉino Apache girl.
apaĉo apache, hood, ruffian, tough.
apalaĉa Appalachian.
apalaĉia Appalachian.
Apalaĉoj Appalachian Mountains.
apanaĝo appanage, perquisite.
aparatadaptilo device driver.
aparat-adaptilo device driver.
aparat-adreso device address.
aparataro equipment, hardware.
aparatbitoko status byte.
aparatiga marko file mark.
aparato apparatus, device, set, appliance, machine, system.
aparatulo apparatchik.
aparta aloof, apart, distinct, distinctive, own, particular, separate, special. **aparta opinio** opposing opinion, minority opinion.
apartaĵo particularity, characteristic.
apartamentaro apartment (building).
apartamento apartment, flat.
aparte apart, separately, aside, asunder, particularly. **aparte de** apart from.
aparteco apartness.
apartema aloof.
aparteme aloofly.
apartena belonging to, appurtenant.
apartenado belonging.
apartenaĵa proprietary.
apartenaĵo belonging, possession.
aparteni to belong to.
aparteno al grupo membership in a group.
apartga separated.
apartiga separated (space). **apartiga marko** file mark.
apartigebla separable (space).
apartigi to detach, divide, separate, put aside, relegate, set apart.
apartigilo separator.
apartigita per separated by.
apartigo separation, partition.
apartiĝi to divide, separate (oneself from someone else), go one's separate ways.
apartiĝo division, separation.

apartismo Apartheid.
apastro apaster.
apatia apathetic.
apatie apathetically.
apatio apathy, nonchalance.
apatito apatite.
apekso apex.
apela appellant, appellate.
apelaci to appeal.
apelacia appellate.
apelacianto appellant.
apelacii to appeal. **apelacii al** to appeal to, make an appeal to.
apelaciinto appellant.
apelacio appeal.
apelacionto appellant.
apelanto appellant.
apeli to appeal.
apelo appeal.
apenaŭ barely, hardly, only just, scarcely, no more than.
apenaŭa bare, meagre.
apendektomio appendectomy.
apendica appendicular.
apendicektomio appendectomy.
apendicito appendicitis.
apendico appendix.
apenina Apennine.
apeninano inhabitant of the Apennines.
Apeninoj Apennines.
apepsio apepsia.
aperaĵo vision, apparition, appearance, occurrence, instance.
apercepti to apperceive.
apercepto apperception.
aperi to appear, come into sight, emerge, materialize, perform, be published.
aperigi to make appear, produce, publish.
aperitivo apéritif.
apero apparition, appearance, phantom.
aperta open.
apertaĵo opening, aperture.
aperte open(ly).
aperteco frankness, openness.
aperti to open.
apertigi to open up.
apertura apertural.
aperturo aperture, opening.
aperturregilo aperture control.
apetaloj Apetalae.
apetenco appetency.
apetita appetizing.
apetitdona appetizing.
apetitdone appetizingly.
apetite appetizingly.
apetitiga appetizing.
apetitige appetizingly.
apetito appetite.
apetitodona appetizing.

apetitveka appetizing.
apetitveke appetizingly.
apetitvekilo appetizer, something that whets the appetite.
apiacoj Apiaceae (family of plants).
apika steep, tilted, sheer, perpendicular.
apikulturo apiculture.
apio (wild) celery.
Apiso Apis.
aplanata aplanatic.
aplanateco aplanatism.
aplanatismo aplanatism.
aplanato aplanatic lens.
aplaŭdado acclamation.
aplaŭdegi to cheer.
aplaŭdego acclamation.
aplaŭdema appreciative.
aplaŭdi to acclaim, applaud, clap.
aplaŭdistaro applauders.
aplaŭdo acclaim, acclamation, approval.
aplaŭdoado applause.
apleto applet.
aplika application. **aplika programaro** application software. **aplika programo** application program. **aplika tavolo** application layer.
aplikado application, employment, use.
aplikaĵo application.
aplikanto applier.
aplikata applied.
aplikebla applicable.
aplikeble applicably.
aplikebleco applicability.
apliki to administer, apply, practice.
aplikilo applicator.
aplikita applied.
apliko application, employment, use.
aplikprogrameto applet.
aplikprogramisto applications programmer.
aplikprogramo application (program).
aplomba unmoved.
aplombo aplomb, self-assurance, nerve.
apneo apnea.
apocinacoj Apocynaceae (family of plants).
apocrypha apocryphal.
apocryphe apocryphally.
apoda apodal.
apodikta apodeictic, apodictic.
apodo apod.
apodoj Apoda.
apodozo apodosis.
apoenzimo apoenzyme.
apofilito apophyllite.
apofiza apophyseal.
apofizo apophysis, process.
apofonio ablaut, apophony.
apoga supporting. **apoga punkto** control point.

apogamio apogamy.
apogarko flying buttress.
apogbrako arm.
apogea apogean, apogeic.
apogei to be in apogee.
apogeo apex, apogee, pinnacle, zenith.
apogeotropa apogeotropic.
apogeotropismo apogeotropism.
apogi to back (up), bolster, buttress, lean, prop, rest, support, sustain, underpin, recline, uphold. **apogi sin** to lean. **apogi sin al** to lean against.
apogiĝi to rest upon, support oneself on.
apogilo prop, support, buttress, pillar.
apogkolono buttress.
apogo backing.
apogpilastro abutment, buttress.
apogpunkto fulcrum.
apografo apograph.
apogseĝo armchair.
apoĝaturo appoggiatura, long grace note.
apokalipsa apocalyptic.
apokalipse apocalyptically.
apokalipso apocalypse.
Apokalipso Apocalypse, Book of Revelation.
apokopeo apocope.
apokopigi to apocopate.
apokopo apocope.
apokrifa apocryphal.
apokrife apocryphally.
apokrifeco apocryphalness.
apokrifo apocrypha.
Apokrifoj Apocrypha.
Apolo Apollo.
apologetiko apologetics.
apologia apologetic. **Apologia Insulo** Vindication Island.
apologiarto apologetics.
apologie apologetically.
apologii to apologize.
apologiisto apologist.
apologio apology, vindication (of one's beliefs), apologia.
apologo apologue, fable.
Apolonia Apollonia.
Apolonio Apollonius.
Apolono Apollo.
apomorfino apomorphine.
aponeŭroza aponeurotic.
aponeŭrozo aponeurosis.
apopleksia apoplectic.
apopleksieca apoplectic.
apopleksiema apoplectic.
apopleksio (apoplectic) fit, seizure, stroke, (stroke of) apoplexy.
apopleksiulo apoplectic.
aporto apport.
aposiopezo aposiopesis.
apostalado apostleship, apostolicity.

apostata

apostata apostate.
apostateco apostasy.
apostatiĝi to apostatize.
apostatiĝo apostacy.
apostato apostate.
aposteriora a posteriori.
aposteriore a posteriori.
apostola apostolic. **apostola patro** church father.
apostoleco apostleship, apostolate.
apostolo apostle, disciple.
apostrofa apostrophic.
apostrofi to apostrophize, elide.
apostrofo apostrophe (').
apotecio apothecium.
apoteka kendulo pot marigold.
apotekisto apothecary, chemist.
apoteko drugstore, pharmacy, chemist.
apotemo apothem, slant height.
apoteozi to apotheosize, deify.
apoteozo apotheosis.
apozemo apozem.
apozicii to appose, juxtapose.
apoziciiĝi to be in apposition.
apozicio apposition.
apozimazo apozymase.
appia Appian.
apra of a wild boar.
apraĵo wild boar (meat).
apraro sounder.
apreci to appreciate, appraise.
apreco appreciation.
apretaĵo dressing, finishing.
apreti to finish.
apreturi to finish.
apreturo starch, dressing, finishing (of fabrics).
aprezi to appreciate, appraise.
aprezo appreciation.
aprido young of a wild boar.
Aprilo April.
aprila April.
Aprilstultulo April fool.
aprino female (wild) boar.
apriora a priori, predefined, intrinsic, standard.
apriore a priori.
aprioreco apriority.
apriorismo apriorism.
apro wild boar.
aproba approving, favourable.
aprobebla plausible.
aprobeble plausibly.
aprobi to approve, authorize, countenance, endorse, sanction, ratify, hold with, tolerate.
aprobinda reasonable.
aprobo acclaim, approval, approbation.
aproĉasado boar hunting.
aproksima approximate.

Arakno

aproksimado approximation.
aproksimaĵo approximate value.
aproksimato approximated quantity.
aproksimi to approximate.
aproksimiĝi to approach, draw nearer.
aproksimo approximation.
apsaro Aspara.
apsido apse, apsis.
aptenodito penguin.
aptera apterous.
apterigo kiwi.
apud at, beside, by, near (to), nearby, next to.
apuda adjacent, adjoining, contiguous, next to, neighbouring.
apudaĵo neighbourhood, vicinity.
apudborda beachfront.
apude nearby. **apude de** next to, adjacent to.
apudeco contiguity, proximity.
apudesti to be present.
apudesto presence.
apudi to be near to, close to.
apudiĝi to approach, come closer.
apudlita bedside.
apudmara seaside, beside the sea.
apudmeti to juxtapose.
apudmeto juxtaposition.
apudnomo nickname.
apudo (near, close) presence.
apudtera near land.
apudvoja fosaĵo roadside ditch.
Apulio Apulia.
apunto change, small money.
apuso swift (bird).
araba Arabian, Arab, Arabic. **araba cifero** Arabic digit. **Araba Duoninsulo** Arabian Peninsula. **Araba Maro** Arabian Sea.
arabalesto crossbow.
arabe in Arabic.
arabeca Arabian.
arabeska arabesque.
arabesko arabesque.
arabeskosegilo jigsaw.
Arabia Arabian, Arabic.
arabidopso thale cress.
arabino Arabian woman.
arabinozo arabinose.
Arabio Arabia.
arabismo arabism.
arabo Arab.
Arabujo Arabia.
araĉo band, gang.
aragona Aragonese.
aragonito aragonite.
Arakano Arakan.
arakida acido arachidic acid.
arakido peanut, groundnut.
Arakna Arachne.
Arakno Arachne.

araknoidito

araknoidito arachnoiditis.
araknoido arachnoid.
arako rack, arrack.
araliacoj Araliaceae (family of plants).
aralio aralia.
Arallago Aral Sea.
Aralo Aral Sea, Lake Aral.
aramea Aramaic.
arameismo Aramaism.
arameo Aramaic.
aranaĵo spider web.
aranea of a spider. **aranea kleomo** spider flower.
araneaĵa sempervivo cobweb houseleek.
araneaĵo spider web.
araneedoj Araneidae.
araneo spider.
araneoido arachnoid, arachnoid membrane.
aranereto cobweb.
araneulo arachnid.
araneuloj Araneae (order containing spiders).
aranĝaĵo arrangement, set-up, permutation, device.
aranĝema ingenious, resourceful.
aranĝi to arrange, adjust, array, fix up. **aranĝi florojn** to arrange flowers. **aranĝi la liton** to make the bed.
aranĝita arranged.
aranĝitaĵo arrangement.
aranĝo accommodation, arrangement, adjustment, layout, format.
aranĝsistemo (system of) arrangement.
Arano Arran.
arao macaw.
Ararato Ararat.
araŭkariacoj Araucariaceae (plant family).
araŭkario araucaria, monkey puzzle (tree).
arba arboreal, tree, of a tree.
arbaĵeto small grove.
arbaĵo tree trunk, tree limbs (used for wood).
arbalestisto archer.
arbalesto bow, crossbow.
arbara forest, of a forest.
arbarbrulego forest-fire.
arbarego large forest, great forest.
arbareto wood.
arbargardisto forester.
arbarigi to afforest.
arbarigo afforestation.
arbarincendio forest-fire.
arbaristo woodsman, forester.
arbarizi to afforest.
arbarkulturo forestry.
Arbarlago Lake of the Woods.
arbarlimo edge of the woods, edge of the forest.
arbaro forest, woods.
arbarpolicisto park ranger.
arbarriĉa woody.

arde

arbarstepo wooded steppe.
arbarvojeto forest path.
arbeca arborescent.
arbeda bushy.
arbedo bush, shrub.
arbego large tree.
arbejo arboretum.
arbetaĵaro brush, brushwood.
arbetaĵlimo edge of a small grove.
arbetaĵo bush, thicket, shrub.
arbetaro thicket, copse, grove.
arbeto bush, shrub, little tree.
arbisto arborist, arboriculturalist.
arbitra arbitrary, despotic.
arbitraciantino arbitress.
arbitracianto arbiter, arbitrator, referee, umpire.
arbitraciebla arbitrable.
arbitracii to arbitrate, referee.
arbitraciinto arbiter, arbitrator.
arbitraciisto arbitrator, referee.
arbitracio arbitrage, arbitration.
arbitracionto arbiter, arbitrator.
arbitraciulo arbiter, arbitrator, referee, umpire.
arbitraĝo arbitrage.
arbitraĵo arbitrary act.
arbitratorino arbitress.
arbitratoro arbiter, arbitrator.
arbitre arbitrarily.
arbitreco arbitrariness.
arbitro arbiter, arbitrator.
arbo tree.
arboĝardeno arboretum.
arbohakado logging.
arbohakisto woodcutter.
arbokulturisto tree-nurseryman.
arbokulturo arboriculture.
arbombraĵo shade of a tree.
arboplena full of trees.
arboŝelo bark.
arbotrairo tree traversal, tree walking.
arbotrunko stem, trunk, tree trunk.
Arbroto Arbroath.
arbsupro top of a tree.
arbtrunko bole, stem, tree-trunk, trunk.
arbustaĵo shrubbery.
arbustaro shrubbery.
arbusto bush, shrub, shrubbery.
arbuto arbutus.
arbutujo arbutus, strawberry tree.
Arĉibaldo Archibald.
arĉinstrumento bow instrument.
arĉkordo bowstring.
arĉo bow (violin).
arĉostango bowstick.
arda ablaze, afire, aflame, aglow, ardent.
ardaĵo embers, coals.
arde ardently.

ardeco

ardeco ardor, glow, heat, passion.
ardeedoj herons.
ardejo kiln.
Ardenoj Ardennes.
ardeo heron.
ardeta almost red-hot, burning hot.
ardeza slate.
ardezo slate.
ardezotabulo slate.
Ardgajo Ardgay.
ardi to be ardent, burn, glow, glow with heat.
ardiferenco set difference.
ardilo kiln.
ardo glow, heat, passion, ardor.
Ardrio Airdrie.
Ardrosano Ardrossan.
are in a group, en masse.
areaĵo area.
arealo area, natural habitat.
arege en masse, as a group.
arego multitude, mass.
arekarbo Areca.
areknukso betel nut.
areko betel palm.
arekosinuso arc cosine.
arekotangento arc cotangent.
arekujo Areca.
arenatero tall oat-grass.
areno arena, (boxing) ring.
areo area.
areolo aureolus, ring around the moon.
areometro aerometer, densitometer, hydrometer.
Areopago Areopagus.
Areso Ares.
arestado apprehension, arrest, detention.
arestejo jail.
aresti to apprehend, arrest, detain.
arestiĝo arrest.
arestinto arrester, arrestor, arresting officer.
arestisto arrester, arrestor, arresting officer.
arestito arrested person, prisoner, arrestee, detainee.
aresto apprehension, arrest, custody, detention.
arestodono arrest warrant.
arestordono warrant.
areto small group, small number.
argano crane (mechanical), oil well derrick.
argentano (new, nickel) silver.
argentina Argentine, Argentinean.
argentinanino Argentinean woman.
argentinano Argentine.
Argentino Argentina.
argila earthen, clay, stone.
argilaĵo clay object, crockery, earthenware, pottery.
argileca argillaceous.
argilo clay.

arĥimandrito

argiloza argillaceous.
argiltabulo clay tablet.
argilujo (earthenware) pot, jar, jug, crock.
argilvazo (earthenware) vase.
argironeto water spider.
Argo Argus.
Argolando Argus.
Argonaŭto Argonaut.
argonaŭto Argonaut; paper nautilus. **argonaŭtoj** Argonauts.
argono argon.
argoto argot.
argumentado argumentation.
argumentema argumentative.
argumenti to argue, maintain.
argumento argument, plea, operand.
Arguso Argus.
arĝenta silver, silvery.
arĝentaĵo item made of silver.
arĝentano argentan, German silver.
arĝentaro silverware.
arĝenti to silver plate.
arĝentika argental, argentic, argent, argentine.
arĝentisto silversmith.
arĝentitaĵo silver-plated article.
arĝentizi to silver.
arĝentkolora silver-coloured.
arĝentmevo herring gull.
arĝento silver.
arĝentoza argentiferous, argentous.
arĝentriĉa argentiferous, argentous.
arĝentumi to silver.
arĝirolo colloidal silver.
arhato Arhat.
arĥaika archaic.
arĥaike archaically.
arĥaismo archaism.
arĥaja antiquated, archaic, obsolete.
arĥaje archaically.
arĥeologia archaeological, archeological.
arĥeologiisto archaeologist.
arĥeologio archaeology.
arĥeologo archaeologist, archeologist.
arĥeopterigo archeopteryx.
Arĥeozoiko Archaeozoic, Archaeozoic era.
arĥetipo archetype.
arĥianĝelo archangel.
arĥidiakona archidiaconal.
arĥidiakono archdeacon.
arĥiduko archduke.
arĥiepiskopa archiepiscopal.
arĥiepiskopejo archbishopric, archepiscopality.
arĥiepiskopo archbishop.
arĥifripono archfiend.
arĥimandrito archimandrite.

44

arĥimeda Archimedean. **arĥimeda spiralo** Archimedes spiral. **arĥimeda ŝraŭbo** Archimedean screw.
Arĥimedo Archimedes.
arĥipelago archipelago.
arĥitektaĵo building.
arĥitekto architect.
arĥitektura architectural.
arĥitekture architecturally.
arĥitekturisto architect.
arĥitekturo architecture.
arĥitravo architrave.
arĥivejo archive.
arĥivisto archivist, keeper of the records.
arĥivo archive, archives, files, records.
arĥivolto archivolt.
arĥonto archon.
aria aryan.
Ariadna Ariadne.
Ariadno Ariadne.
arianisma Arian.
arianismo Arianism.
arianisto Arian.
ariano Arian.
arida arid.
aride aridly.
arieca arioso.
ariecaĵo arioso.
ariece arioso.
Arielo Ariel.
ariera back.
ariergardo rear, rearguard.
ariero rear (military).
arierulo full-back.
Arieso Aries (zodiac).
arieto arietta.
arigi to amass, put together.
arigo round-up.
ariĝi to come together, form a group.
arila arillate.
arilo aril.
ario air, aria, tune.
arista aristate.
Aristido Aristides.
aristo arista, awn, beard, bristle.
aristofano Aristophanes.
aristokrata aristocratic.
aristokrataro aristocracy.
aristokrate aristocratically.
aristokrateco aristocracy.
aristokratia aristocratic.
aristokratie aristocratically.
aristokratio aristocracy.
aristokratismo aristocracy.
aristokrato aristocrat.
aristolokiacoj Aristolochiaceae (plant family).
aristolokio clematis, birthwort.
aristotelianismo Aristotelianism.
aristotelisma Aristotelian.
aristotelisto Aristotelian.
Aristotelo Aristotle.
Aristoto Aristotle.
aritenoida arytenoid.
aritenoido arytenoid.
aritmetika arithmetic. **aritmetika meznombro** arithmetic average, arithmetic mean. **aritmetika mezumo** arithmetic mean. **aritmetika operacio** arithmetic operation. **aritmetika progresio** arithmetic progression, arithmetic sequence. **aritmetika reĝistro** accumulator, arithmetic register, operand register. **aritmetika ŝovo** arithmetic shift. **aritmetika vico** arithmetic progression, arithmetic sequence.
aritmetike arithmetically.
aritmetiki to perform arithmetic, calculate (arithmetic functions).
aritmetikilo arithmetic and logical unit.
aritmetiko arithmetic, number theory.
aritmio arrhythmia.
aritmo arithmetic mean.
aritmomancio arithmomancy.
arizona Arizonan.
arizonano Arizonan.
Arizono Arizona.
arja Aryan.
arjo Aryan.
arka arched.
arkadaro portico, arcade.
arkadia Arcadian.
arkadiano Arcadian.
Arkadio Arcadia.
arkado archway.
Arkadujo Arcadia.
arkaika archaic, obsolete.
arkaikaĵo archaism.
arkaike archaically.
arkaikeco archaism.
arkaikigi to antiquate.
arkaismo archaism.
arkaja antiquated, archaic, obsolete.
arkaĵaro arcade.
arkaĵo arch, vault.
arkana arcane, esoteric.
arkanĝelo archangel.
arkano arcanum, secret.
arkansa Arkansan.
arkansano Arkansan.
arkansasano Arkansan.
Arkansaso Arkansas.
arkaro arcade.
arkeano Archean.
arkebuzo arquebus.
arkefleksi to arch.
arkeo ark.
arkeobotaniko archaeobotany.
arkeocito archeocyte.

arkeologia archaeological.
arkeologiisto archaeologist.
arkeologio archaeology.
arkeologisto archaeologist.
arkeologo archaeologist.
arkeomagnetismo archaeomagnetism.
arkeopterigo archaeopteryx.
arkeopteriko archaeopteryx.
arkeozoika archaeozoic.
arkeozoiko Archaeozoic Era.
arketipa archetypical.
arketipo archetype.
arkforma arcuate.
arki to arch.
arkianĝelo archangel.
arkidiakona archidiaconal.
arkidiakono archdeacon.
arkiduklando archduchy.
arkiduko archduke.
arkiepiskopejo archbishopric, archepiscopality.
arkiepiskopo archbishop.
arkifripono archfiend.
arkigi to arch, camber, bend, hump, curve.
arkiĝi to arc, arch.
arkimandrito archimandrite.
Arkimedo Archimedes.
arkipelago archipelago.
arkisto archer, bowman.
arkitekta architectural.
arkitektaĵo building.
arkitekto architect.
arkitektura architectonic, architectural.
arkitekturaĵo building, edifice.
arkitekturisto architect.
arkitekturo architecture.
arkitravo architrave.
arkivadiko archive administration, archive science.
arkivado archiving.
arkivejo archive, records office.
arkivekzemplero archival copy.
arkivistiko archive administration, archive science.
arkivisto archivist, keeper of the records.
arkivo archive, record(s), file(s).
arkivolto archivolt.
arkkosekanto arc cosecant.
arkkosinuso arc cosine.
arkkotangento arc cotangent.
arklampo arc lamp.
Arklovo Arklow.
arko arc, bow, arch, buttress.
arkokosekanto arc cosecant.
arkokosinuso arc cosine.
arkokotangento arc cotangent.
arkonstruilo set constructor.
arkonto archon.
arkopafado archery.

arkopafisto archer, bowman.
arkopafo archery.
arkopasejo arched passage(way), archway.
arkoponto arch bridge.
arkotangento arctangent.
arkozo arcose.
arkpafado archery.
arkpafanto archer.
arkpafi to shoot a bow and arrow.
arkpafisto archer.
arksekanto arc secant.
arksinuso arc sine.
arkta arctic. **arkta aŭroro** northern lights, aurora borealis. **Arkta Cirklo** Arctic Circle. **Arkta Oceano** Arctic Ocean.
arktangento arc tangent.
arktangento arctangent.
arktika arctic. **Arktika Oceano** Arctic Ocean.
Arktiko Arctic, the Arctic.
arktio burdock.
Arkto Arctic, the Arctic.
arktostafilo bearberry.
arktoto arctotis.
Arkturo Arcturis.
arkuso angle.
arlekena zany.
arlekenadi to clown.
arlekenaĵo buffoonery.
arlekeno buffoon, clown, harlequin, jester.
Armadalo Armadale.
armadeleto armadillo.
armadelo armadillo.
armadilo armadillo.
armado armament.
Armagedono Armageddon.
Armaho Armagh.
armaĵo armour.
Armando Armand.
armaturi to provide.
armaturo armature, framework, formwork, shuttering.
armea military. **armea pastro** chaplain, army chaplain, padre.
armeestro general (of an army).
armejo arsenal, weapons storage.
armena Armenian.
Armena Armenian.
armenino Armenian woman.
Armenio Armenia.
armeno Armenian.
Armenujo Armenia.
armeo army.
armerio sea pink, thrift.
armi to arm (weapons), reinforce (concrete).
armiĝi to bear arms.
armilaro armament, equipment.
armilejo armoury, arsenal, weapons storage.
armilfaristo armourer, gunsmith.

armilisto

armilisto armourer.
armilito armed man.
armilo armament, weapon.
armiloj arms, weapons.
armilpaĝio armour bearer.
armilportisto armour bearer.
armilprovizejo arsenal, armoury.
armiltenejo arsenal, weapons storage.
armistico armistice.
armita armed. **armita betono** (iron-)reinforced concrete.
armito armed man.
armo arm, armament.
armoracio horseradish.
armorika Armorican.
Armoriko Armorica.
armorio coat-of-arms, symbol.
Arnaldo Arnold.
Arnhejmo Arnhem.
Arnhemo Arnhem.
arniko arnica, leopard's bane.
Arnoldo Arnold.
aro[1] collection, group, set, bunch, cluster, file. **aro de ĉiuj subaroj** set of all subsets.
aro[2] are (100 square metres.)
arobo arroba (old unit of weight or volume).
aroga arrogant.
aroganta arrogant, haughty.
arogantaĵo arrogance.
aroganteco arrogance, overbearingness, presumption.
aroge arrogantly.
arogi to arrogate, presume to.
arogo arrogance, arrogation.
aroki to castle (in chess).
aroma aromatic, fragrant, nutty.
aromaĵo aromatic.
aromata aromatic.
aromherbo aromatic herb.
aromi to smell.
aromigi to aromatize.
aromo aroma, flavour, fragrance, smell.
aromoterapio aromatherapy.
arondismento district.
aronganteco arrogance.
Arono Aaron.
aroruto arrowroot.
aroteorio set theory.
arpeĝi to sing arpeggios.
arpeĝo arpeggio.
arpento arpent.
arpio harpy eagle.
arsena arsenic, arsenical. **arsena acido** arsenic acid.
arsenaĵo arsenical.
arsenalo armoury, arsenal.
arsenata acido arsenic acid.
arsenatacido arsenic acid.
arsenato arsenate.

artikdoloro

arsenido arsenide.
arsenika arsenic.
arseniko (white) arsenic.
arsenita arsenious.
arsenito arsenite.
arsenizi to arsenicate.
arseno arsenic.
arsenoksido arsenic.
arsenoza arsenious.
arsinio arsine.
arsino arsine.
arŝino arshin (аршин, an obsolete Russian unit of length, 71.1 cm or 28 inches).
arta artificial, artistic. **arta horizonto** artificial horizon. **arta rezino** synthetic resin.
artaĵo work of art.
arte artfully.
arteca artistic.
artece artistically.
artefakto artifact.
artefarita artificial, man-made. **artefarita intelekto** artificial intelligence. **artefarita lingvo** artificial language. **artefarita satelito** earth satellite.
artefaritaĵo artefact.
artefarite artificially.
artemido Artemis.
Artemisa Artemis.
Artemiso Artemis.
artemizio absinth, mugwort.
Artemo Artemis, Phoebe.
arteoria set theoretical.
arteorio set theory.
arteria arterial.
arterieta arteriolar.
arterieto arteriole.
arterio artery.
arterioskierozo arteriosclerosis.
arteriovejna arteriovenous.
arteza artesian. **arteza puto** artesian well.
artfajraĵo firework.
artgalerio art gallery.
artidaktiloj Artiodactyla.
artifika contrived, sophisticated, complex, tricky.
artifike artfully.
artifikeco artfulness, trickiness.
artifikema artful, tricky.
artifikeme artfully.
artifikemo artfulness.
artifiki to concoct, contrive.
artifikistino con woman.
artifiko artifice, shenanigan, stunt, subterfuge, trick, wile.
artifikoeco deceit.
artifikulo hacker.
artika articulated, jointed.
artikado articulation.
artikdoloro arthralgia.

47

artikframa articulated.
artiki to articulate.
artikiga punkto articulation point.
artikigi to articulate, utter.
artikigita articulated.
artikigo articulation.
artiklo article, commodity.
artiko articulation, joint, hinge.
artikohava articulated.
artikolaro set of articles.
artikolo article (grammatical or newspaper).
artikpieduloj arthropods.
artikulacia articulatory. **artikulacia punkto** articulation point.
artikulacii to articulate.
artikulacio articulation.
artikulo arthropod, articulate.
artileria taĉmento battery.
artileriano artilleryman, gunner.
artileriisto artilleryman, gunner.
artilerio artillery, ordnance.
artiodaktilo artiodactyl.
artipo set type.
artisma artistic.
artisme artistically.
artismo virtuosity, artistic taste.
artista artistic.
artistagento artist agent.
artisto artist.
artiŝoko artichoke.
artlaborejo atelier, studio, work-room, workshop.
artlaboristo artisan, craftsman, tradesman.
arto art.
artobjekto objet d'art, work of art.
artodanco artistic dance.
artokarpo breadfruit tree.
artoplena artistic.
artralgio arthralgia.
artrita arthritic.
artritismo arthritism.
artrito arthritis.
artritulo arthritic.
artrologio arthrology.
artropodo arthropod.
artrozo arthritis.
artsento artistic talent, artistry.
artskribado artistic writing.
artskribo artistic writing.
Arturo Arthur.
artverko a work of art.
aruba Aruban.
arubanino Aruban woman.
arubano Aruban.
Arubo Aruba.
arumo arum, cuckoo-pint.
arvikolo vole.
arvorto mass noun.
asafetido asafoetida.

asalto assault, bout.
Asamo Assam.
asaro farthing.
asaseno assassin.
asasini to assassinate.
asasino assassin.
asbesto asbestos.
asbestozo asbestosis.
ascenda ascending.
ascendanto ascendant.
ascendi to go up, ascend.
ascendo ascension, ascent.
ascensio ascension, ascent.
ascidio ascidian.
ascito ascites.
asekura insurance. **asekura agento** insurance agent. **asekura makleristo** insurance broker. **asekura statistikisto** actuary.
asekurado assurance, insurance.
asekuratesto insurance certificate.
asekurato policyholder.
asekuri to assure, insure, underwrite.
asekuristo insurer.
asekurlibro insurance book.
asekuro assurance, insurance.
asembla lingvo assembler language.
asembleanino assemblywoman.
asembleano assemblyman.
asembleo assembly.
asemblero assembler.
asembli to assemble.
asemblilo assembler.
asemblilprogramo assembler program.
Aseno Assen.
asepsa aseptic.
asepsi to use asepsis in, use asepsis on.
asepsigi to asepticize.
asepso asepsis.
aserta assertive.
asertaĵo assertion.
aserte by all accounts.
asertebla arguable.
aserteble arguably.
asertema assertive.
aserteme assertively.
aserti to affirm, allege, assert, aver, claim, state.
aserto contention, assertion.
asesoro advisor, assessor.
asfalta asphaltic.
asfalti to asphalt, lay asphalt.
asfaltkartono asphalt-impregnated paper.
asfaltmiksatoro asphalt mixing plant.
asfalto asphalt.
asfaltpapero asphalt paper.
asfaltujo asphalt bin.
asfiksii to asphyxiate.
asfiksiiĝi to asphyxiate.

asfiksiiĝo asphyxiation.
asfiksio asphyxia.
asfodelo asphodel.
asidua assiduous.
asidue assiduously.
asidueco assiduity.
asigna appointive.
asignaĵo allocation, allotment.
asignato assignat.
asigni to assign, summon, earmark.
asignisto bailiff.
asignito appointee.
asigno assignment, subpoena, summons.
asimetria asymmetric, asymmetrical, dissymmetric.
asimetrie asymmetrically.
asimetrio asymmetry.
asimilado assimilation.
asimili to assimilate.
asimiliĝi to become assimilated.
asimiliĝo assimilation.
asimilo assimilation.
asimptoto asymptote.
asindeto asyndeton.
asira Assyrian.
asiria Assyrian.
asiriano Assyrian.
Asirio Assyria.
asiriologiisto Assyriologist.
asiriologio Assyriology.
asiriologo Assyriologist.
Asiro Ashur, Assur.
Asirujo Assyria.
asista auxiliary, subsidiary.
asistado assistance, help.
asistantaro company, escort.
asistantino assistant, lady help.
asistanto aid, assistant, helper.
asistato beneficiary.
asistento assistant lecturer, instructor.
asisti to abet, aid, assist, help, attend to, support.
asistinto assistant.
asisto aid, help.
asistolio asystoly.
asistolo asystole.
asistonto assistant.
asiza assize.
Asizo Assisi.
asizo assizes.
askalono shallot.
askaridedoj roundworms.
askarido (intestinal) roundworm.
askario askari.
askaro ascarid.
asketa ascetic.
asketado asceticism.
asketeco asceticism.
asketema ascetic.

asketismo asceticism.
asketo ascetic.
askiigi to convert into ASCII.
Askio ASCII.
asklepiado asclepiad (verse); milkweed.
Asklepio Asclepius.
asko ascus.
askorba acido ascorbic acid.
askorbata acido ascorbic acid, vitamin C.
askorbato ascorbate.
askoto ascot.
Asnato Asenth.
aso ace (cards, etc.).
asocia allied, associated, associative. **asocia atingo** associative access, associative addressing. **asocia memoro** content-addressable memory.
asociacio association.
asociado association.
asociano partner, associate.
asocianto business relation.
asocieca associative. **asocieca memorilo** associative store.
asociece associatively.
asocieco associativity.
asocii to associate.
asociigi to associate.
asociigo association.
asociiĝi to affiliate, associate.
asociiĝo association.
asociito partner, associate.
asocio association.
asonanca assonant.
asonanci to make assonant.
asonancigi to alliterate.
asonanciĝi to be assonant.
asonanco alliteration, assonance.
asparago asparagus.
aspartamo aspartame.
aspektaĵo aspect, characteristic.
aspekte in appearance.
aspekti to appear, look, seem.
aspektigi to design.
aspektigisto layout designer.
aspektismo aspectism.
aspekto appearance, aspect, look, sight, view.
aspergi to asperse, atomize, spray, sprinkle, water.
aspergilo atomizer, sprayer.
aspergilozo aspergillosis.
asperulo asperula, woodruff, squinancywort.
aspidio buckler fern.
aspidistro aspidistra.
aspido asp.
aspiko aspic.
aspiracia aspirate, aspirated.
aspiracii to aspirate.

aspiraciigi to aspirate.
aspiracio aspiration.
aspirado aspiration.
aspiranto aspirant, candidate.
aspiratoro aspirator.
aspiri to aspire (to), hope for, be ambitious of, be eager for, desire earnestly, seek after.
aspirino aspirin.
aspiro ambition, aspiration.
asporto asport.
aspra rough, harsh.
aspre roughly, harshly.
assorbema adsorbent, adsorptive.
astakedoj Astacidae.
astako crayfish, crawdad.
astata astatic.
astateno astatine.
astato astatine.
asteka Aztec.
astenio asthenia.
asteracoj asteraceae.
asterio starfish.
asterisko asterisk (*).
astero aster, Michaelmas daisy.
asteroido asteroid.
astigmata astigmatic.
astigmateco astigmatism.
astigmatismo astigmatism.
astilbo astilbe.
astma asthmatic, wheezy.
astmeco asthma, shortness of breath.
astmo asthma, shortness of breath.
astmulo asthmatic, asthmatic patient.
astra astral.
astragalo astragalus, ankle bone; milk vetch; astragal.
astragalomancio astragalomancy.
astrakano astrakhan wool.
astrala astral.
astralo astral body.
astreca astral.
Astreo Astraea.
astro celestial body, heavenly body.
astrobiologio astrobiology.
astrocito astrocyte.
astrodinamiko astrodynamics.
astrofizika astrophysical.
astrofizikisto astrophysicist.
astrofiziko astrophysics.
astrofloro aster.
astrogeologio astrogeology.
astrohemio astrochemistry.
astroido asteroid.
astrokemio astrochemistry.
astrokupolo astrodome.
astrolabo astrolabe.
astrologia astrological.
astrologiisto astrologer.
astrologio astrology.
astrologo astrologer.
astronaŭtika astronautical.
astronaŭtiko astronautics.
astronaŭto astronaut, spaceman.
astronomia astronomic, astronomical. **astronomia observejo** astronomical observatory. **astronomia unuo** astronomical unity.
astronomiisto astronomer.
astronomio astronomy.
astronomo astronomer.
asturia Asturian.
asturiano Asturian.
Asturio Asturias.
Asturujo Asturias.
asulo ace.
Aŝintono Ashington.
aŝkenaza Ashkenazic.
aŝkenazo Ashkenazic Jew.
aŝkenazoj Ashkenazim.
Aŝoko King Ashoka (ruled northern India in the third century BCE).
aŝramo ashram.
Atabasko Athabasca.
Atabaskolago Lake Athabasca.
ataka aggressive, offensive.
atakadi to harass, press hard.
atakanta aggressive.
atakanto aggressor, assailant, attacker.
atakegi to charge (attack).
atakema aggressive, belligerent, pugnacious, bellicose.
atakeme aggressively.
atakemo aggression.
ataketi to snap.
ataketo attack, fit.
atakhelikoptero (helicopter) gunship.
ataki to assail, assault, attack, storm.
atakinto assailant.
atakita attacked.
atakito assault victim, attack victim.
atako attack, assault, fit, onset.
atakonto assailant.
ataksio ataxia.
atakzono attack zone.
atalanto red admiral.
atamano ataman.
atanazia Athanasian.
ataraksia ataractic, ataraxic.
ataraksio ataraxia.
ataro attar.
ataŝeo attaché.
atavisma atavistic.
atavismo atavism, throw-back.
atavo ancestor.
ateisma atheistic.
ateismano atheist.
ateismo atheism.
ateista atheistic.

ateisto

ateisto atheist.
ateliero atelier, studio, workroom, workshop.
atena Athenian.
atenano Athenian.
atencanto assailant, assaulter.
atence violently.
atenci to assault, violate, attempt (to kill someone).
atencinto assailant, assaulter.
atencisto hitman.
atenco assault, outrage, violation.
atenculo assailant, assaulter.
atendado expectation.
atendanto someone who is waiting, something that is waiting.
atendbudo shelter.
atendebla awaited.
atendejo waiting room.
atendemo expectancy.
atendi to abide, expect, wait (for), await.
  atendi sian vicon to wait one's turn.
atendigi to make someone wait, keep someone waiting.
atendo expectation.
atendoĉambro waiting room.
atendovico waiting line.
atendovico (waiting) line, queue.
atendvica teorio queueing theory.
atendvico queue.
ateneo atheneum.
Ateno Athens.
atenta attentive, heedful, wary.
atente attentively.
atentege very attentively, very studiously.
atentema attentive, watchful.
atenteme carefully, closely, intently.
atentemo attentiveness, care.
atenti to pay attention (to), watch out for, heed, mind. **atenti be** to attentive, be attentive to, heed, mind, pay attention, pay attention to, watch out. **atenti pri** to pay attention to, take account of, take into account. **atentu!** take care!
atentigi to draw attention to, point out.
  atentigi min to bring to my attention.
  atentigi pri to advance, put forward.
atentigo drawing attention.
atentinda notable, noteworthy, striking.
atentinde significantly, strikingly.
atentindeco relevance.
atento advertency, attention, application.
  atenton! attention! look out!
atentokapta conspicuous.
atenui to attenuate.
atenuiĝi to attenuate.
atenuiĝo attenuation.
atenuilo attenuator.
atenuo attenuation.
ateo atheist.

atleto

ateromo atheroma.
aterosklerozo atherosclerosis.
atestado certification, verification.
atestaĵo deposition, evidence.
atestanto witness. **atestanto de Jehovo** Jehova's witness.
atestejo witness box, witness stand.
atesti to affirm, attest, (bear) witness, testify, certify, give evidence, vouch.
atestilo attest, voucher.
atesto affirmation, attestation, certificate, testimony, witness, voucher, certification, evidence.
atestoilo certificate.
atika Attic.
atikeco Atticism.
atikismo Atticism.
atiko attic.
Atiko Attica.
Atilo Atilla.
atingaĵo acquirement.
atingebla accessible.
atingebleco attainability.
atingi to accomplish, achieve, attain, get, reach, overtake, obtain.
atinginstrukcio access instruction.
atingo accomplishment, achievement, attainment, access.
atingodistanco range, reach.
atingokontrolo access control.
atingomaniero access method.
atingopermeso access permission, file mode.
atingopermesoj mode.
atingopovo range, reach.
atingorajto access right.
atingotempo access time.
atlanta Atlantean.
atlantida Atlantean.
atlantidano Atlantean.
Atlantido Atlantis.
atlantika Atlantic.
Atlantiko Atlantic (Ocean).
atlantino Atlantean woman.
Atlantio Atlantis.
Atlanto Atlas.
atlanto telamon; Atlantean.
Atlantujo Atlantis.
atlasa satin, satiny, satin-smooth.
Atlaso Atlas.
atlaso atlas; (type of) satin.
atlazo atlas.
atleta athletic.
atlete athletically.
atleteco athletics, track and field.
atletika athletic.
atletiko athletics.
atletismo athleticism, athletics.
atleto athlete.

Atlono

Atlono Athlone.
atm. → **antaŭtagmeze.**
atmano atman.
atmo atman.
atmometro atmometer.
atmosfera atmospheric. **atmosfera premo** atmospheric pressure, barometric pressure.
atmosferaĵoj atmospherics.
atmosfere atmospherically.
atmosfero atmosphere.
atmosferologio atmospherology.
atolo atoll.
atoma atomic. **atoma horloĝo** atomic clock.
atombombo atom bomb, atomic bomb.
atomcentralo atomic power station.
atome atomically.
atomeco atomicity.
atomelektrejo nuclear power plant.
atomenergio atomic energy.
atomero subatomic particle.
atomfendado fission.
atomfiziko atomic physics.
atomfuzio atomic fusion.
atomhorloĝo atomic clock.
atomigi to atomize.
atomisma atomist.
atomismo atomism.
atomisto atomist.
atomkerno atomic nucleus, atomic core.
atommaso atomic.
atomnumero atomic number.
atomo atom.
atompezo atomic weight.
atompilo atomic pile.
atomreaktoro atomic reactor.
atomteorio atomic theory.
atonala atonal.
atonale atonally.
atonia atonic.
atonie atonically.
atonio atony.
atrabila atrabilious.
atrabilo atrabiliousness.
atrakcio (tourist) attraction.
atrakto attraction.
Atreĥto Arras.
atrepsio athrepsia.
atrezio atresia.
atria atrial.
atribuado attribution.
atribuebla attributable.
atribui to accredit, ascribe, assign, attach, award, bestow, attribute. **atribui lokon** to allocate store.
atribuo assignment.
atributo attribute.
atricio attrition.
atrikapilo blackcap.

aŭd-vida

atrio atrium.
atriplo orache.
atrofia atrophied.
atrofii to atrophy, be atrophied.
atrofiigi to cause atrophy.
atrofiiĝi to atrophy, undergo atrophy.
atrofiiĝinta atrophied.
atrofiita atrophied.
atrofio atrophy.
atropino atropine.
atropismo atropism.
atuti to play the trump card, trump.
atuto trump.
audiĝi to be heard.
aŭ either, or. **aŭ ... aŭ** either ... or. **aŭ ĉio aŭ nenio** all or nothing.
aŭbado aubade.
aŭbrietio aubrieta, aubretia, lilac bush.
aŭbrieto aubretia.
aŭda auditory. **aŭda osteto** anvil, incus.
aŭdaca audacious, bold, daring, intrepid.
aŭdace boldly.
aŭdaci to dare, have the audacity (to).
aŭdaco audacity, boldness, daring.
aŭdado listening.
aŭdantaro audience, congregation.
aŭdante hearing, while hearing.
aŭdanto listener.
aŭdavida audio-visual.
aŭdebla audible.
aŭdeble audibly, able to be heard.
aŭdebleco audibility.
aŭdi to hear.
aŭdicio audition.
aŭdiencejo audience chamber.
aŭdienco audience (official reception).
aŭdigi to make a sound.
aŭdiĝi to be heard.
aŭdilo hearing aid.
aŭdio audio.
aŭditorio assembly, audience, auditory, auditorium.
aŭditoro auditor.
aŭdkapablo hearing.
aŭdlibro audio book.
aŭdnervo auditory nerve.
aŭdo hearing.
aŭdogramo audiogram.
aŭdokapablo hearing.
aŭdologio audiology.
aŭdologo audiologist.
aŭdometro audiometer.
aŭdosignalo audio signal.
aŭdovida audiovisual.
aŭdpovo hearing, ability to hear.
aŭdsenso hearing.
aŭdsentumo hearing.
aŭdvida audio-visual.
aŭd-vida audio-visual.

Aŭgia

Aŭgia Augean. **aŭgia stalo** Augean stable.
Aŭgio Augeas.
aŭgita augitic.
aŭgito augite.
aŭgmentativa augmentative.
aŭgmentativo augmentative.
aŭgmentigi to augment.
aŭgmento augment.
Aŭgosto August.
aŭgosto August.
aŭgurado augury, divination.
aŭguri to augur, forecast, foretell, prophesy, foreshadow, predict.
aŭguristino fortune teller.
aŭguristo diviner, fortune teller, soothsayer.
aŭguro augury, indication, omen, presage, portent, sign.
aŭgustena Augustinian.
aŭgustenismo Augustinism.
Aŭgusteno Augustine.
aŭgusto August, Augustus.
aŭkcia vendo auction.
aŭkcidomo auction house.
aŭkcie at auction.
aŭkciejo auction-room, auction-rooms, saleroom.
aŭkcii to auction (off).
aŭkciisto auctioneer.
aŭkcio auction.
aŭkedoj auks.
Aŭklando Auckland.
aŭko razorbill.
aŭkoformaj Alciformes.
aŭksino auxin.
aŭksokroma auxochromic.
aŭksokromo auxochrome.
aŭkubo aucuba, Japanese laurel.
aŭkuparii to rowan.
aŭkupario rowan.
aŭkuparo sorb (apple).
aŭlo auditorium, hall.
aŭo conjunction.
aŭra aural.
aŭreliano Aurelian.
Aŭrelio Aurelius.
aŭreolo aura, aureole, halo.
aŭreomicino aureomycin.
Aŭrignacio Aurignacian.
aŭrikla auricular.
aŭriklo auricle.
aŭrikolo auricula, bear's ear.
aŭrikulo bear's-ear, primrose, auriculo.
aŭrinio aurinia.
aŭro aura.
aŭrokso aurochs, urus.
aŭrora Aurora.
aŭrori to dawn.
Aŭroro Aurora.
aŭroro aurora, dawn, polar light.

aŭti

aŭskultadi to keep listening, continue to listen.
aŭskultado listening, auscultation.
aŭskultantaro audience, auditory.
aŭskultanto hearer, listener.
aŭskultejo auditorium.
aŭskulti to listen (to). **aŭskultu!** hark!
aŭskultilo earphone.
aŭskulto auscultation.
aŭskultumi to auscultate (heart).
aŭspicia auspicious.
aŭspicie auspiciously.
aŭspicio auspice(s), patronage, protection, support, good omen, harbinger, precursor.
aŭspicioj auspices.
aŭstenito austenite.
aŭstera austere, Spartan.
aŭstere austerely.
aŭstereco austerity.
aŭstero austerity.
aŭstra Austrian.
aŭstrala austral. **Aŭstrala Krono** Corona Australis.
Aŭstralazio Australasia.
aŭstralia Australian.
aŭstralianino Australian woman.
aŭstraliano Australian.
Aŭstralio Australia.
aŭstraloida Australoid.
aŭstraloido Australoid.
aŭstralopiteka australopithecine.
aŭstralopiteko australopithecine.
aŭstria Austrian.
aŭstriano Austrian.
Aŭstrio Austria.
aŭstro Austrian.
Aŭstronezio Austronesia.
Aŭstrujo Austria.
aŭta automotive.
aŭtarcia autarkic(al).
aŭtarcio economic autarchy.
aŭtarkia autarkic(al).
aŭtarkio autarchy, autarky, self-sufficiency.
aŭte by car.
aŭtejo carport, garage.
aŭtenta authentic.
aŭtente authentically.
aŭtenteco authenticity.
aŭtentigi to authenticate.
aŭtentika authentic, genuine.
aŭtentike authentically, genuinely.
aŭtentikeco authenticity.
aŭtentikigi to authenticate.
aŭtentikigo authentication.
aŭtentiko authenticity.
aŭtentoindiko authentication code.
aŭtentokontrolo authentication.
Aŭteo Great Barrier Island.
aŭti to drive (a car, automobile).

aŭtisma autistic.
aŭtismo autism.
aŭtisto motorist, driver.
aŭto automobile, car.
aŭtobiografia autobiographical.
aŭtobiografie autobiographically.
aŭtobiografio autobiography.
aŭtobusa bus, coach. **aŭtobusa haltejo** bus stop. **aŭtobusa stacio** bus station.
aŭtobushaltejo bus stop.
aŭtobuso bus, coach.
aŭtobusstacio bus station.
aŭtoĉaro coach, motor-coach.
aŭtodafeo burning at the stake, auto-da-fé.
aŭtodidakta autodidactic.
aŭtodidakte autodidactically.
aŭtodidakto autodidact, self-taught person.
aŭtofabrikejo car factory.
aŭtofabriko car factory.
aŭtofloto rolling-stock.
aŭtogamia autogamic.
aŭtogamio autogamy.
aŭtogena autogenous.
aŭtogenado self-actualization.
aŭtogene autogenously.
aŭtogenveldado autogenous soldering.
aŭtogiro autogyro.
aŭtografi to autograph.
aŭtografia autographic.
aŭtografio autography, facsimile.
aŭtografo autograph.
aŭtogramo autograph.
aŭtoĥtona autochthonous, indigenous.
aŭtoĥtono native.
aŭtoimuna autoimmune.
aŭtoimuneco autoimmunity.
aŭtoinfektado autoinfection.
aŭtoinfekto autoinfection.
aŭtokataliza autocatalytic.
aŭtokatalizo autocatalysis.
aŭtokavalkado motorcade.
aŭtoklavi to autoclave.
aŭtoklavo autoclave, pressure cooker.
aŭtokonkurso auto race.
aŭtokonservado auto-save.
aŭtokorno horn (of an automobile).
aŭtokrata autocratic, overbearing.
aŭtokrataro autocracy.
aŭtokrate autocratically.
aŭtokrateco autocracy, autocratship.
aŭtokratieca authoritarian.
aŭtokratio absolute power, absolute rule, autocracy.
aŭtokratismo autocracy.
aŭtokrato absolute ruler, autocrat.
aŭtoktona indigenous, native, autochthonous.
aŭtoktone indigenously, natively.
aŭtoktono native, autochthon.

aŭtokuri to taxi (plane).
aŭtolitotrajno car sleep train.
aŭtolitvagonaro car sleep train.
aŭtolizo autolysis.
aŭtoluigado car hire.
aŭtomacii to automate.
aŭtomacio automation.
aŭtomata automatic. **aŭtomata fininstalaĵo** intelligent terminal.
aŭtomataĵo automatism.
aŭtomate automatically.
aŭtomateco automatism.
aŭtomatigi to automate.
aŭtomatigo automation.
aŭtomatismo automatism.
aŭtomatizi to automate.
aŭtomatizo automation.
aŭtomato automate, automaton.
aŭtomekanisto auto mechanic.
aŭtomobila automotive. **aŭtomobila pneŭmatiko** automobile tyre.
aŭtomobilejo garage.
aŭtomobilismo motoring.
aŭtomobilisto motorist.
aŭtomobilo automobile, car.
aŭtomobilvojo expressway, freeway.
aŭtomorfa automorphic.
aŭtomorfio automorphism.
aŭtomorfismo automorphism.
aŭtonoma autonomic, autonomous.
aŭtonome autonomously.
aŭtonomia autonomic, autonomous.
aŭtonomie autonomously.
aŭtonomio autonomy.
aŭtonomisto autonomist.
aŭtopneŭmatiko automobile tyre, motor tyre.
aŭtopneŭmo automobile tyre, motor tyre.
aŭtopordo car door.
aŭtopsio autopsy.
aŭtora authorial. **aŭtora rajto** copyright.
aŭtoradio car radio.
aŭtoreco authorship.
aŭtori to author.
aŭtorino authoress, writer, woman writer.
aŭtoriparejo auto repair shop, garage.
aŭtoriparilo automotive tool.
aŭtoriparisto auto mechanic.
aŭtoritata authoritative.
aŭtoritate authoritatively.
aŭtoritateca authoritative.
aŭtoritatece authoritatively.
aŭtoritateco authority.
aŭtoritatismo authoritarian.
aŭtoritato authority.
aŭtoritatulo authority figure.
aŭtorizi to authorize.
aŭtorizo authorization.

aŭtoro author.
aŭtorrajto copyright.
aŭtorsigno author's signature.
aŭtoservado automotive servicing.
aŭtosomo autosome.
aŭtostiranto motorist.
aŭtostirlernejo driving school.
aŭtostrada alveturejo access road.
aŭtostrado motor road, motorway.
aŭtosugesto autosuggestion.
aŭtosôseego motorway, turnpike, super-highway.
aŭtosôseo motor road, motorway.
aŭtotipio half-tone block.
aŭtotoksado autointoxication.
aŭtotomio autotomy.
aŭtotrofa autotrophic.
aŭtotrofia autotrophic.
aŭtotrofo autotroph.
aŭtovetkuristo racing driver, racing motorist.
aŭtovojo expressway, freeway, motorway, interstate, highway.
aŭtovrakejo junk yard.
aŭtovrako car wreck.
aŭtuna autumn. **aŭtuna ekvinokso** autumn equinox. **aŭtuna kolĉiko** meadow saffron.
aŭtunaraneajô air-threads.
aŭtuneca autumnal.
aŭtunfino last days of autumn.
aŭtuno autumn, fall.
ava bird, bird's, of a bird.
avali to back.
avalo guarantee (of payment), backing.
avalokiteŝvaro Avalokiteśvara.
avancado advancement.
avancego breakthrough.
avanci to advance, be promoted.
avancigi to advance.
avanco advancement.
avangarda avant-garde.
avangardo avant-garde, scout party, vanguard.
avano van (military).
avantaĝa advantageous.
avantaĝe advantageously, to one's advantage.
avantaĝo advantage, benefit.
avanularo attacker.
avanulo forward.
avara avaricious, miserly, stingy, greedy, mean, greedy.
avare avariciously.
avarea Avar.
avareco avarice, miserliness, stinginess.
avareo Avar.
avari to be greedy, penny-pinch.
avaro avarice.

avarulo miser, niggard, skinflint.
avataro avatar; transformation.
avêjo grandpa, granddad.
avelarbedo common hazel-tree, filbert, hazel, hazel-tree.
avelarbo hazel tree.
avelo hazelnut.
avelujo hazel tree.
avenkaĉo oatmeal porridge.
aveno oats.
Aventino Aventine.
aventura adventurous.
aventuranto adventurer.
aventure adventurously.
aventurema adventurous.
aventureme adventurously.
aventuremulo thrill seeker.
aventurino aventurine.
aventuristino adventurer, female adventurer.
aventuristo adventurer, mercenary.
aventuro adventure.
aventuroplena adventurous.
aventurriĉa adventurous.
aventurromano adventure novel.
aventurulo adventurer.
avenuo avenue.
averaĝa (mathematical) average, mean.
averaĝi to average.
averaĝigi to average.
averaĝo (mathematical) average, mean.
averii to break down, suffer damage.
averio damage.
Averno Avernus.
averso medal etc., head of coin.
averta warning.
avertanto monitor.
averteto broad hint.
averti to alert, caution, (fore)warn.
avertilo alarm.
avertkonuso cone.
averto warning.
avertulo monitor.
avesta Avesta.
avesto Avesta.
avia aviational.
aviada aeronautical. **aviada regantaro** air traffic control. **aviada reganto** air traffic controller.
aviadelektroniko avionics.
aviadi to aviate, fly.
aviadila homekipo aircrew.
aviadilaro air fleet.
aviadilbileto air ticket.
aviadile by plane.
aviadilejo airport.
aviadilhomekipo aircrew.
aviadilo aeroplane, airplane, aircraft.
aviadilportanto aircraft-carrier.

aviadilŝipo aircraft carrier.
aviadistaro aircrew.
aviadistino aviatrix.
aviadisto airman, aviator, pilot.
aviadmekanikisto flight engineer.
aviado aeronautics, aviation.
Aviceno Avicenna.
avida avid, eager, greedy.
avidadile by plane.
avide eagerly, avidly. **avide trinki** to booze (it up).
avideco avidity, covetousness, eagerness, greediness, lust.
avidega voracious.
avidi to be avid, covet, crave, lust, want greatly, desire, yearn (for). **avidi spiron** to gasp, pant for breath.
avido avidity, covetousness, eagerness, greediness, greed.
avidulo greedy person.
aviejo airport.
avigruo aircraft crane.
avii to fly.
avikulario bird spider.
avikulturo aviculture.
avilifto aircraft elevator.
Avimoro Aviemore.
avinejo mother-in-law apartment.
avinjo granny.
avino grandmother.
avio aircraft.
aviomotoro aircraft engine.
aviportanto aircraft carrier.
aviso dispatch boat.
aviŝipo aircraft carrier.
avitaminozo avitaminosis.
aviza advisory.
avizi to advise, counsel, notify.
avizo notification, notice, advice.
avizotabulo bulletin board.
aviztabulo notice board, announcement board, bulletin board.
AVL-arbo AVL tree.
avo grandfather.
avoceto avocet (bird).
avoĉjo granddad.
avokadarbo avocado, avocado-tree.
avokado avocado.
avokadoarbo avocado, avocado-tree.
avokadujo avocado.
a-vorto adjective.
azagajo assagai.

azaleo azalea.
azaraĵo asarum.
azaro ginger, asarabacca.
azarolo azarole.
azena ass's, donkey, of an ass.
azenaĵo blunder, boner, bungle.
azenbleki to bray.
azenĉevalo hinny.
azeneca asinine, donkey-like.
azeni to act like an ass.
azenido baby donkey, donkey foal.
azenigi to make a fool of.
azenino female donkey.
azenisto donkey driver.
azeno ass, donkey.
azenviro jackass.
azera Azerbaijan.
azerbajĝana Azerbaijan, Azerbaijani.
azerbajĝanano Azerbaijani, Azeri.
Azerbajĝano Azerbaijan.
azerino Azerbaijan woman.
Azerio Azerbaijan.
azero Azerbaijani, Azeri.
Azerujo Azerbaijan.
azia Asian, Asiatic.
azianino Asian woman.
aziano Asian.
Aziano Asiatic.
azido azotite.
azigosa azygos, azygous.
azilo asylum, sanctuary.
azilpetanto asylum seeker.
azilrajto right to asylum.
azimuta angulo azimuth angle, polar angle.
azimuto azimuth, bearing.
Azio Asia.
azoa azoic.
azoika Azoic.
Azoiko Azoic, Azoic era.
azolo mosquito, fern.
azota azotic.
azotacido nitric acid.
azotemio azotemia.
azoto azote, nitrogen.
azoturio azoturia.
Azova Maro Sea of Azov.
Azovmaro Sea of Azov.
Azovo Azov.
azteka Aztec.
azteko Aztec.
azuleĥo glazed tile.
azurito azurite.

B

B si (music).
Baalo Baal.
babao sponge cake.
Babelo Babel, Babylon.
Babelturo Tower of Babel.
babila flippant.
babilaĉi to chat offensively.
babiladi to have long talk, banter, chat.
babilado chat.
babilaĵo chat, gossip, verbiage, wordiness.
babile flippantly.
babilejo chat room, chat line, channel.
babilema talkative.
babilemo talkativeness.
babilemulino gossipy or chatty woman.
babilemulo chatterbox, tattler, telltale.
babili to babble, blab, chatter, prattle, shoot the breeze, chat.
babilo chat.
babilona Babylonian.
babilonia Babylonian.
babiloniano Babylonian.
Babilonio Babylonia.
Babilono Babel, Babylon.
babiltruo mouth (pejorative), trap, gob.
babilulo chatterbox, tattler, telltale.
babiruso babirusa, deer hog.
babito babbitt.
babordo port side.
babuŝo slipper, babouche.
bacila bacillary.
bacilo bacillus.
baco old German coin.
Baĉano Bachan.
baĉo batch.
Badao Bath.
baden-virtembergano resident of Baden-Württemberg.
Baden-Virtembergo Baden-Württemberg.
badmintono badminton.
bafina Baffin. **Bafina Golfo** Baffin Bay. **Bafina Insulo** Baffin Island.
Bafingolfo Baffin Bay.
Bafinlando Baffin Island.
bagaĝisto baggage handler, baggage loader.
bagaĝkupeo baggage compartment.
bagaĝlifto baggage elevator.
bagaĝo baggage, luggage.
bagaĝoĉaro baggage cart.
bagaĝvagono baggage car.
bagaso bagasse.
bagatela insignificant, trifling, marginal, trivial.
bagatelaĵo bagatelle, something unimportant.
bagatelema frivolous.
bagateli to underestimate.
bagateligi to marginalize.
bagatelo bagatelle, bauble, trifle, unimportant thing.
Bagavadgito Bhagavad-Gita.
Bagdado Baghdad.
bagelo bagel.
bagno house of correction.
bagro excavator.
Bahaa Bahá'í faith.
Bahaano member of the Bahá'í faith.
Bahaismo Bahá'íism, the Bahá'í faith.
bahama Bahamian.
bahamanino Bahamian woman.
bahamano Bahamian.
Bahamoj Bahama Islands, Bahamas.
Bahao Bahá'í.
Bahio Bahia.
baĥanalo bacchanalia.
baĥanto bacchant.
Baĥo Bacchus.
baĥrajna Bahraini.
baĥrajnanino Bahraini woman.
baĥrajnano Bahraini.
Baĥrajno Bahrain.
bajadero bayadère, (Indian) dancing-girl.
Bajelo Bailleul.
Bajkallago Lake Baikal.
Bajkalo Baikal.
bajoneta fermilo bayonet catch, bayonet joint.
bajoneti to bayonet.
bajoneto bayonet.
Bajramo each of the two celebrations after Ramadan.
bajronismo Byronism.
Bajrono Byron.
Bajruto Beirut.
bajto byte.
bakado baking, the act of baking.
bakaĵo baked goods.
bakalaŭra baccalaureate.
bakalaŭreco holding a bachelor's degree, baccalaureate.
bakalaŭro baccalaureate, bachelor's degree holder.
bakalo wide-mouthed, short-necked bottle or jar.
bakanalo Bacchus festival, bacchanalia, drunken orgy.
bakango type of popular South African music.
bakarato baccarat.
bakejo bakery.

bakelito

bakelito bakelite.
bakfaruno flour.
bakforno oven, baking oven.
bakgamono backgammon.
bakĥa bacchanal.
bakĥanalio bacchanal.
Bakĥanalio Bacchanalia.
bakĥanalo bacchanal, Bacchanalia.
bakĥanino bacchanal.
Bakĥanino Bacchanalian person.
bakĥano bacchanal, bacchant.
Bakĥano Bacchanalian person.
Bakĥantino Bacchanalian woman.
bakĥantino bacchantine.
Bakĥanto Bacchanalian person.
bakĥanto bacchant.
Bakĥo Bacchus.
Bakĥofesto Bacchanal party, celebration.
baki to bake, cook in an oven.
bakiĝi to bake, become baked.
bakista baker's.
bakistestro chief baker, head baker.
bakisto baker.
bakistoknabo baker's helper.
bakita baked.
bakitaĵo baked good.
bakka bacchanalian.
bakkanino bacchanal.
bakkano bacchanal, bacchant.
Bakko Bacchus.
baklavo baklava.
bakmidisko bakmi disc.
bakmio bakmi.
bakpleto baking sheet, baking tray, pizza pan.
bakpulvoro baking powder.
baksodo baking soda.
bakŝiŝo baksheesh.
bakteria bacterial.
baktericida bactericidal.
baktericido bactericide.
bakterio bacterium.
bakteriofagio bacteriophagy.
bakteriofago bacteriophage.
bakteriofaĝo bacteriophage.
bakterioliza bacteriolytic.
bakteriolizo bacteriolysis.
bakteriologia bacteriological.
bakteriologiisto bacteriologist.
bakteriologio bacteriology.
bakteriologo bacteriologist.
bakteriostazo bacteriostasis.
baktria Bactrian. **baktria kamelo** Bactrian camel.
Baktrio Bactria, Bactriana.
bakujo oven.
Bakuo Baku.
bakupi to backup.
bakupo backup.

baledjupo

balaado sweeping, the act of sweeping.
balaaĵo sweepings.
balaaĵujo dustpan.
balaaŭto street cleaner.
balado ballad, ballade.
balafono balaphone.
Balaĥuliŝo Ballachulish.
balai to sweep, whisk.
balailo broom, sweeper.
balailstango broomstick.
balailŝranko broom closet.
balailtenilo broomstick.
balaisto sweep, sweeper.
balakeno canopy, baldaquin.
balaklavo balaclava.
balalajko balalaika.
balancado balancing, the act of balancing.
balancelo balancelle.
balanci to balance, rock, swing, sway, nod.
balanciero balance, fly.
balanciĝi to balance, poise, oscillate, swing.
balanciĝo balancing.
balancilo seesaw, swing.
balanco nod.
balancoseĝo rocking chair.
balano acorn barnacle.
balantidio balantidium.
balantidiozo balantidiasis.
balasti to ballast.
balasto ballast.
balatarbo balata.
Balatero Ballater.
balato balata.
balboo balboa.
balbuta faltering, haltingly, hesitant, inarticulate.
balbutado mumble, gibberish.
balbute falteringly, haltingly, hesitantly.
balbuti to falter, stammer, stutter.
balbuto stammer, stutter.
balbutulo stammerer, stutterer.
balĉambro ballroom.
baldakeno baldachin, canopy.
baldaŭ soon.
baldaŭa approaching, approximate, nigh (time), speedy.
baldaŭege very soon, very quickly, right away.
baldaŭigi to bring near.
baldaŭo near future.
baldriko baldric.
baldueno Baudouin.
Balduro Bald, Balder.
Baleraj Insuloj Balearic Islands.
Balearoj Balearic Islands.
baleda balletic.
baledestro ballet master.
baledistino ballerina, ballet dancer.
baledjupo ballet skirt.

baledo

baledo ballet.
balejo ball-room.
balena cetaceous.
balenaĵo baleen, whalebone.
balenbarko whaleboat.
balenĉasado whaling.
balenĉasisto whaler.
balenedoj whales.
Balengolfo Walvis Bay.
balenido baby whale.
balenisto whaler.
balenkaptado whaling.
balenlameno baleen, whalebone.
Baleno Cetus.
baleno whale.
balenoleo train-oil, whale-oil.
balenoptero blue whale.
balenosto baleen, whalebone.
balenŝarko whale shark.
balenŝipo whaler.
baleta balletic.
baletaro choreography.
baletestro ballet master.
baletistaro ballet company.
baletistino ballerina, ballet dancer, ballet girl.
baletisto ballet dancer.
baletjupo ballet skirt.
baletmastro ballet master.
baleto ballet.
baletŝuo ballet shoe.
balgo bellows.
balgoblovilo bellows.
balgopedalo bellows pedal.
balia Balinese.
balianino woman of Bali.
baliano Balinese.
Balimeno Ballymena.
Balimonio Ballymoney.
Balingrio Ballingry.
Balino Ballina.
Balintreo Ballintrae.
Balio Bali.
balista ballistic.
balistika ballistic.
balistiko ballistics.
balisto ballista, catapult.
Baliŝanono Ballyshannon.
Balivagano Ballyvaghan.
Balivodo Rothesay.
balkana Balkan.
balkanigi to balkanize.
balkanigo balkanization.
Balkanio Balkan States.
Balkano Balkan Mountains, Balkans.
Balkanoj Balkans.
Balkaŝo Balkhash, Balqash.
balkonkoridoro access balcony.
balkono balcony, verandah.

banado

balkonpordo balcony door.
balo ball, party, dance.
Baloĥo Balloch.
balonaviado ballooning.
balonbalasto ballast.
balonbarilo balloon barrage.
baloneto balloon.
balonfiguro balloon figure.
balonisto balloonist.
balonkorbo balloon basket.
balono balloon, flask.
balotado ballot, balloting, voting by ballot, vote, election.
balotanto voter.
balotejo polling place.
baloti to ballot, poll, vote, elect.
balotilo ballot.
balotilujo ballot-box.
balotkesto ballot box.
baloto election, vote.
balotpapero ballot slip.
balotrajta having the right to vote.
balotrajtiga karto voter (identification) card.
balotrajto right to vote, suffrage.
balotujo ballot box.
baloturno ballot-box.
balsalonego ballroom.
balsalono ballroom.
balsamo balsam.
Balta Baltic. **Balta Maro** Baltic Sea. **Balta-Slava** Balto-Slavic, Balto-Slavonic.
baltazaro Balthazar.
balteo baldric, shoulder belt.
baltika Baltic.
Baltiko Baltic Sea.
Balto Baltic, Balt.
balustrado balustrade, banisters, parapet, railing.
balustraro banister.
balustro baluster.
balzama balm, balsam, balmy, balsamic.
balzamado to balm, embalm.
balzamarbo balm of Gilead, balsam.
balzami to embalm.
balzaminacoj Balsaminaceae.
balzamino balsam.
balzamisto embalmer.
balzamito alecost.
balzamizi to embalm.
balzamo balm, balsam.
balzamumi to embalm.
balzo balsa.
balzoligno balsa, balsa-wood, cork-wood.
bambua bamboo.
bambuo bamboo.
bambuŝosoj bamboo shoots.
banado bathing.

banaĥa Banach. **banaĥa algebro** Banach algebra. **banaĥa spaco** Banach space.
Banaĥo Banach.
banakvo bath water.
banala banal, commonplace, dismal, trite.
banalaĵo banality, platitude.
banaleco banality, triteness, triviality, platitude.
banaligi to make banal, turn into a cliché.
bananarbo banana tree.
bananaro bunch of bananas.
bananfolio banana leaf.
bananmuŝo drosophila, fruit-fly.
banano banana.
bananplanto banana tree.
bananŝelo banana peel.
bananŝtopilo banana plug.
bananujacoj musaceae.
bananujo banana plant, banana tree.
banbudo bathing box.
banĉambro bathroom.
banĉapo bathing-cap.
banĉelo bathroom.
banĉkostumo bathing suit.
bandaĉo band, troop (of thugs, hooligans, etc.).
bandaĝi to bandage, bind, dress (wound).
bandaĝilo ligature.
bandaĝo bandage.
Bandamaro Banda Sea.
bandano band member.
banderilisto banderillero.
banderilo banderilla.
banderolo paper band, wrapper (for mailing, etc.).
bandestro band leader.
bandiĝi to band together.
bandikuto bandicoot.
bandito bandit.
bando band, bevy, gang, posse.
bandoliero bandoleer, shoulder belt.
bandomo bath house.
bandonio bandoneon.
bandurio bandurria.
banduro bandura.
banejgardisto bath superintendent.
banejo bathroom.
bangalo bungalow.
bangalparko bungalow park.
bangaltendo frame tent.
bangasto seaside visitor.
bangastoj bathers.
bangladeŝa Bangladesh.
bangladeŝanino Bangladeshi, Bangladeshi lady, Bangladeshi woman.
bangladeŝano Bangladeshi.
Bangladeŝo Bangladesh.
Bangoro Bangor, Bangor Erris.
banĝo banjo.

Banĝulo Banjul.
bani to bathe, rinse, wash (over), submerge.
bani sin to bathe, have a bath.
baniĝi to take a bath.
banilo bath.
banjanarbo banyan tree.
banjano banyan.
banĵo banjo.
banka bileto banknote.
bankaĝio bank rate.
bankajuto bathing box.
bankalsono bathing suit, swimming trunks, swimsuit.
bankbileto bank note, paper money.
bankdiskonto bank discount, bank rate.
bankedĉambro banquet room.
bankedejo banquet hall.
bankedi to banquet, feast.
bankedo banquet, dinner. **bankedo por la okuloj** a feast for the eyes.
bankejo bank branch.
bankestro bank director, bank manager, banker.
banketalo bank statement.
bankiero banker.
bankismo banking.
bankisto banker, bank clerk, bank official.
bankizo ice cap, pack-ice, ice-floe.
bankkliento bank customer.
bankkomizo bank clerk.
bankkonto bank account, banking account.
banklibro bank-book.
banknoto bank note, paper money, bank bill, bill of money.
banknotoj paper money.
banko bank.
bankoficisto bank officer.
bankokano Bangkokian.
Bankoko Bangkok.
bankokonto bank account, banking account.
bankonumero bank account, banking account.
bankostumo bathing suit, swimsuit.
bankposedanto banker, bank manager.
bankrota bankrupt.
bankrotaranĝo bankruptcy agreement.
bankroti to be bankrupt, go broke, fail.
bankrotigi to bankrupt.
bankrotinto bankrupt.
bankroto bankruptcy, failure.
bankrotoproceso bankruptcy proceedings.
bankrotulo bankrupt.
banksaldo balance, balance with a bank.
banksekreto banking secret.
banksio banksia.
bankuracejo health resort.
bankuvo bath, bathtub.
banloko springs.
banmantelo bathrobe.

banmato

banmato bath mat.
bano bath.
banpantoflo bath slipper.
bansapo bath soap.
banseĝo beach chair.
banspongo bathing sponge.
banŝaŭmajo bath foam.
banŝio banshee.
banŝorteto bathing briefs.
banŝorto bathing trunks.
bantamo bantam.
bantapiŝo bath mat.
bantermometro bath thermometer.
bantigi to knot.
bantkravato bow tie.
banto bow, knot, loop, rosette, pom-pom.
Bantrio Bantry.
bantua Bantu.
bantuko bath towel.
bantuo Bantu.
banujo bathtub.
banurbo spa, town known for its mineral baths, springs.
banuso ban.
banvesto bathing costume, bathing suit.
Banvo Banff.
baobabo baobab.
bapta baptismal.
baptado christening.
baptakvujo font.
baptano co-sponsor, crony, mate.
baptanto baptizer.
baptato person to be baptized.
baptejo baptistery.
bapti to baptize, christen.
baptinfano godchild.
baptisterio baptistery.
baptisto Baptist.
bapto baptism, christening.
baptofesto baptism, baptism party.
baptofilino goddaughter.
baptofilo godson.
baptokapelo baptistery.
baptokuvo baptismal font.
baptonomo baptismal name, Christian name, first name.
baptopatrino godmother.
baptopatro godfather.
baptopatroino sponsor.
baptopelvo baptismal font, baptistery.
baptovesto christening robe, chrisom.
baptujo font, baptismal font.
barado blockade, blockage, blocking.
baraĵilo barrier.
baraĵo blockage, dam, obstruction.
barakaro camp.
barako barrack, barn, shack, shanty, shed.
baraktado struggle.

barelforma

barakti to struggle (against), writhe, wrestle, move convulsively, convulse, flounder.
baraktisto wrestler.
barakto struggle, fight.
baramundo barramunda.
barata Indian (of Asia).
baraterio barratry.
Barato India.
barba bearded. **barba dianto** sweet William.
Barbado Barbados.
barbadosa Barbadian.
barbadosanino Barbadian woman.
barbadosano Barbadian.
Barbadoso Barbados.
barbakano barbican.
barbara barbaric.
barbaraĵo barbarity.
barbare barbarically.
barbareco barbarity.
barbareo winter-cress.
Barbario Barbary.
barbarismo barbarism.
barbaro barbarian.
barbedo gun-turret, turret.
barbfadeno barbel.
barbfiŝo barbel, catfish.
barbhava bearded.
barbikano barbacab, barbican.
barbio barbel.
barbira barber's.
barbirejo barber shop.
barbirhelpanto barber's assistant.
barbiro barber.
barbisto barber.
barbitura acido barbituric acid.
barbiturato barbiturate.
barblano fuzz.
B-arbo B-tree.
barbo beard.
barbofiŝo barbel.
barbohava bearded.
Barbra Barbara.
Barbro Barbara.
barbulo a bearded man.
barbumo barb.
Barcelono Barcelona.
barĉirkaŭi to pen, enclose.
barĉo beet soup, borscht.
bardo bard, minstrel.
Bardzdalo Bardsdale.
barelbendo band.
barelego tun.
barelejo barrel factory, cooper's shop.
bareleto keg, barrel, chamber.
barelfarado cooperage.
barelfarejo barrel factory, cooper's shop.
barelfaristo cooper.
barelforma barrel-shaped.

bareliefo bas-relief, low relief.
bareliĝi to put on weight.
barelista barrel maker's. **barelista metio** cooperage.
barelisto cooper.
barelo barrel, cask.
barelringego band.
barelringo hoop.
bareltruo bore hole.
barelvolbo barrel vault.
baremo (arithmetic) table.
Barenca Maro Barentsz Sea.
Barencmaro Barents Sea.
barfermi to barricade.
barĝestro bargemaster.
barĝisto bargee, bargeman.
barĝo barge.
bari to bar, block, obstruct.
baria baric. **baria spato** barytes. **baria sulfato** barytes.
bariergardisto signalman.
bariero barrier, barricade.
barihidroksido baryta.
barikadi to barricade.
barikado barricade.
barila digo dam.
barilo barrier, fence, obstruction.
barilpordo gate.
bario barium.
barioksido baryta.
bariono baryon.
barisfero barysphere.
barita bounded, cordoned off, fenced off. **Barita Mozo** Dammed Meuse. **barita serĉo** bounded search.
barito barite, barium oxide.
baritona baritone.
baritono baritone.
baritonulo baritone (singer).
baritpapero glossy paper.
bariumo barium.
barjono baryon.
barkarolo barcarole.
barketo wherry.
barko bark, boat, small ship.
barlistigi to blacklist.
barlisto blacklist.
Barnabaso Barnabas.
Barnabo Barnabas.
baro bar, barrier, impediment, obstacle, obstruction, bound.
barografo barograph.
barogramo barogram.
baroka baroque.
baroko baroque.
barokstila baroque.
barometra barometric. **barometra alto** barometer reading, height of the barometer.
barometrio barometry.

barometro barometer.
barona baron's.
baroneco baronage.
baronedzino baroness.
baroneteco baronetcy, baronetage.
baroneto baronet.
baronino baroness.
baronlando barony.
barono baron.
baroskopo baroscope.
barto busk, steel, whalebone.
Bartolomea Nokto Massacre of Saint Bartholomew.
Bartolomeo Bartolomew.
barzojo wolfhound.
basa deep, low, bass.
basbalejo baseball field.
basbalisto baseball player.
basbalo baseball.
basbutono bass button, bass stud.
basebakĉapelo baseball cap.
baseneto basin.
baseno basin, pool, reservoir.
basetkorno basset horn.
basfluto bass flute.
basiero bear.
basieroj bears (financial markets).
basigisto bear.
basineto basinet.
basio butter tree (of Nepal).
basisto bassist.
baska basque.
basketbalejo basketball court.
basketbalisto basketball player.
basketbalo basketball.
basklarneto bass clarinet.
basklavo bass button, bass stud.
basklefo bass clef (𝄢).
basko coattails, train (of a dress or robe).
baskuli to toggle.
baskulkamiono dump truck.
baskulludo waffling, seesaw, teeter-totter.
baskulo seesaw, teeter-totter, lever, toggle, trigger, weighing machine.
baskulponto bascule bridge, drawbridge.
baskulŝaltilo toggle-switch.
baskulŝalto toggle switch.
basludanto bass player.
baso bass, bass voice.
baspilkĉapelo baseball cap.
baspilkejo baseball field.
basregilo bass control.
basregistro bass coupler, bass register, bass stop.
Basro Basrah.
bastamburo bass drum.
bastarda bastard.
bastardeco bastardy.
bastardiĝi to bastardize, become inferior.

bastardo

bastardo bastard.
bastfibro bast fibre.
bastiono bastion.
basto bast, inner bark.
bastonadi to beat, beat up, flog, thrash, whack.
bastonbato blow with a stick.
bastone with a stick.
bastonego bludgeon, club, thick stick, cudgel.
bastoneto stick, little stick, chopstick.
bastoni to club.
bastonmarŝado Nordic Walking.
bastono baton, cane, staff, stick, rod.
bastrumpeto bass trumpet.
bastŝuo clog, sabot.
bastubjo bombardon.
basulo bass (singer).
basviolono bass-viol, violoncello.
basvjolo bass viol, bass viola, bass fiddle.
baŝibazuko bashi-bazouk.
baŝibozuko bashi-bazouk.
baŝo tarpaulin.
batadi to clatter.
batado barrage, beating.
bataĵo black-and-blue mark, bruise.
batala battle, of a battle.
batalaĉo affray.
batalado warfare.
batalakiro booty.
batalanto combatant.
batalegi to fight a great battle.
batalego great battle.
batalejo battlefield, battleground.
batalema aggressive, bellicose, combative, militant, pugnacious, truculent.
batalemo militancy.
batalemula militant.
batalemulo hawk, militant.
batalestra bastono mace.
bataleto skirmish.
batalhakilo pole-axe.
batalhalto truce, cease-fire.
batali to (do) battle, combat, contend, fight, struggle, engage in combat.
bataligi to pit.
batalilo weapon.
bataliloj arms, weapons.
bataliono battalion.
batalisto warrior.
batalkampo battlefield.
batalkorno battle horn.
batalkrio battle cry.
batalkrozoŝipo battle cruiser.
batalkrozŝipo battle cruiser.
batalo[1] action, battle, scuffle, struggle, combat, fray, fight.
batalo[2] sweet potato, yam.
batalpartiano warrior, champion, fighter.

bavuro

batalpreta up in arms.
batalŝipo battleship.
batalŝminko war paint.
bataltaĉmento militia, armed group, gang of henchmen, thugs.
batalvola up in arms.
batanto batter.
batato sweet potato.
batava Batavian. **Batava Respubliko** Batavian Republic.
Batavio Batavia.
batavo Batavian.
bategi to belabour, maul, thrash, thump.
batejo batting area.
baterio battery.
bateriujo battery compartment.
batesa Batesian.
batetado beating.
bateti to tap.
bateto dab.
batfermi la pordon to slam the door shut.
bati to beat, hit, strike, smack, beat, lash. **bati iun ĝismorte** to beat someone to death.
batiĝo affray.
batiki to batik.
batiko Batik.
batilo bat, racquet etc.
batisfero bathysphere.
batiskafo bathyscaphe.
batisto batiste, cambric, lawn.
batita having been hit, struck. **batita kremo** whipped cream.
batmakulo bruise.
batmiksi to whip.
batmortigi to finish off.
bato blow, stroke, hit.
batoado throbbing.
batolito batholith.
batometria bathometric, bathymetric.
batometrio bathometry, bathymetry.
batometro bathometer.
batoso bathos.
batraka batrachian.
batrako batrachian.
batrakoj anura.
batsono (sound of) striking (of a clock).
batuo battue, hunt, shoot.
Batuo Batu.
baŭdo baud.
baŭdruĉo goldbeater's skin.
baŭksito bauxite.
baŭmi to buck (as a horse).
baŭo bow.
bavara Bavarian.
Bavario Bavaria.
bavaro Bavarian.
Bavarujo Bavaria.
bavi to dribble, slobber.
bavuro burr.

baza basic. **baza adreso** base address. **baza ĉeno** terminal string. **baza linio** baseline.
baza salajro basic wage.
bazado basing.
bazaj datenoj data base.
bazalta basaltic.
bazalto basalt.
bazamento base.
bazanito basanite.
bazaro bazaar, fair, market, department store, mall.
bazbalĉapelo baseball cap.
bazbalejo baseball field.
bazbalisto baseball player.
bazbalo baseball.
baze basically, essentially.
bazeco basicity.
bazedova Basedow's. **bazedova malsano** Basedow's disease.
Bazelo Basel, Basle.
bazfolio basal leaf.
bazgardanto baseman.
bazi to base.
bazidia basidial.
bazidio basidium.
bazidiomiceto basidiomycete.
bazidiosporo basidiospore.
bazidisporo basidiospore.
baziĝi to be based (upon). **baziĝi sur** be based on.
bazilara basilar.
bazilika basilic, basilican.
baziliko basilica.
bazilio basil.
bazilisko (American) basilisk.
bazlatero base.
bazlinio baseline.
baznivela basic.
baznumero basicity.
bazo base, basis, footing, ground, platform, stem. **bazo de naturaj logaritmoj** base of natural logarithms.
bazoadreso base address.
bazopilkado baseball.
bazopilkejo baseball field.
bazopilkisto baseball player.
bazopilkludo baseball.
bazopilko baseball.
bazoregistro base register.
bazpilkisto baseball player.
bazpilko baseball.
bazreĝistro base register.
bazroko bedrock.
bazuko anti-tank gun, bazooka.
bazvektoro basis vector.
BEA → **Brita Esperantista Asocio**.
beata beatified, blessed, blissful.
beate blessedly.
beateco blessedness, bliss.

beatiga beatific.
beatigi to beatify.
beatigo beatification.
Beatrico Beatrice.
beatulo beatus.
beba baby's.
bebĉareto stroller.
bebmurdo infanticide.
bebo baby.
bebobanujo baby bath.
bebocareto baby carriage, stroller.
beboĉaro baby carriage.
bebofono baby intercom, baby phone.
bebogardantino babysitter.
bebogardanto babysitter.
bebokaĝo playpen.
bebokovrilo baby blanket.
beboliteto baby's crib.
bebomarŝigilo walker.
bebomurdintino baby killer (female).
bebomurdinto baby killer.
bebopomado baby powder.
bebopupo baby doll.
beboŝtrumpetoj baby bootees.
beboŝuo baby's shoe.
bebovartantino baby sitter.
bebovartanto baby-sitter.
bebzorgado babysitting.
bebzorgantino babysitter.
bebzorganto babysitter.
bebzorgi to babysit.
bedaŭinde unfortunately, regrettably.
bedaŭratone in a regretful tone (of voice).
bedaŭre regretfully, regrettably.
bedaŭregi to deplore, rue, grieve.
bedaŭri to be sorry about, regret, lament, pity.
bedaŭriga miserable, lamentable, regrettable, unfortunate.
bedaŭrinda lamentable, pitiable, regrettable, sad, unfortunate. **bedaŭrinda knabino!** poor girl!
bedaŭrindaĵo (a) pity, (a) shame.
bedaŭrinde alas, regrettably, unfortunately.
bedaŭro regret, remorse, sorrow.
bedelio bedellium (an aromatic gum).
bedo bed (garden), plot.
beduena Bedouin.
bedueno Bedouin.
beginejo beguinage.
begino beguine.
begoniacoj begonias.
begonio begonia.
behaviorismo behaviourism.
Behemoto behemoth.
bei to baa, bleat.
beja reddish brown, bay, sorrel.
bejlo bail.
bejo bey.

bejrumo

bejrumo bay rum.
Bejruto Beirut.
bejulo sorrel.
bekabungo brooklime.
bekerelo becquerel.
bekero beaker.
bekfluto recorder.
bekforme beak-shaped.
beki to peck.
beko beak, bill.
bekvadrato natural symbol.
bela beautiful, fine, handsome, lovely, good-looking, pretty. **bela literaturo** belles lettres.
beladono belladonna, deadly nightshade, devil's cherry.
belaĵo beautiful sight.
belarta fine arts.
belartaĵo object d'art, work of fine art.
belarto fine arts.
belartoj fine arts.
belaspekta attractive, beautiful.
belaspekte attractively, beautifully.
belaspekto beauty, attraction.
bele beautifully.
beleco beauty.
beleco-kremo beauty cream.
belecreĝino beauty queen.
belega exquisite, gorgeous, lovely, magnificent, splendid. **belega sedo** showy stonecrop, ice plant, butterfly stonecrop.
belegaĵo beauty, cute thing, trinket, bauble.
belege very beautifully.
belegeco splendor.
belegi to be beautiful.
belego beauty.
belemnito belemnite.
belenofobia belenophobic.
belenofobio belenophobia.
belenofobiulo belenophobic.
beleta attractive, bonny, pretty, comely, cute.
beletaĝo bel étage, ground floor, main storey.
beletraĵo literary work.
beletre klera well-read.
beletristiko belles-lettres, belletristic literature.
beletristo author, man of letters, writer.
beletro belles lettres, literature.
Belfasto Belfast.
Belfegoro *Belfagor Arcidiavolo* (a novella by Niccolò Machiavelli).
belfigura curvaceous, shapely.
belforma nicely shaped, well-formed.
belfrido belfry, bell tower.
belga Belgian.
belgino Belgian, Belgian woman.
Belgio Belgium.
Belgo a Belgian.

bendbremso

belgo Belgian.
Belgrado Belgrade.
belgrajno beauty mark.
Belgujo Belgium.
beli to be beautiful.
beliga beautifying.
beligado adornment, beautification.
beligadsalono beauty parlour.
beligaĵo cosmetic.
beligejo beauty-parlour.
beligi to beautify.
Beligi to embellish.
beligistino beautician, beauty specialist.
beligisto beautician.
belino beautiful girl.
beliso daisy.
beliza Belizean.
belizanino Belizean, Belizean lady, Belizean woman.
belizano Belizean.
Belizo Belize.
belkolora beautifully coloured.
belkreska beautifully developed.
belliteraturo fiction, literary fiction.
Belmopano Belmopan.
Belmuleto Belmullet.
Belo Bell. **belo** bel (unit of intensity).
belo beauty.
belomancio belomancy.
Belono Bellona.
belorusa Belarusian, White Russian.
Belorusio Belarusia, White Russia.
Beloruslando Belarusia, White Russia.
beloruso Belarus, Belarusian.
Belorusujo Belarus, White Russia.
belskribado calligraphic writing.
belskribisto calligrapher.
belskribo beautiful lettering.
belsona euphonious, tuneful, sonorous, pretty-sounding.
belstatura well-built, well-proportioned.
belucâ Baluch, Baloch.
belucô Baluch, Baloch.
belulino beautiful woman, beauty, belle.
belulo attractive person.
belvedero scenic overlook, viewing platform.
belvesti to wear one's best (clothes).
belvidejo belvedere, scenic overlook, viewing-platform, viewpoint.
belviro good-looking man.
belvizaĝa having a pretty face.
bemolo flat (music) (♭).
bena blessed.
benadi to keep blessing, continue to bless.
benado blessing.
benaĵo blessing, benediction.
benanto blesser, person giving a blessing.
Benbekulo Benbecula.
bendbremso band brake.

bendi

bendi to tape.
bendkapacito bandwidth.
bendlarĝo bandwidth.
bendo binding, strip, tape.
bendobremso band brake.
bendosegilo band-saw.
benediktano Benedictine, Benedictine monk.
benediktanto Benedictine.
benediktino benedictine.
Benedikto Ben, Benedict.
benefico benefit performance.
beneficulo beneficiary.
Benelukso Benelux.
bengala Bengal, Bengali. **bengala fajro** bengal-light. **Bengala Golfo** Bay of Bengal.
Bengalio Bengal.
bengalo Bengali.
Bengalujo Bengal.
beni to bless.
benigna benign.
benigne benignly.
beniĝi to become blessed.
benina Beninese.
beninanino Beninese woman.
beninano Beninese.
Benino Benin.
benita blessed.
benito blessed one.
Benjameno Benjamin.
benjeto doughnut.
benkaro bleachers.
benketo small bench, stool.
benklito berth.
benko bench, form.
benkseĝaro lounge suite, three-piece suite.
beno benediction, blessing, boon.
benoado blessing.
benplena blessed.
bentonito bentonite.
benzalo benzal.
benzeno benzene.
benzenserio benzene series.
benzilo benzyl.
benzina gasoline, gas.
benzinbombo Molotov cocktail.
benzincisterno fuel tank.
benzinejo filling station, petrol station, gas station.
benzinindikilo petrol gauge, gas gauge.
benzinkruĉo petrol can, gas(oline) can.
benzinmezurilo petrol gauge, gas gauge.
benzinmotoro petrol engine, gas engine.
benzinnivela indikilo gas(oline) gauge, fuel gauge.
benzino petrol, gasoline.
benzinpumpejo filling station, petrol station, gas station.
benzinpumpilo petrol pump, gas pump.

berniklo

benzinstacio filling station, petrol station, gas station.
benzinujo petrol tank, gas tank.
benzoa acido benzoic acid.
benzoarbo benjamin tree.
benzoata acido benzoic acid.
benzodiazepino benzodiazepine.
benzoino benzoin.
benzokaino benzocaine.
benzolo heating oil.
benzoo benzoate.
beo baa (sound made by a sheep).
Beogrado Belgrade.
Beotio Boeotia.
beoto Boeotian.
Beotujo Boeotia.
Beovulfo Beowulf.
berarbedo berry bush.
berarbeto berry tree.
berarbusto berry bush.
beraro cluster (of berries), bunch.
berbera Berber.
Berberio Barbary.
berberiso berberis.
berbero Berber.
Berberujo Barbery.
berdona baccate, bacciferous.
bereca baccate.
Berenica Hararo Coma Berenices.
bereto beret.
bergamotarbo bergamot tree.
bergamoto bergamot.
bergamotoleo bergamot.
bergamotpiro bergamot pear.
bergamotujo bergamot tree.
Berheno Mons.
beribero beriberi.
berilio beryllium.
berilo beryl.
berilŝtono beryl.
Beringa Markolo Bering Strait.
Beringa Maro Bering Sea.
Beringo Bering.
Beringomaro Bering Sea.
berkelio berkelium.
berlina Berlin.
berlinanino Berliner, Berlin lady, Berlin woman.
berlinano Berliner.
berlineano Berliner.
Berlino Berlin.
bermanĝa baccivorous, berry-eating.
bermo shoulder, verge, verge of a road.
Bermudo Bermuda.
Bermudoj Bermudas.
berna Bernese.
Bernano Bernese.
Bernerajo Berneray.
berniklo brent goose.

66

Berno

Berno Bern, Berne.
bero berry.
berserka berserk.
berserke amok.
berserko berserk, berserker.
Berviko Berwick. **Berviko ĉe la Tvido** Berwick upon Tweed.
Bes si (flat) (♭).
Besarabio Bessarabia.
Besarabujo Bessarabia.
besta animalistic, beastly, bestial.
bestaĉa bestial.
bestaĉo horrid creature, monster.
bestaĵo bestiality.
bestama animal loving.
bestaro cattle, fauna.
besteca beastly, bestial.
besteco beastliness.
bestega bestial, brutal, savage.
bestejo cattle pen, pen, sty.
bestetaĉoj vermin.
besteto animalcule.
bestia beastly, bestial, brutal, brutish.
bestiala beastly.
bestialo beastly person, brute.
bestigi to animalize, bestialize.
bestiĝi to besot.
bestio beast, brute, wild animal.
bestkuracisto veterinarian.
bestnutraĵo provender.
besto animal, beast. **bestoj** Animal kingdom.
bestoĝardeno zoo.
bestokuracisto veterinarian, veterinary surgeon.
bestopatrino dam.
beŝamelo bechamel sauce.
beta¹ beet, of a beet, of beetroot.
beta² beta (Bβ). **beta-globulino** beta globulin. **beta-partiklo** beta particle. **beta-radiado** beta radiation. **beta-radio** beta ray. **beta testado** beta testing.
betaĵo beet salad, beets.
betao beta (Bβ).
betatrono betatron.
betelfolio betel leaf.
betelo betel pepper.
betelonukso betel areca.
betelopalmo betel areca.
Betihilo Bettyhill.
betkampo beet field.
betkolora beet-red, claret.
Betleĥemo Bethlehem.
betlo betel, betel pepper.
beto¹ beet, beetroot.
beto² beta (Bβ).
betona concrete.
betonfero ferro-concrete, reinforced concrete.

bidkalkulilo

betoni to concrete.
betoniko betony, stachys.
betonmiksatoro cement mixer.
betonmiksilo concrete mixer.
betonmiksmaŝino concrete mixer.
betono concrete.
betosukero beetroot sugar, beet sugar.
betrikoltatoro beet harvester.
betsukero beet sugar, beetroot sugar.
betula birchen.
betulacoj birches.
betularo birch forest, birch grove.
betulejo birch forest, birch grove.
betulo birch (tree).
beveli to bevel.
bevelilo bevel.
bevelita beveled.
bevelo beveled edge.
bezigo bezique.
bezoaro bezoar.
bezona necessary, needful, requisite, needed.
bezonaĵo requisite, need.
bezonaĵoj materials, necessaries, requisites.
bezonata necessary.
bezoni to need, require, want.
bezono need, want, lack, requirement.
biatlonisto biathlete.
biatlono biathlon.
Biblia biblical.
biblia biblical.
bibliaĵo Biblicism.
Biblio Bible.
bibliofilio bibliophilia.
bibliofilo bibliophile.
bibliografia bibliographical.
bibliografiisto bibliographer.
bibliografio bibliography.
bibliografo bibliographer.
bibliomanio bibliomania.
bibliomaniulo bibliomaniac.
bibliotekadministrado library maintenance system.
bibliotekisto librarian.
biblioteko book case, library.
bicepsa bicipital.
bicepso biceps.
biciklado cycling.
biciklanto bicycle rider, cyclist.
bicikli to cycle.
biciklisto cyclist, biker.
biciklo bicycle, bike, cycle.
biciklokaravano bicycle caravan, cycling caravan.
biciklosako cycle bag.
biciklovego bicycle track.
bidaro beads.
bidento beggar's lice.
bideo bidet.
bidkalkulilo abacus.

bidkolĉeno

bidkolĉeno (strand of) beads.
bido bead.
bielo connecting-rod.
bienalo biennial.
bienaŭto station wagon.
biendomo farmhouse.
bienetato land register, official real estate register, register of title deeds.
bieneto smallholding.
bienetulo peasant.
bienhavanto landholder, landowner.
bienisto farmer, rancher.
bienkorto farmyard.
bienmastro farmer, landlord, squire.
bieno domain, estate, farm, property, ranch, land, ground(s).
bienoaĵo demesne.
bienposedanto farmer, landlord, squire.
bienulo property owner, landlord.
biera beery.
bierbarelo beer barrel.
bierbotelo beer bottle.
bierĉaro beer wagon.
bierejo beer-bar.
bierfareja brewer's, brewing.
bierfarejo brewery.
bierfari to brew.
bierfaristo brewer.
bierglasego beer mug.
bierglaso beer glass.
bierhordeo malt.
bierkruĉeto beer mug.
bierkruĉo beer pitcher.
biero ale, beer.
bierskatolo beer can.
biertrinkejo beer room.
biervarmigilo beer warmer.
biervendejo alehouse, beerhouse, pub.
bifaco biface.
bifadena bifilar.
bifida bifid.
bifilara bifilar.
biforkiĝa bifurcate.
biforkiĝo bifurcation.
bifsteko steak, beefsteak.
bigamia bigamous.
bigamio bigamy.
bigamiulo bigamist.
biglo beagle.
bigoso sauerkraut stew.
bigota bigoted, fanatical.
bigoteco hypocrisy.
bigotismo bigotry.
bigoto bigot, fanatic.
bigotulo bigot.
bijekcia bijective, one-to-one.
bijekcio bijection, biunique correspondence, one-to-one mapping.
bijeto bijection.

biletisto

bikarbonato bicarbonate.
bikino bikini.
biklorido bichloride.
bikornino chichevache.
bikorno bicorn.
bikso achiote, annatto, lipstick-tree.
biksotinkturo anatta, anatto.
bikŝuo bhikshu, bhikku.
bikvadrata biquadratic.
bilabiala bilabial.
bilabialo bilabial.
bilabongo billabong.
bilanci to reconcile, balance.
bilanciĝi to balance out.
bilancita balanced.
bilanco annual accounts, (annual) financial statement, balance sheet, statement of conditions, balance.
bilarda globo billiard ball.
bilardanto billiards player.
bilardbastono billiard cue.
bilardejo billiards hall, pool hall.
bilardeto bagatelle.
bilardglobo billiard-ball.
bilardi to play billiards.
bilardludi to play billiards.
bilardo billiards, billiards table, pool, pool table.
bilardsalono billiards parlour.
bilardtablo billiard table.
bilardtapiŝo billiards room.
bilaterala bilateral.
bilboko cup-and-ball game.
bilda esprimo figurative expression.
bildaĉo kitschy painting.
bildaro image set (of a mapping).
bildbendo video.
bildekrano screen.
bildero pixel.
bildigi to depict, visualize, render.
bildigo mapping.
bildkarto picture postcard.
bildkaseto videocassette.
bildo image, picture.
bildodetruo iconoclasm.
bildolibro album, picture book.
bildosimbolo icon.
bildotubo cathode tube.
bildrakonto comic (strip, book), graphic novel.
bildsimbolo icon.
bildstrio comic strip.
bildtubo cathode tube.
bildvalvo cathode tube.
bildvico slideshow.
bildvortaro picture dictionary.
biletejo box office.
biletgiĉeto booking office.
biletisto ticket collector.

biletkiosko

biletkiosko ticket window.
bileto bill, ticket, note, docket.
biletujo wallet.
biletvendejo box office.
bilĝakvo bilge water.
bilĝkilo bilge keel.
bilĝo bilge.
bilharzio bilharzia, bilharziasis, schistosomiasis, snail fever.
biliono trillion, billion.
bilionono billionth.
bilmakleristo stockbroker.
bilo negotiable document of value, negotiable security, negotiable instrument.
biloborso stock exchange.
bilokacio bilocation.
bilomakleristo stock broker.
bilono small change, coins.
bimetala bimetallic.
bimetalismo bimetallism, double standard.
binara binary. **binara arbo** binary tree. **binara dosiero** binary file. **binara kodo** binary code. **binara nombro** binary number. **binara nombrosistemo** binary number system. **binara serĉarbo** binary search tree. **binara serĉo** binary search.
binare binarily.
binarkodo de dekumnombro binary code decimal.
bindado bookbinding.
bindaĵo binding, cover.
bindarto bookbinding.
bindejo bindery.
bindi to bind, link (a program).
bindilo binder, linkage editor, linker.
bindista bookbinder's.
bindisto bookbinder.
bindita bound.
binditaĵo hardback.
bindmarĝeno binding offset, gutter (margin).
bindo binding, cover.
bingo bingo.
binoklo binoculars.
binomo binomial.
bioakumula bioaccumulative.
bioakumulado bioaccumulation.
bioakustika bioacoustic.
bioakustiko bioacoustics.
bioastronaŭtiko bioastronautics.
biocida biocidal.
biocido biocide.
biodanĝera biohazardous.
biodanĝero biohazard.
biodinamika agrikulturo biodynamic agriculture.
biodinamiko biodynamics.
biodisiĝiva biodegradable.
biodisiĝiveco biodegradability.
biodisiĝo biodegradation.

biopsio

biodiverseco biodiversity.
bioekologio bioecology.
bioelektra bioelectric.
bioelektro bioelectricity.
bioenergetiko bioenergetics.
biofizika biophysical.
biofizikisto biophysicist.
biofiziko biophysics.
biogaso biogas.
biogeneza biogenetic.
biogenezo biogenesis.
biogeografia biogeographic, biogeographical.
biogeografio biogeography.
biogeohemia biogeochemical.
biogeoĥemio biogeochemistry.
biogeokemia biogeochemical.
biogeokemio biogeochemistry.
biografia biographic.
biografie biographically.
biografiisto biographer.
biografio biography.
biografo biographer.
biohemia biochemical.
bioĥemiisto biochemist.
bioĥemio biochemistry.
biokataliza biocatalytic.
biokatalizilo biocatalyst.
biokemia biochemical.
biokemio biochemistry.
bioklimatologia bioclimatic.
bioklimatologio bioclimatology.
biolizo biolysis.
biologia biological.
biologie biologically.
biologiisto biologist.
biologio biology.
biologo biologist.
biolumineska bioluminescent.
biolumineskо bioluminescence.
biomaso biomass.
biomatematiko biomathematics.
biomedia environmental.
biomedicina biomedical.
biomedicino biomedicine.
biomedie environmentally.
biomedio environment.
biomeĥanika biomechanical.
biomeĥaniko biomechanics.
biomekanika biomechanical.
biomekaniko biomechanics.
biometeorologio biometeorology.
biometria biometric.
biometrio biometrics.
bionikisto specialist in bionics.
bioniko bionics.
biontologio biontology.
biopolimero biopolymer.
biopsio biopsy.

bioritma   **blablai**

bioritma biorhythmic.
bioritmo biorhythm.
biosfera biospheric.
biosfero biosphere.
biosinteza biosynthetic.
biosintezo biosynthesis.
biostatistiko biostatistics.
bioteknologio biotechnology, biotech.
bioterorismo bioterrorism.
biotito biotite.
biotopo biotope.
biotrono biotron.
biplano biplane.
birda avian, bird, bird's, of a bird.
birdaĵo fowl, poultry.
birdaraneo bird spider.
birdaro avifauna, ornis, birds.
birdejo aviary.
birdeto little bird.
birdido nestling.
birdkaĝo bird cage.
birdkanto bird's song.
birdkaptisto bird-catcher.
birdmigrado bird migration.
birdnesto bird nest.
birdnestosupo bird's nest soup.
birdo bird.
birdobredado aviculture.
birdobservanto birdwatcher.
birdodomo aviary.
birdogluo birdlime.
birdokaĝo bird cage.
birdokorto barnyard.
birdologio ornithology.
birdomigrado bird migration.
birdonesta supo bird's nest soup.
birdonesto bird's nest.
birdonutrejo bird feeder.
birdostarejo perch.
birdotimigilo scarecrow.
bireto beret, biretta.
biri to sound, take a bearing.
Birkenhedo Birkenhead.
birma Burmese.
birmanino Burmese woman.
birmano Burmese.
Birminhamo Birmingham.
Birmo Burma, Union of Myanmar.
biro (directional) bearing.
bis encore, one more time, again.
Bisaŭo Bissau.
bisekanto bisector, bisectrix.
bisekcado bisection.
bisekcanto bisector.
bisekci to bisect.
bisekcii to bisect.
bisekco bisection.
biseksa bi, bisexual.
bisi to demand an encore, play an encore.

bisina byssal, fine linen.
bisino byssus, fine linen.
Biskajio Biscay.
Biskajujo Biscay.
biskoto biscuit.
biskvito biscuit, cookie, zwieback, cracker.
bismuto bismuth.
biso (interjection) encore.
bistorto bistort.
bistra bistre brown.
bistro bistre, brown wash.
bisturio lancet, surgeon's knife.
bisulfato bisulfate.
bisulfido bisulfide.
bisulfito bisulfite.
bisusa byssal.
bisuso byssus.
bitbildo bitmap.
bitĉeno bit string.
biteto cleat, lug.
bitlibro e-book, digital book.
bitmapa ekranbloko bitmap display.
bitmapo bitmap.
bitmatrico bitmap.
bitniko beatnik.
bito bit.
bitoko byte.
bitokvaro nibble.
bitŝablono bit mask.
bituma bituminous, bituminoid, bitumen.
bitumeca bituminous, bituminoid.
bitumi to cover or smear with bitumen.
bitumizi to bituminize.
bitumo bitumen.
bitumoza bituminous, bituminoid.
bivaki to bivouac.
bivako bivouac.
bivalenta bivalent.
bivalenteco bivalency.
bivalvo bivalve.
bivo biwa.
bizanca Byzantine. **Bizanca Imperio** Byzantine Empire. **bizanca monero** bezant (coin).
bizancano Byzantine.
Bizancio Byzantium.
Bizanco Byzantium.
bizanto bezant.
bizara bizarre, odd, weird, eccentric, strange, odd.
bizare bizarrely, strangely.
bizari to be bizarre.
bizariĝi to become bizarre.
bizarulo weirdo.
bizono bison, buffalo.
Bjelorusio White Russia.
Bjelorusujo White Russia.
bĵura abjuratory.
blablai to chatter, babble, jabber, blab.

blablao chatter, prattle, jabber, babble.
blaga humorous, playful, mischievous.
blagi to joke, kid, pull someone's leg.
blago joke, nonsense.
blagrakonto yarn.
Blakpulo Blackpool.
blamanĝo blancmange.
blanka blank, white. **blanka abio** silver fir. **blanka argilo** white clay. **blanka elfluo** leucorrhoea. **Blanka Insulo** White Island. **blanka libro** blank book. **blanka linio** blank line. **Blanka Maro** White Sea. **blanka materio** white matter. **Blanka Nilo** White Nile. **blanka nimfeo** white water-lily. **blanka poplo** abele. **blanka sangoĉelo** leukocyte, white blood cell, white blood corpuscle. **blanka simforikarpo** common snowberry. **blanka spaco** white space. **blanka urso** polar bear. **Blanka Voltao** White Volta.
blankaĵo white.
blankarda ashen.
blankdorsa buntpego white-backed woodpecker.
blanke whitely.
blankeco whiteness, white.
blankedo blank check, carte blanche.
blankega snow white.
blanketa whitish.
blanketo blank check, carte blanche.
blankfiŝo bleak.
blankflugila white-winged. **blankflugila alaŭdo** white-winged lark. **blankflugila mevo** iceland gull.
blankgorĝa emberizo white-throated sparrow.
blankhara white-haired.
blankhaŭta pale-skinned, white-skinned.
blankhaŭtulo white-skinned person, Caucasian.
blankigado blanching.
blankigejo bleach-field.
blankigi to blanch, whiten, bleach.
blankigilo bleach.
blankigo blanching.
blankiĝi to become white, turn white.
blankkapa emberizo pine bunting.
blankkola maraglo pallas's fish eagle.
blanklume in white light.
blanko white.
blankspegula maranaso velvet scoter, white-winged scoter.
blankulo European, white man.
blankurso polar bear.
blankverso blank verse.
blankverta emberizo white-crowned sparrow.
blankvizaĝulo pale face.
blankvosta maraglo white-tailed eagle.

Blaratolo Blair Atholl.
blasfema blasphemous.
blasfemanto blasphemer.
blasfeme blasphemously.
blasfemi to blaspheme, cuss, curse, swear.
blasfemisto blasphemer.
blasfemo blasphemy, oath (curse).
blasfemulo blasphemer.
blastemo blastema.
blastocero marsh dear.
blastodermo blastoderm.
blastodisko blastodisk.
blastomero blastomere.
blastulo blastula.
blato cockroach, chip.
blaua blue.
blaziga blistering.
blazo blister.
blazoni to emblazon.
blazono blazon, coat of arms, heraldry, symbol.
blazonoscienco heraldry.
blazonŝildo escutcheon, heraldic shield.
blefarito blepharitis.
blekadi to growl.
blekado bleating, grunting, making animal sounds.
blekegi to bellow, roar.
blekego great cry, loud grunt.
bleketi to squeak, purr, whine.
bleketo small cry, small grunt.
bleki to cry (of animals), bellow, bleat, neigh, grunt.
bleko cry, animal sound.
blendi to armour, armour-plate.
blendo[1] armour-plate, armour-plating.
blendo[2] blende, sphalerite, zinc sulfate.
blenio blenny.
blenoragio blennorrhagia, gleet.
blenoreo blennorrhoea, gleet.
blesboko blesbok.
blimpo blimp.
blinda blind, sightless.
blinde blindly. **blinde imiti** to blindly imitate.
blindeco blindness.
blindiga blinding.
blindige blindingly.
blindigi to dazzle.
blindigilo blinder, blindfold.
blindiĝi to become blind.
blindkaptado blindman's buff.
blindludo blindman's buff.
blindokaze by blind chance.
blindpalpe feeling blindly.
blindtuko blindfold.
blindule blindly.
blinduliga tuko blindfold.
blinduligi to blindfold.

blindulo blind, sightless person.
blindumi to dazzle.
blito Indian paint, strawberry blite, strawberry pigweed.
blizardo blizzard.
blogo blog, weblog.
blokadi to blockade.
blokado blockade.
bloke all in one piece.
blokestro warden.
bloketo bit.
blokhaŭso blockhouse, log cabin.
bloki to block, blockade.
bloklitero block letter.
bloko block, boulder, chunk, unit.
bloksekcio block section.
bloksistemo block system.
blokstano block-tin.
blokŝtupo block step.
blonda blond, fair, fair-haired. **blondaj haroj** blond hair.
blondeco blondness.
blondhara blonde-haired.
blondigi to dye blond.
blondulino blonde (woman).
blondulo blond.
blovadi to keep blowing, continue blowing.
blovado gale.
blovaĵo smell, waft.
blovatoro blower.
blovega blustery, boisterous.
blovego blast.
bloveksciti to fan, blow, stir up.
blovestingi to blow out.
bloveti to waft.
bloveto breeze, small movement of air.
blovharmoniko harmonica, harp.
blovi to blow, puff.
blovilo bellows.
blovinstalaĵo air blower.
blovinstrumento wind instrument.
blovisto blower.
blovmuzikisto blower.
blovo blowing, movement of air.
blovpafilo blowpipe.
blovŝalmo blowpipe.
blua blue. **blua cirkuo** hen harrier. **Blua Nilo** Blue Nile. **blua paruo** blue tit. **Blua Rivero** Chang Jiang, Yangtze Kiang.
bluaĵo blue.
blualgo blue-green alga.
Blubarbo Bluebeard.
Blubarbulo Bluebeard.
blubero blueberry, whortleberry.
blueska bluish.
blueta light blue.
blufanto bluffer.
blufi to bluff, brag.

bluflugila blue-winged. **bluflugila anaso** blue-winged teal.
blufo boasting.
blufulo braggart.
blugriza blue-grey.
bluigaĵo bluing.
bluigi to make (something) blue.
blukopio blueprint.
blunderbuzo blunderbuss.
bluo blue.
bluokula blue-eyed.
bluradia disko Blu-ray Disc.
bluso blues.
bluŝtrumpulino bluestocking.
bluti to sift.
bluvanga abelmanĝulo Madagascar Bee-eater, Olive Bee-eater.
bluverda blue-green.
bluzo blouse.
bo name of the letter B.
bo- (denotes in-law, relatives by marriage).
boa by marriage.
boaco caribou, reindeer.
Boacolago Reindeer Lake.
boacosledo reindeer sleigh.
boao boa (snake).
boardi to manoeuvre, to tack.
boata of a boat.
boatado boating.
boatano shipmen, crew (of a boat).
boataro fleet of boats.
boate by boat, on a boat, with a boat.
boatego large boat.
boatejo boathouse.
boateto little boat, skiff.
boatferdeko boat deck.
boatflanko side of a boat.
boatforma boat-shaped.
boatgardo ship's watchmen.
boatisto boatman.
boatkondukisto waterman.
boato boat, vessel, ship.
boatoponto pontoon.
boatremizo boathouse.
boatveturado boat journey.
bobado bobsledding.
bobejo bobsled run, bobsled course.
bobelado bubbling.
bobeli to bubble.
bobelmetoda ordigo bubble sort.
bobelnivelilo spirit level.
bobelo bubble.
bobenego spool, reel.
bobenfarilo reel.
bobeni to spool, wind.
bobenilo bobbin-winder.
bobeningo bobbin holder.
bobenistino bobbin winder.

bobeno

bobeno bobbin, coil, reel, spool, choke, inductor, reactor.
bobenpunto bobbin lace.
bobenrako bobbin creel.
bobenstango spindle.
bobenumi to wind (on spool).
bobenvindilo bobbin-winder.
bobisto bobsledder.
bobo bobsled.
bobolinko bobolink, a songbird related to meadowlarks.
bobsledanto bobsledder, bobsleigher.
bobsledisto bobsledder, bobsleigher.
bobsledo bobsled, bobsleigh.
bobvego bobsled run, bobsled course.
bocaĵo beef.
Bocvano Bechuanaland, Botswana.
boĉianto bocce player.
boĉio bocce ball.
Bodenlago Bodensee, Constance.
bodiarbo bodi tree.
bodisatvo bodhisattva.
bofilino daughter-in-law.
bofilo son-in-law.
Boformaro Beaufort Sea.
bofratino sister-in-law.
bofrato brother-in-law.
bogefratoj brother- and sister-in-law.
bogepatroj in-laws, parents-in-law.
boĝio bogie, truck.
bohema Bohemian.
bohemia Bohemian.
bohemiano bohemian.
Bohemio Bohemia.
Bohemo bohemian.
Bohemujo Bohemia.
Bohidro Balquhidder.
bojadi to bark (continuously).
bojado barking.
bojaro boyar, boyard.
bojegi to bark, bay.
bojeti to yap.
bojeto yap.
boji to bay, bark.
bojkotado boycott, boycotting.
bojkoti to boycott.
bojkoto boycott.
bojminaci to bay at, bark at.
bojo bark (of a dog).
bokado bucking.
bokalo jar.
boko ram, vaulting-horse.
boksado boxing.
boksareno boxing ring.
boksarto boxing.
boksbato blow.
boksero boxer.
boksganto boxing glove.
boksi to box.

bombasta

boksisto boxer.
boksito bauxite.
bokso boxing, pugilism.
boksoganto boxing glove.
boksomaĉo boxing match.
boksopilko punching-bag.
bokstrejnado boxing training.
bolado ebullition.
bolanata boiling.
bolao bola, bolas.
bolardo bollard, mooring-post.
bolaso bola, bolas.
bolea Boolean.
bolegi to boil over, boil rapidly.
bolegilo boiler.
bolero bolero.
boleti to simmer, stew, poach.
boleto boletus.
bolgrado boiling point.
boli to boil, seethe.
bolido bolide, fireball, meteor.
boligi to boil (something).
boligilo boiler, kettle.
bolilo kettle.
bolivia Bolivian.
bolivianino Bolivian woman.
boliviano Bolivian.
Bolivio Bolivia.
bolkruĉo kettle.
bolkuiri to boil, cook by boiling.
bolo boil.
bolometro bolometer.
bolonjo baloney.
bolpoto boiler (saucepan).
bolpunktleviĝo boiling point elevation.
bolpunkto boiling point.
bolŝevika bolshevist.
bolŝeviko Bolshevik.
bolŝevismo bolshevism.
bolŝevisto Bolshevik.
bolti to bolt.
boltilo wrench.
boltingo nut.
bolto bolt.
bolujo boiler.
boluso bolus.
bolvarma boiling hot.
bolveziko bump.
bomao boma.
bombado bombardment, bombing.
Bombajo Bombay.
bombardado cannonade.
bombardi to bombard.
bombardilo howitzer, mortar.
bombardisto artilleryman, gunner, bombardier.
bombardo shelling.
bombardono bombardon.
bombasta showy, bombastic.

bombasto bombast.
bombatenco bomb attack.
bombaviadilo bomber.
bombavio bomber.
bombazino bombasine.
bombĉambro bomb bay.
Bombejo Bombay.
bombflugilo bomber, bomber plane.
bombi to bomb.
bombicilo Bohemian Waxwing.
bombiksedoj Bombycidae.
bombikso bombyx, silkworm.
bombilio bee-fly.
bombilo bomber.
bombo bomb, shell.
bombokanono mortar.
bombono bonbon, piece of candy, sweet.
bombonujo candy dish.
bombopafilo mortar.
bomborezista bomb-proof.
bombrezista bomb-proof.
bomerango boomerang.
bona good, nice, okay, kind, nice. **bona ordo** well-ordering. **bonaj manieroj** good manners. **bonan matenon!** good morning! **bonan nokton!** good night! **bonan posttagmezon!** good afternoon. **bonan ŝancon** good luck! **bonan tagon** good day! **bonan versperon!** good evening!
Bonaero Buenos Aires.
bonafida bonafide.
bonafide in good faith.
bonaĵo good thing.
bonamiko good friend.
bonanima good-hearted.
bonanime good-heartedly.
bonanzo bonanza.
bonaspekta good-looking.
bonaspektigi to flatter.
bonaŭgura of good omen.
bonazio hazel hen.
boncelite well-aimed.
bondezirbileto greeting card.
bondeziro good wishes, goodwill.
bondeziroj good wishes.
bone well. **bone!** fine! OK! all right! well! **bone edukita** accomplished, cultivated, cultured, educated. **bone posedi** to have mastery of.
boneco excellence, goodness, kindness.
bonedo bonnet.
bonedukiteco well-breeding.
bonefika salutary.
bonega excellent, fine, great, very well.
bonege excellently. **bonege!** excellent!
bonego excellence.
Bonespera Kabo Cape of Good Hope.
boneta nice, so so.
bonfama of good repute.

bonfara beneficent, beneficial, charitable, humanitarian, welfare. **bonfara societo** charity. **bonfara vendo** bazaar.
bonfarada charitable.
bonfarado charity.
bonfaraĵo good work, good dead.
bonfaranto benefactor, humanitarian, charitable person, do-gooder.
bonfarema charitable.
bonfaremulo philanthropist.
bonfari to benefit, do good.
bonfaristo benefactor.
bonfaro benevolence, boon, good work, good deed, good turn.
bonfarta (doing) well, fine, comfortable.
bonfartanta well.
bonfarti to be well, feel fine.
bonfarto well-being.
bonfido good faith.
bonformigi to place in good form.
bongoj bongo drums.
bongusta luscious, nice, tasty, savory, succulent.
bongustaĵo delicacy.
bonguste with, in good taste.
bongusteco good taste.
bongustega delicious.
bongusto good taste.
bonhava in easy circumstances, well-to-do, well off.
bonhavaĵo asset, easy circumstances.
bonhaveco affluence.
bonhavo assets, credit.
bonhumora gay, merry.
bonhumore cheerfully, merrily.
bonhumoreco cheerfulness.
bonhumoro good humour.
boni to be good, be okay, be nice.
bonifiko bonus.
bonigi to improve, make good.
boniĝi to become good.
bonintenca well-intentioned.
Bonito Bonita.
bonito bonito.
bonkaraktera good-hearted.
bonkondiĉa well-conditioned.
bonkonduta sweet.
bonkora good-hearted, kind.
bonkore goodheartedly.
bonkoreco kindness.
bonkvalita high-quality.
bonkvaliteco virtue.
bonloko a good place, a good location.
bonmanĝaĵo good food.
bonmaniera courteous, polite, well-mannered, refined.
bonmaniereco good breeding, refinement.
bonmetiista workmanlike.
bonmora decorous, mannered.

Bonno

Bonno Bonn.
bonnovaĵo (piece of) good news.
bono good.
bonodora fragrant, good-smelling, nutty.
bonodoreco fragrance.
bonodorfumaĵo air freshener.
bonodorfumilo censer.
bonodorfumo incense.
bonodoro nice smell, sweet smell.
bonokaza fortunate, lucky.
bonokaze fortunately, luckily.
bonorda well-ordered.
bonorde neatly, orderly, tidily, trimly.
bonordeco tidiness.
bonordigi to trim.
bonordo good order.
bonsajo bonsai.
bonsani to heal, recover, get better (health).
bonsona euphonic.
bonsorta fortuitous, fortunate, lucky.
bonsorte fortuitously, fortunately, happily, luckily.
bonstata in good condition.
bonstatigaĵo conditioner.
bonstato good, welfare, well-being.
bonstila good style.
bonŝanca lucky.
bonŝance fortunately, luckily.
bonŝanci to be lucky, have luck.
bonŝanco luck.
bonŝancon good luck.
bonŝanculo lucky devil.
bonteboko bontebok.
bontona well-mannered.
bontrovi to approve of, think fit.
bontrovo discretion.
bonulo nice guy.
bonvena welcome.
bonveni to welcome. **bonvenu!** welcome!
bonvenigi to welcome.
bonvenigo greeting, salutation.
bonveno welcome. **bonvenon!** welcome!
bonvivo good life.
bonvola genial, well-wishing.
bonvolanta well-wishing.
bonvole please.
bonvolema of good will.
bonvoli to condescend, deign; welcome.
  bonvolu be so good as to, please. **bonvolu turni** to please turn over, P.T.O.
bonvolo affection.
bonzo bonze.
boparenceco affinity, alliance.
boparenciĝi to become someone's in-law.
boparenco in-laws.
bopatrino mother-in-law.
bopatro father-in-law.
bopo bop.
borago borage.

Bosporo

boraĵo bore hole.
boraĵoj borings.
borakso borax.
borata acido boracic acid, boric acid.
boratacido boracic acid, boric acid.
boratingi to bore, broach, sink, strike, tap.
borato borate.
borda adjacent, adjoining, bordering.
bordano beach-dweller.
bordelo bordello, brothel.
borderaĵo border.
borderi to border, fringe, hem.
bordero border, hem.
bordi to border.
bordiĝi to board, get on board.
bordmarŝejo embankment, quay.
bordo bank, border, edge, coast, shore.
Bordozo Bourdeaux.
borduno bourdon.
boreala boreal. **boreala aŭroro** aurora borealis. **Boreala Krono** Corona Borealis.
borela sigmaalgebro Borel's field.
Borelo Borel.
Borglono Looz.
bori to bore, drill.
borilego auger.
borileto awl, gimlet.
borilingo shank.
borilo bore, borer, drill.
bormaŝino power drill.
bornego bushing.
Borneo Borneo.
borno electrical terminal.
boro boron.
borsa makleristo stock broker.
borsisto broker.
borso money market, stock exchange, stock market.
borstacio oil rig.
bortruo borehole, drill-hole.
borturo derrick.
bosanovo bossa nova.
bosi to boss.
bosketo bosket.
bosko copse, grove.
bosna Bosnian.
bosnia Bosnian.
bosnianino Bosnian woman.
bosniano Bosnian.
bosnino Bosnian woman.
Bosnio Bosnia. **Bosnio kaj Hercegovino** Bosnia and Herzegovina.
Bosnio-Hercegovino Bosnia-Herzegovina.
bosno Bosnian.
Bosnujo Bosnia. **Bosnujo kaj Hercegovino** Bosnia and Herzegovina.
boso boss.
bosono boson.
Bosporo Bosporus.

Bostono

Bostono Boston.
bostono boston.
boŝmano Bushman.
botanika botanical. **botanika ĝardeno** botanical garden.
botaniki to botanize.
botanikisto botanist.
botaniko botany.
botaŭro bittern.
botelarbo bottle palm, elephant-foot tree, pony-tail palm.
botelbiero bottled beer.
botelbretaro bottle rack.
botelbroso bottlebrush.
botelĉapeto bottle cap.
botelego flagon, jar.
boteletikedo bottle label.
boteleto flask, phial, vial.
botelkolo bottleneck.
botelkorbo bottle basket.
botelkorko bottle cork.
botelkukurbo bottle gourd.
botelmalfermilo bottle opener.
botelo bottle.
botelpurigatoro bottle washing machine.
botelrako bottle rack.
botelskrapilo bottle scraper.
botelujo bottle-holder, bottle-straw.
botelverdaĵo bottle green.
botelvino bottled wine.
boteto hiking boot, short boot, work boot.
botisto bootmaker.
Botna Golfo Gulf of Bothnia.
boto boot.
botono bud.
botoŝtipo boot-tree.
bototirilo bootjack.
botsvana Botswanan.
botsvananino Botswanan woman.
botsvanano Botswanan.
botŝtipo boot-tree.
bottirilo bootjack.
botulino botulin.
botulismo botulism.
boŭlanto bocce player.
boŭlo bocce, bowls.
bova bovine, cow. **bova spongeca encefalopatio** Bovine Spongiform Encephalopathy (BSE).
bovaĵo beef.
bovaĵraguo beef stew.
bovaĵtranĉo beefsteak.
bovaro cattle.
bovedoj bovids.
bovejo byre, cowhouse, cowshed.
bovgardisto cowherd.
bovida calf's. **bovida viando** veal.
bovidaĵo veal.
bovidino heifer.

brakumo

bovido calf.
bovidviando veal.
bovina bovine.
bovinejo cow shed.
bovino cow, bovine animal, head of cattle, ox.
bovintritiko cow-wheat.
bovisteo puff-ball.
Bovisto Boötes.
bovlingo cow-tongue.
bovlo bowl.
bovo cow, ox. **Bovo** Taurus (zodiac).
bovokulo porthole.
bovorabanto cattle-lifter, cattle-stealer.
bovorabisto cattle thief, rustler.
bovostalo shed.
bovoviro bull. **Bovoviro** Minotaur.
brabanta Brabantine.
brabantano Brabantine.
Brabanto Brabant.
bracelethorloĝo watch, wrist-watch.
braceleto bracelet.
braĉo breeches.
bradipo sloth, three-toed sloth.
brago type of homemade beer.
braĝo charcoal.
braĥicefalo brachycephalic.
braĥiskomo brachyscome.
braĥiuro crab.
brajli to brail (up), clew up, draw in, haul up.
brajlilo brail.
brajlo Braille.
braka arm, of an arm.
brakapogilo arm, armrest.
brakbendo armband, brassard.
brake by the arm, with one's arm.
brakforto arm strength.
brakhorloĝo watch, wristwatch.
brakicefalo brachycephalic.
brakiopodo brachiopod.
brakiosaŭro brachiosaurus.
brakkiraso brassard.
brako arm (of the body), upper arm. **brako ĉe brako** arm in arm.
brakocefala brachiocephalic.
brakocefalika brachiocephalic.
brakpiedulo brachiopod.
brakpleno (an) armload.
brakprotezo arm prosthesis, artificial arm.
brakringo bracelet.
brakseĝo armchair.
brakŝloso bar arm.
braktea bracteal. **braktea eternfloro** bracted strawflower, golden everlasting.
brakteato bracteate.
brakteno arm hold.
brakteo bract.
brakumi to embrace, hug.
brakumo embrace, hug.

bramanismo

bramanismo Brahminism.
bramano Brahmin.
Bramaputro Bramaputra.
bramari to bell.
bramo bream, topgallant mast.
Bramoputro Brahmaputra.
bramvelo top-gallant.
branĉa ordono conditional statement.
branĉajo faggot.
branĉaro network of branches.
branĉbalailo besom.
branĉbarileto hurdle.
branĉetaĵo dry twigs, dry sticks.
branĉetfasko bundle of sticks.
branĉeto shoot (tree), twig, sprig.
branĉfasko brushwood, bundle of sticks.
branĉhakileto billhook.
branĉido shoot, sprout.
branĉiĝi to branch off.
branĉkorno antler.
branĉnesto nest of branches.
branĉo bough, branch.
branĉoplanti to propagate by cuttings.
branĉoplena branchy.
branĉoriĉa branchy.
branĉotondilo pruning shears.
branĉotranĉilo bill, billhook, pruning-knife.
branĉrivero affluent.
branĉvojo by-way, side-way.
brandejo bar.
brandfaristo distiller.
brando brandy.
brandofarejo brandy distillery.
brandoglaso brandy glass.
brankardo stretcher.
brankiostomo amphioxus.
branko gill.
brano bran.
branopano wholemeal bread.
branpano whole-grain bread.
braserio brasserie.
brasi to brew.
brasiknapo swede (vegetable).
brasiko brassica, cabbage, cole.
brasiksalato coleslaw.
brasikstumpo stalk of cabbage.
braso brace, guy.
brava brave, gallant, good, honest, stalwart, staunch, valiant, valorous, worthy.
bravaĉa impudent.
bravaĉo impudence.
bravaĵo bravery.
brave bravely.
Brave! Bravo!
braveco bravery, valor.
bravega very brave.
bravege very bravely.
bravegeco temerity.
bravo bravery, gallantry, valor.

brevo

bravulo brave.
bravura bravura.
bravuro bravura.
brazi to braze, hard-solder.
brazila Brazilian.
brazilanino Brazilian woman.
Brazilano Brazilian.
Brazilo Brazil.
breco pretzel.
breĉeti to nick, notch.
breĉetigi to nick, notch.
breĉeto indentation, notch.
breĉi to breach.
breĉigi to breach.
breĉio breccia.
breĉo breach, gap.
bredado breeding.
bredi to breed, farm, keep, raise, rear.
bredisto breeder.
bredo breeding.
bredreaktoro breeder reactor.
Brejo Bray.
breloko charm, trinket.
Bremara Distrikto Braemar.
Bremaro Braemar.
bremsado brakeage, braking capacity.
bremsbendo brake band.
bremsbudo braking booth.
bremsdisko brake pulley.
bremsi to brake.
bremsilo brake.
bremsisto brakesman.
bremskablo brake cable.
bremskonuso brake cone.
bremslampo brake light.
bremslevumilo brake lever.
bremsmagneto brake magnet.
bremsmanometro brake pressure gauge.
bremso brake.
bremsokapablo brakeage, braking capacity.
bremsopedalo brake pedal.
bremsostango brake lever.
bremsoŝuo brake-block, brake-shoe, drag, skid.
bremspedalo brake.
bremspezaĵo brake weight.
bremsregvalvo brake valve.
bremsŝafto brake axle.
bremsŝuo brake block, brake shoe.
bremsujo brake casing.
bretaro set of shelves, cabinet, shelves, shelving, bookcase.
breto shelf.
Bretonio Bretagne, Brittany.
bretono Breton.
Bretonujo Bretagne, Brittany.
breveco brevity.
breviero breviary.
brevo breve.

brevosigno

brevosigno breve (˘).
brezi to stifle.
bridi to bridle, check, restrain.
Bridlintono Bridlington.
brido bridle, check, restraint.
bridrimeno bridle strap.
brigadestro brigade commander.
brigado brigade.
brigantino brigantine.
brigo brig.
brigskuno brigantine.
briĝi to play bridge (the card game).
briĝisto bridge player.
briĝo bridge.
brika brick.
brikabrako bric-à-brac.
brikejo brick-field, brick works, brickyard.
brikero brickbat.
briketo bar (candy etc.).
brikfabriko brick works, brickyard.
brikfarejo brick works, brickyard.
brikkolora brick-red.
brikmetisto bricklayer.
brikmuro brick wall.
briko block. **briko da tualetsapo** bar of toilet soap.
brikportisto brick carrier.
brikruĝa brick red (the colour).
briktranĉilo brick cutter.
brila bright, brilliant, shining.
briladi to keep shining, keep glowing.
brilaĵeto spangle.
brilanta aglitter.
brilantino brilliantine.
brilanto diamond.
brilaspergi to spangle.
brile brightly, brilliantly.
brileco brilliance.
brilega very bright, glaring.
brilegi to glitter.
brilego flare, glare.
briletado glitter, sparkle.
briletaĵo spangle.
brileti to scintillate, twinkle.
brileto twinkle (of light).
brili to glisten, glow, shine, sparkle.
brilianto gem, jewel.
briligi to brighten.
briliĝi to become resplendent.
brilo brightness, gloss, sheen, lustre, shine, brilliance.
briloraĵo tinsel.
brilpura sparkling clean.
brilstriaĵo tinsel.
brilŝtono shining stone, glittering rock.
brilvidaĵo shining image, brilliant image.
brioĉo brioche.
briofita bryophytic.
briofito bryophyte.

bromuso

briologia bryological.
briologio bryology.
briologisto bryologist.
brionio bryony.
Brisbejno Brisbane.
Bristola Markolo Bristol Channel.
Bristolo Bristol.
brita British. **Brita Esperantista Asocio** British Esperanto Association, BEA. **Brita Insularo** British Islands. **Brita Kolombio** British Columbia. **Britaj Insuloj** British Isles. **Britaj Virgulinaj Insuloj** British Virgin Islands.
Britio Britain, Great Britain.
brito Briton.
britujano Brit.
Britujo Britain, Great Britain.
brizo breeze.
broĉo brooch, safety pin.
brodado embroidering, embroidery.
brodaĵo embroidery.
brodfadeno embroidering thread.
brodi to embroider.
Brodiko Brodick.
brodkastejo broadcasting station.
brodkasti to broadcast.
brodkasto broadcast.
brodteksi to brocade.
brogaciebla abrogable.
brogaĵo broth.
brogi to scald.
brogvundo scalding wound.
brokaĵo brocade.
brokanta second hand, secondhand.
brokantado bartering.
brokantaĵo second-hand good, used product.
brokanti to buy and sell used (second-hand) products.
brokantisto buyer and seller of used (second-hand) products.
brokanto bartering.
brokato brocade.
broki to brocade.
brokolio broccoli.
brokolo broccoli.
broma bromic.
bromata acido bromic acid.
bromatacido bromic acid.
bromato bromate.
bromido bromide.
bromika bromic.
bromismo bromism.
bromizi to brominate.
bromizo bromination.
bromo bromine.
bromoformo bromoform.
bromumado bromination.
bromumi to brominate.
bromuso brome.

bronka bronchial.
bronketa bronchiolar.
bronketo bronchiole.
bronkito bronchitis.
bronko bronchial tube.
bronkopulma bronchiopulmonary.
bronkoskopio bronchoscopy.
bronkoskopo bronchoscope.
brontosaŭro brontosaur.
bronza bronze. **Bronza Epoko** Bronze Age.
bronzaĵo bronze.
bronzepoko bronze age.
bronzfrunta brazen-faced.
bronzi to bronze.
bronzkolora bronze, brown.
bronzkoloro brown.
bronzo bronze.
bronzumi to bronze.
bronzvizaĝa brazen-faced.
Broro Brora.
brosado brushing.
brosi to brush.
broso brush.
brostiro brushstroke.
broŝura paperbacked.
broŝureto small brochure, small pamphlet.
broŝuri to bind in paper.
broŝurita paperbacked.
broŝuritaĵo paperback.
broŝuro brochure, leaflet, pamphlet, paperback.
brovo brow, eyebrow.
brua noisy.
bruâci to make a racket.
bruado hubbub.
brucino brucin.
brue loudly, noisily.
bruegadi to rumble.
bruegado clatter, din.
bruegi to blare, clamour.
bruego clamour, racket, row, noise, turmoil, uproar, tumult.
brueti to rustle.
brufermi to bang, slam.
Brugo Bruges.
Bruĝo Bruges.
brui to make a noise.
brula burning, combustible.
brulado combustion, conflagration.
brulaĵcisterno fuel tank.
brulaĵo brand, embers, fuel.
brulaĵujo bunker.
brulalarmo fire-alarm.
brulalkoholo methylated spirit.
brulanta afire, burning.
brulasekuro fire insurance.
brulavertilo fire alarm.
brulbombo incendiary bomb.
brulbotelo Molotov cocktail.

brulbriketo briquette.
bruldifekti to burn.
bruldolora inflamed.
brule varmega burning hot.
brulebla combustible.
brulego inferno.
brulema combustible, flammable, volatile.
brulestingisto fireman.
bruletado smoldering.
bruleti to char, scorch, smoulder, singe.
bruletigaĵo scorch.
bruletigi to scorch, sear.
bruleto glimmer.
brulgluiĝi to burn.
brulgusta burnt.
bruli to burn, be on fire, sting. **bruli de dezirego** to burn with desire.
bruligaĵo fuel.
bruligebla combustible.
bruligi to burn, sear.
bruligo arsonism.
bruliĝema inflammable.
bruliĝo combustion.
brulilo burner.
brulimuna fireproof, incombustible.
brulkonsumiĝi to be burnt down.
brulkrimo arson.
brulkrimulo incendiary.
brulligno firewood.
brulmarki to brand.
brulmarkilo branding iron.
brulmarko brand.
brulmortigi to burn to death.
brulo combustion.
brulofera holocaustal.
brulofero burnt offering.
bruloftero burnt offering.
brulpretigi to bake something into something, prepare by baking.
brulpumpilo fire engine.
brulsigni to brand.
brulstampi to brand.
brulstampilo branding iron.
brulstampo brand.
brulŝirmilo fire screen.
brulŝtiparo faggot.
brulumi to be inflamed.
brulumo inflammation.
brulvundi to burn.
brulvundo burn.
brumarŝi to clatter, clump.
brumo haze.
bruna brown. **bruna urso** brown bear.
Brunajo Brunei.
brunalgo brown.
brunalgoj brown algae.
bruneja Bruneian.
brunejanino Bruneian woman.
brunejano Bruneian.

Brunejo

Brunejo Brunei.
brunelo all-heal, self-heal.
bruneta brownish.
brunflava dun.
brungriza dark dun, dark grey.
brunhara brown-haired, brunette.
brunharulino brunette.
Brunhildo Brunhild, Brünnhilde.
brunigi to tan (the skin).
bruniĝi to tan.
brunkapa brown-headed. **brunkapa anaso** pochard. **brunkapa emberizo** red-headed bunting.
brunkarbo brown coal, lignite.
bruno brown.
Bruno Bruno.
brunokula brown-eyed.
brunruĝa fawn-coloured.
Brunsviko Brunswick.
brunulino brunette.
bruo ado, din, noise.
brusela Brussels. **brusela brasiko** Brussels-sprouts.
bruselbrasiketo brussel sprout.
bruselbrasiko Brussels-sprouts.
Bruselo Brussels.
bruska abrupt, blunt, brusque.
bruske abruptly, gruffly.
bruskeco brusqueness, grimness.
bruski to be sharp with.
brustaĵo breast, chest, brisket.
brustangino angina pectoris.
brustangoro angina pectoris.
brustaŭskulti to auscultate.
brustkesto thorax.
brustkiraso breastplate.
brusto bosom, breast, chest.
brustonaĝado breaststroke.
brustopeco bib.
brustopoŝo breast pocket.
brustorimeno breast collar, breast strap.
brustosto sternum.
brustoŝirmilo plastron.
brustotuko bib.
brustpoŝo breast pocket.
brusttenilo brassiere, bra.
bruta beastly, brutal, brute, harsh.
brutala brutal, violent.
brutalaĵo atrocity.
brutale brutally, violently.
brutaleco brutality.
brutali to bully, maltreat.
brutalo barbarian, inhuman, thug, wretch.
brutaro drove, herd, livestock, flock.
brute brutally.
bruteca inhuman, thuggish, vicious.
brutece viciously.
bruteco vicissitude.
brutedukisto animal herders.

budho

brutejo barn.
brutforta metodo brute force.
brutigi to brutalize, dull.
brutiĝi to become dull.
brutisto farmer, stockman.
brutkondukisto drover.
Bruto[1] Brutus.
bruto[2] brute, beast, head of cattle, farm animal.
brutulo brute, boor.
b.t. → **bonvolu turni**.
bubaĉo naughty boy, pickle.
bubaĵo prank.
bubalkrono buffalo horns.
bubalo buffalo.
bubaro bunch of kids.
bubego boob, bumpkin.
bubeto toddler bubo brat, urchin.
bubino hussy, wench.
bubo brat kid, urchin, jack (cards).
bubona bubonic. **bubona pesto** bubonic plague.
bubono bubo.
bubonpesto bubonic plague.
bucero hornbill.
buĉadi to slaughter (animals).
buĉado butchery, slaughter, carnage, massacre.
buĉbruto animal for slaughter.
buĉejo abattoir, butcher's shop, slaughterhouse, killing field.
buĉhelpisto butcher's assistant.
buĉi to butcher, slaughter, kill (animals).
buĉista butcherly.
buĉistbutiko butcher's shop.
buĉisto butcher.
buĉita butchered.
buĉtranĉilo butcher's knife.
budaano Buddhist.
budaisma Buddhist.
budaismo Buddhism.
budaista pastro Buddhist priest, bonze.
budaisto Buddhist.
Budao Buddha.
budao Buddha.
Budapeŝto Budapest.
budaro group of vending stalls, bazaar.
buddhisma erao Buddhist Era.
buddismo Buddhism.
buddisto Buddhist.
Buddo Buddha.
budeno blood sausage.
budeto sentry box.
budĝeto budget.
budhano Buddhist.
budhisma Buddhist.
budhismo Buddhism.
budhisto Buddhist.
budho Buddha.

budi

budi to pout, sulk.
budleo buddleia.
budo barn, shed, stand, stall, hut, booth, cabana, kiosk.
buduaro boudoir.
bufago beefeater.
bufalo buffalo.
bufedejo buffet hall.
bufedistino barmaid.
bufedisto barman, barkeeper, bartender.
bufedo buffet.
bufo toad.
bufona zany.
bufonado tomfoolery.
bufonaĵo tomfoolery.
bufono fool, freak, zany.
bufri to buffer, bump into.
bufro buffer, bumper.
bufrodisko buffer disk.
bufroŝtato buffer state.
bufrozono buffer zone.
bugenvilo bougainvillaea.
bugio buggy.
Bugo Bug.
bugri to bugger, sodomize.
bugro anal sex.
buĝerigo budgerigar.
buĝeta budgetary. **buĝeta deficito** budgetary deficit. **buĝeta jaro** budget year. **buĝeta juro** budget law. **buĝeta konsilaro** budget committee. **buĝeta superresto** budget surplus. **buĝetaj elspezoj** budget expenditure. **buĝetaj reguloj** budget regulations.
buĝeti to appropriate.
buĝeto budget.
buĝio bougie.
Buhoro Bukhara, Buxoro.
bujabeso bouillabaisse.
bukako bukkake.
bukanisto buccaneer.
Bukareŝto Bucharest.
bukceno whelk.
bukcinatoro buccinator muscle.
bukdorno buckle pin.
bukedo bunch, bouquet.
bukfermi to buckle, fasten.
buki to buckle.
bukla curly (of hair), loopy.
bukli to curl.
bukligi to curl.
bukligilo curling-tongs.
buklilo curler.
buklo curl, lock (hair), loop, lock, wisp.
bukmekro bookie, bookmaker.
buko buckle, clasp.
bukolika bucolic.
bukoliko bucolic.
bukramo buckram.

bumerango

bukrimeno buckle strap.
buksa ligno boxwood.
bukskino buckskin.
bukso box (shrub, tree), boxwood.
Bukureŝto Bucharest.
bulado bowling.
bulba bulbous.
bulbero clove.
bulbeto onion.
bulbkulturisto bulb farmer.
bulbo bulb, dome.
bulbokampo bulb field.
bulbokulturisto bulb farmer.
bulbulo bulbul.
bulcerastio sticky mouse-ear.
bulĉapo bowler.
buldogo French bulldog.
buldogteriero bull terrier.
buldozi to bulldoze.
buldozo bulldozer.
Bulea Boolean, logical. **Bulea algebro** Boolean algebra. **Bulea esprimo** Boolean expression. **Bulea funkcio** Boolean function. **Bulea operacio** Boolean operator, logical operator. **Bulea valoro** Boolean value.
buleca lumpy.
bulejo bowling green.
buleno bowline.
Buleo[1] Boole.
buleo[2] papal bull.
buleto pellet, small ball.
bulgara Bulgarian.
bulgarino Bulgarian woman.
Bulgaria Bulgaria.
bulgaro Bulgarian.
Bulgaro Bulgarian.
Bulgarujo Bulgaria.
buligi to ball up, wad.
buliĝi to ball up.
bulimia bulimic.
bulimio bulimia.
buljonkubo bouillon cube.
buljono bouillon, broth.
bulkego loaf.
bulketo roll.
bulko bun, roll.
bulkokorbo bread basket.
bullo bull.
bulmarko bullet (•).
Bulo[1] Buhl.
bulo[2] ball, chunk, clod, hunk, lump, wad.
buloaĵo clod.
bulrulejo bowling green.
bulteno bulletin, newsletter.
bulvardo boulevard.
bulvolvi to wind up.
bumbramvelo royal.
bumerango boomerang.

bumlifto boom topping lift.
bumo boom.
bungalo bungalow.
bunkro bunker, shelter.
bunrako bunraku.
bunsenbruligilo Bunsen burner.
bunta colourful, multicoloured.
buntaĉa garish.
buntpego spotted woodpecker.
buo buoy.
burbono bourbon whiskey.
burbonviskio bourbon, bourbon whiskey.
burdado buzzing.
Burdegalo Bordeaux.
burdo bumblebee, drone.
burdono bourdon.
bureo bourrée.
bureto burette, chalice.
burgero burger.
burgestro burgrave.
Burghedo Burghead.
burgmajstro burgomaster.
burgo burgess.
Burgonjo Burgundy.
Burgoponto Boroughbridge.
burgrafo viscount.
burgunda Burgundian. **burgunda vino** burgundy.
Burgundio Burgundy.
burgundo Burgundian.
Burgundujo Burgundy.
burĝa bourgeois, middleclass.
burĝaro bourgeoisie.
burĝo bourgeois, commoner, middle-class citizen.
burĝonbrasiko Brussels sprout.
burĝoni to bud.
burĝono bud.
burho burka, burqa.
burjata Buryatian.
burjato Buryat.
Burjatujo Buryatia.
Burkinafaso Upper Volta.
Burkino Burkina Faso.
burleska burlesque.
burleskaĵo antic, farce.
burlesko burlesque.
burleskulo fool, jester.
burma Burmese.
burmanino Burmese woman.
burmano Burmese.
Burmo Burma.
burnuso burnous.
buro Afrikaner, Boer.
burokrata bureaucratic.
burokrataro bureaucracy, officialdom, bureaucracy.
burokrateco bureaucracy, red tape.
burokratisma bureaucratic.
burokratisme bureaucratically.
burokratismo bureaucracy.
burokrato bureaucrat.
buroo bureau.
bursito bursitis.
burso bursa.
burundia Burundian.
burundianino Burundian woman.
burundiano Burundian.
Burundio Burundi.
Burundo Burundi.
busa bus. **busa haltejo** bus stop. **busa stacio** bus station.
busbileto bus ticket.
bushaltejo bus stop.
buso bus, omnibus.
busprito bowsprit.
buspritstajo bobstay.
busstacidomo bus station.
busstacio bus station.
busŝoforo bus driver.
busto bust, torso.
buŝa oral. **buŝa seksumo** oral sex.
buŝakviga mouthwatering.
buŝe orally.
buŝego jaws, mouth, muzzle, jowl, maw, gullet.
buŝelo bushel.
buŝelujo bushel.
buŝfermulo quiet, closed-mouth person, silent type, someone who doesn't talk much.
buŝfreŝigenzo breath freshener.
buŝfreŝigilo breath freshener.
buŝharmoniko harmonica, harp.
buŝmano Bushman.
buŝmeno Bushman.
buŝo mouth, orifice.
buŝoŝtopilo gag (to stop someone from speaking).
buŝpleno morsel, mouthful.
buŝpreno bite.
buŝtuko napkin, serviette.
buŝumi to gag, muzzle.
buŝumilo bit.
buŝumo muzzle (for a dog).
buŝveziketo aphtha.
butana Bhutanese.
butananino Bhutanese woman.
butanano Bhutanese.
Butano Bhutan.
butano butane.
butanoa acido butyric acid.
butanoata acido butyric acid.
butanoato butyrate.
butanolo butanol.
buteo buzzard.
butera buttery, buttered.
buteracido butyric acid.
buterbuklo brioche.

buterfari

buterfari to churn.
buterfloro hawkbit. **buterfloro de la diablo** buttercup.
buteri to butter.
buterigi to churn.
buterigilo butter-churn.
buterilo churn.
buterizi to butter.
buterlakto buttermilk.
butero butter.
buterpano bread and butter.
butertrançilo butter knife.
buterujo butter dish.
buterumi to butter.
buti to earth, earth up, hill, hill up.
butika shopping, for shopping. **butika centro** shopping centre. **butika strato** shopping street.
butikaro mall.
butikego department store, store, warehouse.
butikisto merchant, retailer, shopkeeper, tradesman.
butiko boutique, shop, store.
butikŝtelado shoplifting.
butikŝtelanto shoplifter.

bv.

butiktablo counter.
butikumado shopping.
butikumi to go shopping, shop.
butikumlisto shopping-list.
butila alkoholo butyl alcohol.
butilato butylate.
butileno butylene.
butira butyric. **butira acido** butyric acid.
butiracido butyric acid.
butirata acido butyric acid.
butirato butyrate.
butirino butyrin.
butlero butler.
Buto Bute.
butomo flowering rush.
butoni to button.
butono bud, button, knob, stud.
butonŝaltilo button switch.
butontruo button-hole.
butonumata button-through.
butonumhoko buttonhook.
butonumi to button.
butonumilo button-hook.
butoro bittern.
bv. → **bonvolu**.

C

cara tsar's. **cara reĝimo** tsarism.
carido tsarevich.
carino tsarina.
carismo tsarism.
carista tsarist.
caro tsar.
cebo capuchin monkey.
ceceo tsetse fly.
cedado compliance.
cedaema compliant.
cedajo concession.
cedajˆricevanto abandonee.
cedanto ceder.
cedema yielding, accommodating.
cedeme yieldingly, accommodatingly.
cedemo accommodation, concession.
cedi to cede, give in, yield, comply, concede, grant, accommodate. **cedi al siaj pasioj** to yield to one's passions.
cedigi to soften up.
cedilo cedilla.
cedo abandonment, cession, concession.
cedra cedar, of a cedar.
cedrato citron.
cedro cedar.
cefalantero helleborine.
cefalo brain.
cefalopodo cephalopod.
cefeido cepheid.
Cefeo Cepheus.
cejana cyan.
cejano cornflower.
cejlona Ceylonese.
cejlonano Ceylonese.
Cejlono Ceylon.
cekumo cecum.
cela aimed, apt. **cela aro** codomain, target set.
celado endeavour.
celaĵo target.
celakanto coelacanth.
celanta al bound for.
celaro codomain.
celatinga purposeful, intentional.
celdirekti to aim, level, train.
celdisko target.
celdosiero output, output file, target file.
cele effective, telling.
Celebesmaro Celebes Sea.
Celebeso Celebes.
celebrado celebration.
celebranto celebrant.
celebri to celebrate.
celeco usefulness, purposefulness.
celegi to make great efforts (to do something).

celerio celery.
celesto celesta.
celgrajno front sight.
celi to aim (at, for), mean, target, intend, aspire, strain after.
celibato celibacy.
celigi to aim.
celilo sight, gun sight.
celintenco purpose.
celkodo object code.
celkomputilo target machine.
celkonforma purposeful, intentional.
celkonformeco effectiveness.
celkonscia purposeful.
cellingvo object language, target language.
cellinio finish line.
celmodulo object module.
celo aim, goal, purpose, target, purpose, objective, aspiration, goal. **celo por si mem** an end in itself.
celofana cellophane.
celofano cellophane.
celoidino celloidin.
celozio celosia, cockscomb, woolflower.
celprogramo object program, target program.
celpunkto bull's-eye.
celsia Celsius.
Celsio Celsius.
Celsiuso Celsius.
celtabulo target.
celto Celt.
celtrafa effective.
celtrafe effectively.
celtuŝi to finish.
celulito cellulite.
celuloido celluloid.
celulozo cellulose.
celumado aim, aiming.
celumaparato aiming mechanism.
celumi to aim, level, train.
celumo aim, goal, purpose.
celzia centigrade.
Celzio Celsius.
cembro stone-pine.
cementado cementing.
cementi to carburize, case-harden.
cemento cement.
cendo cent.
Cenomano Cenomanium, Cenomanian.
cenotafo cenotaph.
censisto censor.
censo census.
cent hundred, one hundred.
centaŭreo knapwood.

centaŭro centaur.
centavo centavo.
centerco centrality.
centerjo centre.
Centerŭropo Central Europe.
centestro centurion.
centezimala centesimal.
centfoje one hundred times.
centfunto hundredweight, quintal.
centiaro centare, centiare.
centigrada centesimal.
centigramo centigram.
centilitro centilitre.
centimetro centimetre.
centimo centime.
centjara one hundred year. **centjara festo** centenary.
centjaro century.
centjarulo centenarian.
centmil hundred thousand.
centmilo hundred thousand.
centmiloj hundreds of thousands.
cento quantity of a hundred.
centobla one hundred times.
centoble hundred-fold.
centona bado one hundredth of a baht, satang.
centono hundredth.
centope by hundreds.
centra central. **centra angulo** central angle. **centra aparato** central processing unit. **centra hejtado** central heating. **centra memorilo** main memory. **centra projekcio** central projection.
centrafrika Central African. **Centrafrika Respubliko** Central African Republic.
Centrafriko Central Africa(n Republic).
centrala central. **centrala hejtado** central heating.
centralismo centralism.
centralizado centralization.
centralizi to centralize.
centraliziĝi to be centralized.
centralo central office, exchange (telephone), power station.
Centrameriko Central America.
centre centrally.
centrejo headquarters, head office.
centri to centre, centralize, concentrate.
centrifuga centrifugal.
centrifugilo centrifuge.
centrigi to centre, centralize, concentrate.
centrigo centralization.
centriĝi to centre.
centripeta centripetal.
centro centre. **centro de grupo** centre (of a group).
Centroburgo Middlesbrough.
centuma centesimal.

cenzura censorious.
cenzurebla correct, proper.
cenzuri to censor, censure.
cenzuristo censor.
cenzuro censor.
cenzuso qualification, requirements, census.
cepo onion.
cerambicido longhorn beetle, long-horned beetle.
ceramika ceramic.
ceramikaĵo ceramic art, ceramic object.
ceramikisto ceramic artist, ceramist, potter.
ceramiko ceramics, pottery.
cerastio mouse-ear.
cerasto cerastes, horned (desert) viper.
ceratofilo hornwort.
cerba brain.
cerbaĵo brains.
cerbaro brain trust.
cerbatano blowpipe.
cerbelo cerebellum.
Cerbero Cerberus.
cerbeto cerebellum.
cerblaboristo brain worker.
cerbo brain.
cerboforfluo brain drain.
cerbohormono brain hormone.
cerbolabora white-collar.
cerbolaboristo brain worker.
cerbomorta brain dead.
cerbomorto brain death.
cerboondo brain wave.
cerboparaliza spastic.
cerboparalizulo spastic.
cerboskuo concussion.
cerboŝtopi to brainwash.
cerboza brainy.
cerbujo cranium.
cerbularo brain trust.
cerbumaĵoj worries.
cerbumi to puzzle over, rack one's brains, think hard, brood.
cerciso cercis.
cerealaĵo cereal.
cerealo cereal.
cerebelo cerebellum.
cerebrospina cerebrospinal.
cerefolio chervil.
ceremonia ceremonious, formal, measured, stiff.
ceremoniaĵoj ceremony, formalities.
ceremoniaro rite.
ceremonie ceremonially.
ceremonieco ceremony, solemnity.
ceremoniestro master of ceremonies.
ceremonio ceremony, observance.
ceremonioado observance (rite).
Cereso Ceres.
cerezino ceresine.

cerio

cerio cerium.
cerkopitekedoj old world monkeys.
cerkopiteko meercat.
ceroskopio ceroscopy.
certa certain, sure, unerring. **certa okazo** certain event.
certagrade to a certain degree.
certaĵo certainty, certitude.
certe certainly, surely.
certeca assured.
certeco certainty, certitude.
certege most certainly, very surely.
certgrade to a certain degree.
certi to be certain.
certigi to assure, affirm, assert, certify, make certain, certify, support.
certigo affirmation, confirmation.
certiĝi to ascertain.
certio creeper, tree-creeper.
cerumeno ear wax.
cerva deer, deer-, of a deer. **cerva skarabo** stag-beetle.
cervaĵo venison.
cervelaso cervelat.
cervido fawn.
cerviko cervix.
cervino doe, hind.
cervo deer, hart, stag.
cervokolora fawn.
cervoparko deer-park.
cervoskarabo stag beetle.
cervrapide as quick as a deer.
cesalpinio brazilwood.
cetaco cetacean.
cetera additional, remaining, rest of. **ceteraj** remaining, other.
cetere as for the rest, besides, for the rest, moreover, what's more, otherwise. **cetere...** aside from that..., I might add...
cetero remainder.
cezare by C-section.
Cezaro Caesar.
cezio caesium.
cezuro caesura.
ci thou, you (familiar form).
cia thine, thy, your (familiar form).
ciana acido prussic acid.
cianacido prussic acid.
cianido cyanide.
ciano cyanogen.
Cibelo Cybele.
cibernetika cybernetic.
cibernetiko cybernetics.
ciberspaco cyberspace.
cibetkato civet.
cibeto civet.
ciborgo cyborg.
ciborio ciborium.
Cicero Cicero.

ciklopa

Cicerono Cicero.
cico nipple.
cicumo nipple (artificial).
cidaro cidaris.
cidimetro acidimeter.
cidiri to say "ci", to use the familiar form.
cidonio quince.
cidro cider.
cifera digital.
ciferdisko CD, a disk that stores digital data.
cifere digitally.
cifereca numerical, digital. **cifereca komputilo** digital computer. **cifereca mono** digital cash. **cifereca prezento** digital representation. **cifereca stirado** numeric control, numerical control.
ciferece numerically, digitally.
ciferecigi to digitize.
ciferecigilo analogue-to-digital converter, digitizer.
ciferi to figure.
ciferigo digitization.
cifero cipher, digit, figure, numeral.
ciferplato clock face, dial (telephone).
cigana Gypsy, Romany.
cigano Gypsy, Romany.
cigardrestaĵo cigarette butt.
cigaredingo cigarette holder.
cigaredo cigarette.
cigaredostumpo cigarette-end, stub.
cigaredstumpo cigarette-end, stub.
cigaredujo cigarette box.
cigareto cigarillo.
cigaringo cigar holder.
cigaro cigar.
cigarstumpo cigar-end, cigar-stub.
cigarujo cigar box.
cignido baby swan.
cigno swan. **Cigno** Cygnus.
cii to use the familiar form of 'you' (**ci**).
cikado cicada.
cikatrigi to scar.
cikatriĝi to form a scar.
cikatro scar.
cikla cyclic. **cikla listo** circular list. **cikla permuto** cyclic permutation. **cikla ŝovo** circular shift, cyclic shift.
Cikladoj Cyclades.
ciklameno cyclamen.
cikle cyclically.
cikli to cycle.
ciklismo bicycling.
ciklisto cyclist.
ciklo cycle, bicycle, bike.
ciklogiro chopper, helicopter.
cikloido (common) cycloid.
ciklometria cyclometric.
ciklono cyclone.
ciklopa cyclopean.

ciklopo

ciklopo Cyclops.
ciklostili to cyclostyle.
ciklostilo cyclostyle.
ciklotempo cycle time.
ciklotimio cyclothymia.
ciklotrono cyclotron.
cikonio stork.
cikorio Belgian endives, chicory.
cikuto water hemlock, cowbane.
cilindra cylindrical. **cilindra ĉapelo** top-hat, topper. **cilindra koordinato** cylindrical coordinate, semi-polar coordinate.
cilindrakso axon.
cilindro cylinder, roller, stack, cylindrical surface.
cilindrobloko cylinder block.
cilindrokapo breech, cylinder-head.
cilio cilia.
cimatio cyma, picture rail.
cimbalisto cymbalist.
cimbalo cymbal.
cimento cement.
cimo (software) bug, bedbug.
cinabra vermilion.
cinabro cinnabar, vermilion.
cinabrruĝa brilliant red.
cinamo cinnamon.
cinamujo cinnamon tree.
cinanko vincetoxicum.
cincino cincinus.
cindra ashen. **Cindra Merkredo** Ash Wednesday.
cindrejo ashery.
cindrigi to incinerate, reduce to ashes.
 cindrigi kadavron to cremate.
cindrigo incineration.
cindro ash(es), cinder.
cindroblonda ash-blond.
cindrogriza ashen.
cindrokesto ash box, ash can.
cindrokolora ash.
Cindromerkredo Ash Wednesday.
cindropolvo ash.
cindrotelero ashpan, ashtray.
cindrourno ash urn.
cindrujego ash pit.
cindrujo ash pan, ashtray.
Cindrulino Cinderella.
cinerario cineraria.
cinika cynical.
cinike cynically.
cinikeco cynicism.
cinikismo cynicism.
cinikisto cynic.
cinikulo cynic.
cinkenito zinkenite.
cinkikulo cynic.
cinklo dipper.
cinocefalo baboon.

cisoido

cionisma Zionist.
cionismo Zionism.
Cionismo Zionism.
cionisto Zionist.
Ciono Zion.
cipra Cypriot, Cypriote.
cipranino Cyprian woman.
ciprano Cypriot, Cypriote.
cipresacoj Cupressaceae, cypress (family of trees).
cipreseŭforbio cypress spurge.
cipreso cypress.
ciprino carp.
Cipro Cyprus.
cipselo swift.
ciri to polish.
cirila Cyrillic.
Cirilo Cyril.
ciripedo barnacle.
ciristo bootblack, shoeblack.
cirkaeto short-toed eagle.
cirkareno ring.
cirkelo (pair of) compasses.
Cirkelo Circinus.
cirkelujo case of mathematical instruments.
cirkeo enchanter's-nightshade.
cirkla circular. **cirkla funkcio** circular function.
cirkle circularly.
cirklego great circle.
cirklo circle, disc.
cirko circus.
cirkonferenca angulo angle at circumference.
cirkonferenco circumference.
cirkonstancaro circumstances, conditions, state of things, conjecture, situation.
cirkonstanco circumstance.
cirkulado circulation, traffic. **cirkulado de de narkotaĵoj** drug traffic.
cirkulanta about, abroad.
cirkulero circular.
cirkuli to be about, circulate, get about.
cirkuligi to circulate, get about, move about.
cirkumcidi to circumcise.
cirkumcidiĝi to become circumcised.
cirkumcido circumcision.
cirkumfleksa circumflexed.
cirkumflekso circumflex (ˆ).
cirkuo harrier, kite.
cirkvitero logic element.
cirkvitkarto circuit board.
cirkvito circuit.
ciro polish, wax.
cirozo cirrhosis.
ciruso cirrus.
cis on this side of.
cisalpa cisalpine.
cisoido cissoid.

cisternaŭto fuel truck.
cisterno cistern, reservoir, tank.
cistito cystitis.
cisto cyst.
citadelo citadel.
citado citation, quotation.
citaĵo citation, quotation.
citaro zither.
citato summons.
citi to cite, quote, mention.
citilo inverted comma, quotation mark, quote. **citiloj** quotation marks, quotes ('); (" "); („ "); (« »).
citmarko quotation mark.
cito quotation.
citoplasmo cytoplasm.
citozino Cytosine.
citrato citrate.
citro zither.
citrolo water-melon.
citrona papilio brimstone butterfly.
citronarbo lemon tree.
citronelo citronella, citronella grass.
citronflava lemon yellow.
citrongreso lemon grass.
citronkolora lemon-coloured.
citronmeliso lemon balm.
citrono citron, lemon.
citronpremilo lemon squeezer.
citronsuko lemon juice.
citronujo lemon-tree.
citruso citrus fruit.
citsignoj inverted commas, quotation marks, quotes ('); (" "); („ "); (« »).
civeto civet.

civila civil, civilian, non-military, secular.
 civila stato civil status.
civiliza civilized.
civilizacia civilized.
civilizacio civilization.
civilizado civilization.
civilizeco civilization.
civilizi to civilize.
civilizita civilized.
civiliziteco civility.
civilizo civilization.
civilulo civilian.
civita civic.
civitaneco citizenship.
civitanigi to naturalize.
civitanismo sense of public responsibility.
civitano citizen.
civitismo civic virtue, good citizenship.
civito citizenry, city state, incorporated town, polity.
cizeli to emboss, tool.
co name of the letter C.
codorom-legilo CD-ROM drive.
codoromo CD-ROM, compact disc.
coizito zoisite.
coldika tabulo one-inch plank.
colmezurilo folding rule.
colo inch.
colsigno inch sign (").
conga lingvo Tsonga, Tsonga language.
congo Tsonga.
cunamo tsunami.
cvano Tswana.
cviterjona zwitterionic.
cviterjono zwitterion.

Ĉ

ĉ. → ĉirkaŭ.
ĉabrako saddle blanket.
Ĉada Lago Lake Chad.
Ĉadio Chad.
Ĉado Chad.
Ĉadolago Lake Chad.
ĉadoro chador.
Ĉagosinsuloj Chagos Islands.
ĉagrena deplorable, pitiable, sad, peevish.
ĉagrenaĵo annoyance, irritant.
ĉagrene deplorably.
ĉagrenega disconsolate, woeful.
ĉagrenegi to perplex, trouble.
ĉagreni to aggravate, annoy, distress, vex, worry, grieve. ĉagreni sin to worry oneself.
ĉagrenigi to distress.
ĉagreniĝi to be vexed.
ĉagreniĝo vexation.
ĉagrenita sad, sorrowful.
ĉagreno annoyance, disappointment, grief, chagrin, worry.
ĉagrino shagreen.
ĉajoto chayote, chocho, christophine, merliton.
ĉako shako.
ĉakro chakra.
ĉaledo chalet.
ĉaleto chalet.
ĉambelano chamberlain.
ĉambra of a room, chamber.
ĉambraĉo dirty room, poor quality room.
ĉambraro apartment.
ĉambrego large room.
ĉambreto cabin, cabinet (room).
ĉambristino chambermaid, maid.
ĉambristo man-servant, servant, valet.
ĉambro chamber, room. Ĉambro de komerco Chamber of Commerce.
ĉambroarango furnishing.
ĉambroj quarters.
ĉambroluiganto room lessor.
ĉambromuziko chamber music.
ĉambronumero room number.
ĉambroplanto houseplant.
ĉamo chamois.
ĉampana champagne, of champagne.
ĉampanjo champagne.
ĉampano champagne.
ĉampinjono mushroom.
ĉampioneco championship.
ĉampioniĝo championship.
ĉampiono champion.
ĉano cock, trigger, hammer.
ĉantaĝi to blackmail, extort.
ĉantaĝisto blackmailer.

ĉantaĝo blackmail, extortion.
ĉanti to chant.
ĉanto chant.
ĉapdosiero header file.
ĉapelino bonnet.
ĉapelistino milliner.
ĉapelo caret, hat, circumflex.
ĉapitro chapter.
ĉapo beret, cap, cover, bonnet.
ĉapobeko visor.
ĉar as, because, for, since, whereas.
ĉardaŝo czárdás.
ĉarego waggon.
ĉareto carriage, pushcart; typewriter carriage.
ĉaretreveno carriage return.
Ĉaristo Auriga.
ĉarlatanaĵo con, flimflam, rip-off.
ĉarlatani to bilk, cheat, take in.
ĉarlatanino conwoman.
ĉarlatanismo quackery.
ĉarlatano charlatan, imposter.
Ĉarlestono Charleston.
Ĉarlotmalio Charlotte Amalie.
ĉarma attractive, charming, lovely, pleasing, alluring.
ĉarme charmingly.
ĉarmeco charm.
ĉarmega delightful.
ĉarmegi to captivate (charm).
ĉarmeta attractive.
ĉarmi to charm, entrance.
ĉarmo charm, spell.
ĉarniro hinge.
ĉaro car, cart, chariot.
ĉarpentaĵo carpentry, framework, structure.
ĉarpenti to build, build from wood, construct.
ĉarpentisto carpenter.
ĉarpentligno lumber, timber.
ĉarpio lint.
ĉarti to charter.
ĉarto charter.
ĉarumo wheelbarrow.
ĉasadi to chase, hunt.
ĉasado chase, pursuit.
ĉasaĵo game, venison.
ĉasaĵujo game-bag.
ĉasalpelanto beater.
ĉasanto hunter.
ĉasaviadilo fighter plane.
ĉasavio fighter.
ĉasdometo hunting-lodge.
ĉasgardisto gamekeeper.

ĉashundo

ĉashundo hunting dog, hunting hound. **Ĉashundoj** Canes Venatici.
ĉasi to chase, hunt, pursue, seek after.
ĉasidamaĝo bodywork damage.
ĉasio chassis.
ĉasisto hunter.
ĉasjeto jet fighter.
ĉaskorno hunting horn.
ĉaskuri to chase, hunt for.
ĉasleopardo cheetah.
ĉaso chase.
ĉasoŝteli to poach.
ĉasoŝtelisto poacher.
ĉasputoro ferret.
ĉasta chaste, pure.
ĉaste chastely, purely.
ĉasteco chastity, purity.
ĉastigi to bowdlerize, chasten, expurgate, purify.
ĉasto chastity, purity.
ĉastranĉilego cutlass.
ĉasvagi to prowl.
ĉatnio chutney.
ĉatrio chatri.
ĉaŭ ciao.
ĉaŭĉaŭo chow, chow chow.
ĉaŭo chow, chow chow.
ĉe at (house of), beside, with. **ĉe ĉiuj stratanguloj** on every street corner. **ĉe la freŝa faro** in the act, red-handed. **ĉe la komenco de** at the start of. **ĉe la penso ke** at the thought that. **ĉe la reto** on the (inter)net. **ĉe la sojlo de** on the brink of. **ĉe la unua ekvido** at first sight. **ĉe sia posteno** at one's post. **ĉe tiuj vortoj** at those words. **ĉe unu ekstremaĵo** at one end. **ĉe vi** to at your house.
ĉebeko xebec.
Ĉeĉena Chechen.
Ĉeĉenio Chechenia.
Ĉeĉeno Chechen.
Ĉeĉenujo Chechenia, Chechnya.
ĉeestado presence.
ĉeestanta present.
ĉeestantaro those present.
ĉeestanto present one.
ĉeesti to attend, be present, witness. **ĉeesti festenon** to attend a party, feast.
ĉeesto presence.
ĉef- arch-, chief-.
ĉefa cardinal, chief, main, major, principal, premier. **ĉefa celo** main goal. **ĉefa etikedo** header label.
ĉefabato prior (title).
ĉefafero main point.
ĉefaĵo main thing, main idea, important thing.
ĉefakcento main accent.
ĉefanĝelo archangel.

ĉefornamaĵo

ĉefartikolo leading article.
ĉefbaziliko archbasilica.
ĉefcirklo great circle.
ĉefĉeno backbone.
ĉefdekoracio centrepiece.
ĉefdiagonalo main diagonal.
ĉefdiakona archidiaconal.
ĉefdiakono archdeacon.
ĉefdioceza archdiocesan.
ĉefdiocezo archdiocese.
ĉefdosiero master file.
ĉefduka archducal.
ĉefdukejo archduchy, archdukedom.
ĉefdukino archduchess.
ĉefduklando archduchy.
ĉefduko archduke.
ĉefe chiefly, mainly.
ĉefeligujo standard output.
ĉefenigujo standard input.
ĉefepiskopa archiepiscopal.
ĉefepiskopejo archbishopric, archiepiscopality.
ĉefepiskoplando archbishopric.
ĉefepiskopo archbishop.
ĉefepiskopujo archbishopric, archiepiscopate.
ĉeffripono archfiend.
ĉefgeneralo commander in chief, generalissimo, supreme commander.
ĉefgitaristo lead guitarist.
ĉefherezulo arch-heretic.
ĉefi to lead, be the boss of.
ĉefideala principal ideal (ring).
ĉefindekso main index, master index, primary index.
ĉefinstiginto mastermind.
ĉefkarto mother board.
ĉefkasisto archtreasurer.
ĉefkomercaĵo chief trade good.
ĉefkomputilo host, host computer, mainframe.
ĉefkonsulo consul general.
ĉefkuiristo chef.
ĉeflibro main book.
ĉeflitero capital letter, initial (letter).
ĉefmago archimage, archimagus.
ĉefmanĝo dinner.
ĉefmarŝalo chief marshal.
ĉefmasto mainmast, maintop.
ĉefmatroso botswain.
ĉefmemoro main store, primary memory, main memory.
ĉefministrejo chancellery.
ĉefministro premier, prime minister.
ĉefo boss, chief, leader, headman, chieftain.
ĉefoficejo headquarters, head office.
ĉeforgano mainframe.
ĉefornamaĵo centrepiece.

ĉefparte   **Ĉestro**

ĉefparte for the greater part, for the most part.
ĉefparto body.
ĉefpastro hierarch, high priest, pontiff.
ĉefplado main course.
ĉefpordo main door.
ĉefpresbitero archpriest.
ĉefprimaso archprimate.
ĉefprinco grand duke, grand prince.
ĉefprocesoro central processing unit, central processor, CPU.
ĉefprogramo main program.
ĉefpulso downbeat.
ĉefredaktoro editor in chief.
ĉefreto backbone, spin.
ĉefretregiono top level domain.
ĉefrolanto star.
ĉefroli to feature, star.
ĉefroligi to star.
ĉefrolulino leading actress.
ĉefrolulo protagonist.
ĉefservisto butler.
ĉefstrato main street.
ĉefsubtenantilo mainstay.
ĉefsubtenanto mainstay.
ĉefŝaltilo main switch.
ĉefŝlosilo primary key.
ĉefŝtono keystone.
ĉeftablo head table.
ĉefteksto main body, main text.
ĉeftendenca mainline.
ĉeftermino keyword.
ĉeftero mainland.
ĉeftitolo headline.
ĉeftrabo supporting beam.
ĉefurbo capital (city), metropolis.
ĉefuzanto root, superuser.
ĉefvelo main sail.
ĉefverko masterpiece.
ĉefvojo major road.
ĉefvorto keyword.
ĉeĥa Czech.
Ĉeĥino Czech woman.
Ĉeĥio Czech Republic.
Ĉeĥoslovakio Czechoslovakia.
Ĉeĥo Czech.
Ĉeĥoslovaka Czechoslovak, Czechoslovakian.
Ĉeĥoslovakino Czech woman.
Ĉeĥoslovakio Czechoslovakia.
Ĉeĥoslovako Czechoslovak, Czechoslovakian.
Ĉeĥoslovakujo Czechoslovakia.
Ĉeĥujo Czech Republic.
ĉekamene at the fireside, by the hearth.
ĉekaro checkbook.
ĉekastela at a castle, at the castle.
ĉeklibro check-book.
ĉeko check.

ĉela cellular.
ĉelaro honeycomb.
ĉeldividiĝo cell division.
ĉelemajlo cloisonné.
ĉelime at the limit.
ĉelita bedside.
ĉelite at the bedside.
ĉelito cellulitis.
ĉelo cell.
ĉeltelefono cellphone.
ĉelveturilo paddy waggon.
ĉemane at hand, handy.
ĉemizino blouse.
ĉemizo chemise, shirt.
ĉena frakcio continued fraction.
ĉenbutiko chain store.
ĉene by chain, in chains.
ĉenero link (in a chain).
ĉeneto chain.
ĉenfinilo string terminator.
ĉenfrakcio continued fraction.
ĉeni to chain.
ĉeniljo chenille.
ĉenlaboro assembly line work.
ĉenligata chained, bound in chains.
ĉenligi to bind in chains, chain (someone).
ĉenligita chained, bound in chains.
ĉeno chain, sequence.
ĉenringo link.
ĉensegilo chainsaw.
ĉenstablo assembly line.
ĉenujo chain-guard, gear-case.
ĉepobe abaft.
ĉerizarbo cherry-tree.
ĉerizo cherry.
ĉerizujo cherry-tree.
ĉerka sepulchral.
Ĉerkesio Circassia.
Ĉerkesujo Circassia.
ĉerko coffin.
ĉerkokovrilo pall.
ĉerkoportilo bier.
ĉerkveturilo hearse.
ĉerpado bailing.
ĉerpaĵo bucketful.
ĉerpeto spoonful.
ĉerpi to bail, draw (water), excerpt, extract, spoon. **ĉerpi akvon** to draw water.
ĉerpilo dipper.
ĉerpo extraction.
ĉervonco chervonets.
ĉesado cessation.
ĉesi to cease, stop, leave off, desist, quit, end.
ĉesigi to stop. **ĉesigi malamikecon** to create hostilities.
ĉesigo prorogation, stop.
ĉeso break.
ĉesrefuta refuting any inclination to stop.
Ĉestro Chester.

ĉetable at the table.
ĉetabliĝi to draw up to the table, sit down to table.
ĉevala equestrian, horse, horse-, of a horse.
   ĉevala neĝplugilo horse-drawn snowplough.
ĉevalaĵo horsemeat.
ĉevalaro stud.
ĉevalbastono hobby-horse.
ĉevalbleketo whinny.
ĉevalbleki to neigh.
ĉevalbredejo stud farm.
ĉevaldente horse-toothed.
ĉevaldresisto horsebreaker.
ĉevalejo corral, stable.
ĉevalestro riding-master.
ĉevaleto hobbyhorse, pony.
ĉevalforto horsepower.
ĉevalidino filly.
ĉevalido colt, foal, filly.
ĉevalidoino foal.
ĉevalino mare.
ĉevalisto groom, stableman.
ĉevalkaŝtano buckeye, horse-chestnut.
ĉevalo horse, steed.
ĉevalpiedo coltsfoot.
ĉevalpovo horsepower.
ĉevalrajda equestrian.
ĉevalrajdantino horsewoman, lady equestrian.
ĉevalrajdanto horseback rider.
ĉevalŝanĝo relay (horses).
ĉevaltrio team of three horses.
ĉevalviro stallion.
ĉevalvojo bridle path.
ĉevalvosto horsetail ensign, panache.
Ĉeviota Montaro Cheviot Hills.
ĉevrono rafter, support beam.
ĉi here (denotes proximity). **ĉi-foje** this time. **ĉi-hore** at this hour, at this time. **ĉi-kaze** in this case. **ĉi-kune** attached (to this), herewith. **ĉi-kunteksto** in this context. **ĉi-momente** at this moment. **ĉi-suba** below. **ĉi-sube** below. **ĉi-supre** above. **ĉi tie** here, in this place. **ĉi tien** here, hither, this way. **ĉi tio** these, this, this here. **ĉi tiu** the latter, this one. **ĉi tiuj** these. **ĉi tiun nokton** tonight. **ĉi-transen** across to this side. **ĉi-vespere** this evening.
ĉia all, every kind of, each. **ĉiaj aĵoj** all sorts of things.
ĉiaforme in all forms, of all shapes. **ĉiaforme elpenseble** of all imaginable shapes.
ĉial for every reason.
ĉiam all the time, always, ever. **ĉiam batadi la saman ambozon** always harp on the same string. **ĉiam plu** more and more.
ĉiama everlasting, permanent, constant.

ĉiamdaŭra eternal, everlasting, perpetual.
ĉiamdaŭre eternally, everlastingly, perpetually.
ĉiame of all times, at all times.
ĉiameco permanence.
ĉiamjuna ever young.
ĉiamverda evergreen.
ĉiaokaze in all (kinds of) cases, in any event.
ĉiapreze at any price.
ĉiaspeca all kinds of.
ĉiavetera all-weather.
ĉiĉerono cicerone, tour guide, docent.
ĉie all about, everywhere. **ĉie densa** everywhere dense (subset). **ĉie en la** all over the, throughout the.
ĉiea omnipresent.
ĉieesta omnipresent, ubiquitous.
ĉieestado omnipresence.
ĉieesto omnipresence, ubiquity, ubiquitousness.
ĉiekonata universally known, well-known.
ĉiel every manner, every way, in every way.
ĉiela celestial, heavenly.
ĉielarbo tree of heaven.
ĉielarka emberizo painted bunting.
ĉielarko rainbow.
ĉielblua sky blue.
ĉielbluo sky blue.
ĉiele heavenly.
ĉielece like heaven.
ĉielen towards heaven, upwards.
ĉielenpremo assumption.
Ĉielenpreno Assumption.
ĉielglora heavenly, glorious.
Ĉieliro Ascension (feast of).
ĉieliro ascension, assumption.
Ĉielirtago Ascension Day.
Ĉielirtago Ascension Day.
ĉielkorpo celestial body, heavenly body, star.
ĉielo heaven, sky.
Ĉieloj! Heavens!
ĉielosfero coelosphere.
ĉielruĝo aurora.
ĉielskrapulo skyscraper.
ĉies everyone's.
ĉiesaĵo freeware.
ĉiesulino hooker, prostitute, whore.
ĉiesvoĉa unanimous.
ĉiesvoĉe unanimously.
ĉifaĵo wad.
Add
ĉifalo cifal (head of Volapük movement)
ĉifbulo wad.
ĉifĉafo chiff-chaff.
ĉifi to crease, crumble, crumple, rumple, wrinkle.
ĉifona ragged.
ĉifonaĵo tatter.
ĉifoneco shabbiness.

ĉifonfiguro scarecrow.
ĉifonisto ragman, rag picker.
ĉifonkolektisto ragpicker.
ĉifono rag, scrap, tatter, shred.
ĉifonujo chiffonier.
ĉifonulo ragamuffin.
ĉifrado encryption.
ĉifri to encrypt, encode.
ĉifro cipher, code, secret code, secret writing.
ĉifroŝlosilo encryption key, key.
ĉigongo chi gong, qigong.
ĉijara this year's.
ĉijare this year.
ĉikagano Chicagan, Chicagoan.
Ĉikagano Chicagoan.
Ĉikago Chicago.
ĉikanado hair-splitting.
ĉikanema censorious.
ĉikanemo censoriousness.
ĉikaneti to carp.
ĉikaneto quibble, trifle.
ĉikani to nit-pick, quibble, split hairs, badger, bait.
ĉikano quibble.
ĉikanulo hair-splitter, nit-picker.
Ĉiko Chic.
ĉiko chigger, jigger, sand flee.
ĉikune herewith.
ĉilia Chilean.
ĉilianino Chilean woman.
ĉiliano Chilean.
Ĉilio Chile.
ĉilo chyle.
ĉimo chyme, chymus.
ĉimomente at the moment, at this moment.
ĉimpanzo chimpanzee.
ĉina Chinese. **ĉina inko** Indian ink. **ĉina lingvo** Chinese, Chinese language. **Ĉina Novjaro** Chinese New Year.
ĉinĉilo chinchilla.
Ĉingiŝhano Genghis Khan.
Ĉinio China.
ĉino Chinese. **Ĉino** Chinese, Chinaman.
ĉinokte tonight.
ĉinujano Chinese (citizen).
Ĉinujo China.
ĉio all, altogether, everything.
ĉiofaranta almighty.
ĉiofarulo busy-body.
ĉiokapabla all-round.
ĉiokaze on this occasion.
ĉiom all, all of it, the full amount, the whole quantity.
ĉioma full-scale, total.
ĉiomjare all the years.
ĉioninkluda across the board.
ĉionpova almighty, omnipotent.
ĉionpove almightily, omnipotently.
ĉionriskema desperate, frantic.
ĉionriskeme desperately, frantically.
ĉionriskemo desperation.
ĉionsciado omniscience.
ĉiopardona all-forgiving.
ĉiopermesa permissive.
ĉiopermese permissively.
ĉiopotenca all powerful, almighty.
ĉiopova almighty, all-powerful, omnipotent.
ĉiopove almightily, all-powerfully, omnipotently.
ĉiopoveco omnipotence.
ĉiopovo omnipotence.
ĉioscia all-knowing, omniscient.
ĉiosciulo wiseacre.
ĉiotaŭga all-purpose.
ĉiovendejo bazaar, department store.
ĉiovida all-seeing.
ĉipa cheap, inexpensive.
ĉipe cheaply.
ĉipo chip.
ĉipso crisp, potato chip.
ĉirckaŭaĵo surrounding(s).
ĉirkaue around, on all sides of.
ĉirkaŭ about, round, around, towards, round, circa. **ĉirkaŭ la mateno** around morning (time).
ĉirkaŭa ambient, surrounding, neighbouring.
ĉirkaŭaĵa ambient.
ĉirkaŭaĵo environment, environs, surroundings, neighbourhood, outskirts, surroundings.
ĉirkaŭantaro attendants.
ĉirkaŭbarejo corral, enclosure.
ĉirkaŭbari to fence off, surround.
ĉirkaŭbraki to embrace, hug.
ĉirkaŭbrako armlet, bracelet.
ĉirkaŭĉizi to chip, chip off.
ĉirkaŭdigi to embank.
ĉirkaŭe about, around, roundabout, thereabout, thereabouts. **ĉirkaŭe de** around.
ĉirkaŭejo environment, environs, lap, neighbourhood, surroundings.
ĉirkaŭen around.
ĉirkaŭfermi to enclose.
ĉirkaŭflugi to fly around.
ĉirkaŭfrazo circumlocution, paraphrase.
ĉirkaŭhaki to lop, prune, trim (shape by cutting around the edges).
ĉirkaŭi to beset, encompass, surround.
ĉirkaŭigi to surround.
ĉirkaŭiri to circulate, circumvent, go around.
ĉirkaŭkaprioli to frolic about.
ĉirkaŭkolo collar, necklace.
ĉirkaŭkuri to run around.
ĉirkaŭligaĵo bandage.
ĉirkaŭligi to garrote.
ĉirkaŭligo band, restraint.

ĉirkaŭlimi to surround.
ĉirkaŭmano bracelet.
ĉirkaŭmetro perimeter.
ĉirkaŭmurigi to wall.
ĉirkaŭo circuit, circumference, periphery.
ĉirkaŭpalpi to fumble.
ĉirkaŭparoli to beat about the bush.
ĉirkaŭplekti to twine around.
ĉirkaŭpremi to embrace, hug.
ĉirkaŭprenegi to hug.
ĉirkaŭpreni to embrace, hug.
ĉirkaŭpreno embrace.
ĉirkaŭrando brim.
ĉirkaŭrigardegi to stare all around.
ĉirkaŭrigardi to look all around.
ĉirkaŭsieĝi to blockade, blockage.
ĉirkaŭskribi to circumscribe.
ĉirkaŭskribita circumscribed.
ĉirkaŭstaranto bystanders, people standing around.
ĉirkaŭstari to stand around.
ĉirkaŭteksto context.
ĉirkaŭtranĉi to trim.
ĉirkaŭumi to encircle, round up.
ĉirkaŭumo encirclement, round up.
ĉirkaŭurbo suburbs.
ĉirkaŭvagadi to wander around.
ĉirkaŭvagi to roam around.
ĉirkaŭveturi to drive around.
ĉirkaŭvojo roundabout way.
ĉirkaŭvolvi to wind, wrap.
ĉirkaŭzoni to belt.
ĉiro tendril, runner.
ĉirpa squeaky, strident, stridulous.
ĉirpi to chirp.
ĉisupre above.
ĉitalo chital, chital deer, spotted deer.
ĉiu all the, each, every, everybody, every one. **ĉiu ajn** absolutely everyone. **ĉiu el ni** all of us. **ĉiun duan tagon** every other day.
ĉiuebla every possible, all possible.
ĉiuflanke in all aspects, on every side.
ĉiufoja invariable.
ĉiufoje always, each time, every time, invariably.
ĉiuhoma universal (of all people).
ĉiuhore every hour, hourly.
ĉiuj all.
ĉiujara annual, yearly.
ĉiujare every year, each year, annually, yearly.
ĉiukaze in any case.
ĉiulaboraĉfaranto bottle washer.
ĉiulanda international, of every country.
ĉiulandano citizen of all nations, world citizen.
ĉiulande internationally.
ĉiuliteraĵo pangram.
ĉiuloke everywhere.

ĉiumaniere in all ways.
ĉiumatene every morning.
ĉiuminute every minute.
ĉiumomente any time, momentarily.
ĉiumonate every month, monthly.
ĉiunokta nightly.
ĉiunokte every night.
ĉiuokaze in any event.
ĉiuparte everywhere.
ĉiupaŝe at every step.
ĉiurilate in all respects, in every respect, in every way.
ĉiuriska asekuro comprehensive insurance.
ĉiusemajna weekly, hebdomadally.
ĉiusemajne weekly, every week.
ĉiusense in every sense.
ĉiusezona perennial.
ĉiusezone perennially.
ĉiuspeca all sorts, all sorts of, miscellaneous, of all sorts.
ĉiuspecaj of all kinds.
ĉiuspeco all kinds, all manner.
ĉiutaga casual, daily, everyday. **ĉiutaga pano** daily bread. **ĉiutaga vivo** everyday life.
ĉiutage daily, every day.
ĉiuterena all-terrain.
ĉiuvespere every evening.
ĉiuvoĉa unanimous.
ĉiuvoĉe unanimously.
ĉizi to carve, chisel.
ĉizileto mini-chisel.
Ĉizilo Caelum.
ĉizilo chisel, graving tool, chiseling tool.
ĉizojo clippers, nippers, shears.
ĉo name of the letter Ĉ.
ĉokolada chocolate.
ĉokoladbriketo bar of chocolate.
ĉokoladkovrita pufkuko chocolate éclair.
ĉokoladlakto chocolate milk.
ĉokolado chocolate.
ĉonmago chonmage (Japanese haircut).
ĉopsuo chop suey.
ĉoto bullhead, sculpin.
ĉu either, if, is it, whether, (asks a question). **ĉu ... aŭ** whether ... or. **ĉu ... ĉu** whether ... or, whether ... whether. **ĉu mi estas prava?** am I right? **ĉu mi rajtas?** may I? **ĉu ne?** isn't that so? **ĉu pluan?** one more? (drink, etc.). **ĉu vere?** really? **ĉu vi estas certa, ke...** are you sure that... **ĉu vi iam konsideris...** have you ever considered... **ĉu vi ne kredas, ke...** don't you think that... **ĉu vi neniam pripensis...** haven't you ever thought about... **ĉu vi opinas?** do you think?, is it your opinion? **ĉu vi perdis la saĝon?** have you lost your mind? **ĉu vi volos...** won't you...

Ĉukĉa

Ĉukĉa Chukchi. **Ĉukĉa Duoninsulo** Chukot(ski) Peninsula. **Ĉukĉa Maro** Chukchi Sea.
ĉukĉo Chukchi man.
ĉuko chuck, mandrel.
ĉurado cumming, ejaculating.
ĉurasko churrasco.

Ĉurĉa tezo Church thesis.
ĉuri to cum, ejaculate.
ĉuro cum, semen, ejaculate.
ĉurovoj balls.
ĉusigno question mark (?).
ĉuvaŝa Chuvash.
ĉuvaŝo Chuvash.

D

da (quantity) of.
dabi to dab.
dadaismo Dadaism.
daero daerah.
Dafno Daphne.
dafodilo Lent lily, wild daffodil.
dagerotipo daguerreotype.
dagestana Dagestan.
Dagestano Dagestan.
Dagono Dagon.
daĝeta adagietto.
Dahomeo Dahomey.
daimio daimyo.
dajako Dayak.
dajkirio daiquiri.
dajmjo daimyo.
dajmono daemon.
Dakaro Dakar.
Dakko Dacca.
Dako Dacca.
dakoto Sioux.
daktilarbo date palm.
daktiliomancio dactyliomancy.
daktilo dactyl, date (fruit).
daktilogio sign language.
daktilografado typing.
daktilografio typing.
daktilologio sign language.
daktiloskopio dactyloscopy.
daktilpalmo date-palm.
daktilujo date palm.
Dalajlamao Dalai Lama.
Dalaso Dallas.
Dalekarlio Dalecarlia.
dalio dahlia.
Dalketo Dalkeith.
Dalmacio Dalmatia.
Dalmacujo Dalmatia.
Dalmalo Dalmally.
dalmatiko dalmatic.
Dalmatio Dalmatia.
dalmato Dalmatian.
Dalmatujo Dalmatia.
dalo daal.
daltonismo colour blindness.
Daltono Dalton.
Dalvino Dalwhinnie.
dama tabulo draughtboard, checkerboard.
damaĝi to damage, harm, hurt, injure.
damaĝo damage.
damaledo doeskin.
damao fallow deer.
damaskeni to damascene.
damaski to damask.
Damasko Damascus.

damasko damask.
damcervo fallow-deer.
damdisko checker.
damigi to crown a man, go king.
damludo draughts, checkers.
damne damn.
damni to damn.
damnita accursed.
damno damnation.
damo dame, queen, king, lady.
damoj checkers, draughts (pieces).
Damokleso Damocles.
dampeco checker.
dampi to dampen, muffle, deaden.
dampilo dampener.
damtabulo draughtboard.
dana Danish. **dana lingvo** Danish, Danish language. **Dana Markolo** Denmark Strait.
dancadi to dance, keep dancing.
dancado dancing.
dancantino dancer.
dancanto dancer.
dancaranĝa choreographic.
dancaranĝo choreography.
dancareno dance floor.
dancarto (art of) dancing.
dancejo ballroom, dance hall.
danceti to hop, skip.
danchalo ballroom.
danci to dance.
dancigi to make someone dance.
dancinstruisto ballet master.
dancistino (female) dancer.
dancisto dancer.
dancjupeto ballet skirt.
dancleciono dancing lesson.
dancmuzika dance music.
dancmuziko dance music.
danco dance.
dancopaŝo dance step.
dancpaŝo dance step.
dancŝuo dance shoe.
danctrupo dance troupe.
dando dandy, dude, fop, fashionista.
danĝa dangerous.
danĝe dangerously.
danĝera dangerous, insecure, hazardous.
danĝerbremso communication-cord.
danĝere dangerously, perilously, treacherously.
danĝereco danger.
danĝerhava unsafe.
danĝeri to be dangerous.
danĝero danger, hazard, jeopardy, peril.
danino Danish woman.

Danio

Danio Denmark.
dank' → **danke**.
danka thankful, grateful. **danka pro** grateful for.
dankado thanking, thanksgiving.
danke thankfully. **danke al** thanks to.
dank' al thanks to. **dank' al Dio** thank God.
dankeco gratitude, thankfulness.
dankegi to thank greatly.
dankegon thank you very much.
dankema grateful, thankful. **dankema pro** grateful for.
dankeme gratefully, thankfully.
dankemeco thankfulness.
dankemo gratitude, thankfulness.
dankesprimo acknowledgement.
dankhimni to sing a hymn of thanks.
danki to thank. **danki pro** to acknowledge, thank for.
dankinde worthy of thanks.
danko gratitude, thanks. **dankon!** thank you! thanks!
Dankofesto Thanksgiving Day.
dankopruvo acknowledgement.
Danlando Denmark.
Dano a Dane.
Danubo Danube River.
Danujo Denmark.
Danuo Don.
Dardanelo Dardanelle.
Dardaneloj Dardanelles.
darfi to be able, be entitled to, have the right to.
darkemono daric (Persian coin).
darkrumo darkroom.
Darlintono Darlington.
darmo dharma.
dartro acne, scurf.
darvinismo Darwinism.
Darvino Darwin.
dasiprokto agouti.
datagramo datagram.
datao data.
datena data. **datena akirilo** data capture device. **datena akiro** data acquisition. **datena ĉenado** data chaining. **datena eliro** data output. **datena enmeto** data input. **datena fininstalaĵo** terminal. **datena gardo** data protection. **datena interŝanĝregilo** data exchange control. **datena konservilo** data carrier. **datena kontrolado** data verification. **datena nomo** data name. **datena redukto** data reduction. **datena sekurigo** back up. **datena skemo** data flow chart. **datena transsendo** data communication. **datena vico** array.
datenaro data file.

daŭrigebla

datenbanko data bank, database.
dateno datum.
datenoj data.
datfalo deadline.
datfesto anniversary.
dati to (assign, set a) date.
datiĝi to begin on, date from.
dativo dative.
dato date (time).
datreveno birthday, anniversary.
datumano data item.
datumaro data set, document.
datumbanko data bank.
datumbaza lingvo data base language.
datumbaz-manipulilo data base management system.
datumbazo data base.
datumbloko data block.
datumbuso data bus.
datumflua diagramo data flow chart.
datuminterkomunikiĝo data communication.
datumkohero data consistency.
datumkontrolo data validation.
datummanipula lingvo data manipulation language.
datumo data, datum.
datumoj data.
datumportilo data medium, data volume.
datumprilaboro data processing.
datumprotekto data protection, security.
datumreduktado data reduction.
datumredukto data reduction.
datumregistrado data recording.
datumsekurigo data protection, security.
datumstrio data stream.
datumstrukturo data structure.
datumtipo data type.
datumtrafiko data traffic, traffic.
datumtraktado data processing.
datumtraktilo processor.
datumtransmeto data transmission.
daturo jimson weed, thorn apple.
daŭbo stave.
Daŭdeĝingo Tao Te Ching.
daŭfeno dauphin.
daŭo dhow.
daŭra abiding, lasting, enduring, continuous, permanent. **daŭra planto** perennial plant.
daŭradi to continue, hold, last.
daŭre constantly, continually, continuously.
daŭre plialtiĝi to keep going up.
daŭreco endurance.
daŭrema durable, lasting.
daŭri to continue, endure, keep on, last, go on, persist.
daŭrigado maintenance.
daŭriganto maintainer.
daŭrigebla sustainable.

daŭrigeble

daŭrigeble sustainably.
daŭrigi to continue, carry on, go on, proceed with, perpetuate, resume, continue, prolong.
daŭrigo continuation.
daŭrigota to be continued. **daŭrigota deklaro** forward declaration.
daŭro duration, space (time), lapse (of time).
Davido David.
davito davit.
dazibaŭo wall journal, wall poster.
dazipo armadillo.
de by, from, of, on, since. **de ĉi tie** from here, hence. **de du jaroj** for two years. **de jaro al jaro** from year to year. **de kiam** since (the time when). **de kie** from where, whence. **de kie vi havas tiun ideon?** where did you get that idea? **de kiu** of which. **de la jaro** of the year. **de loko al loko** from place to place. **de mia flanko** on my part. **de nun** from now on, hence, henceforth, hereafter. **de post** since. **de post kelkaj semajnon** for the past several weeks. **de supre ĝis malsupre** from top to bottom. **de tago al tago** from day to day. **de tempo al tempo** from time to time, now and then, occasionally. **de tiam** since then. **de tie** from there, thence. **de tie ĉi** from here, hence. **de tiu tago** since that day. **de tiu tempo** since that time, since then.
deadmoni to advise against, dissuade from.
deadmoni de to warn (someone) away from.
debatado debate.
debatanto debater.
debati to beat off, knock off, strike off, debate.
debatisto debater.
debato debate.
debeti to debit.
debetkarto debit card, check card, bank card.
debeto debit.
debila feeble, weak, feebleminded.
debile weakly, feebly.
debileco weakness.
debitejo retail store.
debiti to sell individually, sell at retail.
debitisto retailer.
debito debit, demand, sale, turnover.
debitoro account receivable, debtor.
deblovaĵo windfall.
debrustigi to wean (a child).
debuta maiden.
debutanta junior, future, young.
debutanto debutante.
debuti to debut, make ones debut.
debuto debut.
debutonumi to unbutton.

dediĉi

deca becoming, decent, fitting, proper, suitable, seemly, neat.
dece decently, properly. **dece kunmeti** to assort.
dececo decorum, neatness.
Decembro December.
decembro December.
decentrokura centrifugal.
deci to befit, be fitting.
decibelo decibel.
decida decided, decisive, determined, resolute. **decida konkurso** decider, play-off.
decide critically, decisively.
decidebla aro recursive set.
decideco decision, firmness, peremptoriness, resolution, determination.
decidega unbending, resolute.
decidema decisive, determined, resolute, unflinching, unhesitating.
decideme decisively, resolutely, unflinchingly, unhesitatingly.
decidemo decisiveness, determination, resolution, willpower.
decidi to choose, decide, determine, resolve, settle. **decidi alie** to decide otherwise. **decidi pri** to decide on.
decidiga decisive.
decidige conclusively, convincingly, decisively.
decidigi to induce.
decidiĝi to make up one's mind.
decidiĝo decision-making.
decidita accomplished.
decido decision.
decidofarado decision-making.
decidrajto dispositional right.
decidtabelo decision table.
decidua deciduous.
decidvoĉe in a determined voice.
decigramo decigram.
decilitro decilitre.
decimala decimal.
decimalo decimal, digit after the radix point.
decimetro decimeter.
decmora modest.
deco decency, propriety.
deĉerpi to draw (water), ladle, scoop.
deĉevaliĝi to dismount.
deĉifraĵo decrypt.
deĉifri to decipher, decode.
dedekinda Dedekind. **dedekinda tranĉo** Dedekind cut.
Dedekindo Dedekind.
dedica decisive.
dedice decisively.
dediĉi to consecrate, dedicate, devote, set aside, vow. **dediĉi atenton al** to pay attention to.

dediĉita dedicated.
dediĉo dedication.
dedukta deductive.
dedukti to deduce, gather.
deerigi to split off.
defalaĵejo dump, refuse dump, tip, rubbish tip.
defalaĵo clippings, cuttings, parings, refuse, rubbish, waste, windfall.
defali to fall, fall off, tumble down.
defalo decline, downfall, drop, fall.
defaŭlta default.
defaŭlte by default.
defaŭlto default.
defelisto knacker.
defenda defensive.
defendanto defender.
defende defensively.
defendi to defend.
defendilo (instrument of) defence.
defendisto advocate.
defendo defence.
defensiva defensive.
defensive defensively.
defensivo defensive.
defetismo defeatism.
defia challenging.
deficito deficiency, deficit.
defii to challenge, defy.
defilado march, marching, parade.
defili to march in file, march past, parade.
definitiva definite, definitive.
definitive definitely, positively.
definitivigi to confirm, ratify.
defio challenge.
deflacio deflation.
deflanki to move to the side.
deflankiĝi to go astray, get off the subject.
deflori to deflorate.
defluado efflux.
defluejo drain.
deflui to flow away.
defluiga tubo drain-pipe, outlet-pipe, waste-pipe.
defluilego sewer.
defluilo ditch, eaves, gutter.
defonta source.
defora remote. **defora atingo** remote access. **defora stirado** remote control.
defore remotely.
deformi to contort, deform, disfigure, distort, pervert, twist.
defraŭdi to misappropriate.
defrotaĵo excoriation.
defroti to rub off.
degelado thaw.
degeli to melt, thaw.
degeligi to thaw.
degeliĝo melting, thaw.

degelo melting, thaw.
degenera matrico singular matrix.
degenerado degradation, deterioration.
degeneri to degenerate, degrade, deteriorate.
degenerigi to degrade.
degenerita degenerate.
degenero degradation, deterioration.
degliti to slide off.
degna condescending.
degne condescendingly.
degni to condescend, deign, vouchsafe.
degno condescension.
degradado demotion, downgrading.
degradi to degrade, demote, downgrade.
degradiĝo demotion.
degrado degradation, demotion, reduction in ranks, relegation.
degrati to scrape, scrape off, scratch off.
deguti to drain, drip down, trickle down.
dehaki to chop down, cut off, hew.
dehiskado dehiscence.
dehiski to dehisce.
deigi to detach.
deiĝi to become dislodged.
deiri to leave (depart).
deiro departure.
deirpunkto starting point.
deismo deism.
Dejmo Deimos.
dejni to condescend, deign, vouchsafe.
dejeti to cast off, fling off, throw off.
deĵorado serving, performing one's duty.
deĵoraĵo corvée.
deĵoranto person on duty.
deĵorejo place of duty, workplace, post, position.
deĵori to be on duty, serve.
deĵoro duty.
dek ten. **dek du** twelve. **dek kvar** fourteen. **dek kvin** fifteen. **dek naŭ** nineteen. **dek ok** eighteen. **dek sep** seventeen. **dek ses** sixteen. **dek tri** thirteen. **dek unu** eleven.
deka tenth.
dekaaro decare.
dekadenca decadent.
dekadenci to be decadent.
dekadencigi to make decadent.
dekadenco decadence, decline, decay.
dekado decade.
dekagramo decagram.
dekalitro decaliter.
dekalkulebla deductible.
dekalkuli to count down.
dekalkulo allowance (ac).
dekalogo Decalogue, the Ten Commandments.
dekametro decameter.
dekano dean (college, etc.).
dekanti to decant, pour off.

99

dekatlono decathlon.
dekdisciplino decathlon.
dek-dua twelfth.
dekduedro dodecahedron.
dek-duedro dodecahedron.
dekduhore for twelve hours.
dekdujara twelve-year old.
dek-dulatero dodecagon.
dekduo dozen.
dek-duo a dozen.
deke tenthly.
dekedro decahedron.
dekfoje ten times.
dekjara ten year-old.
Dekkano Deccan.
dekkelkjarulo teenager.
dek-kvara fourteenth.
dek-kvina fifteenth.
dekkvinjara fifteen year-old.
deklamado declamation, recital.
deklamanto reciter.
deklami to declaim, recite. **deklami monotone** to rattle off, reel off.
deklamo declamation.
deklamoado recitation.
deklaracio announcement, declaration, proclamation, manifesto.
deklarado assertion.
deklaraĵo assertion.
deklarema lingvo declarative language, non-procedural language.
deklari to declare, state, proclaim. **deklari invalida** to reject. **deklari netaŭga** to declare unfit for use, condemn, scrap.
deklarilo tax form.
deklaro declaration, proclamation, statement.
deklatero decagon.
deklinacii to decline (grammar).
deklinacio declension, declination.
deklini to decline.
deklinigi to ward, turn aside.
dekliniĝi to deviate.
dekliniĝo declination, deflection, deviation.
dekliva sloping.
deklivaĵo bank.
dekliveco declivity, inclination, slant, slope.
deklivi to slope (down).
deklivirejo ramp d.
deklivo declivity, gradient, hillside, side, slant, slope, incline.
dekmil ten thousand.
dekmilo ten thousand.
dek-naŭa nineteenth.
deko (count of) ten.
dekobla tenfold.
dekoble ten-fold.
dekodigi to decode.
dek-oka eighteenth.

dekokjara eighteen year-old.
dekokti to boil, decoct.
dekokto decoction.
dekoltaĵo cleavage, décolletage.
dekolti to cut low, expose neck and shoulders.
dekoltita bare-necked, décolleté, low-cut.
dekomence from the beginning.
dekonaĵo a tenth, tithe.
dekonduki to lead away.
dekoneco tithing.
dekono tenth, tithe.
dekonsili to advise against, dissuade from.
dekontigi to transfer.
dekope by tens.
dekoracii to decorate.
dekoracio décor, decoration, theatre set.
dekori to adorn, decorate, ornament.
dekoro décor, decoration.
dekpieda decapod. **dekpieda krustulo** decapod.
dekrementi to decrement.
dekremento decrement.
dekrepito decrepitation.
dekreti to decree.
dekreto decree, edict.
dekroĉi to unhook.
dek-sepa seventeenth.
dek-sepono a seventeenth.
dek-sesa sixteenth.
deksesuma hexadecimal. **deksesuma nombrosistemo** hexadecimal notation. **deksesuma sistemo** hexadecimal system.
dekstra right, right-hand. **dekstra duonglobo de la cerbo** right hemisphere of the brain. **dekstra flanko** right-hand side. **dekstra klaso** right coset.
dekstrakorna acute.
dekstre on the right. **dekstre de** at the right hand of.
dekstremigo right alignment, right justify.
dekstremularo right.
dekstren right, to the right.
dekstrino dextrin.
dekstro starboard.
dekstrozo glucose.
dekstrula rightist, right-wing.
dekstrulo right-hander.
dekstruma positively oriented (basis).
dekstrume clockwise.
dek-tria thirteenth.
dekuma decimal. **dekuma frakcio** decimal fraction. **dekuma logaritmo** common logarithm. **dekuma nombrosistemo** decimal notation.
dekunu eleven.
dek-unua eleventh.
dek-unulatero hendecagon.
dekuri to run off, run away.

dekutimigi to break of a habit, teach.
dekutimiĝi to break oneself of a habit, get out of a habit, unlearn.
Del. → **Delegito**.
delasi to abandon.
delaso abandonment, drop.
delavaria Delawarean.
delavariano Delawarean.
Delavario Delaware.
Delavaro Delaware.
delegacio delegation.
delegado delegation, deputation.
delegato delegate, deputy, representative.
delegi to delegate.
delegitaro delegation, deputation.
delegitino (female) delegate.
delegito delegate, local representative.
delego assignment.
delekti to delight.
delfa Delphic.
Delfeno Delphinus.
delfeno dolphin.
delfinio larkspur.
Delfio Delphi.
Delfo Delphi.
delfta Delft.
Delfto Delft.
Delhio Delhi.
delico delight, bliss.
delicumi to delight in.
delikata delicate, fine, refined, gentle, sensitive, fragile, dainty, awkward.
delikataĵo delicacy.
delikate delicately.
delikateco tact, tenderness.
delikatmove with a delicate movement.
delikattuŝe with a light touch.
delikto offence, misdemeanor.
deliktulo delinquent.
delikveska deliquescent.
delinkvento delinquent.
delira delirious.
deliradi to be delirious, be crazy.
deliraĵo crazy talk, madness, delirium.
delire deliriously.
deliri to be delirious, wander, rave.
deliro delirium.
delkredero guarantee.
deloga wheedling.
delogi to beguile, seduce, decoy, lead astray.
delogisto cajoler, wheedler.
delogiteco infatuation.
deloka instrukcio shift instruction.
deloki to displace.
delokigo (proper) motion, (proper) movement, displacement.
delokiĝo displacement.
delonga long-standing.
delonge for a long time.

deltametalo iron brass.
deltaplano hang glider.
delto delta ($\Delta \delta$).
deltoido deltoid, kite.
demagogeco demagogy.
demagogio demagoguery, demagogy.
demagogo demagogue.
demamigado ablactation.
demamigi to ablactate, wean.
demamigo ablactation.
demanda interrogatory.
demandado questioning.
demandante while asking.
demandanto enquirer.
demandaro questionnaire.
demandi to ask, inquire, demand, interrogate, question. **demandi al si** to ask oneself, wonder. **demandi sin** to ask oneself, wonder.
demandilo form.
demando inquiry, query, question.
demandoekzerco question exercise.
demandosigno question mark (?).
demandsigno question mark (?).
demarĝenigi to indent.
demarĝenigo indentation.
demarkacii to demarcate.
demarkacio demarcation.
demarŝo advance.
demenca demented.
demence dementedly.
demenco dementia.
dementi to officially deny, repudiate.
demetebla disko removable disk.
demeti to put down, take off, put off, lay (eggs). **demeti dosiersistemon** to unmount a file system. **demeti la reĝecon** to abdicate. **demeti ovojn** to lay eggs.
Demetro Demeter.
demimondo demimonde.
demisia under resignation.
demisii to resign.
demisiigi to dismiss, oust, remove.
demisiigo dismissal, removal.
demiurgo demiurge.
demografia demographic.
demografie demographically.
demografiisto demographer.
demografio demography.
demokrata democratic.
demokrataro democracy.
demokrate democratically.
demokratia democratic.
demokratiana democratic.
demokratiano democrat.
demokratie democratically.
demokratiigi to democratize.
demokratiiĝo democratization.
demokratio democracy.

demokrato

demokrato democrat.
demona demonic.
demone demonically.
demonhavanta possessed (by a demon).
demoniako demoniac.
demono demon.
demonologiisto demonologist.
demonologio demonology.
demonologo demonologist.
demonomancio demonomancy.
demonstra demonstrative.
demonstracii to demonstrate.
demonstracio demonstration, proof.
demonstranto demonstrator.
demonstrativa demonstrative.
demonstrativo demonstrative, demonstrative pronoun.
demonstre demonstratively.
demonstrebla provable.
demonstreble provablely.
demonstri to demonstrate, prove, show.
demonstro demonstration, proof.
demoraliza bad for morale.
demoralizi to demoralize.
demordi to bite off.
Demorganaj leĝoj de Morgan's laws.
demotiko demotic.
denaro denarius.
denaska congenital, inborn, innate, native.
denaske congenitally, inherently, innately.
denaskeco inherence.
denaskulo native.
denaturi to denature.
dendrito dendrite.
denombrado enumeration.
denombri to enumerate.
denominatoro denominator.
denova another.
denove again, anew, once again.
densa compact, concentrated, dense, thick, condensed. **densa alspiro** rough breathing.
dense densely, thickly.
denseco density.
densejo thicket.
densigi to condense.
denso density.
denta dental, jagged, toothed.
dentalo dental.
dentalveolo socket.
dentaro teeth.
dentbroso toothbrush.
dentdoloro toothache.
dentego tusk.
denteto baby tooth.
dentgrincado grinding of the teeth.
denti to indent, tooth.
dentigi to indent, tooth.
dentingo tooth socket.

deporti

dentino dentin, dentine.
dentisto dentist.
dentkarno gingiva, gum.
dentkuracisto dentist.
dentligneto toothpick.
dento tooth, cog, prong.
dentobroso tooth-brush.
dentodoloro toothache.
dentokarno gum, gums.
dentopasto toothpaste.
dentopikilo toothpick.
dentopinglo toothpick.
dentorado gear.
dentpasto tooth-paste.
dentpikilo toothpick.
dentpingilo toothpick.
dentpinglo toothpick.
dentradeto sprocket, sprocket-wheel.
dentrado cogwheel, gear.
dentskrapi to gnaw off, pick.
denudi to expose.
denuncado tirade.
denuncanto accuser, denouncer.
denunci to accuse, denounce, impeach, inform against.
denuncisto informer, snitch, snout, whistleblower.
denunco accusation, denouncement, denunciation.
denuncoado denunciation.
depaganta tributary.
depago contribution, tribute, rent, toll.
departementa departmental.
departemento (administrative) department.
dependa dependent. **dependa de** dependent on. **dependa variablo** dependent variable. **dependas de tio, ĉu...** it depends on whether ...
depende de according to. **depende de la konteksto** depending on context.
dependeco dependence.
dependi to depend. **dependi de** to be dependent on, depend on.
dependulo addict.
depeŝi to dispatch.
depeŝigi to hand in.
depeŝo dispatch, message.
depinĉi to pinch off.
deploji to deploy.
deplojo deployment.
deponaĵo deposit.
deponanto depositor.
deponatesto warrant.
deponejo depository.
deponi to deposit, dump, bank, file, lodge, store.
deponitaĵo deposit.
deportado deportation.
deporti to deport.

depost

depost since, ever since. **depost kiam** since.
depost tiu tempo since that time.
depoto depot.
depozicio testimony.
depravacio depravation.
depreci to deprecate.
depremi to depress, press, push.
depreni to deduce, deduct, take away, take off, subtract. **depreni de** break into.
depreno deduction, demand, sale, subtraction.
depresaĵo print, imprint.
depresia depressive.
depresio depression.
deprezi to write off.
deprimi to depress.
deprimita depressed.
deprimiteco dejection, depression.
deprimo depression.
deprunti to borrow.
depruntinto borrower.
deprunto loan.
depuŝi to knock off, push down, push off, thrust down.
depuŝo shove.
deputado delegation, deputation, delegate, deputy, representative.
deputato delegate, deputy, representative.
deputi to depute.
deputilaro delegation, deputation.
deputitaro assembly, deputation.
deputito delegate, deputy, representative.
derazi to shave, shave off.
Derbio Derby.
Derio Derry, Londonderry.
deriso derris.
derivaĵo derivation, derivative.
derivarbo parse tree.
derivebla differentiable.
derivi to derive, differentiate.
derivregulo production.
dermatito dermatitis.
dermatologiisto dermatologist.
dermatologio dermatology.
dermatologo dermatologist.
dermito dermatitis.
dermo dermus.
dermologio dermatology.
derompaĵo wreckage.
derompi to break, break off.
derompiĝi to break, break off.
deruladi to roll away, roll aside.
deruli to roll off, roll away, roll aside.
deruliĝi to roll off.
derviŝo dervish.
des all the more, so much the more. **des pli** to all the more.
desalti to dismount, jump down, jump off, leap down.

detaleco

desaponti to disappoint, disabuse, set straight.
desapontiĝi to become disillusioned.
descendi to descend, go down.
descendo descent.
desegna papero construction paper.
desegnado design.
desegnaĵo design, drawing.
desegni to design, depict, draw, sketch.
desegniĝi to be outlined, stand out.
desegnilo plotter.
desegnisto draughtsman.
desegno design, drawing.
desegnopapero drawing-paper.
desertforko dessert fork.
deserto dessert.
desfili to cover, defilade.
desinfektaĵo disinfectant.
desinfekti to disinfect.
desinfektilo disinfector.
desintegratoro disintegrator.
deskampsio hair-grass.
deskrapi to erase.
deskvamiĝi to flake off, peel off, scale off.
desmodio telegraph-plant, tick trefoil.
despota despotic.
despote despotically.
despoteco despotism.
despotismo despotism.
despoto despot.
destini to assign, consign, designate, destine, dispose, earmark, ordain. **destini por** to destine for. **destinita al malsukceso** destined for failure. **destinita por** intended for. **destinita por morto** destined for death.
destino destiny, fate.
destinprojekto development plan.
destrojero destroyer.
destruado destruction.
desubtrahata nombro minuend.
desuĉilo hood, suction apparatus.
desupra top-down. **desupra analizo** top-down analysis, top-down parsing. **desupra konstruado** top-down development. **desupra projektado** top-down design.
deŝiraĵo tear (a rent).
deŝiri to pick, pluck, tear off. **deŝiri sin de iu** to get rid of someone.
deŝovi to abdicate, indent.
deŝovo displacement, indent, indention, offset, paragraph break.
detala descriptive, detailed, elaborate, retail (trade).
detalado specification.
detalaĵo detail, retail.
detale (by) retail, in detail. **detale vendi** to sell by retail.
detaleco prolixity.

detalemo attention to detail.
detaleto details, minutiae.
detali to detail.
detalisto retailer.
detalkomercisto retailer.
detalkomerco retail.
detalo detail.
detalvendisto retailer.
detavolaĵo flake.
detavoliĝi to exfoliate.
detavoliĝo exfoliation.
detekti to detect.
detektilo detector.
detektivo detective, private eye, investigator.
detektoro detector.
detemiĝi to stray from one's subject, wander from one's subject.
detemiĝo digression, straying, wandering from the point.
detempe since (the time of).
detempro distemper, tempera.
detenebla preventable.
detenema abstinent.
deteni to abstract, restrain, detain. **deteni sin** to abstain. **deteni sin de** to abstain from.
deteniĝo abstention.
deteno abstinence.
detergaĵo detergent.
detergento cleanser, detergent.
determinaĵo determinant.
determinanto determinant.
determini to decide, determine, fix, set, settle.
determinilo determiner.
determinisma deterministic.
determinisme deterministically.
determinismo determinism.
deterministo determinist.
determino determination, setting.
detonacii to detonate.
detonacio detonation.
detondi to cut off.
detrancaĵo cut.
detranĉi to carve, cut (off), amputate, clip off.
detranĉiĝo abscission.
detranĉo abscission, cut, cutback, cutting, slash.
detriki to cast off.
detroni to depose, dethrone.
detronigi to depose, dethrone.
detrua destructive. **detrua povo** destructive power.
detruado destruction, havoc, mayhem.
detruanta subversive.
detruante subversively.
detruanto destroyer.
detrue destructively.
detruegi to demolish.
detrui to destroy, quash.
detruiĝi to be destroyed.
detruiĝo devastation.
detruo destruction.
detrupovo destructiveness.
deturna manovro diversion, red herring, smoke screen.
deturni to avert, lead astray, turn away, ward off. **deturni iun de la ĝusta vojo** to lead someone astray.
deturniĝi to turn.
deturniĝo divergence, diversion.
deturno diversion.
deŭterio deuterium, heavy hydrogen.
deŭterono deuteron.
devaluti to devalue (currency).
devalutiĝi to devalue.
devaluto devaluation.
devanci to overhaul, overtake, pass.
devao deva.
devena coming. **devena de** a native of, coming from.
deveni to come (from), derive (from), originate, result (from).
devenigado derivation.
devenigi to derive.
devenigiĝi to originate.
deveno beginning, origin, extraction, lineage, source, parentage, pedigree.
deverŝi to pour off, strain off.
devi to be obliged to, have to, must, ought to, should. **devas esti** (there) must be.
devia deviant.
deviacio deviation.
devianta aberrant.
devie deviantly.
deviga obligatory, mandatory, binding, compulsory.
devigata compulsive.
devigate compulsively.
devigebla forcible.
devigeble forciblely.
devigi to compel, force, coerce, oblige.
devigo coercion, compulsion, constraint, force, pressure.
devii to aberrate, deviate, turn.
deviigi to deflect.
devio aberrance, aberration.
deviznegoco currency trade.
devizo[1] device, motto, watchword, slogan, rallying cry.
devizo[2] draft on foreign bank.
devo duty, obligation.
devojigi to sidetrack.
devojiĝanta aberrant.
devojiĝi to go astray, stray off.
devojiĝo detour, deviation from a path or way.
Devonio Devonian.

Devono

Devono Devon, Devonian period.
devontigi to obligate.
devontigo determination, liability, resolve, resolving.
devota devoted, obsequious.
devote devotedly, obsequiously.
devoteco piety.
devotulo zealot, churchy person, pietist.
dezerta desolate, dreary, gaunt.
dezerteco abandonment, bleakness, void.
dezertigi to devastate.
dezertiĝi to become deserted, become a wasteland.
dezertiĝo desertification.
dezerto desert, wilderness.
dezertulo anchorite.
dezinfekti to disinfect.
deziregi to ache, hanker, yearn.
dezirego strong, feverish desire.
deziregoado yearning.
deziri to desire, wish, want.
dezirinda desirable.
deziro desire, want, wish.
dia divine. **Dia volo** God's will.
diabeta diabetic.
diabeto diabetes.
diabetulo diabetic (person).
diabla devilish, diabolical, damned, diabolic, satanic. **Diabla Insulo** Devil's Island.
diablaĵo devilry.
diable diabolically.
diable! darn!
diableca devilish.
diablece devilishly, fiendishly.
diableto imp, little devil.
diablino she-devil.
diablo devil.
diablosigno devil's mark.
diabolo diabolo, yo-yo.
diademo diadem.
diafana diaphanous, pellucid, semi-transparent, translucent, transparent.
diafaneco transparency.
diafilmo film strip.
diafizo diaphysis.
diafonio dissonant.
diafragmo diaphragm.
diagnoza diagnostic.
diagnoze diagnostically.
diagnozi to diagnose.
diagnozo diagnosis.
diagonala diagonal, transverse. **diagonala matrico** diagonal matrix.
diagonalado diagonalization.
diagonale diagonally.
diagonaligebla diagonalizable.
diagonaligo de matrico matrix diagonalization.
diagonalo diagonal.

diboĉi

diagramo diagram.
diaĵo deity.
diakilo adhesive plaster.
diakilono adhesive plaster, diachylon, lead-plaster.
diaklazo diaclase.
diakoneco diaconate.
diakonino sick-nurse.
diakono deacon.
diakrita diacritical.
diakritaĵo accented letter.
diakriti to add a diacritic.
diakritilo diacritic mark.
diakrito accent, accent mark.
diakrona diachronous.
dialektiko dialectic(s).
dialekto dialect.
dializi to dialyse.
dializo dialysis.
dialoga proceso foreground process.
dialoga ŝelo interactive shell.
dialogi to hold a dialogue.
dialogkomputado conversational mode.
dialogo dialogue.
dialogujo dialogue box.
diamagneta diamagnetic.
diamagnetismo diamagnetism.
diamagneto diamagnet.
diamanta diamond.
diamanteca adamantine.
diamanti to adorn with diamonds.
diamanto diamond.
diamanttajlisto diamond cutter.
diametro diameter.
dianetiko dianetics.
Diano Diana.
dianto carnation (flower), pink.
diapazono tuning fork, diapason.
diapozitivo slide, transparency.
diarea loose.
diareo diarrhoea.
diartro diarthrosis.
diartrozo diarthrosis.
diasporo diaspora.
diastazo diastase.
diastola diastolic.
diastolo diastole.
diatermo diathermy.
diatezo diathesis, disposition, predisposition.
diatomeo diatom.
diatona diatonic.
diatribo bitter criticism.
diboĉa dissolute, ribald.
diboĉado abandonment.
diboĉeco abandonment, debauchery.
diboĉejo bawdy-house, house of ill repute.
diboĉema abandoned.
diboĉeto binge.
diboĉi to debauch, revel, wallow.

diboĉigi to corrupt, debauch.
diboĉo dissipation, debauchery.
diboĉoaĵo ribaldry.
diboĉulino wanton.
diboĉulo dissolute person, swinger, debauchee, profligate.
dicentro bleeding heart.
didaktika didactical, pedagogical.
didaktike didactical,ly pedagogically.
didaktiko didactics, pedagogy.
didelfo kangaroo, opossum.
dido dodo (extinct bird).
die in a god-like manner.
dieco divinity.
dielektrika dielectric.
dielektriko dielectricum.
dierezo diaeresis (¨).
diesa sharp (music) (♯).
dieso grid, hash, number sign, pound sign (#); sharp (music) (♯).
dieta dietary.
dieti to be on a diet.
dietisto dietitian.
dieto diet.
difavoro grace.
difekta broken, out of order, defective.
difektado damaging.
difektaĵo damage, imperfection, injury.
difekteto defect.
difekti to damage, harm, hurt, impair, injure, mutilate, spoil, mar.
difektiga injurious.
difektiĝadi to deteriorate.
difektiĝema perishable.
difektiĝi to break down, deteriorate.
difektiĝinta broken (down).
difektiĝo deterioration.
difektita broken, damaged.
difekto damage, flaw, defect, imperfection.
difektoaĵo defect.
difektohava rejective, defective, faulty, deficient.
diferenca different. **diferenca ekvacio** difference equation.
diference differently. **diference de** unlike.
diferenci to be different, differ, disagree.
diferenciala differential. **diferenciala ekvacio** differential equation. **diferenciala ekvacio en partaj derivaĵoj** partial differential equation. **diferenciala formo** differential form. **diferenciala kalkulo** differential calculus.
diferencialado differentiation.
diferencialebla differentiable.
diferenciali to differentiate.
diferencialkvociento differential quotient.
diferencialo differential.
diferencigi to differentiate.
diferencigo differentiation, distinguishing.
diferenciĝi to differ.
diferenco difference.
diferencoperatoro difference operator.
difina defining, determining. **difina artikolo** definite article. **difina modulo** definition module.
difinebla definable.
difineble definably.
difini to allot, define, determine.
difinita definite. **difinita integralo** definite integral. **difinita por** to be appropriate for.
difinitiva affirmative, decided, decisive, definite, definitive, final, firm, positive.
difino definition.
difrakti to diffract.
difrakto diffraction.
difterio diphtheria.
difterito diphtheria.
diftongo diphthong.
diftonogo diphthong.
difuza diffuse.
difuze diffusely.
difuzi to diffuse.
difuzilo diffusor.
difuzo diffusion.
digamo digamma (Fϝ).
digestado digestion.
digesti to digest.
digesto digestion.
digi to stop, dam up, form an embankment, halt.
digitalino digitalin.
digitalo foxglove.
digitoksino digitalin.
digna dignified.
digneco dignity.
digno dignity, respect, self-worth, self-respect, worth.
digo dam, dike, embankment, jetty, mound.
digramo digraph.
diĝesto digest.
diĝita digital. **diĝitaj datenoj** digital data.
diĝite digitally.
dihotomio dichotomy.
diigi to deify.
diigo apotheosis.
diino goddess.
diismo deism.
diisto deist.
dika thick, corpulent, fat, stout, plump. **dika fingro** thumb. **dika intesto** large intestine.
dikaĉa bloated.
dike thickly.
dikeco bulk, plumpness, stoutness, thickness, volume.
diketa plump.
dikfigura buxom.
dikfingro thumb.
Dikfingrulo Tom Thumb.

dikhaŭta thick-skinned.
dikhaŭtulo pachyderm.
dikhornŝafo bighorn, mountain sheep.
dikigi to fatten, thicken.
dikiĝi to thicken.
dikkorpa squat, thick-set.
diklina diclinous.
diklitera bold, boldface.
diko thickness.
dikpuga steatopygous.
Diksilando Dixie, Dixieland.
diktado dictation.
diktafono dictaphone.
diktaĵo dictation.
diktamno dittany.
diktato dictation.
diktatora dictatorial.
diktatore dictatorially.
diktatoreca dictatorial.
diktatorece dictatorially.
diktatoreco dictatorship.
diktatorema dictatorial.
diktatoreme dictatorially.
diktatoro dictator.
diktatura dictatorial.
diktaturo dictatorship.
dikti to dictate.
dikto dictate.
diktrunka squat.
dikulo fat person.
dikventra fat (stomached).
dikventro paunch.
dikventrulo chubby, fatso.
dikvoĉe thickly (voiced).
dilati to dilate, expand.
dilatiĝi to expand.
dilatiĝo expansion.
dilato expansion.
dilemo dilemma.
dileta amateurish.
diletanta amateurish, dilettantish.
diletanteca amateurish, small-time.
diletanteco amateurism, dilettantism.
diletantismo amateurism, dilettantism.
diletanto amateur, dabbler, dilettante.
dileteco amateurism, amateurishness.
diligenta assiduous, diligent, hardworking, industrious, earnest.
diligente diligently.
diligenteco industry.
diligenti to apply oneself.
diligentiĝi to plod on.
diligento diligence.
diligentulo hard worker.
diliĝenco diligence, stage-coach.
dilui to adulterate, dilute.
diluva of a flood. **diluva akvo** floodwater(s).
Diluvio Diluvium.
diluvo deluge, flood.

dimanĉa Sunday, of Sunday.
dimanĉe on Sunday(s).
Dimanĉo Sunday.
dimanĉo Sunday.
dimensinombro dimensionality.
dimensio dimension, measurement, order, size.
diminuendo diminuendo.
diminui to diminish.
diminutivo diminutive.
dimorfoteko African daisy.
dinamika dynamic. **dinamika datuminterŝanĝo** Dynamic Data Exchange (DDE). **dinamika ekzemplero** generation, instance. **dinamika memorareo** dynamic area, heap. **dinamika memordisponigo** dynamic allocation. **dinamika tabelo** dynamic array.
dinamike dynamically. **dinamike bindebla biblioteko** dynamic link library (DLL), shared library.
dinamiko dynamics.
dinamismo dynamism (philosophy).
dinamito dynamite.
dinamo dynamo.
dinamometro dynamometer.
dinamotoro dynamotor.
dinaro dinar.
dinastia dynastic.
dinastio dynasty.
dinatrono dynatron.
Dinbiĥo Denbigh.
dineo Navajo.
Dinglo Dingle.
dingo dingo.
Dingvalo Dingwall.
dino dyne.
dinornito moa.
dinosaŭro dinosaur.
dinoterio dinothere, dinotherium.
dio deity, divinity, god. **Dio** God. **Dio benu vin!** God bless you!
dioceza diocesan.
diocezo diocese.
diodo diode.
Diogeno Diogenes.
dioika dioecious.
diomedeo albatross.
Dionizo Dionysus.
dioptriko dioptrics.
dioptrio dioptre.
dioramo diorama.
Dioservo divine service.
dioskoreo yam.
diotropo trinity (of gods).
Dipatrino Mother of God.
dipleksa duplex.
diplodoko diplodocus.
diplomado certification.

diplomata

diplomata diplomatic.
diplomateco diplomacy.
diplomatia diplomatic. **diplomatia noto** diplomatic note.
diplomatie diplomatically.
diplomatiisto diplomat.
diplomatio diplomacy.
diplomato diplomat.
diplomi to certify.
diplomiĝi to graduate.
diplomita certificated, graduate.
diplomitiĝi to graduate.
diplomitino alumna.
diplomitita certified, having a certificate.
diplomito graduate.
diplomo certificate, degree, diploma.
dipodo jerboa.
dipolo dipole.
diporto backwardation.
dipsako teasel.
dipsomanio dipsomania.
diptiko diptych.
dirado saying.
diraĵo saying.
diraka Dirac. **diraka combilo** Dirac's comb. **diraka distribucio** Dirac distribution. **diraka kombilo** Dirac comb. **diraka mezuro** Dirac measure.
Dirako Dirac.
dirante while saying.
diregi to say loudly, strongly.
direkcio directorate.
direkta directional. **direkta eĝo** directed edge. **direkta grafeo** directed graph.
direktado steering.
direktalo tail fin.
direktanta leading.
direktanto director, manager.
direkte directly.
direktebla docile.
direkterono rudder.
direkti to conduct, direct, drive, guide, manage, refer, steer, govern. **direkti al** to head for, make for. **direkti sin** to bear down, make. **direkti sin al** to break down upon, make for, head for. **direkti sin laŭ** to abide by.
direktiĝi to direct oneself towards, head towards.
direktilisto driver, helmsman, steersman.
direktilo handlebars, helm, rudder, tiller.
direktilstango tiller.
direktisto director.
direktivo directive.
direkto direction.
direktoraro board, directorate.
direktoreco directorate, directorship.
direktorino manageress.
direktorio directorate.

diserigi

direktoro director, manager.
diri to say, tell, state. **diri sensencaĵon** to talk nonsense. **diru al mi!** tell me!
dirigento conductor.
dirigi to have someone say, make someone say.
dirmaniero expression, turn of speech, way of speaking.
diro statement.
dis- (denotes dispersal or separation).
disa disjoint. **disa datumbazo** distributed data base. **disa dosiersistemo** distributed file system. **disa komputilsistemo** distributed system. **disa kunlaboro** distributed processing. **disa tradukado** separate compilation. **disaj aroj** disjoint sets.
disafiŝi to spam.
disapartiĝi to become separated.
disatomi to split the atom.
disaŭ XOR, exclusive or.
disaŭdiganto broadcaster.
disaŭdigi to broadcast.
disaŭdigo broadcast.
disaŭo exclusive disjunction, XOR operator.
disbabili to babble away.
disbari to segregate.
disbati to dash to pieces, knock down, smash.
disblovi to blow apart, scatter (by blowing). **disblovi la nazon** to blow one's nose.
disbranĉigi to branch.
disbranĉigo branching.
disbranĉiĝi to branch off.
disbruligilo bubbler.
disbuki to unfasten.
discenterco eccentricity.
discentreco eccentricity.
disciplina disciplinary.
disciplinemo obedience.
disciplini to discipline.
disciplino discipline.
disĉiplo adherent, disciple, follower.
disde out of.
disdividi to cut up, partition.
disdonado distribution.
disdoni to deal out, distribute, dispense, give out, share.
disdono distribution.
disduigi to cut in two.
disduiĝi to split apart, become split, split into two.
disduiĝo bifurcation.
dise spread about, here and there. **dise de** apart from, away from.
diseco divergence, dispersal.
diselo diesel.
disenterio dysentery.
diserigebla biodegradable.
diserigi to disintegrate, separate into elements, decompose, disassemble.

108

diseriĝi to fall apart.
disertacio dissertation.
disertaĵo dissertation.
diserti to dissertate, discuss.
diserto dissertation.
diserva devotional.
diservo (religious) service, worship service, church service, divine service.
disetendi to expand, open, spread, spread-eagle.
disetendiĝi to expand, open.
disfadenigi to unravel.
disfadenigo multi-threading.
disfaldi to spread out.
disfalema crumbling.
disfali to collapse, fall to pieces.
disfaligi to demolish.
disfalo collapse, disintegration.
disfamigi to spread the fame of.
disfandi to melt, melt away.
disfendiĝi to split apart.
disfolido boomslang.
disforkiĝi to fork.
disfrakasi to crush, shatter.
disfrakasiĝi to shatter.
disgutigi to atomize.
disgutigilo atomizer.
dishaki to chop, chop up.
disi to be separate.
disidento dissident.
disiernomo file name.
disiga konjunkcio disjunctive conjunction.
disigi to disband, disconnect, disintegrate, divide, separate, disunite, sever.
disigilo delimiter, separator.
disiginta schismatic.
disigita dispersed.
disignifo double meaning.
disigo disjunction, schism, separation.
disiĝema loose, sandy.
disiĝi to separate, part.
disiĝo disunion, break up (of a relationship).
disipi to waste.
disiri to break up, separate.
disirigi to break up.
disjunkcio disjunction.
disĵeta injective.
disĵeti to (broad)cast, scatter, strew.
disĵeto injection.
diskaparato hard disk.
diskarabo ladybird.
diskedo floppy, diskette.
diskestro disc jockey (DJ).
disketingo floppy drive.
disketo diskette, floppy disk.
diskettenilo diskette drive, diskette drive.
diski to dial (telephone).
diskilo disk drive.
diskingo disk drive.

diskingolitero drive letter.
diskĵokeo disc jockey.
diskmemoro disk space.
disko dial, disc, disk, record, circle.
diskodancejo disco, discothèque.
diskodrajvo disk drive.
diskombi to card.
diskonigi to publicize.
diskonigisto publicist.
diskonti to discount.
diskontisto bill-broker.
diskonto discount.
diskontprocento bank rate.
diskordo disagreement, discord, dissension.
diskosegilo buzz saw.
diskostako disk stack.
diskoteko discothèque.
diskoturnisto disc jockey.
diskrediti to discredit.
diskreditigi to cry down, cut up, demolish, pull to pieces, run down, write down.
diskredito discredit.
diskreski to grow apart, grow across.
diskreta discrete, countable, denumerable.
  diskreta topologio discrete topology.
diskrete discretely.
diskreteco modesty.
diskretigo discretization, sampling.
diskreto discretion.
diskriminacia discriminatory.
diskriminacii to discriminate.
diskriminacio discrimination.
diskriminanto discriminant.
diskrimini to discriminate.
diskrimino discrimination.
diskturnila niĉo drive bay.
diskturnilo disk unit.
diskuri to run about.
diskurso discourse.
diskutado discussion.
diskutema argumentative.
diskuti to discuss.
diskutigi to raise the subject of, bring up.
diskuto discussion.
diskutrondo discussion circle.
disleksia dyslexic.
disleksio dyslexia.
disleksiulo dyslexic.
disligi to disjoin.
dislimi to delimit.
dislimo demarcation, divide, division, parting.
dismalĉasta promiscuous.
dismalĉasteco promiscuity.
dismaŝiĝi to ladder.
dismaŝiĝo ladder.
dismeti to decompose, take apart.
dismordi to bite apart, bite off.
disnodiĝo the coming undone of a knot.

disocii to dissociate.
disonanco dissonance.
disondaĵo wake.
disondo wake.
disparceligi to divide into lots.
dispartigi to partition.
dispartigo partition (of a set).
dispecetiĝi to crumble.
dispecigi to parcel out, take apart, break into pieces.
dispeciĝi to break into pieces.
dispeco shred.
dispeli to disperse.
dispensario dispensary, public dispensary, welfare centre.
dispepsio dyspepsia, indigestion.
dispersi to disperse, scatter.
dispisti to crush.
disponado disposal, care.
disponaĵa komando device control.
disponaĵo device.
disponebla available, disposable. **disponebla por tuja uzo** available for immediate use.
disponebleco availability.
disponeblo availability.
disponi to absorb, have at one's disposal, dispose (of), have available.
disponigi to make available, provide.
disponiĝi to be available.
dispono disposition.
dispostenigi to deploy.
dispostenigo deployment.
dispoŝtaĵo cross-post.
dispoŝti to cross-post.
dispozicii to predispose, dispose.
dispozicio predisposition, tendency.
dispremi to crush, squash.
disproporcio imbalance.
disprozio dysprosium.
disputa disputatious.
disputaĉi to squabble, wrangle.
disputaĉo wrangle.
disputado controversy, wrangle.
disputebla moot.
disputego large argument, disagreement.
disputema argumentative, confrontational, contentious.
disputeti to bicker.
disputi to argue, dispute, bicker, contest, wrangle, contend.
disputiga contentious, controversial.
disputo contest, debate, dispute, quarrel, polemic, strife.
disradiado radiance.
disradii to emit.
disreferenca bildo clickable image map.
disreviĝo disappointment, disenchantment, disillusionment.

disrompaĵo wreckage.
disrompi to break off, smash.
disrompiĝi to break, fall apart.
dissalti to burst apart, fly asunder.
dissekcii to dissect.
dissekcio dissection.
dissemado propagation.
dissemi to disseminate, scatter, sow, spread (seed).
dissemigi to disseminate, sow.
dissemiĝado propagation.
dissemiĝi to disseminate, propagate, scatter.
dissendata broadcasted.
dissendi to distribute, circulate, broadcast, send out.
dissendilo transmitter.
dissendita broadcasted.
dissendo transmission.
dissendoanteno broadcast antenna.
dissendolisto mailing list.
disskvamiĝi to flake off, peel off.
disspecigi to sort.
disstari to straddle.
dissterni to strew.
dissterniĝi to sprawl.
dissterniĝo sprawl.
dissurĵeta bijective, one-to-one.
dissurĵeto bijection, biunique correspondence, one-to-one mapping.
disŝiri to rend, tear (in pieces).
disŝiriĝi to tear apart.
disŝirita tattered.
disŝiro rending.
disŝovreĝimo insert mode.
disŝuti to distribute (scatter).
dista distant, remote.
distanca aloof.
distance at a distance.
distancema aloof.
distancigi to distance.
distanciĝi to distance.
distanco distance, offset. **distanco laŭ Hamming** Hamming distance.
diste at a distance.
distetendiĝo expansion.
distetendo expansion.
distiko distich, couplet.
distilado distillation.
distilaparato alembic, still.
distilejo distillery.
distili to distil.
distililo still (distilling).
distilisto distiller.
distinga distinctive.
distingaĵo peculiarity.
distinge distinctively.
distingebla distinguishable.
distingeble discernibly, distinctly.
distingebleco distinctness.

distingeco distinctiveness.
distingema discerning.
distingi to differentiate, discern, discriminate, distinguish, mark.
distingiga distinctive.
distingiĝa distinctive.
distingiĝi to distinguish oneself.
distingilo feature, trait, attribute, character.
distingita distinguished.
distingivo resolution.
distingo distinction, renown.
distomo fluke, liver-fluke.
distopia dystopia, anti-utopia.
distopio dystopian, anti-utopia.
distopiulo dystopian (person), anti-utopian.
distordi to skew, twist, wrench.
distordiĝi to sprain.
distordiĝo skewing, sprain.
distordo distortion, skewing, wrench.
distra entertaining. **distra vespero** evening, party.
distrado distraction, diversion.
distraĵo distraction, diversion.
distranĉi to cut up.
distre entertainingly.
distreco distraction.
distri to amuse, distract, divert, entertain, unbend, relax.
distribua funkcio (probability) distribution function.
distribua servo parcels delivery, parcels service.
distribuado delivery, distribution.
distribuanto carrier.
distribucio distribution, generalized function.
distribueca distributive.
distribuece distributively.
distribueco distributivity.
distribui to allocate, apportion, distribute.
distribuilo distributor.
distribuisto distributor.
distribuo distribution.
distriĝema absent-minded, distracted.
distriĝemo absence of mind.
distriĝi to distract.
distriĝo absence of mind.
distrikta tribunalo county court.
distriktestro bailiff.
distrikto circuit, district, zone.
distrita absent-minded, distracted.
distriteco absence of mind.
distro distraction, diversion.
distrofio dystrophy.
distrumpeti to trumpet.
disurio dysuria.
disvagi to straggle.
disvastigi to spread abroad, promulgate.
disvastigo diffusion, dispersion, dissemination, expansion, propagation.
disvastiĝi to spread, become widespread.
disvastiĝo dispersion, expansion, propagation, spreading.
disverŝi to spill.
disvojo branch (in roads).
disvolva developmental.
disvolvi to develop.
disvolviĝi to develop.
disvolviĝo development, unrolling.
ditirambo dithyramb.
diurezo diuresis.
diurna diurnal.
diurno day, period of twenty-four hours.
divano couch, divan, ottoman.
diveni to divine, guess (correctly).
diveno conception, estimate, guess.
diverĝa divergent.
diverĝe divergently.
diverĝeco divergence.
diverĝenco divergence (of a field).
diverĝi to diverge.
diverĝo divergence.
diversa different, diverse, varied, various, sundry, miscellaneous.
diversaĵa miscellaneous.
diversaĵaro miscellany.
diversaĵoj miscellany, sundries.
diverse severally.
diverseco diversity, variety, variation.
diversgrade to varying degrees.
diversi to vary.
diversigi to diversify.
diversigo diversification.
diversiĝi to diversify.
diversiĝo diversification.
diverskolora many-coloured, multicolored.
diverslanda from many countries.
diverslingveco diversity of languages.
diversmaniere in various ways.
diversspeca different kinds of.
divida divisive. **divida signo** division sign (÷).
dividado division.
dividaĵo part.
dividanto divider, divisor.
dividato dividend.
dividebla divisible.
dividebleco divisibility.
divideblo divisibility.
dividendo dividend, share profits.
dividi to divide, separate, share. **dividu kaj regu** divide and conquer.
dividiĝi to become divided.
divido division, partition. **divido kun resto** division with remainder.
dividonto divisor.
dividooperacio division.

dividostrekado hyphenation.
dividostreko hyphen (-).
dividrezultato quotient.
dividsigno division sign (÷).
dividstreko break, hyphen (-).
divizio division, military division.
divizorhava non-prime. **divizorhava divizoro** non-prime divisor.
divizori to divide, go into.
divizoro divisor.
divorci to divorce.
divorco divorce.
dizajni to design.
dizajnisto designer.
dizajno design.
dizela diesel.
dizelo diesel.
dizeloleo diesel.
dizeltrajno diesel train.
dizerti to desert, run away from.
dizertinto deserter.
dizerto desertion.
D-kordo D-chord.
Dnepro Dnieper.
do[1] accordingly, so, then, therefore.
do[2] name of the letter D.
Dobroĝo Dobruja.
docento docent, university teacher.
dogana customs.
doganejo customs office.
doganisto customs officer.
dogano customs (duty at border).
doganoficejo custom-house.
doganpago customs duties.
dogma dogmatic.
dogmaro doctrine, dogma.
dogmema dogmatic.
dogmemo dogmatism.
dogmismo dogmatics.
dogmo dogma, tenet.
dogo bulldog, mastiff.
doĝo doge.
dojeno doyen.
dokisto dockworker, longshoreman.
doklaboristo docker.
doko dock, dockyard.
doksologio doxology.
dokta learned, erudite.
doktora doctor's, of a doctor.
doktoreco doctorate.
doktoriĝanto candidate for a doctor's degree.
doktoriĝi to graduate with a doctorate.
doktoriĝo doctorate.
doktorino doctor.
doktoro doctor (title). **doktoro de la eklezio** doctor of the church.
doktrina doctrinal.
doktrinano adherent of a doctrine.

doktrino doctrine.
dokumentado documentation.
dokumentaro documentation, dossier.
dokumentfilmo documentary (film).
dokumenti to document.
dokumentlegilo document reader.
dokumento document, paper, certificate.
dolaro dollar.
dolĉa gentle, soft, sweet, tender, mild. **dolĉa akvo** fresh water.
dolĉacida bittersweet, sweet-and-sour.
dolĉaĵo candy, sweet.
dolĉaĵvendejo sweet shop, confectioner's shop.
dolĉamara bittersweet, sweet-and-sour.
dolĉamaro bittersweet, woody nightshade.
dolĉe gently. **dolĉe!** take it easy!
dolĉeco mildness, sweetness.
dolĉega pleasant (manner).
dolĉigi to alleviate, assuage.
dolĉiĝi to relent.
dolĉodora sweet-smelling.
dolĉulino sweetheart.
dolĉulo sweetie, sweetheart.
doliĥocefalo dolichocephal.
dolikocefalo dolichocephal.
dolio dolly.
dolmeno dolmen.
Dolomitoj Dolomites.
dolora aching, anguished, pained, painful, sore.
dolore with pain, achingly.
doloreca achy.
dolorega poignant.
doloregi to agonize.
doloregiĝi to agonize.
dolorego anguish.
dolorema afflictive.
dolorestinga anodyne.
doloreti to smart (to suffer).
dolorĝemi to groan with pain.
dolori to ache, be painful, hurt.
doloriga agonizing, painful.
dolorige painfully.
dolorigi to cause pain, hurt, inflict pain.
dolorigo affliction.
doloriĝi to ache, feel pain, suffer.
doloro ache, pain, pang, tribulation, anguish, hurt.
doma domestic, of a house.
domaĉo hovel.
domaĝa regrettable.
domaĝe regrettably. **domaĝe!** that's too bad! what a pity!
domaĝi to be anxious about, be concerned for, begrudge, not want to spend, regret, be sorry about, fear for.
domaĝo pity, something regrettable.

domajna domain. **domajna nomsistemo** domain name system.
domajno domain (internet).
domanaro household.
domano cohabitant, housemate, roommate.
domaresto house arrest.
domaro cluster of houses, settlement.
domaŭto camper (vehicle).
dombesto domestic animal.
dombloko block (of houses).
dome at home.
domego mansion.
domeno domino(es), masquerade dress.
dometo cottage, lodge, small house.
domfronto house front.
domgardistino caretaker.
domgardisto caretaker.
domhirundo barn swallow.
domicilo abode, dwelling place, residence.
dominanto dominant.
Domingo Dominican Republic.
domini to dominate.
Dominika Respubliko Dominican Republic.
dominikana Dominican.
Dominikanio Dominican Republic.
dominikano Dominican.
dominikia Dominican.
dominikiano Dominican.
Dominikio Dominican Republic.
Dominiko Dominic, Dominica.
dominio dominion.
domino domination.
domkolombo pigeon.
domkolorigisto house-painter.
domkonstruejo building site.
dommakleristo real estate agent.
dommastrino homemaker, housewife.
dommastro househusband.
dommuŝo house-fly.
domnumero number, number of the house.
domo house, villa, building, home.
domorabisto burglar.
dompasero house sparrow.
dompastro chaplain.
dompordo house door.
domposedanto homeowner.
domprizorgisto janitor.
dompropriulo house owner.
dompurigo housecleaning.
domtegmento roof (of a house).
domuzurpinto squatter.
donacado donation, presentation.
donacanto donor.
donace as a gift, gratis.
donacema generous.
donaceme generously.
donaceto little present.
donaci to donate, give, grant, present, bestow.
donacio donation.
donaco gift, present, donation.
donadi to keep giving, continue to give.
donaĵo gift.
donaĵoj data.
donanto donor.
Donegalo Donegal.
donema bountiful.
donĥuano Don Juan, woman-chaser.
doni to give, administer, afford, allow, confer, grant, impart, provide, spare, yield. **doni klarigon** to account for. **doni loĝejon** to accommodate. **doni sian moralan apogon al iu** to give one's moral support to someone. **doni sin** to devote one's self.
donitaĵo datum, something taken for granted.
Donjeco Donetz.
Donjuano Don Juan, woman chaser.
Donĵuano Don Juan, woman chaser.
Donkastro Doncaster.
donkiĥoto Don Quixote.
dono giving, provision.
dopado dope.
dopelgangero double.
doria Dorian, Doric.
dorika Dorian, Doric.
Dorio Doris.
dorlotbesto pet.
dorloti to coddle, pamper, pet, fondle.
dorlotigi to domesticate, turn into a pet.
dorlotiĝi to be pampered.
dorma drowsy.
dormadi to sleep (for a while).
dormado sleeping.
dormanta asleep, inactive, sleeping.
dormante asleep.
dormanto sleeper, one who is sleeping.
dormĉambro bedroom.
dormĉapo nightcap.
dormĉemizo night shirt.
dorme in (one's) sleep.
dormegi to sleep heavily.
dormejo bedroom, dormitory, sleeping place.
dormema drowsy, sleepy.
dormeme sleepily.
dormemo sleepiness.
dormemulo sleepyhead, someone who likes to sleep.
dormetema drowsy.
dormeti to doze, nap, slumber.
dormeto nap.
dormi to be asleep, sleep. **dormi la tutan nokton** to sleep all night long. **dormi sur** to sleep on.
dormiga soporific, sleep-inducing.

dormigi to put to sleep.
dormigilo soporific.
dorminklina drowsy, sleepy.
dormiranto sleep-walker.
dormo sleep.
dormoĉambro bedroom.
dormomuso dormouse.
dormosako sleeping bag.
dormrobo night dress, night gown, nightie.
dormsako sleeping bag.
dorna thorny. **dorna krono** crown of thorns.
dornarbusto thorn bush.
dornbarilo barbed-wire fence.
dornbranĉaro brushwood.
dorndrato barbed wire.
dorneca thorny.
dornfiŝo stickleback.
dornhava bristly.
dornkrono crown of thorns.
dorno thorn, prickle, spine.
dornofiŝo stickleback.
Dornoĥo Dornoch.
dornoplena thorny.
Dornorozeto the Sleeping Beauty.
Dornorozulino Sleeping Beauty.
dornoza bristly.
dornplena bristly.
doroniko false leopard's bane.
dorsa dorsal.
dorsantaŭa backwards.
dorsantaŭe backwards.
dorsantaŭen backwards.
dorsapogilo backrest.
dorsbendo backband.
dorsdirekte back.
dorse at the back.
dorsen backward, on one's back.
dorseskribi to indorse.
dorsflanko back, reverse, reverse side.
dorskorbo basket carried on one's back.
dorso back (of body).
dorsobroso back-scrubber.
dorsodoloro backache.
dorsosako rucksack, pack, backpack.
dorsparto back piece.
dorssako backpack.
dorstabulo backboard.
dosiera historio history.
dosieradministrado file management.
dosieradministrilo file manager, file system, filer.
dosierarangô file organization.
dosierfino end of file, EOF.
dosierflegado file maintenance.
dosiernumero file descriptor, file handle.
dosiero dossier, file.
dosiersistemo file system.
dosiertipo file type.
dosierujo directory, folder.

Dosonkriko Dawson Creek.
doti to endow.
dotita blessed.
doto dowry, portion.
Dovero Dover.
dozado dosage.
dozeno dozen.
dozi to measure out, dose.
dozo dose, portion, quantity.
drabo whitlow-grass.
dragaĵo dredgings.
dragi to drag, dredge.
dragmaŝino dredger.
dragono dragoon.
draĝeo dragée.
drahmo drachma.
drajvi to drive.
drajvo drive.
draĵo sucker.
drakino virago (fig).
drakmo drachma.
Drakmontaro Drakensberg Mountains.
Drako Draco.
drako dragon.
drakona draconian.
drakunkolo tarragon.
drama dramatic.
dramaturgio dramaturgy.
dramaŭtoro dramatist.
drameca dramatic.
dramece dramatically.
dramigi to dramatize.
dramisto playwright.
dramo drama, thriller.
dramverkado dramaturgy, playwriting.
dramverkisto playwright.
drankona leĝo Draconian law.
drapego heavy, woollen cloth.
drapiraĵo drapery, draping.
drapiri to drape.
drapiro drape, drapery.
drapo cloth, woollen cloth, sheet.
drappendaĵo tassel.
drapvendisto draper.
drasta drastic.
draste drastically.
drastika drastic.
draŝado bashing, beating, hammering, thrashing.
draŝejo threshing floor.
draŝi to thresh, thrash, hammer, wallop.
draŝilo flail.
draŝmaŝino threshing machine, thresher.
draŝulo thresher (person).
dratado wiring.
drataro wiring.
dratbaraĵo barbed-wire fence.
dratbarilo barbed-wire fence.
drateca wiry.

dratgazo screen (mesh).
drati to wire.
dratigi to wire.
dratkonektita wire connected.
drato wire.
dratprovizado wiring.
dratretaĵo wire mesh screen.
dratreto wire-netting.
drattondilo wire shears.
Dravo Drava.
drednaŭto dreadnought.
dreliko denim.
drenado draining.
dreni to drain.
dreniĝi to drain.
drenilo drain.
drenkanalo drainage-canal.
drenkrano drain cock.
dresado taming, training.
dresi to tame, train (an animal).
dresisto trainer.
dresrajdado breaking in.
driado dryad.
driaso mountain avens.
dribli to dribble.
drili to drill.
drilo drill.
drinkadi to keep drinking, continue to drink.
drinkado drinking, boozing.
drinkaĵo (alcoholic) drink, booze.
drinkantaro bunch of drunks.
drinkĉambro bar, pub.
drinkegi to swill.
drinkejmastro publican.
drinkejo bar, pub, canteen, tavern, saloon.
drinkema alcoholic.
drinkemo alcoholism.
drinkemulo boozer, alcoholic, drunkard, drunk.
drinkfesteno binge.
drinki to drink (to excess).
drinkulo boozer, alcoholic, drunkard, sot.
driopterido buckler fern.
drivado drifting.
drivangulo angle of swerve.
drivanta adrift.
drivi to drift, be adrift.
drivo drift.
drivtabulo driftwood, flotsam.
drizelo drizzle.
D-ro → **Doktoro**.
droga drug.
Drogedo Drogheda.
drogejo drugstore.
drogekscitita high.
drogi to dope, drug.
drogisto druggist.
drogo drug, pharmaceutical.
drogstimulado dope.
drogvendejo drugstore.
drola funny, funny-looking, queer.
dromajo emu.
dromedaro dromedary.
dromiceo emu.
dromo racing track.
droni to drown, sink. **droni en detaloj** to drown in details. **droni en ŝuldoj** to be drowning in debt.
dronigi to drown.
droniĝo drowning.
droninto drowned body.
dronmarĉejo quicksand.
droso rudder-chain, tiller-rope.
droŝko drosky.
drozero sundew.
druido druid.
drumisto drummer.
Drumnadroĥito Drumnadrochit.
drumo drum set.
drumonda flokso annual phlox, Drummond phlox.
drupo drupe, stone fruit.
D-trajno corridor train, corridor-train.
du two. **du semajnoj** fortnight, two weeks.
dua second (order). **dua mondmilito** Second World War, World War II. **dua persono** second person.
duafoje twice.
duagrada indifferent, mediocre. **duagrada lernejo** secondary school.
duagradeco mediocrity.
duagradulo mediocrity.
duakanona deuterocanonical.
duaksa biaxial.
duala dual. **duala bazo** dual basis.
dualeco duality.
dualismo dualism.
dualo dual.
duaranga secondary.
duargumenta rilato binary relation.
duatoma diatomic.
duba doubtful, dubious, questionable, precarious.
dubanto doubter.
dubasenca ambiguous.
dubasence ambiguously, equivocal.
dubasenco ambiguity.
dube in doubt, doubtfully.
dubeblanka whitish.
dubeble in a doubtful manner.
dubeblua bluish.
dubebruna brownish.
dubeflava tawny, yellowish.
dubekolora drab.
dubelo dowel.
dubeluma dim.
dubelume dimly.
dubema dubious.

dubeme dubiously.
dubemolo double flat symbol (♭).
dubenigra blackish.
duberuĝa reddish.
dubeverda greenish.
dubi to doubt, question.
dubinda doubtful.
dubinde worthy of doubt, doubtful.
dublado dubbing.
dublanto double.
dubleo gold plate.
dubli to dub.
Dublino Dublin.
dublo dowel.
dublono doubloon.
dubo doubt, misgiving.
dubsenca ambiguous.
dubsenceco ambiguity.
ducelkarto dual card.
ducent two hundred.
ducentjara bicentenary.
duciklo bicycle.
duĉambra bicameral.
dudek twenty. **dudek unu** twenty-one.
dudeka twentieth. **dudeka jarcento** twentieth century.
dudekdua twenty-second.
dudekdujara twenty-two-year-old.
dudekedro icosahedron.
dudekjara twenty two year-old.
dudekjarulo twenty year-old (person).
dudeko score.
dudekope twenty together.
dudieso double sharp symbol (⋈).
dudualo double dual.
due secondly.
dueco duality.
duedro dihedron.
duelanto dueler, duelist.
duelbirdo fighting cock, gamecock, ruff.
duelementa binary.
dueli to duel.
duelo duel.
duenjo chaperone.
duentranĉa bifid.
duera binary.
duetaĝa domo two-story house.
dueto duet.
dufadena bifilar.
duflanka bilateral, two-sided.
duflanke bilaterally.
dufoje twice. **dufoje ĉiutage** twice a day.
dufokusa bifocal.
dufolia bifoliate.
duglasio Douglas-fir.
Duglaso Douglas.
dugongo dugong.
duĝemina bigeminate.
duhore for two hours.

duhufa cloven-footed.
duiliono billion, trillion.
duilo median.
dujara biennial, two-year, two-year-old.
dujare for two years.
dujarulo biennial.
duka ducal.
dukapa vico double-ended queue.
dukato ducat.
Dukbosko Bois-le-Duc.
dukino duchess.
duklando duchy, dukedom.
duko duke.
dukolora bicolour, bicoloured, of two colours.
dukomponenta binary.
dukorna bicorn, bicornuate, bicornuous.
dukotiledona dicotyledonous.
dukrono 2-crown piece (Swedish coin).
dukto duct, pipeline, tube; pipe (|).
dukujo duchy.
dukultura bicultural.
dulineara bilinear.
dulingismo bilingualism.
dulingva bilingual.
dulingve bilingually.
dulingvismo bilingualism.
dulipa bilabial, bilabiate.
duliteraĵo digraph.
dulito bunk beds.
duloba bilobate.
duloĝia bilocular.
duloka dyadic, binary. **duloka operacio** binary operation.
dulorneto binoculars.
duluta Duluthian.
dulutano Duluthian.
dum during, while, for, whereas, whilst. **dum centoj da jaroj** for hundreds of years. **dum iom da tempo** for a (little) while. **dum kelka tempo** for some (period of) time, for a while. **dum kelkaj horoj** for several hours. **dum la taglumaj horoj** during daylight hours. **dum la tuta jaro** all year long. **dum la tuta nokto** all night long. **dum lastatempaj jaroj** in recent years. **dum longa tempo** for a long time. **dum multe de semajnoj** for many weeks. **dum pliaj du jaroj** for two more years. **dum senfinaj horoj** for countless hours. **dum tempo** at times, for a time.
duma momentary, temporary, short-lived, transient.
Dumbartono Dumbarton.
dumdorme in one's sleep.
dume all the time, in the meantime, meanwhile, while, for the time being.
dumetala bimetallic.
dumetalismo bimetallism.

Dumfriso

Dumfriso Dumfries.
dumil two thousand.
dummomenta momentary, temporary, short-lived, transient.
dummomente for the moment.
dumnokte at night, during the night.
dumodala bimodal.
dumolekula bimolecular.
dumonata bimonthly.
dumpingi to dump.
dumpingo dumping.
dumtage by day, during the day.
dumtempa temporary.
dumtempe for the time being, meanwhile.
dumviva lifelong. **dumviva malliberiĝo** life imprisonment.
dumvivo lifetime.
dumvoje on the way, on the road.
dunaskito twin.
dunaskitoj twins.
Dunblano Dunblane.
Dundalko Dundalk.
Dundino Dunedin.
Dundio Dundee.
Dunfarlino Dunfermline.
dungado hiring.
dunganto employer.
Dungarvano Dungarvan.
dungato mercenary.
dungi to employ, engage, hire.
dungiĝa job, labour.
dungiĝado employment.
dungiĝi to be hired.
dungiĝo job.
dunginto employer.
dungitaro labour force, personnel, staff, workforce.
dungito employee.
dungo the act of hiring someone, employment.
dungokontrakto labour agreement, labour agreement, labour contract.
dungolisto muster roll.
dungosoldato mercenary soldier, soldier of fortune.
dungperejo employment exchange, labour exchange.
Dunkeldo Dunkeld.
Dunkerko Dunkirk.
Dunkirko Dunkirk.
duno dune.
Dunono Dunoon.
duo couple, pair.
duobla double, dual. **duobla dualo** double dual. **duobla implico** equivalence. **duobla klako** double click. **duobla mentono** double chin. **duobla obeluso** double dagger (‡). **duobla precizeco** double precision. **duobla vo** name of the letter W.

duonkonduktanto

duoblaĵo duplicate.
duoble twice, doubly. **duoble pli facile** twice as easy.
duobligi to double, duplicate, redouble.
duobligo duplication.
duobliĝi to duplicate.
duoblo aŭ nenio double or nothing.
duodeno duodenum.
duoedzineco bigamy.
duokula binocular.
duokuleco binocularity.
duona half. **duona rideto** half-smile.
duonacida bittersweet.
duonblanka whitish.
duonboli to parboil.
duonboto buskin.
duonbruna brownish.
duonbuŝe inarticulately.
duondia of a demigod.
duondiametro radius.
duondiino demigoddess.
duondio demigod.
duondiri to allude, hint, refer to, insinuate, suggest.
duondorma dozy, drowsy.
duondormi to doze, drowse.
duonduto semitone.
duone by halves.
duonebeno half plane.
duonebria tipsy.
duonesvenigi to daze, stun.
duonetaĝo mezzanine.
duonfali to stumble.
duonfermi to half close (eyes).
duonfermita ajar.
duonfilino step-daughter.
duonfilo stepson.
duonfratino half-sister.
duonfrato half-brother.
duonfreneza half-crazy.
duonglobo hemisphere.
duongrasa marbled.
duongrupo semigroup.
duonhisita half-raised, half-staff (flag). **duonhisita flago** a flag at half-staff.
duonhisite at half mast.
duonhore for half an hour.
duonhoro half hour, thirty minutes.
duoniga serĉo binary search.
duoniganto bisector.
duonigi to cut in half, halve.
duoniĝi to halve.
duoninsulo peninsula.
duonjara biannual.
duonjaro midsummer.
duonkapono capon.
duonkodo byte-code.
duonkonduktanto semiconductor.

duonkonduktila memoro semiconductor memory.
duonkonduktilo semiconductor.
duonlevi to tilt.
duonlineara antilinear, semilinear.
duonluma dim.
duonlume in the half-light, half-lit, dimly.
duonlumo dusk, half-light.
duonmalplena half-empty.
duonmaratono half marathon.
duonmatura half-baked.
duonmejlo half mile.
duonmonato fortnight.
duonmondumo demimonde.
duonmorta half-dead.
duonmorte pro soifo half dying of thirst.
duonnormo pseudonorm, semi-norm.
duono half.
duonpalto short coat.
duonpatrino stepmother.
duonpatro stepfather.
duonplena half-full.
duonposedanto half owner.
duonpreta almost ready.
duonrekto half-line, ray.
duonrideto half-smile.
duonringo semiring.
duonrondo semicircle.
duonsfera hemispheric, hemispherical.
duonsfero half sphere, hemisphere.
duonsumilo half-adder.
duonsurda half-deaf.
duonŝtrumpo sock.
duontono halftone (music). **duontono sube** flat (♭). **duontono supre** sharp (♯).
duontuŝi to touch lightly.
duonvoĉe inarticulately.
duonvoja halfway.
duonvoje half the way, halfway (there). **duonvoje al** halfway to.
duonvokalo semivowel.
duopa binary, double, dual, duplex.
duope by twos, two together.
duopo ordered pair, couple.
duopolo duopoly.
duopsonio buyer's duopoly.
duorela binaural.
duparta two-part.
duparteca bipartite.
dupartia bilateral.
dupartohava bipartite.
dupersona lito double bed.
dupieda bipedal, two-footed.
dupiedulo biped.
dupleksa full duplex.
duplikati duplicate.

duplikato duplicate.
dupo dupe.
dupolusa bipolar.
dupoluso dipole.
dupunkto colon (:).
dura hard, major (mus.).
duraluminio duralumin.
duramatro dura mater.
durdisko hard disk, hard drive.
durega adamant.
Durhamo Durham.
durifrukto durian.
duro douro.
durtolo buckram.
dusekcanto bisector.
dusekci to bisect.
dusemajna fortnightly.
dusemajne fortnightly.
dusenca ambiguous, equivocal.
dusencaĵo ambiguity.
dusenceco ambiguity.
dusignifa ambiguous.
dustabila bistable. **dustabila cirkvito** bistable circuit, flip flop.
dustilusa kratago midland hawthorn.
Duŝanbeo Dushanbe.
duŝĉapo shower cap.
duŝejo shower stall.
duŝi to shower. **duŝi sin** to take a shower.
duŝilo showerhead.
duŝkapo showerhead.
duŝkurteno shower curtain.
duŝo douche, shower.
dutermo binomial.
duto second (musical interval).
duuma binary. **duuma arbo** binary tree. **duuma dosiero** binary file. **duuma frakcio** dyadic fraction. **duuma kodo** binary code. **duuma nombrosistemo** binary number system. **duuma operacio** binary operation. **duuma serĉarbo** binary search tree. **duuma sistemo** binary system.
duum-dekuma prezento binary-coded decimal notation.
duvalenta bivalent.
duvalenteco bivalency.
duvalva bivalve.
duvalvulo bivalve.
duvalvuloj bivalves.
duveto duvet.
duzo nozzle, jet.
DVD-disko DVD disc.
dzeta zeta (Zζ).
dzeto zeta (Zζ).
Dzungario Dzungaria.
Dzungarujo Dzungaria.

E

e name of the letter E.
Eako Aeacus.
easto east.
ebeeco compliance.
ebena even, flat, level, smooth. **ebena angulo** plane angle. **ebena grafeo** planar graph. **ebena kurbo** plane curve.
ebenaĵeto level spot, level area.
ebenaĵo plain.
ebenavoje smoothly (of a path, road).
ebenbatita beaten flat.
ebene evenly.
ebenejo plain.
ebenigi to even, level, (make) smooth.
ebenigilo roller.
ebeniĝi to flatten.
ebeno plane (geom.).
ebi to ebb.
eblas it is possible.
eble maybe, mayhap, perchance, perhaps, possibly. **eble jes** perhaps so. **eble ne** perhaps not.
ebleco possibility.
ebli to be possible.
ebligi to enable, render possible.
ebligo allowance.
eblo possibility.
ebo ebb (of tide).
ebona ebony.
ebonarbo ebony tree.
ebonito ebonite.
ebonkolora ebony.
ebono ebony.
ebonujo ebony.
ebria drunk, intoxicated, tipsy, inebriated.
ebrie drunkenly.
ebrieco drunkenness, intoxication.
ebrieta buzzed, slightly drunk, tipsy.
ebrigaĵo intoxicating liquor.
ebrii to be drunk.
ebriiga intoxicating.
ebriigaĵo intoxicating substance.
ebriige intoxicatingly.
ebriigi to intoxicate, make (someone) drunk.
ebriiĝi to get drunk.
ebrio drunkenness, intoxication.
ebriulo drunk person, drunk(ard).
Ebro Ebro.
ebulo danewort, dwarf elder.
ebura ivory. **Ebura Marbordo** Ivory Coast. **ebura turo** ivory tower.
Ebur-Bordo Ivory Coast.
Eburio Ivory Coast.
eburkolora ivory-coloured.
eburmevo ivory gull.
eburo ivory.
ecidio aecidium, aecium.
ecigi to qualify.
eco property, quality, attribute, qualification.
eĉ even. **eĉ iom ne** not at all, by no means, anything but. **eĉ ne unu** not a single. **eĉ se** even if.
Edamo Edam.
edelvejso edelweiss.
edemo edema.
Edeno Eden.
edeno paradise.
Edgaro Edgar.
edifi to edify.
edikto decree, edict.
edilo aedile.
Edinburgo Edinburgh.
editisto editor.
editoro editor.
Edmundo Edmund.
edro face.
Eduardo Edward.
eduka educational.
edukado education, upbringing.
edukarto pedagogy.
edukato boarder (school).
edukejo boarding school.
eduki to breed, bring up, educate, raise.
edukiĝi to be educated.
edukisto educator.
edukita raised, trained, educated.
edukiteco education (received).
eduko education, upbringing.
Edvardinsulo Prince Edward Island.
edzeca marital.
edzeco marriage, matrimony, wedlock.
edziga of a wedding. **edziga ceremonio** wedding ceremony. **edziga ringo** wedding ring.
edzigebla marriageable.
edzigi to marry, wed.
edziĝa nuptial. **edziĝa festo** wedding, wedding party.
edziĝanonco banns, wedding announcement.
edziĝanto bridegroom.
edziĝfesto wedding feast, wedding-party.
edziĝi to get married, marry, wed.
edziĝinta married.
edziĝo marriage, wedding.
edziĝofesto wedding.
edziĝonto husband-to-be, future husband.
edziĝopropono offer of marriage, proposal.
edziĝovojaĝo honeymoon.
edziĝpeto offer, offer of marriage.

edziĝpropono offer of marriage, proposal.
edzineco marriage.
edzinigi to marry, wed.
edziniĝantino bride.
edziniĝi to get married, marry, become married.
edziniĝinta married.
edziniĝo marriage.
edzinmurdinto wife killer.
edzino wife.
edzo husband, mate, spouse.
EEU → **Eŭropa Esperanto-Unio**.
efekta showy.
efekti to be effective.
efektiĝi to come to pass, come true.
efektiva actual, real, effective, effectual, true.
  efektiva adreso actual address.
efektivaĵo reality, fact.
efektive absolutely, actually, in fact, effectively, really, as a matter of fact.
efektiveco actuality, truth, reality.
efektivigaĵo fait accompli.
efektivigebla achievable.
efektivigi to accomplish, achieve, act out, effect, realize, perform, bring about.
efektivigita completed.
efektivigo accomplishment, execution, implementation.
efektiviĝi to come about, come to pass, come true.
efekto effect, impression.
efemera ephemeral.
efemeraĵo bubble, ephemeron.
efemereco ephemerality.
efemeredoj dayflies, mayflies.
efemerido astronomical table, ephemeris.
efemermemorilo scratch-pad memory.
efemero mayfly.
efermera ephemeral.
eferverska bubbly.
eferveska effervescent, fizzy.
eferveski to effervesce, fizz, bubble.
efervesko effervescence.
Efeso Ephesus.
efezano Ephesian.
Efezo Ephesus.
efika effective, effectual, efficacious.
efikado action.
efike decisively, effectively.
efikeco effectiveness, efficacy.
efiki to act, be effective, have effect, work, effect.
efikilo agent.
efikita affected.
efiko effect, result.
efloreski to effloresce.
efluvo effluvium, discharge.
efodo ephod.
efrito ifrit, afreet, afrit.

ega considerable, major, great, enormous, intense, extreme.
egala equal, even, level.
egalaĵo equation.
egalanima even-tempered.
egalanimeco equanimity.
egalbone equally good.
egale alike, all the same, equally.
egaleco draw, equality, parity.
egalforta well-matched.
egali to equal.
egaligi to equalize, even, level, match.
  egaligi konton to settle an account.
egallarĝa fixed-width, monospaced.
egallatera equilateral.
egallonga kodo fixed-length code.
egalpezi to balance.
egalpezigi to balance.
egalpezo equilibrium.
egalrajta equal, having equal rights.
egalrajteco equality (of rights).
egalrajtismo egalitarianism.
egalsenca synonymous.
egalsence synonymously.
egalsenco synonym.
egalsigno equals sign (=)
egalulo equal (person), match.
egalvalora al tantamount to.
egalvenko draw.
egardema attentive, watchful.
egardo attention.
ege extremely, greatly.
egea Aegean. **Egea Maro** Aegean, Aegean Sea. **Egeaj Insuloj** Aegean Islands.
egeco intensity.
egeja Aegean. **Egeja Maro** Aegean Sea.
egido aegis, protection, shield, auspices, sponsorship.
egipta Egyptian.
Egiptio Egypt.
Egipto Egyptian.
egiptujano Egyptian.
Egiptujo Egypt.
Egiro Aegir.
eglanterio eglantine.
eglefino haddock.
egocentra egocentric.
egocentre egocentrically.
egocentrismo egocentrism.
egoisma self-interested, selfish, egoistical.
egoisme selfishly, egoistically.
egoismo egoism, self-interest, selfishness.
egoismulo egoist, egotist.
egoista egoistical, egotistical, self-interested, selfish.
egoiste selfishly, egoistically.
egoisto egoist, egotist.
egoo ego.
egopodio bishop's weed.

egretardeo aigrette.
egreto aigrette, tuft.
egzameni to investigate, study, do research, examine, explore.
egzerci to make exercises, master.
egzilito exile.
egzilo exile.
eĝo arc (of a graph), mountain ridge, edge.
ehe aha.
eĥi to echo.
eĥidno spiny ant-eater.
eĥino sea urchin.
eĥo echo. **Eĥo** Echo.
eĥolokalizilo echolocation, sonar.
eĥosondilo sonar.
eĥosanĝo ĉiujaŭde The quick brown fox jumps over the lazy dog.
Eiffel-turo Eiffel Tower.
eiskoplando diocese.
ej! *interjection* (mild disapproval or protest) eh! (enquiry, surprise, or inviting assent) eh?
Ejfelturo Eiffel Tower.
ejlo ale.
ejnstejnio einsteinium.
ejnstejno Einstein.
ejnŝtejnio einsteinium.
Ejnŝtejno Einstein.
ejo place.
Ejro Ireland.
ek away we go, let's start. **ek de** starting from.
ek- (denotes an action which begins or is of short duration).
eka abrupt.
ekaboni to subscribe, subscribe to.
ekamasiĝi to boom.
ekamasiĝo boom.
ekami to fall in love.
ekaperi to emerge.
ekapero emergence.
ekarto approximation error, deviation.
ekaŭdatoj anurans, batrachians, salientians.
ekaŭdi to catch the sound of, descry, perceive.
ekaŭdiĝi to make a noise, make a sound.
ekbalbuti to blurt.
ekbatali to begin fighting, commence hostilities.
ekbatalo engagement.
ekbatejo tee.
ekbati to lash out.
ekbato throbbing.
ekblovi to start to blow, begin blowing.
ekboji to start barking.
ekboli to start to boil, begin boiling.
ekbrileti to twinkle, sparkle.
ekbrili to flash.
ekbrilo flash.
ekbrui to bang.

ekbruli to (begin to) burn, catch, flash on, strike, take fire.
ekbruligi to ignite, kindle, light, set fire to, strike, spark.
ekbruligo lighting.
ekbruo bang.
ekceli to aim, take aim.
ekdanci to start to dance, begin dancing.
ekde from, since, right from. **ekde hieraŭ** since yesterday. **ekde la komenco** from the beginning. **ekde la tempo kiam** from the time when. **ekde tiu momento** from that moment.
ekdeĵori to accede.
ekdeĵoro accession.
ekdetrui to zap.
ekdiskuti pri to bring up.
ekdisputi to start arguing.
ekdorma dormant.
ekdormi to fall asleep, drop off to sleep.
ekeliĝi to emerge from, poke out of, come out of.
ekenui to bore, make someone become bored.
ekesti to arise, start to be. **ekestis ventego** a storm blew up.
ekestiĝi to commence, start.
ekestiĝo commencement, start.
ekesto commencement, start.
ekfali to dip, slump.
ekfalo dip, downturn, slump.
ekfari to make or do suddenly.
ekfarti to start feeling, start faring.
ekfiaski to go under.
ekfiniĝi to wane.
ekfiniĝo decline.
ekflagri to burst into flames.
ekflama volatile.
ekflamejo flashpoint.
ekflami to catch fire, flare up, take fire, enkindle.
ekflamigi to set fire to.
ekflamigo lighting.
ekflamiĝema passionate.
ekflamiĝi to flame, flare.
ekflori to come into bloom.
ekflugi to take wing, take flight, take off.
ekflugo take-off.
ekforkuri to start to run away, suddenly run away.
ekfrotadi to start to rub.
ekfuĝi to flee, take to flight, take to one's heels.
ekfulmeti to flash.
ekfulmeto flash.
ekfulmi to flash.
ekfulmo flash, thunderbolt.
ekfunkcii to set going.

ekfunkciigi to put on, start, switch on, turn on.
ekfunkciigo activation.
ekgardi to secure.
ekgenui to kneel down.
ekgliti to skid, slip.
ekĝemi to sigh.
ekĝemo moan, groan.
ekĝoji to become joyful.
ekhalti to stop suddenly.
ekhalto stand.
ekhavi to get.
ekhejmporti to start carrying home.
eki to begin, come on, set in, start.
ekidno spiny ant-eater.
ekigi to begin, commence, start.
ekimozo ecchymosis.
ekino sea urchin.
ekinopso globe-thistle.
ekinospermo bur-seed.
ekinsulti to become abusive.
ekinteresiĝi to begin to be interested.
ekio viper's bugloss.
ekipaĵo accoutrement, accoutrements, equipment.
ekipestro boatswain.
ekipi to equip, outfit.
ekipo equipment.
ekirangulo angle of departure.
ekire going out, leaving.
ekirejo starting-point.
ekiri to get out, set off, start (out).
ekirigi to get something going. **ekirigi motoron** to start an engine.
ekkanti to intone, raise, strike up singing.
ekkapti to clutch, grab, grasp, grip, seize, apprehend, grapple, lay hold of.
ekkaptigi to clutch.
ekkapto seizure.
ekkati to catch, seize, grab hold of, take hold of, catch hold of.
ekkaŭzi to trigger.
ekkiam as soon as.
ekkolerema irascible.
ekkoleremulo hot-head.
ekkoleri to get angry.
ekkompreni to begin to understand.
ekkompreno grasp, insight.
ekkonebla recognizable.
ekkoneble recognizablely.
ekkoni to get to know, become familiar. **ekkonu vin mem!** know thyself!
ekkono notion.
ekkonscii to become aware of, realize.
ekkonscio realization.
ekkonstrui to start to build, begin to build.
ekkonsumi to break into, broach, cut into.
ekkontakti to contact.

ekkonteorio epistemology, theory of knowledge.
ekkrampo open (left) parenthesis (( ).
ekkreski to start to grow.
ekkriegi to begin to shout, start to shout.
ekkrii to call out, cry out, exclaim, shout out.
ekkrio ejaculation, yell.
ekkuri to start running, take to one's heels.
ekkuro run.
ekkuŝi to lie down.
ekkuŝiĝi to lie down.
ekkutimi to take to (something).
eklabori to start work(ing).
eklampsio eclampsia.
eklektika eclectic.
eklektike eclectically.
eklektikismo eclecticism.
eklektikulo eclectic.
eklerni to begin learning.
eklero éclair.
eklevi to hitch, jerk.
eklevo jerk.
eklezia ecclesiastic, ecclesiastical. **eklezia regulo** canon.
ekleziano church member, churchgoer, churchman, ecclesiastic.
eklezimajstro Teacher of the Faith.
eklezio church (institution, not building).
ekleziologia ecclesiological.
ekleziologio ecclesiology.
ekleziulo chaplain, clergyman, ecclesiastic, cleric, priest.
eklipsi to surpass, eclipse.
eklipso eclipse.
ekliptiko ecliptic.
eklogo eclogue.
ekloĝi to take up one's residence, settle in. **ekloĝi en** to live in.
ekludi to kick off, start to play.
ekludo kick off.
eklumigi to light. **eklumigi la laternon** to light the lantern.
ekmalbonfarti to start feeling badly.
ekmalfortiĝi to decline (health).
ekmalsati to get hungry.
ekmalsukcesi to go under.
ekmanĝi to start to eat.
ekmanki al to fall short of.
ekmarŝi rapide to mend one's pace, step out.
ekmemori to remember, come to mind.
ekmorti to be dying.
ekmovi to begin to move, start to move.
ekmoviĝi to begin to move.
ekmultiĝi to boom.
ekmultiĝo boom, upsurge.
eknaĝi to begin to swim, start to swim.
eko beginning, commencement, inception, opening, outset, start.

ekokazo

ekokazo emergency.
ekokupado invasion.
ekokupo inroad.
ekologia ecological. **ekologia legomo** organic vegetable.
ekologie ecologically.
ekologiismo ecological movement, environmental movement, environmentalism, green movement.
ekologiisto ecologist, environmentalist.
ekologio ecology.
ekologo ecologist.
ekonmortigi to decimate.
ekonometrio econometrics.
ekonomia economic. **ekonomia ekspansio** economic expansion.
ekonomie economically.
ekonomiisto economist.
ekonomika economical.
ekonomike economically.
ekonomikisto bailiff, steward.
ekonomiko economics.
ekonomio economics, economy.
ekonomo bailiff, bursar, estate manager, manager, steward, treasurer.
E-kordo E-chord.
ekpafi to discharge, fire, fire off.
ekpago initial deposit, installment, down payment, first installment.
ekparoli to begin speaking, utter. **ekparoli pri** to bring up.
ekparolo utterance.
ekpaŝi to step out, take a first step.
ekpensi to have an idea, occur to (one).
ekpliiĝo upsurge.
ekplori to burst into tears.
ekpluvema showery.
ekpluvi to start raining.
ekpluvo shower.
ekposedi to take possession of.
ekpreni to grasp, snatch.
ekpreno grasp.
ekprocesi to begin a lawsuit. **ekprocesi kontraŭ** to prosecute, sue.
ekprovi to tackle.
ekpuŝi to jog, nudge.
ekpuŝo push.
ekrana butono screen button.
ekranbloko monitor, visual display unit.
ekrankurteno screen saver.
ekrano screen.
ekransavilo screen saver.
ekranumi to screen.
ekregi to take command of, take power over.
ekrego accession, ascendancy.
ekrideti to titter.
ekridi to burst out laughing.
ekrigardi to glance (at).
ekrigardo glance.

eksigo

ekrimarki to descry, perceive.
ekrodi to gnaw.
ekronĝi to gnaw.
ekronki to snort.
eks- late, former, ex-.
eksa former, ex-.
eksagi to dart off, dart away.
eksalti to leap, spring up, start.
eksalto spike.
eksamantino ex-lover.
eksarko exarch.
ekscelenco excellency.
Ekscelenco Excellency.
ekscenterga way-out.
ekscentra eccentric.
ekscentre eccentrically.
ekscentrika eccentric.
ekscentrike eccentrically.
ekscentriko eccentric.
ekscepsio exception.
ekscesa excessive, inordinate, immoderate, too much.
ekscese excessively.
eksceso excess.
ekscii to get to know, find out, learn, realize.
ekscita exciting.
ekscitaĉo ballyhoo.
eksciteco excitement.
eksciti to agitate, arouse, excite, rouse, stir, stir up.
ekscitiĝeta shivery.
ekscitiĝeto frisson, shiver.
ekscitiĝi to become excited.
ekscitiĝo agitation, excitement.
ekscitita agitated.
ekscititeco agitation, excitement.
ekscito excitation, excitement.
eksdosiero backup file.
eksedzigi to divorce.
eksedzigo divorce.
eksedziĝi to get a divorce, get divorced.
eksedziĝinta divorced.
eksedziĝo divorce (judicial).
eksedziniĝi to get a divorce.
eksedziniĝinta divorced.
eksedziniĝo divorce.
eksedzino ex-wife.
eksedzo ex-husband.
eksekvi to begin to follow.
eksenti to begin to think, start to think.
eksento emotion.
ekshibicii to exhibit.
ekshibicio exhibitionism.
eksidi to sit down.
eksigeco exclusion.
eksigi to discharge, dismiss, fire, sack, exclude, recall, prevent. **eksigu** exclude.
eksigii to fire (discharge).
eksigo dismissal, removal.

eksiĝdato purge date.
eksiĝi to quit, resign, withdraw from office, retire.
eksiĝo renunciation, resignation.
eksjuĝisto former judge.
eksĵurnalisto former newspaperman.
eksklavo exclave.
ekskludi to bar, exclude.
ekskludo ban, bar.
ekskluziva exclusive. **ekskluziva aŭ-operacio** exclusive-or operation. **ekskluziva disjunkcio** exclusive disjunction.
ekskluzive exclusively.
ekskluzivema exclusivist.
ekskluzivi to exclude.
ekskluzivigo exclusion.
ekskomuniki to excommunicate.
ekskomuniko anathema, ban, excommunication.
ekskoriacii to abrade.
ekskoriacio abrasion, excoriation, graze, scratch.
ekskorii to abrade.
ekskreci to excrete.
ekskrecia excretal.
ekskrecii to excrete, secrete.
ekskrecio excretion.
ekskrementa excremental.
ekskremento excrement.
ekskui to jerk, jolt, shake.
ekskuo jerk.
ekskursafiŝo poster about an excursion.
ekskursi to go on an excursion.
ekskurso excursion, outing, trip.
ekskuzi to excuse. **ekskuzi sin** to apologize.
ekskuzo apology.
ekslernanto alumnus.
ekslibriso ex libris.
eksloĝejo former place of residence.
ekslojaliĝi to defect.
ekslojaliĝinto defector.
ekslojaliĝo defection.
eksmembriĝi to withdraw one's name, withdraw one's subscription.
eksmilitisto veteran.
eksmoda old-fashioned, out of date.
eksoficiro ex-officer.
eksoni to resound, become audible.
eksp exp.
ekspansia expansive.
ekspansie expansively.
ekspansii to expand.
ekspansiismo expansionism.
ekspansio expansion.
ekspansionismo expansionism.
ekspastrigi to defrock, unfrock.
ekspeda servo parcels delivery, parcels service.
ekspedaĵo consignment.

ekspeddato shipping date.
ekspedi to dispatch, send off, ship, expedite, forward, dispatch.
ekspedicio expedition.
ekspedinto sender.
ekspedisto shipper.
ekspedo dispatch.
ekspekto expectation (of a random variable).
eksperimenta experimental.
eksperimentado experimentation.
eksperimente as an experiment.
eksperimente experimentally.
eksperimentĝardeno botanical garden.
eksperimenti to experiment.
eksperimento experiment.
eksperta expert. **eksperta sistemo** expert system.
eksperte expertly.
ekspertisto expert.
ekspertizado appraisal.
ekspertizi to appraise, assess, survey, value (as an expert).
ekspertizisto appraiser.
ekspertizo assessment, expertise.
eksperto expert, specialist.
eksplicita explicit.
eksplicite explicitly.
ekspliciteco explicitness.
ekspliki to account for, explain, explicate.
ekspliko account, explanation.
eksploda explosive. **eksploda substanco** explosive.
eksplodaĵo explosive (substance).
eksplodbrui to blast.
eksplodbruo detonation.
eksplodi to explode, blow up.
eksplodigi to blow up.
eksplodilo explosive device.
eksplodkonsonanto plosive.
eksplodmotoro internal combustion engine.
eksplodo explosion.
eksplodsono report (of gun, etc.).
ekspluatado exploitation.
ekspluatanto exploiter.
ekspluati to exploit, leverage, take advantage of, utilize, work.
ekspluatisto exploiter.
ekspona tempo exposure time.
eksponado exposure.
eksponanto exhibitor.
eksponadŭro exhibition length.
ekspondeklami to hawk, hype.
eksponejo show-room.
eksponenciala exponential.
eksponenciale exponentially.
eksponencialo exponential.
eksponenta funkcio exponential function.
eksponento exponent.

eksponi

eksponi to demonstrate, exhibit, expose, showcase, display.
eksponisto stall-holder.
eksponmezurilo exposure meter.
ekspono exposure.
eksportado exportation.
eksportaĵo export.
eksportebla exportable.
eksporti to export.
eksportisto exporter.
eksportmonopolo export monopoly.
eksporto export, exportation.
ekspoŝisto ex-postman.
ekspoziciaĵo exhibit, show.
ekspozicii to exhibit.
ekspozicio exhibition, exposition.
ekspresa express.
ekspresi to express.
ekspreso express (train, messenger), special delivery.
eksproprietigi to expropriate.
ekssklavo ex-slave.
ekssoldato ex-soldier.
eksstudentino alumna.
eksstudento former student.
ekstari to get up, rise, stand, stand up.
ekstaza ecstatic.
ekstazi to be ecstatic.
ekstazo ecstasy, rapture, delight.
ekstemporalo test paper, unprepared composition.
ekster aside from, apart from, out, outside (of), beyond. **ekster si de eksciteo** beside oneself with excitement. **ekster via scio** beyond your knowledge.
ekstera external, outer, outside. **ekstera interrompo** external interrupt. **ekstera memorilo** external memory. **ekstera memoro** external memory. **ekstera operacio** external composition law.
ekstera ordigo external sort.
eksteraĵo exterior, outer part.
eksterdanĝera out of danger.
eksterduba definite, outright, undoubted, unmistakable, unquestionable.
eksterdube undoubtedly.
ekstere abroad, out, outside.
eksteredzeca out of wedlock, outside of marriage, illegitimate (of a child). **eksteredzeca infano** illegitimate child.
eksteren out, outside, outward. **eksteren sendi** to export.
ekstereŭropano non-European (person).
ekstergeedziĝa illegitimate.
eksterhavene off the harbour.
eksterlanda alien, foreign.
eksterlandanino foreigner, foreign lady, foreign woman.
eksterlandano foreigner.

ekstreme

eksterlande abroad.
eksterlanden abroad.
eksterlando abroad, foreign country.
eksterleĝulo outlaw, criminal.
eksterloka position-independent.
ekstermi to exterminate, wipe out.
ekstermiĝi to become exterminated.
ekstermino extermination.
ekstermo annihilation.
Eksternaj Hebridoj Outer Hebrides.
eksternatura unnatural.
eksternature unnaturally.
eksternorma abnormal, abnormous.
eksternorma abnormal.
eksternormaĵo abnormality.
eksternorme abnormally.
ekstero exterior.
eksterorda extraordinary.
eksterorde extraordinarily.
eksterordinara extraordinary, formidable, out of the ordinary. **eksterordinara dividendo** bonus.
eksterordinare exceedingly, extraordinarily.
eksterordinarega extraordinary.
eksterpartia neutral, independent, impartial.
eksterpoli to extrapolate.
eksterregula irregular.
eksterregule irregularly.
ekstersezona out of season.
ekstersunsistema planedo exoplanet.
eksterŝtatano alien.
ekstertera alien, extraterrestrial.
eksterterano alien.
eksterterulo alien, extraterrestrial.
eksterulo outsider.
ekstervarieja out of range.
ekstervoje off the road.
ekstra additional, extra, spare.
ekstradi to extradite.
ekstradicia extradition.
ekstradicii to extradite.
ekstradicio extradition.
ekstraĵo accessory, extra.
ekstraktado abstraction, extraction.
ekstrakti to extract.
ekstrakto extract.
ekstrapoli to extrapolate.
ekstravaganca extravagant, high-flown.
ekstravaganco extravagance.
ekstravaganculo oddball, weirdo.
ekstravertita extroverted.
ekstravertito extrovert.
ekstrema extreme, utmost. **Ekstrema Oriento** the Far East.
ekstremaĵo end, tip, extremity.
ekstremdekstra far right.
ekstreme extremely.

ekstremeco extremity.
ekstrementbulo piece of droppings.
ekstremisma extremist.
ekstremismo extremism.
ekstremisto extremist.
ekstremmaldekstra far left.
ekstremo extreme.
ekstremofilo extremophile.
ekstremumiganto position of an extremum.
ekstremumo extreme value, extremum.
ekstrulo supernumerary.
ekstudentiĝi to finish studying, graduate.
eksudi to exude.
eksvalida invalid.
eksvalidiĝi to expire, invalid.
eksvalidiĝo expiry.
ekŝanĝiĝema volatile.
ekŝuldi to incur.
ektagiĝo sunrise.
ektedi to begin to tire, start to bore.
ekteni to clutch, grapple.
ekteno grasp.
ektimegi to begin to panic, start to panic.
ektimi to begin to fear.
ektimigita startled.
ektiminta startled.
ektimo alarm.
ektiregi to wrench.
ektiri to jerk, pull, tug.
ektiro yank.
ektondro thunderclap.
ektopio ectopia.
ektoplasmo ectoplasm.
ektranĉi to cut into.
ektremi to start, startle.
ektremigi to begin to scare, start to frighten.
ektropio ectropion.
ektuŝegi to hit against, run against.
ektuŝi to touch upon.
ektuŝmaniero touch.
ektuŝo brush.
ekumena ecumenic(al). **ekumena koncilio** ecumenical council. **ekumena majstro** Teacher of the Faith.
ekumenismo ecumenicism, ecumenism.
ekumenisto ecumenist.
ekuzi to start to use, start using.
ekvaciaro system of equations.
ekvaciigi to put into an equation.
ekvacio equation.
ekvadora Ecuadorian.
Ekvadoro Ecuador.
ekvatora equatorial. **Ekvatora Gvineo** Equatorial Guinea.
ekvatorialo equatorial.
ekvatoro equator.
ekventego gust.
ekvento gust (of wind).
ekverviĝi to fire.
ekveturi to depart, leave, sail, start.
ekvidi to catch sight of, perceive, spy.
ekvidiĝi to suddenly become visible.
ekvido glimpse.
ekvigligi to galvanize.
ekvigliĝi to boom.
ekvigliĝo boom.
ekvilibra balanced. **ekvilibra arbo** balanced tree.
ekvilibri to be in balance, be in equilibrium, poise.
ekvilibriga faktoro balance factor.
ekvilibrigi to balance, stabilize.
ekvilibrigo counterbalance.
ekvilibristo acrobat, equilibrist.
ekvilibro balance, equilibrium.
ekvinoksa punkto equinoctial point.
ekvinokso equinox.
ekvipolenta equipollent.
ekviseto horsetail.
ekvivalenta equivalent.
ekvivalenteco equivalence.
ekvivalentklaso equivalence class.
ekvivalento equivalence, equivalent.
ekvivalentoklaso equivalence class.
ekvivalento-klaso equivalence class.
ekvivalento-operacio equivalence operation.
ekvivalentorilato equivalence relation.
ekvivalento-rilato equivalence relation.
ekvivalentrilato equivalence relation.
ekvizeto horsetail.
ekvojaĝi to depart, leave, set out.
ekvolo caprice.
ekz. → **ekzemple**.
ekzakta exact.
ekzakte exactly.
ekzakteco accuracy, exactitude, precision.
ekzakto accuracy.
ekzalti to exalt.
ekzameni to examine, inspect, verify, question, scrutinize, survey.
ekzameniĝi to be examined.
ekzameno exam, examination, investigation, review, test.
ekzamentablo examining table.
ekzamento examination.
ekzantemo eruption, exanthema, rash.
ekz-e → **ekzemple**.
ekzegeza exegetical.
ekzegezisto exegete.
ekzegezo exegesis.
ekzekucii to execute.
ekzekuciisto sequestrator.
ekzekucio sequestration.
ekzekuti to execute (criminal).
ekzekutisto hangman, executioner.
ekzekuto execution.

ekzekvaturo exequatur.
ekzekvi to execute.
ekzemo eczema.
ekzempla exemplary.
ekzemple for example, e.g.
ekzemplero copy (of book, etc.), exemplar.
ekzempli to be an instance of, exemplify, illustrate.
ekzempligi to exemplify.
ekzemplo copy, example, instance.
ekzemplodoni to instance.
ekzercado practice, exercise, training.
ekzercaro exercise book, practice book, problem book.
ekzercejo range.
ekzerci to exercise, practise, train, drill, rehearse. **ekzerci sin** to practise.
ekzerciĝi to exercise, practise.
ekzerciĝo work-out.
ekzercita experienced, expert, skilful, skilled, practised.
ekzerciteco expertness, skill, skilfulness, facility (through practice).
ekzerclibro exercise book.
ekzerco drill, exercise, practice.
ekzercokarto flashcard.
ekzercolibro exercise-book.
ekzergo exergue.
ekzibi to exhibit.
ekzilejo exile.
ekzili to ban, banish, exile.
ekziliĝi to exile.
ekzilito exile.
ekzilloko place of exile.
ekzilo exile, outcast.
ekzistadismo existentialism.
ekzistado existence.
ekzistaĵo existence.
ekzistanta extant.
ekzisteca existential.
ekzistencialismo existentialism.
ekzisti to exist.
ekzistigi to bring into existence.
ekzisto existence.
ekzistorajto raison d'être, right to exist.
ekzoftalmio exophthalmia.
ekzogamio exogamy.
ekzorci to exorcise.
ekzorcizi to exorcise.
ekzorco exorcism.
ekzota exotic.
ekzotaĵo exotic.
ekzotika exotic.
ekzotikaĵo exotic.
ekzotiko exoticness.
ekzotikulino exotic.
ekzoto exoticness.
ekz-ro → **ekzemplero**.

el from, (out) of. **el alia perspektivo** from another point of view. **el kie vie estas?** where are you from?
elaĉeta redemptive. **elaĉeta mono** ransom.
elaĉeti to ransom, redeem.
Elaĉetinto Redeemer, Savior.
elaĉeto redemption.
elaĉetsumo ransom, redemption money.
elafuro Père David's deer.
elajosomo elaiosome.
el-Aksa-moskeo Al-Aqsa Mosque.
elaktori to act out.
elamano Elamite.
Elamo Elam.
elano élan.
elartikigi to disjoint, dislocate, sprain.
elartikigo dislocation.
elartikiĝi to become dislocated.
elartikiĝo dislocation.
elasta elastic, springy.
elastaĵo elastic.
elastano elastane, lycra, spandex.
elasteco elasticity.
elaterido wireworm.
elaterio claterium.
elatro click beetle.
elaŭtiĝi to get out, get out of a car.
elaŭtobusiĝi to alight, get out, debus.
elaviadiliĝi to get out.
elbabili to blab, blurt out.
elbareligi to decant.
elbari to shut out.
elbati to strike out.
elblovi to blow off, blow out.
Elbo Elba.
elbruli to go out (of a light).
Elbruso Mount Elbrus.
elbufrigi to flush.
elburĝoniĝi to bud, sprout.
elbusiĝi to alight, get out, debus.
elcentaĵo percentage.
elcento per cent, per centum, percent, percentage.
elcentosigno percent sign (%).
elcentra eccentric.
elcentre eccentrically.
elĉenigi to unchain.
elĉerpa exhaustive. **elĉerpa serĉo** exhaustive search.
elĉerpe exhaustively.
elĉerpi to ladle out, scoop out, exhaust, use up, consume.
elĉerpiĝi to exhaust.
elĉerpita exhausted, used up, out of print.
eld. → **eldonis**, **eldono**.
eldetrui to raze, raze to the ground.
eldevigado enforcement.
eldevigi to extort, wrest, wring.
eldevigo exaction, extortion.

eldirado

eldirado airing, delivery.
eldiri to articulate, put, state, utter, voice, enunciate. **eldiri verdikton** to pronounce a verdict.
eldiro articulation, statement.
eldonaĵo publication.
eldonejo publisher, publishing house.
eldoni to issue, publish, edit. **eldonis** he published.
eldoninto publisher.
eldonisto editor, publisher.
eldonkvanto circulation (number), number of issues.
eldono edition.
Eldorado El Dorado.
eleagno oleaster.
elefanta elephant, elephant's, elephantine, of an elephant.
elefantaro a herd of elephants.
elefantiazo elephantiasis.
elefantido baby elephant.
elefanto elephant.
elefantosto ivory.
eleganta elegant, smart. **eleganta klarkio** elegant clarkia, woodland clarkia. **elegantaj manieroj** good manners.
elegante elegantly, smartly.
eleganteco elegance.
elegia elegaic.
elegio elegy.
elejo egress, exit, outlet, way out.
elektada electoral.
elektado election.
elektaĵo choice.
elektanto elector.
elektaro selection.
elektebla eligible.
elektebleco eligibility.
elekteco alternative.
elektema picky.
elekti to choose, elect, pick (out), select.
elektita elected.
elektitaĵo flower.
elekto appointment, choice, election.
elektoaĵo option.
elektodistriktano constituent.
elektodistrikto constituency, electorate.
elektosekcio constituency, electorate.
elektpromeso election promise.
elektra electric. **elektra kampo** electric(al) field. **elektra luno** electric light. **elektra pilo** pile (electric).
elektre electrically.
elektrejo power-plant.
elektrigi to electrify.
elektrika kurento electrical current.
elektrizi to electrify.
elektro electricity.
elektroadaptilo adaptor.

elevatoro

elektrocentralo power station.
elektrodinamika electrodynamic.
elektrodinamiko electrodynamics.
elektrodinamismo electrodynamicism.
elektrodinamometro electrodynamometer.
elektrodo electrode.
elektroekzekuti to electrocute.
elektrofono record player.
elektroĥemia electrochemical.
elektroĥemie electrochemically.
elektroĥemio electrochemistry.
elektroinĝeniero electrical engineer.
elektrokemio electrochemistry.
elektrokonduktilo electrical conductor.
elektrolito electrolyte.
elektrolizi to electrolyse.
elektrolizo electrolyse.
elektromagneta electromagnetic. **elektromagneta kampo** electromagnetic field. **elektromagneta ondo** electromagnetic wave.
elektromagnete electromagnetically.
elektromagnetismo electromagnetism.
elektromagneto electromagnet.
elektromova forto electromotive force.
elektrona electronic. **elektrona mikroskopo** electron microscope.
elektronika electronic.
elektronike electronically.
elektronikisto electronics engineer.
elektroniko electronics.
elektronmikroskopo electron microscope.
elektrono electron.
elektroproduktado generation of power.
elektroskopo electroscope.
elektrostacio power station, electrical station.
elektrostatika electrostatic.
elektrostatike electrostatically.
elektrostatiko electrostatics.
elektroŝoko electric shock.
elektrotekniko electrical engineering.
elektroterapio electroshock therapy.
elektrotipo electrotype.
elekzameni to scan.
elelekto selection.
elementa elemental, elementary, primary. **elementa funkcio** elementary function. **elementa geometrio** elementary geometry. **elementa instruado** elementary education. **elementa lernejo** primary school. **elementa okazo** simple event.
elementaĵo ingredient, rudiment, element.
elemente elementally, elementarily, primarily.
elemento coefficient, element, entry.
Elenhaveno Port Ellen.
elevatoro grain elevator.

elfa

elfa elfin, elfish; (Tolkien) elvish.
elfali to crumble.
elfalo drop out.
elfandi to smelt.
elfarajo output, performance.
elfaranto performer.
elfari to accomplish, achieve, finish (off), finalize.
elfarigi to make, produce, manufacture.
elfarita accomplished, completed.
elfaro achievement.
élfeca elfin, elfish.
elfini to finish.
elflari to nose out.
elfleksiteco curvature.
elflosigi to unload, remove from a raft.
elfluejo spillway.
elflui to flow out, issue.
elfluilo drain.
elfluo outflow, spillover.
elfo elf.
elfosado excavation.
elfosajo excavation.
elfosatajo fossil.
elfosi to dig out, dig up, excavate, grub.
elfosita excavated.
Elgino Elgin.
elgutigilo colander, strainer.
elĝemi to bellow.
elhaki to cut off.
Elicinsuloj Ellice Islands.
eliga organo output device.
eligajo output data.
eligejo vent.
eligi to discharge, express, utter, output.
eligilo output device.
eligo output.
eliĝi to withdraw.
eliksiro elixir.
eliminado elimination.
elimini to eliminate, eradicate.
eliminiĝi to drop out.
elimino elimination (of unknowns).
elimo lyme grass.
elimplikaciigo modus ponens.
elingigi to draw.
Elinjo Lizzie, Liz.
Elio Elias.
elipso ellipse.
elipsoido ellipsoid.
elira duongrado demi-degree outward, out-degree.
elira karttruilo card punch.
elira kondiĉo postcondition.
elirado exodus.
elirante while doing out.
elirejo exit, way out.
eliri to come out, make one's debut, go out, exit.

ellacigi

elirigi to deprive, dismiss.
eliriĝi to come from, emerge from, arise from.
elirlagro bossing.
elirmalpermeso curfew.
eliro egress, exit, outlet, way out, exodus.
Eliro Exodus.
elirpunkto starting-point.
elirstato exit status, return status, termination code.
elirvojo exit ramp.
elita élite.
elitismo elitism.
elito elite.
elitro wing-case.
Elizabeto Elizabeth.
elizea blissful, blessed. **Elizeaj Kampoj** Champs-Élysées, Elysian Fields.
Elizeo Elysium.
elizeo paradise.
elizii to elide.
elizio elision.
eljetajo refuse, rubbish, waste, garbage, trash.
eljeti to cast out, eject, spurn, throw out, spew, spit out.
eljetiĝi to become dislodged, ejected.
eljetindajo waste.
elkarcerigi to free.
elkarceriĝi to be released from prison.
elkatenigi to free, loose, loosen.
elkavatoro excavator.
elkavigi to excavate, groove.
elkeligi to remove from the cellar, take out of the cellar.
elkestigi to unpack.
elkonduki to lead out.
elkora hearty, cordial, warm.
elkore absolutely, deeply, greatly, heartily, warmly, wholeheartedly.
elkovi to give birth to, hatch out, give rise to.
elkoviĝi to hatch.
elkrani to draw off, tap.
elkreskajo excrescence.
elkreski to sprout (bud).
elkribri to screen.
elkriptaĵo decrypt.
elkriptigi to decipher, decode, decrypt.
elkulerigi to spoon out.
elkuri to run out.
elkursigi to demonetize, divert.
elkursigo demonetizing.
ellaborado development, elaboration.
ellaborajo work, elaboration.
ellaboranto developer.
ellabori to elaborate, finish, work out (in detail), treat at length, develop.
ellacigi to fatigue, jade, overdrive, override, tire out.

ellaciĝo

ellaciĝo exhaustion.
ellasa loose.
ellasi to emit, loosen, release. **ellasi informojn** to leak information.
ellasilo trigger.
ellasita left out, omitted.
ellaso vent.
ellastruo vent hole.
ellastubo exhaust-pipe.
ellegi to peruse.
ellerni to master, learn completely.
ellerninta accomplished.
elligigi to free.
ellitiĝi to get out of bed, get up.
ellogi to draw out, elicit.
elloĝigi to evict.
elloĝigo eviction.
elloĝiĝi to move out (dwelling).
elmergiĝi to emerge.
elmetadi sin to expose oneself.
elmeti to eliminate, expose, show goods.
elmigrado emigration.
elmigranto emigrant.
elmigri to emigrate.
elmontrado manifestation.
elmontraĵo display, exhibit.
elmontrema showy.
elmontreme showily.
elmontremo showiness.
elmontri to exhibit, manifest, show, display.
elmontristo demonstrator.
elmontro display.
elmortigi to massacre.
elmortigo massacre. **elmortigo de la inocentoj** massacre of the innocents.
elmoviĝi to exit, move out, leave.
ELNA → **Esperanto-Ligo por Norda Ameriko**.
elnaĝi to flow down.
elnodiĝo denouement.
elnutri to bring up, nurture, rear (a child).
elnutrita nourished, fed.
elo ale.
elodeo waterweed, pondweed, ditchmoss.
eloficigi to depose, dismiss, oust, remove, unseat.
eloficigo deposition, dismissal, removal.
eloficiĝi to deposition.
eloficiĝo deposition.
elokventa eloquent, fluent, rhetorical.
elokvente eloquently.
elokventeco eloquence, oratory.
elokventi to be fluent.
eloviĝi to hatch.
elpagi to defray, discharge, pay (in full), pay off, redeem, settle an account.
elpago expiation.
elpaki to unpack.
elparolado pronunciation.

elreviĝo

elparoli to articulate, pronounce, enunciate, speak clearly.
elparolo pronunciation.
elpaŝi to make a statement, step out.
elpaŝo advance.
elpeli to dislodge, drive out, expel. **elpeli de la urbo** to drive out of town, run out of town. **elpeli demonojn** to drive out demons.
elpelito outcast, outlaw.
elpelo expulsion.
elpendaĵo signboard.
elpendigi to hang out, suspend.
elpensaĵo contrivance, idea, invention.
elpenseble conceivable.
elpensema innovative.
elpensemo innovativeness.
elpensemulo innovator.
elpensi to contrive, devise, think up, invent.
elpensinta thought up, thought out.
elpensinto mastermind.
elpensita invented, made up, thought out.
elpenso conception, idea, invention.
elperfidi to betray.
elpetigi to implore, invoke.
elpoenti to beat, win.
elportebla can be carried away, portable.
elporti to bear, carry out, endure, put up with, suffer.
elpoŝigi to take from the pocket.
elpremi to extort, extract, squeeze out.
elpremo exaction, extortion.
elpreni to subtract.
elproklami to proclaim to the world.
elprovi to try out, test.
elprovilo tester, touchstone.
elprovita approved, tried, well-tried.
elprovo agony.
elpumpi to pump.
elpuŝi to push aside.
elrabi to ravage.
elradii to radiate.
elradiki to root up.
elradikigi to eradicate, extirpate, uproot, root out.
elradikiĝi to become uprooted.
elregistri sin to log out.
elreligi to derail.
elreliĝi to derail, run off rails.
elreliĝo derailment.
elrenversi to tumble.
elreta offline.
elrevigi to bring someone out of a dream, bring someone back to reality, disappoint, disenchant, disillusion.
elrevigo disappointment.
elreviĝi to be disappointed, disillusioned.
elreviĝo disappointment, disenchantment, disillusionment, disillusion.

elrigardi

elrigardi to look out.
elsalti to jump out.
elsaltulo parvenu, start, upstart.
elsaluti to log out.
elsalvadora Salvadorian.
elsalvadoranino Salvadorian, Salvadorian lady, Salvadorian woman.
elsalvadorano Salvadorian.
Elsalvadoro El Salvador.
elsarkado extermination.
elsarki to weed out.
elsciado insight.
elsekigi to desicate, parch, wither.
elseligi to cast, shed, broadcast, send out, emit, transmit.
elsendado airing, broadcasting.
elsendanto broadcaster.
elsendi to broadcast.
elsendo airing, broadcast, transmission.
elserĉi to seek out.
elservigi to decommission.
elskuo shakeout.
elsorbiĝi to exude.
elspezado expenditure.
elspezi to disburse, expend, pay out, spend.
elspezo disbursement, expense, outlay, expenditure.
elspezoj expenses.
elspirado sighing.
elspiraĵo breath.
elspiri to aspirate, exhale, expire, breathe out.
elspiro aspiration.
elspiroado aspiration (breathing).
elspirtesto breath test.
elstakigi datumon to pop.
elstara outstanding. **elstara pozicio** prominent position.
elstaraĵo landmark, projection, prominence, protrusion.
elstare prominently.
elstareco brilliance, prominence.
elstari to project, protrude.
elstarulo ace.
elstera outer.
elstreki to expunge, strike out, cross out.
elsuĉi to deplete, suck out.
elsuĉo aspiration.
elsvenigi to revive, rouse.
elŝalti to turn off.
elŝeligi to hatch.
elŝipejo wharf.
elŝipiĝi to debark, disembark, land, go ashore, land.
elŝiri to tear out.
elŝiriĝi to be torn out.
elŝovi to thrust out.
elŝpruci to spurt, squirt.

elvolvanto

elŝprucigi to inject, splash, spout, spray, sprinkle, spurt, squirt.
elŝprucigilo squirt.
elŝutebla downloadable.
elŝuti to download.
elteneblo stamina.
eltenema patient.
eltenemo endurance.
elteni to abide, endure, hold out, withstand.
elterigi to dig, dig up, lift, pull up, exhume.
eltiraĵo extract.
eltiregi to extort.
eltiri to elicit, pull out, reclaim, extract.
eltirilo extractor.
eltiro pull.
eltiroaĵo extract.
eltondaĵo clipping.
eltondi to clip, cut out.
eltordi to twist off.
eltordo extortion.
eltranĉi to cut out, slope.
eltrinki to drink up.
eltrovaĵo invention.
eltrovema ingenious, inventive, resourceful.
eltroveme ingeniously, resourcefully.
eltrovemo ingenuity, resourcefulness.
eltrovi to detect, discover, invent, find out.
eltrovo discovery, invention.
eltrudi to extort.
elturniĝema elusive, resourceful, slippery, wily.
elturniĝeme resourcefully.
elturniĝemo resourcefulness.
elturniĝi to wangle, contrive, manoeuvre.
elturniĝo artifice, ruse, pretext.
eluza threadbare.
eluzi to make full use of, take advantage, use up, wear out.
eluziĝi to wear away, wear off, wear out.
eluziĝo wear.
eluzita shabby, worn out, threadbare, used up.
elvagoniĝi to get out.
elveni to come out.
elvenki to rout, trounce.
elvenko rout.
elveno outcome.
elverŝado outpouring.
elverŝi to pour out.
elvidi to survey.
elvido view.
elviŝi to obliterate.
elviŝo obliteration.
elvojiri to aberrate, go astray, stray off.
elvoka evocative.
elvoki to evoke.
elvolvaĵo expansion.
elvolvanto evolvent, involute. **elvolvanto de cirklo** evolvent of circle.

elvolvato evolute.
elvolvi to expand.
elvolviĝi to expound, open, unwind, unwrap.
Elzaco Alsace, Elsass.
elzasa Alsatian.
elzasano Alsatian.
Elzaso Alsace.
elzeviro Elzevir.
ema inclined to.
emajli to enamel.
emajlo enamel.
emancipi to emancipate.
emancipiĝi to be emancipated.
emancipiĝo emancipation.
emancipo emancipation.
emani to emanate.
embarasa cumbersome, embarrassing, troublesome, awkward.
embarasaĵo strait (difficulty).
embarasi to embarrass, encumber, hamper, perplex, inconvenience, hinder, impede.
embarasiĝi to be embarrassed, become embarrassed.
embarasita in distress.
embaraso abashment, embarrassment, perplexity, difficult situation, quandary, complication, difficulty.
embargi to embargo.
embargo embargo.
emberizo bunting.
emblemo emblem, suit (of cards), logo.
embolio blood-clot, embolism.
embolo clot.
embolozo blood-clot, embolism.
embrazuro embrasure.
embria embryonic.
embrio embryo.
embriologiisto embryologist.
embriologio embryology.
embriologo embryologist.
embuski to ambush.
embuskigi to ambush.
embusko ambuscade, ambush.
ementalo Emmental, Emmentaler.
emerĝi to emerge.
emerita retired.
emeritiĝi to retire.
emerito emeritus, ex-official, retired person, retiree, pensioner.
emetiko emetic.
emfaza emphatic.
emfaze emphatically.
emfazi to accent, accentuate, emphasize.
emfazo accent, emphasis.
emfazosigno accent, accent mark.
emfizemo emphysema.
emi to be inclined to, have a tendency to.
emigracio emigration.
emigri to emigrate.

eminenta distinguished, eminent, prominent.
eminente eminently, fine, very well.
eminenteco distinction, eminence, position, prominence, stature.
eminentularo elite.
eminentulo celebrity, distinguished personality, V.I.P., star.
emirlando emirate.
emiro emir.
emirujo emirate.
emisario emissary.
emisii to emit, issue.
emisio issue.
emo inclination, tendency, propensity.
emocia affecting, moving, touching, emotional.
emocie emotionally.
emocii to affect, move, stir.
emociiĝi to feel emotion.
emociiĝo affect.
emociita seized with emotion.
emociite moved, touched.
emocio emotion.
empeno empennage, tail unit.
empiemo empyema.
empirea empyreal, empyrean.
empireo empyrean.
empiria empirical, objective.
empirie empirically, objectively.
empiriismo empiricism, objectivism.
empiriisto empiricist, objectivist.
empirio empery.
empiriulo empirikus (ember), gyakorlatias ember.
empiro Empire style.
emulatoro emulator.
emulsino emulsin.
emulsio emulsion.
emuo emu.
en in, into, within. **en akompano de** accompanied by. **en alia maniero** differently, otherwise. **en ambaŭ okazoj** in both cases. **en certaj okazoj** on certain occasions. **en ĉeesto de** in the presence of. **en ĉiu kazo...** in any case..., in all events..., at any rate... **en ĉiu okazo** in any event. **en ĉiuj aliaj okazoj** in all other cases. **en Esperanteca maniero** in an Esperanto-like way. **en foresto** in absentia, in one's absence. **en fulma rapideco** lightning fast. **en grandaj amasoj** in great numbers. **en ia ajn ordo** in any order. **en ia maniero** in some way, in some manner, in some fashion. **en ies ĉeesto** in someone's presence. **en ies foresto** in someone's absence. **en kelkaj maloftaj okazoj** on rare occasions. **en kio** wherein. **en kiu** in which, wherein. **en kolera**

humoro in a bad mood, in an angry mood.
en konsento in (by) agreement. **en la baldaŭa estoneco** in the near future. **en la daŭro de** in a period of (time). **en la dua okazo** in the second place. **en la floro de la juneco** in the flower of youth. **en la komenco** at first, at the outset, in the beginning. **en la lasta signifo** in the latter sense. **en la mezo de** amid, among, in the middle of. **en la nomo de** in the name of. **en la okazo se** in case. **en la plej multaj okazoj** in most cases. **en la praktiko** in practice. **en la tria potenco** to the third power, cubed. **en la tuta** all over the, throughout the. **en la unua okazo** in the first place. **en la ventonta semajno** in the coming week. **en la vico de** in the ranks of. **en natura grandeco** actual size. **en naŭ el dek okazoj** nine out of ten times. **en nenatura maniero** in an unnatural way. **en okaze de** if. **en okaze de bezono** when needed. **en okazo de vera bezono** when really need, when truly necessary. **en plena korpeco** in the flesh, in person. **en preparo por** in preparation for. **en rilato kun** relative to. **en stoko** stocked. **en ŝipo** aboard. **en tago** a day. **en tio** therein. **en tiu kazo...** in that case... **en tiu relato, mi supozus...** in that connection I would suppose... **en tiu sama momento** at that very moment. **en tiu senco, oni povus diri...** in that sense you could say... **en tre maljuna aĝo** at a very young age. **en tute alia mondo** in a completely different world.
ena inside, inner. **ena operacio** internal composition law.
enabismiĝi to fall into the abyss.
enadaptiĝi ĝuste fit together.
enaera aerial, aeriform.
enakva aquatic.
enakvigi to immerse.
enakvigo immersion.
enakviĝi to immerse.
enakviĝo immersion.
enamiĝi to fall in love. **enamiĝi al** to fall in love with. **enamiĝi en** to fall in love with.
enamiĝinta enamored.
enamiĝinteco falling in love.
enanime in one's thoughts, feelings, soul.
enarĥivigi to archive.
enarkivigi to archive.
enarmeigo forced conscription.
enartikigi to set a bone.
enartrozo ball-and-socket joint.
enaŭtiĝi to get in, get into a car.
enaŭtobuse aboard.
enaŭtobusiĝi to get on the bus.
enbalzamigi to embalm.

enbankigi to bank.
enbareligi to load into a barrel.
enbati to drive in.
enblovi to blow in.
enboata onboard.
enboatiĝi to board, get on a ship.
enboteligado bottling, bottling up.
enboteligi to bottle.
enboteligo bottling, bottling up.
enbrakigi to hug.
enbruste in one's chest.
enbuse aboard.
enbusiĝi to get on the bus.
enbuŝaĵo bit (horse).
enbuŝe inarticulately.
enbuŝigi to put in one's mouth.
encefalito encephalitis.
encefalo encephalon.
encefalogramo encephalogram.
encefalopatio encephalopathy.
encerbigi to inculcate.
encikliko encyclical.
enciklopedia encyclopaedic.
enciklopedio encyclopaedia.
enĉenigi to chain.
enĉifri to encipher, encode.
endanĝerigi to endanger.
endanĝerita specio endangered species.
endemia endemic.
endemie endemically.
endemio endemic.
endi to be compulsory.
endigi to embank.
endigigi to embank.
endivio endive.
endogamio endogamy.
endokardio endocardium.
endokardo endocardium.
endokarpo endocarp.
endokiĝi to dock.
endokrina endocrine.
endoma indoor.
endomadi to keep someone indoors.
endome indoors.
endomorfio endomorphism.
endoplasmo endoplasm.
endormiĝi to fall asleep, go to sleep.
endormiĝo Dormition.
endoskopio endoscopy.
endoskopo endoscope.
endosmozo endosmosis.
endoterma endothermic.
ene inside, within.
Eneado Aeneid.
Eneido Aeneid.
eneliga dosiero I/O file.
eneligo I/O, input-output.
enen inwards.
enen-klavo Enter key.

Eneo Aeneas.
energetiko energy, energetics.
energia energetic, strenuous.
energi-dependa memoro volatile memory.
energie energetically.
energiemulo hustler.
energifonto energy source.
energi-nedependa memoro non-volatile memory.
energio energy, spirit.
enestanto occupant.
enesti to be inside, be enclosed or contained.
enfali to cave in, fall in.
enfalo drop in.
enfalujo pitfall, trap, snare.
enfendiĝi to fall into a rift or crack.
enfermi to confine, enclose, put away, stow, pen.
enfermito inmate.
enfiksi to embed, implant.
enfiksitaĵo implant.
enfili to enfilade, rake, strafe.
enflari to sniff.
enfluejo mouth.
enflui to pour in.
enfluo mouth (of river).
enfokusigi to focus.
enfosi to bury.
Engadino Engadin.
engaĝi to engage, involve.
engaĝiĝi to become involved.
engaĝiĝo engagement, involvement.
engaĝo assignment.
engla Anglian.
englavingi to sheath (a sword).
englo Angle.
englosaksa Anglo-Saxon.
engluteco voracity.
englutema ravenous, voracious.
engluti to engulf, swallow up, gulp.
engraŭlo anchovy.
engrunda below-ground.
enhavebleco capacity, tonnage.
enhaveco capacity, tonnage.
enhaveniĝi to come into port, dock.
enhavi to comprise, contain, include, hold.
enhavigi to store (something in something).
enhavmarko label.
enhavo assets, contents, property.
enhejma at home.
enhejmi at home.
enhorarigi to schedule.
enhospitaligi to hospitalize.
enhospitaligo hospitalization.
eniga organo input device.
enigaĵo input data.
enigi to put in, insert, enter, input.
enigilo input device.
enigma enigmatic.

enigme obscurely, enigmatically.
enigmeco enigmatic character, mysteriousness.
enigmo enigma, puzzle, riddle.
enigo ingress, put, input.
eniĝi to get in, enter, insert, put in.
enimpeto irruption.
eningigi to nest.
enira duongrado demi-degree inward, in-degree.
enira kondiĉo precondition.
enirbileto admission ticket.
enirejo entrance, portal, entry.
eniri to enter, go in. **eniri ĉe** to call at someone's house, call on.
enirigi to let in.
enirkarto admission pass.
eniro access, admission, admittance.
enirpago admission, admission fee.
enirŝakto access shaft.
enirvojo entrance ramp.
Enistimo Ennistimon.
enjekcia injective.
enjekcio injection.
enjetiĝi to be injected.
enkadraĵo panel.
enkadrigi to frame.
enkadrigo incorporation.
enkaĝigi to cage, confine, encage.
enkalkuli to take into account, allow for.
enkanonigi to canonize.
enkapigi to get into one's head.
enkapiĝi al iu to come to someone's mind, enter someone's head, occur to someone.
enkapsuligo encapsulation, hiding.
enkapti to capture, entangle.
enkarcerigi to imprison.
enkarcerigo imprisonment.
enkarnigi to embody.
enkarnigo embodiment.
enkarniĝo incarnation.
enkasigi to encase, pay in, take in, collect.
enkasigisto bank messenger.
enkatenigi to restrain, fetter, shackle, handcuff.
enkaviĝi to penetrate.
enkaviĝinta hollow.
enketi to inquire, investigate, make an inquiry, survey.
enketisto coroner, investigator, magistrate.
enketo inquiry, investigation, survey.
enklasigi to classify.
enklavo enclave.
enklitiko enclitic.
enkodigi to encode.
enkonduka introductory.
enkonduki to introduce.
enkonduko introduction, forward, preface.
enkonstrui to build in.

enkonstruita

enkonstruita built-in.
enkorpigi to embody.
enkorpigo embodiment.
enkorpiĝi to impersonate.
enkorpiĝo incarnation.
enkrasikolo anchovy.
enkrusti to encrust, incrust.
enkudriligi fadenon to thread a needle.
enkulturigi to inculturate.
enkulturiĝo inculturation.
enkursigilo router.
enkursigo routing.
enladigejo cannery.
enladigi to can (food, etc.).
enlanda aboriginal, domestic, indigenous, native.
enlandano inhabitant, native.
enlandulo aboriginal.
enlasejo intake.
enlasi to leave inside.
enlaso admission, admittance.
enlistigi to list.
enlitigi to put to bed.
enlitiĝa horo bedtime.
enlitiĝi to go to bed.
enlitiĝtempo bedtime.
enlogi to lure in.
enloĝado indwelling.
enloĝantaro inhabitants, people.
enloĝanto inhabitant.
enloĝebla habitable.
enloĝejo accommodation, residence, place where one is staying.
enloĝi to inhabit, move in (dwelling).
enloĝigi to accommodate.
enloĝigo accommodation.
enloĝiĝi to settle in, take up residence.
enmagazenigi to store.
enmane in hand.
enmanigi to hand something to someone, put something in someone's hand. **enmanigi ion al iu** to put something in someone's hand.
enmarĉiĝi to sink.
enmare in the ocean.
enmemorigi to store.
enmenti to enclose.
enmeta adreso load address.
enmetaĵo enclosure.
enmeti to insert, put in, put away, stow, deposit.
enmeto inclusion, introduction.
enmetu insert.
enmigrado immigration.
enmigranto immigrant.
enmigri to immigrate.
enmigrinto immigrant.

enrompo

enmiksi to mix in, embroil. **enmiksi sin en ion** to get involved in something, get tangled up in something.
enmiksigi to tangle (entangle).
enmiksiĝema meddlesome.
enmiksiĝemo meddlesomeness.
enmiksiĝemulo busybody, meddler.
enmiksiĝi to intermeddle, meddle. **enmiksiĝi en** to interfere with. **enmiksiĝi pri** to tamper.
enmiksiĝo interference, involvement.
enmiksiigi to shuffle (cards).
enmurigi to wall.
eno yen.
enoficado incumbency.
enoficanto incumbent.
enoficigi to appoint, inaugurate, commission.
enoficigo appointment, appointment to office.
enoficiĝi to install.
enoficiĝo accession.
enokulumi to peek in.
enordigi to arrange, put in sequence.
enorma enormous.
enorme enormously.
enotero evening primrose.
enpaĝigo lay-out.
enpaki to pack, package, wrap up.
enpeli to drive into.
enpenetri to invade, overrun.
enpiki to stab, sting, puncture.
enplanti to implant.
enplekti to introduce, entwine.
enporti to bring in, import.
enporto introduction.
enpoŝigi to pocket, put something in one's pocket.
enpoŝtigi to post, mail.
enpoziciigo positioning, seek.
enpremi to push in.
enpreni to take along.
enpresaĵo insertion.
enpresi to insert (print).
enprizonigi to jail, imprison, incarcerate.
enprizonigo imprisonment.
enpuŝi to thrust.
enradiki to implant, inculcate, take root.
enradikigi to implant, inculcate.
enradikiĝi to root, strike.
enradikita inveterate.
enregistri sin to log in.
enregistrigi to register.
enreta on-line.
enrete on-line.
enretigo round-up.
enrigardo glance.
enritigi to ritualize.
enrompo break-in, burglary.

ensakigi

ensakigi to bag.
ensaluti to log in.
enscenigi to present, stage, direct.
enseliĝi to mount up.
ensemado sowing.
ensemblo ensemble.
ensemi to instil, sow.
enskribi to enter, inscribe, register.
enskribigi to register.
enskribigo entry.
enskribita inscribed.
enskribo record.
ensorbado assimilation, digestion.
ensorbi to absorb.
ensorbiĝi to absorb.
ensorĉi to bewitch, delude, fascinate.
ensorĉiga enchanting.
ensorĉige enchantingly.
ensorĉo bewitchment, delusion, spell, enchantment, fascination.
enspaci to fill, take up, occupy.
enspermigi to inseminate.
enspermigo insemination.
enspezi to receive, take in.
enspezimposto income tax.
enspezo income, revenue, proceeds.
enspezoj income, receipts.
enspiri to inhale, inspire.
enspiro inspiration (breath).
enstaligi to stable.
enstampado stamping.
enstampi to stamp.
enŝalti to turn on.
enŝipe aboard, on board. **enŝipe de** aboard.
enŝipi to take on board (a ship).
enŝipigejo pier, wharf.
enŝipigi to ship.
enŝipiĝi to embark, go aboard, go on board.
enŝipiĝinta aboard (a ship).
enŝlimiĝi to wallow, welter.
enŝlosi to lock up, shut up.
enŝlosita locked in.
enŝovi to insert, shove in.
enŝoviĝi to worm.
enŝprucigi to inject.
enŝprucigilo syringe.
enŝteliĝi to creep in.
entabeligi to tabulate.
entabeligo tabulation.
entablemento entablature.
Entempligo Presentation.
entenaĵo contents.
enteni to hold, contain.
enteriga burial. **enteriga entreprenisto** mortician, undertaker. **enteriga entrepreno** undertaker's business.
enterigejo cemetery, graveyard.
enterigi to inter, bury.
enterigiro funeral.

enumeracio

enterigo burial, funeral, interment.
enteriĝi to be buried.
enteriĝo burial.
enterito enteritis.
enterolito enterolith.
enterpreni konversacion to make conversation.
entiri to draw, pull.
entjera integer, integral. **entjera parto** integer part, integral part.
entjeriko number theory.
entjero integral number, integer.
ento entity.
entombigi to bury, entomb, inter.
entombigo burial, funeral, interment.
entomologiisto entomologist.
entomologio entomology.
entomologo entomologist.
entordita hernio strangulated hernia.
entranĉi to cut into, engrave.
entranĉo engraving, cutting into.
entreprena aktivado trade and industry.
entreprenaro trade and industry.
entrepreneca enterprising.
entreprenece enterprisingly.
entreprenema enterprising.
entrepreneme enterprisingly.
entreprenemo entrepreneurship.
entrepreni to undertake (take it upon oneself to do).
entreprenisto contractor, entrepreneur.
entrepreno enterprise, undertaking.
entropio entropy.
entrudiĝi to intrude.
entrudiĝo incursion, infringement.
entrudinto intruder.
entuta overall.
entute altogether, as a whole, on the whole, in short.
entuziasma enthusiastic, rapt.
entuziasme eagerly, enthusiastically.
entuziasmega lyrical.
entuziasmi to be enthusiastic about something.
entuziasmiga rousing.
entuziasmigi to enthuse, inspire.
entuziasmo alacrity, enthusiasm,.
entuziasmulo enthusiast.
enua boring, weary, wearisome, tiresome.
enui to be bored, be tired, be weary, bother, pester, tire.
enuiga boring, stodgy, wearisome, irksome.
enuige tiring, boring.
enuigi to bore, harass, worry, vex.
enuigita bored.
enuigo making tired, making bored.
enuiĝi to get bored.
enuklei to enucleate.
enumeracio enumerated type.

enuo annoyance, boredom, worry, weariness.
enurezo bed wetting, enuresis.
envagone aboard.
envejna intravenous.
envelopo envelope.
enveni to come in, enter.
envenigi to bring.
enveno entrance.
enverguro wingspan.
enverŝi to pour in.
enveturejo driveway.
enveturi to drive in.
envia envious.
enviciĝi to fall in, fall into line, form up, line up, rank (among), be in a list of.
envie enviously.
enviema envious.
envieme enviously.
envii to envy.
enviinda enviable.
envio envy.
envolvaĵo envelope.
envolvi to envelop, muffle, swathe.
envulti to put a hex on, hoodoo, voodoo.
enzimo enzyme.
Eoceno Eocene.
eola Aeolian.
eolia Aeolian.
eoliano Aeolian.
Eolio Aeolia.
Eolo Aeolus.
eono con.
Eoso Eos.
eosto east.
eozino eosin.
epakto epact.
eparĥiestro eparch.
eparĥio eparchy.
eparkiestro eparch.
eparkio diocese.
ependimo ependyma.
eperlano smelt.
epicikloido epicycloid.
epidemia epidemic.
epidemio epidemic.
epidermo epidermis.
epidiaskopo overhead projector.
Epifanio Epiphany, Twelfth-night.
epifito epiphyte.
epifizo epiphysis.
epigastro epigastrium.
epigloto epiglottis.
Epigono Epigonus.
epigono epigone, successor, descendant.
epigrafo epigraph, inscription.
epigramo epigram.
epikarpo epicarp.
epikura epicurean.
epikurano epicure, epicurean.
epikurisma epicurean.
epikurismo Epicureanism, Epicurism.
epikuristo epicure.
Epikuro Epicure.
epilepsia epileptic.
epilepsio epilepsy.
epilepsiulo epileptic (person).
epilobio willowherb.
epilogo epilog, epilogue.
epimedio epimedium.
epinefrino adrenaline, epinephrine.
epiornito aepyornis.
epipakto helleborine.
epipogio ghost orchis.
episkopa Episcopal. **episkopa bastono** crosier. **episkopa moŝto** monsignor.
episkopara Episcopal.
episkoparo episcopate.
episkopeco episcopacy.
episkopejo diocese, episcopate.
episkoplando diocese.
episkopo bishop, prelate.
episkopujo bishopric, diocese.
epistemologia epistemological.
epistemologio epistemology.
epistolo epistle, letter.
epistrofo axis.
epitafo epitaph.
epitelio epithelium.
epiteto epithet.
epitomigi to abridge.
epitomo epitome, abridgement.
epitroĥoido epitrochoid.
epitrokoido epitrochoid.
epizoda episodal, incidental.
epizodo episode, occurrence, event.
epizootio epizootic.
epoĥo epoch, era, period.
epokfara epoch-making.
epoko age, epoch, era, period.
epokspirito spirit of the age, spirit of the time, zeitgeist.
epoleto epaulet, epaulette.
epopea epic.
epopeo epic, epic poem.
eposa epic.
eposo primitive narrative poetry.
epriskribebla indescribable.
epriskribeble indescribably.
epsilono epsilon (Εε).
erantido wolfsbane.
erao era.
erara erratic, erroneous, mistaken, wrong.
eraralmeti to misapply.
eraranta wandering.
erare by mistake, erratically, erroneously, mistakenly.
erarego blunder.
erarema errant, fallible.

erari

erari to err, make a mistake, go astray, wander.
erariga deceptive, delusive, fallacious.
erarigi to mislead, mislay.
erariĝi to stray, go astray.
erarkompreni to misapprehend, mistake, misunderstand.
erarkredi to fancy.
erarlumo ignis fatuus, will-o'-the-wisp.
erarmesaĝo error diagnostics, error message.
eraro aberration, error, mistake, erratum, fault.
erarpaŝo aberration.
erarserĉilo debugger.
erarvaga stray.
erarvagi to go astray, stray.
erarvojo the wrong way.
Eratostena kribrilo Eratosthenes' Sieve.
erbino erbia, erbium oxide.
erbio erbium.
erco ore.
erekti to erect.
erektiĝi to become erect.
erektiĝo erection.
erektive actually.
ergo erg.
ergonomia ergonomic.
ergonomio ergonomics.
ergotino ergotine.
ergoto ergot.
erigerono fleabane.
erikejo heath, moor.
eriko heath, heather (plant).
erinacedoj hedgehogs (family).
erinaco hedgehog.
eringio eryngo.
Erino Erin.
Erio Lake Erie, Lake Eyre.
erioforo cotton grass.
erisipelo erysipelas.
Eriskajo Eriskay.
Eriso Eris.
Eritreo Eritrea.
erizimo treacle mustard.
erizipelo erysipelas.
Ermelo Ermelo.
ermenfelo ermine (fur).
ermeno ermine (animal).
ermitejo hermitage.
ermitludo solitaire.
ermito hermit, recluse.
ero[1] element, fragment, item, particle, item, unit, piece, grain, component.
ero[2] era.
eroda abrasive.
erodi to wear down, wear off, wear out.
erodio stork's-bill.
erodo erosion.

eskarpo

erofilo common whitlow-grass.
erospaco aerospace.
erotika erotic.
erotike erotically.
erotiki to act erotically.
erotomanio erotomania.
erozii to erode.
erozio erosion.
erpado harrowing.
erpebla arable.
erpi to harrow, rake, till, plough.
erpilo harrow.
erudi to educate, enlighten.
erudicia scholarly.
erudicio erudition, scholarship.
erudiciulo erudite person, scholar.
erudito guru, scholar.
eruidiciulo learned one.
eruko rocket.
erupcii to erupt.
erupcio eruption, rash.
erupti to erupt.
erupto eruption.
esameno swarm of bees.
escepta exceptional. **escepta raportado** exception reporting.
escepte apart from, but, except, other than, except, by way of exception. **escepte de** with the exception of.
escepti to except, exclude.
esceptinte with the exception of. **esceptinte ke** unless.
escepto exception, exclusion.
esceptokaze apart from, aside from, but, except, exceptionally, other than, except in the case but.
eseisto essayist.
esenca essential.
esence basically, essentially, inherently, innately, intrinsically.
esenceco essentiality, inherence.
esenco essence, gist, substance.
eseo essay.
Eŝilo Aeschylus.
eskadro squadron (naval).
eskadrono squadron.
eskaladi to climb, scale.
eskalado climb, escalation.
eskalatoro escalator.
eskali to scale (walls, etc.).
eskalo ladder.
eskalopo escalope, scallop.
eskapi to escape, flee.
eskapisma escapist.
eskapismo escapism.
eskapklavo escape key.
eskapo escape.
eskapsigno escape character.
eskarpo escarp, escarpment.

eskima Eskimo, Inuit.
eskimo Eskimo, Inuit.
Eskineso Aeschines.
eskortanto escort.
eskorti to escort.
eskorto escort.
eskudo escudo.
Eskulapo Aesculapius.
eskviro equerry, squire.
esotera esoteric.
esotere esoterically.
esoterismo esotericism.
espanjoleto espagnolette, window catch.
esparto esparto, esparto-grass.
esperantaĵoj Esperanto things.
esperante hoping.
esperanteca Esperanto-like.
esperantigi to Esperantize, turn into Esperanto.
esperantigo Esperanto localization.
esperantiĝi to become an Esperantist.
esperantismo Esperantism.
esperantista Esperantist.
esperantistaro all Esperantists, the "Esperanto World".
esperantistino Esperantist (female).
esperantisto Esperantist.
esperantlingva in Esperanto, Esperanto-language.
Esperanto Esperanto. **Esperanto-Ligo por Norda Ameriko** Esperanto League for North America.
esperanto optimist.
Esperantolando Esperanto-land.
esperantologiisto esperantologist.
esperantologio Esperantology.
esperantologo esperantologist.
Esperantujo Esperanto-land.
esperantumi to do the Esperanto thing, spend time with Esperanto.
esperdona hopeful, promising.
espere in a hopeful way.
espereble hopefully.
esperema hopeful.
esperemulo hopeful person.
esperi to hope.
esperiga hopeful, promising.
esperigi to give hope to.
espero hope.
esperplena sanguine.
esplanado esplanade.
esplora scientific, exploratory, research.
esplorada exploratory.
esplorado exploration, research, investigation.
esploranto explorer.
esplordemandi to interrogate, question.

esplori to examine, explore, investigate, prospect, research, study, survey. **esplori la pacienton** to examine the patient.
Esplorilo Internet Explorer.
esploristo explorer.
esploro exploration, investigation, research.
esplorvojaĝisto explorer, prospector.
espozi to demonstrate, exhibit, expose, showcase, display.
esprimante expressing.
esprimi to express, state. **esprimi penson** to express a thought. **esprimi sin** to express oneself.
esprimilo expressive means, feature.
esprimo expression.
esprimplena expressive.
esprimplene expressively.
esprimpleneco expressiveness.
esprimriĉa expressive.
establi to erect, establish.
establiĝi to become established.
establo establishment.
estado being, entity, existence, stay.
estafeto courier, dispatch-rider, relay, relay racer, relay rider, runner.
estaĵo being, creature, entity.
estanta tempo present time.
estante (while) being, when one was.
estanteco present (time).
estejo abode.
estero ester.
Estero Estero.
estetika aesthetic.
estetike aesthetically.
estetiko aesthetics.
estetikulo aesthete.
estezo aesthesia.
esti to be. **esti adepto de** to adhere to. **esti angilglata** to be as slippery as an eel. **esti bona kontraŭ iu** to be good to someone. **esti bone nutrita** to be well-fed, well nourished. **esti bonhava** to be in easy circumstances, be well off, be well-to-do. **esti bonŝanca** to be lucky, have good luck. **esti certa je tio** to be certain of that. **esti ĉe la limo de sia pacienco** to be at the end of one's patience. **esti de la skolo** to be of a school of thought. **esti deponita** to be deposited, be in the keeping, rest. **esti domaĝo** to be a pity, to be a shame. **esti ebla** to be possible. **esti en bonaj manoj** to be in good hands. **esti en bono sano** to be in good health. **esti en la kaĉo** to be in a mess. **esti en ŝercema humoro** to be in a joking mood. **esti eraro diri** to be incorrect to say. **esti grava** to signify (to matter). **esti kapabla je ĉio** to be capable of anything. **esti konforma** to be correct, be right. **esti konforma al** to answer,

estigi

answer to, come up to. **esti konforma laŭ** to correspond to. **esti konsiderata** to be considered, count. **esti la plena potreto de** to be the picture of. **esti laŭ** to correspond to. **esti laŭmezura** to fit. **esti malaj unu al la alia** to be opposites (of each other). **esti malbonŝanca** to have bad luck. **esti maldungata iom post iom** to be discharged gradually. **esti malfermetita** to be ajar. **esti malsana** be sick. **esti maniulo** to be addicted. **esti menciinde ke...** to be worth mentioning that... **esti parenco de** to be related to. **esti pli forta ol** to be able to match with, be stronger than. **esti preskaŭ** to abut (on) to. **esti pura de peko** to be free from sin. **esti samaĝa kiel** to be the same age as. **esti samnivela kun** to keep abreast of. **esti simila al** to be similar to. **esti sklaviĝinta** to be addicted. **esti ŝparema pri** to be sparing with. **esti traktata kiel** to be treated as. **esti unu el** to belong to, be one of. **esti vere ke...** to be true that... **estas vere ke...** admittedly... **estis necese, ke mi...** I had to... **estu** should be. **estu kiel estos** whatever will be, will be. **estus plej bone, se** it would be better if.
estigi to bring into being, develop, make, create.
estiginto creator, originator.
estigo creation.
estiĝi to arise, come into being.
estiĝo commencement, start.
estimado estimation.
estimata dear, esteemed. **Estimata Sinjoro** Dear Sir.
estimebla reputable.
estimi to esteem, think well of, have esteem for, respect, regard.
estiminda estimable, respectable, worthy.
estimo esteem, regard, respect.
estingado extinction.
estingaparato fire-extinguisher.
estingi to extinguish, put out, put out, quench.
estingiĝi to go out (of a light).
estingiĝo extinguishing, extinction.
estingilo extinguisher.
estingita extinct.
estingkamiono fire truck.
estingo extinction.
estinta former, past.
estinteco past.
estinto past.
esto being, entity.
estona Estonian.
estonino Estonian woman.
Estonio Estonia.

etendo

estono Estonian.
estonta future, about to be, prospective.
estontece hereafter.
estonteco future.
estonto future, hereafter.
Estonujo Estonia.
estra bastonego mace, baton.
estrado platform, stage.
estrarano board member.
estrarejo boardroom.
estraro board of directors, staff, authority, authorities.
estre as a leader.
estreco authority.
estrema bossy, masterful.
estri to govern, head up, restrain. **estri unu lingvon** to master a language.
estrino matron, mistress.
estro boss, chief, leader, manager, head.
estrogeno oestrogen.
estuario estuary.
estuaro estuary.
estulo being, creature.
eŝafodo scaffold (for hangings, executions).
eta tiny. **eta kriaglo** lesser spotted eagle. **eta mono** small change, coins.
etaĝero set of shelves.
etaĝo floor, storey, story.
etalono benchmark.
etanima petty, small-minded.
etanime petty, small-minded.
etanimeco pettiness, small-mindedness.
etano ethane.
etanolo ethanol.
etao eta (Hη).
etapo period, stage, phase, distance covered, halting place, length covered, stage, stopover, lap.
etato account, inventory, report, list, register, return (financial), statement (financial), table (data).
etbienulo yeoman.
etburĝa lower class.
etburĝaro petty bourgeoisie.
etburĝo petit bourgeois.
etenda adresado extended addressing.
etendaĵo extension.
etendebla ductile, malleable.
etendebleco ductility.
etendeblo extensibility.
etendeco expanse.
etendi to extend, stretch out, expand. **etendi la manojn al** to reach for.
etendiĝi to run. **etendiĝi antaŭen** to reach forward.
etendiĝo expansion, extend, extension, reach.
etendilo extension.
etendo extension.

etera

etera ethereal.
eterizi to anaesthetize.
eterna endless, eternal, everlasting, perpetual.
eterne forever, eternally.
eterneco eternity.
eternfloro everlasting.
eterno eternity.
Eternulo Lord.
etero ether.
eterreto Ethernet.
etfingro little finger.
etflora small-flowered.
etigi to belittle, shrink, dwarf.
etika ethical.
etike ethically.
etikedi to label, tag.
etikedo label, tag. **etikedo de HTML** HTML tag.
etiketo code of conduct, etiquette, protocol, rules of behaviour; label, tag.
etiko ethic, ethics, morals.
etileno ethylene.
etilo ethyl.
etimo etymon.
etimologia etymological.
etimologie etymologically.
etimologiisto etymologist.
etimologio etymology.
etimologo etymologist.
etindustrio small industry.
etinvestanto small investor.
etiologiisto aetiologist.
etiologio etiology.
etiologo aetiologist.
etiopa Ethiopian.
etiopino Ethiopian woman.
Etiopio Abyssinia, Ethiopia.
etiopo Abyssinian, Ethiopian.
Etiopujo Abyssinia, Ethiopia.
etkuraĝa pusillanimous.
etlitero lower case letter, minuscule, small letter.
etmakleristo small-time broker.
etmoido ethmoid bone.
etna ethnic. **etna dialekto** ethnic dialect.
etnika ethnic.
etnike ethnically.
etnismo ethnism.
Etno Etna.
etno ethnos, ethnic group.
etnogenezo ethnogenesis.
etnografiisto ethnographer.
etnografio ethnography.
etnografo ethnographer.
etnologiisto ethnologist.
etnologio ethnology.
etnologo ethnologist.
eto eta (Ηη).

Eŭropo

etologio ethology.
etoso atmosphere, environment, ethos, mood.
etosplena atmospheric.
etrioskopo aethrioscope.
etruska Etrurian, Etruscan.
Etruskio Etruria.
etrusko Etrurian, Etruscan.
Etruskujo Etruria.
etskala small scale.
etspirita petty, small-minded.
etudo etude, study, sketch.
etulino tot, little girl.
etullernejo nursery school.
etulo little fellow, little one.
europa European.
eŭdiometrio eudiometry.
eŭdiometro eudiometer.
eŭfemisma euphemistic.
eŭfemisme euphemistically.
eŭfemismo euphemism.
eŭfonio euphony.
eŭforbio spurge.
eŭforio euphoria.
Eŭfrato Euphrates.
eŭfrazio eyebright.
eŭgeniko eugenics.
eŭgenio allspice tree.
Eŭharistio Eucharist.
eŭkalipto eucalyptus, jarrah.
eŭkaristia eucharistic.
eŭkaristio Eucharist.
Eŭkaristo Eucharist.
eŭklida Euclidean. **eŭklida algoritmo** Euclid algorithm. **eŭklida divido** division with remainder. **eŭklida geometrio** Euclidean geometry. **eŭklida ringo** Euclidean ring. **eŭklida spaco** Euclidean space.
Eŭklido Euclid.
eŭlera Euler, Eulerian. **eŭlera cirklo** Euler circle, nine-point circle. **eŭlera rekto** Euler line.
Eŭlero Euler.
eŭnuko eunuch.
eŭpatorio thoroughwort.
eŭrazia cervo red deer.
Eŭrazio Eurasia.
eŭro euro.
eŭroo euro.
Eŭropa European. **Eŭropa bizono** European bison, wisent. **Eŭropa cifero** European digit. **Eŭropa Esperanto-Unio** European Esperanto Union, EEU. **Eŭropa evonimo** common spindle, European spindle (tree). **Eŭropa Unio** European Union.
Eŭropano European.
eŭropio europium.
Eŭropo Europe.

eŭroskeptika eurosceptic.
eŭroskeptikulo eurosceptic.
eŭska Basque.
eŭsko Basque.
eŭtamio chipmunk.
eŭtanazio euthanasia.
Eva Eve.
evakui to evacuate.
evakuiĝi to be evacuated.
evakuo evacuation.
evangelia evangelic, evangelical.
evangeliano evangelical.
evangeliisto evangelist.
evangelikredo belief in the Gospel.
evangelilibro book of Gospels.
Evangelio gospel.
evangelizado evangelization.
evangelizanto evangelizer.
evangelizi to evangelize.
eventaro programme.
evento event.
eventuala contingent, eventual.
eventuale if the occasion arises.
eventualeco potential.
eventualo contingency, eventuality.
Everesto Everest.
Evergreno Evergreen.
evidenta evident, obvious, manifest, unmistakable, clear.
evidentaĵo something obvious.
evidente apparently, obviously, evidently.
evidenteco evidence, obviousness.
evidentigi to manifest.
evidentiĝi to become evident.
evikcii to evict.
evikcio appropriation.

evitado shirking.
evitanto shirker.
evitebla avoidable, preventable.
evitema cautious, evasive, noncommittal, oblique.
eviteme cautiously.
eviti to avoid, evade, eschew, keep aloof, shirk, shun.
evitigi to ward, turn aside.
evitilo loophole.
evitinda to be avoided.
evito avoidance.
Evo Eva.
evolua evolutionary.
evoluada evolutionary.
evoluado development, evolution.
evolucia evolutionary.
evolucii to evolve.
evoluciismo evolutionism.
evoluciisto evolutionist.
evolucio development, evolution.
evolui to develop, evolve.
evoluigi to develop, direct.
evoluintaj landoj developed countries.
evoluismo evolutionism, theory of evolution.
evolulando developing country, developing nation.
evoluo development, evolution.
evoluto evolute.
evolvento evolvent, involute.
evonimo euonymus, spindle-tree.
e-vorto adverb.
ezofago esophagus, gullet.
ezoko pike (fish).
Ezopo Aesop.
ezotera esoteric.

F

fabansero bean goose.
fabela fabulous.
fabelaro book of fairy tales.
fabelaŭtoro fabulist.
fabele fabulously.
fabelisto fabulist.
fabelo bedtime story, fairy tale, story, tale.
fabelverkisto fabulist.
fabla fabulous.
fablisto fabulist.
fablo fable.
fabloverkisto fabulist.
fabo bean, broad bean, fava bean.
fabostango beanpole.
fabotrunko beanstalk.
fabrika marko brand name.
fabrikado fabrication, making, manufacture.
fabrikejo factory, works.
fabriki to fabricate, manufacture.
fabrikinto maker.
fabrikista prezo recommended price.
fabrikisto manufacturer.
fabriklaboristo shop worker.
fabriklaboro factory work.
fabriko fabric, factory, manufacture.
facetaĵo flake.
faceti to facet.
faceto facet.
facila easy, facile.
facilanima flighty, impulsive, light-hearted, flippant, frivolous.
facilanimaĵo frivolity.
facilanime airily.
facilanimeco flippancy, light-mindedness, frivolity.
facile easily. **facile farite** easily done, piece of cake.
facileco ease, facility.
faciligaĵoj accommodation.
faciliganto facilitator.
faciligi to make easy, facilitate.
faciligo ease.
faciliĝi to ease.
facilkomprenebla for obvious reasons, understandably.
facilmova agile.
facilmoveco agility.
facilo facility.
facilpieda easy-going.
facilriska overconfident.
facilrompa brittle, fragile.
facilrompebla fragile.
faco face.
fadenaro skein.
fadenbulo thread ball, yarn ball.

fadendrapa worsted.
fadendrapo worsted.
fadenero ply, strand.
fadenfasko hank, skein.
fadenglobo ball of string.
fadenigi to draw into a thread.
fadenisto haberdasher.
fadenmontra threadbare.
fadeno strand, thread.
fadenpupo marionette.
fadensekura thread-safe.
fadenvolvaĵo ball of thread.
fadi to fade.
fado fading.
faduo fado.
faetono phaeton.
Faetono Phaeton.
Fafno Fafnir, Fafner.
faga ligno beech, beech wood.
fagaro beech forest, beech grove.
fagejo beech forest, beech grove.
fago beech (tree).
fagocito phagocyte.
fagofrukto beech nut.
fagonukso beech nut.
fagopiro buckwheat.
fagoto bassoon.
fajencaĵo china, faience.
fajenco crockery, earthenware, pottery.
fajfado whistling.
fajfanaso wigeon.
fajfi to whistle.
fajfilego fog horn.
fajfilo whistle.
fajfo whistle, toot.
fajfosignalo por ludokomenco a whistle signal to begin the game.
fajfspiri to wheeze.
fajlaĵo filing.
fajli to file (down).
fajlilo file (tool).
fajna fine.
fajne finely.
fajneco fineness.
fajnigi to refine.
fajo faille.
fajra burning, fiery.
fajraĵo fireworks.
fajrejo hearth, fireplace.
fajreri to spark, sparkle.
fajrero spark.
fajrestingilo fire extinguisher.
fajrestingistino firewoman.
fajrestingisto fireman.
fajrfungo tinder.

fajrgardo fender.
fajri to burn.
fajrigi to ignite, kindle, light. **fajrigi la cigaredon** to light the cigarette.
fajrilo lighter.
fajrincitilo poker.
fajro fire, ardor, enthusiasm, fervor.
fajroalarmo fire-alarm.
fajrobapto baptism by fire, baptism of fire.
fajrobirdo firebird, phoenix.
fajrobrigadano fire fighter.
fajrobrigadejo firehouse.
fajrobrigadisto firefighter, fireman.
fajrobrigado fire brigade.
fajrobulo fireball.
fajrodanĝero risk of fire.
fajroestingilo fire extinguisher.
fajrofarilo lighter.
fajrokraĉisto fire eater.
fajrokrano fire-plug.
Fajrolando Tierra del Fuego.
fajrolilio orange lily, fire lily.
fajrolumo firelight.
fajromuro firewall.
fajroplanto dittany.
fajroprenilo fire tongs.
fajroprovo acid test.
fajropumpilo fire engine.
fajrorezista fire-resistant.
fajroruĝa fire-red.
fajrostango poker.
fajroŝirmilo fender.
fajrprenilo fire tongs.
fajrŝtono brick (fire).
fajrujo brasier, firebox, grate, hearth, fireplace, firebox.
faka specialized, departmental.
fakaro file(s), pigeonholes.
fakcio faction.
fakdelegito special delegate
fakego compartment (train).
fakestro head of a department.
faketaro pigeon-hole (for papers, etc.).
fakiro fakir.
fakista unuiĝo trade union.
fakisto specialist.
fa-klefo bass clef (𝄢).
faklernejo special school.
faklibro technical book.
fako area of expertise, branch, compartment, department, section, speciality, subject, discipline.
fakoĉero warthog.
fakoĥero warthog.
faksaado fax.
faksaĵo fax.
fakseno minnow.
faksi to fax.
faksilo fax machine.

faksimila redaktado WYSIWYG, what you see is what you get.
faksimilo facsimile.
faksnumero fax number.
fakso fax message.
fakta actual, factual, real. **fakta adreso** actual address, effective address, machine address. **fakta parametro** actual parameter.
fakte actually, as a matter of fact, indeed, in fact.
faktermino technical term.
faktitiva factitive.
faktitivo causative, factitivity.
fakto fact.
faktoreca factorial.
faktorgrupo factor group, quotient group.
faktorialo factorial.
faktorio (trading) agency.
faktoro agent, factor, steward.
fakturado billing.
fakturi to invoice.
fakturo account, bill, invoice.
fakularano panelist.
fakularo panel.
fakulo expert, specialist.
fakultatano faculty.
fakultativa optional, facultative.
fakultato faculty (university, etc.).
fakultestro dean.
fakulto faculty.
faladi to keep falling, fall continually.
falaĵo rock-fall.
falakvo waterfall, cascade.
falangio harvester.
falango phalanx.
falangulo angle of descent.
falaro canary grass.
falaropo phalarope.
falbalo flounce, furbelow, trimming, frill, ruffle.
falĉado mowing.
falĉaĵo swath.
falĉeti to trim fame famously.
falĉi to cut, mow, reap.
falĉilanaso falcated duck.
falĉileto sickle.
falĉilo scythe.
falĉisto reaper.
faldaĵo fold.
faldata folded, furled.
faldebla folding.
faldi to fold, wrap.
faldo fold.
faldseĝo folding chair.
faldumi to pleat.
falego blow, strike, downfall.
faleno phalaena.
faleti to slip, stumble, trip.

faleto slip, stumble.
fali to drop, fall, topple. **fali dorsen** to fall backwards. **fali en la manojn de** to fall into the hands of. **fali surgenuen** to fall to one's knees.
faligi to drop, overthrow, fell, knock down, make fall.
faligo overthrow, subversion.
falilo snare, stumbling block.
Falkirko Falkirk.
falko falcon.
falmenuo drop-down menu.
falo fall.
falopio bindweed.
falsa counterfeit, fake, false, spurious, forged, wrong. **falsa amiko** false friend. **falsa ĵuro** perjury.
falsado falsification.
falsaĵo counterfeit.
falsbrilaĵo tinsel.
falsdentaro dentures.
false falsely, wrongly.
falsema false, insincere.
falseto falsetto.
falsgesto affected manner, false gesture.
falsi to counterfeit, fake, falsify, counterfeit, forge. **falsi ies subskribon** to forge someone's signature.
falsigi to adulterate, counterfeit, fake, falsify, forge.
falsigo falsification.
falsinto falsifier.
falsisto counterfeiter, forger.
falsluksa tawdry.
falso falsification.
falsofari to adulterate, counterfeit, fake, falsify, forge.
falsreprezenti to misrepresent.
falstelo shooting star, falling star.
falŝanceliĝi to stumble.
falti to wrinkle.
faltiĝi to fault, wrinkle.
falto crease, wrinkle.
faluso phallus.
fama famous, celebrated, illustrious, notable.
famaĵo something famous.
fame famously.
fameco fame, renown.
fami to be famous.
famigi to make famous.
familia domestic. **familia ĉambro** living room. **familia nomo** surname.
familiano family member.
familiara familiar, informal, intimate, friendly.
familiare colloquially, familiarly.
familiareco familiarity.
familiestro head of family.
familio family.

famkonata famous.
famo fame, hearsay, renown, repute, rumour, reputation.
famulo celebrity, famous person.
fanatika fanatical.
fanatike fanatically.
fanatikeco bigotry, fanaticism.
fanatikigi to infuriate.
fanatikulo bigot, fanatic.
fandado melting, fusion.
fandaĵo casting, ingot, bullion.
fandango fandango.
fandebla meltable, fusible.
fandejo foundry.
fandfermi to seal shut with heat, fuse shut.
fandfornego blast furnace.
fandforno melting furnace.
fandgardilo fuse.
fandi to case, fuse, melt, smelt.
fandigi to melt, fuse, flux.
fandiĝi to melt.
fandiĝo fusion.
fando melting, fusion.
fandodrato fuse.
fandopunkto melting point.
fandujo crucible, melting pot.
fandvazo crucible.
fanfaro fanfare, flourish.
fanfaronado fanfaronade, ostentation.
fanfaronaĵo boast.
fanfaroneco boastfulness.
fanfaronema affected.
fanfaroni to bluster, boast, brag, swagger, boast.
fanfarono boast.
fanfaronulo boaster, braggart.
fano fan.
fantasmagorio phantasmagoria.
fantasta fantastic, fantasy.
fantaste fantastically.
fantasto fantasy.
fantazia fantastic, imaginary.
fantazie fantastically.
fantazii to fantasize.
fantazio fantasy, imagination.
fantaziulo visionary.
fanto jack, knave.
fantoma ghostly, phantom, spectral.
fantomi to haunt, phantom.
fantomo ghost, phantom, spectre, spirit.
far by (in passive constructions).
faraĉaĵo botch.
faraĉi to botch.
faraĉita botchy.
faraĉulo botcher.
faradi to wage.
faradizi to faradize.
Farado Faraday.
farado making, manufacture.

farajô

farajô creation.
farandolo farandole.
faranto performer.
faraono pharaoh.
farbi to paint.
farbisto painter.
farbo dye, paint.
farbopistolo airbrush.
farboplato palette.
farbopulvoro toner.
farĉajô stuffing.
farĉi to stuff (cooking).
farĉo mincemeat, stuffing.
fare in doing, having been done, having been made. **fare de** made by, done by.
farebla achievable, feasible.
fareble feasibly.
farebleco feasibility.
farenda called for, to be done.
farendajô a thing that needs to be done.
farendajôj things that need to be done, to-do list.
farenhejta Fahrenheit.
Farenhejto Fahrenheit.
Fareso Forres.
fari to achieve, act, do, make, perform. **fari bieron** to brew. **fari diklipon** to pout. **fari distingon inter** to make a distinction among. **fari du aferon je unufojo** to do two things at once. **fari el muso elefanton** to exaggerate, make a mountain out of a molehill. **fari ion je propra risko** to do something at one's own risk. **fari komplezon** to oblige (render service). **fari krimon** to commit a crime. **fari kurson** to run a race. **fari la dikan lipon** to pout. **fari servon** to accommodate, render a service. **fari signon de kruco** to make the sign of the cross. **fari uzon de** to turn to (good) account. **fari uzon el** to make use of.
farigi to make, create, manufacture.
fariĝado incident.
fariĝi to become, come about, grow, happen. **fariĝi ekskutima** to fall into abeyance.
fariĝo event.
farinda worth doing.
faringo pharynx, gullet.
farinto maker.
fariseo Pharisee.
faristo maker.
farita done, made.
faritajô accomplishment, achievement, deed, act, creation, thing made.
farite done, finished.
farito feat.
farizeo Pharisee.
farma mastro farmer.
farmaciajô pharmaceutical(s), medicine.
farmaciejo pharmacy (place).

fatalismo

farmaciisto apothecary, chemist, pharmacist.
farmacio pharmaceutics, pharmacy (science).
farmakobezoaro pharmacobezoar.
farmakologiisto pharmacologist.
farmakologio pharmacology.
farmakologo pharmacologist.
farmakopeo pharmacopoeia.
farmanto farmer.
farmbieno farm.
farmdomo farmhouse.
farmi to farm, lease.
farmigi to farm out.
farmilaro farming tools, farming implements.
farmisto farmer.
farmkorto barnyard.
farmo farm.
farmodomo farmhouse.
farmulo farmer.
faro accomplishment, achievement, act, action, deed.
farotajô thing to be done, chore.
farsisto buffoon.
farso farce.
farti to be, fare (as to health).
farto state.
farunajô baked goods, pastry.
farunbatajô batter.
faruneca mealy.
faruno flour, meal.
fasado façade, front, interface.
fascina absorbing, fascinating.
fascinado fascination.
fascini to fascinate.
fascinita fascinated, gripped.
fascino fascination.
fascio fascia.
fasĉino faggot (of brushwood), fascine.
faskigado bunching together, bundling.
faskigi to bind, bunch.
fasko bunch, bundle, cluster, sheaf.
fasmo stick-insect.
fasoni to cut, fit, make to measure, fashion, tailor.
fasono cut, fashion, style, make, tailoring, model.
fasta tago fast day.
fasti to fast.
fastinte fasting.
fasto fast.
faŝisma fascist.
faŝismo fascism.
faŝisto fascist.
fatala fated, fateful, ill-fated, inevitable, ruinous.
fatalajô calamity.
fatale fatally.
fatalismo fatalism.

fatalo

fatalo fatality, fate, ill fate.
fatamorgano Fata Morgana.
fato destiny, fate, ill fate, fortune.
fatraso jumble, junk, trash.
faŭki to gape, yawn.
faŭko jaws, maw.
faŭli to commit a foul.
faŭlo foul.
faŭno faun, fauna.
Faŭsto Faust.
fava scabby, verminous, scurvy.
favo favus, ringworm.
favora advantageous, auspicious, favourable.
favora aĉetpropono bargain, special offer.
favoraĵo boon, favour, grace, kindness.
favoranto patron.
favorata favourite.
favoratino favourite.
favorato favourite.
favore advantageously, auspiciously, favourably. **favore surprizita** pleasantly surprised.
favorema benign, biased.
favoremo bias.
favori to favour, patronize.
favorigi to propitiate.
favorkora good-hearted, benevolent.
favorkore good-heartedly, benevolently.
favorkoreco grace.
favoro favour.
favulo scurvy rascal.
fazanejo pheasantry.
fazano pheasant.
fazeolo bean, green bean, haricot. **fazeolo granda** butter bean.
fazeolstango beanpole.
fazo phase, stage, aspect.
FD → **Fakdelegito**.
fea faerie, fairy, spirit.
Feba Phoebe.
febla feeble.
Febo Phoebus.
febra febrile, feverish.
febre feverishly.
febreto ague.
febri to have a fever.
febro fever.
Februaro February.
februaro February.
feĉo dregs, scum, sediment.
federa federal, federative.
federacia federal.
federacii to federate.
federaciismo federalism.
federacio federation.
federala federal.
federalismo federalism.
federi to federate.

femuro

federismo federalism.
federo federation.
feina fairy.
feino elf, fairy, sprite.
feinrakonto fairy tale.
feka fecal.
fekado defecation.
fekaĵo defecation, dung, excrement, shit.
fekaĵputo cesspit, cesspool.
fekegala not making a damn bit of difference.
feki to defecate, shit.
feko defecation, dung, excrement, shit. **fek! crap! shit!**
fekopelvo bed pan.
fektema affected.
fekunda fertile.
fekundeco fertility.
fekundigi to fertilize.
fekundigo fertilization.
fela furry.
felaho fellah.
feldspato feldspar.
feliĉa fortunate, happy, lucky. **Feliĉan Kristnaskon!** Merry Christmas! **Feliĉan Novjaron!** Happy New Year!
feliĉe fortunately, happily, luckily.
feliĉeco felicity, happiness.
feliĉega ecstatic.
feliĉegeco beatitude, bliss.
feliĉego ecstasy, great joy.
feliĉi to be happy.
feliĉiga delightful, pleasing.
feliĉige pleasingly.
feliĉigi to delight.
feliĉiĝi to become happy.
feliĉo happiness.
feliĉulo lucky person, happy person.
felietono feuilleton, serial, serial feature.
Felikso Felix (name).
feliso feline.
felisto furrier, skinner.
felo fur, hide, skin, pelt.
felpo sweatshirt.
felpreparadi to taw.
felŝuo moccasin.
felta felt, made of felt.
felti to cover with felt.
feltizi to cover with felt.
felto felt.
feluko felucca.
femalo female.
femdofobio xenophobia.
feminismo feminism.
feministino feminist.
feministo feminist.
femuraĵo leg, drumstick.
femuralo femur.
femuro femur, thigh, leg, upper leg.

femurosto thigh bone.
fenacetino phenacetin.
fendaĵo crack, crevice, crevice, chink.
fendata cracked, split.
fendego chasm, divide, gulf, ravine.
fendethava chapped.
fendeto fissure.
fendi to cleave, crack, split. **fendi haron** to split hairs.
fendiĝi to burst, split.
fendiĝinta cracked.
fendiĝo split.
fendilo cleaver.
fendo cleft, crack, crevice, rift, slit.
fendoaĵo crevice.
fendohava cracked.
fendpeceto splinter.
fendro fender, fireguard.
fenestra window, of a window. **fenestra kovrilo** window shutter. **fenestra vitro** window glass.
fenestrado window technique, windowing.
fenestraĵo widget.
fenestreto air hole, dormer window, skylight.
fenestro window.
fenestrobreto window sill.
fenestrokadro frame, window frame.
fenestrokovrilo blind.
fenestrokruceto mullion, transom.
fenestrokruco mullion, transom.
fenestropordo window.
fenestrosistemo window system.
fenestrumo shutter.
fenica Phoenician.
fenico Phoenician.
fenikoptero flamingo.
fenikso phoenix.
fenilamino aniline.
fenkolo fennel.
feno chinook (wind).
fenolo carbolic acid, phenol.
fenomena phenomenal.
fenomene phenomenally.
fenomenisma phenomenalistic.
fenomenismano phenomenalist.
fenomenismo phenomenalism.
fenomeno phenomenon.
fenomenologia phenomenological.
fenomenologio phenomenology.
fenomenologo phenomenologist.
fenotipo phenotype.
Fenro Fenrir, Fenris.
fenugreko fenugreek.
feo fairy, spirit.
fera iron. **fera kurteno** iron curtain.
feraĵisto ironmonger.
ferakonto fairy story.
ferbetono (iron-)reinforced concrete.

ferdeko deck (ship).
ferdekseĝo lounge chair.
Ferdinando Ferdinand.
ferdrato wire, iron wire.
ferepoko iron age.
ferfandaĵo cast-iron.
ferganto gauntlet.
feria aŭtobuso holiday coach.
ferianto holidaymaker.
feriaŭtobuso holiday coach.
ferika ferric.
ferio holiday, vacation.
ferioj vacation.
feritkerna memorilo ferrite core.
ferlada tin.
ferladisto tinsmith, whitesmith.
ferlado tin.
ferli to furl, roll up, take in.
ferma krampo end (close) parenthesis ( )).
fermaĵo closure.
fermata closed.
fermato fermata, hold.
Fermdigo IJsselmeer Dam.
fermegi to bang, slam.
fermenta zymotic.
fermentado fermentation.
fermentaĵo dough (starter).
fermentema fermentable.
fermenti to ferment.
fermentigi to ferment, leaven.
fermentilo leaven, yeast.
fermentita brasiko sauerkraut.
fermento enzyme, ferment.
fermi to close, shut, adjourn. **fermi dosieron** close a file. **fermi vian klapon!** shut your trap! shut up! **fermu la faŭkon!** shut up! shut your trap!
fermiĝi to close, be closed, become closed.
fermiĝo closure.
fermilo fastener, latch.
fermio fermium.
fermiono fermion.
fermita closed, shut. **fermita proceduro** closed subroutine. **fermita societo** clique. **fermita vojo** closed path, loop.
fermo closure.
fermpinĉi to squeeze.
fermplato cover, lid.
fero iron.
Feroaj Insuloj Faeroes.
feroca fierce.
feroce fiercely.
feroco ferociousness.
ferolo devil's dung, giant fennel, stinking gum.
feromono pheromone.
Ferooj Faroe Islands.
feroza ferrous.
ferskatolo can, tin, tin can.

fertila fertile.
ferumi to shoe.
fervoja railroad, railway.
fervoja stacidomo railway station.
fervojisto railroad employee, railroad worker.
fervojkompanio railroad company.
fervojo railroad, railway.
fervora ardent, fervent, full of zeal, zealous.
fervore earnestly.
fervoreco fervency.
fervorega fiery.
fervorege officiously.
fervoregeco officiousness.
fervori to be zealous.
fervoro fervor, zeal, mettle.
fervorulo zealot.
festa festal.
festado celebration.
festanto reveler.
festena festive.
festenado banquet.
festenanto reveler.
festene festively.
festeneco conviviality.
festenego revel.
festenejo banquet hall.
festeni to banquet, feast.
festeno banquet, feast.
festenoĉambro banquet room.
festeto party.
festi to celebrate, party.
festi sian naskiĝtagon to celebrate one's birthday.
festivalo festival.
festlibro commemorative publication, festschrift.
festo celebration, festival, party, holiday.
   Festo de Ĉiuj Sanktuloj All Saints' Day.
   Festo de la Sankta Triuno Trinity Sunday. **Festo de Laŭboj** Feast of Tabernacles. **Festo de Sankta Patriko** St. Patrick's Day.
festoni to festoon.
festono festoon.
festosalono assembly hall.
festotago holiday.
festparolado address, (keynote) speech.
festuko fescue.
feta foetal.
fetiĉismo fetishism.
fetiĉisto fetishist.
fetiĉo fetish.
feto foetus.
fetora bad-smelling, stinking, odorous.
fetoranta bad-smelling, stinking, odorous.
fetoreco smelliness.
fetori to reek, smell, smell bad, stink.
fetoro fetor, stench, stink.

feŭda feudal.
feŭdala feudal.
feŭdaleco feudality.
feŭdalismo feudalism.
feŭdestro feudal lord.
feŭdismo feudalism.
feŭdo feud, fief.
feŭdoĉefo feudal lord.
feŭdulo vassal.
fezo fez.
fi to shame. **fi!** shame! **fi al vi!** shame on you!
fi- (denotes lack of morals, principles).
fia base, disgusting, nasty, shameful, filthy, dirty, vile.
fiaga abusive.
fiagado abuse.
fiago abuse.
fiajo nastiness, something disgusting.
fiakristo cab driver.
fiakro cab, carriage for hire, coach for hire, fiacre.
fianciniĝo engagement.
fianĉamiko best man.
fianĉeco betrothal.
fianĉigi to betroth, become engaged, get engaged.
fianĉiĝi to get engaged.
fianĉiĝinta engaged.
fianĉiĝo betrothal, engagement.
fianĉina bridal.
fianĉinbukedo bridal bouquet.
fianĉiniĝi to become engaged.
fianĉiniĝinta engaged.
fianĉiniĝo betrothal, engagement.
fianĉino bride, fiancée.
fianĉo betrothed, fiancé, sweetheart.
fiaska abortive.
fiaski to abort, fail.
fiaskigi to abort, quash.
fiasko abortion, failure, fiasco.
fiaŭdaca outrageous.
fiberca fibrous.
fibero muskrat.
fiberto fibril.
fibestoj vermin.
fibolo safety pin.
Fibonaĉi Fibonacci.
Fibonaĉia sekvenco Fibonacci series.
fibra fibre.
fibriĝi to fray.
fibrino fibrin.
fibro fibre, filament.
fibromo fibroma.
fibuba loutish.
fibubo lout.
fibulo fibula, safety pin.
fibuŝo dirty mouth.
fiĉefo instigator.

fidebla dependable, reliable, responsible, trusty.
fideble dependably, reliably.
fidela accurate, exact, faithful, loyal, staunch, trusty, trustworthy.
fidele faithfully.
fideleco adherence, allegiance, fealty, fidelity, loyalty.
fidelo adherence, allegiance, faithfulness, fidelity.
fidelrompo breach of faith.
fidelulo believer.
fidema confident, trusting.
fideme confidently.
fidi to have faith, have faith in, trust. **fidi al** to rely on, trust in. **fidi je** to have faith in, rely on, trust in.
fidinda reliable, trustworthy, dependable.
fidinde dependably, faithfully.
fidindeco reliability.
fidindo reliability.
fido confidence, faith, trust.
fidro feeder, feeder-cable.
fie grossly.
fiera proud, haughty.
fieraĵo pride.
fiere proudly.
fiereco pride.
fierega overbearing.
fierege overbearingly.
fierego arrogance, haughtiness.
fiereta perky.
fieri to be proud. **fieri pri** to be proud of. **fieru pri ŝi!** be proud of her!
fieriĝi to be proud.
fierinda glorious, illustrious.
fiero pride.
fierulo proud person.
fifama of ill repute.
fifame notoriously.
fifamiga smear.
fifamigi to smear.
fifamigo smear.
fifamo infamy.
fifari to commit, perpetrate.
fifarinto perpetrator.
fiflata adulatory.
fiflatado adulation.
fifro fife.
figarbo fig tree.
figazeto dirty magazine.
figo fig.
figringo thimble.
figujo fig tree.
figura figurative. **figura esprimo** figurative expression, figure of speech.
figurado depiction, representation.
figuranto extra (performer in a play, etc.).
figure figuratively.
figuri to depict, represent, figure.
figuro configuration, diagram, figure, image, picture, representation.
figvidanto instigator.
Fiĝiinsuloj Fiji Islands.
Fiĝio Fiji.
fihelpanto abetter, accessory, accomplice.
fihelpo abetment.
fiherbo weed.
fihomo evil person, bad person.
fihumila obsequious.
fihumile obsequiously.
fihumileco obsequiousness.
fiigi to pervert.
fiinsektoj pests, vermin.
fikado fucking.
fikampanjo agitation.
fikario lesser celandine.
fikcia fictional, fictitious.
fikcie fictionally, fictitiously.
fikcio fiction.
fiki to fuck, screw.
fiko (a) fuck.
fikomerci to traffic.
fikomercisto trafficker.
fikomerco traffic.
fikopii to crib.
fiksa fixed. **fiksa memorilo** read-only store. **fiksa memoro** read-only memory, ROM. **fiksa punkto** fixed point.
fiksado setting.
fiksbano fixing agent.
fikseco fixity.
fiksi to attach, determine, fasten, fix, affix, make fast, secure. **fiksi doganon** clear.
fiksiĝi to attach, be stranded, stick.
fiksiĝo adhesion.
fiksilo fixer.
fiksita fixed, hard. **fiksita disko** fixed disk, hard disk. **fiksita programo** firmware. **fiksita punkto** fixed-point.
fikskoma fixed-point.
fikso fixing.
fikspunkta fixed-point. **fikspunkta nombro** fixed-point number. **fikspunkta prezento** fixed-point representation.
fiksrigardi to gaze.
fiksrigardo stare.
fikssignara reĝimo text mode.
fikstempo deadline.
fiktiva fictitious.
fiktive fictitiously.
fikuso banyan, banian.
fikutimo vice.
filakterio phylactery.
filaktero phylactery.
filamenteca filament.
filamento filament.
filandro gossamer.

filanto phyllanthus.
filantropeco philanthropy.
filantropia philanthropic.
filantropie philanthropically.
filantropio philanthropy.
filantropo philanthropist.
filario guinea-worm.
filatela philatelic.
filatelio philately, stamp collecting.
filatelisto philatelist.
filatelo philately, stamp collecting.
fileo fillet.
filerte craftily.
filharmonia philharmonic.
filia filial.
filieco affiliation.
filigi to adopt (child).
filigo adoption.
filigrani to filigree.
filigrano filigree, watermark.
filiigi to affiliate.
filiigo affiliation.
filiiĝi to affiliate.
filiiĝo affiliation.
filiko fern.
filikoplantoj ferns.
filino daughter.
filio affiliate, affiliation, branch, affiliated body.
filipina Philippine. **Filipina Maro** Philippine Sea.
filipinanino Philippine woman.
filipinano Filipino.
Filipinoj Philippine Islands, Philippines.
filistro philistine.
filiŝto Philistine.
filmaktoro film actor.
filmarkitekto art director.
filmfaristo film maker.
filmi to shoot (a film), film.
filmisto film maker.
filmitaĵero clip.
filmitaĵo footage.
filmkamerao film camera.
filmkaseto film cartridge.
filmo film, motion picture, movie.
filmprojekciilo film projector.
filmruleto film.
filmteatro cinema, movie theatre, theatre, the pictures.
filo son.
filogenezo phylogenesis.
filoj sons.
filologia philological.
filologie philologically.
filologiisto philologist.
filologio philology.
filologo philologist.
filono phylum, sub-kingdom.

filoskopo warbler, willow-warbler.
filozofe philosophically.
filozofi to philosophize.
filozofia philosophic.
filozofie philosophically.
filozofiema philosophical.
filozofii to philosophize.
filozofiisto philosopher.
filozofio philosophy.
filozofo philosopher.
filtri to filter.
filtriĝi to filter.
filtrilo filter.
fimbrio fimbria.
fimensa foul minded.
fina final. **fina parto** back part, hind part. **fina prilaborado** finishing off. **fina rando** terminal vertex (of an arc). **fina uzulo** end user. **fina valoro** final value.
finaĵo ending.
finalano finalist.
finalisto finalist.
finalo decider, playoff, finale.
financa financial.
financado finance, financing.
finance financially.
financi to finance.
financisto financier.
financo finance.
finaranĝi to conclude, dispatch, expedite, finish, settle.
finaranĝo completion, settlement.
findecidi to compose, conclude, dispatch, settle, make up one's mind.
fine at last, finally, ultimately, finally, in the final analysis, when all is said and done. **fine de** at the end of, in the end, finally.
finfara bato coup de grace.
finfari to complete, finish (off), finalize.
finfina ultimate.
finfine after all, at last, at long last, when all is said and done.
finfineco finality.
fingra digital.
fingringo thimble.
fingro finger, digit.
fingrofrapo touch.
fingropremaĵo fingerprint.
fingrospuro fingerprint.
fingrumi to finger, handle.
fini to accommodate, end, finish, terminate, close, conclude. **fini fuŝrapide** to bungle one's work.
finia finite. **finia aŭtomato** finite automaton. **finia vico** finite sequence.
finialo finial.
finidimensia finite-dimensional.
finiĝi to finish.
finiĝanta ending.

finiĝi to end up, come to an end, expire, wind up. **finiĝi je** to end in.
finiĝo end, terminate.
finilo terminating symbol, terminator.
finilonga vico finite sequence.
finio finite object.
finita completed, done, finished, over, through.
finitivo finite, finite form.
finkondiĉa iteracio REPEAT-loop, REPEAT-statement.
finkrampo end (close) parenthesis ( )).
finkunsidi to finish a meeting.
finlabori to finish.
finlegi to read, read out.
finletero final letter.
finludiĝi to play itself out, come to an end.
finmanĝi to finish eating.
finna Finnish. **Finna Golfo** Gulf of Finland. **finna lingvo** Finnish, Finnish language.
finnino Finnish, Finnish lady, Finnish woman.
Finnio Finland.
Finnlando Finland.
finno Finn.
Finnujo Finland.
F-ino → **Fraŭlino**.
fino end, ending.
finofara finished.
finomi to brand.
finpagi to pay off.
finpago acquittal, payment, full payment.
finparoli to finish speaking.
finpretigi to finish, get finished.
finpretigo accomplishment.
finsigno end character.
finstacio end-of-the-line.
finstudi to finish one's studies.
finti to feint.
finto ruse, feint.
finuzitajo cast-off.
finveni to end up.
finvorto final word.
fio phi (Φφ).
fiolo phial, vial.
fiparolado filthy talk.
fipetola wanton.
fipetolemo wantonness.
fiprofiti to take advantage of.
firakonto dirty story, smutty story.
firma fast, firm, stable, staunch, unshaken.
firmaĵo dry land, firmament.
firmamento firmament.
firmao company, firm.
firme firmly.
firmeco firmness.
firmeto partnership, small business, small company, small firm, sole proprietorship.
firmigi to congeal, fasten, fix, affix, secure.

firmigilo splint.
firmiĝi to firm.
firmo company, firm, enterprise, business.
firmvaro firmware.
firsto coping.
fisio fission.
fiska fiscal. **fiska jaro** fiscal year.
fisko exchequer, state treasury.
fiskribi to scrawl.
fistuleno beef-steak fungus.
fistulo fistula.
fiŝa vosto fish tail.
fiŝado fishing.
fiŝaglo osprey.
fiŝaĵo fish meat.
fiŝanto angler, fisher.
fiŝaro shoal.
fiŝĉasi to angle, fish.
fiŝejo fishing spot, fishing hole, fishing ground(s).
fiŝfadeno fishing line.
fiŝgluaĵo kaid.
fiŝgluo kaid.
fiŝhoki to fish with a line.
fiŝhoko fishhook.
fiŝi to fish. **fiŝi nase** to fish with a fish trap. **fiŝi rete** to fish with a net.
fiŝidaĵo whitebait.
fiŝilaro fishing-tackle.
fiŝisto fisherman.
fiŝistvilaĝo fishing village.
fiŝkapta fishing.
fiŝkaptada fishing. **fiŝkaptada ŝipeto** fishing boat.
fiŝkaptado angling, fishing, fishery.
fiŝkaptejo fishery.
fiŝkapti to (catch) fish, go fishing, angle. **fiŝkapti nase** to fish with a fish trap or net.
fiŝkaptisto angler, fisher, fisherman.
fiŝlageto fish pond.
fiŝmanĝaĵo fish.
fiŝmiksaĵo fish mixture, fish stew.
fiŝo fish. **Fiŝoj** Pisces (zodiac)
fiŝodoro fish smell, fish odour.
fiŝoleo fish oil.
fiŝosteko steak.
fiŝosto fish-bone.
fiŝreto fishing net.
fiŝsemo spawn.
fiŝvendejo fish market.
fiŝvendisto fishmonger.
fiŝvergo fishing rod.
fiteŭmo rampion.
fitobezoaro phytobezoar.
fitogeografia phytogeographical.
fitogeografie phytogeographically.
fitrakta abusive.
fitraktado abuse, mistreatment.
fitrakti to abuse.

fitrakto

fitrakto abuse.
fiulo immoral person, evil person.
fiuza abusive.
fiuzanto abuser.
fiuzi to abuse.
fiuzo abuse.
fivirino slut, bad woman.
fiviro cheat, crook, rascal, rogue, swindler, trickster.
fivoleptemo concupiscence.
fivorto bad, foul word.
fizalido physalis.
fizalio bladder.
fizika physical. **fizika adreso** physical address. **fizika geografio** physical geography, physiography. **fizika memoro** physical storage. **fizika tavolo** physical layer.
fizike physically.
fizikeca programado physical programming.
fizikisto physicist.
fiziko physics.
fiziologiisto physiologist.
fiziologio physiology.
fiziologo physiologist.
fizionomio physiognomy (face).
fizioterapiisto physical therapist.
fizioterapio physiotherapy.
fjordo firth, fjord, inlet, loch.
F-klefo bass clef (𝄢).
flagaĵo bunting.
flagelo flagellum.
flageto pennant.
flagi to deck with flags.
flago banner, flag, banner.
flagornami to deck with flags.
flagranta flagrant.
flagrante flagrantly.
flagretado flicker.
flagreti to flicker.
flagri to flare, flare up, flicker.
flagstango flag staff.
flagŝtofo bunting.
flaĝoleto flageolet.
Flajfiŝkovo Flying Fish Cove.
flakeniri to swerve.
flako puddle, pool.
flakono flacon, flask.
flama fervent, flaming.
flamando Fleming.
flamanta ablaze.
flambergo dress-sword.
flamegi to blaze.
flamejo burner.
flamema passionate.
flamengo flamingo.
flameti to singe.
flami to burn, flame.

flatanto

flamiga inflammatory.
flamigi to inflame, kindle, light.
flamiĝema flammable, inflammable.
flamiĝi to catch fire, enkindle, flare up, take fire.
flamiĝo outburst, passion.
flamingo burner (gas).
flamkapa hot-headed.
flamlume by firelight, by the light of a flame.
flamo flame.
flanaĵo custard.
flandra Flemish. **Flandraj Ardenoj** Flemish Ardennes.
Flandrio Flanders.
flandro Flemish, Fleming.
Flandrujo Flanders.
flanela flannel.
flanelo flannel.
flanĝo flange.
flanka incidental, side, lateral, incidental. **flanka branĉo** collateral branch, sidebranch. **flanka klaso** coset.
flankafero accessory.
flankaĵo accessory matter, side issue, sideshow, wing.
flankblindigilo blinder.
flankĉaro sidecar.
flankdoloro stitch.
flanke at the side, on the side. **flanke de** at the side of, beside, alongside, next to.
flanken aside, to the side. **flanken rigardi** to leer.
flankeniĝi to deflect, diverge, wander.
flankenpuŝi to overshadow.
flanketo side.
flankiĝi to go astray, stray off.
flanknavo aisle.
flanko flank, side, lateral surface. **flanko ĉe flanko** abreast, side by side. **flankon ĉe flanko** abreast.
flankokupo hobby, sideline.
flankprodukto by-product.
flankvalo side valley.
flankvelo studding sail.
flankvojo by-way, side-way.
flano flan, tart, pancake, thin flat pastry.
flaresplori to smell at, sniff at.
flari to scent, smell. **flari tabakon** to take snuff.
flaro smell.
flaroado smell (sense).
flarsento sense of smell.
flarsentumo smell.
flartabako snuff.
flarumi to snuffle.
flataĉi to brown-nose.
flatado flattery.
flataĵo flattery.
flatanto flatterer.

flate

flate coaxingly.
flategi to adulate.
flatema flattering.
flati to flatter.
flato flattery.
flatulo flatterer.
flaŭro flora.
flava yellow. **flava emberizo** yellowhammer. **flava febro** yellow fever. **flava kupro** brass. **Flava Maro** Yellow Sea. **Flava Rivero** Huang He, Yellow River.
flavbeka albatroso yellow-nosed albatross.
flavbekulo greenhorn.
flavbrova emberizo yellow-browed bunting.
flavbruna fawn.
flaveca yellowy.
flaveta yellowish.
flavgriza beige.
flavigi to yellow.
flaviĝi to yellow.
flaviĝinta yellowed.
flaviĝo jaundice.
flavkrura mevo lesser black-backed gull.
flavmalsano acute hepatitis A, jaundice.
flavo yellow.
flavroza carnation (colour).
flavruĝa russet.
flavulo yellow man.
flebito phlebitis.
flebo seam, vein.
flegado care, nursing.
flegi to attend, nurse, tend to, mind, take care of, see to.
flegistino nurse.
flegisto nurse.
flegma impassive, passive, stolid, indifferent, calm.
flegme passively, calmly, indifferently.
flegmo apathy, indifference, phlegm, stolidity, composure, calmness.
flegmono phlegmon.
flegmulo phlegmatic.
fleksa flexible.
fleksado bending.
fleksaĵo bend.
fleksebla flexible, pliable, pliant, supple.
flekseble flexibly.
fleksebleco flexibility.
flekseblo flexibility.
fleksi to bend, flex, inflect.
fleksiaĵo inflexion.
fleksigilo bender.
fleksigo bend.
fleksiĝema flexible.
fleksiĝemo flexibility.
fleksiĝi to bend.
fleksiĝo curve.
fleksii to inflect.

floristo

fleksiilo inflexion.
fleksio flexion, inflexion.
fleksita bent.
flekso flexion.
fleo timothy-grass.
fleso flounder.
flibustro freebooter, privateer.
flikaĉi to patch things up.
flikado darning.
flikaĵaro patchwork.
flikaĵo patch, patchwork.
flikeca patchy.
fliki to darn, mend, patch, patch up.
fliko (software) patch.
flikteno bleb, vesicle.
Flinto Flint.
flinto flint-glass.
flirtegi to hover.
flirtema volatile (fickle).
flirtemulo philanderer.
flirti to flirt, flit, flutter.
flirtigi to wave.
flirto flirt.
flirtumi to flirt, spend time flirting.
Flisingo Flushing.
Flitvudo Fleetwood.
floemo phloem.
flogistonismo phlogistonism.
flogistono phlogiston.
flogo phlox.
floko flake, flock, wisp.
flokso phlox.
flora floral.
florado efflorescence.
floraĵo blossom.
floranta abloom.
florbedo flower bed.
florbranĉeto spray.
florbrasiko cauliflower.
florbroĉo corsage.
florbulbkulturejo bulb field, bulb-growing field.
florbulbo flower bulb.
florburĝono bud.
florbutiko florist.
floreca flowery.
florejo flower garden.
florenca Florentine.
Florenco Florence.
floreno florin (f).
florfolieto petal.
florfolio petal.
Florfontano Bloemfontein.
florĝardeno flower garden.
flori to bloom, blossom, flower.
florida Floridian.
floridano Floridian.
Florido Florida.
floristo florist.

154

florkaliko calyx.
florkrono crown, garland, wreath.
florkulturejo nursery (horticulture).
floro bloom, flower.
floroleo attar.
florparado flower parade.
florpoto flowerpot.
florsemo pollen.
florujo flower pot, vase.
flosanta doko floating dock.
flosbazaro floating market.
flosbueto buoy.
flose afloat.
floseco buoyancy.
flosi to float.
flosigi to float.
flosilo float.
flosilênuro buoy rope.
floslinio Plimsoll line, waterline.
floso raft.
flosponto pontoon bridge.
flotanta afloat.
floteto flotilla.
flotforto buoyancy.
flotkapabla able to float.
floto fleet.
flua fluent, fluid.
fluadi to flow, keep flowing.
fluado flowing.
fluaĵa fluid, liquid.
fluaĵo fluid, liquid.
fluanta flowing, fluent.
fluante flowingly, fluently.
fluantparola talkative.
flue fluently, fluidly.
flueca fluid, liquid.
flueco fluency.
fluegi to stream.
fluego spate.
fluejo bed, watercourse.
fluemo fluidity.
flugado flight (birds).
flugaparato flying machine.
flugarmea bazo air base.
flugarmeisto airman.
flugarmeo air force.
flugbileto air ticket.
flugboato sea-plane.
flugdrako kite.
flugeti to flutter.
flugfolio flier, leaflet.
flughavena busstacidomo air terminal.
flughavenimposto airport tax.
flughaveno airport.
flugi to flee, fly.
flugigi to let fly, make fly.
flugila alar.
flugileca alar.
flugilhava alar, alate.

flugilo pinion (feather), wing.
flugisto flier.
flugiva able to fly.
flugkampo airfield.
flugkapabla airworthy.
flugkatastrofo air crash.
flugludilo kite (toy).
flugmaŝino aircraft.
flugo flight.
flugpasaĝero airline passenger.
flugpendi to float, hang, hover, waft.
flugporti to waft.
flugpova airworthy.
flugsciuro flying squirrel.
flugtaŭga airworthy.
flugtuŝi to touch lightly.
flui to flow, run, stream.
fluida fluid, liquid. **fluida oksigeno** liquid oxygen, LOX.
fluidaĵo fluid, liquid.
fluidiĝi to melt, liquefy.
fluido fluid, liquid.
flukso flux.
fluktui to fluctuate.
flulavi to flush.
flulinia streamlined.
fluo current, flow, stream.
fluorborato borofluoride.
fluoreska fluorescent.
fluoreski to fluoresce.
fluorido fluoride.
fluoro fluorine.
fluparola glib.
fluparoleco fluency.
flusa flood.
flusablo quicksand.
flusego spring-tide.
flusejo foreshore, intertidal zone, littoral zone.
fluskemo flow chart.
fluso flood, high tide.
flustrado whisper.
flustri to whisper. **flustri dolĉaĵojn al** to whisper sweet nothings to.
flustro whisper.
fluteto piccolo.
fluti to pipe.
flutludi to pipe.
fluto flute.
FM-dissendilo FM transmitter.
FM-ricevilo FM receiver.
fo name of the letter F.
fobio phobia.
Fobo Phobos.
foceno porpoise.
foino stone-marten.
foirejo fairground, marketplace.
foirkomercisto market trader.
foiro fair, bazaar, (street) market.

foja occasional.
foje on occasion, sometimes.
fojfoje sometimes, occasionally, from time to time.
fojnamaso haystack.
fojnbalao whisk.
fojnejo barn, hay loft.
fojno hay.
fojnoforkego pitchfork.
fojnostako haystack.
fojnujo hay rack.
fojo occasion, time.
fokedoj earless seals.
foko seal (animal).
fokseno porpoise.
fokstroto foxtrot.
fokusa focal.
fokusdiseco eccentricity.
fokuso focus.
fola zany.
foldi to groove, slot.
foldo slot.
foliaro foliage.
folibeto Chard.
folieto blade.
folii to browse.
foliklo follicle.
folikrono acanthus.
folilaŭso aphid, aphis, greenfly, plant-louse.
folio leaf, sheet, page.
foliolo leaflet (botany).
foliumebla browseable.
foliumi to browse, leaf through.
foliumilo browser.
folklora folkloric.
folkloristo folklorist.
folkloro folklore.
folriĉa leafy, rich in leaves.
fomenti to foment.
fomento heating.
fomoro Fomorian.
fona background. **fona procezo** background process. **fona reĝimo** background processing. **fona tasko** background task.
fonbruo background noise.
fonda foundational.
fondaĵo establishment, foundation.
fondi to erect, establish, form, found, institute.
fondiĝo foundation.
fondintino foundress.
fondinto founder.
fondo establishment.
fonduso fund.
fonemo phoneme.
fonetika phonetic. **fonetika alfabeto** phonetic alphabet.
fonetike phonetically.
fonetiko phonetics.
fonetismo pronunciation.
fonkuliso backdrop.
fono background.
fonoforo hearing aid.
fonografo (cylinder) phonograph.
fonologiisto phonologist.
fonologio phonology.
fonometro phonometer.
fonpeniko background brush.
fonta source. **fonta aro** domain. **fonta programo** source program.
fontakvo spring water.
fontanelo fontanel(le).
fontano fountain.
fonti to spring, well up.
fontkodo source code.
fontlingvo source language.
fonto fountain, fount, source, spring.
fontolingvo source language.
fontoplumo fountain pen.
fontplumo fountain pen.
fontprogramo source program.
fontserĉisto water-diviner.
fontteksto source text.
for away, distant, far (off, away), forth, gone. **for de la okuloj, for de la koro** out of sight, out of mind. **for de mia vido!** get out of my sight! **for de tie ĉi!** begone! **for la away with. for por aferoj** away on business.
fora distant, far, remote. **fora lando** far away land. **fora multipleksoro** remote multiplexer. **fora terminalo** remote terminal. **fora uzanto** remote user.
foraĉeti to corner, corner the market, monopolize.
foraĉeto buyout.
forbagateli to while away.
forbalai to sweep away.
forbari to ward off.
forbati to beat back, beat off, knock off, strike off.
forblovi to blow away.
forbloviĝi to be blown away.
forbrili to burn away.
forbrosi to brush away, brush out.
forbruli to be burnt down.
forbruligi to burn down.
forbruligilo incinerator.
forbruligo incineration.
forbruliĝi to be consumed in flames, burn up.
forcedi to relinquish, yield.
forceja efiko greenhouse effect.
forcejo greenhouse, hothouse.
forcepso forceps.
forci to grow in a greenhouse.
forĉerpi to exhaust, use up, consume.
fordiboĉi to throw away, squander.

fordoni to abandon, give away, give up. **fordoni sin** to abandon oneself. **fordoni sin al** to indulge in, abandon oneself to.
fordoniĝi to abandon oneself.
fordono abandonment, renunciation.
fordrinki to drink away.
fordrivi to drift away.
fore afar, afield, far, far away, remotely.
foreco remoteness.
foresi to be absent.
foresta absent.
forestanta absent.
forestantado absenteeism.
forestanteco absenteeism.
forestantismo absenteeism.
forestantlisto attendance register.
forestanto absentee.
foreste in one's absence. **foreste de** in the absence of.
foresteco absence, non-attendance.
foresti to be absent, be missing, be away.
forestigi to remove, send away, make absent.
foresto absence.
forestoado absence.
forfali to drop out (of a course).
forfandi to melt, melt away.
forfandiĝi to melt, melt away.
Forfaro Forfar.
forfikolo earwig.
forfikulo earwig.
forflankiĝi to go astray, stray off.
forflugi to fly away.
forflui to flow down, flow off.
forfluo receding tide, reflux. **forfluo kaj alfluo** ebb and flow.
forforeski to phosphoresce.
forfosi to dig off, level.
forfrotiĝo attrition.
forgesa forgetful, oblivious.
forgese forgetfully.
forgeseco forgetfulness.
forgesema forgetful.
forgesi to forget.
forgesigi to make someone forget.
forgeso oblivion.
forgluti to swallow.
forĝejo forge, smithy.
forĝi to forge. **forĝu feron dum ĝi estas varmega** strike while the iron is hot.
forĝista blacksmith's.
forĝisto blacksmith, smith.
forĝmartelo blacksmith's hammer.
forĝofera wrought iron.
forĝofero wrought iron.
forĝotranĉilo blacksmith's chisel.
forhavi to do without.
fori to absent oneself, be away.
forigi to do away with, get rid of, remove, estrange, discard, wean, deface, omit, put away. **forigi la manĝilaron** to clear the table (of eating utensils, etc.).
forigilo repellent.
forigo abolition.
foriĝi to wean (alienate).
forinto forint.
foriri to absent oneself, depart, go away, leave, set out. **foriri malfiere** to slink off.
foriru! be off!
foriro departure.
forjetaĵo rubbish.
forjetaĵo refuse, rubbish, waste, trash, refuse.
forĵeti to discard, throw away.
forĵetindaĵo garbage, leavings, refuse, rubbish, waste.
forĵeto disposal.
forĵetulo castaway.
forĵuri to abjure.
forĵuro abjuration, disavowal, repudiation.
forkaptanto abductor.
forkapti to hijack, kidnap. **forkapti garantiulojn** to take hostages.
forkaptinto abductor, kidnapper.
forkapto abduction.
forkaŝi sin to abscond.
forke astride.
forkego hay fork, pitchfork, prong.
forki to fork.
forkiĝi to bifurcate, branch (off), split (off).
forklini to parry, ward off.
forkliniĝo aversion.
forko fork.
forkomenti to comment out.
forkomerci to buy, purchase, take over.
forkomuniigi to excommunicate.
forkondukado carrying off, discharge.
forkonduki to divert.
forkonduko carrying off, discharge.
forkonfesi to abjure, renounce, give up.
forkonsenti to relinquish, renounce, waive.
forkonsumi to use up.
forkonsumo depletion.
forkosto wishbone.
forksileno forked catchfly.
forkuranteto truant.
forkuranto fugitive, runaway.
forkuregi to rush away.
forkuri to abscond, elope, escape, run away.
forkurigi to make someone run away.
forkurinto deserter.
forkuro evasion, flight.
forkvosta mevo sabine's gull.
forlasaĵo omission.
forlasavizo eviction notice.
forlasi to abandon, forsake, desert, leave, quit, give up, relinquish, vacate, disown, renounce. **forlasi ĵure** to abjure, forswear, swear off, renounce.
forlasinto abandoner.

forlasita abandoned.
forlasiteco abandonment.
forlaso abandonment, renunciation.
forlavi to wash away, wash off.
forlesivi to wash off.
forloga repellent, repelling, repulsive.
forlogaĵo decoy.
forlogata de lured away by.
forlogi to decoy, lead astray.
forma formative.
formacio (geological, military) formation.
formado fashioning, forming.
formala formal. **formala lingvo** artificial language, formal language. **formala parametro** formal parameter. **formala polinomo** formal polynomial. **formala potencoserio** formal power series, formal series. **formala serio** formal power series, formal series.
formalaĵo formality.
formaldehido formaldehyde.
formale formally.
formalino formalin.
formalismaĵo technicality.
formalismo formalism.
formalisto bureaucrat.
formalparametra listo formal parameter list.
formanĝi to eat up, finish eating.
formati to format.
formatigitaj datenoj data structure.
formato format, size (of a book).
forme in form.
formetado omission.
formetejo shed.
formeti to put away, store, omit.
formi to fashion, form, shape.
formigo formation.
formiĝi to form, take shape.
formiĝo formation.
formikaro ant colony, army of ants.
formikejo ant hill, ant mound.
formikerinaco spiny ant-eater.
formiki to have pins and needles.
formikleono antlion.
formikmanĝanto anteater.
formikmanĝulo anteater.
formiko ant.
formikurso anteater.
formilo mould.
formingo phorminx.
formo form, shape, formation. **formo de Backus-Naur** Backus-Naur form, BNF.
formodifekti to deform.
formolo formalin.
formorekono format recognition, pattern recognition.
formortado dying.
formortanta dying out, becoming extinct.

formorti to become extinct, die (away, off, out) fail.
Formoso Formosa.
formovi to remove.
formovo shift.
formujo mould.
formulario blank, form.
formularo blank, form.
formuli to formulate.
formulo formula.
fornaĝi to swim away.
fornego furnace.
fornei to deny.
fornejo bake house, bakery.
forneo disavowal, disclaimer.
fornikso dome, fornix.
Forno Fornax.
forno furnace, kiln, oven, stove.
fornoganto pot holder.
fornomi to disown.
foroferi to relinquish, offer up.
forpasadi to fade.
forpasi to march off, retreat, withdraw, pass away, die.
forpaso disappearance, expiry.
forpeladi to pursue.
forpeli to banish, send away, chase away, drive away, expel, dispel.
forpelito outcast.
forpermesi to dismiss.
forpermeso furlough, leave, pass (from military service).
forporti to bring away, carry away.
forprenebla detachable, removable.
forpreni to abstract, take away, remove. **forpreni la jungilaron de** to unharness.
forpreno seizing, seizure.
forpuŝi to push aside, repel, disgust.
forpuŝo repulse.
forrabi to abduct, carry off (by force).
forrabita kidnapped.
forrabo abduction, rape.
forreagado abreaction.
forreagi to abreact.
forregali to put off, send about his business.
forresti to absent oneself.
forrevi to dream away.
forsalti to bound off, jump away.
forsendi to dismiss, turn away, send away, dispatch, send off. **forsendi ĝentile** to put off, rebuff, stall. **forsendi pretekste** to put off, rebuff, stall.
forsendo deportation.
forsitio forsythia.
forskrapi to erase.
forskui to shake off.
forstari to stand away, stand back (from).
forstkultivo forestry.
forstkulturo forestry.

forsto cultivated forest.
forstreki to make out, strike out.
forstreko deletion.
forstumi to afforest.
forstumo forestry.
forsveni to faint away.
forŝovi to move.
forŝoviĝo shift.
forŝovo shift.
forŝteli to kidnap.
forŝteliĝi to abscond.
forŝuti to pour out.
forta strong.
fortakvo aqua fortis.
Fortaŭgusto Fort Augustus.
forte strongly, earnestly.
forteco force, strength.
fortega lusty, vigorous.
fortege very strongly, violently.
fortegeco vigor.
fortego violence.
fortegulo weight-lifter.
fortelo stall (theatre), armchair.
fortempiĝi to expire, run out, terminate.
fortempiĝo expiry.
forteni to keep at a distance, keep at bay.
fortepiano grand piano, piano, pianoforte.
forti to outrage.
fortigi to consolidate, fortify.
fortigilo tonic, restorative.
fortiĝi to become strong, strengthen (oneself).
fortika able-bodied, durable, firm, robust, sturdy, strong, solid, stable, substantial, rugged, fortified. **fortika tolo** sturdy cloth.
fortikaĵeto fort.
fortikaĵo citadel, fortification, fortress, stronghold, fort.
fortike solidly.
fortikeco firmness, robustness, solidity, stability.
fortikigi to fortify.
fortikulo hunk.
fortimiga deterrent, forbidding.
fortimigi to deter, discourage, scare (away).
fortimigo deterrence.
fortiri to withhold.
forto force, strength, vigor, power.
fortomanko helplessness, powerlessness.
fortostreĉo exertion.
fortranĉi to be subtended by, intercept, cut off.
fortransi to pass away.
fortreso fortress.
fortulo strong person.
fortuna fortunate.
fortune fortunately.
fortuno fortune.
forturni to turn away.
forumaro netnews, Usenet.

forumo forum, newsgroup.
foruzi to use up.
foruzita used up.
forvagi to stray.
forvaginto maverick, stray.
forvaporiĝi to evaporate.
forvelki to abort.
forveturi to drive away, drive off.
forveturo departure.
forviŝi to delete, wipe away, erase.
forviŝiĝi to be expunged, be wiped away.
forviŝita wiped away, obliterated.
forvojaĝi to depart, leave, set out.
fosado digging.
fosaĵo excavation, hole, ditch, pit, moat, trench.
fosbesto burrowing animal.
fosejo pit.
fosfata acido phosphoric acid.
fosfato phosphate.
fosfaturio phosphaturia.
fosfito phosphite.
fosforeska phosphorescent.
fosforeski to glow in the dark, phosphoresce.
fosforesko phosphorescence.
fosforo phosphorus.
fosi to dig, grub, spade, excavate.
fosiliiĝi to fossilize.
fosilio fossil.
fosilo digging implement, shovel, spade.
fosmaŝino backhoe.
foso ditch.
fosto pole, post, stanchion, stake, upright, upright beam, upright support, vertical support, pier.
fotado photography.
fotaĵo photo, photograph.
fotaparato camera.
fotelo armchair, easy chair.
fotema fond of taking photos.
foti to photograph.
fotilo camera.
fotisto photographer.
foto photo, photograph.
fotocelilo viewfinder.
fotoĉelo photoelectric cell.
fotodermatito photodermatitis.
fotografa photographic. **fotografa aparato** camera.
fotografado photography.
fotografaĵo photograph.
fotografarto photography.
fotografi to photograph.
fotografilo camera.
fotografio photography.
fotografisto photographer.
fotografo act of taking a photograph.
fotographo photograph.
fotogravuro collotype.

fotokopii to photocopy.
fotokopiilo photocopier.
fotokopio photoprint.
fotokromio colour photography.
fotometro photometer.
fotono photon.
fotosfero photosphere.
fotosintezo photosynthesis.
fotostato photostat.
fototerapio phototherapy.
fototipio collotype.
fraĉjo bro.
fragila fragile.
fragileco fragility.
fragmenta fragmentary.
fragmenti to fragment.
fragmentigi to break into fragments.
fragmentigo fragmentation.
fragmentiĝi to fragment.
fragmentiĝo fragmentation.
fragmento bit, fragment, lump, piece, scrap, shred, splinter.
fragmito reed.
frago strawberry.
fragomarko birthmark.
fragopotentilo barren strawberry.
fragospinaco Indian paint, strawberry blite, strawberry pigweed.
frajejo breeding pond.
fraji to spawn.
frajo fish eggs, spawn, fry, roe.
frajti to freight.
frajtletero official list of quotations, list of prices, way-bill.
frajto freight.
frakasi to crush, shatter, smash, break to pieces, shatter.
frakasiĝebla breakable, fragile.
frakasiĝema brittle.
frakasiĝo break, fracture.
frakcia parto fractional part.
frakcii to crack, fractionate, split up.
frakciigi to crack, fractionate, split up.
frakcikorpo fraction field, quotient field.
frakcio faction, fraction.
frakcistreko forward slash, fraction bar.
frako dress coat, evening dress, tails.
frakseno ash (tree).
fraksinelo dittany.
fraktalo fractal.
frakturo fracture.
framasona Masonic.
framasono Freemason, Mason.
frambezio yaws.
frambo raspberry.
framboarbusto raspberry, raspberry bush.
frambujo raspberry bush.
framo frame, framework, substructure, skeleton.

franca French. **Franca Giano** French Guiana. **Franca Gujano** French Guiana.
franca lingvo French, French language.
Franca Polinezio French Polynesia.
France in French.
francino Frenchwoman, French lady.
Francio France.
francio francium.
franciskano Franciscan.
Francisko Francis.
franciumo francium.
Franclando France.
franclingva French-language.
franclingvano French speaker.
Franco Frenchman.
Francujo France.
franda alluring, attractive, enticing, tempting, appetizing, delicious, tasty.
frandaĵejo delicatessen.
frandaĵo delicacy, titbit, sweet, rarity, tidbit.
frandema dainty, sweet-toothed.
frandi to eat for pleasure, relish, enjoy.
frandulo epicure.
frangolo glossy buckthorn, breaking buckthorn, black dogwood.
franĝharoj bangs.
franĝi to fringe.
franĝipano almond paste.
franĝo fringe.
franka Frankish.
frankfurta of Frankfurt.
Frankfurto Frankfort, Frankfurt. **Frankfurto ĉe la Majno** Frankfort upon the Main. **Frankfurto ĉe majno** Frankfurt am Main. **Frankfurto ĉe odro** Frankfurt an der Oder.
franko franc.
frankolino francolin.
Frankonio Franconia.
franzi to eat cunt.
frapegi to thump.
frapego great blow.
frapeti to pat, tap, rap. **frapeti sur** to tap at, tap on.
frapeto rap.
frapfermi la pordon to slam the door (shut).
frapfrazo catchphrase.
frapi to hit, knock, strike. **frapi ĉe la pordo** to knock at the door. **frapi laŭte** to knock loudly. **frapi sur la pordon** to knock at the door, rap at the door.
frapiĝi to strike.
frapinstrumento percussion instrument.
frapmildigilo bumper.
frapo knock, shock.
frata brotherly, fraternal.
frataro brotherhood, confraternity, fraternity.

frateca brotherly, fraternal.
frateco brotherhood, fraternity.
fratedzino brother's wife, sister-in-law.
frateraro brotherhood, fellowship.
fraterkulo puffin.
frateto little brother.
fratidino niece.
fratido nephew.
fratigi to unite.
fratiĝi to fraternize.
fratino sister.
fratmortiga fratricidal.
fratmortiginto fratricide.
fratmortigo fratricide.
fratmurda fratricidal.
fratmurdinto fratricide.
fratmurdo fratricide.
frato brother.
fratrio phratry.
fratula fraternal.
fratuleco fellowship.
fratulo friar.
fraŭda fraudulent.
fraŭde fraudulently.
fraŭdi to defraud, swindle.
fraŭdo fraud.
fraŭdulo hacker.
fraŭla single, unmarried.
fraŭleca celibate.
fraŭleco bachelorhood, celibacy, unmarried state.
fraŭlina single, unmarried.
fraŭlino maiden, Miss, unmarried woman, young lady.
fraŭlo bachelor.
frazaro phrase-book.
frazeologio phraseology.
Frazerburgo Fraserburgh.
frazero phrase.
frazisto coaxer, flatterer.
frazo expression, sentence, statement, phrase.
Frederiko Frederick.
fregatkapitano commander.
fregato frigate, frigate bird.
frekvenco frequency.
frekventanto patron, frequenter, denizen.
frekventi to frequent, visit regularly, habitually visit.
fremburi to stuff.
fremda alien, foreign, strange.
fremde strangely, in a foreign way.
fremdigi to abalienate, alienate.
fremdigo abalienation.
fremdlanda alien, foreign, offshore, overseas.
fremdlandano foreigner, alien.
fremdlande abroad.
fremdlando foreign country.
fremdolando strange land, foreign country.
fremdulino stranger, female stranger.
fremdulo foreigner, stranger.
fremdvorto loanword.
freneza crazy, insane, mad, nuts.
frenezaĵo madness, folly.
freneze madly.
frenezeco craziness, insanity, lunacy, madness, frenzy, insanity.
frenezeta crack-brained, daft, loopy, nuts, weird.
frenezi to act crazy, rave.
frenezigi to madden.
freneziĝi to go crazy.
freneziĝo frenzy.
frenezo craziness, insanity, lunacy, madness.
frenezulejo insane asylum.
frenezulino madwoman.
frenezulo lunatic, madman, maniac.
frenologio phrenology.
freono freon.
fresko fresco.
freŝa fresh, new, recent, raw.
freŝbakita freshly-baked.
freŝcerba adroit.
freŝdata recent.
freŝdate recently.
freŝe freshly. **freŝe bakita** freshly baked.
freŝeco airiness.
freŝiganta refreshing.
freŝviando fresh meat.
fretita banded.
freto collar, ferrule, fret.
freŭda Freudian.
freŭdismo Freudianism.
Freŭdo Freud.
frezi to mill-cut, mill.
frezilo router.
frezio freesia.
fri including. **fri dogana** including duties.
frida cold, frigid.
fridigi to refrigerate.
fridigujo refrigerator.
fridkesteto cooler.
fridujo refrigerator.
friganeo caddis-fly.
frigano caddis-fly.
frikandelo frikandel (Dutch snack).
frikasaĵo fricassee.
frikasi to fricassee.
frikativo fricative.
fringelo siskin.
fringo chaffinch, finch.
fripona nasty, roguish.
friponaĵo con, scam.
friponeco knavery.
friponego great scoundrel.
friponeto little rascal.
friponi to cheat, trick, do something crooked, swindle, con, scam.

fripono

fripono cheat, crook, rogue, rascal, villain, swindler.
frisa Frisian.
frisino Frisian, Frisian woman.
Frisio Frisia.
friska chilly.
Frislando Friesland, Frisia.
friso frieze.
Friso Frisian.
Frisujo Frisia.
fritaĵo fritter.
Fritaŭno Freetown.
friti to fry.
fritiĝi to fry.
fritilario fritillary.
fritilo frying pan.
fritita ovo boiled egg.
frito French fry, potato chip.
frituri to deep-fry.
friula Friulian.
frivola frivolous.
frivolaĵo trifling.
frivoleco frivolity.
frivolo frivolity.
friza crisp.
frizaĵo hairdo, frizz.
frizejo hairdressing salon.
frizi to curl, frizz.
frizilo curler (hair).
frizistino hairdresser, female hairdresser.
frizisto barber, hairdresser, hair stylist.
frizo hairdo.
frizona Frisian.
frizonino Frisian, Frisian woman.
Frizonio Friesland.
frizono Frisian.
Frizonujo Friesland.
frogo frog.
fromaĝo cheese.
fromaĝotrançilo cheese slicer.
frondo frond.
frontartikolo editorial, leading article.
fronte in front. **fronte al** across from, opposite to, facing.
fronti to confront, face (toward).
frontispico frontispiece, title-page.
frontmasto foremast.
fronto front, battlefront, frontage.
frontono pediment.
frosta freezing, frosty, raw, chilly.
frostabsceso chilblain.
frostas it's freezing.
frostfako freezing department.
frosti to freeze.
frostigi to freeze.
frostigilo freezer.
frostigita frozen.
frostigujo freezer.
frostiĝi to freeze.

fruktovendejo

frostiĝinta frozen.
frostkesto freezer.
frosto freezing cold, frost.
frostotremi to shiver.
frostotremiga chilling.
frostotremo chills.
frostotremoj creeps, chills, shivers.
frostovundo frostbite.
frostŝvelo chilblain.
frostujo freezer.
frostvundo frostbite.
frota abrasive.
frotadi to rub, keep rubbing.
frotado friction.
frotbroso scrubbing-brush.
froteluza abrasive.
froteti to strike.
frotflamigi to strike.
froti to grate, rub, stroke.
frotiadi to rub.
frotlavi to scour, scrub.
frotlavilo scouring pad.
froto friction.
frotokesto freezer.
frotpeco brake block, brake shoe.
frotpuriga abrasive.
frotpurigi to polish, rub, scrub.
frotpurigilo abrasive.
frotskrapi to abrade.
frotumi to grind, polish smooth.
frotvundi to graze.
frotvundo abrasion, excoriation, graze, scratch.
frua early.
frue early, shortly, soon.
frugilego rook.
frui to be early, be fast.
fruigi to hasten, advance.
fruktabro fruit tree.
fruktaĵo jam, marmalade.
fruktarbaro orchard.
fruktarbejo orchard.
fruktarbo fruit tree.
fruktejo fruit garden.
fruktgrapolo berry cluster.
frukti to yield, bear fruit.
fruktigi to fertilize.
frukto fruit.
fruktodona fertile, fruitful. **fruktodona interŝanĝo** fruitful exchange.
fruktodoneco fruitfulness.
fruktodoni to fructify.
fruktofolio carpel.
fruktoĝardeno orchard.
fruktoj benefits.
fruktoporta fruitful, productive, prolific.
fruktoriĉa bearing much fruit.
fruktosukero fructose, laevulose.
fruktovendejo fruitier's.

fruktozo fructose, laevulose.
fruktsuko fruit juice.
fruktuzo usufruct.
frumatene early in the morning.
frumatura precocious.
frumaturoeco precocity.
fruntaĵo pediment.
frunto brow, forehead.
fruntosto frontal bone.
fruntrimeno brow band.
frustracia frustrating.
frustri to frustrate.
frustro frustration.
frutempe early, soon.
ftiza phthisical.
ftizo consumption, tuberculosis, phthisis.
ftizulo consumptive, pulmonic person.
FTP-ejo archive, FTP site.
fueli to fuel.
fuelo fuel.
fugo fugue (mus.).
fuĝanto fugitive.
fuĝi to flee, run away.
fuĝkoridoro firebreak.
fuĝo flight, run.
Fuji-monto Fujiyama.
fuko jetsam, wrack.
fuksino fuchsine, magenta.
fuksio fuchsia.
fulardo foulard.
fulgeca black as soot.
fulgi to be sooty.
fulgigi to blacken (with soot).
fulgo soot.
fulgokolora black as soot.
fulgonigrigi to blacken.
fulgoro firefly.
fulgosimila black as soot.
fuli to full.
fuligulo tufted duck.
fuliko coot.
fulma lightning.
fulmaro fulmar.
fulmas lightning is flashing.
fulmeti to sparkle.
fulmi to lighten.
fulmkotono guncotton, nitrocellulose.
fulmlumilo flash.
fulmo lightning.
fulmofermilo fastener, zip, zip fastener, zipper.
fulmoforigilo lightning-rod.
fulmofrapa thunderstruck.
fulmomilito blitzkrieg.
fulmoŝirmilo lightning conductor.
fulmotondro thunderstorm.
fulmrapida lightning-speed.
fulmrapide as fast as lightning, lightning-fast.

fulmŝirmilo lightning-rod.
fuma smoky, of smoke.
fumadi to smoke, continue to smoke.
fumado smoking.
fumaĵi to smoke (fish, etc).
fumaĵita smoked. **fumaĵita haringo** red herring.
fumamanto smoker.
fumanto smoker.
fumario fumitory.
fumdetektilo smoke detector.
fumi to smoke.
fumigado smoking.
fumizi to fumigate.
fumkupeo smokers.
fumo fume, smoke.
fumsuĉi to take a drag (on a cigarette).
fumtabako smoking tobacco.
fumtubo chimney, smokestack.
fumturo smokestack.
fumujo smokestack.
funda thorough, painstaking.
fundamenta foundational, fundamental, base, basis. **fundamenta grupo** fundamental group.
fundamente basically, fundamentally.
fundamenteco fundamentality.
fundamenti to base, establish, found.
fundamentismo fundamentalism.
fundamentisto fundamentalist.
fundamento element, foundation.
funde from A to Z, thoroughly. **funde de** at the very bottom of.
fundo bottom, foundation, ground.
funebra dismal, doleful, funereal, mournful, sinister, gloomy. **funebra kanto** dirge. **funebra kovrilo** shroud, pall. **funebra procesio** funeral procession. **funebra sonorado** knell. **funebra vesto** mourning (dress).
funebraĵo funeral service.
funebraĵoj funeral (services).
funebranto mourner.
funebri to bewail, mourn, grieve, weep.
funebro grief, mourning (band, garments).
funebrulo mourner.
funeli to funnel.
funelo funnel.
fungo fungus, mushroom, toadstool.
fungoatakita attacked by fungus.
funiklo umbilical chord.
funkcia functional. **funkcia klavo** function key. **funkcia programlingvo** functional language.
funkciado action, functionality, operation, performance, workings.
funkciadsistemo operating system.
funkcianta active.
funkciĉapeto function identification.

funkciĉapo function heading.
funkcideklaro function declaration.
funkcie functionally. **funkcie ekvivalenta** functionally equivalent.
funkcieco functionality.
funkcii to function, operate, run, work.
funkciigi to control, operate, work.
funkciigo implementation, operation.
funkciklavo function key.
funkcinomo function identifier.
funkcio function.
funkcionalo functional.
funkcipreta in working order.
funkciserio function series.
funkciteno maintenance.
funkciulo functionary.
funkcivico function sequence, sequence of functions.
funkcivoko function designator.
funto pound (weight or money).
funtocento centner, hundredweight, cental, quintal.
fuorto stronghold, fort.
furaĝi to fodder, forage.
furaĝo fodder, forage.
furiero quartermaster (sergeant).
furio fury, goddess of vengeance.
furioza desperate, frantic, furious, raging.
furioze furiously, wildly, ferociously.
furiozeco rage, fury.
furiozegiĝi to run amuck.
furiozi to be furious, rage.
furiozigi to enrage, incense.
furioziĝi to run amuck.
furiozo fury.
furiozulo madman.
furo ferret.
furora hit, best-selling.
furori to be all the rage, be a hit.
furorkanto hit (song).
furorlibro bestseller.
furoro blockbuster, craze, hit, fad.
furunko boil (blain), furuncle.
furzadi to fart.
furzado breaking of wind.
furzi to fart.
furzo fart.
fusilisto rifleman.
fusilo gun, rifle.
fusteno fustian.
fusto shaft, stock.
fuŝ- (denotes bungling, incompetence).
fuŝa clumsy, half-arsed, half-assed, ham-fisted, inept, messy.
fuŝado blundering.
fuŝaĵo blunder, bungle, mess, screw-up.
fuŝanto bungler.
fuŝe clumsily, ineptly.
fuŝema errant, inclined to mistakes.
fuŝformi to deform, distort.
fuŝfotografisto a bungling photographer.
fuŝi to botch, bungle, screw up, spoil, make a mess of, muddle.
fuŝisto a bumbler, a botcher, one who screws things up.
fuŝita spoiled.
fuŝkompreni to misunderstand.
fuŝkontakto short circuit.
fuŝlingvaĵo gibberish.
fuŝludi to strum.
fuŝmetiisto botcher.
fuŝnodo granny knot.
fuŝoado daubing.
fuŝpalpi to fumble, touch, grope.
fuŝparoli to misspeak.
fuŝparolo gibberish.
fuŝpentraĵo daub, kitschy painting.
fuŝpentri to daub.
fuŝskribi to scrawl.
fuŝtranĉi to mangle.
fuŝulo bungler, bumbler, unskilled person.
futbalejo gridiron.
futbali to play football or soccer.
futbalo football, soccer.
futo foot (12 inches).
futsigno foot sign (′).
futurismo futurism.
futuristo futurist.
futuro future, future tense.
fuzaĵo rocket.
fuzaviadilo rocket-plane.
fuzelaĝo fuselage, hull.
fuzeo fuse.
fuzi to fizz, burn slowly.
fuziliero fusilier.
fuzio fusion.

G

G sol (music).
gabardino gabardine.
gabaro lighter.
gabio gabion.
gablo gable.
Gabono Gabon.
Gaborono Gaborone.
gadmeso dildo.
gado cod.
gadolinio gadolinium.
gaela Gaelic.
gaelo Gael.
gafo gaff.
gagato jet.
gago gag.
gaino sheath petticoat.
gaja cheerful, gay, merry, happy.
gajado merrymaking.
gajakligno lignum-vitae.
gajako lignum vitae.
gajakolo guaiacol.
gajanima cheerful, cheerful.
gajanimeco cheerfulness.
gaje cheerfully, happily, gaily.
gajeco cheerfulness, gaiety, merriment, mirth.
gajega jolly.
gajegeco exuberance.
gajema cheerful.
gajeme cheerfully.
gajemo cheerfulness.
gajhumora cheerful, gay, merry.
gaji to be gay.
gajiga amusing.
gajigi to enliven.
gajiĝi to become happy, turn cheerful.
gajlardio gaillardia, blanketflower.
gajlardo galliard.
gajlo gall-nut, oak apple, gall.
gajna winning.
gajnado accrual.
gajnanto winner.
gajni to gain, earn, profit, win. **gajni monon** to make money. **gajni sian porvivon per** to live on, live upon.
gajniga remunerative.
gajniĝi to accrue.
gajninto winner.
gajno benefit, gain, profit, boon.
Gajo Caius, Gaius.
gajulo fun guy, jolly fellow.
gaki to cackle.
gala bilious.
galacido bile acid.
galago bushbaby.

galaksia galactic.
galaksio galaxy.
galanta gallant.
galante gallantly.
galanterio millinery, toilet accessories.
galantino galantine.
galanto snowdrop.
Galapagoinsuloj Galápagos Islands.
Galapagoj Galápagos Islands.
Galaŝilzo Galashiels.
galato Galatian.
galbano galbanum.
galbuledoj jacamars.
galbulo jacamar.
galdukto bile duct.
galeaso galleass, galliass.
galega Galician.
Galegio Galicia.
Galegujo Galicia.
galeno galena.
galeopiteko colugo, flying lemur.
galeopso hemp-nettle.
galerio gallery.
galero galley.
galeza Galois. **galeza grupo** Galois group. **galeza korpo** Galois field. **galeza superkorpo** Galois extension.
Galezo Galois.
galgo gallows.
galica Galician.
galicia Galician.
Galicio Galicia.
galicismo Gallicism.
Galicujo Galicia.
galilea Galilean.
galileano Galilean.
Galileo Galilee.
Galilio Galilee.
Galilujo Galilee.
galimatio balderdash, farrago, nonsense, gibberish.
galinago snipe.
galino fowl.
galinolo moorhen.
galinulo moorhen.
galio bedstraw.
galiono galleon.
galiumo gallium.
galjono galloon, gold braid, stripe.
galkrevi to burst for biliousness.
Gallo Gaul.
galo bile, gall.
galono galloon, piping, ribbon, tinsel, trim, cord, lace, stripe.
galope galloping.

galopege

galopege at a full gallop.
galopegi to gallop along, go at a gallop, ride at a gallop.
galopego gallop.
galopeti to canter.
galopi to gallop.
galopo gallop.
galoŝo galosh, overshoe.
galoza biliary, bilious. **galoza ŝtono** biliary stone.
galŝtona malsano cholelithiasis.
Galvajo Galway.
galvana galvanic.
galvanaplastiko electroplating.
galvanismo galvanism.
galvanizi to galvanize.
galvanoplastiko electroplating.
gamao gamma (Γγ).
gamaŝeto spat.
gamaŝo gaiter.
Gambilando Gambia.
Gambio Gambia.
gambito gambit.
gambo leg.
gambovjolo bass viol, bass viola, bass fiddle.
gamelo mess tin.
gameto gamete.
gamo[1] gamma (Γγ).
gamo[2] gamut, key, (musical) scale, range.
gana Ghana.
ganaa Ghanaian.
ganaano Ghanaian.
ganano Ghanaian.
Ganao Ghana.
gandarvo gandharva.
ganglio ganglion.
gangliono ganglion.
Gango Ganges.
gangreni to mortify.
gangreniĝi to become gangrene.
gangreno gangrene.
gangstero gangster, hoodlum.
Ganĝeso Ganges.
Ganimedo Ganymede.
Gano Ghana.
ganstero gangster, hoodlum.
ganto glove, mitten.
gantpupo glove puppet, hand puppet.
gantujo glove compartment.
gapanta thoughtless, unthinking, mindless, wanton.
gapi to gape, gawk. **gapi al** to gape at.
gapulo loafer, simpleton, gawk.
gapvagi to dawdle, moon about.
garaĝi to dock, put away.
garaĝo garage.
garantiaĵo bail, lien, pawn, pledge, security, guarantee, surety.
garantianto bondsman, surety, voucher.

gasforma

garantii to guarantee, warrant, vouch, be responsible for.
garantiita letero bill of lading.
garantio guarantee, warrant, voucher.
garantiulo hostage.
garbaro stack (straw).
garbejo barn, granary.
garbigi to bind into sheaves.
garbigilo baler.
garbo bunch, bundle, sheaf, cluster, shock.
garda protective.
gardado security, vigil.
gardanĝelo guardian angel.
gardanto custodian, guard, guardian, watch, warder, keeper.
garde protectively.
gardeco ward (care).
gardema careful, vigilant, watchful.
gardeme carefully.
gardemo vigilance, watchfulness.
gardenio gardenia.
gardhundo guard dog.
gardi to guard, keep, look after, watch over, escort, retain. **gardi sin** be careful. **gardu vin!** look out!
gardilo safeguard.
gardistaro escort.
gardisto curator, guard, jailer.
gardo guard, vigil, watch.
gardohundo watchdog.
gardostaranto sentinel, sentry.
gardostari to stand guard.
gardotempo watch.
gardoturo watch-tower.
gargarajo gargle.
gargari to gargle, rinse.
gargojlo gargoyle.
Gario Gary.
garlando wreath.
Garloĥo Gairloch.
garnaĵo equipment, accessories, fittings.
garni to decorate, embellish, equip, fit out, furnish, garnish, trim, reinforce, strengthen, adorn. **garni tablon** to set the table.
garnilo equipment, accessories, fittings.
garnituri to decorate, embellish, fit out, furnish, garnish, trim.
garnituro accessories, fittings, garniture, kit, trimmings.
garnizoni to garrison.
garnizono garrison.
garolo jay.
Garvo Garve.
gasa gaseous.
gasbotelo gas canister, gas cylinder.
gasdukto gas pipeline.
gaseca gaseous.
gaseldukto bustle pipe.
gasforma gaseous.

gasigi to aerate.
gaskomputilo gas meter.
Gaskona Golfo Bay of Biscay.
Gaskonio Gascony.
gaskono Gascon.
Gaskonujo Gascony.
gasmasko gas mask.
gasmezurilo gas meter.
gasmufo mantle.
gaso gas.
gasojlo kerosene, mineral oil, oil.
gasometro gasometer.
gaspedalo accelerator, accelerator pedal.
gaspremo gas-pressure.
gastama hospitable.
gastameco hospitality.
gastamo hospitality.
gastejestrino hostess, landlady.
gastejestro host, innkeeper, landlord.
gastejo guest house, hostel, inn.
gasterosteo stickleback.
gasti to be a guest of, stay with, receive hospitality.
gastiga komputilo host, host computer.
gastigantino hostess.
gastiganto host.
gastigema hospitable.
gastigi to accommodate, entertain, put up.
gastlibro guestbook.
gastloĝi to be on a visit, stay, stop.
gasto guest, sojourner.
gastornito gastornis.
gastra gastric.
gastroladi to play the guest.
gastronomiisto gastronome, gourmet.
gastronomio gastronomy.
gastronomo gastronome.
gastropiedulo gastropod.
gastropodo gastropod.
gastrostomio gastrostomy.
gasujo gas-holder.
gaŭĉo cowboy, gaucho.
gaŭĝi to gauge.
gaŭĝo gauge.
gaŭla Gallic, Gaulish.
Gaŭlio Gaul.
Gaŭlo Gaul.
gaŭlterio gaultheria, wintergreen.
gaŭlto gault.
Gaŭlujo Gaul.
gaŭro gaur.
gaŭsa Gaussian. **gaŭsa eliminado** gaussian elimination. **gaŭsa entjero** Gaussian integer. **gaŭsa kurbo** bell-shaped curve, Gaussian curve.
Gaŭso Gauss.
gavialo gavial.
gavio diver, loon.
gavoto gavotte.

gazanio gazania.
gazelo gazelle.
gazetara konferenco press conference.
gazetaro press, newspapers, printing.
gazetistino journalist, female journalist.
gazetisto journalist.
gazetkapo banner.
gazeto gazette, magazine, newspaper, periodical.
gazo gauze.
gazonero sod, sod of grass, turf.
gazonfalĉilo lawn mower.
gazono lawn.
gazpaĉo gazpacho.
ge- (persons of both sexes taken together).
geadoptintoj adoptive parents.
geaktoroj actors and actresses.
geamantoj lovers.
geavo grandparent.
geavoj grandparents.
gebani to bathe together.
geedza spousal. **geedza paro** married couple.
geedzeca marital, matrimonial.
geedzeco marriage, matrimony.
geedzigi to marry (unite).
geedziĝa nuptial. **geedziĝa ceremonio** wedding. **geedziĝa festo** wedding, wedding party.
geedziĝanonco banns, wedding-announcement.
geedziĝantoj bride and groom.
geedziĝi to marry, be married, get married.
geedziĝinta married.
geedziĝo marriage, wedding.
geedzo spouse.
geedzoj couple, married people.
geedzoringo wedding ring.
geesperantistoj Esperantists (of both sexes).
geezdiĝa marital.
gefianciĝo engagement.
gefianĉiĝi to become engaged.
gefianĉiĝo betrothal, engagement.
gefiloj sons and daughters.
gefrateca brotherly.
gefrato brother, sibling, sister.
gefratoj brothers and sisters, siblings.
gefraŭloj single people.
geheno Gehenna.
Geheno Gehenna, hell.
gejo homosexual, gay.
gejsero geyser.
Gejsersvilo Geysersville.
gejŝo geisha.
gejunularo youth, young people.
gejunuloj boys and girls.
gekedoj geckos.
geknaboj boy(s) and girl(s).
geko gecko.

Gelaso Galashiels.
gelatenaĵo jelly.
gelateno gelatine.
Gelderlando Guelderland, Guelders.
geldra Guelders.
Geldrio Guelderland, Guelders.
Geldrujo Guelderland, Guelders.
gelignito gelignite.
gelo frost.
gemisto gem worker, jeweller.
gemo gem, jewel.
gemuta agreeable.
genaro genome.
genciano gentian.
genealogia genealogical. **genealogia arbo** genealogical tree. **genealogia tabelo** family tree, pedigree.
genealogiarbo genealogical tree.
genealogie genealogically.
genealogiisto genealogist.
genealogio family tree, genealogy, pedigree, genealogy.
genealogo genealogist.
genepo grandchild.
genera generative, genital.
generaciaro family tree, genealogy, pedigree.
generacio generation.
generado generation.
generaj operacisimboloj polymorphism.
generalisimo generalissimo.
generalo general.
generatorejo electrical generator.
generatoro generator.
generi to beget, generate, spawn.
generilo genitals.
genero clan, ethnic group, family, kin, kind, people, race, stock, tribe.
genetika genetic.
genetike genetically.
genetikisto geneticist.
genetiko genetics.
Genezo Genesis.
genia brilliant, gifted, ingenious, masterly, of genius.
genie brilliantly.
genio genius.
genisto broom.
genitivo genitive.
geniulo genius, man of genius.
geno gene.
genocido genocide.
genomo genome.
genotipo genotype.
genoto genet.
genro gender, genus.
genta sistembendo master tape.
gento clan, ethnic group, genus, tribe, family, kin, race, people.

Gento Ghent.
genue on the knees.
genufleksi to genuflect, kneel.
genui to kneel.
genuiĝi to kneel.
genukavo back of the knee, hock.
genuo knee.
genuosto kneecap, patella.
geocentra geocentric.
geocentre geocentrically.
geocentrismo geocentrism.
geodeziko geodesic.
geodezio geodesy.
geofiziko geophysics.
geognozio geology.
geografia geographic, geographical. **geografia karto** map.
geografie geographically.
geografiisto geographer.
geografikarto map.
geografio geography.
geografo geographer.
geokaŝludo geocaching.
geokomputiko geomatics.
geologia geological.
geologie geologically.
geologiisto geologist.
geologio geology.
geologo geologist.
geometria geometric. **geometria figuro** figure (geometric shape). **geometria meznombro** geometric average, geometric mean. **geometria progresio** geometric progression, geometric sequence. **geometria serio** geometric series. **geometria vico** geometric progression, geometric sequence.
geometrie geometrically.
geometriisto geometer, geometrician.
geometrio geometry.
geometro geometer moths, Geometra; geometer, geometrician.
geopolitika geopolitical.
geopolitike geopolitically.
geopolitiko geopolitics.
georgia Georgian.
georgiano Georgian.
georgino dahlia.
Georgo George.
geoterma geothermal. **geoterma energio** geothermal energy.
geotrupo dor beetle, earth-boring dung beetle.
gepardo cheetah.
gepatra parental. **gepatra lingvo** mother tongue.
gepatreco parenthood.
gepatro parent. **gepatroj** parents.
gepraavo great-grandparent.

geranio geranium.
gerbilo gerbil.
gerila guerilla.
gerilano guerilla.
gerilisto guerrilla.
gerilo guerilla war.
gerleno warp.
Germana German. **Germana Demokratia Respubliko** East Germany, GDR. **Germana Federacia Respubliko** German Federal Republic. **germana lingvo** German, German language.
germanaĉo Hun, Jerry, Kraut.
germanema pro-German.
germanino German, German lady, German woman.
Germanio Germany.
germaniumo germanium.
Germanlando Germany.
germanlingva German-language.
germanlingve in German.
germano German.
Germanujo Germany.
gerundio gerund.
gesamideanoj fellow Esperantists.
gesinjoroj ladies and gentlemen, Mr and Mrs.
gesta lingvo sign language.
gestadi to make gestures, gesticulate.
gestema demonstrative, gesticulating.
gesti to gesticulate, gesture.
gestlingvo sign language.
gesto gesture.
gestolingvo sign language.
getao geta (Japanese shoe).
geto ghetto.
Getshedo Gateshead.
getto ghetto.
geumo avens.
gevolapukistoj Volapükists (of both sexes).
gibi to jibe.
gibono gibbon.
Gibraltaro Gibraltar.
giĉeto window, ticket window.
Gideono Gideon.
gigabajto gigabyte.
gigabito gigabit.
gigaherco gigahertz.
giganta gigantic, huge, giant.
gigante gigantically.
giganto giant.
gigatuno gigaton.
gigavatto gigawatt.
Gigo Gigha.
Gilbertinsuloj Gilbert Islands.
Gilberto Gilbert.
gildestro guildmaster.
gildo guild.
gilgameŝ Gilgamesh.
Gilgameŝo Gilgamesh.
giloŝi to guilloche.
gilotini to guillotine.
gilotino guillotine.
gimastika gymnastic.
gimnasti to exercise.
gimnastika gymnastic.
gimnastikejo gym, gymnasium.
gimnastiki to do gymnastics, exercise.
gimnastikisto gymnast.
gimnastiko exercise, gymnastics.
gimnastikulo gymnast.
gimnasto gymnast.
gimnaziano pupil, student.
gimnazio grammar school, high school, secondary school, middle school.
gimnospermo gymnosperm.
gimnoto eel.
gineceo gynoecium.
ginekologia gynaecological.
ginekologiisto gynaecologist.
ginekologio gynaecology.
ginekologo gynaecologist.
gineo guinea.
Ginevro Guinevere.
gingamo gingham.
gingiva gum.
gingivalo palato-alveolar.
gingivo gum (mouth).
ginodioika gynodioecious.
ginoika gynoecious.
ginomonoika gynomonoecious.
ginostemo gynostemium.
gipaeto bearded vulture, lammergeier.
gipsbandaĝo cast.
gipsi to plaster.
gipso gypsum, plaster (of Paris).
gipsofilo baby's breath, chalk plant, gypsophila, soapwort.
gipsoŝtono gypsum.
giri to gyrate.
girlandi to wreathe.
girlando garland, wreath.
giroskopo gyroscope.
gisfero cast iron.
gisforno blast furnace.
gisi to cast.
giso alloy of carbon with a metal.
gisto yeast.
gistpulvoro baking powder.
gitaro guitar.
G-klefo treble clef (𝄞).
glabelo glabella.
glacaĵo ice cream.
glacea glossy.
glaceo icing.
glacia icy.
glaciaĵbombo bombe.
glaciaĵejo ice cream shop.

glaciaĵo ice cream.
glaciaro glacier.
glacibalaisto sweeper.
glacie icily.
glaciejo glacier.
glaciepoko ice age.
glacierego iceberg.
glacihokeo ice hockey.
glaciiga frigid.
glaciigi to freeze.
glaciiĝi to freeze.
glaciinsulo iceberg.
glacikompreso ice pack.
glacikubfarilujo ice tray.
glacimalvarma ice-cold.
glacimevo glaucous gull.
glacimonto iceberg.
glacio ice.
glacipluvo sleet.
glacirompiĝo break in ice.
glacirompilo icebreaker.
glaciso glacis.
glacisranko cold store, freezer, ice box, ice cellar, ice chest.
glacitenejo cold store, freezer, ice box, ice cellar, ice chest.
glaciujo cold store, freezer, ice box, ice cellar, ice chest.
glaciumi to glaze.
glaciurso polar bear.
glaciviro iceman.
glacmonto iceberg.
glaco pane (of glass), plate glass.
glacosprucigilo windscreen washer.
glacovisilo screen wiper, windscreen wiper.
glaĉero glacier.
gladi to iron (clothes).
gladiatora gladiatorial.
gladiatoro gladiator.
gladilo iron (for clothes).
gladiolo gladiolus.
gladistino ironer (fem).
gladotabulo ironing board.
glamora glamorous.
glamore glamorously.
glamorulino glamour girl.
glanarbo oak.
glandinflamo adenitis.
glando gland.
glaningo acorn cup.
glankukurbo acorn squash.
glano acorn, glans.
glareolo pratincole.
glasa glass.
glasego mug.
Glasgovano Glaswegian.
Glasgovo Glasgow.
glaso glass (a vessel).
glata sleek, slippery, smooth, slick.

glate smoothly, sleekly.
glatigi to smooth, make smooth, smoothen.
glatigo anti-aliasing, smoothing.
glatiĝi to flatten.
glatumi to pet, rub soothingly, stroke.
glaŭcio yellow horned poppy.
glaŭka blue-green.
glaŭkomo glaucoma.
glaŭkonito glauconite.
glave with a sword, using a sword.
glavego large sword.
glavgluisto sword swallower.
glavingo scabbard.
glavisto swordsman.
glavo sword. **Glavo de Damoklo** Sword of Damocles. **glavo dutranĉa** double-edged sword.
glavofiŝo swordfish.
glazuri to glaze.
glazuro glaze.
glebo clod of earth, lump of earth.
glediĉio locust-tree.
glekomo ground ivy.
Glenjuho Linlithgow.
Glenko Glencoe.
glicerino glycerine.
glicerio flote-grass.
glicerolo glycerine.
glicirizaĵo liquorice.
glicirizo liquorice.
glifosato glyphosate.
glikolo glycol.
glikozo glucose.
glimbrili to gleam.
glimi to gleam.
glimo mica.
gliptiko glyptics.
gliptodonto glyptodon.
gliptoteko sculpture gallery.
gliredoj dormice.
gliro dormouse.
glisadi to glide.
glisado glide, gliding.
glisaviadilo glider, sailplane.
glisi to glide, plane.
glisilo glider, sailplane.
glita slick, slippery.
glitadi to glide.
glitado glide, gliding.
glitbobeno shuttle.
glitejo slide.
glitfali to slip.
gliti to glide, slide, slip, skate.
glitiga slick, slippery.
glitigi to scroll, slide, slip.
glitiĝi to slide.
glitilo skate.
glitiloj skates.
glitkalkulilo slide rule.

glitkuranto

glitkuranto skater.
glitkuri to go skating, skate.
glitkurilo skate.
glitkuristo skater.
glito slide, slip.
glitpilko hockey.
glitpunkta floating-point. **glitpunkta prezento** floating-point representation.
glitveturi to sled, sledge.
glitveturilo sledge, sleigh, toboggan.
glitvojo rink, slide.
globa globular.
globartiko ball-and-socket joint.
globetlagro ball bearing.
globeto bead, corpuscle, marble, globule, corpuscle.
globetringo bearing cup.
globforma globular.
globkalkulil abacus.
globkrajono ballpoint pen.
globlagro ball-bearing.
globludado bowling.
globludanto bocce player.
globludisto bocce player.
globludo bowling.
globmartelo ball hammer.
Globo Globe.
globo ball, ball bearing, globe, billiard ball, sphere.
globokardo globe-thistle.
globringo bearing cup.
globskribilo ballpoint, ballpoint pen.
globtavolo spherical layer.
globtrotulo globetrotter.
globulario globe-daisy, globularia.
globuso globe.
glora famous, glorious.
glorama vainglorious.
gloramo ambition.
gloranto eulogist, encomiast.
gloravida thirsting for glory.
gloravido ambition.
glore famously, gloriously.
glori to commend, glorify, laud, praise, glorify. **glori sin** brag, boast.
glorigi to put on the map.
glorigo glorification.
gloriĝi to glorify.
gloriĝo glorification.
glorkanto paean, song of glory.
glorkrono nimbus.
gloro fame, glory, renown.
glorplena glorious, illustrious.
glosaro glossary.
glosi to gloss.
glosino tsetse fly.
gloso gloss.
glota plosivo glottal plosive.
gloto glottis.

golfejo

glua adhesive, clammy.
gluaĵo glue.
gluanta glutinous, sticky, viscous.
glubendo (adhesive) tape.
glubildo collage.
glucinio beryllium.
glueca sticky.
glueco adhesiveness.
glueto size.
glugli to burble, gurgle.
glui to glue, stick.
gluiĝi to stick.
gluilo adhesive.
glukozo glucose.
glumarko sticker.
glumo glume.
gluo glue.
glutaĵo bite.
glutamato glutamate.
glutega binge.
glutegi to gulp down, quaff, swill.
glutego binge.
glutejo maw, gullet.
glutema voracious, gluttonous, piggish.
gluteno gluten.
gluteo buttock.
gluti to swallow.
gluto draught, sip, mouthful, gulp, swallow, sup.
gnafalio balsamweed, cudweed.
gnejso gneiss.
gneto gnetum.
gnoma gnomish.
gnomo brownie, gnome, goblin; (Tolkien) dwarf.
gnomono gnomon.
gnostika gnostic.
gnostikisma gnostic.
gnostikismo gnosticism.
gnostiko gnostic.
gnostikulo gnostic.
gnozo gnostic.
GNUa Ĝenerala Publika Permesilo GNU General Public Licence.
gnuo gnu, wildebeest.
go name of the letter G.
gobio gudgeon.
gobiuso goby.
godetio godetia, satinflower, farewell-to-spring.
goeleto schooner.
gofri to ave with a hot iron.
Gogo Gog.
gojo goy.
goldveno bonanza.
golejisto goalie.
golejlinio goal line.
golejo goal.
golfejo course.

golfeto bay (geography).
golfludado golfing.
golfludanto golfer.
golfludejo course.
golfludisto golfer.
golfludo golf.
golfo bay, golf, gulf.
golfpilko golf ball.
Golgoto Calvary, Golgotha.
goli to score.
Goliato Goliath.
golo goal.
Golspio Golspie.
golulo goalie.
gombo okra.
gonado gonad.
gondolisto gondolier.
gondolo gondola.
gongo gong.
goniometria trigonometric.
gonokoko gonococcus.
gonoreo gonorrhoea, the clap.
goo go (board game).
gorda Gordian.
gordia Gordian.
Gorgono Gorgon.
gorĝdoloro pain in the throat, sore throat.
gorĝinflamo laryngitis.
gorĝnodo Adam's apple.
gorĝo throat.
gorĝotranĉi to cut the throat of.
gorĝpendaĵo wattle.
gorĝŝire throat-splittingly.
gorilecvizaĝa gorilla-faced.
gorilo gorilla.
gosipio cotton plant, gossypium.
Gotaburgo Gothenburg, Göteborg.
Gotamo Gautama, Gotama.
Gotenburgo Gothenburg, Göteborg.
gotika Gothic.
gotiko gothic style.
goto Goth.
graceco grace(fulness).
gracia graceful, gracious, slender, slim.
gracie gracefully, graciously.
gracieco grace, gracefulness.
gracileco graceful slenderness.
gracio grace.
graco grace (of God), gracefulness, mercy.
grada gradual.
gradaltigo promotion.
grade gradually.
gradeco gradation.
gradiento gradient.
gradigi to graduate.
gradigo graduation.
grado degree, grade.
graduso grade.
grafa of a count, of an earl.

grafeiko graph theory.
grafemo grapheme, written symbol.
grafeno graphene.
grafeo graph (of a relation).
grafeteorio graph theory.
grafika graphic. **grafika disponaĵo** graphic device. **grafika fasado** graphical user interface, GUI. **grafika prezento** graphic representation, image curve, plot (of a function). **grafika redaktilo** graphics editor. **grafika reĝimo** graphic mode. **grafika signo** drawing character, graphic character, linedraw character. **grafika uzulinterfaco** Graphical User Interface, GUI.
grafikaĵo graph.
grafike graphically.
grafikilo graphics editor.
grafikisto graphic designer, commercial artist.
grafiko graphic arts, graphics.
grafino countess.
grafismo written form of a word or words (as compared to the sound).
grafito graphite.
graflando county, earldom, shire, landgraviate.
grafo[1] count, earl.
grafo[2] graph.
grafologia graphological.
grafologiisto graphologist, handwriting analyst, handwriting expert.
grafologio graphology, handwriting analysis.
grafologo graphologist, handwriting analyst, handwriting expert.
grafteorio graph theory.
grafujo county, earldom.
Grajaj Alpoj Graian Alps.
grajlo sleet.
grajna granular.
grajnaĵo granule.
grajneca granular.
grajnero (individual) grain.
grajneto granule, tiny particle.
grajnigi to granulate.
grajniĝi to be granulated.
grajno grain, granule, pip (of fruit), stone (of fruit), particle, speck, seed.
grajnpinto bead.
grajnumo pericarp, seed case, seed vessel.
graki to caw, croak, rasp.
Gralkavaliro Grail Knight.
Gralo Grail.
gramatika grammatical. **gramatika sekso** grammatical gender.
gramatike grammatically.
gramatikisto grammaticist, grammarian.
gramatiko grammar.
gramo gram (weight).

gramofonaŭtomato jukebox.
gramofondiskejo disco, discothèque.
gramofondisko gramophone disc.
gramofono gramophone, phonograph, record player, turntable, stereo.
Gramonto Grammont.
Granado Granada.
granatarbo pomegranate tree.
granato pomegranate.
granda big, great, large, tall. **Granda Bernero** Great Bernera. **Granda Bulgarujo** Great Bulgaria. **granda buntpego** great spotted woodpecker. **granda duko** grand duke. **granda duonakso** semi-major axis. **Granda Fasto** Lent, Ramadan. **Granda Fiŝista Benko** Great Fisher Bank. **Granda Frato** Big Brother. **granda kriaglo** spotted eagle. **granda litero** capital letter. **granda nigrakapa mevo** great black-headed gull. **granda otido** great bustard. **granda paruo** great tit. **granda plano** long shot. **granda rabmevo** great skua. **Granda Sklavolago** Great Slave Lake. **Granda Ursino** Great Bear, Greater Bear. **Granda Ursolago** Great Bear Lake. **Grandaj Antiloj** Greater Antilles.
grandaĝa aged, elderly, grown-up, old, of great age.
grandaĝulo elder, person of great age.
grandanima magnanimous.
grandanime magnanimously.
grandanimeco magnanimity.
grandare in a big group.
grandbildo close-up.
grandduklando grand duchy.
grande large (adv.).
grandeco greatness, magnitude, size.
grandega considerable, enormous, huge, immense, tremendous.
grandege enormously, largely.
grandegeco enormity, enormousness, hugeness, immensity.
grandegula giant.
grandegulo giant.
grandflora epimedio longspur epimedium.
grandflora lavatero annual mallow, regal mallow, rose mallow, royal mallow.
grandfolia hortensio bigleaf hydrangea.
grandiga vitro magnifying glass.
grandigi to amplify.
grandiĝi to grow.
grandindustrio big industry.
grandioza grand, grandiose, magnificent, superb, sublime, splendid.
grandioze magnificently.
grandiozeco grandeur, grandiosity, magnificence.
grandiozo grandeur, grandiosity, magnificence.
grandkvanta abundant.
grandmagazeno department store.
grandmama large-breasted.
grandmasto mainmast, maintop.
grando magnitude, size.
grandparte for the greater part, for the most part.
grandparto majority, larger part, greater part.
Grandpolujo Great Poland, Greater Poland.
grandsinjoro gentleman.
grandskala large scale.
grandskale on a large scale.
grandspaca capacious, commodious, roomy, spacious.
grandsume heavily.
grandula suitable for a large person.
grandulo big person.
grandvalora costly, valuable.
grandvolumena bulky.
granita granite.
granito granite.
grano grain.
grapfrukto grapefruit.
grapli to dredge.
graplo grapnel, grappling iron.
graplohoko dragging hook.
grapolo cluster.
grasa bold(face), fat, fatty, greasy, stout. **grasa tiparfasono** boldface.
graseco greasiness, fattiness.
grasega obese.
graseta light.
grasherbo butterwort.
grashisto adipose tissue.
grasi to grease.
grasigi to fatten.
graso fat, grease.
grasoĉelo fat cell.
grasumi to fertilize.
gratado scrabble.
grataĵo scratch.
grateca scratchy.
gratenado au gratin baking.
gratene au gratin.
grati to scratch.
gratifi to tip.
gratifikacio gratuity.
gratifiki to tip, leave a tip.
gratifiko gratuity.
gratifo gratuity.
grato scratch.
gratuli to felicitate, congratulate.
gratulo congratulation.
gratvundi to scratch.
gratvundiĝo scarification.

gratvundo abrasion, scratch, scrape (wound).
graŭli to growl.
graŭlo whirr, whir, throb, hum, drone.
graŭvako greywacke.
grava important, serious, grave, notable, important.
gravaĵo engraving.
gravaspekta important-looking.
grave seriously, importantly.
graveco concern, gravity, importance, weight.
graveda pregnant, with young.
gravedeco pregnancy.
gravedigi to impregnate, make pregnant.
gravedigo insemination.
gravediĝi to conceive (a child), get pregnant.
gravedulino pregnant woman.
gravega momentous, ominous.
gravegaĵo enormity.
gravegeco enormity.
gravi to be serious, be important.
gravigi to make a fuss about, make a big deal of.
graviĝi to become serious.
gravita gravitational.
gravitacio gravitation, gravity.
graviti to gravitate.
gravito gravitation, gravity.
gravitono graviton.
gravitotiro gravitational attraction.
gravmiena serious-faced.
gravmiene with a serious, solemn expression.
gravo engraving.
gravtone in a serious tone.
gravulo important person.
gravuraĵo engraving, print.
gravurĉizilo burin.
gravuri to engrave.
gravurilo engraving tool, graver.
gravuristo engraver.
grebo grebe.
greftado grafting.
greftaĵo graft.
grefti to graft, transplant.
greftilo budding knife.
grefto graft.
grega herd.
gregejo pasture.
grego flock, herd.
gregoria Gregorian.
grejhundo greyhound.
grejo gray (SI unit of the absorbed dose of ionizing radiation). **Grejo** (Louis H.) Gray.
grejsa poto Cologne pot, stone jar.
grejso sandstone.
greka Greek.
grekino Greek woman.
Grekio Greece.
Greklando Greece.
Greko Greek.
Grekujo Greece.
grenadiro grenadier.
grenadisto grenadier.
Grenado Grenada.
grenado grenade.
grenatkolora garnet-coloured, deep red.
grenato garnet.
grencirklo crop circle.
Grendlo Grendel.
grenejo granary, loft.
grenkampo (wheat) field.
grenkesto bin.
grenlanda Greenland. **Grenlanda Maro** Greenland Sea.
grenlandano Greenlander.
Grenlando Greenland.
greno corn, grain, cereal.
grenskarabo corn weevil.
grenventumaĵo chaff, husks.
greso grass.
griaĵo porridge.
grifelo pencil, stylus, pen.
grifo griffin, vulture.
grifono griffon.
grilo cricket (insect).
grimaci to grimace, grin.
grimaco grimace.
grimpi to climb.
grimpkreskaĵo climber, climbing-plant.
grimpmasto pole.
grimpoplanto climber, climbing- plant.
Grimzbio Grimsby.
grincado grating.
grinci to creak, gnash, grate, grind, grate, make a grinding sound, squeak.
grinco scratch, scratching, scraping, grating.
Grinoko Greenock.
grio coarse meal, grits, meal, oatmeal.
grioto morello.
gripo flu, influenza.
griza grey. **griza cirkuo** montagu's harrier. **griza gisfero** grey cast iron. **griza klavo** grey key. **griza materio** grey matter. **griza mevo** common gull, mew gull. **griza pego** grey-headed woodpecker.
grizeco dullness.
grizhara grey-haired.
griziĝi to (turn) grey.
grizo grey.
grizuo fire-damp.
groco gross, 144.
groenlanda Greenland.
groenlandano Greenlander.
Groenlando Greenland.
grogo grog.
grondi to beach, run aground, strand.

gronlanda Greenland. **Gronlanda Maro** Greenland Sea.
gronlandano Greenlander.
Gronlando Greenland.
gropeĝo arris.
grosiero wholesaler.
grosisto wholesaler.
groso gooseberry.
grosujo gooseberry.
groŝo groschen (low value coin).
groteska grotesque, ludicrous.
groteske grotesquely.
groteskulo freak, weirdo.
groto cave, grotto.
grubrako boom.
gruedoj cranes (family).
grujero gruyère.
grumblema morose.
grumblemulo complainer, grumbler.
grumbli to growl, grumble.
grumblulo grouser, grumbler.
grumo bellhop, groom, stableman, page boy, stable boy, servant.
grunda disfalo landslide.
grundakvo groundwater.
grundi to strand.
grundigi to run aground, strand.
grundo ground, soil. **Grundo-Nulo** Ground Zero.
grundoscienco soil science.
grundostato condition of the soil.
grundtavolo layer, layer of earth.
gruntbovo yak.
grunti to grunt.
grunto grunt.
gruo crane (bird).
Gruo Grus.
gruobrako boom.
gruobumo boom.
grupano group member.
grupe in a group.
grupeto small group, circle.
grupigi to group (together).
grupiĝi to form a group, group.
grupnumero group id, group identifier.
grupo group. **grupo de n-modulaj resto-klasoj** residue class group.
grupoido groupoid.
grupope by groups.
gruza gravelly, gritty.
Gruzio Georgia.
gruzmalsano disease characterized by kidney stones or similar.
gruzo gravel, grit.
Gruzujo Georgia.
guano guano.
guaŝo gouache.
gubernatoro governor.
guberniestreco governorship.
guberniestro governor.
gubernio (administrative) province.
gudjero creeping lady's-tresses.
gudri to tar.
gudro pitch, tar.
gudrotuko tarpaulin.
gufo (eagle) owl.
gufujo owlery; tea bar at Esperanto events.
gugli to google.
Guglo Google.
Gujano Guyana.
gujavarbo guava.
gujavo guava.
gulago gulag.
gulaŝo goulash, stew.
guldeno guilder, gulden.
gulo glutton, wolverine.
gumbo gumbo, okra, okra plant.
gumi to erase, gum, smear (with gum).
gumiguto gamboge.
gumo eraser, gum. **gumo araba** akacia.
gupio guppy.
gurdi to grind out.
gurdinsto organ grinder.
gurdisto organ grinder.
gurdita corny, hackneyed.
gurdo barrel-organ, hurdy-gurdy, organ.
gurnardo grey gurnard.
guruo guru.
gusti to taste.
gustigi to flavour, season.
gusto flavour, relish, savoir, taste, zest.
gustumi to taste (food, drink).
gustumo taste, sense of taste.
guŝo husk, pod.
gutaperko gutta-percha.
gute by drops.
guteti to drip, leak, patter, trickle, exude.
guteto droplet.
gutflui to trickle.
guti to drip, drop.
gutigilo medicine dropper.
gutmalsekigi to baste.
guto drip, drop.
gutope nonstop, continuously.
guturala guttural.
guturale gutturally.
guturalo guttural.
guverni to coach, tutor, teach privately.
guvernistino governess.
guvernisto preceptor, tutor.
guzlo gusla.
Gvadelupo Guadalupe.
Gvajanio Guyana.
Gvajano Guyana.
gvalo Welshman.
Gvamo Guam.
gvardiano guard.

gvardio guard (elite military corps, not sentry).
gvatanto lookout, watcher.
gvatemala Guatemalan.
gvatemalano Guatemalan.
gvatemalia Guatemalan.
gvatemaliano Guatemalan.
Gvatemalio Guatemala.
Gvatemalo Guatemala. **Gvatemalo-urbo** Guatemala City.
gvati to be on the watch, on the lookout, keep an eye on, spy on.
gvatisto lookout, watcher.
gvato watch, lookout.
gvatsekvi to tail, shadow.
gvatturo watch-tower.
gverilo guerrilla war.
gvida leading. **gvida ideo** leitmotif, leitmotiv.
gvidantaro leadership.
gvidanteco leadership.
gvidanto leader.
gvidi to conduct, direct, drive, guide, lead, show the way.
gvidilo guidebook.
gvidisto guide.
gvidlibro handbook, guide, guidebook.
gvidmarki to beacon.
gvidmarkilo beacon.
gvido guide, pilot.
gvidstelo lodestar.
gvidvoĉo guiding voice.
gvinea Guinea.
Gvineo Guinea. **Gvineo-Bisaŭo** Guinea-Bissau.

Ĝ

ĝainismo Jainism.
ĝaino Jaina.
Ĝakarto Djakarta, Jakarta.
ĝangalo jungle, rain forest.
ĝardena (having to do with a) garden, gardening. ĝardena kosmoso garden cosmos, Mexican aster.
ĝardenbrasiko cabbage.
ĝardenestro head gardener.
ĝardeneto little garden.
ĝardenilaro garden equipment, garden tools.
ĝardenisto gardener, groundskeeper, landscaper.
ĝardenkoboldo garden gnome.
ĝardenkulturo horticulture.
ĝardenlaborado gardening.
ĝardeno garden.
ĝardenumado gardening.
Ĝardenurbo Garden City.
ĝartero garter belt.
Ĝavo Java.
ĝazbando jazz band, jazz ensemble.
ĝazo jazz.
Ĝedburgo Jedburgh.
ĝelateno jelly.
ĝelo gel.
ĝemadi to moan, groan.
ĝemado groaning, moaning.
ĝeme while groaning.
ĝemegi to wail.
ĝemela twin.
ĝemelduo twins.
ĝemelo twin; Ĝemelo a Gemini. ĝemeloj twins. Ĝemeloj Gemini (zodiac).
ĝemi to groan, moan.
ĝemo¹ groan, moan.
ĝemo² gem.
Ĝemstaŭno Jamestown.
ĝena inconvenient, nasty, troublesome, troubling.
ĝenadi to harass.
ĝenado harassment, hassling.
ĝenajo inconvenience, trouble.
ĝenata bothered.
ĝenateco bother.
ĝendarmo constable, gendarme, patrolman.
ĝene inconveniently, troublingly.
ĝeneco bashfulness.
ĝenega burdensome.
ĝenerala general, usual, rife, prevalent.
Ĝenerala Publika GNU-Permesilo GNU General Public Licence. ĝenerala termo general term.
Ĝeneralaj Ŝtatoj States General.

ĝeneralaĵo generality.
ĝeneralcela komputilo general purpose computer.
ĝenerale generally, in general. ĝenerale akceptita accepted.
ĝeneraleco generality, universality.
ĝeneraligi to generalize.
ĝeneraligita funkcio distribution, generalized function.
Ĝenevo Geneva. Ĝeneva Lago Lake of Geneva.
Ĝengis Genghis.
ĝeni to bother, disturb, hinder, trouble, make uncomfortable. ĝeni sin to go to the bother of, go to the trouble of.
ĝeno nuisance, inconvenience, trouble.
ĝenova Golfo Gulf of Genoa.
Ĝenovo Genoa. Ĝenova Golfo Gulf of Genoa.
ĝenro genre.
ĝentila polite, gentle, civil, courteous, well-mannered, polished, refined. ĝentilaj manieroj good manners.
ĝentilaĵo courtesy.
ĝentile gently, politely.
ĝentileco civility, courtesy, politeness.
ĝentilhomeca gentlemanlike, ladylike.
ĝentilhomo gentleman.
ĝentlemaneca gentlemanlike.
ĝentlemanineca ladylike.
ĝentlemanino lady.
ĝentlemano gentleman.
ĝenulo pain in the ass, pest, nuisance.
Ĝeponto Bridge of Dee.
ĝerboso jerboa.
ĝermana Germanic, Teutonic. ĝermanaj lingvoj Germanic languages.
Ĝermanio Germania.
ĝermanismo Germanism.
ĝermanistiko Germanistic, German Studies.
ĝermanisto Germanist, student of German Studies.
ĝermano German, Teuton.
Ĝermanujo Germania.
ĝermeto gamete.
ĝermi to germinate, shoot, bud.
ĝermo germ.
ĝermoi to germinate.
ĝeto jetty, protecting mole, pier.
ĝi it. ĝi estas por mi volapukaĵo it's all Greek to me.
ĝia its. ĝia la nuna tempo until the present time, up until now.
ĝiaflanke on its side.
ĝiasone at its sound.

ĝiavoje

ĝiavoje on its way.
ĝiba gibbous, hunch-backed.
ĝibaĵo hump, bump.
ĝibeto bump.
ĝibhava hunch-backed.
ĝibigi to arch, stoop, hunch one's back.
ĝibo bump, hump.
ĝibobovo zebu.
Gibraltaro Gibraltar. **Ĝibraltara Markolo** Strait of Gibraltar.
ĝibulo humpback, hunchback.
Gibutio Djibouti.
ĝigo jig.
gigolo gigolo.
ĝihado jihad.
ĝimkano gymkhana.
ĝinfizo Gin Fizz.
Gingiso Genghis.
Ĝinĝis Genghis.
ĝinismo Jainism.
ĝino gin (drink).
ĝinzo jeans.
ĝirafedoj Giraffidae.
ĝirafido baby giraffe.
ĝirafo giraffe.
ĝiranto endorser.
ĝirato endorsee, holder (in due course).
ĝirebla endorsable.
ĝiri to endorse, transfer.
ĝirilo commercial paper, negotiable instrument.
ĝirindikilo blinker.
ĝiro endorsement.
ĝis till, until, up to, as far as. **ĝis!** so long! goodbye! **ĝis antaŭnelonge** until recently. **ĝis kia grado** to what extent. **ĝis la** so long, (see you) later, bye. **ĝis la revido** goodbye, so long. **ĝis malfrua nokto** until late at night. **ĝis malfrue en la nokto** until late at night. **ĝis nun** up to now, yet. **ĝis profunda nokto** until late at night. **ĝis revido** bye, goodbye, so long. **ĝis tia grado ke** to such an extent that.
ĝisatendi to bide, abide, stay for, await, wait (for).
ĝisbaza komplemento radix complement.
ĝisdata up-to-date.
ĝisdatigi to update.
ĝisdatigo update. **ĝisdatigo de dosiero** file updating.
ĝisdektage up to ten days.
ĝisfunda thorough.
ĝisfunde thoroughly.
ĝisgenua to the knees, knee-length.
ĝisgenue up to one's knees, knee-deep.
ĝisi to say goodbye.
ĝisiri to arrive at.
ĝiskole up to one's neck.
ĝiskore right to the heart, thoroughly.

ĝuinde

ĝislimi to extend to.
ĝismentone up to one's chin.
ĝismorte until death.
ĝisnaŭze ad nauseum.
ĝisnombrado countdown.
ĝisnuna present.
ĝisnune until now, until this day.
ĝiso goodbye, farewell.
ĝisosta diehard, dyed-in-the-wool, to the bone.
ĝisoste to the bone.
ĝisostulo die-hard.
ĝispinte to the top of.
ĝisrandigo alignment. **ĝisrandigo dekstren** right alignment, right justify.
ĝisrandiĝi to brim.
ĝis-streko en dash (–). → **streko**.
ĝistalia waist-high.
ĝistalie up to one's waist, waist-deep.
ĝistiam until that time.
ĝistombe to the grave.
ĝisvivi to go through, live to see.
ĝiuĝico jiu-jitsu.
ĝo name of the letter Ĝ.
Goĉia apanaĝo the Ulus of Jochi.
Ĝoĉio Jochi.
ĝogi to jog.
ĝoja happy, glad, joyful, joyous.
ĝojado jubilation, rejoicing.
ĝoje joyfully, happily.
ĝojeco gladness, joy.
ĝojega jovial, jubilant.
ĝojege very joyfully.
ĝojegi to exult.
ĝojego exultation.
ĝojfajro bonfire.
ĝojfrapo burst of joy.
ĝoji to be glad, enjoy, rejoice.
ĝojiga joyful. **ĝojiga pilolo** happy pill.
ĝojige joyfully.
ĝojigi to gladden, make glad, make joyful.
ĝojiĝi to become happy, become joyful.
ĝojkaŭzo reason for joy, cause of joy.
ĝojkriegi to shout with joy.
ĝojkrii to shout with joy.
ĝojkrio shout of joy.
ĝojo gladness, joy, glee.
ĝojplena full of joy.
ĝojvenki to overcome with joy.
Gon John.
ĝonko junk.
ĝuadi to continually enjoy.
ĝuado enjoyment.
ĝuamo hedonism, wanton pleasure.
ĝuegi to relish.
ĝuego delight, relish.
ĝui to delight in, enjoy, relish.
ĝuinda worth enjoying, enjoyable.
ĝuinde enjoyably.

Ĝungario

Ĝungario Dzungaria.
ĝuo delight, joy. **ĝuo por la okuloj** eye candy.
ĝuplena blissful, blessed.
ĝusta correct, exact, proper, right.
ĝustateme on the right topic.
ĝustatempa opportune, seasonable, timely, punctual.
ĝustatempe at the right time, in time, just in time, timely.
ĝustatempeco timeliness.
ĝuste correctly, just, exactly, okay, right, precisely. **ĝuste li** to exactly he, he of all people.

ĝustokaze

ĝusteco accuracy, exactitude, exactness, rightness.
ĝusti to be right, be correct, be proper.
ĝustiga corrective.
ĝustigi to adjust, put right, correct, make adjustments.
ĝustigilo balance wheel.
ĝustigo amendment, correction.
ĝustiĝi to adjust.
ĝustokaze in that case.

H

Ha lo? Hello? (telephone).
habitato habitat.
haĉi to hatch, shade.
Hadeso Hades.
hadiso hadith.
hadrono hadron.
hafnio hafnium.
haga Hague, of The Hague.
hagano inhabitant of The Hague.
hagiografio hagiography.
Hago The Hague.
haĝo hajj.
haĝulo hajji.
haitano Haitian.
haitia Haitian.
haitiano Haitian.
Haitio Haiti.
Haito Haiti.
hajko haiku.
hajlas it hails.
hajlero hailstone.
hajli to hail.
hajlneĝo sleet.
hajlo hail.
hajpo hype.
hakbloko chopping-block.
hakbovaĵo ground beef.
haketado hashing.
haketfunkcio hash function.
haketi to chop, dice, mince.
haketilo hatchet.
hakglavo sabre.
haki to chop, cut, hack, hew.
hakileto hatchet.
hakilo axe, chopper, hatchet.
hako chop, hack.
hakŝtipego chopping-block.
hakviando hamburger meat.
haladza fetid, fumy, gassy, reeking, stinking.
haladzi to fume, reek, stink.
haladzo bad smell, fume(s), stink, stench.
halanĝo baloney, garbage, rubbish, shit.
halebardo halberd.
haleluja alleluia, hallelujah.
halelujo alleluia, hallelujah.
halfo halfback.
haliaeto sea eagle.
haliotiso abalone, ear shell, ormer, haliotis.
halioto abalone, ear shell, ormer.
halo hall (great room).
halogeno halogen.
haloo halo.
Haloveno Halloween.
Halovino Halloween.
halso tack.

haltadi to halt, remain halted.
haltejo halting-place, stop.
halterego barbell.
haltereto dumb-bell.
haltero dumbbell.
halteti to sleep, suspend.
halti to halt, come to a halt, stop. **halti en** to call at.
haltigaĵo obstacle, obstruction.
haltigi to (bring to a) halt, make stop, check, restrain, curb, repress.
haltigilo brake, stopping device.
haltigisto brakesman.
haltigo arrest, obstacle, obstruction, stop, stoppage.
haltigŝuo brake-block, brake-shoe, drag, skid.
halto stop.
haltoloko breakpoint.
haltostreko break, dash; em dash (—). → **streko**.
haltstreko break, dash; em dash (—).
halucinacio hallucination.
halucino hallucination.
halukso big toe.
hamako hammock.
hamamelido witch-hazel.
hamamelo hamamelis, witch-hazel.
hamburgero hamburger.
Hamburgo Hamburg.
hamburgro hamburger.
Hamiltona problemo Hamilton's problem.
Hamiltono Hamilton.
Hamleto Hamlet.
hamstri to hoard.
hamstro hamster.
handbalo handball.
handikapaĵo handicap.
handikapi to handicap.
handikapito disabled person.
handikapo handicap.
handikapula handicapped.
handikapulo disabled person, handicapped person.
hangaro hangar.
Hanibalo Hannibal.
hanlingvo Mandarin.
hannacio Han (principle ethnic group of China).
Hanojaj turoj towers of Hanoi.
Hanojo Hanoi.
Hanovro Hanover.
hansa Hanseatic.
Hanso Hanse, Hanseatic League.
hanti to haunt.

hapakso hapax legomenon.
hapalo marmoset.
hapsburga Hapsburg.
haraĵa hairy.
harakiri to commit harakiri.
harakiro harakiri.
hararangô hair style, hairdo.
Harareo Harare.
hararo coat (animal), hair (head of).
hararsekigilo dryer.
hararzono hair ribbon, fillet.
harbendo sweatband.
harbroso hairbrush.
harbulo hairball.
harda hardy, sturdy.
hardado hardening, seasoning.
harde hardily, sturdily.
hardi to harden, season, steel, temper, toughen.
hardiĝi to harden (to become hardy).
hardita hardy.
hardluti to braze, hard-solder.
hardvaro hardware.
harego bristle.
haremo harem.
harfasko ponytail.
harfendado hair-splitting.
harfendemulo hair-splitter, nit-picker.
harhava hairy.
haringo herring.
Hariso Harris.
harkovrita hairy, hirsute.
Harlemo Harlem.
harleto ringlet.
harligaĵo chignon.
harligo plait, tress (hair).
Har-Magedon Armageddon.
harmona harmonic (function). **harmona meznombro** harmonic average, harmonic mean. **harmona progresio** harmonic progression, harmonic sequence. **harmona serio** harmonic series. **harmona vico** harmonic progression, harmonic sequence.
harmonia harmonious.
harmonie harmoniously.
harmonii to accord, fit together, harmonize.
harmonii kun to accord with.
harmoniigi to harmonize.
harmoniigo harmonization.
harmoniko accordion, harmonica, harp, harmonics.
harmonio harmony.
harmoniumo harmonium.
harmono harmonic.
harneso loom.
harniso harness.
harnodo bun.
haro (single) hair.
haroj (head of) hair.

harperdo alopecia, baldness, loss of hair.
harpi to play the harp.
harpio harpy (eagle).
harpisto harpist.
harplektaĵo braid.
harplena shaggy.
harpo harp.
harpuni to harpoon.
harpuno harpoon.
harsapo shampoo.
harsekigilo hair dryer, blow dryer.
harsplitado hair-splitting.
harstariga eerie, grisly, gruesome, macabre.
hartondisto barber.
hartubero bun.
hartufo forelock, lock (of hair), tuft (hair).
haspelo reel.
hasta hurried.
haste hastily, hurriedly, in a hurry.
hasti to hurry.
hasto haste.
haŝio chopstick.
haŝiŝo hashish, marijuana.
hati to hate.
haŭbizo howitzer.
haŭli to drag, haul, tow.
haŭsieroj bulls (financial markets).
haŭso boom.
haŭta cutaneous.
haŭtbrulumo dermatitis.
haŭtero scurf, dandruff.
haŭtinflamo dermatitis.
haŭtkoloro skin colour.
haŭtmakulo blemish.
haŭto hide, skin.
haŭtveziketo blister.
havaja Hawaiian.
havajano Hawaiian.
Havajo Hawai'i.
havaĵo asset, possession, property.
Havano Havana.
havebla available.
havebleco availability.
havema acquisitive.
havenda essential, indispensable, integral, irreplaceable.
havendaĵo requisite.
havenimposto anchorage, harbour dues, port charges, port dues.
havenisto docker, dockworker, longshoreman.
havenkvartalo water-front.
haveno harbour, port, haven, seaport.
havenurbo harbour town, port (city), seaport.
havi to have, own. **havi aferon** to have to do (with). **havi aliron al** to have access to. **havi deĵoron** to be on duty. **havi diareon** to have diarrhoea. **havi febron** to have a

fever. **havi forton por fari ion** to have the strength to do something. **havi intereson pri** to be interested in, have an interest in. **havi koro el ŝtono** to have a heart of stone. **havi malbonŝancon** to have bad luck. **havi miksitajn sentojn pri** to have mixed feelings about. **havi nenion komunan kun** to have nothing in common with. **havi permeson** to be allowed to, may. **havi plurajn kromajn uzojn** to have many other uses. **havi sin gardon** to take care, look out. **havi sperton en** to have experience with. **havi sufiĉon** to have enough (of something). **havi ŝtonon por koro** to have a heart of stone. **havi tri manĝojn ĉiutage** to eat three meals a day.
havigebla available.
havigi to get, procure. **havigi al si** to buy, get, procure.
havigo delivery.
Haviko Hawick.
havinda worth having.
havo possession.
Havro Havre.
hazarda accidental, adventitious, chance, random, rash, hazardous. **hazarda variablo** random variable, variate.
hazardaĵo accident.
hazarde by accident, by chance, at random.
hazardeco rashness.
hazardi to hazard, venture, risk, gamble.
hazardluda turbo put-and-take top, teetotum.
hazardludo game of chance, gambling.
hazardnombra generatoro random number generator.
hazardo accidence, chance, hazard.
H-bombo H-bomb.
he! eh! hey! say!
hebraj literoj Hebrew letters.
hebrea Hebrew, Jewish. **hebrea lingvo** Hebrew, Hebrew language.
Hebreino jewess.
Hebreismo Hebraism.
hebrelingva Hebrew.
Hebreo Hebrew.
Hebridoj Hebrides, Western Islands. **Eksternaj Hebridoj** Outer Hebrides. **Internaj Hebridoj** Inner Hebrides.
hedero ivy.
hedisaro sainfoin.
hedonisma hedonism.
hedonismo hedonism.
hedonisto hedonist.
hegemonia hegemonic.
hegemonii to dominate.
hegemonio dominance, hegemony, supremacy.
heĝado hedging.

heĝanto hedger.
Heĝiro Hegira.
heĝligustro garden privet.
heĝo hedge.
heĝtondilo hedge clippers, hedge shears.
hejma domestic. **hejma dosierujo** home directory, login directory. **hejma preĝejo** (private) oratory.
hejmbazo home base.
hejmbesto domestic animal.
hejme domestically, at home.
hejmeca homey.
hejmen home(wards).
hejmeniri to go home.
hejmen-klavo home key.
hejmenporti to carry home.
hejmenreveni to come home, return home.
hejmenveni to come home.
hejmforlaso leaving home, departure from home.
hejmi to dwell.
hejmiri to go home.
hejmlaboro housework, homework.
hejmlando homeland, motherland, fatherland.
hejmo home.
hejmolando homeland, mother country, native land.
hejmpaĝo home page.
hejmporti to carry home.
hejmsida sedentary.
hejmsidema stay-at-home.
hejmsopira homesick.
hejmsopiro homesickness.
hejmtasko homework.
hejmurbo hometown.
hejmveo homesickness.
hejmvesto dressing gown.
hejta heating.
hejtado heating.
hejtaĵo fuel.
hejtaparato hot air stove.
hejtejo boiler house.
hejtforno stove.
hejti to heat, stoke.
hejtilo heater.
hejtisto fireman, stoker.
hejtlignejo woodpile.
hejtligno firewood.
hejtmaterialo fuel.
hejtoleo fuel oil.
Hekato Hecate.
hekatombo hecatombe.
heksaedro hexahedron.
heksagono hexagon.
heksametro hexameter.
heksano hexane.
hektaro hectare.
hektoaro hectare.

hektografi to hectograph.
hektografo hectograph.
hektogramo hectogram.
hektolitro hectoliter.
hektometro hectometer.
Hektoro Hector.
hela bright, brilliant, clear, light, vivid.
Helaso Hellas.
helblua bright blue.
heldenso brightness.
hele brightly, clearly.
heleboro hellebore.
heleco brightness, brilliance.
helena Hellenic.
helenio sneezeweed.
Helenismo Hellenism.
Heleno Helen.
helero heller (monetary unit).
Helesponto Dardanelles, Hellespont.
heliantemo rock-rose.
helianto sunflower.
helice axially.
helico helix, propeller.
heligi to brighten up.
heliĝi to clear, get bright.
helika konko snail shell.
helikforma spiral.
heliko snail, at sign (@).
helikopterejo helipad.
helikoptero helicopter.
helikso helix.
heliocentra heliocentric.
heliocentrismo heliocentrism.
heliografo heliograph.
heliopso heliopsis, ox-eye.
heliostato heliostat.
heliotropo heliotrope.
heliptero paper daisy.
heliumkerno alpha ray.
heliumo helium.
helminto helminth.
Helmsdalo Helmsdale.
helo brightness, brilliance.
heloto helot.
helpa auxiliary, helpful. **helpa lingvo** auxiliary language. **helpa mono** bounty, subsidy, subvention.
helpado helping, relief.
helpantaro auxiliary.
helpantino assistant, lady help.
helpanto aid, helper, assistant, auxiliary.
helpe helpfully.
helpejo helpdesk.
helpema accommodating, helpful.
helpemo helpfulness, readiness to help.
helpfonduso assistance fund.
helpi to accommodate, aid, assist, help. **helpi al si** to look after oneself. **helpi malsupreniri** to help down, help off.
helpilo aid.
helpinto assistant.
helpistino aid, female aid.
helpisto aid, helper.
helpkameraisto assistant cameraman.
helpmilitista paramilitary.
helpmono benefit.
helpo aid, help, assistance, relief.
helpocentro aid centre.
helponto assistant.
helpopreta constructive, helpful.
helpopreteco helpfulness, readiness to help.
helposigno punctuation.
helppredikisto curate.
helprimedo aid.
helpverbo auxiliary verb.
Helsinko Helsinki.
helvelo helvella.
Helvetio Helvetia.
helveto Helvetian.
helviolkolora mauve.
hematito hematite.
hematofobia haematophobic, haemophobic.
hematofobio haematophobia, haemophobia.
hematopo oyster-catcher.
hematurio blood in urine.
hemeralopio night-blindness.
hemerokalido day-lily.
hemerokalo day-lily.
hemikranio migraine.
hemiono Mongolian wild ass, khulan, chigetai, dziggetai.
hemisfero hemisphere.
hemistiko half-line, hemistich.
hemofilio haemophilia.
hemoglobino haemoglobin.
hemoragio haemorrhage.
hemoroido haemorrhoid, pile.
hemoroidoj haemorrhoids.
hemorojdo haemorrhoids, piles.
henao henna.
Henegovio Hainault, Henegovia.
heni to whinny, neigh.
heno whinny.
henoteismo henotheism.
Henriko Henry.
henrio henry.
henro henry.
hepata hepatic. **hepata cirozo** cirrhosis of the liver.
hepataĵo liver.
hepatiko hepatica.
hepatito hepatitis.
hepatkolbaso liver sausage.
hepato liver.
heptalonisto heptathlete.
heptano heptane.
heptatlono heptathlon.

herakleo cow parsnip, hogweed.
heraldika heraldic.
heraldiko heraldry.
herba grassy, herbal.
herbaĉo weed.
herbario herbarium.
herbebenaĵo grassland.
herbeca verdant.
herbejo lawn, meadow, prairie, pasture.
herbero blade of grass.
herbicido herbicide, weed-killer.
herbkuracisto herbalist.
herbo grass, herb.
herbobedo lawn.
herbokolektaĵo herbarium.
herbokolekto herbarium.
herbolibro herbal.
herbomanĝanta herbivorous.
herbovendisto herbalist.
herboverda grass green.
Hercegovino Herzegovina.
herco hertz.
herdo drove, flock, herd.
hereda hereditary. **hereda propraĵo** patrimony.
heredado inheritance.
heredaĵo bequest, inheritance, legacy, heritage, heirloom.
heredantino heiress.
heredanto heir, inheritor.
herede by inheritance.
heredebla hereditary.
heredeco heredity.
heredi to inherit.
heredigi to bequeath, leave.
heredimposto inheritance tax.
heredita eraro inherited error.
heredo heritage.
Herefordo Hereford.
hereza heretical.
herezi to commit heresy.
herezo heresy.
herezulo heretic.
herklua laboro Herculean labour.
Herkulo Heracles, Hercules.
hermafrodita hermaphroditic.
hermafroditeco hermaphroditism.
hermafrodito hermaphrodite.
hermeneŭtika hermeneutic, hermeneutical.
hermeneŭtiko hermeneutics.
Hermeso Hermes.
hermeta hermetic.
hermetika hermetic, airtight.
hermetikigi to seal.
herminio musk orchid.
hermita Hermitian. **hermita formo** Hermitian form. **hermita produto** Hermitian (scalar)product. **hermita skalara produto** Hermitian (scalar)product. **hermita spaco** Hermitian space.
Hermito Hermite.
Hermo Hermes.
hernio hernia, rupture.
Hero Hera.
heroa heroic. **heroa morto** heroic death, hero's death.
heroaĵo act of heroism, exploit, feat, heroic deed, heroic act.
Herodoto Herodotus.
heroe heroically.
heroeco heroism.
heroeno heroin.
heroino¹ heroine.
heroino² heroin.
heroldi to herald.
heroldo herald.
heroo hero.
herpesto ichneumon, mongoose.
herpeto herpes.
Hespero Hesperus.
Hestio Hestia.
Hesujo Hesse.
hetajro hetaera, hetaira.
heterodoksa heterodox.
heterogena heterogeneous.
heterogene heterogeneously.
heterokira heterochiral.
heteroseksa heterosexual, straight.
hetmano hetman.
heŭristiko heuristics.
heŭristika heuristic.
hevisida Heaviside. **hevisida funkcio** Heaviside function.
Hevisido Heaviside.
hezitado hesitation, wavering.
hezitanta hesitant.
hezitante while hesitating, hesitatingly.
hezitema irresolute, undecided.
heziteme haltingly, hesitantly, hesitatingly, irresolutely.
heziti to hesitate.
hezito hesitation.
hiacinto hyacinth.
hiato gap, hiatus.
hibaĉo hibachi.
hibisko hibiscus.
hibrida hybrid, mongrel. **hibrida integra cirkvito** hybrid integrated circuit. **hibrida komputilo** hybrid computer.
hibrido hybrid.
hida hideous.
hidalgo hidalgo.
hide hideously.
hidranto hydrant.
hidrargaĵo tinfoil.
hidrargo mercury, quicksilver.
hidrato hydrate.

hidraŭlika hydraulic.
hidraŭlike hydraulically.
hidraŭliko hydraulics.
hidrido hydride.
hidro hydra.
Hidro Hydra.
hidroaeroplano sea-plane.
hidrocefalo hydrocephalus.
hidroelektra hydroelectric.
hidroelektre hydroelectrically.
hidrofito aquatic plant.
hidrofobio hydrophobia.
hidrogenbombo H-bomb, hydrogen bomb.
hidrogeno hydrogen.
hidrohero capybara.
hidrokarbido hydrocarbon.
hidrokarbonido hydrocarbon.
hidrokarido frogbit.
hidrokorako cormorant.
hidrokotilo marsh pennywort.
hidrolizi to hydrolyse.
hidrologo hydrologist.
hidrometrio hydrometry.
hidrometro hydrometer.
hidroplano seaplane.
hidropso dropsy.
hidrostatika hydrostatic.
hidrostatike hydrostatically.
hidrostatiko hydrostatics.
hidroterapio hydrotherapy.
hieno hyena.
hieracio hawkweed.
hierarĥia hierarchical.
hierarĥie hierarchically.
hierarĥio hierarchy.
hierarkia hierarchical.
hierarkie hierarchically.
hierarkio hierarchy. **hierarkio laŭ Ĉomski** Chomsky hierarchy.
hieratika hieratic.
hieraŭ yesterday. **hieraŭ vespere** last night.
hieraŭa yesterday, of yesterday.
hieroglifa hieroglyphic.
hieroglifo hieroglyph.
Hieronimo Jerome.
higiena hygienic, sanitary.
higiene hygienically.
higieno hygiene.
higrometrio hygrometry.
higrometro hygrometer.
hiki to hiccup, hiccough.
hikorio hickory.
hilberta Hilbert. **hilberta spaco** Hilbert space.
Hilberto Hilbert.
hilumo hilumo.
Himalajo Himalayas.
Himalajoj Himalayas.

himenio hymenium.
himeno hymen.
himnaro hymnal, hymnbook.
himnego anthem.
himno anthem, hymn, canticle.
hinda Indian, Hindu. **Hinda Oceano** Indian Ocean.
hindeŭropa Indo-European.
hindino Indian, Indian lady, Indian woman.
Hindio India.
Hindo Hindu, Indian.
hindo Indian (Asia).
Hindoĉinio Indo-China.
Hindoĉinujo Indo-China.
hindoeŭropa Indo-European.
hindoeŭropano Indo-European.
hindoĝermana Indo-European, Indo-Germanic.
hindua Hindu.
hinduismo Hinduism.
Hindujo India.
Hindukuŝo Hindu Kush.
hinduo Hindu.
hingo hinge.
hino hinny.
hiosciamino hyoscyamine.
hiperaktiva hyperactive.
hiperbola hyperbolic. **hiperbola funkcio** hyperbolic function. **hiperbola kosinuso** hyperbolic cosine. **hiperbola kotangento** hyperbolic cotangent. **hiperbola sinuso** hyperbolic sine. **hiperbola spiralo** hyperbolic spiral. **hiperbola tangento** hyperbolic tangent.
hiperbolo hyperbole.
hiperboloido hyperboloid.
hiperebeno hyperplane.
hiperelipso hyperellipse.
hiperiko Saint John's wort.
hiperligilo hyperlink.
hiperligo hyperlink.
hiperono hiperon, hyperon.
hiperteksta hypertextual.
HiperTeksta MarkLingvo hypertext markup language, HTML.
hiperteksto hypertext.
hipertensio high blood pressure.
hipertrofio hypertrophy.
hipio hippie.
Hipno Hypnos.
hipnota hypnotic.
hipnote hypnotically.
hipnotigi to hypnotize.
hipnotiĝi to become hypnotized.
hipnotismo hypnotism.
hipnotisto hypnotist.
hipnotizi to hypnotize.
hipnoto hypnosis, hypnotic trance.
hipnozo hypnosis.

hipocikloido hypocycloid.
hipodromo hippodrome, racecourse.
hipoelipso hypoellipse.
hipofeo sea-buckthorn.
hipofizo hypophysis, pituitary, pituitary gland.
hipogeo hypogeum.
hipogloso halibut.
hipogrifo hippogriff, hippogryph.
hipoĥondrio hypochondria.
hipoĥondriulo hypochondriac.
hipokampo seahorse.
hipokaŝtanacoj Hippocastanaceae (family of trees).
hipokaŝtano horse chestnut.
hipokondrio hypochondria.
hipokondriulo hypochondriac.
Hipokrato Hippocrates.
hipokrita hypocritical.
hipokritaĵo hypocrisy.
hipokritanto hypocrite.
hipokrite hypocritically.
hipokriteco hypocrisy.
hipokriti to dissemble.
hipokritismo hypocrisy.
hipokrito hypocrisy.
hipokritulo hypocrite.
hipolito Hippolytus.
hipopotamedoj hippos.
hipopotamo hippo, hippopotamus.
hipostaza hypostatic.
hipostazo hypostasis.
hipoteki to mortgage.
hipoteko mortgage.
hipotenuzo hypotenuse.
hipoteza hypothetical.
hipoteze hypothetically.
hipotezi to hypothesize.
hipotezo hypothesis.
hipotroĥoido hypotrochoid.
hipotrokoido hypotrochoid.
hipurido mare's-tail.
hiraganao hiragana (Japanese writing system).
hirako coney.
hirta bristling, bristly, standing on end, untidy.
hirti to bristle (hair, etc.).
hirtigi to tousle.
hirudo leech.
hirundaro flock of swallows.
hirundo swallow (bird).
hisi to hoist, hoist up, run up, wind up. **hisi la flagon** to hoist the flag.
hisilo halyard.
hiskiamino hyoscyamine.
hiskiamo henbane.
hisopo hyssop.

hispana Spanish. **hispana artiŝoko** cardoon. **hispana lingvo** Spanish, Spanish language.
hispanino Spanish woman.
Hispanio Spain.
Hispaniolo Hispaniola.
Hispanlando Spain.
Hispano Spaniard.
Hispanujo Spain.
histamino histamine.
histerezo hysteresis.
histeria hysterical.
histerie hysterically.
histerio excitement, hysteria, hysterics.
histeriulo hysteric (person).
histo tissue.
histologio histology.
historia historical. **historia materiismo** historical materialism.
historie historically.
historieto story, anecdote.
historiisma historicist.
historiismano historicist.
historiismo historicism.
historiisto historian.
historio annals, history, story.
historiono harlequin.
historiplena full of history, historic.
historiskribanto historian.
histriko porcupine.
histriono ham, bad actor, third-rate actor.
Hiŝamo Heysham.
ho name of the letter H.
hobalo myrrh.
hobie as a hobby.
hobio hobby.
hobito hobbit.
hobojo oboe.
hodiaŭ today. **hodiaŭ matene** this morning. **hodiaŭ posttagmeze** this afternoon. **hodiaŭ vespere** this evening.
hodiaŭa actual, current, present, present-day.
hoj! ahoy!
hoji to hail.
hojli to howl (wolf).
hoka hooked, crooked.
Hokajdo Hokkaido.
hokedisko puck.
hokeo hockey.
hoketo breve.
hokfadeno fishing line.
hokfiŝado angling.
hokfiŝanto angler.
hokfiŝi to fish with a line.
hokfiŝilo fishing rod.
hokfiŝkaptanto angler.
hokfiŝkapti to fish with a line.
hoki to hook.

hokmuntaĵo bait.
hoko caron, háček, hook, inverted circumflex, inverted hat, wedge (ˇ).
hokstango boat hook, gaff.
hokŝnuro fishing-line, line.
hoktenilo angle tongs.
hola hey, stop.
Hola! Hold on!, Hey!
holanda Dutch. **Holanda Angulo** Hook of Holland.
Holandano Dutchman, Hollander.
Holando Holland.
holdfako coal-hold.
holdo hold.
holdofako coal-hold.
Holihedo Holyhead.
holisma holistic.
holisme holistically.
Holivudo Hollywood.
holmio holmium.
holmo hill.
holografiaĵo hologram.
holografio holography.
holografo holograph.
holokaŭsto holocaust.
holomorfa holomorphic.
holoturio sea cucumber.
homa human. **homa lingvo** natural language.
homama benevolent.
homamasiĝo affray.
homamaso crowd, mass, multitude.
homamo charity, love of one's neighbour.
homaranismo Zamenhofan humanism.
homaro human race, mankind, humanity.
homaŭtomato android.
hombuĉado massacre.
home humanly.
homeco humanity.
homekipi to man.
homekipo crew.
homeomorfia homœomorphic.
homeomorfieco homœomorphism.
homeomorfio homœomorphism.
homeopatia homœopathic.
homeopatiisto homœopath.
homeopatio homœopathy.
homeopato homœopath.
homeostazo homœostasis.
Homero Homer.
hometo little person.
homevita antisocial.
homevitema antisocial.
homevitulo misanthrope.
homfarita manmade.
homforma man-shaped, hominoid.
homformiĝo anthropomorphosis.
homforto manpower, human power.
homfrato fellow human being, neighbour.

homhava peopled.
homhelpa philanthropic, humanitarian.
homido child.
homlaŭso body louse.
homlevilo lift.
hommanĝanto anthropophagite, anthropophagus.
hommanĝulo cannibal.
hommortiga homicidal.
hommortige homicidally.
hommortigo homicide.
hommulto mass of people.
homo human being, man.
homofono homophone.
homogena homogeneous.
homogene homogeneously.
homogenigo homogenization.
homogeniĝo homogenization.
homoj people.
homokira homochiral.
homokireco homochirality.
homologa homologous.
homomorfa homomorphic.
homomorfia homomorphic.
homomorfio homomorphism.
homonimigo overloading.
homonimigode operacisimboloj polymorphism.
homonimo homonym.
homoseksuala gay, homosexual, queer.
homoseksualeco homosexuality.
homoseksualulo queen, queer, homosexual, (offensive) faggot.
homotetia homothetic.
homotetiaĵo homothetic figure.
homotetio homothety.
homotopa homotopic.
homotopeco homotopy.
homplena crowded, full of people.
homportilo stretcher.
homrabanto abductor.
homrabi to abduct.
homrabo abduction.
homroboto android.
homscienco anthropology.
homsimio ape, primate.
hondurasa Honduran.
hondurasanino Honduran woman.
hondurasano Honduran.
Honduraso Honduras.
Honduro Honduras.
honesta above-board, honest, incorrupt, upright. **honesta ludo** fair play.
honeste honestly, uprightly.
honesteco honesty, rectitude, uprightness.
honesto honesty.
honestulo honest person.
Honkongo Hong Kong.
Honolulo Honolulu.

honora honorary. **honora legio** Legion of Honour. **honora protektanto** patron.
honorado accolade.
honorarii to pay a fee, pay a honorarium, remunerate.
honorario fee, honorarium, remuneration.
honore honorarily, with honour.
honorego accolade.
honorfraŭlino maid of honour.
honori to honour.
honorinda honourable.
honorindeco honourableness, respectability, venerability.
honoro honour.
honta ashamed.
honte ashamedly. **honte al** shame on.
honteco shyness.
hontema bashful, shy.
honti to be ashamed.
hontiga humiliating.
hontige disgracefully.
hontigi to abash, put to shame, shame.
hontigita ashamed.
hontigo disgrace.
hontinda shameful.
hontindaĵo vileness.
honto abashment, shame.
hontosigni to stigmatize.
hontosigno stigma.
hopi to hop.
Horacio Horace, Horatio.
horaro schedule, timetable.
horde by hordes.
hordea barley.
hordeo barley. **hordeo trempita** malt.
hordeolo sty.
hordo band, horde, troop.
hore hourly, per hour.
horizonta kotoneastro wall cotoneaster, rockspray cotoneaster, rock cotoneaster.
horizontala horizontal, level. **horizontala formato** landscape.
horizontale horizontally, across.
horizontalo horizontal line, row.
horizonto horizon.
horkvaronon poste fifteen minutes later.
horlibro timetable.
horloĝbombo time bomb.
horloĝeto watch.
horloĝisto clock maker, watchmaker.
horloĝo clock, watch, timepiece.
Horloĝo Horologium.
hormino horminum.
hormono hormone.
hormontrilo hour hand.
horo hour, o'clock, time. **horon post horo** hour by hour, hourly, on the hour.
horora chilling, ghastly, grisly, gruesome, horrendous, horrid, horrific.
horore ghastly, horrifically.
horori to be horrified.
hororo horror.
horoskopo horoscope.
horplano schedule, timetable.
horrori to be horrified.
horsignalo time signal.
hortabelo timetable.
hortensio hydrangea.
hortikulturisto gardener, groundskeeper, landscaper.
hortikulturo horticulture.
hortulano ortolan.
Horuso Horus.
horzono time zone.
hoso hose, tube.
hospico hospice.
hospitalo hospital.
hostimontrilo monstrance.
hostio wafer, host (Eucharist).
hostiujo pyx.
hostivazo ciborium.
hotelo hotel.
hotentoto Hottentot.
hotonio water-violet.
HTML-etikedo HTML tag.
htŝu sound of sneezing.
hu boo.
Huberto Hubert.
hubo croft, hide.
Hudsongolfo Hudson Bay.
Hudsonkolo Hudson Strait.
hufferaĵo horseshoe.
hufferi to shoe.
hufferista blacksmith's.
hufferisto blacksmith.
huffero horseshoe.
hufo hoof.
hufoferi to shoe.
hufulo steed.
hufumo horseshoe.
hugenoto Huguenot.
hui to boo, hoot.
hukero hooker.
Hulfordo Haverfordwest.
huli to surge.
huligana loutish.
huligano hooligan, punk.
hulo hull, swell, surge (of the sea).
humana humane, humanitarian.
humane humanely.
humaneco humanity.
humanigi to humanize.
humanigo humanization.
humanisma humanistic.
humanismo humanism.
humanisto humanist.
Humbro Humber.
humero humerus.

humida damp, humid, moist.
humideco damp.
humidigi to dampen.
humila humble, lowly, submissive.
humile humbly.
humileco humility, lowliness.
humilega abject, meek.
humili to demean.
humiliga humiliating.
humiligego abjection, abjectness.
humiligi to abase, humble, humiliate.
humiligo abasement.
humiligsento abashment.
humiliĝi to abase oneself, humble oneself.
humiliĝo abasement.
humilulo humble person.
humo humus.
humora humorous.
humore humorously.
humori to be in a mood.
humoro humour, mood, temper, wit.
humura humorous, witty.
humuro humour, wit, mood.
hunda canine. **hunda rozo** brier.
hundaĉo cur, mutt, pooch.
hundarejo kennel.
hundaro pack (hounds).
hundblekegi to howl.
hundbleki to yelp.
hundbleko bark.
hundbredado dog breeding.
hundbredisto dog breeder.
hundego large dog.
hundejo kennel, dog kennel.
hundema fond of dogs.
hundeto small dog.
hundfilo son of a bitch.
hundherbo cocksfoot, couch-grass.
hundido pup, puppy.
hundino bitch.
hundo dog, hound.
hundobleki to bay (bark).
hundobleko bark (of dog).
hundodometo doghouse.
hundoj dogs.
hungara Hungarian.
hungarino Hungarian, Hungarian woman.
Hungario Hungary.
Hungarlando Hungary.
hungaro Hungarian.
Hungarujo Hungary.
huntuno wonton.
huo hoot.
hupi to hoot.
hupilo horn.
hupo hooter.
hura hurrah, hurray, yea.
huraadi to cheer.
huraado cheering.
hurai to cheer, exult, rejoice.
hurao cheer.
hurdo hurdle, wattle.
huri to cheer.
hurio houri.
hurlado howling.
hurli to howl.
hurlo howl.
huro hurrah.
husaro hussar, light cavalry soldier.
hutuo Hutu.
huzo beluga, (European, white) sturgeon, hausen.

Ĥ

Ĥabakuko Habakkuk.
ĥaldea Chaldean.
ĥaldeano Chaldean.
Ĥaldeio Chaldea.
Ĥaldeo Chaldea.
Ĥaldeujo Chaldea.
ĥalifo caliph.
ĥalkogeno chalcogen.
ĥameleonedoj chamaeleonidae.
ĥameleono chameleon.
ĥamemoro cloudberry.
ĥamida Hamitic.
Ĥamo Ham.
ĥano khan.
ĥanoh Enoch.
ĥanto Khanty, Ostyak.
ĥanujo khanate.
Ĥanuko Chanukah, Hanukkah.
ĥaosa chaotic.
ĥaose chaotically.
ĥaosigi to cause chaos.
ĥaoso chaos, tangle.
ĥaradriedoj plovers.
ĥaradrio plover.
Ĥarkovo Harkow.
Ĥarono Charon.
Ĥartumo Khartoum.
ĥasidismo Hasidim.
ĥasido Hasid.
ĥato hut.
ĥazaro Khazar.
Ĥazarujo Khazar Empire, Khazaria.
ĥelonio green sea turtle.
ĥemia chemical.
ĥemiaĵo chemical.
ĥemiaĵoj chemicals.
ĥemie chemically.
ĥemiinstruisto chemistry teacher.
ĥemiisto chemist.
ĥemio chemistry.
ĥemiterapio chemotherapy.
Ĥeopso Cheops, Khufu.
Ĥeroneo Chaeronea.
ĥilo chyle.
ĥimera chimerical, shadowy.
Ĥimero Chimera.
ĥimero chimera, chimaera.
ĥimerulo freakish man.
ĥimo chyme, chymus.
ĥina Chinese. **ĥina inko** Indian ink. **ĥina lingvo** Chinese, Chinese language. **ĥina novjaro** Chinese New Year.
ĥinino[1] Chinese, Chinese lady, Chinese woman.
ĥinino[2] quinine.
Ĥinio China.
Ĥinlando China.
Ĥino Chinese (man).
Ĥinujo China.
Ĥio Chios.
ĥio chi (Χχ).
ĥiragro arthritis, arthritism.
ĥiromanciisto palmist.
ĥiromancio palmistry.
ĥironekto water opossum, yapok.
Ĥirono Chiron.
ĥiroptero bat.
ĥirurga surgical.
ĥirurgia surgery.
ĥirurgie surgically.
ĥirurgiejo surgery.
ĥirurgiisto surgeon.
ĥirurgio surgery (the science).
ĥirurgo surgeon.
ĥitino chitin.
ĥo name of the letter Ĥ.
ĥolecistito cholecystitis.
ĥolera hot-tempered, fiery, choleric.
ĥolero cholera.
ĥolesterolo cholesterol.
ĥora choral.
ĥoraĵo carol, choral.
ĥoralkanto chant.
ĥoralo choral.
ĥoranino choirgirl.
ĥorano choir singer, choirboy.
ĥoraro chorus.
ĥordo notochord.
ĥordulo chordate.
ĥorduloj chordates.
ĥore in unison, as a chorus, as a group (speaking or singing).
ĥorejo chancel, choir loft.
ĥoreo (Sydenham's) chorea, Saint Vitus's dance.
ĥoreografio choreography.
ĥorestro choir director, choirmaster.
ĥoristo chorister.
ĥorjambo choriamb.
ĥorkanto chorale.
ĥoro chorus, choir.

I

i name of the letter I.
ia any, some (kind of). **ia ajn** any kind of.
i.a. → **inter aliaj**.
iafoje sometimes.
iagrade to some extent.
iai to bray.
ial for some reason.
iam at any time, at some time, ever, sometime, once upon a time, formerly. **iam ajn** any time. **iam pli malfrue** sometime later.
iama of a time, former, previous, one-time.
iama amikeco former friendship. **iama amo** former love.
iamaniere anyway.
iamo yore.
iao hee-haw, braying of a donkey.
ibekso ibex.
ibera Iberian.
ibisedoj Threskiornithidae (bird family).
ibiso ibis.
IBM-a kodo IBM code.
icingo chip socket.
ico integrated circuit, chip.
iĉi to devote.
iĉo male of a species.
ida dosiero son file.
idaha Idahoan.
idahano Idahoan.
idaro descendants, issue, offspring, posterity, progeny, young.
idea imaginary.
ideala ideal.
ideale ideally.
idealigi to idealize.
idealismo idealism.
idealisto idealist.
idealo ideal.
idearo ideas, body of thought.
ideismo idealism.
ideisto idealist.
idekonfuzo confusion of ideas.
idemo ditto.
identa identical.
identaĵo identity.
identeco identity.
identigaĵo ID, signature.
identiganto spotter.
identigi to identify.
identigilo identifier.
identigo identification.
identiĝi to identify oneself.
identiĝo identification.
idento identity.
identobildigo identity mapping.
idento-bildigo identity mapping.

identorilato identity.
ideo idea.
ideografiaĵo written Chinese character, ideogram.
ideografio ideography, picture writing.
ideogramo ideogram.
ideologia ideological.
ideologie ideologically.
ideologiisto ideologue.
ideologio ideology.
ideologo ideologist.
ideoriĉa full of ideas.
idiferenteco apathy.
idilia idyllic.
idilie idyllically.
idilio idyll.
idioma idiomatic.
idiomaĵo idiomatic expression.
idiome idiomatically.
idiomo idiom, tongue, language, vernacular.
idiosinkrazio idiosyncrasy.
idiota idiotic.
idiote idiotically.
idioteco idiocy.
idiotismo idiom, idiomatic expression.
idioto idiot.
idiotulo idiot, oaf.
Ido Ido (constructed language derived from Esperanto).
ido child, offspring, young, progeny, descendent.
idolano heathen, idolater, pagan.
idolejo shrine, temple.
idolfiguro idol.
idolismo idolatry, idol worship.
idolkulto idolatry, idol worship.
idolo idol.
idolservado idolatry.
idolservanino idolatress.
idolservano idolater.
idolservo heathenism, idolatry, idol worship.
iduo ides.
ie anywhere, somewhere. **ie ajn** anywhere.
iel anyhow, anyway, somehow, some way. **iel ajn** anyway at all, anyway you like.
ien somewhere, to some place. **ien ajn** anywhere, anywhere at all.
ieporhundo greyhound.
ies anyone's, somebody's, someone's. **ies ajn** anyone's you like.
Igdrasilo Yggdrasil, Yggdrasill.
igi to cause to become, get, make.
iglo igloo.
igluo igloo.
ignamo sweet potato, yam.

ignorema

ignorema cavalier.
ignoreme cavalierly.
ignori to ignore, leave out of account.
iguamo yam.
igumenino hegumene, hegumeness, hegumenia.
igumeno hegumen, igumen.
igvano iguana.
igvanodonto iguanodon.
iĝebleco probability.
iĝi to become, get, grow. **iĝi la edzino de** to become the wife of, marry. **iĝi la edzo de** to become the husband of, marry. **iĝi la fianĉino de** to become engaged with, become the fiancée of. **iĝi la fianĉo de** to become engaged with, become the fiancé of.
iĥneŭmono ichneumon.
iĥtiokolo isinglass.
iĥtiologio ichthyology.
iĥtiosaŭro ichthyosaurus.
ikneŭmonoido ichneumon, ichneumon fly.
ikonismo iconolatry.
ikonisto iconolater.
ikono icon.
ikonoklasto iconoclast.
ikonostazo iconostasis.
ikonrompado iconoclasm.
ikonrompismo iconoclasm.
ikonrompisto iconoclast.
ikskromosomo X-chromosome.
ikskruroj knock-kneed legs, turned-in legs.
ikso name of the letter X.
iksodo tick.
iksrada x-ray.
iksradioj X-rays.
iktero jaundice.
iktiokolo isinglass, fish glue.
iktiologio ichthyology.
iktiosaŭro ichthyosaurus.
ikto attack.
I.L. → **Internacia Lingvo**.
il. → **illustrita**.
ilarejo tool closet.
ilaro gear, tackle, apparatus, equipment.
ilejo tool shed.
ilekso holly.
ileo ileum.
ilfako tool bar, tool pane.
ilgarnituro tool box, toolkit.
ilgimnastiko apparatus gymnastics.
ilgimnasto apparatus gymnast.
ili they. **ili ne kuraĝus** they wouldn't dare.
ilin them.
ilia their, theirs. **ilia tuta mono** all their money.
Iliado Iliad.
iliaflanke on their side, for their part.
ilialingve in their language.
ilicio star anise.

impito

ilio theirs.
iliumo ilium.
ilkesto toolbox.
ilkomputilo host, host computer.
ilo agent, means, tool, implement, instrument.
ilobreto tool bar.
iloj means.
ilpanelo toolbar.
ilprogramo tool program.
ilrimedo tool.
iluminado illumination.
ilumini to enlighten, illuminate.
iluminiĝi to become enlightened.
iluminmarŝo tattoo.
ilustraĵo illustration.
ilustri to illustrate.
ilustrita illustrated, pictorial. **ilustrita poŝtkarto** picture postcard.
iluzia misleading.
iluzii to delude, mislead.
iluziisto magician.
iluzio illusion.
ilzono tool bar.
imaga fanciful, imaginary.
imagaĵo (mental) image.
imagebla imaginable.
imageble conceivably.
imagema imaginative.
imagi to fancy, imagine.
imaginara imaginary. **imaginara parto** imaginary part. **imaginara unuo** imaginary unit.
imaginaro complex number, imaginary number.
imagipovo imaginativeness.
imagitaĵo conception.
imago imagination.
imagopovo imagination.
imamo imam.
imanenta immanent, indwelling, inherent (in), intrinsic.
imanenteco immanence.
imanentisma immanentist.
imanento immanence.
imertinenteco arrogance, insolence.
Imhotepo Imhotep.
Imiro Ymir.
imitaĉado mockery.
imitaĉi to ape, mock.
imitado imitation.
imitaĵa fake.
imitaĵo imitation.
imitemulo copycat.
imiti to imitate, emulate, fake, mimic, counterfeit.
imitilo emulator.
imitisto imitator, mimic.
imitita counterfeit, faked, forged.
imito imitation.

impedanco impedance.
imperativa imperative.
imperativo imperative.
imperfekto imperfect, imperfect tense.
imperia imperial. **imperia aglo** imperial eagle.
imperialismo imperialism.
imperialisto imperialist.
imperialo top deck of vehicle.
imperie imperially.
imperiestra imperial.
imperiestrino empress.
imperiestro emperor.
imperii to rule.
imperiisma imperialist.
imperiismo imperialism.
imperiisto imperialist.
imperio empire.
imperiumo empire.
impertinenta impertinent, impudent, insolent.
impertinentaĵo impertinence, impudence, insolence.
impertinente impudently.
impertinenteco impertinence.
impertinenteta perky.
impertinento impertinence, rudeness.
impertinentulo boor, cheeky rascal, saucy fellow.
impeta impetuous.
impeti to be impetuous, bound, dash, spring, leap, rush. **impeti al** to rush at.
impetigino impetigo.
impeto impetus, rush, impulse.
implica implicit, implicative. **implica difino** implicit definition. **implica funkcio** implicit function.
implice implicitly.
implici to imply.
implicita implied.
implico implication.
implikacia implicative.
implikacio implication.
implikaĵo tangle.
implikanta confusing.
impliki to entangle, implicate, infer.
implikiĝi to be implicated, become tangled up.
implikiĝo involvement.
impona imposing, impressive.
imponeco airs, impressiveness.
imponega awesome, formidable, sublime.
imponegeco awe.
imponegi to awe, overawe.
imponi to impress forcibly, strike.
imponisto tax collector.
importa import.
importado importation.
importaĵo import.

importi to import.
importisto importer.
importmonopolo import monopoly.
importo import, importation.
imposta fiscal, tax.
impostado taxation.
impostdeklarilo taxpayer.
impostdeklaro tax (return), tax declaration.
impostdepreno tax deduction.
impostebla taxable, subject to tax.
impostejo tax-collector's office.
impostenda assessable.
impostevitulo tax dodger.
imposti to assess, charge a tax, levy a tax, tax.
impostisto revenue agent, tax collector.
impostkonsilisto tax consultant.
impostkvoto assessment.
impostlibera duty-free, tax-free.
impostmalplialtigo tax abatement, tax reduction, tax relief.
imposto duty, impost, tax.
impostodeva assessable.
impostoficejo tax collector's office.
impostoŝarĝo tax burden.
impostpaganto ratepayer, taxpayer.
impostplialtigo tax hike, tax increase.
impostpremo tax burden.
impostsistemo fiscal system, system of taxation, tax system.
imposttaksado assessment.
impotenta impotent.
impotente impotently.
impotenteco impotence.
impozi to impose.
impregni to impregnate.
impresa impressive.
impresario impresario.
imprese impressively.
impresebla accessible, impressible, sensitive, impressionable.
impresebliĝema impressionable.
impresema impressionable, sensitive.
impresi to impress, make an impression on.
impresiĝema impressible, sensitive.
impresiĝemo susceptibility.
impresionismo impressionism.
impresionisto impressionist.
impresismo impressionism.
impreso impression. **impreso pieda** footprint.
improveekzameni to revise.
improviza ad lib.
improvizaĵo improvisation.
improvize extemporaneously.
improvizi to improvise.
improvizisto improviser.
improvizita ad-lib.
improvizo ad-lib.

impulsa

impulsa impulsive.
impulse impulsively.
impulsema impulsive.
impulseme impetuously, impulsively.
impulsemo impetuosity.
impulsi to impel.
impulsiĝema impulsive.
impulso access, impetus, impulse.
imputi to blame, hold against.
imputo imputation.
imuna exempt, immune. **imuna sistemo** immune system.
imuneco immunity.
imunigi to immunize.
imunigo immunization.
imunohemio immunochemistry.
imunologiisto immunologist.
imunologio immunology.
imunologo immunologist.
imunsistemo immune system.
ina female, feminine. **ina genro** feminine gender.
inaŭgura inaugural.
inaŭguracia inaugural.
inaŭguracii to inaugurate.
inaŭguracio inauguration.
inaŭgurado inauguration.
inaŭguri to inaugurate.
inaŭguro inauguration, opening.
incendia incendiary.
incendiado arson.
incendio conflagration, fire.
incensi to burn incense.
incensilo censer, incensory, thurible.
incenso incense.
incensujo censer, incensory.
incesta incestuous.
incesto incest.
incida incident. **incida angulo** angle of incidence.
incidento incident.
incidi to fall on (a surface).
incido incident.
incitado abetment.
incitanto firebrand, instigator.
incitebla irritable.
incitegi to aggravate, provoke.
incitegoado provocation.
inciteti to tease, worry, vex.
inciti to abet, excite, incite, provoke, rouse, stimulate, stir up, irritate. **inciti la fajron** to stir up, stoke the fire.
incitiĝi to get riled, become upset.
incitita actuated.
incitnudiĝo striptease.
incito abetment, incitement.
incizado incision.
incizaĵo incision.
incizivo incisor.

indiĝena

incizo incision.
inĉapelo bonnet.
inĉemizo blouse.
inda deserving, worthy. **inda je** worthy of.
indas ripeti, ke... it bears repeating that...
inde worthily. **inde je me** worthy of me.
indeco dignity.
indeksa indexed. **indeksa atingo** indexed access method. **indeksa registro** index register.
indekshava dosiero indexed file.
indeksi to index.
indeksnodo inode.
indekso index.
indeksseria memorilorganizo index sequential organization.
indeksvica atingo index-sequential access method.
indento indent, indention.
indi to be worth, be worthy of, be deserving.
indiana Indian.
indianano Hoosier.
indianino squaw.
indiano Indian, American Indian.
Indiano Indus.
indichava indexed, **indichava adresado** indexed addressing. **indichava variablo** indexed variable.
indico index, indicant.
indicreĝistro index register.
indictipo index type.
indieno chintz, calico.
indiferenta immaterial, indifferent.
indiferente indifferently. **indiferente al** indifferent to.
indiferenteco indifference.
indiferentismo indifferentism.
indiga indigo.
indigestio dyspepsia, indigestion.
indigi to dignify.
indigna indignant.
indigne indignantly.
indignema resentful, touchy.
indigni to be indignant, be irritated, resent.
indigni pri to resent, take exception to, take offence at. **indigni pro** to be indignant with, take offence at.
indigniga aggravating.
indignigi to aggravate, annoy.
indignigo provocation.
indignindaĵo affront, indignity.
indigno offence, scandal.
indigo indigo.
indigujo indigo.
indiĝena aboriginal, native, indigenous. **indiĝena aŭstraliano** Australian aborigine. **indiĝena lingvo** native language. **indiĝena prezento** native format.

indiĝena reĝimo native mode. **indiĝena tradukilo** native compiler.
indiĝenaŭstralia (Australian) aboriginal.
indiĝenaŭstraliano (Australian) aboriginal.
indiĝeno aborigine, native, indigenous person.
indiĝenulo aboriginal.
indika indicative.
indikaĵo (circumstantial) evidence.
indikativa frazo clause of statement, narrative sentence.
indikativo indicative, indicative mood.
indiki to indicate, suggest.
indikilo indicator.
indikita indicated.
indiko flag, indication.
indio indium.
indiumo indium.
individua individual.
individualisma individualistic.
individualismo individualism.
individualisto individualist.
individue individually.
individueco individuality.
individuisma individualistic.
individuismo individualism.
individuisto individualist.
individuo individual.
indo value, worth.
indonezia Indonesian.
indonezianino Indonesian woman.
indoneziano Indonesian.
Indonezio Indonesia.
Indro Indra.
induki to induce.
indukta inductive.
induktanco inductance.
indukti to generalize, induce, infer, reason.
indukto inductance, induction.
indulga lenient.
indulgema indulgent, lenient, magnanimous, merciful.
indulgenco indulgence (religious).
indulgi to be lenient with, indulge, spare.
indulgigi to make someone be lenient, force someone to be indulgent.
indulgiĝi to indulge (one's self).
indulgo clemency, forbearance, indulgence.
Induso Indus.
industria industrial. **industria fako** industrial branch. **industria revolucio** industrial revolution.
industriigo industrialization.
industriiĝo industrialization.
industriisto industrialist.
industrio industry.
industristo industrialist.
industriulo industrialist.
Industriurbo City of Industry.

ineco femininity.
inercia inertial. **inercia forto** inertial force.
inercio inertia.
inercirado fly-wheel, inertia wheel.
inerciuma inertial.
inerta inert. **inerta gaso** noble gas.
inerte inertly.
inerteca inertial.
inerteco inertia.
inerto inertia.
inertoforto inertial force.
inertorado inertia wheel.
infamio blame.
infana childish, infantile.
infanaĉo brat.
infanaĝo childhood, infancy (age).
infanaĵo childishness.
infanĉambro nursery.
infanĉareto baby carriage.
infanĉaro baby carriage.
infane childishly.
infaneca childish.
infaneco childhood, infancy.
infanejo nursery.
infaneto babe, baby, infant.
infangardejo crèche.
infanĝardeno kindergarten, nursery school.
infaniĝi to become childish.
infanistino nursemaid.
infankuracisto pediatrician.
infanlito child's bed, cot.
infanludejo playground.
infanmedicino paediatrics.
infanmiena with a childish expression.
infanmurdo infanticide.
infano child, infant.
infanparalizo polio, poliomyelitis.
infanprostituado child prostitution.
infanseĝo child's seat.
infanŝteli to kidnap.
infanŝtelinto kidnapper.
infanŝtelo kidnapping.
infanteamano Little Leaguer.
infanteca child-like.
infanteriano foot soldier, infantryman.
infanterio infantry.
infanvartanto babysitter.
infanvartejo crèche.
infanvarti to babysit.
infanvartisto babysitter.
infanveturilo perambulator.
infanvoĉo childish voice.
infanzorgado childcare.
infarkto infarct.
infekta catching, contagious, infectious.
   infekta centro source of infection.
infektado contagion, contamination, infection.
infektaĵo infection.

infekti to infect.
infektiĝi to become infected.
infektita contaminated, infected.
infekto infection.
infera hellish, infernal.
inferinda abominable.
inferno Hell.
infero hell, underworld.
infesti to infest.
infestiĝo infestation.
infesto infestation.
infikso infix.
infimo greatest lower bound.
infinita infinite.
infinite infinitely.
infinitezima infinitesimal. **infinitezima kalkulo** infinitesimal calculus.
infinitezimo infinitesimal.
infinitiĝi to approach infinity.
infinitivo infinitive.
infinito infinity.
inflacia inflationary.
inflacio inflation.
inflama inflamed.
inflami to be inflamed.
inflamigi to inflame, irritate (medical).
inflamiĝi to act up, inflame.
inflamo inflammation.
infleksa (point) of inflection, flex (point).
infloresko inflorescence.
influa influential.
influebla amendable.
influega seminal.
influejo inflow area, intake area.
influenco flu, grippe, influenza.
influgrupo lobby.
influi to act, affect, influence, have influence on, shape, sway.
influo action, influence.
informa informative.
informadiko information science, computer science.
informado information, publicity.
informaĵo information, inquiry office.
informatiko computer science, informatics, information science.
informejo inquiry-office.
informfonto source.
informi to acquaint, inform, report, make known.
informiĝi to be advised, find out, enquire, learn.
informiĝo enquiry, quest.
informilo informational publication, brochure.
informinto informant, source.
informisto informer.
informita informed.
informivo information, information content.

informletero news letter.
informmendo enquiry, inquiry, query.
informo account, information.
informoŝoseo information superhighway.
informpanelo notice-board.
informpeto inquiry.
informsigno information character.
informtabulo notice-board.
informteorio information theory.
infraruĝa infrared. **infraruĝa radiado** infrared radiation.
infrastrukturo infrastructure.
infre at the bottom, below.
infuzado infusion.
infuzaĵo extract, infusion.
infuzi to infuse, instil.
infuziĝi to draw.
ingadnivelo nesting level.
ingado nesting.
ingenra feminine.
ingenro feminine gender.
ingi to nest.
ingiĝo nesting. **ingiĝo de subaj rutinoj** nesting of subroutines.
ingita nested. **ingita iteracio** nested loop. **ingita proceduro** nested procedure.
ingo case, holder, socket, sheath.
ingoto ingot.
ingredienco component, element, ingredient, part.
Inguŝio Ingushia.
inguŝo Ingush.
Inguŝujo Ingushia.
ingveno groin.
ingvenzono athletic supporter.
Inĝ. → **Inĝeniero**.
inĝenia ingenious.
inĝenie ingeniously.
inĝenierarto engineering.
inĝeniero engineer.
inhali to inhale.
inhalilo inhalator.
inhibi to inhibit.
inhibicii to inhibit.
inhibicio inhibition.
inhibo inhibition.
inici to introduce to, let into, initiate.
inicialo initial.
inicialvorto acronym.
iniciatado introduction.
iniciatema innovative, inventive, proactive, visionary.
iniciateme proactively.
iniciatemo enterprising.
iniciatemulo innovator.
iniciati to initiate, start.
iniciatinto instigator.
iniciativo initiative.
iniciato initiative.

iniciatoro initiator, promoter.
inicito initiate.
inico initiation.
Iniso Ennis.
injektaĵo injection.
injekti to inject.
injektilo (hypodermic) needle, syringe, injector.
injekto injection.
inkaano Incan, Inca.
inkandeska incandescent.
inkao Inca.
inkĵeta printilo inkjet printer.
inklina inclined, prone.
inklineco inclination.
inklinema prone, inclined to.
inklini to be inclined (to do something, toward something).
inklinigi to induce.
inkliniĝi to become inclined.
inklino disposal, inclination, tendency, inclination, predisposition, proneness, propensity, tendency, slope.
inklinoemo penchant.
inklude including, inclusively.
inkludi to include, incorporate.
inkluziva inclusive. **inkluziva aŭ-operacio** inclusive-or operation.
inkluzive including, inclusively. **inkluzive de** including.
inkluziveco inclusion (of sets).
inkluzivi to include.
inkluzivigo incorporation.
inkluzivo inclusion.
inko ink.
inkognito incognito.
inkrustaĵo inlay work.
inkrusti to encrust, incrust, inlay.
inksorbilo blotting paper.
inkuba nightmarish.
inkubacio incubation.
inkubatoro incubator.
inkubo incubus, nightmare.
inkubsonĝo nightmare.
inkudo anvil, incus.
inkujo well, inkpot, ink well.
inkuso anvil, incus (small bone in the middle ear).
inkviziciisto inquisitor.
inkvizicio inquisition.
inkvizitoro inquisitor.
ino female, feminine.
inocenta blameless, guiltless, innocent.
inocente innocently.
inocento innocent.
inokuli to inoculate, vaccinate.
inokuliĝi to be inoculated.
inseksa female.
insektforpelilo repellent, insect repellent.

insekticido insecticide, pesticide.
insekto bug, insect.
insektoj insects, vermin.
insektosciencisto entomologist.
insepkisto inspector.
insertaĵo insert.
inserti to insert.
insida insidious, treacherous.
insidanto attacker, enemy.
inside insidiously. **inside ataki** to waylay.
insideco insidiousness, stealthiness.
insidema insidious, treacherous.
insidemo snare.
insidi to lay a snare, plot against, set a trap (for). **insidi kontraŭ** to threaten.
insido ambush, snare, trap.
insigno badge, insignia, coat-of-arms.
insili to ensile.
insista emphatic, insistent.
insistadi to persevere, persist, pursue one's point, insist.
insistado insistence, pressure, urgency.
insistanto stickler.
insiste insistently. **insiste peti** to beg, implore.
insistema insistent.
insisti to insist.
insisto insistence, pressure, urgency.
inskripcio inscription.
insolacio sunstroke.
insolenta arrogant, haughty, proud, insolent, overbearing, supercilious.
insolente arrogantly, insolently.
insolventa bankrupt.
inspekado inspection.
inspekisto inspector.
inspeko inspection.
inspektado inspection.
inspektatesti to certify.
inspektatesto certification.
inspekti to inspect.
inspektistaro inspectorate.
inspektisto inspector.
inspekto inspection.
inspektoro inspector, overseer.
inspira inspiring.
inspirado inspiration.
inspiraĵo inspiration.
inspiri to imbue, inspire, suggest.
inspiriĝi to be inspired.
inspiro inspiration.
instalaĵa infrastructural.
instalaje infrastructurally.
instalaĵo installation.
instali to install.
instaliĝi to install.
instalilo installer.
instalo implementation.
instanca authoritative.

instanco authoritative source, court, (competent official) authority, instance, jurisdiction, body.
instepo instep.
instiga inducing. **instiga kaŭzo** inducement, occasion, motive. **instiga okazaĵo** inducement, motive, occasion.
instigado abetment, prodding.
instigaĵo enticement, incitement, stimulus.
instiganto ringleader.
instigi to encourage, impel, instigate, spur on, stimulate, urge, incite. **instigi je** to bring about, urge (people) on to. **instigi la scivolemon** to arouse one's curiosity.
instigilo goad, prompt.
instiginto abetter.
instigisto whip, hortator.
instigo impetus, incitement, stimulus.
instigulo ringleader.
instinkta instinctive.
instinkte instinctively.
instinkto instinct.
institucia institutional.
instituciigi to institutionalize.
institucio institution.
instituto institute.
instrua instructional, instructive, teaching.
instruado education, instruction, teaching.
instruanto teacher.
instruejo school.
instruema fond of teaching.
instrui to instruct, teach, train.
instruiĝi to become educated, learn.
instruistekzameno exam to become a teacher.
instruistino instructor, female teacher, schoolmistress.
instruisto instructor, teacher, schoolmaster.
instruita erudite, learned.
instrukciado instruction.
instrukciaro instruction set.
instrukcii to instruct.
instrukcinombrilo instruction counter.
instrukcio command, directions, instruction, orders.
instrumenta instrumental.
instrumentalo instrumental.
instrumenti to orchestrate.
instrumentisto instrumentalist.
instrumento instrument.
instruo instruction.
instruoado teaching.
instruplana curricular.
instruplano curriculum, syllabus.
insuficienco inadequacy, insufficiency, scarcity.
insula insular.
insulano islander.
insularo archipelago.

insulino insulin.
insulo island, isle.
insulta insulting, offensive, opprobrious.
insultado abuse.
insultaĵo insult.
insultanto abuser.
insulte abusively, harshly, insultingly, roughly.
insulteco abusiveness.
insultegi to outrage.
insultema insolent, saucy.
insulti to abuse, insult, offend.
insulto affront, verbal abuse.
insultvorto invective, term of abuse.
intajlo intaglio.
integra integral. **integra cirkvito** integrated circuit. **integra komputado** integrated data processing.
integrado integration.
integraĵo integral.
integrala integral (math). **integrala ekvacio** integral equation. **integrala kalkulo** integral calculus.
integraligo integration.
integralato integrand.
integralebla integratable.
integralhava integratable.
integrali to integrate.
integralo integral.
integralsigno integral sign ($\int$).
integreco integrity.
integri to integrate.
integrigi to integrate.
integrigo integration.
integriĝi to integrate.
integriĝo integration.
integrismo fundamentalism.
integrita integrated. **integrita cirkvito** integrated circuit.
intelekta intellectual.
intelekte innately, intellectually.
intelektema intellectual.
intelektismo intellectualism.
intelekto intellect, mind, understanding.
intelektula highbrow.
intelektularo intellectuals.
intelektulo intellectual.
inteligencio intelligentsia.
inteligenta intelligent, sagacious. **inteligenta terminalo** intelligent terminal, smart terminal.
inteligente intelligently.
inteligenteca kvociento I.Q., intelligence quotient.
inteligenteco intellect, intelligence.
inteligento intelligence.
inteligentulo clever person.
intenca intentional. **intenca murda** (premeditated) murder.

intence deliberately, on purpose, intentionally.
intenci to intend, mean, purpose.
intenco intention, meaning, plan, design.
intendanteco stewardship.
intendantino matron.
intendanto administrator, agent, steward, superintendent, curator, manager.
intensa acute, intense, intensive.
intense intensely.
intenseco intensity.
intensigi to intensify.
intensigo intensification.
intensiĝi to intensify.
intensiĝo intensification.
intensive intensively.
intensivigi to intensify.
intensivigo intensification.
inter among, between. **inter ... kaj** , from ... to, of ... to. **inter aliaj** inter alia, among other things. **inter aliaj aferoj** among other things. **inter martelo kaj amboso** between a rock and a hard place. **inter niaj amikoj** among our friends.
intera intermediate.
interaga interactive.
interagado interactive mode, interface.
interage interactively.
interagi to interact.
interago interaction.
interakordi to agree.
interakto entr'acte, interlude, intermezzo, intermission.
interalie among others, inter alia.
interamikiĝi to become friends (with each other).
interargumenti to discuss.
interatendo deadlock, deadly embrace.
interbatado affray, fight.
interbatalado affray.
interbatali to be at loggerheads, tussle.
interbatigo brawl, fight.
interbatiĝi to fight.
interbatiĝo scuffle.
interbloko block gap.
intercivitana milito civil war.
interdependa interdependent.
interdependeco interdependence.
interdigigi to dam in, dam up, embank.
interdikti to interdict.
interdikto interdict (Catholic).
interdisciplina interdisciplinary.
interefiko interaction.
interesa interesting.
interesaspekta interesting-looking.
interesato interested party.
interese interestingly.
intereseco curiosity, curiousness.
interesega absorbing.

interesegi to fascinate.
interesi to interest.
interesiĝi to be interested, take an interest. **interesiĝi je** to interest oneself in, become interested in. **interesiĝi pri** to be interested in, take an interest in.
interesiĝo interest.
interesita gripped, interested.
interesite interestedly.
intereskomunumo community of interests.
intereso interest.
interesto interest.
interetaĝo mezzanine.
interezo interest.
interfaco interface.
interferi to cause interference.
interfingrigi la manojn clasp the hands.
interfono intercom.
interfrapo collision.
interfratigi to unite.
interfratiĝo fraternization.
intergenta communal.
interhelpo mutual aid.
interhoma interpersonal.
interigo interment.
interjekcio interjection.
interkapti to intercept.
interkolega collegial.
interkompreniĝi to communicate, understand each other.
interkompreno mutual understanding.
interkomunikiĝi to communicate.
interkomunikiĝo communication.
interkona getting-acquainted.
interkonatiĝi to meet, get to know one another.
interkonatiĝo acquaintance.
interkonekteco interconnection.
interkonekti to interconnect.
interkonekto interconnection.
interkonfesa interfaith.
interkonfesia interconfessional, interdenominational, ecumenical.
interkonsenti to agree, come to an understanding with, come to terms with. **interkonsenti pri** to have an understanding. **interkonsenti rendevuon** to make an appointment.
interkonsento accommodation, accord, agreement, covenant, transaction.
interkonsiliĝi to deliberate.
interkonsiliĝo consultation, deliberation.
interkontaktulo contact (person).
interkonveneco compatibility.
interkrampigi to parenthesize.
interkruciĝo intersection.
interkrurigi to bestride, straddle.
interkrutejo defile.
interkultura intercultural.

interkvereli to be at loggerheads, tussle.
interligi to ally, connect, join.
interligiteco connection, interconnectedness.
interligo alliance, covenant, connection.
interlingvistiko interlinguistics.
interlingvo interlingua, interlanguage.
interlinie between the lines.
interlinii to interline.
interludo interlude.
intermaniera intermodal.
intermeti to interpose. **intermeti sin** to intervene.
intermeto intervention.
intermeza intermediate.
intermeze de amid, amidst.
intermezo intermezzo, interlude.
intermiksi to mix up, confuse.
intermiksiĝi to intermingle.
intermiksita pell-mell.
interministra interministerial.
intermita intermittent. **intermita febro** tertian fever.
intermite intermittently.
intermiti to be intermittent, occur intermittently.
intermito intermission.
intermontaĵo ravine.
intermonto defile, mountain pass.
interna domestic, inner, inside, internal.
interna aŭtomorfio inner automorphism. **Interna Azio** Central Asia. **Interna Mongolio** Inner Mongolia. **Interna Mongolujo** Inner Mongolia. **interna operacio** internal composition law. **interna ordigo** internal sort. **interna rilato** relation on a set. **interna rimo** internal rhyme.
internacia international. **internacia juro** international law. **Internacia Labour Organizaĵo** International Labour Organization. **Internacia Lingvo** International Language. **Internacia Mona Fonduso** International Monetary Fund. **internacia rapidtrajno** international express, international express train. **internacia respondkupono** international reply coupon.
internacie internationally.
internacieco internationality.
internaciigi to internationalize.
internaciigo internationalization.
internaciiĝo internationalization.
internaciismo internationalism.
Internaciisto internationalist.
internacismo internationalism.
Internaj Hebridoj Inner Hebrides.
internaĵo bowels, core, entrails, inside, intestine, viscera, interior.

interne in, inside, internally, within. **interne de** in, inside, within.
internen inside, inwards.
Internet-adreso Internet address.
internigi to insert, internalize, confine.
internigito internee.
internlando back country.
interno inside, interior.
internulejo boarding school.
internulo boarder.
interokazaĵo incident.
interorda trairo inorder traversal.
interpaciga peace.
interpaciganto mediator, peacemaker.
interpacigi to mediate.
interpacigo peacemaking.
interpaco armistice, cessation (of hostilities), truce.
interparoladi to converse.
interparolado conversation.
interparolanto interlocutor.
interparoleti to chat.
interparoleto chat.
interparoli to converse, discuss.
interparolo conversation.
interpelacii to interpolate.
interpelacio interpolation.
interpelaco interpellation, intervention.
interplaneda interplanetary. **interplaneda vojaĝo** interplanetary travel.
interplekti to intersperse, interweave.
interplektiĝi to interweave.
interpolado interpolation.
interpoli to interpolate.
interpopola people-to-people.
interpremi to squeeze together.
interpreta interpreting.
interpretado interpreting.
interpretanto interpreter.
interpreti to interpret.
interpretilo interpreter.
interpretisto interpreter.
interpreto interpretation.
interpunkcii to punctuate.
interpunkcio interpunction, punctuation.
interpuŝiĝi to scuffle.
interpuŝiĝo mêlée, scramble, scuffle.
interpuŝo scuffle.
interrasa interracial.
interregiona interregional.
interregistrara intergovernmental.
interregno interregnum.
interreligia interreligious.
interresponda interactive.
interreta Internet.
interreto Internet.
Interret-peranto Internet provider.
interrilati to interact, interrelate. **interrilati kun** to associate with.

interrilato intercourse, relation, understanding.
interrimi to rhyme.
interrompi to break in, interrupt, disturb.
interrompigi to cut off, disconnected.
interrompiĝi to be cut off, disconnected.
interrompiĝo break, interruption, stop.
interrompita koito coitus interruptus.
interrompo discontinuance, interruption, interrupt.
interrompotraktilo interrupt handler.
interrompregistro interrupt register.
intersekci sin to intersect.
intersekcii to intersect.
intersekcio intersection.
intersekco intersection.
intersekva consecutive, successive. **intersekva adreso** chain address.
intersekve consecutively, successively.
intersekvo order, run, sequence, series, succession.
intersezono off-season.
intersoldata intersoldier.
interspacigi to space.
interspaco distance, interval, space.
interstacia bloko section.
interstela interstellar.
intersulko balk.
interŝanĝado sharing.
interŝanĝe interchangeably.
interŝanĝi to barter, exchange, interchange, swap, invert.
interŝanĝo exchange, permutation.
interŝaniĝi to trade.
interŝtata international.
interŝtate internationally.
intertempa interim, temporary.
intertempe all the while, meanwhile, in the meantime.
intertempo interval (time).
intertraktado involvement, negotiation.
intertraktanto negotiator.
intertrakti to negotiate.
interuptoro circuit breaker.
intervalo interval.
intervenĝado vendetta.
interveni to intervene.
interveno intervention.
intervidiĝi to get to see between, come to see between.
intervidiĝo interview.
intervjuanto interviewer.
intervjui to interview.
intervjuisto interviewer.
intervjuo interview.
intervorte between words.
intestaro intestines.
intesto intestine.
intestotubo gut.

intima close, intimate. **intima interparolo** private talk.
intimaĵo intimacy.
intime intimately.
intimeco intimacy.
intimiĝi to become intimate.
intimulo soul-mate.
intonacio intonation.
intramuskola intramuscular.
intramuskule intramusculary.
intrareto intranet.
intravejna intravenous.
intrigado intriguing.
intriganto intriguer, schemer.
intrigemulo intriguer, schemer.
intrigi to intrigue, scheme, plot.
intrigo intrigue, scheme; plot, story (of a novel, play).
intrigulo intriguer, schemer.
introspekto introspection.
introvertito introvert.
intua intuitive.
intue intuitively.
intuicia intuitive.
intuicii to intuit.
intuicio intuition.
intuitiva intuitive.
intuitive intuitively.
intuo intuition.
inuita Eskimo, Inuit.
inuito Eskimo, Inuit.
inundebenaĵo flood plain.
inundejo floodplain.
inundi to flood. **inundi la merkaton per** to flood the market with.
inundo flood.
invadi to invade.
invado invasion.
invalida disabled.
invalideco disability, infirmity.
invalido disabled person, invalid.
invarianta invariant.
invariante invariantly.
invarianto invariant.
invariantokorpo fixed field.
inventado invention.
inventaĵo invention.
inventarado stock-taking.
inventari to do inventory, take stock.
inventaro inventory, stocklist.
inventarregistrado stock-taking.
inventema inventive.
inventi to invent.
inventinto inventor.
inventisto inventor.
invento invention.
Inveraro Inveraray.
Invergaro Invergarry.
Invergordono Invergordon.

inversa inverse, inverted, reverse, reversed.
inversa bildigo inverse mapping. **inversa bildo** inverse image. **inversa ekranbildo** reverse video. **inversa hiperbola funkcio** inverse hyperbolic function. **inversa hiperbola kosinuso** inverse hyperbolic cosine. **inversa hiperbola kotangento** inverse hyperbolic cotangent. **inversa hiperbola sinuso** inverse hyperbolic sine. **inversa hiperbola tangento** inverse hyperbolic tangent. **inversa rilato** inverse relation. **inversa trigonometria funkcio** inverse trigonometric function.
inversaĵo reverse.
inverse vice-versa.
invershava invertible.
inversi to invert.
inversigebla invertible.
inversigi to turn.
inversigo inversion (with respect to a circle).
inversio inversion (gram.).
inverso inverse.
inversvica memoro LIFO queue, LIFO stack, push-down list, stack.
inverti to invert.
Inveruro Inverurie.
investado investment.
investaĵo investment.
investanto investor.
investi to invest.
investituro investiture.
investo investment.
Invirĥeto Inverkeithing.
Invirnarano Nairn.
Invirniso Inverness.
inviti to invite.
invitiĝi to be invited.
invitilo invitation.
invito bidding, invitation.
involucia involuntary.
involucie involuntarily.
involucio involution.
io anything, something. **io ajn** anything. **io tia** something like that.
iofoje sometimes.
iom a little, rather, some, somewhat, to some extent, a bit. **iom ajn** any amount. **iom aparta** somewhat special. **iom da** a little of. **iom da tempo** for a little while. **iom de vero** some truth. **iom freneza** nutty, goofy. **iom post iom** bit by bit, gradually, little by little. **iom-post-ioma** gradual. **iom simila** somewhat similar.
ioma slight, minor.
iomajn anything, whatever.
iometa slight. **iometa da vojo** a little way.
iomete a little, rather. **iomete da** very little of, only a trace.
iometo handful.

iompostioma gradual.
iompostiome little by little.
iomproksime somewhere nearby, in the vicinity.
iomvorte in a few words.
ion anything.
ionia Ionic. **Ionia Maro** Ionian Sea.
ionika Ionian.
Ionio Ionia.
Iono Iona.
ionosfero ionosphere.
iova Iowan.
iovano Iowan.
ipekakuano ipecacuanha.
ipeko ipecacuanha.
iperito mustard gas.
ipo bark beetle.
ipomeo morning glory.
Ipro Ypres.
ipsilonkromosomo Y-chromosome.
ipsilono name of the letter Y.
iraĉi to go badly, go terribly.
iradi to go along, keep on going.
irado gait.
iraka Iraqi.
irakano Iraqi.
Irako Iraq.
irana Iranian.
irananino Iranian woman, Persian woman.
iranano Iranian, Persian.
Irano Iran, Persia.
iranta sampaŝe abreast.
irbileto ticket.
irebla passable, practicable.
iredenta unliberated.
iredentismo irredentism.
irejo path, road, way.
Ireno Irene.
iri to go, walk. **iri al kinejo** to go to the cinema, go to the movies. **iri antaŭe** to go first, go on ahead. **iri en diversajn flankojn** to go in different directions. **iri kun** to go with, accompany. **iri plue** to pass on. **iri rekte al** to go straight to. **iri sub** to go under.
iridio iridium.
irido iris (flower).
irigacii to irrigate.
irigacio irrigation.
irigaco irrigation.
irigi to cause to go, propel.
irilo stilt pole, stilt. **iriloj** stilts.
iriso iris (anat.).
iritaĵo irritant.
iriti to irritate.
irito irritation.
iriza iridescent.
irizi to make iridescent.
Irkucko Irkutsk.

irlanda Irish. **Irlanda Maro** Irish Sea.
irlandanino Irishwoman.
Irlandano Irishman.
Irlando Ireland.
irmallongigo shortcut.
irmaniero gait, manner of walking.
iro course, operation, run.
ironia ironic, ironical.
ironie ironically.
ironii to speak ironically.
ironio irony.
irorevena bileto return ticket.
irorevenbileto return-ticket.
irpasejo aisle.
irpreni to fetch, get, pick up.
irrapido pace, pacing.
irsulkaĵo wake.
Irtiŝo Irtysh.
irvojeto path.
irvojo road, path.
isato woad.
Isido Isis.
iskiatalgio sciatica.
iskiatiko sciatic nerve.
iskio ischium.
islama Islamic.
islamanigi to convert to Islam.
islamano Muslim, Moslem.
islamigi to Islamize, Islamicize, make Islamic.
islamismo Islamism.
islamisto Islamist.
Islamo Islam.
islanda Icelandic.
Islandano Icelander.
islandlingva Icelandic language.
Islando Iceland.
Islolago IJsselmeer.
ismo doctrine, ism.
ISO-kodo ISO code.
israela Israeli.
israelanino Israeli woman.
israelano Israeli.
israelida Israelite.
israelido Israelite.
Israelo Israel.
Isro IJzer.
Istanbulo Istanbul.
istempo past, preterite.
istmo isthmus.
isto professional.
Istrio Istria.
Iŝtaro Ishtar.
Itako Ithaca.
itala Italian. **itala kukurbo** courgette, zucchini. **itala lingvo** Italian, Italian language.
itale in Italian.
italia Italian. **italia kukurbo** courgette, zucchini.
italino Italian woman.
Italio Italy.
Italo Italian.
Italujo Italy.
iteraciĉapo loop header.
iteraciero iteration.
iteraciilo iterator.
iteracikorpo loop body.
iteracinombrilo control variable.
iteracio iteration.
iterbio ytterbium.
iteropara iteroparous.
itinero itinerary, route.
itrio yttrium.
iu anybody, anyone, somebody, someone. **iu ajn** any(one). **iu alia** someone else. **iuj** a few, some. **iun nokton** one night. **iun tagon** one day, someday.
iufoje at some time.
iuloke anyplace, anywhere, someplace, somewhere.
iusence in some sense.
iuspeca some type of.
iutage one day, someday.
iutempa sometime, temporary.
iutempe anytime, at some time, eventually, ever, once, sometime, someday.
izatido woad.
izobaro isobar.
izocela isosceles.
izola isolated, secluded. **izola vertico** isolated vertex.
izolado insulation, isolation.
izolaĵo insulation.
izolbendo electrical tape.
izole apart.
izoleco isolation, separation.
izoli to insulate, isolate, seclude.
izoliĝi to be isolated.
izoliĝo isolation.
izolilo insulator.
izolismo isolationism.
izolita isolated, remote.
izolite out of the way. **izolite staranta** detached, free-standing. **izolite staranta domo** detached house.
izoliteco isolation, separation.
izomero isomer.
izometria isometric.
izometrio isometry.
izomorfa isomorphic.
izomorfia isomorphic.
izomorfio isomorphism.
izoterma isothermal, isothermic.
izotermo isotherm.
izotopo isotope.
izotropa isotropic.

izotropeco isotropy.
izraela Israeli.
izraelano Israeli.
izraelia Israeli, Israelian.

izraelianino Israeli woman.
izraeliano Israelian.
Izraelido Israelite.
Izraelo Israel.

J

j. → **jaro**.
ja certainly, indeed, rather, surely, in fact.
jacinto jacinth.
jada jade.
jado jade.
jaguaro jaguar.
jahurto yogurt.
jaĥtisto yachtsman.
jaĥto yacht.
jakarando jacaranda.
Jakelino Jacqueline.
jaketo jacket, vest.
Jako Jack. **Jako de Ĉiametio** Jack-of-all-trades (person who can do many things).
jako jacket, coat.
jakobeno extreme radical.
jakobia Jacobian. **jakobia determinanto** Jacobian determinant. **jakobia matrico** Jacobian matrix.
jakobiano Jacobian.
Jakobio Jacobi.
Jakobo Jacob.
jaktisto yachtsman.
jakto yacht.
jakuta Yakut.
Jakutio Yakutia.
jakuto Yakut.
Jakutujo Yakutia.
jakvarbo breadfruit tree.
jakvo breadfruit.
jakvujo breadfruit tree.
Jalto Yalta.
jam already, by now, yet. **jam de** since. **jam ne** no longer, no more. **jam nun** right now.
jama already achieved.
Jamajko Jamaica.
jambo iamb.
jambosfrukto rose apple.
jamboso rose apple.
Janceo Yangtze (River).
Jangzio Yangtze.
janiĉaro janizary.
jankia Yankee.
jankio Yankee.
Jano Janus.
jansenismo Jansenism.
jansenisto Jansenist.
januara January, of January, January's.
Januaro January.
januaro January.
japana Japanese. **japana kenomelo** Japanese flowering quince, Japanese quince. **japana lingvo** Japanese, Japanese language. **Japana Maro** Sea of Japan.
japanaĉo Jap.
japanbilardo bagatelle.
japanino Japanese woman.
Japanio Japan.
Japanlando Japan.
japano Japanese.
Japanujo Japan.
japio yuppie.
jara annual.
jarabono yearly subscription.
jarcenta centennial.
jarcentiĝo centenary.
jarcento centennial, century.
jardaĵo yardage.
jardaŭra annual.
jardaŭrulo annual.
jardbrako yardarm.
jardeko decade.
jardo yard (3 feet, 0.9144m), spar.
jardpinto yard-arm.
jarduono half year, semester.
jare yearly, annually.
jarfina tago New Year's Eve.
jargono gibberish, jargon, lingo.
jarkolektaĵo annual, volume.
jarkolekto one-year collection.
jarkroniko annals.
jarkvarono quarter.
jarlibro annual (publication), yearbook.
jarlibroj annals.
jarmeza midyear.
jarmila millennial.
jarmilo millennium.
jaro year; vintage (of wine). **jaron post jaro** year after year.
jarpago annuity.
jarraporto yearly report.
jarringo annual ring.
jartempo season (of the year).
jasmeno jasmine.
Jasono Jason.
jaspiso jasper.
jaspo jasper.
jaŝmako yashmak.
jatagano yataghan.
java Javan, Javanese.
javanino Javanese woman.
javano Javanese.
Javo Java.
Javomaro Java Sea.
jazo jazz.
Jazono Jason.
je (preposition with no fixed meaning). **je bezono** when needed, as needed. **je Dio** by God. **je eterne** for evermore. **je favora aĉetpropono** on offer. **je iuj momento**

Jehovo   **judaro**

at times, sometimes. **je kioma horo** at what time. **je kioma kosto** at what cost. **je la fino** at the back, behind, in the rear. **je la konvena tempo** at the appropriate time, at the proper time, at the right moment. **je la lasta fojo** for the last time. **je la sunleviĝo** at sunrise. **je la unua fojo** at first. **je la unua rigardo** at first glance, at first sight. **je la vido de** at the sight of. **je lundo** on Monday. **je mia aĝo** at my age. **je mia miro** to my surprise. **je reala tempo** in real time. **je tagiĝo** at dawn, at daybreak. **je tiu aĝo** at that age. **je via sano** cheers, good health.
Jehovo Jehovah.
jejuno jejunum.
jeĵuri to conspire.
jelpi to yelp.
jelpo yelp.
jemena Yemeni.
jemenanino Yemeni woman.
jemenano Yemeni.
Jemeno Yemen.
jen behold, here is, here are, look, there. **jen ... jen** now ... now, sometimes ... sometimes. **jen alia!** here's another! **jen estas** here is, here are. **jen kaj jen** here and there, now and again.
jena that which follows.
jene thus.
jeno[1] this, the following.
jeno[2] yen (Japanese money, ¥).
jeremiado jeremiad.
jeriĥa rozo jericho rose.
Jeriĥo Jericho.
jeriĥorozo jericho rose.
Jerusalemo Jerusalem.
Jeruzalemo Jerusalem.
jes yes.
jesa affirmative.
jese affirmatively.
jesemulo yes-man, yes-person.
jesi to affirm, assent, say yes, reply in the affirmative.
jesigi to certify, confirm.
jesigo affirmation.
jesja but yes.
jeso affirmation, assent.
Jesuo Jesus. **Jesuo Kristo** Jesus Christ.
jetavio jet plane.
jeti to jet.
jetio Abominable Snowman, Yeti.
jetmotoro jet engine.
jeto jet (plane), jet propulsion.
Jezuito Jesuit.
Jezuo Jesus.
jida Yiddish.
Jido Yiddish.
jo name of the letter J.

Joakimo Joachim.
Joĉjo Johnny.
jodli to yodel.
jodlo yodel.
jodo iodine.
jodoformo iodoform.
jogano yogi.
jogio yogi.
jogo yoga.
jogurto yogurt.
Johana John.
Johanesburgo Johannesburg.
Johanino Joan, Joanna, Joanne.
Johano John.
johimbo yohimbe-tree.
jokero wild card.
jokersigno wild card.
Jokohamo Yokohama.
jolo yawl.
jomkipuro Yom Kippur.
jonigi to ionize.
Jonika Maro Ionian Sea.
jonio yoni.
jonizi to ionize.
jonkvilo jonquil.
jono ion.
jonosfero ionosphere.
jordanĝero danger of skidding.
jordania Jordanian.
jordaniano Jordanian.
Jordanio Jordan (country).
Jordano Jordan.
jori to skid.
jorigi to yaw.
Jorko York.
joro skid, yaw.
Joŝuo Joshua.
joto iota, jot (Iι).
Jozefo Joseph. **Jozef el Arimateo** Joseph of Arimathea.
ju ... des the ... the. **ju malpli ... des malpli** the less ... the less. **ju malpli ... des pli** the less ... the more. **ju pli ... des malpli** the more ... the less. **ju pli ... des pli** the more ... the more.
juano yuan.
jubeo rood loft, rood screen.
jubila jubilant.
jubilado jubilation, rejoicing.
jubile jubilantly.
jubilea jubilee.
jubileo jubilee.
jubileulo person celebrating an anniversary.
jubili to exult.
jubilo exultation, jubilation.
juda Jewish. **juda preĝejo** synagogue.
judaismo Judaism.
judaro Jewry.

206

Judaso

Judaso Judas. **Judaso Iskariota** Judas Iscariot.
judeco Jewishness.
judgermana Yiddish.
judismo Judaism.
judkvartalo Jewish quarter.
Judo Jew.
Judujo Judea.
jufto leather.
jugi to yoke, subjugate.
juglanda walnut.
juglandarbo walnut (tree).
juglando walnut.
juglandujo walnut (tree).
jugo subjugation, yoke.
jugoslava Yugoslav, Yugoslavian.
jugoslavino Yugoslav woman.
Jugoslavio Yugoslavia.
jugoslavo Yugoslav, Yugoslavian.
Jugoslavujo Yugoslavia.
juĝa judicial. **juĝa decido** decision, judgement. **juĝa persekutisto** bailiff (legal).
juĝa preno attachment, seizure.
juĝado adjudication, trial.
juĝafero case, lawsuit.
juĝalvoki to subpoena, summon.
juĝalvoko summons.
juĝantaro jury.
juĝantino arbitress.
juĝanto judge.
juĝantoisto umpire.
juĝato defendant.
juĝejo court(room), tribunal.
juĝfarado adjudication, hearing, judgement, trial.
juĝi to judge, sentence. **juĝi en foresto** to try in absentia. **juĝi laŭ** to go by, rely on, trust.
juĝista magisterial.
juĝistaro bench (of judges), tribunal.
juĝisto judge (legal).
juĝo judgement, sentence, verdict.
juĝokunsido hearing.
juĝordoni to order.
juĝordono order.
jujubarbo jujube.
jujubo jujube.
jujubujo jujube.
jukao yucca.
juki to itch.
juko itch, itching.
jukoniano Yukoner.
Jukono Yukon.
juli to scull.
Julio July.
julio July.
Julo Yule.

Jutio

juna young, youthful, juvenile. **juna angilo** elver. **juna arbo** sapling. **juna bovoviro** bullock. **juna bovviro** steer.
junaĝo (time of) youth, childhood.
junarbaro forest of young trees.
juneca young-looking, youthful.
juneco youth, youthfulness.
jungaĵo harness.
jungi to harness, yoke.
jungilaro harness, yoke.
jungitaro team.
junigi to rejuvenate.
juniĝi to grow young.
Junio June.
junio June.
juniperbrando gin.
junipero juniper.
junka rush (grassy plant).
junko rush (grassy plant).
junkro junker, squireen.
Juno Juno.
junto seam.
juntopremilo C-clamp.
juntskatolo plug-socket.
junula of a young person, youth, juvenile.
junulara youth.
junulargastejo youth hostel.
junularo youth (collectively).
junuleca youthful.
junuleco youthfulness.
junulgastejo lobsterman.
junulino young woman, girl, gal.
junulo lad, young person, youngster, youth, young man.
junuloino youngster.
jupeto ballet skirt.
Jupitero Jupiter.
jupitra Jovian.
Jupitro Jove, Jupiter.
jupo skirt.
jura legal. **jura persono** juridical person.
jure legally.
jurisdikcio jurisdiction.
jurisprudenco jurisprudence.
juristo jurist, lawyer.
Juro Jura.
juro jurisprudence, law.
juroscienco legal science.
jurto yurt.
justa fair, just, righteous, equitable. **justa puno** just punishment.
juste fairly, justly, rightly.
justeco equity, justice, righteousness.
justico justice system.
Justitio Justice.
justo equity, justice, righteousness.
justulo just person.
juta Jutish.
Jutio Jutland.

Jutlando

Jutlando Jutland.
juto jute, Jute.
Jutujo Jutland.
juvelaĵo bauble, tinsel, jewellery.
juvelaro jewellery.
juvelejo jewellery shop.
juveleto bijou.

jŭano

juvelisto jeweller.
juvelo jewel.
juveloeto trinket.
juvelŝtono stone.
juvelujo jewel box, jewel case, jewellery box.
jŭano yuan.

Ĵ

ĵaboto jabot.
ĵaketo jacket.
ĵako jack, topcoat, tunic.
ĵaluza jealous.
ĵaluze jealously.
ĵaluzi to be jealous.
ĵaluzio jalousie, Venetian blind.
ĵaluzo jealousy.
ĵamboreo jamboree.
ĵami to jam.
ĵargono jargon, lingua franca, pidgin.
ĵaro stone jar.
ĵartelo garter, (woman's) suspender.
ĵaŭde on Thursdays.
Ĵaŭdo Thursday. **ĵaŭdo** Thursday.
ĵazbando jazz-band.
ĵazisto jazz musician.
ĵazkantisto jazz singer.
ĵazo jazz.
ĵaztrupo jazz-band.
ĵeleo jelly.
Ĵerzo Jersey.
ĵerzo cardigan, jersey, sweater.
ĵetadi to throw, keep on throwing.
ĵetado de monero join toss.
ĵetaĵo projectile.
ĵetarmilo missile.
ĵetaro over.
ĵetbulo bocce ball, boule, bowl, bowling ball.
ĵetdisko disc, discus, frisbee.
ĵetegi to hurl.
ĵeteti to toss.
ĵetfermi to bang, slam.
ĵetfermo bang.
ĵeti to cast, fling, throw, toss, pitch. **ĵeti la kulpon sur iun** to place the blame on someone. **ĵeti sin sur** to leap upon, pounce upon, spring upon, rush. **ĵeti sur** abdicate to.
ĵetiĝadi to pace, roll.
ĵetiĝante plunging.
ĵetiĝi to get thrown.
ĵetilo sling.
ĵetisto pitcher.
ĵetita thrown.
ĵetkaptilo bola, bolas.
ĵetkovri to sprinkle, strew.
ĵetkubludo dice game.
ĵetkubo die (cubical object).
ĵetlanco javelin, spear.
ĵetmaŝino catapult.
ĵeto throw, toss, pitch.
ĵetono chip, disc, token.
ĵetonvendejo token booth.
ĵetponardo javelin.
ĵibo jib.

ĵigo jig.
ĵino genie.
ĵinrikŝo rickshaw.
ĵinso jeans.
ĵinzo jeans.
ĵipo jeep.
ĵo name of the letter Ĵ.
ĵogado jogging.
ĵogi to jog.
ĵokeo jockey.
ĵokero joker, wildcard.
ĵokersigno wildcard, wildcard character.
ĵokervorto wildcard, wildcard character.
ĵonglado jugglery.
ĵongli to conjure, juggle.
ĵonglisto conjurer, juggler.
ĵonko junk (type of ship).
ĵosaĵo ball.
ĵosi to earth, earth up, hill, hill up.
ĵudi to practice judo.
ĵudisto judo wrestler.
ĵudo judo.
ĵulo joule.
Ĵuno Juneau.
ĵura sworn. **ĵura forlaso** abjuration, renunciation.
ĵurasa Jurassic.
Ĵuraso Jurassic.
ĵuratesti to adjure.
ĵurdeklaranto affiant.
ĵurdeklarinto affiant.
ĵurdeklaro affidavit.
ĵurdeklaronto affiant.
ĵuri to affirm, pledge, swear, take an oath, vow.
ĵurigi to swear (in).
ĵurigo administration of the oath.
ĵurintaro jury.
ĵurintino jurywoman.
ĵurinto juror, juryman.
ĵurio jury.
ĵurligi to bind by oath.
ĵurligita bound by oath.
ĵurnalaĉo 'rag' (publication).
ĵurnalismo journalism.
ĵurnalistino journalist, female journalist.
ĵurnalisto journalist.
ĵurnalo daily paper, journal, newspaper.
ĵurnalvendejo paper shop.
ĵuro oath.
ĵurpeti to petition.
ĵurrompi to commit perjury, perjure.
ĵurrompo perjury.
ĵus just (now), a moment ago.
ĵusa recent.

K

k. → **kaj**.
k.a. → **kaj aliaj**.
kaba Cape. **kaba emberizo** Cape bunting.
kabalo cabal.
Kabalo Cabbala.
kabangrupo group of cabins, settlement.
kabano cabin, hut, shack.
kabaredo cabaret.
kabareto cabaret.
kabei to suddenly leave the Esperanto movement, having been active within it.
kabineto cabinet (ministry), gallery.
kabinetula nerdish, nerdy.
kabinetulo cabinet secretary, minister.
kabla televido cable television.
kablero strand.
kableto wire.
kablingo cringle, eyelet.
kablisto linesman.
kablo cable.
kablogramo cablegram.
kablotramo funicular.
kabo cape, promontory, headland. **Kabo de Bona Espero** Cape of Good Hope.
Kaboprovinco Cape Province.
Kaboverdo Cape Verde.
kabrioleto cabriolet, chaise, convertible, hansom.
Kabulo Kabul.
kaburbano Capetonian.
Kaburbo Cape Town.
kaco cock, prick, dick (vulgar terms for penis).
kacosuĉado cock-sucking.
kaĉaloto cachalot, sperm whale.
kaĉo gruel, mess, mush, porridge, puree, slush, hodgepodge, hotchpotch.
kadastro cadastral survey, land registry.
kadavra cadaverous. **kadavra graso** adipocere.
kadavraĵo carrion.
kadavro cadaver, corpse.
kadavrogrifo vulture.
kadavromuŝo bluebottle, meat-fly.
Kadelo Cadell.
kadenco cadence.
kadeto cadet.
kadio cadi, kadi.
kadisto treasurer.
kadmio cadmium.
kadraĵo box, cadre, context, frame, framework, level, official, parameters.
kadrato quad, quadrant.
kadre de in the framework of.
kadri to frame.

kadro backdrop, cadre, frame, framework, setting.
kaduceo caduceus.
kaduka decayed, decrepit, dilapidated, rickety, frail, fragile, inoperative.
kadukaĵo ailment, sign of decay.
kaduke feebly.
kadukeco decadence, decay.
kadukega senile.
kadukegeco senility.
kadukigi to bring down.
kadukiĝema memoro dynamic memory.
kadukiĝi to be on the decline, go downhill, go off.
kadukiĝo decay.
kadukulo elderly.
kafeino caffeine.
kafejestro pub-keeper.
kafejo café, coffeehouse, coffee shop.
kafeterio cafeteria.
kafkeska Kafkaesque.
kafkruĉo coffee pot.
kafo coffee.
kafpulvoro coffee grounds, ground coffee.
kafro Kaffir.
Kafrujo Kaffraria.
kafskatolo coffee canister, coffee tin.
kaftano caftan (Oriental garment).
kafujo coffee bush, coffee plant, coffee pot, coffee canister, coffee tin.
kaĝego coop.
kaĝigi to coop.
kaĝo cage.
kaĝobirdo cage bird.
kaheli to tile.
kahelo flag, paver, paving block, tile.
Kahero Caher.
Kahersiveno Cahersiveen.
kaido qaid, kaid, caïd.
kaiko caique.
Kaino Cain.
kainsigno brand of Cain, mark of Cain.
Kairo Cairo.
kaj and. **kaj ... kaj** both ... and. **kaj aliaj** et al., and others. **kaj ankaŭ** and also, and ... as well, as well as, together with. **kaj cetere** etc. **kaj sekve** and as follows, and the following. **kaj simile** etc. **kaj tamen** and yet. **kaj tiel plu** and so on, et cetera.
Kajafo Caiaphas.
kajako kayak.
kajaŭ and/or.
kajaŭo disjunction.
kajero copybook, exercise book, folder, notebook, pamphlet.

Kajleakino

Kajleakino Kyleakin.
kajmano cayman.
kajo[1] pier, platform, quay, wharf.
kajo[2] conjunction.
kaj-operacio and-operation.
kajovo Kiowa.
Kajrvirdino Carmarthen.
kajsigno ampersand (&).
kaj-signo ampersand (&).
kajto kite.
kajuto cabin (ship, etc.), hovel.
kaĵoli to cajole, coax, wheedle.
kakaarbo cocoa tree.
kakao cocoa.
kakaoarbo cocoa tree.
kakapulvoro cocoa powder.
kakatuo cockatoo.
kakaujo cocoa tree.
kakemono kakemono.
kakia khaki.
kakio khaki.
kakodemono cacodemon.
kakofonia cacophonous.
kakofonio cacophony.
kakto cactus.
kala callous.
kalabaseto courgette, zucchini.
kalabaso calabash, gourd.
Kalabrio Calabria.
Kalabrujo Calabria.
kalaftri to caulk.
kalaĵo corn.
kalambako agarwood, aloeswood, eagle wood.
kalamino calamine, carbon deposit.
kalamo calamus.
kalandrao corn weevil.
kalandri to mangle.
kalandrilo mangle.
kalandro corn weevil, mangle.
kalankoo kalanchoe.
kalao bog arum, water arum.
kalcedono chalcedony.
kalceolario calceolaria, lady's purse, pocketbook flower, slipper flower, slipperwort.
kalcini to calcine.
kalcio calcium.
kalcito tiff.
kalcitri to recalcitrate, kick.
kalcitro kick.
kaldronegejo boiler house.
kaldronego boiler, steam boiler.
kaldronfaristo tinker.
kaldronisto tinker.
kaldrono boiler, cauldron, kettle.
kaledona Caledonian.
kaledonia Caledonian.
Kaledonio Caledonia.
kaledono Caledonian.

kalkulema

Kaledonujo Caledonia.
kalejdoskopo kaleidoscope.
kalemburo pun.
kalendaro calendar.
kalendo calend.
kalendulo marigold.
kaleŝaĵo chassis.
kaleŝeto buggy.
kaleŝisto carriage maker, coachman.
kaleŝo carriage, coach.
kalfatri to calk, caulk, pitch.
kalibri to calibrate.
kalibrigi to recalibrate.
kalibro bore (of a gun), calibre.
kalibrocirkelo callipers.
kalifo caliph.
kalifornia Californian. **Kalifornia Golfo** Gulf of California.
kaliforniano Californian.
Kalifornio California.
kalifornio californium.
kaliforniumo californium.
kaliforo blowfly, blue-bottle.
kalifujo caliphate.
kaligrafio calligraphy.
kalikfolio sepal.
kaliko chalice, goblet, tankard, grail.
kalikoto calico.
kalio potassium.
Kalipso Calypso.
kalistefo china aster.
kalistegio bindweed.
kalistemo bottlebrush.
kalisteniko calisthenics.
kalisteno calisthenics.
Kalisto Callisto.
kalitriko water-starwort.
kalkaĵo whitewash.
kalkaneo heel bone.
kalkano heel (foot).
kalkansidi to sit on one's heels, squat.
kalkanumo heel.
kalkargilo marl.
kalkedonio chalcedony.
kalki to whitewash.
kalko lime. **kalko estingita** slack lime, slaked lime. **kalko kaŭstika** burnt lime, quicklime.
kalkoŝtono limestone.
kalkotofo Travertine.
kalkŝmiri to plaster.
kalkŝtono limestone.
kalkulado calculation, computation.
kalkulaĵo account, bill, reckoning.
kalkularo accounts.
kalkulatoro adding-machine.
kalkulbastono slide rule.
kalkulebla calculable.
kalkulema calculating.

kalkuleraro miscalculation.
kalkuli to calculate, count, figure, work out, compute, reckon. **kalkuli je** to count on. **kalkuli kun** to take into account. **kalkuli perfingre** to count on one's fingers.
kalkuli proksimume to approximate.
kalkuliĝi to amount.
kalkulilo calculator.
kalkulisto accountant.
kalkullibro reckoner (book).
kalkulmaŝino calculator.
kalkulo account, bill, calculation, computation, reckoning, check, accounting, tab, calculus.
kalkulscio numeracy.
kalkuluso calculus.
kalkumi to lime.
kalmaro squid.
kalmuko Kalmuck.
kalo callus, corn (on foot).
Kalokalŝo Kyle of Lochalsh.
kalomelo calomel.
kalorio calorie.
kaloto spherical cap.
kalpako bearskin, bearskin cap.
kalsoneto bottom half of bikini, briefs.
kalsono drawers, panties, underpants, undershorts.
kalto kingcup, marsh-marigold.
kalumnia defamatory, slanderous.
kalumnianto detractor, slanderer.
kalumnii to defame, libel, malign, slander, vilify, bad-mouth.
kalumnio false charge, malicious misrepresentation, scandal, slander.
kaluno heather.
kalva bald(-headed), hairless.
kalvaria vojo Calvary, stations of the cross.
Kalvario Calvary, Golgotha.
kalveco baldness.
kalviĝi to become bald, be balding.
kalvinano Calvinist.
kalvinisma Calvinistical.
kalvinismo Calvinism.
kalvinisto Calvinist.
Kalvino Calvin.
kalvulo bald man.
kamaradeco comradeship.
kamaradi to be chummy with.
kamaradino comrade.
kamarado buddy, companion, comrade, pal, mate, chum.
kamarilo camarilla.
Kamarilo Campbelltown.
Kambeltaŭno Campbelltown.
kambia makleristo bill broker.
kambio bill of exchange, draft, letter of exchange.
kambiono cambion.

kamboĝa Cambodian.
kamboĝanino Cambodian woman.
kamboĝano Cambodian.
Kamboĝo Cambodia.
Kambriĝo Cambridge.
kambrio Cambrian (period).
Kambuslango Cambuslang.
Kamĉatko Kamchatka.
kameciparo cedar, false cypress.
kameleono chameleon.
kamelino she-camel.
kamelio camelia.
kamelo camel.
Kameloto Camelot.
kamemberto camembert.
kamenbreto mantel, mantelpiece.
kamenfajro fire on the hearth.
kameno fireplace, hearth, fireside.
kamenpurigisto sweep.
kamenskrapisto chimney sweep.
kamenstableto fire dog.
kamentubisto chimney sweep.
kamentubo chimney, smokestack, stack, flue.
kameo cameo.
kamerai to film.
kameraisto cameraman, cinematographer, cameraperson.
kamerao (film, movie, video) camera.
kameristo cameraman.
kamerlingo camerlengo.
kamero chamber, darkroom, small room.
kameruna Cameroon.
Kamerunio Cameroon.
Kameruno Cameroon.
kamforarbo camphor tree.
kamforo camphor.
kamforujo camphor tree.
kamioneto van.
kamionisto truck driver.
kamiono lorry, truck.
kamizolo camisole, doublet, jerkin, undershirt.
Kamlopso Kamloops.
kamloto camlet.
Kamo Kama.
kamomilo chamomile.
kampa pastoral, rural. **kampa konvolvulo** lesser bindweed.
kampadejo camping ground, camping site.
kampadi to camp, be encamped, lie encamped, camp out.
kampado camping.
kampadveturilo caravan.
Kampalo Kampala.
kampanilo bell tower, clock tower.
kampanjanto campaigner.
kampanji to campaign.
kampanjo campaign, drive.

kampanulo

kampanulo bellflower, campanula, harebell, Canterbury bell.
kampara rural. **kampara domo** country house.
kamparana peasant's.
kamparanido country lad.
kamparano countryman, peasant, farmer.
kampare in the country.
kampareca rustic.
kamparo country, countryside.
kampatingo field designator.
kampeĉo campeachy, logwood.
kampejo camp, campground, camping ground, camping-site.
kampeto paddock.
kampfesteno picnic.
kamphirundo barn swallow.
kampi to camp out.
Kampino Kempenland.
kampkardo creeping thistle.
kamplaboristo agricultural worker.
kamplisto field list.
kamploĝejo camp, encampment.
kamploĝi to camp out.
kampo field.
kampodometo villa.
kampodomo country house.
kampokorvo rook.
kampomuso grass vole.
kampuĉea Cambodian.
kampuĉeanino Cambodian woman.
kampuĉeano Cambodian.
Kampuĉeo Cambodia.
kampularo peasantry.
kampulino country-woman.
kampulo country dweller, peasant, farmer.
kampulservisto hand.
kampumi to camp out.
kamuflaĵo camouflage.
kamufli to camouflage.
kamuflilo camouflage material.
kamuflo camouflage.
kana cane.
Kanaanio Canaan.
Kanaanujo Canaan.
kanaba hemp.
kanabeno linnet.
kanabo cannabis, hemp.
kanada Canadian. **kanada cervo** elk, wapiti. **kanada elodeo** American waterweed, Canadian waterweed.
kanadanino Canadian woman.
Kanadano Canadian.
kanadia Canadian.
kanadianino Canadian woman.
kanadiano Canadian.
Kanadio Canada.
Kanado Canada.
kanajla villainous.

kankrogenta

kanajlaĵo villainy.
kanajlaro rabble, riff-raff.
kanajleco baseness.
kanajlo blackguard, knave, rogue, scoundrel, scamp, villain.
kanala tavolo data link layer.
kanaligi to sewer, canalize, canal.
kanalizi to canalize, ditch.
kanalo canal, channel, gutter.
kanapo couch, sofa.
kanaria Canary. **Kanaria Insularo** Canary Islands. **Kanariaj Insuloj** Canary Islands.
kanariino hen canary.
kanario canary.
kanato canoe, pleasure-boat.
Kanbero Canberra.
kancelario chancellery, chancery, office of public records, reception, waiting room.
kanceliereco chancellorship.
kancelierejo chancellery.
kanceliero chancellor.
kancero cancer, canker.
kandelabro candelabrum.
kandeleto taper.
Kandelfesto Candlemas.
kandelingo candlestick, sconce.
kandellumo candlelight.
kandelo candle.
kandidataro ticket.
kandidateco candidature.
kandidati to apply for, aspire to (an office), run for election, seek (to obtain honour or office), stand as a candidate for.
kandidatigi to nominate.
kandidatigo nomination.
kandidatiĝi to apply, stand.
kandidatlisto nomination, recommendation.
kandidato applicant, aspirant, candidate.
kandidatpropono recommendation.
kanditatiĝo application.
kandizi to crystallize, candy.
kando candy, crystallized sugar, sugar candy.
kanejo cane field.
kanelaĵo groove.
kaneli to chamfer, groove, rifle.
kanelo slot, groove, fluting, rifling.
kanguruo kangaroo.
kanibalismo cannibalism.
kanibalo cannibal.
kanino canine (tooth), eye tooth.
kanistro fuel tank.
Kanjo Cathy.
kanjono canyon.
kankano cancan.
kankro crab, crayfish. **Kankro** Cancer, the Crab (zodiac).
kankrogenta crustaceous.

kankromo boat-bill.
kano cane, reed.
kanona canonical. **kanona bazo** canonical basis. **kanona juro** canon law. **kanona projekcio** canonical projection. **kanonaj horoj** canonical hours.
kanonadi to shell.
kanonado shelling.
kanonaro artillery.
kanonigi to canonize.
kanonigo canonization.
kanoniko prebendary, canon.
kanonisto artilleryman, gunner, bombardier.
kanonizi to canonize.
kanono cannon, big gun.
kanonŝipo gunboat.
kanoto canoe.
kansasa Kansan.
kansasano Kansan.
kantabra Cantabrian.
kantadi to sing (continually), keep singing.
kantado chant, singing.
kantaĵo act of singing.
kantalupo cantaloupe.
kantarelo chanterelle, cantharides, Spanish fly.
kantarido sailor beetle, soldier beetle.
kantaro songbook.
kantarto singing (the art).
kantato cantata.
kantbirdo singing bird, songbird.
Kanterburgo Canterbury.
kanteti to hum.
kanteto ditty.
kanti to sing.
kantia Kantian.
kantiko canticle.
kantilevro cantilever.
kantino cafeteria, canteen.
Kantio Kant.
kantistino singer, female singer.
kantisto minstrel, singer, songster, vocalist.
kantlibro songbook.
kanto song.
kantona Cantonese.
kantonigo block system.
kantonlingva Cantonese.
kantonmento billet.
Kantonmento Cantonment.
kantono canton, county (USA).
kantoro cantor, choir member.
kantraŭi to oppose.
kanuado canoeing.
kanulo cannula.
kanuo canoe.
kanvaso canvas.
kanzono ballad, chanson, song.
kaosa chaotic.

kaose chaotically.
kaosigi to disarrange, disarray.
kaoso chaos, tangle.
kapabla able, capable, apt.
kapable ably, aptly.
kapableco ability, aptitude, capability.
kapabli to be able, be able to.
kapabligi to enable, habilitate.
kapabligo en la entrepreno on-the-job training.
kapablo ability, capability, capacity, competence, competency, faculty.
kapacitanco capacitance.
kapacito capacity.
kapadoca Cappadocian.
kapadoco Cappadocian.
kapaĵo head-piece, headset.
kapapogilo headrest.
kapaŭdilo headphone.
kapaŭskultilo headphone.
kapaŭskultiloj headphones.
kapdetenilo martingale.
kapdolori to have a headache.
kapdoloro headache.
kapei to lie to.
kapeigi to heave to.
kapelestro choirmaster.
kapelo chapel.
kaperanto hijacker, pirate.
kaperi to absorb, assimilate, hijack, take over.
kaperisto buccaneer, freebooter, pirate, corsair.
Kapernaumo Capernaum.
kaperŝipo privateer.
kapeto head. **kapeto lega-skriba** read/write head.
kaphararo hair of the head.
kaphaŭteroj dandruff.
kapibaro capybara.
kapilara capillary.
kapilareco capillarity, capillary action.
kapilaro capillary.
kapitaligi to capitalize.
kapitalisma capitalist.
kapitalismo capitalism.
kapitalisto capitalist.
kapitalo capital (money).
kapitano captain.
kapitelo capital (of a column).
Kapitolo Capitol, Capitoline.
kapitulaci to capitulate, surrender, yield, give up, resign.
kapitulaco capitulation.
kapitulo capitulum.
kapjesi to nod (in agreement).
kapkosta krimo capital crime.
kapkuseno bolster, pillow.
kapneadi to shake one's head.

kapnei

kapnei to shake one's head (no).
kapnomancio capnomancy.
kapo[1] head, cape, cranium, promontory.
  kapo de la pafilo butt (end of gun).
kapo[2] kappa (Кк).
kapobanto topknot.
kapobati to head-butt.
kapoko kapok.
kapokujo kapok tree.
kapolo cabochon.
kapono capon, castrated cock, castrato, eunuch.
kapopiede end-to-end, head-to-toe.
kapopieduloj cephalopods.
kaporalo corporal.
kaporo caper bush.
kapoto bonnet, hood, capote.
kappo kappa.
kapra goat's, of a goat.
kaprajô goat meat.
kapraro flock of goats.
kapreolido fawn.
kapreolo roe, roebuck.
kaprica capricious, fitful, whimsical.
kaprice on a whim.
kapricemo capriciousness.
kaprici to act up.
kaprico caprice, whim, fad.
kapridajô kid.
kaprido kid.
kaprifolio honeysuckle.
Kaprikorno Capricorn (zodiac).
kaprimulgo nightjar.
kaprinaro herd of (female) goats.
kaprino she-goat.
kaprioladi to frolic, gambol.
kapriolado frolic, gambol.
kaprioli to caper, frolic about, frisk, leap about, prance, romp.
kapriolo caper.
kapristo goatherd.
kapro goat.
kaprobleki to bleat.
kaprofela goatskin.
kaprofelo goatskin.
kaprograsa goat fat.
kaprograso goat fat.
kaproledo goatskin.
kaprompa fatal.
kaprompilo billy club.
kaproviro billy-goat, he-goat.
kapselo shepherd's-purse.
kapsiketo chili.
kapsiko chili, pepper.
kapstano capstan, winding gear.
kapsulo capsule, firing cap.
kapŝirmilo head protector.
kaptado capture.
kaptajô prey.

karakterizajô

kaptanto catcher.
kaptema avid, eager, greedy.
kapti to capture, catch, grapple, trap, ensnare, clutch, grasp. **kapti sin** to seize, grasp, grab hold of.
kaptiĝi to be captured, get caught.
kaptilo decoy, snare, trap.
kaptinto one who has captured.
kaptipova prehensile, adapted for grasping, grabbing, grappling.
kaptisto catcher.
kaptita caught. **kaptita ĉe la freŝa faro** caught in the act, caught red handed.
kaptitajô capture.
kaptiteco captivity.
kaptito prisoner.
kapto catch, prey.
kaptoganto catcher's mitt.
kaptoŝnuro lasso.
kaptuko kerchief, scarf.
kapturna dizzy.
kapturne dizzily.
kapturniga dizzying.
kapturnigi to make giddy.
kapturniĝo dizziness, vertigo.
kapturno dizziness, giddiness, swimming (in head), vertigo.
kapuceno Capuchin monk.
kapuĉino cappuccino.
kapuĉmantelo cape, cloak.
kapuĉo capuche, cowl, hood.
kapuĉpalto parka.
kapuslinio zero alignment.
kaputa broken down, decrepit.
Kapverdaj Insuloj Cape Verde Islands.
kapvesto head dress, headwear.
kapvorto headword.
kapvualo wimple.
kara beloved, cherished, dear, expensive, valuable, precious, costly, high-priced.
karabeno carbine.
karabo ground-beetle.
karadrio ringed plover.
Karadromo Carrick-on-Shannon.
karafi to decanter.
karafo carafe, decanter.
karaiba Caribbean. **Karaiba Maro** Caribbean Sea.
karakoli to caracole, prance about.
karaktera characteristic.
karakteranalizo profile.
karakteristiko characteristic.
karakteriza characteristic. **karakteriza funkcio** characteristic function. **karakteriza polinomo** characteristic polynomial. **karakteriza vektoro** characteristic vector.
karakterizado characterization.
karakterizajô characteristic.

karakterize characteristically.
karakterizi to characterize.
karakterizo profile.
karaktero character, nature, personality, temper, habitual conduct, individuality, moral strength, personality, reputation.
Karaljo Crail.
karambolfrukto carambola, star-fruit.
karamboli to strike, collide.
karambolo strike, collision.
karamelo caramel.
karaokeo karaoke.
karapaco carapace, shell.
karaso crucian carp.
karateisto karate practitioner.
karateo karate.
karato carat.
karavanejo caravansarai, caravansary.
karavano caravan.
karavelo caravel.
karbardaĵo charcoal.
karbejo colliery.
karbfosisto collier.
karbo coal.
karbobriketo briquette.
karbolo carbolic acid, phenol.
karbominejo coal mine.
karbomino coalmine.
karbona carbon.
karbonhidrato carbohydrate.
karbonido carbide.
Karbonifero Carboniferous.
karbonigra coal-black.
karbonkopio carbon copy.
karbono carbon. **karbono-14** carbon-14.
karbonpapero carbon paper.
karbopapero carbon paper.
karborundo carborundum.
karboskorio cinder.
karbpapero carbon paper.
karbujo coal scuttle.
karbujoeto coal scuttle.
karbunklo boil, carbuncle.
karbunkolo carbuncle.
karburaĵo fuel.
karburatoro carburettor, carburator.
karburi to carburet, carburate, vaporize.
karburilo carburettor, carburator.
karcero jail cell, prison.
karcinomo cancer.
kardamino bittercress.
kardamomo cardamom.
kardano universal joint.
kardario hoary cress.
kardaro thistle field.
kardelo goldfinch.
kardi to card.
Kardifo Cardiff.
Kardigano Cardigan.

kardinalbirdo cardinal.
kardinalo cardinal.
kardio cockle.
kardiogramo cardiogram.
kardioido cardioid.
kardjo cardia.
kardo thistle.
kardono artichoke thistle, cardoon.
kardopapilio painted lady.
kareaĵo curry.
kareco love, value, worth.
karega darling.
karegulo darling.
karekso sedge.
Karelio Karelia.
karenasekuro hull insurance.
karenco malnutrition.
karenforma boat-shaped.
Kareno Carina.
kareno hull.
kareo curry.
karesa wheedling.
karese caressingly, tenderly.
karesema affectionate, caressing, cuddlesome, cuddly.
kareseme softly, tenderly.
karesemo softness, tenderness.
karesi to caress, fondle, stroke.
karesiga cuddly.
karesindaĵo knick-knack, trinket, bauble.
Karesmo Lent.
karesnomo nickname.
kareso caress, stroke, endearment.
karespremi to cuddle, hug.
karganto consignor, shipper.
kargboato freight boat, freighter.
kargi to freight.
kargisto shipping agent.
kargo cargo, freight, lading.
kargoatesto bill of lading.
Karia Maro Karian Sea.
kariatido caryatid.
kariba Caribbean. **Kariba Maro** Caribbean Sea.
Karibdo Charybdis.
Karibio Caribbean.
Karibuo Caribou.
karibuo caribou.
karierismo careerism.
karieristo careerist.
karier-konsilisto career counsellor, guidance counsellor.
kariero career.
karierresumo résumé.
kariertabelo curriculum vitae.
karikaturi to caricature.
karikaturisto caricaturist.
karikaturo caricature.
Karikfergo Carrickfergus.

kariko papaya.
kariljonisto carillonneur.
kariljono carillon, chimes.
kario caries, tooth decay.
kariofila fromaĝo clove-cheese.
kariofilo clove.
kariofilujo clove tree.
kariokinezo mitosis.
kariolo dog cart, trap.
karisma charismatic.
karismo charisma.
karitado charity, love of one's neighbour.
karitata charitable.
karitato charity, benevolence, goodwill.
karito benevolence, goodwill, charity, love of one's neighbour.
Karlajlo Carlisle.
karlino carline thistle.
Karlo Charles.
Karlourbo Charlestown.
Karlovo Carlow.
karmelanino Carmelite.
karmelano Carmelite.
karmelo burnt sugar.
karmemora lamented, deceased.
karmezina crimson.
karmezino crimson, deep red.
karmina carmine.
karmino carmine.
karmo karma.
karna carnal, fleshy.
Karnarvono Caernarvon.
karnavalo carnival.
karnejo charnel house.
karnevalo carnival.
karno flesh, meat.
karnokolora flesh-coloured.
karnomanĝa carnivorous.
karnomanĝulo carnivore.
karnovora carnivorous.
karnovoro carnivore.
karnulo mortal man.
karobarbo algarroba.
karobo carob, St. John's bread.
karobujo carob tree.
karolida skribo minuskla Carolingian minuscule.
karolo carol.
Karono Charon.
karoo diamond (cards).
karoserio body, coach work.
karoteno carotene.
karotido carotid.
karoto carrot.
Karpatoj Carpathians, Carpathian mountains.
karpelo carpel.
karpeno hornbeam, yoke elm.
karpeo wrist-bone.

karpo carp.
karsto karst.
kartaga Carthaginian.
kartagano Carthaginian.
Kartago Carthage.
kartaro card deck, card file.
kartavi to make a uvular R.
kartego placard, poster.
kartelo cartel, bulletin.
karteto card (visiting), docket.
kartezia Cartesian. **kartezia folio** Cartesian folium. **kartezia koordinato** Cartesian coordinate. **kartezia ovalo** Cartesian oval. **kartezia prisigna regulo** Descartes rule of signs. **kartezia produto** Cartesian product. **kartezia produto** Cartesian product.
Kartezio Descartes.
kartilago cartilage.
kartingo card slot.
kartludi to play cards.
kartludo card game.
karto card, map, menu. **karto geografia** (geographic) chart.
kartoĉego shell.
kartoĉo cartridge, shell, shot shell, shotgun shell.
kartoĉozono bandoleer.
kartoĉujo cartridge box.
kartografia cartographic.
kartografiisto cartographer.
kartografio cartography.
kartomancio cartomancy.
kartona cardboard.
kartonalumetaro book.
kartono cardboard, pasteboard.
kartoteko card-file.
karttradukilo card interpreter.
kartujo card cage.
kartunisto cartoonist.
kartuno cartoon.
kartuŝo cartouche, scroll.
kartuziano Carthusian.
kartuzio Chartreuse.
kartvela Georgian.
Kartvelio Georgia.
kartvelo Georgian.
Kartvelujo Georgia.
karula dear.
karulino darling.
karulo darling, dear (person).
karuselo carousel, carrousel, merry-go-round.
karvibrando kümmel.
karvio caraway.
kasacii to quash, vacate, overturn.
kasacio annulment.
Kasandro Cassandra.
kasavo cassava.

kasedmagnetofono cassette.
kasedo cassette.
kasejo cash desk, cashier's office, cashpoint.
kaserolo casserole, saucepan, stew pan.
kaseto cassette.
kasio cassia.
Kasiopeo Cassiopeia.
kasiso cassis.
kasistino cashier.
kasisto cashier, treasurer, paymaster.
kaskado cascade, waterfall.
kaskaro cascara.
kaskedo cap (with visor).
kasko helmet.
kaskofloro aconite, monkshood, wolfsbane, leopard's bane.
Kaslebajo Castlebay.
kaslibro account book.
Kaslobaro Castlebar.
kaso cash box, money box, till, cashier.
kasono caisson.
Kaspia Maro Caspian Sea.
Kaspio Caspian Sea.
kastanjeto castanet.
kastego ark.
Kastelburgo Castlebury.
kastelestro castellan.
kastelgrafo viscount.
kastelo castle, citadel, fort, stronghold, mansion.
kastila Castillian.
kastilia Castilian.
kastiliano Castilian.
Kastilio Castile.
kastilo Castilian.
Kastilujo Castile.
kastismo caste system.
kasto caste.
kastora beaver, of a beaver.
kastoredoj beavers.
kastoro bearer.
Kastoro Castor.
kastrado castration.
kastri to castrate.
kastrita castrated, gelded. **kastrita virĉevalo** gelding.
kastro castration.
kasuarino beefwood.
kasuaro cassowary.
kaŝa surreptitious, veiled, stealthy.
kaŝado hiding.
kaŝanta hiding.
kaŝata occult.
kaŝaŭskulti to bug, eavesdrop, listen in, monitor, tap.
kaŝe clandestinely, secretly, by stealth.
kaŝeco secrecy.
kaŝejo hiding place.
kaŝema sly, underhand.

kaŝeme furtively, slyly.
kaŝemo dissimulation.
kaŝgardi to hold back, keep back, withhold.
kaŝgastigi to harbour.
kaŝhelpilo cheat sheet.
kaŝi to conceal, hide, veil. **kaŝi sin** to hide (oneself). **kaŝu kaj serĉu** hide and seek.
kaŝiĝi to hide, skulk.
kaŝiri to steal.
kaŝita hidden, latent.
kaŝitaĵo mystery.
kaŝite behind one's back, underhand.
kaŝiteco secrecy.
kaŝludi to play hide-and-seek.
kaŝludo hide-and-seek.
kaŝmemoro cache.
kaŝmikrofono bug, hidden microphone.
kaŝmiksi to scramble.
kaŝmira Kashmiri.
kaŝmirano Kashmiri.
Kaŝmiro Kashmir.
kaŝnomo pseudonym, pen name, nom de guerre.
kaŝobservanto spy.
kaŝobservi to peep, peep upon, spy, spy upon.
kaŝpafisto sniper.
kaŝpasaĝero stowaway.
kaŝprovokisto agent-provocateur.
kaŝridi to giggle, snigger.
kaŝrigardi to peep.
kaŝtanarbo chestnut tree.
kaŝtanbruna chestnut.
kaŝtano chestnut, edible chestnut, horse chestnut.
kaŝtanujo chestnut tree.
kaŝtanurbo chestnut-tree.
kaŝvesti to disguise.
kaŝvesto disguise.
kaŝvojaĝanto stowaway.
kata feline.
katafalko catafalque, open hearse.
kataklismo cataclysm.
katakombo catacomb.
katalepsio catalepsy, trance.
katalizi to catalyse.
katalizilo catalyser.
katalogi to catalogue.
katalogo catalogue, directory, inventory, schedule.
kataluna Catalonian.
Katalunio Catalonia.
Katalunujo Catalonia.
katamarano catamaran.
kataplasmo plaster, poultice.
katapulti to catapult.
katapulto catapult.
katarakto cataract (eyes).
Katarino Catherine.

katario catmint, catnip.
Kataro Qatar.
kataro catarrh.
katartedoj New World vultures.
katastro land register, official real estate register, register of title deeds.
katastrofa calamitous, catastrophic, miserable, disastrous.
katastrofo calamity, catastrophe, disaster.
katatonio catatonia.
katbleki to mew.
kateca feline, cat-like.
kateĉuareko betelnut palm.
kateĉuo catechu, cutch.
kateĉupalmo betelnut palm.
katedralo cathedral.
katedro cathedral, professorial chair or platform, pulpit, lecturer's desk, professorship.
Kategato Kattegat.
kategoria categorical, firm, peremptory, resolute.
kategorie categorically.
kategorio category.
kateĥismo catechism.
kateĥisto catechist.
kateĥiza catechetical.
kateĥizado confirmation classes.
kateĥizato catechumen.
kateĥizi to catechize.
kateĥizisto catechist.
kateĥizo catechetics.
katekismo catechism.
katekisto catechist.
katekiza catechetical.
katekizado confirmation classes.
katekizato catechumen.
katekizi to catechize.
katekizisto catechist.
katekizo catechetics.
kateni to fetter, shackle, restrain, handcuff.
kateno chain, fetter, shackle, restraint, restriction.
katetero catheter.
kateto kitty.
katherbo allheal, valerian.
katido kitten.
katino female cat, she-cat.
katio catty.
katizi to glaze, gloss.
katizo gloss, lustre.
katjono cation.
kato cat.
katodo cathode, negative electrode.
katodradia ekrano cathode ray screen.
katolika Catholic.
katolikeco catholicity.
katolikismo Catholicism.
katoliko Catholic.
katuna cotton.

katuno cotton (cloth, fabric).
katviro tom cat.
kaŭĉukfloso inflatable raft.
kaukazo Caucasus.
kaŭcie under bond, on bail.
kaŭcii to (post) bail.
kaŭcio bail.
kaŭĉuka rubber.
kaŭĉukarbo rubber tree.
kaŭĉuko rubber.
kaŭkalido bur-parsley.
kaŭkaza Caucasus, Caucasia. **Kaŭkaza montaro** Caucasus Mountains. **kaŭkaza skabiozo** Caucasian pin-cushion flower, Caucasian scabious.
Kaŭkazo Caucasus, Caucasia.
Kaŭkazoj Caucasus.
kaŭri to cower, crouch, squat.
kaŭriĝi to crouch, squat.
kaŭsalgio burning pain.
kaŭstika burning, caustic, corrosive.
kaŭstikaĵo caustic (substance), cautery.
kaŭstikeco causticity.
kaŭteri to cauterize.
kaŭterizi to cauterize, sear.
kaŭterizilo cautery.
kaŭtero branding-iron, cautery.
kaŭza causal. **kaŭze de** because of, on account of.
kaŭzeco causality.
kaŭzi to activate, cause, give rise to. **kaŭzi malprofiton** to harm, hurt, injure, prejudice. **kaŭzi malutilon al** to harm, hurt, injure, prejudice. **kaŭzi skandalon** to create a scandal, give offence.
kaŭzo cause, reason, incentive, motive.
kava concave, hollow.
kavaĵo cavity.
kavaleriano cavalryman.
kavalerio cavalry.
kavalira chivalrous, gallant, knightly.
kavaliraĵo gallant act, gallant deed.
kavalire chivalrously, gallantly.
kavalireca chivalrous, knightly, gallant.
kavalireco chivalry, knighthood.
kavalirigo accolade.
kavaliro cavalier, knight, chevalier.
kavalirsprono larkspur.
kavalkado cavalcade.
Kavano Cavan.
kaveca hollow.
kaverna cavernous, hollow.
kaverneto small cave.
kavernhomo caveman.
kaverno cave, cavern, den.
kavernulo cave-dweller, caveman, troglodyte.
kaveta concave.
kaveto indentation.

kavi to dig out, excavate.
kaviaro caviar.
kavigi to burrow, excavate, hollow.
kavio guinea pig.
kavo cave, cavity, groove.
kavokula hollow-eyed.
kaza ordono case statement.
kazaĥa Kazak, Kazakh.
Kazaĥio Kazakhstan.
kazaĥo Kazakh.
Kazaĥujo Kazakhstan.
kazako colours, smock.
kazeigaĵo rennet.
kazeigilo rennet.
kazeiĝi to curdle.
kazeino casein.
kazemato casemate.
kazerno curd.
kazerno barracks, soldiers' quarters.
kazetikedo tag field.
kazfrazo case.
kazigilo rennet.
kazino casino.
kazo affair, case, matter.
kazuaro cassowary.
kazublo chasuble.
kazuistiko casuistry.
kazuisto casuist.
kazuo difficulty of conscience.
k.c. → **kaj cetere**.
k-do → **kamarado**.
K.E. CE (Common Era).
ke that. **ke mi iru** that I should go.
kecalo quetzal.
keĉua Quechua.
keĉupo ketchup.
kefiro kefir.
kegio skittle.
keglado bowling.
keglanto bowler.
keglaro ninepins, skittles, bowling.
keglejo bowling-alley.
keglisto bowler.
keglo bowling pin, ninepin, pin, skittle.
kegloj skittles.
kegloludanto bowler.
kegloludejo bowling-alley.
kegloludo bowling.
keiranto wallflower.
kejli to peg, pin.
kejlo peg, pin.
Kejto Keith.
kekso biscuit, cookie.
keletaĝo cellar, basement.
kelfenestro basement window.
kelidonio greater celandine.
kelisto butler, cellar man.
kelka a little, some. **kelkaj** a few, any, some, several. **kelkaj homoj** some people.

kelkafoje a few times.
kelkatage for a few days.
kelkatempa temporary.
kelkatempe for a (short) time, temporarily.
kelke some. **kelke da** a few, some.
kelkfoja occasional.
kelkfoje several times, sometimes.
kelkmonate for a few months.
kelkoblo several times.
kelkokaze sometimes.
kelkope several together.
kelktempe a little time, temporarily.
kelneri to wait.
kelnerino waitress.
kelnero waiter.
kelo basement, cellar.
kelonio turtle.
kelŝtuparo basement stairs.
kelta Celtic. **kelta lingvo** Celtic language.
   Kelta Maro Celtic Sea.
kelto Celt, Kelt.
Kelvino Kelvin.
kemia chemical.
kemiaĵo chemical.
kemie chemically.
kemiisto chemist.
kemio chemistry.
kemiterapio chemotherapy.
kenja Kenyan.
kenjanino Kenyan woman.
kenjano Kenyan.
Kenjo Kenya.
Kenmaro Kenmare.
keno resin-wood, resinous wood.
kenomelo dwarf quince.
kenopodiacoj goosefoot.
Kenozoiko Cenozoic.
kenta Kentish.
kentukia Kentuckian.
kentukiano Kentuckian.
keo kea.
Keopso Cheops.
k.e.p. → **kiel eble plej**.
keplera Kepler, Keplerian. **kepleraj leĝoj** Kepler's laws.
Keplero Kepler.
kepo cap (military).
kepro twill.
Kerbero Cerberus.
Kerero Kerrera.
Kergeloj Kerguelen.
kerio Japanese yellow rose.
kerkedulo garganey.
kermeso country fair, fair, kermis, village fair.
kerna central, crucial, key.
kerneca pithy.
kerneco centrality.
kerneto pit.

kernfrukto drupe.
kerno core, nucleus, kernel, pit, stone.
kernovoko supervisor call, system call.
kernrompulo hawfinch.
kero heart (cards).
kerofilo chervil.
kerosena kerosene.
keroseno kerosene.
kerubo cherub.
kesteto cassette.
kestkaptilo box trap.
kesto box, chest, coffer, case, trunk, crate.
Kesto de Interligo Ark of the Covenant.
kestoŝranko buffet.
kia what a, what kind of, what sort of. **kia ajn** any at all, whatever, whatever kind of, whatsoever. **kia blago!** you're pulling my leg! you've got to be kidding! **kia ĝi estis** such as it was. **kia ideo** what an idea. **kia patro, tia filo** like father, like son. **kia sensancaĵo!** what a bunch of baloney!
kiagrade to what extent.
kial what for, why, for what reason.
kialo account, reason.
kiam as, when. **kiam ajn** whenever.
kiamaniere how, in what way.
kian what kind of, what sort of.
kiberkosmo cyberspace.
kibernetika cybernetic.
kibernetiko cybernetics.
kibico busybody, meddler.
Kiblo Qibla (in Mecca).
kibucano kibbutznik.
kibuco kibbutz.
kiĉa kitschy.
kiĉo kitsch.
kie where. **kie ajn** wherever. **kie diable** where in the dickens.
kiel as, like, such as, how, in what way; such a, what a. **kiel antaŭe** as before. **kiel ĉiam** as always. **kiel dirite** that said, having said that, as was mentioned. **kiel eble plej** as … as possible. **kiel eble plej anglamaniere** in as English a manner as possible. **kiel eble plej baldaŭ** as soon as possible. **kiel eble plej frue** as early (as soon) as possible. **kiel eble plej multe** as much as possible. **kiel eble plej rapide** as quickly as possible. **kiel eble pli malofte** as seldom as possible. **kiel fiŝo ekster akvo** like a fish out of water. **kiel jam dirite** as already mentioned. **kiel komenci?** how should I begin? **kiel longe** how long. **kiel mallerte!** how clumsy (of me)! **kiel malproksima** how far. **kiel mi ĵus diri...** as I just said... **kiel ofte okazas** as often occurs. **kiel oni scias...** as you know... **kiel ordinare** as usual. **kiel plaĉas al vi...?** how do you like...? **kiel**

se as if. **kiel tutaĵo** as a whole. **kiel vi fartas?** how are you? **kiel vi fartas?** how are you? how do you do? **kiel vi nomiĝas?** what are you called? **kiel vi pravas en tio!** how right you are (about that)! **kiel vi sanas?** how are you? how do you do?
kiele in what way, how.
kien where to.
kieo whereabouts.
kies of which, which one's, whose.
Kieva Regno Kievan Rus'.
Kievo Kiev.
Kijevo Kiev.
kikero chickpea.
Kilarnio Killarney.
Kilimanĝaro Kilimanjaro.
Kilino Killin.
Kilkenio Kilkenny.
Kilmarnoko Kilmarnock.
kilo keel.
kilobajto kilobyte.
kilobito kilobit.
kilociklo kilocycle.
kilogramo kilo, kilogram.
kiloherco kilohertz.
kiloĵulo kilojoule.
kilolitro kiloliter.
kilometro kilometre.
kilomolo kilomole.
kiloneŭtono kilonewton.
kilonutono kilonewton.
kiloomo kilo-ohm, kilohm.
kiloparseko kiloparsec.
kilopaskalo kilopascal.
Kilorglino Killorglin.
kilotuno kiloton.
kiloŭato kilowatt.
kilovathoro kilowatt-hour.
kilovato kilowatt.
kilovatto kilowatt.
kilovolto kilovolt.
Kilruŝo Kilrush.
Kilsido Kilsyth.
kilsono centreboard.
kilto kilt.
Kimberlio Kimberley.
kimono kimono.
kimra Welsh. **kimra lingvo** Welsh, Welsh language.
Kimrio Wales.
Kimro Welshman.
Kimrujo Wales.
kinaĵo (cine) film.
kinazo kinase.
Kinegado Kinnegad.
kinejo cinema, movie theatre, movie house.
kinejvizitanto moviegoer.
kinematiko kinematics.

kinematografejo cinema, movie theatre, theatre, the pictures.
kinematografio cinematography.
kinematografo film projector, movie projector.
kineta kinetic.
Kinguso Kingussie.
kinino quinine.
kinisto filmmaker.
Kinkardino Kincardin.
kinkonino cinchonine.
kinkono cinchona (bark, tree).
Kinlohbervo Kinlochbervie.
kino cinema, cinematography.
kinofilmo movie.
kinono quinone.
kinoteatro cinema, movie house, movie theatre.
Kinroso Kinross.
Kinstono ĉe la Hulo Kingston upon Hull.
Kintajlo Kintail.
kio that, which. **kio ajn** whatever. **kio ajn okazos** at all events. **kio estas al vi** to what's the matter. **kio estas al vi?** what's the matter with you? **kio estas la nomo de...?** what is ... called? **kio estas?** what's wrong? **kio estis pruvota** quod erat demonstrandum, QED. **kio plu estas...** what's more... **kion ajn** anything, whatever. **kion fari?** what could I do? **kion signifas...?** what does ... mean? **kion vi faras?** what did you do? **kion vi havas por diri** what do you have to say. **kion vi opinias pri...** what do you think about... **kion vi volas diri?** what do you mean? **kion? kion vi diris?** what? what did you say?
K-io → Kompanio.
kiom how many, how much. **kiom ajn** however much. **kiom da** how many, what quantity of? **kiom da tempo** how long. **kiom eble** as far as possible. **kiom oni volas** as much as one wishes. **kiom pagi?** how much do I owe you?
kioma how many, what number. **kioma horo** what time. **kioma horo estas?** what time is it?
kiomgrade to what extent.
kiomjara how old.
kiomo amount, quantity; what, which.
kiosko gazebo, kiosk.
Kioto Kyoto.
kipĉako Kipchak, Qypchaq.
kipo kip.
Kipro Cyprus.
kirasa armoured.
kirasaŭto armoured car.
kirasglaso armour glass.
kirasi to armour.
kiraso armour, cuirass, breastplate.
kiraspiko armour-piercing.
kirasŝipo armoured ship.
kirgiza Kyrgyz.
Kirgizio Kirghizia.
Kirgizujo Kirghizia.
Kiribato Kiribati.
Kirkaldo Kirkcaldy.
Kirko Circe.
kirko[1] church (building).
kirko[2] harrier, kite.
Kirkudbrito Kirkcudbright.
Kirkvalo Kirkwall.
kirlakvo maelstrom, whirlpool.
kirlakvoj rapids.
kirli to curl, froth, stir, whip, whirl.
kirliĝi to swirl.
kirlilo whisk.
kirlita whipped, frothed.
kirlo curl.
kirlovaĵo scrambled eggs.
kirloventego cyclone.
kirlovento whirlwind.
kirmeso kermes.
kiromancio chiromancy, palmistry.
kiromiso aye-aye.
kiroptero bat.
kirŝo cherry brandy, kirsch.
kirurga surgical. **kirurga operacio** surgical operation, operation, surgery.
kirurgia surgery.
kirurgie surgically.
kirurgiejo surgery.
kirurgiisto surgeon.
kirurgio surgery.
kirurgo surgeon.
kisi to kiss.
kisinde kissable.
kisinto one who has kissed.
kisito one who has been kissed.
kiso kiss.
kisonto one who will kiss.
kisoto one who will be kissed.
kisto cyst (medical).
kiŝo quiche.
kitelo blouse, overalls, smock, frock.
Kitimato Kitimat.
kitino chitin.
kitio kittywake.
kitivako kittywake.
kiu that, which (one), who. **kiu ajn** any, whichever, whoever, whosoever. **kiu pli frue venas, pli bonan lokon prenas** first come, first served. **kiuj** that, which, who.
kiucele why, for what purpose.
kivifrukto kiwi.
kivio kiwi.
kivo kiwi.

klabfungoj

klabfungoj club fungi.
klabi to bludgeon.
klabo bludgeon, club, mace.
klabujo golf bag.
klaĉado gossip, gossiping.
klaĉemulino yenta.
klaĉgazetaro tabloids.
klaĉgazeto tabloid.
klaĉi to gossip, prate, make small talk, prattle.
klaĉisto gossip (person).
klaĉo gossip, prattle, babble, chitchat.
klaĉulino gossip (person).
klaĉulo gossip (person).
klado phylum, sub-kingdom.
kladonio reindeer-moss.
klafto fathom.
klakĉapelo high hat, top hat.
klakdanco tap dance.
klakfermi to bang, slam.
klakfermiĝi to slam shut.
klaki to chatter, clap, click, rattle, flap, slap, smack. **klaki per butono de muso** to click.
klakileto castanet.
klakilo rattle (noisemaker).
klako click, snap.
klangulo long-tailed duck.
klano clan.
klapeto tab.
klapkonko bivalve.
klaplito crib.
klapo flap, valve, half shell.
klappordo trap door.
klapseĝo folding chair.
klara clear, distinct, plain, explicit, lucid, manifest.
klaraŭdebla audible.
klaraŭdeco clairaudience.
klare clearly, plainly.
klareco clarity, clearness.
klarega limpid, self-evident.
klaresprima articulate.
klaresprime articulately.
klareto claret (wine).
klariga explanatory.
klarigebla accountable.
klarigi to account for, clarify, explain, elucidate, make clear. **klarigi per ekzemploj** to clarify by examples.
klarigo account, explanation.
klariĝi to clear.
klariona clarion.
klarioni to sound.
klarionisto bugler.
klariono bugle, clarion.
klarkio clarkia.
klarneto clarinet.
klarsento clairsentience.
klarvida clairvoyant.

klerigi

klarvideco clairvoyance.
klasado sorting.
klasamiko classmate.
klasano grader.
klasbatalo class struggle.
klasĉambro classroom.
klasejo classroom, schoolroom.
klasi to sort.
klasifika datenaro sort file.
klasifikado classification.
klasifiki to classify, sort.
klasifiko classification.
klasigi to classify.
klasigo classification.
klasika classic, classical.
klasikaĵo classic.
klasike classically.
klasikeco classicalness.
klasikismo classicism.
klasikisto classicist.
klasikulo classical (composer, author, etc.).
klaskonscio class consciousness.
klaso class.
klaŭnaĵo antic.
klaŭni to clown around.
klaŭno clown.
klaŭstro cloister.
klaŭstrofobio claustrophobia.
klaŭzo clause.
klavareto keypad.
klavaristino keyboard player.
klavaro keyboard.
klavceno harpsichord.
klavi to hit, type.
klaviceneto ottavino, spinet, virginal.
klaviceno harpsichord.
klaviklo clavicle, collar bone.
klavikordo clavichord.
klavkomando hot key.
klavo button, key (piano, typewriter, etc.).
klavpremo keystroke.
klefo clef.
klejdomancio cleidomancy.
klematido clematis, old man's beard, traveller's joy.
klementino clementine.
klemo terminal (electrical).
kleo clef.
kleomo spiderflower, cleome.
Kleopatro Cleopatra.
klepsidro sandglass, hourglass, water clock.
kleptomanio kleptomania.
klera cultured, educated, learned, well-informed, talented, enlightened.
kleraĉa academic.
klereco scholarship.
klerega profound, learned.
klerigado education, enlightenment.
klerigi to educate, enlighten.

223

klerijuo clerihew.
klerika clerical.
klerikala clerical, clericalist.
klerikaro clergy.
klerikino clergywoman.
kleriko clergyman, cleric.
klerismo Age of Reason, Enlightenment.
kleromancio cleromancy.
klerulo erudite (person), scholar, learned (man).
klevinkulo accolade.
Klevlando Cleveland (city in Ohio, USA).
klientaro clientele, patrons, clients.
klienta-servila arkitekturo client-server architecture.
klientino customer.
kliento client, customer, patient.
Klifdeno Clifden.
klifo cliff, crag, headland.
klikhorloĝo stop-watch.
kliko[1] (safety) catch, click, set.
kliko[2] clique, coterie.
klimaksa climactic.
klimaksi to climax.
klimakso climax.
klimaktera climacteric.
klimakteriko climacteric.
klimaktero climacteric.
klimata climatic.
klimatizado air-conditioning.
klimatizi to air-condition.
klimatizilo air conditioner.
klimatizita air conditioned.
klimatizo air conditioning.
klimato climate.
klimatologio climatology.
klimatologo climatologist.
klinĉo deadlock, deadly embrace.
klingo blade (knife, etc.), cutting edge.
klini to bend, incline, tilt, lean, slope, tilt.
klini sin to bend, stoop, bow.
kliniĝi to stoop. **kliniĝi antaŭen** to bend over.
kliniĝinte stealthily, furtively.
kliniĝo inclination, pitch, slant, slope, stoop, tilt.
kliniigi to tilt.
klinika clinical.
kliniko clinic.
klinko latch, spring bolt.
klino bending, bow.
klinrando beveled edge.
klipo clasp, clip.
klipso adjusting clip.
klisterilo enema.
klistero clyster, injection (medical), douche, enema.
kliŝaĵaro plate (stereotype).
kliŝajo cliché, stereotype.
kliŝi to stereotype.
kliŝo cliché, cut, half-tone, negative, stereotype.
klitoro clitoris.
klivi to cleave, split.
kloakaĵo sewage.
kloakfaŭko drain.
kloako cesspit, cesspool, latrine, septic tank, sewer.
Kloĥo Clough.
kloni to clone.
klonigi to clone.
klonigo cloning.
klonika clonic. **klonika spasmo** clonic spasm.
Klonmelo Clonmel.
klono clone.
klonulo clone (a cloned person).
klopodado bustle, exertion, proceedings, striving.
klopodema assiduous, bustling.
klopodi to aim, attempt, endeavour, take steps, undertake, try.
klopodo attempt, effort.
kloralo chloral.
klorido chloride.
kloro chlorine.
klorofilo chlorophyll.
kloroformi to chloroform.
kloroformo chloroform.
kloroza anemic.
klorozo chlorosis, iron-deficiency anaemia.
klorpromazino chlorpromazine.
klostro cloister.
klostrofobio claustrophobia.
kloŝforma bell-shaped. **kloŝforma kurbo** bell-shaped curve, Gaussian curve.
kloŝo bell jar, cloche, frame.
kloŝoĉapelo bowler.
kloŝopo closed shop.
klozeto toilet.
klozoneo cloisonné.
klubaneco club membership.
klubano club member.
klubejo clubhouse.
klubo club, society.
kluĉi to clutch.
kluĉilo clutch.
kluĉopedalo clutch pedal.
kluĉorisorto clutch return spring.
kluĉstango clutch arm, clutch lever.
kluki to cluck.
klukkluki to gurgle.
klupeo clupeoid.
kluso hawse hole, hawse pipe.
kluzo gateway, lock, sluice.
knaba boyish.
knabaĉo brat.
knabaĝo boyhood.

knabeca

knabeca boyish.
knabeco boyishness.
knabego big boy.
knabeto little boy.
knabina girlish. **knabina nomo** maiden name.
knabineca girlish.
knabineto little girl.
knabino girl, lass.
knabo boy, lad.
knabulino tomboy.
knali to bang, explode, burst, make a loud sound.
knaligi to bang.
knalo backfire, bang.
knara strident.
knaranaso gadwall.
knari to creak, screech, grate, grind, scratch, squeak, scrape.
knarilo clack.
knaro scratch, scratching, scraping, grating.
knedaĵo dough.
knedi to form, give form to, knead, mix.
knedliko dumpling.
knedpasto plasticine.
knedujo kneading bowl, kneading trough.
knelo dumpling.
kniki to buckle.
knikiĝi to buckle.
knikiĝo buckling.
knokaŭto knock-out.
knuto knout.
ko name of the letter K.
koagulaĵo clot.
koaguli to coagulate.
koaguliĝi to coagulate.
koaguliĝo blood clump.
koakso coke.
koaliciano ally.
koalicii to form a coalition.
koalicio coalition.
koalo koala.
koano choana.
kobajo Guinea pig.
kobalto cobalt.
Kobeo Kobe.
kobitidedoj loach.
kobitido loach.
koboldo (hob)goblin, gnome, imp, sprite, elf, kobold.
kobro cobra.
koĉenilo cochineal.
koĉero coachman. **Koĉero** Auriga (constellation).
koĉo coccus.
koda coded.
kodado coding, encoding, encryption.
kodako snapshot camera.
kodeino codeine.

kokejo

kodekso codex, pharmacopoeia.
kodi to code, encode.
kodicilo codicil.
kodigi to codify, encode.
kodigo codification.
kodiĝo coding, encoding.
kodilo coder.
kodisto coder.
kodo code. **kodo de signaro** code, coded character set.
kodogenerilo code generator.
kodono bit combination, code element.
kodoprezento encoding.
kodpaĝo code page.
kodranto quadrant.
kodrompisto cracker.
kodteorio coding theory.
kodumi to hack.
kodumulo hacker.
kodvorto code word.
koeficiento coefficient.
kofaktoro cofactor.
kofro chest, coffer, suitcase, trunk.
kofrujo trunk (of car).
kohera coherent, connected, consistent, stuck together.
kohere coherently.
kohereco coherence.
koheri to cohere.
kohero cohesion.
kohorto cohort.
koincida coincident.
koincidi to coincide, concur.
koincidigebla superposable.
koincido coincidence.
koiti to copulate, make love.
koito coitus.
kojlo colon.
kojna dento fang.
kojnforma skribo cuneiform.
kojni to wedge.
kojno block, chock, wedge.
kojnodento canine (tooth).
kojnoforma cuneiform.
kojnoskribo cuneiform.
kojono ball, nut, testicle.
kojonoj balls.
kojoto coyote, prairie wolf.
kojpo coypu.
koka ovo hen's egg.
kokaino cocaine.
kokaĵo chicken, hen.
kokao coca bush.
kokardo bow, cockade.
kokbatalo cockfight.
kokcigo coccyx.
kokcinelo lady beetle, ladybird, ladybird beetle, ladybug.
kokejo chicken house, coop.

Kokenzo

Kokenzo Cockenzie ([ko'kɪni]).
kokeriki to cock-a-doodle-doo, crow.
kokeriko cock-a-doodle-doo, crow.
koketa coquettish.
koketeco coquetry, flirtation.
koketi to coquette, flirt.
koketulino coquette, flirt.
koketulo beau.
kokidaĵo chicken.
kokideto baby chicken.
kokidino pullet.
kokido chick, chicken, fowl, hen.
kokinaĵo chicken, hen.
kokino hen.
kokleario scurvy-grass.
kokluŝo pertussis, whooping cough.
koko chicken, fowl, cock, rooster.
kokono cocoon.
kokosarbo coconut palm.
Kokosinsuloj Cocos Islands.
kokoslakto coconut milk.
kokosnukso coconut.
kokoso coconut.
kokospalmo coconut palm.
kokospulpo coconut pulp.
kokossuko coconut water.
kokosujo coconut palm.
kokotraŭsto hawfinch.
kokri to be unfaithful, be unfaithful to, cuckold.
kokrito cuckold, deceived husband.
koksalgio coxalgia.
kokso haunch, hip.
koktelo cocktail.
kolapsi to collapse.
kolapso collapse.
kolardo collard.
kolbasbulko hot dog bun.
kolbaseto sausage.
kolbaso sausage, salami.
kolbo stock, butt, grip.
kolbrido halter.
kolĉeno necklace.
kolĉikino colchicine.
kolĉiko meadow saffron.
koldkremo cold cream.
koldoloro stiff neck.
kole by the neck, around the neck.
koledoko bile duct.
kolega fraternal.
kolegaro band of coworkers.
kolegeca fraternal.
kolegeco good fellowship.
kolegema fraternal.
kolegemo good fellowship.
kolegieco collegiality.
kolegio college, trade school.
kolego associate, classmate, coworker, colleague, companion, comrade, schoolmate.

koliziigi

kolektado collection.
kolektanto accumulator, collector.
kolekti to collect, gather, pick up, congregate, rally, assemble.
kolektiĝi to collect, get together, gather together.
kolektiĝo parade, roll call.
kolektisto receiver, collector (of taxes).
kolektiva collective, joint.
kolektive collectively.
kolektivigi to collectivize.
kolektivismo collectivism.
kolektivo collective.
kolekto collection, gathering.
koleo coleus.
koleoptera coleopterous.
koleoptero beetle.
koleopteroj beetles.
kolera angry, cross, choleric. **kolera je** mad (angry) at.
Kolerajno Coleraine.
kolere angrily.
kolereco anger, choler, ire, wrath.
kolerega furious, wrathful, wroth.
kolerege extremely angry, furious.
koleregi to be in a rage.
koleregigi to exasperate.
koleregiĝi to become furious, very angry.
kolerego anger, rage, wrath.
kolerema passionate, testy.
koleremo temper.
kolereta sullen.
kolereti to pout, sulk.
koleri to be angry. **koleri kontraŭ iu** to be mad at someone, get angry at someone.
koleriga exasperating.
kolerigi to anger.
kolerigi to get angry.
kolerika choleric.
kolerikulo hothead, hot-tempered, choleric person.
kolero anger, ire, resentment, wrath.
kolerpreta quick to anger.
kolesterolo cholesterol.
kolhararo mane.
kolharoj mane.
Kolĥido Colchis.
kolĥozo collective farm, kolkhoz.
kolibro hummingbird.
koliero necklace.
koliko colic, gripes.
koliksorpujo chequer tree, wild service-tree.
kolimati to adjust.
kolimbo diver (bird), loon.
kolirio eye drops, eye salve, eye wash.
kolizii to collide (with), crash into, run into, clash. **kolizii kontraŭ** to collide with.
kolizii kun to collide with, crash into.
koliziigi to crash.

226

kolizio collision.
kolizo collision.
Kolo Coll, Kola Peninsula.
kolo neck.
kolocinto bitter apple, colocynth, colocynth apple.
kolodio collodion.
kolofono colophony, rosin, resin.
koloida colloidal, gluey, colloid.
koloido colloid.
kolokvo colloquium.
kolomba of a dove, pigeon.
kolombejo dovecot, pigeon house.
kolombia Colombian.
kolombianino Colombian woman.
kolombiano Colombian.
kolombino dove, female pigeon.
Kolombio Colombia.
Kolombo Columba.
kolombo dove, pigeon.
kolombumi to coo.
kolonaro colonnade.
kolonelo colonel.
kolonia colonial.
koloniado colonization.
koloniano colonial.
kolonii to colonize.
koloniigi to colonize.
koloniiĝi to be settled.
koloniisma colonialist.
koloniismo colonialism.
koloniisto colonist.
kolonio colony, settlement. **kolonio de abeloj** bee colony.
Kolonjo Cologne, Köln.
kolono column, pillar, file, stack.
Kolonsajo Colonsay.
kolora coloured.
koloradia Coloradan.
koloradiano Coloradan.
koloraĵo colour, colouring, tinge.
koloraro colour, colouring.
koloraturo coloratura.
kolorblindeco achromatopsia, colour-blindness.
koloreco colouration, colouring.
koloretigi to tinge, tint.
kolori to colour, paint.
kolorigaĵo paint.
kolorigi to colour, paint, dye.
kolorigilo dye, paint.
kolorigisto dyer, painter.
koloriĝi to colour.
kolorilo crayon, paint.
koloristo colourist.
kolorita coloured.
kolorivo colour depth.
kolornuanco hue, dye.
koloro colour, dye.
kolorpendinta pale, sallow.
kolorplena colourful.
kolorplene colourfully.
kolosa colossal, huge.
kolose colossally.
koloso colossus.
kolostro colostrum.
kolporti to peddle, sell door-to-door, hawk.
kolportisto hawker, peddler.
kolrimeno collar.
kolrompa fatal.
kolskarpo shawl.
koltuko neckcloth, scarf.
kolubro adder, colubrid.
Kolumbo Columbus.
kolumĵerzo polo neck.
kolumno column.
kolumo collar.
koluzio collusion.
Kolvinbajo Colwyn Bay.
kolzo colza, winter rape.
komanda peremptory. **komanda dosiero** command file. **komanda historio** history. **komanda linio** command line.
komandanta in charge, in command.
komandanto commandant, commander.
komandaro instruction set.
komandejo bridge.
komandema peremptory.
komandeta arkitekturo RISC architecture.
komandi to command, be in command, order.
komandita ordered, commanded.
komanditanto silent partner, sleeping partner.
komandito limited partnership.
komandlinia command line. **komandlinia interfaco** command line interface. **komandlinia parametro** command line parameter.
komando command, instruction, mandate, order.
komandociklo instruction cycle.
komandodosiero batch file.
komandoformo instruction format.
komandonombrilo instruction counter, program counter.
komandoro commander.
komata comatose.
komato coma.
komatulo feather star.
komatuloj feather star.
kombajno combine.
kombi to comb.
kombilo comb.
kombinado combination.
kombinaĵo combination, compound.
kombinato combine.

kombinatorikaĵo

kombinatorikaĵo choice.
kombinatoriko combinatorial analysis, combinatorics.
kombineo body suit.
kombini to combine.
kombiniĝemo affinity.
kombiniĝi to combine.
kombino combination, compound.
kombisto barber.
komedia comedic.
komedianto comedian.
komediisto actor (drama), comedian.
komedio comedy.
komedono acne.
komenca initial. **komenca krampo** open (left) parenthesis (( ). **komenca litero** initial. **komenca periodo** initial stage. **komenca rando** initial vertex. **komenca salajro** commencing salary. **komenca valoro** initial value. **komencaj kostoj** initial cost, initial costs, start-up costs.
komencantklaso class for beginners.
komencanto beginner.
komence at first, at the outset, in the beginning, to begin with. **komence de** at the beginning of, in the beginning.
komenci to begin, commence, start.
komenci de to start with.
komenciĝi to begin, commence, start.
komenciĝo beginning, commencement, start.
komenckondiĉa iteracio WHILE-loop.
komenclitero initial.
komencloko starting point.
komenco beginning, commencement, start, debut, outset.
komencrapido initial velocity.
komencvalorizi to initialize.
komentarii to comment on.
komentariisto commentator.
komentario annotation, note, commentary.
komentaro commentary.
komenti to comment (on).
komento comment.
komerca mercantile. **komerca agento** commercial agent. **komerca amiko** business friend. **komerca kaj** ampersand (&). **komerca konato** business relation. **komerca saĝeco** business acumen.
komercado trading.
komercaĵo article, commodity, goods, merchandise, wares.
komercebla tradable.
komerci to deal, do business, trade.
komercistino businesswoman.
komercisto commercial man, dealer, merchant, businessman, tradesman.
komerco business, commerce, trade.
komercocentro business centre.

komparado

komercŝipo bulk carrier, cargo ship, container ship, freighter, merchant vessel, tanker.
Komercurbo Commerce City.
kometo comet.
komforta at ease, comfortable, cozy, snug.
komforte comfortably.
komforteco comfort.
komforti to comfort, solace.
komfortigi to make comfortable.
komforto comfort, ease, sense of well-being.
komika comic, comical, funny, facetious, humorous, laughable, ludicrous, witty.
komike comically.
komikeco comedy, comicalness, funniness, humorousness, wittiness.
komikso comic (strip, book), graphic novel.
komikulo comedian, comic.
Komino Comine.
komisario commissioner.
komisaro commissar, commissary, commissioner.
komisia agento commission agent.
komisiano commissioner.
komisii to appoint, assign, authorize, charge, entrust, instruct, commission.
komisiitaro commission.
komisiito commissioner.
komisiknabo errand boy.
komisio commission, appointment, authorization, charge, entrustment, errand, job, mandate, trust.
komisiono commission.
komitatano committee member.
komitatkunsido committee meeting.
komitato committee. **komitato de sindikataj delegitoj** shop stewards.
komizo clerk, office assistant, salesman, shop assistant.
komo comma (,).
komodo chest of drawers, dresser, commode (furniture).
komodoro commodore.
Komoroj Comoro Islands, Comoros.
kompakta compact, dense. **kompakta histo** compacta.
kompaktdiskilo CD player.
kompaktigi to compress.
kompaniano associate.
kompanio company. **kompanio kun limigita respondeco** company with limited liability, limited liability company, LLC.
kompaniulo companion.
kompano buddy, companion, comrade, pal.
kompara comparative. **kompara kvalitprovo** benchmark. **kompara operacio** comparison operation.
komparacio comparison.
komparado comparison.

komparaĵo parable, similitude.
komparativo comparison.
kompare comparatively. **kompare kun** compared with.
komparebla comparable.
kompari to compare. **komparu** compare, cf.
komparo comparison.
kompartimento compartment.
kompasdirekto compass direction.
kompaso compass.
kompataema merciful.
kompatema charitable, merciful, compassionate, tenderhearted, sympathetic.
kompatemo charity, mercifulness, mercy.
kompati to be sorry for, commiserate with, feel compassion for, feel sorry for, have compassion, pity, have mercy on, have pity for, pity.
kompatigi to excite pity, move to compassion.
kompatinda deplorable, dismal, miserable, pitiful, poor, piteous, pitiable.
kompatindulo poor person.
kompato compassion, pity, mercy, sympathy.
kompatoeco mercy.
kompendio abridgement, compendium.
kompensa compensatory.
kompensaĵo amends, compensation, reparation, satisfaction.
kompensatoro compensator.
kompense as compensation. **kompense al** as compensation to.
kompensi to atone, balance, compensate, indemnify, counterpoise, make amends for, make up for, offset, restore equilibrium.
kompensilo compensator.
kompenso amends, compensation, reparation, satisfaction, indemnity.
kompensodevo liability.
kompetenta able, accomplished, competent, proficient, adept, capable, efficient, qualified.
kompetente capably, efficiently.
kompetenteco ability, competence, qualification.
kompetento ability, competence, qualification.
kompetentulo expert, connoisseur.
kompilado compilation, compiling.
kompilaĵo compilation.
kompilanto compiler.
kompilero compiler.
kompili to compile.
kompililgeneratoro compiler.
kompililo compiler.
kompilo compilation.
kompleksa complex.

komplekseco complexity.
kompleksо complex.
komplementa complementary, complemented. **komplementa prezento** complement representation. **komplemento** adjunct, complement. **komplemento ĝis dek** ten's complement. **komplemento ĝis du** two's complement. **komplemento ĝis naŭ** nine's complement. **komplemento ĝis unu** one's complement.
kompleta absolute, complete. **kompleta sumilo** full adder.
komplete completely, entirely, through.
kompleteco completeness, wholeness.
kompletiga complementary, supplementary.
kompletigeco complementariness.
kompletigi to (cause to be) complete.
kompletigo replacement, replenishment, supplement.
kompletiĝi to become complete.
kompletiĝo completion, consummation.
kompletiva completive.
kompleto outfit, set, suit.
kompleza friendly, kind, benevolent, courteous, good natured, kindly, obliging, willing.
kompleze kindly.
komplezema benevolent, courteous, good natured, obliging, willing, friendly, kind, obliging.
komplezemo kindness, benevolence, good will.
komplezi to be so kind as to, do a favour, oblige.
kompleziĝema easily accommodated.
komplezismo appeasement.
komplezo courtesy, favour, complacency, kindness, service.
kompliceco abetment.
komplico abettor, accessory, accomplice.
komplika complex, complicated, intricate, involved.
komplikaĵo complication.
komplike intricately.
komplikeco complexity, intricacy.
kompliki to complicate.
komplikiĝo complexity.
komplikiteco complexity.
kompliko complexity.
komplikteorio complexity theory.
komplimentado giving compliments.
komplimentema complimentary.
komplimenti to compliment.
komplimento compliment.
komploti to plot, scheme.
komploto conspiracy, plot, intrigue, scheme.
komponado composition.
komponaĵo composition.
komponanto constituent, component.
komponi to combine, compose, conjoin.

komponisto composer.
kompono composition.
komposta grafiko character graphics.
kompostado typesetting.
kompostaĵo type.
komposti to typeset.
kompostisto compositor (printer).
komposto compost.
kompoto compote.
kompozicio composition (music).
kompozito composite material.
komprenaĵo conception, idea, notion.
komprene understandably.
komprenebla comprehensible, understandable.
kompreneble of course, naturally.
komprenebleco comprehensibility, intelligibility.
kompreneblo comprehensibility, intelligibility.
kompreneco comprehension.
komprenema understanding.
komprenemo understanding.
kompreni to comprehend, realize, understand.
komprenigi to explain.
komprenigo comprehension.
komprenita understood.
kompreno notion, sense, realization.
komprenpovo understanding.
kompreso compress, gauze pads.
kompresoro compressor.
kompromisi to compromise.
kompromiso accommodation, compromise.
kompromiti to compromise, endanger, imperil, jeopardize, prejudice.
komputa sistemo computer system.
komputada stato processor state.
komputado data processing. **komputado oficejo** bureau.
komputebla computable. **komputebla aro** effectively computable set, recursively enumerable set. **komputebla funkcio** computable function, effectively computable function.
komputeblo effective computability.
komputejo computer centre, data centre.
komputemulo avid computer user.
komputera computer.
komputerdisketo diskette.
komputero computer.
komputeroscienco computer science.
komputerprogramisto computer programmer.
komputerprogramo computer program.
komputi to compute.
komputiko computer science, information technology.

komputila computer. **komputila arkitekturo** computer architecture. **komputila reto** computer network.
komputilego mainframe computer.
komputilizita computer-aided. **komputilizita fabrikado** computer aided manufacturing. **komputilizita instruado** computer aided learning, computer assisted learning. **komputilizita programarinĝenierado** computer aided software engineering, CASE. **komputilizita projektado** computer aided design.
komputil-nedependa machine independent.
komputilo computer.
komputilreta poŝto computer mail, e-mail, electronic mail.
komputilscienco computer science.
komputisto programmer.
komputivo computer power, computing power.
komputo calculation, computation.
komputoscienco computing science.
komputsistema system.
komuna common, joint, shared. **komuna prudento** common sense.
komunaĵo common property, community, intersection (of sets).
komune jointly, mutually.
komunejo green (village).
komunestro mayor.
komunii to administer Holy Communion.
komuniiĝanto communicant.
komuniiĝi to receive Holy Communion.
komunikadisto communicator.
komunikado communication.
komunikaĵo communication, message, communiqué.
komunikebla contagious.
komunikema communicative, talkative.
komuniki to communicate, report, impart.
komunikiĝado communication.
komunikiĝantaj verticoj connected vertices.
komunikilo means of communication.
komuniko account, communication.
komuniksistemo communication system.
komunikteorio communication theory.
komunio communion.
komunisma communist.
komunismo communism.
komunista communist.
komunisto communist.
komunuma buĉejo abattoir, slaughterhouse.
komunumaro community.
komunumo commune, community.
komuta commutative.
komutatoro switch.

komutebla commuting.
komuteca commutative.
komuteco commutativity.
komuti to commute, commute.
komutiĝanta commuting.
komutiĝi to commute (be permutable).
komutilaro switchboard.
komutilo switch.
komutisto switchboard operator.
konarligno zebrawood.
konaro zebrawood.
konata (well) known.
konateco acquaintance, conversance, familiarity, notoriety.
konatigi to acquaint, make known.
konatiĝi to be acquainted with. **konatiĝi kun** to make someone's acquaintance.
konatiĝo acquaintance.
konato acquaintance.
koncedi to admit, concede, grant.
koncedo concession.
koncenterjo concentration camp.
koncentra concentric.
koncentratoro concentrator.
koncentri to concentrate. **koncentri sin** to concentrate.
koncentrigi to concentrate.
koncentriĝi to become concentrated, concentrate.
koncentriĝo concentration.
koncentrita concentrated, strong.
koncepcii to become pregnant.
koncepti to conceive.
koncepto concept, idea.
koncerna concerned, in question.
koncernato stakeholder.
koncerne about, concerning, as to. **koncerne min** as far as I am concerned.
koncerneco relevance.
koncerni to concern.
koncerno concern.
koncertado performance.
koncertejo concert hall, concert room.
koncerti to give a concert, play a concert.
koncertino concertina.
koncertisto performer.
koncerto accord, concert, harmony, agreement.
koncesii to concede, franchise, licence.
koncesio concession, franchise.
koncesiulo licensee.
koncilio council.
koncipa conceptual.
koncipe conceptually.
koncipi to become pregnant, conceive.
koncipo conception.
konciza concise, brief and comprehensive, pithy, terse, succinct.
koncize briefly.

koncizeco brevity, briefness, conciseness.
koncizigi to abridge.
konĉerto concerto.
kondamna proscriptive.
kondamnato convict.
kondamni to condemn, sentence, damn, convict, find guilty.
kondamno condemnation, conviction, doom.
kondamnulo convict (man).
kondensaĵo moisture.
kondensatoro capacitor, condenser lens.
kondensi to compress.
kondensiĝi to condense.
kondenskovriĝi to get blurred, dim.
kondicionalo conditional tense.
kondiĉa conditional. **kondiĉa asemblado** conditional assembly. **kondiĉa modo** conditional mood. **kondiĉa probablo** conditional probability.
kondiĉe conditionally.
kondiĉi to set conditions, stipulate.
kondiĉigi to stipulate.
kondiĉo condition, stipulation, terms.
kondimento condiment.
kondolenca sympathetic.
kondolence sympathetically.
kondolenci to commiserate, condole, express condolences.
kondolenco condolence(s).
kondomo condom, rubber.
kondoro condor.
kondotiero condottiere.
kondukado charge, lead, leadership.
kondukantino usher.
kondukanto conductor, leader.
konduki to conduct, guide, lead, drive (vehicle).
kondukilo rein (of a horse).
kondukisto conductor, driver.
konduklernejo driving school.
konduko conduct, lead, leadership.
kondukpermesilo driver's licence.
kondukrimeno reins.
konduktanco conductance.
konduktanto conductor.
kondukti to conduct.
konduktilo conductor, conduit.
konduktokodo code of conduct.
konduktoro conductor, fare collector, guard, ticket checker.
konduta behavioural.
konduti to behave, act, conduct (oneself).
kondutmaniero policy.
konduto behaviour, conduct, deportment, manners.
koneksa connected. **koneksa al** connected to, related to. **koneksa komponanto** connected component. **koneksa memoreareo** contiguous area.

koneksega strongly connected (graph).
konekseta grafeo weakly connected graph.
konektejo port.
konekti to connect, connect up, plug in.
konektiĝi to connect.
konektilo connector.
konektingo socket.
konektite on-line.
konektloko interface.
konekto connection. **konekto per komutebla lineo** dial-up account.
konektoskatolo socket.
konektotabulo switchboard.
konfederacii to confederate.
konfederaciiĝi to confederate.
konfederacio confederation.
konfederi to confederate.
konfedero commonwealth, confederation.
konfekcio confection (clothing), ready-made clothes.
konferenci to have a conference.
konferenco conference.
konferenseo entertainer.
konfermi to confirm.
konfervo conferva.
konfesanto penitent.
konfese admittedly.
konfesejo confessional.
konfesi to acknowledge, admit, confess, profess, avow. **konfesi sian kulpon** to confess one's guilt.
konfesia confessional.
konfesinto confessor.
konfesio confession.
konfeso acknowledgement, admission, confession, avowal.
konfesprenanto confessor.
konfespreni to shrive.
konfeto confetti.
konfida trusting.
konfidatesto power (of attorney).
konfidatisto procuration.
konfide confidently.
konfidema confident, trustful.
konfidenca confidential.
konfidence confidentially.
konfidencio confidence.
konfidenco confidence, secret.
konfidi to confide, have confidence in, trust, entrust, rely. **konfidi al** to count upon, rely on, trust in.
konfidinda reliable.
konfido confidence, reliance.
konfigurajo configuration.
konfirma affirmative.
konfirmacii to confirm.
konfirmacio confirmation.
konfirmado affirmation.
konfirme affirmatively.

konfirmi to acknowledge, confirm, corroborate.
konfirmo confirmation.
konfisiki to confiscate.
konfiski to confiscate.
konfisko confiscation.
konfitaĵo preserve, jam.
konfiti to preserve with sugar.
konfitisto confectioner.
konflikti to be at odds with, clash.
konflikto clash, conflict, antagonism.
konforma compliant, conforming, (well-)fitting.
konforme in conformity. **konforme al** in accordance with. **konforme al tio** accordingly.
konformeco conformity.
konformi to be in line with, conform, fit (in).
konformigi to fit, adhere, conform.
konformiĝi to conform. **konformiĝi al** to abide by.
konformismo conformism.
konformisto conformist.
konfrontado confrontation.
konfronti to confront.
konfronto confrontation.
konfuceanismo Confucianism.
konfuceano Confucian.
Konfuceismo Confucianism.
Konfuceo Confucius.
konfuza confused, jumbled (up).
konfuzaĵo hotchpotch, medley.
konfuzakapa addle-brained, addle-pated.
konfuzanta confusing.
konfuzeco perplexity.
konfuzegi to confound, puzzle.
konfuzego disarray.
konfuzi to bewilder, confuse, puzzle, disconcert, perplex, trouble, perturb, unsettle, disturb.
konfuziĝi to be confused.
konfuzita dazed, perplexed, upset.
konfuziteco perplexity.
konfuzo commotion, confusion, muddle.
konfuzoado confusion.
kongano Congolese.
kongao conga.
kongeli to deep-freeze.
kongesta congestive.
kongesti to overcharge with blood.
kongesto congestion.
konglomeraĵo conglomerate, conglomeration, pudding-stone.
konglomerato conglomerate.
konglomeri to conglomerate.
konglomeriĝi to fuse.
Kongo Congo, Zaire. **Kongo Brazavila** Republic of the Congo. **Kongo Kinŝasa** Democratic Republic of the Congo.

Konglando

Kongolando Congo.
kongregacio congregation.
kongresa congressional.
kongresanino congresswoman.
kongresano congress participant, conventioneer.
kongresejo conference centre, convention hall, exposition centre.
kongresi to convene, hold or attend a congress.
kongreso conference, congress, convention.
kongresraportoj actae, actas.
kongro conger-eel.
kongrua compatible, congruent. **kongrua malplien** downward compatible. **kongrua plien** forward compatible, upward compatible.
kongrueco congruence (of numbers).
kongrui to agree, be compatible, coincide, fit together, match.
kongruo agreement.
konĥoido conchoid. **konĥoido de rekto** conchoid of Nicomedes.
koni to be acquainted with, know.
koniferaro conifer forest.
konifero conifer.
konigi to divulge, let know, reveal. **konigi sin** to acquaint oneself. **konigi sin pri** to acquaint oneself with.
konigilo key.
konigi pri to get acquainted with.
koniko conic section.
konio hemlock.
koniozo coniosis.
konita known.
konizo fleabane.
konjakglaso brandy glass.
konjako brandy, cognac.
konjekta speculative.
konjektebla presumable, supposable.
konjekti to (make a) conjecture, surmise, suppose, guess.
konjekto conjecture, guess, guesswork, supposition, surmise. **konjekto pri la kvar koloroj** four-colour conjecture.
konjugacii to conjugate.
konjugacio conjugation.
konjugi to conjugate, pair.
konjugita conjugate.
konjuglineara antilinear, semilinear.
konjugo conjugation.
konjunkcii to be in conjunction.
konjunkcio conjunction.
konjunktivito conjunctivitis.
konjunktivo subjunctive, subjunctive mood.
konjunkturo conjuncture.
konkava concave.
konkeraĵo loot.
konkeranto conqueror.

kono

konkeri to bring to subjection, conquer, gain, win, overcome by force, subjugate.
konkerinto conqueror.
konkero conquest.
konklavo conclave.
konklude as a conclusion.
konkludi to abstract, induce, gather, infer, conclude, deduce.
konkludiga clinching, conclusive, convincing, decisive.
konkludige conclusively.
konkludo conclusion, inference, deduction.
konko shell.
konkoido conchoid.
konkorda concordant, harmonious.
konkordanco concordance.
konkordato concordat.
konkorde harmoniously.
konkordi to agree.
konkordo accord, concord, harmony, agreement.
konkreta concrete, not abstract, perceptible, real, positive.
konkretaĵo something concrete.
konkrete concretely.
konkreteco concreteness.
konkretigi to put into concrete form.
konkubeco concubinage.
konkubino concubine.
konkura kontraktkomisiado public tender.
konkurado competition, rivalry.
konkurantaro competition.
konkuranto competitor, rival.
konkure competitively.
konkurema competitive.
konkuremeco competitiveness.
konkurencantaro competition.
konkurencanto competitor.
konkurencebla competitive.
konkurenceblo competitiveness.
konkurencema competitive.
konkurenci to compete.
konkurenco competition (business, etc.).
konkuri to compete, contend, rival, vie.
konkuro competition, rivalry.
konkuroeco rivalry.
konkursa competitive.
konkursado competition, form.
konkursaga reprezento action replay.
konkursanto competitor, contender, contestant.
konkursebleco competitiveness.
konkursejo venue.
konkursero event, match.
konkursi to compete, contend.
konkurso bout, competition, contest, match.
konkursoserio league.
kono acquaintance, knowledge.

konoido conoid.
konosamento bill of lading, consignment note, waybill.
konringio hare's-ear mustard.
konscia aware, conscious.
konscidubo qualm.
konscie consciously, lucidly.
konscienca conscientious, scrupulous, faithful, upright, honourable.
konsciencdubo scruple.
konscienco conscience, inner voice, moral sense.
konsciencriproĉo remorse.
konscii to appreciate, be aware of, be conscious of, realize, see. **konscii pri** to be aware of.
konsciigi to make aware.
konsciiĝi to become aware.
konscio awareness, consciousness.
konsekri to consecrate, coronate, dedicate, devote, hallow, sanctify, ordain.
konsekriĝo consecration.
konsekvenca consequent, consistent, logically following.
konsekvence accordingly, consequently, consistently, logically, therefore. **konsekvence de** as a consequence of, as a result of.
konsekvenco consequence, consistency.
konsentado agreement, assent.
konsentebla admissible, accommodating, good-hearted.
konsentema agreeable, good-hearted.
konsentemo accommodation.
konsenti to agree, consent, concur, admit, approve, be in accord (with), be in harmony with, comply with. **konsenti neesprimite** to acquiesce. **konsenti pri** to agree to.
konsentinta consenting, agreeing.
konsentite agreed, OK.
konsento acceptance, accord, agreement, consent, permission, approval, assent, concurrence.
konservado conservation, maintenance, preservation, retention.
konservajfabriko canning-factory.
konservaĵo canned food, preserves.
konservatismo conservatism.
konservativa conservative.
konservativismo conservatism.
konservativulo conservative, Tory.
konservatorio academy of music, conservatory.
konservejo box room, storage room.
konservema conservative.
konservemulo conservationist, conservative.
konservi to conserve, keep, maintain, preserve, save (a file).
konserviĝi to be preserved.
konservisma conservative.
konservismo conservatism.
konservisto conservator.
konservo conservation, maintenance, preservation, retention.
konservospaco storage, storage space.
konservujo bin.
konservulo conservative.
konsiderada deliberative.
konsiderado deliberation.
konsidereco considerateness.
konsiderema considerate, reflective, thoughtful.
konsideri to account, consider, esteem, regard, take into account.
konsiderinda considerable, sizeable.
konsiderinde considerably.
konsidero consideration, deliberation.
konsila advisory.
konsilado advice.
konsilantara salono boardroom.
konsilantaro council.
konsilanto advisor, counsellor.
konsilebla advisable.
konsilejo boardroom.
konsileto hint, tip.
konsili to advise, counsel.
konsilia conciliar.
konsiliĝi to deliberate. **konsiliĝi kun** to consult with.
konsiliĝo consideration, deliberation, consultation.
konsililo expert system.
konsilinda advisable.
konsilinde advisable.
konsilindeco advisability.
konsilio advisory board, advisory committee, council.
konsilistaro advisory board, advisory committee.
konsilisto adviser.
konsilo advice, counsel.
konsistenco consistency.
konsisti to consist. **konsisti el** to consist of.
konsistiga constituent, constitutive.
konsistigaĵo component, element, ingredient, part.
konsistigi to account for, constitute, make up.
konsisto consistency.
konsistorio consistory.
konskripcii to conscript.
konskripcio conscription.
konskripto conscript.
konsolado consolation, solace.
konsolanto comforter.
konsoli to cheer, comfort, console, soothe, solace.
konsoliĝi to get over, be consoled. **konsoliĝi pri** to get over.

konsolo comfort, consolation, solace.
konsomeo clear soup.
konsonanco chord.
konsonanto consonant.
konsorcio consortium.
konspiranto conspirator.
konspiri to conspire, plot.
konspiro conspiracy, plot.
konstanta constant, continual, permanent, sustained, steadfast. **konstanta kurento** direct current. **konstanta memoro** read-only memory, ROM. **konstantaj datenoj** constant data.
konstantaĵo feature.
konstante constantly, continuously.
konstanteco constancy, consistency.
Konstanteno Constantine.
Konstantinopolo Constantinople.
konstanto constant.
konstantodeklaro constant definition.
konstati to ascertain to be true (a fact), establish, take note, prove.
konstatigi to perpetuate.
konstato finding, statement.
konstelacio constellation.
konsterna alarmed, dismayed, dumbfounded, put out of countenance.
konsternanta startling.
konsterni to alarm, dismay, puzzle, appall.
konsterniĝinta upset.
konsterniĝo alarm, consternation.
konsternita aghast, taken aback, upset.
konsterno alarm, consternation.
konstipeco constipation.
konstipi to constipate.
konstipiĝi to become constipated.
konstipilo astringent.
konstipita blocked, clogged, constipated.
konstipo constipation.
konstitucia constitutional.
konstitucie constitutionally.
konstitucio constitution.
konstitui to account for, constitute, make up.
konstriktoro boa.
konstrua constructive.
konstruado building.
konstruaĵaro complex.
konstruaĵideo constructive idea.
konstruaĵo building, structure, construction, edifice.
konstruanto builder.
konstruareo building plot, building site.
konstruarto architecture.
konstruejo construction site.
konstruelementaro construction box.
konstruentreprenisto builder, contractor, building contractor, master builder.
konstruestro builder, architect.

konstrui to build, construct, craft, erect, establish.
konstruigi to contract, have built.
konstruiĝi to be constructed, become built.
konstruilo constructor.
konstruisto builder.
konstruita built, constructed.
konstrukcii to build.
konstrukesto construction box.
konstrukompanio building company.
konstrulaboristo construction worker.
konstruligno building material.
konstrumaterialo building material.
konstrumetio building trade.
konstruo construction, erection.
konstrupermeso building permit.
konstruplaco construction site.
konstruplano specifications.
konstruskatolo box of bricks.
konstrustilo building style.
konstruŝtono building block, building stone.
konstrutereno building plot, building site.
konstumo costume.
konsulejo consulate.
konsulo consul.
konsulta advisory, consultative.
konsultado consultation.
konsultejo consultancy.
konsulti to consult.
konsultiĝa advisory.
konsulto consultation.
konsumado consumption.
konsumaĵo article of consumption.
konsumantligo consumers' union.
konsumanto consumer.
konsumi to consume, use up, exhaust.
konsumiĝi to pine, languish, wear away, decline, waste (away). **konsumiĝi de tristo** to be consumed by sadness.
konsumiĝo consumption.
konsumismo consumerism.
konsumite consumed. **konsumite pro timego** consumed by fear.
konsumiteco exhaustion.
konsumo consumption.
kontado accounting.
kontaĝa catching, contagious, infectious.
kontaĝi to communicate.
kontaĝo contagion, contamination, infection.
kontakti to contact.
kontaktiĝi to come into contact.
kontaktlenso contact lens.
kontaktloko point of contact.
kontakto contact.
kontaktoskatolo outlet, socket.
kontaktpunkto point of contact.
kontaktujo socket.
kontaktulo contact.
kontanta cash, in cash.

kontantajo cash.
kontante in cash, paid immediately.
kontantigi to cash.
kontanto cash (money).
kontekspertizisto accountant.
konteksto context.
kontekzameni to audit.
konteltiro statement of account.
kontempla contemplative.
kontemplado contemplation.
kontempli to consider, contemplate, envisage, look at, regard, view.
kontenero container.
kontenta content, contented, gratified, happy, pleased, satisfied, happy.
kontenteco contentedness, contentment.
kontenti to be content.
kontentiga satisfactory.
kontentige satisfactorily.
kontentigi to meet with, satisfy.
kontentigo gratification, satisfaction.
kontentiĝi to be satisfied.
kontentiĝo gratification.
kontento contentment, satisfaction.
kontestado controversy.
kontestanto protestor.
kontestebla debatable, questionable.
kontesti to call into question, challenge, question, debate, deny the truth of, contest.
kontesto contest.
kontinenta continental.
kontinentano mainlander.
kontinento continent, mainland.
kontinentodrivo continental drift.
kontingento contingent.
kontinua lasting, continuous. **kontinua formuladpapero** continuous document. **kontinua paperbendo** continuous stationery.
kontinue continuously.
kontinueco continuity.
kontinuega uniformly continuous.
kontinui to be continuous, continue, last.
kontinuigi to continue.
kontinuigo continuance, perpetuation.
kontisto accountant.
kontjaro financial year.
kontnero (freight) container.
konto account. **konto kuranta** account (current).
kontonumero account number.
kontorbezonaĵbutiko stationer's shop.
kontoristo clerk.
kontoro bureau, office (business).
kontoroficiro yeoman.
kontoscienco accountancy, accounting.
kontrabandado smuggling.
kontrabandaĵo contraband.
kontrabandi to smuggle.
kontrabandisto smuggler.
kontrabando contraband, prohibited traffic, smuggling.
kontrabaso bass viol, counter-bass, double bass.
kontradanco contra-dance, country-dance.
kontradmiralo commander.
kontrakta contractual.
kontrakti to enter into a contract with, make a contract. **kontrakti prunton** contract a loan.
kontraktita job-.
kontrakto (binding, legal) agreement, compact, contract, treaty, deal, pact, covenant, pact.
kontrakturo contracture.
kontralto alto, contralto.
kontramarko counter-mark, pass-out ticket.
kontrapunkto counterpoint.
kontrasta contrasting.
kontraste by contrast, in contrast. **kontraste kun** compared to, contrasted with.
kontrasti to contrast, exhibit contrast, show difference, stand out.
kontrastigi to compare, point out difference between, set off.
kontrasto contrast, difference, opposition.
kontraŭ across from, against, in exchange for, opposed to, opposite, upon, in return for. **kontraŭ la fluado** against the current. **kontraŭ la suno** towards the sun, facing the sun.
kontraŭa adverse, alien, contrary, opposite, untoward, hostile, perverse. **kontraŭa al** alien to.
kontraŭabortiga anti-abortion, "pro-life".
kontraŭabortigulo anti-abortion activist, "pro-lifer".
kontraŭacida antacid.
kontraŭacido antacid.
kontraŭaerataka ŝirmejo air-raid shelter.
kontraŭagaca soothing.
kontraŭagi to counteract.
kontraŭajo disappointment, obstacle.
kontraŭamerika anti-American.
kontraŭargumento objection.
kontraŭastma anti-asthmatic.
kontraŭavia anti-aircraft.
kontraŭaviadila anti-aircraft. **kontraŭaviadila artilerio** anti-aircraft artillery.
kontraŭaviadila defendo air-defence, anti-aircraft defence(s).
kontraŭbakteria antibacterial.
kontraŭbalistika antiballistic.
kontraŭbatali to combat, contend with, fight (against), resist, withstand, do battle with, oppose.
kontraŭbataliagi to react.
kontraŭciklono anticyclone.

kontraŭdeprimilo antidepresant.
kontraŭdiagonalo secondary diagonal.
kontraŭdira contradictory.
kontraŭdiradi to recriminate.
kontraŭdirado recrimination.
kontraŭdiri to contradict, gainsay.
kontraŭdiro contradiction.
kontraŭdiskriminacia anti-discrimination.
kontraŭdiskutebla debatable, questionable.
kontraŭdolorilo pain remedy, painkiller, analgesic.
kontraŭe on the contrary, otherwise, opposite facing, vice versa. **kontraŭe al** against.
kontraŭe de opposite.
kontraŭeco adversity.
kontraŭegala opposite.
kontraŭegaligebla (element) with an opposite.
kontraŭegalo additive inverse, opposite element.
kontraŭekzameni to cross-examine.
kontraŭekzemplo counter-example.
kontraŭflua upstream.
kontraŭflue upstream.
kontraŭflugilarmilo anti-aircraft warfare, ackack.
kontraŭfolia opposite-leaved.
kontraŭfrostaĵo antifreeze.
kontraŭglita ĉeno non-skid chain.
kontraŭhelikso anthelix.
kontraŭhoketo barb.
kontraŭi to oppose, be against.
kontraŭjudismo anti-Semitism.
kontraŭjora non-skid.
kontraŭkirasa armour-piercing.
kontraŭkloraĵo antichlor.
kontraŭkoloniismo anticolonialism.
kontraŭkoncipa contraceptive.
kontraŭkoncipado contraception.
kontraŭkoncipilo contraceptive.
kontraŭkopia protekto copy protection.
kontraŭkrima anti-crime.
kontraŭlabori to work against.
kontraŭlatera opposite.
kontraŭleĝa illegal.
kontraŭleĝeco illegality.
kontraŭlineara antilinear, semilinear.
kontraŭlogaritmo antilogarithm.
kontraŭmalaria anti-malarial.
kontraŭmarki to check.
kontraŭmendi to cancel, countermand.
kontraŭmeta konjunkcio adversative conjunction.
kontraŭmeti to oppose.
kontraŭmetoado opposition.
kontraŭmikroba antiseptic.
kontraŭmilitarismo antimilitarism.

kontraŭmini to countermine, sap, undermine.
kontraŭmisila antimissile.
kontraŭmoskita anti-mosquito. **kontraŭmoskita gazo** mosquito net, mosquito netting. **kontraŭmoskita vualo** mosquito net.
kontraŭnatura unnatural.
kontraŭnaturaĵo abnormality, perversion.
kontraŭnature unnaturally.
kontraŭneŭtrino antineutrino.
kontraŭo aversion.
kontraŭpapo antipope.
kontraŭparoli to object, speak against.
kontraŭparolo objection.
kontraŭpartiklo antiparticle.
kontraŭparto counterpart.
kontraŭpersona ad hominem.
kontraŭpersone ad hominem.
kontraŭpezi to counterbalance, offset.
kontraŭpezo counterbalance.
kontraŭpostulo counterclaim, countersuit.
kontraŭpozicio contrapositive.
kontraŭprotono antiproton.
Kontraŭreformacio Counter-Reformation.
kontraŭregula undue.
kontraŭregule unduly.
kontraŭreligia antireligious.
kontraŭrevolucio counter-revolution.
kontraŭrusa anti-.
kontraŭsemidismo anti-Semitism.
kontraŭsemitismo anti-Semitism.
kontraŭsenco misinterpretation.
kontraŭsepsa antiseptic.
kontraŭsepso antisepsis.
kontraŭsigna opposite-signed.
kontraŭsimetria matrico skew-symmetric matrix.
kontraŭsklaveca movado abolitionism.
kontraŭsklavecisto abolitionist.
kontraŭskriba protekto write protection.
kontraŭsocia antisocial, unsocial.
kontraŭspionado counter-espionage.
kontraŭstarema intractable, obstinate, refractory, stubborn.
kontraŭstari to confront, stand up to, withstand, be opposed to, weather, defy, oppose, resist. **kontraŭstari al** to brave, face, stand up to.
kontraŭstarigi to confront.
kontraŭstaro contention, resistance.
kontraŭsuna kremo sunscreen.
kontraŭŝtata anti-state.
kontraŭtanka antitank. **kontraŭtanka artilerio** antitank artillery.
kontraŭterorisma antiterrorist.
kontraŭtinea sako mothproof storage bag.
kontraŭtrusta antitrust.

kontraŭtusa antitussive.
kontraŭtutmondiĝa anti-globalization.
kontraŭulo adversary, opponent, antagonist, foe.
kontraŭutopia dystopian, anti-utopian.
kontraŭutopio dystopia, anti-utopia.
kontraŭutopiulo dystopian (person), anti-utopian.
kontraŭvenana antivenin.
kontraŭvenena antidotal.
kontraŭveneno antidote, anti-venom.
kontraŭvermaĵo vermifuge.
kontraŭvermilo vermicide.
kontraŭvirusa antivirus.
kontraŭvola against one's will.
kontraŭvole against one's will, unwillingly.
kontreo country music, country and western.
kontrevizori to audit.
kontrevizoro accountant.
kontribuaĵo contribution.
kontribuanto contributor.
kontribucio reparations.
kontribui to contribute.
kontribuo contribution.
kontricio compunction, contrition, remorse, repentance.
kontrola supervisory. **kontrola bito** check bit.
kontrolado checking, supervision.
kontrolanto moderator.
kontrolcentro control centre.
kontrolcifero check digit.
kontrolejo checkpoint.
kontroli to audit, check (up on), supervise, verify.
kontrolisto checker, controller.
kontrolkarto hash total card.
kontrolkonsilio board of directors.
kontrollisto checklist.
kontrolo check, oversight, scrutiny, verification.
kontrolpunkto breakpoint, checkpoint, watchpoint.
kontrolsumo checksum.
kontulo account-holder.
kontumace in one's absence.
kontura tiparo outline font.
konturi to delineate, draw.
konturo contour, outline.
kontuzaĵo bruise.
kontuzblua black-and-blue.
kontuzi to bruise, contuse.
kontuziĝi to bruise.
kontuziĝo bruise, bruising.
kontuzo bruise.
konuro conures.
konusa conical.
konuso cone.
konustrunko frustum of cone.

konusturo steeple.
konvalo lily of the valley.
Konvejo Conway.
konveksa convex.
konvekti to convect.
konvektilo convector.
konvekto convection.
konvena appropriate, becoming, seemly, suitable, proper, becoming.
konvencia conventional.
konvencio agreement, convention, general usage.
konvene appropriately.
konveneco propriety.
konveni to be appropriate, suit, be suitable.
konvento convent.
konvergi to converge.
konverĝa convergent. **konverĝa en distribuo** convergent in distribution. **konverĝa en mezuro** convergent in measure. **konverĝa en probablo** convergent in probability.
konverĝi to be concurrent, converge.
konverĝintervalo interval of convergence.
konverĝo convergence.
konverĝocirklo circle of convergence.
konverĝoradiuso radius of convergence.
konverĝradiuso radius of convergence.
konversacii to chat, converse, talk.
konversacio chat, talk, conversation.
konversado conversation.
konversi to chat, converse, talk.
konverso conversion.
konverteblo convertibility.
konverti to convert, proselytize, transform.
konvertiĝi to convert.
konvertiĝo conversion.
konvertilo converter.
konvertito convert, proselyte.
konverto conversion.
konvikti to convict.
konvinka persuasive.
konvinke convincingly.
konvinki to convince, persuade.
konvinkiĝi to be convinced.
konvinko belief, conviction.
konvojo convoy.
konvolvadoaĵo convolution.
konvolvulo bindweed, convolvulus, morning glory.
konvulsii to convulse.
konvulsio convulsion.
konvulso convulsion.
konzerno concern, corporation.
konzolo console.
koopera cooperative.
kooperativo cooperative.
koopti to co-opt.
koordinata akso coordinate axis.

koordinatakso coordinate axis.
koordinato coordinate.
koordinatsistemo coordinate system.
kopalo copal.
kopeko kopeck.
Kopenhago Copenhagen.
koperniciumo Copernicium.
Koperniko Nicolaus Copernicus.
kopiaĵo copy, reproduction.
kopii to copy.
kopiilo copier.
kopiisto copier.
kopio copy.
kopirajto copyright.
kopli to connect, couple.
kopo koppa, qoppa (Ϙϙ, Ҷҷ).
kopro copra.
kopta Coptic.
kopto Copt.
kopulo copula.
kora cardiac, cordial, hearty, warm. **kora inklino** fondness. **korajn salutojn** cordial greetings, sincerely yours.
koracio roller.
koraklo coracle.
korako raven.
korala coral.
koralinsulo atoll.
koralmevo Larus audouinii.
koralo coral.
koralorizo coral-root orchid.
koralrifo atoll.
koramikeco relationship (emotional).
koramikino girlfriend.
koramiko boyfriend.
Korano Koran.
Korantino Corantin.
koraŭriklo auricle.
korbatado heartbeat, pulse.
korbati to palpitate.
korbato heartbeat.
korbatoado palpitation.
korbat-regulilo (cardiac) pacemaker.
korbego car (of balloon), pannier.
korbelo corbel.
korbeto small basket.
korbfarado basket-making, basket-weaving.
korbfaristo basket-maker, basket-weaver.
korbo basket, hamper.
korbopilkado basketball.
korbopilkejo basketball court.
korbopilkisto basketball player.
korbopilko basketball.
kordinstrumento string instrument.
kordito cordite.
kordo cord, string.
kordobo cordoba.
kordono cordon.
kordurojo corduroy.

kore cordially, heartily. **kore afabla** cordial, hearty, warm.
korea Korean.
korega hearty.
koregidoro Spanish mayor.
koregono cisco, whitefish.
koregrafio choreography.
koreino Korean woman.
Koreio (the peninsula of) Korea.
korekta correct, right, corrective.
korektado correction.
korekte correctly.
korekteco correctness.
korekti to correct, revise.
korektisto proof-reader.
korekto correction.
korelacii to correlate.
korelacio correlation coefficient.
korelativa correlated, correlative. **korelativaj konjunkcioj** adversative conjunction.
korelativeco correlation.
korelativigi to correlate.
korelativo correlative.
Koreo Korea.
koreo Korean.
koreopso tickseed, coreopsis, calliopsis.
korespondado correspondence.
korespondadreso accommodation-address.
korespondaĵo piece of correspondence.
korespondamiko pen-friend, pen-pal.
korespondanto correspondent, pen-pal.
korespondi to correspond.
korespondisto correspondent.
korespondkurso correspondence course.
korespondo correspondence.
Koreujo Korea.
korfavora charitable, merciful.
korfavoro charity, mercifulness, mercy.
korfbalo korfball.
korfloro man's trousers, lyre flower, old-fashioned bleeding heart.
korforto strength of heart, courage.
korĝojiga heartwarming.
korĝojige heartwarmingly.
koriandro coriander.
korido bullfight, bullfighting.
koridora corridor.
koridoro corridor, passage, hallway, hall, lane, passageway.
korifeo chorus leader, coryphaeus.
korimbo corymb.
korinklino affection, fondness.
korinta Corinthian.
korintika Corinthian.
korinto Corinthian.
korizo cold.
korkflosilo float.
korki to cork (up).

korko

korko cork, stopper.
korkokverko cork oak.
korktirilo corkscrew.
korlando heartland.
korligita attached, close, dear to the heart.
kormalsano heart disease.
kormo corm.
kormorano cormorant, shag.
kornaro antlers.
kornaŭza disturbing, unsettling, upsetting (one's emotions).
kornaŭzigi to disturb, unsettle, upset (one's emotions).
kornblovego loud trumpeting, loud blow (of a horn).
kornblovi to trumpet, blow on a horn.
kornbranĉo antler.
kornbruo sound of trumpet, blow of a horn.
kornbruto horned animal.
korneca horny.
kornemuzo bagpipe.
korneo cornea.
korneto cornet.
korni to honk.
kornico cornice.
korniko (hooded) crow.
korno hooter, horn, klaxon.
kornobati to buck.
kornobranĉaro antlers.
kornuso cornel, dogberry.
kornvala Cornish.
kornvipuro cerastes, horned viper.
koro heart. **koro ĉe koro** heart to heart.
koroda corrosive.
korodado corrosion.
korodema corrosive.
korodi to corrode, eat away.
korodiĝi to corrode.
korodimuna stainless.
korodo corrosion.
koroido choroid.
korolario corollary.
korolo corolla.
koronaria coronary.
koronilo axseed.
korono corona.
korpa bodily, body, corporal, corporeal, of the body, physical.
korpaĉo bulk, hulk.
korpe physically.
korpeca bodily, physical, corporal.
korpego bulk, hulk.
korperdi to lose heart.
korpeto corpuscle.
korphararo body hair.
korpigi to embody, incarnate.
korpiĝi to impersonate.
korpiĝo incarnation.
korplingvo body language.

korto

korpo body. **korpo de makroodifino** macro expansion.
korpodamaĝo bodily harm, body damage.
korpodifekto bodily harm, body damage.
korpodoro body smell.
korpoforto body strength, vigor.
korpogardisto bodyguard, lifeguard.
korpoparto body part.
korporacia corporate.
korporaciestro guildmaster.
korporacio company, corporation, trade union.
korporalo corporal.
korposana able-bodied.
korprema distressing, oppressing.
korpremita dejected, depressed.
korpremiteco dejection, depression, oppression.
korpremo heartache.
korpstato physique.
korpulenta corpulent, fat, stout, fleshy, obese, beefy.
korpusklo corpuscle.
korpuso (army) corps.
korsaĵo bodice, body, corsage.
korsaro corsair, privateer.
korseto corset.
korsika Corsican.
korsikanino Corsican woman.
korsikano Corsican.
korsikia Corsican.
korsikianino Corsican woman.
korsikiano Corsican.
Korsikio Corsica.
Korsiko Corsica.
korso broadway, mall.
korŝira heart-rending.
korŝiranta heartrending.
korŝireco poignancy.
korŝiri to break heart.
kortaderio pampas grass.
kortbirdara of poultry.
kortbirdaro poultry.
kortbirdejo poultry yard.
kortbirdo fowl (domestic).
kortega spritulo court jester.
korteganaro royal household.
korteganino lady-in-waiting.
kortegano courtier.
kortego court (royal).
kortegulo courtier.
korthundo mastiff.
kortiko cortex.
kortikosurrena adrenocortical.
kortikotropa adrenocorticotrophic, adrenocorticotropic.
kortizono cortisone.
korto court, yard, courtyard, enclosed area, quadrangle.

kortobirdo domestic fowl, farm bird.
Kortrajo Courtrai.
Kortrejko Courtrai.
kortuma judicial.
kortumo court of law.
kortumoficisto court official.
kortuŝa affecting, moving, touching.
kortuŝanta affecting, touching, pathetic.
kortuŝeco emotion.
kortuŝi to affect, agitate, move, touch (emotionally).
kortuŝiĝi to be moved (emotionally).
kortuŝita seized with emotion, moved.
kortuŝite seized with emotion, moved.
kortuŝo emotion.
korundo corundum.
korupta corrupt.
koruptado corruption, graft, subornation.
koruptanto choir, chorus.
korupteco corruption.
korupti to bribe, taint, corrupt.
koruptilo bribe.
korupto bribery, corruption, graft.
koruso choir.
Korveno Corwen.
korvestiblo auricle, auricula.
korvetkapitano lieutenant commander.
korveto corvette.
korvo crow, raven.
kosa Xhosa. **kosa lingvo** Xhosa, Xhosa language,.
kosekanto cosecant.
kosino Xhosa woman.
kosinuso cosine.
kosma cosmic. **kosma spaco** outer space.
kosmetikaĵo cosmetics.
kosmetiko cosmetics.
kosmo (outer) space, cosmos, universe.
kosmodromo space centre.
kosmogonio cosmogony.
kosmografiisto cosmographer.
kosmografio cosmography.
kosmografo cosmographer.
kosmologio cosmology.
kosmonaŭto cosmonaut.
kosmonavigado astrogation.
kosmonavigi to astrogate.
kosmonavigisto astrogator.
kosmopolita cosmopolite.
kosmopoliteco cosmopolitanism.
kosmopolitismo cosmopolitanism.
kosmopolito cosmopolite, cosmopolitan.
kosmoso cosmos.
kosmosondilo space probe.
kosmoŝipo spaceship.
koso Xhosa.
Kosovo Kosovo.
kosta dear, expensive, costly, expensive, high-priced.
Kostabravo Costa Brava.
kostarika Costa Rican.
kostarikano Costa Rican.
Kostariko Costa Rica.
koste de at the cost of, at the price of.
kostega priceless, invaluable.
kostelportebla affordable.
kosti to cost.
kosto charge, price, cost.
kostoj charge, cost, expense.
kostpago charge.
kostumo costume, outfit, suit, dress, garb.
koŝera kosher.
koŝia Cauchy. **koŝia vico** Cauchy sequence, fundamental sequence.
Koŝio Cauchy.
Koŝivico Cauchy's sequence, fundamental sequence.
Koŝi-vico Cauchy sequence, fundamental sequence.
koŝmaro nightmare.
koŝo thimble.
kota dirty, muddy, filthy, mucky, muddy.
kotangento cotangent.
kotanimulo low-minded person.
kotejo mudhole.
koterio coterie, exclusive circle, set.
koti to defecate, shit.
kotigi to dirty. **kotigi la akvon de** to muddy the waters of.
kotiledono cotyledon.
kotiljono cotillion.
kotisto dustman.
kotizi to contribute, subscribe.
kotizo contribution, dues, subscription, share, quota.
kotiztabelo subscription table, dues table.
kotkovrita muddy, mud-stained.
kotleto chop, cutlet.
kotligita dear to the heart.
koto dirt, mire, mud, muck, filth.
kotona cotton.
kotonarbo cotton plant, cotton.
kotoneastro cotoneaster.
kotonkampo cotton field.
kotono cotton (raw).
kotonrubando tape.
kotonujo cotton plant, cotton.
kotoo koto.
kotorno buskin, cothurnus.
kotŝirmilo fender, mudguard.
kotujo mud-hole, muddy place.
koturno quail (bird).
kovaĵo brood.
kovalento covalency.
Kovalo Cowal.
kovarianco covariance.
kovĉelo brood cell.
kovejo birth place, nesting place, nest.

koverto envelope.
kovi to brood (over), hatch (up), incubate, watch over.
koviĝi to incubate.
kovilo incubator.
kovitaro covey.
kovotempo breeding season.
kovra protective.
kovrajo cover.
kovri to cover, veil, wrap, cover. **kovri iun per kisoj** to cover someone in kisses. **kovri parte** to overlay.
kovriĝi to be covered.
kovrilego tilt (an awning).
kovrilo cover, hood, lid, wrapper.
kovrita covered.
kovro cover, covering.
kovropapero wrapping paper.
kovrotuko veil.
kozakestro ataman.
Kozako Cossack.
kp. → **komparu**.
krabli to sidle (like a crab).
krabo crab.
krabro hornet.
kraĉajo saliva, spittle.
kraĉeti to drivel (to slaver).
kraĉi to expectorate, spit.
kraĉo spittle.
kraĉospiri to wheeze.
kraĉotusi to clear one's throat, ahem, wheeze.
kraĉujo cuspidor, spittoon.
kradajo grate, grating, railing, trellis.
kradi to fence in, fence off, rail in, rail off.
kradita plaid.
krado lattice, crossbars, grate, grid, grill, grating; hash, pound sign, number sign (#); sharp sign (♯).
kradrostado barbecue.
kradrosti to barbecue, grill.
kradrostilo barbecue, gridiron, grill.
krajono pencil.
krajonpintigilo pencil sharpener.
krakado crunch, scrunch, grating noise, grinding noise, scratch, scratching, scraping, grating.
krakeno cracker.
kraketa brittle, crisp, crunchy.
kraketado grating.
kraketi to crackle, pop, snap, rattle (a toy).
kraketigi to munch, crunch, crack.
kraki to bang, clap, crack, snap (noise).
krakmaĉa brittle.
krakmaĉi to munch, crunch, crack.
krako crack (sound).
Krakovo Krakow.
kraksoni to crunch, scrunch, grate, grind.
kraktiko butcher bird.

krambo sea kale.
kramfo cramp.
krampfo cramp.
krampi to clamp, staple.
krampilo stapler.
krampo clamp, staple, bracket; brace, bracket, parenthesis. **ekkrampo** open (left) parenthesis (( ). **ferma krampo** close (right) parenthesis ( )). **finkrampo** close (right) parenthesis ( )). **komenca krampo** open (left) parenthesis (( ). **krampoj** brackets, parentheses. **angulaj krampoj** angle bracket (⟨ ⟩). **kunigaj krampoj** curly brackets ({ }). **rektaj krampoj** square brackets ([ ]). **rondaj krampoj** round parentheses (( )).
kranio cranium, head, skull, pate.
kranko crank, starter handle.
krano cock, faucet, tap, spigot.
krasulo crassula, mossy stonecrop.
kraŝi to crash.
kraŝo crash.
kratago hawthorn.
kratero crater.
kravali to riot.
kravato necktie, tie.
krea creative. **Krea Komunajo** Creative Commons.
kreado creation.
kreajo creature, creation.
kredado belief, believing.
kredanto believer.
kredartikolo article of faith.
kredebla believable, credible, probable, plausible.
kredeble probably.
kredebleco probability.
kredema credulous, naïve.
kredemo credulity.
kredenci to believe.
kredenco credence-table.
kredi to account, accredit, believe, deem. **kredi al** to believe in. **kredi je** to believe in. **kredi pri** to believe in. **kredas ke ne** don't think so.
krediga convincing, persuasive.
kredige convincingly.
kredigi to pretend, induce to believe.
kredinda plausible.
kredinde credibly, reliably.
kredindeco credibility, believability.
kredite on credit.
krediti to arrange a credit to, credit to, enter on the credit side.
kreditigi to accredit.
kreditkarto credit card.
kreditletero letter of credit.
kredito credit.
kreditoro account payable, creditor.

kredkonfeso creed.
kredo belief, credence, creed, tenet. **kredo je** belief in.
kredu-ne-kredu believe it or not.
kreema creative.
kreemo creativeness, creativity.
krei to create, produce.
kreiĝi to be created, come into being.
kreintismano creationist.
kreintismo creationism.
kreinto creator.
kreismo creationism.
kreitaĵo creation, creature.
kreito creature, creation.
krekso corn-crake.
krema cream.
kremaciejo crematory.
kremacii to cremate.
kremacio cremation.
kremaĵo (beauty, cold) cream.
krematorio crematory.
kremkolora cream, crème.
kremkruĉo creamer.
Kremlo Kremlin.
kremo cream, choicest part.
kremondo creation of the world.
krenela crenate, crenellated, notched, scalloped, toothed.
kreneli to crenellate.
krenelo crenel, crenellation.
kreno horseradish.
krensaŭso horseradish (sauce).
kreo creation.
kreola Creole.
Kreolo Creole.
kreozoto creosote.
krepido hawksbeard.
krepiti to crackle, crepitate.
krepo crepe.
kreppapero crepe paper.
krepuska dim.
krepuski to dawn, become daytime.
krepuskiĝi to dusk has fallen.
krepusko dawn, dusk, twilight.
krescento crescent.
kresĉendo crescendo.
kreska rising, ascending. **kreska diftongo** rising diphthong. **kreska ordigo** ascending sort. **kreska ordo** ascending order.
kreskado growth.
kreskaĵado vegetation.
kreskaĵbarilo hedge.
kreskaĵo plant, seedling.
kreskanta increasing (mapping).
kreskanta luno waxing moon.
kreski to accrue, grow, increase. **kreski per ŝlimo** to silt up.
kreskigi to cultivate, grow, make grow, raise.
kreskiĝi to accrue, increase, grow.

kresko accretion, growth, stature. **kresko per ŝlimo** accretion.
kreso cress.
krespo crepe, pancake.
kresteto wale.
kresto (cock's) comb, (mountain) ridge, crest.
krestomatio chrestomathy.
kresĉendi to swell.
kreta chalk. **Kreta Maro** Sea of Crete.
Kretaceo Cretaceous.
kretano Cretan.
kreteca chalky.
kreteno cretin.
Kreto Crete.
kreto chalk.
kretobreto chalk tray.
kretono cretonne.
kretskribi to chalk.
krevaĵo burst, crack, flaw.
krevi to burst.
krevigi to burst.
kreviĝo blow-out.
krevinta cracked.
krevmaizo popcorn.
krevo burst, crack.
kriaĉi to scream terribly.
kriado shouting, clamour.
Krianlariko Crianlarich.
kribri to sift, strain, filter.
kribrilo colander, sieve, strainer.
kriĉi to screech.
kriĉo screech.
kridemandosigno interrobang (‽); (?!)
krie screamingly.
kriega vociferous.
kriegado howling, shouting.
kriegi to bawl, roar, scream, shout, shriek, yell.
kriego scream, yell.
kriegulino termagant.
krieti to squall.
krieto squeal.
krifo claw, talon.
krii to call (out), cry (out), scream, shout.
kriketo cricket (sport).
kriko (lifting) jack.
krima criminal, felonious.
krimbruliganto arsonist.
krimbruligi to commit arson.
krimbruligisto arsonist.
krimbruligo arson.
krimea Crimean. **krimea tataro** Crimean Tatar.
krimeco criminality, iniquity.
krimego atrocity, outrage.
Krimeo Crimea.
krimeto misdemeanor.
krimi to commit a crime.

kriminala criminal. **kriminala kodo** penal law. **kriminala leĝo** criminal law.
kriminale criminally.
kriminaleco criminality.
kriminto offender, perpetrator.
krimo crime, felony, offence.
krimpago blood-money.
krimromano crime novel, detective novel, murder mystery.
krimulo criminal, felon, malefactor, wretch.
kringo ring-shaped roll, biscuit.
krinolino crinoline.
krio cry, shout.
kriogeniko cryogenics.
kripla crippled, infirm, handicapped.
kriplaĵo deformity, impairment, infirmity.
kripli to disable.
kripliga disabling.
kripligi to cripple, handicap.
kripligo maiming, mutilation.
kripliĝi to be crippled, become handicapped.
kriplulo cripple.
kripta cryptic.
kriptaĵo cryptogram.
kriptaĵoscienco cryptology.
kriptigado encryption.
kriptigi to encrypt.
kripto crypt, underground cell, vault.
kriptogamo cryptogam.
kriptografio cryptography.
kriptogramo cryptogram.
kriptonimo alias, pseudonym.
kriptono krypton.
kriptorkidio cryptorchidia.
krisigno exclamation mark, exclamation point (!).
krisolo crucible.
krispa crimped, crinkled, wavy. **krispa potamogeto** curly-leaf pondweed.
krispaĵo crinkle, kink.
krispigi to crimp, wave, curl.
krispiĝi to become crinkled.
krispo frill, ruffle, frilled collar.
kristala crystal. **kristala mezembriantemo** common ice plant, crystalline ice plant.
kristaligi to crystallize.
kristaliĝi to crystallize.
kristalo crystal.
kristalografia crystallographic.
kristalografio crystallography.
kristalomancio crystallomancy, scrying.
Kristalveno Advent.
kristana Christian. **kristana erao** Christian Era.
Kristanaro Christendom.
kristanaro Christiandom.
kristaneco Christianity.
kristanigi to Christanize.
kristaniĝi to become a Christian.
Kristanismo Christianity.
kristanismo Christianity.
Kristano Christian.
kristano christian.
Kristanujo Christendom.
kristarbo Christmas tree.
kristismo Christianity.
kristnaska Christmas, of Christmas, Christmas-time. **Kristnaska arbeto** Christmas tree. **Kristnaska Festo** Christmas, Christmas feast. **Kristnaska Insulo** Christmas Island. **Kristnaska piceo** Christmas tree. **Kristnaska Tago** Christmas Day. **Kristnaska vespero** Christmas Eve. **Kristnaska Viro** Father Christmas, Santa Claus.
kristnaskarbo Christmas tree.
Kristnaskdono Christmas box.
kristnaski to spend Christmas.
Kristnaskinsulo Christmas Island.
Kristnasko Christmas, Yule.
kristnaskokanto carol.
Kristo Christ.
kristologio Christology.
Kriŝno Krishna.
krita critical. **krita risurco** critical resource. **krita sekcio** critical section. **krita vojo** critical path.
kriterio criterion, rule, touchstone, measure.
kriticismo criticism.
kritika critical.
kritikaĉi to cavil, carp.
kritikado flak.
kritikanto judge.
kritike critically.
kritikema critical.
kritikeme critically.
kritiki to censure, criticize, knock.
kritikismo criticism.
kritikisto critic.
kritiko criticism.
kriza critical.
krizalido chrysalis, pupa.
krizantemo chrysanthemum.
krize critically, desperately.
krizi to be in critical condition.
krizo crisis, depression, emergency, depression, critical situation.
krizofriso goldfish.
krizokalo pinchbeck.
krizolito chrysolite, olivine, peridot.
krizosplenio golden saxifrage.
krizotorĉo flare.
kroata Croatian.
Kroatio Croatia.
kroato Croat.
Kroatujo Croatia.
kroĉi to concatenate, hook.
kroĉiĝi al to board, clutch.

kroĉiĝo adhesion.
kroĉilo hook, peg.
kroĉo concatenation.
krokedo croquette.
kroketo croquet.
krokizi to outline sketch.
krokizo design, outline, sketch, storyboard, plan.
krokodili to speak one's national language among Esperantists.
krokodilklemo alligator clip.
krokodilo crocodile.
krokosmio montbretia.
krokuso crocus.
krom apart from, besides, except, except for. **krom se** unless. **krom tio** besides, in addition, moreover. **krom tio ke** except for the fact that.
kroma accidental, additional, spare. **kroma ŝlosilo** spare key.
kromaĵo extra, something else.
kromakcento secondary accent, secondary stress.
kromaltarejo aisle, side-chapel.
kromartikuloj Xenarthra.
kromata chromatic.
kromateco chromaticity.
kromatografio chromatography.
krombaloto by-election.
kromcelo hidden agenda.
kromĉaro sidecar.
kromdomo outbuilding, outhouse.
krome besides, in addition, moreover.
kromefiki to cause side effects.
kromefiko side-effect.
Kromero Cromer.
kromgusto additional flavour.
kromi to chrome(-plate).
kromindekso secondary index.
kromintenco hidden agenda.
kromio chromium.
kromizi to chromium-plate.
kromkarto plug-in card.
kromklapo tab.
kromleciono additional lesson.
krommarĝeno indentation.
kromnomo byname, nickname, sobriquet.
kromo chromium.
kromofotografio colour photography.
kromolitografio chromolithography.
kromosfero chromosphere.
kromosomo chromosome.
krompagi to pay extra.
krompago additional payment.
kromperiodo overtime.
kromposteno moonlight job.
kromprocesoro coprocessor.
kromprodukto by-product, waste product.
kromprogramo plug-in.

kromrado spare time.
kromrolanto extra.
kromrolulo extra.
kromsigno accent mark, accidental.
kromspongo (mop) refill.
kromŝlosilo secondary key.
kromtubo spare tyre.
kromvagono trailer.
kromvirino concubine.
kromviroino paramour.
kronado coronation, crowning.
kroneto corolla.
kroni to crown.
kronika chronic, lingering.
kronikisto chronicler, historian.
kroniko annals, chronicle.
Krono Cronus.
krono crown (money).
Krono Kronos.
kronologia chronological.
kronologio chronology.
kronometri to time.
kronometria chronometric.
kronometrio chronometry.
kronometristo timekeeper.
kronometro chronometer.
kropo craw, crop, goitre, gullet, pouch.
krotalo rattlesnake.
krotofago ani.
krozadi to cross.
krozado cruise.
krozanto cruiser.
krozi to cruise.
krozilo browser.
krozisto cruiser.
krozŝipo cruiser.
kruca crucial, cruciform. **kruca militiro** crusade.
krucarmo cross-arm.
krucbekulo crossbill.
krucforme across.
kruci to cross.
krucifikso crucifix.
krucigi to cross.
krucigo crossing.
kruciĝe across.
kruciĝi to cross.
kruciĝo intersection.
krucisto crusader.
kruckontrolo cross-check.
krucmarki to check off, mark with a cross, put a cross against, tick off.
krucmasto driver, mizzen mast.
krucmilitiro crusade.
krucmilito crusade.
kruco cross. **Kruco** Crux (constellation).
krucosigni to make the sign of the cross.
krucplakaĵo plywood.
krucreferenco cross-reference.

krucumi to crucify.
krucumo crucifixion.
krucvortenigma crossword.
krucvortenigmo crossword puzzle.
kruĉego ewer.
kruĉeto ampoule.
kruĉo cruse, ewer, jug, pitcher, pot, vessel.
kruĉoforma ascidiform.
kruda crude, raw, rough, unbleached, uncooked, uncut, virgin, natural, primitive.
kruda datumo raw data. **kruda petrolo** crude oil. **kruda skizo** adumbration, shadow. **krudaj materialoj** raw materials.
krudaĵo commodity.
krude in the rough.
krudeco crudity.
krudfero pig iron.
krudlanŝtofa baize.
krudlanŝtofo baize.
krudmaterialo raw material.
krudulaĉa loutish, yobbish.
krudulaĉo lout.
krudulo boor, churl.
kruela cruel, fierce.
kruelaĵo atrocity, act of cruelty.
kruele cruelly.
krueleco cruelty.
kruelega atrocious, ferocious, fierce, heinous, horrible, ruthless.
kruelegaĵo atrocity.
kruelege atrociously, ferociously.
kruelegeco ferocity.
kruelego atrocity, ferocity.
krueloeco cruelty.
kruelulo brute.
krupiero croupier.
krupo croup.
kruraĵo leg meat.
krurbraceleto anklet.
kruro leg, paw, limb.
kruroprotezo artificial leg.
krurrompo fracture of the leg.
krurungo spur.
krurvindaĵoj leggings, gaiters.
krurvindo puttee.
krurzono garter.
krustaco crustacean.
krusto crust, deposit, hard outer covering, rind, scab, casing, scale.
krustulo crustacean.
krustuloj crustacean.
kruta abrupt, steep, sheer.
krutaĵo bluff, cliff, precipice, escarpment.
krute steeply.
kruteco steepness.
krutegaĵo escarpment, precipice.
krutigi to steepen.
krutiĝi to steepen.
kruzero cruzeiro.

k.s. → **kaj simile**.
ksantato xanthate.
ksantelasmo xanthelasma.
ksanteno xanthin.
ksantino xanthine.
ksantofila xanthophyllic, xanthophyllous.
ksantofilo xanthophyll.
ksantomo xanthoma.
ksantomozo xanthomatosis.
ksantosomo yautia.
Ksavero Xavier.
ksenio xenia.
ksenobiologio exobiology, xenobiology.
ksenofobia xenophobic.
ksenofobio xenophobia, hostility to or fear of foreigners.
ksenofobiulo xenophobe.
ksenofobo xenophobe.
ksenogamia xenogamous.
ksenogamio xenogamy.
ksenogeneza xenogeneic.
ksenogenezo xenogenesis.
ksenogrefto xenograft.
ksenologio xenology.
ksenonlampo xenon lamp.
ksenono xenon.
ksera xerographic.
kserazo xerasia.
ksero xerography.
kserodermo xeroderma.
kserofila xerophilous.
kserofito xerophilous plant, xerophyte.
kseroftalmio xerophthalmia.
kserografia xerographic.
kserografio xerography.
kserokopio xerographic copy.
kseroradiografio xeroradiography.
kseroradiogramo xeroradiogram.
ksifio swordfish.
ksifisterno xiphisternum.
ksifoida xiphoid.
ksifoido xiphoid.
ksifosura xiphosuran.
ksilano xylan.
ksilemo xylem.
ksileno xylene.
ksilofaga xylophagous.
ksilofonisto xylophonist.
ksilofono xylophone.
ksilografaĵo woodcut.
ksilografi to xylograph.
ksilografia xylographic, xylographical.
ksilografiaĵo wood-cut, xylograph.
ksilografiisto wood-engraver, xylographer.
ksilografio xylography.
ksilografo wood-engraver, xylographer.
ksilotoma xylotomous.
ksilozo xylose.
ksio xi (Ξξ).

ksisto

ksisto xyst, xystus.
ktp. → **kaj tiel plu**.
k.t.p. → **kaj tiel plu**.
Kualalumpuro Kuala Lumpur.
kuba¹ Cuban.
kuba² cubic, cubical.
kubano Cuban.
kube in the Cuban way.
kubika metro cubic metre.
kubĵeto roll, throw of the dice.
Kubo Cuba.
kubo cube.
kubutlibereco elbow room.
kubuto elbow.
kudrado needlework.
kudraĵo needlework.
kudrero stitch.
kudri to stitch, sew, tack.
kudrilarkorbo sewing basket, work basket.
kudrilaro sewing things.
kudrilarujo sewing box.
kudrilkuseno pincushion.
kudrilo needle.
kudristino dressmaker, seamstress.
kudrofadeno sewing thread.
kudrokurso sewing class.
kudromaŝino sewing machine.
kufo bonnet, cap.
kuglaĵo (canon)ball, shot.
kuglego shell, bomb.
kugletaĵo grapeshot.
kugletarpafilo shotgun.
kugleto pellet.
kuglingo case, casing.
kuglo ball, bullet, shot.
kuirado cookery.
kuiraĵo cooking.
kuirarta culinary.
kuirarto cooking, cuisine.
kuirbanano plantain.
kuireja kitchen, of a kitchen.
kuirejo kitchen.
kuirejstablo dresser.
kuirforno cooker, stove.
kuiri to cook.
kuiriĝi to cook.
kuirilaro kitchen utensils.
kuirilvendisto hardwareman.
kuirista cook's. **Kuirista Markolo** Cook Strait. **Kuirista Monto** Mount Cook.
kuiristino cook, female cook.
kuiristo cook.
kuirita cooked.
kuirpoto cooking pot.
kukaburo kookaburra.
kukaĵo pastry.
kukbakejo confectionery.
kukbakisto confectioner.

kultivebla

kukejo bakery, confectioner's, confectioner's shop, pastry shop.
kuketo little cake, cupcake.
kuketujo biscuit tin.
kuko cake.
kukolhorloĝo cuckoo clock.
kukolo cuckoo.
kukumeto gherkin, cucumber.
kukumo cucumber.
kukurbacoj curcurbits.
kukurbeto zucchini.
kukurbo gourd, pumpkin, squash.
kulako kulak.
kulasbloko breech block.
kulaso breech of gun.
kulasriglilo breech bolt.
kuleranaso shoveler.
kulerĉerpi to dish up.
kulerego scoop, large spoon.
kulerkavo bowl of a spoon.
kulero spoon.
kulinara culinary.
kulinario art of cooking.
kulio coolie.
kuliso flat (theatre), slip, wing.
kulisoŝovisto stage-hand.
kulmina climactic, ultimate.
kulmini to climax, culminate.
kulmino acme, climax, culmination, peak, point.
kulmo blade, stalk.
kulo gnat, mosquito.
Kulombo Charles de Coulomb.
kulombo coulomb.
kuloto short pants, shorts.
kulpa culpable, guilty, to blame.
kulpatesto admission of guilt.
kulpeco culpability.
kulpi to be guilty.
kulpiga accusatory.
kulpiganto accuser.
kulpigi to accuse, (place) blame, arraign, incriminate, indict, impeach. **kulpigi pri** to accuse of, charge with, impeach of, indict for, tax with.
kulpigito accused, defendant.
kulpigo accusation, charge, complaint, indictment.
kulpiĝi to be guilty.
kulpiko gnat-bite, midge-bite.
kulpo fault, offence, guilt, failing.
kulposente guiltily, with feelings of guilt.
kulpulo culprit, delinquent.
Kulroso Culross.
kulŝirmilo mosquito net.
kulti to idolize, venerate, worship, exalt, glorify.
kultivado cultivation, tillage.
kultivebla arable.

kultivejo

kultivejo plantation.
kultivi to cultivate.
kultivisto grower, cultivator.
kultivo cultivation, growing.
kulto cult (system of religious worship), homage, devotion.
kultura cultural.
kulturado cultivation.
kulture culturally.
kulturejo plantation, tillage.
kulturhomo cultured person, educated person.
kulturi to cultivate, grow.
kulturiĝi to become cultivated.
kulturkampo farmland.
kulturo culture.
kulturologio humanities.
kulvualo mosquito net, mosquito netting.
kumano Cuman.
Kumarado Cumbrae.
Kumbernaŭldo Cumbernauld.
kuminfromaĝo cumin-seed cheese.
kumino cumin.
kumiso koumiss.
kumkvato kumquat.
kumulado cumulation.
kumuli to cumulate.
kumuluso cumulus, woolpack.
kun with. **kun escepto de** with the exception of. **kun la fluado** with the current. **kun la spiro retenita** holding one's breath. **kun la tempopaso** over the course of time. **kun matematika precizeco** with mathematical precision. **kun respekto** with respect. **kun rezervo pri** to bar, barring, except for, subject to, without prejudice. **kun senpacienco** impatiently. **kun sopiro** longingly. **kun ŝvitanta frunto** with a sweating forehead. **kun tempo** with time.
kun- co-, fellow.
kuna joint, combined, together.
kunagi to cooperate.
kunaĵo union (of sets).
kunalie with others.
kunaŭtoro co-author.
kunbatalanto fellow fighter.
kunbati to beat together.
kunbekiĝi to peck, squabble, wrangle.
kuncelebri to concelebrate.
kuncentrigi to centre, centralize, concentrate.
kuncentrigo centralization.
kuncivitano fellow citizen.
kundancantino dance partner.
kundancanto dance partner.
kundecido co-decision.
kune jointly, together. **kune kun** along with, together with.

kuniri

kuneco togetherness.
kunefrapi to clap together (hands).
kunegali to tally.
kunekzistado co-existence.
kunekzisti to coexist.
kunenzimo coenzyme.
kunestado coexistence, time together, being together.
kunesti to be with.
kunesto meeting.
kunfandaĵo alloy.
kunfandema lingvo inflective language.
kunfandi to collate, merge, fuse (together).
kunfandiĝi to fuse, coalesce.
kunfandiĝo fusion, merger.
kunfando fusion.
kunfaranto accessory.
kunfinanci to co-finance.
kunflue downstream.
kunfluiĝo confluence.
kunforĝi to weld.
kunfrato confrère.
kunfripono accomplice.
kunfunkciebla interoperable.
kunfunkcieblo interoperability.
kunglui to agglutinate.
kungluiĝemo adhesiveness.
kungrefti to graft.
kunhava proporcio a share.
kunhavi to have (with oneself), share.
kunhelpa cooperative.
kunhelpanto accessory, helpmate.
kunhelpe cooperatively.
kunhelpi to abet, cooperate, help together.
kunhelpinto abetter.
kunhelpo assistance, help, aide.
kunhelpoado cooperation.
kunhomo fellow human being, neighbour.
kuni to conjoin, put together.
kuniga connecting. **kuniga histo** connective tissue. **kuniga krampo** curly bracket, brace. **kunigaj krampoj** curly brackets ({ }).
kunigi to annex, connect, unite, join together, couple, splice. **kunigi siajn ideojn** to collect one's thoughts.
kunigo annexation, conjunction, joining, connection, union.
kunigado convergence.
kunigĝi to associate, come together, join, pool, coalesce, unite, become joined.
kunigo coalition, joining, junction, joint (carpentering), docking.
kuniklejo rabbit hutch, warren.
kunikleto bunny.
kuniklo rabbit.
kuniranto companion (on a trip, journey), fellow traveller.
kuniri to go with.

kunjungitaĵo set of draught horses.
kunĵuri to conspire.
kunkantado sing-along.
kunkanti to accompany, sing along with.
kunkateni to shackle.
kunkrimulo accomplice.
kunkudraĵo seam.
kunkudri to sew together.
kunkudro seam.
kunkulpa accessory.
kunkulpeco complicity.
kunkulpulo abettor, accessory, accomplice.
kunlabora collaborative, cooperative.
kunlaborado collaboration.
kunlaboranto fellow worker, co-worker.
kunlabore cooperatively.
kunlabori to collaborate, cooperate.
kunlaboro collaboration.
kunlernanto schoolfellow.
kunligaĵo composition product.
kunligi to bind (together), connect, join, tie together, unite.
kunligo coherence, connection, composition.
kunloĝantejo dormitory.
kunloĝanto co-occupant.
kunloĝi to cohabit, live together.
kunludanto fellow player.
kunludi to accompany.
kunmanĝanto messmate.
kunmanĝi to mess.
kunmetado building, construction.
kunmetaĵo assemblage, build, combination, compound, construct, construction.
kunmeti to add together, compound, put together.
kunmetita assembled.
kunmetitaĵo combination.
kunmeto composition (mixture).
kunmezurebla commensurable.
kunmiksi to combine.
kunmunti to assemble.
kunnaskita congenital, inborn, inbred, innate, native.
kunnomumi to duplicate.
kunokazeco coincidence.
kunordiga coordinating. **kunordiga klasifiko** merge sorting. **kunordiga konjunkcio** coordinating conjunction.
kunordigi to coordinate, merge.
kunordigo coordination.
kunparolanto conversation partner, interlocutor.
kunparoli to speak together.
kunplekti to entwine, interweave.
kunporti to bring along, take along.
kunpremado constriction, squeeze.
kunpremebla compressible.
kunpremegi to squash, squeeze.
kunpremi to compress, squeeze together.
kunpremilo compressor.
kunpremo compression.
kunpreni to bring along, take (with oneself).
kunproksimiĝi to huddle.
kunpuŝiĝi to collide.
kunpuŝiĝo collision.
kunrespondi to correspond.
kunrespondo connection.
kunrimi to rhyme.
kunrula concurrent. **kunrulaj procezoj** concurrent processes.
kunrulo concurrency.
kunsenco connotation.
kunsendaĵo attachment.
kunsendi to enclose.
kunsenta sympathetic.
kunsente sympathetically.
kunsenti to feel together.
kunsento sympathy.
kunsidantaro assembly.
kunsidi to meet.
kunsido session, meeting.
kunŝovi to kern.
kuntara gross. **kuntara pezo** gross weight.
kunteksteco contextuality.
kuntekstigi to contextualize.
kunteksto context.
kuntekstohava gramatiko context-sensitive grammar.
kuntekstohava lingvo context-sensitive language.
kunteniĝi to hold together, cohere.
kunteniĝo cohesion.
kuntira astringent.
kuntiri to draw together, pull together.
kuntiriĝi to contract, cower, shrink.
kuntiro contraction.
kuntreni to bring with it.
kuntreniĝi to involve.
kuntreniĝo involvement.
kuntuŝiĝi to adjoin, touch.
kunularo company.
kunuleco companionship, comradeship, fellowship.
kunulo associate, companion, consort, mate, partner.
kunumado being together.
kunuzi to share.
kunvarianco covariance.
kunvenejo meeting place, rendezvous, resort.
kunveni to assemble, congregate, gather, meet.
kunvenigi to muster, take along.
kunvenintaro assemblage.
kunveno assemblage, gathering, meeting, assembly.
kunveturi to travel together.
kunvivado cohabitation.

kunvivantino cohabitee, partner.
kunvivanto cohabitee, partner.
kunvivi to cohabit, live together.
kunvojaĝanto companion (travelling).
kunvojaĝi to travel together.
kunvoki to assemble, call together, convoke.
kunvoko convocation, parade, roll call.
kunvulsio convulsion.
kuo name of the letter Q.
Kuparo Cupar.
kupeo compartment, coupé.
kupido cupid.
kuplado feedback.
kupleto couplet.
kupli to couple, join up, unite.
kuplilo coupler, coupling.
kupliretro feedback.
kupo cupping glass.
kupokso cowpox.
kupolo cupola, dome.
kupono coupon, stub.
kupra copper.
kupraĵo brassware.
kupreca coppery.
kuprepoko copper age.
kupri to copperplate.
kupristo coppersmith.
kupro copper (metal).
kuproepoko copper age.
kuprokolora copper, coppery.
kupromonero copper.
kupropirito chalcopyrite.
kupulo cupule.
kuraca medical. **kuraca gimnastiko** physiotherapy.
kuracado (course of) treatment.
Kuracao Curaçao.
kuracarto therapeutics.
kuracato sick person, patient.
kuracebla curable.
kuracejo health resort, nursing home, sanatorium.
kuracherbo medicinal herb.
kuraci to care for, cure, heal, remedy, treat.
kuraciĝi to heal.
kuracilejo dispensary.
kuracilo cure, remedy, drug, medicine, pharmaceutical.
kuracisto doctor, physician.
kuracloko spa, health resort.
kuraco cure (act of curing).
kuracplanto medicinal plant.
kuradi to keep on running.
kurado running.
kuraĝa audacious, bold, brave, courageous, valiant, daring, fearless, intrepid.
kuraĝanima brave.
kuraĝanime bravely, boldly.
kuraĝe courageously.

kuraĝeco fortitude.
kuraĝega intrepid.
kuraĝege fearlessly.
kuraĝegeco prowess.
kuraĝi to be bold enough (to), dare, have courage, venture to. **kuraĝi batali kontraŭ** dare to fight, stand up to. **kuraĝi entrepreni** to dare, venture.
kuraĝiga heartening, supportive.
kuraĝige supportively.
kuraĝigi to cheer on, hearten, encourage, inspire.
kuraĝigo encouragement.
kuraĝiĝi to embolden, encourage.
kuraĝo audacity, boldness, bravery, courage, mettle, fortitude, valor, spirit.
kuraĝulo brave person.
kuraĝus would dare to.
kuraho currach.
kuranta actual, current.
kuranto runner.
kuraro curare.
Kuraso Curaçao.
kurataki to assault, storm.
kuratako assault, charge, storming.
kuratoreco curatorship, trusteeship.
kuratoro conservator, curator, guardian, trustee.
kurba bandy, bent, curved, bow(ed), winding. **kurba krampo** brace.
kurbbastono Episcopal staff.
kurbeco curvature, curve.
kurbecocentro centre of curvature.
kurbecocirklo circle of curvature.
kurbecoradiuso radius of curvature.
kurbecradiuso radius of curvature.
kurbflugo curving flight.
kurbigi to arch, bend, curve, turn, warp.
kurbiĝadi to twist.
kurbiĝi to bend, loop.
kurbiĝo bend, crook, curve, turn.
kurbkrua bow-legged.
kurbo bend, curve.
kurboplena twisting.
kurĉatovio Kurchatovium.
kurĉevalo racehorse.
kurda Kurdish.
Kurdio Kurdistan.
kurdo Kurd.
Kurdujo Kurdistan.
kuregado stampede.
kuregi to race, run.
kuregisto runner.
kurego dash, race, stampede.
kurejo course, racecourse, track, running track.
kuremulino woman who likes to run.
kuremulo person who likes to run.
kurentintenseco amperage.

kurentintenso electric current.
kurento current (electric).
kurhundeto whippet.
kuri to run.
kuriero bishop (chess), courier, runner, messenger.
kurierŝipo packet boat, transporter.
kurigi to cause to run, make run.
kurilo cooker.
Kuriloj Kurile Islands.
kurio curia.
kurioza curious, interesting, quaint, rare, odd, strange.
kuriozaĵo curio, curiosity, oddity.
kuristo runner.
kuriumo curium.
kurkulio curculio, weevil.
kurkumino curcumin.
kurkumo turmeric.
kurlingisto curler.
kurlingo curling.
kurlo curlew.
kuro course (race). **kuro de la rivero** course of the river.
kursadi to circulate.
kursado circulation, run.
kursano course participant.
kursaviadilo air liner.
kursgvidanto teacher of a course.
kursilo router.
kursiva italic (writing). **kursive presita** printed in italics.
kursivigi to italicize.
kursivo cursive, italic.
kurso class, course.
kursoro cursor.
kurspaĝaro course website.
kursvaro courseware.
kurta short.
kurtaĝo broker commission, broker fee, brokerage.
kurteno curtain, screen, veil.
kurtenstango curtain rod.
kurtigi to abbreviate, shorten.
kurtino curtain.
kurtonda short-wave.
kuruko garden warbler.
kurvo curve.
kurvojo jogging path.
kurzo exchange rate, rate of exchange, quotation, rate, price.
kusenego thick comforter used as a bed covering.
kuseneto pad.
kusenlito pillow.
kuseno cushion, pillow.
kusensako cushion cover, pillow case.
kusentegilo cushion cover, pillow case.
kusentego cushion cover, pillow case.
kusenveturilo hovercraft.
kusineto bolster, bush.
Kusko Cuzco.
kuskuso couscous.
kuskuto dodder.
kuspi to brush against the grain, roll up.
kuspnaza snub-nosed.
kustardo cream, custard.
kuŝa recumbent.
kuŝbenko bunk.
kuŝe secretly, secretively, in secret, in hiding.
kuŝejo couch, berth (ship), litter (animals), lair.
kuŝemulo truant.
kuŝi to lie, recline, rest on. **kuŝi dise sur la table** to lie scattered on the table. **kuŝi supre sur** be on top of, lay on top of.
kuŝigi to lay, lay out.
kuŝiĝeti to nestle.
kuŝiĝi to go to bed, rest, lie down.
kuŝoseĝo couch, divan.
kuŝujo bed (river).
kutima accustomed, customary, used to, usual, conventional, familiar, habitual, usual.
kutime ordinarily, usually.
kutimeto familiarity.
kutimi to accustom, be accustomed to, be in the habit of.
kutimigi to accustom, familiarize, habituate, inure.
kutimiĝi to accustom oneself, get used to.
kutimiĝo adjustment.
kutimo custom, habit, way, practice, routine.
kutimulo (a) regular (guest, customer, etc.).
kutro cutter.
kuvajta Kuwaiti.
kuvajtano Kuwaiti.
Kuvajto Kuwait.
kuvego vat.
kuveto basin, bowl.
kuvo bath, tub, vat.
kuvoeto tub.
kuzino (female) cousin.
kuzo (male) cousin.
kvadranto quadrant.
kvadrata quadrate, quadratic, square. **kvadrata matrico** square matrix. **kvadrata metro** square metre. **kvadrata mezumo** quadratic mean.
kvadratangule in a square (pattern).
kvadrategala idempotent.
kvadratigi to square (make square).
kvadratita checked, chequered.
kvadratmejlo square mile.
kvadrato quadrate, quadrature, square.
kvadraturo quadrature.
kvadrigo chariot, quadriga.
kvadriko quadric.

kvadrilo quadrille.
kvadro ashlar.
kvadroŝtono ashlar.
kvago quagga.
kvajzoj chopsticks.
kvakado honking.
kvakera Quaker.
kvakero Quaker.
kvaki to croak, quack.
kvako croak, honk, squawk.
kvalifi to qualify.
kvalifika qualified, qualifying.
kvalifiki to qualify.
kvalifikiĝi to be eligible.
kvalifikita able.
kvalifiko ability, qualification.
kvaliteco qualification.
kvalitigi to qualify.
kvalito property, quality.
kvankam albeit, though, although.
kvanteca quantitative.
kvantesprimo expression of quantity.
kvanto quantity.
kvantoro quantifier.
kvantummeĥaniko quantum mechanics.
kvantummekaniko quantum mechanics.
kvantumo quantum.
kvantumteorio quantum theory.
kvar four.
kvara fourth.
kvarangula quadrangular.
kvarangulaĵo quadrangle.
kvarangulo quadrangle.
kvaranteni to be quarantined.
kvaranteno quarantine.
kvarco quartz, rock-crystal.
kvardek forty.
kvardeka fortieth.
kvare fourthly.
kvaredro tetrahedron.
kvarfoje four times.
kvarko quark.
kvarlampa four-tube.
kvarlatero quadrilateral.
kvarliteraĵo tetragraph.
kvarmonate four-monthly.
kvaro foursome.
kvarobla quadruple.
kvarobligi to square (math).
kvarona noto crotchet.
kvaronarierulo quarterback.
kvaronbuŝelo quarter bushel.
kvaronhoro quarter of an hour.
kvaronjara quarterly.
kvaronjare quarterly.
kvaronjaro quarter.
kvarono fourth, quarter.
kvaronujo quarter.
kvaronumi to quarter.

kvarope by fours, by fourths.
kvaropo quadruple, quadruplet(s).
kvarpieda quadruped.
kvarpiede on all fours.
kvarpiedulo quadruped.
kvarrada four-wheel.
kvartalaĉo back street, slum.
kvartalo district, neighbourhood, quarter, ward.
kvartermo quadrinomial.
kvarteto quartet.
kvartiro billet.
kvarto fourth.
kvasio quassia.
kvaso kvass.
kvassupo kvass (soup).
kvasto tassel.
kvaternara Quaternary.
kvazaro quasar.
kvazaŭ as if, as though, in a way. **kvazaŭ sur la manplato** as though on the palm of my hand. **kvazaŭ tondrofrapita** (as if) thunderstruck.
kvazaŭa seeming, quasi-.
kvazaŭĉasta demure.
kvazaŭdecmora demure.
kvazaŭdiri to insinuate, suggest.
kvazaŭe almost, as it were.
kvazaŭfreneza nutty.
kvazaŭhomo manikin.
kvazaŭkompakta quasi-compact (space).
kvazaŭkunrulo quasi-concurrency.
kvazaŭparalelado quasi-parallel processing.
kvazaŭpruda demure.
kvazaŭstokasta pseudorandom.
kvazaŭstokasto pseudorandom number.
kvazaŭvokalo semivowel.
kverelado altercation, dispute, quarreling, squabbling, wrangling.
kverelema cantankerous, quarrelsome.
kvereli to quarrel, wrangle.
kvereliga contentious, controversial.
kverelo quarrel.
kverelulo brawler.
kveri to coo.
kverka oak, oaken.
Kverkaro Oak Forest.
kverkejo oak-wood.
kverko oak.
kverkoligno oak, oak-wood.
kvestisto mendicant friar.
kvestoro quaestor.
kvieta calm, quiet, placid.
kviete quietly, leisurely, softly, tamely.
kvietebla placable.
kvieteco calmness, quietness, retirement, rest.
kvietega impassive.

kvietema placable.
kvietiga soothing.
kvietigi to allay, calm, lull, quench (thirst), quiet, soothe, tame.
kvietigo abatement, alleviation, appeasement.
kvietiĝi to abate, subside, compose one's self, relent.
kvietiĝo abatement, respite.
kvietismo quietism.
kvietmaso rest mass.
kvieto calm, quiet, silence, rest.
kviettemperamenta staid.
kvikstepo quickstep.
kvin five.
kvina fifth.
kvinangulo pentagon.
kvinanokte on, during the fifth night.
kvincent five hundred.
kvindek fifty.
kvindekjara fifteen year-old.
kvine fifthly.
kvinedro pentahedron.
kvinjambo iambic pentameter.
kvinkunkso quincunx.
kvinlatero pentagon.
kvinoble five times, fivefold.
kvinono fifth.
kvinoo quinoa.
kvinope by fives.
kvinopo quintuple.
kvintalo quintal.
kvintesenca quintessential.
kvintesenco quintessence.
kvinteto quintet.
kvinto fifth.
kvislingo quisling.
kvita debt-free, even, paid up, paid-up, free and clear.
kvitanca acknowledging. **kvitanca reĝimo** handshaking. **kvitanca signo** acknowledge character, ACK.
kvitanci to acknowledge receipt of something.
kvitanco quittance, (acknowledgment of) receipt.
kvitigi to clear, release from debt.
kvitigo acquittal.
kvitiĝi to settle, square up.
kvitiĝo account, settlement.
kviviti to chatter, twitter, warble, peep, tweet, pipe, chirp.
kvizo quiz.
kvocienta quotient. **kvocienta aro** quotient set. **kvocienta frakcio** common fraction, vulgar fraction. **kvocienta grupo** factor group, quotient group. **kvocienta ringo** quotient ring.
kvociento quotient, ratio.
kvodlibeto medley, potpourri, quodlibet.
kvorumo quorum.
kvotigi to allocate.
kvotigo allocation, allotment.
kvoto quota, share.
kvotovirino token woman.

L

la the. **la 10-an** on the 10th. **la afero estas, ke...** the thing is that... **la afero ne brulas** it's not urgent, the matter is not urgent. **la afero ne tuŝas min** the matter doesn't concern me. **la afero ne urĝas** it's not urgent, the matter is not urgent. **la aferoj** business, commerce. **la antaŭan semajnon** last week. **la batetadon de mia koro** the beating of my heart. **la batsono de la horloĝo** the striking of the clock. **la bela sekso** the fairer sex. **la Blanka Domo** the White House. **la ceteraj** the rest, remainder. **la cia** yours. **la demando estas...** the question is... **la Dia juĝo** God's judgement. **la Dipatrino** Our Lady. **la dua matene** two in the morning. **la ferioj** vacation. **la Fremda Legio** the Foreign Legion. **la hieraŭan nokton** last night. **la hodiaŭ tago** the present day, this day. **la hodiaŭa tempo** nowadays. **la ilia** theirs. **la irado de la konversacio** the course of the conversation. **la jena...** the following... **la jena ekzemplo** the following example, this example. **la ĵurio konsideradas** the jury is still out. **la katolika tempo** Catholic times. **la konita mondo** the known world. **la lia** his. **la malfacilaĵo estas, ke...** The trouble is that... **la malplej** the least. **la mia** mine. **la nia** ours. **la novaĵoj** the news. **la okazintaĵoj de la tago** the events of the day. **la ora proporcio** the golden ratio, psi. **la pasintan nokton** last night. **la pasintan semajnon** last week. **la plej** the most. **la plej bona** best. **la plej bone** best. **la plej efika maniero fari ion** the most effective way of doing something. **la plej juna** youngest. **la plej sube** undermost. **la plej supra** uppermost. **la plejmalbonaĵo** the worst (thing). **la plejparto de** most of. **la pordo staris aperte** the door stood open. **la postan tagon** (on) the next day. **la presarto** the art of printing. **la proksiman semajnon** next week. **la Ruĝa Muelejo** the Moulin Rouge (club in Paris). **la sama** the same. **la Sankta Virgulino** the Blessed Virgin. **la Sinjoro** the Lord. **la sorto destinis, ke** fate destined that. **la ŝia** hers. **la tempoj aliiĝas** the times are changing. **la trejntendaro de rekrutoj** boot camp. **la tuja plenumo de mia deziro** the immediate fulfilment of my wish. **la tutan** all, throughout the. **la Tutpotenculo** the All Powerful, God. **la urbo Rotterdam** the city of Rotterdam. **la usona revo** the American dream. **la venonta** the coming, next. **la venonta tempo** coming times, times to come. **la venontan semajnon** next week. **la via** yours.
labdo lambda (Λλ).
laberdano Aberdeen fish, salted cod.
labialo labial.
labio lipped corolla.
labirinto labyrinth, labyrinth, maze.
labora toilsome.
laborabelo worker (bee).
laboradi to work, keep working, work continuously.
laborado work, toil.
laboraĵo result of work.
laborakcidento work accident, accident in the workplace.
laborakiri to accrue.
laborantaro manpower.
laboranto worker.
laboratoria asistanto laboratory assistant.
laboratorio laboratory.
laborborso employment exchange, labour exchange, labour exchange.
laborĉambro work room.
labordivido division of labour, division of labour.
labordonanto employer.
laborega arduous.
laboregado drudgery.
laboregi to drudge, work hard.
laborego graft, labour, toil.
laborejo workplace, workshop, laboratory, studio.
laborema active, hardworking, diligent, laborious, industrious.
laboremo activity.
laborenskribo tender.
laborenspezo pay, salary, wage, wages.
laborestro foreman, overseer.
laboreto trifle.
laborevita work-shy, unwilling to work.
labori to labour, work.
laboriga arduous.
laborigi to cause to work, make work, put to work, force to work.
laborilo tool.
laborinta having worked.
laborintensiva labour-intensive.
laborista worker. **laborista klaso** working class, working classes. **laborista movado** labour movement.
laboristara working-class.
laboristaro labour force, work force.

laboristino female labourer, female worker.
laboristo labourer, operative, worker, working man, workman.
laboristoj labourers, workers, workmen.
laborkapabla able-bodied.
laborkapitalo working capital.
laborkondiĉoj terms of employment, working conditions.
laborkonflikto labour dispute.
laborloko place of employment.
labormaltaŭga disabled, unfit for work.
labormanko unemployment.
labormemoro working memory, RAM.
labormerkato labour market.
labornekapabla disabled, unfit for work.
labornekapablo inability to work.
laboro job, work, labour, toil. **laboro abundas** there was plenty of work. **laboroj** labours, work.
laboroado work (physical).
laborpago pay, remuneration, salary, wage, wages.
Laborpartio Labour-Party.
laborplanado job scheduling.
laborplano work-plan.
laborposteno job.
laborpostula laborious.
laborprenanto employee.
laborpreta in working order.
laborstacio workstation.
laboratablo desk, desktop, workspace.
labortago work day.
laborulo labourer, worker.
laborvestoj work(ing) clothes.
labrako European sea bass.
laburno laburnum, golden chain tree, golden chain.
laca tired, weary, fatigued.
lace wearily.
laceco fatigue, weariness.
lacega exhausted, tired out, worn out.
lacegiga exhausting.
lacegigi to fag out, jade, overdrive, override.
lacegiĝo exhaustion.
lacego exhaustion.
lacerto lizard.
laciga fatiguing.
lacigadi to jade (tire).
lacigi to fatigue, make tired, tire, harass, molest.
lacigita tired, fatigued.
laciĝi to get tired.
laciĝo lassitude.
laculo tired person.
laĉboto shoe.
laĉi to lace.
laĉo lace, shoelace.
laĉtirilo bodkin.
lada sheet metal, tin, tin plate.

ladaĵisto tinker.
ladaĵo tinware.
ladbotelo flask.
ladbovaĵo canned beef.
ladfruktoj canned fruit.
ladisto tinsmith.
ladlegomoj canned vegetables.
lado sheet metal, tin, tin plate.
Ladono Ladon.
ladskatolo can, tin, tin can.
ladsupo canned soup.
ladurbo slum.
Laerto Laertes.
lafa lava.
lafo lava.
lageto pond.
lago lake, loch. **Lago Arala** Aral Sea.
lagopo (willow) grouse, willow ptarmigan.
lagro bearing, bushing.
laguno lagoon.
laguro hare's-tail.
laika lay, secular, non-professional.
laikaro laity.
laikeco lay status.
laikino laywoman.
laiko non-professional, layman.
Lakadivoj Laccadives.
lakeeto page boy.
lakeo flunkey, footman, knave (cards), lackey, valet, servant.
laki to lacquer, varnish.
lakmusa papero litmus paper.
lakmuso litmus.
lako lacquer.
lakoaĵo varnish.
lakona brief, laconic, concise, succinct.
lakonismo laconism.
lakono Laconian.
laksa lax, loose.
laksigi to purge.
laksigilo laxative, purgative.
laksileto aperient.
laksilo laxative.
lakso diarrhoea.
Lakta Vojo Milky Way.
laktajfabriko dairy.
lakteca milky.
lakti to lactate.
lakto milk.
laktobovino dairy cow, milk cow.
laktodento milk tooth.
laktodona milch.
laktoliveristo milkman.
laktolo oilcloth.
laktovendejo dairy.
laktozo lactose, milk sugar.
laktuko lettuce, milt, roe.
laktumo roe.
lama feeble, hobbling, lame, weak.

lamaestro

lamaestro abbot.
lamao lama.
lambastono crutch.
lambdo lambda (Λλ).
lambdokalkulo lambda calculus.
lambrekino drapery.
lame limpingly.
lamelibrankio clam.
lamelibranko lamellibranch.
lamelikorno lamellicorn.
lamenbrankulo lamellibranch.
lamenigi to laminate.
lameno lamina, layer, plate.
lamenti to grieve, mourn, lament, wail.
lamentinda lamentable.
lamento lament, wail.
lameti to limp.
lami to limp, be lame.
lamigi to lame.
laminario brown seaweeds.
laminati to flatten, roll.
lamio dead-nettle, nettles.
lamiri to hobble.
lamo llama.
lampa petrolo kerosene.
lampeto little lamp.
Lampetro Lampeter.
lampingo bulb holder.
lampiono dim lamp, fairy lamp.
lampiro firefly, glow-worm.
lamplumo lamplight.
lampo lamp.
lampolumo lamplight.
lampoŝirmilo lampshade.
lampŝaltilo light switch.
lampŝirmilo lampshade.
lamulo lame person.
lana wool.
lanaĵo woollen stuff.
lanaĵoj woollens.
lanario merlin, stone falcon.
lanbulo ball of wool.
lanceto lancet, scalpel.
lancisto spearman.
lanco lance, spear.
lancpiki to spear.
lancpinto spearhead.
lanĉa rulponto launch gantry.
lanĉejo launch site, launch pad.
lanĉi to launch.
lanĉilo launcher.
landano compatriot, native.
landaŭo landau.
landestro sovereign.
landgrafo landgrave.
landido aboriginal, aborigine, native.
landinterno hinterland.
landkartaro atlas.
landkarto map.

Laponio

landlimo border, frontier, boundary.
lando country, land.
Landovero Llandovery.
landsinjoro landlord.
landstrato major highway.
laneca fleecy, woolly.
Lanelo Saint Asaph.
lanfadenaĵo yarn.
lanfadeno worsted.
langeto tab.
lango tongue.
langopinto tip of one's tongue.
langotrinki to lap up.
langtrinki to lap (up), drink using one's tongue.
langusto lobster.
langvori to languish.
langvoro languor.
lanherbo cotton-grass.
laniario guard dog.
lanio shrike.
lankasko balaclava helmet.
Lankastro Lancaster.
lankovrilo blanket.
lano wool.
lanolino lanolin.
Lanrago Lanark.
lanta slow.
lantanido lanthanide.
lantano lanthanum.
lante slowly.
lanternego beacon light.
lanterno lantern.
lanti to delay, tarry.
lanuga downy.
lanuglito down bed.
lanugo down, fluff, nap.
lanugovesto down vest.
Laocio Lǎozi, Lao-tzu.
laosa Laotian. **laosa lingvo** Lao, Laotian language.
laosano Laotian.
Laoso Laos.
laparatomio laparotomy.
laparotomio laparotomy.
lapis lazuro lapis lazuli.
lapiso lunar caustic.
laplaca Laplace. **laplaca operatoro** Laplace operation, Laplacian.
Laplaco Laplace.
laplacoperatoro Laplace operation, Laplacian.
lapo burdock, burr.
lapona Sami; (dated) Lapp, Lappish. → **samea**.
laponino Sami woman; (dated) Lappish woman. → **sameino**.
Laponio Lapland.

lapono Sami, Laplander; (dated) Lapp. → **sameo**.
Laponujo Lapland.
lapsano nipplewort.
Lapteva Maro Laptev Sea.
Laptevmaro Sea of Laptev.
lardhaŭto bacon-rind.
lardi to lard.
lardo bacon.
Largado Largs.
Largo Largo.
larĝa wide, broad.
larĝanima open-minded.
larĝanimeco open-mindedness.
larĝaŝultra broad-shouldered.
larĝbenda broadband.
larĝe widely.
larĝeco breadth, width, wideness.
larĝeŝultra broad-shouldered.
larĝfolia broad-leaved.
larĝhakilo broadaxe.
larĝigado broadening.
larĝigi to widen.
larĝigo broadening.
larĝmaneco bounty.
larĝo width.
larika larch.
lariko larch.
laringito laryngitis.
laringo larynx.
larma guto teardrop.
larmi to cry, shed tears, weep.
larmo tear (from eye).
larmoguto teardrop.
Larno Larne.
laro (sea)gull.
larvo grub, larva.
lasante leaving.
lasciva carnal, horny, hot, sensual, sensuous, voluptuous.
lasera laser. **lasera lokalizilo** LIDAR, optical radar, optical ranger. **lasera printilo** laser printer.
lasero laser.
lasi to allow, leave, let, release, quit. **lasi eniri** to admit. **lasi flanke** to leave out of account.
Lasso Lhasa.
lasta hindermost, last, ultimate.
lastatempa recent, of late.
lastatempe lately, recently.
laste at the last, ultimately. **laste sed ne balaste** last but not least.
lastfoje (at) the last time.
lastjare last year.
lastminuta last-minute.
lastmomente at the last moment.
lastnomita last (named).
Las-vegaso Las Vegas.

lataro battens.
latekso latex.
latenta dormant, hidden, latent.
lateralo lateral.
laterito laterite.
latero arm, side.
Laterono Latheron.
Latia ligo Latin League.
latina Latin. **latina alfabeto** Latin alphabet. **Latina Biblio** Vulgate.
latinida Romance. **Latinida Ameriko** Latin America. **latinida lingvo** Roman language, language derived from Latin.
latinidaj lingvoj Romanic languages.
Latino Latin.
latiro everlasting pea, meadow pea.
latiso lattice.
latitudo latitude.
latkrado trellis.
latkurteno Venetian blind.
lato batten, lath, slat.
latreo toothwort.
latrino latrine.
latrono thief.
latuna brass.
latuno brass.
latva Latvian, Lettish.
latvino Latvian woman.
Latvio Latvia.
latvo Latvian, Lett.
latvuja Latvian.
latvujano Latvian.
Latvujo Latvia.
laudinda praiseworthy.
laŭ according as, according to, as, by, along, in accordance with. **laŭ alia maniere** in another way. **laŭ bova rapideco** ploddingly, at ox speed. **laŭ ĉiuj informoj** by all accounts. **laŭ ĉiuj scigoj** by all accounts. **laŭ deziro** at choice, at pleasure, at will. **laŭ diversaj manieroj** in different ways. **laŭ insisto de** at the instance of. **laŭ la cirkonstancoj** in the circumstances, under the circumstances. **laŭ la fluado** with the current. **laŭ la karto** à la carte. **laŭ la kunteksto** from context. **laŭ la leĝo** by law. **laŭ la ŝajno** according to appearance(s). **laŭ li mem** by his own account. **laŭ mi...** as far as I'm concerned. **laŭ mi scio** as far as I know. **laŭ mia opinio** in my opinion. **laŭ mia sperto** in my experience. **laŭ nia dirmaniero** as we say. **laŭ niaj ebloj** to be best of our abilities. **laŭ onidiroj** it is understood that, it is rumoured that. **laŭ ordono de iu** at someone's order(s). **laŭ peto de iu** at someone's request. **laŭ rekomendo de** on the recommendation of. **laŭ sia bontrovo** as one sees fit. **laŭ sia eblo** to be best of

laŭa

one's ability. **laŭ sia ekstero** by its appearance. **laŭ sia kapablo** to be best of one's ability. **laŭ tiu vidpunkto...** according to that point of view. **laŭ via diro** according to you. **laŭ via opinio** in your opinion. **laŭ via propra diro** as you yourself have said. **laŭ vico** in rotation.
laŭa similar, like; transverse, cross-.
laŭalfabeta alphabetic.
laŭbaŭe abeam.
laŭbaŭen abeam.
laŭbezona personalized.
laŭbezone as needed, where needed, as need be.
laŭbita operacio bitwise operation.
laŭbo arbor, bower, summerhouse, booth, shady retreat.
laŭbone as well.
laŭcela adequate.
laŭcele deliberately, intentionally, on purpose.
laŭceleco functionality.
laŭcifera komplemento radix-minus-one complement.
laŭda praiseful.
laŭdado ovation.
laŭdano laudanum.
laŭdanto eulogist, encomiast.
laŭde glowingly.
laŭdebla laudable.
laŭdegi to eulogize, exalt, extol.
laŭdegisto panegyrist.
laŭdego eulogy, laudation.
laŭdeve obediently.
laŭdi to acclaim, commend, laud, praise. **laŭdi sin** to brag, boast.
laŭdifine by definition.
laŭdinda commendable, praiseworthy, laudable.
laŭdira alleged, so-called.
laŭdire allegedly, as is being said, by all accounts.
laŭdo commendation, praise.
laŭe accordingly, in the same way, similarly.
laŭebla as much as possible, as far as possible.
laŭeble if possible, as much as possible, when possible. **laŭeble simple** as simply as possible.
laŭfaktora integralado integration by parts.
laŭfame by hearsay.
laŭfari to do the same as, imitate.
laŭflua downstream.
laŭflue downstream.
laŭforme in form.
laŭgrada gradual, transverse.
laŭgrade gradually, little by little.
laŭgrupe by groups, in groups.
laŭigi to adapt, bring into line.

laŭsupozeble

laŭiri to travel.
laŭkanona canonical.
laŭkanone canonically.
laŭkape by headcount.
laŭkontrakta contractual.
laŭkronike chronologically.
laŭkutima conventional.
laŭkutime customarily, as is the custom.
laŭlarĝa transverse.
laŭlarĝe across, crossways. **laŭlarĝe de** across.
laŭlegenda legendary.
laŭleĝa legal, legitimate. **laŭleĝa filo** legitimate son.
laŭleĝe legally.
laŭleĝeco legality.
laŭlime along the border, edge, shore.
laŭliniigi to line up, align.
laŭlitere literally, to the letter.
laŭlonge lengthwise, in length. **laŭlonge de** along (the length of).
laŭlongiri to travel along something.
laŭmendigi to customize.
laŭmendigo customization.
laŭmezura to measure.
laŭmoda fashionable.
laŭnature naturally, according to nature.
laŭnecese as needed, when necessary.
laŭnome named, by name, namely.
laŭnominala at par.
laŭnormigi to calibrate.
laŭofice officially.
laŭordone as ordered.
laŭplaĉe as desired, as one pleases, as one wishes.
laŭplaĉigi to customize.
laŭplaĉigo customization.
laŭpove as one is able, as possible, to the best of one's ability.
laŭrajta rightful.
laŭraporte according to reports.
laŭrdire alleged, according to what people say.
laŭreato laureate, winner.
laŭregula due.
laŭregule duly.
laŭrekta programado unwound programming.
Laŭrenco Lawrence.
laŭrencio lawrencium.
laŭro bay tree, laurel.
laŭrofolio bay leaf.
laŭsage like an arrow.
laŭsezona seasonal.
laŭsignifie in meaning.
laŭsistema systematic.
laŭso louse.
laŭstatuta statutory.
laŭsupozeble as expected.

**laŭŝajne according to appearances, as it appears.
laŭta** aloud, loud.
laŭtage per day.
laŭte aloud, loudly.
laŭteco loudness.
laŭtege very loudly.
laŭteksta textual.
laŭtema pertinent, relevant.
laŭteme by subject, by topic.
laŭtemeco relevance.
laŭtiĝi to become loud.
laŭtlegi to read aloud.
laŭtparolilkesto box.
laŭtparolilo loudspeaker.
laŭtvoĉe aloud, in a loud voice.
laŭvalora ad valorem.
laŭvalore ad valorem.
laŭvica sequential. **laŭvica atingo** sequential access, serial access.
laŭvice in order, in rotation, in turn.
laŭvide according to appearance, as far as can be seen, by sight. **laŭvide koni** to know by sight.
laŭvile at will.
laŭvola free, freestyle, optional, voluntary.
laŭvole as one pleases, as you wish, at will.
laŭvorta literal, word-for-word. **laŭvorta tradukado** literal translation.
laŭvorte verbatim, word-for-word. **laŭvorte traduki** to translate literally.
lavabo hand-basin, sink.
lavado ablution, cleaning, laundering, washing.
lavaĵpinĉilo clothes peg, clothespin.
Lavalo The Valley.
lavangbarilo avalanche wall.
lavangi to avalanche.
lavango avalanche.
lavatero tree mallow.
lavaŭtomatejo laundromat.
lavaŭtomato washing machine.
lavbluo bluing.
Lavdo The Lothian.
lavejo laundry, lavatory, washroom.
lavendo lavender.
laveti to rinse.
lavi to wash. **lavi la manĝilaron** wash up. **lavi sin** to wash one's self.
laviĝi to be washed.
lavistino laundress, washerwoman.
lavkuvo washing-up bowl.
lavmaŝino washing machine.
lavo the act of washing.
lavoĉambro lavatory, washroom.
lavpelvo wash-basin.
lavpulvoro detergent, soap powder.
lavpurigebla washable.
lavpurigi la manĝilaron to wash up, do the dishes.
lavsodo washing soda.
lavtablo washstand.
lavtuko washcloth.
lavurso raccoon, washing-bear.
lazanjo lasagna.
lazareto quarantine station, military hospital.
lazi to lasso.
lazo lasso.
lazura sky blue, azure. **Lazura Bordo** Riviera, French Riviera.
lazurito azurite.
lazuro azure, sky blue.
lazurŝtono azurite.
LDA acid, LSD.
Lebanono Lebanon.
lebega Lebesgue. **lebega integralo** Lebesgue integral. **lebega mezuro** Lebesgue measure.
Lebego Lebesgue.
leciono lesson.
lecitino lecithin.
Leĉestro Leicester.
leda leather.
ledaĵoj leather goods.
Ledao Leda.
ledo leather.
ledosako wine skin.
ledplando sole (of boot, etc).
ledpretigisto currier.
ledrimeno thong.
ledtubo hose.
lefta left, left-hand.
lefte on the left, left.
legacio legation.
legadi to peruse.
legado perusal, reading.
legaĵaro lectionary.
legaĵo reading matter.
legantaro readership, readers.
legante reading (while reading).
leganto reader.
legato legate.
legebla legible.
legemulo avid reader.
legenda legendary.
legendaro lore.
legendo legend, myth.
legendulo legend.
legi to read.
legiano legionary.
legilo reader.
leginda readable, worth reading.
legio legion.
legisto lawyer.
legitimaĵo ID, pass.
legitimi to legitimize, prove identity.
legitimilo ID, identification.

legolibro reader (book for reading).
legoma ĝardeno kitchen garden, vegetable garden.
legomĝardenisto kitchen gardener.
legomĝardeno vegetable garden.
legomisto greengrocer.
legomo vegetable.
legomvendisto greengrocer.
legoscia literate.
legoscio literacy.
legosigno bookmark.
legpupitro lectern.
legscio ability to read, reading ability.
legumeno legume, pod.
legumino legumin.
leĝa lawful, legal, valid.
leĝaro code, laws, statutes.
leĝdona legislative.
leĝdoni to legislate.
leĝe legally.
leĝeco legality.
leĝera light(weight).
leĝeranima light-hearted.
leĝere lightly.
leĝfarajo act.
leĝfaranto legislator.
leĝfaristo lawmaker, legislative.
leĝiganta legislative.
leĝigi to give laws to, legalize.
leĝigo enactment.
leĝisto lawyer.
leĝo law, principle. **leĝo pri ofertado kaj mendado** law of supply and demand.
leĝodona potenco legislative power.
leĝofara legislative.
leĝoforta by force of law.
leĝoforte by force of law.
leĝoscienco jurisprudence, law, legal science.
lejdena kondensoro Leyden jar.
Lejdeno Leyden.
lekanteto (English) daisy.
lekanto daisy, marguerite.
lekcii to lecture.
lekciisto lecturer.
lekcikotizo lecture fee.
lekcio lecture.
leki to lick, lap.
leksemo lexeme.
leksika lexical. **leksika analizilo** lexical analyser, scanner. **leksika analizo** lexical analysis, scan.
leksiko vocabulary.
leksikografia lexicographic. **leksikografia ordigo** lexicographic sort. **leksikografia ordo** lexicographic order.
leksikografiisto lexicographer.
leksikografo lexicographer.
leksikologia lexical.
leksikologio lexicology.

leksikono lexicon.
lektoro lector, lecturer, instructor.
lekumi to lap.
lemingo lemming.
lemniskato lemniscate.
lemno (ivy, star) duckweed.
lemo lemma.
lempiro lempira.
lemuria Lemurian.
lemuriano Lemurian.
lemuro lemur.
Leningrado Leningrad.
Leno Lena.
lenso lens.
lento lentil.
lentuga freckled.
lentugo freckle.
Leominstro Leominster.
leona lion, of a lion, lion's.
leonfaŭko snapdragon.
leonido cub (of lion).
leonino lioness.
leono lion. **Leono** Leo (zodiac).
leontodo dandelion.
leontopodo edelweiss.
leopardo leopard.
lepismo silverfish.
leporfela rabbit skin.
leporhundo greyhound, harehound, harrier (dog).
leporo hare, rabbit.
Leporo Lepus.
lepra leprous.
leprekano leprechaun, clurichaun.
lepro leprosy.
leprulo leper.
lepto mite (coin).
leptono lepton.
lerna scholastic.
lernado apprenticeship, learning.
lernanto apprentice, scholar, pupil.
lernebla learnable.
lernega profound, learned.
lerneja school, of a school, school's. **lerneja knabino** schoolgirl. **lernejaj ferioj** school holidays.
lernejanino schoolgirl.
lernejano pupil, scholar.
lernejestrino headmistress.
lernejestro headmaster, head of a school.
lernejinstruisto schoolmaster.
lernejo school.
lernema studious.
lernenda has to be learned.
lerni to learn. **lerni parkere** to memorize, learn by heart.
lernigi to teach.
lernilo tutorial.
lernita acquired, learnt.

lerniteco learning, scholarship.
lernjaroj apprenticeship.
lernojarano former.
lernojaro form.
lernojaroj apprenticeship.
lernoknabo apprentice.
lernolibro manual, textbook.
lernoservi to work as an apprentice.
lerta able, adroit, clever, dexterous, skilful, expert, talented, handy.
lertaĵo trick, (act of) cleverness, skill.
lerte cleverly. **lerte eviti** to elude.
lerteco ability, adroitness, cleverness, dexterity, expertness, skill, skilfulness, ingenuity, knack.
lertega consummate, sophisticated.
lertego excellence.
lertigi to make exercises, master.
lertiĝi to become skilled.
lertulo adept.
Lerviko Lerwick.
lesba Lesbian.
lesbanina lesbian.
lesbanino lesbian.
lesbo lesbian.
lesivakvo lather.
lesivejo laundry.
lesivi to wash. **lesivi vestojn** wash clothes.
lesivistino laundress.
lesivo lye.
lesivomaŝino washing-machine.
lesivpulvoro washing powder.
Lesoto Lesotho.
leŝmanio leishmania.
leŝmaniozo kala-azar.
letala fatally.
letargio apathy, drowsiness, inertness, lethargy, stupor, torpidity.
letera epistolary.
leterbloko notepad.
letere by letter.
letereto note, letter.
leterfino letter ending.
leteristo letter carrier, postman.
leterkesto letterbox, mailbox.
leterkolombo carrier pigeon, messenger pigeon.
letero epistle, letter, missive.
leterpapero writing paper.
leterpesilo letter balance.
leterportisto postman.
letersekreto confidentiality of the mail.
letertranĉilo paper-knife.
leterujo letter case.
leterumi to spell.
Leto Lethe.
letona Latvian, Lettish.
letono Latvian, Lett.
leŭcisko dace.

leŭgo league (unit of distance).
leŭkemio leukaemia.
leŭkocito leukocyte, white blood cell, white blood corpuscle.
leŭkojo snowflake.
leŭkomo leucoma.
leŭkoreo leucorrhoea.
leŭso loess.
leŭtenanto lieutenant.
levanta Levantine.
levantano Levantine.
Levanto Levant.
levi to lever, lift, raise. **levi sin** to arise.
levido Levite.
leviero joystick.
leviĝi to arise, ascend, get up, go up, lift, rise, arise.
leviĝo rise.
levilbrako lever arm.
levilo crowbar, lever.
levitacio levitation.
levjatano leviathan.
levkojo gilliflower, wallflower.
levo elevation, erection, uplift, rising, improvement, increase, ascension, raise, exaltation, state, lift.
levrelo greyhound.
levstango crowbar, lever.
levulozo fructose, laevulose.
lezi to harm, hurt, injure.
lezo harm.
Lhasao Lhasa.
li he. **li atendu** let him wait. **li faras mienon ke li laboras** he acts (or pretends) to be working. **li faras mienon kvazaŭ li laboras** he acts (or pretends) to be working.
lia his.
liakoste at his expense.
lialingve in his language.
lialoke in his place.
liano bind-weed, liana, tropical climbing vine.
liaso blue limestone, lias.
Liaso Lias.
libana Lebanese.
libanano Lebanese.
Libano Lebanon.
libelo dragonfly.
libera exempt, free, unrestrained, spare, unchecked. **libera interŝanĝado** free trade. **libera merkato** free market. **libera programaro** free software. **libera variablo** free variable.
liberala liberal.
liberaligi to liberalize.
liberaligo liberalization.
liberaliĝo liberalization.
liberalismo liberalism.
liberbatalanto freedom fighter.

liberdonaco bonus.
libere freely.
libereco freedom, liberty.
liberege very freely.
liberia Liberian.
liberianino Liberian woman.
liberiano Liberian.
liberiga liberating, liberatory.
liberiganto rescuer.
liberigi to release, set free, liberate, disengage, disentangle, emancipate. **liberigi de respondeco** to acquit. **liberigi iun kaŭcie** to release someone on bond, on bail. **liberigi sin de** to get rid of.
liberigo liberation.
liberigota to be freed, released (in the future).
liberiĝi to become free, get free.
Liberio Liberia.
libero freedom, liberty.
liberpensulo free thinker.
libertempa recreational.
libertempi to spend one's free time.
libertempo free time, holiday, leisure, spare time, time off, vacation, leave (time).
libertempulo holidaymaker.
libertino freethinker, libertine.
liberulo free man, free person.
libervola voluntary, of one's own will.
libervole voluntarily.
libervolulo volunteer.
libia Libyan.
libianino Lybian woman.
libiano Libyan.
libido libido, sex drive.
Libio Libya.
libraj scioj book-learning, book-knowledge.
librapogilo book-end.
libraro book collection (private library).
librejo library.
libreto booklet, libretto.
libristo bookseller.
libro book.
libroamanto bibliophile.
libroapogilo book-end.
librobindado bookbinding.
librobindejo bookbindery.
librobindisto bookbinder.
librobretaro bookcase.
librobreto bookshelf.
librobutiko bookshop, bookstore.
librokovrilo cover.
librolerno book learning.
librolisto reading list.
libromagazeno book storage area.
libromanio bibliomania.
libromaniulo bookworm.
libromarko bookmark.
libromeblo bookshelf.
librosako schoolbag.
libroservo book service.
librostako book stack.
libroŝatanto bibliophile, book lover, bookworm.
libroŝranko bookcase.
librotenado accounting, bookkeeping.
librotenanto bookkeeper, accountant.
librotenejo book storage area, bookkeeping, accountancy.
libroteni to keep account.
librotenisto bookkeeper.
librotitolo book title.
librovendado bookselling.
librovendejo bookshop, bookstore.
librovendisto bookseller.
librujo schoolbag.
librulo book louse, bookworm.
lica licit.
liceano pupil, student.
licencato licentiate.
licenci to authorize, license.
licenciato licentiate.
licencio licence (academic title in some countries).
licenciulo licentiate.
licenco licence.
licencplato number plate, licence plate.
licentiato licentiate, university degree.
liceo grammar school, high school, secondary school, lyceum.
lici to be permitted, be allowed.
licia Lycian.
licianino Lycian woman.
liciano Lycian.
licio boxthorn.
Licio Lycia.
liĉiarbo lychee.
liĉio lychee.
liĉiujo lychee.
lidia Lydian.
lidiano Lydian.
Lidio Lydia.
Lieĝo Liège.
lieno milt, spleen.
Liero Lyra.
lifto elevator, lift.
liftoŝakto elevator shaft.
ligaĵo braid, fillet, string, tie.
ligamento ligament.
ligano leaguer.
ligatoro linkage editor.
ligaturo ligature.
ligenzo binder, binding agent.
ligfermi to ligature, tie, tie up.
ligi to bind, connect, join, tie, tie up.
ligiĝi to be attached, link up.
ligillisto linked list.

ligilo

ligilo band, strap, bond, tie, leash, tether, linker, link (WWW).
ligita bound, tied up. **ligita variablo** bound variable.
ligna wooden. **ligna najlo** spile. **ligna ŝuo** sabot. **ligna tegaĵo** camp-shedding, camp-sheeting, camp-shot.
lignaĵisto carpenter, cabinet-maker, joiner.
lignaĵo timber.
lignanajlo peg, hook.
lignejo woodhouse.
lignero splinter.
lignito brown coal, lignite.
ligno timber, wood. **ligno martelo** gavel.
lignobloko block of wood.
lignogarni to board, wainscot.
lignoglavo wooden sword.
lignogravuraĵo wood-cut.
lignokarbigi to make into charcoal.
lignokarbo charcoal.
lignolaboristo wood worker.
lignonajlo hobnail, hob, stud, brad, clout-nail, peg.
lignopeco log.
lignoskarabo wood-boring beetle.
lignosplito (wooden) splinter.
lignotelero trencher.
lignotubero knot (in wood).
ligo connection, league. **Ligo de Nacioj** League of Nations.
ligotubero noose.
ligpakaĵo bundle.
ligtubero knot.
ligulo ligule.
ligura Ligurian. **Ligura Maro** Ligurian Sea.
liguro Ligurian.
Ligurujo Liguria.
ligustro ligustrum, privet.
ligverbo copula, link verb.
liĥtenstejnano Liechtensteiner.
liĥtenŝtejnano Liechtensteiner.
Liĥtenŝtejno Liechtenstein.
likantropa lycanthropic.
likantropio lycanthropy.
likantropiulo lycanthrope.
likeno lichen.
liki to leak.
likimuna watertight.
liknido ragged robin.
liko leak.
likoperdo puff-ball.
likopodio clubmoss.
likopodioplantoj club-mosses.
likopso bugloss.
likva liquid. **likva petrolgaso** liquefied petroleum gas, LPG.
likvaĵo liquid.
likvakristala ekrano liquid crystal display, LCD.

limnomo

likvida liquid.
likvidanto liquidator.
likvidi to liquidate.
likvidiĝi to disband.
likvido liquidation.
likvigi to liquefy.
likvigilo blender.
likvo liquid.
likvoro liqueur.
lila lilac, lavender.
lilako lilac.
liliblanka lily-white.
lilio lily.
liliputa diminutive, Lilliputian, tiny, dwarf.
Lilito Lilith.
lilo lily.
Lilongvo Lilongwe.
lima bounding.
limakedoj slugs.
limaki to go at a snail's pace.
limako slug, snail.
limando dab.
limao lima.
limbo limb.
Limburgo Limburg.
limdato deadline.
limdifini to mark out, trace, trace out.
limedo lime, sweet lime.
Limeriko Limerick.
limesinfimo inferior limit, lower limit.
limeso limit.
limesosupremo superior limit, upper limit.
limeto lime, sweet lime.
limetujo lime-tree.
limfa lymphatic.
limfatismo lymphatism.
limfo lymph.
limfocito lymphocyte.
limfoida lymphoid.
limhava finite, limited.
limhaveco finiteness.
limhoro deadline.
limi to be a boundary of, bound.
limiga restrictive.
limige restrictively.
limigi to abridge, confine, limit, restrict, circumscribe.
limigita confined, limited, restricted.
limigo limitation, restriction.
limiĝi to be bounded by, be limited to.
limiĝo limit, limitation.
limimposta customs.
limimpostisto customs officer.
limimposto duty.
limito limit.
limlando borderland.
limlinio borderline.
limnomo bound identifier.

limo boundary, frontier, limit. **limo suba** infimum. **limo supra** supremum.
limokazo borderline case.
limonado lemonade.
limonelo sour lime.
limonito limonite.
limono lemon.
limozo godwit.
limsigno landmark.
limŝtono border marker, border stone, boundary marker, boundary stone.
limtempo deadline, time limit.
limtuŝanta adjacent, adjoining.
limtuŝi to abut, adjoin, be next to.
limurbo border town.
limuzino limousine.
linaĝo linen.
linaĵo linen.
linario toadflax.
linĉado lynching.
linĉi to lynch.
linda charming, lovely, pretty.
linde prettily.
lineadaptilo line adapter.
lineara linear. **lineara algebro** linear algebra. **lineara gramatiko** linear grammar. **lineara kombinaĵo** linear combination. **lineara ordo** linear order. **lineara programado** linear programming.
lineare linearly. **lineare dependa** linearly dependent. **lineare nedependa** linearly independent. **lineare sendependa** linearly independent.
lineo line (of communication).
lingva linguistic. **Lingva Komitato** Linguistic Committee.
lingvaĵo language, wording.
lingvano speaker.
lingve linguistically.
lingvistika linguistic.
lingvistike linguistically.
lingvistiko linguistics.
lingvisto linguist.
lingvo language, tongue.
lingvobarilo language barrier.
lingvofamilio language family.
lingvohelpanto language helper.
lingvoiteracio iteration.
lingvokapablo fluency.
lingvolaboratorio language lab.
lingvonivelo language level.
lingvoscienco linguistics.
linia linear. **linia listo** linear list.
liniaro staff, stave.
liniavanco line feed.
linifaldo line wrap, word wrap.
linifinilo end-of-line marker, line separator, newline.
linifino end of line.

linii to line.
liniigi to align.
liniilo ruler, straight-edge.
linimento liniment.
linio curve, line.
linipaŝo baseline skip.
liniprintilo line printer.
linko lynx.
Linkolno Lincoln.
lino flax.
linolea tolo linoleum.
linoleo linseed oil.
linoleumo linoleum.
linotipo linotype.
lintelo lintel.
Linukso Linux.
Lio Lee.
Liono Lyons.
lipdenta labio-dental.
liphararo moustache.
lipharoj moustache.
lipido lipid.
lipmieni to pout.
lipo lip.
lipresino lypressin.
lirforma lyrate.
lirika lyrical.
lirikeco lyricism.
lirikisto lyric poet.
liriko lyric, lyric poetry, lyrical poem.
lirismo lyricism.
lirli to burble, gurgle, murmur, purl.
liro[1] lyre. **Liro** Lyra.
liro[2] lira.
Lisbono Lisbon.
Lisburno Lisburn.
Lismoro Lismore.
lisolo lysol.
lispi to lisp.
listelo fillet.
listero twayblade.
listigi to list, make a list.
listo list.
listrosaŭro lystrosaurus.
lita superkovrilo bedspread, counterpane, coverlet.
litaĵo bed linens, bedding.
litanio litany.
litargiro litharge.
litbarilo bumper (in a bed, crib).
litbenko bunk.
litcimo bedbug.
lite in bed.
litera alphabetic.
literalo literal.
literatoro littérateur.
literatura literary.
literaturisto litterateur (person).
literaturo literature.

litercifera

litercifera alphanumeric.
literi to spell.
litero letter (alphabet). **literoj de Esperanto** Esperanto letters. **literoj grekaj** Greek letters.
litertipo type, typeface.
literumi to spell (a word).
literumilo spell-checker.
literumo spelling.
liteto cot.
litframo bed frame.
litino lithia.
litio lithium.
litkadro bed, bedstead.
litkapo headboard.
litkovrilo blanket, quilt.
litkuseno pillow.
litlaŭso bedbug.
litmalsana bedridden, confined to one's bed, laid up.
lito bed, couch.
litofino footboard.
litografarto lithography.
litografi to lithograph.
litografio lithography.
litografisto lithographer.
litorino winkle, periwinkle.
litorno fieldfare.
litospermo gromwell.
litoto understatement.
litotuko sheet.
litova Lithuanian.
litovino Lithuanian woman.
Litovio Lithuania.
litovo Lithuanian.
Litovujo Lithuania.
litpisado bed-wetting, enuresis.
litro litre.
litrumo loosestrife, lythrum.
litsako sleeping-bag.
litŝranko cupboard-bed.
litto lytta.
littuko sheet (bed).
liturgia liturgical.
liturgio liturgy.
liturinado bed-wetting, enuresis.
liturinanto bedwetter.
litvagono sleeping car.
liuto lute.
liva left.
livemigo left alignment, left justify.
livera servo parcels delivery, parcels service.
liverado delivery, purveying.
liveraĵo consignment.
liveranto purveyor, supplier.
liveraŭto delivery van.
liveraŭtomobilo delivery van.
liveri to deliver, furnish, supply.
liveristo delivery person.

logogrifo

livero delivery, uniform.
Liverpulo Liverpool.
livertipo result type.
livio rock dove.
livona Livonian.
Livonio Livonia.
livono Livonian.
Livonujo Livonia.
Livorno Leghorn.
livreo livery.
livro pound (sterling).
lizino lysine.
lizoklino lysocline.
lizosoma lysosomal.
lizosomo lysosome.
lizostafino lysostaphin.
L.K. → **Lingva Komitato**.
LKK → **Loka Kongresa Komitato**.
lo name of the letter L.
Loaso Lewis.
lobelio lobelia.
lobiado lobbying.
lobianto lobbyist.
lobii to lobby.
lobio lobby.
lobo lobe.
lobulario alyssum.
lodiklo lodicule.
lodo lot.
Lodzo Łódź.
loeso loess.
lofflanka windward.
lofflanko windward.
lofi to luff.
lofio angler.
Lofotoj Lofoten Islands.
logado enticement, inducement.
logaĵo attraction, bait.
logaritma logarithmic. **logaritma derivaĵo** logarithmic derivative. **logaritma spiralo** logarithmic spiral.
logaritmo logarithm.
logi to allure, entice, attract, decoy, lure, coax.
logika logical. **logika cirkvito** logic circuit. **logika elemento** gate, logic element. **logika operacio** logical operation. **logika ŝovo** logical shift.
logike logically.
logikeca programado device-independent mode.
logiko logic.
logilo bait.
logistiko mathematical logic.
Loglano Loglan.
loglibro logbook.
lognutraĵo bait.
logo[1] allurement, bait, enticement.
logo[2] log.
logogrifo logogriph, riddle.

logotipo

logotipo logo, logotype.
loĝadejo abode.
loĝado habitation.
loĝanta housed.
loĝantardenseco density of population.
loĝantaro population.
loĝantejo boarding house.
loĝanto dweller, inhabitant, inmate, resident, occupant.
loĝatigi to populate.
loĝaŭto camper, motor home.
loĝdomo apartment building.
loĝebla habitable, inhabitable.
loĝeja residential.
loĝejo abode, accommodation, dwelling, residence, domicile, dwelling, habitation, lodgings.
loĝi to dwell, live, inhabit, reside. **loĝi en luitaj ĉambroj** to live in lodgings.
loĝigejo housing.
loĝigi to accommodate, give a home to, house, install.
loĝigo accommodation.
loĝiĝi to settle.
loĝio box (opera), lodge (freemason, etc.).
loĝistika logistical.
loĝistiko logistics.
loĝkajuto living quarters.
loĝlando country of residence.
loĝloko abode, dwelling place, residence.
loĝoĉambro living room, sitting room.
loĝrifuĝejo dormitory.
Lohalino Lochaline.
Loĥbosdalo Lochboisdale.
Loĥgilphedo Lochgilphead.
Loĥgojlhedo Lochgoilhead.
Loĥinvero Lochinver.
Loĥkarono Lochcarron.
Loĥmado Lochmaddy.
lojala faithful, loyal.
lojale loyally, staunchly.
lojaleco adherence, loyalty.
lojalulo loyalist, stalwart.
lojto burbot, eel pout.
Lojbano Lojban.
loka local. **loka anestezilo** local anaesthetic. **loka disponaĵo** local device. **loka ekstremumo** local extremum. **Loka Kongresa Komitato** Local (Congress) Organizing Committee. **loka metodo** local method. **loka objekto** local object. **loka reto** local area (computer) network, LAN. **loka variablo** local variable.
lokado relocation.
lokadverbo local adverb.
lokaĵaro locale.
lokaĵo locale category.
lokalizi to confine, localize, locate.
lokalizilo locator.

longatempe

lokalo premises, location.
lokaro geometric locus.
lokativo locative.
lokaŭto (industrial) lockout.
loke locally.
loki to locate, place.
lokiĝi to be placed, be positioned.
Lokio Loki.
lokkazo locative case.
loknombro arity, adicity.
loknomo place name.
loko locality, location, place, spot.
lokomobilo traction engine.
lokomotivestro engineer.
lokomotivo engine, locomotive.
loksidiĝi to remain in a place.
loksio crossbill.
loksodromio rhumb line, loxodrome, rhumb-line.
lokucio expression, phrase.
lokumi to place, put (someone in a location). **lokumi bebon en infanvartejon** to put a child in daycare.
lokuso locus.
lokusto grasshopper, locust.
loligo squid.
lolio rye-grass.
lolito lolita.
lolo rye grass.
lombarda Lombard, Lombardic.
lombardejo pawnshop.
lombardi to borrow money on, pawn, hock.
Lombardio Lombardy.
lombardisto pawnbroker.
lombardo credit against pledge of chattels, pawning.
lombardoj Lombards.
Lombardujo Lombardy.
lomo loam.
Lomondo Loch Lomond.
Londo London.
Londona London, of London. **Londona Akciborso** London Stock Exchange, LSE, Lombard Street. **londona biblio** London Bible.
Londonano Londoner.
Londone in London.
Londono London.
Lonforto Longford.
longa long. **longa fingro** middle finger.
longaĵo length, section (of something).
longanarbo Longan tree, euphoria longana.
longano longan.
longanujo Longan tree, euphoria longana.
longaspace for a long way, distance.
longatempa long, of long standing, prolonged, protracted.
longatempe long time, long while.

longbarbulo bearded man, man with a beard.
longboato longboat.
longdaŭra long (of time), long-duration, long-time, long-lasting, enduring.
longdistance by long distance.
longdormulo late sleeper.
longe a long time, for a long time, long.
longeco length.
longedaŭra long-lasting, enduring, protracted.
longedaŭre perennially.
longega very long, lengthy.
longeluda disko LP (record).
longetempa long, of long standing, prolonged, protracted.
longetempe at great length, for a long time.
longforma oblong.
longigi to lengthen.
longigita prolate. **longigita cikloido** prolate cycloid. **longigita epicikloido** prolate epicycloid. **longigita hipocikloido** prolate hypocycloid.
longigkablo extension cord.
longiĝi to lengthen.
longitudo longitude.
longo length, longitude.
longoforma elongated, oblong.
longtempa long (of time), long-duration, long-time.
longtempe for a long time.
longtrafa artilerio long-range artillery.
lonicero honeysuckle.
lontana remote, distant.
lopi to loop the loop.
lorantacoj mistletoe.
lordo lord.
Lorelejo Lorelei.
Loreno Lorraine, Lothringen.
loriso loris.
lorneto opera glass.
lorno binoculars, field glasses, spyglass.
lotado drawing (lots).
lotaĵo allotment, lot.
loteca random. **loteca variablo** random variable, variate.
loterio lottery, raffle.
loti to cast lots, draw lots.
lotumi to allot, apportion.
lotuso lotus.
Loveno Louvain.
loza loose.
lozanĝo lozenge, rhombus.
luado rental, renting.
luanto lodger, renter, tenant.
lubrikaĵo lubricant.
lubriki to lubricate.
lubrikilo oilcan.
lubriko lubrication.

lucerno hanging lamp in church.
lucida lucid.
lucide lucidly.
lucideco lucidity.
Lucifero Lucifer.
luĉambrano boarder.
ludadi to fiddle.
ludado enactment, playing.
ludantaro playgroup.
ludanto player.
ludbobeno yo-yo.
ludĉambro playroom.
ludegi to romp.
ludejo playground.
ludema playful.
ludeti to play about.
ludi to play, enact, perform. **ludi globetojn** to play marbles. **ludi la rolon de** to act as. **ludi nenian rolon** to play no role. **ludi per kanonpulvo** to play with gunpowder. **ludi sur** to play on. **ludi ŝakon** to play chess.
ludilaro toys.
ludilkesto toy chest.
ludilo plaything, toy.
ludiltrajno toy train.
ludkarto playing card.
ludkradejo playpen.
ludkuboj dice.
ludloto raffle.
Ludlovo Ludlow.
ludmarko counter (token).
ludo game (play).
ludomo apartment building.
ludoni to lease, let, rent.
Ludoviko Ludwig.
ludspektaklo game show.
ludtempo playtime, recreation.
ludtintilo rattle.
ludvaro gameware.
luebla for rent. **luebla domo** house to let.
lufo Chinese okra, luffa.
lugro lugger.
lugrovelo lugsail.
luĝi to luge.
luĝo luge.
lui to hire, rent.
luidoro Louis d'or.
luiganto lessor.
luigi to hire, let, rent, rent out.
luigita hired out.
luita hired. **luita domo** hired house, rented house.
luiziana Louisianan.
luizianano Louisianan.
lukano stag beetle.
luko porthole, skylight.
lukontrakto lease.
lukra lucrative.

lukrado accrual.
lukranto breadwinner.
lukri to make money, earn.
lukriĝi to accrue.
luksa deluxe, luxurious, sumptuous.
luksacio dislocation.
luksaĵo luxury.
lukseco luxury.
luksema gaudy.
luksemburgano Luxembourger.
luksemburgia Luxembourg, Luxemburg.
luksemburgiano Luxembourger.
Luksemburgio Luxembourg, Luxemburg.
Luksemburgo Luxembourg, Luxemburg.
luksnutraĵvendotablo deli counter.
lukso luxury.
Luksoro Luxor.
luktado wrestling.
luktejo arena.
lukti to struggle, wrestle.
lukto struggle, tussle.
lukumo Turkish delight.
lulado rocking.
luleti to dandle.
luli to cradle, rock, sooth, lull.
lulilo cradle.
lulkanto lullaby.
lulseĝo rocking chair.
luma bright, light, luminous.
lumba lumbar.
lumbaĵo fillet, loin.
lumbildo slide, transparency.
lumbo haunch, loin, small of the back, loin.
lumboj loins.
lumbriko earthworm.
lumdiodo light emitting diode, LED.
lumdiskego compact disc, optical disc, CD, DVD.
lumdiskingo CD-ROM drive.
lumdisko optical disc.
lumeco light.
lumecreguligilo dimmer.
lumego large light.
lum-eliganta diodo light emitting diode, LED.
lumeno lumen.
lumetadi to glimmer, shimmer.
lumetado glimmer, shimmer, shimmering.
lumeti to gleam.
lumeto gleam, glimmer.
lumfibro optical fibre.
lumfonto light source.
lumĝeni to dazzle.
lumhoro light-hour.
lumi to light, light up, shine.
lumiga luminous.
lumigi to illuminate, light.
lumigilo luminary.
lumigo lighting.
lumiĝi to become (grow) light.
lumilo luminary.
lumineska luminescent.
lumineski to luminesce.
luminesko luminescence.
lumjaro light year.
lumĵetilo spotlight.
lummarkilo light pen.
lumminuto light minute.
lumo light.
lumoserĉanto searchlight.
lumplumo light pen.
lumpulsi to blink.
lumrapido velocity of light.
lumredukti to dim.
lumsekundo light second.
lumserĉanto searchlight.
lumŝaltilo light switch.
lumŝanceli to flicker.
lumŝirmilo lampshade, shade, screen.
lumtago light day.
lumtubo fluorescent lamp.
lumturo beacon, lighthouse.
lumvermo firefly.
luna lunar. **luna kalendaro** lunar calendar.
lunario lunaria, money plant.
lunatika lunatic.
lunatikeco lunacy.
lunatiko lunatic, sleepwalker.
lunatikulo lunatic.
lunbrilo moonlight.
lunĉkamiono lunch truck.
lunĉo lunch, snack.
lunde on Mondays.
Lundo Monday.
lundo Monday.
lundomateno Monday morning.
lunfazo moon phase.
lunjaro lunar year.
lunkalendaro lunar calendar.
lunlume by the light of the moon.
lunlumo moonlight.
luno moon.
lunsurfaco lunar surface, surface of the moon.
lunŝtono adularia.
luo hire, rent, rental.
lupago rent.
lupanaro bordello, brothel.
lupeo magnifying glass.
luphomo werewolf.
lupido brownie, cub scout.
lupinino lupinine.
lupino lupine, she-wolf.
lupo wolf.
lupolejo hop-field.
lupolisto hop grower.
lupolkampo hop-field.
lupolkulturisto hop grower.

lupolo hop, hops.
lupreni to rent.
luprezo rent, rent money.
lupuso lupus.
Lurgo Lairg.
Lusako Lusaka.
lusoldato mercenary soldier, soldier of fortune.
luspezo rent cost.
lustro chandelier, lustre (lamp).
lutajô solder.
lutecio lutetium.
luteolo weld.
luterana Lutheran.
luteranismo Lutheranism.
luterano Lutheran.
Lutero Luther.
luti to solder.
lutilo soldering iron.
luto solder.
lutreolo mink.
lutro otter.
luvi to beat (up against the wind), tack (about).
luzerno alfalfa, lucerne.

M

MA → **Membro-Abonanto**.
maato mate (ship).
macedona Macedonian.
Macedonio Macedonia.
macedono Macedonian.
Macedonujo Macedonia.
maceri to macerate.
maco matzo, unleavened bread.
maĉado mastication.
maĉeto machete.
maĉgumo chewing gum.
maĉi to chew, masticate, munch.
maĉo match.
madagaskara Madagascan.
madagaskarano Madagascan.
Madagaskaro Madagascar.
Madejro Madeira.
madjaro Magyar.
Madono Madonna.
Madrido Madrid.
madrigalo madrigal.
madura Madurese.
mafia mafia.
mafio mafia.
Mag. → **Magistro**.
magarino margarine.
magazenego department store.
magazeno big store, department store, warehouse.
magazino magazine.
Magdalenio Magdalenian.
Magdaleno Magdalena.
mageneta magnetic.
magenetigi to magnetize.
magia magical. **magia lanterno** magic lantern.
magiisto magician.
magio magic.
magistrata domo town hall.
magistratano alderman.
magistrato city council, town council, magistrate.
magistro master, master's degree.
magmo magma.
magnato magnate.
magneta magnetic. **magneta disko** magnetic disk. **magneta kontokarto** magnetic ledger card.
magnetbendmemorilo magnet tape storage.
magnetbendregilo magnetic tape controller.
magnetcilindra memorilo magnetic drum storage.
magnetdiska memorilo magnetic disk storage.
magnete magnetically.
magneti to magnetize.
magnetigi to magnetize.
magnetismo magnetism.
magnetito magnetite.
magnetizi to magnetize.
magnetkapo magnetic head.
magnetkarta aŭtomato magnetic ledger card reader/encoder.
magnetkarta memorilo magnetic card storage.
magneto loadstone, magnet.
magnetofono tape deck, tape player, tape recorder, stereo (system).
magnetoskopo video recorder.
magnetstrio magnetic strip.
magnettavola memorilo fixed-head memory.
magnezio magnesium.
magnezito magnesite.
magnezo magnesia, magnesium oxide.
magnolio magnolia.
mago magus.
Magogo Magog.
magra gaunt, lean, meagre, skimpy, skinny, thin.
magreco meagerness.
maĝango mah-jongg.
mahagono mahogany.
mahalebo mahaleb, mahaleb cherry.
maharaĝo maharajah.
mahatmo mahatma.
mahometana Islamic. **mahometana terorismo** Islamic terrorism.
mahometanismo Islam.
mahometano Mohammedan, Moslem, Muslim.
Mahometo Muhammad, Mohammed, Mahomet.
maĥinacio machination.
maĥo Mach (aerospace).
maizfloko cornflake.
maizflokoj corn flakes.
maizkrakeno taco.
maizo (Indian) corn, maize.
maizospadiko cob.
maizpano cornbread.
maizviskio bourbon whiskey.
majaa Maya, Mayan.
majantemo may lily.
majao Maya.
majesta majestic.
majeste majestically.

majesteco majesty.
majesto majesty.
majfloro lily-of-the-valley.
majnano Mainer.
Majno Maine.
Majo May.
majo May.
majoliko majolica.
majonezo mayonnaise.
majorano marjoram.
majoratbieno entailed estate.
majorato birthright, primogeniture.
majoritato majority.
Majorko Majorca, Mallorca.
majoro major (rank).
majskarabo may-bug.
majstra masterful.
majstraĵo masterpiece, masterwork.
majstrata magisterial.
majstre masterfully.
majstreco mastership.
majstri to master.
majstro adept, maestro, master, maestro.
majstroverko masterpiece, masterwork.
majuscule uppercase.
majuskla capital, uppercase.
majuskligo capitalization.
majusklo capital (upper case) letter.
maĵora major.
Makabeoj Maccabees.
makabra macabre.
makadami to macadamize.
makadaminukso Bauple nut, macadamia nut, popple nut, Queensland nut.
makadamio macadamia, macadamia tree.
makadamo macadam.
makako macaque.
Makao Macau.
Makaronezio Macaronesia.
makaronio macaroni.
makarono macaroon.
Makaŭo Macao.
makedona Macedonian.
Makedonio Macedonia.
makedono Macedonian.
Makedonujo (Republic of) Macedonia.
makiavela Machiavellian.
makiavelismo Machiavellianism.
Makiavelo Machiavelli.
Makintoŝo Macintosh.
makiso maquis.
makisumume to the maximum.
makleraĵo brokerage, commission.
makleri to act as a middleman, act as broker, broker.
makleristo broker, commission agent.
maklero broker, brokerage, commission.
Makmuro MacMurray.
makro macro.

makroa generado macro expansion, macro generation.
makrobiotika macrobiotic.
makrobiotiko macrobiotic.
makrocefaledoj sperm whale.
makrocefalo cachalot, sperm whale.
makroekonomia macroeconomic.
makroekonomiko macroeconomics.
makroklavo key sequence, macro, programmed key.
makrokodo macroassembler.
makrokomando macro command, macro instruction.
makroo macro.
makroodifino macro declaration, macro definition.
makroogenerilo macro generator, macro processor.
makropedoj kangaroos.
makropo kangaroo, macropus.
makroskopa macroscopic.
maksimo maxim, principle.
maksimuma maximal, maximum.
maksimume at most.
maksimumiganto point of maximum.
maksimumigi to maximize.
maksimumigo maximizing.
maksimumo maximum.
Makso Max.
Maksvelo Maxwell.
makulaturo scrap paper.
makulaturtraktado garbage collection.
makuleca patchy.
makuleto speck, spot.
makulhara multi-coloured.
makuli to soil, spot, stain.
makulita blotchy.
makulo blemish, blot, spot, stain.
makzela maxillary.
makzelo jaw, jawbone.
makzelosto jawbone.
mal- (prefix used to form word of opposite meaning).
mala contrary, opposite, converse. **mala okazo** complementary event.
malaboni to unsubscribe.
malabunda in short supply, scanty, scarce.
malabunde scantily.
malabundeco scarcity.
malabundo shortage.
malacida sweet.
malaerobia anaerobic.
malafabla blunt, brutal, gruff, harsh, rough, sour, surly, unkind, unpleasant, rude.
malafable bluntly, unkindly.
malafableco peevishness.
malafablega grim.
malafrodizio (sexual) frigidity.
Malagasio Madagascar.

malagnoski to disavow.
malagrabla bleak, dismal, dreary, horrible, ghastly, grisly, nasty, unpleasant. **malagrabla laboreto** bad job.
malagrablaĵo bad job.
malagrafi to unclamp.
malaja Malay.
malajala Malayalam.
Malajgo Mallaig.
malajo Malay.
Malajujo Malaysia.
malajzia Malaysian.
malajziano Malaysian.
Malajzio Malaysia.
malakceli to decelerate, slow down, abate, lag, relax, slacken.
malakcelo skid.
malakcepti to reject. **malakcepti voĉdone** to reject by voice vote.
malakcepto rejection.
malakito malachite.
Malako Malacca.
malakordo discord (music).
malakra dull, blunt, obtuse.
malakrigi to blunt.
malaktiva passive.
malaktivigi to deactivate.
malaktuala out-of-date, dated.
malakuta obtuse.
malalta low (not high). **malalta lernejo** grammar school, primary school. **malalta tajdo** low tide.
malalte low, below.
malaltega prezo fire sale price, rock-bottom price.
malaltgermana Low German.
malaltigi to abase, decrease, lower. **malaltigi la prezojn de** to mark down the prices of.
malaltigo abasement, decrease, lowering.
malaltiĝi to sink.
malaltmaro low tide.
malalto low.
malaltreliefo bas-relief, low relief.
malaltvalora inferior.
malamata accursed, hated.
malambigua unambiguous.
malameco grudge, rancour.
malamegi to abhor, loathe.
malamego abhorrence.
malameti to dislike.
malami to detest, hate.
malamika adverse, hostile.
malamikeco animosity, enmity.
malamikema antisocial.
malamikiĝi to become enemies.
malamiko adversary, enemy, foe.
malaminda hateful, nasty, odious.
malamo hate, hatred, spite.

Malamsemjano Hate Week.
malamuza boring.
malamuzi to bore.
malamuzo boredom.
malankri to weigh anchor.
malankriĝi to weigh anchor.
malankrumi to weigh anchor.
malantaŭ behind, after, posterior.
malantaŭa after, back, later, rear. **malantaŭa akso** back axle, hind axle, rear axle. **malantaŭa benko** back seat, rear seat. **malantaŭa elirejo** rear exit. **malantaŭa ferdeko** after-deck. **malantaŭa flanko** back, reverse, reverse side. **malantaŭa glaco** rear window. **malantaŭa kovrilo** back cover. **malantaŭa lampo** rear-lamp, rear-light, taillight. **malantaŭa parto** back, rear. **malantaŭa plano** background. **malantaŭa platformo** rear platform. **malantaŭa pordo** back door. **malantaŭa rado** back wheel, hind wheel, rear wheel.
malantaŭaĵo rear, stern.
malantaŭe behind, in arrears.
malantaŭen backwards.
malantaŭenigi to back up, reverse, move back, draw back.
malantaŭgusto aftertaste.
malantaŭiĝi to fall behind.
malantaŭiri to trail.
malantaŭkorto backyard.
malantaŭo back, behind, rear, stern.
malantaŭplano background.
malaperantaj bestoj endangered species.
malaperi to disappear.
malaperigi to liquidate.
malaperigo annihilation.
malaperinda unwanted.
malaperinta having disappeared.
malaperinto disappeared person.
malapero disappearance.
malapostrofo back quote.
malaprobegi to do down, slash, slate.
malaprobi to condemn, disapprove, disapprove of, rebuke.
malaprobinda blameworthy, censurable, condemnable, objectionable.
malaprobo censure, condemnation, disapprobation, disapproval.
malapud far (from), not near.
malaranĝi to put into disarray, disarrange.
malario malaria.
malarmado disarmament.
malarmi to disarm.
malarmiĝo disarmament.
malasidua truant, absent.
malatenta negligent.
malatenteco inadvertence.
malatentema inattentive, lax.

malatenti

malatenti to neglect, overlook.
malatentiga distracting.
malatentigi to distract.
malatentigo distraction.
malatento negligence.
malaŭo anti-alternative.
malavanco backtracking.
malavantaĝa adverse, detrimental, disadvantageous, prejudicial.
malavantaĝe detrimentally, disadvantageously, prejudicially.
malavantaĝigi to disadvantage.
malavantaĝo disadvantage.
malavara bountiful, generous, liberal, munificent.
malavare generously, unstintingly.
malavareco generosity, munificence.
malavari to be generous with something.
malavia Malawian.
malaviano Malawian.
Malavilago Lake Malawi.
Malavio Malawi, Nyasaland.
malbagatela significant.
malbari to unbar.
malbela nasty, ugly, plain.
malbelaĵo eyesore, monstrosity, ugly thing, ugliness.
malbeleco ugliness.
malbelega dismal, dreary, horrible, nasty, hideous, repulsive.
malbelforma deformed.
malbeli to be ugly.
malbeligi to deface, mutilate.
malbeligo mutilation.
malbeliĝi to grow ugly.
malbelo ugliness.
malbelulino hag.
malbelulo ugly person, unattractive person.
malbena accursed.
malbenegi to execrate.
malbeni to curse.
malbenita accursed.
malbenite! damn!
malbeno malediction, curse.
malblindigi to open somebody's eyes.
malbloki to clear.
malbobenado unrolling, unwinding.
malbobeni to unroll, unwind, wind off.
malbona bad, miserable, nasty, poor, naughty, evil, wicked. **malbona digestado** indigestion. **malbona traktado** abuse.
malbonaĝo bad thing.
malbonaĵo abuse.
malbonaŭgura of ill omen.
malbone badly, ill.
malboneco wickedness, iniquity, mischief.
malbonega villainous, terrible.
malbonege very badly.

malcedema

malbonego atrocity.
malbonema mischievous.
malboneta mediocre.
malbonfama ill-famed.
malbonfamigi to defame.
malbonfamo infamy.
malbonfarado evil doing.
malbonfaraĵo trick.
malbonfaranto evildoer, malefactor, wrongdoer.
malbonfari to harm, do evil or harm to.
malbonfaro misdeed, outrage.
malbonfarta unwell.
malbonfartanta not well, unwell.
malbonfarto disease, illness, sickness; disorder, condition.
malbonformigi to deform, mar.
malbongusta bad-tasting; in bad taste.
malbonherbo weed.
malbonhumora cross, peevish, pettish, petulant.
malboniga virulent.
malbonigi to botch, spoil.
malboniĝi to go bad, spoil.
malboniĝo corruption, decay, depravation, taint, worsening.
malbonintence with malice aforethought.
malbonkonduta badly behaved.
malbonkonduti to misbehave, misconduct.
malbonkvalita inferior.
malbonmora immoral, licentious, obscene.
malbonmoreco immorality.
malbonnovaĵo (piece of) bad news.
malbono ill.
malbonodora fetid.
malbonodoreco smelliness.
malbonodori to stink.
malbonodoro stench.
malbonokazo misfortune.
malbonorda messy.
malbonskribi to scribble.
malbonsona bad sounding.
malbonsoneco cacophony.
malbonsorte unhappily.
malbonŝanca unlucky, unfortunate.
malbonŝance unfortunately.
malbonŝanco bad luck.
malbonulo miscreant, ruffian, wretch.
malbonuzi to misuse.
malbonvola unwilling.
malbonvolaonta reluctant.
malbonvole unwillingly.
malbonvolo malevolence.
malbrila dull (unpolished).
malbrile dully.
malbuki to unfasten.
malcedado confrontation.
malcedema inexorable, intransigent, obdurate, relentless, uncompromising.

malcedeme inexorably, relentlessly, uncompromisingly, unyieldingly.
malcedemigi to harden.
malcedemiĝi to harden.
malcedemo relentlessness.
malcedemulo hardliner.
malcedi to confront.
malcentralizi to decentralize.
malcentralizo decentralization.
malcerta uncertain.
malĉarma unattractive.
malĉasta lewd, obscene, ribald.
malĉaste lewdly.
malĉasteco licentiousness.
malĉastejo house of ill-repute, brothel.
malĉasti to commit sexual improprieties.
malĉastigi to assault.
malĉastigo assault.
malĉastulino slut, trollop.
malĉastulo libertine, rake, profligate.
malĉifri to decrypt, decode.
maldankema ungrateful.
maldaŭra fleeting.
maldaŭrigi to interrupt.
maldaŭrigo interruption.
maldeca indecent, scurrilous.
maldece indecently.
maldeco indecency.
maldekstra left. **maldekstra flanko** left, left side. **maldekstra klaso** left coset.
maldekstraflanke on the left, to the left.
maldekstrano leftist.
maldekstre on the left.
maldekstren left, to the left.
maldekstrula leftist, left-wing.
maldekstrulo left-hander.
maldekstruma negatively oriented (basis).
maldekstrume counterclockwise.
maldelikata boorish, coarse, crude, harsh, gross, vulgar. **maldelikata ceratofilo** common hornwort, rigid hornwort.
maldelikataĵo vulgarity.
maldelikateco vulgarity.
maldelikatulo crude person, vulgar person.
maldensa airy, sparse. **maldensa tabelo** sparse matrix.
maldense thinly.
maldensejo clearing (in a forest), glade.
maldensigi to thin out.
malderivaĵo indefinite integral, primitive, anti-derivative.
maldetala general, vague.
maldiafana opaque.
maldika gaunt, lean, slender, thin, lank. **maldika intesto** small intestine. **maldika muro** partition wall.
maldikbeka mevo slender-billed gull.
maldikega emaciated.
maldikigi to taper.

maldikiĝi to become thin.
maldikuleto skinny little person.
maldiligenta lazy.
maldiligente lazily.
maldiligenteco laziness.
maldiligenti to idle, slack.
maldiligento laziness.
maldiligentulo lazy person.
maldilui to concentrate.
maldiskreta continuous, indiscreet, meddlesome. **maldiskreta topologio** indiscrete topology, trivial topology.
maldiskreteco meddlesomeness.
maldiskretemo indiscretion.
maldiskreti to do something indiscreet.
maldiskreto meddlesomeness.
maldisponebla unavailable.
maldisponebleco unavailability.
maldistingi to addle, baffle, bemuse, bewilder, confuse, disarrange, disarray, perplex, puzzle.
Maldivoj (Republic of) Maldives.
maldolĉa acerbic, bitter, harsh, rough.
maldolĉe bitterly.
maldolĉeco acerbity, bitterness.
maldolĉigi to make bitter.
maldorma awake.
maldormeco wakefulness.
maldormemo insomnia.
maldormi to be awake, stay awake.
maldormigi to cause someone to sleep badly, disturb someone's sleep.
maldormo vigil, wake.
maldubema unquestioning.
maldunga severance. **maldunga aranĝo** redundancy pay, redundancy scheme, severance scheme.
maldungi to discharge, dismiss, fire, lay off.
maldungiĝo unemployment.
maldungo firing, discharge, dismissal, layoff.
male (on the) contrary, conversely, vice versa. **male al** contrary to, opposite of, opposed to, unlike.
malebena bumpy, rugged, rough.
malebenaĵo bump.
malebla impossible.
maleblaĵo impossibility.
malebleco impossibility.
malebligi to bar, inhibit, prevent, hinder, make impossible.
malebligo denial.
malebria sober.
malebriiĝi to sober up.
malebriiĝo sobering up.
malediva Maldivian.
maledivano Maldivian.
Maledivoj Maldive Islands, Maldives.
maledukita ill-bred.

malegala different.
malegaleco disparity, inequality.
malegoismo altruism.
malegoisto altruist.
malekvilibrigi to destabilize, unbalance.
malekvilibro unbalance.
maleleganta coarse, crude.
malelegata coarse.
malelokventa inarticulate.
malema averse.
malembarasi to rid.
malemi to be reluctant or disinclined to do something.
maleminentulo nobody.
malemo aversion.
malen astern.
malenui to be amused.
malenuigi to amuse, distract, divert, entertain.
malenuo amusement.
maleo mallet.
maleolo ankle, anklebone.
malepilkado polo.
malerekti to be flaccid.
malerektiĝi to become flaccid.
malesekiĝi to become wet.
malesotera exoteric.
malespera desperate.
malespere despairingly.
malespereco hopelessness.
malesperi to despair, despond.
malesperigi to dash the hopes.
malespero despair.
malesta absent.
malesti to not exist.
malestima contemptible.
malestimanto detractor.
malestime contemptuously, disdainfully.
malestimeco abjection.
malestimi to despise, underrate, disdain, disrespect, hold in contempt.
malestimigo derogation.
malestiminda abject.
malestiminde despicably.
malestimindeco abjection, abjectness.
malestimo contempt, scorn.
malesto non-existence.
maleŝarko hammerhead, hammerhead shark.
malfacila difficult, hard, inconvenient, troublesome. **malfacila spirado** asthma.
malfacilaĵo difficulty, trouble.
malfacile hardly, not easily, with difficulty.
malfacileco difficulty.
malfacilega challenging, daunting.
malfacili to be difficult.
malfaciligi to hamper, hinder, thwart.
malfaciliĝi to become difficult.
malfajneco crudeness, roughness.

malfaldi to spread out, unfold, unfurl, unroll.
malfalsa authentic, genuine.
malfama infamous.
malfamo infamy.
malfari to undo.
malfaro undoing.
malfavora unfavourable.
malfavore unfavourably.
malfavoreco adversity.
malfavori to look askance at.
malfavoro disfavor.
malfaza out of phase, phase-delayed.
malfekunda barren, infertile.
malfekundeco infertility.
malfeliĉa hapless, unfortunate, unhappy.
  malfeliĉa je amo unlucky in love.
malfeliĉaĵo misfortune, unhappy event.
malfeliĉe unfortunately.
malfeliĉeco infelicity, unhappiness.
malfeliĉego disaster.
malfeliĉiga miserable.
malfeliĉigi to make someone sad, sadden.
malfeliĉo accident, mischance, misfortune, mishap.
malfeliĉulino sad person (female).
malfeliĉulo unfortunate.
malferli to unfurl.
malferma open. **malferma parolado** opening speech.
malfermaĵo aperture, interior.
malferme openly.
malfermeco openness.
malfermegi to throw open. **malfermegi la buŝon** to open one's mouth wide.
malfermeti to open a little.
malfermetita ajar.
malfermi to open (up), unbar. **malfermi dosieron** open a file.
malfermiĝi to open (itself), become open.
malfermiĝi svinge to swing open.
malfermilo opener.
malfermita open. **malfermita proceduro** inline subroutine.
malfermo opening.
malfervora cold, cool, indifferent.
malfervore coldly.
malfervoro coldness, coolness.
malfesta sombre.
malfeste sombrely.
malfestiga sobering.
malfevore indifferently.
malfida suspicious.
malfidela disloyal, unfaithful.
malfidelaĵo act of disloyalty.
malfideleco infidelity.
malfideliĝi to apostatize, desert, secede.
malfideliĝo apostasy, defection.
malfidelo disloyalty.
malfidelulo deserter, renegade.

malfidema

malfidema distrustful, suspicious.
malfidi to distrust, suspect.
malfido distrust, mistrust, suspicion.
malfiera humble.
malfieriĝi to back down, climb down.
malfiero humility.
malfiksi to detach, unfasten.
malfinia infinite.
malfinidimensia infinite-dimensional.
malfinio infinity.
malfirma unstable, loose.
malfirme loosely.
malflosi to sink.
malflua ebb.
malfluemo viscosity.
malfluidiĝi to solidify.
malfluido solid.
malfluo ebb, low tide.
malfoldi to unfold.
malfono foreground.
malfora ĉenero weak link (in a chain).
malforprenebla irremovable.
malforta faint, light, weak, feeble, infirm, frail. **malforta topologio** weak topology.
malfortaĵo weakness.
malforte lightly, weakly. **malforte konverĝa** weakly convergent.
malforteco debility, feebleness, infirmity, weakness.
malfortiga enervating.
malfortigi to weaken. **malfortigi iom** tone down.
malfortiĝi to abate, weaken, languish.
malfortiĝo abatement.
malfortika languid, puny.
malfortike feebly.
malfortikeco fragility, frailty.
malfortikulo weakling.
malforto weakness, lack of strength.
malfortulo weakling, weak person.
malfortuna unfortunate.
malfreŝa musty, stale.
malfreŝaera airless, close, frowsy, stuffy.
malfreŝiĝi to age.
malfrivola staid.
malfrostiĝi to thaw (out).
malfrua late, tardy, slow.
malfrue late.
malfrueco lateness.
malfrui to be late, dally, tarry, be slow.
malfruigi to delay.
malfruiĝi to get, become late.
malfruiĝo delay, retardation.
malfrumatene late in the morning.
malfrunokte late at night.
malfruo delay.
malfruposttagmeze late in the afternoon.
malfunkciĝi to break down, not work.

malgrandega

malfunkciigi to shut off, stop, switch off, turn off.
malfunkciigo disabling.
malfunkciiĝi to malfunction.
malfunkcio downtime, outage.
malfuŝebla foolproof.
malgaja bleak, dismal, dreary, gaunt, miserable, sad, sombre.
malgaje sadly, drearily.
malgajeco grief, sadness, sorrow, moroseness.
malgajhumora fretful, morose, peevish, sullen, surly.
malgaji to be sad, be unhappy.
malgajiga miserable.
malgajigi to sadden, make unhappy.
malgajiĝi to become sad.
malgajnaĵo loss.
malgajni to lose (a game).
malgajninto loser.
malgajno loss.
malgajo gloom (sadness).
malglata coarse, rough, uneven, unpolished (surface).
malglataĵo bump, hump.
malglateco roughness.
malglatigi to roughen.
malglatiĝi to become rough, become uneven.
malglora notorious, infamous.
malgloro opprobrium, infamy.
malgluiĝi to become unglued.
malgracia awkward, clumsy.
malgracieco awkwardness.
malgracio awkwardness.
malgraciulo nerd.
malgranda diminutive, little, small, puny. **Malgranda Azio** Asia Minor. **malgranda buntpego** lesser spotted woodpecker. **malgranda ĉimpanzo** dwarf chimpanzee. **malgranda duonakso** semi-minor axis. **malgranda emberizo** little bunting. **malgranda kriaglo** lesser spotted eagle. **malgranda lemno** common duckweed, lesser duckweed. **malgranda litero** small letter. **malgranda otido** little bustard. **Malgranda Ursino** Little Bear, Little Dipper, Ursa Minor. **Malgrandaj Antiloj** Lesser Antilles.
malgrandaeta diminutive.
malgrandampleksa tight, cramped, confined.
malgrandanima mean (paltry).
malgrandanimeco pettiness, small-mindedness.
Malgrand-Azio Asia Minor.
malgrandeca smallish.
malgrandeco littleness, smallness.
malgrandega minute, tiny.

malgrandegulo dwarf.
malgrandeta tiny.
malgrandigi to restrict.
malgrandigo decrease, diminishment, diminution.
malgrandiĝi to decrease, decline, wane, dwindle.
malgrandiĝo decline, decrease, diminishment, diminution.
malgrandioza squalid.
malgrandmama small-breasted.
Malgrandpolujo Lesser Poland, Little Poland.
malgrandspaca tight, cramped, confined.
malgrandulo small person.
malgrasa gaunt, thin, lean.
malgrasega emaciated.
malgrasiĝi to grow lean, waste, grow thin.
malgrasulo thin, sickly person.
malgraŭ despite, in spite of, notwithstanding. **malgraŭ ke** in spite of the fact that, notwithstanding the fact that. **malgraŭ tio** nevertheless. **malgraŭ tio ke** despite the fact that.
malgraŭe nevertheless.
malgrava unimportant.
malgravajo trifle, unimportant thing.
malgravuleto whippersnapper.
malĝentila discourteous, gruff, impolite, rude, uncivil, uncouth, unruly.
malĝentilajo vulgarity.
malĝentile impolitely, rudely.
malĝentileco rudeness, vulgarity.
malĝentilega as bold as brass, incredibly insolent, shameless.
malĝentilulo rude person.
malĝoja dismal, gaunt, miserable, sad.
malĝojaeta sorry.
malĝoje sadly.
malĝojeco dejection, sadness.
malĝojego great sadness, depression.
malĝojeta tiny unhappiness.
malĝoji to be grieved, be sad, be sorrowful, grieve, mourn.
malĝojiga dismal, miserable.
malĝojigi to afflict, cause pain, cause pain to, distress, give pain to, sadden.
malĝojiĝi to mope.
malĝojo grief, sadness, sorrow, tribulation.
malĝusta incorrect, wrong, inexact.
malĝustajo wrong.
malĝuste incorrectly.
malĝusteco error.
malhardi to annealing (metallurgy).
malharmonia ajar, discordant.
malharmonio discord, disunity.
malhavebla unavailable.
malhavebleco unavailability.
malhavi to lack, be wanting, lack, miss.

malhavigo denial.
malhela bleak, dark, dismal, dreary, dusky, obscure, sombre, murky, dull. **malhela materio** dark matter. **malhelaj okuloj** dark eyes.
malhelblua dark blue.
malhele darkly, bleakly, obscurely. **malhele blua** dark blue.
malheleco dimness, gloom, obscurity.
malhelige in the dark(ness).
malheligi to tarnish.
malheligo tarnish.
malheliĝi to darken.
malhelo darkness.
malhelpa detrimental, unhelpful.
malhelpajo handicap, impediment, obstacle, hitch.
malhelpema obstructive.
malhelpi to bar, hinder, inhibit, prevent, conflict with, counteract, deter, frustrate, detain, hamper, thwart, impede.
malhelpilo obstruction, obstacle, hindrance.
malhelpo hindrance, retardation, impedance.
malhelruĝa beet-red, claret.
malhisi to lower (a flag). **malhisi la flagon** to lower the flag, retrieve the colours.
malhonesta crooked, dishonest, nasty, unfair, unprincipled.
malhonesteco dishonesty.
malhonesto deceit, dishonesty.
malhonora dishonourable. **malhonora kolono** pillory.
malhonorajo indignity.
malhonore disgracefully, dishonourably, shamefully.
malhonoreco stigma.
malhonori to disgrace, dishonour, stigmatize.
malhonorigi to dishonour.
malhonoro dishonour.
malhumana inhumane, inhuman.
malhumila arrogant, haughty, proud.
malhumileco pride.
malhumilo hubris.
malhundema having an aversion to dogs.
mali to curse.
malia Malian.
malianino Malian woman.
malica malevolent, malicious, mischievous, nasty, vicious, wanton, spiteful.
malicaĵo nastiness, malicious act.
malice maliciously. **malice ruza** shrewd.
maliceco malice.
malicema malignant.
maliceta ill-natured.
malico craft, craftiness, cunning, guile.
maliculo malicious person, trouble-maker, rascal.
maligna vicious.

malimpliki to untie, take apart.
malimpliko extraction.
malinda undignified, unworthy.
malindulga adamant.
malinfekti to disinfect.
malinflacio deflation.
malingi to draw.
malinhibicio abandon.
malinklina averse, disinclined.
malinkliniga repugnant, repulsive.
malinklino aversion, reluctance, repugnance.
malinsisti to relent.
malinstali to uninstall.
malinstalilo uninstaller.
malinstiga discouraging, inhibiting.
malinstigi to dissuade.
malinstigilo disincentive.
malinstigo deterrent, discouragement.
malinteligenta obtuse.
malintenci to overlook.
malinteresa boring.
malinterese uninterestingly.
malinteresi to be boring, be uninteresting, bore.
malintereso boredom.
malintima distant.
malintimema aloof.
Malio Mali.
maljesi to say no.
maljuna aged, old.
maljunaĝo age, old age.
maljuneco old age.
maljungi to unharness, unyoke.
maljunigi to make old, age.
maljuniĝanta ageing.
maljuniĝi to age, grow old. **maljuniĝi je pluraj jaroj** to age by several years.
maljuniĝo ageing.
maljunula hejmo old people's home.
maljunulejo almshouse, old people's home.
maljunulino gammer, old woman.
maljunulo old person, old man.
maljusta unjust.
maljustaĵo injustice.
maljuste unjustly.
maljusteco iniquity, injustice.
maljusto injustice.
malkajo NAND function.
malkapabla disabled.
malkapabligi to disqualify.
malkapablo disability.
malkara cheap, inexpensive.
malkare cheaply.
malkaŝa above-board.
malkaŝe frankly, openly, publicly. **malkaŝe fumi** to smoke in public. **malkaŝe, mi kredas ke...** frankly, I think...

malkaŝeco explicitness, frankness, openness, transparency.
malkaŝema above-board, communicative, free, outspoken.
malkaŝeme freely.
malkaŝemeco openness.
malkaŝemo candour, outspokenness.
malkaŝi to disclose, reveal, unfold.
malkaŝiĝi to come to light.
malkaŝinto revealer.
malkateni to free, unshackle, release, unfetter, unchain.
malkava spherical.
malkaveta convex.
malkiel unlike.
Malkintiro Mull of Kintyre.
malklara cloudy (not clear), indistinct, overcast.
malklaraĵo ambiguity.
malklare unclearly, opaquely, dimly.
malklareco dimness, turbidity.
malklaresprima inarticulate.
malklarigi to muddle (of liquors).
malklariĝi to blur, fade.
malklera dull, stupid, ignorant, illiterate, uncultured, uneducated, simple.
malklereco lack of education.
malklerulo dunce.
malkodaĵo decrypt.
malkodi to decode.
malkodigi to decode.
malkodilo decoder.
malkohera inarticulate.
malkoloniigo decolonization.
malkombi to dishevel, tousle.
malkombini to break up.
malkombiniĝi to break up.
malkomenti to uncomment.
malkomforta uncomfortable.
malkomforto discomfort.
malkompakta loose, sandy.
malkompatema hard, harsh, implacable, pitiless, hard-hearted, merciless, ruthless, uncompassionate, unfeeling.
malkompateme harshly.
malkomponaĵo decomposition.
malkomponebla decomposable.
malkomponi to decompound, resolve, dissect.
malkomponilo parser.
malkompreni to misapprehend, misunderstand.
malkompreno misapprehension.
malkomprenoeco misconception.
malkoncentri to disperse, dilute, rarefy, thin.
malkonciza long-winded, wordy.
malkoncizeco prolixity.

malkondamni to absolve, acquit, find not guilty.
malkondamno pardon, absolution.
malkondensi to uncompress.
malkonekti to cut, cut a connection.
malkonektiĝi to disconnect.
malkonfesi to disavow, disclaim, recant, renounce, retract, abjure, disown, deny.
malkonfeso abjuration, denial, disavowal, recantation, refusal.
malkonfirmi to contest, deny, refute.
malkonfuza clear (mental).
malkongrui to disagree.
malkonkorda discordant.
malkonkordo disagreement, discord, dissension.
malkonsekvenca inconsistent.
malkonsenti to deny, disagree, dissent, refuse.
malkonsento disagreement, discord, dissension.
malkonsentulo dissenter, dissident.
malkonservi to uncache.
malkonsili to advise against, dissuade from.
malkonstruado demolition.
malkonstrui to break down, demolish, pull down, take down.
malkonstruigebla destructible.
malkonstruilo destructor.
malkonstruo demolition.
malkontenta discontented, displeased, dissatisfied.
malkontenteco discontent, discontentedness, displeasure, dissatisfaction.
malkontentiga displeasing.
malkontentigi to disappoint.
malkontentigo disappointment.
malkontentiĝi to become disaffected.
malkontentulo malcontent.
malkonulo stranger.
malkonvena not fitting, unseemly, unbecoming.
malkonvene inappropriately.
malkonveni to disagree.
malkonvergi to diverge, pervert.
malkonverĝa divergent.
malkonverĝi to diverge.
malkonverto perversion.
malkorekta incorrect.
malkorektaĵo error.
malkorki to uncork.
malkorpulenta emaciated, scrawny, skinny.
malkovranima open-hearted.
malkovri to discover, uncover, lay open, unburden, reveal, tell.
malkovro discovery.
malkredeco unbelief.
malkredi to disbelieve.
malkreditigi to discredit.

malkredulo unbeliever.
malkreska falling, descending. **malkreska diftongo** falling diphthong. **malkreska ordigo** descending sort. **malkreska ordo** descending order.
malkreskado attrition.
malkreskanta decreasing (mapping). **malkreskanta luno** waning moon.
malkreski to abate, decrease, diminish.
malkresko abatement, decrease, diminution, wane.
malkroĉi to unhook.
malkuna separate.
malkune separately.
malkunigi to separate.
malkuniĝi to separate, part.
malkunvoki to dissolve.
malkupli to uncouple.
malkuraĝa afraid.
malkuraĝeco cowardice.
malkuraĝi to be afraid of, fear, dread.
malkuraĝigi to dishearten, unnerve.
malkuraĝiĝi to be discouraged, become demoralized.
malkuraĝo cowardice.
malkuraĝulo coward.
malkutimiĝi to break oneself of a habit, get out of a habit, unlearn.
malkvalifiki to disqualify.
malkvalifiko disqualification.
malkvieta restless, noisy, unquiet.
malkviete restlessly, roughly, turbulently, violently.
malkvieteco agitation, alarm.
malkvietiga unsettling.
malkvietigi to discompose, ruffle, agitate.
malkvietiĝi to fret.
malkvieto concern, anxiety.
mallaboreco laziness.
mallaborema lazy, slothful.
mallaboremo sloth.
mallaboremulo sluggard.
mallaborulo sluggard.
mallaksa constipated.
mallaksigilo astringent.
mallakso constipation.
mallarĝa narrow, strait.
mallarĝaĵo bottleneck.
mallarĝanima narrow minded.
mallarĝe narrowly.
mallarĝeco narrowness.
mallarĝigi to straiten.
mallarĝigo stricture.
mallaŭda deprecatory.
mallaŭdegado tirade.
mallaŭdegi to revile, traduce.
mallaŭdema dismissive.
mallaŭdeme dismissive.

mallaŭdi to blame, dispraise, reproach, rebuke, reprove, scold, upbraid, reprimand, condemn.
mallaŭdinda blamable, blameworthy, culpable.
mallaŭdo censure, observation, remark, reproof, reprimand.
mallaŭta low, soft (not loud).
mallaŭte softly.
mallaŭteco softness.
mallaŭtigi to soften.
mallaŭtiĝi to decrease in volume.
malleĝa illegal.
mallerni to unlearn.
mallerta awkward, backward, slow, clumsy, unhandy, unskilful.
mallertaĵo blunder.
mallerte ineptly, unskilfully.
mallertulo clumsy person.
malleveti to depress.
mallevi to abate, lower, let down, subside.
mallevigi to lower (something).
malleviĝi to descend, go down.
malleviĝo descent.
mallibera captive.
mallibereco captivity.
malliberejo dungeon, jail, prison.
malliberigi to imprison, jail, lock up.
malliberigo imprisonment.
malliberiĝo captivity.
malliberulejo jail, prison.
malliberulo captive, prisoner.
malligi to disconnect, undo, unfasten, untie.
mallofi to bear away.
malloga repellent, repelling, repulsive.
mallogi to be repugnant, deter, repel.
mallogika illogical.
mallojala disloyal.
malloka global. **malloka optimigo** global optimization. **malloka reto** wide area network, WAN. **malloka variablo** global variable.
mallonga brief, short, concise, curt, succinct. **mallonga akto** brief. **mallongan tempon** a while, momentarily.
mallongdaŭra ephemeral, short-lived.
mallongeco brevity.
mallongedaŭra ephemeral, transitory.
mallongigaĵo abbreviation, abridgement.
mallongigi to abbreviate, abridge, shorten, curtail.
mallongiginto abridger.
mallongigita condensed. **mallongigita cikloido** curtate cycloid. **mallongigita epicikloido** curtate epicycloid. **mallongigita hipocikloido** curtate hypocycloid.
mallongigo abbreviation.
malluksa Spartan, frugal.
malluma dark, dim, gloomy, murky.
mallumĉambro darkroom.
mallume in the dark(ness).
mallumeco darkness, obscurity.
mallumejo darkroom.
mallumigi to darken, obscure, turn out the lights.
mallumiĝe at dusk.
mallumiĝi to dark (to become).
mallumiĝo eclipse.
mallumo darkness, murk, gloom.
malmanka abundant, affluent, ample, aplenty, copious, plentiful, profuse, rich.
malmarki to uncheck.
malmasiva hollow.
malmendi to cancel an order, countermand.
malmergi to raise.
malmergiĝi to emerge.
malmerĝiĝi to resurface.
malmilda bleak, stringent, severe, hard, harsh.
malmilitistigi to demilitarize.
malmiopa far-sighted, long-sighted.
malmobilizado demobilization.
malmobilizi to demobilize.
malmobiliziĝi to be released, demobilize.
malmobilizo demobilization.
malmodera immoderate.
malmodereco excess.
malmoderna antiquated, obsolete, old-fashioned, out-of-date.
malmodesta arrogant, conceited.
malmodeste pretentiously.
malmodesteco arrogance, high-handedness, presumption, pretence, conceit.
malmodestemo pretension, pretentiousness.
malmola hard, tough. **malmola kiel ŝtono** hard as a rock.
malmoleco hardness.
malmolega adamant.
malmoligi to harden, make hard.
malmoliĝi to become cold.
malmolnuka intransigent, mulish, stiff-necked, obstinate, stubborn.
malmorala abandoned, nasty.
malmoralaĵo vice.
malmorale abandonedly.
malmoraleco immorality, vice.
malmulta little.
malmultaj few. **malmultaj okazoj** rare occasions.
malmulte little, not much. **malmulte da** a small quantity of, little.
malmulteco scarcity.
malmultekosta cheap, inexpensive.
malmultekoste cheaply.
malmultidea of few ideas.
malmultiĝi to decline, dwindle.

malmultiĝo decline.
malmulto few, not many, not much.
malmuntebla detachable.
malmunti to dismantle, take apart.
malnaiva sophisticated.
malnegliĝa tidy.
malnegliĝeco tidiness.
malnepra parametro optional parameter.
malneta[1] draft.
malneta[2] gross. **malneta enlanda produkto** gross domestic product, GDP. **malneta nacia produkto** gross national product, GNP.
malnete roughly.
malneteco roughness.
malnetigi to draft.
malneto first draft, rough draft.
malnobelo plebeian, commoner.
malnobla abject, base, low, nasty, vile, mean, despicable, ignoble.
malnoblaĵo meanness, villainy.
malnoble vilely.
malnobleco abjection, ignominy.
malnobligi to debase.
malnobliĝo degradation.
malnoblulo knave, scoundrel.
malnodi to untie.
malnova old (not new). **Malnova Testamento** Old Testament.
malnovaĵo old thing, antique.
malnovangla Old English. **malnovangla lingvo** Old English.
Malnovbavarujo Old Bavaria.
malnoveco oldness.
malnovegipta ancient Egyptian.
malnoviĝi to age.
malnoviĝo ageing.
malnovmoda old fashioned.
malnovulo veteran.
malnutri to starve.
malnutriĝi to starve, be hungry, be malnourished.
malo opposite.
malobea disobedient, insubordinate.
malobeado defiance, flouting, insubordination.
malobee defiantly.
malobeema disobedient, insubordinate, undisciplined.
malobeeme defiantly.
malobeemo defiance, insubordination.
malobei to disobey.
malobeo disobedience, contravention.
maloblikvo backslash (\ ).
malobservi to violate, disregard.
malobservo infringement, violation.
malobstrukci to clear.
malofta infrequent, rare, seldom, unusual.
maloftaĵo rarity.

malofte infrequently, rarely, seldom, infrequently.
malofteco rareness, rarity.
malokupi to deallocate, dispose, free.
malokupiĝo disengagement.
malonlajna off-line.
maloportuna inconvenient.
maloportunaĵo flaw, inconvenience.
maloportuneco inconvenience.
maloportuni to disturb, incommode, trouble.
malorda bedraggled, chaotic, disheveled.
malordema disorderly.
malordeme unsystematically, untidily.
malordigi to derange, disarrange, unsettle, disturb, throw into disorder, upset.
malordigo disruption.
malordo confusion, disorder, mess.
malorganizi to disorganize.
malorganiziteco anomie.
maloriginala banal, trivial, commonplace.
Malovo Mallow.
malpaca factious, discordant.
malpacado wrangle.
malpacego brawl, feud.
malpaceti to squabble.
malpaci to dispute, quarrel, fall out, disagree.
malpacienca impatient.
malpacience impatiently.
malpacienco impatience.
malpacigi to set at variance.
malpaciĝi to get in a quarrel.
malpaco altercation, difference, dispute, discord, quarrel, strife.
malpacula contentious.
malpaki to unpack.
malpala dark (colour).
malpaleco swarthiness.
malpara odd (numbered).
malparalela serial.
malpardonema implacable, resentful.
malpardonemo grudge, rancour, resentment.
malparolema taciturn, quiet.
malpermanenta temporary.
malpermesa proscriptive.
malpermesi to forbid, prohibit, interdict, disallow.
malpermesita forbidden, prohibited, illicit, unlawful. **malpermesita elirtempo** curfew.
malpermesite forbidden, prohibitively.
malpermeso prohibition, veto.
malpeza light (weight). **malpeza artilerio** light artillery.
malpeze lightly.
malpezigi to lighten.
malpia godless, impious, irreligious, profane, ungodly.

malpiaĵo sacrilege.
malpie wickedly.
malpieco impiety, profanity.
malpiegaĵo desecration, profanation.
malpiulo unbeliever, infidel, heathen.
malplaĉa nasty, unpleasant.
malplaĉi to displease.
malplaĉo displeasure.
malplej fewest, least.
malpleje at least, least often, minimally.
malplekti to unbraid, take apart.
malplena empty, void, vacuous. **malplena aro** empty set.
malplenaĵo vacancy, vacuum, void, emptiness.
malplene emptily.
malpleneco emptiness.
malplenejo emptiness, empty area.
malplenigi to empty, evacuate.
malpleniĝi to become empty.
malpleno emptiness.
malplenumi to fail.
malplenumo failure.
malplezuro displeasure.
malpli fewer, less. **malpli... ol** less than. **malpli bona** worse. **malpli kaj malpli** to less and less. **malpli konata fakto estas ke** it's a little know fact that.
malplia lesser.
malplialtigi to decrease, lower.
malplialtigo abasement, abatement.
malplialtiĝi to go down.
malplialtiĝo descent.
malpliboniĝi to decline, go back, fall off.
malplifortiĝi to abate, settle.
malpligrandiĝi to become smaller.
malpligravigi to alleviate, ease, relieve.
malpligravigo alleviation, relief.
malpligraviĝi to ease.
malpligraviĝo relief.
malpliigebla abatable.
malpliigi to abate, abridge, decrease, lessen, reduce, relax.
malpliigo abatement, curtailment, retrenchment. **malpliigo de laborhoroj** reduced hours, shortening of working hours.
malpliiĝi to abate, decrease, diminish, drop, fall, shrink.
malpliiĝo abatement.
malplikariĝo decline, fall (in price).
malplilongiga abbreviatory.
malplilongigaĵo abbreviation, abridgement.
malplilongigi to abbreviate, abridge, curtail, shorten.
malplimulta minority.
malplimulto minority.
malplipeziĝi to fall away, lose, lose flesh, lose in weight.
malpliseverigo abatement.

malplisigno less-than sign (<).
malplivarmigi to cool, cool down.
malplivarmiĝi to get cold.
malplivarmiĝo cooling.
malpluirado deadlock, impasse, stalemate, standstill.
malpolurita frosted.
malprava wrong.
malprave wrongly.
malpraveco mischief, wrong.
malpravi to be wrong.
malpravigebla indefensible.
malpravigi to negate.
malpravigo negation.
malpreciza vague.
malpreferi to subordinate.
malprefero neglect, slighting.
malpremi to release.
malpremiĝo respite.
malpreteco unreadiness.
malpretendi to renounce.
malpretendo disclaimer.
malprivilegia disadvantaged.
malprofani to consecrate.
malprofite at a loss.
malprofitema disinterested.
malprofito loss, detriment.
malprofunda shallow, superficial.
malprofundaĵo bank, shoal.
malprofundejo bank, shoal.
malprogresemulo Luddite.
malprogresi to decline, recede.
malprogresigi to back up, reverse, move back, draw back.
malprokrasti to advance.
malprokrastiĝi to advance.
malproksima distant, far, remote. **Malproksima Oriento** Far East.
malproksime afar, far, far away, remotely, in the distance.
malproksimeco distance.
malproksimege in the far distance.
malproksimejo backwoods.
malproksimigi to distance.
malproksimiĝi to blow over, recede.
malproksimo distance (from).
malpromocii to degrade.
malpropra another man's, other people's.
malprospera downhill.
malprosperi to decline, recede, fail.
malprosperigi to impoverish, retard, ruin.
malprosperigo impoverishment.
malprosperiĝo impoverishment.
malprospero adversity, failure, reverse.
malprotesto acquiescence, resignation, submission.
malpruda unabashed, lewd, ribald.
malprudenta imprudent.
malprudente unadvisedly.

malprudenteco foolishness.
malprudentulo fool.
malprunto carry.
malpruvi to confute.
malpura dirty, filthy, nasty, soiled, unclean, foul, impure.
malpuraĵo dirt, filth.
malpureco dirtiness, untidiness, grime, impurity, uncleanness.
malpurega filthy, nasty, sordid.
malpuregeco squalor.
malpurigaĵo contaminant, pollutant.
malpuriganto polluter.
malpurigi to contaminate, defile, dirty, pollute, soil.
malpurigo contamination, pollution.
malpuriĝi to become dirty, get dirty.
malpuriĝo contamination.
malracia irrational.
malraciemo irrationalism, irrationality.
malrajta illegitimate, unfair, dishonest.
malrajte wrongfully, wrongly.
malrapida slow, tardy.
malrapide leisurely, slowly.
malrapideco slowness.
malrapidema sluggish.
malrapideme deliberately.
malrapidi to lose time (e.g. a watch).
malrapidigi to slow.
malrapidiĝi to slow.
malrapidiĝo slowdown.
malrapidiri to saunter.
malrapido slowness.
malrapidtrajno slow train.
malrapidvagonaro slow train.
malrava uncool.
malrefi to unreef.
malrefleksiva anti-reflexive.
malregula irregular.
malreguligo deregulation.
malrekta awry, devious, indirect, crooked.
malrekta adreso indirect address.
malrekte crookedly, deviously.
malrektiĝi to deviate, swerve.
malrektiĝo deviation.
malrelativa absolute, unconditional.
malrespekta impertinent, pert.
malrespekte disrespectful.
malrespekti to disrespect, violate.
malrespektigi to abase. **malrespektigi sin** to abase oneself.
malrespektigo abasement.
malrespekto disrespect, rudeness, violation.
malriĉa indigent, miserable, poor, needy.
malriĉeco need, poverty.
malriĉega destitute.
malriĉigi to impoverish.
malriĉigo impoverishment.
malriĉiĝi to grow poor.

malriĉularo the poor, poor people, the destitute.
malriĉulejo almshouse, almonry, workhouse.
malriĉulo pauper, poor man.
malriĉulprizorgado almonership.
malriĉulprizorgisto almoner.
malriĉulzorgisto almoner, distributor of alms.
malrigi to dismantle, unrig.
malrigida limp.
malrigide limply.
malrigidiĝi to relax.
malriverenco irreverence.
Malrozo Melrose.
malruli to unroll.
malsaĝa foolish, unwise.
malsaĝaĵo an unwise thing.
malsaĝe foolishly, unwisely.
malsaĝeco foolishness, silliness, nonsense.
malsaĝigi to trick, deceive, fool.
malsaĝo foolishness.
malsaĝulo blockhead, dolt, fool.
malsama different, dissimilar, distinct.
malsame differently, dissimilarly.
malsameco difference.
malsami to differ, disagree.
malsamkreda dissenting.
malsamopinia at variance, disagreeing.
malsamopinii to differ, disagree.
malsamopinio difference, disagreement.
malsana ill, sick, unhealthy, unwell, unwholesome.
malsane unhealthily.
malsaneca unhealthy.
malsaneco unhealthiness.
malsanejo hospital.
malsanema ailing, sickly. **malsanema infano** sickly child.
malsanemulo weakling.
malsaneta indisposed, not well, upset.
malsaneto a slight indisposition.
malsanetulo invalid.
malsani to ail, be ailing, be ill.
malsaniga causing illness, pathogenic, unhealthy, unwholesome.
malsanigi to make ill.
malsaniĝi to be taken ill, fall ill, sicken.
malsano ailment, disease, illness, malady, sickness.
malsanoego disease.
malsanulejo ambulance (place), hospital, infirmary.
malsanulino sick person (female).
malsanulistino nurse (hospital).
malsanulo invalid, sick person, patient.
malsanuloino patient.
malsanulveturilo ambulance.
malsata hungry.

malsatega famished.
malsategi to be famishing.
malsategigi to starve.
malsatego famine.
malsateta peckish.
malsati to be hungry.
malsatigi to starve, make hungry.
malsato hunger, famine.
malsatostriko hunger strike.
malsciigi to misinform.
malscio ignorance.
malseka damp, humid, wet. **malseka doko** wet dock. **malseka sezono** wet season.
malsekaĵo damp.
malsekeco damp, humidity, wetness, dampness.
malsekega soaking wet.
malsekejo bog, marsh, swamp, quagmire.
malseketa moist.
malseketaĵo moisture.
malseketigi to dampen, moisten, wet.
malseketiĝi to become damp, become moist.
malsekigi to wet.
malsekiĝi to get wet.
malsentema insensitive.
malsentimentala hard-headed.
malserena agitated, dismal, dreary, stormy.
malserenigi to disturb, ruffle, trouble.
malsereniĝi to cloud over.
malserioza frivolous.
malseriozaĵo old wives' tale.
malserioze airily.
malseriozeco levity.
malseriozo levity.
malseriozulo whippersnapper, whipster.
malservi to be detrimental to, detract from, do harm to.
malsevera lenient.
malsevere indulgently.
malsevereco clemency, leniency.
malseveriĝi to relent.
malsimetria antisymmetric, asymmetric, asymmetrical, dissymmetric. **malsimetria rilato** asymmetric relation.
malsimetrio asymmetry.
malsimila different.
malsimile dissimilarly.
malsimileco dissimilarity.
malsimpatia nasty.
malsimpatie coldly, uncongenially.
malsimpatii to antipathize.
malsimpatiigi to alienate.
malsimpatiiĝo alienation.
malsimpatio antipathy.
malsimpla complex, complicated, intricate.
　malsimpla tipo structured type.
malsimpleco complication.
malsimpligi to complicate.

malsincera underhanded.
malsindona selfish.
malsindone selfishly.
malsingardema unwary.
malsinkigebleco unsinkability.
malsobra intemperate.
malsobreco insobriety, intemperance.
malsocietema antisocial.
malsorbiĝi to exude.
malsovaĝa tame.
malsovaĝigi to tame.
malsovaĝiĝi to become tame, domesticated.
malsperteco inexperience.
malspirita clumsy, klutzy, gauche.
malspiritulo bungler, loser, klutz, milksop.
malsprita dull, stupid, slow-witted, witless.
malspriteco folly, stupidity.
malspritigi to stupefy.
malspritulo imbecile, slow-witted person, stupid person, fool, blockhead.
malstabila unstable.
malstabileco instability.
malstabiliga destabilizing.
malstabiligi to destabilize.
malstabiligo destabilization.
malstabiliĝo destabilization.
malstreĉa slack.
malstreĉe loosely.
malstreĉi to slacken (loose).
malstreĉiĝi to relax.
malstreĉiĝo relaxation, slackening.
malstreĉilo trigger.
malstreĉita loose.
malstreĉo détente, relaxing, loosening (up).
malstrikta loose.
malsubstanca insubstantial, light.
malsufiĉa scarce.
malsufiĉega scanty.
malsufiĉo scarcity.
malsukcesa abortive.
malsukcesego failure, flop.
malsukcesi to abort, fail, miscarry. **malsukcesi pro** to be foiled by, be frustrated by.
malsukcesigi to abort, quash, wreck.
malsukcesinta unsuccessful, off-the-mark, abortive.
malsukceso abortion, failure.
malsuper below.
malsupera inferior.
malsupereco inferiority.
malsupra bottom. **malsupra flanko** bottom. **malsupra najbaro** neighbour on the lower story.
malsupre below, downstairs, underneath.
malsupre de below, beneath, under.
malsupren downwards.
malsuprengliti to slide down.
malsuprengrimpi to climb down.

malsuprenigi to let down, lower.
malsupreniĝi to descend, go down.
malsuprenirejo slope.
malsupreniri to descend, get off, go down.
malsupreniro descent.
malsuprenĵeti to throw down.
malsuprenpendi to depend, hang down.
malsuprenrigardi to look down(wards).
malsuprensalti to jump off, leap down.
malsuprenstreko backslash, reverse solidus (\ ).
malsuprentiri to pull down.
malsuprenveni to come down, descend.
malsupro bottom.
malsvenigi to revive, rouse.
malŝalti to shut off, stop, switch off, turn off.
malŝanĝebla immutable.
malŝanĝeble immutably.
malŝanĝebleco immutability.
malŝargi to discharge, fire, fire off, let off, unload.
malŝargiĝi to go off.
malŝarĝi to unload.
malŝarĝo acquittal.
malŝatema fastidious.
malŝati to disdain, dislike.
malŝato disdain, dislike.
malŝirmo exposure.
malŝlosi to unlock.
malŝloso unlock.
malŝminki to take off make-up.
malŝpara lavish, prodigal.
malŝparema extravagant, wasteful.
malŝparemeco bounty.
malŝparemo prodigality.
malŝpari to dissipate, squander, waste.
malŝparita spoiled, wasted.
malŝparo dissipation, extravagance, waste.
malŝparulo spendthrift.
malŝraŭbi to unscrew.
malŝtatigi to privatize.
malŝtatigo privatization.
malŝtopi to uncork, open, unplug, unstop.
malŝtopilo plunger.
malŝuldigo remission.
malŝvela flat.
malŝveli to collapse, deflate, flatten, reduce, subside.
malŝveligi to deflate, flatten, reduce, subside.
malŝveligo reduction.
malŝvelo collapse, reduction.
malta Maltese.
maltaksigi to depreciate.
maltano Maltese.
maltegmenti to unroof.
malteni to release.
maltima bold, daring.
maltimega audacious.

maltimego audacity.
maltimema daring.
maltimeme fearlessly, unflinchingly.
maltimemo boldness, hubris.
maltimi to dare.
maltimo boldness.
malto malt.
Malto Malta.
maltolerema bigoted, intolerant.
maltoleremo intolerance.
maltoleremulo bigot.
maltordi to unravel.
maltrafa unsuccessful, off-the-mark, abortive.
maltrafi to miss.
maltrankvila agitated, anxious, restless, uneasy, fitful.
maltrankvile anxiously.
maltrankvileco anxiety, inquietude, uneasiness.
maltrankviliga alarming, grave, serious.
maltrankviligi to agitate, alarm, disquiet.
maltrankviligo alarm.
maltrankviliĝi to be anxious, fret, worry.
maltrankviliĝo worry.
maltrankvilo agitation, anxiety, concern, disquiet, fear, trouble, unease.
maltroigi to understate.
maltroigo understatement.
maltroo underflow.
maltujulo lingerer.
malunueco disunity.
malutila adverse, harmful, hurtful, prejudicial, unavailing.
malutile detrimentally, disadvantageously, prejudicially.
malutilega pernicious.
malutili to harm, hurt.
malutilo detriment, disadvantage, harm.
malutopia dystopian, anti-utopian.
malutopio dystopia, anti-utopia.
malutopiulo dystopian (person), anti-utopian.
maluzi to misuse.
malva mauve.
malvacoj mallow family.
malvalida void.
malvalidigi to cancel, disable, turn off.
malvarma bleak, chilly, cold. **malvarma ĝis dentoklakado** so cold one's teeth are chattering. **malvarma milito** Cold War. **Malvarma Rojo** Coldstream.
malvarme coldly.
malvarmeco coldness.
malvarmeta cool. **malvarmeta sezono** cool season.
malvarmeteco coolness.
malvarmetigi to cool.
malvarmetiĝi to cool, cool down.
malvarmeto coolness.
malvarmiga chilling.

malvarmigi to chill.
malvarmigilo radiator, cooler.
malvarmiĝejo cold store.
malvarmiĝi to get cold.
malvarmiĝo chill.
malvarmo chill, cold.
malvarmsanga cold-blooded, ectothermal, ectothermic, ectothermous.
malvarmsango presence of mind, sang-froid, composure, equanimity.
malvarmtone diri to speak coldly.
malvarmulo a cold, chill.
malvarmumi to catch a cold.
malvarmumo cold.
malvasta close, cramped.
malvaste narrowly.
malvastejo narrow space.
malvastigaĵo partial mapping, restriction (of a mapping).
malvastigi to restrict.
malvastigo constriction.
malvastiĝi to contract.
malvastiĝo contraction.
malvazio malmsey.
malvenkego rout.
malvenki to lose, be defeated.
malvenkigi to discomfit.
malvenkismo defeatism.
malvenkita worsted.
malvenko defeat.
malvenkoego defeat.
malvera false, untrue.
malveraĵo untruth.
malvere untruthfully, not reality.
malverema deceitful.
malverigi to pervert.
malverigo perversion.
malveriĝi to prevaricate.
malveriĝo perversion.
malvero untruth.
malversacio embezzlement, misappropriation.
malverva lifeless, stolid, wooden.
malverve lifelessly, stolidly.
malverveco lifelessness, stolidity.
malvesti to undress (one's self).
malvigila apathetic.
malvigileco apathy.
malvigla sluggish, indolent, slack. **malvigla sezono** off-season, low season, slack season.
malvigle lifelessly, listlessly.
malvigleco indolence, lifelessness.
malvirgigi to deflower.
malvirgiĝi to lose one's virginity.
malvirta corrupt, vicious, wicked.
malvirte evilly, wickedly.
malvirteco wickedness.
malvirtigi to deprave.
malvirto depravity, vice.
malvirtulo evil-doer.
malviŝi to undelete, unerase.
malviva lifeless, dead.
malvivulo corpse.
malvo mallow.
malvola grudging, unwilling.
malvole against one's will, forcefully, reluctantly, unwillingly.
malvoli to refuse.
malvolonte unwillingly.
malvolvado unwinding.
malvolvi to unfold (open), unfurl, unroll.
malvolvo bootstrap, bootstrapping, expansion. **malvolvo de makroo** substitution.
malvorto antonym.
malvulgareco distinction.
malzipi to unzip.
malzomi to zoom out.
malzorga careless, neglectful, negligent, remiss.
malzorge carelessly.
malzorgeco carelessness, negligence, remissness.
malzorgema careless.
malzorgeme carelessly.
malzorgemo carelessly.
malzorgi to neglect.
malzorgo carelessly.
mambesto mammal.
mambestoj mammals.
mambo mambo.
mamego udder.
mameto nipple.
mammezuro breast size.
mamnutrado breast feeding.
mamnutri to nurse, suckle.
mamo breast, chest, teat, udder.
Mamono Mammon.
mampinto nipple, teat.
mamsuĉbesto mammal.
mamsuĉi to suck, suckle.
mamsuĉigi to breast-feed.
mamtenilo bra.
mamula mammalian.
mamulo mammal.
mamuloj mammals.
mamuta mammoth.
mamuto mammoth.
mamzono bra, brassiere.
mana manual.
manaĝera managerial.
manaĝero manager.
manakas kaŭzo fari ion there's no reason to do something.
manao manna.
manapteko first-aid kit.
manartiko wrist.
manato manatee.
manbati to spank.

mancinelo manchineel.
manĉestrano Mancunian.
Manĉestro Manchester.
manĉua Manchurian.
manĉuo Manchurian.
manĉura Manchurian.
Manĉurio Manchuria.
manĉuro Manchurian.
Manĉurujo Manchuria.
mandalo mandala.
mandarena mandarin.
mandarenanaso mandarin duck.
mandareno mandarin.
mandarino mandarin, tangerine.
mandato mandate, order (postal, money).
mandiblo mandible.
mandolino mandolin.
mandorsa backhand.
mandorso back of the hand.
mandragoro mandrake.
mandreno mandrel.
mandrilo baboon.
mane by hand.
maneĝo breaking in (horse), riding school, manège.
manekeno fashion model, mannequin.
manenmane kun hand in hand.
manepiede on all fours, on hands and feed.
manfarado handicraft.
manfarita handmade.
manfaritaĵo handiwork.
manfrapi to clap.
mangano manganese.
mangao manga.
manglo mangrove-fruit.
mangloarbo mangrove.
manglujo mangrove.
mango mango.
mangoarbo mango-tree.
mangostano mangosteen.
mangujo mango tree.
manĝado repast.
manĝaĵejo larder, pantry.
manĝaĵo food, viands, victuals, provision.
manĝaĵoŝranko larder, pantry, store-cupboard.
manĝante while eating.
manĝavida voracious.
manĝavide voraciously.
manĝbastoneto chopstick.
manĝebla edible.
manĝegema gluttonous, greedy.
manĝegeme gluttonously, greedily.
manĝegemo gluttony.
manĝegi to devour.
manĝegulo glutton, gourmand.
manĝeĵo dining hall, cafeteria, dining room.
manĝetaĵo snack.
manĝeti to snack, nibble.

manĝeto refection.
manĝetobudo refreshment stand.
manĝi to eat, feed.
manĝigi to feed.
manĝilara lavilo detergent, washing-up liquid.
manĝilaro eating utensils.
manĝinda edible, worth eating.
manĝmeto course.
manĝo meal.
manĝobastoneto chopstick.
manĝobastonetoj chopsticks.
manĝobruo noise made while eating.
manĝoĉambro dining room.
manĝokarto menu, bill of fare.
manĝometo meal.
manĝoprovizejo pantry.
manĝosalono dining-room.
manĝoskatolo lunch box.
manĝrestaĵo leavings, remains, scraps (food).
manĝtuneleto burrow.
manĝujo manger, nosebag.
Manĝurio Manchuria.
mania addicted.
manieraĵo mannerism.
maniero fashion, manner, mode, way.
maniero de pretigado manner of preparation.
manieto fad.
manifestacianto demonstrator.
manifestacii to demonstrate.
manifestacio demonstration.
manifestaĵo manifestation.
manifesti to (make) manifest, demonstrate, show. **manifesti sin** to manifest (itself).
manifestiĝi to manifest itself.
manifesto manifest, manifesto.
maniĥeano Manichaean.
maniĥeisma Manichaean.
maniĥeismo Manichaeism.
maniiga addictive.
maniigi to addict.
maniiĝi to become addicted.
Manika Kolo Strait of Dover. **Manikaj Insuloj** Channel Islands.
manikhava sleeved.
maniko sleeve. **Maniko** the Channel, the English Channel.
Manikuagano Manikuagan.
manikuri to manicure.
manikuro manicure.
manila fibraĵo abaca.
Manilo Manila.
manilo handle.
manio addiction, mania, passion.
maniohava nutty, goofy.
manioko cassava, manioc.
manipulado treatment.

manipulanto

manipulanto manipulator, operator.
manipulatoro key.
manipuli to handle, manipulate, manage.
manipulilo key.
manipulo adjustment.
maniso pangolins, scaly anteater.
Manitobolago Lake Manitoba.
maniuligi to addict.
maniulo maniac.
Manjo May.
manka missing.
mankanta absent.
mankantlisto attendance register.
mankanto absentee.
mankateni to handcuff, manacle.
mankateno handcuffs, manacles.
manke de in the absence of.
mankhava faulty.
manki to be lacking, be missing, fail, miss.
mankigi to drop, omit.
Mankinsulo Isle of Man.
mankiso hand-kiss.
manko absence, lack, shortage, shortcoming, gap, lapse.
mankohava rejective, defective, faulty, deficient. **mankohava ajo** defective product.
mankoloko lacuna.
mankonduki to lead someone by the hand.
manksa Manx.
mankso Manxman.
manlaboro manual labour.
manlerteco workmanship.
manlibro handbook.
mano hand. **mano en mano** hand in hand.
manobuso hand grenade.
manometro manometer.
manovrejo apron.
manovri to manoeuvre.
manovro manoeuvre.
manpilkado ballgame.
manpilkludo ball game.
manpilko handball.
manplata frapado applause.
manplato palm (of hand).
manplekti to join hands.
manplena handful. **manplena da** handful of.
manpleno fistful, handful.
manportebla handheld.
manpremi to shake hands, handshake.
manpremo handshake.
manpreni to handle, wield.
manradiko wrist.
manregi to wield.
mansaketo handbag.
mansako handbag.
mansardo attic, garret.
mansigni to wave.
mansupro back of the hand.

marcipano

manteleto pelerine, tippet.
manteliĝi to cloak.
manteliĝo cloaking.
mantelo cape, cloak, mantle, coat.
manteni to have got hold of.
mantenilo grip, handle.
mantilo mantilla.
mantiso mantissa.
manto mantis.
mantro mantra.
mantuko towel.
manufakturo factory, manufactory, works.
manumo cuff.
manuskripto manuscript.
manuzi to handle, manipulate, use.
manveturilo truck.
maoisma Maoist.
maoismo Maoism.
maoisto Maoist.
maora lingvo Maori, Maori language.
maoria Maori. **maoria lingvo** Maori, Maori language.
maorio Maori.
maparo atlas.
mapi to map.
mapisto cartographer.
mapo map.
mara maritime, sea, of the sea. **mara lobulario** sweet alison, sweet alyssum.
marabuo marabou stork.
maraglo sea eagle, white-tailed eagle.
maralgo seaweed.
maranaso scoter.
maranemono actinia, sea-anemone.
marangilo conger-eel.
marano seaman.
marant-amelo arrowroot.
maranto arrowroot.
mararaneo spider crab.
mararmea naval.
mararmeano sailor.
mararmeo navy.
maraskino maraschino.
marasmo emaciation, marasmus, stagnation.
marasmulo weakling.
maratio Marathi.
maratono marathon.
marbano bath taken in the sea.
marborda coast, coastal, of the coast, beach, seaside, shore.
marborde on the shore, at the shore, shoreside.
marbordo seashore, beach, shore.
marbovo sea-cow, sea-pig.
marbranĉo arm of the sea, estuary, firth.
marcipano marzipan.

marĉa quaggy. **marĉa cirkuo** marsh-harrier. **marĉa kalitriko** vernal water-starwort.
marĉanaso garganey.
marĉandado bargaining, haggling.
marĉandaĵo bargain, special.
marĉandi to bargain, haggle.
marĉeca boggy, marshy, swampy.
marĉeco marshiness.
marĉego bog.
marĉejo fen, quagmire, swamp.
marĉejoaĵo morass.
marĉlageto pool.
marĉo marsh, swamp.
marĉoplena muddy, sludgy.
marde at Tuesdays.
Mardo Tuesday.
mardo Tuesday.
mare at sea.
marenporti to carry (out) to sea.
marerinaco sea urchin.
marestaĵo sea creature.
marfundo bottom of the sea, sea-bottom.
Margareto Margaret.
margarino margarine.
margarito daisy.
marglano acorn barnacle, acorn-shell.
marĝena marginal.
marĝeno margin.
marĝenulo fringe existence, marginalized person.
marhordeo sea barley, squirrel-tail grass.
marhundo seal.
Maria Mary.
mariaista Marist.
mariaisto Marist.
Marianoj Mariana Islands.
marihuano marijuana.
marilandano Marylander.
marini to marinate.
Mario Mario, Marius, Mary.
marioneto marionette, puppet.
marirebla seaworthy.
marista seaman's, of a sailor. **marista bluo** navy blue.
maristaro crew.
mariste blua navy blue.
maristo mariner, sailor, seaman.
markado markup.
markaĵo markup.
markankreto shrimp.
markaŝtano sea urchin.
marketraĵo marquetry.
marketri to inlay.
markezo marquee, penthouse, shed.
marki to mark.
markilo marker.
Markisoj Marquesas Islands.
markizino marchioness.
markizo marquis.
Markizo marquis.
Marko Marcus.
marko mark, stamp.
markobutono check box, choice button.
markolbaso sea cucumber.
markolo channel, strait. **Markolo de Forto** Firth of Forth.
markompaso compass.
markosensado mark sensing.
markoti to layer.
markoto layer.
Markova kateno Markov chain.
marksisma Marxist.
marksismo Marxism.
marksisto Marxist.
Markso Marx.
marleono sea-lion.
marmalsano motion sickness, sea sickness.
marmanĝaĵo seafood.
marmejlo nautical mile, sea-mile.
marmelado jam, marmalade.
marmeze at see, in the middle of the sea.
marmito (cooking) pot, casserole.
marmonstro sea-monster.
marmora marble.
marmoranaso teal.
marmoro marble.
marmoto groundhog, marmot, woodchuck.
marmova tidal.
marni to marl.
marnivelo sea level.
marno marl.
maro sea. **Maro Arkta** Arctic Ocean.
marodi to maraud, plunder, raid.
marodisto marauder, raider.
maroka Moroccan.
marokanino Moroccan woman.
marokano Moroccan.
marokeno Moroccan leather.
Maroko Morocco.
maronarbo chestnut tree.
marono chestnut.
maronujo chestnut tree.
maroto eccentricity, quirk.
marovasto vastness of the sea.
Marovino Maroni.
marplaŭdejo strand.
marporko porpoise.
marrabisto buccaneer, pirate, privateer.
marraboado piracy.
marrodo way (sea).
marrozo actinia, sea anemone.
marrulado rolling (of ships).
marsa Martian.
marsano Martian.
Marseljezo Marseille.
marsilko byssus.
marskareto tidal wave.

Marso Mars.
marsoldato marine (soldier).
marspertulo sea-dog.
marstelo starfish.
marsupio marsupium, pouch.
marsupiulo marsupial.
marsupiuloj marsupials.
marŝado march.
Marŝalinsuloj Marshall Islands.
marŝalo marshal.
Marŝaloj Marshall Islands.
marŝaŭmo foam (sea), surf.
marŝi to march, walk.
marŝinta having marched, having walked.
marŝo march, walk.
marŝtono pebble.
marŝtopilo anchor.
martagono martagon lily.
martaŭga seaworthy.
martelado hammering.
martelborilo jackhammer.
martelego mallet.
marteli to hammer.
martelo hammer.
martelumi to hammer.
marteso marten.
Martiniko Martinique.
martinio martini.
martino martini.
martirigo martyrdom.
martirino martyr, female martyr.
martiro martyr.
Marto March.
marto March.
maruno Maroon.
marverda glaucous (colour).
marveturado navigation.
marveturarto seamanship.
marveturi to navigate.
marveturisto mariner, sailor, seafarer, seaman.
marvojaĝo ocean voyage, sea voyage.
masaĝi to massage.
masaĝistino masseuse.
masaĝisto masseur.
masaĝo massage.
masakrado massacre.
masakri to massacre.
masakro massacre.
Masero Maseru.
masiva large, massive, heavy.
maskado masquerade.
maskajo travesty.
maskareto bore, tidal wave.
maskaro mascara.
maskerado masquerade.
maski to mask.
maskitaro masquerade.
maskla male.

masklo male.
masko mask.
maskobalo masked ball.
maskofesto mummery, masquerade.
maskovesti to disguise.
maskvesto disguise.
maso lump, mass, pile, heap.
masoĥismo masochism.
masoĥisto masochist.
masonaĵo masonry.
masonfermi to brick in, brick up.
masonhelpisto bricklayer's labourer.
masoni to build (with stone), mason.
masonilo bricklayer's tool.
masonista bricklayer's.
masonisto mason.
masoristo masorete.
masoro Masora(h).
mastaro spar.
mastiki to fill in, stop (hole), putty.
mastiko mastic, putty.
mastmeze at half mast.
masto mast.
mastodonto mastodon.
mastoido mastoid.
mastraĵo housekeeping.
mastrema domineering, overbearing.
mastri to be master over, dominate.
Mastriĥto Maastricht.
mastrino housewife, mistress.
mastro boss, lord, master, manager.
mastrostriko lockout.
mastruma household. **mastruma sistemo** operating system.
mastrumada kaslibro account book.
mastrumado housekeeping, management.
mastrumaĵo household affairs.
mastrumi to keep house, manage.
mastrumistino housekeeper.
mastrumisto housekeeper.
mastrumsistemo operating system.
masturbi to masturbate.
maŝaro mesh, net.
maŝina automatic.
maŝinaro machinery.
maŝineca programadlingvo computer oriented language.
maŝinfusilo machine gun.
maŝinisto machinist.
maŝinkodo machine code, machine language.
maŝinlingvo computer language, machine language.
maŝino engine, machine.
maŝinpafilo automatic rifle, machine gun.
maŝinskribado typewriting.
maŝinskribi to type.
maŝkiraso chainmail.
maŝkruco ankh, ansate cross.

maŝnodo

maŝnodo noose.
maŝo knot, link, loop, mesh, mail (armour).
matadoro matador.
matĉo game, match. **matĉo de bokso** boxing match.
matearbo yerba mate.
matematika mathematical. **matematika logiko** mathematical logic. **matematika programado** mathematical programming.
matematike mathematically.
matematikisto mathematician.
matematiko mathematics.
matena morning, of morning. **matena bano** morning bath. **matena krepusko** dawn, daybreak.
matene in the morning.
matenhoro morning time.
mateniĝo dawn, becoming morning.
matenkoncerto aubade.
matenmanĝi to breakfast.
matenmanĝo breakfast.
mateno morning.
matenon in the morning.
matenruĝo red of dawn.
matenstelo morning star.
mateo yerba mate.
Materhorno Matterhorn.
materia material.
materiala material.
materialisma materialistic, worldly.
materialismo materialism.
materialisto materialist.
materialo data, material, matter.
materie tangibly.
materiiĝi to materialize.
materiismo materialism.
materiisto materialist.
materio matter.
mati to checkmate.
matineo matinée.
mato checkmate, mate.
matraco mattress.
matriarko matriarch.
matrica matrix. **matrica adicio** matrix addition. **matrica multipliko** matrix multiplication. **matrica nulo** null matrix. **matrica unuo** identity matrix, unit matrix.
matrico matrix. **matrico de vektora homomorfio** matrix of a linear mapping.
matrikario chamomile, mayweed.
matrikulo roll, list of members.
matrono matron.
matura mature, ripe, full-grown, mature.
maturaĝa adult.
matureco maturity, ripeness.
maturigi to mature, bring to maturity.
maturigiĝi to mature.
maturiĝi to mature, ripen.
maturiĝo maturation, maturity.

medio

maturiĝrito rite of passage.
maturulo adult.
matutino matins.
maŭra Mauretanian, Moorish, Moresque.
Maŭricio Mauritius.
maŭritania Mauritanian.
maŭritaniano Mauritanian.
Maŭritanio Mauritania.
maŭro Mauretanian, Moor.
Maŭrolando Mauritania.
Maŭrujo Mauritania.
maŭzoleo mausoleum.
mava bad.
mazamo brocket deer.
Mazurio Masuria.
mazurko mazurka.
mazuto fuel oil, mazut.
meandri to meander.
meandro meander.
meblaĵo furnishing.
meblaro furniture.
mebli to furnish.
meblisto cabinetmaker, upholsterer.
meblita furnished.
meblo piece of furniture.
meblobutiko furniture store.
meblofarado cabinet-making.
meblofaristo upholsterer.
mebloj furniture.
meblokamiono moving van.
meblokatuno chintz.
mebloportisto (re)mover.
mebraro membership.
mecenateco patronage, support.
mecenati to support.
mecenato patron, supporter.
meĉaĵo tinder.
meĉo fuse, wick.
meĉoaĵo wick.
meĉotondi to mechanics.
medalgajninto medalist.
medali to decorate.
medaliono locket, medallion.
medalo medal.
media ambient.
mediacii to mediate.
mediacio mediation.
medialo middle, middle voice.
mediano median.
medicina medical, medicinal.
medicinaĵo drug, medicine, pharmaceutical.
medicino medicine (practice of).
medicinŝranko medicine chest.
medikamenta pharmaceutical.
medikamento drug, medicine, pharmaceutical, medication.
Medino Medina.
medio environment, medium. **medio rultempa** run-time environment.

meditadi

meditadi to meditate.
meditado meditation.
meditema thinking, thoughtful, meditative, pensive.
mediteme meditatively.
mediteranea Mediterranean.
Mediteraneo Mediterranean.
mediti to meditate, think to oneself.
medito meditation.
mediumo medium (spiritualism).
medivariablo environment variable.
medo mead.
medolo medulla, pith, marrow.
meduzo jellyfish.
Meduzo Medusa.
Mefisto Mephistopheles.
Mefistofelo Mephistopheles.
mefito skunk.
megabajto megabyte.
megabito megabit.
megafono megaphone.
megaherco megahertz.
megaĵulo megajoule.
megalito megalith.
megalomanio megalomania.
megalosaŭro megalosaurus.
megaomo megaohm.
megatuno megaton.
megaŭato megawatt.
megavatto megawatt.
megavolto megavolt.
megera bitchy, shrewish.
megero bitch, shrew, vixen.
Megero Megaera.
megero shrew.
megomo megohm.
meĥanika mechanical.
meĥanikaĵo mechanism.
meĥanike mechanically.
meĥanikisto mechanic (engineer).
meĥaniko mechanics.
meĥanismo mechanism.
Meĥleno Malines, Mechlin.
Meĥlino Malines, Mechlin.
mejlo mile. **mejloj hore** miles per hour.
mejloŝtono landmark, milepost, milestone.
mekanika mechanical.
mekanikigo mechanization.
mekanikisto mechanic.
mekaniko mechanics.
mekanisma mechanistic.
mekanismo action.
meki to bleat.
Mekko Mecca.
Mekongo Mekong River.
meksikia Mexican. **Meksikia Golfo** Gulf of Mexico.
meksikianaĉo greaser, taco, wetback.
meksikianino Mexican woman.

membriĝo

meksikiano Mexican.
Meksikio Mexico.
Meksiklando Mexico.
Meksiko Mexico.
Meksikurbo Mexico City.
melampiro cow wheat.
melanezia Melanesian.
melaneziano Melanesian.
Melanezio Melanesia.
melanino melanin.
melanito scoter.
melankolia bleak, dismal, dreary, gaunt, melancholy, dejected, depressed, gloomy.
melankolie in a melancholy way.
melankolio dejection, gloom, melancholia, melancholy, depression.
melankoliulo melancholic.
melaso golden syrup, molasses, treacle.
melduo mildew.
meleagra fritilario fritillary.
meleagraĵo turkey.
meleagro turkey.
melhundo dachshund.
meliko melick.
meliloto melilot.
melinito melinite.
melino badger sow.
meliso balm-mint.
melitido bastard balm.
melki to milk.
melo badger.
melodia melodic, melodious, tuneful.
melodio melody, tune.
melodrama melodramatic.
melodramo melodrama.
melolonto may bug.
melonarbo papaw, papaya.
melongeno eggfruit, eggplant.
melono melon.
melopeo recitative chant.
melopepo spaghetti squash, summer squash, yellow squash.
melopsitako budgerigar.
mem self, (puts emphasis on the noun or pronoun it follows).
memabsorbiĝo introversion.
memabsorbo self-absorption.
memadjunkta matrico self-adjoint matrix.
memalkremento autoincrement.
memamo self-love.
membiografio autobiography.
memblokamiono furniture van, moving van.
membraneto pellicle.
membrano film, membrane.
membreco membership.
membriĝi to accede.
membriĝo membership.

membro

membro limb, member, term. **Membro-Abonanto** subscribing member.
membrokarto membership card.
membroŝtato member state.
memcerta self-assured.
memdaŭriga self-perpetuating.
memdecido self-determination.
memdefendo defence.
memdekremento autodecrement.
memdigno dignity, self-worth, self-respect.
memdisciplino self-discipline.
memdungato freelancer.
memdungiĝi to freelance.
memestimo self confidence, self esteem, self respect.
memevidenta self-evident.
memevidente obviously.
memevoluigado self-actualization.
memfarita home-made, self-produced. **memfarita homo** self-made man.
memfida confident, self-assured.
memfide confidently.
memfido self-confidence, self-reliance.
memforgeso abnegation, self-denial.
memhumiligo abasement.
meminstruita self-taught.
meminstruito autodidact, self-taught (person).
memkatalizo autocatalysis.
memkomprenebla self-evident.
memkompreneble of course.
memkonfese avowedly.
memkonjugita distinguished, invariant, self-conjugate.
memkontenta self-content, self-satisfied.
memkontente smugly.
memkontraŭa inconsistent.
memkontraŭdira contradictory, inconsistent, self-contradictory.
memkontraŭdiro contradiction.
memkontraŭo inconsistency.
memkritiko self-criticism.
memlaŭda boastful, bragging.
memlaŭdo vaunt, brag.
memlernilo teach-yourself book.
memlerninta self-taught.
memlerninto autodidact, self-taught person, self-learner.
memmallaŭda deprecatory.
memmallaŭde deprecatingly.
memmallaŭdi to deprecate.
memmallaŭdo deprecation.
memmortiga suicide.
memmortigi to commit suicide. **memmortigi sin** to commit suicide.
memmortigo suicide.
memo ego, self.
memoradministrado storage management.

memvole

memoradministrilo storage management system, storage manager.
memoraĵo keepsake, memento, souvenir, memorial.
memorando memorandum.
memorareo area, storage area.
memorarto art of memorization.
memorcikla daŭro memory cycle.
memorĉelo memory cell.
memorero byte.
memorfesta poŝtmarko commemorative stamp.
memorgenerado memory allocation.
memorhava cirkvito sequential circuit.
memorhierarkio memory hierarchy.
memori to recall, recollect, remember.
memorigaĵo keepsake, memento, souvenir.
memorigi to commemorate, make remember, remind.
memorigisto prompter.
memorigo relic, reminder.
memoriladreso storage address.
memorilero partition.
memorilo storage.
memorilŝirmilo memory protect.
memorinda memorable.
memorkapablo memory.
memorkapacito memory size.
memorlibro agenda.
memorlikado memory leak.
memoro memory, recollection, storage.
memorperdo amnesia.
memorprotekto memory protection.
memortabulo plaque.
memortago anniversary.
memorunuo byte.
mempensi to commune.
mempligrandigo self-aggrandizement.
memregado restraint, self-command, self-control, self-possession, self-rule.
memriproĉa remorseful.
memriproĉe remorsefully.
memriproĉo compunction, remorse, self-reproach.
memserva self-service. **memserva vendejo** supermarket.
memskribo autograph.
memstara free-standing, independent, stand-alone.
memstare independently, self-assuredly.
memstareco independence.
memstiranta self-guided. **memstiranta raketo** self-guided rocket.
memsufiĉa self-sufficient.
memŝaltilo automatic switch.
memuaro memoir (scholarly paper).
memvola of one's own will, wayward, willing, voluntary.
memvole willingly, of one's own (free) will.

memvolulo volunteer.
menaĝerio menagerie, zoo, zoological garden.
mencii to mention. **mencii mallonge** touch lightly on, touch on.
menciinda worth mentioning.
mencio mention.
mendanto applicant.
mendelevio mendelevium.
Mendelevo Mendeleyev.
mendelismo Mendelism.
mendi to book, order, reserve.
mendilo order form.
mendo order (for goods).
mendoformularo application form, form of application.
mendoslipo call slip.
menestrelo minstrel.
menhiro menhir.
menianto bogbean.
meningito meningitis.
meningo meninges.
menisko meniscus.
menopaŭzo menopause.
mensa mental. **mensa postrestanteco** backwardness.
mense mentally. **mense postrestanta** backward, mentally deficient, retarded.
mensmalsano mental illness.
mensmalsanulo mentally ill person.
menso mind.
mensoga lying, untruthful.
mensoge lyingly, untruthfully.
mensogeco mendacity.
mensogemo mendacity.
mensogeto story (untruth).
mensogi to lie, tell a lie.
mensogisto cheat, deceiver, imposter.
mensogo falsehood, lie.
mensogulo liar.
mensosensentiga mind-numbing.
mensosensentige mind-numbingly.
mensostato mentality, state of mind.
mensstuporiga mind-numbing.
mensstuporige mind-numbingly.
menstruo menstrual flow, menstruation.
mento mint (plant, flavour).
mentolo menthol.
mentono chin.
mentora advisory.
mentoro mentor.
menueto minuet.
menuo menu.
menuro lyrebird.
menuzono menu bar.
mercero haberdashery.
merdo shit.
mergado immersion.
merganaso tufted duck.
mergi to immerse.
mergiĝi to submerge.
mergulo dovekie, little auk.
merĝo merganser.
meridiano meridian (line).
merina merino.
meringelo meringue.
meringo meringue.
merino merino.
merinolano merino (wool).
merita meritorious, worthy.
meritaĵo appropriate compensation, just desserts, reward, punishment.
meriti to be worthy of, deserve, merit. **meriti la morton** to deserve death.
merito merit, worth.
merizarbo bird cherry.
merizo wild cherry.
merizujo mazzard, mazzard cherry, sweet cherry.
merkantilismo mercantilism.
merkatado marketing.
merkatekonomio market economy.
merkato market, sales activity.
merkatoekonomio market economy.
merkatumado marketing.
merkatumi to market.
merkatvaloro market value.
merkrede on Wednesdays.
Merkredo Wednesday.
merkredo Wednesday.
Merkura Mercurial.
merkurialo dog's mercury.
Merkurio Mercury.
Merkuro Mercury.
merlango whiting.
merlo blackbird.
merluĉo hake.
meromorfa meromorphic.
meropo bee-eater.
mesaĝaro thread.
mesaĝi to send a message.
mesaĝisto messenger.
mesaĝo errand, message.
meseno Messenian.
mesianismo messianism.
mesiismo messianism.
Mesino Messina.
mesio messiah.
meskalino mescaline.
meslibro missal.
meso mass (religious).
mesoservanto acolyte, altar boy, altar server.
mespilarbo medlar.
mespilo medlar.
mespilujo medlar.
mestizo mestizo.
mesvesto chasuble.

metabola metabolic.
metabolo metabolism.
metaesprimo meta-expression.
metafaktoro meta-factor.
metafizika metaphysical.
metafizikisto metaphysician.
metafiziko metaphysics.
metafora figurative.
metafore figuratively.
metaforo metaphor.
metaforriĉa full of images.
metahistoria metahistorical.
metakarpeo metacarpal.
META-klavo META key.
metaksileno metaxylene.
metala metal, metallic. **metala ŝaŭmo** dross, slag.
metaldehido methaldehyde.
metaldetektilo metal detector.
metaleca metallic.
metalfadeno (metal) wire.
metalfolio sheet metal, tinplate, tin.
metalgarnaĵo ironwork, mounting, studs.
metalingvo metalanguage.
metalo metal.
metaloida metalloid.
metaloido metalloid.
metalroko metal music.
metalsegilo hacksaw.
metalurgio metallurgy.
metalurgo metallurgist.
metamatematiko metamathematics.
metamorfa metamorphic.
metamorfozi to transform.
metamorfozo metamorphosis, recreation, regeneration, transformation.
metano methane.
metapsikio psychics, parapsychology.
metatarso metatarsal.
metateorio metatheory.
metatezo metathesis.
metejo environment.
metempsikozo metempsychosis, transmigration of souls.
meteo atmospheric phenomenon.
meteologiisto meteorologist.
meteologio meteorology.
meteologo meteorologist.
meteorismo meteorism, hoove (abdominal gas).
meteorito meteorite.
meteoro atmospheric phenomenon, meteor, shooting star.
meteorologiisto meteorologist.
meteorologio meteorology.
meteorologo meteorologist.
meteorŝtono aerolite, meteorite.
meti to lay down, place, put, put down, set.
meti en prezkonkurado to invite tenders for, put out to tender. **meti finon al** to put an end to. **meti iun sub gardo** to put someone under guard. **meti la kulpon sur iun** to place the blame on someone. **meti laŭ ĝusta ordo** to put in the correct order, put in proper order. **meti supre sur** to superimpose on. **meti sur la karton** to put (risk) on the (turn of a) card.
metiaĵo craftwork.
metiejo jobsite, workplace, workshop.
metiere workmanlike.
metiistarto workmanship.
metiiste workmanlike.
metiisteco workmanship.
metiisto artisan, mechanic, operative, blue-collar worker.
metilaboristo artisan, craftsman, tradesman.
metileno methylene.
metilernanteco apprenticeship.
metilernantigi to apprentice.
metilernanto apprentice.
metilo methyl.
metio handicraft, occupation, trade, profession.
metiservi to be apprenticed.
metiservo apprenticeship.
metita placed, laid down, put down.
metoda methodical.
metodaro methodology.
metode methodically.
metodika methodological.
metodiko methodology.
Metodio Methodius.
metodista Methodist.
metodisto Methodist.
metodo method.
metodologio methodology.
metonimio metonymy.
metopo metope.
metra metric.
metrigi to covert to the metric system.
metrika metrical. **metrika spaco** metric space.
metriko metric.
metro metre, meter.
metroa metro (railway). **metroa haltejo** underground station. **metroa stacio** underground station.
metrohaltejo underground station.
metronimiko metronymic.
metronomo metronome.
metroo metro, subway, underground.
metropolito archbishop.
metropolo metropolis.
metrostacio underground station.
Metuŝelaĥo Methuselah.
mevo gull, seagull.

meza average, mean, middle, medium, central. **meza kvanto** average. **meza lernejo** intermediate school (a kind of university). **meza masto** mainmast, maintop. **Meza Oriento** Middle East. **meza punkto** middle dot (·).
mezaere in mid-air.
mezafrika Central African. **Mezafrika Respubliko** Central African Republic.
Mez-Afriko Central Africa.
Mezafriko Central Africa.
mezaĝa middle-aged.
mezaĝulo middle-aged person.
mezakvanto mean (math).
mezalianco misalliance - marriage into lower class.
Mez-Ameriko Central America.
Mezameriko Central America.
mezanto median.
mezaranĝo accommodation.
mezazia Central Asian.
Mez-Azio Central Asia.
Mezazio Central Asia.
mezdaŭra intermediate.
meze amid, amidst, rather. **meze de** among, amidst, in the middle of. **meze en** amid, among, in the middle of. **meze inter** amid, among, in the middle of.
mezembriantemo ice plant.
mezembrianto ice plant.
mezentero mesentery.
mezepoka mediaeval.
mezepoko Middle Ages.
mezereo mezereon.
Mezeŭropo Central Europe.
mezfingro middle finger.
mezgranda medium-sized. **mezgranda buntpego** middle spotted woodpecker. **mezgranda videbliga komputilo** visible record computer.
mezkampo midfield.
mezkampulo midfielder.
mezklasa bourgeois.
mezklaso middle classes.
mezkvalita mediocre.
mezkvanto arithmetical mean, average.
mezlernejo secondary/high school.
mezlinio axis, axis deer.
mezmalnovnederlanda Middle Dutch.
mezmara Mediterranean.
Mezmaro Mediterranean Sea.
mezmaste at half mast.
meznederlanda Middle Dutch.
meznivela intermediate, medium.
meznokta midnight, of midnight.
meznokte in the middle of the night.
meznokto midnight.
meznombra average, mean.
meznombre on the average.
meznombro average, mean.
mezo average, mean, middle.
mezogastro abdomen.
Mezolitiko Mesolithic, Mesolithic Age.
Mezomaro Mediterranean.
mezono meson, mesotron.
mezonombro average, mean.
mezopotamia Mesopotamian.
Mezopotamio Mesopotamia.
Mezoriento Middle East.
mezortanto mid-perpendicular (of a segment).
mezotinto mezzotint.
mezozoika Mesozoic.
mezozoiko Mesozoic.
Mezozoiko Mesozoic, Mesozoic era.
meztagmanĝi to lunch, eat the midday meal.
meztagmanĝo dinner, lunch, snack.
mezumo mean.
mezurado measurement.
mezuraĵoeco measurement.
mezurbando measuring tape.
mezurbendo tape measure.
mezurcilindro graduated cylinder.
mezurebla measurable (mapping).
mezurhava spaco measure space.
mezuri to gauge, measure.
mezuriĝi to measure.
mezurilo measure, meter.
mezurita measured. **mezurita ĝuste** adjusted.
mezuro bar, measure, measurement.
mezurrubando measuring tape, tape-measure.
mezurstango yardstick.
mezurunuo unit.
mezvaloro average.
mezvarma lukewarm.
mezvintre in the middle of winter.
mezvoje halfway.
mi I. **mi ankoraŭ kredas, ke...** I still think... **mi devas iri** to I must go. **mi dubas pri tio** I doubt that. **mi jam remarkigis, ke...** I've already pointed out that. **mi konsentas** I agree. **mi kredas, ke jes** I think so. **mi ne havas apetiton** I'm not hungry. **mi nur ripetu, ke...** let me just say again that... **mi opinias same** I'm of the same opinion. **mi opinias, ke...** I think that... **mi pensu** let me think. **mi petas** please, you're welcome. **mi povas** I can. **mi volas diri ...** I mean... **mi volus aldoni, ke...** I'd like to add that...
mia my, mine. **mia iama memo** my former self. **mia kara** my dear, my good fellow.
mia opinie in my opinion.
miadoma of one's home.
miaflanke on my part, for my part.

miakrede in my belief, according to my belief.
miaopinie in my view, in my opinion, to my thinking.
miaparte for me, for my part.
miarasa of my (own) race.
miasmo miasma.
miasperte in my experience.
miaŭi to meow, mew.
miaŭo meow, mew.
miavejne in my veins.
micelio mycellium, spawn.
Miĉelo Mitchell.
miĉigana Michiganite.
miĉiganano Michigander, Michiganite.
Miĉjo Mickey. **Miĉjo Muso** Mickey Mouse.
Midaso Midas.
midŝipmano midshipman, naval cadet.
midzado fellatio.
midzi to perform oral sex on, fellate.
midzo blow job, fellatio.
miela honeyed, saccharine, sweet. **miela monato** honeymoon.
mielĉelaro honeycomb.
mielkuko gingerbread.
mielluno honeymoon.
mielmonato honeymoon.
mielo honey.
mielsiropo molasses.
mieltavolo honeycomb.
mieltrinkaĵo mead.
mielvoĉa mellifluous.
mieneto smiley.
mieni to appear.
mieno air, appearance, expression, look, face, mien, aspect.
migdala almond-like.
migdalarbo almond tree.
migdalkukaĵo almond pastry.
migdalo almond.
migdalokula almond-eyed.
migdaloleo almond oil.
migdalujo almond tree.
migra itinerant. **migra kato** stray cat.
migrado migration; hiking.
migranta nomadic.
migranto migrant, hiker, wanderer, nomad.
migregi to mass-migrate.
migrema fond of travelling, footloose, migrant.
migremo wanderlust.
migreno migraine.
migri to migrate, roam, wander, wander about, travel about.
migrinto migrant.
Mihaelo Michael.
mikado Mikado.
Mikeno Mycenae.
mikozo mycosis.

mikroampero microampere.
mikrobiologio microbiology.
mikrobo germ, microbe.
mikrocirkvito chip.
mikroekonomiko microeconomics.
mikroelektronika microelectronic.
mikroelektroniko microelectronics.
mikrofarado microfarad.
mikrofilmi to microfilm.
mikrofilmkarto microfilm card.
mikrofilmo microfilm.
mikrofono microphone.
mikrogramo microgram.
mikrokanela disko long-playing record, LP.
mikrokanelo microgroove.
mikrokoko micrococcus.
mikrokomputilo microcomputer.
mikrokredito microcredit.
mikrometro micrometer.
Mikronezio (Federated States of) Micronesia.
mikrono micrometer, micron.
mikroonda microwave.
mikroondo microwave.
mikroprocesoro microprocessor.
mikroprogramado microprogramming.
mikroprogramo microprogram.
mikrorganismo microorganism.
mikrosekundo microsecond.
mikroskopa microscopic.
mikroskopo microscope.
Mikroskopo Microscopium.
mikroto grass vole.
mikrotomo microtome.
mikrovatto microwatt.
mikrovolto microvolt.
miksa promiscuous. **miksa frakcio** mixed fraction.
miksado admixture, mixing.
miksaĵo admixture, mixture, mash.
miksamaso hodgepodge, medley, mess.
miksbatalo affray.
miksedziĝo mixed marriage.
miksegi to scramble.
miksi to blend, mingle, mix, shuffle.
miksiĝi to blend, mingle, mix.
miksilo mixer.
miksita miscellaneous.
mikso mix.
miksomatozo myxomatosis.
miksomo myxoma.
mikspoto miscellany, potpourri.
miksta desegregated(racially), mixed, coeducational.
mil thousand, one thousand.
mila thousandth.
Milano Milan.
milda gentle, mild.

milde mildly.
mildeco balminess, gentleness, leniency, meekness, mildness.
mildigi to soften, alleviate.
mildigo abatement, alleviation, relief.
mildiĝi to become soft, mild.
mildiĝo relief, respite.
milfoje a thousand time, thousands of times.
milfolio common yarrow, gordaldo, milfoil.
miliampero milliampere.
miliardo billion.
miliardulo billionaire.
milibaro millibar.
milicio militia.
milico militia.
miligramo milligram.
mililitro millilitre.
milimetro millimetre.
milio millet.
miliona millionth.
miliono million.
milionono millionth.
milionulo millionaire.
milisekundo millisecond.
milita militant, military. **milita potenco** big stick. **milita trumpeto** clarion.
militado warfare.
militago act of war.
militakiri to conquer.
militakiro booty, loot, plunder.
militama warlike.
militamaema martial.
militantaro militia.
militarto strategy.
militaviadilo warplane.
militdeklaro declaration of war.
militema inclined to war, martial, warlike.
militemulo warmonger.
militforto military force.
milithakilo battle-axe.
milithalto armistice, truce.
militi to make war, wage war. **militi kontraŭ** to make war on, wage war against.
militiro campaign, expedition.
militista military. **militista vesperkoncerto** tattoo.
militistaro army.
militisto military man, warrior.
militkaptitino captive woman.
militkaptito prisoner of war.
milito war.
militoado war.
militotaŭga fit for military service.
militpastro chaplain, army chaplain, padre.
militpaŭzo truce.
militservi to serve in the military.
militservo military service.
militservorezistanto conscientious objector.

militŝiparego armada.
militŝiparo navy.
militŝipo military ship, warship.
milivatto milliwatt.
milivolto millivolt.
miljaro millennium.
Milngavio Milngavie.
milo thousand.
miloble thousand-fold.
miloj thousands.
milono thousandth.
milvo kite (bird).
mimeografi to mimeograph, stencil.
mimeografo mimeograph.
mimi to mime.
mimiko mime.
mimo dumb-show, mime.
mimozo mimosa, sensitive plant.
minaca imminent, menacing, threatening. **minaca timigo** intimidation.
minacado intimidation.
minacanta menacing, threatening.
minace imminently, threateningly.
minaci to impend, menace, threaten, intimidate.
minacletero threatening letter.
minaco menace, threat.
minacordono exhortation, warning.
minado mining.
minaĵo ore.
minareto minaret.
minbalaa ŝipo mine sweeper.
minbalai to sweep.
minbalaŝipo minesweeper.
minbarita tereno minefield.
minca slender.
minĉaro shuttle car.
Minĉo Minch.
mineapolano Minneapolitan.
minejo mine.
minejoligno pit-props, pitwood.
minekspluatado mining.
minerala mineral.
mineralakvo mineral water.
mineralo mineral.
mineralogiisto mineralogist.
mineralogio mineralogy.
mineralogo mineralogist.
Minervo Minerva.
minesotano Minnesotan.
mingalerio gallery of a mine.
mingaso fire-damp.
mini to mine.
miniatura miniature.
miniaturigi to miniaturize.
miniaturo miniature.
minibuso mini-bus.
minikamerao minicamera.
minimuma minimal, minimum.

minimume

minimume at (the) least.
minimumejo point of minimum.
minimumiganto point of minimum.
minimumigi to minimize.
minimumigo minimizing.
minimumismo minimalism.
minimumisto minimalist.
minimumo least, minimum.
mininĝeniero mining engineer.
minio lead tetroxide, minium, red lead, triplumbic tetroxide.
ministeria departmental.
ministerio (cabinet) department, ministry.
ministo miner.
ministra ministerial.
ministraro cabinet, government, ministry, department.
ministrejo ministry.
ministro minister (head of govt. dept.).
ministroprezidanto premier, prime minister.
minkarbo coal.
minlampo safety lamp.
mino mine (pit).
minoa Minoan.
minora minor.
minoritata minority.
minoritato minority.
minoro minor (subdeterminant).
minosano Minoan.
minotaŭro minotaur.
minsema ŝipo minelayer.
minsemŝipo minelayer.
minserĉilo mine-detector.
minstrelo minstrel.
minterneo minefield.
minus minus.
minusa minus.
minuskla lowercase, minuscule, small.
minuskligi to lowercase.
minusklo lower case letter, small letter.
minuskomplekso inferiority complex.
minuso minus sign (−).
minus-signo minus sign (−).
minuto minuet (time).
mio (the) self, one's self.
Mioceno Miocene.
miogalo desman, muskrat.
miopa myopic, near-sighted, short-sighted.
miopeco shortsightedness.
miopema myopic.
miopsito monk parakeet, quaker parrot.
miosotono water chickweed.
miozoto forget-me-not, myosotis.
mira astonishing.
mirabelo mirabelle.
miraĝo mirage.
miraĵo wonder.
mirakla miraculous.

misfaro

mirakle miraculously.
miraklo miracle.
miraklofaranto wonderworker, miracle man.
mire amazingly, astonishingly.
mirege very amazingly.
miregi to astound, be stupefied.
miregiga astonishing, astounding.
miregigi to amaze.
miregiĝi to be amazed.
mireginda prodigious, stupendous.
miregindaĵo prodigy.
mirego amazement, stupefaction, wonder.
mirho myrrh.
miri to be amazed, be astonished, marvel (at), wonder, be surprised.
miriado myriad.
miriametro myriameter.
miriapodo centipede.
mirido sweet cicely.
miriga amazing, astonishing.
mirige astonishing, surprising.
mirigi to astonish, amaze, surprise.
miriko bog myrtle, sweet gale.
mirinda amazing, astonishing, marvelous, wonderful.
mirindaega wonderful.
mirindaĵo marvel, wonder.
mirinde marvelously, wonderfully.
mirinfano child prodigy.
miriofilo water-milfoil.
Mirlando Wonderland.
mirmekofago anteater.
mirmeleono ant lion, doodle bug.
miro amazement, astonishment, wonder, surprise.
mirrakonto fairy tale.
mirtelbero blueberry.
mirtelo blueberry.
mirto myrtle.
mis- (denotes an error).
misa incorrect, amiss.
misago misdeed.
misagorda out of tune.
misagordi to put out of tune.
misalo missal.
misalproprigi to misappropriate.
misapliko misapplication.
misatento diagnostic error.
misaŭdi to mishear.
misciti to misquote.
miscito misquote.
misdecidi to make a bad decision.
misdigesto dyspepsia, indigestion.
mise wrongly.
misekvilibro imbalance.
misfamigi to defame.
misfari to trespass.
misfaro misdeed.

misfino abnormal end, abnormal termination, failure.
misformajô abnormality, abnormity.
misformeco abnormality, abnormity.
misformi to deform, misform.
misformita deformed.
misformiteco abnormality, abnormity.
misformo distortion.
misfunkciado malfunctioning.
misfunkcii to malfunction.
misfunkcio malfunction.
misgvida misguided.
misgvidi to misguide.
mishumoreco resentment, spite.
misidentigi to confuse.
misigi to distort.
misigo distortion.
misiĝi to go awry.
misiista mission. **misiista pozicio** missionary position.
misiisto missionary.
misila missile.
misilo missile.
misinformi to misinform.
misinterpreto misinterpretation.
misio mission.
misiri to go awry.
misisipia Mississippian.
misisipiano Mississippian.
Misisipo Mississippi.
misisto missionary.
misĵeto wide pitch, wild pitch.
miskalkuli to miscalculate.
miskalkulo miscalculation.
miskompreni to misunderstand.
miskompreniĝo miscomprehension.
miskompreno misunderstanding.
miskondiĉa ill conditioned.
miskonduti to act up.
miskonduto misconduct.
miskreditigi to discredit.
miskreska weedy.
misloki to misplace, mislay.
mismalkuli to miscalculate.
misnomi to misname.
miso evil, fault, foul.
misopinia wrong-headed.
misordo mess, disorder, disarray, chaos.
misortografii to misspell.
mispaŝi to tread wrongly, misstep.
mispaŝo aberration, false step, misstep.
mispensi to think wrongly, misthink.
mispercepto misperception.
misprezenti to misrepresent.
misprononci to mispronounce.
misproporcia disproportionate.
misproporcie disproportionately.
misproporcio imbalance.
misruliĝejo gutter.
missignalo glitch.
mistaksi to misjudge.
mistera abstruse, mysterious.
mistere mysteriously.
mistereco mysteriousness.
mistero mystery.
mistifi to fool, hoax, mystify, trick.
mistifika tricky.
mistifikaĉi to cheat, defraud, fool, swindle.
mistifiki to fool, hoax, mystify, trick.
mistifiko hoax, mystification, trick.
mistifo mystification.
mistika mystic, mystical.
mistikismo mysticism.
mistikisto mystic.
mistiko mysticism, mystique.
mistikulo mystic.
mistraduki to mistranslate.
mistrafo blunder.
mistraktado mistreatment.
mistrakti to mistreat, abuse.
mistrakto abuse.
mistralo mistral.
misuria Missourian.
misuriano Missourian.
misurinado strangury.
Misurio Missouri.
misuza abusive.
misuzado abuse.
misuzanto abuser.
misuzi to abuse, misuse.
misuzo abuse.
misvojo unbeaten track, wilderness.
mita mythical.
mitaro myths, mythology.
mitingo meeting, political meeting.
mito myth.
mitokondria mitochondrial.
mitokondrio mitochondrion.
mitologia mythological.
mitologiisto mythologist.
mitologio mythology.
mitozo mitosis.
mitraisma Mithraic.
mitraismo Mithraism.
mitraleto machine pistol, submachine gun.
mitrali to fire, shoot (a machine gun).
mitralnesto machine gun nest.
mitralo machine gun.
mitro mitre (headdress).
mitulejo mussel-bank, mussel-bed.
mitulo mussel.
mizantropa misanthropic.
mizantropo misanthrope.
mizera abject, dismal, meagre, miserable, wretched. **mizera salajro** starvation wage.
mizeraj nobeloj small freeholders.
mizeraspekta pathetic.
mizere miserably, wretchedly.

mizereco wretchedness.
mizerego want.
mizeri to be miserable, wretched.
mizerigo distress.
mizeriĝi to become miserable, wretched.
mizerikordo mercy.
mizero misery, wretchedness.
mizeruleto waif.
mizerulo pauper, poor devil, poor man, wretch.
mizogino misogynist.
Mjanmao Myanmar "(former Burma)".
mjelencefalo afterbrain.
mjelo spinal cord.
mnemonika mnemonic. **mnemonika simbolo** mnemonic symbol.
mnemoniko mnemonics.
mnemotehniko mnemonics.
mo name of the letter M.
mobilizado mobilization.
mobilizi to mobilize.
mobilizo mobilization.
mobilo mobile.
moda fashionable.
modala modal. **modala logiko** modal logic. **modalaj verboj** modal verbs. **modalaj vortoj** modal words.
modalo modality.
modbutiko fashion boutique.
modela model, typical.
modelado model building, model, modelling.
modelfolio pattern.
modeli to model.
modeligi to model.
modelilo mould.
modelino model.
modelo model, specimen, standard, type, pattern.
modemo modem.
modera moderate, reasonable.
modere modestly.
modereco moderation.
moderigi to mitigate, moderate, mollify, reign in.
moderiĝi to abate, moderate.
moderkosta reasonable.
moderna modern.
moderneco modernity.
modernigi to modernize.
modernismo modernism.
moderno modernity.
modero moderation.
moderpreza reasonable.
moderulo moderate.
modesta bashful, demure, modest, unassuming, moderate.
modeste modestly, unassumingly, unpretentiously.

modesteco modesty.
modesto modesty.
modifado alteration, modification.
modifi to modify.
modifiki to alter, amend, modify.
modifiko amendment.
modifilo modifier.
modifo amendment.
modistino milliner.
modkanto hit (song).
modli to model, mould.
modlopasto plasticine.
modluro (ornamental) modelling, moulding.
modo fashion, mode, mood.
modulado modulation.
module modulo.
modulema programado modular programming.
moduli to modulate.
modulo module, modulus.
mogola Mogul.
mogolo Mogul.
mohajro angora, mohair.
Mohamedo Muhammad, Mohammed.
mohavka Mohawk.
mohavko Mohawk.
mohîto mojito.
moka scornful.
mokadi to jeer.
mokado derision, mockery, ridicule.
mokaĵo mockery.
mokanto detractor, scoffer.
mokao mocha.
mokaseno moccasin.
moke scornfully.
mokegi to deride.
mokema scornful.
mokeme scornfully.
moketi to tease.
mokfajfi to whistle, whizz.
moki to mock, deride, jeer at, poke fun at, ridicule, taunt.
mokimiti to echo, repeat parrot-like.
mokinsulti to jeer, jeer at, taunt.
mokinsulto scoffing.
moknomo nickname.
moknono (unflattering, teasing, mocking) nickname.
moko mockery.
mokoeco mockery.
mokridi pri to laugh at.
mokturdo mocking-bird.
mola gentle, soft, tender, minor (music). **mola histo** soft tissue.
molaĉulo sissy.
molaĵo pulp. **molaĵo de frukto** pulp.
molanaso eider-duck.
molanimeco soft-heartedness.
molaro molar.

moldava Moldavian.
Moldavio Moldavia.
moldavo Moldavian.
Moldavujo Moldavia.
moldisko floppy disc.
Moldo Mold.
mole gently, softly, tenderly.
moleco mellowness, softness, tenderness.
molega limp.
molege limply.
molekula molecular.
molekulo molecule.
moleo breakwater, mole.
molesti to badger, molest.
molibdeno molybdenum.
moligi to soften up.
moligilo softener.
molinio purple moor-grass.
molkoreco tenderness.
molmatura overripe.
molo minor (music).
Moloĥo Moloch.
molotovkoktelo Molotov cocktail.
moluka Moluccan.
molukano Moluccan.
Molukoj Moluccas.
molusko mollusc. **moluskoj** mollusca, molluscs.
momanto moment.
momenta momentary.
momentaĵo quickie.
momente for the moment, in an instant, momentarily.
momenteto short moment, instant.
momentfoto snapshot.
momento instant, moment.
momordiko balsam pear, bitter gourd.
mona monetary, pecuniary. **mona kolektado** offertory. **mona puno** fine (penalty).
monado monad.
monaĥa monastic.
Monaĥano Monaghan.
monaĥaro abbey.
monaĥejestrino mother superior.
monaĥejestro (Father) Superior.
monaĥejo monastery.
monaĥestro archimandrite.
monaĥinaro abbey.
monaĥinejestrino (Mother) Superior.
monaĥinejo abbey, convent, nunnery.
monaĥino nun.
monaĥismo monasticism.
monaĥo friar, monk.
monaka Monegasque.
monakano Monacan.
monakejo monastery.
monakinejo convent.
monakino nun.
Monako Monaco.

monalo monal.
monardo bee balm, fragrant balm.
monarĥejo monarchy.
monarĥio monarchy.
monarĥismo monarchism.
monarĥisto monarchist.
monarĥo monarch.
monarkio monarchy.
monarko monarch.
monasignaĵo allowance.
monasigni to appropriate.
monasigno allocation, allowance, appropriation.
monata monthly. **monata abonbileto** monthly season ticket, monthly subscription.
monataĵo period, menses.
monatkomenco beginning of the month.
monato month.
monaŭtomato ATM.
monavido avarice.
monavidulo money-grubber.
monbileto bank note, paper money.
monbiletujo wallet.
moncelante for money, for profit.
monda mundane, secular, temporal, worldly, earthly, worldwide. **Monda Banko** World Bank. **Monda Naturfonduso** World Wildlife Fund. **Monda Organizaĵo pri Meteologio** World Meteorological Organization, WMO. **Monda Organizaĵo pri Sano** World Health Organization, WHO. **Monda Organizaĵo pri Turismo** World Tourism Organization, WTO.
mondaĝo epoch, period (geological).
mondamilito world war.
mondanimo anima mundi.
mondcivitaneco cosmopolitanism, world citizenship.
mondcivitano cosmopolitan, world citizen.
mondegrino mondegreen.
mondfama world-famous.
mondkoncepto world view.
mondliteraturo world literature.
mondmilito world war.
mondo world.
mondoceano global ocean, world ocean.
mondoparto part of the world, continent.
mondoskua earth-shaking.
mondperspektivo view of the world, Weltanschauung.
mondpokalo world cup.
mondrigardo worldview.
monduma sophisticated, worldly. **monduma vivo** worldly life.
mondumo high society.
monedo jackdaw.
monereta mono change.
monereto mite (coin).
monerfiguro effigy, head.

monero

monero coin.
monfarejestro Master of the Mint, mint-master.
monfarejo mint.
monfari to coin, mint.
monforte an Italian family name, the name of a town in Italy.
mongajniga lucrative.
mongajnigo remuneration.
mongola Mongolian.
mongoleda Mongolian.
Mongolio Mongolia.
mongolo Mongol, Mongolian.
Mongolujo Mongolia.
monhava rich, wealthy.
monhelpato beneficiary.
monhelpo assistance.
monherbo honesty.
monitoro (computer) monitor.
monkesto safe (money).
monkolektado collection.
monkolektanto collector of donations.
monkolekti to collect money.
monkolekto collection (of money).
monludi to gamble.
monludisto gambler.
monmandato warrant (money).
mono cash, money.
monobileto paper money.
monoferado subscription.
monoferi to subscribe (money).
monofilona holophyletic, monophyletic.
monogamio monogamy.
monografio monograph.
monografo monograph.
monogramo monogram.
monoido monoid.
monoika monoecious.
monokesteto till, money box.
monoklina monoclinous.
monoklo monocle.
monolatrismo monolatrism.
monolito monolith.
monologi to make a monologue.
monologo monologue, soliloquy.
monomanio monomania.
monomero monomer.
monomo monomial.
monoplano monoplane.
monopola vendo sole agency, sole sale.
monopoligi to monopolize.
monopolo monopoly.
monopresi to strike (coins).
monopsonio buyer's monopoly, monopsony.
monoskatoleto money box.
monoŝranko strongbox.
monoteisma monotheistic.
monoteismo monotheism.
monoteisto monotheist.

montodeklivo

monotipo monotype.
monotona monotone, monotonic, monotonous.
monotropo yellow bird's-nest.
monpaperujo wallet.
monperdo loss.
monpoŝo money pocket.
monprovizi to bankroll.
monpuni to fine.
monpuno fine.
Monrovio Monrovia.
monseratano Montserratian.
monsinjoro monsignor.
monsistemo monetary system.
monspeco type of money.
monstra monstrous.
monstranco monstrance.
monstreco monstrosity.
monstro monster.
monsumo sum of money.
monŝanĝejo money exchange.
monŝanĝisto money-changer.
monŝranko strongbox.
monta mountainous. **monta lagopo** rock ptarmigan.
montana Montanan. **montana bastono** axe-like staff, alpenstock.
montanano Montanan.
montano highlander, mountaineer.
montara mountain, of a mountain.
montara aero mountain air. **montara ĉeno** chain of mountains, mountain chain, mountain range.
montarhorizonto mountain range skyline.
montaro chain of mountains, mountain range.
montbastono alpenstock.
montbretio montbretia.
montenegra Montenegrin.
montenegrano Montenegrin.
Montenegro Montenegro.
monteta hill, small mountain. **monteta deklivo** hillside.
monteto hill, mount.
montfendo chasm, cleft, gorge, gully, ravine.
montflanko mountainside.
montgrimpado mountaineering.
montgrimpanto Alpinist, mountaineer, (mountain) climber.
montgrimpo mountain climbing.
montkabano Alpine hut, climber's hut, mountain hut.
montkolo pass, defile, creek, notch, saddle.
montkorvo chough.
montkresto mountain ridge.
monto mountain.
montoĉeno chain of mountains, mountain chain, mountain range, rand.
montodeklivo mountain slope.

montodorso mountain ridge.
montofringo brambling.
montoprediko Sermon on the Mount.
montpasejo (mountain) pass.
montra demonstrative. **montra pronomo** demonstrative, demonstrative pronoun.
montrado manifestation.
montraĵo display.
montrebla apparent.
montri to indicate, point out, show, denote, expose. **montri sin inda je** to show oneself worthy of.
montriĉa mountainous.
montriĝi to appear, show oneself, turn out to be. **montriĝis ke...** it turned out that...
montriĝo display.
montrilo hand (of a clock), pointer, indicator.
montro sign.
montrofenestro show window.
Montrozo Montrose.
montspino mountain ridge.
montsuben down the slope, downhill.
montsupro mountain peak, mountain top, pinnacle.
montŝuo mountaineering boot.
montvojeto mountain path.
monujo purse, wallet.
monumenta monumental.
monumente monumentally.
monumento monument.
monunio monetary union.
monunuo currency unit, monetary unit.
monvalorperdiĝo inflation.
mopedisto moped rider.
mopedo moped.
mopseto pug dog.
mopso pug.
morala moral.
moralaĵo moral.
morale morally.
moraleco morality.
moralinstruo moral.
moralisto moralist.
moralo morals.
moratorio moratorium.
moravia frato Moravian brother.
Moravio Moravia.
morbila measles.
morbilo measles.
morbo disease.
morda mordant, pungent.
mordaĵo mordant, stain, wood dye, wood stain.
mordanta biting.
mordema scathing, biting.
mordeti to corrode, gnaw, nibble.
mordeto nip.
mordi to bite.
mordo bite.
mordovundo bite.
mordpeco morsel.
morelo poker.
moreno moraine.
morfemo morpheme.
morfemscienco morphology.
Morfeo Morpheus.
morfinmaniulo morphine addict.
morfino morphia, morphine.
morfio morphism.
morfologia morphological.
morfologie morphologically.
morfologio morphology.
morganata morganatic, morganatical.
morgaŭ tomorrow. **morgaŭ matene** tomorrow morning. **morgaŭ posttagmeze** tomorrow afternoon. **morgaŭ vespere** tomorrow evening.
morgaŭa of tomorrow.
morgaŭo tomorrow.
morgaŭtage the next morning.
morgaŭtagmeze the next afternoon.
morgaŭtago morrow.
morhelo morel.
Morifirto Moray Firth.
morkelo morel.
mormona Mormon.
mormonismo Mormonism.
mormono Mormon.
morna desolate, dismal, dreary, gaunt, gloomy, mournful.
morneco gloom.
moro custom, mores, morals.
moroj manners.
moroza fretful, morose, peevish, sullen.
morsa Morse code. **morsa alfabeto** Morse alphabet. **morsa klavo** Morse key.
morsi to send in Morse code.
Morso Morse.
morta dead. **morta malamiko** archenemy. **Morta Maro** Dead Sea. **morta peko** mortal sin.
mortaĉi to croak (die).
mortado mortality (effect).
mortaĵo carrion.
mortanoncisto undertaker's man.
mortanto dying (person).
mortbati to beat to death.
mortbato manslaughter.
morte terminally. **morte malsana** deathly ill.
mortebria dead drunk.
morteco mortality (state).
mortema mortal.
morteristo bricklayer.
mortero mortar (building).
morterportisto bricklayer's labourer.
morterujo hod.
mortezi to mortise, slot.

mortezo mortise, slot.
mortfesto wake.
morti to die, expire, pass away. **morti de malsato** to die of hunger. **morti per natura morto** to die a natural death. **morti pro sangelfluo** to bleed to death.
mortideva mortal.
mortiga deadly, mortal. **mortiga bato** fatal blow.
mortiganto assassin, murderer.
mortigi to kill, liquidate, slay, murder. **mortigi sin** to commit suicide, kill oneself.
mortigiloj instruments of murder.
mortigisto murderer.
mortigo murder.
mortigulo assassin.
mortiĝi to die, pass away. **mortiĝi de malsato** to die of hunger.
mortinta dead.
mortintaĵo carrion.
mortintejo dead house.
mortinto defunct, late, deceased.
mortkialo cause of death.
mortkitelo shroud, winding sheet.
mortkonduko leading someone to their death.
mortkovrilo shroud, pall.
mortmalsana deathly ill.
mortmalsato starvation.
mortmerita krimo capital crime.
mortnaskito stillborn (child).
morto death, demise.
mortobato death blow.
mortokvanto mortality.
mortominaci to threaten with death.
mortotuko shroud.
mortpafi to shoot dead, shoot to kill, shoot to death.
mortpafita shot dead.
mortpala deathly pale.
mortpeko cardinal sin.
mortpiki to stab.
mortpuno death penalty, punishment by death.
mortsciigisto undertaker's man.
mortsimila silento deathly silence.
mortsonorado knell.
mortsopiri to breathe one's last.
morttuko winding sheet.
mortulejo morgue.
mortverdikto death sentence.
mortvesto shroud.
Morua Benko Dogger Bank.
moruaĵo cod.
moruo cod, codfish.
moruoleo codfish oil.
morusarbo mulberry tree.
moruso mulberry.
morusujo mulberry tree.

morvo glanders.
Mosea pertaining to Moses, Mosaic.
Moseo Moses.
moska musky, smelling of animal musk.
moskatelo muscatel.
moskeo mosque.
moskfrago hautbois strawberry.
moskitforpelilo mosquito repellant.
moskito mosquito.
mosko musk.
moskobesto musk-deer.
moskobovo musk ox.
moskodoro musky smell.
moskorato muskrat.
moskulo musk deer.
moskva Muscovite.
moskvano Muscovite.
Moskvo Moscow.
moslema Muslim, Moslem.
moslemo Muslim, Moslem.
mosto must, new wine, unfermented grape juice.
moŝta honorary.
moŝte komplezi to condescend.
moŝto (general title for persons of high rank).
moŝtulo bigwig.
motacilo wagtail.
motelo motel.
moteto motet.
motivado motivation.
motivi to motivate.
motivigi to justify.
motiviĝo motivation.
motiviteco motivation.
motivo account, motive, reason, goal, purpose, incentive, motif, motivation, cause.
moto motto.
motociklo motorbike.
motorbiciklo motorcycle.
motorboato motorboat.
motorcikla policisto motorcycle policeman, police motorcyclist.
motorciklisto motorcyclist.
motorciklo motorcycle.
motorfiakro cab, taxi.
motoristo machinist, mechanic, motorist.
motorizi to motorize.
motoro engine, motor.
motoroleo motor oil.
motorŝipo motor ship.
motorveturilo motor vehicle.
mova locomotive, moving.
movadiĝi to fidget.
movado movement.
movebla mobile, movable.
movebleco mobility.
movetadi sin to bestir one's self.
moveti to move slightly, nudge.

movi

movi to move, shift, stir. **movi en la poŝon** cut.
moviga motive.
moviĝado motion.
moviĝema active.
moviĝemo agility.
moviĝi to (make) move.
moviĝo motion, move, shift. **moviĝo al** movement towards.
movilo motor, movement mechanism.
movimento movement.
movinta having moved.
movlerta agile.
movlibero elbow-room.
movo move, motion, movement.
movoplena animated, bustling.
movsablo quicksand.
mozaiko mosaic, mosaic work.
mozaikplanko mosaic floor.
mozambika Mozambican.
mozambikano Mozambican.
Mozambiko Mozambique.
Mozelo Moselle.
mozelvino moselle.
Mozo Meuse.
muara moiré.
muari to moiré.
mucida foul, mouldy, musty.
mucilago mucilage.
mueldento molar.
muelejo mill, millhouse.
mueli to grind, pulverize.
muelilo mill.
muelisto miller.
muezino muezzin.
mufganto mitt.
muflo muffle.
muflono mouflon.
mufo gas mantle, mitten, muff.
muftio mufti.
mugiledoj mullets (family).
mugilo mullet.
muĝado growling, roaring, howling.
  muĝado venta howling of the wind.
muĝi to bellow, howl, roar, low, moo, roar.
muĝo rage, roar.
Muhamado Muhammad, Mohammed.
muka mucous.
muko mucus, phlegm.
mukozo mucous membrane.
mulao mullah.
mulatino mulatto, female mulatto.
mulato mulatto.
mulĉo mulch.
muldaĵo cast.
muldi to cast, mould.
muldilo mould.
muldorso back of a mule.
mulera Müllerian.

multipleksa

Mulinkaro Mullingar.
mulisto muleteer.
Muljo Mull.
mulo mule.
mulpelisto muleteer.
Mulranio Mulranny.
mult- multi-.
multa a lot of, much, numerous. **multaj** many, several.
multampleksa comprehensive.
multamplekse comprehensively.
multangulo polygon.
multcela multimission, multipurpose, multicellular.
multdiismo polytheism.
multdika bulky, voluminous.
multe a lot, many, much. **multe da** a lot of, much, plenty of, many of.
multeco multiplicity, plurality, size.
multedzineco polygamy.
multega huge, tremendous.
multege immensely, numerously.
multego infinity.
multekosta costly, dear, expensive, pricey, precious, valuable, expensive, high-priced.
multekoste expensively.
multemova animated, busy, full of traffic.
multenombra manifold.
multenombro plural.
multepeza burdensome, ponderous, weighty.
multepezeco heaviness.
multepova powerful.
multesona vibrant.
multetaŭga multipurpose.
multevalora very valuable, precious.
multeventa tumultuous.
multflanka many-sided, multi-faceted.
multfoje many times.
multforma multiform.
multfunkcia multifunctional.
multhoma crowded, populous.
multigado multiplication.
multiganto multiplier.
multigato multiplicand.
multigi to multiply, propagate.
multigita multiplied.
multigo multiplication.
multiĝi to increase, multiply.
multiĝo proliferation.
multiiĝo multiplication.
multinfana prolific.
multipleksorado multiplexing.
multipleksoro multiplexer.
multiplika multiplicative. **multiplika grupo** multiplicative group.
multiplikanto multiplier.
multiplikato multiplicand.
multiplikeska simbolo multiplying operator.

multipliki to multiply.
multipliko multiplication.
multjara multi-year.
multjarcenta age-old.
multkolora multicolored, variegated.
multkolorigi to variegate.
multkultura multicultural.
multlingva multilingual.
multlingveco plurality of languages.
multlingvigi to multilingualize.
multlingvigo multilingualization.
multmaniere in many ways.
multnacia multinational.
multnombra numerous, plural.
multnombro plural.
multo a lot, many; mass, large quantity.
multobla multiple.
multobligi to duplicate, multiply.
multoblo multiple.
multokupita busy.
multpaperujo ring binder.
multpartia multilateral.
multpeza weighty.
multpieda having many feet.
multpieduloj myriapods.
multsignifa significant.
multsilaba multi-syllable.
multspeca diverse, of many types.
multvalora of great price.
multvojaĝinta travelled, widely-travelled.
multvorta long-winded, wordy.
multvorteco prolixity.
mumiigo mummification.
mumio mummy.
mumo mummy.
mumpso mumps.
munano Moonie.
mungo mongoose.
mungoto mongoose.
municiejo ammunition dump, magazine.
municio munition, ammunition.
municipo municipality.
Munkeno Munich.
muntado assemblage, assembly, composing, erecting, fitting up, mounting.
muntadohalo assembly hall, assembly shop.
muntaĵo base, setting.
muntbendo assembly line conveyor belt.
muntejo assembly room.
Muntenio Greater Wallachia, Muntenia.
munti to assemble, link, mount, set.
muntiako barking dear, muntjac.
muntilo linker.
muntisto assembler, fitter.
muntita foto photomontage.
muntkadro frame-work.
muntodosiero makefile.
muntumo setting.
muo mu (Mμ).

muono muon.
murapogilo abutment.
murbalo squash.
murda murderous.
murdanto killer, murderer.
murdema bloodthirsty.
murdemo bloodthirstiness.
murdento "arch" battlement, pinnacle.
murdi to murder.
murdilo murder weapon.
murdintino murderess.
murdinto murderer.
murdisto murderer.
murdo murder.
murego rampart, (large) wall.
mureno moray.
murhorloĝo wall clock.
muria briny.
Murihiko Invercargill.
murio brine.
murkahelo wall tile.
murkolorigisto house painter.
murkrampo brace.
Murmansko Murmansk.
murmurado babble, murmur.
murmuregi to growl.
murmurego growl.
murmureti to murmur softly, purr.
murmureto soft murmur.
murmuri to murmur, mutter.
murmuro murmur, whisper.
muro wall.
murpapero wallpaper.
murpentraĵo mural, mural painting, wall painting.
murpilkadejo handball court.
murpilko handball.
murŝranko cabinet.
murŝtupo stile.
murtapiŝo tapestry, wall-hanging.
musbutono mouse button.
musido baby mouse.
muska mossy.
muskaptilo mousetrap.
muskario grape hyacinth.
muskatarbo nutmeg tree.
muskato nutmeg.
muskatvino muscat wine, muscatel.
muskedisto musketeer.
muskedo musket.
musketero musketeer.
musketisto musketeer.
musketo musket.
musko moss.
muskoj mosses.
muskola brawny, muscular.
muskolaro musculature.
muskoleca hunky, muscular.
muskolo muscle.

muskoplantoj mosses.
muskursoro mark, mouse pointer.
muskuseneto mouse-pad.
muskverda moss-green.
muslino muslin.
muslio muesli.
Musloburgo Musselburgh.
musmato mouse-pad.
muso mouse.
musono monsoon.
mustango mustang.
mustarda saŭco mustard sauce.
mustardo mustard.
mustardujo mustard pot.
mustelkato stone-marten.
mustelo marten, weasel.
musveneno rat poison.
muŝbirdo hummingbird.
muŝo fly.
muta dumb, mute, speechless, silent. **muta cigno** mute swan.
mutacii to mutate.
mutacio mutation.
mutaciulo mutant.
muteco dumbness.
mutigi to mute.
mutiĝi to be struck dumb.
mutili to mutilate.
mutlkultureco multiculturalism.
mutuala friendly, mutual.
mutulo mute.
muzelingo muzzle.
muzelo muzzle, snout.

muzeo museum.
muzika musical. **muzika komedio** musical comedy, musical. **muzika prezentaĵo** musical performance. **muzika societo** musical club, musical society. **muzika vespero** musical evening.
muzikaĵo piece of music.
muzikamanto music lover.
muzikema musical.
muzikemo musicality.
muzikestro band leader.
muzikgrupo band, music group.
muziki to make music.
muzikilo musical instrument.
muzikinstruado musical instruction.
muzikinstrumento musical instrument.
muzikistaro band.
muzikisto musician.
muzikkesto music box.
muzikkiosko bandstand.
muzikleciono music-lesson.
muziklernejo school of music.
muziklibro music-book.
muziko music.
muzikologio musicology.
muzikpodio bandstand.
muzikportilo music-stand.
muziktalento musical aptitude.
muzikteatraĵo musical.
muzikteorio theory of music.
muzikverko piece of music.
muzo muse.
muzulmano Muslim, Moslem.

N

n- the variable n. **n-argumenta funkcio** function of n variables. **n-argumenta rilato** n-ary relation. **n-ciklo** n-cycle. **n-dimensia** n-dimensional. **n-edro** n-hedron. **n-grafeo** n-graph. **n × p matrico** (= **n kontraŭ p**) n-by-p matrix. **n-latero** polygon of n sides. **n-lineara** n-linear. **n-modula restoklaso** residue class (modulo n). **n-obla** n-fold. **n-opo** n-tuple. **n-uma prezento** representation (of a number in base n).
n-a (= **noa**) nth. **n-a centra momanto** nth central moment. **n-a momanto** nth moment. **n-a potenco** nth power. **n-a radiko** n-th root. **n-a termo** nth member, nth term. **n-a-grada** nth-degree, of the nth degree.
nababo nabob.
nabo hub, nave.
nabocâpo hubcap.
nacelo nacelle.
nacia national. **nacia sanservo** national health service.
naciaĵo national idiom.
nacianigi to nationalize.
naciano national.
nacie kaj internacie nationally and internationally.
nacieco nationality.
naciigi to nationalize.
naciigo nationalization.
naciismo nationalism.
naciisto nationalist.
nacilingva national-language.
nacimalplimulto national minority.
nacio nation, nationality.
nacionalismo nationalism.
nacisocialismo national socialism.
nadiro nadir.
nadla acicular.
nadlara printilo dot matrix printer.
nadlo indicator, pointer, needle (compass, phonograph), hand (watch, clock).
nadloforma acicular.
naftaleno naphthalene.
naftalino naphthalene.
nafto crude oil.
naftodukto oil pipeline.
naftofonto oil well.
naftolo naphthol.
naftoputo oil well.
naftorafinejo oil refinery.
naftoŝipo oil tanker.
Nagasako Nagasaki.
Nagojo Nagoya.

naĝa potamogeto broad-leaved pondweed, floating-leaf pondweed.
naĝadi to keep on swimming.
naĝado swimming.
naĝanto swimmer.
naĝarto swimming.
naĝbarelo buoy.
naĝbaseno swimming pool.
naĝe afloat.
naĝejo pool, swimming pool.
naĝema buoyant.
naĝi to float, swim.
naĝigi to make someone swim.
naĝilo fin.
naĝisto swimmer.
naĝkostumo bathing suit.
naĝmovo stroke.
naĝobarelo buoy.
naĝokapablo ability to swim.
naĝosigno buoy.
naĝtabulo kickboard.
naiva artless, candid, naïve, simple, innocent, unaffected, unsophisticated, natural.
naive naïvely.
naiveco naïvety.
naivega silly, simple, foolish.
naivegrideti to simper.
naivegulo simpleton.
naivulo naïve person.
najado naiad, water nymph.
najbara adjacent, nearby, neighbouring, adjoining, consecutive.
najbaraĵo neighbourhood, vicinity, surroundings.
najbare de adjacent to, next to, in the vicinity of.
najbareco neighbourhood, neighbourliness, vicinity.
najbarejo neighbourhood.
najbarfilino girl next door.
najbarino female neighbour.
najbaro neighbour.
najlborilo bradawl.
najlego spike.
najleti to tack.
najleto tack.
najlforma nail-shaped, pointed.
najli to nail.
najlo nail.
najlofajlilo nail file.
najlofiksita fixed with nails.
najlotirilo pincers.
najlpinta pointed (like a nail).
najlturnilo bradawl.
Najrobio Nairobi.

Najrobo Nairobi.
najtingalo nightingale.
Nakso Naxos.
Nameno Namur.
namibia Namibian.
namibianino Namibian woman.
namibiano Namibian.
Namibio Namibia.
Namuro Namur.
nana dwarf, midget.
nanduo American ostrich, nandu.
nanigi to stunt.
nankeno nankeen.
Nankino Nanking.
nano dwarf, midget, little person.
nanofarado nanofarad.
nanometro nanometer.
nanosekundo nanosecond.
nanoteknologio nanotechnology.
nanplanedo dwarf planet.
napalmi to napalm.
napalmo napalm.
Napiero Napier.
napo[1] rapeseed, canola.
napo[2] turnip.
napola Neapolitan.
napolano Neapolitan.
napoleona Napoleonic.
Napoleono Napoleon.
Napolo Naples.
narcisismo narcissism.
narciso daffodil, narcissus.
Narciso Narcissus.
nardo matgrass, spikenard.
nargileo hookah, water pipe.
narkoanalizo narco-analysis.
narkolepsio narcolepsy.
narkotado doping.
narkotaĵo drug.
narkotejo a shop where drugs are sold.
narkoti to drug, narcotize.
narkotiĝo narcosis, stupor.
narkotiko narcotic.
narkotikoj drugs.
narkotilo drug, narcotic.
narkotismo drug abuse, drug addiction.
narkotiulo drug addict.
narkoto drug.
narkotulo drug addict.
nartecio bog asphodel.
narvalo narwhal.
Nasaŭo Nassau.
Naserlago Lake Nasser.
naska sezono breeding season.
naskado giving birth.
naskakto birth certificate.
naskantino a female who is giving birth.
naskanto generator.
naskatesto birth certificate.
naskdoloroj birth pains, labour pains, pains of childbirth, throes.
naskema having many children.
naski to bear, give birth to, bring forth, generate, spawn. **naski bovidon** calve. **naski ĉevalidon** bear foal.
naskigi to beget.
naskigo procreation.
naskiĝa of one's birth. **naskiĝa lando** land of one's birth, homeland.
naskiĝanonco birth announcement.
naskiĝatesto birth certificate.
naskiĝdato date of birth, birthday.
naskiĝdomo birthplace, childhood home.
naskiĝejo cradle, place of birth.
naskiĝi to arise, be born.
naskiĝlando land of one's birth, homeland.
naskiĝloko birthplace.
naskiĝo birth, nativity, parentage.
naskiĝotago birthday.
naskiĝpezo birth weight.
naskiĝtaga birthday. **naskiĝtaga kuko** birthday cake.
naskiĝtago birthdate, birthday.
naskiĝurbo city of birth.
naskita born.
naskitaro brood.
naskito new-born.
nasko childbirth, delivery.
naskokvanto birthrate.
naskolando native country, country of one's birth.
naskoloko place of birth.
naskoregulado birth control.
naskotago birthdate, birthday.
naskurbo hometown, city in which one was born.
naso crayfish net, eel pot, eel trap, fish trap, fishing basket, hoop net, lobster trap.
nasturcio watercress.
natalitato birthrate.
Natalo Natal.
natria bikarbonato bicarbonate of soda.
natrio sodium.
natro caustic soda, lye, niter.
natura natural. **natura entjero** natural number. **natura leĝo** natural law. **natura logaritmo** natural logarithm. **natura nombro** natural number. **natura persono** natural person.
naturaleco naturalness.
naturalismo naturalism.
naturalisto naturalist.
naturdotita gifted, talented.
naturdoto aptitude, disposition, talent, turn.
nature naturally.
natureco abandonment.
naturesploristo naturalist.

naturismo naturism, living according to nature, nudism.
naturkatastrofo act of God.
naturkuraco natural healer.
naturleĝo law of nature, natural law.
naturo character, nature.
naturparko natural park.
naturponto wildlife crossing.
naturscienco natural science, physics.
naturspirito elemental, nature spirit.
Nauro (Republic of) Nauru.
naŭ nine.
naŭa ninth.
naŭcent nine hundred.
naŭcenta nine hundredth.
naŭdek ninety.
naŭdeka ninetieth.
naŭdekkelkjara nonagenarian.
naŭdekkelkjarulo nonagenarian.
naŭe ninthly.
naŭlatero enneagon, nonagon.
naŭno ninth.
naŭoble ninefold.
naŭono ninth.
naŭtika nautical.
naŭtilo nautilus.
naŭto ninth.
naŭza abhorrent, abominable, alien, disgusting, nasty, nauseous.
naŭze vilely.
naŭzeco nastiness.
naŭzi to disgust, nauseate.
naŭziĝema squeamish.
naŭziza loathsome.
naŭzo disgust, nausea.
navaha Navaho.
Navaho Navaho.
navedo shuttle.
naveta shuttle.
navetanto commuter.
naveti to commute, shuttle.
naveto shuttle.
naviga navigation.
navigacia navigation(al). **navigacia sputniko** navigation(al) satellite.
navigaciado navigation.
navigaciejo chart house.
navigacii to cruise, lay a course, navigate, voyage, sail.
navigacio navigation.
navigado navigation.
navigebla navigable.
navigebleco navigability.
navigejo bridge.
navighaltejo landing stage, pier.
navigi to navigate.
navigilo navigator.
navigisto navigator.
navo nave (church).

naza nasal.
nazalo nasal consonant.
nazaretano Nazarene.
Nazareto Nazareth.
nazego snout.
nazeto neck (of vase), nozzle.
nazia Nazi.
naziismo Nazism.
nazio Nazi.
nazkataro cold in the head.
nazlobo nostril.
nazmuko mucus, phlegm, snot.
nazo nose.
nazosangado bloody nose.
nazotruo nostril.
nazparoli to snuffle, speak through the nose.
nazradiko bridge (of nose).
naztabako snuff, sniffing tobacco.
naztruo nostril.
naztuko handkerchief, tissue.
nazumi to nuzzle.
nazumo pince-nez.
nazuo coati, coatimundi.
N.B. → **notu bone**.
ndebela lingvo Ndebele, Ndebele language.
ndebelo Ndebele.
N.d.l.R. → **Noto de la Redakcio**.
ne no, not. **ne atendite** unexpectedly. **ne atentante** apart from. **ne ĉio brilanta estas diamanto** all that glitters is not gold. **ne dankinde** don't mention it, you're welcome. **ne eblas** it's not possible. **ne eble!** impossible! **ne efektiviĝi** to break down, come to nothing. **ne estas deviga** it is not necessary, obligatory, mandatory. **ne estas maloftajo ke** It's not uncommon that. **ne estas vere, ke...** It's not true that... **ne estis daŭronta** was not meant to last. **ne fari** to fail, neglect, omit. **ne fumi** to no smoking. **ne gravas** It doesn't matter. **ne havi kaŭzon por** to have no reason to. **ne havi tempon por ion** to not have time for something. **ne kapabli** to be unable. **ne konsideri** to leave out of account. **ne malbone** so-so. **ne mirinde ke** it's not surprising that. **ne ofendiĝu** don't be offended. no offence (intended). **ne okazi** to fail to appear. **ne parolu al mi pri...** Don't talk to me about... **ne plu** no longer. **ne plu paroli pri** to leave in abeyance. **ne ridigu min** Don't make me laugh. **ne sole ... sed ankaŭ** not only . but also. **ne temas pri tio** That's not the point. **ne troigu** don't exaggerate. **ne trovi dormon** to not find sleep, be unable to sleep. **ne tuŝi** to keep one's hands off. **ne tute** not quite. **ne unufoje** more than once. **ne utilas** it's no use. **ne zorgi pri** to neglect. **ne zorgu vi** don't worry.

ne- not-, un-, dis-, il-, im-, in-, un-.
nea negative.
neaĉetita uncorrupted (moral).
neado denial, negation.
neaerobia anaerobic.
neafekta unaffected.
neafektema unassuming, unpretending, unvarnished, plain.
neagema passive.
neagemo indolence.
neakcentita unaccented, unstressed.
neakceptebla inadmissible, unacceptable.
neakcepteble unacceptably.
neakordigebla incompatible, irreconcilable.
neaktiva inactive.
neaktiveco inactivity.
neakurata inaccurate.
nealirebla inaccessible.
nealirebleco inaccessibility.
neallasebla inadmissible.
neallaseble unacceptably.
nealloga unattractive.
neamika unfriendly.
neamikiĝema unsociable.
neandertala Neanderthal. **neandertala homo** Neanderthal man.
Neandertalo Neanderthal.
neandertalulo Neanderthal man.
neanstataŭigebla irreplaceable.
neantaŭdirebla unpredictable.
neantaŭdireble unpredictably.
neantaŭvidebla unforeseeable.
neantaŭvidita unforeseen.
neapartigebla indissoluble, inseparable.
nearmita unarmed.
neatakebla unassailable.
neatendebla unforeseeable.
neatendi to not expect.
neatendita abrupt, unexpected.
neatendite unexpectedly.
neatenta careless, negligent.
neatenteco inattention.
neatenti to not expect, not be waiting for.
neatingebla inaccessible.
neatingeble unattainably.
neaŭdebla inaudible.
neaŭdeble inaudibly.
neaŭdita unheard of.
nebaptita unbaptized.
nebarita unbounded.
nebatalanto civilian.
nebela homely.
nebezona unneeded, unnecessary.
nebindita unbound (book).
nebona passable.
nebone poorly.
nebonkora unkind.
nebonkore unkindly.
nebonkoreco unkindness.

nebonvola unkind, unobliging.
nebonvole unkindly.
nebonvoleco unkindness.
nebraska Nebraskan.
nebraskano Nebraskan.
Nebrasko Nebraska.
nebridebla indomitable.
nebrila dim.
nebruligebla fire proof.
Nebukadnecaro Nebuchadnezzar.
Nebukadnezo Nebuchadnezzar.
nebula dull, sombre, fuzzy, misty, nebulous.
nebulastro nebula.
nebuleco nebulosity.
nebuleta hazy, misty.
nebuleto haze, mist.
nebuligi to befog, cloud, dim.
nebuligilo atomizer.
nebuliĝi to become steamy, get covered with, get dim.
nebulo fog, mist.
nebulozo nebula.
neceda unbending, resolute.
necedema adamant.
necedeme firmly, resolutely, unflinchingly, unyieldingly.
necedemo firmness, resolution.
necedigebla adamant.
necerta precarious, uncertain.
necerte uncertainly.
necerteco suspense (uncertainty).
necesa necessary, needful, requisite. **necesa kondiĉo** necessary condition.
necesaĵo necessary thing. **necesaĵoj** materials, necessaries, requisites.
necese necessary.
neceseco necessity, requirement.
necesega indispensable, vital.
neceseja toilet. **neceseja broso** toilet brush. **neceseja papero** toilet paper. **neceseja seĝo** toilet bowl, toilet seat.
necesejo bathroom, lavatory, toilet, restroom, WC.
necesejpapero toilet paper.
necesi to be needed; to use the toilet.
necesas it is necessary. **necesas ankaŭ diri, ke...** it must also be said that.
necesigi to make necessary.
neceso necessary (thing).
necesseĝo toilet bowl, toilet seat.
necesujo dressing case, workbox.
necikla acyclic.
necivilizita uncivilized.
neciviliziteco want of civilization.
neĉeesto absence.
neĉefa accessory.
neĉiameco impermanence.
nedanka ungrateful.
nedankema ungrateful.

nedankinde don't mention it, you're welcome.
nedaŭra fleeting, temporary.
nedaŭre temporarily.
nedaŭrigebla unsustainable.
nedaŭrigeble unsustainably.
nedaŭrigebleco unsustainability.
nedeca improper, inappropriate, indecent.
nedece improperly, ineptly.
nedececo impropriety.
nedecida irresolute.
nedecideco indecision.
nedecidema indecisive.
nedeklinaciebla indeclinable.
nedemokratia undemocratic.
nedependa independent. **nedependa variablo** independent variable.
nederlanda Dutch. **nederlanda lingvo** Dutch, Dutch language. **Nederlanda Suda Maro** Zuider Zee. **Nederlandaj Antiloj** Netherlands Antilles. **Nederlandaj Indioj** Dutch East Indies.
nederlandaneco Dutch nationality.
nederlandanino Dutch woman.
nederlandano Dutch. **Nederlandano** Dutchman.
Nederlando the Netherlands, Holland.
Nedertaŭno Nethertown.
nedetena unrestrained.
nedeterminita fluganta objekto unidentified flying object, UFO.
nedeviga optional.
nedezirinda undesirable.
nedifina undefined. **nedifina artikolo** indefinite article.
nedifinebla indefinable.
nedifini to undefine.
nedifinita indefinite, indeterminate. **nedifinita integralo** antiderivative, indefinite integral.
nedigestebla indigestible.
nedirebla unspeakable.
nedireble unspeakably.
nedirektebla uncontrollable.
nedirekteble uncontrollably.
nedisigebla inseparable. **nedisigebla ago** atomic transaction, inseparable action.
nedisigeble indivisibly, inseparably.
nedisigeblo inseparability.
nedisputebla incontestable, indisputable.
nedisputeble indisputably, overwhelmingly.
nedistingebla indistinguishable.
nedistingeble indistinguishably.
nedividebla indivisible.
nedivideble indivisibly.
nedizirinde undesirably.
Nedo Neath.
nedresebla indomitable, intractable.
neduba indubitable.

nedubebla undoubted.
nedubeble undoubtedly.
nee negatively.
neebena uneven.
neebena kurbo space curve.
neebla impossible. **neebla okazo** impossible event.
neeblaĵo impossibility.
neeble impossibly.
neebleco impotence, inability.
neebli to be impossible.
neebligi to make impossible.
neeblo impossibility.
needukita uneducated.
neefektivigebla unachievable.
neefektiviĝi to come to nothing.
neegala unequal.
neegalaĵo inequality.
neegaleco disparity, inequality.
neekonomia inefficient.
neekonomie inefficiently.
neekvacio inequality.
neekvilibra arbo skewed tree, unbalanced tree.
neekzakta inaccurate.
neekzakteco inaccuracy.
neelĉerpebla inexhaustible.
neeldirebla ineffable, unutterable.
neeldireble ineffably.
neeldonita unpublished.
neelektebla ineligible.
neelparolata silent (letter).
neeltenebla overwhelming, unbearable.
neenloĝebla uninhabitable.
neensorba non-absorbent.
neentuziasma cold.
neentuziasme coldly.
neerara unerring.
neerarebla infallible.
neerareble infallibly.
neerarebleco infallibility.
neerarema infallible.
neesperantisto non-Esperantist.
neesprimebla inexpressible.
neesprimeble inexpressibly.
neesprimita implied, unexpressed, tacit. **neesprimita konsento** acquiescence.
neestaĵo nonentity.
neestimi to make no account of.
neesto non-existence.
neeŭklida geometrio non-Euclidean geometry.
neevitebla inevitable.
neeviteble unavoidably.
neeviteblo inevitability.
nefalsita unadulterated.
nefarebla impracticable.
nefari to fail, neglect, omit.
nefaritaĵo arrears.

nefavora inauspicious.
nefermi to open.
nefermita open.
nefervora lukewarm.
nefidebla irresponsible.
nefidinda unreliable.
nefidindeco untrustworthiness.
nefiksita loose.
nefila unfilial.
nefinia infinite.
nefinio infinity.
nefinita infinite, immense.
nefirma loose.
nefirme loosely.
nefleksebla inflexible.
nefokusiva astigmatic.
nefokusiveco astigmatism.
neforgesebla unforgettable.
neforgesumino forget-me-not.
neforigebla unremovable, indelible.
neforlasebla indispensable.
neformala informal.
neformale informally.
neforprenebla inalienable.
neforta faint.
nefrito nephrite.
nefruktodona barren, infertile, sterile, unfruitful.
nefumanto non-smoker.
nega negative.
negacio negation.
negativa negative. **negativa kvitanco** negative acknowledgement, NAK.
negative negatively.
negativo negative.
negatono negaton, negatron.
negatrono negaton, negatron.
negeedza extramarital.
negi to deny, reject.
neglektebla negligible.
neglektema careless, neglectful, negligent, remiss.
neglektemo carelessness, negligence, remissness.
neglekti to neglect.
neglektinda negligible.
neglekto neglect, slighting, negligence.
negliĝa untidy (dress). **negliĝa robo** dressing gown. **negliĝa vesto** dressing gown.
negliĝo housedress, negligee, undress.
negliĝulino slut.
negliĝulo sloven.
nego negation.
negoca business, commercial.
negocado negotiation, trading.
negoceca businesslike.
negoci to do business, engage in business, negotiate, deal, trade.
negocisto businessman, merchant, trader.

negoco business, trade, commerce, transaction.
negocperisto broker.
negra Negro.
negraĉo nigger.
negranda minor.
negrava immaterial, unimportant.
negravaĵo accessory.
negravas it doesn't matter.
negraveco insignificance, unimportance.
negrino black woman.
negro Negro.
negroido negroid.
neĝa snowy.
neĝado snowfall, snowing.
neĝamaso mass of snow.
neĝas it's snowing.
neĝblanka snow white.
Neĝblankulino Snow White.
neĝbloko block of snow.
neĝborulo snowdrop.
neĝbuli to throw snowballs.
neĝbulo snowball.
neĝero snowflake.
neĝhomo snowman.
neĝi to snow.
neĝkovrita snowy, snow-covered.
neĝo snow.
neĝobulo snowball.
neĝoŝtormo blizzard.
neĝtabulado snowboarding.
neĝtabulanto snowboarder.
neĝtabuli to snowboard.
neĝtabulisto snowboarder.
neĝtabulo snow board.
Neĝulino Snow White.
neĝusta incorrect.
neĝustatempa inopportune.
neĝuste incorrectly.
neĝustloka misplaced.
neĝustmeti to mislay.
nehaltigebla irrepressible.
nehaltigeble unstoppably.
neharmonia anharmonic.
nehavi to be wanting, lack, miss.
nehebreo Gentile.
nehejitita unheated.
nehumana inhuman.
nei to deny, say no, disown, repudiate, negate.
neigebla deniable.
neigi to negate.
neimagebla inconceivable, unimaginable.
neimageble unimaginably, unthinkably.
neinda unworthy.
neinteligenta dim, obtuse, unintelligent.
neintence unintentionally.
neintima detached.
neintimigita undaunted.
neinvershava non-invertible.

neinversigebla non-invertible.
neizotropio anisotropic.
nejuna old, not young.
nek neither, nor.
nek ... nek neither ... nor.
ne-kaj-operacio nand-operation.
nekalkulebla incalculable, innumerable.
nekapabla incapable.
nekapable inefficiently.
nekapableco incapacity.
nekaptebla uncapturable, elusive.
nekartografia uncharted.
nekaŝa overt.
nekaŝebla apparent, obvious.
nekaŝema open (candid).
neklara unclear.
neklarajo ambiguity.
neklare abstrusely, ambiguously, obscurely.
neklareco abstruseness, obscurity.
neklarigebla inexplicable, unaccountable.
neklarigeble inexplicably.
nekombita unkempt.
nekomparebla incomparable, matchless, peerless.
nekompareble incomparably, uniquely.
nekompetenta incompetent.
nekompetente inefficiently.
nekompetenteco inefficiency.
nekompleta incomplete.
nekomprenebla incomprehensible, inconceivable, unintelligible.
nekompreneble incomprehensibly.
nekomprenebleco abstruseness, obscurity.
nekomuna uncommon.
nekomunikema uncommunicative.
nekonata ulterior, unknown.
nekonataita unknown.
nekonateco obscurity.
nekonato stranger, unknown person.
nekoncerna irrelevant, unrelated.
nekondiĉa unconditional.
nekonformisma unorthodox.
nekonformismo non-conformism.
nekonformisto nonconformist.
nekonformulo maverick.
nekoni to not know, not be familiar with.
nekonscia unconscious.
nekonscie unconsciously.
nekonsekvenca inconsistent.
nekonsekvenco inconsistency.
nekonsiderema thoughtless, unthinking, mindless, wanton.
nekonsiderita thoughtless, unthinking, mindless, wanton.
nekonsilebla opinionated, pigheaded.
nekonsilinda ill-advised.
nekonsolebla inconsolable.
nekonstanteco inconsistency, inconstancy.
nekonsternita unmoved.

nekonsumebla inexhaustible.
nekontenta discontented, not content.
nekontente unhappily.
nekontentiga unsatisfactory, unsatisfying.
nekontestebla undisputed, unquestioned, undeniable.
nekontinua discrete, non-continuous.
nekonvena inexpedient.
nekonvencia unconventional.
nekonvene unduly.
nekonverĝa divergent.
nekorektebla incorrigible.
nekorpa non-corporeal.
nekoruptebla incorruptible.
nekredanto unbeliever.
nekredebla incredible.
nekredeble incredibly.
nekredema incredulous. **nekredema Tomaso** doubting Thomas.
nekredemo disbelief, lack of faith.
nekredinda incredible, untrustworthy.
nekredindeco untrustworthiness.
nekristala amorphous.
nekristalizita sukero caster sugar, castor sugar.
nekritikema uncritical, indiscriminate.
nekrofilio necrophilia.
nekroforo burying beetle.
nekrologio necrology, obituary.
nekrologo necrology, obituary.
nekromancio necromancy.
nekromancisto necromancer.
nekropolo catacombs, necropolis.
nekropsii to autopsy, necropsy.
nekropsio autopsy.
nekrozo necrosis.
neksta next.
nektarino nectarine.
nektaro nectar.
nekuirita raw, uncooked.
nekulturita dreary.
nekunigebla incompatible.
nekunigita unconnected.
nekunmezurebla incommensurable.
nekuracebla incurable.
nekutima unusual, unwonted.
nekutime unusually.
nelacigebla indefatigable, tireless, untiring.
nelaŭleĝa illegitimate, unlawful, illegible.
nelegitima extramarital.
nelegoscia illiterate.
nelegoscio illiteracy.
neleĝa illegal, unlawful, illegitimate. **neleĝa infano** illegitimate child.
neleĝeco illegality.
nelga recent.
nelge not long ago, recently.
nelibervola involuntary.
nelibervole involuntarily.

nelimigita absolute.
nelimigiteco absoluteness.
nelogika illogical.
neloĝata empty, uninhabited.
neloĝebla uninhabitable.
nelonga not long, short.
nelonge briefly.
nelongtempe not for long, for a short time.
Nelsono Nelson, Nelson River.
nemalhavebla indispensable.
nemalimplikebla inextricable.
nemalimplikeble inextricably.
nemalmulte quite.
nemalplektebla inextricable.
nemalplilongigita unabbreviated.
nemaltrankvila unruffled.
nemankipova crucial, indispensable.
nemanregebla unwieldy.
nematodo eelworm, nematode.
nematura immature, unripe, not ripe. **nematura frukto** unripe fruit.
nememorebla impossible to remember, immemorial.
Nemeso Nemesis.
nemetiisto amateur.
nemetiulo amateur, layman.
nemezio nemesia.
nemezurebla immeasurable.
nemezurebleco infinity, immensity.
nemiksita unalloyed.
nemilita civilian.
nemilitisto civilian.
ne-mio non-self.
nemodesta immodest.
nemorala amoral.
nemovebla immovable.
nemoveblaĵo estate.
nemulta not many, few.
nemulteco scarcity.
Nenago Nenagh.
nenatura artificial.
nenature abnormally, unnaturally.
nenecesa needless, inexpedient.
nenecese unnecessarily.
nenegativa non-negative.
nenia no kind of, no ... whatsoever.
neniaĵo nothing, trifle.
nenial for no cause, for no reason, on no account.
neniam at no time, never, not ever. **neniam antaŭe** never before. **neniam ĝis nun** never before.
nenie nowhere.
nenieco nothingness.
neniel by no means, in no way, not at all, not on any account.
nenies no-one's.
neniesa no man's, belonging to no one.
neniesa tereno no man's land.

nenieslando no man's land.
neniestereno no man's land.
nenifarado inaction.
nenifaranto loafer.
nenigi to annihilate.
neniigi to abolish, annihilate, rescind.
neniigilo annihilator.
neniigo annihilation.
neniigulo annihilator.
neniiĝi to be destroyed, become nothing, vanish.
nenio naught, none, not any thing, nothing. **nenion oni hazardu** Nothing must be left to chance.
neniom no amount, none.
neniu neither, nobody, none, no-one. **neniu el ni** neither of us, none of us.
nenoca harmless.
nenocivo harmlessness.
nenombrebla countless.
nenorma abnormal.
nenormaĵo abnormality, abnormity.
nenormala abnormal.
nenormalaĵo abnormality.
nenormale abnormally.
nenormaleco abnormality.
nenormeco abnormality, abnormity.
neo denial.
neobeebla impermissible.
neobeema disobedient.
neobservi to ignore.
neodimo neodymium.
neofendema inoffensive.
neoficiala unofficial.
neofito neophyte.
neofrono Egyptian vulture (Neophron percnopterus).
neofta infrequent, uncommon.
neofte infrequently.
neokupata empty (unoccupied).
neokupita free, unoccupied, vacant.
neolitika Neolithic.
Neolitiko Neolithic.
neologismemo tendency to use neologisms.
neologismemulo someone who frequently uses neologisms.
neologismo neologism.
neologo neologism.
neona neon.
neono neon.
neoplasmo neoplasm, tumor.
neoplazio neoplasia, formation of new tissue.
neoportuna inconvenient, inopportune.
neopreno neoprene.
neordinara unusual, out of the ordinary.
neordinare unusually.
neorganika inorganic.
neorientita grafeo non-directed graph, non-oriented graph.

neoriginala unoriginal.
neornitoj Neornithes (subclass of birds).
neortodoksa maverick, unorthodox.
neotena neotenic.
neoteneco neoteny, juvenilization.
neotio Neottia (genus in the orchid family).
nepagebla unaffordable.
nepageble unaffordably.
nepagipova insolvent, incapable of paying.
nepagita unpaid, outstanding, overdue, back.
nepagokapabla insolvent.
nepala Nepalese.
nepalano Nepalese.
Nepalo Nepal.
nepalpebla intangible.
nepara odd (number).
nepardonebla unpardonable.
nepardonema unforgiving.
neparhufuloj perissodactyls.
nepartia neutral.
nepenetrebla impenetrable, impermeable, waterproof.
nepensebla unthinkable.
nepera Napierian. **nepera logaritmo** Napierian logarithm.
neperceptebla imperceptible.
nepercepteble imperceptibly.
nepereema imperishable.
neperfekta imperfect.
neperfektaĵo defect, flaw, imperfection.
Nepero Napier, Neper.
nepersona impersonal.
nepino granddaughter.
nepiva not found in the PIV (*Plena Ilustrita Vortaro*).
neplena incomplete.
neplenaĝa junior, minor (age), under age.
neplenaĝo minority (age).
neplenaĝulo (law) minor.
neplenkreskulo minor, underage person.
neplenumebla unfulfillable.
neplibonigebla incorrigible.
nepo grandson.
nepopulara unpopular.
nepostulema undemanding.
nepostumela reasonable.
nepotismo nepotism.
nepozitiva non-positive.
nepra absolute. **nepra parametro** mandatory parameter.
nepraĵo necessity.
nepraktika academic, impractical, unworkable.
neprava incorrect, invalid.
nepraveco invalidity.
nepravigebla unjustifiable.
nepravigeble unjustifiably.
nepravigita groundless, unfounded, baseless.

nepre absolutely, definitely, without fail, certainly, surely. **nepre ne** definitely not.
nepreciza inaccurate.
neprecizeco inaccuracy.
nepreco absoluteness.
neprege most certainly.
nepri to be absolute, definite.
nepridubebla undisputed, unquestioned, undeniable.
nepriresponda not responsible.
nepriskriba nondescript.
nepriskribebla indescribable.
nepriskribeble indescribably.
neprofesiulo amateur.
neprofita bootless.
neprofitema disinterested.
neprogresema backward.
neprokrastebla pressing, urgent.
nepropra frakcio improper fraction.
neprospera unsuccessful.
neprospere unsuccessfully.
neprudenta cavalier, impetuous, imprudent, reckless, unwise.
neprudente cavalierly, impetuously, recklessly.
neprudenteco recklessness.
nepruvebla unprovable.
neptuna Neptunian.
neptunio neptunium.
Neptuno Neptune.
nepublika private. **nepublika kompanio** company, limited liability.
nepunita unpunished.
nepura rimo approximate rhyme, assonant rhyme, imperfect rhyme, near rhyme, oblique rhyme, off rhyme, slant rhyme.
neputrebla incorruptible.
neputrigita uncorrupted (phys).
neracia irrational.
neraciemo irrationalism, irrationality.
neracionala irrational.
neracionalo irrational number.
nerakontebla indescribable.
nerapida leisurely, slow, not fast.
nerapide not fast, slowly, leisurely, without haste.
nerealigebla unachievable, unworkable.
nerealisma unrealistic.
nerebonigebla incorrigible.
nereduktebla irreducible. **nereduktebla frakcio** reduced fraction.
nerefutebla irrefutable, unanswerable.
nerefutebla fakto irrefutable fact.
nerefuteble irrefutably, unanswerably.
neregebla ungovernable.
neregula abnormal, irregular.
neregulaĵo irregularity.
neregule irregularly.
nereguleco abnormality.

nerehavebla

nerehavebla irreplaceable.
nerekonebla unrecognizable.
nerekta indirect. **nerekta aparato** off-line device. **nerekta funkciado** off-line operation. **nerekta parolo** indirect speech.
nerekte indirectly.
nereligia non-religious.
nereligiulo layman.
nereligiuloj laity.
neresanigebla incurable.
nerespekta disrespectful.
nerespektaĵo irreverence.
nerespekteco irreverence.
nerespondebla unanswerable.
nerespondeble unanswerably.
nerespondeca nonaccountable, unaccountable.
neretenebla uncontrollable.
nerevenigebla irretrievable.
nerevenigeble irrevocably.
nerevokebla irrevocable.
nerevokeble irrevocably.
nerezerva unreserved.
nerezistebla irresistible.
nerezisteble irresistibly, overwhelmingly.
nerimarkebla unremarkable.
nerimarkeble unremarkably.
nerimarki to not notice.
neriparebla beyond repair, irreparable. **neriparebla eraro** fatal error.
neripozema restless.
neripozemo restlessness.
neriproĉebla irreproachable.
neriproĉeble irreproachably.
neriproĉinda irreproachable.
neriproĉinde irreproachably.
nerompebla unbreakable. **nerompebla spaceto** no-break space.
nerva agitated, nervous.
nervaro nervous system.
nerve nervously.
nerveco nervousness.
nervo nerve.
nervodoloro neuralgia.
nervosistemo nervous system.
nervotransigilo neurotransmitter.
nervoza agitated, nervous.
nervoze nervously.
nervozeco nervousness.
nervuro veining, rib.
nesaĝema impolitic.
nesala akvo fresh water, sweet water.
nesama different, unlike.
nesame dissimilarly.
nesameco dissimilarity.
nesana unhealthy, not healthy.
nesatigebla insatiable.
nescia unknowing, unwitting, witless.
nescii to be ignorant of.

neŝirmata

nescio ignorance.
neseksa asexual.
nesekse asexually.
neserĉebla inscrutable, unsearchable.
neserĉita unsearched for.
neserioza lighthearted.
neservema disobliging.
nesfera aspherical.
nesignifa insignificant.
nesignifa cifero non-significant digit.
nesimetria asymmetric, asymmetrical, dissymmetric.
nesimila dissimilar.
nesimile dissimilarly.
nesimileco dissimilarity.
nesincera insincere.
nesingardema imprudent.
nesinkigebla unsinkable.
nesinkigebleco unsinkability.
nesinkrona asynchronous.
nesintaksa asyntactic.
neslio ball mustard.
nesocietamoemo unsociableness.
nesocietema unsociable.
nesolvebla indissoluble, insoluble.
nesondebla abysmal.
nesondeble inscrutably, unfathomably.
nesonĝita undreamt of, unimaginable.
nesorba non-absorbent.
nesperta inexperienced, inexpert, unskilled, untrained.
nestabila unstable.
nestabileco instability.
nestarema shaky, rickety, wobbly, loose.
nestego lair, den, nest.
nesti to nest.
nestiĝi to nest.
nesto nest, den, lair.
nesubtenebla unsustainable.
nesubteneble unsustainably.
nesuferebla insufferable, unendurable.
nesufiĉa insufficient.
nesufiĉe insufficiently.
nesufiĉeco inadequacy, insufficiency, scarcity.
nesufiĉo shortfall.
nesuperebla insuperable.
nesurirebla impassable.
nesurpaŝita untrodden.
neŝancelebla steady.
neŝanceleble unshakably.
neŝanceliĝa unshaken, unwavering.
neŝanĝebla immutable, invariable, unalterable, unchangeable.
neŝanĝi to not change.
neŝanĝiĝema constant, continual, lasting, steady, stable, unchanging.
neŝatinda uncool.
neŝirmata bleak.

neta

neta cleanly cut, neat, precise, net (weight, etc.), distinct.
netaksebla inappreciable, inestimable, invaluable, priceless.
netaŭga inappropriate, inept, unfit, unsuitable, unsuited, worthless.
netaŭge inappropriately, ineptly.
netaŭgeco unsuitability.
netbalo netball.
nete carefully prepared, in the final analysis.
netigi to finalize, put in finished form.
netipa pneŭmonio severe acute respiratory syndrome, SARS.
neto corrected copy, final copy.
netolerebla intolerable, unbearable.
netolereble intolerably.
netolerema intolerant.
netransitiva intransitive, non-transitive.
netrovebla missing.
netuŝebla untouchable.
netuŝeblulo untouchable.
netuŝenda inviolable.
netuŝi to not touch.
netuŝumino touch-me-not.
netute not entirely.
neutila not useful.
neutiligebla useless.
neuzebla unusable.
neuzindigi to deprecate.
neuzindigo deprecation.
neuzita unused.
Neŭmana arkitekturo von Neumann architecture.
neŭra neural.
neŭralgio neuralgia.
neŭrastenio neurasthenia.
neŭrenberga Nuremberg.
Neŭrenbergo Nuremberg.
neŭrologia neurological.
neŭrologiisto neurologist.
neŭrologio neurology.
neŭrologo neurologist.
neŭrono neuron.
neŭroza neurotic.
neŭrozo neurosis.
Neŭtona metodo Newton's method.
Neŭtonabio Newtonabbey.
Neŭtonmoro Newtonmore.
Neŭtono Newton.
neŭtra neuter, neutral. **neŭtra elemento** neutral element. **neŭtra genro** inanimate gender, neuter gender.
neŭtrajo neutral element.
neŭtrala impartial, neutral.
neŭtraleco neutrality.
neŭtraligi to neutralize.
neŭtralulo neutralist, opponent of political involvement.
neŭtriga elemento reciprocal element.

nigra

neŭtriganto reciprocal element.
neŭtrigebla invertible. **neŭtrigebla elemento** invertible element.
neŭtrino neutrino.
neŭtrono neutron.
neŭtronstelo neutron star.
nevada Nevadan.
nevadano Nevadan.
nevendebla unsaleable.
nevenkebla insurmountable, invincible.
nevera false, untrue.
neverŝajna improbable, unlikely.
neverŝajne unlikely.
nevidata unseen.
nevidebla invisible. **nevidebla signo** unprintable character.
nevideble invisibly.
nevidi to not see.
nevino niece.
nevivipova unviable.
nevivipoveco unviability.
Nevo Neva River.
nevo nephew.
nevola involuntary, unwilling.
nevole involuntarily, unwillingly.
nevolemo reluctance.
nevoli to be unwilling, not want to.
nevundebla invulnerable.
nevundi to not injure, not wound.
nevuro vein of leaf, rib of vault.
nevuso birthmark.
nezorgema unconcerned.
nezorgita neglected, unheeded.
ngunio Nguni.
ni we. **ni iru** Let's go. **ni iru returen** Let's go back. **ni naĝu** let's swim.
nia our(s). **Nia Sinjorino** Our Lady. **niaj vojoj disiĝas** our paths go separate ways.
niavoje (on) our way.
Niêjo la Dormigulo the Sandman, Wee Willie Winkie.
niĉo niche, nook.
nielo niello.
niesperteco inexperience.
nifo UFO.
nifologio ufology.
nigelo devil-in-the-bush, fennel flower.
nigeria Nigerian.
nigerianino Nigerian, Nigerian lady, Nigerian woman.
nigeriano Nigerian.
Nigerio Nigeria.
Nigero Niger.
nigra black. **nigra araneo** black widow spider, button spider. **Nigra Arbaro** Black Forest. **nigra arto** black magic. **nigra biero** stout (beer). **nigra cigno** black swan. **nigra heleboro** Christmas rose. **nigra humuro** black humour. **nigra kesto** black

nigrabrova   **nocio**

box. **nigra magio** black magic, dark magic. **nigra maranaso** black scoter, common scoter. **Nigra Maro** Black Sea, Euxine Sea. **nigra merkato** black market. **nigra pego** black woodpecker. **nigra pino** black pine. **nigra ribo** black currant. **nigra skatolo** black box. **nigra skribtabulo** blackboard. **nigra tabulo** blackboard. **nigra truo** black hole, collapsar. **nigra urso** black bear. **Nigra Voltao** Black Volta.
nigrabrova black-browed. **nigrabrova albatroso** black-browed albatross.
nigraflugila black-winged. **nigraflugila mevo** Larus atricilla, laughing gull.
nigraĵo black.
nigrakapa black-headed. **nigrakapa emberizo** black-headed bunting. **nigrakapa mevo** Mediterranean gull.
nigramantela mevo great black-backed gull.
nigravizaĝa swarthy.
nigre blackly.
nigrebruna dark brown, black-brown.
nigreco blackness.
nigrega pitch black.
nigreta somewhat black, darkish.
nigrharulino brunette.
nigrharulo dark-haired man.
nigrigi to blacken.
nigriĝi to become black, darken (oneself).
Nigrinsulo Black Isle.
nigro black.
nigrulo black, black person, negro.
nigrumi to black-out.
nigrumo black-out.
niĝeria Nigerian.
niĝerianino Nigerian woman.
niĝeriano Nigerian.
Niĝerio Niger, Nigeria.
Niĝero Niger.
nihilisma nihilistic.
nihilismo nihilism.
nihilisto nihilist.
nikandro apple of Peru, shoo-fly plant.
nikaragva Nicaraguan.
nikaragvano Nicaraguan.
Nikaragvo Nicaragua.
nikeli to nickel plate.
nikelo nickel.
Nikobaroj Nicobar Islands.
Nikolao Nicholas, Nicolas.
Nikosio Nicosia.
nikotiano tobacco plant.
nikotino nicotine.
nikso water-sprite.
niktereŭto raccoon dog.
Nilo Nile.
nilona nylon.

nilono nylon.
nilpotenta nilpotent.
nimbo halo, nimbus.
nimbuso nimbus, rain cloud.
Nimego Nimeguen, Nimwegen.
nimfeo waterlily.
nimfo labia minora, nymph.
nimfomanio nymphomania.
Nimrodo Nimrod.
niobio niobium.
niobo niobium.
niplo nipple.
nirvano Nirvana.
Nirvano nirvana.
nisano Abib.
Niso Loch Ness.
niti to rivet.
nitilo riveter.
nitisto riveter.
nitjunto rivet(ed) joint.
nito rivet.
nitono radon.
nitrata acido azotic acid.
nitratacido aqua fortis.
nitrato nitrate.
nitrita acido nitrous acid.
nitrito nitrite.
nitrobenzeno nitrobenzene.
nitrogeno nitrogen.
nitroglicerino nitroglycerin.
Niuo Niue.
nivela level.
nivelado alignment.
niveli to level.
nivelilo level (instrument).
nivelo level.
nizo sparrow hawk.
NLM read-only memory, ROM.
no name of the letter N.
noa radiko nth root.
Noaĥo Noah.
nobela noble. **nobela klaso** nobility.
nobelaro nobility, peerage.
nobele nobly.
nobeleco nobility.
nobeligi to ennoble.
nobelino peeress.
nobelio nobelium.
nobelo noble, nobleman.
Nobelpremio Nobel Prize.
Nobel-premio Nobel Prize.
nobla great, noble, honourable. **nobla gaso** inert gas, noble gas.
noble nobly.
nobleco loftiness (character), nobleness.
nobligi to ennoble.
noca harmful.
noci to harm.
nocio notion, concept.

noĉo notch. **noĉo de prestipo** nick.
nodeca knotty.
nodi to knot.
nodligi to tie up.
nodo knot, node.
nokaŭti to knock-out, knock unconscious.
nokaŭto knock-out.
noksobruna chestnut.
nokta nightly, nocturnal. **nokta besto** nocturnal animal. **nokta deĵoro** night duty, night service, night shift. **nokta flugo** night flight. **nokta frosto** ground frost, night frost. **nokta lampo** night lamp. **nokta papilio** moth. **nokta papilo** moth. **nokta patrolo** night watch. **nokta ripozo** night's rest. **nokta servo** night duty, night service, night shift. **nokta skipo** night shift. **nokta trajno** night train.
noktblinda night blind.
noktblindeco night blindness.
nokte at night, by night, during the night.
noktfesteni to make a night of it.
noktgardisto watchman.
noktgardo night watch.
nokti to it's night out.
noktiĝi to night is falling.
noktiĝo evening twilight.
noktmeza meso midnight mass.
noktmeze in the middle of the night.
noktmezo midnight.
nokto night.
noktoĉemizo night shirt.
noktogardo nightwatch.
noktohirundo nightjar.
noktoklubo night club, night spot.
noktomanĝi to take supper.
noktomanĝo supper.
noktomeza midnight, of midnight, midnight's.
noktomeze at midnight.
noktomezo midnight.
noktoŝranko pedestal cupboard.
noktotablo night table.
noktotarifo night rate, night tariff.
noktovazo pot, chamber pot.
noktpapilio moth, night moth.
noktseruro double lock.
noktŝirmo night covering, night shelter.
noktŝranko pedestal cupboard.
noktuo little owl, screech owl.
nokturno nocturne.
noktvazo chamber pot.
noktvestaĵo night attire.
noma appelative. **noma akcio** registered share.
nomada nomadic, wandering.
nomadejo lair, encampment, bivouac.
nomadi to wander, be a nomad.
nomadismo nomadism.

nomado[1] nomenclature, denomination.
nomado[2] nomad.
nomadulo wanderer.
nomaro index (names), list of names, nomenclature.
nombra numerical. **nombra klavaro** number pad, numeric pad, numerical pad. **nombra metodo** numerical method.
nombrametoda numeric, numerical.
nombre numerically.
nombrebla countable, denumerable, discrete.
nombri to count.
nombriĝi to number, be of a certain number.
nombrila iteracio FOR-loop, FOR-statement.
nombrilo counter, meter.
nombro amount, number, quantity.
nombrosistemo number system.
nome namely, viz., that is, to be precise. **nome de** by the name of.
nomenklaturo nomenclature.
nomfesto name day, saint's day.
nomhava named. **nomhava dukto** named pipe. **nomhava konstanto** named constant.
nomi to appoint, nominate, call, mention, name, designate.
nomigo christening.
nomiĝi to be called.
nominala nominal.
nominalismo nominalism.
nominalvalora at par.
nominativo nominative.
nomita named.
nomizi to assign, name.
nomkarto business card.
nomkonflikto names conflict.
nomlisto identifier list.
Nomo Nome.
nomo name, appellation, denomination, noun.
nomplato name plate.
nomŝildo name badge, name shield, name tag.
nomtago name day.
nomumi to appoint, nominate.
nomumiĝo designation.
nomumo appointment, nomination.
nomuskla title case.
norda northerly, northern. **norda cervo** reindeer. **norda duonglobo** northern hemisphere. **Norda Dvino** Northern Dvina. **Norda Insulo** North Island. **Norda Markolo** North Channel. **Norda Maro** North Sea. **Norda Palmerstono** Palmerston North. **norda stelo** north star.
nordafrika North African.

nordafrikano North African.
Nord-Afriko North Africa.
Nordafriko North Africa.
nordamerika North American.
nordamerikano North American.
Nord-Ameriko North America.
Nordameriko North America.
Nord-Atlantika Traktat-Organizaĵo North Atlantic Treaty Organization, NATO.
Nordbrabanto North Brabant.
norddakotano North Dakotan.
norde in the north, northerly. **norde de** above.
norden north, northward, northwards.
nordeosta northeastern.
Nord-Holando North Holland.
Nordholando North Holland.
Nord-Irlando Northern Ireland.
Nordirlando Northern Ireland.
nordkorea North Korean.
nordkoreano North Korean.
Nord-Koreio North Korea.
Nordkoreio North Korea.
Nord-Koreujo North Korea.
Nordkoreujo North Korea.
nordlumo aurora borealis, northern lights.
nordo north.
nordokcidenta northwesterly.
nordokcidento northwest.
nordorienta northeastern.
nordoriente north-east.
nordoriento the Northeast.
nordpolusa arctic.
Norduvisto North Uist.
Nordvjetnamo North Vietnam.
norio bucket-chain.
norma normal, standard. **norma vortsignifo** acceptation.
normala normal.
normale ordinarily.
normaleco normalcy.
normaligi to adjust, regulate, set.
normaligo adjustment.
normana Norse.
normanda Norman.
Normandio Normandy.
normando Norman.
Normandujo Normandy.
normano Dane, Northman, Norseman.
norme normally.
norme konverĝa normally convergent.
normhava standardized.
normi to standardize, norm.
normigado standardization.
normigi to standardize.
normigita normed.
normigo standardization.

normita normed. **normita skribo** standard font. **normita spaco** normed space.
normo norm, standard.
normohava normed. **normohava spaco** normed space.
norvega Norwegian.
norvegino Norwegian woman.
Norvegio Norway.
Norveglando Norway.
Norvego a Norwegian.
norvego Norwegian.
Norvegujo Norway.
nostalgia nostalgic.
nostalgie nostalgically.
nostalgio nostalgia.
notacio notation.
notaĵo annotation, remark.
notario notary.
notbloka komputilo notebook computer, notebook.
notbloko notepad.
notfoliaro notepad.
noti to annotate, note, make a note, write down. **notu bone** nota bene, N.B.
notico notice.
notinda noteworthy.
notkanti to solfa (a method for teaching sight-singing).
notkanto solfa, solfège, solfeggio (a method for teaching sight-singing).
notlibreto notebook.
notlibro notebook.
notliniaro staff-lines.
noto annotation, note, grade, memorandum, bulletin, mark. **noto de la redakcio** editor's note. **notoj** music.
notonekto water-boatman.
noumeno noumenon.
nova new, novel, recent. **nova balailo bone balaas** new broom sweeps clean. **Nova Epoko** New Age. **Nova Gvineo** New Guinea. **Nova Kaledonio** New Caledonia. **nova linio** line feed. **nova paĝo** form feed. **Nova Plimuto** New Plymouth. **Nova Rosso** New Ross. **Nova Sudkimrio** New South Wales. **Nova Sudkimrujo** New South Wales. **Nova Testamento** New Testament. **Novaj Hebridoj** New Hebrides.
novaĵagentejo news agency.
novaĵaro news-file.
novaĵeco newness.
novaĵgrupo newsgroup.
novaĵleganto newscaster.
novaĵlegilo newsreader.
novaĵletero news letter.
novaĵo news, novelty, something new.
novaĵoj news.
novala fallow.

novalaro soil bank.
novalo fallow land.
novalveninto newcomer.
Nov-Anglio New England.
Novanglio New England.
novao nova.
Novdelhio New Delhi.
nove newly.
noveco newness.
novedzino bride.
novedzo bridegroom.
noveleto short story.
novelo novelette, short story.
Novembro November.
novembro November.
noveno novena.
novgreka lingvo Modern Greek.
Novhaveno Newport.
novhebrea lingvo Modern Hebrew.
noviceco noviceship, novitiate.
novicejo novitiate (place).
novicino novice.
novico novice.
novigado innovation.
novigi to renovate, renew.
novjara tago New Year's Day.
Novjare at New Year's.
novjaro New Year.
Novjartago New Year's Day.
Novjorka Akciborso New York Stock Exchange, NYSE.
novjorkano New Yorker.
novjorkiano New Yorker.
Nov-Jorko New York.
Novjorko New York, New York City.
novkaledona New Caledonian.
Novkaledonio New Caledonia.
novkaledono New Caledonian.
Novkaledonujo New Caledonia.
Novkastelo Newcastle.
novlatina neo-Latin.
novluno new moon.
Nov-Meksikio New Mexico.
novnaskito newborn.
novokaino Novocain.
Nov-Orleana ĵazo New Orleans jazz.
novorleanano New Orleanian.
Novosibirsko Novosibirsk.
novplatonismo Neo-Platonism.
novriĉulo newly-rich, nouveau riche.
Novsudkimrio New South Wales.
Novtero Newfoundland.
novulo new person, newcomer, novice.
Novurbo Newtown.
novzelanda New Zealand.
novzelandanino New Zealand woman.
Nov-Zelandano New Zealander.
novzelandano New Zealander.
Nov-Zelando New Zealand.

Novzelando New Zealand.
n-ro → **numero**.
nu now, well, well then. **nu, ni vidos** well, we'll see. **nu, se vi volas mian konsilon...** well, if you want my opinion...
nuanci to shade.
nuancigi to nuance.
nuanco hue, nuance, shade, tint.
nuba cloudy, overcast, gloomy, obscure, unclear.
nube cloudily.
nubeto small cloud.
nubia Nubian.
nubiano Nubian.
nubiĝi to become cloudy, become overcast.
Nubio Nubia.
Nubkolektano the Cloud Gatherer (Zeus).
nubkovrita cloudy.
nubkurteno curtain of clouds.
nubo cloud.
nuboplena cloudy, full of clouds.
nuboza cloudy.
nuda bare, naked, nude. **nuda vertico** isolated vertex.
nudaĵo nude.
nudbruste topless.
nude barely, nakedly.
nudeco nakedness, nudity.
nudelo noodles.
nudigi to undress, strip (someone, something).
nudiĝi to strip.
nudismo nudism.
nudisto nudist.
nudkape bareheaded.
nudpieda barefoot.
nudpiede barefoot.
nudrivela striptease.
nudrivela danco striptease.
nudrivelado striptease.
nufaro yellow waterlily.
nugato nougat.
nuklea[1] nuclear. **nuklea energio** nuclear energy.
nuklea[2] nucleic. **nuklea acido** nucleic acid.
nukleacido nucleic acid.
nukleo nucleus.
nukleono nucleon.
nukleotido nucleotide.
nuko back of the neck, nape, scruff.
nuksa nutty.
nukso nut.
nuksrompilo nutcracker.
nul null, nil, zero, naught.
nula invalid, null, zero.
nuldivizoro zero divisor.
nulgrafeo null graph.
nuliga null, void.
nuliganto null (of a function).

nuligebla revocable.
nuligi to abjure, abolish, abrogate, annul, cancel, remit, invalidate, nullify. **nuligi telefone** to cancel by telephone, countermand by telephone.
nuligo abolition, abrogation, revocation.
nuliĝi to vanish.
nulizi to zero fill, zeroize.
nulizotermo zero isotherm.
nulmatrico null matrix.
nulmezura null (set).
nulo zero, naught, null.
nulpolinomo null polynomial.
nulpotenca nilpotent.
nulpunkto zero.
nulredukto zero suppression.
nulvektoro null vector.
numenio curlew.
numera numeric, numerical. **numera adreso** numeric address.
numerado numbering.
numeralo numeral.
numeraro directory.
numeratoro numerator.
numerebla countable. **numerebla** countable, denumerable, discrete. **numerebla aro** countable set, denumerable set. **numerebla tipo** ordinal type.
numeri to (assign a) number.
numero number, house number, issue number, number in a series, numeral.
numerplato number plate, licence plate.
numido guinea-fowl.
numismatikisto numismatist.
numismatiko numismatics.
numismato numismatist.
nun at present, now. **nun ankoraŭ** still, yet. **nun estas via vico** Now it's your turn.
nuna actual, current, present.
nunatempe modern, current, of the present (time).
nunciejo nunciature.
nuncio nuncio.
nune at present, currently, nowadays.

nuneco actuality.
nunmomente at the moment.
nuno the present (as opposed to the past or future).
nuntempa current, present.
nuntempe at present, at the present time, currently, nowadays, these days.
nuntempo current times, modern times, the present (day, time).
nuo nu (Nv).
nupta danco display.
nupto nuptials, wedding.
nur exclusively, just, only, simply. **nur se** only if. **nur unu** just one, one only, only one.
nura mere, solitary, sole.
nure merely.
Nurenbergo Nuremberg.
Nurio Newry.
nurlega read-only.
nurlegebla komputila lumdisko compact disc read-only memory, CD-ROM. **nurlegebla memoro** read-only memory, ROM.
nurskriba write only.
nutono newton.
nutra nourishing, nutritious, nutritional.
nutrado nourishing, feeding.
nutradoaĵo board (food).
nutraĵo food, nourishment, sustenance. **nutraĵo ĝisdektage** food for up to ten days, up to ten day's (worth) of food. **nutraĵo kortbirdara** bird food, poultry feed.
nutramono alimony.
nutri to feed, nourish, foster.
nutrigi to feed, nourish.
nutristino nurse.
nutrita fed, nourished.
nutro nourishment, food.
nutroaŭtomato automatic feeder.
nutrobloko power supply unit.
nutromanko malnutrition.
nutromono alimony.
nutropago alimony.

O

o name of the letter O.
oazo oasis.
Obano Oban.
obdukcio autopsy, necropsy.
obea docile, obedient.
obeado compliance.
obee obediently.
obeema obedient.
obeeme obediently.
obeemo docility, obedience.
obei to obey.
obeigema authoritative, peremptory.
obeigeme authoritatively.
obeigi to train, bring into allegiance, bring to heel, subdue.
obelisko obelisk.
obeluso dagger (†). **duobla obeluso** double dagger (‡).
obeo obedience.
Oberono Oberon.
obeza obese.
obio obi (Japanese belt).
objekta lingvo object language.
objektema object-oriented. **objektema programado** object-oriented programming. **objektema programlingvo** object-oriented programming language, OO language.
objektiva objective.
objektive objectively.
objektiveco objectivity.
objektivo objective.
objekto article, object, thing, subject.
objeti to object.
oblato seal, wafer.
oble times, multiplied by.
obleco multiplicity.
obligacihavanto bond holder.
obligacio bond.
obligaciulo bond holder.
obligi to multiply.
oblikva oblique, slanting. **oblikva projekcio** skew projection.
oblikveco obliquity.
oblikvo diagonal, forward slash, fraction bar; (/).
oblo multiple.
oblonga oblong.
obloprefikso magnifying prefix.
Obo Ob.
obolo obolus (a Greek silver coin worth a sixth of a drachma).
obscena obscene.
obscenaĵo obscenity.
obscisa akso axis of abscissae.

obsedato obsessed.
obsede obsessively.
obsedi to obsess.
obsedo obsession.
observa observation.
observadi to (continue to) observe.
observado observation, monitoring, watching.
observaĵo perception.
observanto observer.
observatorio observatory.
observebla observable.
observejo observatory.
observema observant.
observemo compliance, watchfulness.
observi to observe, abide by, comply, mind, obey, respect, watch, follow, take notice of. **observi kaŝe** to spy (on).
observisto look out (man), watch(man), overseers.
observo observation.
observoado observation.
observulo lookout, observer, watcher.
obsidiano obsidian.
obskura dark, obscure, unclear, unknown.
obskurantismo obscurantism.
obskuranto obscurantist.
obskure obscurely.
obskureco obscurity.
obskuro obscurity.
obstaklo obstacle.
obstina dogged, headstrong, obstinate, stubborn.
obstine obstinately.
obstineco obduracy, obstinacy, stubbornness.
obstinega stubborn.
obstinegeco stubbornness.
obstinema contumacious.
obstini to be obstinate, be stubborn, persist.
obstino obstinacy, obstinence, stubbornness.
obstinulo stubborn person.
obstrukca inhibiting.
obstrukcema obstructive.
obstrukci to hamper, hinder, impede, obstruct, stand in the way of.
obstrukcio impediment, obstruction, stoppage.
obstrukco impediment, obstruction, congestion, filibuster.
obturatoro shutter, throttle.
obturi to seal.
obturilo shutter.
obtuza dull, obtuse.
obtuzangula obtuse (obtuse-angled).

obtuze obtusely.
obtuzigi to dull, muffle.
obuso artillery shell.
oceana oceanic. **oceanaj abismoj** ocean depths.
Oceanio Oceania, Oceanica.
oceannivelo sea level.
oceano ocean.
oceanografio oceanography.
oceanologiisto oceanologist.
oceanologio oceanology.
oceloto ocelot.
ocimo basil (herb).
oĉjo uncle.
odalisko odalisque.
odekolono cologne, eau de cologne, toilet water.
Odino Odin.
Odiseado Odyssey.
Odiseo Odysseus, Ulysses.
odo ode.
odora odorous.
odoraĉi to reek, smell bad, stink.
odoraĉo smell, stench, stink.
odoreto whiff.
odori to give off an odour, reek, smell. **odori kiel** to smell of.
odoro odour, scent, smell.
Odro Oder.
oero öre (Swedish unit of currency, ¹/₁₀₀ of a krona).
ofenda abusive, nasty, offensive.
ofendanto offender, transgressor.
ofende offensively.
ofendeco offensiveness.
ofendega obnoxious.
ofendegi to outrage.
ofendego outrage.
ofendi to abuse, insult, offend, transgress.
ofendiĝema easily offended, touchy.
ofendiĝemo touchiness.
ofendiĝi to take offence. **ofendiĝi pro** to resent, take exception to, take offence at.
ofendiĝo pique, umbrage.
ofendinto offender.
ofendita affronted, aggrieved, insulted, offended, hurt.
ofendo abuse, transgression, offence, trespass.
ofendoturmentado abuse.
ofendsenteco touchiness.
ofendsentema touchy.
ofensiva aggressive, offensive. **ofensiva milito** war of aggression.
ofensivo offensive.
oferado offering, sacrifice.
oferaĵo offering.
oferaltaro altar of sacrifice.
oferbuĉi to immolate.
oferdoni to offer, offer up, sacrifice.

oferdono donation, offering.
ofere as an offering.
oferejo altar.
oferema generous, self-denying, self-giving, self-sacrificing.
oferi to offer, offer up, sacrifice.
ofero oblation, sacrifice.
ofertado bidding.
ofertanto bidder.
oferti to bid, offer, make an offer of.
oferto offer.
ofertorio offertory.
oferverŝo libation.
ofica official. **ofica kostumo** robes of office. **ofica krimo** abuse of power, misfeasance. **ofica loĝejo** official residence. **ofica periodo** term of office.
oficdaŭro term (of office).
oficdono appointment, nomination.
oficeja office.
oficejkonstruaĵo office building.
oficejlaboro office work.
oficejo bureau, office, place of work, workplace, office space.
ofici to hold office.
oficiala officer, official.
oficiale officially.
oficialema bossy.
oficialigi to appoint.
oficina officinal. **oficina kalendulo** pot marigold, Scotch marigold. **oficina peonio** common peony, European peony.
oficinala officinal.
oficio situation (post).
oficirejo wardroom.
oficiro officer.
oficirservisto camp follower.
oficistaro bureaucracy, staff.
oficisto functionary, officer, official, office-holder, overseer.
oficĵuro oath of office.
ofico capacity, function, job, office, position, post, employment.
oficperiodo term of office.
oficpreskribo official regulation.
oficsekreto official secret.
ofiogloso adder's tongue fern.
oflajne off line.
ofseto offset printing.
ofta frequent, often. **ofta gasto** patron, frequenter, denizen.
oftalmito ophthalmia.
oftalmologiisto ophthalmologist.
oftalmologio ophthalmology.
oftalmologo ophtalmologist.
oftalmoskopo ophthalmoscope.
ofte commonly, frequently, often, oftentimes, regularly.
ofteco frequency.

oftiĝi to become frequent.
ofto frequency.
ogivo ogee, ogive.
ognostiko agnostic.
ogrino ogress.
ogro ogre.
oguzo Oguz.
ohia Ohioan.
ohiano Ohioan.
Oĥocka Maro Sea of Okhotsk.
Ojdipo Oedipus.
ojstra larvo bot (larva of the botfly).
ojstro gadfly, hornet, sheep fly, warble fly.
ok eight.
oka eighth.
okangula octagonal.
okangulo octagon.
Okao Oka.
okapio okapi.
okaza accidental, casual, occasional, chance.
okaza mortigo manslaughter.
okazado incident.
okazaĵo event, occasion, occurrence, opportunity, incident, happening.
okazalgebro algebra of events, field of events.
okazantaĵo event.
okaze by chance, on occasion, casually, in that case. **okaze de** in case of, on the occasion of.
okazejo setting, locale, scene.
okazi to come about, happen, occur, befall, chance, happen, take place, transpire, arrange, bring about. **okazu kio okazas** whatever will be will be, *que será será*. **okazu kio okazos** come what may, no matter what happens.
okazigi to cause to take place, give rise to.
okazigo event.
okazintaĵo event.
okazo accident, chance, event, occurrence, opportunity, occasion.
okazontaĵo event.
okazoplena eventful.
okazplena eventful.
okcent eight hundred.
okcidenta westerly, western. **Okcidenta Azio** Middle East, Near East. **Okcidenta Dvino** Western Dvina. **Okcidenta Flandrio** West Flanders. **Okcidenta Flandrujo** West Flanders. **Okcidenta Germanujo** West Germany. **Okcidenta Kongo** Republic of the Congo. **okcidenta kristanismo** Western Christianity. **Okcidenta Skeldo** Western Skeldt. **Okcidentaj Indioj** West Indies.
okcidentano Westerner.
Okcidentaŭstralio West Australia.
okcidente westward. **okcidente de** west of.

okcidenten west, westward, westwards.
okcidenteŭropa Western European, West European.
okcidentgermana West German.
okcidentindia West Indian.
okcidento West.
okcidentparto western part.
okcipitalo occipital bone.
okcipito back of the head, occiput.
okcipitosto occipital bone.
okcitana Occitan.
okdek eighty.
okdeka eightieth.
oke eighthly.
Okeano Oceanus.
okedro octahedron.
okej agreed, okay.
okera voko (the) eightfold path (of Buddhism).
Okinavo Okinawa.
oklahoma Oklahoman.
oklahomano Oklahoman.
Oklahomo Oklahoma.
oklatero octagon.
oko number of eight.
okobla eightfold, octuple.
okono eighth, eighth part.
okopo octuple.
okotono cony, pika.
okro ochre.
oksalido oxalis, wood-sorrel.
Oksfordo Oxford.
okshofto hogshead.
oksidigi to oxidize.
oksido oxide.
oksigeni to oxygenate.
oksigenizi to oxygenate.
oksigeno oxygen.
oksikoko cranberry.
oksimoro oxymoron.
okso ox.
okspelisto oxherd.
oktano octane.
oktanto octant.
oktavo octave, octavo.
Oktobro October.
oktobro October.
oktopuso octopus.
okula ocular.
okuladi to peep, peek.
okulado budding.
okulario eyepiece.
okulbendo blindfold.
okule with the eye, visually.
okulfrapa striking.
okulfrape prominently.
okulglobo eyeball, eye.
okulharnigrigilo mascara.
okulharo eyelash. **okulharoj** eyebrows.

okuli

okuli to ogle.
okulinflamo eye inflammation.
okulisto optician, ophthalmologist.
okulĵeti to cast a glance, look at.
okulkavo cavity of the eye, eye socket.
okulklapo blinder.
okulkontako eye contact.
okulkuracisto ophthalmologist.
okullenso lens.
okulmezure by eye, more or less.
okulo eye.
okulrigardi to look at, observed.
okulsigni to wink.
okulsigno wink.
okulŝminko eye shadow.
okulta occult.
okultismo occultism.
okultisto occultist.
okultruda tawdry.
okulumi to make eyes at, ogle, stare at.
okulvidanto eyewitness.
okulvindaĵo blindfold.
okulvitroj eyeglasses, spectacles, glasses.
okuma octal. **okuma nombrosistemo** octal representation. **okuma sistemo** octal system.
okupa busy.
okupacii to occupy.
okupacio occupation.
okupado occupation.
okupanto occupant.
okupata occupied, busy.
okupateco business.
okupi to occupy, employ, engage. **okupi sin** to be busied.
okupiĝi to be concerned, keep busy. **okupiĝi pri** to be concerned with, occupied with.
okupiĝo occupation.
okupita occupied, busy.
okupo activity, occupation.
okzalo sorrel.
ol than.
Olavo Olav.
olda old.
oldulo old man.
oleacoj Oleaceae.
oleandro oleander.
oleastro oleaster.
olei to oil.
olekuvo sump.
oleo oil.
olesemo oilseed.
oleujo cruet.
olibano frankincense.
oligarĥio oligarchy.
oligarĥo oligarch.
oligarkio oligarchy.
oligarko oligarch.

ondetigi

Oligoceno Oligocene.
oligopolo oligopoly.
oligopsonio buyer's oligopoly, oligopsony.
olimpia Olympian, Olympic. **Olimpiaj Ludoj** Olympic Games.
olimpiado Olympiad.
olimpika Olympic.
olimpikano Olympian.
Olimpikoj Olympics.
Olimpo Olympus.
olivarbo olive tree.
Olivero Oliver.
olivforma olive-shaped.
olivkolora olive.
olivo olive.
olivoleo olive oil.
olivujo olive tree.
oma ohmic.
omaĝi to pay homage to.
omaĝo homage.
Omaho Omagh.
Omana Golfo Gulf of Oman.
Omano Oman.
omaro lobster.
omaso omasum, psalterium.
ombra shady.
ombraĵo shade, umbrage.
ombreca shadowy.
ombreco shadiness.
ombrelo umbrella.
ombri to cast a shadow.
ombriĝi to be darkened.
ombro shade, shadow, umbra.
ombroplena shady, shaded, shadowy, shade-giving, giving shade.
ombrostreko hatching.
ombrumi to hatch, shade.
omego omega (Ωω).
omeno bad sign.
omeroo omer.
omikrono omicron (Οο).
omleto omelette.
omnibuso omnibus.
omo Ohm.
onagro onager, wild Asian ass (equus hemionus).
onajdo Oneida.
onani to masturbate.
onanismo onanism.
onanulo onanist.
onda of a wave. **onda lado** corrugated iron, corrugated sheet metal.
ondadi to surge, undulate.
ondado swell.
ondatro muskrat.
ondegi to be rough.
ondego billow, surge.
ondeti to ripple.
ondetigi to ripple, ruffle.

ondetiĝi to ripple, ruffle.
ondeto ripple, wavelet.
ondi to undulate.
ondiĝi to surge, undulate.
ondiĝo swell.
ondo wave.
ondobrila moiré.
ondoforto strength or power of a wave.
ondofrapado surf.
ondokondukilo waveguide.
ondolinia undulating.
ondolinii to undulate.
ondolinio undulation.
ondolongo wavelength.
ondoresalto surf.
ondorompilo breakwater.
ondosekcio wave-band.
ondostrio bend sinister wavy.
ondrompilo breakwater.
ondumi to corrugate, wave.
oneco divisibility.
oni one, they, people. **oni ĝojas des pli** to one is all the gladder.
onia one's.
onidire according to rumour, supposedly, people say (that), allegedly.
onidiro hearsay, rumour.
onikso onyx.
onisko woodlouse.
onjo auntie.
onkla avuncular.
onkleca avuncular.
onklido first cousin.
onklinjo auntie.
onklino aunt.
onklo uncle.
onkomo radix point.
onlajna on-line.
ono decimal digit, fraction, unit fraction.
onobriko sainfoin.
onomatopeo onomatopoeia.
onono rest-harrow.
onpunkto radix point.
ontogenezo ontogenesis, ontogeny.
ontologia ontological.
ontologie ontologically.
ontologio ontology.
ontologo ontologist.
Onufrio Humphrey.
oolito oolite.
opa collective, joint.
opaka opaque.
opalo opal.
opcio option.
ope at a time, collectively, together.
opera operatic.
operacia operational. **operacia enketado** operations research. **operacia semantiko** operational semantics.

operacianto operator.
operaciato operand.
operaciendo operand.
operaciesploro operational research.
operacii to operate.
operaciilo operator.
operaciindika parto operating part.
operacio operation, surgical operation.
operacisimbolo operator.
operaciuma system.
operaciumkraŝo system crash.
operaciumo operating system.
operaco operation.
operacosistemo operating system.
operando argument, operand.
operati to operate.
operatoro operator.
operejo opera house.
opereto operetta.
opero opera.
opiaĵo opiate.
opinienketo opinion survey.
opinii to account, deem, opine, think, believe, have an opinion.
opinio opinion, sentiment.
opinisondisto pollster.
opio opium.
oponado opposition.
oponanto opponent.
oponi to oppose.
oponii to opine.
oponulo opponent.
oportuna convenient, handy, opportune.
oportunaĵo convenience.
oportunaĵoj things of convenience.
oportune advantageously, comfortably, conveniently, usefully, opportunely, handy.
oportuneco convenience.
oportunisto opportunist.
oportuno convenience, ease, handiness.
opozicii to be in opposition, oppose.
opozicio opposition.
opoziciulo anti, member of opposition.
optativo optative.
optika optical. **optika fibro** fibre optics, optical fibre. **optika lokalizilo** optical radar, optical ranger, LIDAR (light detection and ranging). **optika signorekono** optical character recognition.
optikisto optician.
optiko optics.
optima optimal.
optimigi to optimize.
optimisma optimistic.
optimismo optimism.
optimisto optimist.
optimumigi to optimize.
optimumo optimum.
opulo Guelder rose.

opuntio prickly pear.
opuza shared.
ora golden. **ora aglo** golden eagle. **Ora Bordo** Gold Coast. **ora dispartigo** golden section. **Ora hordo** Golden Horde. **Ora Lanfelo** Golden Fleece. **Ora Marbordo** Gold Coast.
oracio oration.
oraĵisto goldsmith.
oraklo oracle.
orakolo oracle, revelation.
orangutango orangutan.
oranĝa orange.
oranĝarbo orange tree.
oranĝerio orangery.
oranĝkolora orange-coloured. **oranĝkolora hieracio** orange hawkweed.
oranĝo orange.
oranĝosuko orange juice.
Oranĝrespubliko Orange Free State.
oranĝujo orange tree, orange tree.
orato aurate.
oratora oratorical.
oratoraĵo oration, speech.
oratori to deliver an oration.
oratorio oratorio.
oratoro orator, spokesperson, speaker.
orbataĵo rolled gold.
orbito eye socket, field, orbit.
orblonda golden.
orbo orb.
orbruna auburn.
orcino grampus, killer whale, orca.
orda orderly, tidy, organized, systematic. **orda arbo** ordered tree, plane tree. **orda aro** ordered set.
orde orderly, in order.
ordema orderly, methodical, neat, tidy.
ordeme neatly, tidily.
ordemeco tidiness.
ordemo orderliness.
ordenemo officiousness.
ordeni to decorate, ordain.
ordeno badge, decoration, fraternity, order.
ordenvesto habit (clothing).
ordi to arrange, categorize, collate, order, put in order, sort, tidy.
ordigi to arrange, put in order, tidy, class, classify, sort.
ordigita ordered.
ordigo arrangement, sort.
ordinacii to ordain.
ordinacio ordination.
ordinado ordination.
ordinara common, ordinary, usual. **ordinara acero** sycamore. **ordinara cikorio** chicory. **ordinara dipsako** common teasel, Fuller's teasel, wild teasel. **ordinara dosiero** ordinary file, regular file. **ordinara hipurido** common mare's-tail. **ordinara laburno** common laburnum. **ordinara logaritmo** common logarithm. **ordinara paduso** common birdcherry. **ordinara utrikulario** common bladderwort.
ordinare commonly, usually.
ordinarulo ordinary person.
ordinata akso axis of ordinates, y-axis.
ordinato ordinate, y-coordinate.
ordini to ordain, consecrate, confer holy orders, admit into a holy order.
ordinitino clergywoman.
ordinito clergyman.
ordino holy order, ministry.
ordizi to order.
ordo order, sequence, arrangement.
ordomanko lack of order, disorder.
ordona imperative. **ordona modo** imperative mood.
ordonema authoritarian, dictatorial, domineering, imperious, magisterial. **ordonema lingvo** imperative language. **ordonema programlingvo** procedural programming language, procedure-oriented language.
ordoneme authoritatively, imperiously, officiously.
ordonemo imperiousness.
ordoni to command, order, tell, direct, prescribe. **ordoni skribe** to order in writing.
ordonita ordered, commanded.
ordonkambio bill of exchange.
ordono command, order, commandment, edict, ordinance, precept.
ordorilato order relation.
ordo-rilato order relation.
oreamnoso mountain goat.
orela aural, auricular, ear. **orela lobo** earlobe, lobe of the ear.
orelinflamo ear inflammation, otitis.
orelisto aurist.
orelkonko auricle.
orelo ear.
orelpendaĵo earring.
orelringo earring.
orelstrigo long-eared owl.
orelŝtopilo ear plug.
oreltamburo eardrum, tympanum.
orelumo earphone.
oreotrago klipspringer.
orepoko golden age.
orfa orphan.
orfejo orphanage.
Orfeo Orpheus.
orfigi to orphan.
orfiĝi to become an.
orfino orphan.
orfiŝo goldfish.
orflava golden yellow.

orfo orphan.
orfoino orphan.
orfolio gold foil.
orfopatrino foster mother.
organa organic.
organdio organdie.
organika organic. **organika ĥemio** organic chemistry.
organisma organic.
organismo organism.
organiza organizational. **organiza programo** supervisor.
organizacio organization.
organizado organization.
organizaĵo organization. **Organizaĵo de Petrol-Eksportaj Landoj** Organization of Petroleum Exporting Countries, OPEC. **Organizaĵo por Ekonomiaj Kunlaboro kaj Evoluigo** Organization for Economic Cooperation and Development, OECD.
organizi to organize.
organizilo supervisor.
organizinto organizer.
organizo organization.
organo organ.
orgasmo orgasm.
orgeno organ.
orgia orgiastic.
orgio orgy.
orgojla arrogant, proud, vain.
orgojlo arrogance, pride.
orhava auriferous.
ori to gild.
orienta easterly, eastern, Oriental. **Orienta Azio** East Asia, Far East, Southeast Asia. **Orienta Ĉina Maro** East China Sea. **orienta doroniko** leopard's bane, Oriental leopard's bane. **orienta duonglobo** eastern hemisphere. **Orienta Flandrio** East Flanders. **Orienta Flandrujo** East Flanders. **Orienta Frislando** East Friesland. **Orienta Frizonio** East Friesland. **Orienta Frizonujo** East Friesland. **Orienta Kongo** Democratic Republic of the Congo. **orienta kristanismo** Eastern Christianity. **Orienta Skeldo** East Skeldt. **Orienta Timoro** (Democratic Republic of) Timor-Leste, East Timor.
orientalismo orientalism.
orientalisto orientalist.
Orientazio East Asia.
Orientĉina Maro East China Sea.
oriente easterly, in the east. **oriente de** east of, eastward of, to the east of.
orienten east, eastward, eastwards.
orientflanke on the east side.
orientgermana East German.
orienthinda East-Indian.

orienti to orient, orientate.
orientiĝi to orient(ate) oneself.
orientiĝo orientation.
orientita oriented. **orientita arbo** oriented tree. **orientita grafeo** digraph, directed graph, oriented graph.
oriento East, Orient.
Orientsiberia Maro East Siberian Sea.
origamio origami.
origano marjoram, oregano, origanum.
origi to gild.
origina aboriginal, original.
originala original, primitive.
originale originally.
originaleco originality.
originalo original.
originalteksto original text.
originalulo nut, eccentric.
origine originally.
origini to originate.
origino origin.
orika auric.
orikteropo aardvark.
orioledoj orioles (family).
oriolo oriole.
Oriono Orion.
oritaĵo gold plate.
Orkadoj Orkney Islands, Orkneys.
orkadra gold-edged. **orkadraj paĝoj** gold-edged pages.
orkestrejo bandstand.
orkestrestro choir master.
orkestreto band.
orkestriono orchestrion.
orkestro orchestra.
orkestrogvidanto conductor.
orkestrumi to orchestrate.
orkideo orchid.
orkido orchid; testicle.
Orkniinsularo Orkney Islands, Orkneys.
orko grampus, killer whale, orca.
orkolora gold-coloured, golden.
orkrona koreopso goldenmane coreopsis, goldenmane tickseed.
orli to hem.
orlo hem.
orlono orlon.
orminejo gold mine.
ormonero gold coin.
ornama ornamental.
ornamado adornment, decoration.
ornamaĵo adornment, decoration, ornament, finery, ornamentation.
ornami to adorn, decorate, ornament, embellish.
ornamisto decorator.
ornamita adorned.
ornamo adornment, ornament.
ornamoplena flowery.

ornato

ornato clerical robe, robes of office, vestment.
ornito bird.
ornitologiisto ornithologist.
ornitologio ornithology.
ornitologo ornithologist.
ornitopo bird's foot.
ornitorinko duck-billed platypus.
orno flowering ash, manna ash.
oro gold.
orobanko broomrape.
orografio orography.
oroza aurous.
orpolvo gold-dust.
orriĉa auriferous.
orta orthogonal, right-angle, square, perpendicular. **orta matrico** orthogonal matrix. **orta projekcio** orthogonal projection. **orta triangulo** right triangle.
ortangula right-angled.
ortangulo rectangle.
ortanto normal, perpendicular.
ortilo carpenter's square, T-square.
orto right angle.
ortocentro orthocenter.
ortodoksa orthodox.
ortodoksa kristanismo orthodox Christianity.
ortodokseco orthodoxy.
ortodoksismo orthodoxy.
ortodoksulo orthodox person.
ortografia orthography.
ortografii to spell.
ortografiilo spellchecker.
ortografio orthography.
ortopediisto orthopedist.
ortopedio orthopedics.
orumi to gild.
Osako Osaka.
oscedegi to gape.
oscedi to yawn.
oscedo yawn.
oscedoado yawn.
oscilado oscillation.
oscili to oscillate.
oscililo oscillator.
oscilo oscillator.
oscilografo oscilloscope.
osciloskopo oscilloscope.
Osetio Ossetia.
oseto Ossetian.
Osetujo Ossetia.
Osiro Osiris.
Oslo Oslo.
osmero smelt.
osmio osmium.
osmozo osmosis.
osmundo royal fern.

ovolado

osta bone, bony, large-boned, large-framed, thick-boned.
ostaĝi to be a hostage, be held hostage.
ostaĝigi to take someone hostage.
ostaĝmono ransom.
ostaĝo hostage.
Ostara Marbordo Skeleton Coast.
ostaro skeleton.
osteca bony.
ostempo future.
Ostendo Ostend, Ostende.
ostero boner.
ostfiŝa osteichthian.
ostfiŝo bony fish, osteichthian, osteichthian.
ostiĝi to ossify.
osto bone.
ostocerbo marrow.
ostoĉizilo bone chisel.
ostohisto bone tissue.
ostopatiisto osteopath, osteopathist.
ostpulvoro bone dust.
ostracismo ostracism.
ostro oyster.
ostrobirdo oyster-catcher.
ostrogoto Ostrogoth.
Osvestro Oswestry.
Otaŭtaho Christchurch.
Otelo Othello.
Oterburno Otterburn.
otido bustard.
otiso bustard.
otito otitis.
otomana Ottoman.
otomano Ottoman.
otorinolaringologiisto ear, nose, and throat specialist.
otorinolaringologio otorhinolaryngology.
otorinolaringologo ear, nose, and throat specialist, otorhinolaryngologist.
otuso long-eared owl.
ova of an egg.
ovacii to applaud.
ovacio ovation.
ovaĵo eggs (food), omelette.
ovala oval.
ovalo oval.
ovario ovary.
ovblanko egg white, the white.
ovibovo musk ox.
ovingo eggcup.
ovio ovine.
ovo egg.
ovoblanko egg-white.
ovobrando eggnog.
ovoĉelo ovule, ovum.
ovoflavaĵo yolk.
ovoflavo yolk of egg.
ovoforma egg-shaped.
ovolado ovulation.

ovolo

ovolo ovule, ovum.
o-vorto noun.
ovri to clear, open, open up.
ovujo ovary.

ovulo ovum, ovule.
ozeno ozaena.
ozono ozone.

P

p. → **paĝo**, **pencoj**.
p.a. → **per adreso**.
p.K. → **post Kristo**.
p.s. → **postskribo**.
paca peaceful.
pacama peaceful, peace loving.
pace amicably, peaceably, peacefully.
pacema conciliating, pacific, peaceable, peaceful.
paceme peacefully.
pacflago flag of truce, flag of peace.
pacgarda peacekeeping.
pacgardado peacekeeping.
pacgardisto peacekeeper.
pacienca patient.
pacience patiently.
pacienci to be patient.
pacienco patience.
paciento patient.
pacifika Pacific.
Pacifiko Pacific, Pacific Ocean.
pacifismo pacifism.
pacifisto pacifist.
pacigi to appease, conciliate, reconcile, make peace, pacify.
pacigo pacification, reconciliation.
paciĝi to calm (oneself) down, be reconciled.
paciĝo to make peace.
pacismo pacifism.
pacisto pacifist.
packontrakto peace treaty.
paco peace.
pacperado peacemaking.
pactraktato peace treaty.
paĉjo dad, daddy, pa, papa.
paĉulo patchouli.
padeli to paddle.
padelo blade, paddle.
pado path.
Pado Po.
paduso bird-cherry, hagberry, hagberry tree.
paeljo paella.
pafadi to be shooting, keep shooting.
pafado firing (of guns), fusillade, shooting.
pafaĵo projectile.
pafaĵprovizo ammunition, ammo.
pafanto gunman, shooter.
pafarke with a bow, along a bow.
pafarkisto archer.
pafarko bow.
pafarmilo firearm.
pafatingi to command, cover, sweep.
pafbruo sound of a (gun)shot.
pafĉesigo ceasefire.
pafdistanco range.

pafego large shot.
pafejo firing range, shooting range.
paffaligo shoot-down.
pafforigi to shoot off.
pafforto firepower.
pafi to fire, shoot (a gun). **pafi al** to fire at, fire upon. **pafi korpotuŝe** to fire at point-blank range. **pafi sagojn al** to shoot arrows at.
pafiĝi to become shot.
pafilado gunnery, volley (gun firing).
pafilbatalo shoot-out.
pafilbati to club with a rifle.
pafilbato blow with a rifle.
pafilbruo sound of a gunshot.
pafilegado cannonade.
pafilego cannon.
pafileto pistol.
pafilisto gunman, shooter.
pafilkape with the butt of a rifle.
pafilkapo butt, grip.
pafilo gun, musket, rifle, firearm.
pafilpafo gunshot.
pafiltenile with the butt of a rifle.
pafiltenilo butt, stock (of a rifle).
pafiltureto gun turret.
pafilujo holster.
pafisto marksman. **Pafisto** Sagittarius (zodiac).
paflertulo marksman, sharpshooter.
pafludo shoot-em-up game, shooter game.
pafmortigi to shoot dead.
pafo shot.
pafspaco shooting distance, firing range.
paftruo bullet hole.
pafvundi to wing, wound.
pafvundita winged, wounded.
paga remunerative.
pagadmoni to dun, dun for payment.
pagado payment.
pagaji to paddle.
pagajo paddle.
pagana pagan.
paganismo paganism.
pagano pagan.
paganto payer.
pagatesto bill of sale.
pagebla payable.
pagegi to pay.
pagenda payable, due, has to be paid.
pagi to pay. **pagi kontante** to pay in cash. **pagi la kostojn de** to bear the cost of, defray the cost of, pay the expenses of. **pagi la unuan parton** to make a deposit, make

pagigi

a down payment. **pagi parte** to pay on account.
pagigi to charge.
pagigo levy.
pagilo means of payment.
pago payment, wages.
pagodo pagoda.
pagokapabla solvable (payable).
pagokapableco solvability, solvency.
pagokapablo solvent.
pagokesto fare box.
pagprokrasto moratorium.
pagpromeso acceptance.
pagumo masked palm civet.
paguro hermit crab, soldier crab.
paĝaro website.
paĝavanco form feed.
paĝio page (person).
paĝo page (book, etc.).
paĝosigni to bookmark.
paĝosigno bookmark.
paĝotitolo page footer, page header.
paĝumebla browseable.
paĝumi to browse, surf.
paĝumilo browser.
pahidermo pachyderm.
pajaca zany.
pajaceca zany.
pajaco buffoon, clown, fool, jester.
pajla straw, of straw. **pajla matraco** palliasse. **pajla tegmento** thatch.
pajlaĵo bed (horse), litter.
pajlero piece of straw.
pajlo straw.
pajlohomo stooge.
pajloplekti to plait (with straw).
pajlrestaĵo chaff.
Pajno Pan.
pajnto pint.
pajro peer.
pakado package.
pakaĵbileto luggage ticket.
pakaĵejo cloakroom, parcels office.
pakaĵo baggage, luggage, package, parcel.
pakaĵoj goods.
pakaĵospaco baggage hall.
pakaĵrako luggage rack.
pakaĵujo cargo area.
pakego bale.
paketo packet, parcel.
paki to pack.
pakidermo pachyderm.
pakistana Pakistani.
pakistananino Pakistani, Pakistani lady, Pakistani woman.
pakistanano Pakistani.
Pakistano Pakistan.
pakisto packer.
paklitakselo paclitaxel.

palisplektaĵo

pako pack, parcel.
pakoaĵo packet.
pakto pact.
pakumo packaging.
pakvagono luggage van.
pala pale, sallow, wan. **pala cefalantero** white helleborine.
palaceto mansion.
palaco palace.
paladio palladium.
palankeno palanquin, litter.
palata palatal.
palatalo palatal.
palato (hard) palate.
Palaŭo Palau.
palavri to palaver.
palavro palaver.
Palco Palatinate.
pale palely.
paleco paleness.
paledo pallet.
palega ghastly, pallid, wan.
palemono prawn.
paleoantropologiisto palaeoanthropologist.
paleoantropologio palaeoanthropology.
paleoantropologo palaeoanthropologist.
Paleoceno Palaeocene.
paleografiisto palaeographer.
paleografio palaeography.
paleografo palaeographer.
Paleolitiko Palaeolithic.
paleontologiisto palaeontologist.
paleontologio palaeontology.
paleontologo palaeontologist.
Paleozoiko Palaeozoic.
palestina Palestinian.
palestinano Palestinian.
Palestino Palestine.
paletro painter's palette.
palflava dun.
paliativa palliative.
paliativo palliative.
paligi to pale.
paliĝi to blanch, fade, grow pale, become pale.
palimpsesto palimpsest.
palindromo palindrome.
palinuro crayfish, spiny lobster, rock lobster, sea crayfish.
Palio Pali.
palisandro rosewood.
palisaro fence, palisade.
palisaroaĵo paling, palisade.
paliseti to stump.
paliseto lath, stamen.
palisigi to stake.
paliso post, stake, pile, support, stick.
palisoŝtupo stile.
palisplektaĵo lattice, trellis.

palisumi to impale.
palmarbo palm tree.
palmo palm, palm tree.
palmobranĉo palm frond.
Palmodimanĉo Palm Sunday.
Palmofesto Palm Sunday.
palmoj palms.
palmopieda palmiped, web-footed bird.
palpado palpation.
palpe by feel, by touch.
palpebla palpable, tangible, perceptible.
palpeble tangibly.
palpebrito blepharitis.
palpebro eyelid.
palpebruma blinking.
palpebrumi to blink, wink.
palpeti to feel one's way, grope.
palpi to feel, grope, touch.
palpilo antenna.
palpitacio palpitation.
palpiti to palpitate, throb.
palpo feeling, touch.
palto coat, overcoat.
palumbo pigeon.
pamfletisto pamphleteer.
pamfleto pamphlet, lampoon, satire.
pampelmo grapefruit.
pampelmuso pomelo.
pampo pampa, pampas.
panaceo panacea.
panakiranto breadwinner.
panama Panamanian. **Panama Golfo** Gulf of Panama.
panamanino Panamanian woman.
panamano Panamanian.
Panamo Panama.
panarbo breadfruit tree.
panaricio whitlow.
panariso whitlow.
panbakujo bread oven.
panbulo bread roll, bap, bun.
panbutiko baker's shop.
pandemio pandemic.
pandemonio pandemonium.
pandiono osprey.
pandito pundit.
pando panda.
pandonanto employer, meal ticket.
Pandoro Pandora.
panegira panegyrical.
panegiro panegyric.
panei to break down, malfunction.
paneinta broken down.
panejo bakery.
paneli to wainscot.
panelo control panel, dashboard, panel, wainscot.
paneo breakdown.
panero bread crumb.

panetolero fault tolerance.
panfermentilo yeast.
panfrukto breadfruit.
panĝaba Punjabi.
panĝabano Punjabi.
panherbo cereal.
panika frantic.
panike frantically.
paniketo flap.
paniki to panic.
panikiganto alarmist.
panikla flokso fall phlox, garden phlox, perennial phlox.
paniklo panicle.
paniko panic.
panisto baker.
panjo mom, mommy.
pankaĉo bread pudding.
pankorbeto bread basket.
pankovraĵo sandwich filling.
pankraco pancratium.
pankreaso pancreas.
pankreato pancreas.
pankrusto bread crust.
panmolaĵo crumb (bread).
pano bread, loaf.
panoramo panorama, view.
panrostilo toaster.
pansaĵo bandage.
pansako haversack.
pansbendo bandage, swathe.
pansi to bandage, put a band-aid on, dress (wound).
panskatolo bread bin.
pansobendo plaster, adhesive bandage, band-aid.
pansurmetaĵo sandwich filling.
pantabulo bread board.
pantaflo slipper.
pantaloneto pantaloon, short pants, shorts.
pantalono pants, trousers.
pantalonportanta trousers wearing.
pantalonpoŝo pants pocket.
pantalonzono belt.
panteisma pantheist.
panteismo pantheism.
panteisto pantheist.
panteono pantheon.
panterino female panther.
panterkato ocelot.
pantero leopard, panther.
pantofleto sandal.
pantoflo slipper.
pantoflofloro calceolaria, lady's purse, pocket-book flower.
pantografo pantograph.
pantomimi to pantomime.
pantomimisto mime.
pantomimo pantomime.

pantranĉilo bread knife.
panujo bread basket, bread pan.
panumi to bread.
panumo breading.
panvendejo baker's shop.
papa papal.
papageto parakeet.
papago parrot.
papagumi to parrot.
papaino papain.
papajo papaya.
papajoarbo papaya, pawpaw.
papajobero papaya, pawpaw.
papajofrukto papaya, pawpaw.
paparaco paparazzo.
papaŭto popemobile.
papaveto poppy, red poppy, corn poppy, field poppy, Flanders poppy.
papavo poppy.
papeco papacy.
papera of paper, paper, (made) of paper.
paperaĉo scrap of paper.
paperaĵo stationery.
paperbulo ball of paper.
paperfarejo paper manufactory, paper mill.
paperisto paper maker.
paperkorbo paper basket.
paperkovristo paper hanger.
papermovo paper feed.
papero (piece of) paper.
paperpremilo paperweight.
paperstrio streamer.
papertapeto wallpaper.
paperujo file, folder, portfolio.
papervendisto stationer.
papilikolekto butterfly collection.
papilio butterfly.
papiruso papyrus.
papisto papist.
papo pope.
papriko paprika, red pepper.
papua Papua. **Papua Nova Gvineo** Papua New Guinea.
papumi to act like the Pope, issue edicts, make proclamations.
papuo Papuan.
para even (numbered).
parabolo parable, parabola.
paraboloido paraboloid.
parada pretentious.
paradema showy.
parademe showily.
parademo showiness.
paradi to display, parade.
paradigma paradigmatic.
paradigmo paradigm.
paradilo float.
paradiza paradisiac, paradisiacal.
paradizbirdo bird of paradise.

paradizeo bird of paradise.
paradizludo hopscotch.
paradizo paradise, Eden, Heaven.
paradmarŝo parade.
parado display, parade, review, show, pageant.
paradoksa paradoxical.
paradokse paradoxically.
paradokso paradox.
parafi to initial.
parafilona paraphyletic.
parafina paraffin.
parafino paraffin.
parafo initials; flourish after signature, paraph.
parafrazi to paraphrase.
parafrazo paraphrase.
paragrafo paragraph, section.
paragvaja Paraguayan.
paragvajanino Paraguayan woman.
paragvajano Paraguayan.
Paragvajo Paraguay.
Parakleto Paraclete, Holy Spirit.
paraksileno paraxylene.
paralakso parallax.
paralela parallel. **paralela projekcio** parallel projection. **paralela serĉo** parallel search. **paralela sumilo** parallel adder. **paralela universo** parallel universe.
paralelado parallel processing, parallelism.
paralele al parallel to.
paralele kun parallel with.
paralelepipedo parallelepiped.
paralelo parallel line.
paralelogramo parallelogram.
paralelprojekcio parallel projection.
paralimpikano paralympian.
Paralimpiko Paralympic Games.
paraliza paralytic.
paralizeto palsy.
paralizi to paralyse.
paraliziĝi to be paralysed.
paraliziĝinta paralysed.
paralizo paralysis.
paralizoado paralysis.
paralizulo paralysed person, quadriplegic.
paralogismo fallacy.
parametra parametric. **parametra prezento** parametric representation.
parametro parameter.
parametropasigo parameter passing.
paranoia paranoid.
paranoja paranoid.
paranojo paranoia.
parapentanto paraglider.
parapenti to paraglide.
parapentilo paraglider.
parapeto parapet.
paraplegio paraplegia.

parapsiĥologio parapsychology.
parapsikologio parapsychology, psychics.
paraŝuta airborne, parachute.
paraŝuti to parachute.
paraŝutigi to airdrop, drop, parachute.
paraŝutigo airdrop, drop.
paraŝutisto parachutist.
paraŝuto parachute.
paratifo paratyphoid.
parazita parasitic. **parazita rabmevo** arctic skua, parasitic jaeger.
paraziteca parasitical.
paraziteco parasitism.
paraziti to freeload, leech (off of).
parazito cadger, parasite, sponger, freeloader.
parceligi to parcel out.
parcelo lot, parcel.
parcimonio parsimony.
parco Parca.
pardonebla excusable, pardonable, venial.
pardonemo clemency.
pardoni to forgive, pardon, reprieve, excuse, overlook. **pardonu!** excuse me! sorry! forgive me! **pardonu min!** pardon me!
pardoniĝi to be pardoned.
pardonipeti to ask forgiveness.
pardono absolution, pardon, forgiveness. **pardonon peti** to apologize.
pardonpeti to ask forgiveness, excuse oneself.
pardonpeto apology.
parecbito parity bit.
pareckontrolo parity check.
pareco parity.
parenca affined, akin, related.
parencaro connections, kindred, kinsfolk, relations, relatives.
parenceco affiliation, blood relationship, affinity, relationship.
parenciĝi to become related.
parencino relative, female relative.
parenco kinsman, relation, relative.
parenkimo parenchyma.
parenteze by the way.
parentezo parenthesis.
pareo pareu.
parfumfarado perfumery (manufactory).
parfumi to perfume.
parfumisto perfumer.
parfumĵetilo atomizer.
parfumo perfume.
pargeto parquet, wood flooring.
parhufulo artiodactyl.
parhufuloj artiodactyls.
parietalo parietal bone.
parieto inner surface, lining.
parietosto crown of the head, sinciput.
parigi to couple, match, pair, unite.
pariĝi to mate.
pariĝo mating.
pario outcaste, pariah, untouchable.
Pariso Paris.
pariza Parisian.
Parizano Parisian.
Parizo Paris.
parkadgaraĝo parking garage.
parkejo car park, parking garage, parking place.
parkere by heart, from memory.
parkeri to memorize, learn by heart.
parkerigi to memorize.
parkhorloĝo parking meter.
parki to park.
parko park.
parkumejo car park, parking place.
parkumi to park.
parlamenta parliamentary.
parlamentano member of parliament.
parlamentejo house of parliament.
parlamento parliament.
parnasio grass-of-Parnassus.
Parnaso Parnassus.
parneteze... by the way...
parnombro even (number).
paro brace, couple, pair.
parodii to parody.
parodio burlesque, parody.
paroĥa parochial.
paroĥanaro parishionership.
paroĥano parishioner.
paroĥejo parish.
paroĥestrejo vicarage.
paroĥestro pastor, vicar, rector.
paroĥismo parochialism.
paroĥo parish.
paroka parochial.
parokano parishioner.
parokestro pastor, vicar.
paroko parish.
paroksismo fit, paroxysm, seizure.
parola oral, spoken, verbal. **parola Esperanto** spoken Esperanto.
parolaĉi to speak badly, murder (a language).
paroladeto allocution.
paroladi to be talking, parley.
parolado discourse, harangue, lecture, oration, speech.
paroladoskribisto speech-writer.
parolante pri... speaking of...
parolanto speaker, spokesman.
parolarto rhetoric.
parolata spoken.
parole orally, verbally.
parolegeco verbosity.
parolegema verbose.
parolejo parlour.
parolelemento part of speech.

parolema

parolema loquacious, talkative.
paroleme volubly.
paroleti to whisper.
parolflueco speaking fluency.
parolfluega voluble.
paroli to speak, talk. **paroli angle** to speak English. **paroli per lingvoj** to speak in tongues. **paroli sensancaĵon** to talk nonsense. **paroli sensence** to ramble, rant, rave (in speech), talk nonsense. **paroli sensensaĵon** to talk nonsense.
paroligi to cause to speak, make to talk.
parolisto orator, spokesperson, presenter, speaker.
parolkapablo speaking ability.
parolmaniero manner of speaking, speech.
parolo speech, word (spoken). **parolo je la honoro** parole.
parolrajto right to speech.
parolscienco elocution.
parolturno turns of phrase.
paronico whitlow.
paroniĥio whitlow.
paronimo paronym.
paronomazio paronomasia.
parotidito mumps, parotitis.
parseko parsec.
Parta Parthian.
parta partial. **parta derivaĵo** partial derivative. **parta eklipso** partial eclipse. **parta ordo** partial order. **parta sumo** partial sum (of a series).
parte partially, partly. **parte orda aro** partially ordered set, poset.
partenogenezo parthenogenesis.
partero ground floor, parterre, pit (lower floor of theatre).
parteto chip, particle.
partia biased, partial, partisan.
partianeca partisan.
partianeco partiality, partisanship.
partianiĝi to take sides. **partianiĝi kun** to side with.
partiano advocate, member, supporter, partisan, party member.
partianoj adherents, disciples, followers, party members.
participo participle.
partieca partisan.
partieco partiality.
partiema biased.
partigvardio militia, armed group, gang of henchmen, thugs.
partiklo particle.
partikloakcelilo particle accelerator.
partikulara particularist, particular.
partikulo particle.
partio faction, party, side, game, match.
partituro partition, score (musical).

pasintjara

partiuniforma party uniform.
partizana partisan.
partizano partisan.
partnero partner.
parto behalf, part, share, portion, section, quota.
partopago installment payment.
partopeni to participate in.
partoprenanto participant, partner.
partopreni to take part, share, partake, participate.
partopreno participation.
partpage on account.
partpago installment payment.
partprenado participation.
partprenanto participant, party, sharer.
partpreni to participate. **partpreni ies sentojn** to sympathize with someone's feelings.
partpreno part.
partumo fraction.
paruo titmouse.
parvenuo parvenu.
parvolo wren.
pasado passing, passing by, transit.
pasaĝera passenger.
pasaĝeraviadilo airliner.
pasaĝeri to travel as passenger.
pasaĝerigi to convey as passenger.
pasaĝero passenger.
pasamentaĵo braid, braiding.
pasamenti to trim, braid.
pasamento braid, lace, trimming, trim.
pasanta passing.
pasanto passer-by.
pasejo gate, gangway, passage, passageway.
pasema transient, ephemeral, transitory.
paseo past.
pasero sparrow.
pasi to pass. **pasi preskaŭtuŝe** to skim. **pasi preskaŭtuŝe super** to skim over. **pasi preter** to pass over, not stop at.
pasia passionate.
pasie passionately.
pasiggrupo formal parameter section.
pasigi to cause to pass, make pass by.
pasigo a call. **pasigo per algoritmo** call by name. **pasigo per referenco** call by reference, parameter passed by reference. **pasigo per rezulto** call by result, parameter passed by result. **pasigo per valoro** call by value, value parameter. **pasigo per valorrezulto** call by value-result.
pasilibereco abandon.
pasinta previous, last.
pasinteca past.
pasintece historically, in the past.
pasinteco past.
pasintjara last year's.

339

pasintjare last year.
pasinto past.
pasio lust, passion.
Pasiono Passion.
pasiva passive.
pasive passively.
pasivo debts, liabilities, passive voice.
paska Paschal. **Paska Insulo** Easter Island. **Paska semajno** Easter Week, Octave of Easter.
paskala Pascal. **paskala limako** Pascal limaçon. **paskala triangulo** binomial array, Pascal triangle.
Paskalo Pascal.
Pasko Easter, Passover.
Paskoleporo Easter bunny.
paskvila satirical, spoof.
paskvile satirically.
paskvili to lampoon, satirize, spoof.
paskvilo lampoon, satire.
Pasligo Paisley.
pasloĝanto sojourner, temporary dweller, temporary resident.
pasmovo pass.
paso pass.
paspermeso pass.
pasporto passport.
pasrajto way-leave.
pastabulo gangway.
pastaĵo pasta.
pasteco pastry.
pasteĉo pâté, pie.
pastelo lozenge, pastille.
pasteŭrizi to pasteurize.
pastiĉo pastiche.
pastinako parsnip.
pasto dough, paste.
pastocilindro rolling pin.
pastoralo pastoral.
pastoro pastor.
pastra sacerdotal. **pastra domo** parsonage, rectory. **pastra vesto** cassock.
pastrado ministry.
pastraro clergy, priesthood.
pastre pastorally.
pastreco priesthood, ministry.
pastrejo presbytery, rectory.
pastriĝi to become a minister, become a priest.
pastriĝo ordination.
pastrino clergywoman.
pastro clergyman, pastor, priest, minister, parson.
pastromonaĥo monk-presbyter.
pastujo mixing bowl.
pasumi to dawdle, lounge, lounge about, stroll.
pasvorto password.
paŝado pace, pacing.

paŝao pasha.
paŝegi to stalk, stride.
paŝego stride.
paŝegulo strider.
paŝetulo toddler.
paŝi to pace, stalk, step, stride, tread.
paŝo pace, step, stride. **paŝo paŝe** step by step. **paŝo post paŝo** step by step.
paŝtabulo gangway.
paŝtaĵo pasturage, grazing ground, meadow, pasture.
paŝtejo meadow, pasture.
paŝtelaĵo pastel.
paŝtelo crayon, pastel.
paŝteni to keep up with.
paŝti to (take to) pasture, feed, shepherd. **paŝti sin** to browse, graze.
paŝtiĝejo meadow, pasture.
paŝtiĝi to graze.
paŝtista bucolic.
paŝtisto herder, herdsman, shepherd.
Patagonio Patagonia.
patato sweet potato.
patelo kneecap, patella.
patenta patent.
patenti to patent.
patentito patentee.
patento patent.
paternalisma paternalistic.
paternalismo paternalism.
patinigi to weather.
patiniĝi to weather.
patino patina.
patkuko griddle cake, pancake.
pato frying pan.
patogena pathogenic.
patologia pathological.
patologie pathologically.
patologiisto pathologist.
patologio pathology.
patologo pathologist.
patosa emphatic.
patoso bombast, expression, feeling, fervor, passion, pathos, rant, emphasis.
patra fatherly, paternal.
patreca fatherly, paternal.
patreco fatherhood, paternity.
patreto pa, papa.
patriarĥo patriarch.
patriarka patriarchal.
patriarkeco patriarchate.
patriarkejo patriarchate.
patriarko patriarch.
patricio patrician.
patrico die, stamp, hallmark.
Patriko Patrick.
patrina maternal.
patrineca maternal, motherly.
patrineco maternity, motherhood.

patrineto little mother, mama.
patrinflanka maternal, mother's side. **patrinflanka avino** maternal grandmother. **patrinflanka avo** maternal grandfather. **patrinflanka onklino** aunt, maternal aunt. **patrinflanka onklo** uncle, maternal uncle. **patrinflankaj geavoj** maternal grandparents.
patrinflanke on the mother's side.
Patrinfonto Motherwell.
patrini to mother.
patrino matron, mother.
patrinujo motherland.
patriota patriotic.
patriotisma patriotic.
patriotismo patriotism.
patrioto patriot.
patro father, sire. **patroj** fathers.
Patro Kristnasko Father Christmas, Santa Claus.
patroflanka paternal, father's side. **patroflanka avino** paternal grandmother. **patroflanka avo** paternal grandfather. **patroflanka onklino** aunt, paternal aunt. **patroflanka onklo** uncle, paternal uncle. **patroflankaj geavoj** paternal grandparents.
patrolando fatherland.
patroli to patrol.
patrolingve in one's native language, in one's father's language.
patrolo patrol.
patromortiginto parricide.
patrona sanktulo patron saint.
patronado sponsorship.
patroneco sponsorship.
patroni to act as patron.
patronimiko patronymic.
patronino matron.
patrono patron, pattern.
patrujo fatherland, native land, motherland.
patvendisto ironmonger.
Paŭla Paula, Pauline.
Paŭlino Paula, Pauline.
Paŭlo Paul.
paŭperismo pauperism.
paŭsaĵo calque.
paŭsi to slavishly reproduce, trace.
paŭso tracing.
paŭspapero tracing paper.
paŭta dismal.
paŭti to pout, sulk.
paŭto pout.
paŭzi to pause, take a break, take a rest.
paŭzigi to suspend.
paŭzigo suspension.
paŭzo break, intermission, pause, recess, interval, rest, stop.
pavezo bulwarks, topsides.
pavi to show off, strut, swagger.
paviano baboon.
paviliono pavilion.
pavilono pavilion.
pavima stone-paved.
pavimado paving.
pavimero paving stone.
pavimi to pave.
pavimo paving, pavement.
pavimŝtono cobblestone.
pavo peacock.
pazigrafio pasigraphy.
pĉk → **poŝta ĉekkonto**.
peano paean.
pecego large piece.
pecereto particle.
pecero particle.
pecetiĝi to crumble, crumble away, crumble off.
peceto morsel, scrap.
pecigi to take apart.
peco bit, lump, piece, shred. **peco post peco** piecemeal.
peĉi to pitch.
Peĉjo Pete.
peĉo pitch.
pedagoga pedagogical.
pedagogia pedagogical.
pedagogiisto pedagogue.
pedagogio pedagogy.
pedagogo pedagogue, teacher.
pedalboato pedal boat.
pedali to pedal.
pedalo pedal, treadle.
pedaltaksio pedicab, trishaw.
pedanta pedantic.
pedanti to be pedantic.
pedanto pedant.
pedantulo pedant, wiseacre.
pedelo apparitor, beadle, usher, verger.
pederastio pederasty.
pederastiulo pedophile.
pederasto pederast.
pedia lingvo Pedi, Pedi language.
pediatra paediatric.
pediatriisto paediatrician.
pediatrio paediatrics.
pediatro paediatrician.
pedika lousy.
pediko louse.
pedikovo nit (of louse).
pedio Pedi.
pedofilio paedophilia.
pedofilo paedophile.
pedologio paedology.
pedomorfa paedomorphic.
pedunklo flowerstalk, peduncle.
Pegaso Pegasus.
pegedoj woodpeckers (family).

pego woodpecker.
pejzaĝisto landscape painter.
pejzaĝo landscape, scenery.
peka evil, sinful.
pekanto sinner, transgressor.
pekario peccary.
pekeco sinfulness.
pekema sinful.
pekemo sinfulness.
peketo peccadillo, offence.
peki to sin, transgress. **peki kontraŭ** to violate (something), sin against (something).
Pekino Peking, Beijing.
peklaĵo salt meat.
peklakvo brine.
pekli to pickle (in salt).
pekliberigi to absolve (a sinner).
pekliberigo pardon.
pekliberiĝi to atone.
peklita viando salt meat, salted meat.
peknaskito illegitimate child.
peko evil, sin, transgression.
pekofera kapro scapegoat.
pekpardono indulgence.
pekporta kapro scapegoat.
pekteno pecten, scallop.
pektinea potamogeto fennel pondweed, ribbonweed.
pektino pectin.
pekulo sinner.
pelagro pellagra.
pelargonio geranium.
pelĉasado beating.
pelĉaso battue.
pelerino cape, pelerine, tippet.
peli to chase, drive, drive on, impel, shoo, expel, dispel, propel. **peli piedbate malsupren** to kick down, kick off.
peliĝi to be driven (to).
pelikano pelican.
pelilo driver.
pelmelo pell-mell.
pelmenoj meat dumplings.
Peloponezo Peloponnese, Peloponnesus.
pelta made of fur, made of skin.
peltisto furrier, peltmonger.
peltkolumo fur collar.
peltmantelo fur coat.
pelto fur, fur coat, fur piece, pelisse, pelt.
peltoĉapo bearskin, bearskin cap.
pelvo basin, bowl, pelvis.
pemikano pemmican.
penadi to strive.
penado efforts, toil.
penakiri to procure.
penakiro procurement.
penalo penalty.
Penarlago Hawarden.
penco penny.

penda seruro padlock.
pendaĵo pendant.
pendeti to dangle.
pendglacio icicle.
pendglisilo hang glider.
pendi to droop, hang.
pendigado hanging (as in, hanging things up).
pendigi to hang, suspend.
pendigilo gallows.
pendigita hung, hanging.
pendigo hanging, suspending.
pendigŝnuro clothesline.
pendkolumo bands.
pendlito hammock.
pendofervojo aerial tramway.
pendoli to swing.
pendolilo swing.
pendolo pendulum.
pendolvaonaro commuter train.
pendŝnuro noose.
pendumi to hang (execute).
pendumilo gallows.
pene with difficulty, with effort. **pene labori** to work hard.
penegadi to make great efforts (to do something).
penegi to make great efforts (to do something).
penego labour, toil.
Penelopo Penelope.
penema assiduous.
penetra penetrating.
penetrebla penetrable, permeable.
penetrema bright, smart, clever.
penetri to penetrate, pervade, pierce.
penetro penetration.
peni to aim, attempt, endeavour, try.
Penibonto Bridgend.
penicilino penicillin.
penicilio penicillium.
peniga hard, laborious, irksome.
penigaĵoj fuss, to-do.
penigo challenge.
peniki to paint, use a paintbrush.
peniko brush, paintbrush.
penikotiro brushstroke.
Peninoj Pennines.
penio penny.
penisa penile.
peniseto peter, willy.
peniso penis.
peno effort, endeavour.
penplena strenuous.
pensa pensive.
pensadi to be thinking.
pensado thought.
pensanta wistful.
pensante while thinking.

pense

pense in one's thoughts.
pensema pensive, thoughtful.
penseo pansy.
pensi to think, deem. **pensi nur pri si** to think only of oneself. **pensi pri** to think about.
pensiga thought-provoking.
pensigi to remind, cause to think, suggest.
pensiĝi to go on pension, retire.
pensii to pension.
pensiiĝi to go on pension, retire.
pensilvania Pennsylvanian.
pensilvaniano Pennsylvanian.
pensio pension, retirement.
pensionano boarder.
pensiono boarding house, boarding school.
pensiulo pensioner, retiree.
pensmaniero way of thinking.
penso thought.
Penspolico Thought Police.
pensrapide as quick as thought.
pensrompo anacoluthon, break in train of thought.
penstemono beard-tongue, penstemon.
pensu think.
pensulo thinker.
penta contrite, penitent.
pentagono pentagon.
pentagramo pentacle, pentagram.
pentametro pentameter.
pentanta contrite, penitent, repentant.
Pentateŭko Pentateuch.
pentatlono pentathlon.
pentekosta Whit.
pentekostano Pentecostal.
pentekostismo Pentecostalism.
pentekostisto Pentecostal.
Pentekosto Pentecost, Whitsunday.
pentema apologetic.
pentfarejo penitentiary.
penti to repent. **penti pri** to feel sorry for, regret, repent, repent of.
pentigi to regret, repent, repent of.
pento penance, penitence, repentance, regret, remorse.
pentoado repentance.
pentodo pentode.
pentoeco contrition.
pentofara penitential.
pentofarado penance, penitence.
pentofaranto penitent.
pentofari to do penance.
pentoplena fill of regret.
pentpago expiation.
pentrado painting.
pentraĵaĉo daub, kitschy painting.
pentraĵkadro frame, picture frame.
pentraĵo painting, picture.
pentrarto painting, portraiture (art).

perdi

pentrejo artist's studio.
pentri to paint.
pentrinda picturesque.
pentristo painter (artist).
pentrita painted.
pentrotekniko brushwork.
Penvro Pembroke.
peonio peony.
peono pawn (chess).
pepegadi to hoot (of owl).
pepegi to cackle, hoot (owl).
peperomio peperomia.
pepi to chirp, peep, twitter, warble.
peplomo quilt.
pepo chirp.
pepsino pepsin.
peptido peptide.
peptono peptone.
pepulo warbler.
per by means of, through, with. **per adreso co**, care of. **per helpo de** with the help of, by means of. **per kia maniero** in what way, how. **per kio** whereby. **per la ŝvito de mia frunto** by the sweat of my brow. **per la unua rigardo** at first glance. **per laŭta voĉo** in a loud voice. **per malmultaj vortoj** in a few words. **per si mem** by itself, by themselves, in (and of) itself. **per tio** thereby. **per unu spiro** in one breath. **per vojo natura** in a natural way.
pera indirect.
perado mediation.
peramelo bandicoot.
peranti to act as agent.
peranto agent.
perbuŝe by mouth.
percepta discerning.
perceptebla appreciable, discernible, distinct, noticeable, palpable, perceptible.
percepteble discernibly, distinctively, tangibly.
perceptebleco distinctness.
perceptema discerning.
percepti to discern, find, notice, perceive.
percepto perception.
perceptorgano sense.
perĉo ruff (fish).
perdadi to go on losing.
perdaĵo wastage.
perdata lost.
perdego perdition.
perdi to lose. **perdi ĉian tempkalkulon** to lose all track of time. **perdi la ekvilibron** to lose one's balance. **perdi la fadenon** to lose the train of thought, lose the thread. **perdi la orientiĝon** to lose one's orientation, lose one's bearings. **perdi sian paciencon** to lose one's patience. **perdi sian virgecon** to lose one's virginity.

perdido betrayal.
perdigi to cause to lose, make to lose.
perdiĝi to be lost, get lost, lose one's self.
perdinto loser.
perdita lost.
perdo detriment, loss.
perdriko partridge.
pere indirectly (through an intermediary). **pere de** per.
pereema perishable.
pereemo frailty.
perei to perish.
pereiga deadly, ruinous, overwhelming.
pereigi to destroy, ruin.
pereigo bane, destruction.
pereigonto nemesis.
pereiĝo destruction.
pereo destruction, doom, downfall, fall, perdition, ruin, wreck.
perfekta perfect. **perfekta modelo** paragon. **perfekta vaskulo** perfect vacuum.
perfektaĵo paragon.
perfekte perfectly.
perfekteco perfection.
perfektigi to perfect.
perfektigo consummation.
perfektiĝi to become perfect.
perfektmodelo paragon.
perfekto perfect.
perfektulo perfect person.
perfida perfidious, traitorous, treacherous.
perfidaĵo betrayal.
perfide basely.
perfideco baseness, treachery.
perfidema treacherous.
perfidi to betray.
perfido betrayal, treachery, treason.
perfidulo betrayer, traitor.
perflati to wheedle, win by flattery.
perfolia perfoliate.
perforta boisterous, vehement, violent.
perforte by force, violently.
perforteco vehemence.
perforteniri to raid.
perforti to assault, force, violate.
perforto outrage, violence.
perfortulo thug.
pergameno parchment.
peri to act as agent, act as go-between, mediate.
peridoto peridot.
periferia peripheral. **periferia aparato** peripheral, peripheral device.
periferiaĵo peripheral.
periferio outskirts, periphery.
perigeo perigee.
perihelio perihelion.
perikardo pericardium.
perikarpo seed case, seed vessel.

perilo agency, agent, medium.
perimetro circumference, perimeter.
perineo perineum.
perioda periodic (function). **perioda gazeto** periodical. **perioda pozicia frakcio** periodic fraction. **Perioda tabelo** Periodic Table.
periodaĵo periodical.
periode periodically.
periodeco periodicity.
periodo period.
periosto periosteum.
periplo circumnavigation, periplus.
periskopa periscopic.
periskopo periscope.
peristalta peristaltic.
peristilo peristyle.
peristo agent, broker.
peritoneo peritoneum.
perkalo cotton cambric, percale.
perko bass, perch (fish).
perkomputila grafiko computer graphics.
perkudrila laboro needlework.
perkuti to percuss.
perkutilo firing-pin, percussion pin.
perkutinstrumento percussion instrument.
perkuto clash.
perla pearly.
perlaboraĵo earning.
perlabori to earn.
perlamoto mother of pearl.
perlikve by fluid.
perlo pearl.
perlueto ampersand (&).
permana done by hand. **permana skribado** handwriting, writing by hand.
permane manually.
permanenta abiding, constant, continual, continuous, enduring, lasting, permanent, standing, steadfast. **permanenta konekto** dedicated line.
permeabla permeable.
permesa permissive.
permesebla admissible.
permesi to accord, admit, afford, allow, permit, authorize, grant.
permesilo licence, permit.
permesita allowed.
permeso licence, permission.
Permo Perm.
permutaĵo permutation (of n things).
permuti to permute.
permuto permutation.
pernio chilblain.
peronisma Peronist.
peronisto Peronist.
perono front steps of a building, stoop, platform, railway platform.
perpendikla perpendicular.

perpendikulara

perpendikulara perpendicular, orthogonal.
perpendikularo perpendicular.
perpleksa perplexed, taken aback.
perpleksigi to perplex, stump.
perreferenca parametro parameter passed by reference.
perrezulta parametro parameter passed by result.
perruzi to wangle.
persa Persian. **Persa Golfo** Persian Gulf.
Persefono Persephone.
persekuta oppressive.
persekutado persecution, pursuit.
persekutanto persecutor, stalker.
persekuti to chase, persecute, prosecute, pursue.
persekutisto prosecutor.
persekuto persecution, pursuit.
Perseo Perseus.
persieno persienne, slatted shutter.
persikarbo peach tree.
persiko nectarine, peach.
persikujo peach tree.
persimono date-plum, persimmon.
persino Persian woman.
Persio Persia.
persista perennial, persistent, retentive.
persistado perseverance.
persiste habitually, persistently.
persisteco persistency, pertinacity, tenacity.
persistema dogged, tenacious.
persisteme tenaciously.
persistemo perseverance.
persisti to abide, persevere, persist.
persisto perseverance.
persistoado persistence.
perso Persian.
persona personal. **persona komputilo** personal computer, PC. **persona nomo** first name.
personaĵo personal trait.
personaĵoj personal details.
personalo work force, labour force.
personaro personnel.
persone personally.
personeco personality.
personigi to personify.
personigo personalization, personification.
personiĝi to personate.
personiĝo personification.
personnumero personal number.
persono character, person, personage.
personoj people, persons.
persontrajno passenger train.
perspektivo perspective, prospect.
Persujo Persia.
persvada compelling, convincing, persuasive.
persvade convincingly, persuasively.

petformularo

persvadi to persuade. **persvadi aĉeti** to palm off on.
persvado persuasion.
Perto Perth.
pertubo interference.
perturbado interference.
perturbi to disquiet, interfere with, perturb.
perturbo disquiet, disturbance, interference, unrest.
perua Peruvian.
peruanino Peruvian woman.
peruano Peruvian.
perubalzamo balsam of Peru.
perukisto wigmaker, perruquier.
peruko hairpiece, wig.
perulo mediator.
Peruo Peru.
pervalora parametro value parameter.
perventa by wind, wind-blown.
perversa perverse.
perverseco perversity.
perversio perversion.
perversiulo pervert.
pesario pessary.
peseto peseta.
pesi to weigh (something).
pesilego weigh-bridge.
pesilo balance, scale.
pesilo scales. **Pesilo** Libra (zodiac).
pesimisma pessimistic.
pesimisme gloomily.
pesimismo pessimism.
pesimisto pessimist.
pesita meznombro weighted average, weighted mean.
pesmaŝino steelyard.
peso peso.
pesta pestiferous.
pestiga pestilential.
pesto pest, pestilence, plague, pestilence.
pestoego plague.
pestulo plague-stricken (person).
petadi to badger.
petado postulate.
petalo petal.
petanto applicant.
petardo detonator, firecracker, petard.
petasito butterbur.
petazito butterbur.
petega solicitous.
petegado pleading.
peteganta imploring.
peteganto supplicant.
petegi to appeal, beg, beseech, implore, plead.
petego appeal, entreaty, supplication.
Peterburgo Petersburg.
petformularo application form, form of application.

peti to ask (for), request, seek, bid, beg. **peti almozon** to ask for alms, ask for a handout. **peti ies manon** to ask for someone's hand. **peti pri la mano de iu** to ask for someone's hand.
peticio petition.
petilo application form, form of application.
petiolo petiole.
peto request.
petola frolicsome, frolic, petulant, playful, saucy.
petoladi to frolic, gambol.
petolado frolic, gambol.
petolaĵo prank, shenanigan, trick.
petoleca impish.
petoleco frolic, petulance.
petolecoaĵo prank.
petolema frolicsome, mischievous, playful.
petolemulino hussy.
petolemulo imp, scamp.
petoli to frolic, horse around, play about.
petolo mischief, prank.
petolulo joker, trickster.
petoluluno mischievous girl.
petra Petrine.
petrelo petrel.
Petro Peter.
Petroburgo Saint Petersburg.
petrolĥemio petrochemistry.
petrolo paraffin oil, petroleum, oil.
petrologio petrology.
petrolŝipo (oil) tanker.
Petromaricburgo Pietermaritzburg.
petromizo lamprey.
petroselo parsley.
petskribinto applicant, petitioner.
petskribo petition.
petunio petunia.
petunklo scallop.
petveturado hitch-hiking.
petveturanto hitchhiker.
petveturi to hitchhike.
peza burdensome, heavy, onerous, weighty. **peza artilerio** heavy artillery. **peza laboro** hard work.
pezaĵo heavy thing.
peze heavily, with weight.
pezega burdensome, weighty.
pezi to be heavy, weigh.
pezigi to weigh down.
peziljetado shot-put.
peziljetisto shot-putter.
pezilo weight.
pezkore with a heavy heart.
pezo weight.
pezocentra koordinato barycentric coordinate.
pezocentro centroid (of n points).
pezoforto gravitation, gravity.

Pfalzo Palatinate.
pfenigo pfennig.
pĝ → **paĝo**.
pia pious, righteous.
piamatro pia mater.
pianisto pianist.
piano piano.
pianolo pianola.
piastro piaster.
pibroĥo pibroch.
picejo pizzeria.
piceo spruce, spruce fir.
pico pizza.
piĉleki to eat cunt.
piĉo cunt, pussy.
pie devoutly.
pieco piety.
pieda of a foot.
piedartiko instep.
piedbatante having struck with foot or paw.
piedbati to kick.
piedbato kick. **piedbato la postaĵon** boot.
piedbenketo footstool.
piede afoot, on foot. **piede de** at the foot of, below.
piedego paw.
piedestalo base, pedestal, stand.
piedfingro toe.
piedfrapadi to stamp with foot.
piedfrapado tramping.
piedfrapi to kick.
piedfrapo kick.
piedingo stirrup, toe-clip.
piediranto pedestrian.
piediri to walk, go on foot.
piednoto footnote.
piedo foot, paw.
piedpasi to pass by on foot, tread.
piedpilkado football, soccer.
piedpilkludo football, soccer.
piedpilko football, soccer ball.
piedplato sole.
piedplika maĉo soccer match.
piedponto foot bridge.
piedpremi to crush underfoot, step on, tread down, trample.
piedsigno footprint, track, trail.
piedungo toenail.
piedvarmigilo foot warmer.
piedvestaĵo footwear.
piedvesto footwear.
piedvojeto footpath.
piedvojo footway.
pierido cabbage white.
pieriso cabbage white.
pieroto pierrot.
pietato pietas, veneration.
pietismo pietism.

pigmea pigmy, of a pygmy. **pigmea mevo** Larus minutus, little gull.
pigmento pigment.
pigmeo pigmy, pygmy.
pigo magpie.
pigra indolent, lazy, slothful.
pigre lazily, slothfully.
pigro idleness, indolence, laziness, sloth, slothfulness.
piĝina pidgin.
piĝino pidgin.
pijamo pyjama.
pika nasty, piquant, prickly, pungent.
pikaĵo spike.
pikbastono skewer, spit.
pikdrataro barbed wire.
pikdrato barbed wire.
pike racily, sharply.
pikeco piquancy.
pikedo guard, outpost, picket, sentry.
pikegi to stab.
pikema pointed, sharp.
pikeme sharply.
pikfosilo mattock, pick, pickaxe.
piki to bite, jab, pick, pierce, prick, puncture, stab, stick, sting.
pikildrato barbed wire.
pikilego pike (tool).
pikilhava prickly.
pikilo awl, dart, prick, sting, pin.
pikkalkanumo stiletto heel.
pikmanĝi to eat by pecking.
pikmortigi to stab.
pikmortigo stabbing.
pikniki to picnic.
pikniko picnic.
piknikokorbo picnic basket.
piknikotablo picnic table.
piko pick, prick, spade, sting.
pikodora acrid.
pikofarado picofarad.
pikokalkanumo high heels.
pikometro picometre.
pikosekundo picosecond.
pikpluki to peck, pick.
pikrato picrate.
pikstango pike, spear.
pikta Pictish.
pikto Pict.
piktogramo icon, pictogram, pictograph.
pikulo picul.
pikvundo stab.
pilafo pilaf.
pilaro battery.
pilastro pilaster.
Pilato (Pontius) Pilate.
pilĉardo pilchard.
pilgrima falko peregrine, peregrine falcon.
pilgrimado pilgrimage.
pilgrimanto pilgrim.
pilgrimi to go on a pilgrimage.
pilgrimo pilgrimage.
pilgrimoado pilgrimage.
pilgrimulo pilgrim.
pilhardo pilchard.
piliero pillar.
pilkego airball (toy).
pilketo little ball.
pilkknabino ball girl.
pilkludi to play ball.
pilko ball (for playing).
pilkoĵeti to bowl.
pilkoknabo ball boy.
pilkoludo ballgame.
pilkraketo battledore.
pilo battery cell, pile.
pilolo pill.
pilono pylon.
pilorio pillory.
pilota permesilo pilot's licence.
pilotado steering.
pilotejo cockpit.
piloti to pilot.
pilotino airwoman.
piloto pilot.
pimento allspice, pimenta.
pimpa chic, smart.
pinaklo pinnacle.
pinakoteko art gallery.
pinarbaro pine forest.
pinarbo fir tree, pine tree.
pinaso jolly-boat, pinnace.
pinĉaĵo da sablo pinch of sand.
pinĉegi to pinch.
pinĉi to nip, pinch.
pinĉileto tweezers.
pinĉilo pincers, tongs.
pinĉpreno bit.
pinĉtenajlo pincers.
pinĉtenilo pair of pincers, pincers, pliers.
pindo pint.
pineala pineal.
pineto evergreen tree.
pingikolo butterwort.
pingikulo butterwort.
pinglarbo conifer.
pinglego belaying pin.
pinglo needle, pin.
pingloarbo conifer.
pinglokuseneto pin-cushion.
pingveno penguin.
pingvino penguin.
pinio pine, silver fir, stone pine, umbrella pine.
pinjakolado piña colada.
pinjato piñata.
Pinjino pinyin.
pinkonuso pine cone.

pino

pino pine (tree).
Pinokjo Pinocchio.
pinta pointed, spiked.
pintaĵo peak.
pintarko ogive.
pintega ultimate.
pintigi to point (to sharpen).
pintingo fingerstall.
pintita pointed.
pinto peak, point, tip, summit, ridge, vertex.
Pinto de Bali to Bali Peak.
pintokonferenco summit.
pintvostanaso pintail.
pio pi (Пп).
pioĉo pick, pickaxe.
pionira groundbreaking, pioneering.
pioniro pioneer.
piono pi-meson, pion.
pioreo pyorrhoea.
pipa tubo stem of a pipe.
pipeto pipette.
pipio pipit.
pipo pipe.
pipri to pepper.
pipro (black) pepper.
pipromento peppermint.
piprujo pepper shaker.
pipso pip (disease in birds).
piramida pyramid-shaped. **piramida kampanulo** chimney bell-flower. **piramida ordigo** heap sort.
piramido pyramid.
piranjo piranha.
pirarbo pear tree.
pirarukuo arapaima.
piratestro pirate chief.
pirato pirate, sea robber.
pirenea Pyrenean.
Pireneoj Pyrenees.
piretro pyrethrum.
piriko dibrach, pyrrhic.
pirito pyrite.
piro pear.
pirogo[1] dumpling, pie, pierogi.
pirogo[2] dug-out canoe.
pirokorako chough.
pirolo bullfinch.
piroteknikaĵo fireworks.
pirotekniko pyrotechnics.
pirozo acid stomach, heartburn, pyrosis.
pirsuko pear juice.
pirueti to pirouette.
pirueto pirouette.
pirujo pear tree.
pisi to piss, urinate.
pispoto chamber pot, toilet.
pistaĵo purée.
pistako pistachio.
pistakujo pistachio.

plaĝseĝo

pisti to crush, pound, grind.
pistilo pestle.
pistolo pistol, spray gun.
pistujo mortar.
piŝto piston.
pitagora Pythagorean. **pitagora teoremo** Pythagorean theorem. **pitagora triangulo** Pythagorean triangle. **pitagora triopo** Pythagorean triple.
pitagorano Pythagorean.
pitagorismo Pythagoreanism.
Pitagoro Pythagoras.
Piterhedo Peterhead.
Pitlokrio Pitlochry.
pitono python.
pitoreska picturesque.
pitoreske picturesquely.
Pitsburgo Pittsburgh.
pituitario hypophysis, pituitary, pituitary gland.
piulo pious person, religious person.
pivoti to pivot, revolve, turn, rotate.
pivoto pivot.
pizango banana.
pizo green pea.
pizosupo pea-soup.
Pjanĝo Pandj.
pk. → **poŝtkarto**.
plabaera open-air.
placeba efiko placebo effect.
placebo placebo.
placeboefiko placebo effect.
placego esplanade.
placento afterbirth, placenta.
placeto patch.
placo place, plaza, square, public square.
plaĉa pleasant, winning, pleasing.
plaĉaspekta pretty.
plaĉaspekte prettily.
plaĉe nicely, pleasantly, pleasingly.
plaĉema coquettish.
plaĉemo coquetry.
plaĉi to be pleasing, please. **plaĉas al mi** I like.
plaĉivola coquettish.
plaĉo pleasure.
pladego platter.
pladeto salver.
plado course, dish, plate, platter, tray.
plafono ceiling.
plagi to afflict, plague.
plagiati to plagiarize.
plagiato plagiarism.
plago calamity, scourge, plague.
plaĝo beach.
plaĝokostumo bathing costume, bathing suit.
plaĝpilko beach ball.
plaĝseĝo beach chair.

plaĝtuko beach towel.
plaki to plate, veneer.
plako plate.
planado planning.
plando sole (foot).
plandumo sole (shoe).
planeda planetary.
planedero asteroid.
planedeto asteroid.
planedo planet.
planeo aerofoil, airfoil.
plani to plan.
planilo organizer, planner.
planimetrio planimetry.
planinto designer.
planisto designer, planner.
planizi to plan.
planke on the floor.
plankhokeo floor hockey.
planko floor.
plankpordo trapdoor.
planktono plankton.
planlingvo planned language, constructed language.
plano design, diagram, plan, plane.
planta plant, vegetable.
plantado planting.
plantago plaintain, plantago.
plantaĵo plantation.
plantaro plantation, planting.
plantejo plantation.
planti to plant.
planto plant, planting.
plasi to invest.
plasma ekrano plasma screen.
plasmekrano plasma screen.
plasmo plasma.
plasmoekrano plasma screen.
plasta plastic.
plastika modelling, moulding, plastic.
plastiko modelling art, moulding art, plastic art.
plasto plastic.
plastro plaster (dressing).
plata flat.
plataĵo landing (place), plateau, platform, level part, shelf.
plataleo spoonbill.
platana acero Norway maple.
platano plane (tree), sycamore.
platantero butterfly-orchid.
platbeka anaso mallard.
platbordo beach.
plateco platitude.
plateno platinum.
plateso plaice.
platfiŝo flatfish.
platformgruo cherry picker.
platformkamiono flatbed.

platformo landing (in a staircase), platform.
platfosilo spade.
platigi to flatten.
platiĝi to flatten.
platnazo pug-nose.
plato board, plate, sheet, slab.
Plato Plato.
platona platonic. **platona solido** Platonic body.
platone Platonically.
platonisma Platonistic.
platonismo Platonism.
Platono Plato.
platpoŝa broke.
platringo washer.
platvagoneto taming, training.
plaŭdado beating.
plaŭdeti to burble, gurgle, murmur, purl.
plaŭdi to beat, flap, lap, plash, splash.
plaŭdigi to clap.
plaŭdo splash.
Plaŭto Plautus.
plebano commoner, plebian.
plebiscito plebiscite.
plebo common people, plebs.
pledado pleading.
pledi to appeal, plea, plead. **pledi por** to advocate, plead.
pledo plea.
Pleistoceno Pleistocene.
plej most. **plej bona** best. **plej bonega** best of all, very best. **plej ekstera** outer. **plej granda komuna divizoro** greatest common divisor. **plej grava** most important. **plej interesa** most interesting. **plej malbona** worst. **plej malgranda komuna oblo** least common multiple. **plej posta** hind, hindmost. **plej proksima** nearest, next. **plej proksimaj parencoj** next of kin. **plej supra** upper.
pleja chief, dominant, overwhelming, ultimate.
Plejado Pleiades.
Plejadoj Pleiades, Seven sisters.
plejaĝulo doyen, elder.
plejalto acme.
plejbonigi to optimize.
plejdo plaid wrap, travel shawl.
pleje at most, mostly, maximally, most often.
plejebla utmost.
plejeblo utmost.
plejekstera outermost.
plejmalbona worst.
plejmalbonaĵo (a) worse thing.
plejmalbone worst.
plejmulte mostly.
plejmulto majority, plurality.
plejofta usual.
plejofte most often.

plejparte for the most part, mostly.
plejparto great majority, greatest part.
plejproksima next (near).
Plejstoceno Pleistocene.
plejsupra topmost.
plejsupriĝi to peak.
plejsupro peak.
plekso plexus.
plektaĵo plait, tress.
plekti to braid, plait, twine, wreathe.
plektisto weaver.
plektita braided. **plektita mato** plaited mat.
plektobarilo hedge, hedge row.
plektri to pick (stringed instrument).
plektro pick, plectrum.
plena complete, full, integral, plenary, thorough, whole. **plena de ĝojo** full of joy. **plena domajnnomo** fully qualified domain name. **plena je** full of. **plena je ĝojo** full of joy. **plena je scivolo** full of curiosity. **plena noto** semibreve.
plenaera kradrostado barbecue.
plenaĝa adult, grown-up, full-grown, over the age of majority.
plenaĝeco adulthood.
plenaĝo majority (age).
plenaĝulo adult.
plenarierulo fullback.
plenblovi to inflate, puff up.
plenbotelo bottleful.
plenbrako armful.
plenbuŝo mouthful.
plenĉarumo barrow-load.
plenĉase in hot pursuit.
plenda complain, plaintive.
plendanto complainant.
plende lamentingly, complainingly.
plendema complaining.
plendi to complain, lament. **plendi kontraŭ** to accuse.
plendinda lamentable, unfortunate.
plendkaŭzo grievance.
plendkriadi to yammer.
plendkriado yammer.
plendmotivo objection.
plendo complaint.
plendomuro Wailing Wall.
plendprotesto appeal.
plendulo suitor.
plendupleksa full duplex.
plenduto whole tone (musical interval).
plene completely, fully. **plene estri** to fully master.
pleneco plenitude, repletion.
plenega copious, exuberant, thorough.
plenegigi to cram.
plenforma ample.
plenglaso bumper.
plengorĝe aloud.
pleni to fill.
plenigadi to cause completion, make full.
plenigi to complete, consummate, fill (up), stuff.
plenigita having caused completion, having made full.
plenigo consummation.
pleniĝi to become full.
plenkalva completely bald.
plenkore with one's whole heart, wholeheartedly.
plenkreska adult, full-grown.
plenkreskeco adulthood.
plenkreski to grow up.
plenkreskula instruado adult education.
plenkreskulo adult, grown-up.
plenkulero spoonful.
plenluna (of a) full moon.
plenluno full moon.
plenmano handful.
plennombro complement.
plenoplena brimful.
plenplena brimming, replete, chock-full, (full to) overflowing, crammed.
plenplene very full.
plenpota brimful.
plenpovo empowerment, legal authority.
plenskala fullscale.
plenŝtopi to stuff, cram.
plenŝuti to fill up.
plenuma potenco executive power.
plenumebla satisfiable. **plenumebla dosiero** executable file.
plenumi to accomplish, achieve, keep, observe, perform, fulfill, abide by. **plenumi la deziron de iu ajn** to fulfill someone's wish.
plenumiĝi to come true, be fulfilled.
plenumiĝo fulfilment.
plenumita completed.
plenumkomitato executive committee.
plenumo accomplishment, fulfillment.
plenumoprovo benchmark.
plenzorga anxious.
plenzorge anxiously.
pleonasma repetitive.
pleonasmo pleonasm, redundancy.
plesiosaŭro plesiosaurus.
pleto tray.
pletoro plethora.
pleŭrito pleurisy.
pleŭro pleura.
pleŭronekto flounder, flatfish.
plezura agreeable, pleasant, pleasurable.
plezure with pleasure.
plezurege very pleasurably, with great pleasure.
plezurego great pleasure.
plezuri to take pleasure in.

plezuriga enjoyable, pleasurable.
plezurigi to gratify.
plezuro fun, pleasure.
pli more. **pli aĝa** elder, older. **pli aŭ malpli baldaŭ** sooner or later. **pli aŭ malpli frue** sooner or later. **pli bona** better. **pli bone** better. **pli bone malfrue ol neniam** better late than never. **pli detala** further. **pli detale** more precisely. **pli fajna** finer (math.). **pli forte ol iam ajn** more strongly than ever (before). **pli granda** bigger. **pli ĝuste** rather. **pli juna fratino** younger sister. **pli juna frato** younger brother. **pli juna gefrato** younger brother, younger sibling, younger sister. **pli kaj pli** to increasingly, more and more. **pli malbona** worse. **pli malfrue** later, later on. **pli maljuna fratino** elder sister. **pli maljuna frato** elder brother. **pli maljuna gefrato** elder brother, elder sibling, elder sister. **pli malpli** to quite. **pli malproksima** farther. **pli malproksime** beyond, farther, further. **pli malproksime ol** beyond, past. **pli malproksimen** farther. **pli ol** above, more than, over. **pli ol en iu alia loko** more than anywhere else. **pli ol ie aliloke** more than anywhere else. **pli poste** later on. **pli proksima** nearer. **pli proksime** nearer. **pli volonte** preferably.
plia another, one more, extra.
pliaĉigi to worsen.
pliaĉiĝi to worsen.
pliaĝa elder, older, senior.
pliaĝi to become older, grow up.
pliaĝigi to age.
pliaĝulo elder.
pliajo extra.
pliaktiviĝi to act up.
plialtigi to advance, increase, raise.
plialtiĝi to accrue, advance, ascend, go up, increase, get higher.
plialtiĝo rising.
pliami to prefer.
pliampleksigi to broaden, expand.
pliampleksigo expansion.
pliampleksiĝi to expand.
pliampleksiĝo expansion.
plibeligi to embellish.
plibeliĝi to grow more beautiful.
pliboniga enhancing.
plibonigejo reformatory.
plibonigi to ameliorate, improve, reform.
plibonigo improvement, reformation.
pliboniĝi to improve, become better, get better.
pliboniĝo progress.
plibonstatiĝo progress.
plibriligi to burnish.

plidaŭrigi to prolong.
plidikigi to thicken.
plidire or rather, in better words.
plie and also, as well as, together with, further, moreover.
plietiĝi to decrease, diminish.
plifaciligi to facilitate.
plifaciligo relief.
plifervorigi to cheer, fire, inspire, stimulate.
plifirmigi to strengthen, reinforce, tighten.
plifortige intensifyingly.
plifortigi to fortify, make stronger, reinforce, strengthen.
plifortigo boost, reinforcement.
plifortiĝi to increase, freshen.
plifruigi to accelerate, advance.
plifruiĝi to advance.
pligrandigaĵo enlargement.
pligrandigi to aggrandize, augment, enlarge, increase, magnify.
pligrandigo aggrandizement, enlargement, increase.
pligrandiĝanta accumulative.
pligrandiĝi to accrue, increase.
pligrandiĝo enlargement, increase.
pligravigi to blow up, heighten.
pligravigo accentuation.
pliigi to augment, increase.
pliigo increase, rise.
pliiĝi to augment, grow, increase.
pliiĝo increase, rise.
pliintensigi to heighten.
plijuna younger.
plijunigi to make younger, rejuvenate.
plikariĝo rise (in price).
pliko Polish plait.
plilarĝigi to dilate, widen, distend. **plilarĝigi la mensan horizonton** to widen the mental horizon.
plilarĝigo expansion.
plilarĝiĝi to expand.
plilarĝiĝo expansion.
plilaŭtiĝi to swell, swell into a roar.
plilongiga extension.
plilongigi to lengthen, make longer, prolong.
plilongiĝi to lengthen.
plilongiĝo elongation.
plimalbona worse.
plimalbone worse.
plimalbonigi to aggravate.
plimalbonigo accentuation.
plimalgrandigi to decrease, lessen.
plimalgrandiĝi to decrease, diminish.
plimalobea incorrigible.
plimalpli more or less.
pli-malpli more or less.
plimalproksima further.
plimulta mainstream, majority.
plimultaĵo overplus.

plimulte

plimulte more (quantity).
plimultigi to enhance, increase, augment.
plimultigo accession.
plimultiĝi to multiple, increase in number.
plimultiĝo increase.
plimulto majority.
Plimuto Plymouth.
Plinio Pliny. **Plinio la Juna** Pliny the Younger. **Plinio la Maljuna** Pliny the Elder.
plinto plinth, wainscot.
Plioceno Pliocene.
plioferi to outbid.
plioftiĝi to become more frequent.
plipago surcharge.
plipeziga aggravating.
plipezigi to aggravate.
plipeziĝi to gain, put on weight.
plipezo excess weight, overload.
pliposte later on.
pliproksimiĝi to advance, come on.
pliproponi to bid (at auction).
plirangigo promotion.
plirapidi to accelerate, speed up.
plirapidigi to accelerate, advance.
plirapidigo acceleration.
plirapidiĝi to accelerate.
plirapidiĝo acceleration.
pliseverigi to exacerbate.
plisi to crease, pleat.
plisigno greater-than sign (>).
plisimpligo simplification.
Plistoceno Pleistocene.
plistreĉi to draw tighter, tighten.
plisupra upper.
plivalorigi to appreciate.
plivaloriĝi to appreciate.
plivastigi to amplify, extend.
plivastiĝi to extend.
plivigligado abetment.
plivigligi to fan, fire, inspire, stimulate, stir up, urge on.
plivigligo abetment.
plivole rather.
plivoli to want more.
ploceido weaver-bird.
plombaĵo (dental) filling.
plombi to fill (a tooth).
plombo dental filling.
plonĝado diving.
plonĝi to dive, plunge.
plonĝigi to plunge.
plonĝisto diver.
plonĝo plunge.
ploradi to cry, weep (constantly).
plorado crying, weeping.
plorboji to yelp.
ploregado howling, wailing.
ploregi to bewail, sob, mourn, wail.

plumono

plorego sob.
plorema tearful.
ploreme tearfully.
ploreti to snivel, whimper, whine.
ploreto whimper.
plorĝemi to sob.
plori to cry, weep, shed tears.
plorigi to make someone cry.
plorkrii to wail.
ploro tear.
plorpeti to beg, implore.
plorplendi to drone, whine.
plorplendo whine.
plorsaliko weeping willow.
plorsingulti to sob.
plosivo plosive.
ploto roach.
plotono platoon.
Plovdiv Plovdiv.
plozivo plosive.
plu else, further, more, on, any more. **plu juna frato** younger brother, little brother.
plua additional, another.
pludaŭrigi to extend.
pludetali to amplify.
plue besides, furthermore, in addition, moreover, further.
plueca memorilo overflow storage.
plugado tillage.
plugebla arable, plowable. **plugebla grundo** arable soil.
plugfero ploughshare.
plugi to plough, till.
plugilbeko ploughshare.
plugilo plough.
plugisto ploughman.
plugo the act of ploughing.
plugoskribado boustrophedon.
plugvidi to refer.
plugvido referral.
plui to further.
pluigi to continue, extend, go on, maintain, proceed with, sustain.
pluiri to continue, go on.
pluki to pick, pluck.
pluklarigi to amplify.
pluko pluck.
plumaro plumage.
plumba lead.
plumbalailo feather duster.
plumbero lead shot.
plumbisto plumber.
plumbo lead.
plumbofadeno plumb line.
plumeraro writing error.
plumfasko plume.
plumingo penholder.
plumo feather, pen, plume, quill.
plumono quilt.

plumpa awkward, lumpish, plump, ungainly.
plumpulino bag.
plumtiregi to pluck (fowl).
plumtufo crest.
plumviŝilo feather duster.
pluparoli to keep talking.
plura plural. **pluraj** more than one, multiple, several.
pluradresa instrukcio multi-address instruction.
plurala plural.
plurale plurally.
pluraligi to pluralize.
pluralismo pluralism.
pluralo plural.
pluratinga sistemo multi-access system.
plurbito byte.
plurcelregistro multipurpose register.
plureco plurality.
pluredro polyhedron.
plurfoja several times.
plurfoje repeatedly.
plurgrafeo multigraph (oriented or non-oriented).
plurisma pluralistic.
plurismo pluralism.
pluristo pluralist.
plurjara perennial.
plurjare perennially.
plurkomputado multiprocessing, multiprogramming.
plurlatero polygon.
plurlineara multilinear.
plurlingva multilingual.
plurlingveco multilingualism.
plurlingvulo polyglot.
plurmedio multimedia.
plurnacia multinational.
plurnombro plural.
plurobla multiple.
plurprocesorado multiprocessing.
plursenca ambiguous.
plursenca funkcio multiple-valued function.
plursilaba polysyllabic.
plurspeca assorted.
plurtaskado multitasking.
plurtaskplenumado multitasking.
plurtavola ligno plywood.
plus plus.
plusendi to forward, relay, retransmit. **plusendi retleteron** forward.
plusendilo broadcast relay station, broadcast translator, relay transmitter, repeater.
plusendinto referrer.
pluskvamperfekto pluperfect.
pluso plus sign (+), surplus.
plus-minus-signo plus-minus sign (±).
plus-signo plus sign (+).

plusvaloro surplus value.
pluŝbesto stuffed animal.
pluŝo plush.
pluŝurseto teddy bear.
pluŝurso teddy bear.
pluta Plutonian, Hadean.
Pluto Pluto.
plutokratio plutocracy.
plutokrato plutocrat.
plutona Plutonian, Hadean.
plutonio plutonium.
Plutono Pluto.
plutrakto follow-up.
pluva rain, of rain, rainy.
pluvalidigi to extend.
pluvarbaro rain forest.
pluvarko rainbow.
pluvas it's raining.
pluvbano shower bath.
pluvegi to pour, rain cats and dogs.
pluvego downpour.
pluvero raindrop.
pluveti to drizzle.
pluveto drizzle, drizzling rain, shower.
pluvguto raindrop.
pluvi to rain.
pluviva subsistent.
pluvivi to subsist.
pluvmantelo raincoat.
pluvo rain.
pluvobano bath taken in the rain.
pluvojaĝo further journey, further trip.
pluvombrelo umbrella.
pluvsezono rainy season.
pluvtubego drain.
pluvtubo downpipe, drainpipe.
pm. → **poŝtmarko**.
pneŭmata pneumatic. **pneŭmata fusilo** airgun, air rifle. **pneŭmata kuseno** air cushion. **pneŭmata martelo** jackhammer.
pneŭmatika matraco airbed, air mattress.
pneŭmatiko pneumatics, tyre.
pneŭmo tyre.
pneŭmokoko pneumococcus.
pneŭmonio pneumonia.
pneŭo tyre.
Pnompeno Phnom Penh.
po[1] a, at, at the rate of, per, each, apiece. **po ... por unu** at ... each.
po[2] name of the letter P.
poa individual.
pobe abaft.
poben abaft.
pobo poop(deck), stern.
pocentaĵo percentage.
pocento percentage.
pocio potion.
poĉi to poach.
podagro gout.

podajro pedal.
podetale retail.
podetalisto retailer.
podicepso grebe.
podicipo grebe.
podio platform, podium.
podkastado podcasting.
podkasto podcast.
podlaĥia Podlachian.
Podlaĥio Podlachia.
poefago yak.
poemaro collection of poetry.
poemeto small poem.
poemo poem.
poentaro score.
poenti to score.
poento point (cards, score).
poentokarto scorecard.
poentotabulo scoreboard.
poeta poetical, of poetry.
poetedzino poet's wife.
poetiko poetics.
poetinedzo husband of a poetess.
poetino poetess.
poeto poet.
poezia poetic.
poeziaĵo poetry.
poezio poetry.
pogoniuleto small woodpecker.
pogoniulo tinkerbird.
pogranda wholesale.
pogrande wholesale.
pograndisto wholesaler.
pogromo pogrom.
pogrupe by groups.
pogute by drops, drop by drop, in drops.
pojnhorloĝo watch, wrist-watch.
pojno wrist.
poka little.
pokaleto mug.
Pokalo Crater.
pokalo fancy cup, goblet, tankard.
pokera vizaĝo poker face.
pokero poker (game).
pola Polish.
polara polar.
polarigi to polarize.
polarimetro polarimeter.
polarizi to polarize (optics).
polarizilo polarizer (optical device).
polarizo polarization.
poldero polder.
polekso thumb.
polemika polemical, controversial.
polemiki to engage in a controversy.
polemiko controversy, polemic, dispute.
polenado pollination.
polenero grain of pollen.
poleni to pollinate.
poleno pollen.
poliandrio polyandry.
polianto polyanthus.
polica police, of police.
policanaro constabulary.
policanino policewoman.
policano policeman.
policejo police station.
policestro chief of police.
polichundo police dog.
policistino policewoman.
policisto policeman.
polico police.
policpatrolo police patrol, squad.
polietileno polyethylene.
polifilona polyphyletic.
polifonio polyphony.
poligamio polygamy.
poligamiulo polygamist.
poligloto polyglot.
poligonato Solomon's-seal.
poligono[1] polygon.
poligono[2] buckwheat, knotgrass, knotweed.
polihetoj polychaete.
polikliniko polyclinic.
polikromio colour illustration, polychromy.
polimero polymer.
polinezia Polynesian.
polinezianino Polynesian woman.
polineziano Polynesian.
Polinezio Polynesia.
polino Polish woman.
polinoma polynomial. **polinoma adicio** polynomial addition. **polinoma funkcio** polynomial function. **polinoma multipliko** polynomial multiplication. **polinoma nulo** null polynomial. **polinoma spaco** polynomial space. **polinoma tempo** polynomial time. **polinoma unuo** unit polynomial.
polinomo polynomial.
polinomringo polynomial ring.
Polio Poland.
poliomjelito polio, poliomyelitis.
polipo polyp, polypus.
polipodio polypody.
polipolo polypoly.
polipsonio polypsony.
polishavanto policyholder.
poliso policy, insurance policy.
polistireno polystyrene.
politeisma polytheistic.
politeismo polytheism.
politeisto polytheist.
politekniko polytechnic.
politika political. **politika ekspansio** political expansion. **politika saĝeco** political acumen. **politika sistemo** political system.
politike politically.

politikero plank.
politikisto politician, statesman.
politiko policy, politics.
polivinilklorido polyvinyl chloride, PVC.
polki to polka.
polko polka.
Pollando Poland.
polma palmtop.
polmflanka bato forehand.
polmo palm (of the hand).
polo Pole.
polonezo polonaise.
polonio polonium.
poloo polo.
polpo octopus.
poltrono coward, poltroon.
poluado pollution.
poluaĵo pollution, polluting substance.
poluciaĵo contaminant, pollutant.
polucii to contaminate.
poluciiganto polluter.
poluciigi to pollute.
poluciigo pollution.
polucio (involuntary) nocturnal emission.
polui to pollute.
Polujo Poland.
poluo pollution, the act of pollution.
polurado hinting.
poluraĵo polish (substance).
poluri to brighten, burnish, glaze, gloss, polish.
poluro lustre, polish.
polurvakso polishing wax.
polusa polar. **polusa akso** polar axis.
  polusa angulo azimuth angle, polar angle.
  polusa aŭroro polar aurora. **polusa distanco** polar distance, polar radius. **polusa glaĉero** polar icecap. **polusa koordinato** polar coordinate. **polusa lumo** polar light.
  Polusa stelo North star, polar star, Polaris.
polusdistanco polar radius.
poluso pole (geography).
polva dusty.
polvero grain of dust.
polvigi to dust.
polvo dust.
polvobroso powder brush.
polvofungo puff-ball.
polvokovri to cover with dust.
polvosuĉi to vacuum clean.
polvosuĉilo vacuum cleaner.
polvoŝovelilo dustpan.
polvotuko dust cloth.
polvoviŝilo dust cloth.
pomado pomade, pomatum, ointment.
pomalgrande at retail, in small quantities.
pomalgrandisto retailer.
pomarbo apple tree.
pomego large apple.

pomejo orchard.
Pomerio Pomerania.
Pomerujo Pomerania.
pometre by the meter.
pomfloro apple blossom.
pomfritpastaĵo apple fritter.
pomgranato pomegranate.
pomhaŭto apple skin.
pomkaĉo applesauce.
pomkerneto apple seed.
pomkomposto apple sauce.
pomkompoto apple sauce.
pomo apple.
pomologio pomology.
pompa pompous, resplendent, showy, splendid.
pompaĉa flashy.
pompaĉo ballyhoo.
pompasteĉo apple turnover.
pompe splendidly.
pompeca glitzy, showy.
pompece showily.
pompeco glitz, glitziness, showiness.
Pompejo Pompeii.
pompi to be resplendent.
pompo display, pomp, splendor.
pomsaŭco apple-sauce.
pomsuko apple juice.
pomŝelo apple peel.
pomtigeto apple stalk, apple stem.
pomtorto apple pie, apple tart.
pomujo apple tree.
pomvango cheek like an apple.
pomvino apple wine, cider.
ponardego pike (weapon).
ponardi to stab.
ponardo dagger, poniard; (typography) dagger († ‡).
ponardvundo stab wound.
pondi to adjust.
poneo pony.
ponevosto ponytail.
ponĝeo pongee.
ponorda neat, tidy.
ponteto jumper.
pontgardisto bridge keeper.
pontifika pontifical.
pontifikeco pontificate.
pontifiko pontifex.
Pontipulo Pontypool.
pontkolono pier (pillar).
pontlingvo bridge language.
ponto bridge.
pontolingvo intermediate language.
pontono pontoon.
Ponturbo Bridgetown.
poo meadow-grass.
poparta integralado integration by parts.

popeca piece-meal, piecewise. **popeca salajro** piecework.
popece piece by piece, piecewise. **popece monotona** piecewise monotonic (function).
poplino poplin.
poplito back of the knee, hock.
poplo poplar.
popo pope.
popola popular, folk; populous.
popolamasano average Joe.
popolamaso masses (the masses).
popoldiraĵo folk saying.
popoldiro popular saying.
popole popularly.
popolĝardeno public park.
popolista populist.
popolisto populist.
popolkanto folk song.
popolleviĝo uprising.
popolnombrado census.
popolo folk, nation, people.
popoloamaso populace.
popolrakonto folk tale.
popolribelo insurgency, insurrection, rebellion.
popolvesto folk costume.
populacio population (e.g. statistical, biological, etc.).
populara popular.
populare popularly.
populareco popularity.
popularigo popularization.
por for, for the sake of, to, in order to, per, so as to. **por ĉiam** forever. **por ĉiu homo de la tago** at all hours of the day. **por diversaj kialoj** for various reasons. **por ia alia kaŭzo** for some other reason. **por ial** for some reason. **por ke** in order that, so, so that. **por kiaj celoj** for what purposes. **por kio** why. **por klareco** for clarity. **por komuna bono** for the common good. **por kvindek centimoj** 50 centimes worth. **por la unua fojo** for the first time. **por lasi tute flanke** let alone, aside from. **por momento** for a moment. **por personaj kialoj** for personal reasons. **por stilaj kaŭzoj** for stylistic reasons. **por tiaj okazoj kiam** for those occasions when. **por tiel diri** to so to speak. **por tio, ĉar** for the reason that. **por unu** one dollar's worth. **por unu minuto** for a minute. **por unu tago** for a day.
poranonca gazeto advertiser.
porbatalanto advocate.
porcelana porcelain.
porcelanaĵo (piece of, item of) china, porcelain.
porcelano china, porcelain.
porcieto whit.
porciigi to ration out.
porcio allowance, portion, ration, share, part, quota.
porciolimigo rationing.
porciumi to ration out.
porĉiama eternal.
porĉiame forever.
pordanso doorknob.
pordaperturo doorway.
pordegejo gateway.
pordego gate, gateway, portal.
pordeto wicket.
pordistino doorwoman.
pordisto doorkeeper, porter, doorman, gatekeeper.
pordmalfermo opening of a door.
pordo door, gate. **pordo kurteno** door curtain.
pordokurteno door curtain.
pordomato doormat.
pordoriglilo door lock.
pordosonorilo door bell.
pordrisorto latch.
poreo leek.
porfiro porphyry.
poriĝo porridge, hot cereal.
porka pig, of a pig.
porkaĵo pork.
porkeja swine, pigs.
porkejo sty.
porkflankaĵo bacon.
porkido piglet, sucking pig.
porkino sow.
porko hog, pig, swine.
porkocervo babirusa, deer-hog.
porkograso lard.
porkostalo sty.
porkstalo sty.
porkviro boar, hog.
pormanĝilara lavmaŝino dishwasher.
pornografaĵo pornography.
pornografia pornographic. **pornografia filmo** adult film.
pornografio pornography.
pornografo pornographer.
pornokte for the night.
poro pore.
porokaza ad hoc.
porokaze ad hoc.
porparolantino spokeswoman.
porparolanto advocate, spokesperson.
Portadaŭno Portadown.
portadi to carry.
portaĵo burden.
portalo portal.
portante while carrying.
portanto carrier, bearer, porter.
Portaskajgo Port Askaig.

portebla portable. **portebla komputilo** laptop computer, notebook, portable computer.
porteblo portability.
portempa provisional, temporary.
portempe temporarily, for a time.
portepeo sword-belt.
portero porter, stout.
porti to bear, carry, wear, bring. **porti ĉemison** to wear a shirt. **porti pantalonon** to wear pants. **porti robo** to wear a dress.
portiĝi to float, hang, hover, waft.
portiko porch, portico.
portilmarko volume label.
portilo carrier, litter, stretcher, sedan chair.
portisto porter.
portita borne.
Portluizo Port Louis.
Porto Oporto.
portoseĝo litter, sedan chair.
portreti to portray.
portreto portrait.
portrimeno strap.
Portrio Portree.
portugala Portuguese. **portugala lingvo** Portuguese, Portuguese language.
portugalino Portuguese woman.
Portugalio Portugal.
portugalo Portuguese.
Portugalujo Portugal.
portulako purslane.
porvesperaj vestoj evening dress.
poseda possessive.
posedaĵo goods, possession, property.
posedaĵoj possessions.
posedanto possessor, proprietor.
posedi to own, possess.
posedkazo possessive case.
posedo possession.
Posejdono Poseidon.
posesivo possessive pronoun.
po-signo at sign (@).
post after, behind, in. **post du semajnoj** in two weeks time. **post iom da tempo** after a little while, after a short period of time. **post kiam** after. **post Kristo** A.D. **post la kulisoj** behind the scenes. **post malmutaj tagoj** in a few days. **post nelonge** soon. **post ok tagoj** a week from now, in a week. **post pliaj du monatoj** after two more months, two months later. **post tio** beyond, next, then, thereafter.
posta hind, hindmost, posterior, ulterior. **posta flanko** back side, reverse side. **posta meditado** commentary. **posta parto** aft, poop, rear, stern (of ship). **posta skribo** postscript, P.S. **posta steveno** stern-post.
postafikso extension, suffix.

postaĵo backside, rump.
postakuŝo post-birth, after-birth, expulsion of the placenta following childbirth.
postalkremento postincrement.
postamento pedestal, stand.
postanto successor.
postbrilado afterglow.
postbrilo afterglow.
postbruligilo afterburner.
postbuŝo pharynx.
postdatigi to reschedule.
postdekremento postdecrement.
postdorse behind one's back.
poste afterwards, next, subsequently, then.
postebrio hangover.
postefiko after-effect.
postekrano backstop.
posten backwards.
posteni to be on duty, stand guard.
postenigi to advance, station.
postenigo appointment, posting.
posteniĝi to go back, go backwards.
posteniri to go back, go backwards.
posteno job, position, post.
postesekvi to pursue.
posteularo offspring, posterity.
posteuliĝo succession.
posteulo descendant, offspring, successor.
posteuloj issue, offspring, posterity, progeny.
postflanko rear side, backside.
postfojno aftermath.
postgusto aftertaste.
postgvardio defence, rearguard.
postĝojo afterglow.
postiĉo postiche.
postiĝi to fall back, get behind.
postiĝinto straggler.
postiljono postilion.
postiri to follow.
postirilo trace program.
postklapo flap.
postkolo withers.
postkomplico accessory after the fact.
postkompreno hindsight.
postkondiĉo postcondition.
postkranio occiput.
postkrii moke to hoot after.
postkritiki to second guess.
postkropo gizzard.
postkuirejo scullery.
postkulisa backdoor, backstage, behind the scenes.
postkuradi to dog.
postkurado chase, pursuit.
postkuri to chase, run after.
postkvarono hindquarter (cut of meat).
postlampo parking lights.
postlasaĵo estate.
postlasi to leave behind.

postlerneja

postlerneja instruado further education, continuing education.
postmangaĵo dessert.
postmasto driver.
postmeta operaciskribo postfix notation.
postmeti to affix, add.
postmilita post-war.
postmilite after the war.
postmorgaŭ day after tomorrow.
postmorta posthumous. **postmorta mondo** hereafter. **postmorta vivo** afterlife.
postmorte after death.
postnaska depresio postnatal depression, baby blues.
postnaskaĵo afterbirth, placenta.
postnepo great-grandson.
posto aft, back.
postoperacia kuracado after-treatment, follow-up.
postpalato muscular palate, soft palate, velum.
postparolo afterword, conclusion, epilogue.
postpenso afterthought.
postpozicio postposition.
postpurigo clean-up.
postraza ŝmiraĵo aftershave.
postrazaĵo aftershave.
postrazpomado aftershave lotion.
postregiono hinterland.
postresta pozicio arrears.
postrestaĵo remnant.
postrestanto laggard, straggler.
postresti to be detained, be kept in, stay on, remain.
postrestigi to keep in.
postrestinto holdover.
postrevolucia post-revolutionary.
postrigardi to follow up with one's eyes, look after.
postrikoltanto gleaner.
postrikolti to glean.
postrikolto aftermath.
postsekva consequent.
postsekvanto successor.
postsekvi to run after.
postsekvoj aftermath.
postsigneto vestige.
postsigno clue, trace, vestige.
postskiada après-ski.
postskribaĵo postscript.
postskribo postscript, P.S.
PostSkripto PostScript.
postsoifo thirst after drinking to excess.
postsoni to resound.
postsono echo, resonance.
poststrio wake, track.
postsulko wake.
posttagmeza afternoon.
posttagmeze in the afternoon.

poŝtekspedado

posttagmezo afternoon.
posttagmezon in the afternoon.
posttempa behind, delayed, expired, late, out of date, overdue, tardy.
posttiri to draw after.
posttraktado preprocessing.
posttraktilo postprocessor.
posttreni to tow, tug.
postula exigent.
postulaĵo requirement.
postulanto claimant.
postulato postulate.
postulema assertive, exacting, insistent, demanding.
postuleme insistently, unreasonably.
postuli to demand, postulate, require, exact.
  postuli klarigon to call to account.
  postuli klarigon de to call to account.
  postuli kontentigon de to demand an account of.
postulo demand, requirement.
postuloeco exigence.
postulspecifo requirement specification.
postumo successor.
postvango buttock.
postveni to come (after), succeed.
postveninta subsequent.
postveninto afterthought.
postveturilo trailer.
postvidado hindsight.
postvivado survival.
postvivanto survivor.
postvivi to outlive, survive.
postvojo rear path, back path.
postzorgo after-care.
poŝa pocket. **poŝa ŝtelisto** pickpocket.
  poŝa tranĉilo pocket knife.
poŝhorloĝo pocket watch.
poŝkalkulilo pocket calculator.
poŝkasedilo walkman.
poŝkomputilo handheld, palmtop, PDA, pocket computer.
poŝlampo flashlight.
poŝlanterno electric torch.
poŝlibro paperback, pocket book.
poŝmelo bandicoot.
poŝmono allowance, pocket money.
poŝo pocket.
poŝoŝtelisto pickpocket.
poŝta postal. **poŝta ĉekkonto** postal checking account. **poŝta karto** post card.
  poŝta kesto letter box. **poŝta oficejo** post office. **poŝta paketo** parcel post.
poŝtaĵo letter, piece of mail.
poŝtĉeko postal check.
poŝte by mail.
poŝtejo post office.
poŝtekspedado delivering mail.

poŝtelefono mobile phone, cell phone, mobile telephone, cellular telephone.
poŝtestro postmaster.
poŝti to post, mail.
poŝtilo e-mailer.
poŝtisto postman, mailman, mail carrier, postal worker.
poŝtkamioneto mail truck.
poŝtkarto postcard.
poŝtkesto postal box.
poŝtkodaĵo postal code, post code, ZIP code.
poŝtkodo postal code, post code, ZIP code.
poŝtmandato money order.
poŝtmarko (postage) stamp.
poŝto mail, post. **Poŝto, Telegrafo, Telefono**. Post, Telegraph, Telephone, PTT.
poŝtoficejo post office.
poŝtranĉilo pen knife.
poŝtrestante poste restante, general delivery.
poŝtsako mailbag.
poŝtstampo cancellation (postage).
poŝtuko handkerchief, tissue.
poŝvortaro pocket-size dictionary.
potaĵo pottery.
potamogeto pondweed.
potaso potash, potassium hydroxide.
potenca dominant, mighty, potent, powerful.
potencado domination.
potencavida power-hungry.
potence powerfully.
potencebla potential.
potenciala potential. **potenciala diferenco** potential difference, tension.
potenciale potentially.
potencialhava potential (field).
potencialo potential.
potenciganto exponent.
potencigato base (of exponential).
potencigi to exponentiate, raise to a power.
potencigo exponentiation, raising to a power, taking a number to a power.
potenciometro potentiometer.
potenco domination, might, potency, power.
potencoserio power series.
potenculo potentate, holder of power.
potentilo cinquefoil.
poteto mug.
potfarado pottery (art).
potfaristo potter, pottery-maker.
potisto potter.
potkovrilo (pot) cover, lid.
potlavejo scullery.
poto jug, pot.
Potsdamo Potsdam.
pottornilo potter's wheel.
pounua interespondo one-one correspondence.
poŭpo poop, poop deck, stern.
pova capable of, able to.

povi to be able, can. **povi fari** to be able to cope with, be able to do. **povi tutfari** to be able to cope with, be able to handle.
poviga potential.
povigi to empower.
povigo empowerment.
povo ability, power.
povoscii to be master of, know.
povra poor.
povrulo poor person.
povumo effect, power.
pozi to pose.
pozicia positional. **pozicia frakcio** systematic fraction. **pozicia nombrosistemo** place value system. **pozicia notacio** positional notation. **pozicia parametro** positional parameter.
pozicidetermino reckoning.
pozicio location, place, position, pose, post, situation, stance, status, posture, rank.
Pozidono Poseidon.
Pozikso POSIX.
pozistino model.
pozisto model.
pozitiva positive.
pozitive positively.
pozitivisma positivist, positivistic.
pozitivismo positivism.
pozitivisto positivist.
pozitivo positive.
pozitono positron.
pozitrono positron.
Poznano Poznań.
pozo pose, posture.
pra great-grand (relationship).
pra- (denotes remoteness in time, distant relationship).
praa ancient, primal, primeval, primitive, primordial.
praantaŭlasta antepenultimate.
praarbaro primeval forest.
praavino great-grandmother.
praavo great-grandfather.
praavoj ancestors.
prabesto prehistoric animal.
prabiciklo primitive bicycle.
prabovo aurochs.
prabulgaro Proto-Bulgarian.
praĉelo archeocyte.
praeksplodo Big Bang.
praformo primitive form.
prafunkcio intrinsic function, predefined function, primitive, standard function.
pragenepo great-grandchild.
pragmatiko pragmatics.
pragmatismo pragmatism.
Prago Prague.
prahistorio ancient history, prehistory.
prahomo prehistoric man, primitive man.

prainfano distant descendant.
prajmi to prime.
prajmo primer, detonator, percussion cap.
praknalo Big Bang.
prakontinento proto-continent.
praktianto trainee solicitor, trainee barrister.
praktika practical.
praktikado practice.
praktikanto practitioner.
praktike in practice.
praktikeco practicality, usefulness.
praktikema practical.
praktiki to exert, practice, put into practice.
praktiko practice.
prakuzino second cousin.
prakuzo second cousin.
pralingvo proto-language.
pralino praline.
praloĝanta indigenous, native.
praloĝanto aborigine, native.
praloĝinto aboriginal.
prameto punt.
prami to ferry.
pramisto ferryman.
pramo ferry boat, pontoon.
pramŝipo ferry, ferryboat.
pranci to balk, buck, prance, rear.
pranepino great-granddaughter.
pranepo great grandson.
pranevino grand-niece.
pranevo grand-nephew.
praonklino great-aunt.
praonklo great-uncle.
prapatra ancestral.
prapatrino foremother.
prapatro forefather.
prapatroj ancestors.
prapeko original sin.
prapraavino great-great-grandmother.
prapranepo great-grandchild.
praproceduro intrinsic procedure, pre-defined procedure, primitive, standard procedure.
praŝargo boot, booting, startup.
pratempa prehistoric, primeval, of ancient times.
pratempo prehistoric time.
pratinkolo stonechat.
pratipo prototype.
praulo ancestor, forbearer.
prava correct, right, just, justified, true.
pravalorizi to initialize.
pravaloro initial value.
prave correctly, rightly.
praveco justice (correctness).
pravi to be right.
pravigebla justifiable.
pravigeble justifiably.
pravigeco vindication.

pravigi to exonerate, justify, vindicate, warrant.
pravigo excuse, justification, vindication.
prazeodimo praseodymium.
prebendo prebend.
precedenco precedence, precedent.
precedento precedent.
precesio precession.
precioza pretentious, affected.
precipa chief, main, predominant, principal.
precipe above all, especially, chiefly, mainly, principally, chiefly, particularly, especially.
precipe in poezio especially in poetry.
precipiti to precipitate.
preciza accurate, precise, exact.
precize exactly, sharp, precisely.
precizecaltigo double precision.
precizeco accuracy, exactness, precision.
precizega pinpoint.
precizema punctilious.
precizigi to define, determine, narrow, pinpoint, state, specify.
precizigo definition, specification.
precizo precision, exactness, accuracy.
predi to plunder, prey (upon), loot.
predikado preaching.
predikativo predicative.
predikato predicate.
predikejo pulpit.
prediki to preach.
predikisto preacher.
prediko sermon.
predikofico benefice.
predikseĝo pulpit.
predikta predictive.
predo booty, loot, prey.
prefaco foreword, preamble, preface.
prefekto commissioner, prefect.
prefektujo prefecture.
prefera preferred.
prefere preferably, rather.
preferi to prefer, like best.
preferinda preferable.
prefero preference.
prefiksi to prefix.
prefikso prefix.
preĝado prayer, praying, recitation.
preĝaro breviary.
preĝbenko pew.
preĝeja turo steeple.
preĝejanaro congregation.
preĝejeto (small) chapel, shrine.
preĝejkorto churchyard.
preĝejo church, place of worship.
preĝejoĉambro vestry.
preĝema prayerful.
preĝemo prayerfulness.
preĝi to pray.
preĝlibro prayer book.

preĝo prayer.
preĝolibro prayer book.
preĝovorto word of prayer.
preigi to have printed.
prelato prelate.
prelegado lecturing.
preleganto lecturer, speaker.
prelegejo lecture hall.
prelegi to address, discourse, lecture.
prelego lecture, talk.
preludo overture, prelude.
prema burdensome, onerous, tight, oppressive, pressing.
premado pressure.
premaera stuffy.
premaĵo tablet.
premateco pressure.
prembutono push-button.
premcilindro barrel.
premdevigi to pressure.
preme tightly.
premeganto oppressor.
premegi to crush, overwhelm, squash, wring, twist.
premego grip.
premejo fruit press.
premfiksi to press, press firmly.
premgrupo lobby.
premi to press, oppress, squeeze, grasp.
premie at a premium.
premiero[1] premier, prime minister.
premiero[2] first run, first night, première.
premii to award a prize.
premilo press (machine).
premio premium, prize, reward.
premiodonado award ceremony.
premisi to assume, premise, take for granted, presuppose.
premiso precondition, premise.
premita oppressed.
premiteco pressure.
premiumo premium.
premmaŝino press.
premmortigi to squeeze to death.
premnecesigi to pressure.
premo press, pressure.
premoado pressure.
premorebla retentive.
premsigno print, imprint.
premsonĝo nightmare.
premtordilo mangle, wringer.
premtrudi to pressure.
preni to get, lay hold of, pick up, take. **preni en konsideron** to take into account. **preni juĝe** to seize. **preni la bovon per la kornoj** to take the bull by the horns. **preni la temperaturon** to take someone's temperature.
prenilego vice (screw press).
prenileto nippers, tweezers.
prenilo pincers, tongs.
preniloeto pliers.
prenipova prehensile.
preno capture, clasp, grasp, trick (at cards).
prepara preliminary, preparatory, prior.
preparado preparation.
preparaĵo preparation.
prepareco preparedness.
prepari to prepare.
prepariĝi to get ready, prepare oneself.
prepariteco fitness.
preparmaniero method of preparation.
preparo preparation.
preparoado preparation.
preposto provost.
prepozicio preposition.
prepozitivo prepositional phrase.
prepucio foreskin, prepuce.
preria prairie.
prerio prairie.
preriomevo Franklin's gull, Larus pipixcan.
prerogativo prerogative.
presa press.
presaĵo print, printed matter.
presarto printing.
presbiopa presbyopic.
presbiteriana Presbyterian.
presbiterianismo Presbyterianism.
presbiteriano Presbyterian.
presbitero church warden, presbyter.
presebla printable.
presejo press, printing house, printing office.
preseraro misprint, printer's error, printing error.
presi to impress, print, type.
presigi to have printed, print.
presilo die, (printing) press.
presisto printer.
presita print. **presita cirkvito** printed circuit.
preskaŭ almost, nearly. **preskaŭ certe konverĝa** almost surely convergent. **preskaŭ ĉie** almost everywhere. **preskaŭ ĉiuj** almost all. **preskaŭ ne falas neĝo** almost no snow falls.
preskaŭtrafo near-miss.
preskorektisto reader (for press).
preskriba prescriptive. **preskriba gramatiko** prescriptive grammar.
preskribanalizatoro entity reader.
preskribe prescriptive.
preskribi to order, prescribe, stipulate.
preskribo directions, orders, regulation, statement, prescription.
preskripti to bar.
preskriptiĝi to prescribe, fall under the statute of limitations.

preskripto bar, prescription, limitation of time.
preskvanto publishing run, printing.
preslaboristo printer.
presliteraro font, fount.
preslitero type.
preso print, printing.
presonigo personification.
prespozicio print position.
prespretigo print editing.
presprovaĵo proof (for press).
presprovo proof.
pressignaro font.
prestidigiti to conjure.
prestiĝa glamorous, prestigious.
prestiĝo glamour, prestige.
prestipo type.
preta finished, ready, through, prepared.
preteco readiness.
preteksti to give as an excuse, pretend.
pretekstо excuse, pretence, pretext.
pretendado application.
pretendanto claimant.
pretendema arrogant.
pretendemo overbearingness, presumption, pretence.
pretendi to allege, claim, presume, maintain, assert.
pretendilo application.
pretendo claim, presumption, pretence.
preter beyond, by, past, straight past. **preter ĉia racio** beyond all reason.
preteraĵo overplus.
preteratenti to overlook.
preteratento oversight.
pretere beyond.
preterflugi to overshoot.
preteriranto passer-by.
preteriri to pass, pass by.
preterito past tense.
preterkuri to outrun, outstrip.
preterlasaĵo omission.
preterlasema careless, neglectful, negligent, remiss.
preterlasi to leave out, omit, overlook, let pass.
preterlasita left out, omitted.
preterlaso omission, oversight.
preternatura preternatural.
preterpasi to go beyond, go by, overtake, pass by.
preterveturi to overhaul, overtake, pass.
pretervidi to neglect, overlook.
pretervido neglect.
pretervojo bypass.
pretervola unintended, accidental.
preti to be ready.
pretiga rutino bootstrap.
pretigi to finish, prepare, get ready.

pretiĝi to get ready.
pretkonstrui to prefabricate.
Pretorio Pretoria.
pretoro praetor.
pretpansaĵo sticking-plaster.
pretparta konstruado prefabrication.
pretro priest.
preventa preventive.
preventebla preventable.
preventi to prevent.
preventilo means of prevention, prophylactic, preservative.
prevento prevention.
Prez. → **Prezidanto**.
prezaro price lists.
prezenco present tense.
prezenta introductory.
prezenta tavolo presentation layer.
prezentado introduction, presentation.
prezentaĵo presentation.
prezentanto introducer, performer, presenter.
prezentata klare clear, graphic.
prezentebla actable.
prezenti to present, offer, tender, give, perform, show, tender.
prezentiĝi to appear, feature, be presented.
prezentiĝi forire to check out.
prezentinda presentable.
prezentisto presenter.
prezento presentation, representation.
prezidanteco presidency.
prezidantino chairwoman, president.
prezidanto chairman, president, chairperson.
prezidenta presidential.
prezidenteco presidency.
prezidento president, chairman.
prezidi to preside, take the chair.
prezidio presidium.
prezindaĵo bargain.
prezindiko ticket.
prezkonjekto budget, estimate, estimates.
prezkonkurado tender.
prezkonkuro (public) tender.
prezlisto price list.
prezmarki to price.
prezo price.
preztrompi to fleece.
preztrompisto extortionist, swindler.
preztrompita taken in.
preztrompo swindle, swindling.
pri about, concerning, upon, on. **pri kio temas?** what's this about? what's the point? **pri tio ĉu ne estus eble** about whether it wouldn't be possible. **pri tio ke** for the fact that.
priapismo priapism.
priatenti to attend to.

priĉerpi to bail out.
pridemandi to interrogate, make inquiries, query, question, quiz.
pridemando query.
pridiri to speak of.
pridiskuti to discuss.
pridisputi to argue, dispute, query, question.
pridubebla doubtful.
pridubi to (cast) doubt (upon).
prienketi to investigate.
prifajfi to boo, hiss at.
prifraŭdi to misappropriate.
prifriponi to cheat, swindle, con, scam.
priinstrua didactic.
prijuĝi to judge.
prijxeti to barrage.
prikalkuli to anticipate.
prikalkulo anticipation.
prikonsiliĝi to deliberate.
prikonsiliĝo deliberation.
prikonstrui to build over.
prilaborado preparation, treatment.
prilaborebla workable.
prilabori to elaborate. **prilabori la teron** to work the soil.
prilaboro process.
priloĝi to inhabit.
prilumi to light up, shine upon.
prima prime (number).
primadono prima donna.
primajstri to master.
primajstro master.
primara primary.
primaseco primacy.
primaso primate.
primato primate.
primavero primavera.
primeti to set, lay.
primico first-fruit.
primitiva primeval, primitive. **primitiva komando** primitive.
primo prime (number), prime (6 a.m. religious service), prime (fencing position).
primoki to deride, mock, quip, ridicule.
primolo primrose.
primuso camp stove, primus.
princa illustrious, princely.
princido prince's son.
princino princess.
principa firm in one's principle, firm in one's principles.
principe in principle.
Principeo Príncipe.
principo principle.
princlando principality.
princo prince.
princujo principality.
prinotado annotation.
prinotaĵo annotation.

prinoti to annotate.
printaĵo hard copy, listing, printout. **printaĵo de fonta programteksto** listing.
printempa spring. **printempa krokuso** spring crocus. **printempa leŭkojo** spring snowflake.
printempo spring, springtime.
printi to print.
printilo printer.
printo print.
priokupado preoccupation.
priokupi to engross (fully occupy).
prioritata priority. **prioritata vicigo** priority scheduling. **prioritata vojo** major road.
prioritatigi to prioritize.
prioritato priority.
prioro prior (ecclesiastical title).
priparolado discussion.
priparoli to discuss, talk about.
priparolo description, reference.
pripensa thoughtful.
pripensado pondering, reflection, premeditation.
pripensema circumspect, considerate, critical, reflective, thoughtful.
pripenseme critically, reflectively.
pripensemo cautiousness.
pripensi to premeditate, reflect on, consider, think about, ponder.
pripensinda worthy of reflection.
pripenso reflection (thought).
pripenstempo time to consider.
priplanti to plant.
priplori to mourn.
priplorinda regretful.
priprograma pruvado verification.
priprograma pruvo verification.
priproprieta juro proprietary law.
prirabi to rob.
prirabo robbery.
priraporti to cover.
priresonda por accountable for.
priresponda accountable, responsible.
prirespondeca accountable, responsible.
prirespondeco responsibility.
prirespondi to account for, be answerable, be liable, be responsible.
prirgardo observation.
prisangi to get blood on.
prisemi to sow.
priserĉado search.
priserĉi to search.
priservi to service.
prisilenti to maintain silence about, conceal.
priskriba descriptive. **priskriba geometrio** descriptive geometry.
priskribi to depict, describe.
priskribiĝi to be described.
priskribo account, description.

prismo prism.
pristudi to study.
pristudo study.
priŝteli to rob, steal.
pritondi to prune.
pritraktado treatment.
pritraktata pending.
pritrakti to cover, go over, treat, act towards.
pritraktigi to bring before, lay before, take up.
privata private.
privateco privacy.
privatulo private person.
priverŝi to water.
priveti to back, bet on.
priveturebla passable, practicable.
priveturi to drive over, ride over.
privilegia privileged.
privilegiado favouring.
privilegii to confer privilege, show favour.
privilegio favour, privilege, special advantage.
privilegiulo privileged user.
prizonestro warden.
prizono jail, prison.
prizonulo inmate, prisoner.
prizorgado attendance, maintenance, upkeep.
prizorgante while worrying about.
prizorganto monitor.
prizorgi to look after, guard, take care of.
prizorgo care.
pro because of, for, for sake of, on account of, owing to, through. **pro ĝentileco** out of courtesy, out of politeness. **pro kio** what for, wherefore, why. **pro kiu kaŭzo** for what reason, why. **pro komercaj kialoj** for commercial reasons. **pro la ĉielo!** for heaven's sake! **pro tie ke** because. **pro tio** on that account, therefore. **pro tio ke** because, for the reason that.
proabortiga "pro-choice".
probabla probable.
probable probably.
probablo probability (of an event).
probablodenso probability density.
probablodistribuo probability distribution.
probablokalkulo probability theory.
probablospaco probability space.
probatalanto champion.
problableco likelihood.
problema problematic.
problemanalizo requirements analysis.
problemaro set of problems.
problemdifino problem definition.
problemeca programado problem-oriented language.
problemeto hitch.
problemigi to problematize.

problemo problem, trouble. **problemo pri kvar farboj** four colour map conjecture. **problemo pri la Konigsbergaj pontoj** Königsberg bridge problem. **problemo pri ok damoj** eight queens problem. **problemo pri vojaĝa komizo** travelling salesman problem.
procedi to act, proceed.
procedo method, procedure, process, proceeding.
procedura procedural.
procedurĉapo procedure heading.
procedurdeklaro procedure declaration.
procedurnomo procedure identifier.
proceduro procedure.
procedurparametra specifo procedural parameter specification.
procedurpreskribo procedure statement.
procedurvoko procedure statement.
procelario shearwater.
procentaĵo commission.
procentdoni to invest (money).
procentegisto usurer.
procentego extortionate interest, usury.
procento interest rate, percent, percentage, rate.
procentsigno percent sign (%).
procesado litigation.
procesebla actionable.
procesema litigious.
procesi to go to court, litigate, sue, plead. **procesi kontraŭ** to sue.
procesia processional.
procesii to go in procession.
procesinda actionable.
procesio procession.
proceso action, lawsuit, case (in court).
procesoado proceedings (law).
procesoro processor.
proczilo processor.
procznumero process identifier, PID.
procezo process.
procezrego process control.
procionhundo raccoon-dog.
prociono raccoon.
prodaĵo feat, act of prowess.
prodigi to lavish, squander.
prodo knight-errant.
produkta productive.
produktado production.
produktaĵo produce, product, yield.
produktanto producer.
produktema productive.
produkti to afford, bear, produce, generate.
produktigi to produce, make productive.
produktisto producer.
produktiva prolific.
produktive gainfully, productively.
produktiveco productivity.

produkto product, production.
produktokvanto yield.
produto product (of multiplication).
proedziĝa by marriage, related by marriage.
Prof. → **Profesoro**.
profana profane.
profanado profanation.
profani to defile, desecrate, profane.
profano layman.
profanulo layman.
profesi to profess.
profesia professional.
profesie professionally.
profesii to practice.
profesiisto professional.
profesio business, calling, profession, occupation, job.
profesiulo professional.
profesorino professor (female).
profesoro professor.
profeta prophetic.
profetadi to predict.
profetado prophesying.
profetaĵi to prophesy.
profetaĵo prophecy.
profeti to forecast, foretell, prophesy.
profetino prophetess.
profeto prophet, seer.
profilaktika prophylactic.
profilaktiko prophylaxis.
profili to profile.
profililo profiler.
profilo profile, side face, silhouette.
profita advantageous, beneficial, credit, surplus, lucrative, profitable.
profitama avaricious.
profitanto beneficiary.
profitavida rapacious.
profitdona profitable.
profitema greedy for profit.
profitemo selfishness.
profiti to profit.
profitiga profitable.
profitigeco profitability.
profitigi to benefit.
profitilo moneyspinner.
profito advantage, gain, profit, benefit.
profitparto share.
profunda deep, profound. **profunda dormo** deep sleep.
profundaĝa aged.
profundaĝulo doyen, elder, person of great age.
profundaĵo depth.
profunde deeply, profoundly.
profundeco depth, profundity.
profundega abysmal, abyssal, bottomless.
profundegaĵo abyss, gulf, precipice.
profundigi to deepen, become deeper.
profundiĝi to submerge, sink.
profundo depth.
profundoaĵo depth.
profundsenca abstruse.
profundsenceco abstruseness.
progesterono progesterone.
prognozi to forecast, predict.
prognozita forecasted.
prognozo forecast, prognosis, prediction.
programa fuŝo bug.
programada programming. **programada lingvo** programming language. **programada medio** development environment.
programada sistemo programming system.
programado programming.
programara programming. **programara medio** programming environment. **programara metiejo** programming environment, software tool environment.
programaringenierado software engineering.
programaro software.
programbiblioteko program library.
programciklo loop.
programebla nurlegebla memoro programmable read-only memory, PROM.
programero program item, program item.
programi to program.
programilo programmer.
programiriga regado job control.
programiriga rutino executive routine.
programiro run.
programisto programmer.
programkontrolo program verification and validation.
programlingvo programming language.
programo declaration of policy, platform, programme, statement of policy.
programprotokolo program diagnostic.
programskemo flow chart.
programverkado programming.
progresa advanced, progressive.
progresado progression.
progrese progressively.
progresema advanced, progressive.
progresemulo progressive.
progresi to advance, progress, proceed. **progresi kun** to keep abreast of.
progresigi to advance.
progresigo advancement.
progresio progression.
progresiva graduated, progressive, sliding-scale.
progreso advance, advancement, progress.
prohibi to ban, disallow, forbid, prohibit, proscribe.
prohibicio prohibition.
projekciaĵo projection.

projekcii

projekcii to project.
projekciilo projector.
projekciisto projectionist.
projekcilo projector.
projekcio projection.
projekcisto projectionist.
projektado planning.
projekti to design, make a project of, plan.
projektinto designer.
projektisto designer.
projekto design document, draft, plan, project, scheme, technical specification.
prokavio hyrax, dassie, cony (biblical).
proklamado proclamation.
proklamaĵo proclamation.
proklami to issue, proclaim.
proklamo proclamation.
proklitiko proclitic.
prokonsulo proconsul.
prokrastadi to delay.
prokrastado procrastinating, procrastination.
prokrastanto procrastinator.
prokrastema dilatory.
prokrastemo procrastination.
prokrastemulo procrastinator.
prokrasti to adjourn, delay, postpone, defer, procrastinate, put off.
prokrastiĝi to linger.
prokrastita in abeyance.
prokrasto adjournment, delay.
proks. → **proksimume**.
proksima close, near, nearby, next, proximate. **Proksima Oriento** Middle East.
proksimaĵo neighbourhood, vicinity.
proksime close, near, nearby. **proksime al** close to, near. **proksime de** close to, near.
proksimeco nearness, proximity, vicinity.
proksimigi to bring near to.
proksimiĝi to advance, approach, come close, come closer, come on.
proksimiĝo approach.
proksimo proximity.
proksimulo fellow-creature, neighbour.
proksimuma approximate. **proksimuma kalkulado** approximation.
proksimumado approximation.
proksimumaĵo approximation.
proksimume about, approximately. **proksimume kie** whereabouts.
proksimumigo approximation.
proksimumiĝo approximation.
proksimumo approximation.
proktektanto patron.
prokura proxy. **prokura kluzo** proxy gateway. **prokura servilo** proxy server.
prokuristo attorney in fact.
prokuro power of attorney.

propetulo

prokuroro district attorney, prosecuting attorney, public prosecutor.
prolapsi to prolapse.
prolapso prolapse.
prolegomeno prolegomenon.
proleta proletarian.
proletaria proletarian.
proletario proletarian.
proletaro proletariat, the proletariat.
proleto member of the lower class, proletarian.
prologo prologue.
promenado stroll, walk.
promenanto stroller, walker.
promenejo parade, promenade.
promeni to go for a walk, stroll, promenade.
promeno stroll, walk.
promesi to promise, vow.
promeso affirmation, promise.
promesplena promising, full of promise.
promesrompi to break one's word.
Prometeo Prometheus.
prometio promethium.
promocii to advance, promote.
promociiĝi to advance.
promocio promotion.
promontoro cape, headland, promontory.
prompta quick, rapid, speedy, fleet, swift, instant, fast.
prompte suddenly.
promulgi to promulgate.
pronelo dunnock, hedge-sparrow.
pronoma pronominal.
pronomo pronoun.
prononcado pronouncing, pronunciation.
prononci to pronounce.
prononcmaniero accent.
prononco pronunciation.
propagandaĵo publicity material.
propagandi to advertise, publicize, propagate.
propagandismo propagandism.
propagandisto propagandist.
propagando propaganda, publicity.
propagi to propagate.
propano propane.
proparoladi to plead.
proparolanto advocate.
proparolo representation.
propedeŭtika propaedeutic.
propedeŭtiko preparatory instruction, propaedeutics.
propeka kapro scapegoat.
propekulo scapegoat.
propeta intercessory.
propetanto intercessor.
propeti to intercede, plead for, mediate.
propeto intercession.
propetulo intercessor.

proponado

proponado offer, tender.
proponanto bidder.
proponeti to hint, insinuate.
proponi to propose, offer, advocate, suggest.
proponi al iu merkaton to offer someone a deal.
propono offer, presentation, proposal, tender, suggestion.
proporcia proportional.
proporcie pro rata. **proporcie kun** proportional to.
proporcio proportion, rate, ratio.
propozicio proposition, sentence, statement.
propra own, personal, proper, very. **propra divisoro** proper divisor. **propra divizoro** proper divisor. **propra frakcio** proper fraction. **propra nomo** proper name.
propradecide on one's own account.
proprajuĝe by one's own judgement.
proprajiĝi to become the property (of someone).
proprajô property.
proprajoj possessions.
proprakoste at one's own expense.
propramana skribaĵo autograph.
propramane with one's own hands.
propramova spontaneous, voluntary.
propramove of one's own accord, spontaneously.
propraokule with one's own eyes.
propravola of one's own will.
propravole of one's own accord, of one's own free will, voluntarily.
propre personally.
propreco property.
preprecoaĵo premises.
proprietaĵo property.
proprieti to own.
proprieto ownership.
proprietulo owner.
proprigi to appropriate. **proprigi al si** to acquire.
proprigo appropriation.
proprulo owner.
proprumi to own, possess.
propulsakso drive shaft, driving axle.
propulsi to actuate, drive.
propulso drive.
prosaĵo prose.
proscenio apron.
proskriba proscriptive.
proskribi to outlaw, proscribe.
proskribo proscription.
proskripcii to outlaw, proscribe.
proskripcio proscription.
proskripciulo exile.
prospekto prospectus, brochure.
prospektori to prospect.
prospektoro prospector.

provaĵo

prospera prosperous.
prospereco prosperity.
prosperi to be successful, prosper, thrive.
prosperigi to advance.
prospero prosperity, success.
prostato prostate gland.
prostituado prostitution.
prostituejo brothel, whorehouse, bordello.
prostitui to prostitute.
prostituisto pander, pimp.
prostituitino escort, hooker, prostitute, whore.
prostituito prostitute.
prostituo prostitution.
protagonisto protagonist.
protaktinio protactinium.
proteinhava albuminous.
proteino protein.
protekta protectionist. **protekta relajso** guard relay.
protektado protection.
protektaĵo protection.
protektanto patron.
protektatino protégée.
protektato protégé.
protekti to protect, back, cover.
protektisma protectionist.
protekto patronage, protection.
protektorato protectorate.
protektspirito guardian angel.
protelo aardwolf.
Proteo Proteus.
proterozoiko proterozoic.
Proterozoiko Proterozoic.
protestado protestation.
protestanta Protestant.
protestanto Protestant.
Protestanto Protestant, evangelic.
protesti to protest.
protesto protest.
proteza artificial.
protezo prosthesis, false limb.
protio, ke for the reason that.
protokolanto minute-taker.
protokoli to give a ticket, take somebody's name.
protokolisto court reporter.
protokolo minutes, protocol, report (official).
protono proton.
protoplasma protoplasmic.
protoplasmo protoplasm.
prototipado prototyping.
prototipo prototype.
protozoo protozoon.
protozoologio protozoology.
protruda protuberant.
protuberanco prominence, protuberance.
prova tentative.
provaĵo test, trial.

provante while trying.
provbudo dressing room (of a clothing store).
prove tentatively.
provenca Provençal.
proverba proverbial.
proverbo adage, proverb, maxim, saying.
provi to attempt, test, try, essay.
proviantado catering.
provianti to supply, provision.
proviantisto supply officer.
provianto provisions, rations.
providenca providential.
providenco providence.
provinca provincial. **provinca lingvaĵo** patois.
provincano provincial.
provincestro provincial governor.
provincialismo provincialism.
provinco province.
provizado arrival, arrivals, supply, provision.
provizaĵestro purser.
provizaĵo supply, provision.
provizanto provider, supplier. **provizanto de retkonekto** Internet access provider, IAP. **provizanto de retservoj** Internet service provider, ISP.
provizejo pantry, storeroom, warehouse, supply area, stock room.
provizi to cater, furnish, provide, supply. **provizi je** to accommodate with. **provizi je drataro** to wire. **provizi per** to accommodate with. **provizi per tavoleto** to coat. **provizi sin je** to store. **provizi sin per** to buy, get, procure.
provizio commission, retainer.
provizisto supplier.
provizo stock, store, supply, provision.
provizora provisional, temporary. **provizora funkciado** graceful degradation.
provizore for the time being, temporarily.
provizumado catering.
provizumi to provision, supply.
provlegi to proofread.
provlegisto proofreader.
provludo rehearsal.
provo assay, attempt, test, trial, ordeal.
provoaĵoado trial (an attempt).
provoka provocative.
provoki to defy, incite, provoke, incite.
provoko challenge, incitement, provocation.
provoso jailer, prison guard.
provtempo probation, trial period.
provtubo test tube.
proza prosaic, prose.
Prozako Prozac.
prozelitigi to proselytize.
prozelitismo proselytism.
prozelito convert, proselyte.
prozo prose.

prozodio prosody.
prozopopeo personification.
prozorgi to look after.
pruda prudish.
prude primly.
prudeco prudery, prudishness.
prudenta judicious, prudent, reasonable, sensible, wise, careful.
prudente intelligently, prudently, sensibly, wisely.
prudentigi to put some sense into.
prudento common sense, good sense, prudence.
prudulino prude.
prudulo prude.
prujna frosted, hoar.
prujno frost.
prunarbo plum-tree.
prunelarbo blackthorn, sloe.
prunelo blackthorn, sloe.
prunelujo blackthorn, buckthorn.
pruno plum.
pruntado loan.
pruntaĵo loan.
pruntanto lender.
prunte as a loan, on loan.
pruntedoni to advance, lend. **pruntedoni al** to lend.
prunteprenanto borrower.
pruntepreni to borrow. **pruntepreni de** to borrow from.
pruntepreninto borrower.
prunti to borrow, lend, loan. **prunti al** to lend. **prunti de** to borrow from.
pruntisto pawnbroker.
prunto loan. **prunto preni** to borrow.
pruntoficejo pawnbroker's, pawnshop.
pruntokarto library card.
pruntotablo checkout desk.
pruntovorto loanword.
prunujo plum-tree.
prunuso plum.
pruo bow, prow (of ship).
prusa Prussian. **prusa bluo** Prussian blue.
prusacido Prussic acid.
prusbluo Prussian blue.
Prusia Prussian.
Prusiano Prussian.
Prusio Prussia.
Pruslando Prussia.
pruso Prussian.
prusuja Prussian.
prusujano Prussian.
Prusujo Prussia.
pruvaĵo piece of evidence.
pruvdevo burden of proof.
pruvebla provable.
pruvi to demonstrate, prove, substantiate.
pruvmaterialo evidence.

pruvo proof, sign, token. **pruvo de ekzisto** proof of existence. **pruvo per indukto** proof by induction. **pruvo per redukto al absurdo** proof by reductio ad absurdum.
pruvpovo evidential value.
psalmaro psalm-book, psalmody, psalter.
psalmisto psalmist.
psalmo psalm.
psalmokantado psalmody.
psalmverkisto psalmodist.
psalterio psaltery.
psaltero psaltery.
psefito psephite.
psefologio psephology.
psefologo psephologist.
pseŭdepigrafio pseudepigraphy.
pseŭdo- pseudo.
pseŭdocugo Douglas-fir.
pseŭdodekumo redundancy character, pseudodecimal.
pseŭdonima pseudonymous.
pseŭdonimo alias, pseudonym.
pseŭdonomo nom-de-plume, pen name, pseudonym.
pseŭdopatriotismo pseudo-patriotism.
pseŭdopodo pseudopodium.
pseŭdoscienca pseudo-scientific.
pseŭdoscienco pseudo-science.
pseŭdosufikso pseudo-suffix.
pseŭdoturka pseudo-Turkish.
psihanalizo psychoanalysis.
Psiĥo Psyche.
psiĥologio psychology.
psiĥozo psychosis.
psika psychic. **psika kolapso** nervous breakdown, mental breakdown.
psikanaliza psychoanalytic.
psikanalizi to psychoanalyse.
psikanalizo psychoanalysis.
psikastenio psychasthenia.
psike kolapsi to have a nervous breakdown.
psikedela psychedelic.
psikiatra psychiatric.
psikiatria psychiatric.
psikiatrie psychiatrically.
psikiatrio psychiatry.
psikiatro psychiatrist.
psiko mind, psyche.
psikodramo psychodrama.
psikokirurgio psychosurgery.
psikologa psychological.
psikologia psychological.
psikologie psychologically.
psikologiisto psychologist.
psikologio psychology.
psikologo psychologist.
psikoneŭrozo psychoneurosis.
psikopatia psychopathic.
psikopatio psychopath; psychopathy.
psikopato psycho, psychopath.
psikopatologio abnormal psychology.
psikoza demented, psychotic.
psikozo psychosis.
psikozulo psychotic.
psikterapio psychotherapy.
psio psi (Ψψ).
psitako grey parrot.
psitakozo psittacosis.
psoaso psoas.
psoko book louse, bookworm.
psoriazo psoriasis.
ptarmiko sneezewort.
pteridio bracken fern.
pterido bracken.
pterodaktilo pterodactyl.
ptialino ptyalin.
ptialismo ptyalism.
ptm. → **posttagmeze**.
ptolemea Ptolemaic.
Ptolemeo Ptolemy.
ptomaino ptomaine.
PTT → **Poŝto, Telegrafo, Telefono**.
puba pubic.
pubereco puberty.
puberta pubescent.
puberto puberty.
publici to publicize, write for the press, write articles.
publicisto author, commentator, correspondent, essayist, journalist, publicist, reporter.
publika public. **publika ĝardeno** park. **publika letero** open letter. **publika sekreto** open secret.
publikaĵo freeware, public domain software.
publikbaro crush barrier.
publike openly, publicly.
publikeco publicity.
publikigado promulgation.
publikigeco publicity.
publikigi to make public, promulgate, publish, reveal.
publikigo proclamation, publication, publicity.
publiko public.
publikulino harlot, prostitute.
publikutila charitable, non-profit.
pubo pubic region.
pubosto pubic bone, pubis.
puĉo coup d'état, putsch.
pudelo poodle.
pudingo pudding.
pudli to puddle.
pudo pood (пуд, an obsolete Russian unit of mass, 16.38 kg or 36.11 lbs).
pudora modest.
pudore with delicacy.
pudoro chaste behaviour, modesty, sense of decency.

pudra powdery.
pudri to powder.
pudro (cosmetic) powder.
puduo pudú.
pueblo Pueblo.
Puertoriko Puerto Rico.
pufa puffed, puffy, stuffed.
pufhava puffed out, bouffant.
pufigi to puff out.
pufiĝi to puff up, puff out, swell.
pufo padding, puff, swelling, stuffing, wad, pad.
pugnebati to box.
pugni to punch.
pugnigi to clench.
pugno fist.
pugnobatalanto boxer.
pugnobatali to box.
pugnobati to punch.
pugnobato boxing.
pugnofrapo punch.
pugnoganto mitten.
pugnolukti to box.
pugnoluktisto boxer, fighter.
pugo arse, ass, backside, behind, bottom, buttocks, butt, rump.
pugtruo asshole.
pulbazaro flea market.
Pulĉinelo Punch.
pulĉinelo punch and Judy.
pulio pulley.
pulko pulque (milky, somewhat viscous alcoholic beverage).
pulma pulmonary.
pulmano Pullman car.
pulminflamo lung inflammation, pneumonia.
pulmo lung.
pulmonario lungwort, pulmonaria.
pulo flea.
pulovero pullover.
pulovro pullover sweater.
pulpo fleshy part, pulp.
pulsado beating, pulsating, pulsation, throb, throbbing.
pulsaro pulsar.
pulsatilo pasqueflower.
pulsbatado pulsation.
pulsi to pulsate, throb.
pulso beat, pulse.
pulsostelo pulsar.
pulvo gunpowder.
pulvopafilo firearm.
pulvora powdery.
pulvorigi to calcine, pulverize.
pulvorigita lakto milk powder, powdered milk.
pulvoro powder (cosmetic).
pulvorsukero powdered sugar.

pulvro powder.
pumiko pumice stone.
pumo cougar, mountain lion, puma.
pumpbalgo bellows.
pumpi to pump.
pumpilo pump.
pumpisto attendant.
puna penal.
punado punishment.
punbatado castigation, chastisement.
punbati to castigate, chastise, punish.
punca flaming red, poppy red, poppy-coloured, crimson red.
punco crimson red.
punĉo punch.
pundo pound (unit of currency £).
pundomo penitentiary, prison.
punebla punishable.
punejo pillory.
punekzili to deport.
punekzilo deportation.
puni to chastise, punish. **puni trafe** to chastise, correct, punish.
punika punic.
puninda punishable, worthy of punishment.
punio punishment.
punkcii to prick, puncture.
punkcio puncture.
punkteto pinpoint.
punkti to punctuate.
punktita polka dot.
punkto dot, point, spot; full stop, period (.). **punkto!** full stop! period! that's all there is to say!
punktodesegni to stipple.
punktokomo semicolon (;).
punktoparo bound vector.
punlaborejo forced-labour camp.
punlaboro penal servitude.
punmono (monetary) fine.
puno chastisement, penance, punishment, penalty. **punon doni** to inflict.
punoado punishment.
punprokrasti to reprieve.
punprokrasto reprieve.
punto lace.
pupdomo doll house.
pupilo pupil (of eye).
pupitro desk, lectern, school desk.
pupo chrysalis, pupa, doll, puppet.
pura clean, pure, neat, unadulterated. **pura rimo** full rhyme, perfect rhyme, true rhyme.
pure purely. **pure imaginara** pure imaginary.
pureco cleanliness, purity, neatness.
purega immaculate.
purema neat, fastidious, tidy.
pureo purée.

purgatorio purgatory.
puriga abluent, sanitary.
purigi to clean, cleanse, make clean, purge, purify, wash. **purigi la nazon** to blow one's nose.
purigo cleaning (up), laundering, purification.
puriĝejo purgatory.
Purimfesto Purim.
purismo purism.
puristo purist.
puritana puritan.
puritanismo Puritanism.
puritano puritan.
purpura purple. **purpura digitalo** foxglove.
purpurbruna puce.
purpurbruno puce.
purpuro purple.
purrasa pedigree, pure-bred.
pursanga pure blood.
puruma potty trained, toilet trained.
pusadi to ooze.
pusi to discharge pus.
puso pus.
pusoaĵo pus.
pustulo pustule.
puŝadi to push.
puŝĉaro wheelbarrow, hand truck.
puŝegi to hustle, jostle, thrust.
puŝeĝi to be pushed.
puŝekfunkciigi to push.
puŝi to push, thrust, shove.
puŝiĝi to thrust. **puŝiĝi kun** collide with, run into.
puŝnajlo thumbtack.
puŝo impulse, push.
puŝpinglo pushpin.
puŝpumpilo pump.
puŝveturilo barrow, hand-barrow, wheelbarrow.
putino hooker, whore.
puto well, pit.
putoro polecat.
putra addled, bad, rotten, decaying, festering, putrefying.
putrado corruption.
putraĵo carrion, decayed matter, filth, putrefaction.
putreco rottenness.
putrema perishable.
putri to decay, decompose, putrefy, rot, fester.
putrigi to corrupt, putrefy.
putriĝema perishable.
putriĝi to rot.
putriĝo decay.
putro corruption.
putroeco putrescence.
puzlo puzzle.

R

rabadega predatory.
rabadi to plunder, sack, pillage.
rabado robbery, looting.
rabaĵo booty.
rabakiro booty.
rabarba rhubarb.
rabarbo rhubarb.
rabataki to mug.
rabate on discount.
rabati to bring down, lower (of prices), deduct a discount, discount, rebate.
rabato abatement, discount, rebate.
Rabato Rabat.
rabato rebate, abatement, discount.
rabbesta predatory.
rabbesto beast of prey.
rabdo divining rod.
rabdomancio dowsing.
rabegi to rob, plunder, loot.
rabegiado pillage.
rabema rapacious.
rabemeco rapacity.
rabena rabbinical.
rabeno rabbi.
rabeti to maraud.
rabeto slot.
rabi to pillage, plunder, rob, take away (by force).
rabia frenzied, furious, raging, mad, rabid.
rabio rabies, frenzy, rage.
rabisto brigand, highwayman, robber. **rabistoj kaj ĝendarmoj** cops and robbers (game).
rabmevo skua (seabird of the family Stercorariidae).
rabo rapine.
rabobesto beast of prey, predator.
rabobestoj carnivores.
rabobirdo bird of prey.
rabobirdoj birds of prey.
rabotaĵo shavings.
raboti to abrade, plane.
rabotilo plane (tool).
raboto abrasion.
rabulo bandit.
racia rational, sane, reasonable.
racie rationally.
racieco reasonableness, sanity, rationality.
raciemo rationality.
raciigi to rationalize.
raciigo rationale, rationalization.
raciismo rationalism.
racio judgement, reason, logical reasoning, sense, rationality.

racionala rational. **racionala frakcio** rational fraction. **racionala funkcio** rational function.
racionalismo rationalism.
racionalisto rationalist.
racionalo rational number.
raciono rational number.
radakso axle.
radaro[1] wheelwork, machinery.
radaro[2] radar.
radbrako arm.
radcentro hub (of wheel).
radeto roller, caster.
radfaristo wheelwright.
radia radio, by radio, over the radio. **radia elsendotempo** air time.
radiado radiance, radiation.
radiano radian.
radiatoro radiator.
radiestezisto water-diviner.
radiestezo dowsing, divination.
radii to radiate, irradiate.
radiigi to make radiate.
radiisto radioman.
radika basic. **radika korpo** root field (of a polynomial).
radikala radical.
radikale radically, thoroughly.
radikaleco radicality.
radikaligo radicalization.
radikaliĝo radicalization.
radikalismo radicalism.
radikalo radical.
radikalulo radical.
radike inherently, innately.
radikeco inherence.
radikhava arbo rooted tree.
radiki to be rooted.
radikigato radicand.
radikigi to take the root.
radikilo radical sign, root sign (√).
radiko radical (grammar), root.
radiksigno radical sign, root sign (√).
radikvorto root word.
radilokalizilo radar set, radio locator.
radiluma effulgent, radiant.
radio beam, radio, radius, ray, wireless; spoke (of wheel).
radioaktiva radioactive.
radioaktiveco radioactivity.
radioaktivigi to activate.
radioamatoro radio amateur, ham.
radioaparato radio.
radioastronomio radio astronomy.
radiobutono radio button.

radiodisaŭdigo radio broadcast.
radiodissendo radio broadcast.
radiofonio radio, wireless telegraph(y).
radiofono radio receiver.
radiofotografio radiography.
radiofrekvenca radio frequency, RF.
radiofrekvenca identigo radio frequency identification, RFID.
radiogoniometro radio goniometer.
radiografa radiographic.
radiografi to X-ray.
radiografio radiography.
radiogramo wireless telegram.
radioizotopo radio isotope.
radiologiisto radiologist.
radiologio radiology.
radiologo radiologist.
radiondoj airwaves.
radioricevilo wireless.
radiosendilo radio transmitter.
radioskopio radioscopy.
radiostacio radio station.
radioŝtono actinolite.
radiotelefonio radiotelephony.
radiotelegrafio radiotelegraph.
radiotelegramo wireless telegram.
radioteleskopo radio telescope.
radioterapio radiation.
raditeleskopo radio telescope.
radiumo radium.
radiuso radius.
radiusvektoro position vector, radius vector.
radkavo rut.
rado wheel.
radokavo rut, groove.
radono radon.
radradio spoke.
radringa deprenilo tyre lever.
radringo cover, outer cover.
radrondo felly, felloe, rim.
radseĝo wheelchair.
radsigno groove, rut.
radŝpinilo spinning wheel.
rafaneto radish.
rafano radish, black radish, horse radish.
rafinado refinement.
rafinaĵo refinement.
rafinejo refinery.
rafini to refine.
rafinisto refiner.
rafinita refined.
rafio raffia.
raglano raglan.
ragtimo ragtime.
raguo ragout, stew.
raĝabo Rajab.
raĝao rajah.
Raĝastujo Rajasthan.

raĝo rajah.
raida swift, fleet.
rajda mounted.
rajdadi to ride, keep riding.
rajdado riding.
rajdanta mounted.
rajdantaro cavalcade.
rajdantino Amazon, horsewoman.
rajdanto cavalier.
rajdarto horsemanship.
rajdĉasisto light cavalryman.
rajdejo riding school.
rajdi to ride. **rajdi sur ĉevalo** to ride a horse.
rajdistarano trooper.
rajdistaro cavalry.
rajdisto jockey.
rajdmastro riding master.
rajdmiliciano yeoman.
rajdmilico yeomanry.
rajdo ride.
rajdosoldato cavalry soldier, cavalryman.
rajdrobo riding habit.
rajdsoldato cavalry soldier, cavalryman.
rajdvojo bridle path.
rajo ray, skate, stingray.
rajono rayon.
rajpi to bind, seize (up).
rajta lawful, legitimate, rightful.
rajte rightly.
rajti to have the right to, be entitled to.
rajtigi to authorize, empower.
rajtigilo authorization.
rajtigito agent.
rajtigo authorization.
rajto entitlement, right, authority.
raĵao rajah.
rakedo racket.
raketaviadilo rocket-plane.
raketi to skyrocket.
raketo flare, missile, rocket.
raketostarto blastoff.
rakito rachitis, rickets.
rako rack.
rakontaĉo boring story.
rakontadi to unfold, relate, tell.
rakontado storytelling.
rakontanto narrator, storyteller.
rakonteto anecdote.
rakonti to narrate, relate, tell, recount, relate. **rakonti ŝercojn** to tell a joke. **rakonti unu la alian** to meet each other.
rakontintrigo plot.
rakontisto storyteller.
rakonto account, narrative, story, tale, recital.
raliko bolt-rope.
ralio rally.
ralo water rail.

ramadano Ramadan.
Ramajano Ramayana.
rambutanarbo rambutan (tropical tree in the family Sapindaceae).
rambutano rambutan (tropical tree in the family Sapindaceae or its fruit).
ramfasto toucan.
ramilego battering ram.
ramna hipofeo common sea-buckthorn.
ramno buckthorn.
ramo[1] battering ram.
ramo[2] RAM (random access memory).
rampaĉa fawning, fulsome.
rampaĉi to cringe, fawn, grovel.
rampaĵo reptile.
rampi to crawl, creep, sneak. **rampi manepiede** to crawl on one's hands and feet.
ramplo ramp.
rampo crawl.
rampulo crawler, reptile.
ranbleki to croak.
ranca rancid.
ranĉo ranch.
randa boundary, frontier.
randaĵo border (edge).
rande de on the brink of.
randiri to circle.
randmuro parapet.
rando border, brim, brink, edge, edging, fringe, rand, rim, boundary.
randodentigi to indent, notch.
randtrua karto edge-punched card.
ranfemuroj frog's legs.
rangaltigi to promote.
rangi to rank.
rangifero reindeer.
rangigi to rank.
rango grade, rank, rate.
rangordo ranking, order.
rangulo dignitary.
ranido tadpole.
rankoro grudge, rancour, resentment.
rano frog.
ranunkolo buttercup, ranunculus.
ranunkulo buttercup, spearwort.
Rao Ra, Re.
rapida brisk, quick, rapid, speedy, swift, hasty, prompt, fast. **rapida ordigo** quick-sort. **rapida vagonaro** express train.
rapidado speeding.
rapide apace, expeditiously, fast, quickly, swiftly, in a rush, rapidly.
rapideco alacrity, briskness, celerity, haste, promptitude, rapidity, speed, swiftness, velocity.
rapidega expeditious.
rapidege most speedily, at considerable speed.
rapidemo haste.

rapidfluo rapids.
rapidi to go fast, hurry, rush.
rapidigi to accelerate, speed up, hasten, quicken.
rapidigo acceleration.
rapidiĝi to become speedy, speed up, make haste.
rapidindikilo speedometer.
rapidlimo speed limit.
rapido speed.
rapidometro speedometer, tachometer.
rapidpieda quick (on foot), fleet-footed.
rapidpresilo line printer.
rapidresponda to the point.
rapidtrajno fast train.
rapidumo gear.
rapidumskatolo gearbox, gear case.
rapidumstango stick shift.
rapidumŝaltilo gear changer.
rapidumŝanĝilo gear shift.
rapidumujo gearbox, gear case.
rapidvagonaro fast train.
rapiro foil, rapier.
rapkantisto rapper.
rapmuziko rap, rap music.
rapo turnip.
raportado coverage.
raportaro coverage.
raportenda which must be reported.
raporti to give an account, report. **raporti pri si** to give an account of oneself.
raportisto reporter.
raporto account, record, report, statement.
rapsodiisto rhapsodist.
rapsodio rhapsody.
rapsodo rhapsode, rhapsodist.
rapunkolo rampion.
rapunkulo rampion.
rara precious, rare.
raraĵo rarity.
rare rarely.
rasa racial. **rasa diskriminacio** racial discrimination.
rasapartigisto segregationist.
rasapartigo apartheid, segregation.
rasisma racist.
rasismo racism.
rasisto racist.
rasli to rattle, rustle.
raso breed, race.
raspa hoarse, husky, rough, coarse, uneven.
raspi to grate, rasp, grate.
raspilo grater, rasp (a tool).
rasti to rake.
rastilo rake (implement).
rastralo music-pen, rastrum, raster.
rastro hoe.
rastruma raster. **rastruma grafiko** raster graphics. **rastruma signobildo** dot

matrix, pixel pattern. **rastruma tiparo** bitmap font.
rastrumero pixel.
rastrumigilo raster processor, rasterizer.
rastrumo bit map, raster.
rastumulto race riot.
Raŝido Rosetta.
ratafio ratafia.
ratifado ratification.
ratifi to ratify.
ratifiki to ratify.
ratifiko ratification.
ratifo ratification.
rato rat.
raŭka harsh, hoarse, raucous, husky.
raŭkiĝi to become hoarse, have a husky voice, have hoarse voice.
raŭkiĝo hoarseness.
raŭko hoarseness, frog in the throat.
raŭndo round.
raŭpo caterpillar.
rava delightful, lovely, exquisite, ravishing.
raveco allure, enchantment.
ravega exquisite, stunning, superb.
ravege exquisitely, superbly.
ravego euphoria.
ravelino ravelin.
ravi to delight, enchant, enrapture.
ravigi to delight.
raviĝi to delight.
raviĝinta delighted.
ravino ravine.
raviolo ravioli.
ravioloj ravioli.
ravita delighted.
raviteco enchantment.
ravo delight, ecstasy, rapture.
razeno lawn.
razeti to trim.
razi to shave.
raziĝi to be grazed, be shorn.
razii to raid.
razilklingo razor blade.
razilo razor.
razio (police) raid.
razisto barber.
razkapulo skinhead.
razklingo razor blade.
razkremo shaving cream.
razoklingo razor-blade.
razpeniko shaving brush.
re- (denotes repetition of an act), re-.
reaboni to renew a subscription, resubscribe.
reaĉeti to buy back, redeem, ransom.
reaĉeto ransom.
readaptado readaptation, rehabilitation.
Readmono Deuteronomy.
reaga interactive.
reagi to react, respond.

reagilo reagent.
reago reaction.
reakcia reactionary.
reakciaviadilo jet, jet plane.
reakcii to react.
reakciilo reagent.
reakcio reaction.
reakciulo reactionary.
reakirebla recoverable.
reakiri to recover.
reakiro recovery, retrieval.
reakordigebla reconcilable.
reakordigi to reconcile.
reaktivigi to resume.
reaktoro core, reactor, jet engine.
reala actual, practical, real. **reala bezono** real need. **reala lernejo** junior high school.
realaĵo reality.
reale genuinely, indeed, really, truly.
realeco actuality, reality.
realiga modulo implementation module.
realigebla able to come true, achievable.
realigeble feasibly.
realigeblo feasibility.
realigi to implement, produce.
realiginto designer.
realigisto designer.
realigo implementation.
realiĝi to come true.
realiĝo realization.
realisma realistic.
realismo realism.
realista realistic.
realisto realist.
realo reality.
realproprigi to reclaim.
realtempa real time. **realtempa reĝimo** real-time mode, real-time operation.
reamikiĝi to be reconciled.
reanimi to reanimate.
reao nandu (fast-running flightless birds similar to the ostrich).
reaperanto apparition.
reaperi to reappear.
reapero comeback.
rearanĝi to rearrange.
reardigi to rekindle.
reatingi to re-reach.
rebakaĵo zwieback.
rebaki to bake a second time.
rebaloto revote.
rebapti to rechristen, rename.
rebati[1] reduce the price.
rebati[2] to hit back, strike back, get even, rebut.
rebato comeback, crackdown, rebuttal.
rebeligo facelift, makeover.
reboko rhebok.

rebonigi

rebonigi to atone, make good, repair, regress, amend.
rebonigo atonement.
reboniĝi to recover.
reboniĝo recovery.
rebonstatigi to repair, put back in good condition.
rebrila reflective.
rebrili to reflect (light), shine back.
rebrililo reflector.
rebrilo reflection (of light).
rebruligi to rekindle.
rebruligo rekindling.
rebuso rebus.
recenzanto reviewer.
recenzi to review.
recenzisto reviewer.
recenzo review.
recepto formula, prescription, recipe.
recevi to receive.
recikligi to recycle.
reciproka mutual, reciprocal.
reciproke mutually, reciprocally, in return, in exchange.
reciprokeco reciprocity.
reciproki to reciprocate.
recitalo recital.
recitativo recitative.
reciti to recite.
Red. → **Redaktoro**.
redakcia editorial.
redakcio editorial office.
redaktado composition, redaction.
redaktanto editor.
redakti to compile, edit.
redaktilo editor, word processor. **redaktilo teksta** word processor.
redaktinto editor.
redaktisto editor.
redakto composition, redaction.
redaktora editorial.
redaktoro editor.
redeklari to restate.
redekoracii to redecorate.
redemandi to reclaim.
Redemptoro Redeemer, Savior.
redifini to redefine.
redingoto frock coat.
rediri to repeat, restate, say again.
redisdoni to redistribute.
redividi to subdivide.
redonado restitution.
redonaĵo return.
redoneco restoration.
redoni to compensate, give back, return, render, restore, pay back, refund, repay, retaliate, return, reflect, reproduce.
redono restitution, restoration, yield.
redrati to rewire.

refleksivo

reduktado simplification.
reduktebla reducible. **reduktebla frakcio** cancelable fraction.
redukti to reduce.
reduktiĝi to fall, recede, be reduced.
reduktiĝo reduction.
reduktisma reductive.
reduktismo reductionism.
redukto reduction. **redukto al absurdo** reductio ad absurdum.
redunda redundant.
redundeco redundancy.
redundo redundancy.
redungigi sin to find a new job.
redunko reedbuck.
reduto redoubt.
ree afresh, again, once more, anew.
reedukado re-education.
reekzameni to re-examine, review.
reekzameno re-examination, review.
reela real. **reela parto** real part.
reeldono new edition, reissue.
reelekti to reelect.
reelo real number.
reen back, backwards, returning.
reenigi to back up, reverse, move back, draw back.
reeniĝi to reenter.
reeniri to reenter.
reenkarniĝo reincarnation.
reenmeti to remand.
reenmetiigi to reinstate.
reenpaŝo withdrawal.
reensocietigo after-care, rehabilitation.
refaldi to refold.
refali to lapse.
refalo relapse.
refarado remaking.
refari to redo, remake, regenerate, restore.
refektorio refectory.
referaĵo paper, scholarly report.
referato paper, report.
referenca reference. **referenca tipo** pointer type.
referencato referenced variable.
referenci to reference.
referencilo symbol.
referenco recommendation, reference, testimonial.
referendumo referendum.
referi to give a report, lecture, present a paper.
refermi to close again, shut once more.
refi to reef (sail).
refleksa reflex.
reflekse reflexively.
refleksiva reflexive. **refleksiva pronomo** reflexive pronoun.
refleksivo reflexive.

reflekso reflex.
reflekti to reflect.
reflektiĝi to be reflected.
reflektilo reflector.
reflekto reflection.
reflektoro headlight (car), reflector, spotlight.
reflori to bloom again, bloom later.
reflugi to fly back.
reflui to ebb.
refluo low tide.
refo reef (sail).
refoje again.
Reformacio Reformation.
reformanto reformer, reformist.
reformatoro reformer, reformist.
reformejo reformatory.
reformi to amend, reform, remodel.
reformisto reformer, reformist.
reformita reformed.
reformo reform, reformation.
reforti to refortify, make stronger again.
refortigilo restorative.
refortiĝi to convalesce, get stronger, grow stronger, recuperate.
refrakti to refract.
refraktiĝi to refract.
refrakto refraction.
refreno chorus, refrain, theme.
refreŝigi to refresh.
refreŝigo refreshment (food).
refreŝiĝi to refresh.
refuĝi to flee back.
refuti to disprove, rebut, refute. **refuti teorion** to refute a theory.
refuto disproof, refutation.
rega prevalent.
regada trukarto control card.
regadi to control.
regado control, reign, rule.
regajnebla recoverable.
regajni to earn back, regain, win back.
regalaĵo fare.
regale heartily.
regali to entertain, treat, regale. **regali per** to treat to.
regalo feast, treat.
regantaro executive.
reganto governor, regent, ruler.
regardi to look at, regard.
regateco subjection.
regato subject.
regebla manageable.
regeco dominion, regency, sovereignty.
regema bossy.
regeneri to regenerate.
regento regent.
regeo reggae.

regi to control, govern, restrain, rule, reign.
  regi sin to control oneself.
regilo controller.
regimento regiment.
reginto ruler.
regio control, management.
regiona regional. **regiona dialekto** local dialect, territorial dialect.
regionkodo area code.
regiono region, district, tract (of land).
  regiono de deklaro visibility region.
  regiono de nomo visibility region.
registara governmental.
registaro administration, government.
registo one who governs.
registrado recording, registration.
registrejo registry.
registri to note, notice, record, register.
registriĝi to enrol, register.
registriĝo admission, enrolment.
registrilo recorder.
registristo registrar.
registrita registered. **registrita letero** registered letter. **registrita seksa kulpulo** registered sex offender.
registro account book, record, register, list, roll, register.
registrolibro list, register (book), roll (book).
registrumo case.
reglamenti to regiment, regulate.
reglamento regulations, rules.
reglui to paste.
regna state, national, royal. **Regna Delegitaro** States General.
regnano subject.
regnestro head of state, ruler, sovereign.
regno dominion, realm, state, sovereign country, kingdom.
rego ascendance, ascendancy, control, mastery.
regolo goldcrest (regulus regulus).
regrado flywheel.
regresa retrograde.
regrese backwards.
regresi to fall back, regress, retrogress.
regreso decline, going down.
regula even, regular. **regula esprimo** regular expression, regexp. **regula lingvo** regular language.
regularo regulations, rules, statutes.
regulatoro regulator.
regule regularly.
regulebla adjustable.
reguleco regularity.
regulesprimo regular expression.
reguli to enact.
reguligado regularization.
reguligi to regulate, rule, put in order.
  reguligi konton to settle an account.

reguligi la konton to settle, square up an account.
reguligo adjustment, regulation, setting.
reguliĝi to adjust.
regulilo control.
regulo rule, enactment, regulation, statute, law.
reĝa regal, royal. **reĝa aglo** golden eagle. **reĝa molanaso** king eider.
reĝakvo aqua regia.
reĝe kingly, royally, regally.
reĝeco kingship, royalty.
reĝi to reign, be king, be in control, rule.
reĝidino princess.
reĝido prince.
reĝimo mode, regime, regimen.
reĝinedzo queen's husband.
Reĝinlando Queensland.
reĝino queen. **Reĝino Ĉarlotinsuloj** Queen Charlotte Islands.
reĝisoro director, stage manager.
reĝistro register.
reĝlando kingdom.
reĝmortiginto regicide.
reĝmortigo regicide.
reĝo king. **reĝo de reĝoj** king of kings.
reĝolando kingdom.
reĝujo kingdom.
reĝustigi to adjust, readjust.
reĝustigo redress.
reĝustiĝi to be corrected.
rehavi to reobtain, have again.
rehavigi to recoup.
rehavigo replenishment, retrieval.
rehejmeniri to return home.
rehejmiĝi to come home, return home.
reigi to reestablish.
reinformado information retrieval.
reinspektado review.
reinspekti to re-examine, review.
reinspekto re-examination.
reinvesto rollover.
reiri to go back, return.
rejesi to reaffirm.
Rejnbarĝo Rhine barge.
Rejnlanda Rhineland. **Rejnlanda vino** Rhine wine.
Rejnlando Rhineland.
Rejno Rhine.
Rejnŝipo barge, Rhine barge.
rejso reis.
rejŝo ratio.
rejunigi to revitalize, make young again.
rejuniĝi to become young again.
rejetadi to bandy.
rejeti to reject, throw back.
rekantaĵo refrain (song).
rekapti to recapture.
rekaŝi to hide again.

reklama advertising. **reklama ĵargono** advertising language, ad-speak.
reklamacii to claim.
reklamacio complaint.
reklamado advertisement, advertising, promotion.
reklamagento advertising agent.
reklamaĵo advertisement.
reklamareo advertising space.
reklamfaco advertising space.
reklami to advertise.
reklamilo advertising tool, advertisement.
reklamindustrio advertising industry.
reklamisto adman.
reklamo ad, advert, advertisement.
reklampanelo billboard.
reklamteksto advertisement text, advertising copy.
reko horizontal bar.
Rekohoj Chatham Islands.
rekomenci to resume.
rekomenciĝi to restart.
rekomenda letero letter of introduction, letter of recommendation.
rekomendado advocacy.
rekomendanto advocate.
rekomendegi to commend highly.
rekomendi to commend, recommend, register. **rekomendi sin** to recommend oneself.
rekomendinda recommendable.
rekomendita recommended, registered. **rekomendita letero** registered letter.
rekomendo recommendation, testimonial.
rekompence as a recompense. **rekompence doni** to give for something (in exchange).
rekompenci to compensate, reward, recompense, remunerate, requite.
rekompenco compensation, reward.
rekonduki to bring back.
rekonebla recognizable.
rekoneble recognizably.
rekonfirmi to reaffirm.
rekoni to recognize.
rekonkeri to recapture.
rekono acknowledgement, recognition.
rekonsciigi to revive, rouse.
rekonsciiĝi to regain consciousness.
rekonsideri to reconsider.
rekonsidero review, revision.
rekonstruado reconstruction.
rekonstrui to reconstruct, rebuild.
rekonstruo reconstruction.
rekopii to recopy.
rekorda record.
rekordo record.
rekordulo record breaker, record holder.
rekrei to recreate.

rekremento dregs, grounds, husks, refuse, residue, waste.
rekrutado recruitment.
rekrutekzameno recruiting exam, entry exam.
rekruti to recruit.
rekrutigado recruitment.
rekrutigi to recruit.
rekrutigo recruit.
rekrutiĝi to be recruited.
rekrutinstruisto drill sergeant, teacher of recruits.
rekrutisto recruiter.
rekruto recruit.
rekta direct, straight, right, upright, erect. **rekta adresado** direct addressing. **rekta atingo** direct access. **rekta funkciado** online operation. **rekta intesto** rectum. **rekta krampo** square bracket. **rekta kurento** direct current. **rekta ligilo** hard link. **rekta matrico** rectangular matrix. **rekta objekto** direct object. **rekta parolo** direct speech. **rektaj krampoj** square brackets ([ ]).
rektangula rectangular.
rektangulilo square (tool).
rektangulo rectangle, right angle.
rektara ruled (surface).
rektatinga direct, random. **rektatinga memorilo** direct/random access store. **rektatinga memorilorganizo** direct organization. **rektatinga memoro** random access memory, RAM.
rekte directly, straight ahead, uprightly. **rekte antaŭen** straight ahead, straight along. **rekte super** directly above. **rekte tra** across, throughout.
rekteco integrity, rectitude, uprightness.
rektifebla rectifiable (curve).
rektifi to rectify.
rektifiki to rectify.
rektigi to align, put right, rectify, make right.
rektigilo rectifier.
rektigo straightening.
rektiĝi to stand upright, straighten.
rektiĝo straightening.
rektilo ruler.
rekto straight line.
rektoradjunkto vice principal.
rektoreco chancellorship, rectorship.
rektoro chancellor, rector (school).
rektumo rectum.
rektvica memoro queue.
rekulpo second offence.
rekulpulo backslider.
rekunigi to reunite, rejoin.
rekunigo reunion.
rekuniĝo reunion.
rekunmeti to replace, put back again.
rekunvenigi to reconvene.
rekunvoki to reconvene.
rekuperi to reuse, reprocess.
rekuraĝigi to cheer up, reassure.
rekursia nesting. **rekursia funkcio** recursive function. **rekursia proceduro** recursive procedure, recursive subroutine. **rekursie generebla aro** recursively enumerable set.
rekursio recursion.
rekurso recursion.
rekuŝiĝi to become reclined again, lay down again, lie back down.
rekviemo requiem.
rekviri to seize peremptorily, requisition.
rekvizicii to exact, requisition, seize.
rekvizicio requisition.
relajbremso servo-brake.
relajo relay.
relajso relay.
relanĉi to relaunch.
relanĉo comeback, relaunch.
relata modo subjunctive (gram).
relativa relative. **relativa adresado** relative addressing. **relativa adreso** relative address. **relativa eraro** relative error. **relativa sonsento** relative pitch.
relative fairly, rather, relatively.
relativeco relativity.
relativisma relativist.
relativismo relativism.
relegi to read again, read over again, reread.
relego review.
relerni to re-learn.
relevi to raise, resurrect, upraise.
relevigi to resurrect.
leveviĝi to get back up, rise again, resurrect oneself.
releviĝo resurrection.
relforko points (railway).
reliefigi to highlight, pinpoint.
reliefiĝi to bevel.
reliefo embossment, relief (raised out).
reliefstrio moulding.
religia religious. **religia promeso** vow (religious).
religiano believer.
religieco religiosity, religiousness.
religiema religious.
religiemo religiosity, religiousness.
religio religion.
religiulo devotee.
relikvo relic.
relikvujo casket, reliquary, shrine.
relo rail.
relokebla relocatable.
relvojo railway, railroad.
remaĉadi to ruminate (to chew the cud).

remaĉi to chew the cud, ponder, reflect on, ruminate.
remaĉulo ruminant.
remaĉuloj ruminants.
remado rowing.
remalfermi to reopen.
remalfermiĝi to reopen.
remanto rower.
remapi to remap.
remarŝi to retreat.
rembato oar stroke.
remboato rowboat.
remburaĵo padding, stuffing.
remburi to pad, upholster, stuff, justify.
remburisto upholsterer.
remburo justification.
remburso COD, collect on delivery.
rememora remembrance.
rememori to recall, recollect, remember.
rememoriga commemorative.
rememorigi to recall, remind.
rememorigilo reminder.
rememorigo recollection.
rememoriĝi to remember, recall.
rememoro recollection.
remendi to give a repeat order for, order a fresh supply of.
remeti to paddle (to row).
remi to row.
remilo oar.
remisto rower.
remizo garage.
remolado remoulade.
remonto remount.
remontri to redisplay.
remorki to tow.
remorko trailer.
remparo battlement, bulwark, rampart, mound.
remparzono enceinte.
rempieda web-footed.
remŝipego galley.
remŝipo galley.
remtero refectory.
rena renal.
renaĝi to swim back.
renaski to regenerate.
renaskiĝi to be born again.
renaskiĝo rebirth, renaissance.
renaskita born-again.
renasko regeneration.
rendevuejo meeting-place, rendezvous.
rendevui to make an appointment, meet, set a date.
rendevuo appointment, date, rendezvous.
rendimenta efficient.
rendimento efficiency, performance.
renedo pippin, reinette apple.
renegato deserter, renegade.

renegoci to renegotiate.
renegoco renegotiation.
Renesanco Renaissance.
renesanco renaissance.
renio rhenium.
renklodo greengage.
renkonita encountered, found, met.
renkonti to come across, encounter, meet, see. **renkonti hazarde** to meet by chance. **renkonti unu la alian** to meet each other, meet one another.
renkontiĝi to come together, meet together.
renkontiĝo meeting.
renkontito acquaintance.
renkonto encounter, meeting.
reno kidney.
renoma famous.
renomi to rename.
renomo fame, renown.
renonci to cancel.
renovigebla renewable.
renovigi to renew, renovate.
renovigo renewal, renovation.
rensebo kidney-suet.
rentgena X-ray.
rentgenilo X-ray screener.
rentgeno roentgen.
rento annuity, dividend, income, return, revenue.
rentulo fund holder, recipient (of income), stockholder.
rentumo interest.
renversado subversion.
renversaĵo inversion (in a permutation).
renverse backwards.
renversema subversive.
renversemulo subversive.
renversi to overthrow, turn, turn over, overturn, upset, reverse. **renversi veturile** to run into.
renversiĝi to upset, capsize, turn over.
renversitaite topsy-turvy.
renversite upside down.
renverso reversal, upheaval, upset.
reokazi to recur.
reokazo recurrence.
reokupado reoccupation.
reokupi to reoccupy.
reokupo reoccupation.
reordigi to put back into order.
reorganizado rationalization, reorganization.
reorganizi to rationalize, reorganize.
reorientiĝo reorientation.
reoriento reorientation.
reostato rheostat.
repacigebla reconcilable.
repacigi to reconcile. **repacigi perkise** to kiss and make up.

repaciĝebla reconcilable.
repaciĝi to make up, reconcile.
repaciĝo repacification.
repagi to reimburse, repay, refund.
repago retribution.
reparacio damages, redress.
reparoli to retort.
repaŝi to retrace.
repeli to drive back, repel, repulse.
repertuaro repertoire.
replandumi to resole (shoes, boots).
replanti to replant.
replenigi to cause to be complete again, make full again, replenish.
replenigo replenishment.
repliki to answer back, reply, retort.
repliko rejoinder, riposte, retort.
repo rap.
repondi to reply, answer.
reporti to carry back.
repostuli to demand back, reclaim.
repreni to abjure.
repreno retrieval.
represaĵo reprint.
representanto representative.
represi to reprint.
represio political repression.
represo reprint.
reprezalio reprisal, retaliation, sanction.
reprezentado representation.
reprezentanto representative, agent, emissary.
reprezenti to act for, represent.
reprezentita produced again, performed again, introduced again.
reproduktado reproduction.
reproduktaĵo reproduction.
reprodukti to render, reproduce.
reproduktiĝa reproductive.
reproduktiĝi to be reproduced.
reprodukto reproduction.
repso rep.
reptilio reptile.
repudii to repudiate.
repuŝado repression.
repuŝi to drive back, repel, repulse, keep at bay.
repuŝo recoil (of a gun, e.g.).
reputacio reputation.
rericevi to regain.
rerigardi to look again.
resaltema springy.
resalti to bounce, jump back, rebound, ricochet.
resaltigi to bank, bounce.
resalto bounce, recoil, ricochet.
resaluto return greeting, an act of greeting in response to an act of greeting initiated by someone else.

resaniga healing.
resanigi to cure, heal, remedy, make well.
resanigilo cure, medicine, remedy.
resanigo healing.
resaniĝanto convalescent (man).
resaniĝi to get better, heal, recover, get well.
resaniĝo convalescence.
Resaniĝu Get well soon.
resedo mignonette.
resekvi to retrace.
resendadreso return address.
resendi to send back.
resendo return.
residigi to seat again, set back down.
residiĝi to settle.
reskribi to rewrite.
reskripto decree, rescript.
resona resonant.
resonado resonance.
resonanci to resonance.
resonanco resonance.
resoni to clank, echo, resound.
resonilo cavity resonator, resonating chamber, resonator.
resono echo, resonance.
resovaĝiĝi to become wild again.
resp. → **respektive**.
respeguli to mirror, reflect.
respeguliĝo reflection.
respekta respectful.
respektatesto accolade.
respektegi to revere, venerate.
respektego deference, veneration.
respektema dutiful.
respekteme respectfully.
respekti to respect.
respektinda respectable, venerable.
respektindeco deference, devotion, respect.
respektiva respective.
respektive as the case may be, respectively.
respekto respect.
respektoj regards (respects).
respeltinda respectable.
resperti to relive.
respiriga kuracado artificial respiration.
responda accountable, responsible, liable, corresponding (angle).
respondado answering, replying.
respondaĵo repartee.
respondantaro panel.
respondanto panelist.
respondaparato answering machine.
responde correspondingly. **responde al** with regards to.
respondeca accountable, responsible. **respondeca pri** accountable for.
respondecasekuro liability insurance.
respondece responsibly.

respondeci to account for, be answerable, be liable, be responsible, bear responsibility.
respondeci pri to be responsible for.
respondecigi to hold responsible, blame.
respondeco liability, responsibility.
respondema sensitive.
respondenda answerable, awaiting reply.
respondi to answer, reply, respond, retort.
respondi al to answer. **respondi jese** to reply affirmatively. **respondi pri** to be accountable for, answerable for.
respondigi to hold responsible. **respondigi pri** to call to account.
respondilo answering machine.
respondinto respondent.
respondkrii to call back, cry back, shout back.
respondkupono reply coupon.
respondo answer, reply, response.
respondotempo response time.
respondsistemo intelligence service.
responsi to account for, be answerable, be liable, be responsible, be responsible for.
respublika republican.
respublikano republican.
respubliko commonwealth, republic.
restadejo abode.
restadi to abide, dwell, reside.
restado stay.
restaĵejo dump, refuse dump, tip, rubbish tip.
restaĵo remainder, rest, remnant, balance, residue, remains.
restanta abiding, left, left over, remaining.
restarigi to restore.
restarigo restoration.
restartpunkto checkpoint.
restartrutino restart routine.
restaŭrado renovation, restoration.
restaŭri to renovate, restore.
restaŭrkopio backup file, recovery file.
resti to remain, stay, be left, stay over, sojourn, stop, rest. **resti anonima** to remain anonymous. **resti brulanta** to stay on (of a light). **resti dome** to stay at home. **resti en sia funkcio** to continue in office, remain in office, stay on. **resti fidela al** to remain faithful to. **resti ĝisdata** to keep abreast of. **resti korekta** to remain correct. **resti malantaŭe** to remain behind.
restigejo parking.
restigi to keep, leave, park.
restigo parking.
restinta remaining.
restloko place to stay.
resto remainder, rest.
restoo de n-modulaj restoklasoj residue class group.
restoraciisto restaurateur.

restoracio restaurant.
restrikti to confine, limit, restrict.
restrukturado restructuring.
restrukturi to restructure.
resumado abstraction, recapitulation.
resumi to abstract, summarize, sum up, recapitulate.
resumo abridgement, abstract, résumé, summary, epitome, synopsis.
resupreniri to reascend.
resurekti to resurrect, rise.
resurekto resurrection.
resuso rhesus.
reŝargi to recharge.
reŝargo reset.
reŝlosi to relock.
reŝtatigi to renationalize.
reŝtatigo renationalization.
reta network. **reta tavolo** network layer. **Reta Vortaro** Internet Dictionary (of Esperanto).
retadreso e-mail address.
retaĵo netting, network.
retamikino online friend.
retamiko online friend.
retanalizo network analysis.
retano netizen (Internet user), netter.
retejestro webmaster.
retejo internet page, web site.
retenado retention.
reteni to detain, hold back, retain.
reteno detention.
retfasonisto web designer.
retikulo graticule, reticle; handbag, purse.
retino retina.
retiri to draw back, withdraw.
retiriĝema unsociable.
retiriĝi to retreat.
retiriĝo retreat.
retiro withdrawal.
retkamerao webcam.
retkomerco e-commerce.
retkrimo cybercrime.
retlando cyberspace.
retletero e-mail.
retligo weblink.
retmesaĝo e-mail.
retmoroj netiquette.
retnodo host, host computer, node.
reto net, network.
retorika rhetorical.
retoriko oratory, rhetoric.
retoro rhetorician.
retorto retort (chemical vessel).
retotaglibro blog, weblog.
retpaĝaro site, website.
retpaĝo webpage.
retpoŝta e-mail. **retpoŝta adreso** e-mail address.

retpoŝt-adreso e-mail address.
retpoŝtajo e-mail.
retpoŝte by e-mail.
retpoŝti to (send an) e-mail.
retpoŝto e-mail.
retra backward.
retraktado reprocessing.
retranĉi to cut back.
retrankviliĝi to become calm again, get calm again.
retrati to withdraw (money).
retre backwards.
retregiono top-level domain.
retregistro weblog.
retren backwards.
retreti to retreat.
retreto retreat.
retro backwards.
retroa backward, backwards.
retroaktiva retroactive.
retroakumulajo backlog.
retroakumuli to backlog.
retroakumuliĝi to backlog.
retroakumuliĝo backup.
retroakvo backwater.
retrodati to antedate, backdate.
retroefika retroactive.
retroefiki to retroact.
retroflekso backbend.
retrofrapi to backlash.
retrofrapo backlash, backwash.
retroigi to backspace.
retroiĝi to backtrack.
retroira backward, retrograde. **retroira klavo** backspace key.
retroiri to backspace, back up, go backward, recede.
retroklavo backspace key.
retroklino backslash.
retrokuplado feedback.
retrokuplo feedback.
retrolaboro backlog.
retromutaciado back-mutation.
retronaĝado backstroke.
retropafi to backfire.
retropafo backfire.
retropaŝi to walk back, walk backwards.
retropaŝo backspace.
retropeli to back water.
retroprojekciilo overhead projector.
retroprojektado reverse engineering.
retroreakcio back reaction.
retroremi to back water.
retrorotacii to backspin.
retrorotaciigi to backspin.
retrorotacio backspin.
retroserĉo backwards search.
retrospegulo driving mirror.
retrospektiva retrospective.
retrospekto retrospect.
retrostebi to backstitch.
retrostebo backstitch.
retrotraduko decompilation, disassembly.
retrotrafi to backfire, ricochet.
retrovebla recoverable.
retrovi to find (again), recover. **retrovi la ekvilibron** to regain one's balance. **retrovi starpozicion** to stand back up.
retroviŝi to backspace.
retrovo recovery.
retumado surfing.
retumanto surfer.
retumi to surf the web.
retumilo browser.
returne back.
returni to return.
returniĝi to turn back.
returniĝo turnaround.
returnite inside out.
retuŝado adjusting.
retuŝi to retouch, touch up.
retuŝo alteration.
Reunio Reunion.
reunuigi to reunite.
reunuigo reunification.
reunuiĝo reunification.
reuzado recycling.
reuzi to recycle, reuse.
reŭmatisma rheumatic.
reŭmatismo rheumatism.
reva dreamy, in a reverie, lost in thought.
revado reverie.
revarmigi to warm up.
revbildo dream.
reve in a dream, dreamily.
reveki to reawaken.
revekiĝi to reawaken.
revelacii to reveal.
revelacio revelation.
revema dreamy, full of dreams.
revenadreso return address.
revendi to resell.
revendisto retailer.
revenĝa retaliatory.
revenĝi to retaliate.
revenĝo reprisals, retaliation, revenge.
reveni to come back, return.
revenigi to fetch, recall, return.
revenigo recall.
revenmarŝo tattoo.
reveno return.
revenordono return, return statement.
reverki to rewrite.
reversi to turn.
reverso back, reversal, reverse; tails, lapel.
revestigi to dress again.
reveti to ponder.
reveturi to travel back, go back.

reveturigi to take back (vehicle).
revi to dream, daydream, fancy, muse.
revidi to see again.
revido seeing again.
revigliga revitalizing.
revigligo revitalization.
revigliĝi to come to life again, revive.
revigliĝo revitalization.
revivigi to resuscitate, revive.
revivigo revival.
revivigoiĝo resurrection.
reviviĝi to return to life, be resurrected.
reviviĝo resurrection.
revizado auditing.
revizi to audit, inspect, overhaul, revise.
revizii to revise.
reviziismo revisionism.
reviziisto inspector.
revizio revision.
revizisto auditor.
reviziti to revisit.
revizo audit.
revizori to audit.
revizoro auditor, government inspector, inspector general.
revlando dreamland.
ReVo → **Reta Vortaro**.
revo dream, daydream, reverie.
revoki to revoke, call back.
revoko recall.
revolando dreamland.
revolucia revolutionary.
revolucio revolution.
revoluciulo revolutionary.
revolvero revolver.
revortigi to rephrase.
revui to review.
revulo day-dreamer, muser, dreamer.
revuo journal, magazine, periodical, review.
rezedo mignonette, reseda (type of fragrant herbaceous plant).
rezerva coy. **rezerva kopio** backup copy.
rezervado retention.
rezervaĵo auxiliary, backlog.
rezervano reservist.
rezerveco coyness.
rezervejo reservation, preserve, reserve.
rezervi to reserve, book.
rezervigi to book, reserve.
rezervigo booking.
rezervilo placeholder.
rezervita nomo reserved identifier.
rezervitarano reservist.
rezervitaro reserve.
rezervito reserve.
rezervo backup, reservation, reserve.
rezervostoki to stockpile.
rezervostoko stockpile.
rezervujo tank.

rezervulo backup.
rezida programo resident program.
rezidejo residence.
rezidi to reside.
reziduo breakdown product.
rezignacii to acquiesce, resign oneself.
rezignacio acquiescence, resignation.
rezignemo acquiescence, resignation, submission, defeatism.
rezigni to abandon, give up, resign, renounce, yield, renounce, surrender. **rezigni pri** to relinquish, renounce, waive.
rezigno cession, relinquishment, renunciation, surrender, resignation.
rezina resinous.
rezino resin.
rezista resistant, resistive, unyielding.
rezistado resistance.
rezistanco resistance.
rezistanto resister.
rezisti to resist, stand, withstand.
rezistlimo yield-point.
rezisto resistance.
rezistpovo stamina.
rezolucio motion, resolution.
rezoluta resolute.
rezolute resolutely.
rezona reasonable.
rezonadi postfakte to hold a post-mortem.
rezonado reasoning.
rezonegi to expostulate.
rezonema argumentative.
rezoni to discuss, argue, reason. **rezoni pri** to argue, discuss, reason about, reason upon.
rezono reasoning, logical argument.
rezultati to result.
rezultatigi to amount, result.
rezultato conclusion, effect, result.
rezulte consequently. **rezulte de** as a result of. **rezulte de kio** as a result.
rezulti to result.
rezultigi to bring about.
rezulto result.
Riado Riyadh.
ribeko rebec, rebeck (bowed string musical instrument).
ribela mutinous, rebellious, riotous.
ribelanto insurgent, mutineer, rebel.
ribelema insubordinate, rebellious.
ribelemulo Person inclined to rebel or revolt.
ribeletoado insubordination.
ribeli to rebel.
ribeligi to incite to rebel, stir up.
ribelo insurrection, mutiny, rebellion, revolt, sedition, riot.
ribeloado rebellion.
ribelulo rebel.
ribgelateno currant-jelly.

ribĝino black currant gin.
ribmarmelado currant jam.
ribo currant.
ribobero currant.
riboflavino riboflavin.
ribofolio currant leaf.
ribokremaĵo currant custard.
ribokustardo currant custard.
ribonuklea acido ribonucleic acid.
ribsuko currant juice.
ribujo currant (bush).
ricelanto receiver (of stolen goods), fence.
riceli to fence, receive (stolen goods).
ricelisto fence, receiver.
ricevanto consignee, receiver, recipient.
ricevatesto acknowledgement, receipt.
ricevavizo letter of advice.
ricevebla available.
ricevejo reception room.
ricevi to get, have, receive. **ricevi erektiĝon** to have an erection.
ricevilo receiver.
ricevinto recipient.
ricevo reception.
ricino castor oil plant.
riĉa affluent, rich, wealthy, well-off, well-to-do. **riĉa je** rich in. **riĉa rimo** rich rhyme.
riĉaĵo wealth. **riĉaĵoj** riches.
riĉe richly.
riĉeco abundance, affluence, wealth, fortune, opulence, riches.
riĉega affluent, immensely rich, rolling in money, very wealthy.
riĉiga enriching.
riĉigi to enrich.
riĉigo enrichment.
riĉiĝi to become rich, grow rich.
riĉo richness, rich thing.
riĉulo rich man, wealthy person.
ridaĉi to titter.
ridaĉo snigger, titter.
ridadi to laugh, keep laughing.
ridado laughter.
Ridamano Ammanford.
ridante laughingly.
ridegi to laugh loudly, roar with laughter.
ridego guffaw.
ridete smiling.
rideti to smile.
rideto smile.
ridi to laugh.
ridiga amusing, comedy.
ridigi to make someone laugh.
ridinda funny, laughable, ludicrous, ridiculous, droll.
ridindaĵo farce, joke, silliness.
ridinde ridiculously.
Ridinde! Ridiculous.
ridindeco risibility.
ridindigi to ridicule. **ridindigi sin** to make a fool of oneself.
ridmevo black-headed gull.
ridmieno smiley face.
ridmoki to sneer.
rido laugh.
rifo dangerous rocks, reef.
rifto rift.
rifugejo place of refuge.
rifuginto refugee.
rifuĝejo place of refuge, shelter, asylum, retreat.
rifuĝi to take refuge.
rifuĝinto refugee.
rifuĝo refuge.
rifuti to confute.
rifuzi to decline, refuse, reject. **rifuzi unu fojon por ĉiam** to refuse once and for all.
rifuzo refusal, rejection.
rigardaĉi to gape at.
rigardadi to contemplate.
rigardado examination.
rigardallogilo eye-catcher.
rigardante kontinenten looking towards the continent.
rigardanto beholder, spectator.
rigardegi to gaze, stare.
rigardeti to peep, pry, take a look at, have a glance at.
rigardi to consider, deem, look, look at, regard, see, view, watch. **rigardi ĉirkaŭen** to look around. **rigardi fikse** to gaze, peer, stare. **rigardi kiel** to consider, deem, see as. **rigardi kontraŭ sudo** to face south. **rigardi malsupren** to look down. **rigardi supren** to look up.
rigardo look.
rigi to rig.
rigida inflexible, rigid, stiff.
rigide rigidly, stiffly.
rigideco numbness, rigidity.
rigidemo rigidity, stiffness.
rigidi aeren to rise stiffly into the air.
rigidigi to numb.
rigidiĝi to stiffen.
rigidiĝo torpor.
rigidmiene starchily, stiffly.
rigidmora straightlaced.
rigidnuka intransigent, mulish, stiff-necked, obstinate, stubborn.
rigli to bolt, fasten.
riglilo bolt.
riglofermi to bar.
rigo rigging.
rigora rigorous, stringent.
rigore rigorously, severely, strictly, stringently.
rigoreco rigorousness, rigour, severity, strictness.

rigoro

rigoro rigour.
Rigvedo Rig-Veda.
rijeto potted mince, rillettes.
rikani to laugh derisively, sneer.
rikano sneer.
Rikardo Richard.
rikecio rickettsia.
rikiŝo rickshaw.
rikoltaĵo harvest.
rikolti to gather, harvest, reap. **rikolti rikoltojn** to harvest crops.
rikoltileto billhook, reaping-hook, sickle.
rikoltilo sickle.
rikolto crop, harvest.
rikoltojaro vintage (wine).
rikoltosezono harvest season.
rikorda kazo variant.
rikordo record.
rikordotipo record type.
rikura recurrent.
rikuro induction.
rilakso relaxation.
rilata relational. **rilata datumbazo** relational data base. **rilata operacio** relational operator.
rilatato antecedent.
rilate as to, as regards, concerning, with respect to. **rilate al** in regard to, referring to, toward, towards, with reference to.
rilateco application, relevance.
rilati to concern, relate.
rilatigi to ally.
rilatigo association.
rilato correspondence, quotient, ratio, relation. **rilato de ekvivalento** equivalence relation.
rilatsimbolo relational operator.
rilatumo proportion, rate, ratio.
Rilo Rhyl.
rilo reel.
rim. → **rimarkigo**.
rimaĉo bad rhyme.
rimana Riemann, Riemannian. **rimana integralo** Riemann integral.
Rimano Riemann.
rimaranĝo rhyme arrangement.
rimarkebla appreciable, marking, noticeable, perceptible.
rimarkeble markedly.
rimarki to note, notice, observe, remark.
rimarkigi to call attention to, observe, remark. **rimarkigi al** to bring to someone's attention. **rimarkigi al mi** to bring to my attention.
rimarkigo remark.
rimarkinda noteworthy, remarkable, prominent.
rimarkinde noticeably, remarkably.
rimarko notice, observation, remark.

ripetita

rimaro rhyming dictionary.
rimedaro pack.
rimedo means, remedy, resources. **rimedoj** means.
rimenligi to strap.
rimeno band, strap, belt.
rimensandalo thong.
rimesi to remit.
rimeso remittance.
rimi to rhyme.
rimigi to rhyme.
rimiĝi to rhyme.
rimo rhyme.
rimoido approximate rhyme, assonant rhyme, imperfect rhyme, near rhyme, oblique rhyme, off rhyme, slant rhyme.
rimorso remorse.
rimvortaro rhyming dictionary.
rinanto rattle.
ringa annular. **ringa eklipso** annular eclipse.
ringeca annular.
ringego hoop.
ringeto annulet.
ringforma annular.
ringo ring. **ringo de n-modulaj restoklasoj** residue class ring.
ringobeka mevo ring-billed gull.
ringofingro ring finger.
ringokajero ring binder.
ringokolombo wood pigeon.
ringokolubro grass-snake, ring-snake.
rinito cold.
rinkani to grin knowingly, sneer.
rinkoforo weevil.
rinocero rhino, rhinoceros.
Rio-de-Ĵanejro Rio de Janeiro.
Riodeĵanejro Rio de Janeiro.
Riogrando Rio Grande.
ripaĵo spare ribs.
riparado repair.
riparebla recoverable.
ripareco restoration.
riparejo workshop.
ripari to fix, repair, mend, redress, amend, restore.
riparisto repairman.
riparo reparation, repair.
riparpago reparation.
ripeta repeating.
ripetadi to reiterate.
ripetado iteration, repetition.
ripetfoje repeatedly.
ripeti to recapitulate, rehearse, repeat, reiterate.
ripetiĝanta recurring.
ripetiĝi to recur, repeat oneself, be repeated.
ripetiĝo pattern.
ripetita repeated.

ripeto repeat.
ripetsigno mark of repetition (⁋, ‖).
ripo rib.
ripoze at ease.
ripozeco rest, quietude.
ripozejo lounge, resting place, waiting room.
ripozeto respite.
ripozi to repose, rest.
ripozigi to rest (something).
ripozo repose, rest.
ripozpurigi to decant.
riproĉa reproachful. **riproĉa rimarko** observation, remark.
riproĉadmono reproof.
riproĉe reproachfully.
riproĉeblinda objectionable.
riproĉegi to scold.
riproĉeti to tweak.
riproĉi to blame, rebuke, reproach, reprove, scold, reprimand. **riproĉi malafable** to snap at, snarl at, snub.
riproĉinda reprehensible.
riproĉinde reprehensibly.
riproĉo censure, rebuke, reproach, reprimand.
riska adventurous, hazardous, risky, venturous.
riskeco riskiness.
riskema risky, hazardous, venturesome, daring.
riski to hazard, risk, venture.
risko hazard, risk, venture.
riskogrupo risk group.
riskoplena adventuresome.
rismo ream (paper).
risolo rissole.
risorteca springy.
risorteco bounce.
risorto spring (mech.).
ristorni to refund, reimburse.
ristorno collateral, dividend, refund, reimbursement, security.
risurco resource.
rita ritual, ritualistic. **rita sinlavo** ablution.
ritaro ritual.
riteca ritualistic.
ritidektomio facelift, rhytidectomy.
ritismo ritualism.
ritlibro ritual, book of devotions, formulary.
ritma rhythmic.
ritme rhythmically.
ritmo rhythm.
rito rite.
rivali to rival.
rivalo rival.
rivelado developing.
riveli to develop, reveal.
riveliĝi to be revealed.

rivera of a river, stream. **rivera cervo** water deer.
riverbano bath taken in a river.
riverbordo riverbank.
riverdelfeno manatee.
riverego large river.
riverenci to bow, curtsy, make reverence to.
riverenco bow, curtsy, obeisance, homage, reverence.
rivereta small river, creek, stream.
rivereto brook, rill, rivulet, stream.
rivermaŝo bayou.
rivero river.
riverujo river-bed.
Rivervalo Riverdale.
Riviero Italian Riviera.
rivolua (body, surface) of revolution.
rivoluo revolution.
rizalkoholaĵo rice wine.
rizero grain of rice.
rizkampo paddy field, rice field.
rizkampulo paddy field, rice field.
rizkulturisto rice-farmer.
rizo rice.
rizokampo rice field.
rizomo rhizome.
rizopelvo rice bowl.
rizoplanto rice plant.
rizoto risotto.
rizpajla (made of) rice straw.
rizpajlo rice straw.
rizvino sake, rice wine.
rizvolvaĵo rice wrap.
ro name of the letter R.
robaio rubaiyat.
robĉambro robing room.
Roberto Robert.
robi to robe.
robinio false acacia.
robo dress, gown, robe.
robotiko robotics.
roboto robot.
robro rubber.
robusta able-bodied, burly, firm, resistant, robust, rugged, solid, strong, sturdy, tough.
Rodano Rhone.
Rodesio Rhodesia.
Rodezio Rhodesia.
rodi to gnaw, nibble.
rodinsulano Rhode Islander.
rodio rhodium.
rodo anchorage, moorage, mooring.
rododendro Alpenrose, rhododendron.
Rodotaŭno Road Town.
Roĝero Roger.
roho roc.
rojalismo royalism.
rojalisto royalist.
rojeto brooklet, rill, rivulet.

rojo brook, stream.
roka rocky, stony.
rokaro group of rocks.
rokego boulder.
rokenrolo rock-and-roll.
rokeroj breccia.
rokgrupo Rock Group.
rok-katedralo rock cathedral.
rokkolombo rock dove.
Rokmontaro Rocky Mountains.
rokmuziko rock music.
roko rock; rock music.
rokoko rococo.
rokrubuso stone blackberry, stone bramble.
roksaksikolo wheatear.
rokuo bixin.
rolado characterization.
rolanto character (in play, etc.).
roli to play a role. **roli kiel** to act as.
rolludaĵo role-play.
rolo character, part, role, rôle (acting).
rolulo character.
rolvorto preposition.
roma Roman. **romaj cifroj** Roman numerals.
romana of a novel, related to a novel.
romancisto ballad-writer.
romanco romance (music, song).
romanĉa Romansch.
romaneco ballad, ballade.
romania Roman.
romaniano Roman.
romanika Romanesque.
romaniko Romanesque.
Romanio Roman Empire.
romanisto fiction writer, novelist.
Romano Roman.
romano novel (romance).
romantika romantic.
romantikisma romantic.
romantikismo romanticism.
romantikisto romantic.
romantiko romanticism.
romantikulo romantic.
romantismo romanticism.
romba argyle.
rombeto brill.
rombfiŝo turbot.
rombforma rhomboid, diamond-shaped.
rombo rhomb, rhombus.
romboedro rhombohedron.
rombofiŝo turbot.
romboido rhomboid.
romia Roman. **romiaj restaĵoj** Roman ruins.
romiano Roman.
Romio Ancient Rome, Roman Empire.
romkatolika Roman Catholic.
Romo Rome.

rompado breach.
rompaĵo bit, wreckage.
rompebla fragile.
rompi to break. **rompi la kruron** to break one's leg. **rompi promeson** to break a promise.
rompiĝaĵo wreckage.
rompiĝema breakable, brittle, fragile.
rompiĝemo brittleness, fragility.
rompiĝi to break.
rompiĝinta broken.
rompiĝo break.
rompilo breaker.
rompita broken. **rompita linio** broken line.
rompitaĵo bit, broken piece.
rompo fracture, rupture. **rompo de la paco** disturbing the peace.
rompoletero "Dear John" letter.
rompopeco wreckage.
rompŝtelisto burglar.
rompŝtelo burglary.
ronda round. **ronda krampo** parenthesis, round bracket. **rondaj krampoj** round parentheses, (( )).
rondbuŝuloj cyclostomes.
rondcifere round numbers (in).
ronde roundly.
rondelo rondel, rondo.
rondeto circle, small group, circlet.
rondfolia round-leaved.
rondforma round (form).
rondigi to round, round off.
rondigo rounding.
rondiri to circle, circumvent, go around, go round.
Rondo Rhondda.
rondo circle, ring, round.
rondodanco round dance.
rondspaco round area, circular area.
rondvojaĝi to tour.
rondvojaĝo tour.
ronĝi to gnaw, nibble.
ronĝulo rodent.
ronka hoarse, husky, harsh.
ronkado snoring.
ronki to snore.
ronroni to purr.
ronrono purr.
roo rho (Ρρ).
rosino raisin.
Roskomono Roscommon.
Roskrio Roscrea.
Roslaro Rosslare.
rosmareno rosemary.
rosmaro sea horse, walrus.
roso dew.
rosrubuso dewberry.
rostaĵo roast (meat).

rostbefo roast beef.
rostbifo roast beef.
rosteti to brown.
rostfesto barbecue.
rosti to broil, roast, toast.
rostiĝi to roast.
rostilo broiler, roaster.
rostita roasted.
rostkrado barbecue grill.
rostofesto barbecue.
rostostango spit, turnspit.
rostpano toast, toasted bread.
rostpato pan, baking pan.
rostreto stigma (botany).
rostro proboscis, snout, trunk, sucker.
rostrofoko sea-elephant.
rostujo baking tin, pan, baking pan.
rotacia (body, surface) of revolution. **rotacia akso** axis of rotation. **rotacia centro** centre of rotation.
rotaciangulo angle of rotation.
rotacii to rotate.
rotaciigi to rotate.
rotacio rotation. **rotacio de kulturoj** crop rotation.
rotango rattan.
Rotario Rotary.
Roterdamo Rotterdam.
rotiĝi to band together.
roto[1] company, gang, squad, detachment.
roto[2] rho (Pρ).
rotondo rotunda.
rotoro rotor.
rovero rover, venturer.
roza pink, rosy. **roza flamengo** flamingo.
rozacoj Rosaceae.
rozalteo hollyhock.
rozarbeto rosebush.
rozarbusto rose bush.
rozario litany, rosary.
rozbero rose hip.
rozeolo measles.
roziĝi to become rosy, blush.
rozkolora pink (colour), rose-coloured.
rozkoloro pink.
rozo rose. **rozo sovaĝa** briar, sweet briar.
rozoleo attar of roses.
rozujo rose.
rpk. → **respondkupono**.
ruanda Rwandan.
ruandano Rwandan.
Ruando Rwanda.
rubanda matrico band matrix, banded matrix.
rubando ribbon.
rubaŭto garbage truck.
rubejo garbage dump.
rubekolo robin.
rubeno ruby.

rubeolo German measles.
rubidio rubidium.
Rubikono Rubicon.
rubio madder.
rubisto sanitation worker.
rublo ruble (Russian unit of currency).
rubo debris, rubbish, rubble, garbage, trash, junk.
ruboaĵo debris.
ruboj rubbish, old materials.
rubrikisto columnist.
rubriko column, header, rubric, section.
rubujo garbage can, trash can.
rubusarbusto bramble.
rubusbero blackberry.
rubuso blackberry, blackberry bush, bramble.
rubusujo bramble.
rudbekio rudbeckia (plant genus in the Asteraceae family).
rudimenta elementary, rudimentary, vestigial.
rudimento rudiment.
Rudolflago Lake Rudolf.
rudro rudder.
rufa ginger, red, russet, rust-coloured, roan.
rufflanka emberizo eastern towhee.
rugbeo rugby.
rugino xyster.
ruĝa red, ruddy, rosy, blushing. **ruĝa alarmo** red alert. **ruĝa anagalo** scarlet pimpernel. **ruĝa cervo** red deer. **Ruĝa Kruco** Red Cross. **Ruĝa Maro** Red Sea. **ruĝa ribo** currant, red currant. **Ruĝa Rivero** Red River. **ruĝa sangoĉelo** erythrocyte, red blood cell.
ruĝalgo red alga. **ruĝalgoj** red algae.
ruĝa-ribgelatenaĵo currant jelly.
Ruĝbarbulo Redbeard, Barbarossa.
ruĝbarbulo red-bearded person.
ruĝbruna auburn. **ruĝbruna emberizo** chestnut bunting.
ruĝbruno auburn.
ruĝebrune reddish brown.
ruĝeco redness, ruddiness.
ruĝega crimson, florid.
ruĝeta reddish.
ruĝgorĝo redbreast.
ruĝgorĝulo redbreast, robin, robin redbreast.
ruĝhaŭtulo redskin.
ruĝigi to blush, redden.
ruĝigiĝi to redden.
ruĝigilo lipstick.
ruĝiĝema bashful.
ruĝiĝi to blush, redden, make red.
ruĝilo paint (rouge).
ruĝkrura tringo redshank.
Ruĝkufulineto Little Red Riding Hood.
ruĝo red.

ruĝsciuro red squirrel.
ruĝulo red(-skinned) man.
ruĝvosta emberizo fox sparrow.
rui to ret, steep.
ruina ruinous.
ruinaĵo ruin, remains.
ruinego perdition.
ruiniga disastrous.
ruinigi to desolate, lay waste, ravage, ruin, devastate.
ruinigo havoc.
ruiniĝi to fall (in ruins).
ruiniĝo decay.
ruino ruin.
ruk heave ho.
rukti to belch, burp.
rukto belch, burp, eructation.
rukuli to coo.
rulado bowling.
rulaĵo volvaĵo coil.
rulata rolled, trilled.
rulbloko block, pulley.
ruldomo camper (vehicle), trailer, mobile home.
rulejo lane.
ruleto roulette.
rulfali to somersault, tumble.
rulfalo somersault, tumble.
rulfari to roll.
ruli to roll, run.
ruliĝado rolling.
ruliĝi to roll, wallow.
rulilo roller, truckle, trundle.
rulknedilo rolling pin.
rulkurteno roller blind, window blind.
rulo roll, run.
rulpapero scroll.
rulpeniko pan.
rulpenikujo roller.
rulpilkludo bowls.
rulpremi to roll.
rulpremilo steam-roller.
rulseĝo wheelchair.
rulsketilo roller skate.
rulŝtuparo escalator.
rulŝuo roller skate.
rultempa run time. **rultempa eraro** run-time error. **rultempa sistemo** run-time system.
rulumi to roll, scroll.
rulumskalo scroll bar.
rumana Romanian.
rumanĉa Romance, Romanche.
Rumanĉa Romanche.
rumanino Romanian woman.
Rumanio Romania.
rumano Romanian.
Rumanujo Romania.

rume with rum, using rum.
rumekso dock (botany), sorrel.
rumio rummy.
rumo rum.
rumoro din, racket, hubbub.
rumpsteko rump steak.
rumsteko rump steak.
runa runic.
runo rune.
rupio rupee.
rura rural.
Ruro Ruhr.
ruro rural areas, countryside.
Rurvalo Ruhr.
rusa Russian. **rusa ekinopso** globe-thistle. **rusa lingvo** Russian, Russian language. **rusa nobelo** boyar, boyard. **rusa trikorda gitaro** balalaika.
ruse in Russian (language).
Rusia Federacio Russian Federation.
rusigi to Russify, make Russian.
rusino Russian woman.
Rusio Russia.
rusko butcher's broom, Ruscus aculeatus.
Ruslanda Russian. **Ruslanda Federacio** Russian Federation. **Ruslanda Imperio** Russian Empire.
Ruslando Russia.
ruso Russian.
rusta rusty.
rustaĵo rust.
rusti to rust.
rustiĝi to rust.
rustika rustic.
rustikeco rusticity, rusticalness.
rustimuna rustproof.
rusto rust.
Rusujo Russia.
ruŝo ruche, ruching.
rutenio ruthenium.
Rutenujo Ruthenia.
ruterfordio rutherfordium.
rutina routine.
rutinhava expert, skilled, proficient, fluent.
rutino routine, habit.
Ruto Ruth.
ruto rue.
Rutuno Ruthin.
ruza artful, crafty, sly, astute, clever, cunning, smart.
ruzaĵo ruse, stratagem, trick.
ruzeco cunning, subtlety, slyness.
ruzi to be crafty.
ruzo craft, cunning, ruse, trick, stratagem, wile.
ruzulo clever person, cunning person, sly person.

S

S-a Tomaso St Thomas Aquinas.
sabate on Saturday.
sabatnokte on Saturday night.
Sabato Saturday.
sabato Sabbath, Saturday.
sabeko sackbut.
sabeliko Savoy (cabbage).
sabla sand, of sand. **sabla horloĝo** sand clock, hour glass. **sablaj montetoj** downs.
sablaĵo sandbank.
sablego grit.
sablero grain of sand.
sabli to sand.
sablo sand.
sablobenko bank, sandbank.
sablocerastio mouse-ear chickweed.
sablofleo sand catstail.
sablohorloĝo hourglass.
sablokastelo sandcastle.
sablokolora sand-coloured.
sabloludejo sandbox.
sablopapero sandpaper.
sabloŝtono sandstone.
sabloŝtormo sandstorm.
sabloŝuti to sand.
saboti to sabotage.
sabri to hack, slash.
sabro sabre.
sabrobati to slash.
sacerdoceco priesthood.
sacerdota priestly.
sacerdotino priestess.
sacerdoto priest.
sadisma sadistic.
sadismo sadism.
sadista sadistic.
sadisto sadist.
sadukeo Sadducee.
safario safari.
safiro sapphire.
safismo lesbianism, sapphism.
safrano saffron.
sagaca acute, astute, shrewd, ingenious, shrewd.
sagace ingeniously, shrewdly.
sagaceco acuity, acumen, acuteness, discernment, shrewdness.
sagao saga.
sagetludo darts.
sageto dart.
sagi to dart.
sagisto archer.
sagitario arrowhead. **Sagitario** Sagittarius (zodiac).
sago arrow, dart.
sagoforma arrowheaded.
sagoklavo arrow key.
sagopinto arrowhead.
sagujo quiver.
saguo sago.
saĝa sagacious, sage, wise, sensible.
saĝe with wisdom, wisely.
saĝeco wisdom.
saĝema wise.
saĝiĝi to become wise.
saĝo wisdom.
saĝodento wisdom tooth.
saĝulo wise person, sage.
saĝumi to act wise, show off, split hairs.
sahara Saharan.
Saharo Sahara.
Saĥaleno Saghalien, Sakhalin.
sairo pacific saury.
Sajgono Saigon.
ŝajnigi to pretend, give the appearance of.
sakarino saccharine.
sakarozo sucrose.
sakego large bag, large sack.
sakeo sake.
saketo pouch, satchel.
sakfajfilo bagpipe(s).
sakfluto bagpipe.
sakfungoj sac fungi.
sako bag, sack, wallet.
sakperuko bag wig.
Sakramenta Tago Corpus Christi.
sakramento sacrament.
sakri to curse, cuss, swear.
sakrilegia sacrilegious.
sakrilegii to commit sacrilege.
sakrilegio sacrilege.
sakrilegiulo sacrilegist.
sakristio sacristy, vestry.
sakro bad language, curse, expletive, obscenity, profanity, sacrum.
saksa Saxon.
saksifragacoj saxifrage.
saksifrago saxifrage.
saksikolo stonechat.
Saksio Saxe, Saxony.
Sakso Saxon.
sakso Saxon.
saksofono saxophone.
sakstrato cul-de-sac, dead-end street.
Saksujo Saxe, Saxony.
sakŝalmi to pipe.
sakŝalmo bagpipes.
saktolo sackcloth.
sakuro cherry blossom.
sakvojo blind alley, cul-de-sac.

sala briny, saline, salty. **sala akvo** salt water.
Saladino Saladin.
salafismo Salafism.
salafisto Salafist.
salajraltigo pay raise.
salajri to employ, pay a salary.
salajro salary, wage, wages, stipend.
salajroĉeko paycheck.
salajrosumo pay rate.
salajrulo employee, salaried person.
salaĵo brine.
salamandro salamander.
salamara brackish.
salamo salami.
salamoniako sal-ammoniac.
salangana supo bird's nest soup.
salato salad.
salatosaŭco salad dressing.
salbovaĵo salted beef.
saldi to balance (account). **saldi konton** to settle an account.
saldo balance (account).
saleco saltiness.
salero grain of salt.
salesiana Salesian.
salesiano Salesian.
saleta brackish.
sali[1] to salt.
sali[2] to leap.
salicilato salicylate.
salikaĵo wicker.
saliko willow.
salikoketo shrimp.
salikoko prawn, shrimp.
salimposto salt duty.
Salisburgo Salisbury.
salita corned.
saliva salivary.
salivi to salivate.
salivo saliva.
salivŝtona malsano sialolithiasis.
salivtuketo bib.
salivtuko bib (for babies).
salivumi to salivate, slobber.
salmo salmon.
salo salt.
Salomono Solomon.
Salomonoj Solomon Islands.
salona danco ballroom dancing.
salono drawing room, living room, parlour, salon, sitting room.
salpetro nitre, saltpetre.
salpigloso salpiglossis.
salpingo Fallopian tube.
saltantilopo springbok.
saltataki to leap upon, pounce upon, spring upon.
saltegi to leap.
saltego great leap, great jump.
saltetadoludo hopscotch.
salteti to frisk, hop, skip.
salteto hop.
salti to jump, leap, spring, bounce, bound, vault.
saltiero Saint Andrew's cross, saltire.
saltmuso jerboa.
salto bound, jump, leap, spring.
saltotabulo diving board, springboard.
salubra healthy, salubrious.
salujo saltshaker.
saluta ŝelo login shell.
salutado greeting, salutation.
saluti to greet, salute, bow. **saluti militiste** to salute.
salutnomo login name.
saluto bow, greeting, salutation, salute.
saluton! hello!
Salvadoro El Salvador.
salvarsano arsphenamine.
salvio sage (botany).
salvo salvo.
Salzburgo Salzburg.
sama same, ditto.
samaĝa of the same age.
samaĝula grupo age bracket, age group, age range.
samaĝulo contemporary, person of the same age.
samaĵo same stuff, same material.
samaksa coaxial.
samamaniere in the same way.
samampleksa of the same size, co-extensive.
samarea of the same area.
samaria Samaritan.
samariano Samaritan.
Samario Samaria.
samario samarium.
samaritano Samaritan.
Samarkando Samarkand.
samaspekta lookalike.
samavedo Samaveda.
sambalo sambal.
sambao samba.
sambuko elder (tree).
samcentra concentric.
samĉambrano roommate.
same equally, likewise. **same ... kiel** as ... as. **same al vi!** the same to you! **same kiel** the same as. **same kiel ni** just like us.
samea Sami; (dated) Lapp, Lappish.
samebena coplanar.
sameco sameness.
sameino Sami woman; (dated) Lappish woman.
sameo Sami, Laplander; (dated) Lapp.
samesenca consubstantial.
samfaza in phase.

samgepatrido sibling.
samgo sangha.
sami to be the same.
samideano fellow-thinker, fellow Esperantist.
samizdato samizdat.
samkiel in the same way as.
samklasano classmate.
samklubano member of the same club.
samlandano compatriot, countryman.
samlatera adjacent (angle).
samlernejano pupil of the same school, schoolmate.
samlima neighbouring.
samlime contiguously.
samlimeco contiguity.
samloke in the same place.
sammaniere in the same way.
sammatene the same morning.
sammomenta contemporary, live, simultaneous.
sammomente at the same time, at that very moment.
samnatureco connaturality.
samnoma homonym.
samnomulo namesake.
samo same.
samoa Samoan.
samoano Samoan.
samoficano counterpart.
samolo brookweed.
Samoo Samoa.
samopinii to agree. **samopinii kun** to agree with.
samopiniiĝo consensus.
samovaro samovar.
sampano sampan.
sampeza of the same weight.
sampio sampi (ϟϞ).
sampoentiĝi to draw.
sampoentiĝo draw.
sampova equipotent.
samprofesiano colleague.
samrange at the same level.
samrekta collinear.
samreligiano co-religionist.
samsanga consanguineous.
samsanguloj blood relatives.
samseksama homosexual, gay, queer.
samseksamo homosexuality.
samseksamulo homosexual.
samseksema homosexual.
samseksemulo homosexual.
samsenca synonymous.
samsencaĵo synonym.
samsigna of the same sign.
samsignifa synonymous, having the same meaning.
samspeca similar.
samstate in the same state, condition.

samtage on the same day.
samtavola komunikado peer-to-peer.
samteamano teammate.
samtempa coincident, contemporary, simultaneous, synchronized, synchronous.
samtempano contemporary.
samtempe at once, at the same time. **samtempe kun** at the same time as.
samtempeco synchronicity.
samtempigo synchronization.
samtempiĝi to draw.
samtempiĝo draw.
samtempulo contemporary.
samtiel kiel in the same way as.
samumo simoom.
samurajo samurai.
samurbano fellow citizen.
samvolumena of the same volume.
sana healthy, well.
sanatorio sanatorium.
sandalo sandal.
sandro pike-perch, zander.
sandviĉo sandwich.
sane healthily.
sanfojno sainfoin.
Sanfrancisko San Francisco.
sanga bloody.
sangadi to bleed.
sangado haemorrhage.
sangadulto incest.
sangalfluo congestion, rush.
sanganalizo blood test.
sangavida bloodthirsty, sanguinary.
sangbulo blood clot.
sange bloodily.
sangelfluo extravasation of blood.
sangellasi to bleed.
sangellaso bleeding, bloodletting.
sangeltiri to bleed.
sangero drop of blood.
Sangero Sanger.
sangi to bleed.
sangigi to bleed.
sangkolbaso black pudding, blood sausage.
sangmanko anaemia.
sango blood.
sangobanko blood bank.
sangocirkulado blood circulation.
sangoĉelo blood cell.
sangoĉesiga styptic.
sangodonaco blood donation.
sangodonanto blood-donor.
sangoglobeto blood corpuscle.
sangogrupo blood type.
sangoguto drop of blood.
sangohaltiga styptic.
sangohundo Saint Hubert hound, bloodhound, sleuth-hound.
sangokolbaso black pudding, blood sausage.

sangokolora blood-red.
sangokovrita blood-stained, covered with blood.
sangomakulita blood-stained, covered with blood.
sangomakulo bloodstain.
sangomanka anemic, bloodless, pale.
sangomanko anaemia.
sangoperdo loss of blood.
sangoplasmo blood plasma.
sangopremateco blood pressure.
sangopremo blood pressure.
sangopuriga blood-cleansing.
sangopurigilo abluent.
sangorezervejo blood bank.
sangoricevanto blood recipient.
sangoruĝa blood red.
sangosuĉa blood-sucking.
sangosukero blood sugar.
sangotesto blood test.
sangotransfuzo blood transfusion.
sangovaskulo blood vessel.
sangovazo blood vessel.
sangovenenigo blood-poisoning.
sangoverŝado bloodbath.
sangoverŝo bloodshed.
sangrero blood cell.
sangtensio blood-pressure.
sangtubo blood vessel.
sangvejno blood vessel.
sangverŝo flow (of blood).
sangverŝoado bloodshed.
sangvina sanguine.
sani to be well.
saniga healthy, healing, salubrious, wholesome.
sanigi to cure, heal, remedy, make well.
sanigilejo drugstore, pharmacy.
sanigilujo first-aid kit.
sanigo healthcare.
saniĝi to become healthy, get well.
saniklo sanicle.
sanilo cure, medicine, remedy.
sanitara concerning health, sanitary.
sanitaristo attendant.
sankciado sanction.
sankcii to authorize, permit, sanction.
sankcio authorization, official approval, penalty, permission, reward, sanction.
sankorpa able-bodied.
sankta holy, sacred, saintly. **Sankta Biblio** the Holy Bible. **Sankta Ĵaŭdo** Maundy Thursday. **Sankta Manĝo** Last Supper. **Sankta Nikolao** Saint Nicholas, St. Nicholas. **sankta oleo** chrism. **sankta restaĵo** relic (sacred). **Sankta Roma Imperio Ĝermana** Holy Roman Empire. **Sankta Semajno** Holy Week. **Sankta Skribaĵo** Holy Scripture. **Sankta Skribo** Holy Scripture. **Sankta Skripto** Holy Scripture. **Sankta Spirito** Holy Ghost, Holy Spirit. **Sankta Vendredo** Good Friday. **Sankta vespermanĝo** Lord's Supper. **Sanktageorga Markolo** Saint George's Channel.
sanktago holy deed.
sanktaĵo holy object, sacred object.
sanktakvujo stoup.
sankteco godliness, holiness, sacredness, sanctity.
sanktejo sanctuary, sanctum, tabernacle.
Sanktgotarda Montpasejo Saint Gotthard pass.
sanktiga sanctifying.
sanktigi to hallow, make holy, sanctify.
sanktigo sanctification.
sanktiĝi to become holy.
sanktoleado administration of the last sacraments.
sanktolei to administer the last sacraments.
sanktoleito annointed one.
Sankt-Peterburgo Saint Petersburg.
sanktproklamo canonization.
sanktrestaĵo holy relic.
sanktula saintly.
Sanktulara Festo All Hallows, All Saints' Day.
sanktuleco saintliness.
sanktuliĝi to become a saint.
sanktuliniĝi to become a saint.
sanktulino saint.
sanktulo saint.
Sanmarino San Marino.
sano[1] health.
sano[2] san (M_M).
s-ano → **samideano**.
sanplena salutary.
Sansalvadoro San Salvador.
sanseviero sansevieria.
Sanskrito Sanskrit.
sanskrito Sanskrit.
sanstato state of health.
santalo sandalwood.
santolino lavender-cotton.
Santomeo São Tomé. **Santomeo kaj Principeo** São Tomé and Príncipe.
sanulo healthy person.
sapei to sap, undermine.
sapejo soap dish.
sapfa Sapphic.
sapindo soapberry.
sapo soap.
saponario soapwort.
saprofito saprophyte.
sapumaĵo lather.
sapumi to lather, soap.
sapveziko soap bubble.
sarabando sarabanda.

sardelo anchovy, sardine (pickled).
sardinia Sardinian.
Sardinio Sardinia.
sardino sardine.
Sardio Sardinia.
Sardlando Sardina.
sardo Sardinian.
sardona sarcastic, sardonic.
Sardujo Sardinia.
sargaso gulf-weed, sargasso.
sario sari.
sariro sarira.
sarkasma sarcastic, sardonic.
sarkasme sarcastically.
sarkasmo sarcasm.
sarki to hoe, weed, weed out.
sarkilo hoe, weeding hook, weeder, weeding tool.
sarkindaĵo garbage, refuse, rubbish, waste.
sarkofago sarcophagus.
sarkomo sarcoma.
Sarlando Saarland.
sarongjupo sarong.
sarongo sarong.
sarotamno broom.
sasafraso sassafras.
saskvaĉo Sasquatch, Bigfoot.
SAT → **Sennacieca Asocio Tutmonda**.
sata full, replete, satisfied.
satana Satanic.
satanismo Satanism.
satanisto Satanist.
satano devil.
Satano Lucifer, Satan.
satano Satan.
satdormi to sleep in, sleep one's fill.
sateco repletion.
satega glutted.
satelito satellite.
satena teksaranĝo satin weave.
sateno satin.
Sati the faithful wife of Shiva.
sati to be full, have enough, sate.
satigi to glut, satiate, satisfy (hunger).
satiĝi to be satisfied.
satio suttee.
satira satirical. **satira poemo** satire.
satire satirically.
satiri to satirize.
satiriazo satyriasis.
satiristo satirist.
satiro lampoon, satire.
satiruso satyr.
satisfakcio satisfaction.
satmanĝi to eat one's fill.
satmanĝi to eat until one is full.
sato glut, satiety.
satparoli to finish talking, have one's say.
satplori to have a good cry.

satrapo satrap.
satureco saturation.
satureo savory.
saturi to saturate.
saturna Saturnian.
Saturnalio Saturnalia.
Saturno Saturn.
Sauda Arabio Saudi Arabia.
Sauda Arabujo Saudi Arabia.
Saud-Arabio Saudi Arabia.
Saud-arabujo Saudi Arabia.
saudiaraba Saudi.
Saudiarabio Saudi Arabia.
saudiarabo Saudi.
Saudiarabujo Saudi Arabia.
saŭco gravy, sauce.
Saŭda Arabujo Saudi Arabia.
Saŭd-arabujo Saudi Arabia.
saŭdado nostalgia, pensiveness, yearning.
saŭno sauna.
saŭrkraŭto sauerkraut.
saŭro saurian.
savado salvage.
savano savanna.
savanto savior.
Savarmeo Salvation Army.
savboato lifeboat.
savbuo life buoy, rescue buoy.
savebla savable, salvageable.
savgardisto lifeguard.
savi to keep, save, rescue.
saviĝi to be saved, be preserved.
saviĝo deliverance, delivery, rescue.
Savinto Savior.
savista rescue.
savisto rescuer.
savita saved.
savjako life jacket, personal floatation device.
savklapo pop-off valve, safety valve.
savkopio backup (copy).
savmono salvage, salvage money.
savo salvage, salvation, recovery.
savojbrasiko savoy, Savoy cabbage.
Savonto messiah.
savoveŝto life jacket.
savringo life preserver.
savŝnuro lifeline.
savzono lifebelt, safety belt.
sbiro cop, pig.
scenaristo scenarist, scriptwriter.
scenaro scenario, screenplay, script.
scenejo scene, stage (theatre).
scenigi to stage.
sceno scene (painted).
sceptro sceptre.
sciado knowledge.
sciaĵo knowledge.
sciama curious, inquisitive.
sciante knowingly.

sciavida inquisitive.
sciavido curiosity.
sciebla knowable.
scieblo knowability.
sciema curious, interested.
sciemo curiosity, curiousness.
scienca scientific. **scienca fikcio** science-fiction.
science scientifically.
sciencfikcio science fiction.
scienc-fikcio science-fiction.
scienciko Scientology.
sciencisto scientist.
scienco science.
scienculo learned (man), savant, scholar.
scientologiano Scientologist.
scientologio Scientology.
scieto inkling.
scigi to advise, let (someone) know.
scii to know, know how.
sciiga informational, informative.
sciigado promulgation.
sciigi to acquaint, let know, inform, give notice, make known, notify, signify, inform.
sciigo advice, announcement, communication, message, notice, report, intelligence, notification, tidings.
sciiĝa cognitive.
sciiĝi to find out, hear, learn of.
sciiĝo cognition, perception.
sciinda worth knowing.
scilo squill, bluebell.
scintigrafio scintigraphy.
scintilografio scintigraphy.
scio knowledge.
sciobazo knowledge base.
scipova brainy, clever, conversant, skilled, smart.
scipovi to know how.
scipovo command, competence, competency, proficiency, skill.
scirpo bulrush.
sciuro squirrel.
sciuroptero flying squirrel.
scivola curious, inquisitive.
scivole inquisitively.
scivoleco curiosity.
scivolema inquisitive.
scivoleme inquisitively.
scivolemo curiosity.
scivolemulo curious person.
scivoli to want to know, wonder.
scivoliga intriguing.
scivoligi to intrigue.
scivolo curiosity.
se if, provided that. **se jes** if so, if you do, if it is. **se kaj nur se** then and only then. **se kaj nur se, se... kaj nur tiam** if and only if. **se kaj nur tiam** then and only then. **se mi ĝuste komprenas...** if I understand correctly... **se ne** if not, if you don't, if it isn't. **se nur** provided that. **se plaĉos al vi** to if you please. **se vi bonvolas** if you please.
seaborgio seaborgium.
seanca tavolo session layer.
seanco performance, seance, sitting, session.
seba kandelo tallow candle.
sebeca sebaceous.
sebo fat, tallow, suet.
seborgio seaborgium.
sebumo sebum.
secesio breakaway, secession, separation.
sed but. **sed aliaj** but others. **sed tamen** and yet. **sed tamen...** however...
sedativa sedative.
sedativo sedative.
sedevigo exemption.
sedimento sediment.
sedo stonecrop.
segaĵo sawdust.
segi to saw.
segilo saw.
segisto sawyer.
segligno lumber, timber.
seglinejo lumber yard.
segmenti to segment.
segmentiĝo segmentation.
segmento segment.
segpolvo sawdust.
segregacio apartheid.
seĝego armchair.
seĝeto baby's chair.
seĝo chair, seat.
Sejĉeloj Seychelles.
Sejno Sein.
sejno seine.
Sejŝeloj Seychelles.
sek. → **sekretario**.
seka arid, dry. **seka doko** dry dock. **seka pruno** prune.
sekaĵo dry land, mainland.
sekalo rye.
sekanto secant.
sekcado autopsy.
sekcanto secant (line).
sekci to cut, dissect, (perform an) autopsy, intersect.
sekciestro head of department.
sekcilaro dissection kit.
sekcilo scalpel.
sekcio branch, chapter, section.
sekco slice.
seke dryly.
sekeco dryness.
sekega bone dry.
sekegeco drought.
sekestri to sequestrate.

sekiga tuko tea towel.
sekigaŭtomato (clothes) dryer.
sekigi to (cause to be) dry. **sekigi sin** to dry oneself.
sekigilo dryer.
sekigita dried (out).
sekigmaŝino dryer.
sekigoŝranko airing cupboard.
sekigtuko dish towel, tea towel.
sekigujo airing cupboard.
sekiĝi to dry up.
sekiĝinta branĉo stalk.
sekiĝita dried (out).
sekojo sequoia, wellingtonia.
sekrecii to secrete.
sekrecio secretion.
sekreta clandestine, secret, stealthy. **sekreta agento** secret agent.
sekretari to work as a secretary.
sekretaria secretarial.
sekretariato secretariat.
sekretariino secretary.
sekretario secretary.
sekrete by stealth, in secret.
sekreteco secrecy.
sekretema discreet.
sekretemo secrecy.
sekretigi to hide away, conceal.
sekreto secret.
seksa generative, sexual. **seksa kulpulo** sex offender.
seksabstinado celibacy.
seksallogo sex-appeal.
seksarda in heat, rutting.
seksardo heat, sexual desire.
seksardotempo mating-season.
seksatencanto abuser.
seksatenci to rape (sexual attack).
seksatencinto rapist.
seksatenco rape (sexual attack).
seksavida horny.
sekseco sexuality.
sekshontemo prudery, Grundyism.
seksilo sex organ, sex toy.
sekskuniĝi to have sexual intercourse, mate.
sekskuniĝo copulation.
seksmatura sexually mature.
sekso gender, sex.
seksogapejo peepshow.
seksperforti to rape.
seksperforto rape (sexual attack).
seksskandalo sex scandal.
sekstanto sextant.
seksto sixth.
seksumi to have sex.
seksumo sex.
sekta sectarian.
sektano member of a sect, sectarian.
sekto faction, sect.

sektora sectoral.
sektoro sector.
sekulara secular.
sekulareco secularity.
sekularigi to secularize.
sekularigo secularization.
sekulariĝo secularization.
sekularismo secularism.
sekularisto secularist.
sekularizi to secularize.
sekularizo secularization.
sekunda second (time).
sekundanto second.
sekundara collateral, secondary.
sekundo second (time).
sekura safe, secure.
sekure safely.
sekureco safety, security.
sekuriga oficisto security officer.
sekurigi to make safe, secure, safeguard.
sekurigilo safeguard.
sekurigo protection.
sekurkopii to backup.
sekurkopio backup.
sekurrimeno safety belt, seat belt.
sekurvalvo safety valve.
sekurzono safety belt, seat belt.
sekva next, subsequent.
sekvado following.
sekvaĵo consequence, fall-out, sequel.
sekvanta following, next.
sekvantaro adherents, disciples, followers, following, party, supporters, retinue.
sekvanto satellite.
sekvantulo next person, following person.
sekve accordingly, consequently, so, subsequently, thus. **sekve de** as a result of, in consequence of, owing to. **sekve de tio** as a consequence, consequently. **sekve, do...** it follows then, that...
sekveco sequel.
sekvenca sequential, serial.
sekvenco sequence, series, array.
sekventaro company, escort.
sekvestri to seize (by officers of the law), sequester.
sekvestro sequester.
sekvi to ensue, follow, succeed (order).
sekvigi to entail.
sekvilo trace program.
sekvinbero raisin.
sekvinta following, next.
sekvinto successor.
sekvo consequence, result, sequel.
sekvojo sequoia, wellingtonia.
sekvonta following, next.
sekvontaĵo follow-up.
sekvonto successor.
sekvulo satellite.

selakto

selakto whey.
Selando Zealand.
selekta kanalo selector channel.
selektado selection.
selekti to pick, select.
selektiva selective.
Seleno Selene.
seleno selenium.
seli to saddle.
selo saddle.
selsako saddlebag.
seltaŝo saddlebag.
sema seminal.
semado sowing.
semaforo semaphore, signal.
semajna weekly.
semajne weekly.
semajnfino weekend.
semajngazeto weekly.
semajno week.
semaĵo seed.
semantemo semanteme, sememe.
semantika semantic. **semantika reto** semantic network.
semantike semantically.
semantiko semantics.
semanto sower.
sembedo seedbed.
semejo granary.
semelpara semelparous.
semestro semester.
semi to sow. **semi malpacon** to sow discord. **semi semojn** to sow seeds.
semida Semitic.
semido Semite.
seminariano seminarian.
seminario seminar.
semiologia semiological, semiotic.
semiologie semiologically.
semiologio semiology, semiotics.
semisto sower (of seeds).
semo seed.
semolino grits, semolina.
semolo grits, semolina.
semotaŭga suitable for sowing (seed).
sempervivo houseleek, hens-and-chicks, live-forever.
semplena seedy.
semriĉa seedy.
semtaŭga arable.
sen without, less. **sen ia averto** without any warning. **sen mia enmiksiĝado** without my involvement. **sen mia scio** without my knowledge. **sen palpebrovibro** without batting an eye. **sen permespeto** without asking permission. **sen tio ke** without (doing something).
sen- -less, un-.
senaera airless.

senbrankulo

senafekta simple, unaffected.
senafekte simply.
senafekteco abandonment.
senafranka unpaid.
senagado inaction.
senaĝa ageless.
senakcenta unaccented, unstressed.
senakompana a capella.
senakompane a capella.
senakva waterless.
senakvigi to concentrate, drain.
senakviĝi to drain.
senala akvo fresh water, sweet water.
senalie and no one else, and nothing else.
senalkohola non-alcoholic.
senama loveless.
senamika friendless.
senanima soulless.
senantaŭjuĝa free of prejudice, unbiased, unprejudiced.
senao senna.
senapetiteco anorexia.
senarbara treeless, woodless, unwooded.
senarbarigo deforestation.
senarbigi to deforest, clear.
senarma unarmed.
senarmigi to disarm (someone).
senarmiĝi to disarm (oneself), lay down one's arms.
senarmila unarmed.
senarmita armless.
senartifika above-board, guileless.
senartifike artlessly, openly.
senartifikeco openness.
senartika inarticulate.
senatano senator.
senatdomo senate house.
senatejo senate house.
senatenta careless, negligent, heedless, unawares, inattentive.
senatente inattentively.
senatenteco carelessness, negligence.
senatento carelessly.
senato senate.
senavantaĝa underprivileged.
senaverte without warning.
senbakteria abacterial.
senbalastigi to release ballast.
senbarba beardless, clean-shaven.
senbariera barrier-free.
senbaza baseless, groundless, unfounded.
senbazeco baselessness.
senbezona needless, unnecessary.
senbezone needlessly, unnecessarily.
senbiena landless.
senbilda unillustrated.
senbraka armless.
senbranka abranchial, abranchiate.
senbrankulo abranchiate.

senbrida lawless, licentious, riotous.
senbride unrestrainedly.
senbrideco abandon, abandonment, debauchery.
senbridigi to unbridle.
senbridulino hoyden, hussy.
senbrila dull, without shine.
senbrileco dimness, dullness.
senbriligi to dull, tarnish.
senbriliĝi to fade, tarnish.
senbrua noiseless.
senbrue noiselessly, quietly, without noise.
senbrueco silence, stillness, quiet.
senbukla loop-free (graph).
senceda inexorable, intransigent, obdurate, relentless, uncompromising.
sencela aimless, pointless.
sencele aimlessly.
sencerba brainless. **sencerba terminalo** dumb terminal.
sencerbulo brainless, empty-headed, imbecile.
senceremonia unceremonious.
senceremonie unceremoniously.
senceremonieco casualness.
sencermonie cavalierly.
sencikla cycle-free (graph).
sencimigi to debug.
sencimigilo debugger.
sencimigo debugging.
senco meaning, sense.
senĉela acellular.
senĉesa constant, lasting, sustained, unremitting, endless, non-stop. **senĉesa luktado** constant struggle.
senĉese all the time, ceaselessly.
senĉeseco persistence.
sendaĵero bag, bale, barrel, package. **sendaĵeroj** bags, bales, barrels, goods, packages.
sendaĵo consignment, submission, item of mail.
sendanĝera non-dangerous, nonhazardous, safe, secure. **sendanĝera pinglo** safety pin.
sendanĝere safely.
sendanĝereco safety, security.
sendanĝerigi to counteract, neutralize, secure.
sendanĝerigo fibula, safety-pin.
sendanĝeriĝi to become safe.
sendanka thankless, unappreciated, ungrateful, unthankful. **sendanka tasko** thankless job.
sendankeco ingratitude.
sendankema ungrateful.
sendankeme ungratefully.
sendanto sender.
sendaŭra fleeting.

sendecida indecisive.
sendecide indecisively.
sendefenda defenceless.
sendenta toothless.
sendependa independent.
sendepende independently. **sendepende de** independent of.
sendependeco independence.
sendependismo secessionism, separatism.
sendependisto secessionist, separatist.
sendependulo maverick.
sendeviga optional.
sendevigi to exempt.
sendi to forward, remit, send, transmit. **sendi vivsignojn** to let someone hear from you.
sendia godless, impious.
sendieco atheism.
sendifekta flawless, intact, unhurt.
sendinto sender.
sendirekta rogue. **sendirekta grafeo** undirected graph.
sendirektebla uncontrollable.
sendisciplina unruly.
sendisiĝa inseparable.
sendisputa undisputed, unquestioned, undeniable.
sendispute indisputably.
sendistinga indiscriminate.
sendistinge indiscriminately, without distinction, regardless.
sendita sent.
senditaro legation.
senditejo legation (place).
sendito ambassador, emissary, envoy, messenger, bearer, representative.
sendiulo atheist.
sendiverĝenca zero-divergence (field).
sendo consignment.
sendolora painless.
sendoloreco absence of pain, analgesia, painlessness.
sendoloriga analgesic.
sendolorigaĵo analgesic.
sendolorigenzo analgesic.
sendolorigilo analgesic, painkiller.
sendoma homeless.
sendorma sleepless.
sendorma nokto sleepless night.
sendormeco sleeplessness.
sendormo insomnia.
sendostacio transmitter.
sendrata wireless. **sendrata telefono** wireless telephone.
sendrogiĝi to kick it.
senduba doubtless, certain, sure.
sendubasenca unambiguous, unequivocal.
sendubasence unambiguously, unequivocally.

sendube doubtlessly, no doubt, undoubtedly.
sendusenca unambiguous.
senecio ragwort.
seneco dearth, want.
senedza single, unmarried.
senedzeca celibate.
senedzeco celibacy.
senedzina single, unmarried.
senedzineco celibacy.
senefika ineffective, ineffectual, toothless, unavailing, to no avail.
senefike to no avail.
senegala unequalled, unique, peerless.
senegale unequally.
senegalia Senegalese.
senegaliano Senegalese.
Senegalio Senegal.
Senegalo Senegal.
seneha anechoic.
seneklezia unchurched.
Seneko Seneca.
senekzempla peerless.
senelirejo blind alley.
senemocia impassive, unmoved.
senemocie impassively, dryly.
senenergia indolent.
senenhava devoid, empty, hollow, vacant.
senerara free of errors, infallible, inerrant, without error.
senerare accurately, infallibly, inerrantly.
senerarigo debugging.
senescepte without exception.
senespera abysmal, desperate, hopeless.
senespere despairingly.
senespereco hopelessly.
senesperema desperate.
senespereme desperately.
senesperemo desperation.
senesperiga hopeless.
senesperiĝi to lose hope, despair.
senespero lack of hope.
senesti to be absent.
senetikeda untitled.
seneventa uneventful.
senfadena wireless. **senfadena reto** wireless network.
senfadenigi to string.
senfama obscure.
senfantazia unimaginative.
senfara idle.
senfeligi to flay, skin, strip.
senfiera humble.
senfina everlasting, interminable. **senfina iteracio** infinite loop.
senfinaĵo infinity, immensity.
senfine ad infinitum, endlessly.
senfineco infinity, limitlessness.
senfleksia indeclinable.
senflora ananthous.

senflugila apterous.
senfolia leafless.
senforma formless.
senforta powerless, feeble, without strength, weak.
senforte weakly.
senforteco helplessness, powerlessness.
senfrukta barren, sterile, unfruitful, unproductive.
senfrukteco barrenness, sterility.
senfunda bottomless.
senfundamenta baseless.
sengardema careless.
sengardeme carelessly.
sengardemo carelessly.
senglora inglorious.
sengravito weightlessness.
sengrunda landless.
sengusta insipid, tasteless, vapid.
sengusteco lack of taste.
senĝeme frankly, unreservedly.
senĝena without ceremony, at ease, unmoved.
senĝenaĉa brazen.
senĝeneco abandon, easiness, casualness, abandonment.
senĝeno abandon.
senĝoja cheerless.
Senĝonso Saint John's.
senhalta continuous.
senhalte at a stretch, on end, without stopping.
senhara bald, hairless.
senhareco baldness.
senhaŭta raw (without skin).
senhaŭtigi to flay, skin.
senhava miserable, needy.
senhaveco destitution, distress, indigence, need, penury.
senhavigi to deprive (of), impoverish.
senhavigo impoverishment.
senhaviĝi to become destitute, lose everything.
senhaviĝo impoverishment.
senhavulo indigent, pauper, poor man, poor person.
senhejma homeless.
senhejmulo homeless person.
senhelpa helpless.
senhelpe helplessly.
senhelpeco helplessness.
senherbigi paŝtiĝe to browse, graze.
senheredigi to disinherit, disown, write out of one's will.
senhezi to not hesitate.
senhezite without hesitation.
senhimenigi to deflower.
senhoma depopulated, empty (of people), uninhabited.

senhomigi to depopulate.
senhomigita emptied of people.
senhonorigi to dishonour, shame.
senhonta shameless, impudent.
senhonte shamelessly.
senhonteco effrontery.
senhonto audacity, hubris.
senhontulo shameless person.
senhumaniga dehumanizing.
senhumanigi to dehumanize.
senida childless, heirless.
senidea clueless.
senidenteco anomie.
senigi to deprive (of). **senigi de** to deprive of. **senigi je** to strip off.
senigo deprivation, privation, taking away, withdrawal, withholding.
senila senile.
seniluzigata disillusioned.
seniluziigi to disappoint, set straight, disillusion.
seniluziigo bummer, disappointment, disillusionment.
seniluziiĝi to become disillusioned.
seniluziiĝo disappointment.
senimposta duty-free, tax-free.
senindulga exacting, hard, implacable, pitiless, severe, stern, unsparing.
senindulge unindulgently.
seninfana childless.
seninfekti to disinfect.
seninfektigi to disinfect.
seninflua without influence.
seninga unsheathed. **seninga sabro** unsheathed sword.
senintenca unintentional, unwitting, unplanned.
senintence by accidence.
seninteresa uninteresting.
seninterese uninterestingly, without interest.
senintereza interest-free.
senintermanka unbroken.
seninterrompa continuous.
seninterrompe at a stretch, on end, ceaselessly, uninterruptedly, without interruption.
senintestigi to gut.
senjoro squire, feudal lord, lord.
senjunta seamless.
senkapa headless.
senkapigi to behead, decapitate.
senkapigisto headsman.
senkapigo beheading.
senkapulo acephalan, acephalous organism.
senkaraktera characterless.
senkarpela acarpellous.
senkaŝa above-board.
senkatenigi to free, release, unshackle.
senkaŭza causeless.
senkernigi to stone.

senkernigo stoning.
senkirla irrotational (field).
senklamida achlamydeous.
senklina aclinic.
senkniduloj Acnidaria.
senkolora achromatic, colourless.
senkolore colourlessly.
senkoloreco achromaticity, achromatism.
senkolorigi to discolour.
senkolorigilo bleaching agent, bleach.
senkoloriĝi to fade.
senkompara incomparable, hard, merciless, ruthless, uncompassionate, unfeeling, implacable, pitiless, harsh.
senkompare ever, incomparably, uniquely.
senkompata merciless, pitiless, ruthless.
senkompateco callousness.
senkompato harshness.
senkondiĉa unconditional.
senkondiĉe unconditionally.
senkonekte offline.
senkonfesa non-denominational, non-religious, agnostic.
senkonfesulo agnostic, irreligious person.
senkonscia unconscious.
senkonscie unconsciously.
senkonscieco unconsciousness.
senkonscienca unprincipled, unscrupulous.
senkonsciigi to stun.
senkonsciigita caused to be without awareness.
senkonsciiĝi to become unconscious, lose consciousness.
senkonsciiĝo faint.
senkonscio unconsciousness.
senkonsekvenco inconsistency.
senkonsidera inconsiderate, ruthless, heedless.
senkonsidere cavalierly, dismissively, offhandedly.
senkonsidero off-handedness.
senkonsila disconsolate.
senkonsola desolate.
senkora heartless.
senkore heartlessly.
senkorpa non-corporal, without a body.
senkosta free, free of charge.
senkostaĵo freebie.
senkoste free of charge, freely.
senkotigi to clean (remove dirt, mud, etc.).
senkotiledona acotyledonous.
senkotiledonulo acotyledon.
senkovrigi to denude.
senkrampa operaciskribo parentheses-free notation.
senkrampigilo staple remover.
senkreditigi to discredit.
senkreditigo derogation.
senkremigi to cream, skim.

senkremigilo separator, skimmer.
senkreskaĵa bleak.
senkritika uncritical.
senkudra seamless.
senkulpa guiltless, innocent. **senkulpa ĝis fine kondamnita** innocent until found guilty.
senkulpe innocently.
senkulpeco innocence.
senkulpigi to absolve, acquit, exculpate, excuse, pardon, overlook. **senkulpigi sin** to apologize.
senkulpigo absolution.
senkulpulo innocent person.
senkultura dreary, uncultivated, waste (untilled).
senkulturega fallow.
senkunkudra seamless.
senkunteksta context-free. **senkunteksta gramatiko** context-free grammar. **senkunteksta lingvo** context-free language.
senkuraĝa disheartened.
senkuraĝeco discouragement.
senkuraĝi to deject.
senkuraĝiga daunting, discouraging, disheartening.
senkuraĝigi to discourage.
senkuraĝigita discouraged.
senkuraĝigo discouragement.
senlabora out of work, unemployed.
senlaboreco idleness, unemployment.
senlaborofico sinecure.
senlaborulo unemployed person.
senlaca indefatigable, tireless, untiring.
senlace tirelessly, untiringly.
senlaciĝa untiring.
senleĝeco lawlessness, anarchy.
senligi to untie, unbind.
senligita untied, unbound.
senlima absolute, infinite, unbounded, unlimited, limitless. **senlima nombro** (an) infinite number.
senlime without limit.
senlimeco absoluteless, limitlessness.
senlimtempa without time limit, of unlimited duration, open-ended.
senluma lightless, dark. **senluma kamero** camera obscura.
senlumeco obscurity.
senlumejo darkroom.
senmakula immaculate, spotless, unspotted, stainless.
senmalica guileless, inoffensive.
senmanika sleeveless.
senmanke without fail.
senmaskigi to unmask.
senmebligi to unfurnish.
senmembrigi to dismember.
senmetia unskilled.
senmezura immeasurable.
senmezure immeasurably.
senmona broke, without money, penniless, moneyless; non-monetary.
senmora abandoned.
senmoreco abandonment.
senmorta deathless, immortal.
senmorteco immortality.
senmorterigi to chip, chip off.
senmotiveco anomie.
senmova immobile, inert, motionless, stagnant, stationary, still, motionless.
senmove motionless, without moving.
senmoveco immobility, stagnation.
senmovigi to immobilize, paralyse.
senmoviĝi to freeze.
senmuskoleca nerveless.
sennacia anational.
sennacieca without (consideration for) nationality. **Sennacieca Asocio Tutmonda** World Non-Nationalist Association.
sennaciismo anationalism.
sennaciisto anationalist.
sennaciulo anational.
sennoma anonymous, nameless, without a name. **sennoma akcio** bearer share, share to bearer.
sennombra countless.
sennombreco infinity, immensity.
sennomeco anonymity.
sennuba cloudless.
senodora inodorous. **senodora matrikario** corn feverfew, scentless chamomile.
senodorigi to deodorize.
senodorigilo deodorant.
senofenda harmless, inoffensive.
senofende harmlessly.
senofica private.
senoksigena anaerobic.
senokupa idle, inactive, unemployed, unoccupied.
senokupeco idleness.
senokupo inaction.
senombra unshaded.
senopone without opposition.
senorda disordered, random, unruly, untidy.
senordaĵo hodgepodge.
senorde disorderly.
senordeco disorder.
senordego anarchy.
senoriginaleco lack of originality.
senornama plain, unadorned.
senpacienca impatient.
senpacience impatiently.
senpacienco impatience.
senpaga free, gratuitous.
senpagaĵo freebie.
senpage for nothing, free, gratis, gratuitously.
senpana unpunished.

senpaneigi to fix.
senpaneigo fix, repair.
senpardona unforgiving.
senparola speechless, wordless.
senparole speechlessly, wordlessly.
senpartia impartial, unbiased, independent, neutral.
senpartieco impartiality.
senpasejo impasse.
senpasia dispassionate.
senpasie dispassionately.
senpaŝa klavo accent key, dead key, mute key.
senpatra fatherless.
senpaŭza incessant, continual, constant, continuous.
senpedikigi to delouse.
senpeka sinless, without sin.
senpekigi to absolve (from sin).
senpekigo absolution (from sin).
senpena effortless.
senpene easily, effortlessly.
senpeneco effortlessness.
senpensa thoughtless, unthinking, mindless, wanton.
senpense thoughtlessly.
senpenseco mindlessness.
senpera direct. **senpera adresado** immediate addressing.
senpere directly, live (TV). **senpere apud** directly beside, right next to.
senperforta bloodless, nonviolent.
senperforte nonviolently.
senperforto non-violence.
senpersona impersonal. **senpersona pronomo** impersonal pronoun. **senpersona verbo** impersonal verb.
senpersonigi to depersonalize.
senperspektiva without any prospects.
senpeza weightless.
senpeze weightlessly.
senpezeco weightlessness.
senpezigi to cause to be weightless, relieve.
senpezigo relief.
senpieda apod, apodal, apodan.
senpiedulo apod.
senpieduloj Apoda.
senpinta blunt.
senpintigi to top, truncate.
senplana unplanned.
senplumigi to pluck (fowl).
senpluveco drought, lack of rain.
senpolvigi to dust.
senpopoligi to depopulate.
senpopoligo depopulation.
senposedigi to deprive, deprive ... of.
senpotenca powerless.
senpotencigi to remove from power.
senpotenco impotence, powerlessness.

senpova powerless, impotent.
senpove helplessly.
senpoveco impotence, incapacity, powerlessness.
senpovigi to disable.
senpovo helplessness.
senprecedenca unprecedented.
senprepara extempore, impromptu.
senpretenda unpretentious, unassuming.
senpretende unassumingly, unpretentiously.
senpretendiĝi to back down, climb down.
senpreza priceless.
senprincipa unprincipled.
senpripensa rash, thoughtless, headlong. **senpripensa decido** rash decision.
senpripense inconsiderately, unthinkingly, without thinking, thoughtlessly.
senpripenseco rashness, thoughtlessness.
senprobleme without problems.
senprogresa stationary.
senprokrasta prompt, speedy.
senprokraste at once, instantly, immediately, without delay, right away.
senprokrasto dispatch.
senpropriula without an owner.
senprudenta imprudent.
senprudente senselessly.
senprudenteco folly, senselessness.
senpteriguloj Apterygota.
senpudora shameless, unblushing.
senpuna unpunished.
senpune unpunished, without penalty.
senpuneco immunity, impunity.
senputreco incorruption.
senradika rootless. **senradika arbo** free tree, unrooted tree.
senrajta without rights.
senrajtigi to disqualify.
senrajtigo disqualification.
senreĝeco anarchy.
senreliefa even, flat.
senreligia non-denominational, non-religious, agnostic.
senreligiulo agnostic, irreligious person, atheist.
senrevena irretrievable.
senrevigi to disillusion.
senreviĝo disappointment, disenchantment, disillusionment.
senrezerve unreservedly.
senrezulta futile.
senrezulteco futility.
senrima verso blank verse.
senringa acyclic, aliphatic.
senripoza without rest, without rest, unresting.
senripoze unrestingly.
senripozo lack of rest.
senriproĉa irreproachable.

senriproĉe unreproachingly.
senriska harmless, safe, sure.
senriske without taking a risk.
senriskeco safety.
senrubigi to clean (grain).
senrubigo garbage collection.
sensacaĵo nonsense.
sensacia lurid, sensational.
sensacio furore, impression, interest, sensation, commotion, perception.
sensala salt-free. **sensala akvo** fresh water.
sensalajra unpaid.
sensama sensual, sensuous.
sensanga anemic, bloodless.
senscia unconscious.
senscie innocently, unwittingly.
senscieco ignorance, innocence.
senscio ignorance.
sensebla appreciable.
senseksa sexless, asexual, neuter.
sensekura insecure, unsafe.
sensekureco insecurity.
sensela bareback.
sensele bareback.
senseligi to unsaddle.
sensema sensual.
sensenca absurd, incoherent, nonsensical, senseless.
sensencaĵo absurdity, nonsense, senselessness.
sensence nonsensical. **sensence paroli** to talk nonsense.
sensenceco absurdity.
sensenco senselessness, silliness.
sensenta insensible, senseless, torpid, unfeeling.
sensenteco torpidity.
sensentema insusceptible.
sensentigi to numb.
sensentigita numbed.
sensentigo anaesthesia.
sensento torpor.
senserifa sans serif.
sensi to perceive, sense.
sensigeligi to unseal.
sensigna unmarked.
sensignifa insignificant, meaningless.
sensignife insignificantly.
sensignuma unsigned. **sensignuma entjero** unsigned integer. **sensignuma nombro** unsigned number. **sensignuma reelo** unsigned real.
sensilo pickup, sensing device, sensor, transducer.
sensimetria asymmetric, asymmetrical.
sensisma aseismic.
sensismo sensualism.
sensiva sensitive.
sensivigi to sensitize.

senskalpigi to scalp.
senskriba blank.
senskrupula unscrupulous.
senskrupule unscrupulously.
senskue unshakingly.
senso sense.
sensobtuzo stupor.
sensoifiga thirst-quenching.
sensoifigi to slake.
sensona soundless.
sensone soundlessly.
sensonigi to silence.
sensorgano sense.
sensperta inexperienced.
senspertulo novice.
senspira breathless, unaspirated.
senspire breathlessly.
senspiriga breathtaking.
sensprita dull, witless, insipid.
senspritiga dispiriting.
senspritulo dullard, witless person.
senspure without a trace.
senstreĉa stretchless, without winding up.
sensualismo sensualism.
sensubskriba anonymous, nameless.
sensuka dry, spiritless, feeble.
sensukcesa unsuccessful.
sensukcese unsuccessfully.
sensukiĝi to wither.
sensuna dull, overcast, sunless.
sensuprigi to top, truncate.
sensuspektiga disarming.
senŝanca luckless.
senŝanceliĝa unhesitating, unswerving.
senŝanĝa unchanged, unchanging.
senŝanĝe unchangingly.
senŝarĝi to unload.
senŝarĝigi to exonerate.
senŝarĝigita relieved.
senŝarĝiĝo relief.
senŝaŭmiga antifoaming.
senŝaŭmigenzo antifoaming agent, antisudsing agent.
senŝaŭmigi to skim.
senŝaŭmigilo skimmer.
senŝeligi to husk, peel, shell, unwrap.
senŝeligita rizo husked rice.
senŝerce all joking aside.
senŝirma bleak.
senŝirmeco exposure (to the elements).
senŝlimigi to dredge.
senŝua barefoot.
senta sensorial, sensual.
sentadi to feel.
sentado sensation.
sentakta tactless.
sentara sentara.
sentaŭga good-for-nothing, useless.

sentaŭgulo good-for-nothing, worthless person.
sentebla palpable, perceptible, sensible.
senteblaema susceptible.
senteble tangibly.
sentegi to resent.
sentema sensitive, sentient.
sentemeco sentimentality.
sentemo sensibility, susceptibility.
sentemplima without time limit, of unlimited duration, open-ended.
sentenco maxim, proverb, wise saying.
Sentendruzo Saint Andrews.
sentestamenta intestate.
Sentheleno Saint Helena.
senti to experience, feel, sense, perceive.
  senti la foreston de to miss. **senti naŭzon** to be nauseated, feel nauseated. **senti sin** to feel.
sentiĝi to be felt.
sentilo pickup, sensing device, sensor, transducer, sensory receptor.
sentima bold, courageous, fearless, dauntless.
sentime fearlessly, without fear.
sentimeco boldness.
sentimenta sentimental.
sentimentala romantic, sentimental.
sentimentaleco sentiment.
sentimentalega schmaltzy.
sentimentalegaĵo schmaltz.
sentimentalo sentimentality.
sentimento sentiment.
sentimiga disarming.
sentimulino fearless woman.
sentimulo fearless man.
sentinelo guard, sentinel, sentry.
sentiva sensitive.
sento feel, feeling, sensation, perception, sentiment.
sentorgano sense.
sentrompa above-board.
sentumo sense.
senutila abortive, useless.
senutilaĵo useless, worthless thing.
senutile uselessly.
senutileco uselessness.
senutilo inutility.
senvalidigi to annul, cancel.
senvalora valueless, worthless.
senvaloraĵo junk, trash, something worthless.
senvalorigi to invalidate.
senvalorigo depreciation.
senvaloriĝi to depreciate.
senvaloriĝo depreciation.
senvantaro entourage.
senventa airless, windless.
senventeco windlessness.

senvertebruloj invertebrates.
senverva dull, lifeless, stodgy.
senvesta naked, unclothed.
senvestigi to take off (one's) clothes, undress, strip. **senvestigi sin** to get undressed.
senvestiĝi to strip, undress.
senvica atingo direct access, random access.
senvice atingebla memoro random access memory, RAM.
senvida blind.
senvideco blindness.
senvigla listless.
senvirusigilo anti-virus software.
senviva dead, lifeless, inanimate.
senvive lifelessly.
senviveco lifelessness.
senvivigi to kill, deprive of life.
senvoĉa voiceless, unvoiced (sound).
senvoĉe voicelessly.
senvoĉeco aphonia.
senvoĉigi to devoice (sound).
senvola involuntary.
senvole unwillingly.
senvoleco abulia.
senvorta speechless, tacit, wordless, without words.
senvorte without a word, wordlessly.
senvosta tailless.
senvostulo anuran.
senvostuloj Anura.
senvualigi to reveal, unveil.
senvunda unhurt, uninjured, unscathed.
senzorga careless, neglectful, reckless, remiss.
senzorge airily.
senzorgeco carelessness, freedom from care, casualness.
seo conditional statement, IF statement.
sep seven.
sepa seventh.
sepalo sepal.
sepangulo heptagon.
separatismo separatism.
separatisto separatist.
separeo booth.
separi to separate.
separo legal separation (of spouses).
sepcent seven hundred.
sepdek seventy.
sepdeka seventieth.
sepe seventhly.
sepedro heptahedron.
sepia sepia.
sepiaĵo sepia.
sepio cuttlefish, sepia.
sepiolito meerschaum, sepiolite.
seplatero heptagon.
sepono seventh.
sepopo septuple.
sepsa infected, septic.

septa

septa septic.
septavola etalona modelo seven-layer reference model, OSI reference model.
Septembro September.
septembro September.
septeto septet.
septimo seventh (music).
septo bulkhead, partition, septum.
Septuaginto Septuagint.
sepultentreprenisto mortician, undertaker.
sepulti to dispose of (the dead in a funeral).
serafo seraph.
serajlo seraglio.
serba Serb.
Serbio Serbia.
serbo Serb.
Serbujo Serbia.
serĉadi to scrutinize.
serĉado quest, search.
serĉanta looking for, seeking.
serĉanto seeker.
serĉarbo search tree.
serĉateco popularity.
serĉe searchingly, in search of.
serĉfosi to excavate.
serĉi to look for, seek, search. **serĉi kontakton** to strike up an acquaintance.
serĉilo finder, search command, search engine.
serĉmandato search warrant.
serĉo quest.
serĉomendo query.
serĉordono warrant.
serena calm, serene, untroubled.
serenado serenade.
serenco serenity.
serene calmly, composedly, peacefully, placidly, serenely.
sereneco calm, composition.
serenigi to calm.
sereniĝi to clear.
sereno calmness, serenity.
Sergio Sergius.
serĝento sergeant.
serĝo serge.
seria serial. **seria atingo** sequential access. **seria memorilorganizo** sequential organization. **seria serĉo** serial search.
seriaĵo serial.
seriatinga memorilo sequential access store.
serifo serif.
serikomedio sitcom.
serio series, set. **serio de funkcioj** function series.
serioza earnest, serious, staid, sober.
serioze seriously.
seriozeco earnestness, seriousness.
seriozege most seriously, very seriously.

servutulo

serioziga sobering.
seriozmiena stern-faced, having a serious expression.
sero serum (blood).
serotonino serotonin.
serpenta serpentine, sinuous, snaky, twisty.
serpentaglo short-toed eagle.
serpentego python.
serpenteno serpentine.
serpenteto snake.
serpentforma anguine.
serpenti to meander, snake, twist.
Serpentisto Ophiuchus.
serpento serpent, snake.
serpentoj serpents.
serpentuma slithering, winding.
serpentumi to meander, twist, wind around.
serpilo Breckland wild thyme.
serpo sickle.
serumo serum (medicine).
seruristo locksmith.
seruro lock.
serva mono house charge, service charge.
servado attendance, service, waiting.
servalo serval.
servanto servant.
servema obliging, serviceable.
servemaĉa obsequious.
servemaĉe obsequiously.
servemaĉo obsequiousness.
servi to attend, serve, wait on. **servi sian patrujon** to serve one's country. **servi sub iu** to serve under someone.
servico crockery set, service.
servigi to engage.
servilo server.
serviri to serve.
servirkadro service court.
servirlinio service line.
servistaro servants, serving staff.
servistino maid, servant.
servisto servant. **servisto de preĝejo** sexton.
servistoino domestic, servant.
servitulo serf.
servleto servlet.
servo service.
servodaŭro seniority.
servodono provision of services.
servokapabla able-bodied.
servopreta obliging, ready, willing.
servosoldato orderly (military).
servotablo credence-table.
servt to serve.
servulo menial.
servuteco bondage, thrall.
servuto bondage, serfdom, servitude, forced labour, slavery.
servutulo bondservant, serf.

ses six.
sesa sixth.
sesangula hexagonal.
sesangulo hexagon.
sesdek sixty.
sesdeka sixtieth.
sesdekona rupio ana, anna.
sesdekuma sexagesimal.
sese sixthly.
sesedro hexahedron.
sesfoje six times.
seshore six hours.
sesio session.
sesjara six year-old.
sesjarrego six-year reign.
seskvilineara sesquilinear.
seslatero hexagon.
seslerio blue moor-grass, blue sesleria.
sesono sixth.
sesope six together.
sesopo sextet, sextuple.
sespenco sixpence.
sestercio sestertium.
sesterco sesterce, sestertius.
Seŝeloj Seychelles.
setario bristle-grass.
setaro sitar.
setero setter.
setlado settlement.
setli to settle.
Seto Seth.
Seulo Seoul.
seurigi to safeguard.
severa harsh, rigid, severe, strict, stringent, rigorous, stern.
severe rigidly.
severeco severity, rigour.
severega hard, severe, harsh, stern, rigorous.
severege very severely.
severmora austere.
severmore austerely.
severmoreco austerity.
sevrugo starry sturgeon.
sezamo sesame.
sezono season (of year).
sfagno peat moss, sphagnum.
sfenisko jackass penguin.
sfenoido sphenoid.
sfera spherical. **sfera koordinato** spherical coordinate.
sferdisko spherical layer.
sferforma spherical.
sfero ball, sphere.
sfigmomanometro sphygmomanometer, blood pressure machine.
sfingo hawk-moth.
sfinkso sphinx.
sfinktero sphincter.
si (reflexive pronoun).

sia its, their, his, hers, one's own.
siabruste in his heart.
siaflanke for his part.
sialingve in his language.
siama Siamese.
siamaniere in his (her, its) way.
Siamo Siam, Thailand.
siaparte for his/her/its part.
siatempe at the time, in his/her/its/their time.
siavice in (his, her, its) turn.
sibarito sybarite.
siberia Siberian. **siberia molanaso** steller's eider.
siberiano Siberian.
Siberio Siberia.
sibilo sibyl.
sibla shrill. **sibla sono** strident, sibilant.
siblado whirl, whirring, whizz, whizzing.
siblaĵo whisper.
sibli to hiss, whistle.
siblo whizz.
Sibrandaboro Sibrandabuorren, Sijbrandaburen.
sicilia Sicilian.
sicilianino Sicilian woman.
siciliano Sicilian.
Sicilio Sicily.
sidaĉi to slouch.
sidadi to be sitting.
sidĉambro sitting room.
sidejo seat.
sidera sidereal.
sidi to sit, be seated. **sidi bone** to fit (well). **sidi ĉetable** to sit at the table.
sidigi to set down, seat.
sidiĝe sitting.
sidiĝi to become seated, sit down. **sidiĝu!** sit down!
sidilo seat.
sidloko place to sit, seat.
Sidnejo Sydney.
sido site, situation.
sidvango buttock.
sieĝanto besieger.
sieĝi to besiege.
sieĝo siege.
sieno sienna.
Sieraleono Sierra Leone.
siesto siesta.
sifiliso syphilis.
sifilo syphilis.
sifono siphon.
sigelaĵo seal.
sigeli to seal.
sigelilo seal, signet.
sigelmarko seal, stamp, sticker.
sigelo seal.
sigeloilo seal.

sigelvakso

sigelvakso sealing wax.
siglingio heath grass.
siglo acronym.
sigma-algebro sigma-algebra.
sigmo sigma (Σσς).
signa fosto signpost.
signaldiro password, signal, watchword.
signalero signal element.
signalfajro beacon.
signalhorloĝeto alarm watch.
signali to point out, signal.
signalilo semaphore.
signalizi to blaze.
signalo mark, sign, signal, token.
signalŝnuro cord.
signalturo beacon.
signaro character set.
signeca character-oriented. **signeca komputado** character-oriented data processing.
signeca komputilo character-oriented computer.
signi to indicate, point out, show. **signi sin kruce** to make the sign of the cross. **signi sin kurce** to cross oneself, make the sign of the cross.
signifa significant. **signifa cifero** significant digit. **signifa ciferpozicio** significant digit.
signife meaningfully.
signifi to imply, mean, signify.
signifo meaning, signification.
signifoplena significant.
signifoplene full of significance, full of meaning.
signiigi to sign.
signo character, mark, sign, signal, token, accent. **signo de egaleco** equals sign (=). **signo demanda** note of interrogation. **signo ekkria** note of exclamation.
signobarelo buoy.
signobildo face, glyph.
signoĉeno character string.
signodenso character density.
signodoni to nod, beckon.
signogenerilo character generator.
signostango beacon.
signoŝanĝo change in sign, sign inversion.
signovico string.
signumo number sign, signum.
signumpluigo sign extension.
signumŝanĝo sign inversion.
siĥo Sikh.
sikho Sikh.
sikismo Sikhism.
siklo shekel.
sikomoro sycamore, sycamore fig, fig mulberry, mulberry fig.
siksta sistine.
silaba syllabic.
silabi to spell.

simboltabelo

silabo syllable.
sileno campion.
silenta silent, tacit. **silenta admiranto** secret admirer.
silentadi to remain quiet.
silentado silence, being quiet, silencing.
silente silently.
silentema moody, reserved, taciturn, uncommunicative.
silenti to be quiet, silent.
silentigi to cause to be quiet, make silent, hush, silence, gag.
silentiĝi to become silent, hold one's tongue.
silentiĝo silence.
silento silence.
silepso syllepsis.
Silezio Silesia.
silfo sylph.
Silicia Valo Silicon Valley.
silicio silicon.
silicitradukilo silicon compiler.
silico silica.
siliko flint, gravel.
silikono silicone.
silikvo pod, siliqua.
silka silk, silken, of silk. **Silka Vojo** Silk Road.
silkeca silky.
silko silk.
silkpapero tissue.
silkraŭpo silkworm.
silksimio marmoset.
silktuko foulard.
silkvermo silkworm.
Silkvojo Silk Road.
silo silo.
silogismo syllogism.
siluetiĝi to silhouette.
silueto outline, silhouette.
Silurio Silurian.
Siluro Silurian.
Silvestro New Year's Eve, Sylvester.
silvikulturo forestry.
silvio hedge sparrow, warbler.
simbioza symbiotic.
simbiozo symbiosis.
simbola symbolic. **simbola adreso** symbolic address. **simbola ligilo** shortcut. **simbola maŝinkodo** assembly language. **simbola programo** symbolic program.
simbolaro notation.
simbole symbolically.
simboleco symbolism.
simboli to be a symbol of, symbolize.
simboligi to symbolize.
simboliko symbolism.
simbolkonflikto names conflict.
simbolo badge, symbol.
simboltabelo symbol table.

simboltraktado symbol manipulation.
simetria symmetric, symmetrical. **simetria diferenco** symmetric difference. **simetria eĝo** undirected edge. **simetria grupo** symmetrical group. **simetria matrico** symmetric matrix.
simetriakso axis of symmetry.
simetricentro symmetry centre.
simetriebeno plane of symmetry.
simetrieco symmetry.
simetrimanka asymmetric, asymmetrical.
simetrimanko asymmetry.
simetrio symmetry.
simfito comfrey.
simfizo symphysis.
simfonia symphonic.
simfonio symphony.
simforikarpo snowberry.
simia apish. **simia viro** ape man.
simieca ape-like, apish, monkey-like.
simii to ape.
simila alike, similar, like. **simila al** like. **similaj matricoj** similar matrices.
similaĵo image, picture, portrait.
similaspekta of similar type.
simildimensia of similar dimensions.
simile likewise. **simile...** similarly, by the same token...
simileco resemblance, similarity, simile, uniformity.
simili to be similar, resemble. **simili laŭkaraktere** to take after.
similigi to assimilate.
similula lookalike.
similulo double, lookalike.
simio ape, monkey.
simioj primates.
simiosimila ape-like, apish, monkey-like.
simonio simony.
simpatia likeable, sympathetic.
simpatie nicely, sensitively, sympathetically.
simpatii to sympathize, condole.
simpatiiĝo chemistry.
simpatio sympathy.
simpato sympathetic nervous system.
simpla simple, straightforward, unaffected, unvarnished, plain, unpretending. **simpla funkcio** simple function. **simpla grafeo** ordinary graph, simple graph. **simpla konverĝa** simply convergent, pointwise convergent. **simpla ordono** simple statement. **simpla soldato** private (soldier). **simpla tago** working day. **simpla tipo** simple type.
simplanima candid, artless.
simplanimulo booby, fool, ninny.
simple simply, plainly. **simple koneksa** simply connected (space). **simple kon-verĝa** pointwise convergent, simply convergent.
simpleco plainness, simpleness, simplicity.
simpligi to simplify.
simpligo simplification.
simpodio pseudaxis, sympodium.
simpozio symposium.
simptomo symptom.
simulado simulation.
simulatoro simulator.
simuli to dissemble, feign, pretend, simulate.
simulilo simulator.
simultana contemporary, live, simultaneous.
sin mem himself.
sinagogo synagogue.
sinaltrudado imposing on one another.
sinapa mustard. **sinapa kataplasmo** mustard plaster. **sinapa semo** mustard seed.
sinapo mustard plant, sinapis.
sinapso synapse.
sincera sincere, above-board, frank, unfeigned.
sincere frankly, sincerely.
sincereco candour, frankness, sincerity, straightforwardness.
sincero sincerity.
sindefendo (self-)defence.
sindetena abstinent.
sindetenanto abstainer.
sindetenemo continence.
sindeteni to abstain.
sindeteno abstention, abstinence.
sindevigo commitment.
sindevontigo commitment, pledge, resolution.
sindikatismo trade-unionism, syndicalism.
sindikato labour union, trade union, syndicate.
sindiko syndic.
sindona affectionate, devoted, selfless, generous, helpful, self-sacrificing.
sindone devotedly, dedicatedly, selflessly.
sindoneco adherence, affection, attachment.
sindonema devoted, selfless, generous, helpful, self-sacrificing.
sindonemo attachment.
sindono attachment, devotion, generosity, helpfulness, selflessness, self-sacrifice.
sindromo syndrome.
sinduŝi to take a shower.
sinedrio Sanhedrin.
sinekdoĥo synecdoche.
sinekuro sinecure.
sinergio synergy.
sinestezio synaesthesia.
sinetio synesis.
sinforgesema altruistic.
sinforgesemo altruism.
singapura Singaporean.

singapurano Singaporean.
Singapuro Singapore.
singarda careful, cautious.
singarde carefully, gently, lightly.
singardeco caution.
singardema careful, cautious, circumspect, wary, prudent.
singardeme carefully, cautiously, gingerly, guardedly, prudently, warily.
singardemo caution, discretion, generalship, prudence.
singardi to be careful, take care.
singardo caution, precaution.
singularo singular.
singulti to hiccup, hiccough.
singulto hiccup, hiccough.
singena abashed, self-conscious, shy.
singenema shy.
singenigi to aback.
singeno bashfulness, shyness, timidity.
sinhalo Singhalese, Sinhalese.
sinhumiligo abasement.
sinistra baleful, sinister.
sinistro misfortune.
sinjoreco distinction.
sinjorino lady, madam, Mrs.
sinjoro gentleman, lord, Mr, Sir.
sinki to sink.
sinkigi to sink.
sinkopo syncopation, syncope.
sinkretismo syncretism.
sinkrona synchronous. **sinkrona transsendo** synchronous transmission.
sinkrone simultaneously.
sinkroneco synchronicity.
sinkronigi to synchronize.
sinkronigo synchronization.
sinkrotrono synchrotron.
sinkulpiga incriminating.
sinmontrema boastful, braggart, bragger, swaggerer.
sinmontreme showily.
sinmontremo showiness.
sinmortiga suicide.
sinmortigo suicide.
sinnekonado not knowing one another, mutual ignorance.
S-ino → **sinjorino**.
sino bosom, breast, lap.
sinoda synodal.
sinodo synod.
sinofero abnegation, self-sacrifice.
sinonima synonymous.
sinonimo synonym.
sinopsiso synopsis.
sinoptika synoptic.
sinovio synovia.
sinpravigo rationalization.
sinrega composed, restrained, self-possessed.
sinregema unflappable.
sinretenema detached.
sinsekva consecutive.
sinsekve consecutively.
sinsekvigi to link together, link up.
sinsekvo order, sequence.
sinsternigo prostration.
sintaksa syntactic. **sintaksa analizilo** parser. **sintaksa analizo** parse, syntactic analysis. **sintaksa diagramo** syntax diagram. **sintaksa eraro** syntactical error, syntax error. **sintaksa kontrolo** syntactic check. **sintaksa variablo** syntactic variable.
sintaksanalizatoro syntax analyser.
sintaksema redaktilo syntax-oriented editor.
sintakso syntax.
sintenado attitude.
sinteno attitude.
sinteza synthetic.
sintezi to synthesize.
sintezilo synthesizer.
sintezo synthesis.
sintonizi to tune.
sinui to meander, snake, weave.
sinuo bend, sinuosity.
sinuso sine.
sinvenga retaliatory.
sinvengo retaliation.
sionismo Zionism.
Sionismo Zionism.
sionisto Zionist.
Siono Zion.
sipajo sepoy.
Sirakuso Syracuse.
Sirdarjo Syr Darya, Jaxartes, Yaxartes.
sireno mermaid, siren.
sirenoj sirens.
siria Syrian. **siria buntpego** Syrian woodpecker. **siria lingvo** Syriac.
siriaka Syriac.
Siriako Syriac.
siriano Syrian.
siringkolora lilac (colour).
siringo lilac, Syringa.
Sirio Syria.
Siriuso Sirius.
sirnio tawny owl.
siroko sirocco.
siropo syrup.
sirtako sirtaki.
sisalo sisal.
sisimbrio hedge mustard.
sisirinkio blue-eyed grass.
sisma seismic.
sismo earthquake, quake.
sismografo seismograph.
sismologio seismology.

sistema systematic. **sistema programaro** system software.
sistematiko systematics.
sistemejo system residence.
sistemelekta analizo systems analysis.
sistemestro system administrator.
sistemgenerado system generation.
sistemgeneratoro system generator.
sistemo system.
sistemprogramada system.
sistemprogramado software engineering, system programming.
sistemprogramaro systems software.
sistemprogramisto systems programmer.
sistolo systole.
sistro sistrum.
sitaro sitar.
sitelego wooden bucket, wooden pail.
sitelo bucket, pail.
sito nuthatch.
situacio circumstances, condition, situation, position, station, site.
situi to be situated.
situo site.
siuo Sioux.
siverto sievert.
sizifa laboro Sisyphean labour.
sizigio syzygy.
skabelo footstool, stool.
skabeno alderman, sheriff, magistrate.
skabio blotch, scab, infection, itch (disease), mange.
skabioso scabious.
skabiozo pin-cushion flower, scabious.
skadro squadron.
skadrono squadron.
skafaldo scaffold, scaffolding.
skafandristo diver.
skafandro diving suit, space suit.
Skajpo Skype.
skalara scalar. **skalara potencialo** scalar potential. **skalara produto** scalar product. **skalara produto de vektoroj** scalar product.
skalaro scalar.
skalebla scalable.
skalena scalene.
skali to rescale.
skalo scale (map, measure, etc.).
Skalpajo Scalpay.
skalpelo scalpel.
skalpi to scalp.
skalpo scalp.
skanado scan.
skandala offensive.
skandali to scandalize.
skandaliĝi to be shocked, be scandalized.
skandalo scandal, shocking occurrence.
skandi to chant, scan.

skandinava Scandinavian.
skandinavino Scandinavian woman.
Skandinavio Scandinavia.
skandinavo Scandinavian.
Skandinavo Scandinavian.
Skandinavujo Scandinavia.
skandio scandium.
skando scan.
skani to scan.
skanilo scanner.
Skanio Scania, Skåne, southernmost province of Sweden.
skapolo scapula, shoulder blade.
skapulario scapular.
skapularo sclerotic.
skarabeo scarab.
skarabo beetle, scarabaeus, scarab.
skarifiki to scarify.
skarlata scarlet.
skarlatino scarlatina, scarlet fever.
skarlato scarlet.
skarolo escarole.
skarpo (woman's) scarf; arm-sling, sash, stole.
skato skat.
skatoleto box, casket.
skatolĝardeneto window-box.
skatolmalfermilo can opener.
skatolo box (small), can.
skeĉo skit, sketch.
Skeldo Scheldt.
skeleta skeletal. **Skeleta Bordo** Skeleton Coast.
skeletkapo skull.
skeleto skeleton.
skema schematic.
skemi to schematize.
skemo diagram, model, pattern, scheme.
skeptika sceptical.
skeptike sceptically.
skeptikismo scepticism.
skeptiko scepticism.
skeptikulo sceptic.
skerco scherzo.
skermado fencing.
skermi to fence (sport).
skermilo foil (weapon).
skermisto fencer.
skermo fencing.
sketi to skate.
sketilo skate.
skeŭkzerio rannoch rush.
skiado skiing.
skianto skier.
skibastono pole.
skiboto ski boat.
skideklivo Ski Slope.
skii to ski.
skiisto skier.
skikuranto skier.

skikuri **skribotablo**

skikuri to go skiing, ski.
skilifto ski lift.
skilio dog-fish, sea-dog.
Skilo Scylla.
skinko skink.
skio ski.
skipo shift, team.
skisma schismatic.
skismi to create a schism.
skismo schism.
skismulo schismatic.
skisto schist, shale.
skistosomozo bilharzia, bilharziasis, schistosomiasis, snail fever.
skiŝuo ski boot.
skita Scythian.
skito Scythian.
skitrako ski track.
Skitujo Scythia.
skiza projekto draft design document.
skizanto butterfly flower, fringe-flower, poor-man's orchid.
skizi to plan, sketch.
skizlibro sketchbook.
skizo design, outline, sketch.
skizofrenio schizophrenia.
skizoida schizoid.
sklareo clary.
sklava servile.
sklavaĉo poor slave.
sklaveco servitude, slavery.
sklavema slavish, subservient.
sklaveme slavishly, subserviently.
sklavemo servility.
sklavemulaĉo ass-kisser.
sklavemulo bootlicker, toady.
sklavi to be a slave.
sklavigi to enslave.
sklaviĝinta addicted.
sklavino bondwoman, slave, female slave.
sklavo slave.
sklavŝipo slave ship.
sklavumado drudgery.
sklavumo drudgery.
sklera sclerosed.
sklero sclera.
skleroto sclerotic.
sklerozo sclerosis.
skolastika pedantic, scholastic.
skolastiko scholasticism.
skolastikulo scholastic.
skoldi to reproach, rebuke, reprove, scold.
skolo school (of art, philosophy, thought, etc).
skolopendro centipede.
skolopo woodcock.
skoltado reconnaissance.
skoltavio spy aircraft.
skolti to reconnoitre, scout.
skoltino girl guide, girl scout.

skoltismo guiding, scouting.
skolto boy scout.
skombro mackerel.
skono scone.
skopofilio scoptophilia, voyeurism.
skoptofilio voyeurism.
skorbuta scorbutic.
skorbuto scurvy.
skoriejo ash-heap.
skorio cinder(s), clinker, scalia, slag.
skorpio scorpion. **Skorpio** Scorpio (zodiac).
skorzonero black salsify.
skota Scottish. **Skota Altmontaro** Scottish Highlands. **Skota Malaltebenaĵo** Scottish Lowlands. **skota skolo** a group of people devoted to the Scottish language.
skotero motor-scooter.
skotino Scotswoman.
Skotio Scotland.
skotlanda Scots, Scottish, scotch.
Skotlando Scotland.
Skoto Scot, Scotsman.
skoto Scotsman, Scot.
Skotujo Scotland.
skovelo cleaning-brush, shale.
Skrablo Scrabble.
Skrabstero Scrabster.
skrapaĵo scrapings.
skrapgumo eraser, rubber.
skrapi to scrape, scratch, dredge.
skrapilego dredger.
skrapileto eraser.
skrapilo scraper.
skrapmanĝi to gnaw, nibble.
skraptapiŝo doormat.
skrapvundo abrasion, scratch.
skriba written. **skriba ordono** warrant, writ.
skribaĉi to scribble, scrawl.
skribado writing.
skribaĵo writing.
skribe in writing.
skriberaro typo.
skribesko calligraphic face, script.
skribi to write.
skribilaro writing instruments.
skribilo writing implement, writing instrument.
skribisto clerk, copyist, scribe, writer.
skribita written.
skribite en la steloj written in the stars.
skribmaniero handwriting.
skribmarko cursor.
skribmaŝina tiparo typewriter face.
skribmaŝino typewriter.
skribo script, writing.
skriboplumo pen.
skribordono mandate.
skribotablo writing table.

skribpapero writing paper.
skribpeniko writing-brush.
skribrulaĵo scroll.
skribtablo desk, writing desk.
skripto batch file, command file, script.
skrofolo scrofula.
skroto scrotum.
skrupula accurate, scrupulous, conscientious.
skrupuleco accuracy.
skrupulo conscientiousness, scrupulousness.
skualo squall.
skuego concussion.
skueta tremulous.
skueto tremor.
skui to agitate, shake, shock, toss.
skuiĝi to shake.
skulpta sculptural.
skulptaĵo sculpture.
skulptarto sculpture (art).
skulpti to carve, sculpt.
skulptilo chisel.
skulptisto sculptor.
skulpturo sculpture.
skuludilo rattle.
skuno schooner.
skuo shaking, shake, shock.
skuondo shockwave.
skurgi to flog, thrash.
skurĝado lashing.
skurĝi to flog, lash, scourge, whip.
skurĝo scourge, whip, lash.
skusorbilo shock absorber.
skutilo scooter.
skvalo dogfish.
skvama scaly, squamous, flaky.
skvamo scale (of fish).
skvaŝo squash.
skvateno angel-fish.
slabo slab.
slalomo slalom.
slango slang.
slava Slavic, Slav. **slava lingvo** Slavic language.
slavo Slav.
slavona Slavonian.
Slavonio Slavonia.
Slavono Church Slavonic, Slavonian, Slavonic.
slavono Slavonian.
Slavonujo Slavonia.
sledeto sled, sledge.
sledi to sled.
sledisto sledder, slider.
sledo sled, sleigh, toboggan.
Sligo Sligo.
sliparo file.
slipo filing card, slip.
slogano catch-cry, catch-phrase, slogan.
slojdo sloyd.
slovaka Slovak.
slovakino Slovak woman.
Slovakio Slovakia.
slovako Slovak.
Slovakujo Slovakia.
slovena Slovenian.
Slovenio Slovenia.
sloveno Slovene, Slovenian.
Slovenujo Slovenia.
smeralda emerald.
smeraldo emerald.
smilako sarsaparilla.
smirga abrasive.
smirgi to abrade, grind (rub, polish) with emery.
smirgo emery.
smokingo dinner-jacket, tuxedo.
smolando Småland.
sms-mesaĝo SMS message.
smuto smut.
Snimo Sneem.
snoba snobbish.
snobo snob.
snufegi to snort.
snufi to snuffle.
so name of the letter S.
sobra abstemious, sober, staid, temperate.
sobreco sobriety, temperance.
sobrema abstemious.
socia communal, social. **socia dialekto** social dialect. **socia kontrakto** social contract. **socia vivo** social life.
sociala communal, social.
sociale socially.
socialisma socialist.
socialismo socialism.
socialista socialist.
socialisto socialist.
sociano citizen.
socie socially.
sociekonomika socio-economic.
societa societal, of society.
societama sociable.
societema extroverted, outgoing, sociable, social.
societemulo extroverted person.
societo association, circle, club, society, company.
socilingvistika socio-linguistic.
socio society.
sociologia sociological.
sociologie sociologically.
sociologiisto sociologist.
sociologio sociology.
sociologo sociologist.
socipolitika socio-political.
sociumi to socialize.
Soĉi Sochi.

sodakvo soda, soda water.
sodo soda.
sodomiano sodomite.
sodomianto sodomite.
sodomio sodomy.
sodomismo sodomy.
sodomisto sodomite.
Sodomo Sodom.
Sofio Sofia.
sofismo fallacy, sophism.
sofisto sophist.
sofo sofa.
softa quiet.
softvaro software.
soifa thirsty.
soife thirstily.
soifi to be thirsty, thirst. **soifi je scio** to be thirsty for knowledge.
soifiĝi to quench one's thirst.
soifo thirst.
sojfabo soybean.
sojkazeo bean curd, tofu.
sojlo sill, threshold.
sojo soy.
soklo base, plinth, supporting base, pedestal.
soko ploughshare.
Sokrato Socrates.
sola alone, only, sole, solitary, single. **sola agento** sole agent.
solano nightshade.
solapersone solely, as a single person.
soldata botelo canteen, water bottle.
soldataro force.
soldatejo barracks.
soldato pawn, soldier.
soldo pay (military).
sole alone, just, only, solely.
soleca lonely, solitary.
solecismo solecism.
soleco loneliness, seclusion, solitude.
solemulo loner.
solena ceremonious, solemn. **solena kunveno** celebration.
solenado celebration.
solenaĵo ceremony.
solene ceremoniously, solemnly.
soleneco ceremony, solemnity.
soleni to celebrate, observe with ceremony.
solenigi to celebrate, solemnize.
soleno ceremony, solemnity.
solenoido solenoid.
soleo sole (fish).
solfeĝo solfeggio.
solicismo solecism.
solicitoro solicitor.
solida firm, solid. **solida angulo** solid angle.
solidago goldenrod.
solidara interdependent, jointly responsible, standing together.

solidareco community of interests, solidarity.
solidariĝi to rally.
solidaro solidarity.
solideco virtue.
solidigi to consolidate.
solidigo consolidation.
solido geometric body, rigid body, solid.
soligi to insulate.
solinfano only child.
solipsismo solipsism.
solisto soloist.
solitero tape worm.
solkanto solo.
solkutivado monoculture.
solludo solo.
solo base, pedestal, plinth.
Solo Seoul.
solo solo (mus.).
solstico solstice.
solula solitary.
solulo single, single man, unattached man.
solvaĵo solution.
solvebla soluble, solvable. **solvebla kafo** instant coffee.
solvebleco solubility, solvability.
solvenda to be solved.
solventa solvent.
solventeco ability.
solvi to dissolve, reduce, solve.
solviĝi to dissolve.
solvivanta living alone, single.
solvo dissolution, solution.
somala Somali.
somalino Somali woman.
Somalio Somalia.
somalo Somali.
Somalujo Somalia.
somaterio cider.
sombra sombre.
sombre sombrely.
somera summer, of summer, summer's. **somera kverko** common oak. **somera tempo** daylight saving time, summer time.
somerdomo summer home, summer house.
somere in the summer.
somerloĝejo country house.
somerloĝo country seat.
somermezo midsummer.
somero summer.
somertago summer day.
somerteatro summer theatre.
somiero box spring, spring-mattress.
somnabulo sleep-walker.
somnambuli to sleepwalk.
somnambulismo sleepwalking.
somnambulo sleepwalker.
somoso SMS, short message service.
sona sonic.

sonado booming.
sonalterno spoonerism.
sonaparato stereo system.
sonaro sonar.
sonato sonata.
sonbendbobeno audio tape reel.
sonbendo audio tape, magnetic tape.
sonbobeno audio tape reel.
sonbrako tone-arm.
sondado plumbing, survey.
sondi to fathom, sound, try depth, probe, plumb, sound out.
sondilo probe, fathom line, plummet.
sondisko gramophone disc, gramophone record.
sondosiero audio file, sound file.
soneti to tingle.
soneto sonnet.
sonforketo tuning fork.
sonforteco volume.
sonĝado dreaming.
sonĝi to dream.
sonĝo dream.
soni to boom, sound.
sonigi to sound.
sonilo bell.
sonizoli to soundproof.
sonkarto sound card.
sonlegilo sound player.
sonlibro sound book.
sonlokalizilo echolocation, sonar.
sono sound.
sonora sonorous.
sonoradi to toll (bell).
sonorado tolling.
sonoreti to chime, clank.
sonoretilo chime.
sonoreto chime, clank.
sonori to peal, ring, strike (clock). **sonori la unua** to strike one (a clock).
sonorigi to give a ring, ring, ring the bell.
sonorigisto bell ringer.
sonorilado chime.
sonorilaristo carillonneur.
sonorilaro carillon, chimes, peal (of bells).
sonorilbutono bell button, bell push.
sonorilego bell.
sonorilejo belfry, spire.
sonorileto bell, little bell.
sonorilforma bell-shaped.
sonorilisto bell-ringer.
sonorilo bell.
sonorilturo steeple.
sonormartelo clapper.
sonoro clang, peal, ringing.
sonregistraĵo audio recording.
sonserpento rattlesnake.
sonsignalo audio signal.
sonsistemo sound system.

sontekniko Sound technology.
sopira longing.
sopirado yearning.
sopiranta anxious, pining.
sopiri to ache, long for, yearn. **sopiri al** to ache for. **sopiri pri** to long for.
sopiro longing.
soprana soprano.
soprane soprano.
soprano soprano.
sopranulino soprano.
sopranulo soprano singer.
sorba absorbent. **sorba papero** blotter, blotting paper.
sorbado absorption.
sorbeco absorbency (for liquids).
sorbema absorbent. **sorbema kajo** logical AND operator. **sorbema operacio** logical operator.
sorbi to absorb (a liquid), sip.
sorbigi to imbibe.
sorbiĝi to absorb.
sorbiĝo absorption.
sorbilo absorbent, blotter.
sorbo absorption.
Sorbono the Sorbonne.
sorbopapero blotting paper.
sorbpapero blotter.
sorĉa magic.
sorĉado enchantment, magic, sorcery, witchcraft, wizardry.
sorĉaĵo witchcraft.
sorĉarto sorcery.
sorĉbastono wand.
sorĉelvoko incantation.
sorĉi to bewitch.
sorĉinfluo spell.
sorĉista bastono wand.
sorĉistino witch.
sorĉisto enchanter, magician, sorcerer, warlock, wizard, necromancer.
sorĉkuracisto witch-doctor.
sorĉo sorcery.
sorĉvorto abracadabra.
sorĉvortoj abracadabra.
sordida dirty, foul, nasty.
sordino mute.
sorgo sorghum.
sori to soar.
sorikedoj shrews.
soriko shrew mouse.
sorparbo sorb.
sorpo mountain-ash berry, rowan berry, sorb (apple).
sorpujo mountain-ash, rowan.
sortbato agony.
sortdifino predestination.
sortimenti to stock.
sortimento assortment, selection, collection.

sorto destiny, fate, fortune, luck, lot.
sortobato stroke of fate.
sortovico vicissitude.
sota lingvo Sotho, Sotho language.
soteriologia soteriological.
soteriologio soteriology.
soto Sotho.
sovaĝa savage, wild, untamed. **sovaĝa anaso** wild duck. **sovaĝa besto** savage beast. **sovaĝa kapro** wild goat. **sovaĝa porko** wild boat. **sovaĝa striko** wildcat strike.
sovaĝĉevalo wild horse.
sovaĝe wildly, savagely.
sovaĝeco fierceness, savageness.
sovaĝejo bush, wilderness, wilds.
sovaĝiĝi to become savage, wild.
sovaĝkato wild cat, feral cat.
sovaĝularo group of savages.
sovaĝulo savage (person).
soveta Soviet.
Sovetio Soviet Union, USSR.
soveto soviet.
Sovet-Unio Soviet Union, USSR.
Sovetunio Soviet Union, USSR.
sozio (someone's) double, lookalike.
spaca spatial.
spacetklavo space bar.
spaceto blank, space (character).
spacetostango space bar.
spackombineo space suit.
spacnavedo space shuttle.
spaco room, space.
spacosondilo space probe.
spacostacio space station.
spacostango space bar.
spacoŝipanaro crew.
spacoŝipo spaceship.
spacŝipo space ship.
spadfiŝo swordfish.
spadiko spadix.
spado court sword, dress sword, dueling sword, epee, rapier, small sword.
spageto spaghetti.
spajro spire.
spaliro gauntlet (two rows of people), rank, row (of standing people).
spamado spamming.
spamaĵo spam.
spamanto spammer.
spami to spam.
spamo spam.
spanielo spaniel.
spano span.
sparadrapo adhesive plaster.
sparganio bur-reed.
sparkado ignition.
sparki to spark.
sparkilo plug, spark plug.
sparko spark.

sparkŝlosilo ignition key.
sparo spar.
sparta Spartan.
spartano Spartan.
Sparto Sparta.
spasma jerky, spasmodic, spastic.
spasme spasmodically.
spasmo spasm.
spatelo spatula.
spato spar (mineral).
speciala particular, special. **speciala dosiero** special device file, special file. **speciala dosiero bajta** character device file. **speciala dosiero bloka** block device file, block special file. **speciala okazo** particular case, special case. **speciala signo** special character.
specialaĵo special, speciality.
specialcela ad hoc.
speciale expressly, particularly, specially.
specialiĝi to specialize.
specialisto specialist.
specialoeco speciality.
specifa specific. **specifa maso** density.
specifado enumeration.
specife explicitly, specifically.
specifeco explicitness.
specifi to specify.
specifika specific.
specifiki to specify.
specifo specification.
specimenaro collection.
specimenboteleto sample bottle.
specimeni to sample.
specimenisto sampler.
specimenkarto sample card.
specimenlibro sample book.
specimeno sample, specimen.
specio species.
speco kind, sort, species.
speguli to reflect (light, sound).
speguliĝi to be mirrored, be reflected.
spegulo mirror.
spektakla showy, spectacular.
spektakle showily, spectacularly.
spektakleco showiness.
spektaklo show, spectacle.
spektantaro audience.
spektantejo stand.
spektanto spectator.
spektantoj audience.
spektejo stand.
spekti to view, watch, witness, be a spectator.
spektro spectrum.
spektroskopo spectroscope.
spekulacii to speculate.
spekulacio speculation.
spekulacisto swindler.
spekulativa speculative.

spekulativi — spliti

spekulativi to speculate.
spekulativo speculation.
spekuli to speculate.
spekulimposto short-term capital gains tax.
speleologio speleology.
spelto spelt.
spergulo spurrey.
spermaceto spermaceti.
spermatozoo spermatozoon.
spermicido spermicide.
spermo sperm.
sperta accomplished, adept, experienced, expert, conversant, skilled.
spertado experience (general, continuous).
sperteco experience.
spertega seasoned.
sperti to experience, go through, live to see.
spertiĝi to become expert.
sperto experience.
spertularano panelist.
spertularo panel.
spertulo expert.
spesmilo spesmilo (S, obsolete decimal international currency).
speso speso (basic unit of the obsolete spesmilo currency).
spezado cash flow.
spezi to transact money.
spezkalkulo budget.
spezo turnover.
spica spicy. **Spica Marbordo** Pepper Coast, Grain Coast.
spicaĵo ragout, seasoning.
spicaro spicery.
spice racily, spicily.
spiceca nutty.
spiceco spiciness.
spici to spice, season.
spicisto grocer.
spico spice.
spika miriofilo spiked water-milfoil, Eurasian water-milfoil.
spiko ear (of corn), spike.
spikumi to glean.
spili to bottle, broach, tap.
spililo augur.
spina spinal. **spina medolo** spinal chord.
spinaco spinach.
Spinbriĝo Spean Bridge.
spindelo spindle.
spindelrado fusee (component of a clock).
spineto spinet, virginal.
spinmomanto spin.
spino backbone, spine, spinal column.
spiona spy.
spionado espionage, spying.
spione spy-like.
spioni to spy, snoop, watch.
spionino spy.
spiono spy.
spionraporto espionage record, report, account.
spira aspirated.
spirado breathing, respiration.
spiraĵo breath.
spirala spiral.
spiralero whorl.
spirali to spiral.
spiralo spiral.
spiraparato artificial respirator.
spirblovi to snuffle.
spirebla respirable.
spiregi to gasp, pant.
spireo spiraea.
spirĝeno tightness of the chest.
spiri to breathe, respire.
spirilo spirillum.
spirita incorporeal, mental, spiritual, witty, smart.
spiritĉeesto spontaneity.
spiriteco spirituality.
spiritforesta absent-minded.
spiritforesto absence of mind.
spiritismo spiritism, spiritualism.
spiritisto spiritist, follower of spiritism.
spirito mind, spirit.
spiritpreteco spontaneity.
spiritstato state of mind, emotional state.
spiritualismo spiritualism.
spiritualisto spiritualist.
spiritvagado aberration.
spirkanalo airway.
spirkapta breathtaking.
spirmanka breathless.
spirmanko dyspnea.
spiro breath.
spiroĥeto spirochete.
spiroketo spirochaete.
spirotruo air hole, blowhole.
spirpaŭzo breather, breathing space.
spirta be no fool.
spirtruo air hole, blowhole.
spirtubo snorkel.
spitado defiance, flouting.
spite defiantly, despite, in spite of. **spite al tio ke** despite that fact that.
spitema irreverent, perverse.
spiteme defiantly.
spitemo defiance, irreverence.
spiti to defy.
spito defiance, spite.
splendi to sparkle, be brilliant.
spleno blues, depression, ill humour, low spirits, melancholy.
splinto splint.
splisi to splice.
splitema splintery.
spliti to splinter, split.

splitigi to splinter.
splitiĝi to splinter.
splito splinter.
spoko spoke.
spondeo spondee.
sponga spongy.
spongeca spongy.
spongi to sponge (down, over).
spongo sponge.
spongoŝvabrilo (sponge) mop.
sponta spontaneous.
spontana spontaneous.
spontane spontaneously.
spontanea spontaneous.
spontaneco spontaneity.
spontanee spontaneously.
spontaneeco spontaneity.
sporada sporadic. **sporada eraro** soft error.
sporklabo basidium.
sporo spore.
sporta sport, sporting.
sportaŭto sports car.
sportĉemizo sports shirt.
sportego great sport, great fun.
sportejo sports ground.
sportema sporting, sporty.
sporthalo sport hall.
sportige hunting.
sportigi to make sport (of something).
sportistinda sportsmanlike.
sportistino sportswoman.
sportisto sportsman, sports enthusiast, athlete.
sportjako blazer.
sporto sport.
sportocentro sport centre.
sportohalo sport hall.
sportŝuo sneaker, tennis shoe.
sportulo sportsman.
sportumi to play sports.
spoto spotlight.
spozo bridegroom.
spraji to spray.
sprinti to sprint.
sprinto sprint.
sprita bright, clever, lively, witty, racy.
spritaĵo flash (of wit), witticism, wisecrack, joke.
sprite witty.
spriteco wittiness.
spritema witty.
spriti to be bright, clever, witty, sprightly.
sprito brightness, cleverness, sprightliness, wit.
spritresponda to the point.
spritulo joker, wag, wit.
sproni to encourage, incite, rouse, spur, stimulate, stir up.
sprono spur, sprat.

sproso shoot, sprout.
sproto sprat.
spurebla traceable.
spurhundo bloodhound.
spuri to trail, track.
spuro trace, track, trail.
spurvojo track, trace, clue.
sputaĵo sputum.
sputeti to sputter.
sputi to spit.
sputniko satellite, Sputnik.
srangoli to strangle.
Sreŭburgo Shrewsbury.
srilanka Sri Lankan.
srilankanino Sri Lankan woman.
srilankano Sri Lankan.
Srilanko Sri Lanka.
S-ro. → **sinjoro**.
S-ta → **Sankta**.
stabejo headquarters.
stabila stable, firm, steady.
stabileco stability.
stabiliga stabilizing.
stabiligi to balance, stabilize, steady.
stabiligilo stabilizer.
stabiliĝi to balance.
stablo bench, easel, workbench, support, stand.
stablolaboristo bench hand, fitter.
stabo commanding officers, general staff.
stacidomo (railway) station house, terminal.
staciestro station master.
stacii to be stationed.
stacio stage, station, stop, terminal.
stadie gradually.
stadio period, phase, stage, stadium (Greek measure).
stadiono arena, ballpark, coliseum, grandstand, grounds, stadium, sports ground.
stafeto courier, dispatch rider, relay racer, relay rider, messenger.
stafetringo token ring.
stafileo bladder-nut.
stafilokoko staphylococcus.
stagna stagnant.
stagnejo backwater.
stagni to stagnate.
staĝanto trainee.
staĝi to serve as a trainee.
staĝo internship, short training course, traineeship.
stahanovismo Stakhanovism.
stahanovisto Stakhanovist.
stajo brace, cramp-iron, guy, stay.
stajvelo staysail.
staka aŭtomato stack automaton.
stakato staccato.
stakejo stacker.
staki to stack.

stakiso woundwort.
stakmaltroo stack underflow.
stako heap, pile, stack.
stakto stacte.
staktroo stack overflow.
stalagmito stalagmite.
stalaktito stalactite.
stalfako stall.
stalkorto barnyard.
stalo stable, stall, sty.
stalono stallion.
stameno stamen.
stamenportilo androphore.
stamfi to paw the ground, stamp.
stamino stamin.
stampado stamping.
stampaĵo stamp (brand).
stampi to mark, stamp. **stampi monerojn** to coin, mint.
stampilo stamp, rubber stamp, stamper.
stampimposto stamp duty, stamp tax.
stampo mark, stamp.
stana tin.
stanaĵo tin.
stanco stanza.
standardeto banderole, banderol, bannerol.
standardisto ensign bearer.
standardo banner, flag, standard.
standardportisto standard-bearer, colours-bearer, ensign-bearer.
stando booth, stall, stand.
stanfolio foil, silver paper, tinfoil.
stangeto stick.
stangiĝi to roost.
stangirilo stilt.
stango bar, handle, pole, rod, shaft, spar, staff, stake, stave, perch.
stangogaŭgo dipstick.
stangohakilo pole-axe.
stangopupo rod puppet.
stangpere using a rod.
stani to tin (plate).
staniolo (tin) foil.
Stanislavo Stanislaus.
stanisto tinsmith.
stano pewter, tin.
Stanraro Stanraer.
stanumi to plate.
stapla reĝimo batch mode, batch processing.
staplada komputado batch processing.
staplado storage.
staplejo store.
stapli to stack, stash, store, warehouse.
staplisto warehouseman.
staplo pile, stack.
staraĉi to slouch.
starejo foothold, footing, stand, station.
starema stable.

starhimno acathistus.
stari to stand. **stari ekster atingodistanco** to be out of range, beyond reach. **stari fidele ĉe siaj principoj** to stand firmly by one's principles. **stari garde** to stand guard.
starigadi to make someone stand up.
starigi to erect, set up, stand.
starigo establishment.
stariĝante standing up.
stariĝi to get up, rise, stand, stand up.
starpunkto angle, outlook, point of view, position, stance, stand, standpoint, viewpoint.
startanto starter.
startejo start.
starti to start (off).
startigi to start.
startigilo starter.
startigo boot, booting, startup.
startkarto begin card.
starto kickoff, start, takeoff.
startomaŝino starting gate.
startsvingilo handle, starting-handle.
stati to be in a state, be in a condition (*intr.*).
statika static. **statika bindado** static binding. **statika memordisponigo** static allocation.
statikisto statistician.
statiko statics.
statisti to play a small part.
statistika statistical.
statistiko statistics.
statisto bit player, supporting actor.
stativo stand, tripod, support.
stato condition, state, situation, station (of life).
statoro stator.
statuaro statuary.
statuarto statuary.
statueca statuesque.
statueto statuette.
statuo statue.
staturo stature. **staturo de prestipo** type height.
statuso status.
statuto by-laws, statute, regulations.
staŭdo hardy perennial (plant).
staŭli to stall (of a plane).
staŭlo stand.
stearato stearate.
stearino stearin.
stebado quilting.
stebero stitch.
stebi to quilt, stitch, sew.
stebilo sewing machine.
stebisto quilter.
Stefano Stephen, Steven.
stefanoto stephanotis.

steganografia steganographic.
steganografio steganography.
stego brace, prop, support.
stegosaŭro stegosaur.
steko steak.
stela sidereal, star, of a star.
stelamasego galaxy.
stelanizo star anise.
stelario stitchwort.
stelaro constellation.
steleco stardom.
steleo stele.
steleto asterisk (*).
stelfiguro constellation.
stelkantanto star-singer.
stellumo starlight.
stelo star.
steloza cielo starry sky.
stelplena starry star-filled. **stelplena ĉiela** starry sky, star-filled sky. **stelplena ĉielo** star-filled heaven.
stelŝipo starship.
stelulineto starlet.
stelulino celebrity, star.
stelulo celebrity, star.
stencili to stencil.
stencilo stencil.
steno shorthand.
stenografi to write shorthand.
stenografiisto stenographer.
stenografio shorthand, stenography.
stenografisto stenographer.
stenografo stenographer.
stenotajpistino stenotypist, female stenotypist.
stenotajpisto stenotypist.
stenotipio stenotypy.
stenotipo stenotype.
stentora stentorian.
stepaglo steppe eagle.
stepo moor, steppe, heath.
steradiano steradian.
stereofonia stereo, stereophonic.
stereofonie stereo.
stereofonio stereo, stereophony.
stereografio stereography.
stereokasedilo cassette player.
stereometrio stereometry.
stereomikroskopo stereomicroscope.
stereoskopio stereoscopy.
stereoskopo stereoscope.
stereotipa stereotyped.
stereotipado stereotyping.
stereotipi to stereotype.
stereotipo stereotype.
sterila sterile.
sterileco sterility.
steriligi to sterilize.
steriligo sterilization.

sterilizado sterilization.
sterilizatoro sterilizer.
sterilizi to sterilize.
sterkado dressing, fertilization, applying of manure.
sterkaĵo dung heap.
sterkakvo liquid manure, muck-water, stale.
sterki to fertilize.
sterko dung, fertilizer, manure.
sterkorario skua.
sterkoskarabo dung beetle.
sterledo sterlet.
sterlinga sterling. **sterlinga funto** pound sterling.
sterlingfunto pound sterling.
sterlingo pound sterling.
sternaĵo blanket, stratum.
sternejo bed.
sterni to lay out, spread, spread out, sprawl.
sterntabelo spreadsheet.
sternumo sternum.
sterolo sterol.
stertora stertorous.
stertori to breathe (heavily).
stertoro rattle in the throat.
stetoskopi to listen with stethoscope.
stetoskopo stethoscope.
stevardino stewardess.
stevardo attendant, steward (ship, plane, etc.).
Stevardurbo Stewarton.
Stevartinsulo Stewart Island.
steveno stem.
stifto peg, pin.
stigmatizi to stigmatize.
stigmato scar, stigma.
stigmo spiracle, stigma.
stiki to propagate plants by cuttings.
stiksa Stygian.
Stikso Styx.
stila stylish.
stilekzerco exercise in style, style exercise.
stileto stiletto.
stilfolio stylesheet.
stilistiko stylistics.
stilo style.
stiluso style.
stilzo wader (bird), stilt.
stilzobirdo wader.
stimula stimulating, stimulative.
stimulado abetment, stimulation.
stimuli to rouse, stimulate, stir up.
stimulilo stimulant.
stimulo impetus, incitement, stimulus.
stinka malodorous, smelly, stinking, stinky.
stinki to smell, stink.
stipendio grant, scholarship, stipend.
stipendiulo exhibitioner, scholar.
stipo stalk.

stipulo

stipulo stipule.
stirado steering.
stiranto driver.
stirbito control bit.
stirebla controllable.
stirejo cockpit, flight deck.
stireno styrene.
stirflua diagramo control flow chart, control flow diagram, flow chart.
stirglobo rolling ball, track ball.
stiri to drive, fly, steer.
stirilo joystick, steering wheel.
Stirio Styria.
stiristo driver.
stirkolono joystick, steering column.
stirkonstruaĵo control structure.
Stirlingo Stirling.
stiroperacio connector, control operator.
stirorgano control unit, processor.
stirpanelo control panel.
stirrado steering wheel.
stirsigno control character.
stirstango joystick.
stirstrukturo control structure.
stirvojo steerage-way.
stivi to stow (cargo).
stivisto stevedore.
stoika impassive, imperturbable, stoic, stoical.
stoike stoically.
stoikeco stoicism.
stoikismo stoicism.
stoikisto stoic.
stoikulo stoic.
stokado storage.
stokasta variablo random variable.
stokasto random number, random variable.
stokejo stock room, storage room, warehouse.
Stokholmo Stockholm.
stoki to stock.
stokisto stockist.
stoko stock, reserves.
stolo stole.
stolono runner, sucker.
stomaka gastric. **stomaka suko** gastric juice.
stomakdoloro stomach ache.
stomako stomach.
stompi to soften off, stump.
stompilo stump.
stono stone.
stop stop.
stoplejo stubble.
stoplo stubble.
Stornovejo Stornoway.
storo memory.
stovo heating stove, stove.
straba cross-eyed, squinting.

strećeco

strabe squintingly.
strabeco strabism.
strabi to be cross-eyed, look askance, squint.
strabismo squint, strabismus.
stramonio apple of Peru, thorn-apple.
strando beach, shore.
strandŝtelisto beachcomber.
stranga odd, peculiar, strange, curious, eccentric, queer.
strangaĵo quirk, oddity.
strange oddly.
strangeco strangeness.
strangega fantastical.
strangi to be strange, be odd.
strangoli to choke, strangle.
strangolilo choke.
strangolo strangulation, stricture.
strangulo eccentric, weirdo, odd person.
Strasburgo Strasbourg.
straso baubles, junk jewellery.
strata stone-paved. **strata lanterno** street light.
stratangulo corner, street corner.
stratbubo ragamuffin.
strategia strategic. **strategia ludo** strategy game.
strategiaĵo stratagem.
strategiisto strategist.
strategiludo strategy game.
strategio strategy.
stratego general, strategist.
strateto alley, lane.
stratioto water soldier.
stratĵurnalo tabloid.
stratkanaleto sewer.
stratkruciĝo intersection.
stratlaboristo road labourer.
stratlampo street light.
stratlanterno streetlamp, streetlight.
stratmuzikisto busker.
strato road, street.
stratonivelo street level.
stratosfero stratosphere.
stratŝildo street sign.
strattelefono pay phone, pay telephone, public telephone.
strattunelo subway, underpass.
stratumo stratum.
stratuso stratus.
strebado striving, aspiration.
strebi to seek, strive for.
strebo effort.
streĉa taut.
streĉado exertion, stretching.
streĉanta hard.
streĉbandaĝo stretch bandage.
streĉe tightly.
streĉeco rigour, strain, stress, strictness, tension.

streĉi

streĉi to stretch, wind up (watch, clock), tense.
streĉiĝi to stretch.
streĉiĝo tension.
streĉilo rack.
streĉita flat, straight, strained.
streĉiteco tightness.
streĉo stress, tension.
streĉopesilo string-balance.
streĉvundi to rick.
strekaro set of strokes.
streketo hyphen (-).
streki to cross out, draw, make a stroke, draw a line, streak, trace.
strekkodo bar code.
strekmarki to check off, tick off.
streko line, line segment, streak, stroke, dash. **dividostreko** hyphen (-). **ĝis-streko** en dash (–). **haltostreko** em dash (—).
streptokoko streptococcus.
streptomicino streptomycin.
stresimuna immune to stress.
streta narrow.
stria striated, striped.
stridi to be strident.
strigedoj true owls, typical owls.
strigli to curry(-comb), rub down, groom.
striglilo currycomb.
strigo owl.
strii to stripe.
striita oficefalo striped snake-head fish.
strikanto striker.
striki to strike (of workmen).
striknino strychnine.
striko strike.
strikodo barcode.
strikrajto right to strike.
strikrompanto strike-breaker.
strikta tight.
strikte strictly, tightly. **strikte monotona** strictly monotonic (mapping).
strikteco strictness.
stringi to hug, squeeze, tighten, draw, constrict.
strio ray, strip, stripe.
striptizo striptease.
strobilo (pine) cone, strobilus.
stroboskopia stroboscopic.
stroboskopo stroboscope.
strofo couplet, stanza, strophe, verse.
strofoido strophoid.
Stromneso Stromness.
stroncio strontium.
struktura structural. **struktura ordono** structured statement.
strukturado structuring.
strukture structurally.
strukturema programado structured programming.

sturme

strukturi to structure.
strukturismo structuralism.
strukturo structure.
struma nemezio Cape jewels, pouch nemesia.
strumo goitre.
struti to bury one's head in the sand.
struto ostrich.
strutoformaj ratites.
stuci to trim.
studado study.
studanto student.
studĉambro studio.
studegi to swot.
studejo study.
studema fond of studying, studious.
studenta student, undergraduate.
studentino (female) student.
studento student (university).
studĝardeno botanical garden.
studi to study.
studio studio (TV, etc.).
studjaro academic year.
studjaroj student years.
studo study.
studobjekto subject, subject of study.
studoĉambro study.
stufaĵo stew.
stufi to braise, simmer, stew.
stufoviando stewing meat.
stufpoto stew-pan.
stufujo stew-pan.
stukaĵo stucco.
stuki to plaster, stucco.
stuko stucco, plaster.
stulta foolish, silly, stupid, dumb.
stultaĵo foolishness, foolish thing, stupidity.
stulte stupidly.
stulteco stupidity.
stultega as stupid as an ass.
stultigi to stultify, make dumb.
stultiĝi to become stupid.
stultulo fool, idiot.
stumbli to miss one's step, stumble, trip, misstep.
stumbligilo stumbling block.
stumblo blunder.
stumpa squat.
stumpeto butt.
stumpigi to top, truncate.
stumpo butt, stub, stump.
stupi to calk.
stupo tow.
stupori to be in a stupor.
stuporo stupor.
stupro ravishment, rape, violation.
sturgo sturgeon.
sturma headlong.
sturme headlong.

422

sturmi to assault, storm, attack, charge.
sturmo assault, storming, attack, charge.
sturno starling.
sub below, beneath, under, underneath. **sub kiu kondiĉo?** under what condition? **sub la influe de** under the influence of. **sub la pretekso de** under the pretext that. **sub lia disponado** at one's disposal. **sub libera ĉielo** under the open sky. **sub unu kondiĉo** on one condition.
suba lower, bottom, under, subordinate.
suba baro lower bound. **suba flanko** underside. **suba fluo** lower course. **suba indico** subscript. **suba najbaro** neighbour on the lower storey. **suba paĝotitolo** footer. **suba parto** lower part. **suba rutino** subroutine.
subaĉetaĵo bribe.
subaĉetebla mercenary.
subaĉeti to bribe, corrupt.
subaĉeto bribery.
subadmiralo rear-admiral, sub-admiral, vice-admiral.
subaĵo underlay.
subakva underwater.
subakvi to submerge.
subakvigata submerged.
subakvigi to dip (in water), immerse, submerge.
subakviĝi to become submerged, dive, sink, plunge.
subakviĝo flood.
subaldo contralto, countertenor.
subalterna subordinate.
subandroika subandroecious.
subarbo subtree.
subaro subset.
subatoma subatomic.
subaŭdi to overhear.
subaŭskulti to bug, eavesdrop, listen in, monitor, tap.
subbildigo partial mapping.
subbrako armpit, underarm.
subĉemizo vest.
subĉeno substring.
subĉiela open-air, outdoor.
subĉiele in the open air.
subdepartemento arrondissement, district.
subdioika subdioecious.
subdisko a partition.
subdividi to subdivide.
subdosierujo subdirectory.
sube below, underneath, under, below.
subekipaĵo undercarriage.
suben down, underneath.
subenfala dropdown.
subenŝargo download.
subenŝargi to download.
subesprimo subexpression.

subetaĝo basement.
subetno ethnic subgroup.
subevoluinta underdeveloped. **subevoluintaj landoj** undeveloped countries.
subfali to succumb.
subfalo slump.
subferigita betono (iron-)reinforced concrete.
subfervojo subway, tube, underground.
subfleksiĝi to bend.
subfosa subversive.
subfosi to mine, sap, undermine, subvert.
subfrazo subclause.
subgenuo hamstring.
subginoika subgynoecious.
subglaso coaster.
subgrafeo partial graph, subgraph.
subgrupo subgroup.
subhaŭta subcutaneous.
subhoko cedilla (¸).
subigi to subdue, overwhelm, subjugate, subject.
subigo subordination.
subiĝi to submit.
subiĝo subordination.
subintervalo subrange.
subiri to set, go down (sun).
subirigi to sink, submerge, subpress.
subita abrupt, sudden, instantaneous. **subita morto** sudden death.
subite all of a sudden, suddenly.
subitventeto whiff.
subjekta subjective.
subjektiva subjective.
subjektive subjectively.
subjektiveco subjectivity.
subjektivisma subjectivist.
subjektivismo subjectivism.
subjekto subject (grammar), topic.
subjugigi to subjugate.
subjunkcio subjunction.
subjunktivo subjunctive.
subjupo petticoat.
subkategorio subcategory.
subklaso subclass.
subkolonelo lieutenant-colonel.
subkomprenigi to imply.
subkonscia subconscious.
subkonscie subconsciously.
subkonscio subconscious, subconsciousness.
subkonstruaĵo foundation.
subkontrakti to subcontract.
subkontrakto subcontract.
subkorpo subfield.
subkulturo subculture.
subleŭtenanto second lieutenant.
sublima elevated, sublime.
sublimato corrosive sublimate, mercuric chloride, sublimate.

sublimi to sublimate.
sublimigi to sublimate.
sublua sublet, subleased.
subluanto lodger, subtenant.
submajstro assistant master, foreman.
submara submarine. **submara arĥeologio** underwater archaeology. **submara arkeologio** underwater archaeology. **submara bombo** antisubmarine bomb.
submarŝipo submarine.
submatrico submatrix.
submergebla ŝipo submersible (ship).
submetaĵo submission.
submeteco subjection.
submeti to overpower, subdue, subjugate, submit, subject. **submeti sin** to submit.
submetigo subjection.
submetiĝi to give in, resign oneself, submit.
submetiĝo submission.
submetiisto journeyman.
submezbranĉo bez antler.
submezpeza welterweight.
submodulo submodule.
subnocio subnotion.
subnorma below standard, substandard.
subnule below zero.
subo bottom.
suboficejo branch.
suboficiro non-commissioned officer.
subofico branch.
subombro shade.
subordiga konjunkcio subordinating conjunction.
subordigi to subordinate.
subpafilego gun carriage.
subparagrafo subsection.
subpasejo subway, pedestrian underpass.
subporti to wear.
subportilo support (prop).
subpostuli to canvass.
subprema repressive.
subpremado oppression, repression.
subpremanto oppressor.
subpremi to oppress, repress, suppress, stifle.
subpremoado repression.
subprogramo routine, subroutine.
subpropozicio dependent clause.
subreto soubrette.
subridi to laugh up one's sleeve.
subrido giggle, snigger.
subringo subring (mathematics).
subrobo slip.
subsabligita buried in sand.
subsekcio subsection.
subsekvenco subsequence.
subskribi to attest (a document), sign, subscribe.
subskribinto signatory.
subskribo signature.

subskriboaĵo sign manual.
subskripcio advance order.
subspeco subtype.
substanca substantial.
substanco matter, stuff, substance.
substantivigi to make into a noun.
substantivo noun, substantive.
substitui to substitute.
substituo permutation, substitution.
substrato substratum.
substreĉi to subtend (an arc).
substreki to emphasize, underline, underscore.
substreko underscore (_).
subŝerifo bailiff.
subŝovi to insinuate.
subŝteli to pilfer, pinch.
subŝtofi to line.
subŝtofo lining.
subŝtupare downstairs.
subtaksi to underestimate.
subtaso saucer.
subtavolaro substratum.
subtavoli to underlie.
subtegmentejo attic.
subtegmento attic, garret.
subtena support, supporting.
subtenado maintenance.
subtenaĵo abutment, strut, prop.
subtenanto carrier (of a function).
subtenebla sustainable.
subteneble sustainably.
subtenebleco sustainability.
subtenema supportive.
subteneme supportively.
subteni to abet, support, sustain, maintain, shore up, underlie.
subtenilo pillar, stay, support, holder.
subteninto abetter.
subteno pile, support, prop, stanchion, stay.
subtera subterranean, underground. **subteraj galerioj** catacombs.
subteraĵo crypt.
subteretaĝo cellar, basement.
subterfervojo subway.
subtervojo tunnel.
subtila subtle.
subtilaĵo fine distinction, subtlety.
subtile lightly, subtly.
subtileco subtlety.
subtitoligado subtitling.
subtitoligi to subtitle.
subtitolo subheading.
subtraha problemo subtraction sum.
subtrahata nombro subtrahend.
subtrahato subtrahend.
subtrahebla deductible.
subtrahi to subtract.
subtraho subtraction.

subtrajno subway, tube, underground.
subulo inferior, subordinate.
suburbo suburb.
subuteo hobby.
subvariejo subrange.
subvencii to subsidize.
subvencio grant, subsidy.
subventra abdominal.
subventro abdomen.
subvestaĵo underwear.
subvesto undergarment.
subvico subsequence.
subvojo subway, tube, underground.
suĉado suction.
suĉbotelo baby's bottle, feeding bottle.
suĉi to suck.
suĉigantino nursing woman.
suĉigi to breast feed, give suck, suckle, nurse.
suĉigistino nurse (wet).
suĉilo comforter, baby's comforter, dummy, pacifier, vacuum cleaner, nipple.
suĉinfano foster child.
suĉinsekto sucking insect.
suda south, southern, southerly. **Suda Azio** South Asia, Southern Asia. **Suda Ĉina Maro** South China Sea. **Suda Insulo** South Island. **Suda Kruco** Southern Cross.
suda vento south wind.
sudafrika South African.
sudafrikano South African.
Sud-Afriko South Africa.
Sudafriko South Africa.
sudamerika South American.
Sud-Ameriko South America.
Sudameriko South America.
sudana Sudanese.
sudananino Sudanese woman.
sudanano Sudanese.
Sudano Sudan.
Sudaŭstralio South Australia.
sudaziano South Asian.
Sudĉina Maro South China Sea.
sude in the south. **sude de** south of.
suden south, southward, southwards.
sudflanko south side.
Sudgeorgio South Georgia.
Sud-Holando South Holland.
Sud-Koreio South Korea.
Sud-Koreujo South Korea.
Sudkoreujo South Korea.
sudlumo aurora australis.
sudo south.
sudokcidenta southwest.
sudoko sudoku.
sudorienta southeast.
Sudorientazio Southeast Asia.
sudoriento south-east.
sudparto south part.
sudpolusa antarctic.

Sudsandviĉinsuloj South Sandwich Islands.
Sudskota Montaro Southern Uplands.
Sudsudano South Sudan.
Suduvisto South Uist.
Sudvjetnamo South Vietnam.
suferado suffering.
suferanta painful, sore, aching. **suferanta pro** affected with, afflicted with, subject to.
suferanto martyr, victim.
suferi to abide, bear, endure, put up with, suffer, undergo. **suferi de** to suffer from. **suferi doloron** to ache. **suferi pro** to suffer from.
suferiga cause suffering.
suferigi to cause to suffer, make endure, victimize.
sufero martyrdom, suffering.
sufiano Sufi.
sufiĉa adequate, ample, enough, sufficient. **sufiĉa kialo** sufficient reason. **sufiĉa kondiĉo** sufficient condition.
sufiĉe enough, quite, rather, sufficiently. **sufiĉe granda** quite big.
sufiĉeco sufficiency.
sufiĉega abundant, redundant, profuse, plenty, ample.
sufiĉege galore, aplenty, in abundance.
sufiĉegi to abound, teem.
sufiĉego abundance.
sufiĉi to suffice, be enough.
sufiĉo enough (of something).
sufiismo Sufism.
sufikso extension, suffix.
sufiksrimo suffix rhyme.
sufleo soufflé.
suflori to prompt (theatre).
sufloro prompter.
sufoka airless, oppressive, stifling, sultry, suffocating.
sufoki to choke, quell, suffocate, suppress, smother, stifle strangle, throttle.
sufokiĝi to suffocate, choke.
sufokiĝo oppression.
sufragano suffragan.
sugesta suggestive.
sugeste as a suggestion.
sugesti to advance, suggest.
sugestii to suggest.
sugestio the power of suggestion.
sugesto suggestion.
suicidi to commit suicide.
suicido suicide.
suikinkuco suikinkutsu (Japanese garden ornament).
suka juicy.
sukcena amber.
sukceno amber.
sukcesa successful.
sukcese successfully.

sukcesi

sukcesi to succeed.
sukceso achievement, success.
sukcesplene successfully.
sukeracero sugar maple.
sukeraĵejo confectionary, candy store.
sukeraĵisto confectioner, pastry cook.
sukeraĵo a sweet, sweetmeat.
sukeraĵoj sweets.
sukerarejo sugar factory.
sukerfabrikado sugar industry.
sukeri to add sugar to, crystallize, candy.
sukerindustrio sugar industry.
sukerkano sugar cane.
sukero sugar.
sukerpalmo sugar palm.
sukerpano Sugarloaf Mountain.
sukerpeco piece of sugar, sugar cube.
sukerpomo custard apple, sugar apple.
sukersciuro sugar glider.
sukerujo sugar bowl.
sukerumi to add sugar to.
suko gravy, juice, sap, pith.
sukubo succubus.
sukurado first-aid, first aid.
sukurejo first aid station.
sukuri to give first-aid, give first-aid to.
sukurismo first aid.
sukuristo first aider.
sukuro first aid.
sulfido sulfide.
sulfura sulphuric.
sulfuro brimstone, sulphur.
sulka rugged.
sulkegiĝi to scowl.
sulketo wrinkle.
sulki to furrow, wrinkle.
sulkigi to furrow, wrinkle, frown. **sulkigi la frunton** frown.
sulkiĝi to shrivel up, wrinkle, furrow.
sulko groove, ridge, wrinkle (facial), furrow (in the earth).
sulo gannet.
sultano sultan.
Sulumaro Sulu Sea.
suma aggregate.
sumako sumac.
sumatra Sumatran.
sumatrano Sumatran.
Sumatro Sumatra.
sume altogether.
sumera Sumerian.
Sumerio Sumer.
sumero Sumerian.
Sumerujo Sumer.
sumi to sum.
sumigi to add up, sum up, (take a) census.
  sumigi la ciferojn to add up the figures.
sumiĝi to amount. **sumiĝi je** to amount to.

superaro

sumilo adder (numbers). **sumilo seria** serial adder.
sumo amount, sum.
sumoisto sumo wrestler.
sumoo sumo.
suna solar, sun, of the sun. **suna kalendaro** solar calender. **suna makulo** sunspot.
sunao Sunna.
sunbanantino sunbather.
sunbankremo suntan lotion.
sunbano sunbath.
sunbaterio solar cell.
sunbrilo sun, sunshine.
sunbruligo sunburn.
sunbruliĝi to sunburn.
sunbrunigi to tan.
sunbruniĝo sun-tan.
sunbruno suntan.
sune sunny.
suneŭforbio sun spurge.
sunfloro sunflower.
sunfrapo sunstroke.
sunhorloĝo sundial.
sunkalendaro solar calender.
sunkolektilo solar collector.
sunleviĝo sunrise.
sunlumo sunlight.
Suno sun.
suno sun.
sunombrelo parasol, sunshade.
sunplena sunny.
sunradio ray of the sun, sunbeam.
sunrobo sundress.
sunsekigi to dry in the sun.
sunsistemo solar system.
sunsubiro sunset.
sunŝirmilego awning.
sunŝirmilo visor.
suntago sunny day.
sunumi to sun, sun oneself, take a sunbath.
sunvitroj sunglasses.
supeo supper.
super above, over, superior. **super ĉio** above all. **super la nivelo de maro** above sea level.
supera superior, supreme, top. **supera baro** upper bound. **supera korpo** extension field.
superabunda superabundant.
superabundeco overabundance.
superabundi to abound, be superabundant.
superabundo cornucopia, superabundance, surfeit.
superaĵo surface.
superakvego deluge, flood.
superakvi to flood, inundate.
superakviĝi to emerge.
superaltara pentraĵo altarpiece.
superaro superset.

superatuti to outdo, surpass, trump.
superba lovely, magnificent, splendid.
superbazaro supermarket.
superbe superbly.
superbela gorgeous, marvelous.
superblufi to abash.
superboli to boil over, boil rapidly.
superbordigo overflow.
superbordiĝi to come out of its banks, overflow.
superbrili to outshine.
superdosierujo superdirectory.
supereco superiority, upper hand.
superega paramount, supreme.
superege extremely.
superegeco supremacy.
superelipso superellipse.
superemi to emulate.
superemo emulation.
superetno ethnic super-group.
superfantazia great.
superfeliĉa overjoyed.
superflua overflowing, superfluous, redundant. **superflua aldonaĝo** superfluous addition.
superfluaĵo surplus.
superflueco redundancy, superfluity.
superflugo view.
superflui to overflow.
superfluiĝi to brim.
superfluo superfluity.
superforti to overpower, prevail over, subdue.
superforto "act of God".
supergrafeo supergraph.
superheroo superhero.
superheterodino superhet.
superhoma superhuman.
Superhomo superhuman.
superhomo superman.
superi to exceed, excel, prevail, surpass, outdo, top, be superior to.
superiĝi to rise to the surface.
superindekso main index, master index, primary index.
superinto beater.
superjaro leap year.
superĵeti to barrage.
superkonduka superconductive.
superkondukanto superconductor.
superkondukeco superconductivity.
superkonduktanto superconductor.
superkonduktiveco superconductivity.
superkorpo extension field.
superkrita above critical.
superlativo superlative.
supermarkto supermarket.
supermezura exorbitant, profuse.

supermezure extraordinarily, tremendously, exceedingly.
supernacia above nations, over nations, supernational.
supernatura supernatural, unearthly.
supernocio supernotion.
supernovao supernova.
supernutrado eutrophication.
supernutriĝo eutrophication.
supero excellence.
superoferi to outbid.
superpago surcharge.
superpendi to overhang.
superpeza preponderant.
superpeze preponderantly.
superpezi to outweigh.
superpezo preponderance.
superplenumiĝo exceeding, going above or beyond.
superplenumo overfulfilment.
superponti to bridge.
superpotenco superpower.
superpunkto dot above (˙).
superreala surreal.
superrealisma surrealist.
superrealismo surrealism.
superrealisto surrealist.
superrega of paramount importance, predominating.
superregado dominance.
superrege dominantly.
superregema dominant, domineering, overbearing, magisterial, supercilious.
superregeme superciliously.
superregi to overrule, predominate.
superrego preponderance.
superrigardi to have an overview of.
superrigardo overview.
superringo superring.
superruzi to outsmart, outwit.
supersati to surfeit.
supersatigi to cram (of food), gorge.
supersigna accented.
supersigno accent (mark), diacritical mark.
superskribi to overwrite.
superskribsegmento overlay.
superstiĉa superstitious.
superstiĉe superstitiously.
superstiĉo superstition.
superstrukturo superstructure.
superŝarĝi to overwhelm.
superŝtato superstate.
superŝtupare upstairs.
superŝultra overarm.
superŝuti to flood, overwhelm.
superŝuto flood.
supertaksi to overestimate, overvalue.
supertakso overcharge, surcharge.
supertera mid-air.

supertere in mid-air.
supertrakpasejo bridge over railway.
supertuto overalls.
superula lofty.
superule loftily.
superulo chief, superior (person).
supervendejo supermarket.
superverŝiĝi to brim.
supervesto outer clothing, overcoat.
supervivi to outlive, survive.
supino supine.
supla supple.
suplementa supplementary.
suplemento adjunct, supplement.
supo soup.
supoza alleged.
supoze allegedly. **supoze ke** supposing that.
supozeble presumably.
supozi to assume, guess, presume, suppose, surmise.
supozigi to cause to suppose, suggest.
supozita supposed, believed.
supozitorio superpository.
supozo supposition.
supra superior, upper, higher. **supra baro** upper bound, upper limit, superior limit. **supra brako** upper arm. **supra etaĝo** upper floor. **supra flanko** upper side. **supra indico** superscript. **supra paĝotitolo** header, heading, headline.
supraĵa superficial.
supraĵe on the surface of, shallowly.
supraĵeco superficiality.
supraĵo summit, surface, top, surface.
suprapinto apex.
supre above, on top, overhead, upstairs, aloft, up, upstairs. **supre menciita** above, above-mentioned. **supre nomita** above, above-mentioned. **supre sur** on top of.
supredirita above-mentioned.
Suprelago Lake Superior.
supremo least upper bound.
supren above, up, uphill, upwards, upstairs. **supren brui** to go noisily up.
suprenceli to aspire.
suprenflugi to fly over.
suprenigi to boost.
suprenira upward.
suprenirado ascension.
supreniri to ascend, climb, go up, mount.
supreniro acclivity, ascent.
suprenĵetegi to hurl upwards.
suprenĵeti to propel to the surface.
suprenkuregi to rush, race over.
suprenkuri to rush, race over.
suprenlevi to hoist.
suprenleviĝi to rise up, rise above.
suprenomito above.
suprenpremi to boost.

suprenrampi to clamber, climb, scramble up.
suprenrigardi to look up.
suprenstreko diagonal, slash, forward slash, solidus (/).
suprenŝargo upload.
suprenŝarĝi to upload.
suprestaranta above.
suprestaranto above.
suprizataki to raid.
supro pinnacle, summit, surface, top, ridge, vertex.
supujo (soup) tureen.
sur on, upon, onto. **sur kiu** upon which. **sur la patra flanko** on the father's side. **sur malplena stomako** on an empty stomach.
Surabajo Surabaya.
surao sura.
surbaze de based on.
surbazigi to base, found, ground.
surbendaĵo tape recording.
surbendigi to record (on tape).
surbendigilo tape recorder.
surbendigo tape recording.
surbordigi to board, put on board.
surbordiĝi to be washed ashore.
surbordo embankment, quay.
surĉevala equestrian.
surĉevaliĝi to mount (a horse).
surda deaf.
surdamutulo deaf-mute.
surdeco deafness.
surdiga deafening.
surdigi to deafen, make deaf.
surdiĝi to go deaf.
surdmuta deaf and dumb.
surdmuteco deaf-muteness.
surdmutulo deaf mute.
surdorse on one's back.
surdulo deaf person.
surfaco surface.
surfadenigi to string, thread.
surfi to (web)surf.
surfo surf.
surfotabulo surfboard.
surfrajdado surfing.
surfrajdanto surfer.
surfrajdi to surf.
surftabulo surfboard.
surfundaĵo deposit, residue.
surfundiĝi to settle.
surgenue on one's knees.
surgenui to kneel.
surgenuiĝi to kneel.
surgrati to scratch all over, scratch over.
surgrimpado ascent, climbing, mounting.
surgrimpebla mountable.
surgrimpi to ascend, climb, scale.
surhavi to have on, wear.

suriĝi to get on top of, raise oneself.
surikato meerkat, suricate.
surinama Surinamese. **surinama lingvo** Surinamese, Surinamese language.
surinamanino Surinamese woman.
surinamano Surinamer, Surinamese.
Surinamo Surinam.
surirado ascension.
surirebla passable, practicable.
suriri to tread, walk, walk upon.
surjekcia surjective.
surjekcio onto function, surjection.
surĵeta surjective.
surĵeto surjection.
surkape on one's head.
surkaseda on cassette.
surkolonaĵo entablature.
surkonstrui to build on.
surkonstruita areo built-up area.
surkontinenta on the continent, continental.
surkreskata covered, grown over, overgrown.
surkreski to overgrow.
surloka on location, upon the spot.
surloke in (on) a place.
surluniĝo Landing on the Moon.
surmara on the sea.
surmare on the sea.
surmarigi to put out to sea.
surmariĝi to put out to sea.
surmariĝo splashdown.
surmeti to cover, put on. **surmeti dosiersistemon** to mount a file system.
surmetingo mount point.
surmeto application.
surnaĝi to sail.
surnaĝigi to make float.
suro calf.
surogato surrogate.
surogatulo surrogate.
surpanaĵo sandwich filling.
surpapera paper.
surpaperigi to print.
surpaperigo print, printout.
surpaŝi to set foot on.
surpentri to paint over.
surpiede on one's feet.
surpiediĝi to stand up.
surplanke on the floor.
surpliso surplice.
surpresi to print.
surpriza startling, surprising, striking.
surprizatako surprise attack.
surprize aback.
surprizega astonishing, staggering.
surprizi to surprise.
surpriziĝi to be surprised.
surprizo surprise.

surprovejo fitting-room.
surprovi to try on.
surradiado irradiation.
surradii to irradiate, shine upon.
surrajdi to ride.
surrampi to scale.
surrealismo surrealism.
surrena adrenal. **surrena glando** adrenal gland.
sursable on the sand.
surscenigi to direct, present, stage.
surscenigisto director.
surscenigo presentation, staging.
sursidi to sit on eggs.
surskribaĵo sign (notice board).
surskribeto label.
surskribi to write upon.
surskribo inscription, notice (public), superscription.
surstrate in the street.
surstrekaĵo erasure.
surstreki to cancel, erase, deface, efface, obliterate, strike out (writing).
surŝipe on board.
surŝipiĝi to board (a ship).
surŝprucigi to spatter, bespatter, splash, sprinkle.
surŝuti to strew.
surtabla desktop. **surtabla komputilo** desktop computer. **surtabla tipografio** desktop publishing.
surtabligi to serve.
surteni to hold, support.
surtera terrestrial, earthly. **surtera paradizo** paradise on earth.
surtere on land.
surterejo landing spot, place to put aground.
surterigi to land, put aground, put ashore.
surteriĝejo airstrip.
surteriĝi to land.
surteriĝo landing.
surteriri to head for shore.
surtero land, dry land.
surtreti to tread upon, walk on, trample.
surtroniganto kingmaker.
surtronigi to enthrone.
surtronigo enthronement.
surtroniĝi to accede, accede to the throne.
surtroniĝo accession.
surtuto coat, overcoat, overall.
survango slap in the face.
surverŝi to baste, water, spray, sprinkle.
surveturi to run over.
survizaĝe on the face.
survoje along the way, on the way. **survoje al** on the way to.
suskribo inscription.
suspekta shady, suspicious.

suspektato suspect, person suspected of wrongdoing.
suspekte suspiciously.
suspektema mistrustful, suspicious (by nature).
suspekti to mistrust, suspect.
suspektigi to cast aspersions to.
suspektinda suspicious.
suspekto suspicion.
suspendi to postpone, suspend (legal).
suspendita in abeyance.
suspenditeco abeyance.
suspendo suspension (legal).
suspensi to be in suspension.
suspensorio jockstrap.
suspirado sighing.
suspiri to sigh.
suspiro sigh.
susuri to rustle, swish.
susuro rustle, swish.
suŝio sushi.
suŝipeco piece of sushi.
sutano cassock, soutane.
sutro sutra.
suturi to seam, suture.
suturo seam, suture.
suverena sovereign.
suvereneco sovereignty.
suvereno sovereign.
svaga vague, fuzzy. **svaga logiko** fuzzy logic. **svaga timo** vague fear.
svahila Swahili.
svahilo Swahili.
Svalbardo Spitsbergen.
svarmi to abound, swarm.
svarmo swarm, horde.
svastiko swastika.
svati to match-make, match.
svatistino match maker.
svatisto match maker.

svazia Swazi. **svazia lingvo** Swazi, Swazi language.
Svazilando Swaziland.
sveda Swedish. **sveda lingvo** Swedish, Swedish language.
Svedio Sweden.
Svedlando Sweden.
svedledo suede.
Svedo a Swede.
svedo Swede.
Svedujo Sweden.
svelta slender, slim.
sveltiĝadi to slim.
svenadego trance.
svenanta unconscious, passed out.
svenfali to faint (and fall down).
sveni to faint, swoon.
sveniga cerefolio hemlock.
svenigi to drug, intoxicate, stun, stupefy.
sveninta unconscious.
sveno faint, swoon, syncope.
svetero (crewneck) sweater.
svingado beating, swinging.
svingeti to wave.
svingi to brandish, fling, swing, wave, wave about.
svingiĝado oscillation, swinging, vibrating.
svingiĝi to sway, swing.
svingiĝo wag.
svingilo clapper, handle, lever, pendulum.
svingo wag, waggle, wave.
svingpendi to swing.
svingsaluti to wave.
svisa Swiss.
Svisio Switzerland.
Svislando Switzerland.
sviso Swiss.
Svisujo Switzerland.
svopo swap.

ŝabano Sha'aban.
ŝabato Sabbath.
ŝablona stereotyped. **ŝablona rekono** pattern matching.
ŝablono pattern, stencil, template.
ŝafa ovine, sheep. **ŝafa fromaĝo** ewe's cheese. **ŝafa viando** mutton, lamb.
ŝafaĵo mutton.
ŝafaro flock of sheep.
ŝafbleki to baa, bleat.
ŝafejo fold, pen (for sheep).
ŝaffemuro leg of mutton.
ŝafgrifo bearded vulture.
ŝafhundo sheep dog.
ŝafida lamb, of lamb.
ŝafidaĵo lamb.
ŝafido lamb.
ŝafino ewe.
ŝafisto shepherd.
ŝaflano fleece.
ŝafo sheep. **Ŝafo** Aries (zodiac)
ŝafoviro ram.
ŝafto arbor, shaft, spindle.
ŝagrino shagreen.
ŝaho shah.
ŝajna seeming.
ŝajnbrilo lustre, glitter.
ŝajne apparently, seemingly.
ŝajneco semblance.
ŝajni to appear (to be), seem. **ŝajnas al mi, ke...** it seems to me that…
ŝajnigaĵo pretence, sham.
ŝajnigi to feign, pretend.
ŝajnigita affected.
ŝajnigo pretending, show.
ŝajniĝi to sham.
ŝajniĝo sham.
ŝajnkuraĝulo griper, grumbler.
ŝajno appearance.
ŝajnpiedo pseudopod.
ŝaĵnigo feint.
ŝaka tabulo chessboard.
ŝakalo jackal.
ŝaki to check (chess). **ŝak!** check!
Ŝakjamunio Shakyamuni.
ŝakludo (game of) chess.
ŝako check, chess.
ŝakoj chess pieces.
ŝakpeco chess piece, chessman.
ŝakri to peddle.
ŝakristo black marketeer.
ŝaktabula memoro interleaved memory.
ŝaktabulo chessboard.
ŝakto shaft (mine, elevator).
ŝalmo bellows, pipe, windbag, stalk.

ŝalo shawl.
ŝalta registro switch register.
ŝalti to switch on, turn on.
ŝaltilo switch.
ŝalto act of turning something on, closing a circuit.
ŝalupego launch, longboat.
ŝalupo sloop, launch (boat), longboat.
ŝamanismo shamanism.
ŝamano shaman.
ŝamiseno samisen, shamisen.
ŝamo chamois, chamois leather, shammy.
ŝampinjono mushroom.
ŝampui to shampoo.
ŝampuo shampoo.
ŝanca lucky.
ŝance by accident.
ŝanceli to shake, totter, waver.
ŝanceligadi to waffle.
ŝanceliĝa irresolute, vacillating.
ŝanceliĝanta hesitant.
ŝanceliĝe falteringly, hesitantly, hesitatingly.
ŝanceliĝema indecisive, rocky, uncertain.
ŝanceliĝemo indecision, irresolution.
ŝanceliĝi to demur, hesitate, lurch, reel, stagger, vacillate, wave, waddle.
ŝanceliĝo hesitation, perplexity.
ŝanceliiĝi to wobble.
ŝanco chance, luck, prospect. **ŝancon favi** to have a chance.
ŝanelo channel.
ŝanĝa variable.
ŝanĝado mutation.
ŝanĝaĵo change.
ŝanĝebla changeable, fickle, variable.
ŝanĝema inconstant, unstable.
ŝanĝi to change, turn, modify. **ŝanĝi felon** to cast (skin, etc). **ŝanĝi plumojn** to moult (birds).
ŝanĝigi to change (something).
ŝanĝiĝema changeable.
ŝanĝiĝi to change.
ŝanĝiĝo alteration, change, conversion, transformation.
ŝanĝmono change.
ŝanĝo about-face, alteration, change, conversion, transformation, variation.
Ŝanhajo Shanghai.
ŝankro canker, chancre, venereal ulcer.
Ŝanona Shannon. **Ŝanona Flughaveno** Shannon Airport. **Ŝanona komunikmodelo** Shannon's model of communication.
ŝanono bit, Shannon.
Ŝanono Shannon.
ŝarado charade.

ŝarga loading. **ŝarga programo** loader program.
ŝarga tiparo downloadable font.
ŝargado loading.
ŝargi to charge, load, burden.
ŝargiĝi to be loaded.
ŝargilo loader.
ŝargmodulo load module.
ŝargo charge.
ŝargokapo warhead.
ŝargomodulo load module.
ŝargujo breech (of gun).
ŝarĝa burdensome.
ŝarĝaĵo charge.
ŝarĝanta carrying, loaded with.
ŝarĝatesto bill of lading, consignment note, waybill.
ŝarĝaŭtisto truck driver.
ŝarĝaŭto lorry, truck.
ŝarĝavio cargo aircraft, freight carrier.
ŝarĝbarko barge.
ŝarĝbesto beast of burden.
ŝarĝbiciklo carrier cycle, carrier tricycle.
ŝarĝe loaded (with).
ŝarĝega burdensome.
ŝarĝi to burden, load.
ŝarĝita burdened, loaded, laden.
ŝarĝlevilo crane.
ŝarĝlifto elevator, hoist.
ŝarĝo burden, charge, load.
ŝarĝoado lading.
ŝarĝobesto beast of burden.
ŝarĝoveturilo cart, tumbrel.
ŝarĝselo pack saddle.
ŝarĝvagono wagon.
ŝarĝventurilo wagon for hauling freight.
ŝarĝveturilo wagon.
ŝarifo sharif, sherif.
ŝario sharia.
ŝarko shark.
ŝatano subject of a state.
ŝatata favourite, liked, appreciated.
ŝatateco esteem, regard, respect, appreciation.
ŝategi to be fond of, love.
ŝati to appreciate, like, prize, value, esteem, think highly of, relish.
ŝatinda likeable, reputable.
ŝato appreciation, high opinion, reputation.
ŝatokupo hobby.
ŝaumsapo shaving cream.
ŝaŭma effervescent, sparkling.
ŝaŭmadi to effervesce.
ŝaŭmaĵo lather.
ŝaŭmamasiĝi to become full of foam.
ŝaŭmi to foam, froth.
ŝaŭmigita volumenaĵo foamed aggregate.
ŝaŭminhibilo antifoaming agent, antisudsing agent.
ŝaŭmkulero skimmer.
ŝaŭmo foam, froth, scum, spume.
ŝaŭmoaĵo foam.
ŝebeko xebec.
ŝedo penthouse, shed.
ŝejko sheik, sheikh.
ŝeketo shoulder-straps.
ŝeklo bow of padlock.
Ŝekspiro Shakespeare.
ŝelaĵo rind.
ŝelako shellac.
ŝeleto film.
ŝeli to pare.
ŝelketo shoulder-strap.
ŝelko braces, suspenders.
ŝelkoj braces, suspenders.
ŝelo bark, husk, peel, shell, pod, rind, skin.
ŝeloaĵo paring.
ŝelvariablo substitution.
ŝenoprazo chive.
ŝeolo abode of the dead.
ŝerca facetious, joking.
ŝercado fun.
ŝercaĵo gag, joke.
ŝercbabilado badinage.
ŝerce jokingly, in jest.
ŝercema playful, witty.
ŝercemulo buffoon, clown.
ŝerci to jest, joke, kid.
ŝerco gag, joke, farce, jest.
ŝercoado drollery.
ŝerculo jokester.
ŝereo sherry.
ŝerifo sheriff.
ŝero offshore reef, islet.
Ŝetlandinsularo Shetland Islands, Shetlands.
Ŝetlando Shetland. **Ŝetlandoj** Shetland Islands, Shetlands.
ŝi she.
ŝia her, hers.
ŝiaco shiatsu.
ŝiboleto shibboleth.
ŝijaismo Shiism.
ŝijaisto Shiite.
ŝika chic.
ŝildeto sign, tag.
ŝildfiliko buckler fern.
ŝildi to shield.
ŝildo buckler, shield, sign, plaque, tag.
ŝilingo shilling.
ŝilo chyle.
ŝima mouldy. **ŝima odoro** mouldy smell.
ŝimi to get mouldy, mould.
ŝimiĝi to get mouldy.
ŝimo mildew, mould.
ŝindo shingle, wood tile.
ŝindoeto shingle.
ŝinko ham.

ŝintoismo Shintoism.
ŝintoo Shintoism.
ŝio hers.
ŝipa nautical, naval.
ŝipalligilo mooring line, fast.
ŝipamiko shipmate.
ŝipanaro crew.
ŝipano crew member, sailor.
ŝiparestro admiral.
ŝipareto flotilla.
ŝiparo fleet, navy.
ŝipbeko bow.
ŝipboato ship's boat.
ŝipbordo edge of a ship.
ŝipe by ship.
ŝipego ark.
ŝipejo dock.
ŝipekipisto boat supplier.
ŝipestro captain (ship), shipmaster.
ŝipeto craft (vessel), yacht, small ship.
ŝipfarejo shipyard.
ŝipfaristo shipwright.
ŝipflago flag.
ŝipflanke alongside (a ship).
ŝipflanko side of a ship.
ŝipi to cruise, navigate, sail, ship.
ŝipintendanto steward (of ship).
ŝipirebla navigable.
ŝipirejo waterway.
ŝipiri to sail.
ŝipisto sailor.
ŝipkipisto shipowner.
ŝipkonstruejo shipyard.
ŝipkonstruisto shipbuilder, shipwright.
ŝipkuirejo galley.
ŝipkurado boat race, regatta.
ŝipkuro regatta.
ŝipmanifesto manifest.
ŝipmeze abeam, amidships.
ŝipmezen abeam.
ŝipo ship, boat, vessel.
ŝipoficiro mate.
ŝipperei to founder, go down (ship).
ŝippereo shipwreck.
ŝippostsigno wake of ship.
ŝiprestaĵo remains of a ship.
ŝipripo frame, timber.
ŝiprompi to be shipwrecked.
ŝiprompiĝulo shipwrecked person.
ŝiprompo shipwreck.
ŝipruino shipwreck, wrecked ship.
ŝipsava salvage, salvaging. **ŝipsava kompanio** salvage company. **ŝipsava ŝipo** salvage vessel.
ŝipŝarĝisto shipping agent.
ŝipŝarĝo ship's cargo.
ŝipvaporo ship steam.
ŝipvelo ship's sail.
ŝipveturebla navigable.

ŝira shrill.
ŝiraĵo tear.
ŝire (by) tearing, (by) ripping.
ŝiri to rip, tear.
ŝiriĝi to become torn, become ripped.
ŝiriĝinta torn.
ŝirita torn.
ŝirma protective.
ŝirmarmaĵo armament.
ŝirmata screened.
ŝirmbutono button.
ŝirmejo shelter.
ŝirmi to protect, shelter, screen, shield. **ŝirmi sin** to shelter oneself. **ŝirmi sin kontraŭ** to protect (oneself) from, ward off.
ŝirmila ringo file protection ring.
ŝirmileto peak (of cap, etc.).
ŝirmilo screen, shelter.
ŝirmkasko hard hat.
ŝirmo protection, shelter.
ŝirmomasko catcher's mask.
ŝirmtegaĵo dust sheet, loose cover.
ŝirnotlibro block, pad.
ŝirpeco de papero scrap of paper.
ŝkoto sheet.
ŝlagro hit song.
ŝlako clinker, dross, slag.
ŝlemo slam (cards).
Ŝlesvigholstinio Schleswig-Holstein.
Ŝlesvigo-Holŝtejno Schleswig-Holstein.
ŝlifa abrasive, gritty.
ŝlifi to abrade, grind, polish, smooth.
ŝlima slimy, turbid.
ŝlimejo slough.
ŝlimhava miry.
ŝlimo mire, mud, slime.
ŝlosi to lock.
ŝlosila key.
ŝlosillango bit of key.
ŝlosilo key, wrench.
ŝlosiltruo keyhole.
ŝlosilvorta parametro keyword parameter.
ŝlosilvorto keyword.
ŝlosita locked.
ŝloso lock.
ŝmaci to smack.
ŝmaco buss, kiss, smack.
ŝminki to put on make-up. **ŝminki sin** to put on make-up.
ŝminko cosmetic, make up, make-up.
ŝmirado application.
ŝmiraĵo ointment.
ŝmiri to anoint, smear, spread, coat, grease, smear.
ŝmirmono bribe.
ŝmiro anointing.
ŝmiroado anointing.
ŝnuraĵo cordage.
ŝnurarmi to rig.

ŝnurarmilaro rigging.
ŝnurdancisto tightrope walker.
ŝnurdescendado abseiling.
ŝnurdescendi to abseil.
ŝnurdescendo abseiling.
ŝnurego cable, rope.
ŝnurero filament, strand, thread.
ŝnureto string, twine.
ŝnuri to string.
ŝnuro cord, rope, string.
ŝnurosalti to skip rope, jump rope.
ŝnursalti to skip rope, jump rope.
ŝnurŝtupetaro accommodating ladder.
ŝnurumi to braid.
ŝnurumo braid.
ŝo name of the letter Ŝ.
ŝofori to chauffeur.
ŝoforo chauffeur, driver.
ŝogio shogi (Japanese chess).
ŝoguno shogun.
ŝoka shocking.
ŝokamortizilo bumper.
ŝokanta offensive.
ŝoke appallingly, awfully, ghastly, stunningly.
ŝoki to shock.
ŝokiĝi to be shocked, take offence, resent, take exception.
ŝokita shocked.
ŝoko shock.
ŝorbeto sherbet, sorbet.
ŝortkalsono boxer shorts.
ŝorto shorts.
ŝoseo highway.
ŝosi to sprout.
ŝoso shoot, sprout.
ŝoti to shoot.
ŝoto shot.
ŝovebla gliding, sliding, moveable.
ŝovelado bailing.
ŝoveli to shovel.
ŝovelilo shovel.
ŝovi to push along, shove, thrust. **ŝovi la nazon en** to stick one's nose in(to).
ŝoviĝi to glide, slide, thrust.
ŝovinisma chauvinistic.
ŝovinismo chauvinism, jingoism.
ŝovinisto chauvinist, jingo, jingoist.
ŝovo thrust.
ŝovreĝistro shift register.
ŝovsulko slot, groove.
ŝpalo rail sleeper, tie.
ŝparado economy, saving.
ŝparaĵo savings.
ŝpareco thrift.
ŝparegi to save, put aside for the rainy day.
ŝparegulo saver, moneygrubber.
ŝparema economical, frugal, saving, thrifty.
ŝpareme economically, sparingly.
ŝparemo economy.

ŝpari to be careful, spare, economize, save, spare, be sparing of, keep for future use.
ŝparigi to save.
ŝparkaso savings bank.
ŝparkonto savings account.
ŝparmonujo piggy bank.
ŝparo economy, saving.
ŝpato spade.
ŝpico Pomeranian.
ŝpini to spin (thread).
ŝpiniĝi to be spun.
ŝpinilo distaff, spindle.
ŝpinistino spinster.
ŝpinrado spinning wheel.
ŝpinturnilo spindle.
ŝproso bar of window sash.
ŝprucado spraying.
ŝprucaĵo gush, spout.
ŝprucaĵujo aerosol.
ŝprucakvumi to water.
ŝprucakvumo watering.
ŝprucamelo spray starch.
ŝpruceti to spray.
ŝprucetigi to atomize, spatter, splatter, spray.
ŝprucetiĝi to spatter.
ŝprucfenestro pop-up window.
ŝprucfluo jet stream.
ŝpruchelpilo tool tip.
ŝpruci to gush, spurt, spurt out, splash, spout.
ŝprucigi to squirt. **ŝprucigi sur** to spray, sprinkle.
ŝprucigilo sprinkler.
ŝprucilo nozzle.
ŝprucmakuli to spatter.
ŝprucmenuo pop-up menu.
ŝprucnebulo spray.
ŝpruco gush, spray, spurt.
ŝprucpistolo spray-gun.
ŝprucujo spray can.
ŝpurcflui to spurt, gush, spew.
ŝpuro gauge, wheel-span, distance between rails.
ŝramano Shramaṇa, Samaṇa.
ŝrankframo cabinet rack.
ŝranklito cupboard bed.
ŝranko cabinet, closet, cupboard, sideboard, wardrobe.
ŝrapnelo shrapnel.
ŝraŭba screw, spiral.
ŝraŭbbolto bolt.
ŝraŭbego helix.
ŝraŭbi to screw. **ŝraŭbi pli firme** to screw home.
ŝraŭbilo screwdriver.
ŝraŭbingo nut (of a screw).
ŝraŭbita bolted.
ŝraŭbkanelo thread.
ŝraŭblevilo screwjack.

ŝraŭbo screw.
ŝraŭbokanelo worm.
ŝraŭbŝlosilo adjustable wrench, spanner.
ŝraŭbtenilo screw clamp, vice, screwdriver.
ŝraŭbturnilo screwdriver.
ŝriki to howl, vociferate, yell.
ŝroto grits, semolina.
ŝrumpa wizened.
ŝrumpi to crumple, shrink, shrivel up, wilt, wrinkle.
ŝrumpigi to shrink.
ŝrumpo contraction.
ŝtala steel, of steel.
ŝtalbetono armoured concrete.
ŝtalejo steelworks.
ŝtalo steel.
ŝtanci to stamp, punch, press.
ŝtata government, state-run, state. **Ŝtata Konsilio** State Council. **ŝtata monopolo** government monopoly.
ŝtataneco nationality.
ŝtatano citizen, national.
ŝtateco statehood.
ŝtatestra gubernatorial.
ŝtatestro head of state.
ŝtatfederaciano federal state.
ŝtatigi to nationalize.
ŝtatigo nationalization.
ŝtatisto statesman.
ŝtato state.
ŝtatoficisto civil servant, government official.
ŝtatperfida treasonable.
ŝtatperfide treasonably.
ŝtatperfido treason.
ŝtatrenverso coup d'état.
ŝtela stealthy.
ŝtelado stealing, theft.
ŝtelaĵo loot, plunder, stolen goods.
ŝtelanto thief.
ŝtelatendi to lurk.
ŝtelĉasi to poach.
ŝtelĉasisto poacher.
ŝtele stealthily.
ŝteleco stealthiness.
ŝtelema thievish.
ŝteleti to pilfer.
ŝteli to rob, steal, thieve, swindle, purloin, filch.
ŝtelimuna burglar-proof.
ŝtelinto thief.
ŝtelire stealthily, furtively.
ŝteliri to steal, sneak. **ŝteliri al** to stalk.
ŝtelista burglar's.
ŝtelistaro gang of thieves.
ŝtelistino (female) thief.
ŝtelisto robber, thief, swindler, cheat.
ŝtelita stolen.
ŝtelmaniera stealthy.
ŝtelmova stealthy.
ŝtelo larceny, theft.
ŝtelpaŝe stealthily (on foot), on tiptoes.
ŝtelrampi al to come over.
ŝtelrigardi to crib.
ŝtelsekvi to tail.
ŝtelŝakrejo black market.
ŝtelumi to go stealthily, skulk, slink, steal.
ŝternmevo sabine's gull.
ŝterno tern.
ŝtiparo woodpile.
ŝtiparumi to burn at the stake.
ŝtipkapulo blockhead, idiot.
ŝtipo billet, block, chunk of wood, log.
ŝtofego sackcloth.
ŝtofmoligilo fabric softener.
ŝtofo cloth, material, matter, stuff, fabric, textile.
ŝtofrando selvage.
ŝtona stone.
ŝtonaĵo piece of stone, collection of stones.
ŝtonaluno alunite.
ŝtonbloko block of stone.
ŝtondometo stone cottage.
Ŝtondomo Stonehouse.
ŝtone by stone, with a stone. **ŝtone fiksita** fixed or written in stone.
ŝtonego boulder, rock.
ŝtonegplena rocky.
ŝtonejo quarry.
ŝtonepoko stone age.
ŝtonetaĵo gravel.
ŝtonetaro broken stones, (stone) chippings, rubble.
ŝtoneto pebble.
ŝtonhakisto stone cutter, stonemason.
Ŝtonhaveno Stonehaven.
ŝtonigi to petrify.
ŝtoniĝi to petrify, turn to stone.
ŝtoniĝinta petrified.
ŝtonĵetilo sling, slingshot.
ŝtonkarbo anthracite, coal.
ŝtonkartono fibreboard.
ŝtonkora adamant.
ŝtonlavujo sink.
ŝtonmortigi to stone to death.
ŝtonmortigo stoning.
ŝtono stone. **ŝtono bazangula** cornerstone.
ŝtonoza stony.
ŝtonpeco block of stone.
ŝtonplato flagstone.
ŝtonplena stony.
ŝtonriĉa stony.
ŝtonumi to stone.
ŝtopado stopping.
ŝtopaĵo blockage, sealant, stuffing.
ŝtopakumuli to back up.
ŝtopakumuliĝi to back up.
ŝtopakumuliĝo backup.

ŝtopi to block, clog, plug up, stop up.
ŝtopiĝi to become stopped up.
ŝtopilego plug.
ŝtopileto peg.
ŝtopilingo electric socket.
ŝtopilo buffer, plug, electric plug, stopper.
ŝtopita blocked.
ŝtopnutri to force-feed.
ŝtopstango bot stick.
ŝtorma stormy.
ŝtormi to be in a fury.
ŝtormo storm.
ŝtrumpaĵo hose.
ŝtrumpeto sock.
ŝtrumpkalsono pantyhose.
ŝtrumpligilo garter.
ŝtrumpo stocking.
ŝtrumpoligilo garter.
ŝtrumpoŝelko garter.
ŝtrumpvendisto hosier.
ŝtupara funkcio step function.
ŝtupare in steps.
ŝtuparejo stairwell.
ŝtupareto stepladder.
ŝtuparlifto escalator.
ŝtuparo staircase, stairs.
ŝtuparplataĵo steps.
ŝtupbenkoj bleachers.
ŝtupe by degrees.
ŝtupetaro ladder.
ŝtupeto rung (of ladder).
ŝtupigi to stagger.
ŝtupo stair, step, rung.
ŝuaĉo clog, sabot.
ŝubremso block brake.
ŝuciristo bootblack.
ŝufaristo shoemaker.
ŝuflikisto shoemaker.
ŝuisto shoemaker.
ŝukorno shoehorn.
ŝulaĉo shoelace.
ŝuldanto debtor.
ŝuldeco indebtedness.
ŝuldi to owe, be indebted.
ŝuldigi to oblige.
ŝuldiĝi to get into debt.
ŝuldo debt.
ŝultrlevi to shrug.
ŝultro shoulder.
ŝultrolevi to shrug.
ŝultrotiri to shrug.

ŝultrozono bandoleer, shoulder belt.
ŝunti to shunt.
ŝunto shunt.
ŝuo shoe.
ŝupurigisto person who shines shoes.
ŝurci to spurt, gush, spew.
ŝuriparisto shoemaker.
ŝuŝnuro shoelace.
ŝutado dumping, pouring.
ŝuti to dump, pour (out), scatter, tip.
ŝutiĝi to be poured, pour in.
ŝutilo bucket.
ŝutro (window) shutter.
ŝutrotiri to shrug, shrug one's shoulders.
ŝutubo top, leg.
ŝvaba Swabian.
Ŝvabio Swabia.
ŝvabo Swabian.
ŝvabri to mop, swab.
ŝvabrileto dish mop.
Ŝvabujo Swabia.
ŝvebi to float in air, float, hover.
ŝvebo waft.
ŝvebŝipo hovercraft.
ŝvebtrajno hovertrain.
ŝvela bulging.
ŝvelabsceso tumor.
ŝvelaĉa bloated.
ŝveladi to balloon.
ŝvelado bulging.
ŝvelaĵo protuberance.
ŝvelanta bulging.
ŝvelforma baggy, bulging.
ŝveli to bloat, swell, inflate, distend.
ŝveligi to inflate.
ŝveliĝi to become swollen.
ŝvelkontuzaĵo dent.
ŝvelo swelling.
ŝvelondado hull.
ŝvelparola bombastic.
ŝvelparolo bombast.
ŝverbi to soar, glide.
ŝvitado sweating.
ŝvitbanejo sauna.
ŝvitbano sauna.
ŝvitĉemizo sweatshirt.
ŝviti to perspire, sweat.
ŝvitiga heavy.
ŝvitiĝi to break out in a sweat.
ŝvito perspiration, sweat.
ŝvitodoro smell of sweat.

T

tabakaĵbutiko tobacconist's.
tabakbutiko tobacco shop.
tabako tobacco.
tabakskatolo tobacco box.
tabakujo tobacco pouch, tobacco box.
tabano gadfly, horsefly.
tabelaro book of tables.
tabelforma tabular.
tabelkalkula programo spreadsheet program.
tabelo array, index, table, tablet, tabulation.
  tabelo de vereco truth table.
tabeltipo array type.
tabernaklo tabernacle.
table table.
tableto bracket.
tablo table.
tabloj tables.
tablojdo tablet, tabloid (pill).
Tablomonto Mensa.
tablomonto mesa.
tablopreĝo grace.
tabloteniso ping pong, table tennis.
tablotuko tablecloth.
tablovino table wine.
tabo tab, tabulation, tabulator.
tabua taboo.
tabula bordkovraĵo camp sheeting, camp shedding, camp shot.
tabulaĵo boarding.
tabulbarilo wooden fence.
tabuleto bar, slab, tablet.
tabuli to board up.
tabulkuŝejo plank bed.
tabulludo board game.
tabulo board, plank.
tabuo taboo.
tabureto stool.
taĉmenti to detach.
taĉmento detachment, squad, gang, shift, team.
Tadeo Thaddeus.
tadorno sheldrake, shelduck.
tafto taffeta.
taga daily, daytime.
tagaloga Tagalog. **tagaloga lingvo** Tagalog language.
tagalogo Tagalog.
tagbileto day ticket.
tage by day, during the day, in the daytime.
  tage de naskiĝo birthday, anniversary.
  tage kaj nokte day and night.
tageksurso day trip.
tageto African marigold.
taggazeto daily paper.

tagiĝe at dawn, at daybreak.
tagiĝi to dawn, become day(time).
tagiĝo dawn, daybreak.
taglaboristo day labourer, journeyman.
taglibro daybook, diary, journal.
taglilio day-lily.
taglumo daylight.
tagmanĝi to dine.
tagmanĝo dinner, midday meal.
tagmeza midday, noonday, noontime.
tagmeze at noon.
tagmezo midday, noon.
tagmezomanĝo lunch.
tagnoktegaleco equinox.
tagnokto 24-hour period, day.
Tago Tagus.
tago day. **Tago de Ĉiuj Sanktuloj** All Saint's Day. **Tago de la Mortintoj** All Souls' Day. **Tago de la Patrinoj** Mother's Day. **Tago de Pekliberigo** Day of Atonement, Feast of Expiation. **Tago de Valenteno** Saint Valentine's Day. **tago post tago** day and day (day after day).
tagolibro diary.
tagolilio Hemerocallis, day lily.
tagordo agenda (at a meeting), order of the day.
tagplado plat du jour.
tagporcio ration.
tagrestaĵe for the remainder of the day.
tagvojo trip.
Taĝikio Tajikistan.
taĝiko Tajik.
Taĝikujo Tajikistan.
tahitia Tahitian.
tahitiano Tahitian.
Tahito Tahiti.
taĥikardio tachycardia.
Taĥo Tagus.
tailo waist.
Taino Tain.
taja Thai. **taja lingvo** Thai, Thai language.
  Taja Novjaro Thai New Year.
tajdo tide.
Tajdromo Tyndrum.
tajfuno typhoon.
tajgo boreal forest, taiga.
tajĝiĉuano Tai Chi (Chuan).
tajino Thai woman.
tajlanda of Thailand. **Tajlanda Golfo** Gulf of Thailand. **tajlanda lingvo** Thai, Thai language.
Tajlando Thailand, Siam.
tajli to carve, cut, polish, sculpt.
tajlo cut.

tajlori

tajlori to tailor.
tajlorino tailor, female tailor.
tajloro tailor.
Tajno Tyne.
Tajnulto Taynuilt.
tajo Thai.
tajpado typing.
Tajpeo Taipei.
tajperaro typo, typographical error.
tajpeska tiparo TrueType font, typewriter face.
tajpi to type (on keyboard).
tajpilo typewriter.
tajpistino (female) typist.
tajpisto (male) typist.
tajvana Taiwanese.
tajvanano Taiwanese.
Tajvano Taiwan.
takelo tackle.
taki to go about, tack, wear.
takigloso spiny ant-eater.
takimetro speedometer, tachometer.
takiono tachyon.
tako taco.
taksa rating.
taksado estimate, appraisement, valuation.
taksaĵo textile.
taksebla rateable.
taksi to appraise, estimate, rate, assess, tax, value.
taksiejo taxi stand.
taksiisto cab driver, taxi driver.
taksimetro taximeter.
taksino taxine.
taksio taxi, taxicab.
taksistacio taxi stand.
taksisto[1] appraiser.
taksisto[2] taxi driver.
taksiŝoforo cab driver, taxi driver.
takso assessment, toll, tax.
taksti to read, say.
taksuso yew (tree).
taktbastoneto baton.
taktbastono baton.
takte rhythmically.
taktika tactical.
taktike tactically.
taktikisto tactician.
taktiko tactic, tactics.
taktilo system clock.
taktmezurado timing.
takto beat, musical time, tact, time.
taktobastono baton.
taktofrekvenco clock cycle, clock rate.
taktoperiodo clock cycle.
taktostreko bar line.
talanto talent.
talaro gown, robe.
talasemio thalassaemia.

tanilo

talenta accomplished, talented, gifted.
talento ability, accomplishment, aptitude, disposition, talent.
talentotesto aptitude test.
talentplena gifted, talented.
talero taler, thaler.
talesa Thales. **talesa teoremo** Thales theorem.
Taleso Thales.
Talibano Taliban.
talibo talib.
taliktro meadow-rue.
talimezuro waist.
Talino Tallinn.
talio waist, waistline.
talismano amulet, charm, talisman.
taliumo thallium.
talizono girdle.
talko talc, talcum.
Talmudo Talmud.
talo thallus.
talono stock.
talpo mole (animal).
talusi to bank.
taluso[1] bank, embankment.
taluso[2] talus, ankle bone.
tamariko tamarisk.
tamarindo tamarind.
tamarisko salt cedar, tamarisk.
tambono tambon.
tamburado roll (of drum).
tamburi to drum.
tamburino tambourine.
tamburisto drummer.
tamburo drum.
tamen but, however, nevertheless, yet, notwithstanding, still.
tamiaso chipmunk.
Tamizo Thames.
tampono plug, tampon.
tamtamado drumming.
tamtami to drum.
tamtamo tamtam.
tamula Tamil.
tamulo Tamil.
tanaceto feverfew, tansy.
tanagro tanager.
tandemo tandem bicycle.
tanejo tannery.
tangentarko arctangent.
tangento tangent.
tango tango.
tanĝa tangent.
tanĝanta tangent.
tanĝanto tangent.
Tanĝero Tangier.
tanĝi to be tangent.
tani to tan.
tanilo tan, tannin.

tanino tannin.
tanisto tanner.
tankao tanka.
tanko tank (mil.).
tantaligi to tantalize.
tantalizi to tantalize.
tantalo tantalum.
Tantalo Tantalus.
tantiemo percentage of profits.
tanzania Tanzanian.
tanzaniano Tanzanian.
Tanzanio Tanzania.
taoismo Taoism.
tapeti to paper.
tapetisto (wall)paper hanger.
tapeto tapestry, wall covering, wallpaper.
tapioko tapioca.
tapiro tapir.
tapiŝeto rug.
tapiŝi to blanket, carpet.
tapiŝo carpet, rug.
taraksako dandelion.
Taranako Mount Egmont.
tarantelo tarantella.
tarantulo tarantula.
Tarberto Tarbert.
tarda late, overdue, tardy.
tarifo list of charges, list of prices, scale of charges, tariff.
taro tare.
taroko tarot, tarock, tarocchi.
tarpano tarpan.
tarsio tarsier.
tarso instep, tarsus.
tartano tartan.
tartrato tartrate.
tartro fur, scale, tartar.
tasego mug.
taskaro workload.
tasketo job.
taski to assign.
tasklaboro task work.
tasko job, task.
taskopleto system tray.
taskostrio task bar.
tasmania Tasmanian. **tasmania lupo** Tasmanian devil.
tasmaniano Tasmanian.
Tasmanio Tasmania.
Tasmanmaro Tasman Sea.
taso cup.
Taŝkento Tashkent.
taŝo bag.
tatamo tatami (Japanese floor mat).
tatara Tartar.
tataro Tartar.
Tatarujo Tartary.
tatuaĵo tattoo.
tatui to tattoo.

taurobatalo bullfight.
taŭga fitting, suitable.
taŭgaĵo qualification.
taŭge duly, expediently.
taŭgeco ability, capability, fitness, suitability.
taŭgi to be fit, be suitable.
taŭgigi to adapt.
taŭgprovaĵo shareware.
taŭo tau (Ττ).
taŭra bull-like.
taŭrbatalo bullfight, bullfighting.
taŭristo bullfighter, toreador, torero.
taŭro bull. **Taŭro** Taurus (zodiac).
taŭrobatala areno bullring.
taŭrobatalejo bullring.
taŭrobatalo bullfight.
taŭtologia tautological, tautologous.
taŭtologio tautology.
taŭtonimo tautonym.
taŭzi to dishevel, tousle, disorder, hustle, jostle, comb, tease (hair).
taŭzita hararo entangled hair.
taverno inn, tavern.
tavola stratified.
tavoletigi to veneer.
tavoleto coating, film, slice, veneer.
tavolforma stratiform.
tavoli to stratify.
tavoliĝi to stratify.
tavoliĝo stratification.
tavolklino angle of dip.
tavolkuko layer cake.
tavolo layer, stratum.
Tbajt terabyte.
T-ĉemizo T-shirt.
t.e. → **tio estas**.
teamano team member.
teamo team.
tearbeto tea plant.
teatra theatrical.
teatraĵo play, piece, theatrical performance, show.
teatramanto theatre lover.
teatreca theatrical.
teatro theatre.
teda boring, stodgy, tiresome, tedious.
tedaĵo bore, bother.
tedaĵoj fuss.
tede banala hackneyed, hard-worked, stale, trite, worn-out.
tedeco tediousness.
tedi to bore, tire.
tediĝi to weary.
tedlaboro grunt work, tiring work, boring work.
tedo distaste.
tedulo bore.
teejo tea house.
teflono Teflon.

tegajô coating, covering, surface.
tegi to coat, cover, overlay.
tegilo (protective) cover, wrapping, coating.
tegmenta roof, of a roof, roof-like. **tegmenta briko** roof tile. **tegmenta supersigno** circumflex (ˆ).
tegmentajô roofing, slates, shingles.
tegmentĉambro attic.
tegmentfenestro roof window.
tegmentisto slater.
tegmentleporo stray cat.
tegmento roof.
tegmenttrabo rafter.
tego covering, surface.
tegoleto tile.
tegoli to shingle, tile.
tegolisto roofer, tiler.
tegolo roofing tile, shingle.
tegumento cover.
Teherano Teheran.
teĥnika technical. **teĥnika projekto** design document.
teĥnikisto technician.
teĥniko technique.
teĥnokrataro technocrats.
teĥnokratio technocracy.
teĥnokratismo technocratism.
teĥnokrato technocrat.
teĥnologia technology.
teĥnologiisto technologist.
teĥnologio technology.
teĥnologo technology.
Teĥo TEX.
Teĥrano Teheran.
teino theine.
teisma theistic.
teismo theism.
teisto theist.
TEJO → **Tutmonda Esperantista Junulara Organizo**.
tekilo tequila.
tekkomputilo notebook, laptop.
teknecio technetium.
teknika technical.
teknike technically.
teknikisto technician.
tekniko technique, technology.
teknokrataro technocrats.
teknokratio technocracy.
teknokratismo technocratism.
teknokrato technocrat.
teknologia technological.
teknologie technologically.
teknologiemulo techie.
teknologiisma technocratic.
teknologiismano technocrat.
teknologio technology.
teknologo technologist.
teknomaniula geeky.

teknomaniulo geek.
teko briefcase, file.
tekokomputilo laptop computer.
tekruĉo teapot.
teksa textile.
teksado weaving.
teksajô fabric, textile, tissue, web.
teksarango weave.
teksasa Texan. **Teksasa komunkarta pokero** Texan.
teksasanino Texan woman.
teksasano Texan.
Teksaso Texas.
teksbazo warp, groundwork, theme, structure.
teksestro webmaster.
teksi to weave.
teksilo loom.
teksisto weaver.
teksrubando webbing.
teksta text, textual. **teksta dosiero** text file. **teksta redaktilo** text editor.
teksti to read, say.
tekstigi to convert to text.
tekstilajôj textile.
teksto lyrics, text.
tekstobloko block of text.
tekstoprilaborilo word processor.
tekstotraktado text processing, word processing.
tekstotraktilo text processor.
tekstparto passage.
tekstprilabora programeto editor.
tekstprilaborilo editor, word processor.
tektono teak tree.
tekulero teaspoon.
tekvondo taekwondo.
tele- tele-.
teleaŭtografo teleautograph.
teleĉeesto telepresence.
teleekrano telescreen.
telefaksajô fax.
telefaksi to fax.
telefaksilo fax.
telefero cableway, teleferic.
telefio orpine.
telefomandebla remote controlled.
telefona telephonic.
telefonbudo telephone booth.
telefonbufro telephone buffer unit.
telefone by telephone.
telefoni to call, telephone, phone.
telefonio telephony.
telefonkarto telephone card.
telefonkodo telephone code.
telefonlibro phonebook, telephone book.
telefonnumero telephone number.
telefono telephone.
telefunkciigo remote control.

telegrafa

telegrafa telegraphic.
telegrafe telegraphically.
telegrafi to telegraph.
telegrafia telegraphic.
telegrafilo telegraph (instrument).
telegrafio telegraphy.
telegrafisto telegraphist.
telegrafo telegraph.
telegrafoficejo telegraph office.
telegramo telegram.
telegvidado radio control.
telegvidata misilo guided missile.
telekasti to telecast, broadcast on TV.
telekommando remote control.
telekomputado teleprocessing.
telekomunika tekniko telecommunications technology.
telekomunikada telecommunication.
telekomunikado telecommunications.
telekomuniko telecommunications.
telekonduki aviadilon to fly a plane by remote control.
telekonferenco teleconference.
telekopie by fax, by wire.
telekso telex.
telematiko telematics.
telemetri to range-find, telemeter.
telemetrio telemetry.
telemetro range-finder, telemeter.
teleobjectivo telephoto lens.
teleobjektivo telephoto lens.
teleologio teleology.
teleostea teleost, teleostean.
teleosteo teleost, teleostean, teleostean fish, teleost fish.
telepatio telepathy.
teleporti to beam.
telera pertaining to plates, plate-like, plate-shaped.
teleregilo remote control.
telereto saucer, small plate.
telerlavilo dishwashing brush.
telerlavisto dishwasher.
telermeblo china closet, sideboard.
telero dish, plate.
telerrako drainer, draining board.
telertuketo serviette.
telertuko dishcloth.
teleskopo telescope.
telespekado watching television.
telespektanto television viewer.
telespekti to watch television.
telestarto remote job entry.
telestirado remote control.
teletajpilo teletype.
teleteksto teletext.
televida television. **televida anteno** television aerial, television antenna. **televida filmo** television film, television movie.

tempopasigo

televidi to watch television.
televidigi to televise.
televidilo television set.
televido television.
televidoprogramo television programme.
televidprogramo television programme.
televizio television, TV.
telfero cableway, teleferic.
teliptero beech fern.
telo tell.
telomero telomere.
telugo Telugu.
teluro tellurium.
tema thematic.
temanĝo tea (as a meal).
tembro timbre.
teme thematically.
temfadeno topic thread.
temi to be about, be on the subject of, deal with, refer to. **temi pri** to be about. **temis pri** the subject was. **temas nur pri tio, ke** it's just that. **temas pri** to it's a matter of. **Temas pri tio, ke...** that point is that...
temo theme, subject, topic. **temo kun variaĵoj** theme with variations.
tempa chronological, temporal. **tempa akuzativo** accusative of time.
tempaĝo epoch, period (geological).
tempe in time, over time.
temperamento temperament.
temperaturo temperature.
temperi to temper.
tempero distemper, tempera.
tempesta stormy, tumultuous, turbulent, tempestuous.
tempestalveno coming of a storm.
tempesto storm, tempest.
tempete in a short time.
tempeto short time, moment.
tempi to be time for.
tempio temple (forehead).
tempkalkulo sense of time, track of time.
templimo deadline, expiration (of time), term, time limit.
templo temple (worship).
tempo beat, tense, time. **tempo por pripensi** to time to consider.
tempodaŭro duration, period, timeframe, timescale.
tempodiseriga sistemo time-sharing system.
tempokalkulo era.
tempomezurado timing.
tempomezuri to clock, time.
tempomezurilo chronometer, timepiece.
tempono slice, time slice.
tempopartigo time sharing.
tempopasigilo pastime.
tempopasigo pastime.

441

tempopaso course of time, passage of time, passing of time.
tempoperdo waste of time, loss of time.
temporaba time-consuming.
temporalo temporal bone.
tempoŝaltilo timer.
tempumilo timer.
tenaca clinging, tenacious.
tenado custody, grip, holding, storage.
tenajli to pincer.
tenajlo pincers, pair of pincers, tongs.
tenaro ball, ball of the thumb.
Tenbio Tenby.
tendarfajro campfire.
tendaro camp of tents, tented camp.
tendarservisto camp follower.
tendenca biased, partisan.
tendenci to tend.
tendenco tendency, bias.
tendeno ligament, sinew, string, tendon.
tendi to camp.
tendo tabernacle, tent, pavilion.
Tendofesto Feast of Tabernacles.
tendokampo camp, camp of tents, tented camp.
tendonajlo stake.
tendro tender.
tendumado camping.
tendumi to camp (in a tent).
tenebro darkness.
tenejisto warehouseman.
tenejo depository, depot, repository, storehouse, warehouse.
tenera affectionate, fond, loving, tender.
tenere affectionately, fondly, lovingly, tenderly.
tenereco tenderness.
tenesia Tennessean.
tenesiano Tennessean.
teni to hang onto, hold, keep, retain. **teni brulanta** to keep something burning. **teni en la kalkulo** to bear in mind.
teniĝi to keep.
teniĝo attitude, bearing, deportment, posture.
tenilo grip, handle, knob, holder, hilt.
tenio tapeworm.
tenisejo tennis court.
tenisema inclined to tennis.
teniso tennis.
tenispartnero tennis partner.
tenispilko tennis ball.
teno grasp, grip, hold.
tenono tenon.
tenora tenor.
tenoro tenor.
tenorulo tenor.
tensio tension, voltage.
tenso tense.
tensoro tensor.

tenta tempting.
tentado enticement, inducement.
tentaĵo enticement, inducement.
tentaklo tentacle.
tentanto tempter.
tenti to entice, induce, tempt.
tentiĝo temptation.
tento temptation.
tentoado temptation.
teo tea.
Teobaldo Theobald, Tedbald.
teodolito theodolite.
Teodoro Theodore.
teogonio theogony. fv
teokratia theocratic.
teokratio theocracy.
teokrato theocrat.
teologia theological.
teologiisto theologist.
teologio theology.
teologisto theologian.
teologo theologian.
teoremo theorem.
teoria abstract, speculative, theoretic, theoretical.
teorie in the abstract.
teorii to theorize.
teoriigi to speculate, theorize.
teoriisto theorist.
teorio theory. **teorio de evoluo** theory of evolution. **teorio de komputado** computing science. **teorio de la aroj** set theory.
teoriulo theorist, theorizer.
teozofio theosophy.
tepelvo tea bowl.
tepida lukewarm, tepid.
tepoto teapot.
tera earthen, earthly, terrestrial. **tera akso** axis of the earth, earth's axis.
terabajto terabyte.
terabito terabit.
teraherco terahertz.
terakota terracotta.
terakotaĵo (piece of) terracotta pottery.
terakoto terracotta.
teralkala alkaline-earth. **teralkala metalo** alkaline earth metals.
terano earthling.
terapeŭtika therapeutic, therapeutical.
terapeŭtiko medicine, therapeutics.
terapeŭto therapeutist.
terapio therapy.
teraso terrace.
Teravado Theravada.
terbio terbium.
terborden landwards, towards land.
terbordo shore, edge of land.
terbulo clod of earth, lump of earth.
terceto trio.

terdisfalo landslip.
terdometo hovel.
terebinto turpentine.
terenbati to beat to the ground.
terenkuŝa prone (downward).
terenkuŝiĝi to prostrate (one's self).
tereno ground, grounds, terrain, campus.
terenporti to carry to the ground.
terenregistro land register, official real estate register, register of title deeds.
teretaĝe on the ground floor.
teretaĝo ground floor.
terfosisto excavator.
tergaso natural gas.
tergloba terrestrial.
terglobo globe (of the world).
tergrundo earth.
terhundo terrier.
teritoria territorial.
teritorio territory.
terkapo cape, promontory.
terkarbo coal.
terkolo isthmus, neck (of land).
terkonekti to earth, ground.
terkonekto earth connection, earth wire, grounding, ground wire.
terkrusto earth's crust.
terkultivisto agrarian, farmer, agriculturist.
terkultivo agriculture.
terkulturista peasant's.
terkulturisto farmer.
terkulturo agriculture, tillage.
terlaboristo agricultural labourer, agricultural worker.
terlimŝtono landmark.
termezuri to survey (land).
termezuristo surveyor.
termika thermic.
terminalo terminal.
terminaro glossary, terminology, nomenclature.
termino name, (technical) term, expression.
Termino Roman god Terminus.
termino term, jargon.
termito termite.
termo term (math), coefficient, element, entry, member.
termodinamiko thermodynamics.
termoelektra thermoelectric.
termometro thermometer.
termoso thermos bottle.
termostato thermostat.
terni to sneeze.
ternivelo first floor, ground floor, ground level.
terno sneeze.
ternukso ground nut.
tero dirt, earth, ground, land, soil.
Tero Earth.

tero soil, earth, land, ground.
terorismo terrorism.
teroristo terrorist.
teroro terror, reign of terror.
terpeco plot (of land).
terpeĉo asphalt, bitumen.
terpeko asphalt, bitumen.
terpinto point of land, tip of land.
terpiro Jerusalem artichoke.
terpoma potato. **terpoma faruno** potato flour. **terpoma kaĉo** mashed potatoes.
terpoma salato potato salad.
terpomfloko crisp, potato chip.
terpomo potato.
terpomsenŝeliga tranĉilo potato peeler.
terpomŝimo potato blight, potato disease, potato rot.
terrato gopher.
terskuo earthquake shock.
Tersolo Tersoal, Terzool.
tersulko furrow.
tersurfaco ground.
terŝoviĝo landslide.
terŝtopaĵo landfill.
tertavolo layer of earth, layer.
tertestudo land tortoise.
Tertiaro Tertiary.
tertremo earthquake.
terura terrible, dreadful, gruesome, horrible, awful, dire, frightful.
terurajô horror.
terure awfully, frightful, terribly.
terureco terribleness.
terurega aghast, hideous, horrible, ghastly, dreadful.
teruregaĵo abhorrence, abomination.
teruregi to appall, horrify.
terurego abhorrence, horror.
teruri to frighten, terrify.
teruriga horrible.
terurigi to terrorize.
teruriĝi to be terrified.
teruriĝinta startled.
terurita aghast, startled.
teruro alarm, terror, panic, awe, dread, fright.
terursonĝo nightmare.
terurstreĉitaj okuloj eyes stretched wide in terror.
tervarma energio geothermal energy.
tervazo pan.
tervermeto grub (insect).
tervermo earthworm.
terzono zone.
tesdalio shepherd's cress.
teslo tesla.
testa funkcio test function.
testado testing.
testamentanto testator.

testamenti to will, bequeath. **testamenti sian tutan havaĵon al** to bequeath one's entire estate to.
testamento testament, will.
testaro test suite.
testhelpilo testing aid.
testi to test.
testiko testicle, testis.
testisto tester.
testo test.
testofunkcio test function.
testosterono testosterone.
testudo tortoise, turtle.
tetablo tea table.
tetano lockjaw, tetanus.
teto theta (Θθ).
tetraedro tetrahedron.
tetrako little bustard.
tetralogio tetralogy.
tetrao hazel hen.
tetrarko tetrarch.
tetrino grey hen, black grouse hen.
tetro black grouse, grouse.
teujo teapot, tea caddy, tea canister.
teumante while drinking tea.
teŭkrio wood-sage.
teŭtona Teutonic.
teŭtono Teuton.
tezaŭro semantic dictionary, thesaurus.
tezio bastard toadflax.
tezo essay, thesis.
tia such, such a, that kind of, so. **tia, kia** such as (it is).
tiaforte with such force.
tiaĝojege with such great joy.
tiaĵo something like that, such a thing.
tial on that account, therefore, for that reason, so. **tial ke** because, for the reason that, in as much as, insomuch, since. **tial mankas kaŭzon por fari ion** thus there is no reason to do something.
tialo account, ground, motive, reason.
tiam then. **tiam kaj tiam** now and then.
tiama of that time.
tiamaniere in that manner, in that way, in this way, like this, thus.
tiamino aneurine, thiamine.
tiamulo a man of that time, contemporary.
tiaro papal crown, tiara.
tiatempe at that time.
Tiberio Tiberius.
Tibero Tiber.
tibeta Tibetan.
tibetanino Tibetan woman.
tibetano Tibetan.
Tibeto Tibet.
tibiingo gaiter, legging.
tibikarno calf.
tibio shin bone, tibia.
tibiosto calf.
tibiviando calf (of leg).
tie there, in that place, over there, yonder. **tie ĉi** here. **tie ĉi aldonita** herewith. **tie ĉi enfermita** enclosed (herewith). **tie kaj tie** here and there. **tie kaj tie ĉi** here and there.
tiea of that place, local.
tiel in that way, so, thus, like, in such a fashion, in that manner. **tiel ... kiel** as ... as, so ... as. **tiel estu** amen. **tiel la afero staras** that's how it is, that's how things are. **tiel longe kiel** as long as. **tiel nomata** so-called.
tiele sic, thus, thusly.
tielnomata so-called.
tien that way, there, thither, yonder. **tien ĉi** to here, hither, this way. **tien kaj reen** back and forth.
ties that one's, of that one, the latter's.
tieulo person of that place.
tifa febro typhoid (fever).
tifaa sumako staghorn sumac.
tifao bulrush, reedmace, cattail, cumbungi, raupo.
tifo typhus.
tifoido typhoid.
tifono typhoon.
tigo stalk, stem.
tigobrasiko kohlrabi.
tigrido baby tiger.
tigrino tigress.
Tigriso Tigris.
tigro tiger.
tigropitono python molure.
tikla ticklish, delicate.
tikli to tickle.
tikliĝema ticklish.
tiklo tickle.
tiklosentema ticklish.
tiko tic, twitch, ticking.
tiktak tick-tock.
tiktaki to tick.
tiktako tick.
tilacino Tasmanian tiger, Tasmanian wolf,.
tildo tilde (~).
tilia lime, of a lime tree.
Tilikoltro Tillicoultry.
tilio lime tree, linden tree, linden.
tima afraid.
timbalo kettledrum, timpani.
time apprehensively, fearfully.
timeco timidity.
timega horrendous, horrific.
timege terrified, with terror.
timegi to be greatly afraid, have great fear, dread.
timegigi to terrify.
timeginda formidable.

timego awe, fright.
timema afraid, timid, faint hearted, timid.
timeme nervously.
timemiĝi to become sacred.
timemo faintheartedness, nervousness, timidity.
timemulo coward, funk.
timeta shy.
timeteco shyness.
timi to be afraid of, fear.
timiano thyme.
timida shy.
timiga frightful, scary, horrible, dreadful.
timigado intimidation.
timige awfully, frightfully, scarily.
timigeta spooky.
timigi to affright, alarm, frighten, intimidate, scare.
timigilo scarecrow.
timigita afraid, fearful.
timigo scare.
timigulo bogey.
timiĝi to become scared.
timinda frightful, awful.
timkrio cry of distress.
timo apprehension, fear, fright, dread.
timolo thymol.
timono drawbar, shaft (of vehicle), beam, pole.
timoplena terrified, full of fear.
Timormaro Timor Sea.
Timoro Timor.
timoteo timothy-grass.
timpano middle ear, timpani, tympanium.
timpanono dulcimer, cimbalom.
timsigniĝi to show signs of fear.
timtremiga gaunt, ghastly, gruesome, horrible.
timtremoj creeps, chills, shivers.
timulo coward.
timuloegulo poltroon.
timuso thymus.
Tinêĵo Tintin.
tindro tinder, punk, touchwood.
tinedifektita moth-eaten.
tineo clothes moth, moth.
tineto firkin, trough.
tingaĵo achievement.
tinko tench.
tinkturi to dye, tint.
tinkturisto dyer.
tinkturmakuli to stain.
tinkturo dye, tint, tincture.
tino[1] tub, vat.
tino[2] tuna, tuna-fish.
tintado ringing, tinkling, clinking.
tinti to chink, clink, jingle, tinkle.
tintigi to clink, jingle, tinkle, ring.
tintilo bell (ornament), jingle bell.

tinto clink, jingle, tinkle.
tinunkolo kestrel.
tinuso tuna, tuna fish.
tio that over there, that, those. **tio aŭ alio** one thing or another. **tio certiĝas pli kaj pli** that is becoming more and more certain. **tio ĉi** this (thing). **tio dependas** that depends. **tio dependas de via vidpunkto** that depends on your viewpoint. **tio estas** i.e., that is. **tio estas alia rakonto** but I digress, that's another story. **tio estas ĝuste kion mi...** that's exactly what I... **tio estas idiota** that's stupid. **tio estas ridinda** that's ridiculous. **tio estas sensenca** that's nonsense. **tio estas stulta** that's foolish. **tio estas (por mi) volapukaĵo** it's all Greek to me. **tio kaj jeno** this and that. **tio memorigas min pri tio, ke...** that reminds me that... **tio montriĝos** we'll see. **tio ne estas fierindaĵo** that's nothing to be proud of. **tio ne estas imitinda** that should not be imitated. **tio ne estas sama afero** that's not the same thing. **tio ne estis daŭronta** it was not (meant) to last. **tio ne gravas** don't mention it, it doesn't matter, never mind, that's all right, you're welcome, that's OK. **tio neniel efikis** it did nothing. **tio plaĉas al mi** I like that. **tio plaĉas min** I like that. **tio pruvas, ke...** that proves (that)...
Tiobrado Tipperary.
tiom as many, so many, so much. **tiom da** so much, so many. **tiom longe kiom** as long as. **tiom pli bone** so much the better. **tiom, kiom** as much as, as many as.
tioma so much.
tiomjare for so many years.
tion farinte having done this.
tipa typical.
tipara of type. **tipara familio** type family. **tipara fasono** typeface. **tipara grado** point size. **tipara pezo** font weight. **tipara stilo** face, style.
tiparo font.
tiparredaktilo font editor.
tipdeklaro type definition.
tipe typically.
tipizema programlingvo typed language.
tipkonverto type conversion.
tipnomo type identifier.
tipo type.
tipografia typographical.
tipografiisto typographer.
tipografio typography.
tipografo typographer.
tipulo crane-fly, daddy-longlegs.
tiradi to drag.
tirado hauling, pulling, tirade.

tiraljorado skirmish.
tiraljori to skirmish.
tiraljoro sharpshooter, sniper.
tiramiso tiramisu.
tirana tyrannical.
tiranaema tyrannical.
tiraneco despotism, tyranny.
tirani to tyrannize.
tiranmortigo tyrannicide.
tirano despot, tyrant, oppressor.
Tirano Tirana.
tirano tyrant.
tiranosaŭro tyrannosaur.
tirata drawn.
tiraviro parbuckle.
tirboji to bay, howl.
tirĉevalo draught horse.
tiregi to wrest.
Tirena Maro Tyrrhenian Sea.
tirharmoniko accordion.
tiri to drag, draw, haul, pull, tug, tow. **tiri profiton el** turn to account, turn to good account.
tiriĝi to be pulled, wear on, drag on.
tirilo trigger.
Tirio Tiree.
tirkamiono tractor trailer.
tirkesto drawer.
tirkestŝranko cabinet.
tirlevi to hoist, hoist up.
tirmenuo pull-down menu.
tiro pull, tug, twitch.
tiroado traction.
tiroido thyroid (gland).
Tirolo Tyrol.
tirstango connecting-rod, drag-link, drawbar, pull-rod.
titana titanic.
titania titanium.
titanio titanium.
Titano Titan.
titano titanium.
Titanoj Titans.
titoli to entitle, name, title.
titolo title, caption, degree, designation, heading, style.
titolpaĝo title page.
titrado assay.
titri to assay, titrate.
titro concentration, fineness, strength, titre.
tiu that (one). **tiu aŭ alia** any. **tiu aŭ alia momento** one moment or another, in any given moment. **tiu ĉi** this. **tiu, kiu** the one who. **tiuj** those. **tiuj ĉi** these. **tiun ĉi nokton** tonight.
tiucele for that purpose.
tiudirekte in that direction.
tiuflanke on that side.
tiufoje this time.

tiukaze in that case.
tiumaniere in that way.
tiumomente at that moment.
tiunokte that night.
tiuokaze then.
tiuparto that part.
tiupense thinking of this, with this thought.
tiurilate with relation to that.
tiuspeca that kind of.
tiustato this state, thus.
tiutage on that day.
tiutempa of that time, at that time.
tiutempe at that time.
tizano infusion (of tea, etc.), tisane.
tjurka Turkic. **tjurka lingvo** Turkic language.
tjurko Turkic person.
tjurkobulgaro Huno-Bulgar, Proto-Bulgar.
tlaspo penny-cress.
t.n. → **tiel nomata**.
to name of the letter T. **To-ĉemizo**, **T-ĉemizo** T-shirt.
toasti to toast.
toastigi to toast.
toasto toast (a health), toast (bread).
Tobago Tobago.
Tobermoro Tobermory.
tobogani to toboggan.
tofeo toffee.
tofo tuff.
tofuo bean curd, tofu.
togo toga.
Togo Togo, Togoland.
Togolando Togo.
tohuo bean curd, tofu.
tohuvabohuo confusion, disorder.
toĥaro Tokhar.
tokato toccata.
Tokelao Tokelau.
Tokia Golfeto Tokyo Bay.
Tokio Tokyo.
Tokjo Tokyo.
toksa toxic.
tokseco toxicity.
toksino toxin.
tokso toxic substance.
toksologiisto toxicologist.
toksologio toxicology.
toksologo toxicologist.
tola linen. **tola teksaranĝo** plain weave, tabby weave.
tolaĵejo linen room.
tolaĵo linen (the washing).
tolaĵokorbo laundry basket.
toleraema tolerant.
tolerebla bearable, tolerable.
tolereble tolerably.
tolereco tolerance, toleration.
tolerema forbearing, tolerant.

tolereme tolerantly.
toleremo tolerance, toleration.
toleri to endure, put up with, tolerate, suffer, bear, stand.
tolero forbearance.
tolkovrilo linen cover.
tolmarkezo awning.
tolmarko laundry mark.
tolo cloth, linen, sheeting.
tolsekigilo dryer.
tolubalzamo balsam of Tolu.
tolueno toluene.
tolupo toe loop.
tomahaŭko tomahawk.
tomahoko tomahawk.
tomano ashrafi (Persian coin).
tomasisma Thomistic.
tomasismo Thomism.
tomasisto Thomist.
tomatino tomatine.
tomato tomato.
tomatpasto tomato paste.
tomatsuko tomato juice.
tomatsupo tomato soup.
tomba of a tomb.
tombako red brass, tombac.
tombejo cemetery, graveyard, necropolis.
tombisto gravedigger.
tombmonteto (burial) mound.
tombo grave, tomb, vault.
tombocâmbro crypt.
tombokelo crypt.
tombolo charity raffle, tombola.
tombomonteto barrow, burial mound, grave mound, tumulus.
tombomonumento mausoleum.
tombopreĝejo tomb church-building.
tomboŝtono tombstone.
tombŝtona tombstone.
tombŝtono tombstone.
Tomintolo Tomintoul.
tomismo Thomism.
tona tonal, toned, tonic.
tonakcento pitch accent, tonic accent.
tonalo key.
tondeti to snip.
tondi to clip, cut, shear.
tondilo scissors, shears.
tondisto clipper.
tondo cut.
tondra thundering, of thunder, thunderous.
  tondraj aplaŭdoj thunderous applause.
tondrado thundering.
tondre thunderingly.
tondri to thunder.
tondro thunder.
tondrobruo (sound of) thunder.
tondronubo thundercloud.
tonelaro tonnage.

tonelo ton, shipping measure (about 2.83 cubic metres).
tonforketo tuning fork.
Tongo Tonga.
tono note, tone (music).
tonoscililo audio oscillator.
tonsilo tonsil.
tonsuri to tonsure.
tonsuro tonsure.
tontino tontine.
tonuso tone, tonus.
topazo topaz.
topmasto top mast.
topo crow's nest.
topografiisto topographer.
topografio topography.
topografo topographer.
topologia topological. **topologia dualo** adjoint space. **topologia dudualo** second adjoint space. **topologia spaco** topological space. **topologia strukturo** topological structure. **topologia subspaco** topological subspace.
topologio topology. **topologio de simpla konverĝo** topology of pointwise convergence. **topologio de unuforma konverĝo** topology of uniform convergence.
toporo (broad) axe, hatchet.
topvelo top sail.
torako chest, thorax.
Torao Pentateuch.
torĉingo torch holder.
torĉo torch.
torda tortuous.
tordaĵo twist.
tordeca tortuous.
tordece tortuously.
tordeco torsion, twist.
tordeti to wriggle.
tordetiĝi to wriggle.
tordi to contort, twist, warp, wind, wring, wriggle, sprain.
tordigi to distort.
tordiĝi to twist.
tordiĝo sprain.
tordilo strainer, tightener, twister.
tordo torsion.
toreado bullfight.
toreadoro bullfighter, toreador.
toreisto bullfighter, toreador, torero.
torenta torrential.
torente nonstop, continuously.
torenti to flow.
torento stream, torrent, volley.
torero bullfighter.
torfejo peat bog.
torfkovrilo turf roof, turf cover, peat roof, peat cover.
torfo peat, turf.

torijo Shinto temple gateway.
torilido bur-parsley.
Torino Turin.
torio thorium.
torni to turn (on a lathe).
tornilo lathe, potter's wheel.
tornisto turner.
tornistro backpack, knapsack, haversack.
tornmaŝino lathe.
toro toroid, torus.
torpedboato torpedo boat.
torpedi to torpedo.
torpedo torpedo.
torporo torpor.
torro millimetre of mercury, torr.
torso torso, trunk (of body).
torto pie, tart, pastry.
torturado torture.
torturejo torture chamber.
torturi to agonize, torture.
torturisto torturer.
torturo torture.
tortvendisto pieman.
toskana Tuscanian.
Toskanio Tuscany.
toskano Tuscan.
Toskanujo Tuscany.
tosti to toast (speech during drink), offer a toast.
tostkanti to wassail.
tosto toast (speech during drink).
totala overall, total. **totala eklipso** total eclipse.
totale altogether, in all.
totaligi to add together, total.
totalisma totalitarian.
totalismo totalitarianism.
totalo total.
totano redshank.
totemismo totemism.
totemo totem.
toŭfuo bean curd, tofu.
tra through. **tra la tuta lando** across the entire country. **tra la tuta nokto** all night long, the whole night through.
traakvigi to irrigate.
traatendi to wait out.
trababili to babble away.
trabaĵo framework, scaffold (for building).
trabanto satellite.
trabaro framework, scaffold, scaffolding.
trabati to blaze a trail. **trabati per la piedoj** to trample.
trabego balk.
trablovo draught.
trabo beam, girder, joist.
trabori to drill through, pierce, perforate, transfix.
trabruli to burn down, burn up.

trabutiki to shop.
traca Thracian. **Traca Maro** Thracian Sea.
Tracio Thrace, Thracia.
Traco Tracy.
traco Thracian.
traĉi to cut.
trad. → **tradukita (de)**.
tradedia tragic.
tradiboĉi to squander.
tradicia traditional.
tradicie according to tradition, traditionally.
tradiciismo traditionalism.
tradicio tradition.
trado trade wind.
tradormi la nokton to sleep through the night.
tradukaĵo translation.
traduki to interpret, translate. **traduki anglen** to translate into English.
tradukilgenerilo compiler generator.
tradukilo compiler, translator.
tradukisto interpreter, translator.
tradukita (de) translated (by). **tradukita programo** object program.
traduko translation, version.
tradukprogramo translation program.
traduktempa compile time.
trafa striking.
trafdistanco range.
trafe accurately, appropriately, graphically, relevant, on target, apt, to the point. **trafe dirita** to the point. **trafe reaganta** to the point.
trafeca fitting, appropriate.
trafeco appropriateness, pertinence, relevance.
trafi to attain, catch, encounter, find, hit, run across, score, strike. **trafi lote** to accrue to.
trafika traffic.
trafikcirkleto traffic circle.
trafikcirklo roundabout, traffic circle.
trafikilo means of transportation.
trafiklumo traffic light.
trafikmonpuno traffic fine.
trafiko traffic.
trafikpolicisto traffic cop.
trafikreguloj traffic rules.
trafikrondeto traffic circle.
trafikrondo roundabout, traffic circle.
trafikstopiĝo traffic jam.
trafikŝtopiĝo traffic block, traffic congestion, traffic jam, traffic tie-up.
traflisto hit-list.
traflueti to seep through.
trafo hit, strike.
trafoliumi to glance through.
trafosi to dig through, spade.
trafpovo range.
trafrejŝo hit rate.

traganto
traganto tragacanth.
tragedia tragic.
tragedie tragically.
tragedieco tragedy.
tragediisto tragedian.
tragedio tragedy.
tragelafo bushbuck.
tragika tragic.
tragikeco tragedy.
tragikomedio tragicomedy.
traguteti to ooze.
traguti to percolate.
trahaki to hack (through).
trahore for hours.
traĥeo trachea, windpipe.
traĥomo trachoma.
traigivo throughput. **traigivo de kanalo** bandwidth.
trairejo passage, thoroughfare, corridor.
trairi to cover, go through, pass through, perambulate, traverse.
trairo passage.
trajektorio trajectory.
trajnbileto railway ticket, train ticket.
trajno (railroad) train.
trajto feature, facial feature, trait.
trakeo windpipe.
trakforko points, switch.
trakino weaver.
traklarĝo gauge.
traknivela pasejo level crossing.
trako rut, track, traffic lane.
trakomo trachoma.
traktadaĉo mistreatment.
traktado abuse, treatment.
traktaĵo treatise, treaty.
traktato pact, tract, treatise, treaty, monograph.
trakti to deal with, handle, treat. **trakti iun per antibiotikoj** to treat someone with antibiotics. **trakti kiel** to treat as. **trakti malbone** to abuse. **trakti per radioterapio** to radiate (as a medical treatment).
traktilo handler, processor.
trakto treatment.
traktorio tractrix.
traktoro tractor.
tralasi to admit, let through.
tralavi to wash.
tralegi to read through, peruse.
Tralio Tralee.
tralumebla translucent.
tramhaltejo streetcar stop, tram stop.
tramo streetcar, tram.
trampo tramp, vagrant.
trampolino trampoline.
tramveturilo tramcar.
tramvojo street car tracks, tramway.
tranci to be in a trance.

transcendi
tranco trance.
trancosimila trancelike.
tranĉa sharp, cutting, trenchant.
tranĉadi to gash, slash.
tranĉaĵo slice.
tranĉanto blade (knife), cutter.
tranĉe cuttingly.
tranĉegi to slash.
tranĉeo trench (military).
tranĉetaĵo clipping.
tranĉeti to nick (notch).
tranĉeto clip.
tranĉi to cut (with knife), slice, carve. **tranĉi oblikve** to bevel.
tranĉiĝi to be cut.
tranĉilakrigilo knife-grinder.
tranĉilego cutlass.
tranĉileto penknife.
tranĉilo knife.
tranĉilvundo cut.
tranĉo incision.
tranĉodento incisor.
tranĉosurfaco cross-cut.
tranĉrando edge (of tools).
tranĉtabulo cutting board.
tranĉvundo cut (wound, injury).
trankvila calm, tranquil, serene, still, quiet, peaceful.
trankvile peacefully, tranquilly, calmly.
trankvileco calmness, composure, quietude, serenity, tranquility.
trankvilema unflappable.
trankviliga tranquilizing, calming.
trankvilige reassuringly.
trankviligi to appease, calm (down), quiet, soothe, still, quell, tranquilize, pacify.
trankviligo appeasement.
trankviliĝi to calm down.
trankviliĝo relief.
trankvilo tranquility, calmness, peacefulness.
trankvilsangeco composure, equanimity, presence of mind, sang-froid.
tranokta overnight.
tranoktado spending the night.
tranoktejo accommodation, place to spend the night.
tranokti to pass the night, spend the night.
tranokto overnight.
trans across, beyond, on the other side of.
transa on the other side (of). **transa flanko** opposite side.
transakcia dosiero transaction file.
transakcio transaction.
transalpa transalpine.
transarka overarching.
transatlantika transatlantic.
transcenda transcendent, transcendental.
transcendeco transcendence.
transcendi to transcend.

transdiri to pass on, transmit, repeat.
transdoni to convey, hand, hand over, pass, give over, transfer.
transdonluko service-hatch.
transdono delivery.
transe across, opposite, on the other side of. **transe de** across. **transe de la rivero** across the river, on the other side of the river.
transen across.
transepto transept.
transfiguri to transfigure.
Transfigurigo Transfiguration.
transfleksiĝa (point) of inflection, flex (point).
transflugi to fly across.
transforma gramatiko transformational grammar.
transformado transformation.
transformatoro transformer.
transformi to transform.
transformigi to transform.
transformiĝi to become transformed, change form.
transformiĝo transformation.
transformilo transformer.
transformo refashioning, transformation.
transfuĝinto refugee.
transfuzi to transfuse.
transfuzo transfusion.
transgena transgenic.
transgene transgenically.
transgrimpi to climb over.
transi to cross.
transiganto transmitter.
transigi to pass, transmit, transport.
transigilo points, switch.
transigo carry, transmission.
Transilvanio Transylvania.
transira transitional. **transira tempo** propagation time.
transirejo crossing place, ford (in a river).
transiri to cross over, cross, go beyond, transfer. **transiri Rubikonon** to cross the Rubicon.
transirigi to transfer.
transirigo transfer.
transiriĝo transfer.
transiro transfer, crossing, transition.
transistoro transistor.
transita transit, transitive. **transita reto** transit network. **transita rilato** transitive relation.
transiti to transit.
transitiva transitive. **transitiva verbo** transitive verb.
transitiveco transitiveness, transitivity.
transito transit.
transjordana Transjordanian.

transĵeti to throw across.
transkapiĝi to somersault.
transkapiĝo somersault.
Transkejo Transkei.
transkuri to flit.
translacio change of place, translation (math.).
translanda cross-national, transnational.
translaso abandonment.
translima cross-border.
translingvigi to translate.
transliterado transliterating, transliteration.
transliteri to transliterate.
transliveri to deliver.
transloĝiga kamiono furniture van, moving van.
transloĝigi to move, change one's dwelling, relocate.
transloĝiĝi to move.
transloĝiĝo removal, move.
translokado relocation, transposition.
transloki to dislodge, displace, move, transfer, transplant, transpose, remove.
translokigi to move from one place to another, relocate.
translokigo transfer.
translokiĝi to move, change residence.
translokiĝo transfer.
transmara overseas, transmarine.
transmare overseas.
transmeta programo copy program.
transmeti to transfer, transpose.
transmeto transposition.
transmetrapido transfer rate. **transmetrapido en baŭdoj** baud rate.
transmisii to transmit.
transmisiilo transmitter.
transmutacio transmutation.
transpago remittance, remittance of money.
transpasi to cross, go beyond, pass over, overstep.
transpaŝi to transgress, step across.
transpaŝilo stepping stone.
transpaŝo transgression, trespass.
transplantado transplant.
transplanti to transplant.
transponaĵo transpose.
transponi to transpose.
transpono transposition.
transponti to bridge.
transporta tavolo transport layer.
transportado transportation.
transportbendo conveyor belt.
transportbiciklo carrier cycle, carrier tricycle.
transporti to convey, take over, shift, transport, transfer.
transportilo transport.
transportisto carrier, transporter.

transporto transport, carriage.
transpoŝigi to cut and paste.
transpreni to take across, take on.
transproprietigi to abalienate.
transproprietigo abalienation.
transproprigo alienation.
transputoro transputer.
transruĝa infrared. **transruĝa pordo** infrared port. **transruĝa radiado** infrared radiation.
transsalti to jump across, jump over.
transsaltludi to vault.
transsenda transfer. **transsenda kontrolo** transfer checking. **transsenda pago** carriage (cost). **transsenda rapido** transfer rate.
transsendi to carry.
transsiberia trans-Siberian.
transskribado transcribing, transcription.
transskribaĵo copy.
transskribi to transcribe, copy.
transskribo transliteration.
transŝarĝi to shift on to.
transŝarĝo transhipment.
transtera in the hereafter, in the next world.
transtomba beyond the grave.
transurania transuranic.
transuranio transuranic (element).
transvala Transvaalian.
Transvalo Transvaal, the Transvaal.
transversa transverse. **transversa fluto** transverse flute.
transversaŝipe abeam.
transverse crosswise, transversely.
transverso transversal.
transverŝi to transfuse.
transviola ultraviolet.
transvivi to outlive, survive.
trapasejo passageway.
trapasi to pass through, slip through, go beyond, traverse.
trapasigi to pass.
trapaso passage.
trapaŝi to step through.
trapenetri to penetrate through.
trapezo trapeze, trapezium, trapezoid.
trapiki to broach, puncture, perforate, transfix.
trapikileto skewer.
trapiko spit (spike).
trapo water chestnut.
trapremi to squeeze through.
trapuŝi to push through.
trarigardi to look through.
trarompi to break through.
trarompo breakthrough.
traserĉi to search.
traserĉo search warrant.
trasorbigi to soak.
trasorbiĝi to seep through.
trastreki to cross out, strike through.
trastreko cancellation.
trastudi to go through.
trasuferi to suffer through.
traŝiri to rend, slit.
traŝovi to draw.
traŝultre across the shoulder.
tratanto drawer.
tratato drawee, something that is drawn.
trati to make a draft.
trato (bank)draft.
tratranĉi to cut through.
traŭbo grape.
traŭmata traumatic.
traŭmato trauma.
traŭmatologiisto traumatologist.
traŭmatologio traumatology.
traŭmatologo traumatologist.
traŭmo trauma.
travadebla fordable.
travadejo ford.
travadi to ford.
travadoŝtono stepping-stone.
traverŝilo colander, strainer.
travestianto transvestite.
travestii to burlesque, parody.
travestio travesty.
traveturi to travel through, drive through.
travidebla transparent.
travideble transparently.
travidebleco transparency.
travideblo transparency.
travidi to look through, see through.
travintri to (spend the) winter.
travivado survival.
travivaĵo experience.
travive throughout life, all one's life.
travivebla survivable.
travivi to experience, live through, survive.
travivo de la plej taŭgaj survival of the fittest.
travojaĝi to tour, travel through.
travojaĝo tour.
tre quite, very, very much. **tre malklara** abstruse. **tre plaĉas al mi** to I like very much. **tre povas esti, ke...** it's very possible that...
tredi to thread.
tredkodo threaded code.
tredo thread.
treega awful, dramatic, extreme, incredible.
treege enormously, extremely, very much.
trefa cloverleaf.
trefkruciĝo cloverleaf (interchange).
trefo club (cards).
trejnado training.
trejnato trainee.
trejnboksi to spar.

trejni to coach, train. **trejni sin** to train (oneself), be in training.
trejnisto coach, instructor, trainer.
trejnita trained.
trema tremulous.
tremado trembling, trepidation.
tremao diaeresis (¨).
trematodo fluke, trematode.
trematodoj trematode.
tremeco trepidation.
tremegadi to shake violently.
tremeri to start, shiver, shudder.
tremeti to quiver, shiver, waver, wince.
tremeto tremor.
tremfebro ague.
tremi to quiver, shiver, tremble, shake, tremble.
tremiegi to quake.
tremiga eerie, grisly, gruesome, macabre.
tremigi to make tremble, shake.
tremo quiver, quivering, vibration.
tremoado trembling.
tremolo aspen.
trempado ducking.
trempaĵo sop.
trempegi to souse.
trempeti to dip.
trempeto dip.
trempi to dip, immerse, plunge, soak, steep.
trempiĝi to be soaked, soak.
trenaĵo train (of a dress).
trenaŭto tow truck.
treni to drag, tow, trail, train.
treniĝi to be dragged, be towed, trail.
trenkablo towing line.
trenstango towbar.
trenstrio wake.
trenŝipo towing vessel, tug, tugboat.
trepani to trepan.
trepano trepan.
treti to trample on, tread.
trezorejo treasury.
trezori to treasure.
trezoristo treasurer.
trezoro treasure.
trezorserĉanto one who seeks treasure.
tri three. **tri kvaronoj** three quarters.
tria third. **tria klasa** third class. **tria mondo** third world. **tria persono** third person.
triado triad.
triafoje three times.
triamonda third-world.
triangula triangular.
triangulo triangle.
triaranga tertiary.
triasa Triassic.
Triaso Triassic.
triatlono triathlon.

triatoma triatomic.
triba tribal.
tribalismo tribalism.
tribano tribe member.
tribestro chief.
tribo tribe.
triborda starboard.
tribordo starboard.
tribrako tribrach.
tribunalo tribunal.
tribuno podium, rostrum, speaker's platform, pulpit, tribune.
tribunuso tribune.
tributi to pay tribute.
tributo tribute.
tricent three hundred.
tricikla taksio pedicab, trishaw.
triciklo tricycle.
tricio tritium.
tridakno giant clam.
tridek thirty.
trideka thirtieth.
tridekjara thirty year-old.
tridento trident.
tridimensia three-dimensional.
trie thirdly.
triedra trihedral.
triedro trihedral (angle).
trientalo chickweed wintergreen.
Triero Treves.
Triesto Trieste.
trietaĝa three-storeyed floor.
trifingra three-toed. **trifingra bradipo** three-toed sloth. **trifingra buntpego** three-toed woodpecker. **trifingra mevo** kittywake.
triflanke on three sides.
trifoje three times, thrice.
trifolio clover, shamrock, trefoil.
triforio triforium.
triglifo triglyph.
triglo gurnard, sea robin.
trigonometria trigonometric. **trigonometria cirklo** unit circle centred at the origin. **trigonometria funkcio** trigonometric function. **trigonometria prezento** trigonometric representation.
trigonometrio trigonometry.
trihore for three hours, in three hours.
triĥino threadworm, trichina.
triĥobezoaro trichobezoar.
triĥofagio trichophagia.
triĥotilomanio trichotillomania.
trijara triennial.
trijare triennially.
trikado knitting.
trikaĵo knitting-work.
trikfadeno worsted.
triki to knit.

trikilo knitting needle.
trikino threadworm, trichina.
trikistino knitter.
trikobezoaro trichobezoar.
trikofagio trichophagia.
trikolora tri-coloured. **trikolora ipomeo** Mexican morning glory.
trikoloreto pansy.
trikorna tricorn.
trikotaĵo singlet, tights.
trikoti to knit.
trikotilo knitting needle.
trikotilomanio trichotillomania.
trikoto sweater (garment).
trikotvesto cardigan, jersey, sweater.
trikromio three-colour process.
triktrako backgammon.
trilatero triangle.
trili to trill, warble.
trilingva trilingual.
triliono quintillion, trillion.
triliteraĵo trigraph.
trilo quaver, trill, warble.
trilobito trilobite.
trilogio trilogy.
trimestra quarterly.
trimestre quarterly.
trimestro term, quarter, trimester.
trimonata quarterly.
trimonoika trimonoecious.
trinaskito triplet.
tringo sandpiper.
Trinidado Trinidad. **Trinidado kaj Tobago** (Republic of) Trinidad and Tobago.
trinkaĉi to booze (it up).
trinkado drinking.
trinkaĵaĉo concoction.
trinkaĵbufedo bar.
trinkaĵo beverage, drink.
trinkakvo drinking water.
trinkbufedo bar.
trinkĉokolado chocolate milk, hot chocolate.
trinkebla drinkable. **trinkebla akvo** drinking water.
trinkeja of a bar or pub. **trinkeja servisto** barman, bartender. **trinkeja tabureto** bar stool.
trinkejestro bar manager.
trinkejo bar, pub.
trinketi to sip.
trinketo small drink, sip.
trinkfonto water fountain.
trinki to drink. **trinki je ies sano** to drink to someone's health.
trinkigi to make someone drink. **trinkigi ĉevalojn** to water the horses.
trinkmono gratuity, tip.
trinko drink, beverage.

trinkujo tankard.
trinomo trinomial.
trio trio.
triobla triple.
trioble triple, three times.
triobligi to treble, triple.
triobligo trebling.
triobliĝi to triple.
trioblo threefold.
triodo triode.
trioika trioecious.
trioleto triolet, triplet.
triono third.
triopa triple.
triope by threes.
triopo trio.
tripango sea-slug, trepang.
tripanosomo trypanosome.
tripiedo tripod.
Tripitako tripitaka.
tripkolbaso chitterling.
tripo tripe.
Tripolo Tripoli.
tripso thrips.
triptiko triptych.
tripunkto ellipsis (...).
trirada three-wheeled.
triremo trireme.
trisemajne for three weeks.
trisilabo trisyllable.
trista dismal, dreary, sad.
triste sadly.
tristigi to afflict, distress, grieve.
tritage for three days.
tritermo trinomial.
tritika pano white bread.
tritikaĵo semolina.
tritikalo triticale.
tritiko wheat.
trito newt.
Tritono Triton.
trituro newt.
triumfa triumphal. **Triumfa arko** Arch of Triumph.
Triumf-arko Arch of Triumph.
triumfarko arch of triumph.
triumfe triumphantly.
triumfi to triumph.
triumfo triumph.
triumviro triumvir.
triunua Trinitarian. **Triunuaj Alpoj** Trinity Alps.
Triunuo Trinity.
trivi to use up, wear out.
triviala commonplace, course, vulgar, paltry, trifling, trivial.
trivialaĵo trifle, triviality.
trivojiĝo three forked road.

tro too (much, many). **tro da kuiristoj kaĉon difektas** too many cooks spoil the broth. **tro malalte taksi** to underestimate. **tro multa** too much. **tro skribema** discursive.
troa excessive, undue. **troa uzado** excessive use.
troabunda overabundant.
troabundeco overabundance.
troabundo overabundance.
troaĵo overabundance.
troaltigi to raise too high.
troantikva obsolete.
trobadoro troubadour.
trockisma Trotskyite.
trockisto Trotskyite.
trodolĉa sentimental.
trodorloti to spoil.
trodorlotita spoiled.
trodozo overdose.
troe excessively.
troentuziasma over enthusiastic.
trofavoremo favouritism.
trofeo trophy.
trofoblasta trophoblastic.
trofoblasto trophoblast.
trofoplasmo trophoplasm.
trofrua premature, untimely.
trofrue prematurely.
trogĉeno bucket chain.
troglodito cave-dweller, caveman, troglodyte.
trogo manger, trough.
trograndaĝi to become too old.
trograndigi to exaggerate.
trograndigo exaggeration.
trograndiĝi to become too old.
trograseco adiposis.
trohasta precipitous.
troĥeo trochee, choree, choreus.
troĥoido trochoid.
troiga exaggerated, fulsome.
troige exaggeratedly.
troigema given to exaggeration.
troigi to exaggerate.
troigo exaggeration, overstatement.
troja Trojan. **Troja ĉevalo** Trojan horse.
trojano Trojan.
trojko troika.
Trojo Troy.
trokeo trochee.
trokoido trochoid.
trolbarko trawler.
trolebuso trolleybus.
troleĉaro trolleybus.
troleo trolley.
troli to troll (internet), trawl.
trolio globe flower.
trolo trawl, troll.

trologata overpopulated.
trolonga prolix.
trolŝipo trawler.
tromalfrui to delay.
trombo column of water, tornado over water, waterspout.
trombono trombone.
trombozo thrombosis.
tromemfida overweening, presumptuous.
tromemfideco presumption.
tromemfido presumption, self-conceit.
tromometro tromometer.
trompa deceitful, fake, fraudulent.
trompado deceit, fraud, duplicity, trickery.
trompaĵo deceit, rip-off, sham, trick, fraud.
trompanto cheat, deceiver, imposter.
trompbrilo lustre, glitter.
trompema deceitful, shifty, tricky.
trompemo duplicity.
trompeti to play little tricks, take in.
trompi to cheat, deceive, mislead, con, fool, trick.
trompiĝi to be deceived, be mistaken.
trompistino con-woman.
trompisto conman, swindler.
trompita cheated, deceived.
trompito deceived person, deceived one.
tromplogi to bamboozle.
trompo cheat, trick, deception, delusion, fraud, swindle.
trompŝteli to pilfer, pinch.
trompŝtelisto fraud.
trompŝtelo fraud.
trompulo con man, swindler.
tromulte too much.
tromultvorta long-winded.
troni to reign, sit enthroned.
trono throne.
tronutri to overfeed.
troo excess.
tropagigi to fleece.
tropasia overheated.
tropeolino tropaeolin.
tropeolo nasturtium.
tropetadi to badger.
tropieco bigotry.
tropika tropical.
tropiko tropics.
tropismo tropism.
tropo figure of speech, trope.
tropofito tropophyte.
tropokolageno tropocollagen.
tropologia tropological.
tropologio tropology.
tropopaŭzo tropopause.
troposfera tropospheric.
troposfero troposphere.
tropostulema extortionate.
troprema tight.

troproduktado overproduction.
trorapida precipitate.
trorapideco precipitancy, precipitation.
trorapidi to gain (of a watch).
trosato excess, overeating.
troservema servile.
troservemo servility.
trosimpliga simplistic.
trosimpligi to oversimplify.
trostreĉi to strain.
trostreĉo strain.
troŝarĝi to overburden, overload.
troŝarĝita overloaded.
Troŝehano Trossachs.
troŝpara mean, stingy.
trotaksi to overestimate, overrate.
troteti to amble.
troti to trot.
trotilo scooter.
troto trot.
trotoado trot.
trotuaro footpath, pavement, sidewalk.
trotuarrando curb.
trouzi to abuse, overuse.
trouzo abuse.
trovadi to keep finding.
trovaĵo a find.
trovebla findable, able to be found.
trovena has to be found.
trovhundo retriever.
trovi to find. **trovi bonan akcepton** to be well-accepted. **trovi eliron el** to find a way out of. **trovi sin** to be found, be located, find oneself.
troviĝi to be found, be located, find oneself. **troviĝi dise** to be scattered around.
troviĝinta having been found.
trovinda worth finding.
trovita found.
trovitaĵo find.
trua detrančaĵo chad.
truadi to riddle.
truado holing.
trubaduro troubadour.
trubendlegilo tape reader.
trubendo punched tape.
truda aggressive, coercive, forceful.
trudado coercion.
trude aggressively.
trudema importunate, obtrusive.
trudeme insistently, intrusively.
trudemega officious.
trudemege officiously.
trudemego officiousness.
trudherbo weed.
trudi to assert, coerce, force, impose, thrust.
trudiĝema forward, importunate, insistent, intrusive, troublesome.
trudiĝi to importune.

trudkitelo strait-jacket.
trudo coercion, imposition, intrusion.
trudoeco obtrusion.
trudpeta pertinacious.
trudpeti to worry (importune).
trudpompa ostentatious.
trudpompo ostentation.
trudulo interloper, intruder.
truebla dokumento punching document.
truego large hole, pit.
trueta porous.
truetaro perforation.
trueto pore.
truflageto flag.
trufo truffle.
trugazoneto green.
truglobeto bead.
trui to perforate, punch, puncture.
truigi to make a hole.
truigilo awl.
truilo card punch.
trukado faking, trick photography.
trukarta of punch cards. **trukarta duobligilo** reproducer. **trukarta kunordigilo** collator. **trukarta zono** curtate.
trukartenirilo hopper.
trukartlegilo card reader.
trukarto punch card.
truki to trick.
truko trick.
trukulo hacker.
trulo trowel.
trumo pier, pier-glass, wall between openings.
trumpetadi to trumpet.
trumpeti to trumpet.
trumpetisto trumpeter.
trumpeto trumpet.
trunketo blade, stalk, stem.
trunki to truncate.
trunko frustum, stem, trunk, torso.
trunkrestaĵo stump.
trunkstumpo tree stump.
truo hole, orifice.
trupano trooper.
truplena full of holes.
trupo company (theatrical), troop, troupe, group.
trusapogilo brace.
truso truss.
trusto business trust.
truto trout.
tsvana lingvo Tswana, Tswana language.
TTF-tiparo TrueType font.
TTT (Tut-Tera Teksaĵo) WWW (Worldwide Web). **TTT-ejo** web site. **TTT-legilo** browser. **TTT-paĝaro** web site. **TTT-paĝo** web page.
tualetejo dressing room.

tualeto toilet.
tualetpapero tissue.
tualettuko (hand) towel.
tualetujo cosmetic case, vanity case.
tubakso bore axis.
tubera gnarled, knobby, knotty, protruding.
  tubera helianto Jerusalem artichoke.
tuberbrasiko broccoli.
tubercelerio turnip-rooted celery.
tuberkulo tubercle (med).
tuberkulozo tuberculosis.
tubero bump, gnarl, knob, knot, lump, protuberance, tuber.
tuberoso tuberose.
tubesplorilo bougie.
tubforma tubular.
tubfungo boletus.
tubisto fitter, plumber.
tubjo tuba.
tubkonduki to pipe.
tubmuntisto fitter.
tubo barrel, channel, pipe, tube, conduit, duct, stem.
tubtuŝe at point blank range, at muzzle-point.
tucio Tutsi.
tuĉo Indian ink.
tufalaŭdo tufted lark.
tufanaso tufted duck.
tufgrebo grebe.
tufo clump, tuft, wisp.
tuj at once, immediately, just, right away, right now. **tuj kiam** as soon as. **tuj post** right after.
tuja immediate. **tuja komputado** real time processing. **tuja superulo** immediate superior.
tujaĵo successor.
tuje straightway.
tujeco promptness.
tujmesaĝilo instant messenger.
tujo arbor vitae, thuja.
tujposta immediately following.
tujpreta instant.
Tukano Toucan.
tukano toucan.
tukblindigi to blindfold.
tuketo piece of cloth.
tuko cloth (material).
tukportilo towel rack.
Tulamoro Tullamore.
tulio thulium.
tulipo tulip.
tulo tulle.
tumoro tumor.
tumulo tumulus.
tumulta tumultuous, turbulent, riotous.
tumultantaro mob.
tumulte turbulently, wildly.

tumultema wanton.
tumultemo wantonness.
tumulteto flap.
tumulti to rage, riot.
tumulto agitation, riot, tumult, disturbance, clamour, racket, row, noise, commotion.
tumultplena stormy, tumultuous, turbulent, tempestuous.
tumultsonorilo alarm bell.
tunaro loading capacity.
tundro tundra.
tuneli to tunnel.
tunelo tunnel.
Tungo Tongue.
tungsteno tungsten, wolfram.
tuniko tunic.
tunisiano Tunisian.
Tuniso Tunis.
tunizia Tunisian.
tunizianino Tunisian woman.
Tuniziano Tunisian.
tuniziano Tunisian.
Tunizio Tunisia.
Tunizo Tunis.
tuno tonne, metric ton (1000 kg).
turbano turban.
turbino turbine.
turbinreaktoro turbo-jet.
turbo spinning top.
turbula turbulent.
turbulado turbulence.
turbule turbulently.
turbulenta turbulent.
turbuli to swirl.
turbulo swirl.
turdo thrush.
tureto turret.
turfalko kestrel.
Turinga aŭtomato Turing machine.
Turingio Thuringia.
Turingujo Thuringia.
turisma klubo touring club.
turismo tourism.
turisto tourist.
turistoficejo tourist bureau.
turistprospekto travel folder.
turka Turkish. **turka lingvo** Turkish language.
turkakafa Turkish coffee.
Turkestano Turkestan.
turkino Turkish lady, Turkish woman.
Turkio Turkey.
turkiso turquoise.
Turkmenio Turkmenistan.
Turkmeno Turkmen.
Turkmenujo Turkmenistan.
Turko Ottoman, Turk. **Turkoj kaj Kajkoj** Turks and Caicos Islands.
Turkujo Turkey.

turmalino tourmaline.
turmenta distressing, painful, unbearable.
turmentadi to pester.
turmentado abuse, perturbation.
turmentanto persecutor.
turmente painfully.
turmentegi to torture.
turmentego torture.
turmenteti to perturb, pester.
turmenti to abuse, agonize, torment, molest.
turmentiĝi to torment.
turmentiĝo agony, anguish, torment.
turmentito martyr.
turmento martyrdom, torment.
turmentoado torment.
turnado rotation.
turnakvo whirlpool, vortex.
turnborilo centre bit.
turnebla rotating.
turnebla ponto rotating bridge.
turnei to go on tour (theatrical).
turneo (theatrical) tour.
turneti to tweak.
turneto tweak.
turnfermi to turn off.
turni to revolve, turn (around). **turni plipreme** to fasten, tighten. **turni sin** to turn (back, around), refer to. **turni sin al** to apply to.
turnigi to wheel (turn).
turniĝadi to eddy, swirl, whirl.
turniĝado rotation, vortex.
turniĝanta ponto rotating bridge.
turniĝi to gyrate, rotate, turn, revolve.
turniĝo turn. **turniĝo de la tajdo** changing of the tide.
turnilo winch, windlass.
turnirero event.
turniro tournament.
turnklini to bank.
turnkliniĝi to bank.
turnkliniĝo bank.
turnkruco swivel, turnstile.
turnludilo spinning top.
turno turn.
turnomovi to stir.
turnopunkto turning point, watershed.
turnovento whirlwind.
turnrostilo kitchen jack, roasting jack, turnspit.
turnuro bustle.
turnventego tornado, whirlwind.
turnvento whirlwind.
turo rook (chess), tower.
turpa nasty, ugly.
turpinto steeple.
turriparisto steeple-jack.
Turso Thurso.
turstrigo screech owl.

turto turtle dove.
tusado coughing.
tusi to cough.
tusilago coltsfoot (plant).
tuso cough.
tuŝado (sense of) touch.
tuŝanta adjacent, adjoining, neighbouring, touching, striking.
tuŝebla palpable.
tuŝeti to graze, touch lightly.
tuŝi to touch. **tuŝi ies fierecon** to hurt someone's pride.
tuŝlegi to browse (through).
tuŝludi to play tag.
tuŝo touch.
tuŝosurfaco tyre tread.
Tut-Tera Teksaĵo Worldwide Web.
tuta all, entire, overall, whole, total, complete.
tutaĵo entirety, whole, sum total, totality.
tutanime with all one's spirit.
tutanokte all night.
tutatage all day.
tutataĵo (a) whole, (a) unit.
tutcerte with absolute certainty.
tutcifero integer.
tute altogether, at all, entirely, quite, wholly, utterly, completely. **tute alia afero** a completely different matter. **tute hazarde** completely by chance. **tute ne** not at all, by no means, anything but. **tute ne!** not at all! **tute senviva** stone-dead.
tuteco completeness, entirety, totality, wholeness.
tutegale all the same, no matter.
tuthavaĵo all of one's property.
tuthora hour-long.
tutjara all-year, year-long, annual, yearly.
tutkora cordial, whole-hearted, openly.
tutkore whole-heartedly, most cordially.
tutlanda countrywide, national, nationwide.
tutlanda balotado nationwide election.
tutlande nationally.
tutmonata month-long.
tutmonda global, worldwide. **Tutmonda Esperantista Junulara Organizo** World Organization of Young Esperantists. **tutmonda varmiĝo** global warming.
tutmondavarmiĝo global warming.
tutmonde globally, worldwide. **tutmonde konata** known around the world.
tutmondigi to globalize.
tutmondigo globalization.
tutmondiĝi to globalize.
tutmondiĝo globalization.
tutmute completely silent.
tutnokta all-night, night-long. **tutnokta lernado** all-nighter.
tutnokte all night.
tutnuda stark naked.

tutnude stark nakedly.
tuto entirety, sum total, totality, whole.
tutprovinca provincial.
tutregiona provincial.
tutsemajna week-long.
tutsimpla perfectly simple.
tutsimple very simply.
tutslavismo Panslavism.
tutspace everywhere.
tutspaco entire space, entire area.
tuttaga whole day.
tutuo ballet skirt.
tutvivado entire life, whole life.
Tuvalo Tuvalu.
Tvido Tweed.
tvisti to twist.
tvisto twist.
Tvitilo Twitter.

U

u name of the letter U.
Uajto Isle of Wight.
ublieto dungeon, oubliette.
udono udon (Japanese noodle).
UEA → **Universala Esperanto Asocio**.
uedo wadi.
uesto west.
uganda Ugandan.
ugandano Ugandan.
Ugando Uganda.
ugviso Manchurian bush-warbler.
Uigo Uig.
Uisto Uist.
ujguro Uighur.
ujo jug, box, container, vessel.
UK → **Universala Kongreso**.
ukazo ukase.
ukelelo ukelele.
ukraina Ukrainian.
ukrainino Ukrainian woman.
Ukrainio Ukraine, the Ukraine.
ukraino Ukrainian.
Ukrainujo Ukraine, the Ukraine.
ukrajna Ukrainian.
ukrajnano Ukrainian.
ukrajnino Ukrainian woman.
Ukrajnio Ukraine.
ukrajno Ukrainian.
Ukrajnujo Ukraine.
ukulelo ukulele.
ulaĉo bad guy, baddie.
ulambano Ullambana.
ulano uhlan, ulan.
Ulapulo Ullapool.
ulcereto sore.
ulceriĝi to fester.
ulcero ulcer, sore.
ulekso gorse, whin.
ulemo ulema.
ulgenro animate gender.
uliko gorse, whin.
ulino chick, gal.
Uliso Ulysses.
Uljanovsko Ulyanovsk.
ulmacoj Ulmaceae (family of flowing plants).
ulmario meadowsweet.
ulmo elm.
ulno arm's length, cubit, ell, ulna.
ulo chap, guy, fellow, person.
ultimata ultimate.
ultimate ultimately.
ultimato ultimatum.
ultimatumo ultimatum.
ultramara ultramarine.
ultramarino ultramarine.

ultramaro ultramarine.
ultrasono ultrasound.
ultraviola ultraviolet.
ultraviolo ultraviolet.
ululado howling, wailing.
ululi to hoot, howl.
ululo howl, wail, yowl.
Ulvo Ulva.
umaĵo thingamajig, whatchamacallit.
umbelaco umbellifer.
umbeliferaco umbellifer.
umbeliferoj Umbelliferae.
umbelo umbel.
umbilika umbilical. **umbilika ringo** belly button. **umbilika ŝnuro** umbilical chord.
umbiliko navel.
Umbrio Umbria.
umearbo Japanese apricot, Japanese plum, ume.
umeo Japanese apricot, Japanese plum, ume.
umiliono zillion.
umlaŭto umlaut (¨).
umo thingamajig, whatchamacallit.
UN → **Unuiĝintaj Nacioj**.
unara unary.
unco ounce.
Unesko UNESCO.
ungeg claw, talon.
ungego claw, talon, fingernail, nail.
ungo nail.
ungobroso nail brush.
ungofajlilo emery board.
ungograti to scratch (claw).
ungokuŝejo nail bed.
ungolako nail polish, nail varnish.
ungoraspilo nail file.
ungotajlilo nail clipper, nail clippers.
ungotondilo nail cutter, nail clipper, nail scissors.
ungoverniso nail polish, nail varnish.
ungozono cuticle.
ungvento ointment, unguent.
uniano uniate (referring to the Eastern Orthodox church).
uniata uniate (referring to the Eastern Orthodox church).
uniato uniate (referring to the Eastern Orthodox church).
uniformo livery.
unika unique.
unikaĵo unique specimen.
unikaspekta unique in appearance.
unike singularly, uniquely.
unikeco uniqueness.
unikoda Unicode.

Unikodo

Unikodo Unicode.
unikorno unicorn.
uniksa Unix. **uniksa laborstacio** Unix workstation. **uniksa servilo** Unix server.
Unikso Unix.
uniksulo Unix person.
unio union. **Unio de Sovetaj Socialismaj Respublikoj** Union of Soviet Socialist Republics, Soviet Union, USSR.
unisono unison.
unita unitary. **unita matrico** unitary matrix.
unitariano Unitarian.
unitigi to norm.
unito unit.
universa universal.
universala general, universal, worldwide. **Universala Esperanto Asocio** Universal Esperanto Association. **Universala Kongreso** (Esperanto) World Congress. **universala kvantoro** universal quantifier. **universala seria buso** universal serial bus, USB. **universala ŝraŭbilo** monkey wrench, shifting spanner. **universala ŝraŭbŝlosilo** monkey wrench, shifting spanner.
universale universally.
universaleco generality, universality.
universalisma universalist.
universalismo universalism.
universalisto universalist.
universitata academic. **universitata areo** campus. **universitata diplomito** academic, university graduate. **universitata parko** (university) campus. **universitata profesoro** academic.
universitato university.
universo universe.
unkario gambier, gambir.
unktado anointing.
unkti to anoint.
unkto anointing.
unu one. **unu flanko al la alia** one side to the other. **unu fojo** once. **unu kaj duona** one and a half. **unu kaj duona horo** an hour and a half. **unu kaj duono** one and a half. **unu la alian** each other, one another. **unu- kaj duontaga** one-and-a-half-day.
unuj some.
unua first, foremost, premier, primary. **unua etaĝo** ground floor. **unua helpo** first aid. **unua mondmilito** first world war, World War I. **unua partpago** down payment, first installment, initial deposit, installment. **unua persono** first person. **unua plano** close-up. **unua vico** first row, front row.
unuaaĵo first fruit (often used as an offering).
unuaeco primacy, first position.
unuafoja first.
unuafoje for the first time.

unuiĝo

unuagrada primary.
unuaĵo unit.
unuaklasa first class. **unuaklasa soldato** first rank soldier, private.
unuakta one-act (e.g. play).
unualoke above all.
unuanaskito eldest (first born).
unuanima unanimous.
unuanime unanimously, with one accord.
unuanimeco unanimity.
unuaranga first-rate, ace.
unuarangulo ace.
unuatoma monatomic.
unuaulo first (person), primus (inter pares).
unuavenaĵo first fruit (often used as an offering).
unuavica primary.
unuavice first and foremost, firstly, primarily.
unuavide at first glance, at first sight.
unubate with one blow.
unucela single-minded, undivided.
unucikli to ride a unicycle.
unuciklisto unicyclist.
unuciklo unicycle.
unuĉelulo single-celled organism.
unudirekta directional. **unudirekta kanalo** channel. **unudirekta trafiko** one way traffic.
unu-du one or two.
unue first, firstly, first of all.
unueca unified.
unuecigi to cement.
unueco oneness, unity.
unuenaskito first-born (child).
unuetaĝa one-floor, one-story.
unuflanka one-sided, unilateral.
unuflanke on one side, on the one hand, one-sided.
unuflankismo unilateralism.
unufoje on one occasion, once, one time.
unuforma consistent, consonant, monotonous, uniform. **unuforme konverĝa** uniformly convergent (function sequence).
unuformeco uniformity. **unuformeco de la stilo** uniformity of style.
unugrafeo graph.
unuĝiba kamelo dromedary.
unuhava with unit.
unuhora marŝo an hour's walk.
unuhufuloj Equidae.
unuigi to join, unite, unify.
unuigite united, joined.
unuigo combination, joining, junction, union, amalgamation, unification.
unuiĝi to associate, join, pool.
unuiĝinta united. **Unuiĝintaj Arabaj Emirlandoj** United Arab Emirates. **Unuiĝintaj Nacioj** United Nations, UN.
unuiĝo unification, union.

unuj some.
unujara yearling.
unujarulo yearling.
unukolora solid.
unukornulo unicorn.
unukotiledonaj monocotyledonous.
unulingva monolingual.
unulingvismo unilingualism.
unuloka monadic, unary.
unuloke in one place.
unumastŝipo single-masted ship.
ununokta amafero one-night stand.
ununokte for one night.
ununombra singular.
ununombro singular.
ununorma normalized.
ununormigi to normalize.
ununura one and only, sole.
unuo unit, element. **unuo de longo** unit of length.
unuobla single.
unuocirklo unit circle.
unuokula one-eyed.
unuomatrico identity matrix, unit matrix.
unuopa single, individual.
unuope individually, one at a time, singly, one by one.
unuopolinomo unit polynomial.
unuopula independent, individual.
unuopulo individual.
unupersona one person.
unuranga first-rate.
unusenca unambiguous, unequivocal; one-way. **unusenca funkcio** single-valued function.
unusignifa unambiguous.
unusignife unambiguous.
unusilabo monosyllable.
unusola one and only, lone.
unutaga one-day, single-day.
unutermo monomial.
unuto unison.
unutona monotone, monotonous.
unuuma nombrosistemo unary number system.
unuvice single-file.
unuvoĉa concordant, unanimous.
unuvoĉe with one accord, unanimously.
unuvorte in short, in a word.
unversala universal, world.
upaniŝado Upanishad.
Upaniŝadoj Upanishads.
upaso upas.
upsilono upsilon (Υυ).
upupo hoopoe (bird).
uragana hurricane.
uragani to rage like a hurricane.
uragano hurricane, tempest.

urala Ural. **urala lingvo** Uralic language.
  urala-altaja lingvofamilio Ural-Altaic language group.
uralano inhabitant of the Ural region.
Uralo Ural (Mountains, River).
urana Uranian.
uranio uranium.
Urano Uranus.
urba civic, municipal, urban. **urba akcizo** local tariff. **urba distrikto** borough. **urba legendo** urban legend.
urbaĉo pitiful town.
urbanaro townsfolk.
urbano citizen.
urbdomo city hall, town hall.
urbego big city, metropolis.
urbestra mayoral.
urbestredzino mayoress.
urbestrino mayoress.
urbestro mayor.
urbeto town, township.
urbiĝado urbanization.
urbo city, town.
urbocentro city centre, downtown.
urbodomo city hall.
urbomezo city centre, downtown.
urbonomo city name.
urbŝtato city state.
urbumi to go into town, browse in town.
urduo Urdu.
Ureksamo Wrexham.
ureo urea.
uretero ureter.
uretro urethra.
urĝa pressing, urgent.
urĝe urgently.
urĝeco urgency.
urĝi to hurry, press, urge. **urĝi sin** to hurry.
urĝigi to hasten, hurry.
urĝiĝi to hurry, rush.
urĝo craving, stress.
Urhiponto Bridge of Orchy.
urina urinal. **urina reteno** anuria.
urinado urination.
urincistito cystitis.
urinejo urinal.
urini to urinate.
urino urine.
urinŝtona malsano urolithiasis.
urinujo chamber pot.
urno urn.
urnoforma ascidiform.
uro aurochs.
urogalo capercaillie.
urotropino hexamine, urotropin.
ursa bear, ursine.
ursejo bear den, bear garden.
ursfelo bearskin.
ursido bear cub.

ursino   **ŭoŭ**

ursino she-bear.
Ursinsulo Bear Island.
urskavo bear cave.
urso bear (animal).
urtikario nettle rash.
urtiko nettle.
urugvaja Uruguayan.
urugvajanino Uruguayan woman.
urugvajano Uruguayan.
Urugvajo Uruguay.
uruŝio Japanese lacquer.
uskleco case.
usklecodistinga case sensitive.
usklo case.
usoano American.
usona American. **usona futbalo** American football. **Usona Samoo** American Samoa. **Usonaj Virgulinaj Insuloj** Virgin Islands of the United States.
usonaĵoj americana.
usonanino American woman.
usonanismo Americanism.
usonano American.
usonigi to Americanize.
Usono United States of America, USA.
ustilago blight.
uŝuisto student or practitioner of wushu.
uŝuo wushu (Chinese martial art).
utaha Utahan.
utahano Utahan.
utao uta.
uteno uten (old Egyptian unit of weight of copper).
utero uterus, womb.
utila advantageous, useful.
utilaĵo utility, utility program.
utile usefully.
utileca utility. **utileca programo** utility. **utileca rutino** utility.
utileco usefulness.
utilega very useful.
utili to avail, be of use.
utiligebla able to be utilized.
utiligi to make use of, turn to good account, utilize.
utiligo application, use of (something).
utilisma utilitarian.
utilismo utilitarianism.
utilo advantage, benefit, usefulness.
utiloeco utility.
utilprogramo utility.
utopia utopian.
utopiismo utopism.
utopiisto utopist.
Utopio Utopia.
utopiulo Utopian.
Utrehto Utrecht.
utrikulario bladderwort.

uverturo overture (music).
uvo grape.
uvulo uvula.
uzadi to use.
uzado practice, usage, use.
uzaĵo utensil.
uzanco usage, custom.
uzante using.
uzantnomo username.
uzanto user.
uzantonumero user id, user identifier, UID.
uzbeka Uzbek.
uzbekino Uzbek woman.
Uzbekio Uzbekistan.
Uzbekistano Uzbekistan.
uzbeko Uzbek.
Uzbekujo Uzbekistan.
uzebla of use, suitable.
uzebleco usefulness.
uzeblo usefulness.
uzi to employ, use, make use of. **uzi figure** to use figuratively.
uziĝi to be used.
uzino factory, mill.
uzinte usefully.
uzita used. **uzita akvo** effluent.
uzo use.
uzoado usage.
uzofini to discard.
uzoprunto free loan.
uzukapi to usucapt.
uzukapo usucaption, usucapion.
uzula user's, users'. **uzula manlibro** user guide, user manual. **uzula medio** user environment.
uzulo user.
uzura usurious.
uzuro usury.
uzurpanto squatter, usurper.
uzurpatoro squatter, usurper.
uzurpi to overpower, usurp, supplant.
uzurpinto squatter, usurp.
uzurpo usurpation.
uzurpoado usurpation.
uzurpulo usurper.
uzvaloro use value.

Ŭ

ŭa! wah! (like a baby).
Ŭajto Isle of Wight.
ŭato watt.
Ŭiko Wick.
ŭo name of the letter Ŭ.
ŭoŭ wow (expression of admiration, wonder)

V

v. → **vidu**.
vaĉo watch.
vadbirdoj wading birds.
vadboto wader.
vadejo ford.
vadi to wade.
vadio wadi.
vadobirdoj Ciconiiformes, wading birds.
vafleto cone, wafer.
vaflo waffle.
vaflobakilo waffle iron.
vaflofero waffle iron.
vaga circuitous.
vagabondo tramp, vagabond.
vagadi to wander.
vagado wandering, roaming.
vaganto wanderer, rover.
vagi to drift, loiter, prowl, ramble, roam, wander, meander, stray.
vagino vagina.
vagiradi to wander around.
vagisto tramp, vagrant, vagabond, wanderer.
vaglumo will-o-wisp, swamp light, marsh light.
vagnera Wagnerian.
vagonaro train (railway).
vagone by rail.
vagonenira vestiblo platform.
vagonfako compartment.
vagono car, carriage, coach, railway carriage, wagon.
vagpensa absent-minded.
vagulo tramp, vagabond, vagrant.
vaĝrajana Vajrayana.
vaĝrajano Vajrayana.
vahabismano Wahhabism.
vahabismo Wahhabism.
vahabisto Wahhabi.
vahabito Wahhabite.
vajco vice.
Vajĉaĉo Whitchurch.
vajroĉano Vairocana.
Vajto Isle of Wight.
vaka vacant.
vakcinado vaccination.
vakcini to vaccinate.
vakcinio bilberry, blueberry, cranberry, huckleberry.
vakcino vaccine.
vakerfilmo cowboy movie, western.
vakero cowboy. **vakeroj kaj indianoj** cowboys and indians (game).
vaki to be vacant.
vakigi to vacate.
vaksa wax.

vaksarbo bayberry tree.
vaksbildo waxwork.
vakseca waxen, waxy.
vaksfiguro waxwork.
vaksflava as yellow as wax.
vaksi to wax.
vakskandelo taper, wax candle.
vakso wax (bees).
vaksopentro wax painting.
vakstabulo wax tablet.
vakstolo oilcloth.
vakua blank, empty. **vakua linio** blank line. **vakua ordono** empty statement.
vakubotelo thermos.
vakuigi to make a vacuum.
vakuo vacuum.
vakuolo vacuole.
valabio wallaby.
Valaĥio Wallachia.
Valaĥujo Wallachia.
Valakio Walachia, Wallachia.
valdana Waldensian.
valdano Waldensian, Waldense, Vaudois.
valego gorge.
Valencia Golfo Gulf of Valencia.
valencieno Valencia.
Valencio Valencia.
Valencujo Valencia.
valenta valent.
Valenteno Valentine.
valento valence.
valeriano valerian.
valeto dale, dell, glen, gully, vale.
valga bowlegged.
Valhalo Valhalla, Walhalla.
valida valid.
valide validly.
valideco validity.
validi to be valid.
validigi to validate.
valizeto handbag.
valizo suitcase, piece of luggage, valise.
valizujo luggage compartment.
valkiro Valkyrie.
Valo Vaal.
valo valley. **Valo de la Reĝoj** Valley of the Kings.
valona Wallonian, Walloon.
Valonio Wallonia.
valono Walloon.
Valonujo Wallonia.
valora valuable.
valoraĵo item of value, valuable.
valoraldona imposto VAT.
valoreco prowess.

valorega

valorega invaluable, precious.
valorego preciousness.
valoreksceso range error.
valori to be of value, be worth. **valori la penon** to be worth the trouble.
valorigi to make valuable.
valoriza ordono assignment statement.
valorizato destination.
valorizi to assign.
valorizo assignment.
valoro value, worth.
valorŝtono gem, precious stone.
valortaksi to appreciate.
valponto viaduct.
valsi to waltz.
valso waltz.
Valtero Walter.
valuto currency (of a country), money.
valvo tube, valve.
vampiro vampire.
vana abortive, futile, useless, vain, fruitless, ineffectual.
vanado vanadium.
Vanaĥino Beauly.
vandalaĵo act of vandalism.
vandalismo vandalism.
vandalo vandal, Vandal.
vando partition, wall.
vane fruitlessly, in vain, vainly.
vaneco futility, vanity.
vanelo lapwing.
vaneteco frivolity.
vanga buccal. **vanga dento** molar.
vanghararo side-whiskers, whiskers, sideboards, sideburns.
vangharo sideburn, whisker.
vangharoj side whiskers, sideburns, whiskers.
vango cheek, jowl.
vangobarbo whiskers, side whiskers.
vangobato affront, slap on the face.
vangofrapi to slap someone (on the cheek).
vangofrapo slap (on the cheek).
vangohararo whiskers, side whiskers.
vangoharoj whiskers, side whiskers.
vangosto cheekbone.
vanigi to foil, thwart, frustrate.
vanilo vanilla.
vanta conceited, frivolous, vain, frivolous.
vantaĵo frivolity, silliness.
vantamo vanity.
vanteco vanity, state of being transitory.
vantema boastful, bragging.
vantemo vanity.
Vanuatuo Vanuatu.
vao wah.
vapora steam, vaporous.
vaporbanejo steam bath.
vaporbano steam bath.
vaporblovi to blow off steam.

variko

vapori to evaporate, steam.
vaporigi to evaporate, vaporize.
vaporigo vaporization.
vaporiĝema volatile.
vaporiĝi to evaporate.
vaporiĝo evaporation.
vaporizi to steam.
vaporkaldrono steam boiler.
vaporkovriĝi to become steamy, get covered with, get dim.
vaporkuiri to steam.
vaporkuirilo steamer.
vapormaŝino steam engine.
vapormotoro steam engine.
vaporo steam, vapour.
vaporplena damp.
vaporpurigejo dry cleaner's.
vaporŝipkompanio steamship company.
vaporŝipo steamboat, steamship, steamer.
vaporumi to atomize, vaporize, steam.
varango floor plate, floor timber.
varano monitor.
varapo rock-climbing, rock-face.
vararo inventory.
varbado campaigning, enrolment, promotion, recruitment.
varbaĵo promo.
varbi to enlist, enrol, recruit.
varbigistaro press gang.
varbiĝi to enlist.
varbito recruit.
varbo enlistment.
varboado recruiting.
vardomo warehouse.
varfo landing stage, pier, wharf.
varia variable.
variabla variable. **variabla datenoj** variable data.
variablo variable.
variablodeklaro variable declaration.
variacio variation.
variadi to fluctuate.
variado change, variation.
variaĵo variation.
varianca devio standard deviation.
varianco variance.
varianta variable.
varianto different form, variable, variant.
varicelo chickenpox.
variebla datenoj variable data.
variejo domain, range.
variema inconstant, shifting, variable.
varieteo variety entertainment, variety show.
varii to vary.
variigi to cause to vary.
variigo de konstantoj variation of constants.
varika ulcero varicose ulcer.
variko varicose vein, varix.

varilonga kodo variable-length code.
vario variety.
varioleto chicken pox.
variolo smallpox, variola.
varipunktas nombro floating-point number.
varlifto elevator, hoist.
varliveristo delivery boy.
varma warm, hot. **varma restartigo** warm reboot, warm restart.
varmaera aerostato hot air balloon.
varmarko brand, trade.
varmbano warm bath.
varmbedo cold frame.
varmbotelo thermos (flask, bottle).
varmdomo hot-house.
varme warmly.
varmeco heat, warmth.
varmega hot, sultry, torrid. **varmega sezono** hot season.
varmege very warmly.
varmegeco great heat.
varmegigi to make very hot.
varmegiĝi to be brewing.
varmego heat.
varmegsanga ardent, fiery, passionate.
varmejo greenhouse, hothouse.
varmeta lukewarm, tepid.
varmete warmly.
varmetigi to warm.
varmfonto hot spring.
varmiga heating.
varmigadi to anneal.
varmigi to warm.
varmiĝi to warm (up), become warm.
varmkopra warm-hearted.
varmkulturejo greenhouse, hothouse.
varmo warmth.
varmogrado level of heat.
varmplantejo greenhouse, hothouse.
varmsanga warm-blooded, haematothermal.
varmvoĉe in a warm (tone of) voice.
varo ware(s), good(s), commodity, merchandise.
varpi to warp.
varpo warp.
varsaĵo bit of verse.
varsendaĵo shipment of goods.
varsoviano inhabitant of Warsaw.
Varsovio Warsaw.
vartado maintenance. **vartado de programaro** maintenance.
vartantino babysitter.
vartejo day-care centre, nursery.
varti to look after, nurse, take care, tend.
vartistino nanny, nurse, nursemaid.
vartrajno freight train.
varvagono freight car.

vasaleco vassalage.
vasalo bondman, retainer, vassal.
vaska Basque. **vaska ĉapo** beret. **vaska lingvo** Basque, Basque language.
Vaskio Basque Country.
vasko Basque.
Vaskujo Basque Country.
vaskulo vessel.
vasta extensive, spacious, vast, wide, immense, roomy. **vasta maro** open sea.
vastaĵo expanse.
vaste widely.
vasteco immensity, vastness.
vastega abysmal, immense.
vastfasona baggy.
vastigaĵo continuation, extension (of a mapping).
vastigi to develop.
vastigo development, diffusion.
vastiĝi to develop.
vastiĝo enlargement, expansion, extension.
vastkorpa corpulent.
vastkorpeco obesity.
vasto vastness, expanse.
Vaŝingtono Washington.
vaŝintona Washingtonian.
vaŝintonano Washingtonian.
vaŝintonia Washingtonian.
vaŝintoniano Washingtonian.
vataĵo wadding.
Vaterfordo Waterford.
vathoro watt-hour.
vati to pad.
Vatikana Vatican.
Vatikano Vatican, the Vatican.
Vatikanurbo Vatican City.
vatkiomo wattage.
Vato Watt.
vato cotton wool, wadding.
vatoaĵo padding.
vatobastoneto cotton swab.
vatthoro watt-hour.
vatto watt.
vattohoro watt-hour.
vavo name of the letter W. → **vo**.
vazaro crockery, dishes, plates, table service.
vazelino Vaseline.
vazlavilo dishwasher.
vazlesivo dishwashing liquid.
vazo vase, vessel, container.
VD → **Vicedelegito**.
ve! woe! alas! (interjection of complaint or menace). **ve al** woe to.
vea woeful.
veaspekta lugubrious, woebegone.
veaspekte lugubriously.
vebero weber.
veblekadi to yelped.
vedismo Vedism.

vedo

vedo Veda.
vee woefully.
vefto weft.
vegana vegan.
veganismo veganism.
vegano vegan.
vegetado growth.
vegetaĵa vegetable.
vegetaĵaro flora, vegetation.
vegetaĵo plant, vegetation.
vegetala plant, vegetable. **vegetala regno** vegetable kingdom.
vegetalaro flora, vegetation.
vegetalo plant.
vegetara vegetarian.
vegetaranismo vegetarianism.
vegetarano vegetarian.
vegetare vegetarian.
vegetarismo vegetarianism.
vegeti to vegetate.
vegeto growth.
vehiklo carrier, vector, vehicle.
vei to lament, wail.
vejĉii to play go.
vejĉio go.
vejna veined.
vejndirekto strike.
vejnego varicose vein.
vejni to grain, vein, marble, mark with veins.
vejno vein.
vejntranĉo blood-letting.
veka awake.
vekhorloĝo alarm clock.
veki to wake (up), awaken, arouse. **veki grandan intereson** to create much interest.
vekigi to wake up (someone).
vekiĝi to wake (up).
vekiĝinta aroused, awake.
vekiĝinto one who as awakened.
vekiĝo awakening, waking time (reveille).
vekiigi to rouse (waken).
vekita aroused, awake.
veko waking.
vekriado yammering.
vekrii to lament, wail, yammer.
vekrio wail.
Veksfordo Wexford.
veksignalo alarm, reveille.
veksonorilo alarm clock bell.
vekto beam (of scales).
vektora vector, vectorial. **vektora ebeno** two-dimensional vector space. **vektora grafiko** vector graphics. **vektora hiperebeno** linear hyperplane. **vektora potencialo** vector potential. **vektora produto** vector product. **vektora projekcio** projector. **vektora rekto** one-dimensional vector space. **vektora rotacio** vector rota-

vendokonto

tion. **vektora simetrio** vector symmetry.
vektora spaco vector space. **vektora subspaco** vector subspace. **vektora tiparo** vectored font.
vektoro vector.
vektorreĝima ekranbloko directed-beam display, vector-mode display.
vela velar.
veladi to sail.
velado sailing.
velaro sails.
velboato sailboat.
veldi to weld.
veldisto welder.
veleno vellum.
velfadeno seaming twine.
veli to sail.
Velingtono Wellington.
Velintono Wellington.
velka faded, withered.
velkanto fading.
velkeco stigma.
velkema drooping.
velki to fade, wither.
velkigi to blight.
velkinta withered.
velo sail (of a ship), velum.
velocipedo velocipede.
velstango mast, spar, yard (of a sailing ship).
velŝipo sailing ship, sailboat.
veltudi to bet, wager, gamble.
velura velvet.
velurbendo velvet ribbon.
veluro velvet.
velurrubando velvet ribbon.
velveturi to sail.
velveturigi to sail, travel by sail.
venadi to keep coming.
vendaa lingvo Venda, Venda language.
vendakto bill of sale.
vendanto seller, vendor.
vendao Venda.
vendatesto bill of sale.
vendaŭtomato vending-machine.
vendebla for sale, saleable.
vendejo market, mart, shop, store.
vendeto vendetta, feud.
vendetto feud, vendetta.
vendi to sell, vend. **vendi podetale** to sell retail. **vendi pograndeto** to sell wholesale. **vendi pomalgrande** to sell retail. **vendi pometre** to sell by the meter.
vendiĝi to be sold, sell (itself).
vendimposto sales tax, turnover tax.
vendistino saleswoman.
vendisto salesman.
vendmaŝino vending machine.
vendo sale.
vendokonto account sales.

vendoplaco   **ventroparolisto**

vendoplaco market, marketplace.
vendosekcio account department.
vendosumo turnover.
vendotablo counter.
vendrede on Friday.
Vendredo Friday.
vendredo Friday.
veneca Venetian.
venecano Venetian.
venecia Venetian.
veneciano Venetian.
Venecio Venetia.
Veneco Venice.
venena noxious, poisonous, venomous, virulent.
venene venomously.
venenega virulent.
veneni to envenom, poison.
venenigi to poison.
veneno poison, venom, virus.
venera venereal.
venerea sexually transmitted, venereal.
   venerea malsano venereal disease.
venezuela Venezuelan. **Venezuela Golfo** Gulf of Venezuela.
venezuelanino Venezuelan woman.
venezuelano Venezuelan.
Venezuelo Venezuela.
venĝa avenging.
venĝado vengeance.
venĝanto one taking or seeking revenge.
venĝema implacable, spiteful, vindictive.
venĝemo grudge, rancour, resentment.
venĝi to avenge (oneself), revenge.
venĝo revenge, vengeance.
veni to come. **veni al mi en la kapon** to come to me, come to mind. **veni de malproksime** to come from far away. **veni el ĉie** to come from everywhere. **veni en akordon** to come to an agreement. **veni en konflikton** to come into conflict. **veni je alia tempo** to come at a different time. **veni kontraŭ iun** to come towards someone. **veni por akompani** to meet, pick up. **veni poste** to arrive afterwards, come afterwards, come later, follow. **venis al mi idea** I've had an idea.
venigi to get, cause to come, send for, summon. **venigu la kuraciston** call the doctors. **venigu lin al mi** have him come to me.
venigo procurement.
veninto one who has come.
venkakiro booty.
venkanto conqueror, vanquisher, victor.
Venkdomegoj Victory Mansions.
venki to conquer, defeat, win over, overcome, vanquish, subdue.
venkiĝi to be beaten, be defeated, lose.

venkinta victorious.
venkinto victor.
venkita beaten.
venkito loser, person vanquished.
venko conquest, victory.
venkobati to conquer, smite.
venksigno trophy.
veno coming.
venonta coming, next.
venontjare next year, in the coming year.
venontnumere in the next issue.
venpreni to meet, pick up, take up.
venta windy.
ventadi to be windy.
ventado blowing of the wind.
Ventangulo Windhoek.
ventanima empty-headed.
ventblovo gust of wind.
ventega of a great wind, hurricane-like.
ventegmeze in the middle of a great wind.
ventego storm, squall, windstorm, gale, tempest.
ventegpelita beaten by high winds.
ventenergio wind energy.
venteto breeze, zephyr.
ventflago weathervane.
venti to blow.
ventkapa airheaded, empty-headed.
ventkapulo airhead, scatterbrain.
ventkrozanto windsurfer.
ventkrozilo sailboard.
ventmaniko wind-sock.
ventmontrilo weather vane.
ventmuelilo windmill.
vento wind.
ventoflago vane, weathercock.
ventogeneratoro windmill.
ventolado fanning, ventilation.
ventolfendo vent.
ventoli to ventilate, winnow.
ventolilo (electric, ventilating) fan, ventilator.
ventoltruo air hole, ventilation hole.
ventomontrilo weather vane.
ventoŝirmilo folding screen.
ventplena windy.
ventpuŝo squall.
ventra abdominal.
ventraĉo beer belly.
ventrego beer belly.
ventregulo chubby, fatso.
ventriklo ventricle.
ventro abdomen, stomach, belly, tummy.
ventrodoloro stomach ache, tummy ache, belly ache.
ventrokuŝe face-down, lying on one's stomach.
ventroparolanto ventriloquist.
ventroparoli to ventriloquy.
ventroparolisto ventriloquist.

ventropleno

ventropleno bellyfull.
ventrorimeno belly-strap.
ventrozo anemone.
ventŝirmilo windscreen, windshield.
ventumi to aerate, fan.
ventumilo fan.
Venusa Venusian.
Venuso Cytherea, Venus, Evening Star.
veo lamentation, plaint.
veprejo scrubland, thicket, bush.
vepro bush, brushwood, scrub.
vera genuine, intrinsic, true, veritable, authentic.
veraĵo truth, truthful item.
verama truth-loving.
verando porch, veranda.
veratro Veratrum.
verba verbal. **verba modalo** mood, verbal modality.
verbasko mullein.
verbenacoj Verbenaceae.
verbeno verbena, vervain.
verbo verb.
verda green. **verda de ĵaluzo** green with jealousy. **verda kverko** holm oak. **verda martestudo** green sea turtle. **verda pego** green woodpecker. **verda stelo** green star (symbol of Esperanto). **verdaj algoj** green algae.
verdaĵo verdure.
verdalgoj green algae.
verdanta verdant.
verde greenly.
verdi to be green.
verdigro verdigris.
verdikti to adjudicate.
verdikto adjudication, verdict, finding, decision.
verdire to tell the truth.
verdiremo candour.
verdo green.
verdulo green; fervent Esperantist.
vere absolutely, genuinely, indeed, really, truly.
vereca manly, masculine.
vereco truth, truthfulness, veracity, verity.
verega authentic.
verema truthful.
verfakte in truth, in fact.
vergado beating.
vergaĵo bundle of sticks.
vergego wand.
vergeto rib, sprig.
vergfasko bundle of sticks.
vergi to beat, cane, flog, take a switch to.
vergilio Vergil.
vergo cane, rod, switch, wand, stick, staff.
veri to be true.

verŝaparato

verigi to authenticate, verify, meet, satisfy, fulfill.
veriĝi to come true.
verkado work, opus.
verkaĵo writing.
verkanto author, creator.
verkaro works (collected).
verketo small work, small creation.
verki to compose, create, write.
verkilo word processor.
verkinto (completed) work; author.
verkista of an artist.
verkistino authoress.
verkisto author, writer, composer.
verko work (literary or artistic).
verkoŝtelisto plagiarist.
vermborita unsound, worm-eaten.
vermiĉelo vermicelli.
vermifugo vermifuge.
vermiljona vermilion.
vermiljono vermillion.
Vermlando Värmeland, a district of Sweden.
vermmortigilo vermicide.
vermo worm.
vermoforma worm-shaped.
vermoj Helminthes.
vermontano Vermonter.
vermplena worm-ridden.
vermujo bait pail.
vermuto bitters, vermouth.
verniero vernier.
vernisi to varnish.
verniso varnish.
vero reality, truth.
veroeco truth.
veronalo veronal.
veroniko speedwell.
verprimolo cowslip.
versaĵo piece of poetry, verse.
versaro canto.
versero foot (of verse).
versi to poetize, make verses.
versimila likely, probable.
versio edition.
versisto versifier.
versitena sistemo version control system.
verso verse, song.
verspermanĝi to dine.
verspermanĝo evening meal, supper.
verspero evening.
verspiedo foot.
versto verst.
verŝajna likely, probable, seeming.
verŝajne apparently, probably, likely, by all accounts. **verŝajne jes** probably so.
verŝajneco appearance (of being true), probability.
verŝajno likelihood.
verŝaparato beverage dispenser.

verŝbufedo bar.
verŝeti to slop.
verŝi to pour out, scatter, shed.
verŝiĝi to be poured out.
verŝilo watering pot.
Verŝisto Aquarius (zodiac).
verŝlumilo floodlight.
verŝtablo bar counter.
verŝtubo spout.
vertabelo truth table.
vertago dachshund.
vertebra vertebral, vertebrate. **vertebra kolono** spine.
vertebraro spine.
vertebro vertebra.
vertebrulo vertebrate.
vertebruloj vertebrates.
verticgrado grade.
verticila whorled. **verticila koreopso** whorled coreopsis.
verticilo whorl.
vertico apex, node, vertex.
vertiĝi to feel dizzy.
vertiĝo dizziness, vertigo.
vertikala erect, vertical, upright. **vertikala formato** portrait. **vertikala streko** vertical bar (|).
vertikale vertically.
vertikalilo plummet.
vertikalo column, vertical line, vertical row (of a matrix).
verto pate, top (of head), crown.
vertoĉapo skull cap, spherical cap.
vertrago greyhound.
verturilo vehicle.
verukapro warthog.
verukherbo greater celandine, tetterwort.
veruko wart.
verva lively, vivacious.
vervaloro truth value.
verve lively, racily, vibrantly.
vervo verve, vivacity, zest.
veselkapitano captain.
veselo ship, vessel.
vesigno bad sign.
veslejana Wesleyan.
veslejano Wesleyan.
vespa waspish.
vespejo wasp's nest.
vespera evening. **Vespera Diservo** vespers. **vespera ĵurnalo** evening paper. **vespera krepusko** evening twilight. **vespera lernejo** evening classes, evening school, night school. **vespera vartantino** babysitter. **vespera vartanto** babysitter.
vespere in the evening.
vesperiĝas night is falling.
vesperiĝe at dusk.
vesperiĝi to become evening.

vesperkunveno evening party, soirée.
vespermanĝi to dine (evening).
vespermanĝo evening meal, supper.
vespero evening, eve.
vesperpreĝo night prayers.
vesperrobo evening frock, evening gown.
vesperruĝo afterglow.
vesperto bat (animal).
vespiri to sigh.
vespo wasp.
vespro evensong, vespers.
Vesta Vesta.
vestaĵeto baby linen.
vestaĵo clothes, article of dress, garment, attire, clothing.
vestalo vestal (virgin).
vestarko clothes-hanger.
vestaro outfit.
vestejo cloakroom, dressing room.
vesterno western.
Vestfalio Westphalia.
vesti to clothe, dress, robe. **vesti prove** to try on (clothes). **vesti sin** to dress (oneself).
vestiblo entrance hall, lobby, porch, vestibule.
vestiĝi to dress, get dressed.
vestmaniero dress.
Vesto Vesta.
vesto apparel, coat, garb, garment, clothing, dress. **vestoj** clothes, clothing.
vestosako garment bag.
vestoŝranko wardrobe (piece of furniture for storing clothes).
vestotenejo wardrobe (place for storing clothes).
vestpediko body louse.
Vestporto Westport.
vestŝranko armoire.
veŝto vest, waistcoat.
vetado betting, wagering.
vetaĵgardanto stakeholder.
vetaĵo bet, stake.
vetanto punter.
vetarmado arms race.
vetboksisto prize-fighter.
vete competitively, emulously.
veteraĉo foul weather.
veterana veteran.
veterano veteran.
veterinara veterinary.
veterinaro veterinarian.
veterinformisto weather forecaster.
veterinformoj weather report.
vetero weather.
veterprognozo weather forecast.
veterŝanĝo change in the weather.
veteto flutter.
veti to bet, wager, gamble. **veti je ĉevaloj** to bet on horses.

vetkurado

vetkurado race.
vetkuranto runner.
vetkuri to race.
vetkuro race.
vetlibro betting book.
vetludanto gambler.
vetludi to gamble.
vetludo gambling game, game of chance.
vetlundanto gambler.
vetmaŝino gaming machine.
vetmono stake.
veto bet, wager, stake.
vetoi to veto.
vetoo veto.
vetperisto bookie, bookmaker.
vetremado boat race.
vetsumo wager, bet.
veturado travelling, journeying.
veturanto passenger, traveller.
veturbileto ticket.
veturejo traffic area.
veturi to drive (a vehicle), go, ride, travel. **veturi malantaŭen** to travel back.
veturigi to drive, transport, convey, cart, carry. **veturigi malantaŭen** to back up. **veturigi posten** to back up.
veturigisto driver, coachman.
veturilaro convoy, train.
veturilego van.
veturileto chaise, little vehicle.
veturilfaristo cartwright, coach maker.
veturilo vehicle, carriage, coach, conveyance.
veturisto driver.
veturo ride, trip, travelling, journeying.
veturprezo fare.
Vezero Weser.
veziketo blister, vesicle.
vezikigilo blister (plaster).
vezikiĝi to blister.
veziklo blister, bladder, bubble, pocket, sack.
veziko bladder, bubble, blister.
veziro Turkish minister, vizier.
Vezuvio Vesuvius.
Vezuvo Vesuvius.
vi you. **vi eraras** You're wrong. **vi mem** yourself. **vi rajtas fumi** to you may smoke. **vi ŝercas!** you're joking! **vi tute pravas** you're entirely right.
via your, yours.
viadukto viaduct.
viaflanke for your part.
viagenta your peoples'. **viagentaj viroj** your people, your folk.
vialanda of your country.
vianda bulko sandwich.
viandaĵo meat dish.
viandejo butcher's shop.
viandhaketaĵo minced meat.

vidakreco

viandistilaro butcher's knives, butcher's tools.
viandisto butcher.
viandmiksaĵo hash.
viandmuŝo bluebottle.
viando meat, flesh.
viandobutiko butcher's shop.
viandomanĝanta carnivorous.
viandomanĝanto carnivore, meat-eater.
viandovendejo butcher's shop.
viatiko last sacrament, viaticum.
vibrado flutter, vibration.
vibrafono vibes, vibraphone.
vibreti to tingle.
vibri to vibrate, oscillate, thrill.
vibrilo vibrator.
vibriono vibrio.
vibro vibration.
vibrosoni to rumble.
viburno guelder rose, viburnum.
vica sequential.
vicatendi to queue.
vicĉifalo vicifal (vice-head of Volapük movement)
vicdanco line dance.
vicdomo terrace house, terraced house.
vice in rows, in succession.
Vicedelegito deputy local representative.
vicfilino step-daughter.
vicfilo step-son, stepson.
vicfratino step-sister.
vicfrato step-brother.
vicgrafo viscount.
vicigi to line up, arrange in a line. **vicigi sin** to line up.
vicigo alignment.
viciĝi to align, line (up) get in line.
viciĝo alignment.
vicio vetch.
vicleŭtenanto second lieutenant.
vico array, file, line, rank, row, turn, sequence. **vico da jaroj** a number of years. **vico de funkcioj** function sequence, sequence of functions.
vicparto spare part.
vicpatrino step-mother.
vicpatro step-father.
vicprezidanto vice-president.
vicrado spare tyre.
vicreĝo viceroy.
vicrisurco backup copy.
vicvoki to call over.
vida visual.
vidadi to survey.
vidado sight, view, vision.
vidaĵo prospect, sight, view, spectacle, sight, parade, display, pageant.
vidakreco visual acuity.

vidalvide facing, across from, vis-à-vis.
   vidalvide al facing towards.
vidangulo angle of sight.
vidanto witness.
vidatestanto eyewitness.
vidbendilo video recorder, VCR.
vidbendo videotape.
vide visually.
videbla visible, apparent, obvious. **videbla signo** graphic character, printable character.
videble visibly.
videbleti to be barely visible.
videbli to be visible.
videbligi to manifest.
videbligilo video display.
videbliĝi to appear, become evident.
videgebla conspicuous.
videkamerao video camera.
videkunveno video conference.
videludo video game.
video video.
videobendo video-tape.
videofilmo video (film).
videokamerao video camera.
videoklipo video clip.
videokonferenco video conference.
videokunveno video conference.
videoludo video game.
videomemoro video RAM, VRAM.
videoregistrilo video recorder.
videotekniko video technology.
videregistrilo video recorder.
videto glimpse.
vidi to see, view, observe. **vidi nudokule** to see with the naked eye. **vidi sin** to see one's self. **vidu** see. **vidu ĉi poste** see below.
vidigi to show, make someone see, display. **vidigi la dentojn** to show or bare one's teeth.
vidigilo viewer.
vidiĝi to appear, seem, be visible.
vidiĝo appearance, aspect.
vidilo spyglass, telescope.
vidinaĵoj sights.
vidinda worth seeing.
vidindaĵo curiosity, place of interest.
vidindaĵoj the sights.
vidkampo field of vision.
vidkapablo power of sight, seeing ability, ability to see.
vidlimigilo blinders.
vido sight, view, vision.
vidokampo field of vision.
vidoserĉilo viewfinder.
vidpovo (power of) sight, vision.
vidpunkto point of view, viewpoint.
vidveco widowhood.
vidviĝi to be widowered.

vidviniĝi to be widowed.
vidvino widow.
vidvo widower.
viena Vienna, Viennese.
vienanino Viennese woman.
vienano Viennese.
Vieno Vienna.
vigili to keep watch, be vigilant.
vigla adroit, agile, alert, brisk, keen, lively, nimble, vigilant, watchful.
vigle vigilantly.
vigleco activity, gusto, spirit, stir, zest.
viglega aggressive.
viglege aggressively.
vigli to flourish, thrive.
vigliga exhilarating, invigorating.
viglige exhilaratingly.
vigligi to encourage, stimulate.
vigliĝi to bestir one's self.
vigliĝo exhilaration.
viglo vigil, watch.
vigvamo tepee, wigwam.
vikario curate, vicar.
vikaro curate.
vikinga Viking.
vikingo Viking.
vikio wiki.
Viklovo Wicklow.
viktimigado victimization.
viktimigi to victimize.
viktimiĝi to become a victim.
viktimo sacrifice, victim.
Viktorilago Lake Victoria.
Viktoro Victor.
vila hairy, shaggy.
vilaĝa village, of a village.
vilaĝano villager.
vilaĝaro collection of villages.
vilaĝeca rustic.
vilaĝestro burgomaster, mayor, provost.
vilaĝeto hamlet, township.
vilaĝo village.
vilajo village.
vilao country cottage, seaside cottage, summer residence, villa.
Vilaparko Villa Park.
Vilĉjo Bill, Billy.
Vilhelmfortikaĵo Fort William.
Vilhelmo William.
vili to be willing to.
viligi to buff.
viliĝana peasant's.
viliĝanaro peasantry.
viliĝanino countrywoman.
vilo tuft of hair, villus.
vimena wicker.
vimenaĵo wattle.
vimenkorbo wicker basket.
vimeno wicker, willow.

vimenvergo withy.
vinagracido acetic acid.
vinagro vinegar.
vinagrujo vinegar bottle.
vinberarbo grapevine.
vinberaro bunch of grapes.
vinberbranĉo vine-branch.
vinberejo vinery, vineyard.
vinbergrapolo bunch of grapes.
vinberĝardeno vineyard.
vinberkultivado viticulture.
vinberkulturo vine culture.
vinbero grape.
vinbersuko grape juice.
vinbertrunko vine stock.
vinberujo grapevine.
vinbotelo wine bottle.
vinĉaparato winding-gear.
vinĉestro Winchester disk.
vinĉi to winch.
vinĉo winch, hoist.
vindaĵo diaper.
vindaso windlass.
vindi to bandage, swaddle, wind, swathe, wrap.
vindiĝi to become coiled, become wrapped.
vindinfano infant in arms.
vindistino nurse, dry nurse, monthly nurse.
vindotuko diaper, swaddling cloth.
vindoza Windows (operating system). **vindoza kliento** Windows client.
Vindozo Windows (operating system).
vindozulo Windows user.
vinfarado wine making.
vinglaso wine glass.
vinilo vinyl.
vinisto vintner.
vinjetaro notation.
vinjeto decorative design, decorative symbol, text illustration, vignette.
vinkelnero wine steward.
vinkesto barrel of wine.
vinko periwinkle.
vinkti to clinch, staple.
vinktilo stapler.
vinkto rivet, fastener, staple.
vinkulo accolade.
vinlisto wine list.
vino wine.
vinrikolto grape harvest, vintage.
vintra winter, of the winter. **vintra erantido** winter aconite, wolfsbane. **vintra ĝardeno** winter garden. **vintra kverko** sessile oak. **vintra olimpiko** winter olympics. **vintra tempo** standard time, winter time.
vintre in winter, during winter.
vintri to spend the winter.
vintro winter.

vintroĝardeno winter garden.
vinvendisto vintner, wine merchant.
vio yours.
viola violet.
violente violently.
violini to play the violin.
violkolora violet. **violkolora ipomeo** beach moonflower, sea moonflower.
violkoloro violet colour.
violo pansy, violet.
violonĉelisto violoncellist.
violonĉelo cello, violoncello.
violoni to play the violin.
violonisto fiddler, violinist.
violonklefo treble clef (♮).
violono fiddle, violin.
viomingano Wyomingite.
vipado flogging, lashing, whipping.
vipero viper.
vipeto riding whip.
vipi to whip.
vipo whip.
vippuno spanking, flogging, whipping, lashing.
vipstrio weal.
vipuridaro viperous brood.
vipuro adder, viper.
vir- (shows male sex).
vira male, masculine, manly, virile. **vira genro** masculine gender.
virabelo drone.
viraĉo asshole, bastard, son-of-a-bitch.
viraĵo manhood.
viranaso drake.
viransero gander.
virarego large group of people, crowd.
viraro group of people, crowd.
virbova bull.
virbovo bull.
vircervo stag.
virĉevalo stallion.
vireca manly, man-like.
virecismo machismo.
vireco manhood, manliness, virility.
vireculo macho.
virego giant.
virelefanto bull elephant.
vireto dwarf.
virga virgin, virginal.
virgeco virginity.
virgenra masculine.
virgenro masculine gender.
virginia Virginian.
virginiano Virginian.
Virgo Virgo (zodiac).
Virgulinaj Insuloj Virgin Islands.
virgulino maiden, virgin. **Virgulino** Virgo (zodiac).
virgulo virgin.

Virhidro

Virhidro Hydrus.
virhundo male dog.
viriĝi to become a man.
viriĝinto adult.
viriĝo puberty.
virina female.
virinaĉo hag, crone.
virinbiciklo ladies bicycle.
virineca womanly.
virineco femininity, womanliness.
virineto little woman.
virinevitulo misogynist.
virinfrizistino ladies' hairdresser.
viriniĝi to become a woman.
virinkalsono knickers.
virino woman.
virinpaĝo women's page.
virinsaketo lady's bag.
virinseksa feminine.
virkapreolo roebuck.
virkapro he-goat.
virkato male cat, tomcat.
virkoko cock, rooster.
virkolombo cock-pigeon.
virkuniklo buck, buck-rabbit.
virleporo buck, buck-hare.
viro man, male.
virorkido early purple orchid.
virpasero cock-sparrow.
virporko boar.
virseksa male, masculine.
virseksulo male.
virŝafo ram, tup.
virta pure, virtuous.
virte virtuously.
virteco decency.
virto morality, vice, virtue.
virtuala virtual. **virtuala adreso** virtual address. **virtuala disko** virtual disk. **virtuala maŝino** virtual machine. **virtuala memorilo** virtual memory. **virtuala memoro** virtual memory, virtual storage. **virtuala realo** virtual reality.
virtuale virtually.
virtulo righteous man, virtuous person.
virtuozeco artistry.
virtuozo virtuoso.
viruso virus.
viscero internal organ.
visigoto Visigoth.
viskio whisky, whiskey.
visko mistletoe.
viskonsinano Wisconsinite.
viskoza viscous.
viskozo viscose.
visterio wistaria, wisteria.
vistko mistletoe.
visto whist.
Vistulo Vistula.

vivero

viŝebla washable. **viŝebla lumdisko** CD RW, erasable optical disc. **viŝebla programebla nurlegebla memoro** erasable programmable read only memory, EPROM.
viŝi to delete, wipe, wipe off.
viŝilo duster, towel.
Viŝnuo Vishnu.
viŝsigno erase character.
viŝtuko dish cloth, dust rag.
vitala vital.
vitalismo vitalism.
vitameno vitamin.
vitamino vitamin. **vitamino C** vitamin C.
vitejo vine.
vitelo yolk.
viterito witherite.
vito vine, grapevine.
vitra glass. **vitra kloŝo** frame of glass.
vitraĵisto glazier.
vitraĵo pane.
vitralo leaded light, stained glass window.
vitreca glassy, vitreous.
vitrektomio vitrectomy.
vitrigi to vitrify.
vitrino showcase.
vitriola vitriolic.
vitriolo sulphuric acid, vitriol.
vitro glass (material).
vitrofarejo glassworks.
vitroida kvarco fused quartz, vitreous quartz.
vitrolano glass wool.
vitrolesivo window cleaner.
vitromeblo glass case.
vitropordo glass door.
vitrorubo broken glass.
vitroserpento blindworm.
vitroviŝilo wiper.
vitrumi to glaze.
viva alive, living, sprightly.
vivadi to live (on).
vivado living.
vivaĵo life form.
vivanta alive.
vivanteco animation.
vivanto living (thing, being).
vivaranĝoj living arrangements.
vivasekuro life insurance.
vivciklo life cycle. **vivciklo de programaro** software life-cycle.
vivdatoj birth and death dates.
vivdaŭro lifespan.
vive lively.
viveca lively.
viveco liveliness, vivacity, animation.
vivega impetuous, vital.
vivema lively.
vivemo vitality.
vivero civet.

473

vivfine at the end of one's life.
vivgajnanto breadwinner.
vivhistorio biography, life history.
vivi to be alive, live. **vivi en ekzilo** to live in exile. **vivi kune** to live together. **vivu!** live long!, long live!
viviga animating.
vivigi to animate, invigorate, quicken.
vivigita animated.
viviĝi to come to live, become alive.
vivipova viable.
vivipoveco viability.
vivipovo ability to live.
vivisekcio vivisection.
viviva able to live.
vivkoncepto concept of living.
vivkuro course of one's life.
vivkutimoj customs, mores.
vivmaniero way of life.
vivmotivo reason for living, raison d'être.
vivnivelo standard of living.
vivo life.
vivodaŭro lifespan, lifetime.
vivoformo life form.
vivoforta full of life, vital.
vivoforto vitality, zing.
vivokapabla able to live.
vivokapablo ability to live.
vivonaska viviparous.
vivoplena full of life.
vivopriskribo curriculum vitae, CV.
vivoprotokolo curriculum vitae, résumé.
vivostilo lifestyle.
vivotasko life's work.
vivotempo lifetime.
vivovera realistic, vivid.
vivoverve vividly.
vivovojo life's path, way of one's life.
vivpano living.
vivpleneco vitality.
vivprotokolo résumé, CV.
vivrestaĵo rest of one's life.
vivsave to save one's life.
vivsigno sign of life.
vivtabelo actuarial table.
vivtempo lifetime.
vivtena subsistent. **vivtena minimumo** subsistence minimum.
vivtenadi to subsist.
vivtenado to maintain one's life.
vivteni to make a living, support, keep alive.
vivteno livelihood, maintenance, subsistence, living.
vivui to cheer, hurrah.
vivukrii to cheer, hurrah.
vivukrio cheer, hurrah.
vivuo cheer, hurrah.
vizaĝa facial. **vizaĝa neŭralgio** facial tic.
vizaĝaĉo mug (face).

vizaĝalvizaĝa face-to-face. **vizaĝalvizaĝa komunikado** face-to-face communication.
vizaĝkoloro complexion.
vizaĝo face, visage, countenance, look. **vizaĝo kontraŭ vizaĝo** face to face.
vizaĝokoloro colour (complexion).
vizaĝoŝirmilo face guard.
vizaĝvualo yashmak.
vizaĵo de vizaĵo face to face.
Vizbadeno Wiesbaden.
vizi to endorse.
vizia visionary.
viziero visor.
vizio vision.
vizitadi to frequent, haunt. **vizitadi lernejon** to attend a school.
vizitado visiting.
vizitanto caller, visitor.
vizitantregistro visitor's register.
vizite as a visitor.
viziteti to drop in, pop in.
viziti to attend, call on, see, visit. **viziti ejon** to visit a place. **viziti personon** to visit a person.
vizitinda worth visiting.
vizitkarto business card, visiting card.
vizito visit.
viziulo visionary.
vizo visa.
vizono (American) mink.
vjelo hurdy-gurdy.
vjetnama Vietnamese.
vjetnamanino Vietnamese woman.
vjetnamano Vietnamese.
vjetnamia Vietnamese.
vjetnamiano Vietnamese.
Vjetnamio Vietnam.
Vjetnamo Vietnam.
Vjetnamujo Vietnam.
vjolo tenor violin, viola.
vo name of the letter V. **duobla vo** name of the letter W. **Ĝermana vo** name of the letter W. → **vavo**.
vobli to wobble.
voĉa oral, vocal, voiced (sound). **voĉa konsonanto** voiced consonant.
voĉdonado poll, polling, voting.
voĉdonanto voter.
voĉdone by vote.
voĉdoni to vote, ballot.
voĉdono voice, suffrage.
voĉdonrajto right to vote.
voĉdonrajtulo voter.
voĉe orally, out loud, vocally.
voĉeco voicing.
voĉeto small voice.
voĉi to vote.
voĉigi to voice (sound).
voĉkordo vocal cord.

voĉlegi

voĉlegi to read aloud.
voĉo voice, vote.
voĉtono tone of voice.
Vodano Woden, Wodan, Wotan, Odin, Oðinn.
vodevilo light comedy, vaudeville.
vodko vodka.
vodui to voodoo.
Voduismo Voodoo.
voduo voodoo.
Vogezoj Vosges.
vojaĝado travelling.
vojaĝagentejo tourist agency, travel agency.
vojaĝagento travel agent.
vojaĝanta itinerant.
vojaĝanto passenger, traveller, voyager.
vojaĝartisto travelling artist.
vojaĝema inclined to travel a lot.
vojaĝeto trip.
vojaĝi to journey, travel, voyage.
vojaĝisto commercial traveller, salesman.
vojaĝkesto trunk (box).
vojaĝo journey, trip, voyage, tour, passage.
vojaĝoeto trip.
vojaĝoprezo fare.
vojaĝplano travel plan.
vojaĝrompi to stopover.
vojaĝrompo stopover.
vojaĝveturilo chaise.
vojbordero shoulder, verge, verge of a road.
vojborilo pneumatic drill.
vojbrako siding.
vojelspezo travel costs.
vojerari to lose one's way.
vojerarinta lost.
vojeto path, track.
vojevodo Polish provincial governor.
vojflanke by the side of the road.
vojflanko wayside.
vojforko fork in the road, intersection.
voji to be on one's way.
vojimposto toll.
vojindikilo signpost.
vojiranto wayfarer.
vojiri to go along, travel.
vojiro voyage, passage.
vojkoneksa path-connected, pathwise connected (space).
vojkonstruado road work.
vojkruciĝo crossroads, intersection, fork (in a road).
vojkurbiĝo turn, curve (in a road).
vojkurbo bend.
vojkuro path of a journey.
vojlinio course.
vojmontrilo signpost.
vojo course, passage, path, pathway, road, route, way.
vojoforko fork in the road, intersection.

volenevole

vojperdi to lose one's way.
vojplano route.
vojponto viaduct.
vojrabisto bandit, gangster, thug.
vojsulko trail.
vojŝildo road sign.
vojtaŭga roadworthy.
vojtaŭgeco roadworthiness.
voka beckoning.
vokala vowel.
vokalo vowel.
vokativa vocative.
vokativo vocative.
vokegi to hail.
voki to call, summon.
vokilo alarm, bird whistle.
vokkrii to call out, cry out, shout out.
voko call.
voksekvenco calling sequence.
voksignalo call-sign.
vokto taskmaster.
vol. → **volumo**.
vola wilful, desired.
volado volition.
volakto act of will.
volanbatilo badminton racket.
volanludo badminton.
volano badminton, shuttlecock.
volapukaĵo gibberish; Volapük things.
volapukeca Volapük-like.
volapukigi to Volapükize, turn into Volapük.
volapukigo Volapük localization.
volapukiĝi to become a Volapükist.
volapukismo Volapükism.
volapukista Volapükist.
volapukistaro all Volapükists, the "Volapük World".
volapukistino Volapükist, Volapük speaker.
volapukisto Volapükist, Volapük speaker.
volapuklingva in Volapük, Volapük-language.
Volapuko Volapük.
Volapukolando Volapükland.
volapukologiisto volapükologist.
volapukologio volapükology.
volapukologo volapükologist.
Volapukujo Volapükland.
volapukumi to do the Volapük thing, spend time with Volapük.
volatila volatile.
volba arched.
volbi to arch.
volbiĝi to arch, bend.
volbiĝo arch, bend.
volbo arched roof, dome, vault, vaulted ceiling.
vole willingly.
volenevole willy-nilly, like it or not.

volesprimo act of will.
volframo tungsten, wolfram.
Volga-Kama Bulgarujo Volga Bulgaria.
Volgo Volga.
Volgogrado Volgograd.
voli to be willing to, want, wish, will. **voli diri** to mean. **voli havi** to want, want to have.
volismo voluntarism.
volitivo subjunctive, subjunctive mood.
volo will, willingness, wish.
volonta voluntary, willing.
volonte readily, willingly.
volonteco willingness.
volontege very gladly.
volonti to be willing.
volonto alacrity.
volontulo volunteer.
volovano vol-au-vent.
voltaa voltaic.
voltaika galvanic.
Voltao Volta.
voltmetro voltmeter.
volto Volt. **volto je metro** volt(s) per meter.
volumena volumetric. **volumena maso** density.
volumenaĵo aggregate.
volumene by volume.
volumeneco bulkiness.
volumeno volume.
volumo tome, volume.
volupta voluptuous.
volupte sensually, sensuously, voluptuously.
volupteco sensuality, voluptuousness.
voluptema lascivious, sensual, voluptuous.
voluptemo lasciviousness.
volupto lust, sexual pleasure.
voluptulo lecher, debauchee.
volus would like.
voluto ornamental scroll-like carving.
volvaĵo ball.
volvekovri to envelop, wrap.
volvi to roll, roll up, wind, wind up, wrap.
volviĝi to twist.
volvita a at sign.
volvo roll.
volvofadeno tendril.
vomado vomiting.
vomaĵo vomit.
vombato wombat.
vomema sick.
vomemo nausea.
vomero vomer.
vomi to throw up, vomit.
vomiga nauseating, sickening.
vomigilo emetic.
vomilo vomitory.
vomitaĵo vomit.
vomnuksarbo strychnine (tree).
vomnukso strychnine (nut).

vori to devour.
vortareto vocabulary.
vortaro dictionary, vocabulary.
vortelekto word choice.
vortfarada lexical.
vortfarado word formation.
vortfino word ending.
vortformo inflexion, word form.
vortgrupo phrase.
vortico vortex.
vortigi to put into words, phrase.
vortkrucenigmo crossword puzzle.
vortkunmeto composition, compounding (of words).
vortlisto vocabulary, wordlist.
vortludo pun.
vorto word.
vortobatali to argue.
vortodeveno etymology.
vortodivido hyphenation.
vortolisto word list.
vortoprovizo vocabulary.
vortordo word order.
vortosimbolo word symbol.
vortospeco part of speech.
vortoŝuta voluble.
vortotrancado hyphenation, word division.
vortotrezoro vocabulary.
vortprovizo word stock, vocabulary.
vortradiko etymology.
vortsinsekvo word-order.
vortumeca komputilo word-oriented computer.
vortumo word.
vosta caudal. **vosta nulo** trailing zero. **vosta spaceto** trailing space.
vosthava caudate.
vosto tail.
vostumi to wag.
vostumo wag.
voti to vow.
voto vow.
vrako wreck.
vringi to wring.
vuali to veil.
vualiĝi to be veiled.
vualo veil.
vulgara coarse, common, vulgar, underbred, rude, everyday, proletarian.
vulgare commonly.
vulgareco vulgarity.
vulgaresprimo slang.
vulgarigi to popularize, vulgarize.
vulgarigo popularization.
vulgarismo vulgarism.
Vulgato Vulgate.
vulkana volcanic. **vulkana elsputo** volcanic eruption.
vulkanizi to vulcanize.

Vulkano

Vulkano Vulcan.
vulkano volcano.
vulpa fox, vulpine.
vulpido baby fox.
vulpino vixen.
vulpo fox.
vulturo vulture.
vulvo vulva.
vunda injurious.
vundebla vulnerable.
vundegi to maim, mutilate.
vundeti to hurt.
vundeto booboo., minor wound.
vundi to hurt, wound, injure.
vundiĝi to be injured, be wounded.
vundita injured, wounded.
vundito injured person.
vundo injury, wound.
vundpostsignoj stigmata.
vuvuzelo vuvuzela.

X Y Z

x-akso axis of abscissae, x-axis.
x-koordinato abscissa, x-coordinate.
x-rada x-ray.
x-radoj X-rays.

y-akso axis of ordinates, y-axis.
y-koordinato ordinate, y-coordinate.

Zagrebo Zagreb, Agram.
zaira Zairian.
zairano Zairian.
zairia Zairian.
zairiano Zairian.
Zairio Zaire.
Zairo Zaïre.
z-akso z-axis.
zambeza Zambezian.
Zambezo Zambezi.
zambia Zambian.
zambiano Zambian.
Zambio Zambia.
Zambujo Zambia.
zamenhofa Zamenhofan, of Zamenhof.
Zamenhofo Zamenhof.
Zamo Zama.
Zamoro Zamora.
zanikelio horned pondweed.
zanŝino zanshin.
zanzibara Zanzibari.
zanzibarano Zanzibari.
Zanzibaro Zanzibar.
Zaragoso Zaragoza.
Zaragozo Zaragoza.
zaratito zaratite.
Zaratuŝtro Zoroaster, Zarathustra.
zeaksantolo zeaxanthin.
zeatino zeatin.
zebro zebra.
zebrostria zebra-striped.
zebrostrioj zebra stripes.
zebuo Brahman, zebu.
zedoario zedoary.
zefira zephyr.
zefiro zephyr.
Zefiro Zephyrus.
zeino zein.
zekeno sequin (coin used in Italy between 13th and 19th centuries).
zekino zecchino, zechin, zequin.
zelanda Zealand. **Zelanda Flandrio** Dutch Flanders. **Zelanda Flandrujo** Dutch Flanders.
zelandano Zealander.
Zelando Zealand, Zeeland.
zelkovo zelkova.

zeloto fanatic, zealot.
zemstvo zemstvo.
zena Zen.
zenano zenana.
zenbudaismo Zen Buddhism.
zenbudaisto Zen Buddhist.
zenda Zend.
Zendavesto Zend-Avesta.
Zendo Zend.
zenismo Zen Buddhism.
zenita zenithal. **zenita distanco** zenithal distance.
zenito zenith.
Zeno Zen.
zeo public monument of place named after Zamenhof or Esperanto.
zeolita zeolitic.
zeolito zeolite.
zepelino zeppelin.
zeta zeta (Zζ).
zeto zeta (Zζ).
zeŭgmo zeugma.
Zeŭso Zeus.
zibela zibeline, zibelline.
zibelkolora sable-coloured.
zibelo marten, sable (animal).
zibeto zibet.
zigapofizo zygapophysis.
zigodaktila zygodactyl.
zigofilaco bean caper.
zigofilacoj family of tropical plants, Zygophyllaceae.
zigoma zygomatic.
zigomiceto zygomycete.
zigomorfa zygomorphic, zygomorphous.
zigomorfismo zygomorphism.
zigospora zygosporic.
zigosporo zygospore.
zigoto zygote.
zigozo zygosis.
zigurato ziggurat.
zigzaga zigzag.
zigzageto squiggle.
zigzagi to zigzag.
zigzago zigzag.
zimazo zymase.
zimbabva Zimbabwean.
zimbabvano Zimbabwean.
Zimbabvo (Republic of) Zimbabwe.
zimbalono dulcimer.
zimo zyme.
zimogena zymogenic.
zimogeno zymogen.
zimologio zymology.
zimoza zymotic.

zimozo zymosis.
zimurgio zymurgy.
zingibracoj family of tropical plants, Zingiberaceae.
zingibro ginger.
zinio zinnia.
zinka zinc, zincic.
zinkato zincate.
zinki to galvanize, hot dip, zinc plate.
zinkisto zinc worker.
zinko zinc.
zinkoblanko zinc white.
zinkoblendo zinc blende.
zinkografia zincographic, zincographical.
zinkografiaĵo zincograph.
zinkografiisto zincographer.
zinkografio zincography.
zinkogravuro zincography.
zinkoksido zinc white, zinc oxide.
zinkpulvoro zinc dust.
zinkriĉa zinciferous.
zinksulfido zinc blend.
zionismo Zionism.
zipfermilo zip, zipper.
zipi to zip.
zipligilo zip, zipper.
zipo zipper.
zipofermi to zip.
zirkalojo zircalloy.
zirkona zirconic.
zirkonia zirconic.
zirkonidioksido zirconia.
zirkonio zirconium.
zirkono zircon.
zitero zither.
zizelo suslik.
zizifo jujube.
z-koordinato z-coordinate.
zl. → **zloto**.
zloto złoty.
zo name of the letter Z.
zoarco blenny.
zoarko blenny.
zodiaka zodiacal.
zodiako zodiac.
zombia zombie.
zombiismo zombism.
zombio zombie.
zomi to zoom (in).
zomo zoom.
zomobjektivo zoom lens.
zona zonal. **zona defendo** zone defence.
zonado zoning.
zonbuko belt buckle.
zonceramikaĵo beaker pottery.
zoneco zonality.
zonerupcio shingles.
zoni to gird.
zonita belted.

zono waist, belt, girdle; zone.
zonovermoj class of worms, Clitellata.
zonsako belt-bag.
zontuko loincloth.
zonulo zonule, zonula.
zoo zoo.
zoofilio bestiality, zoophilia.
zoofito zoophyte.
zooforma zoomorphic.
zoogena zoogenic.
zoogeografia zoogeographic, zoogeographical.
zoogeografio zoogeography.
zoogleo zoogloea.
zooida zooidal.
zooido zooid.
zoologa ĝardeno zoo, menagerie.
zoologia zoologic, zoological. **zoologia ĝardeno** zoo, zoological garden.
zoologie zoologically.
zoologiisto zoologist.
zoologio zoology.
zoologo zoologist.
zoomorfa zoomorphic.
zoomorfismo zoomorphism.
zoono zoön.
zooprizorganto zoo-keeper.
zoosporangia zoosporangial.
zoosporangio zoosporangium.
zoosporo zoospore.
zoosterolo zoosterole.
zootekniko zootechnics, zootechny.
zoo-tekniko zootechnics, zootechny.
zootomio zootomy.
zorga careful, mindful, regardful.
zorgado concern, care.
zorganto caretaker, guardian, protector.
zorgateco ward (care).
zorgato pupil, ward.
zorgatulo ward (a person).
zorge carefully, cautiously.
zorgeco solicitude.
zorgema careful, provident, watchful.
zorgeme carefully.
zorgemo concern, anxiety.
zorgetoj worries.
zorgi to be anxious, be concerned, (take) care, see (to), worry. **zorgi pri** to care about, take care of, see to. **zorgi pri siaj propraj aferoj** to mind one's own business.
zorgiga disturbing, troublesome.
zorgigi to disturb, trouble.
zorgita taken care of, cared for.
zorgitaro flock (congregation).
zorgo care, concern, worry.
zorgoj worries.
zorgoplena full of worry.
zorgoplene full of worry, worriedly.
zorgplena anxious.

zorgplene anxiously.
zorilo zoril.
zorio flip-flop, thong.
zoroastra Zoroastrian.
zoroastrana Zoroastrian.
zoroastrano Zoroastrian.
zoroastrisma Zoroastrian.
zoroastrismo Zoroastrianism.
Zoroastro Zarathustra, Zoroaster.
zostero eel-grass, wrack; shingles.
zosteropso white-eye.
zostro shingles.

zuavo Zouave.
zukino zucchini, aubergine.
zulua Zulu. **zulua lingvo** Zulu (language).
Zululando Zululand.
Zuluo Zulu.
zuluo Zulu.
zumado buzz, hum.
zumi to buzz, hum, roar (traffic).
zumilo buzzer.
zummuŝo bluebottle.
zumo buzz, hum, roar (traffic).
Zurigo Zurich.

www.ingramcontent.com/pod-product-compliance
Lightning Source LLC
Chambersburg PA
CBHW030124240426
43672CB00005B/15